DEVELOPING MANAGEMENT SKILLS

GLOBAL EDITION

EIGHTH EDITION

David A. Whetten
BRIGHAM YOUNG UNIVERSITY

Kim S. Cameron
UNIVERSITY OF MICHIGAN

PEARSON

Boston   Columbus   Indianapolis   New York   San Francisco   Upper Saddle River
Amsterdam   Cape Town   Dubai   London   Madrid   Milan   Munich   Paris   Montreal   Toronto
Delhi   Mexico City   Sao Paulo   Sydney   Hong Kong   Seoul   Singapore   Taipei   Tokyo

Editorial Director: Sally Yagan
Editor in Chief: Eric Svendsen
Acquisitions Editor: Kim Norbuta
Acquisitions Editor, Global Edition: Steven Jackson
Editorial Project Manager: Claudia Fernandes
Director of Marketing: Patrice Lumumba Jones
Marketing Manager: Nikki Ayana Jones
Marketing Manager, International: Dean Erasmus
Senior Marketing Assistant: Ian Gold
Senior Managing Editor: Judy Leale
Senior Production Project Manager: Kelly Warsak
Senior Operations Supervisor: Arnold Vila
Operations Specialist: Ilene Kahn
Senior Art Director: Janet Slowik

Interior Design: Suzanne Duda and Michael Fruhbeis
Permissions Project Manager: Shannon Barbe
Manager, Cover Visual Research & Permissions: Karen Sanatar
Manager Central Design: Jayne Conte
Cover Art: (c) Dklimke/Dreamstime.com
Cover Design: Jodi Notowitz
Lead Media Project Manager: Denise Vaughn
Full-Service Project Management: Sharon Anderson/
  BookMasters, Inc.
Composition: Integra Software Services
Printer/Binder: Edwards Brothers
Cover Printer: Coral Graphics
Text Font: 10/12 Weidemann-Book

Credits and acknowledgments borrowed from other sources and reproduced, with permission, in this textbook appear on appropriate page within text.

This is a special edition of an established title widely used by colleges and universities throughout the world. Pearson published this exclusive edition for the benefit of students outside the United States and Canada. If you purchased this book within the United States or Canada you should be aware that it has been imported without the approval of the Publisher or the Author.

10 9 8 7 6 5 4 3 2

ISBN 10:   0-13-510302-9
ISBN 13: 978-0-13-510302-9

BRIEF TABLE OF CONTENTS

CONTENTS

2 MANAGING PERSONAL STRESS   127

3 SOLVING PROBLEMS ANALYTICALLY AND CREATIVELY   189

PART II   INTERPERSONAL SKILLS   254

4   BUILDING RELATIONSHIPS BY COMMUNICATING SUPPORTIVELY   255

5 GAINING POWER AND INFLUENCE 301

6 MOTIVATING OTHERS   345

9 BUILDING EFFECTIVE TEAMS AND TEAMWORK   511

10 | LEADING POSITIVE CHANGE   555

PREFACE

What's New in This Edition?

Based on suggestions from reviewers, instructors, and students we have made a number of changes in the eighth edition of *Developing Management Skills*.

- Added new skill assessments in Chapter 1 and new cases in Chapters 3, 4, 5 and 9.
- Revised parts of the book to reflect suggestions and feedback from instructors and students.
- Clarified instructions for scoring skill assessments and updated the comparison data for each assessment.
- Updated the research supporting key points in each chapter.
- Added a Resource Locator table at the beginning of each chapter in the Instructors Manual, organized according to a chapter's learning objectives.
- Added new video clips and exercise recommendations in the Instructors Manual.
- Enhanced the test bank by adding more application questions.
- Revised the PowerPoint slides.

A MESSAGE TO STUDENTS:

Why Focus on Management Skill Development?

Given that a "skill development" course requires more time and effort than a course using the traditional lecture/discussion format, we are sometimes asked this question by students, especially those who have relatively little work experience.

Reason #1: It focuses attention on what effective managers actually "do."

In an influential article, Henry Mintzberg (1975) argued that management education had almost nothing to say about what managers actually do from day to day. He further faulted management textbooks for introducing students to the leading theories about management while ignoring what is known about effective management practice. Sympathetic to Mintzberg's critique, we set out to identify the defining competencies of effective managers.

Although no two management positions are exactly the same, the research summarized in the Introduction highlights ten personal, interpersonal, and group skills that form the core of effective management practice. Each chapter addresses one of these skills.

Personal Skills

1. Developing Self-Awareness
2. Managing Personal Stress
3. Solving Problems Analytically and Creatively

Interpersonal Skills

4. Building Relationships by Communicating Supportively
5. Gaining Power and Influence
6. Motivating Others
7. Managing Conflict

Group Skills

8. Empowering and Delegating
9. Building Effective Teams and Teamwork
10. Leading Positive Change

Consistent with our focus on promoting effective management practice, the material in these chapters provides guidance for a variety of contemporary management challenges, including: "How can I help others accept new goals, new ideas, new approaches?" "How can I invigorate those who feel outdated and left behind?" "How do I help the 'survivors' of a downsizing pick up the pieces and move on?" "How do I help people with very different agendas and philosophies work together, especially during periods of high stress and uncertainty?"

Anyone tempted to dismissively argue that the answers to these questions are "common sense" would do well to recall Will Rogers' pithy observation: "Common sense ain't common." In addition, the research reported in the Introduction suggests that, in many cases, managers' "common sense" isn't "good sense."

The premise of this book and associated course is that the key to effective management practice is practicing what effective managers—those with "good sense"—do consistently.

Reason #2: It is consistent with proven principles of effective teaching and learning.

A seasoned university professor advised a young colleague, "If your students aren't learning, you're not teaching—you're just talking!" Here's what some authorities on higher education have to say about how effective teachers foster learning:

"All genuine learning is active, not passive. It is a process of discovery in which the student is the main agent, not the teacher." (Adler, 1982)

"Learning is not a spectator sport. Students do not learn much just by sitting in a class listening to teachers, memorizing pre-packaged assignments, and spilling out answers. They must talk about what they are learning, write about it, relate it to past experiences, apply it to their daily lives. They must make what they learn part of themselves." (Chickering & Gamson, 1987)

In their classic book on active learning, Bonwell and Elson (1991) list seven defining characteristics.

1. Students are involved in more than passive listening.
2. Students are engaged in activities (e.g., reading, discussing, writing).
3. There is less emphasis placed on information transmission and greater emphasis placed on developing student skills.
4. There is greater emphasis placed on the exploration of attitudes and values.
5. Student motivation is increased, especially in adult learners.

6. Students receive immediate feedback from their instructor and peers.
7. Students are involved in higher order thinking (analysis, synthesis, evaluation).

Our goals in writing this book were to bridge the academic realm of theory and research and the organizational realm of effective practice, and to help students consistently translate proven principles from both realms into personal practice. To accomplish these goals we formulated a five-step "active" learning model, described in the Introduction. Based on the positive feedback we've received from teachers and students we can state with confidence that the form of active learning pioneered in this book is a proven pedagogy for management skill mastery.

Tips for Getting the Most Out of This Course

Whether you are an undergraduate or MBA student, or an experienced manager, based on our years of teaching management skills here are some suggestions for making this course a personally meaningful learning experience.

- Read the introduction carefully. Inasmuch as this is not a typical management textbook, it is important that you understand its distinctive learner-focused features especially the five-step learning model: Skill Assessment, Skill Learning, Skill Analysis, Skill Practice, and Skill Application. You'll also find informative research on how much managers' actions impact individual and organizational performance, and the characteristics of effective managers.

- Thoughtfully complete the Skill Assessment surveys in each chapter. These diagnostic tools are designed to help you identify which specific aspects of each skill topic most warrant your personal attention.

- Carefully study the Behavioral Guidelines and the summary model at the conclusion of the Skill Learning section of each chapter before reading that section. These written and graphical summaries are designed to bridge the research-informed description of each topic with the skill development activities that follow. To help you internalize research-informed "good sense" be sure to use the Behavioral Guidelines as your frame of reference when reading and discussing Skill Analysis cases, and participating in Skill Practice and Skill Application exercises.

- Be sure to complete Skill Application exercise in each chapter. Management skill mastery requires out-of-class skill practice. How to do this is pretty straightforward if you are currently working in an organization, regardless of whether you are an experienced manager or a new, part-time employee. Whether or not you are currently employed, we encourage you to seek out skill practice opportunities in all aspects of your life, including working in assigned teams in this and other courses, planning social events for a campus or community organization, counseling a troubled sibling or friend, managing end-of-semester deadlines, or handling a difficult issue with a boy/girlfriend or spouse. The sooner you begin—and the more you persist in—practicing what you learn in this course, the more you'll be able to count on these skills as "automatic responses" when you need them as a manager.

Supplemental Material

PASSWORD-PROTECTED ASSESSMENT WEB SITE

If your instructor has signed up for this object, an access-code-protected Web site is available so you can take the Skill Assessments in the book online and receive immediate, real-time feedback on how your scores compare with those of thousands of other students in our ever-expanding database. (Two assessments in the book—"Source of Personal Stress" in Chapter 2 and the "Best-Self Feedback Exercise" in Chapter 10—are not available online.)

Acknowledgments

In addition to the informal feedback that we have received from colleagues around the world, we would especially like to thank the following people who have formally reviewed material and provided valuable feedback, vital to the revision of this and previous editions:

Richard Allan, University of Tennessee–Chattanooga
Forrest F. Aven, University of Houston
Lloyd Baird, Boston University
Bud Baker, Wright State University
John D. Bigelow, Boise State University
Ralph R. Braithwaite, University of Hartford
Julia Britt, California State University
Tim Bothell, Brigham Young University
David Cherrington, Brigham Young University
John Collins, Syracuse University
Kerri Crowne, Temple University
Todd Dewett, Wright State University
Andrew J. Dubrin, Rochester Institute of Technology
Steven Edelson, Temple University
Norma Givens, Fort Valley State University
Barbara A. Gorski, St. Thomas University
David Hampton, San Diego State University
Stanley Harris, Auburn University
Richard E. Hunt, Rockhurst College
Daniel F. Jennings, Baylor University
Avis L. Johnson, University of Akron

Jay T. Knippen, University of South Florida
Roland Kushner, Lafayette College
Roy J. Lewicki, Ohio State University
Michael Lombardo, Center for Creative Leadership
Charles C. Manz, University of Massachusetts–Amherst
Ralph F. Mullin, Central Missouri State University
Thomas J. Naughton, Wayne State University
J. Randolph New, University of Richmond
Jon L. Pierce, University of Minnesota–Duluth
Lyman Porter, University of California–Irvine
Lyle F. Schoenfeldt, Appalachian State University
Jacop P. Siegel, University of Toronto
Charles Smith, Hofstra University
Noel M. Tichy, University of Michigan
Wanda V. Trenner, Ferris State University
Ulya Tsolmon, Brigham Young University
Kenneth M. York, Oakland University

We especially thank our collaborators who adapted the book for the European and Australian markets, as well as those who translated *Developing Management Skills* into Spanish, Russian, Chinese, and Dutch.

We are grateful for the assistance of many dedicated associates who have helped us continually upgrade and enhance *Developing Management Skills*. These include Nancy Keesham and Don Clement, both of the Fuqua School of Business at Duke University, for their work on the supplement on making oral and written presentations; Gretchen Spreitzer of the University of Southern California for her work on the chapter on gaining power and influence; Richard M. Steers of the University of Oregon for his work on the motivation chapter; Pat Seybolt and Troy Nielsen of the University of Utah for their work on the chapter on managing conflict; Cathy German of Miami University for her assistance in revising Supplement A, and John Tropman, University of Michigan, for taking the lead in revising Supplement C. Special thanks are also due to Susan Schor, Joseph Seltzer, and James Smither for writing the SSS Software In-Basket Exercise. Our long-time collaboration with Sue Campbell-Clark has been particularly fruitful and we anticipate that our work with Jeff Thompson, Brigham Young University, will be equally energizing.

We would especially like to thank Kim Norbuta, Claudia Fernandes, Kelly Warsak, and Judy Leale; and Sharon Anderson of BookMasters for her expert assistance with this edition.

Finally, and most importantly, we express appreciation to our families for their ongoing patience and support, which is reflected in their willingness to share their time with this competing "labor of love" and to forgive our own gaps between common sense and common practice.

David A. Whetten
Kim S. Cameron

Pearson would like to acknowledge and thank the following people for their work on the Global Edition:

Samuel Azasu, Director of Graduate and Undergraduate Studies, Royal Institute of Technology, Sweden.

Dr. Yavuz Günalay, Bahçeşehir University, Istanbul.

Elham S. Hasham, Assistant Professor, Department of Management & Marketing, Faculty of Business Administration, Notre Dame University, Lebanon.

Jon and Diane Sutherland.

Introduction

The Critical Role of Management Skills

No one doubts that the twenty-first century will continue to be characterized by chaotic, transformational, rapid-fire change. In fact, almost no sane person is willing to predict what the world will be like 50, 25, or even 15 years from now. Change is just too rapid and ubiquitous. The development of "nanobombs" have caused some people to predict that personal computers and desktop monitors will land on the scrap heap of obsolescence within 20 years. The new computers will be a product of etchings on molecules leading to personalized data processors injected into the bloodstream, implanted in eyeglasses, or included in wristwatches.

Predictions of the changes that will occur in the future are often notoriously wrong, of course, as illustrated by Thomas Watson's (founder of IBM) prediction that only a few dozen computers would ever be needed in the entire world, Thomas Edison's prediction that the lightbulb would never catch on, or Irving Fisher's (preeminent Yale economist) prediction in 1929 (a month before the crash) that the stock market had reached "a permanently high plateau." When Neil Armstrong walked on the moon in 1969, most people predicted that we would soon be walking on Mars, establishing colonies in outer space, and launching probes from lunar pads. In 1973, with long lines at the gas pumps due to an OPEC-led fuel crisis, economists predicted that oil would sell for $100 a barrel in the United States by 1980. Most notorious of all, of course, was the prediction by the United States patent office in 1896 that it would soon close its doors since "everything that can be invented has been invented."

Warren Bennis, a colleague of ours, half-jokingly predicted that the factory of the future would have only two employees, a person and a dog. The person would be there to feed the dog. The dog would be there to keep the person from touching the equipment! Tom Peters counseled managers that, due to the chaotic pace of change, "If you're not confused, you're not paying attention." And the late Peter Drucker characterized the current environment this way: "We are in one of those great historical periods that occur every 200 or 300 years when people don't understand the world anymore, and the past is not sufficient to explain the future." Almost no one would argue that "permanent white water" best characterizes our current environment. Almost everything is in flux, from our technology and methods of transacting business to the nature of education and the definition of the family.

Despite all this change in our environment, there is something that has remained, and continues to remain, relatively constant. With minor variations and stylistic differences, what has not changed in several thousand years are the basic skills that lie at the heart of effective, satisfying, growth-producing human relationships. Freedom, dignity, trust, love, and honesty in relationships have always been among the goals of human beings, and the same principles that brought about those outcomes in the eleventh century still bring them about in the twenty-first century. Despite our circumstances, in other words, and despite the technological resources we have available to us, the same basic human skills still lie at the heart of effective human interaction.

In fact, human relationships are becoming more important, not less, as the information age unfolds and technologies encroach even more upon our daily lives. Most of us are exposed to more information each day than we can possibly pay attention to. More than 6,000 business books are published each month. Moreover, no mechanism exists to organize, prioritize, or interpret that information, so it is often unclear what is crucial and what can be ignored. Consequently, the relationship we have with the sources of that information is the key sense-making mechanism. Building trusting relationships is a critical part of coping with information overload.

It is a fact that when everything is changing, change becomes unmanageable. No one can manage constant, unorganized change. Think of being a pilot on an airplane. Everything is changing—the entire plane is in constant motion—as the plane moves through the air. Unless you can fix on something that is not changing—for example, the ground or the stars—it is impossible to fly the plane. Tragically, investigators found that John F. Kennedy Jr. unknowingly flew his plane into the Atlantic Ocean killing himself, his wife, and his sister-in-law because he lost sight of land and, consequently, lost perspective. He became unable to manage change because he did not have an established, unwavering point that helped him maintain his bearings.

We make sense of change by being able to identify a fixed, stable, permanent point that provides us with perspective. In our current "white water" environment, the skills discussed in this book serve as fixed points. They have changed very little in their effectiveness and relevance over several thousand years. And their relationship to effective human and organizational performance has been well-documented. Later in this Introduction we share some of the scientific research that confirms the power of these management skills in accounting for effective personal, interpersonal, and organizational performance.

The problem, of course, is that what is known is not always the same as what is demonstrated. Although we have known about the principles of effective relationships for a very long time, the history of humankind illustrates that these principles have not always been practiced. Especially in our current day, what we know and what we demonstrate do not always match. Dr. Bob Moorehead of Seattle's Overlake Christian Church, who resigned his own position under a cloud of accusations, described it this way:

The paradox of our time in history is that we have taller buildings but shorter tempers, wider freeways but narrower viewpoints. We spend more but have less; we buy more but enjoy it less. We have bigger houses and smaller families, more conveniences but less time. We have more degrees but less sense; more knowledge but less judgment; more experts but more problems; more medicine but less wellness. We drink too much, smoke too much, spend too recklessly, laugh too little, drive too fast, get too angry too quickly, stay up too late, get too tired, read too seldom, watch TV too much, and pray too seldom. We have multiplied our possessions, but reduced our values. We talk too much, love too seldom, and hate too often. We have learned how to make a living but not a life; we've added years to life but not life to years. We've been all the way to the moon and back but have trouble crossing the street to meet the new neighbor. We've conquered outer space but not inner space. We've done larger things but not better things. We've cleaned up the air but polluted the soul. We've split the atom but not our prejudice. We write more but learn less. We plan more but accomplish less. We've learned to rush but not to wait. We build more computers to hold more information to produce more copies than ever but have less communication. These are the times of fast foods and slow digestion; tall men and short character; steep profits and shallow relationships. These are the times of world peace but domestic warfare; more leisure but less fun; more kinds of food but less nutrition. These are the days of two incomes but more divorce, of fancier houses but broken homes. These are the days of quick trips, disposable diapers, throw-away morality, one-night stands, overweight bodies, and pills that do everything from cheer to quiet to kill. It is a time when there is much in the show window and nothing in the stockroom. (Moorehead, n.d.)

This book is built on the presumption that developing management skills—that is, the skills needed to manage one's own life as well as relationships with others—is a ceaseless endeavor. These skills were largely the same a century ago as they are today. The basic behavioral principles that lie at the foundation of these skills are timeless. That is one reason why the shelves of bookstores and on-line newsletters are filled with prescriptions of how one more executive or one more company struck it rich or beat out the competition. Thousands of books trumpet some special set of prescriptions for how to be successful in business, or in life. Many of these books have made it to the best-seller lists and have enjoyed lengthy stays.

Our intention in this book is not to try to duplicate the popular appeal of the best-selling books nor to utilize the common formula of recounting anecdotal incidents of successful organizations and well-known managers. We have produced a book that remains true to, and is based on, social science and business research. We want to share with you what is known and what is not known about how to develop management skills and how to foster productive, healthy, satisfying, and growth-producing relationships with others in your work setting. *Developing Management Skills* is designed to help you actually improve your personal management competencies—to change your behavior. This book, therefore, serves more as a practicum or a guide to effective managerial behavior than a description of what someone else has done to successfully manage an organization. It will surely help you think, and it will provide examples of success, but it will have failed if it also does not help you *behave* more competently in your own life.

Whereas the skills focused on in this book are called "management skills," their relevance is not limited just to an organization or work setting. We focus mainly on work settings here because our primary goal is to help you prepare for and improve your own competency in a managerial role. You will discover, however, that these skills are applicable in most areas of your life—with families, friends, volunteer organizations, and your community.

In the next section we review some of the scientific evidence that demonstrates how management skills are associated with personal and organizational success, and we review several studies of the key management skills that seem to be the most important in our modern-day environment. It is those key skills that this book has targeted. We then describe a model and a methodology for helping you to develop management skills. A large number of management fads abound proclaiming a new way to be a leader, get rich, or both, but our intent is to rely on a proven methodology that has grounding in the scientific literature. We present what has been shown to be a superior process for improving management skills, and we base our claims on scholarly evidence. This Introduction concludes with a brief description of the organization of the rest of the book and the importance of keeping in mind individual differences among people.

The Importance of Competent Managers

In the last decade or so, an abundance of evidence has been produced that skillful management—especially those competent in the management of people in organizations—is *the* key determinant of organizational success. These studies have been conducted across numerous industry sectors, international settings, and organization types. The research findings now make it almost unquestionable that if organizations want to succeed, they must have competent, skillful managers.

For example, in one study of 968 firms, representing all major industries in the United States, organizations whose managers effectively managed their people—that is, they implemented effective people management strategies and demonstrated personal competency in management skills—had, on the average, a decrease in turnover of more than 7 percent, increased profits of $3,814 per employee, $27,044 more in sales per employee, and $18,641 more in stock market value per employee, compared to firms that had less effective people management (Huselid, 1995; Pfeffer & Veiga, 1999). In a follow-up study of 702 firms, shareholder wealth was an amazing $41,000 per employee higher in companies demonstrating strong people management skills than in firms that had a lower emphasis on people management (Huselid & Becker, 1997). A study of German firms in 10 industrial sectors produced similar results: "Companies that place workers at the core of their strategies produce higher long-term returns . . . than their industry peers" (Blimes, Wetzker, & Xhonneux, 1997). A study of five-year survivability in 136 nonfinancial companies that issued IPOs in the late 1980s found that the effective management of people was the most significant factor in predicting longevity, even when accounting for industry type, size, and profits. Firms that did a good job of managing people tended to survive; others did not (Welbourne & Andrews, 1996).

A study by Hanson (1986) investigated the factors that best accounted for financial success over a five-year span in 40 major manufacturing firms. The question being addressed was: "What explains the financial success of the firms that are highly effective?" The five most powerful predictors were identified and assessed. They included market share (assuming that the higher the market share of a firm, the higher its profitability); firm capital intensity (assuming that the more a firm is automated and up-to-date in technology and equipment, the more profitable it is); size of the firm in assets (assuming that economies of scale and efficiency can be used in large firms to increase profitability); industry average return on sales (assuming that firms would reflect the performance of a highly profitable industry); and the ability of managers to effectively manage their people (assuming that an emphasis on good people management helps produce profitability in firms). The results revealed that one factor—the ability to manage people effectively—was three times more powerful than all other factors combined in accounting for firm financial success over a five-year period! We repeat, good management was more important than all other factors taken together in predicting profitability.

Even research by the U.S. government confirms this management-effectiveness link. The U.S. Office of the Comptroller of the Currency studied the reasons for the failures of national banks in the United States during the 1980s. Two major factors were found to account for the record number of bank failures during that period: distressed economic conditions and poor management. The relative impact of those two factors, however, was somewhat surprising. Almost 90 percent of the failed banks were judged to have had poor management. Only 35 percent of the failures had experienced depressed economic conditions in the region in which they operated, and in only 7 percent of the cases was a depressed economic condition the sole cause of bank failure (U.S. Office of the Comptroller of the Currency, 1990).

Dramatic anecdotal evidence also abounds regarding the impact of effective management on workers and organizations. One of the most notable, for example, was the General Motors automobile assembly plant in Fremont, California. The plant was built in the 1950s and, at the beginning of the 1980s, was assembling the Chevrolet Nova model. The plant had a history of labor and productivity problems, however, and by the end of 1982 the performance statistics were dismal. Absenteeism was running at 20 percent. The number of formal grievances filed by employees totaled almost 5,000 (an average of more than 20 grievances per day for every workday of the year), and more than 2,000 grievances were still unresolved at year's end. An average of three to four wildcat strikes per year had occurred during the previous few years, and morale, productivity, and quality of production by the 5,000 employees were the worst in the corporation. Costs of assembling the automobile were about 30 percent above the Asian competitors. In light of these data, corporate headquarters issued an order to close the plant and lay off the workers.

Three years later, General Motors signed a joint operating agreement with one of its major competitors: Toyota Motors. Much had been written about the Japanese method of managing, so General Motors asked Toyota to reopen and manage the Fremont plant. Most of the former U.S. autoworkers were rehired, and a new management team was put in place. Workers were exposed to training in high-involvement work practices, and a former Ford Motor Company employee actually became the plant manager. The primary difference between the plant before it closed and after it reopened was that a new management team was in place and employee training had occurred. The workforce, in other words, remained essentially unchanged. One year after reopening, the organization's performance data looked like this:

Absenteeism:	2 percent
Grievances:	2 outstanding
Strikes:	None
Employees:	2,500 (producing 20 percent more cars)
Productivity:	Highest in the corporation
Quality:	Highest in the corporation
Costs:	Equal to those of the competition
Product:	Toyota Corolla—rated AAA's best car in its price range

The remarkable thing about this turnaround is that it did not take five or ten years to produce major improvements in productivity, cohesion, and commitment. It occurred in just over a year simply by changing the way workers were managed.

These studies indicate overwhelmingly that good management fosters financial success, whereas less effective management fosters financial distress. Successful organizations have managers with well-developed people management skills. In surveys of CEOs, executives, and business owners, results consistently show that the factor most responsible for business failure is "bad management" and the best way to ensure business success is to "provide better management." Moreover, the data are clear, management skills are more important than industry, environment, competition, and economic factors combined.

Surprisingly, however, finding people who effectively manage people is not as easy as might be expected. Pfeffer & Veiga (1999) concluded that: "Even as these research results pile up, trends in actual management practice are, in many instances, moving in a direction exactly opposite to what this growing body of evidence prescribes." Common sense and common knowledge are not necessarily common practice. Knowing and doing are not the same things. Being able to analyze a case, identify a problem, or recite a correct answer to a question is not equivalent to being able to actually implement effective management skills.

The Skills of Effective Managers

What, then, differentiates effective managers from less effective managers? If developing management skills is so crucial for organizational success, what skills ought to be the focus of attention?

The management literature is filled with lists of attributes, behaviors, orientations, and strategies for enhancing successful performance. For example, Pfeffer (1998) identified seven key practices associated with managerial and organizational effectiveness: ensure employment security, selectively hire people, foster decentralization and self-managing teams, institute high levels of pay based on performance, train extensively, reduce status differences, and share information. Quinn (2000) identified eight "seeds" of effective management and leadership: "envision the productive community," "first look within," "embrace the hypocritical self," "transcend fear," "embody a vision of the common good," "disturb the system," "surrender to the emergent process," and "entice through moral power." An international study of 6,052 managers from 22 countries focused on differences in managerial attributes and identified attributes such as inspirational, self-sacrificial, integrity, diplomatic, malevolent, visionary, administrative, self-centered, status conscious, autocratic, modest, and autonomous (Brodbeck et al., 2000). Rigby (1998) focused on the 25 most popular management tools and techniques in an investigation of the association between management tools and techniques and organizational performance. According to 4,137 managers in North America, Europe, and Asia, the tools associated with organization success were: strategic planning, pay for performance, strategic alliances, customer satisfaction measurement, shareholder value analysis, mission and vision statements, benchmarking, cycle time reduction, agile strategies, self-directed teams, and groupware.

These kinds of lists are useful, but they do not identify management *skills* per se. Instead, they enumerate organizational strategies, personality orientations, or philosophical approaches to management, and their implementation is usually outside the explicit control of the individual manager. Either they are complex sets of activities in which many people must be involved—for example, "ensuring employment security," "selectively hiring," or "shareholder value analysis"—or they are cognitive activities that are not behavioral in character—for example, "envisioning the productive community," "first looking within," or "avoiding malevolence." Some of the lists enumerate personality characteristics or styles—for example, inspirational, or autocratic—or they enumerate organizational practices—for example, pay for performance, or strategic planning. The effectiveness of the attributes on these kinds of lists depends on the manager's skill in implementing them, and that means being competent in fundamental management skills. Management skills form the vehicle by which management strategy, management practice, tools and techniques, personality attributes, and style work to produce effective outcomes in organizations. Management skills, in other words, are the building blocks upon which effective management rests. That is why the focus of this book is on developing management skills rather than on strategy, tools and techniques, or styles. Management skills are the means by which managers translate their own style, strategy, and favorite tools or techniques into practice.

Essential Management Skills

A variety of investigators have sought to identify what specific skills are characteristic of the most effective managers. In our own investigation, for example, we wanted to identify the skills and competencies that separate extraordinarily effective performers from the rest of us. We identified 402 individuals who were rated as highly effective managers in their own organizations in the fields of business, health care, education, and state government by asking senior officers to name the most effective managers in their own organizations. We then interviewed those people to determine what attributes were associated with managerial effectiveness. We asked questions such as:

❑ How have you become so successful in this organization?
❑ Who fails and who succeeds in this organization and why?

- ❏ If you had to train someone to take your place, what knowledge and what skills would you make certain that person possessed in order to perform successfully as your successor?
- ❏ If you could design an ideal curriculum or training program to teach you to be a better manager, what would it contain?
- ❏ Think of other effective managers you know. What skills do they demonstrate that explain their success?

Our analysis of the interviews produced about 60 characteristics of effective managers. The 10 identified most often are listed in Table 1. Not surprisingly, these 10 characteristics are all behavioral skills. They are not personality attributes or styles, nor are they generalizations such as "luck" or "timing." They also are common across industries, levels, and job responsibilities. The characteristics of effective managers are not a secret.

The management skills derived from our study are similar to those resulting from several other surveys published in the management literature. Table 2, for example, lists a representative sample of surveys that relied on a heterogeneous mix of respondents. Not surprisingly, the two lists are very similar. Regardless of whether respondents are CEOs or first-line supervisors, whether they work in the public sector or the private sector, their skills are quite easily identifiable and agreed upon by observers. It is not hard to recognize and describe the skills of effective managers.

What Are Management Skills?

There are several defining characteristics of management skills that differentiate them from other kinds of managerial characteristics and practices. First, management skills are *behavioral*. They are not personality attributes or stylistic tendencies. Management skills consist of identifiable sets of actions that individuals perform and that lead to certain outcomes. Skills can be observed by others, unlike attributes that are purely mental or are embedded in personality. Whereas people with different styles and personalities may apply the skills differently, there are, nevertheless, a core set of observable attributes in effective skill performance that are common across a range of individual differences.

Second, management skills are *controllable*. The performance of these behaviors is under the control of the individual. Unlike organizational practices such as "selectively

Table 1	Skills of Effective Managers—One Study
1. Verbal communication (including listening)	
2. Managing time and stress	
3. Managing individual decisions	
4. Recognizing, defining, and solving problems	
5. Motivating and influencing others	
6. Delegating	
7. Setting goals and articulating a vision	
8. Self-awareness	
9. Team building	
10. Managing conflict	

Table 2 Critical Management Skills—A Sample of Studies

STUDY ❑ RESPONDENTS • FOCUS

RESULTS

❑ Luthans, Rosenkrantz, and Hennessey (1985)

- 52 managers in 3 organizations
- Participant observation of skills demonstrated by most effective versus least effective managers

Building power and influence
Communicating with outsiders
Managing conflict
Decision making

Communicating with insiders
Developing subordinates
Processing paperwork
Planning and goal setting

❑ Curtis, Winsor, and Stephens (1989)

- 428 members of the American Society of Personnel Administrators in the United States
- (1) Skills needed to obtain employment
- (2) Skills important for successful job performance
- (3) Skills needed to move up in the organization

Employment
Verbal communication
Listening
Enthusiasm
Written communication
Technical competence
Appearance

Job Success
Interpersonal skills
Verbal communication
Written communication
Persistence/determination
Enthusiasm
Technical competence

To Move Up
Ability to work well with
   others one-on-one
Ability to gather information
   and make a decision
Ability to work well in groups
Ability to listen and give counsel
Ability to give effective feedback
Ability to write effective reports
Knowledge of the job

Ability to present a good
   image for the firm
Ability to use computers
Knowledge of management
   theory
Knowledge of finance
Knowledge of marketing
Knowledge of accounting
Ability to use business
   machines

❑ Van Velsor & Britain (1995)

- Summarizes 5 previous studies of "derailment"
- 20 U.S. managers and 42 European managers
- Focus on skills causing "derailment" (the opposite of success)

Problems with interpersonal relationships
Failure to meet business objectives
Inability to build and lead a team
Inability to manage self-development or to adapt

❑ American Management Association (2000)

- 921 managers in the United States

Skill	Importance to Organizations	Managerial Competence	Gap
Customer focus	1 (4.74)	1 (3.90)	22
Ability to use information to solve problems	2 (4.64)	2 (3.71)	15
Recognizing problems and implementing solutions	3 (4.56)	8 (3.52)	7
Credibility among peers, subordinates, colleagues	4 (4.45)	3 (3.69)	18
Ability to transform words into actions	5 (4.44)	5 (3.55)	11
Listening and asking questions	6 (4.40)	13 (3.36)	3
Contributing to firm mission/objectives	7 (4.39)	4 (3.57)	16
Working in teams (cooperation/commitment)	8 (4.34)	11 (3.40)	8
Identifying opportunities for innovation	9 (4.33)	14 (3.35)	4
Setting standards for self and subordinates	10 (4.32)	7 (3.53)	9
Coaching and mentoring skills	15 (4.21)	26 (2.99)	1
Time management	12 (4.27)	25 (3.19)	2
Implementing improvements	11 (4.29)	17 (3.33)	5
Setting priorities	14 (4.24)	20 (3.32)	6

Table 2	Critical Management Skills—A Sample of Studies	
STUDY ❑ RESPONDENTS • FOCUS	**RESULTS**	
❑ Andersen Consulting (2000) • Study of Andersen partners, consultants, and client leaders	*Employee skills* Creativity Team building Resilience/flexibility Technical competence Deal with ambiguity Speed Emotional intelligence Communication skills	*Leadership attributes* Less controlling Shares authority Culturally attuned Encourages challenge Clear vision Comfortable with risk Creates a motivated business Manages intellectual diversity Entrepreneurial

hiring," or cognitive activities such as "transcending fear," skills can be consciously demonstrated, practiced, improved, or restrained by individuals themselves. Skills may certainly engage other people and require cognitive work, but they are behaviors that people can control themselves.

Third, management skills are *developable*. Performance can improve. Unlike IQ or certain personality or temperament attributes that remain relatively constant throughout life, individuals can improve their competency in skill performance through practice and feedback. Individuals can progress from less competence to more competence in management skills, and that outcome is the primary objective of this book.

Fourth, management skills are *interrelated* and *overlapping*. It is difficult to demonstrate just one skill in isolation from others. Skills are not simplistic, repetitive behaviors, but they are integrated sets of complex responses. Effective managers, in particular, must rely on combinations of skills to achieve desired results. For example, in order to effectively motivate others, skills such as supportive communication, influence, empowerment, and self-awareness may be required. Effective managers, in other words, develop a constellation of skills that overlap and support one another and that allow flexibility in managing diverse situations.

Fifth, management skills are sometimes *contradictory* or *paradoxical*. For example, the core management skills are neither all soft and humanistic in orientation nor all harddriving and directive. They are oriented neither toward teamwork and interpersonal relations exclusively nor toward individualism and technical entrepreneurship exclusively. A variety of skills are typical of the most effective managers, and some of them appear incompatible.

To illustrate, Cameron and Tschirhart (1988) assessed the skill performance of more than 500 midlevel and upper-middle managers in about 150 organizations. The most frequently mentioned 25 management skills taken from about a dozen studies in the academic literature (such as those in Table 2) were measured. Statistical analyses revealed that the skills fell into four main groups or clusters. One group of skills focused on participative and human relations skills (for example, supportive communication and team building), while another group focused on just the opposite, that is, competitiveness and control (for example, assertiveness, power, and influence skills). A third group focused on innovativeness and individual entrepreneurship (for example, creative problem solving), while a fourth group emphasized the opposite type of skills, namely, maintaining order and rationality (for example, managing time and rational decision making). One conclusion from that study was that effective managers are required to demonstrate paradoxical skills. That is, the most effective managers are both participative and hard-driving, both nurturing and competitive. They were able to be flexible and creative while also being controlled, stable, and rational (see Cameron, Quinn, DeGraff, & Thakor, 2006). Our objective in this book is to help you develop that kind of behavioral competency and complexity.

Improving Management Skills

It is a bit unnerving that while average IQ scores have increased in the population over the last half-century, social and emotional intelligence scores have actually declined. In the population in general, people are less skilled at managing themselves and managing others than they were 50 years ago (Goleman, 1998). While average IQ scores have jumped approximately 25 points, emotional intelligence scores (EQ) among young people and adults has fallen. Moreover, whereas the "technological float" has shrunk dramatically— that is, the time between the introduction of a new technology and its being copied and revised is constantly decreasing and is now measured in weeks rather than years—the "human float" has changed very little. It still takes about the same amount of time to develop behavioral skills and human competencies as it always has. No shortcuts or quick fixes have emerged, and the effort and practice that are required to become more emotionally intelligent and interpersonally skilled is substantial. Progress regarding how to cope with and manage issues relating to other people has not kept pace with technological progress, and it remains the biggest challenge for managers.

The good news is that improvement in developing management skills has been found in both students and managers who have been exposed to a curriculum such as the one advocated in *Developing Management Skills*. For example, MBA students showed improvement of from 50 to 300 percent on social skills over the course of two years by enrolling in two courses based on the approach to developing management skills presented here. A greater amount of improvement occurred among students who applied these skills to multiple aspects of their lives outside the classroom, and people who were more competent to begin with made the most progress. In addition, a cohort of 45- to 55-year-old executives produced the same results as the MBA students. That is, they also improved dramatically in their management skills even though most were already experienced in senior managerial positions (Boyatzis, 1996, 2000, 2005; Boyatzis, Cowen, & Kolb, 1995; Boyatzis, Leonard, Rhee, & Wheeler, 1996; Leonard, 1996; Rhee, 1997; Wheeler, 1999).

On the other hand, exposure to a traditional cognitive-based curriculum without exposure to management skills development does not correlate with improvements in social competence, management skills, or career success. For example, Cohen (1984) summarized the results of 108 studies of the relationship between performance in college courses (as measured by grade-point average) and subsequent life success. Life success was measured by a variety of factors, including job performance, income, promotions, personal satisfaction, eminence, and graduate degrees. The mean correlation between performance in school and performance in life in these studies was .18, and in no case did the correlation exceed .20. These low correlations suggest that school performance and successful performance in subsequent life activities are related only marginally.

The data, in other words, appear quite compelling. Attending school merely to achieve high grades in cognitive courses—while important—is not sufficient for management, career, or life success. Going into debt for a formal education or achieving an additional set of letters behind your name without also developing and improving your management skills will be an unfortunate lost opportunity. That is why we feel so strongly that in the management curriculum of universities, students should be exposed to a learning model such as the one we describe here. Our strong feelings, of course, are not based on blind optimism. Scientific evidence exists that such exposure can make a difference both to individuals and to the bottom-line performance of companies.

An Approach to Skill Development

Successful management development, of course, is more than just following a cookbook list of sequential behaviors. Developing highly competent management skills is much more complicated than developing skills such as those associated with a trade (for example, welding) or a sport (for example, shooting baskets). Management skills are: (1) linked to a more complex knowledge base than other types of skills and (2) inherently connected to interaction with other (frequently unpredictable) individuals. A standardized approach to welding or shooting free throws may be feasible, but no standardized approach to managing human beings is possible.

On the other hand, what all skills do have in common is the potential for improvement through practice. Any approach to developing management skills, therefore, must involve a heavy dose of practical application. At the same time, practice without the necessary conceptual knowledge is sterile and ignores the need for flexibility and adaptation to different situations. Therefore, developing competencies in management skills is inherently tied to both conceptual learning and behavioral practice.

The method that has been found to be most successful in helping individuals develop management skills is based on social learning theory (Bandura, 1977; Boyatzis et al., 1995; Davis & Luthans, 1980). This approach marries rigorous conceptual knowledge with opportunities to practice and apply observable behaviors. It relies on cognitive work as well as behavioral work. Variations on this general approach have been used widely in on-the-job supervisory training programs, and they are common in executive education programs and corporate universities—less so in business schools.

This learning model, as originally formulated, consisted of four steps: (1) the presentation of behavioral principles or action guidelines, generally using traditional instruction methods; (2) demonstration of the principles by means of cases, films, scripts, or incidents; (3) opportunities to practice the principles through role plays or exercises; and (4) feedback on performance from peers, instructors, or experts.

Our own experience in teaching complex management skills, as well as recent research on management skills development among MBA students (e.g., Boyatzis et al., 1995; Vance, 1993) has convinced us that three important modifications are necessary in order for this model to be most effective. First, the behavioral principles must be grounded in social science theory and in reliable research results. Common sense generalizations and panacea-like prescriptions appear regularly in the popular management literature. To ensure the validity of the behavioral guidelines being prescribed, the learning approach must include scientifically based knowledge about the effects of the management principles being presented.

Second, individuals must be aware of their current level of skill competency and be motivated to improve upon that level in order to benefit from the model. Most people receive very little feedback about their current level of skill competency. Most organizations provide some kind of annual or semiannual evaluation (for example, course grades in school or performance appraisal interviews in firms), but these evaluations are almost always infrequent and narrow in scope, and they fail to assess performance in most critical skill areas. To help a person understand what skills to improve and why, therefore, an assessment activity must be part of the model. In addition, most people find change uncomfortable and therefore avoid taking the risk to develop new behavior patterns. An assessment activity in the learning model helps encourage these people to change by illuminating their strengths and weaknesses. People then know where weaknesses lie and what things need to be improved. Assessment activities generally take the form of self-evaluation instruments, case studies, or problems that help highlight personal strengths and weaknesses in a particular skill area.

Third, an application component is needed in the learning model. Most management skill training takes place in a classroom setting where feedback is immediate, and it is relatively safe to try out new behaviors and make mistakes. Therefore, transferring learning to an actual job setting is often problematic. Application exercises help to apply classroom learning to examples from the real world of management. Application exercises often take the form of an outside-of-class intervention, a consulting assignment, self-analysis through journal writing, or a problem-centered intervention, which the student then analyzes to determine its degree of success or failure.

In summary, evidence suggests that a five-step learning model is most effective for helping individuals develop management skills (see Cameron & Whetten, 1984; Kolb, 1984; Vance, 1993; Whetten & Cameron, 1983). Table 3 outlines such a model. Step 1 involves the *assessment* of current levels of skill competency and knowledge of the behavioral principles. Step 2 consists of the presentation of validated, scientifically based *principles and guidelines* for effective skill performance. Step 3 is an *analysis* step in which models or cases are made available in order to analyze behavioral principles in real organizational settings. This step also helps demonstrate how the behavioral guidelines can be adapted to different personal styles and circumstances. Step 4 consists of *practice* exercises in which experimentation can occur and immediate feedback can be received in a relatively safe environment. Step 5, finally, is the *application* of the skill to a real-life setting outside the classroom with follow-up analysis of the relative success of that application.

Research on the effectiveness of training programs using this general learning model has shown that it produces results superior to those based on more traditional lecture-discussion-case method approaches (Boyatzis et al., 1995; Burnaska, 1976; Kolb, 1984; Latham & Saari, 1979; Moses & Ritchie, 1976; Porras & Anderson, 1981; Smith, 1976; Vance, 1993). In addition, evidence suggests that management skill training can have significant impact on the bottom-line performance of a firm. The U.S. Postal Service completed a study a few years ago in which 49 of the largest 100 post offices in America were evaluated. An important question in the study was, "How can we make post offices more effective?" Productivity and service quality were both monitored over a period of five years. The two major factors that had impact on these effectiveness measures were (1) degree of automation, and (2) investment in training. Two kinds of training were provided: technical training (operating and maintaining the equipment) and management training (developing management skills). The study found that management training was more important than technical training in accounting for improved productivity and service in the post offices, and both kinds of training were more important than having up-to-date

Table 3	A Model for Developing Management Skills	
Components	**Contents**	**Objectives**
1. Skill assessment	Survey instruments Role plays	Assess current level of skill competence and knowledge; create readiness to change.
2. Skill learning	Written text Behavioral guidelines	Teach correct principles and present a rationale for behavioral guidelines.
3. Skill analysis	Cases	Provide examples of appropriate and inappropriate skill performance. Analyze behavioral principles and reasons they work.
4. Skill practice	Exercises Simulations Role plays	Practice behavioral guidelines. Adapt principles to personal style. Receive feedback and assistance.
5. Skill application	Assignments (behavioral and written)	Transfer classroom learning to real-life situations. Foster ongoing personal development.

equipment in the post office. Low-tech offices outperformed high-tech offices when managers were provided with management skill training. In short, its five-year study convinced the U.S. Postal Service that helping employees to develop management skills was the best way to improve organizational effectiveness (Cameron & Ulrich, 1986).

This is consistent with the conclusion drawn by Eric Greenberg, Director of Surveys for the American Management Association, upon summarizing the lessons learned from years of surveys of American managers:

> *Where companies increased their training activity, the chances were much, much better that they were going to increase their operating profits and that they were going to increase their shareholder value. Product quality, market share, and productivity all tend to rise as training budgets go up. Companies that don't make the investment are apt to see disappointing results. (Greenberg, 1999)*

More than thirty years ago, Mintzberg (1975) made a similar point about the curriculum needed in business schools. Things have not changed.

> *Management schools will begin the serious training of managers when skill training takes its place next to cognitive learning. Cognitive learning is detached and informational, like reading a book or listening to a lecture. No doubt much important cognitive material must be assimilated by the manager-to-be. But cognitive learning no more makes a manager than it does a swimmer. The latter will drown the first time he jumps into the water if his coach never takes him out of the lecture hall, gets him wet, and gives him feedback on his performance. Our management schools need to identify the skills managers use, select students who show potential in these skills, put the students into situations where these skills can be practiced, and then give them systematic feedback on their performance. (p. 60)*

A senior executive in a major consulting firm similarly observed:

> *The higher up the organization you go, the less relevant technical knowledge becomes. It is important for your first couple of promotions, but after that, people skills are what count.*

A recent graduate from a Big Ten management school also reported:

> *I can't believe it. I went for my second interview with a company last week, and I spent the first half-day participating in simulation exercises with ten other job candidates. They videotaped me playing the role of a salesman handling an irate customer, a new director of personnel putting down a revolt by the "old guard," and a plant manager trying to convince people of the need to install a radically new production process. Boy, was I unprepared for that!*

The message behind these personal observations is clear: from almost every perspective, competence in personal, interpersonal, and group skills is a critical prerequisite for success in management. Strong analytical and quantitative skills are important, but they are not sufficient. Successful managers must be able to work effectively with people. Unfortunately, interpersonal and management skills have not always been a high priority for business school students and aspiring executives. In a recent survey of 110 *Fortune* 500 CEOs, 87 percent were satisfied with the level of competence and analytic skills of business school graduates, 68 percent were satisfied with conceptual skills of graduates, but only 43 percent of the CEOs were satisfied with graduates' management skills, and only 28 percent were satisfied with their interpersonal skills and EQ!

To assist you in improving your own management skills, this book emphasizes practicing management skills, rather than just reading about them. We have organized the book with this specific approach in mind.

Leadership and Management

Before outlining the organization of this book, we want to discuss briefly the place of leadership in this volume. Some writers have differentiated between the concepts of "leadership" and "management" (Bass, 1990; Katzenbach, 1995; Nair, 1994; Quinn, 2000; Tichy, 1999). Some have wondered why we concentrate on "management" skills instead of "leadership" skills in this book. We have also been asked by professors, business executives, and students why we have not either changed the title of the book to *Developing Leadership Skills*, or at least included one chapter on leadership in this volume. These queries and suggestions are important and have motivated us to clarify at the outset of the book what we mean by management, and why we believe our focus on management skills lies at the heart of leadership as typically defined.

One of the most popular models of leadership is based on the "Competing Values Framework," an organizing framework for leadership and managerial skills. It was developed by examining the criteria used to evaluate organizational and managerial performance (Cameron et al., 2006; Quinn & Rohrbaugh, 1983). Extensive research has been conducted on this framework over the past two decades, and a brief explanation will help clarify the relationship between management and leadership skills. You should be aware that this framework has been used on several continents to help managers and organizations improve their effectiveness, and a database of more than 80,000 managers has now been compiled (Cameron & Quinn, 2006). That research has shown that leadership and management skills fall into four clusters or categories as illustrated in Figure 1. In order to be an effective manager, in other words, individuals must be competent in: (1) clan skills, or a

| Figure 1 | Leadership and Management Skills Organized by the Competing Values Framework |

Flexibility / Change

CLAN SKILLS—COLLABORATE

Communicating Supportively
Building Teams and Teamwork
Empowering

ADHOCRACY SKILLS—CREATE

Solving Problems Creatively
Leading Positive Change
Fostering Innovation

Internal Maintenance - - - - - - - - - - - - - - - - - - - **External Positioning**

HIERARCHY SKILLS—CONTROL

Managing Personal Stress
Managing Time
Maintaining Self-Awareness
Analytical Problem Solving

MARKET SKILLS—COMPLETE

Motivating Others
Gaining Power and Influence
Managing Conflict

Stability / Control

focus on collaboration; (2) adhocracy skills, or a focus on creation; (3) market skills, or a focus on competition; and (4) hierarchy skills, or a focus on control.

Clan skills include those required to build effective interpersonal relationships and develop others (e.g., building teamwork, communicating supportively). Adhocracy skills include those required to manage the future, innovate, and promote change (e.g., solving problems creatively, articulating an energizing vision). Market skills include those required to compete effectively and manage external relationships (e.g., motivating others, using power and influence). Hierarchy skills include those required to maintain control and stability (e.g., managing personal stress and time, solving problems rationally) (see Cameron & Quinn, 2006).

In Figure 1, the two top quadrants in the Competing Values Framework—clan and adhocracy—are usually associated with leadership. The two bottom quadrants—market and hierarchy—are usually associated with management. In other words, traditionally, leadership has been used to describe what individuals do under conditions of change. When organizations are dynamic and undergoing transformation, people at the top are expected to exhibit leadership (i.e., pay attention to clan and adhocracy issues). Management, on the other hand, has traditionally been used to describe what executives do under conditions of stability. Thus, management has been linked with the status quo (i.e., pay attention to market and hierarchy issues). In addition, leadership has sometimes been defined as "doing the right things," whereas management has been defined as "doing things right." Leaders have been said to focus on setting the direction, articulating a vision, transforming individuals and organizations, and creating something new. Managers have been said to focus on monitoring, directing, and refining current performance. Leadership has been equated with dynamism, vibrancy, and charisma; management with hierarchy, equilibrium, and control.

However, the recent research is clear that such distinctions between leadership and management, which may have been appropriate in previous decades, are no longer useful (Quinn, 2000; Tichy, 1993, 1999). Managers cannot be successful without being good leaders, and leaders cannot be successful without being good managers. No longer do organizations and individuals have the luxury of holding on to the status quo; worrying about doing things right but failing to do the right things; keeping the system stable instead of leading change and improvement; monitoring current performance instead of formulating a vision of the future; concentrating on equilibrium and control instead of vibrancy and charisma. Effective management and leadership are inseparable. The skills required to do one are also required of the other. No organization in a postindustrial, hyperturbulent, twenty-first-century environment will survive without executives capable of providing both management and leadership. Leading change and managing stability, establishing vision and accomplishing objectives, breaking the rules and monitoring conformance, although paradoxical, all are required to be successful.

Figure 2 illustrates one major reason for this assertion. By staying the same, we tend to get worse. Because our circumstances are constantly changing and expectations for performance are continually escalating, the traditional definition of management is outmoded and irrelevant today. Effective managers and leaders do much the same things in dealing effectively with constant change and constant stability.

All of us, in other words, need to develop competencies that will enhance our ability to be both leaders and managers. The specific skills in this book represent all four quadrants in the Competing Values Framework of leadership. They serve as the foundation for effective management and for effective leadership. The book could appropriately include the word "leadership" in the title, therefore, based on the skills being covered. *The skills contained in this book cover both the management and the leadership ground.* We have chosen, appropriately or not, to use the label "management skills" to subsume the skills associated with leadership as well as with management.

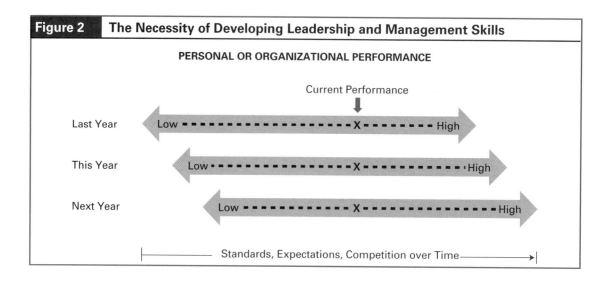

Figure 2 The Necessity of Developing Leadership and Management Skills

Contents of the Book

Again, this book focuses on the skills that research has identified as critically important for successful management and leadership. Part I contains three chapters on personal skills: Developing Self-Awareness, Managing Personal Stress, and Solving Problems Analytically and Creatively. These skills focus on issues that may not involve other people but instead relate to the management of the self—hence they are called personal skills. Each chapter, however, really includes a cluster of related behaviors, not just one single, simple skill. These clusters of interrelated behaviors comprise the overall management skill indicated in the chapter's title. Figure 3 also points out that each skill cluster is related to and overlaps with other personal management skills, so each relies at least partially on the others to be performed successfully.

Part II focuses on interpersonal skills: Building Relationships by Communicating Supportively, Gaining Power and Influence, Motivating Others, and Managing Conflict. These skills focus primarily on issues that arise in your interactions with other people. Overlap exists among these skills, of course, so that you must rely on parts of many skill areas in order to perform any one skill effectively.

Part III includes three chapters on group skills: Empowering and Delegating, Building Effective Teams and Teamwork, and Leading Positive Change. These skills focus on key issues that arise when you are involved with groups of people either as a leader or as a member of the group. As with all the skills in the book, overlap occurs among the group skills as well as with the personal and interpersonal skills. In other words, as you progress from personal to interpersonal to group skills, the core competencies developed in the previous skill area help support successful performance of the new skill area.

In addition to the ten core management skills in Parts I, II, and III, the supplemental Part IV chapters contain three additional communications skills: Making Oral and Written Presentations, Conducting Interviews, and Conducting Meetings. These supplements cover specialized communication skills that are especially relevant for students who have had little managerial experience or skill training. These supplements foster skill development needed to implement assignments typically included in a management skill-building course. Writing reports, giving class presentations, interviewing managers, and conducting group meetings are all prerequisites for building skills in the core management skill areas, so we have provided material on these three topics that students will find helpful.

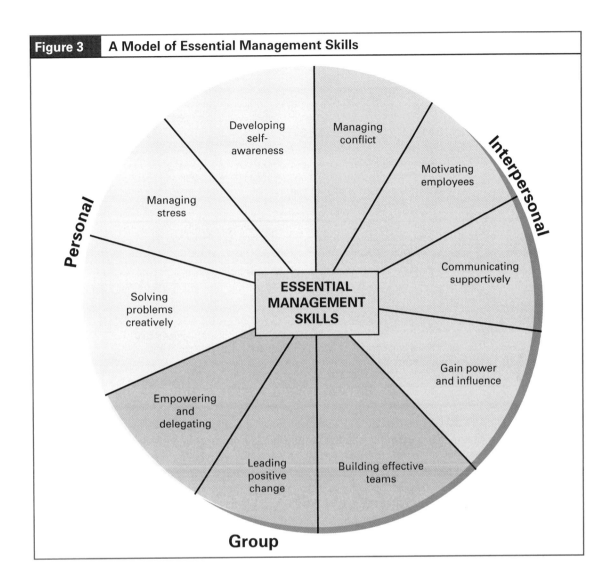

Figure 3 | **A Model of Essential Management Skills**

ESSENTIAL MANAGEMENT SKILLS

Personal

- Developing self-awareness
- Managing stress
- Solving problems creatively

Interpersonal

- Managing conflict
- Motivating employees
- Communicating supportively
- Gain power and influence

Group

- Empowering and delegating
- Leading positive change
- Building effective teams

Appendix I contains a glossary of key terms in the text; and Appendix II lists references for excerpted material in the book.

Organization of the Book

Each chapter is organized on the basis of the learning model summarized in Table 4. Each chapter begins with *Skill Assessment* instruments. Their purpose is to highlight areas of personal competence as well as areas needing improvement in both knowledge and performance. As you complete the instruments in the Skill Assessment section, you will discover areas in which you will want to establish personal learning goals, and areas in which your competency is already well developed. As pointed out earlier, however, research has demonstrated that the most competent managers tend to progress the most when engaging in skill development exercises, so don't dismiss a skill just because you feel that it is an area of strength. We encourage you to take time to complete these assessment instruments. You will be surprised with what you learn if you complete them honestly and as accurately as you can.

Table 4	The Organization of Each Chapter
SECTION	**CONTENTS**
Skill Assessment	Instruments designed to identify your current level of skill competency, your styles, and/or key dimensions of the skill. These instruments can be used to identify individual differences, issues surrounding diversity, and areas for personal improvement plans.
Skill Learning	Behavioral guidelines and key principles associated with the skill are explained. Scientific research is used as the basis for prescribed skill performance. Clarifying how to successfully develop and perform the skill is the purpose of this section.
Skill Analysis	Cases and examples are presented in order to provide examples of successful and unsuccessful skill performance. Analytic problem solving is facilitated as recommendations are made for what the key issues are, how performance might be modified, and why success was achieved.
Skill Practice	Exercises and role plays make it possible for individuals to actually practice the skill. Feedback from peers and the instructor will facilitate improvement of the skill in a setting where failure is not costly.
Skill Application	Suggested assignments are provided so that the skill can be applied in a real-life setting. A feedback mechanism is also suggested so that individuals analyze their own success in applying the skill outside the classroom. Improvement plans should always be associated with the application exercises.

Second, an explanation of the key behavioral guidelines, as well as a rationale for why these guidelines work, is found in the *Skill Learning* section of each chapter. This section explains the core behavioral principles associated with each skill. We present a research-based model of each skill, along with evidence from research that the principles identified are effective in practice. Our objective is to provide a sound rationale for the action guidelines summarized at the end of the section. We have not relied on popular anecdotes or stories from the popular press in presenting these guidelines and principles. Instead, we rely on scientific research that identifies what behaviors must be performed in order to foster effective outcomes.

In the *Skill Analysis* section, you will find brief case histories that illustrate both effective and ineffective applications of the behavioral principles. The purpose of this section is to bridge the gap between intellectual understanding and behavioral application. Critiquing a manager's performance in a real-life case enhances your understanding of the skill learning material. Each case provides a model of effective or ineffective performance and helps identify ways that the skill can be adapted to your personal style. In analyzing these cases, focus less on trying to find a "right" answer and more on determining how you might behave in similar circumstances.

The *Skill Practice* section provides exercises, problems, and role-play assignments. The goal of this section is to provide opportunities to practice the behavioral guidelines in simulated managerial situations and to receive feedback from peers and instructors. Practicing these managerial skills in a classroom setting is not only safer and less costly than in a real-life management job, but others' observation and feedback can be more precise and more timely as well. Many of these types of exercises can seem "gamey" or superficial, of course, unless you take them seriously as ways to improve your skill performance. We encourage you to use the feedback of others to critique your performance and help you find ways to enhance your skill competencies.

The last section of each chapter is *Skill Application*. It contains a form to help you generate your own improvement agenda, as well as assignments and ideas for applying the skill in an out-of-class situation. The purpose of these assignments is to help you transfer behavioral guidelines into everyday practice. You may be directed to teach the skill to someone else, consult with another manager to help resolve a relevant problem, or apply the skill in an organization or family.

Practice and Application

The philosophy of this book is that improvement in management skills is primarily the learner's responsibility. If the application of the principles covered in this book is not conscientiously applied outside the classroom, little or no progress can be achieved. Our intention, therefore, is to have the course carry over into the life activities of learners. Effectiveness in management is no different from effectiveness in most other human enterprises. It requires the same kinds of skills to live a productive and successful life as it does to manage people effectively. That is why, even though some users of this book may not presently be managers of other employees—and indeed may never become managers—they should neither dismiss these skills as irrelevant nor wait until they become managers before attempting to practice them.

Psychological research has confirmed that when we are forced to perform under stress, we rely on what is called a "dominant response pattern" (Staw, Sandelands, & Dutton, 1981; Weick, 1995). That is, we rely on the behavior patterns that are most deeply ingrained in our response repertoire. For example, if a person who has been accustomed to responding to conflict combatively—but who has recently begun practicing a more supportive response pattern—is faced with an intense, emotional confrontation, that person may begin by reacting supportively. But as pressure mounts, he or she is likely to revert to the more practiced, combative style. That is why, it is said, that people always curse in their native language. Stress causes us to revert to our fundamental, most reinforced behaviors.

Thus it is important that learners not make the mistake of thinking they can delay applying skill training until they become managers. When problems and conflicts occur then, it is too late to change behaviors to handle issues effectively. We encourage you, therefore, to practice and apply the skills discussed in this book to part-time jobs, friendships, student organizations, families, church groups, and so forth. If you are in a managerial role, you will want to use the guidelines provided here with your coworkers, managers, subordinates, and customers. With conscientious practice, following the behavioral guidelines will become second nature.

A second reason that nonmanagers should not delay the application of management skills is that we all learn faster and remember better that which we experience emotionally as well as intellectually. That is, people learn best the things that affect them personally, and they feel affected by something if they see an immediate effect on their lives. For example, we can more quickly acquire a working knowledge of a foreign language and retain it longer if we spend a summer living in a country where the language is spoken than if we merely take a language course in our own country. Simply stated, application is a crucial component of the skill improvement process, but it generally takes extra effort and ingenuity to make application exercises effective and worthwhile. We encourage you to put that extra effort into improving your management skills.

Diversity and Individual Differences

One reason developing management skills is difficult is because all of us possess our own unique styles, personalities, and inclinations. We all know that everyone doesn't react in the same way to similar circumstances. We can freely choose to behave differently than expected or than we did in the past. It is impossible, therefore, to manage each relationship in exactly the same way, or even to behave the same way from one encounter to the next. Sensitivity to individual differences is an important part of an effective manager's repertoire.

A great deal of research has been conducted on cultural differences, gender differences, ethnic differences, and age differences in organizations (e.g., Cox, 1994; Cox & Beal, 1997). While we will not summarize that extensive research, we do want to highlight the importance of being sensitive to individuality. Two kinds of sensitivities are necessary: one to the uniqueness displayed by each person, and the other to distinctive but general patterns of behavior that characterize groups of people. For example, it is essential that effective managers not only become aware of, but also value and capitalize on the differences that characterize people with whom they work. In this book we will encourage you to develop sensitivity to the diversity that people display as they interact with you. In addition, you will also become skilled at diagnosing certain generalized patterns of behavior among people with different experiences, nationalities, genders, ethnic backgrounds, and ages. These generalized patterns can be used inappropriately to stereotype or categorize people, of course, and that may lead to deterioration in interpersonal sensitivity and emotional intelligence. On the other hand, being aware of national, cultural, ethnic, gender, or age differences can also be extremely useful to you as you engage in managerial roles.

We have included in each chapter a framework for diagnosing individual differences across cultures and summaries of some extensive crossnational research by Trompenaars and Hampden-Turner (1998). We include this framework to assist you in diagnosing some key differences that affect behavior. Knowing that the general tendency of people is to fear or oppose those who are different from them, our main objective in providing this information is to help us all better understand and appreciate differences. We don't emphasize so much *managing diversity* as we do *diagnosing individual differences* so they can be valued, understood, and appreciated.

In Chapter 1, Developing Self-Awareness, we explain the Trompenaars model, which relies on seven dimensions found to differ across national and cultural boundaries. These dimensions have been found to be very helpful in assisting people to understand key differences in others. They are: universalism versus particularism, individualism versus communitarianism, specificity versus diffuseness, neutral versus affective, achievement versus ascription oriented, internal versus external, and past versus present versus future time emphasis. These dimensions will help you to remain sensitive to the personal variations that may require alternation of some of the ways in which you practice core management skills. Whereas the behavioral principles upon which the management skills are based are applicable across cultures, genders, ethnic groups, and age cohorts, important nuances may be required of you as you practice among people characterized by these differences. Women may not behave the same as men. Japanese colleagues may not respond the same as German colleagues. Individuals in their sixties may not see the world the same as someone in their twenties. Stereotyping based on these categories, of course, is also dangerous and damaging, so being sensitive to and valuing individual differences is the key.

This means that you may want to pay special attention to the results of colleagues' Skill Assessment responses. You can identify the different patterns that arise among your own colleagues as you work your way through the book. Do you detect any general differences among men and women, among old and young, among different nationalities, among ethnic groups, among those with managerial experience and those without? People with high degrees of emotional intelligence have developed the ability to sense and empathize with the differences that are typical of different groups of people. We hope you will improve in this ability as well. Each of the sections of the chapters—Assessment, Learning, Analysis, Practice, and Application—can be useful to you in gaining insight into individual differences.

Summary

In sum, *Developing Management Skills* is not intended just for individuals who plan to enter managerial positions or who currently manage organizations. It is meant to help you better manage many aspects of your life and relationships. It is intended to help you actually change your behavior, to improve your competence, and to be more savvy in your relationships with different kinds of people. It is intended to improve your social and emotional intelligence. John Holt (1964) succinctly summarized our intention by equating management skill to intelligence:

> *When we talk about intelligence, we do not mean the ability to get a good score on a certain kind of test or even the ability to do well in school; these are at best only indicators of something larger, deeper, and far more important. By intelligence we mean a style of life, a way of behaving in various situations. The true test of intelligence is not how much we know how to do, but how we behave when we don't know what to do. (p. 165)*

Fostering the development of such intelligence is the goal of *Developing Management Skills*.

Diagnostic Survey and Exercises

Personal Assessment of Management Skills (PAMS)

Step 1: To get an overall profile of your level of skill competence, respond to the following statements using the rating scale below. Please rate your behavior as it is, not as you would like it to be. If you have not engaged in a specific activity, answer according to how you think you would behave based on your experience in similar activities. Be realistic; this instrument is designed to help you tailor your learning to your specific needs. After you have completed the survey, the scoring key at the end of the chapter will help you generate an overall profile of your management skill strengths and weaknesses.

Step 2: Get copies of the Associates' version of this instrument from your instructor. An alternate version has been provided in the Instructor's Manual that uses "he" or "she" instead of "I" in the questions. Give copies to at least three other people who know you well or who have observed you in a situation in which you have had to lead or manage others. Those people should complete the instrument by rating your behavior. Bring the completed surveys back to class and compare: (1) your own ratings to your associates' ratings, (2) your associates' ratings to the ratings received by others in the class, and (3) the ratings you received to those of a national norm group.

Subsections of this instrument appear in each chapter throughout the book.

Rating Scale

1 Strongly disagree

2 Disagree

3 Slightly disagree

4 Slightly agree

5 Agree

6 Strongly agree

In regard to my level of self-knowledge:

_____ 1. I seek information about my strengths and weaknesses from others as a basis for self-improvement.

_____ 2. In order to improve, I am willing to be self-disclosing to others (that is, to share my beliefs and feelings).

_____ 3. I am very much aware of my preferred style in gathering information and making decisions.

_____ 4. I have a good sense of how I cope with situations that are ambiguous and uncertain.

_____ 5. I have a well-developed set of personal standards and principles that guide my behavior.

When faced with stressful or time-pressured situations:

_____ 6. I use effective time-management methods such as keeping track of my time, making to-do lists, and prioritizing tasks.

_____ 7. I frequently affirm my priorities so that less important things don't drive out more important things.

_____ 8. I maintain a program of regular exercise for fitness.

_____ 9. I maintain an open, trusting relationship with someone with whom I can share my frustrations.

_____ 10. I know and practice several temporary relaxation techniques such as deep breathing and muscle relaxation.

_____ 11. I maintain balance in my life by pursuing a variety of interests outside of work.

When I approach a typical, routine problem:

_____ 12. I state clearly and explicitly what the problem is. I avoid trying to solve it until I have defined it.

_____ 13. I always generate more than one alternative solution to the problem, instead of identifying only one obvious solution.

_____ 14. I keep steps in the problem-solving process distinct; that is, I define the problem before proposing alternative solutions, and I generate alternatives before selecting a single solution.

When faced with a complex or difficult problem that does not have an easy solution:

_____ 15. I try out several definitions of the problem. I don't limit myself to just one way to define it.

_____ 16. I try to unfreeze my thinking by asking lots of questions about the nature of the problem before considering ways to solve it.

_____ 17. I try to think about the problem from both the left (logical) side of my brain and the right (intuitive) side of my brain.

_____ 18. I do not evaluate the merits of an alternative solution to the problem before I have generated a list of alternatives. That is, I avoid deciding on a solution until I have developed many possible solutions.

_____ 19. I have some specific techniques that I use to help develop creative and innovative solutions to problems.

When trying to foster more creativity and innovation among those with whom I work:

_____ 20. I make sure there are divergent points of view represented or expressed in every complex problem-solving situation.

_____ 21. I try to acquire information from individuals outside the problem-solving group who will be affected by the decision, mainly to determine their preferences and expectations.

_____ 22. I try to provide recognition not only to those who come up with creative ideas (the idea champions) but also to those who support others' ideas (supporters) and who provide resources to implement them (orchestrators).

_____ 23. I encourage informed rule-breaking in pursuit of creative solutions.

In situations where I have to provide negative feedback or offer corrective advice:

_____ 24. I am able to help others recognize and define their own problems when I counsel them.

_____ 25. I am clear about when I should coach someone and when I should provide counseling instead.

_____ 26. When I give feedback to others, I avoid referring to personal characteristics and focus on problems or solutions instead.

_____ 27. When I try to correct someone's behavior, our relationship is almost always strengthened.

_____ 28. I am descriptive in giving negative feedback to others. That is, I objectively describe events, their consequences, and my feelings about them.

_____ 29. I take responsibility for my statements and point of view by using, for example, "I have decided" instead of "They have decided."

_____ 30. I strive to identify some area of agreement in a discussion with someone who has a different point of view.

_____ 31. I don't talk down to those who have less power or less information than I.

_____ 32. When discussing someone's problem, I usually respond with a reply that indicates understanding rather than advice.

In a situation where it is important to obtain more power:

_____ 33. I always put forth more effort and take more initiative than expected in my work.

_____ 34. I am continually upgrading my skills and knowledge.

_____ 35. I strongly support organizational ceremonial events and activities.

_____ 36. I form a broad network of relationships with people throughout the organization at all levels.

_____ 37. In my work I consistently strive to generate new ideas, initiate new activities, and minimize routine tasks.

_____ 38. I consistently send personal notes to others when they accomplish something significant or when I pass along important information to them.

_____ 39. I refuse to bargain with individuals who use high-pressure negotiation tactics.

_____ 40. I always avoid using threats or demands to impose my will on others.

When another person needs to be motivated:

_____ 41. I always determine if the person has the necessary resources and support to succeed in a task.

_____ 42. I use a variety of rewards to reinforce exceptional performances.

_____ 43. I design task assignments to make them interesting and challenging.

_____ 44. I make sure the person gets timely feedback from those affected by task performance.

_____ 45. I always help the person establish performance goals that are challenging, specific, and time bound.

_____ 46. Only as a last resort do I attempt to reassign or release a poorly performing individual.

_____ 47. I consistently discipline when effort is below expectations and capabilities.

_____ 48. I make sure that people feel fairly and equitably treated.

_____ 49. I provide immediate compliments and other forms of recognition for meaningful accomplishments.

When I see someone doing something that needs correcting:

_____ 50. I avoid making personal accusations and attributing self-serving motives to the other person.

_____ 51. I encourage two-way interaction by inviting the respondent to express his or her perspective and to ask questions.

_____ 52. I make a specific request, detailing a more acceptable option.

When someone complains about something I've done:

_____ 53. I show genuine concern and interest, even when I disagree.

_____ 54. I seek additional information by asking questions that provide specific and descriptive information.

_____ 55. I ask the other person to suggest more acceptable behaviors.

When two people are in conflict and I am the mediator:

_____ 56. I do not take sides but remain neutral.

_____ 57. I help the parties generate multiple alternatives.

_____ 58. I help the parties find areas on which they agree.

In situations where I have an opportunity to engage people in accomplishing work:

_____ 59. I help people feel competent in their work by recognizing and celebrating their small successes.

_____ 60. I provide regular feedback and needed support.

_____ 61. I try to provide all the information that people need to accomplish their tasks.

_____ 62. I highlight the important impact that a person's work will have.

When delegating work to others:

_____ 63. I specify clearly the results I desire.

_____ 64. I specify clearly the level of initiative I want others to take (for example, wait for directions, do part of the task and then report, do the whole task and then report, and so forth).

_____ 65. I allow participation by those accepting assignments regarding when and how work will be done.

_____ 66. I avoid upward delegation by asking people to recommend solutions, rather than merely asking for advice or answers, when a problem is encountered.

_____ 67. I follow up and maintain accountability for delegated tasks on a regular basis.

When I am in the role of leader in a team:

_____ 68. I know how to establish credibility and influence among team members.

_____ 69. I am clear and consistent about what I want to achieve.

_____ 70. I build a common base of agreement in the team before moving forward with task accomplishment.

_____ 71. I articulate a clear, motivating vision of what the team can achieve along with specific short-term goals.

When I am in the role of team member:

_____ 72. I know a variety of ways to facilitate task accomplishment in the team.

_____ 73. I know a variety of ways to help build strong relationships and cohesion among team members.

When I desire to make my team perform well, regardless of whether I am a leader or member:

_____ 74. I am knowledgeable about the different stages of team development experienced by most teams.

_____ 75. I help the team avoid groupthink by making sure that sufficient diversity of opinions is expressed in the team.

_____ 76. I can diagnose and capitalize on my team's core competencies, or unique strengths.

_____ 77. I encourage the team to achieve dramatic breakthrough innovations as well as small continuous improvements.

When I am in a position to lead change:

_____ 78. I create positive energy in others when I interact with them.

_____ 79. I emphasize a higher purpose or meaning associated with the change I am leading.

_____ 80. I express gratitude frequently and conspicuously, even for small acts.

_____ 81. I emphasize building on strengths, not just overcoming weaknesses.

_____ 82. I use a lot more positive comments than negative comments.

_____ 83. When I communicate a vision, I capture people's hearts as well as their heads.

_____ 84. I know how to get people to commit to my vision of positive change.

What Does It Take to Be an Effective Manager?

The purpose of this exercise is to help you get a firsthand picture of the role of a manager and the skills required to perform that job successfully.

Your assignment is to interview at least three managers who are employed full-time. You should use the questions below in your interviews, plus use others that you think might help you identify effective management skills. The purpose of these interviews is to give you a chance to learn about critical managerial skills from those who have to use them.

Please treat the interviews as confidential. The names of the individuals do not matter—only their opinions, perceptions, and behaviors. Assure the managers that no one will be able to identify them from their responses. Keep written notes of your interviews. These notes should be as detailed as possible so you can reconstruct the interviews later. Be sure to keep a record of each person's job title and a brief description of his or her organization.

1. Please describe a typical day at work. What do you do all day?

2. What are the most critical problems you face as a manager?

3. What are the most critical skills needed to be a successful manager in your line of work?

4. What are the major reasons managers fail in positions like yours?

5. What are the outstanding skills or abilities of other effective managers you have known?

6. If you had to train someone to replace you in your current job, what key abilities would you focus on?

7. On a scale of 1 (very rarely) to 5 (constantly), can you rate the extent to which you use the following skills or behaviors during your workday?

_____ Managing personal time and stress	_____ Fostering continuous improvement and quality
_____ Facilitating group decision making	_____ Making analytical decisions
_____ Creative problem solving	_____ Using interpersonal communication skills
_____ Articulating an energizing vision	_____ Motivating others
_____ Managing conflict	_____ Capitalizing on your self-awareness
_____ Gaining and using power	_____ Facilitating organizational change
_____ Delegating	_____ Setting specific goals and targets
_____ Active listening	_____ Empowering others
_____ Holding interviews	_____ Giving speeches or presentations
_____ Building teams and teamwork	_____ Defining and/or solving complex problems
_____ Conducting meetings	_____ Negotiating

SSS Software In-Basket Exercise

NOTE: *The SSS Software exercise is used with permission. Copyright © 1995 by Susan Schor, Joseph Seltzer, and James Smither. All rights reserved.*

One way to assess your own strengths and weaknesses in management skills is to engage in an actual managerial work experience. The following exercise gives you a realistic glimpse of the tasks faced regularly by practicing managers. Complete the exercise, and then compare your own decisions and actions with those of classmates.

SSS Software designs and develops customized software for businesses. It also integrates this software with the customer's existing systems and provides system maintenance. SSS Software has customers in the following industries: airlines, automotive, finance/banking, health/hospital, consumer products, electronics, and government. The company has also begun to generate important international clients. These include the European Airbus consortium and a consortium of banks and financial firms based in Kenya.

SSS Software has grown rapidly since its inception eight years ago. Its revenue, net income, and earnings per share have all been above the industry average for the past several years. However, competition in this technologically sophisticated field has grown very rapidly. Recently, it has become more difficult to compete for major contracts. Moreover, although SSS Software's revenue and net income continue to grow, the rate of growth declined during the last fiscal year.

SSS Software's 250 employees are divided into several operating divisions with employees at four levels: Nonmanagement, Technical/Professional, Managerial, and Executive. Nonmanagement employees take care of the clerical and facilities support functions. The Technical/Professional staff performs the core technical work for the firm. Most Managerial employees are group managers who supervise a team of Technical/Professional employees working on a project for a particular customer. Staff who work in specialized areas such as finance, accounting, human resources, nursing, and law are also considered Managerial employees. The Executive level includes the 12 highest-ranking employees at SSS Software. An organization chart in Figure 4 illustrates SSS Software's structure. There is also an Employee Classification Report that lists the number of employees at each level of the organization.

In this exercise, you will play the role of Chris Perillo, Vice President of Operations for Health and Financial Services. You learned last Wednesday, October 13, that your predecessor, Michael Grant, had resigned and gone to Universal Business Solutions, Inc. You were offered his former job, and you accepted it. Previously, you were the Group Manager for a team of 15 software developers assigned to work on the Airbus consortium project in the Airline Services Division. You spent all of Thursday, Friday, and most of the weekend finishing up parts of the project, briefing your successor, and preparing for an interim report you will deliver in Paris on October 21.

It is now 7:00 A.M. Monday and you are in your new office. You have arrived at work early so you can spend the next two hours reviewing material in your in-basket (including some memos and messages to Michael Grant), as well as your voice mail and e-mail. Your daily planning book indicates that you have no appointments today or tomorrow but will have to catch a plane for Paris early Wednesday morning. You have a full schedule for the remainder of the week and all of next week.

Assignment

During the next two hours, review all the material in your in-basket, as well as your voice mail and e-mail. Take only two hours. Using the response form below as a model, indicate how you want to respond to each item (that is, via letter/memo, e-mail, phone/voice mail, or personal meeting). If you decide not to respond to an item, check "no response"

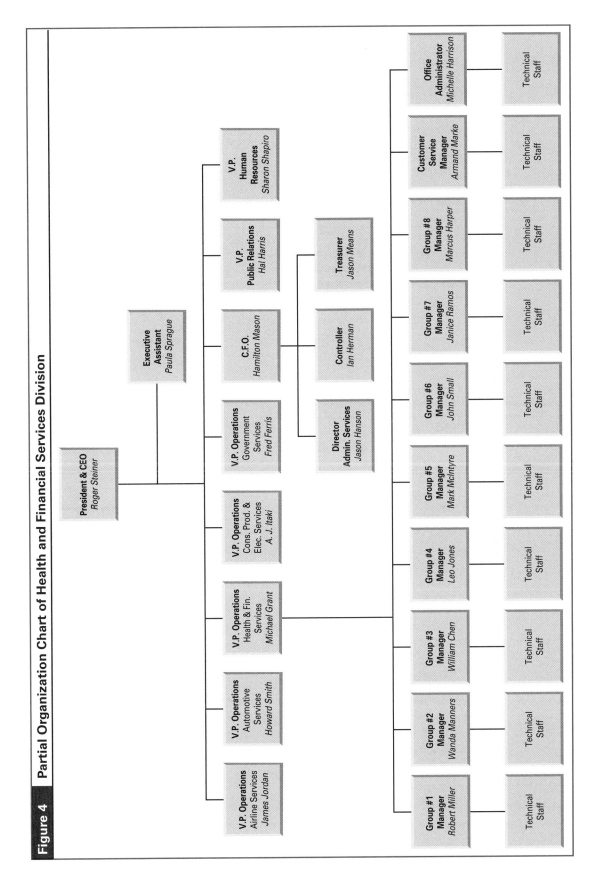

Figure 4 Partial Organization Chart of Health and Financial Services Division

President & CEO
Roger Steiner

Executive Assistant
Paula Sprague

V.P. Operations
Airline Services
James Jordan

V.P. Operations
Automotive Services
Howard Smith

V.P. Operations
Health & Fin. Services
Michael Grant

V.P. Operations
Cons. Prod. & Elec. Services
A. J. Itaki

V.P. Operations
Government Services
Fred Ferris

C.F.O.
Hamilton Mason

V.P. Public Relations
Hal Harris

V.P. Human Resources
Sharon Shapiro

Director Admin. Services
Jason Hanson

Controller
Ian Herman

Treasurer
Jason Means

Group #1 Manager
Robert Miller

Group #2 Manager
Wanda Manners

Group #3 Manager
William Chen

Group #4 Manager
Leo Jones

Group #5 Manager
Mark McIntyre

Group #6 Manager
John Small

Group #7 Manager
Janice Ramos

Group #8 Manager
Marcus Harper

Customer Service Manager
Armand Marke

Office Administrator
Michelle Harrison

Technical Staff

on the response form. All your responses must be written on the response forms. Write your precise, detailed response (do not merely jot down a few notes). For example, you might draft a memo or write out a message that you will deliver via phone/voice mail. You may also decide to meet with an individual (or individuals) during the limited time available on your calendar today or tomorrow. If so, prepare an agenda for a personal meeting and list your goals for the meeting. As you read through the items, you may occasionally observe some information that you think is relevant and want to remember (or attend to in the future) but that you decide not to include in any of your responses to employees. Write down such information on a sheet of paper titled "note to self."

Sample Response Form

Relates to:

Memo # _____   E-mail # _____   Voice mail # _____

Response form:

_____ Letter/Memo   _____ Meet with person (when, where)

_____ E-mail   _____ Note to self

_____ Phone call/Voice mail   _____ No response

ITEM 1 – E-MAIL

TO: All Employees
FROM: Roger Steiner, Chief Executive Officer
DATE: October 15

I am pleased to announce that Chris Perillo has been appointed as Vice President of Operations for Health and Financial Services. Chris will immediately assume responsibility for all operations previously managed by Michael Grant. Chris will have end-to-end responsibility for the design, development, integration, and maintenance of custom software for the health and finance/banking industries. This responsibility includes all technical, financial, and staffing issues. Chris will also manage our program of software support and integration for the recently announced merger of three large health maintenance organizations (HMOs). Chris will be responsible for our recently announced project with a consortium of banks and financial firms operating in Tanzania. This project represents an exciting opportunity for us, and Chris's background seems ideally suited to the task.

Chris comes to this position with an undergraduate degree in Computer Science from the California Institute of Technology and an M.B.A. from the University of Virginia. Chris began as a member of our technical/professional staff six years ago and has most recently served for three years as a Group Manager supporting domestic and international projects for our airlines industry group, including our recent work for the European Airbus consortium.

I am sure you all join me in offering congratulations to Chris for this promotion.

ITEM 2 – E-MAIL

TO: All Managers
FROM: Hal Harris, Vice President, Community and Public Relations
DATE: October 15

For your information, the following article appeared on the front page of the business section of Thursday's *Los Angeles Times*.

In a move that may create problems for SSS Software, Michael Grant and Janice Ramos have left SSS Software and moved to Universal Business Solutions Inc. Industry analysts see the move as another victory for Universal Business Solutions Inc. in their battle with SSS Software for share of the growing software development and integration business. Both Grant and Ramos had been with SSS Software for over 7 years. Grant was most recently Vice President of Operations for all SSS Software's work in two industries: health and hospitals, and finance and banking. Ramos brings to Universal Business Solutions Inc. her special expertise in the growing area of international software development and integration.

Hillary Collins, an industry analyst with Merrill Lynch, said "the loss of key staff to a competitor can often create serious problems for a firm such as SSS Software. Grant and Ramos have an insider's understanding of SSS Software's strategic and technical limitations. It will be interesting to see if they can exploit this knowledge to the advantage of Universal Business Solutions Inc."

ITEM 3 – E-MAIL

TO: Chris Perillo
FROM: Paula Sprague, Executive Assistant to Roger Steiner
DATE: October 15

Chris, I know that in your former position as a Group Manager in the Airline Services Division, you probably have met most of the group managers in the Health and Financial Services Division, but I thought you might like some more personal information about them. These people will be your direct reports on the management team.

Group #1: Bob Miller, 55-year-old white male, married (Anna) with two children and three grandchildren. Active in local Republican politics. Well regarded as a "hands-off" manager heading a high-performing team. Plays golf regularly with Mark McIntyre, John Small, and a couple of V.P.s from other divisions.

Group #2: Wanda Manners, 38-year-old white female, single with one school-age child. A fitness "nut" has run in several marathons. Some experience in Germany and Japan. Considered a hard-driving manager with a constant focus on the task at hand. Will be the first person to show up every morning.

Group #3: William Chen, 31-year-old male of Chinese descent, married (Harriet), two young children from his first marriage. Enjoys tennis and is quite good at it. A rising star in the company, he is highly respected by his peers as a "man of action" and a good friend.

Group #4: Leo Jones, 36-year-old white male, married (Janet) with an infant daughter. Recently returned from paternity leave. Has traveled extensively on projects, since he speaks three languages. Has liked hockey ever since the time he spent in Montreal. Considered a strong manager who gets the most out of his people.

Group #5: Mark McIntyre, 45-year-old white male, married (Mary Theresa) to an executive in the banking industry. No children. A lot of experience in Germany and Eastern Europe. Has been writing a mystery novel. Has always been a good "team player," but several members of his technical staff are not well respected and he hasn't addressed the problem.

Group #6: John Small, 38-year-old white male, recently divorced. Three children living with his wife. A gregarious individual who likes sports. He spent a lot of time in Mexico and Central America before he came to SSS Software. Recently has been doing mostly contract work with the federal government. An average manager, has had some trouble keeping his people on schedule.

Group #7: This position vacant since Janice Ramos left. Roger thinks we ought to fill this position quickly. Get in touch with me if you want information on any in-house candidates for any position.

Group #8: Marcus Harper, 42-year-old black African American, married (Tamara) with two teenage children. Recently won an award in a local photography contest. Considered a strong manager who gets along with peers and works long hours.

Customer Services: Armad Marke, 38-year-old male, divorced. A basketball fan. Originally from Armenia. Previously a Group Manager. Worked hard to establish the Technical Services Phone Line, but now has pretty much left it alone.

Office Administrator: Michelle Harrison, 41-year-old white female, single. Grew up on a ranch and still rides horses whenever she can. A strict administrator.

There are a number of good folks here, but they don't function well as a management team. I think Michael played favorites, especially with Janice and Leo. There are a few cliques in this group and I'm not sure how effectively Michael dealt with them. I expect you will find it a challenge to build a cohesive team.

ITEM 4 – E-MAIL

TO: Chris Perillo
FROM: Wanda Manners, Group 2 Manager
DATE: October 15

CONFIDENTIAL AND RESTRICTED

Although I know you are new to your job, I feel it is important that I let you know about some information I just obtained concerning the development work we recently completed for First National Investment. Our project involved the development of asset management software for managing their international funds. This was a very complex project due to the volatile exchange rates and the forecasting tools we needed to develop.

As part of this project, we had to integrate the software and reports with all their existing systems and reporting mechanisms. To do this, we were given access to all of their existing software (much of which was developed by Universal Business Solutions Inc.). Of course, we signed an agreement acknowledging that the software to which we were given access was proprietary and that our access was solely for the purpose of our system integration work associated with the project.

Unfortunately, I have learned that some parts of the software we developed actually "borrow" heavily from complex application programs developed for First National Investment by Universal Business Solutions Inc. It seems obvious to me that one or more of the software developers from Group 5 (that is, Mark McIntyre's group) inappropriately "borrowed" algorithms developed by Universal Business Solutions Inc. I am sure that doing so saved us significant development time on some aspects of the project. It seems very unlikely that First National Investment or Universal Business Solutions Inc. will ever become aware of this issue.

Finally, First National Investment is successfully using the software we developed and is thrilled with the work we did. We brought the project in on time and under budget. You probably know that they have invited us to bid on several other substantial projects.

I'm sorry to bring this delicate matter to your attention, but I thought you should know about it.

ITEM 5A – E-MAIL

TO: Chris Perillo
FROM: Paula Sprague, Executive Assistant to Roger Steiner
DATE: October 15

RE: Letter from C.A.R.E. Services (copies attached)

Roger asked me to work on this C.A.R.E. project and obviously wants some fast action. A lot of the staff are already booked solid for the next couple of weeks. I knew that Elise Soto and Chu Hung Woo have the expertise to do this system and when I checked with them, they were relatively free. I had them pencil in the next two weeks and wanted to let you know. Hopefully, it will take a "hot potato" out of your hands.

ITEM 5B – COPY OF FAX

C.A.R.E.
Child and Adolescent Rehabilitative and Educational Services
A United Way Member Agency
200 Main Street
Los Angeles, California 90230

DATE: October 11
Roger Steiner, CEO
SSS Software
13 Miller Way
Los Angeles, California 90224

Dear Roger,

This letter is a follow-up to our conversation after last night's board meeting. I appreciated your comments during the board meeting about the need for sophisticated computer systems in nonprofit organizations and I especially appreciate your generous offer of assistance to have SSS Software provide assistance to deal with the immediate problem with our accounting system. Since the board voted to fire the computer consultant, I am very worried about getting our reports done in time to meet the state funding cycle.

Thanks again for your offer of help during this crisis.

Sincerely yours,

Janice Polocizwic

Janice Polocizwic
Executive Director

ITEM 5C – COPY OF A LETTER

SSS SOFTWARE
13 Miller Way
Los Angeles, CA 90224

DATE: October 12

Janice Polocizwic
Executive Director, C.A.R.E. Services
200 Main Street
Los Angeles, California 90230

Dear Janice,

I received your fax of October 11. I have asked Paula Sprague, my executive assistant, to line up people to work on your accounting system as soon as possible. You can expect to hear from her shortly.

Sincerely,

Roger Steiner

Roger Steiner
cc: Paula Sprague, Executive Assistant

ITEM 6 – E-MAIL

TO: Michael Grant
FROM: Harry Withers, Group 6 Technical Staff
DATE: October 12

PERSONAL AND CONFIDENTIAL

Our team is having difficulty meeting the submission deadline of November 5 for the Halstrom project. Kim, Fred, Peter, Kyoto, Susan, Mala, and I have been working on the project for several weeks, but we are experiencing some problems and may need additional time. I hesitate to write this letter, but the main problem is that our group manager, John Small, is involved in a relationship with Mala. Mala gets John's support for her ideas and brings them to the team as required components of the project. Needless to say, this has posed some problems for the group. Mala's background is especially valuable for this project, but Kim and Fred, who have both worked very hard on the project, do not want to work with her. In addition, one member of the team has been unavailable recently because of child-care needs. Commitment to the project and team morale have plummeted. However, we'll do our best to get the project finished as soon as possible. Mala will be on vacation the next two weeks, so I'm expecting that some of us can complete it in her absence.

ITEM 7 – VOICE MAIL MESSAGE

Hello, Michael. This is Jim Bishop of United Hospitals. I wanted to talk with you about the quality assurance project that you are working on for us. When Jose Martinez first started talking with us, I was impressed with his friendliness and expertise. But recently, he doesn't seem to be getting much accomplished and has seemed distant and on-edge in conversations. Today, I asked him about the schedule and he seemed very defensive and not entirely in control of his emotions. I am quite concerned about our project. Please give me a call.

ITEM 8 – VOICE MAIL MESSAGE

Hi, Michael. This is Armand. I wanted to talk with you about some issues with the Technical Services Phone Line. I've recently received some complaint letters from Phone Line customers whose complaints have included long delays while waiting for a technician to answer the phone, technicians who are not knowledgeable enough to solve problems, and, on occasion, rude service. Needless to say, I'm quite concerned about these complaints.

I believe that the overall quality of the Phone Line staff is very good, but we continue to be understaffed, even with the recent hires. The new technicians look strong, but are working on the help-line before being fully trained. Antolina, our best tech, often brings her child to work, which is adding to the craziness around here.

I think you should know that we're feeling a lot of stress here. I'll talk with you soon.

ITEM 9 – VOICE MAIL MESSAGE

Hi, Chris, it's Pat. Congratulations on your promotion. They definitely picked the right person. It's great news—for me, too. You've been a terrific mentor so far, so I'm expecting to learn a lot from you in your new position. How about lunch next week?

ITEM 10 – VOICE MAIL MESSAGE

Chris, this is Bob Miller. Just thought you'd like to know that John's joke during our planning meeting has disturbed a few of the women in my group. Frankly, I think the thing's being blown out of proportion, especially since we all know this is a good place for both men and women to work. Give me a call if you want to chat about this.

ITEM 11 – VOICE MAIL MESSAGE

Hello. This is Lorraine Adams from Westside Hospital. I read in today's *Los Angeles Times* that you will be taking over from Michael Grant. We haven't met yet, but your division has recently finished two large million-dollar projects for Westside. Michael Grant and I had some discussion about a small conversion of a piece of existing software to be compatible with the new systems. The original vendor had said that they would do the work, but they have been stalling, and I need to move quickly. Can you see if Harris Wilson, Chu Hung Woo, and Elise Soto are available to do this work as soon as possible? They were on the original project and work well with our people.

Um . . . (long pause) I guess I should tell you that I got a call from Michael offering to do this work. But I think I should stick with SSS Software. Give me a call.

ITEM 12 – VOICE MAIL MESSAGE

Hi, Chris, this is Roosevelt Moore calling. I'm a member of your technical/professional staff. I used to report to Janice Ramos, but since she left the firm, I thought I'd bring my concerns directly to you. I'd like to arrange some time to talk with you about my experiences since returning from six weeks of paternity leave. Some of my major responsibilities have been turned over to others. I seem to be out of the loop and wonder if my career is at risk. Also, I am afraid that I won't be supported or seriously considered for the opening created by Janice's departure. Frankly, I feel like I'm being screwed for taking my leave. I'd like to talk with you this week.

ITEM 13 – E-MAIL

TO: Michael Grant
FROM: Jose Martinez, Group 1 Technical Staff
DATE: October 12

I would like to set up a meeting with you as soon as possible. I suspect that you will get a call from Jim Bishop of United Hospitals and want to be sure that you hear my side of the story first. I have been working on a customized system design for quality assurance for them using a variation of the J-3 product we developed several years ago. They had a number of special requirements and some quirks in their accounting systems, so I have had to put in especially long hours. I've worked hard to meet their demands, but they keep changing the ground rules. I keep thinking, this is just another J-3 I'm working on, but they have been interfering with an elegant design I have developed. It seems I'm not getting anywhere on this project. Earlier today, I had a difficult discussion with their Controller. He asked for another major change. I've been fighting their deadline and think I am just stretched too thin on this project. Then Jim Bishop asked me if the system was running yet. I was worn out from dealing with the Controller, and I made a sarcastic comment to Jim Bishop. He gave me a funny look and just walked out of the room.

I would like to talk with you about this situation at your earliest convenience.

ITEM 14 – E-MAIL

TO: Chris Perillo
FROM: John Small, Group 6 Manager
DATE: October 15

Welcome aboard, Chris. I look forward to meeting with you. I just wanted to put a bug in your ear about finding a replacement for Janice Ramos. One of my technical staff, Mala Abendano, has the ability and drive to make an excellent group manager. I have encouraged her to apply for the position. I'd be happy to talk with you further about this, at your convenience.

ITEM 15 – E-MAIL

TO: Chris Perillo
FROM: Paula Sprague, Executive Assistant to Roger Steiner
DATE: October 15

Roger asked me to let you know about the large contract we have gotten in Tanzania. It means that a team of four managers will be making a short trip to determine current needs. They will assign their technical staff the tasks of developing a system and software here over the next six months, and then the managers and possibly some team members will be spending about 10 months on site in Tanzania to handle the implementation. Roger thought you might want to hold an initial meeting with some of your managers to check on their interest and willingness to take this sort of assignment. Roger would appreciate an e-mail of your thoughts about the issues to be discussed at this meeting, additional considerations about sending people to Tanzania, and about how you will put together an effective team to work on this project. The October 15 memo I sent to you will provide you with some information you'll need to start making these decisions.

ITEM 16 – E-MAIL

TO: Chris Perillo
FROM: Sharon Shapiro, V.P. of Human Resources
DATE: October 15

RE: Upcoming meeting

I want to update you on the rippling effect of John Small's sexual joke at last week's planning meeting. Quite a few women have been very upset and have met informally to talk about it. They have decided to call a meeting of all people concerned about this kind of behavior throughout the firm. I plan to attend, so I'll keep you posted.

ITEM 17 – E-MAIL

TO: All SSS Software Managers
FROM: Sharon Shapiro, V.P. of Human Resources
DATE: October 15

RE: Promotions and External Hires

Year-to-Date (January through September) Promotions and External Hires

| Level | Race | | | | | Sex | | |
	White	African American	Asian	Hispanic	Native American	M	F	Total
Hires into Executive Level	0 (0%)	0 (0%)	0 (0%)	0 (0%)	0 (0%)	0 (0%)	0 (0%)	0
Promotions to Executive Level	0 (0%)	0 (0%)	0 (0%)	0 (0%)	0 (0%)	0 (0%)	0 (0%)	0

| Level | Race | | | | | Sex | | |
	White	African American	Asian	Hispanic	Native American	M	F	Total
Hires into Management Level	2 (67%)	1 (33%)	0 (0%)	0 (0%)	0 (0%)	2 (67%)	1 (33%)	3
Promotions to Management Level	7 (88%)	0 (0%)	1 (12%)	0 (0%)	0 (0%)	7 (88%)	1 (12%)	8
Hires into Technical/ Professional Level	10 (36%)	6 (21%)	10 (36%)	2 (7%)	0 (0%)	14 (50%)	14 (50%)	28
Promotions to Technical/ Professional Level	0 (0%)	0 (0%)	0 (0%)	0 (0%)	0 (0%)	0 (0%)	0 (0%)	0
Hires into Non-Management Level	4 (20%)	10 (50%)	2 (10%)	4 (20%)	0 (0%)	6 (30%)	14 (70%)	20
Promotions to Non-Management Level	NA	NA	NA	NA	NA	NA	NA	NA

SSS Software Employee (EEO) Classification Report as of June 30

Level	Race					Sex		
	White	African American	Asian	Hispanic	Native American	M	F	Total
Executive Level	11 (92%)	0 (0%)	1 (8%)	0 (0%)	0 (0%)	11 (92%)	1 (8%)	12
Management Level	43 (90%)	2 (4%)	2 (4%)	1 (2%)	0 (0%)	38 (79%)	10 (21%)	48
Technical/ Professional Level	58 (45%)	20 (15%)	37 (28%)	14 (11%)	1 (1%)	80 (62%)	50 (38%)	130
Non-Management Level	29 (48%)	22 (37%)	4 (7%)	4 (7%)	1 (2%)	12 (20%)	48 (80%)	60
Total	141 (56%)	44 (18%)	44 (18%)	19 (8%)	2 (1%)	141 (56%)	109 (44%)	250

SCORING KEY AND COMPARISON DATA

Personal Assessment of Management Skills

Scoring Key

SKILL AREA	ITEMS	ASSESSMENT	
		PERSONAL	ASSOCIATES
Developing Self-Awareness	**1–5**		
Self-disclosure and openness	1–2		
Awareness of self	3–5		
Managing Stress	**6–11**		
Eliminating stressors	6–7		
Developing resiliency	8–9		
Short-term coping	10–11		
Solving Problems Creatively	**12–23**		
Rational problem solving	12–14		
Creative problem solving	15–19		
Fostering innovation and creativity	20–23		
Communicating Supportively	**24–32**		
Coaching and counseling	24–25		
Effective negative feedback	26–28		
Communicating supportively	29–32		
Gaining Power and Influence	**33–40**		
Gaining power	33–37		
Exercising influence	38–40		
Motivating Others	**41–49**		
Managing Conflict	**50–58**		
Initiating	50–52		
Responding	53–55		
Mediating	56–58		
Empowering and Delegating	**59–67**		
Empowering	59–62		
Delegating	63–67		
Building Effective Teams and Teamwork	**68–77**		
Leading teams	68–71		
Team membership	72–73		
Teamwork	74–77		
Leading Positive Change	**78–84**		
Foster positive deviance	78–80		
Lead positive change	81–82		
Mobilize others	83–84		

Comparison Data (N = 5,000 students)

Compare your scores with at least four referents: (1) If you asked others to rate you using the Associates' version, compare how you rated yourself with how your associates rated you. (2) Compare the ratings you received to those received by other students in the class. (3) Compare the ratings you received to a norm group of approximately 5,000 business school students (see the information below). (4) Compare your score against the maximum possible (510).

For the survey as a whole, if you scored

394.35	=	mean
422 or above	=	you are in the top quartile.
395–421	=	you are in the second quartile.
369–394	=	you are in the third quartile.
368 or below	=	you are in the bottom quartile.

What Does It Take to Be an Effective Manager?

This exercise does not have a solution or scoring data. Answers will vary among students.

SSS Software In-Basket Exercise

This exercise does not have a solution or scoring data. Answers will vary among students.

Part I

Personal Skills

CHAPTERS

SKILL *ASSESSMENT* ▶

- Self-Awareness Assessment
- Emotional Intelligence Assessment
- The Defining Issues Test
- Cognitive Style Indicator
- Locus of Control Scale
- Tolerance of Ambiguity Scale
- Core Self-Evaluation Scale (CSES)

SKILL *LEARNING* ■

- Key Dimensions of Self-Awareness
- The Enigma of Self-Awareness
- Understanding and Appreciating Individual Differences
- Important Areas of Self-Awareness
- Summary
- Behavioral Guidelines

SKILL *ANALYSIS*

- Communist Prison Camp
- Computerized Exam
- Decision Dilemmas

SKILL *PRACTICE* ◆

- Through the Looking Glass
- Diagnosing Managerial Characteristics
- An Exercise for Identifying Aspects of Personal Culture:
  A Learning Plan and Autobiography

SKILL *APPLICATION*

- Suggested Assignments
- Application Plan and Evaluation

SCORING KEYS AND *COMPARISON DATA*

1

Developing Self-Awareness

SKILL DEVELOPMENT OBJECTIVES

Increase personal awareness of your:

- SENSITIVE LINE
- EMOTIONAL INTELLIGENCE
- PERSONAL VALUES AND MORAL MATURITY
- COGNITIVE STYLE
- ORIENTATION TOWARD CHANGE
- CORE SELF-EVALUATION

SKILL *ASSESSMENT* ▶

DIAGNOSTIC SURVEYS FOR SCALE SELF-AWARENESS

SELF-AWARENESS ASSESSMENT

Step 1: Before you read the material in this chapter, please respond to the following statements by writing a number from the rating scale below in the left-hand column (Pre-assessment). Your answers should reflect your attitudes and behavior as they are now, not as you would like them to be. Be honest. This instrument is designed to help you discover how self-aware you are so you can tailor your learning to your specific needs. When you have completed the survey, use the scoring key at the end of the chapter to identify the skill areas discussed in this chapter that are most important for you to master.

Step 2: After you have completed the reading and the exercises in this chapter and, ideally, as many of the Skill Application assignments at the end of this chapter as you can, cover up your first set of answers. Then respond to the same statements again, this time in the right-hand column (Post-assessment). When you have completed the survey, use the scoring key at the end of the chapter to measure your progress. If your score remains low in specific skill areas, use the behavioral guidelines at the end of the Skill Learning section to guide further practice.

Rating Scale

1 Strongly disagree
2 Disagree
3 Slightly disagree
4 Slightly agree
5 Agree
6 Strongly agree

Assessment

Pre-	Post-	
_____	_____	1. I seek information about my strengths and weaknesses from others as a basis for self-improvement.
_____	_____	2. When I receive negative feedback about myself from others, I do not get angry or defensive.
_____	_____	3. In order to improve, I am willing to be self-disclosing to others (that is, to share my beliefs and feelings).
_____	_____	4. I am aware of my personal cognitive style and how I process information.
_____	_____	5. I have a good grasp of what it means to be emotionally mature, and I demonstrate that capability.
_____	_____	6. I have a good sense of how I cope with situations that are ambiguous and uncertain.
_____	_____	7. I have a well-developed set of personal standards and principles that guide my behavior.
_____	_____	8. I feel in charge of what happens to me, good and bad.

_____ _____ 9. I seldom, if ever, feel angry, depressed, or anxious without knowing why.

_____ _____ 10. I am conscious of the areas in which conflict and friction most frequently arise in my interactions with others.

_____ _____ 11. I have a close personal relationship with at least one other person with whom I can share personal information and personal feelings.

EMOTIONAL INTELLIGENCE ASSESSMENT

Please reply to each item below by selecting the one alternative that is most likely to be your response. Think about the way you usually respond to these kinds of situations, not the way you would like to respond or the way you think you should respond. No correct answers exist for any of the items, and your scores will be most useful if you provide an accurate assessment of your typical behavior. Mark only one answer per item.

1. When I get really upset, I . . .

   a. _____ Analyze why I am so disturbed.

   b. _____ Blow up and let off steam.

   c. _____ Hide it and remain calm.

2. In a situation in which a colleague takes credit in public for my work and my ideas, I would probably . . .

   a. _____ Let it slide and do nothing in order to avoid a confrontation.

   b. _____ Later—in private—indicate that I would appreciate being given credit for my work and ideas.

   c. _____ Thank the person in public for referencing my work and ideas and then elaborate on my contributions.

3. When I approach another person and try to strike up a conversation but the other person doesn't respond, I . . .

   a. _____ Try to cheer up the person by sharing a funny story.

   b. _____ Ask the person if he or she wants to talk about what's on his or her mind.

   c. _____ Leave the person alone and find someone else to talk to.

4. When I enter a social group I usually . . .

   a. _____ Remain quiet and wait for people to talk to me.

   b. _____ Try to find something complimentary I can tell someone.

   c. _____ Find ways to be the life of the party or the source of energy and fun.

5. On important issues I usually . . .

   a. _____ Make up my own mind and ignore others' opinions.

   b. _____ Weigh both sides, and discuss it with others before making a decision.

   c. _____ Listen to my friends or colleagues and make the same decision they do.

6. When someone that I do not particularly like becomes romantically attracted to me, I usually . . .

   a. _____ Tell that person directly that I am not interested.

   b. _____ Respond by being friendly but cool or aloof.

   c. _____ Ignore the person and try to avoid him or her.

7. When I am in the company of two people who have diametrically opposing points of view about an issue (for example, politics, abortion, war) and are arguing about it, I . . .

   a. _____ Find something upon which they can both agree and emphasize it.

   b. _____ Encourage the verbal battle.

   c. _____ Suggest that they stop arguing and calm down.

8. When I am playing a sport and the game comes down to my last-second performance, I . . .

   a. _____ Get very nervous and hope that I don't choke.

   b. _____ See this as an opportunity to shine.

   c. _____ Stay focused and give it my best effort.

9. In a situation in which I have an important obligation and need to leave work early, but my colleagues ask me to stay to meet a deadline, I would probably . . .

   a. _____ Cancel my obligation and stay to complete the deadline.

   b. _____ Exaggerate a bit by telling my colleagues that I have an emergency that I can't miss.

   c. _____ Require some kind of compensation for missing the obligation.

10. In a situation in which another person becomes very angry and begins yelling at me, I . . .

    a. _____ Get angry in return. I don't take that from anyone.

    b. _____ Walk away. It doesn't do any good to argue.

    c. _____ Listen first, and then try to discuss the issue.

11. When I encounter someone who has just experienced a major loss or tragedy, I . . .

    a. _____ Really don't know what to do or say.

    b. _____ Tell the person I feel very sorry and try to provide support.

    c. _____ Share a time when I experienced a similar loss or tragedy.

12. When someone makes a racist joke or tells a crude story about a member of the opposite sex in mixed company, I usually . . .

    a. _____ Point out that this is inappropriate and not acceptable, and then change the subject.

    b. _____ Ignore it so I don't cause a scene.

    c. _____ Get really upset and tell the person just what I think of what he or she said.

THE DEFINING ISSUES TEST

This instrument assesses your opinions about controversial social issues. Different people make decisions about these issues in different ways. You should answer the questions for yourself without discussing them with others. You are presented with three stories. Following each story are 12 statements or questions. Your task after reading the story is to rate each statement in terms of its importance in making a decision. After rating each statement, select the four most important statements and rank them from one to four in the spaces provided. Each statement should be ranked in terms of its relative importance in making a decision.

Some statements will raise important issues, but you should ask yourself whether the decision should rest on that issue. Some statements sound high and lofty but are largely gibberish. If you cannot make sense of a statement, or if you don't understand its meaning, mark it 5—"Of no importance."

For information about interpreting and scoring the Defining Issues Test, refer to the scoring key at the end of the chapter. Use the following rating scale for your response.

Rating Scale

1	Of great importance	This statement or question makes a crucial difference in making a decision about the problem.
2	Of much importance	This statement or question is something that would be a major factor (though not always a crucial one) in making a decision.
3	Of some importance	This statement or question involves something you care about, but it is not of great importance in reaching a decision.
4	Of little importance	This statement or question is not very important to consider in this case.
5	Of no importance	This statement or question is completely unimportant in making a decision. You would waste your time thinking about it.

The Escaped Prisoner

A man had been sentenced to prison for 10 years. After one year, however, he escaped from prison, moved to a new area of the country, and took on the name of Thompson. For eight years he worked hard, and gradually he saved enough money to buy his own business. He was fair to his customers, gave his employees top wages, and gave most of his own profits to charity. Then one day, Ms. Jones, an old neighbor, recognized him as the man who had escaped from prison eight years before and for whom the police had been looking.

Should Ms. Jones report Mr. Thompson to the police and have him sent back to prison? Write a number from the rating scale on the previous page in the blank beside each statement.

_____ Should report him
_____ Can't decide
_____ Should not report him

Importance

_____ 1. Hasn't Mr. Thompson been good enough for such a long time to prove he isn't a bad person?

_____ 2. Every time someone escapes punishment for a crime, doesn't that just encourage more crime?

_____ 3. Wouldn't we be better off without prisons and the oppression of our legal system?

_____ 4. Has Mr. Thompson really paid his debt to society?

_____ 5. Would society be failing what Mr. Thompson should fairly expect?

_____ 6. What benefit would prison be apart from society, especially for a charitable man?

_____ 7. How could anyone be so cruel and heartless as to send Mr. Thompson to prison?

_____ 8. Would it be fair to prisoners who have to serve out their full sentences if Mr. Thompson is let off?

_____ 9. Was Ms. Jones a good friend of Mr. Thompson?

_____ 10. Wouldn't it be a citizen's duty to report an escaped criminal, regardless of the circumstances?

_____ 11. How would the will of the people and the public good best be served?

_____ 12. Would going to prison do any good for Mr. Thompson or protect anybody?

From the list of questions above, select the four most important:

    _____ Most important
    _____ Second most important
    _____ Third most important
    _____ Fourth most important

The Doctor's Dilemma

A woman was dying of incurable cancer and had only about six months to live. She was in terrible pain, but was so weak that a large dose of a pain killer such as morphine would probably kill her. She was delirious with pain, and in her calm periods, she would ask her doctor to give her enough morphine to kill her. She said she couldn't stand the pain and that she was going to die in a few months anyway.

What should the doctor do? (Check one.)

    _____ He should give the woman an overdose that will make her die
    _____ Can't decide
    _____ Should not give the overdose

Importance

_____ 1. Is the woman's family in favor of giving her the overdose?

_____ 2. Is the doctor obligated by the same laws as everybody else?

_____ 3. Would people be better off without society regimenting their lives and even their deaths?

_____ 4. Should the doctor make the woman's death from a drug overdose appear to be an accident?

_____ 5. Does the state have the right to force continued existence on those who don't want to live?

_____ 6. What is the value of death prior to society's perspective on personal values?

_____ 7. Should the doctor have sympathy for the woman's suffering, or should he care more about what society might think?

_____ 8. Is helping to end another's life ever a responsible act of cooperation?

_____ 9. Can only God decide when a person's life should end?

_____ 10. What values has the doctor set for himself in his own personal code of behavior?

_____ 11. Can society afford to let anybody end his or her life whenever he or she desires?

_____ 12. Can society allow suicide or mercy killing and still protect the lives of individuals who want to live?

From the list of questions above, select the four most important:

    _____ Most important
    _____ Second most important
    _____ Third most important
    _____ Fourth most important

The Newspaper

Rami, a senior in high school, wanted to publish a mimeographed newspaper for students so that he could express his opinions. He wanted to speak out against military build-up and some of the school's rules, such as the rule forbidding boys to wear long hair.

When Rami started his newspaper, he asked his principal for permission. The principal said it would be all right if before every publication Rami would turn in all his articles for the principal's approval. Rami agreed and turned in several articles for approval. The principal approved all of them and he published two issues of the paper in the next two weeks.

But, the principal had not expected that Rami's newspaper would receive so much attention. Students were so excited by the paper that they began to organize protests against the government, hair regulation, and other school rules. Angry parents objected to Rami's opinions. They phoned the principal telling him that the newspaper was unpatriotic and should not be published. As a result of the rising excitement, the principal wondered if he should order Rami to stop publishing on the grounds that the controversial newspaper articles were disrupting the operation of the school.

What should the principal do? (Check one.)

_____ Should stop it

_____ Can't decide

_____ Should not stop it

Importance

_____   1. Is the principal more responsible to the students or to the parents?

_____   2. Did the principal give his word that the newspaper could be published for a long time, or did he just promise to approve the newspaper one issue at a time?

_____   3. Would the students start protesting even more if the principal stopped the newspaper?

_____   4. When the welfare of the school is threatened, does the principal have the right to give orders to students?

_____   5. Does the principal have the freedom of speech to say no in this case?

_____   6. If the principal stopped the newspaper, would he be preventing full discussion of important problems?

_____   7. Would the principal's stop order make Rami lose faith in him?

_____   8. Is Rami really loyal to his school and patriotic to his country?

_____   9. What effect would stopping the paper have on the students' education in critical thinking and judgment?

_____ 10. Is Rami in any way violating the rights of others in publishing his own opinions?

_____ 11. Should the principal be influenced by some angry parents when it is the principal who knows best what is going on in the school?

_____ 12. Is Rami using the newspaper to stir up hatred and discontent?

From the list of questions above, select the four most important:

_____ Most important

_____ Second most important

_____ Third most important

_____ Fourth most important

SOURCE: *Adapted from Rest, 1979.*

COGNITIVE STYLE INDICATOR

This instrument assesses the way you gather and evaluate information and make decisions. There are no right or wrong answers, and the accuracy of your results will depend on the extent to which you honestly answer each question. Please use the following scale in responding to each item:

Rating Scale

1 Totally disagree
2 Disagree
3 Neither agree nor disagree
4 Agree
5 Totally agree

_____ 1. Developing a clear plan is very important to me.

_____ 2. I like to contribute to innovative solutions.

_____ 3. I always want to know what should be done when.

_____ 4. I prefer to look at creative solutions.

_____ 5. I want to have a full understanding of a problem.

_____ 6. I like detailed action plans.

_____ 7. I am motivated by ongoing innovation.

_____ 8. I like to analyze problems.

_____ 9. I prefer a clear structure to do my job.

_____ 10. I like a lot of variety in my life.

_____ 11. I engage in detailed analyses.

_____ 12. I prefer well-planned meetings with a clear agenda.

_____ 13. New ideas attract me more than existing solutions.

_____ 14. I study each problem until I understand the underlying logic.

_____ 15. I make definite appointments and follow-up meticulously.

_____ 16. I like to extend the boundaries.

_____ 17. A good task is a well-prepared task.

_____ 18. I try to avoid routine.

SOURCE: *Cognitive Style Indicator, Cools, E. and H. Van den Broeck. (2007) "Development and Validation of the Cognitive Style Indicator."* Journal of Psychology, *14: 359–387.*

LOCUS OF CONTROL SCALE

This questionnaire assesses your opinions about certain issues. Each item consists of a pair of alternatives marked with *a* or *b*. Select the alternative with which you most agree. If you believe both alternatives to some extent, select the one with which you most strongly agree. If you do not believe either alternative, mark the one with which you least strongly disagree. Since this is an assessment of opinions, there are obviously no right or wrong answers. When you have finished each item, turn to the scoring key at the end of the chapter for instructions on how to tabulate the results and for comparison data.

This questionnaire is similar, but not identical, to the original locus of control scale developed by Julian Rotter. The comparison data provided in the scoring key comes from research using Rotter's scale instead of this one. However, the two instruments assess the same concept, are the same length, and their mean scores are similar.

1. a. Leaders are born, not made.
   b. Leaders are made, not born.

2. a. People often succeed because they are in the right place at the right time.
   b. Success is mostly dependent on hard work and ability.

3. a. When things go wrong in my life, it's generally because I have made mistakes.
   b. Misfortunes occur in my life regardless of what I do.

4. a. Whether there is war or not depends on the actions of certain world leaders.
   b. It is inevitable that the world will continue to experience wars.

5. a. Good children are mainly products of good parents.
   b. Some children turn out bad no matter how their parents behave.

6. a. My future success depends mainly on circumstances I can't control.
   b. I am the master of my fate.

7. a. History judges certain people to have been effective leaders mainly because circumstances made them visible and successful.
   b. Effective leaders are those who have made decisions or taken actions that resulted in significant contributions.

8. a. Avoiding punishing children guarantees that they will grow up irresponsible.
   b. Spanking children is never appropriate.

9. a. I often feel that I have little influence over the direction my life is taking.
   b. It is unreasonable to believe that fate or luck plays a crucial part in how my life turns out.

10. a. Some customers will never be satisfied no matter what you do.
    b. You can satisfy customers by giving them what they want when they want it.

11. a. Anyone can get good grades in school by working hard enough.
    b. Some people are never going to excel in school no matter how hard they try.

12. a. Good marriages result when both partners continually work on the relationship.
    b. Some marriages are going to fail because the partners are just incompatible.

13. a. I am confident that I can improve my basic management skills through learning and practice.
    b. It is a waste of time to try to improve management skills in a classroom.

14. a. More management skills courses should be taught in business schools.
    b. Less emphasis should be put on skills in business schools.

15. a. When I think back on the good things that happened to me, I believe they happened mainly because of something I did.
    b. The bad things that have happened in my life have mainly resulted from circumstances outside my control.

16. a. Many exams I took in school were unconnected to the material I had studied, so studying hard didn't help at all.
    b. When I prepared well for exams in school, I generally did quite well.

17. a. I am sometimes influenced by what my astrological chart says.

 b. No matter how the stars are lined up, I can determine my own destiny.

18. a. Government is so big and bureaucratic that it is very difficult for any one person to have any impact on what happens.

 b. Single individuals can have a real influence on politics if they will speak up and let their wishes be known.

19. a. People seek responsibility in work.

 b. People try to get away with doing as little as they can.

20. a. The most popular people seem to have a special, inherent charisma that attracts people to them.

 b. People become popular because of how they behave.

21. a. Things over which I have little control just seem to occur in my life.

 b. Most of the time I feel responsible for the outcomes I produce.

22. a. Managers who improve their personal competence will succeed more than those who do not improve.

 b. Management success has very little to do with the competence possessed by the individual manager.

23. a. Teams that win championships in most sports are usually the teams that, in the end, have the most luck.

 b. More often than not, teams that win championships are those with the most talented players and the best preparation.

24. a. Teamwork in business is a prerequisite to success.

 b. Individual effort is the best hope for success.

25. a. Some workers are just lazy and can't be motivated to work hard no matter what you do.

 b. If you are a skillful manager, you can motivate almost any worker to put forth more effort.

26. a. In the long run, people can improve this country's economic strength through responsible action.

 b. The economic health of this country is largely beyond the control of individuals.

27. a. I am persuasive when I know I'm right.

 b. I can persuade most people even when I'm not sure I'm right.

28. a. I tend to plan ahead and generate steps to accomplish the goals that I have set.

 b. I seldom plan ahead because things generally turn out OK anyway.

29. a. Some things are just meant to be.

 b. We can change anything in our lives by hard work, persistence, and ability.

TOLERANCE OF AMBIGUITY SCALE

Please respond to the following statements by indicating the extent to which you agree or disagree with them. Fill in the blanks with the number from the rating scale that best represents your evaluation of the item. The scoring key is at the end of the chapter.

Rating Scale

1 Strongly disagree
2 Moderately disagree
3 Slightly disagree
4 Neither agree nor disagree
5 Slightly agree
6 Moderately agree
7 Strongly agree

_____ 1. An expert who doesn't come up with a definite answer probably doesn't know too much.

_____ 2. I would like to live in a foreign country for a while.

_____ 3. There is really no such thing as a problem that can't be solved.

_____ 4. People who fit their lives to a schedule probably miss most of the joy of living.

_____ 5. A good job is one where what is to be done and how it is to be done are always clear.

_____ 6. It is more fun to tackle a complicated problem than to solve a simple one.

_____ 7. In the long run it is possible to get more done by tackling small, simple problems rather than large and complicated ones.

_____ 8. Often the most interesting and stimulating people are those who don't mind being different and original.

_____ 9. What we are used to is always preferable to what is unfamiliar.

_____ 10. People who insist upon a yes or no answer just don't know how complicated things really are.

_____ 11. A person who leads an even, regular life in which few surprises or unexpected happenings arise really has a lot to be grateful for.

_____ 12. Many of our most important decisions are based upon insufficient information.

_____ 13. I like parties where I know most of the people more than ones where all or most of the people are complete strangers.

_____ 14. Teachers or supervisors who hand out vague assignments give one a chance to show initiative and originality.

_____ 15. The sooner we all acquire similar values and ideals the better.

_____ 16. A good teacher is one who makes you wonder about your way of looking at things.

Source: _Tolerance of Ambiguity Scale, S. Budner (1962), "Intolerance of Ambiguity as a Personality Variable,"_ from Journal of Personality, _30: 29–50. Reprinted with the permission of Blackwell Publishing, Ltd._

CORE SELF-EVALUATION SCALE (CSES)

Below are several statements with which you may agree or disagree. Using the response scale below, indicate your level of agreement or disagreement with each statement.

Rating Scale

1 Strongly disagree
2 Disagree
3 Neutral
4 Agree
5 Strongly agree

_____ 1. I am confident I get the success I deserve in life.

_____ 2. Sometimes I feel depressed.

_____ 3. When I try, I generally succeed.

_____ 4. Sometimes when I fail I feel worthless.

_____ 5. I complete tasks successfully.

_____ 6. Sometimes, I do not feel in control of my work.

_____ 7. Overall, I am satisfied with myself.

_____ 8. I am filled with doubts about my competence.

_____ 9. I determine what will happen in my life.

_____ 10. I do not feel in control of my success in my career.

_____ 11. I am capable of coping with most of my problems.

_____ 12. There are times when things look pretty bleak and hopeless to me.

SOURCE: *Judge, Erez, Bono, and Thoreson, 2003. Courtesy of* Personnel Psychology.

Key Dimensions of Self-Awareness

For more than 300 years, knowledge of the self has been considered to be at the very core of human behavior. The ancient dictum "Know thyself" has been variously attributed to Plato, Pythagoras, Thales, and Socrates. Plutarch noted that this inscription was carved on the Delphic Oracle, that mystical sanctuary where kings and generals sought advice on matters of greatest importance to them. As early as 42 B.C., Publilius Syrus proposed: "It matters not what you are thought to be, but what you are." Alfred Lord Tennyson said: "Self-reverence, self-knowledge, self-control, these three alone lead to sovereign power." Probably the most oft-quoted passage on the self is Polonius' advice in Hamlet: "To thine own self be true, and it must follow as the night the day, thou canst not then be false to any man."

Messinger reminded us: "He that would govern others must first master himself." **Self-awareness** lies at the heart of the ability to master oneself, but it is not sufficient. While self-management depends first and foremost on self-awareness, as illustrated in Figure 1.1, other self-management skills are closely linked to and build upon self-awareness. Developing self-control, for example, and clarifying priorities and goals, help individuals create direction in their own lives. Effectively managing time and stress make it possible for individuals to adapt to and organize their surroundings.

This chapter centers on the core aspects of self-management and serves as the foundation for the following chapter on stress and time management. Moreover, as Figure 1.1 illustrates, when problems arise in personal management, the easily recognized symptoms are often time pressures or experienced stress. However, those symptoms are often linked to more fundamental problems with self-awareness and out-of-balance priorities so we begin with a focus on enhancing knowledge of oneself.

Despite the research cited above, students of human behavior have long known that knowledge of oneself—self-awareness, self-insight, self-understanding—is essential to one's productive personal and interpersonal functioning, and in understanding and empathizing with other people. A host of techniques and methods for achieving self-knowledge have long been available—including group methods, meditation techniques, altered consciousness procedures, aromatherapy, assorted massages, physical exercise regimens, and biofeedback. It is estimated that Americans alone spend between $30 billion and $50 billion on such therapies. In this chapter we do not summarize those various approaches to enhanced self-awareness, nor do we espouse any one procedure in par-ticular. Instead, our objective is to help you understand the importance of self-awareness if you are to be a suc-cessful manager—or a successful individual—and to provide you with some powerful self-assessment instruments that are related to managerial success. Our emphasis is on scientifically validated information linking self-awareness to the behavior of managers, and we try to avoid generalizations that have not been tested in research.

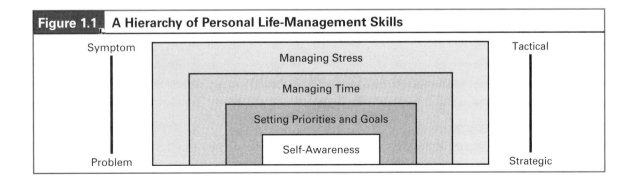

Figure 1.1 **A Hierarchy of Personal Life-Management Skills**

Symptom · Tactical

Managing Stress

Managing Time

Setting Priorities and Goals

Self-Awareness

Problem · Strategic

The Enigma of Self-Awareness

Erich Fromm (1939) was one of the first behavioral scientists to observe the close connection between one's self-concept and one's feelings about others: "Hatred against oneself is inseparable from hatred against others." Carl Rogers (1961) later proposed that self-awareness and self-acceptance are prerequisites for psychological health, personal growth, and the ability to know and accept others. In fact, Rogers suggested that the basic human need is for self-regard, which he found to be more powerful in his clinical cases than physiological needs. Brouwer (1964, p. 156) asserted:

> The function of self-examination is to lay the groundwork for insight, without which no growth can occur. Insight is the "Oh, I see now" feeling which must consciously or unconsciously precede change in behavior. Insights—real, genuine glimpses of ourselves as we really are—are reached only with difficulty and sometimes with real psychic pain. But they are the building blocks of growth. Thus, self-examination is a preparation for insight, a groundbreaking for the seeds of self-understanding which gradually bloom into changed behavior.

There is little question that the knowledge we possess about ourselves, which makes up our self-concept, is central to improving our management skills. We cannot improve ourselves or develop new capabilities unless and until we know what level of capability we currently possess. Considerable empirical evidence exists that individuals who are more self-aware are more healthy, perform better in managerial and leadership roles, and are more productive at work (Boyatzis, 1982; Cervone, 1997; Spencer & Spencer, 1993).

On the other hand, self-knowledge may inhibit personal improvement rather than facilitate it. The reason is that individuals frequently evade personal growth and new self-knowledge. They resist acquiring additional information in order to protect their self-esteem or self-respect. If they acquire new knowledge about themselves, there is always the possibility that it will be negative or that it will lead to feelings of inferiority, weakness, evilness, or shame. So they avoid new self-knowledge. As Maslow (1962, p. 57) notes:

> We tend to be afraid of any knowledge that would cause us to despise ourselves or to make us feel inferior, weak, worthless, evil, shameful. We protect ourselves and our ideal image of ourselves by repression and similar defenses, which are essentially techniques by which we avoid becoming conscious of unpleasantness or dangerous truths.

We avoid personal growth, then, because we fear finding out that we are not all that we would like to be. If there is a better way to be, our current state must therefore be inadequate or inferior. The realization that one is not totally adequate or knowledgeable is difficult for many people to accept. This resistance is the "denying of our best side, of our talents, of our finest impulses, of our highest potentialities, of our creativeness. In brief, this is the struggle against our own greatness" (Maslow, 1962, p. 58). Freud (1956) asserted that to be completely honest with oneself is the best effort an individual can make, because complete honesty requires a continual search for more information about the self and a desire for self-improvement. The results of that search are usually uncomfortable.

Seeking knowledge of the self, therefore, seems to be an enigma. It is a prerequisite for and motivator of growth and improvement, but it may also inhibit growth and improvement. It may lead to stagnation because of fear of knowing more. How, then, can improvement be accomplished? How can management skills be developed if the self-knowledge necessary for the development of those skills is resisted?

THE SENSITIVE LINE

One answer relies on the concept of the **sensitive line**. This concept refers to the point at which individuals become defensive or protective when encountering information about themselves that is inconsistent with their self-concept or when encountering pressure to alter their behavior. Most people regularly experience information about themselves that doesn't quite fit or that is marginally inconsistent. For example, a friend might say, "You look tired today. Are you feeling okay?" If you are feeling fine, the information is inconsistent with your self-awareness. But because the discrepancy is relatively minor, it would not be likely to offend you or evoke a strong defensive reaction. That is, it would probably not require that you reexamine and change your self-concept.

On the other hand, the more discrepant the information or the more serious its implications for your self-concept, the closer it would approach your sensitive line, and you would feel a need to defend yourself against it. For example, having a coworker judge you incompetent as a manager may cross your sensitive line if you think you have done a good job as a manager. This would be especially true if the coworker was an influential person. Your response would probably be to defend yourself against the information to protect the image you hold of yourself.

This response is known as the **threat-rigidity response** (Staw, Sandelands, & Dutton, 1981; Weick, 1993). When individuals are threatened, when they encounter uncomfortable information, or when uncertainty is created, they tend to become rigid. They hunker down, protect themselves, and become risk averse. Consider what happens when you are startled or suddenly shocked by something unexpected. Physically, your body tends to become rigid in order to protect itself. It tightens up to safeguard stability. Similarly, individuals also become rigid—psychologically and emotionally—when they encounter information that is a threat to their self-concept. They tend to redouble their efforts to protect what is comfortable and familiar (Cameron, 1994; Cameron, Kim, & Whetten, 1987; Weick & Sutcliffe, 2000). They rely on first-learned or most reinforced behavior patterns and emotions. When discrepancies in the self-image are encountered, in other words, the validity of the information or its source is denied, or other kinds of defense mechanisms are used to ensure that the self-concept remains stable. Crossing the sensitive line creates rigidity and self-preservation.

In light of this defensiveness, then, how can increased self-knowledge and personal change ever occur? There are at least two answers. One is that information that is verifiable, predictable, and controllable is less likely to cross the sensitive line than information without those characteristics. That is, if an individual can test the validity of the discrepant information (for example, if some objective standard exists for evaluating the accuracy of the information), if the information is not unexpected or "out-of-the-blue" (for example, if it is received at regular intervals), and if there is some control over what, when, and how much information is received (for example, if it is requested), the feedback is more likely to be heard and accepted. The information you receive about yourself in this chapter possesses those three characteristics. You have already completed several self-assessment instruments that have been used extensively in research. Their reliability and validity have been established. Moreover, they have been found to be associated with managerial success. Therefore, as you analyze your scores and seek honestly to understand more about your underlying attributes, you can gain important insight that will prove to be very useful.

A second answer to the problem of overcoming resistance to self-examination lies in the role other people can play in helping insight to occur. It is almost impossible to increase skill in self-awareness unless we interact with and disclose ourselves to others. Unless one is willing to open up to others, to discuss aspects of the self that seem ambiguous or unknown, little growth can ever occur. **Self-disclosure**, therefore, is a key to improvement in self-awareness. Harris (1981) points out:

> In order to know oneself, no amount of intro-spection or self-examination will suffice. You can analyze yourself for weeks, or meditate for months, and you will not get an inch further—any more than you can smell your own breath or laugh when you tickle yourself.
>
> You must first be open to the other person before you catch a glimmering of yourself. Our self-reflection in a mirror does not tell us what we are like; only our reflection in other people. We are essentially social creatures, and our personality resides in association, not in isolation.

As you engage in the practice exercises in this chapter, therefore, you are encouraged to discuss your insights with someone else. A lack of self-disclosure not only inhibits self-awareness but also may affect adversely other aspects of managerial skill development. For example, several studies have shown that low self-disclosers are less healthy and more self-alienated than high self-disclosers. College students give the highest ratings for interpersonal competence to high self-disclosers. Individuals who are high self-disclosers are liked best, and excessive or insufficient self-disclosure results in less liking and acceptance by others (see, for example, Covey, 1989; Goleman, 1998b; Kelley, 1999).

Some of the exercises in this chapter will require you to discuss your experiences with others. This is because involving others in the process of self-understanding will be a critical aspect of your personal growth. These interactions, of course, should be sincere, honest, and motivated by self-understanding and self-improvement. Never should the information you share or receive be used to judge or wound another person. Maintaining a trusting relationship with someone with whom you can share is a critical prerequisite to self-understanding.

The enigma of self-awareness can be managed, then, by exercising some control over when and what kind of information you receive about yourself, and by involving others in your pursuit of self-understanding. The support and feedback individuals receive from others during the process of self-disclosure, besides helping to increase feedback and self-awareness, helps information contribute to greater self-awareness without crossing the sensitive line.

Understanding and Appreciating Individual Differences

Another important reason for focusing on self-awareness is to help you develop the ability to diagnose important differences among others with whom you interact. There is considerable evidence that an individual's effectiveness as a manager is closely related to his or her ability to recognize, appreciate, and ultimately utilize key, fundamental differences among others. This topic is commonly discussed in the management literature under the subject of "managing diversity." The diversity literature has progressed through a series of stages, beginning with a plethora of statistics demonstrating the extent to which, and the specific ways in which, the workforce is becoming more diverse. This was followed by evidence-based arguments touting the merits of a diverse group of workers contributing to the performance of a work group (Cox, 1994). The primary sources of diversity discussed in this literature are gender, age, culture, and ethnicity.

In this chapter, and throughout the book, we use broader, more inclusive, and less ambiguous terminology that is more conducive to skill development. Whereas it is difficult, for example, to understand all the ramifications of "managing diversity," it is not difficult to be sensitive to certain important differences that affect the way you manage others. In other words, this chapter has two objectives: (1) to help you better understand your own uniqueness as an individual—to become better equipped to manage yourself—and (2) to help you diagnose, value, and utilize the differences you find in other people.

Self-knowledge will help you understand your own taken-for-granted assumptions, trigger points, sensitive line, comfort zone, strengths and weaknesses, and so forth. This knowledge is useful for all of us, not because we can or should change fundamental dimensions of ourselves, but because it helps make our interactions with others more effective and insightful. It also helps us gain a more complete understanding of our potential for contributing value in our future career roles and our special strengths relative to others. It is not unusual for many of us to feel intimidated at times, for example, by heroic or luminary figures whose suc-

cess is attributed to charisma, intelligence, or style. We feel we are somehow diminished and less able because of what we see in others. Self-knowledge allows us to recognize our own special gifts and strengths and to capitalize on our talents.

Diagnosing fundamental differences in others is, similarly, an important part of being an effective manager. Being aware of, and empathetic toward, the different perspectives, needs, and inclinations of other people is a key part of emotional intelligence and interpersonal maturity. Most people, however, have a tendency to interact with individuals who are like themselves, to choose similar people to work with them, and to exclude others who seem to be different (Berscheid & Walster, 1978). The history of human warfare and conflict testifies to the fact that differences are usually interpreted as frightening or threatening. However, although fostering similarity seemingly makes it easier to interact with other people, especially in a work setting, it also reduces creativity, complex problem solving, and the likelihood that working colleagues will challenge the perspective of the authority figure. Research on organizational failure has repeatedly demonstrated that a lack of diversity in the composition of key decision-making bodies makes it difficult for them to recognize changes in their environment and to respond in appropriately new and novel ways (Cameron, Kim, & Whetten, 1987).

One key to helping individuals feel comfortable discussing ways in which they are different is by sharing a commitment to focusing on *differences* not *distinctions*. We observe differences; we create distinctions. Differences help us understand potential sources of misunderstanding between people and give us clues for how we can work together more effectively. Distinctions create social barriers between people for the express purpose of creating (or reinforcing) advantages and disadvantages. When someone discounts the opinion of a coworker, for example, on the grounds that the person is "a member of the old boys' club," "from marketing," "a woman," or "doesn't have a college degree," he or she is creating a distinction that is not only potentially hurtful on a personal basis but ineffective for the organization.

The creation of such distinctions destroys trust among people, even if the distinctions refer to individuals who are not present. If you were to apply distinctions that belittled someone in another group, for example, that action plants a seed of mistrust in the minds of people who are present regarding what distinctions you may be privately using to discount them. The point is, recognizing differences is not the same as evaluating distinctions. One is helpful; the other is hurtful. Moreover, when others feel that self-disclosing information could be used against them—that is, they could be placed on the disadvantaged side of a distinction—they will be reluctant to participate in any self-discovery process, especially one that requires them to share information about their personal characteristics.

To repeat, self-awareness and understanding differences cannot occur without self-disclosure, sharing, and trusting conversations. Self-knowledge requires an understanding and valuing of differences, not the creation of distinctions. We encourage you, therefore, to use the information you discover about yourself and others to build, grow, and value both of you in your interactions.

Important Areas of Self-Awareness

Of course, an innumerable quantity of personal dimensions is available to explore if one is to develop in-depth self-awareness. For example, numerous aspects of cognitive style have been measured; authors have identified more than a dozen "intelligences" (ranging from social and practical to cognitive and creative); literally hundreds of personality factors have been investigated in the psychological literature; the mapping of the human chromosome has raised the possibility that hundreds of physiological differences may be crucial in understanding behavior; gender, age, cultural, ethnic, and experience differences all develop individually over time. It is impossible, of course, to accurately select the few best or most central aspects of self-awareness because the alternatives are just too numerous. On the other hand, we focus here on five of the most critical areas of self-awareness that have been found to be key in developing successful management. They are: emotional intelligence, personal values, cognitive style, orientation toward change, and core self-evaluation. These areas represent a limited set of factors, of course, but they have been found to be among the most important predictors of various aspects of effective managerial performance—including achieving life success, performing effectively in teams, competent decision making, life-long learning and development, creativity, communication competency, job satisfaction, and job performance (Allan & Waclawski, 1999; Atwater & Yammarino, 1992; Goleman, 1998b; Judge et al., 2003; Parker & Kram, 1993; Sosik & Megerian, 1999; Cools & Van den Broeck, 2007).

Research on the concept of **emotional intelligence**—the ability to manage oneself and to manage relationships with others—has been identified as among the most important factors in accounting for success in leaders and managers (Boyatzis, Goleman, & Rhee, 2000; Goleman, 1998a). In particular, self-awareness has been identified as a crucial aspect of emotional intelligence, and it is more powerful than IQ in predicting success in life (Goleman, 1995). One study, for example, tried to identify differences between star performers and average managers in 40 companies. Emotional intelligence competencies, including self-awareness, were *twice* as important in contributing to excellence as cognitive intelligence (IQ) and expertise (Goleman, 1998a). In a study of a multinational consulting firm, superior performing partners were compared to average performing partners. Superior performers—who had significantly higher emotional intelligence and self-awareness scores—contributed more than twice the revenues to the firm and were four times more likely to be promoted than those with low self-awareness and emotional intelligence (Boyatzis, 1998).

Personal values are included here because they are "the core of the dynamics of behavior, and play so large a part in unifying personality" (Allport, Gordon, & Vernon, 1931, p. 2). That is, all other attitudes, orientations, and behaviors arise out of an individuals' values. Two major types of values are considered: *instrumental* and *terminal* (Rokeach, 1973). We present research findings that relate personal development in these two types of values to successful managerial performance. The assessment instrument that assesses your values development is discussed, along with information concerning the scores of other groups of people. You will want to compare your scores with individuals who are close to you, as well as with successful managers. Some comparison data is provided for that purpose. Because this discussion of values development is connected to ethical decision making, the implications of managerial ethics are also discussed in this section.

A third area of self-awareness is **cognitive style**, which refers to the manner in which individuals gather and process information. Researchers have found that individual differences in cognitive style influence perception, learning, problem solving, decision making, communication, and creativity (Cools & Van den Broeck, 2007; Hayes & Allinson, 1994; Kirton, 2003). A large number of dimensions of cognitive style have been identified, but we have selected an instrument in this chapter that captures the most frequently studied dimensions (Cools & Van den Broeck, 2007). A discussion of the critical dimensions of cognitive style is presented, and it will assist you in learning more about your own style based on the assessment instrument that you have completed. Empirical research linking cognitive style to successful managerial behavior is also discussed.

Fourth, a discussion of **orientation toward change** focuses on the methods people use to cope with change in their environment. In the twenty-first century, of course, all of us will be faced with increasingly fragmented, rapidly changing, tumultuous conditions (Peters, 1987). It is important that you become aware of your orientation toward adapting to these conditions. Two important dimensions—*locus of control* and *intolerance of ambiguity*—have been measured by two assessment instruments. Research connecting these two dimensions to effective management is discussed in the sections that follow.

Finally, **core self-evaluation** is a recently developed construct that captures the essential aspects of personality. More than 50,000 studies have been conducted on what has been referred to as "the Big Five" personality dimensions—neuroticism, extroversion, conscientiousness, agreeableness, and openness—but an underlying factor has been found to account for the effects of these personality dimensions. It is referred to as core self-evaluation (Judge et al., 2003), and we provide an instrument that assesses your core self-evaluation. Some important research on this construct is explained in this chapter relating to how scores correlate with success at work and in life. By analyzing your scores, you not only learn about your underlying personality dimensions, but you also will learn about how they are associated with other important behaviors such as motivation, problem solving, creativity, life satisfaction, and work performance.

These five areas of self-awareness—emotional intelligence, personal values, learning style, orientation toward change, and core self-evaluation—constitute the very core of the self-concept. Emotional intelligence identifies the extent to which people are able to recognize and control their own emotions, as well as to recognize and respond appropriately to the emotions of others. Values identify an individual's basic standards about what is good and bad, worthwhile and worthless, desirable and undesirable, true and false, moral and immoral. Cognitive style identifies individual thought processes, perceptions, and methods for acquiring and storing information. It determines not only what kind of information is received by an individual, but how that individual interprets, judges, and responds to the information. Orientation toward change identifies the adaptability of individuals. It includes the extent to which individuals are tolerant of ambiguous, uncertain conditions, and the extent to which they are inclined to accept personal responsibility for their actions under changing conditions. Core self-evaluation identifies the general personality orientation that guides behavior. It

uncovers levels of self-esteem, self-efficacy, emotional stability, and self-control that have important effects on individuals' happiness as well as managerial effectiveness. Figure 1.2 summarizes these five aspects of self-awareness, along with their functions in defining the self-concept.

Again, many other aspects of self-awareness could be considered in this chapter, but all these aspects of the self are related fundamentally to the five core concepts discussed here. What we value, how we feel about ourselves, how we behave toward others, what we want to achieve, and what we are attracted to all are strongly influenced by our emotional intelligence, values, cognitive style, orientation toward change, and core self-evaluation. These are among the most important building blocks upon which other aspects of the self emerge.

On the other hand, if you want to do a more in-depth analysis of multiple aspects of self-awareness, instruments such as the Strong-Campbell Vocational Inventory, the Minnesota Multiphasic Personality Inventory, the Myers-Briggs Type Indicator, the Stanford-Binet Intelligence Test, and a host of other instruments are available in most college counseling centers or testing centers. Be careful, however, of the multiple assessment instruments you can find on numerous Web sites. Most are not reliable or valid. On the other hand, no one, it should be emphasized, can get too much self-knowledge.

EMOTIONAL INTELLIGENCE

Emotional intelligence has become a very popular topic that, unfortunately, suffers from the problem that almost all trendy concepts encounter. Its meaning and measurement have become very confusing and ambiguous. Emotional intelligence has come to encompass almost everything that is noncognitive—including social, emotional, behavioral, attitudinal, and personality factors—so the extent to which it can be adequately measured and predictive of outcomes remains cloudy. Since the publication of Daniel Goleman's book *Emotional Intelligence* in 1995, interest in the concept of emotional intelligence has mushroomed (even though the concept was introduced in 1990 by Salovey and Mayer). Several thousand books have been published on the topic, and scores of consulting companies and executive coaches now advertise themselves as experts in helping others develop emotional intelligence. The number of instruments available to assess emotional intelligence is voluminous (more than 100), although only three or four have been scientifically validated and used in any systematic investigations.

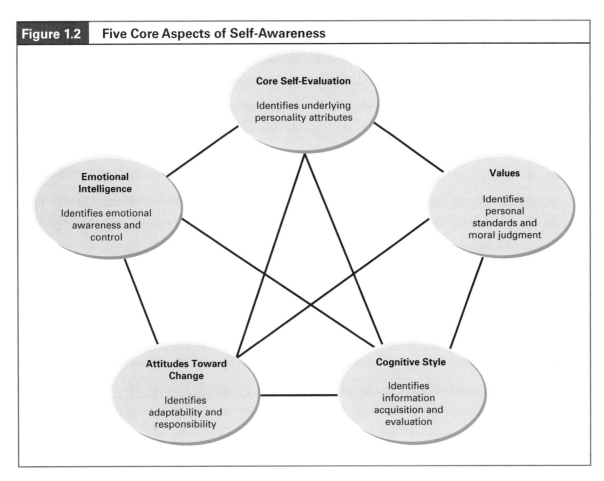

Figure 1.2   Five Core Aspects of Self-Awareness

Core Self-Evaluation

Identifies underlying personality attributes

Emotional Intelligence

Identifies emotional awareness and control

Values

Identifies personal standards and moral judgment

Attitudes Toward Change

Identifies adaptability and responsibility

Cognitive Style

Identifies information acquisition and evaluation

In particular, only Bar-On's *EQ-I* measure (Bar-On, 1997)—a self-report instrument that defines emotional intelligence as an array of noncognitive skills; Salovey's *Multifactor Emotional Intelligence Scale* (Salovey & Mayer, 1990)—a behavioral assessment that defines emotional intelligence as "a form of social intelligence that involves the ability to monitor one's own and others' feelings and emotions, to discriminate among them, and to use this information to guide one's thinking and action"(p. 185); and Goleman and Boyatzis' *Emotional Competence Inventory* (Boyatzis et al., 2000)—a 360-degree assessment that defines emotional intelligence as "the composite set of capabilities that enable a person to manage himself or herself and others," (p. 344) have been scientifically validated. The trouble is, each of these instruments is far too lengthy to be included in this text, and each is protected under copyright. Virtually all other instruments, including the one included in this book, are designed merely to provide a general estimate of particular dimensions of emotional intelligence, and extensive research has not yet been published.

As you can tell by the widely differing definitions associated with the three major assessment instruments described above, the concept of emotional intelligence has been defined as embracing almost everything. A scan of the scientific and popular writing on emotional intelligence confirms this conclusion—almost everything and anything is defined as an aspect of emotional intelligence. Our colleagues Richard Boyatzis and Daniel Goleman, for example—two of the chief researchers in the field of emotional intelligence—explicitly include all capabilities that help people manage themselves and others. These include, for example, leadership, influence, conflict management, communication, self-confidence, and teamwork. Other scholars limit emotional intelligence to a much narrower set of factors. Mayer, Caruso, and Salovey (1998) for example, reduce emotional intelligence to the ability to adequately diagnose and react to emotions.

One way to clarify this problem of multiple definitions is to differentiate between *emotional intelligence* and *emotional competence.* Emotional intelligence refers to the ability to diagnose, understand, and manage emotional cues. Emotional competence refers to the noncognitive capabilities and skills—including social skills—that affect human functioning. The first definition is the one we have adopted in this chapter because the remainder of this book is focused on helping you develop competency and capability in skills that some would include under the emotional competence umbrella. That is, the management skills covered in this text—which have been well-researched and found to predict the success of managers and leaders—are sometimes included in discussions of the impact of emotional intelligence. In this regard, we agree that they are critical. These noncognitive skills and abilities are, in fact, among the most important factors in explaining why some people succeed as leaders and managers and others do not.

On the other hand, a much narrower treatment of emotional intelligence limits it to *emotions*, not to social or interpersonal skills. This is the position we adopt in this chapter. We will help you assess, in an in-depth and rigorous way, other social and behavioral skills throughout the remainder of the book. It is important to point out that a certain degree of emotional *intelligence* is necessary in order for people to develop emotional *competencies* (i.e., social and behavioral competencies), so this aspect of self-awareness is an important prerequisite to your developing other management skills.

Emotional intelligence, then, refers to: (1) the ability to diagnose and recognize your own emotions, (2) the ability to control your own emotions, (3) the ability to recognize and diagnose the emotions displayed by others, and (4) the ability to respond appropriately to those emotional cues. These abilities are not in-born but can be developed and improved. Unlike IQ, for example, which remains relatively constant over a lifetime, emotional intelligence can be enhanced with practice. With concerted effort, people can change their levels of emotional intelligence. The instrument you completed in the Pre-assessment section assesses these four dimensions, and we briefly explain them below.

One of our acquaintances, who now readily admits having made progress in developing emotional intelligence, had a great deal of difficulty recognizing and diagnosing her own emotions. When something seemed to go wrong and she was asked, "Are you upset?" she would invariably deny her feelings—"No, I'm fine." She had never learned to accurately diagnose her own emotional state. This ability is simply the capacity to identify and label your own emotions. Try, for example, to identify the emotion you are feeling right now. Can you label it? Emotionally intelligent people are able to get in touch with and accurately *diagnose* their own internal feelings.

Emotionally intelligent people are also able to *regulate* and control their emotions. They are less likely to blow up and lose control, less likely to experience debilitating depression and anxiety, and more likely to manage their own emotional states than those with less emotional intelligence. Think of how you behave in a sporting event, for example, when the officials make a bad call; when someone gets angry at you and berates you; when you are criticized for something you did; or, alternatively, when you receive special accolades and recognition. Emotionally intelligent people remain in control of their emotions, whereas less emotionally intelligent people lose control. This ability does not mean being bland or even-tempered all the time—emotionally intelligent people may display a wide range of emotions and intensity. Instead, it means that a person can control his or her emotions so that they are not unrestrained.

Emotionally intelligent people are also able to accurately diagnose and empathize with the feelings of others. They are sensitive to what others are experiencing, and they can share in those feelings. Empathy refers to the ability to understand and connect with others' feelings. It does not mean sympathizing or adopting the same feelings, and it is not based on a memory of having experienced the same emotions. If someone has experienced a tragedy or loss, for example, emotionally intelligent people can empathize, share in, and understand those feelings even if they have never experienced something similar. They need not be depressed themselves, for example, in order to understand the depression of others.

Emotionally intelligent people also *respond* appropriately to the emotions of others. Their responses match the intensity of the emotions other people feel, and they support and encourage emotional expressions. That is, if others are excited and happy, they do not remain aloof and withdrawn. They endorse the expression of emotions in others, rather than suppressing or censoring those emotions. On the other hand, they are not merely manipulated in their feelings and responses by the emotions of others. They don't respond merely on the basis of others' feelings. Rather, they remain in personal control of their responses. They advance a sense of caring for, and acceptance of, the other person by means of their emotional responses.

One reason emotional intelligence is so important is that general competency levels seem to have deteriorated over time. Whereas average IQ points have increased almost 25 points over the last 100 years—people tend to be smarter now than 100 years ago—emotional intelligence scores have actually declined (Goleman, 1998a). Think, for example, of the amount of litigation, conflict, disrespect, and divorce that characterizes our society. Less emphasis is placed on emotional intelligence development now than in the past. This is a problem because emotional intelligence has strong predictive power regarding success in management and in work setting—much stronger, in fact, than IQ scores. For example, it is estimated that IQ accounts for only about 10 percent of the variance in job performance and in life success (Sternberg, 1996), but by adding emotional intelligence (EQ) to the equation, we can account for four times more variance.

For example, a study was conducted of 450 boys who grew up in a small town in Massachusetts. Two thirds of the boys lived in welfare families and one third had IQ scores below 90. They were followed over 40 years, and it was found that IQ had almost nothing to do with life success. Emotional intelligence, on the other hand, was the most predictive factor (Snarey & Vaillant, 1985). Another study of 80 PhDs in science who attended the University of California at Berkeley in the 1950s found that what accounted for life success 40 years after graduation was mainly emotional intelligence scores. Emotional intelligence was four times more important than IQ in determining who had achieved in their careers, were evaluated by experts as being highly successful, and were listed in sources such as *Who's Who* and *American Men and Women of Science* (Feist & Barron, 1996). A study of workers followed over 20 years found that employees who were better at empathizing with others—that is, demonstrating a key aspect of emotional intelligence—were more successful in their work, as well as in their social lives (Rosenthal, 1977).

Emotional intelligence has also been found to be an important predictor of managerial success. In a study of managers on three continents, for example, 74 percent of successful managers had emotional intelligence as their most salient characteristic, whereas this was the case in only 24 percent of the failures. A study at PepsiCo found that company units headed by managers with well-developed emotional intelligence skills outperformed yearly revenue targets by 15 to 20 percent. Those with underdeveloped skills underperformed their targets by about the same amount (Goleman, Boyatzis, & McKee, 2002). A McBer study comparing outstanding managers with average managers found that 90 percent of the difference was accounted for by emotional intelligence. In a worldwide study of what companies were looking for in hiring new employees, 67 percent of the most desired attributes were emotional intelligence competencies (Goleman et al., 2002). In a study of highly emotionally intelligent partners in a consulting firm, in which they were compared to partners with average

emotional intelligence, 41 percent of the high emotional intelligence group had been promoted after two years whereas only 10 percent of the low emotional intelligence partners had been promoted. More importantly, high emotional intelligence partners contributed more than twice as much revenue to the company as did the low emotional intelligence partners (Boyatzis, 1982). The point should be clear: effective managers have developed high levels of competency in emotional intelligence.

The Emotional Intelligence Assessment instrument that you completed in the Pre-assessment section provides an evaluation of your competency in the four general areas of emotional intelligence—emotional awareness, emotional control or balance, emotional diagnosis or empathy, and emotional response. Of course, a fully accurate and valid measure of these factors would require an instrument many times longer than the one included here, so this assessment merely provides a glimpse or an incomplete evaluation of your emotional intelligence capability. Your scores should help you identify areas of strength but also motivate you to pursue the development of your emotional intelligence. This may effectively be done by consciously practicing emotional diagnosis, control, and response in yourself and others, but, especially, it may also be significantly enhanced by learning, and improving the skills discussed in this book. They are, according to a variety of writers (e.g., Goleman, 1998b; Boyatzis et al., 2000), critical components of the broad definition of emotional intelligence.

VALUES

Values are among the most stable and enduring characteristics of individuals. They are the foundation upon which attitudes and personal preferences are formed. They are the basis for crucial decisions, life directions, and personal tastes. They help define our morality and our conceptions of what is "good." Much of what we are is a product of the basic values we have developed throughout our lives.

The trouble with values, unfortunately, is that they are taken for granted, and people are often unaware of them. Unless a person's values are challenged, the values being held remain largely undetected. People especially are not aware that they hold some values as being more important than others. This unawareness leads to actions or behaviors that are sometimes contrary to values, or even to confusion about values. Until people encounter a contradiction or a threat to their basic values, they seldom articulate their values or seek to clarify them.

The values held by each of us are affected by a variety of factors, and a number of ways have been used to measure and describe values. We point out several ways in this chapter—each of which has been widely used in research and in management circles. The first is a framework for describing the broad, general value orientations that characterize large groups, such as nationalities, ethnic groups, industries, or organizations. Much research has been done, for example, on identifying the differences in values that arise across cultural groups. The point of this research is to identify ways in which nationalities differ from one another, since almost all managers now face the need to manage across national boundaries. In your own life, it is likely that you will interact more and more with individuals who do not share your birth country, and knowing something about their value orientations will help your interactions be more effective. It has been discovered that values differ systematically across national cultures, and these differences are a strong influence in predicting the values each of us hold ourselves. At least some of our values are affected significantly by the country and culture in which we are raised.

Cultural Values

Trompenaars (1996; Trompenaars & Hampden-Turner, 1998) identified seven value dimensions upon which significant differences exist among national cultures. Data are based upon 30,000 managers in 55 countries, and results show that certain cultures emphasize some values more than others do. Table 1.1 identifies Trompenaars' seven dimensions, and we provide examples of countries that represent each of the value dimensions. No national culture emphasizes one of these dimensions to the exclusion of another, but there are clear differences in the amount of emphasis placed on each dimension.

The first five dimensions of the model refer to how individuals relate to other people. For example, some

Table 1.1	Cultural Values Dimensions	
VALUE DIMENSIONS	**EXPLANATION**	**EXAMPLE OF COUNTRIES WITH DOMINANCE**
Universalism	Societal rules and norms are valued.	United States, Switzerland, Norway, Sweden
Particularism	Individual relationships are valued.	Korea, Venezuela, China, Indonesia
Individualism	Individual contributions are valued.	United States, Nigeria, Denmark, Austria
Collectivism	Team contributions are valued.	Mexico, Indonesia, Japan, Philippines
Affective	Showing emotions is valued.	Iran, Spain, France, Switzerland
Neutral	Unemotional responses are valued.	Korea, Ethiopia, China, Japan
Specific	Segregating life's roles is valued.	Holland, Sweden, Denmark, United Kingdom
Diffuse	Integrating life's role is valued.	China, Nigeria, Singapore, Korea
Achievement	Personal accomplishment is valued.	United States, Norway, Canada, Austria
Ascription	Inherent attributes are valued.	Egypt, Indonesia, Korea, Czech Republic
Past and Present	Past is tightly connected to future.	France, Japan, United Kingdom
Future	Future is disconnected but valued.	United States, Holland
Internal	Individual control is valued.	United States, Canada, Austria, United Kingdom
External	Control comes from outside forces.	Czech Republic, Japan, Egypt, China

SOURCE: *C. Hampden-Turner and F. Trompenaars, (1998). "Riding the waves of culture." Reprinted with the permission of the McGraw-Hill Companies.*

countries (e.g., the United States, Norway, Sweden, Switzerland) emphasize a value of **universalism**, in which other people's behavior is governed by universal standards and rules—e.g., do not lie, do not cheat, do not run a red light, even if no one is coming the other way. General societal rules govern behavior. Other countries (e.g., Korea, China, Indonesia, Singapore) hold a value of **particularism**, in which the relationship with an individual governs behavior—e.g., is the other person a friend, a family member, a relative? To illustrate the differences, consider your answer to this question: *You are driving in a car with a close friend who hits a pedestrian while going 40 miles an hour in a 25-mile-an-hour zone. There are no witnesses, and your friend's lawyer says that if you'll testify that he was only traveling 25 miles an hour, he'll get off. Will you lie for him?* People in universalistic cultures are more likely to refuse than people in particularistic cultures. For example 97 percent of the Swiss and 93 percent of North Americans (Canada and the United States) would refuse to testify, whereas 32 percent of Venezuelans and 37 percent of South Koreans would refuse.

A second value dimension differentiates cultures that value **individualism**—an emphasis on the self, on independence, and on uniqueness—versus **collectivism**—an emphasis on the group, the combined unit, and on joining with others. Individualistic values hold the contributions of individuals to be most valued, whereas collectivism values team contributions. In general, individual responsibility dominates much more in Western cultures than in Eastern cultures. For example, consider your answer to this question: *What kind of job is found most frequently in your organization, one where everyone works together and you do not get individual credit, or one where everyone is allowed to work individually and you receive individual recognition?* Eastern Europeans (e.g, Russia, Czech Republic, Hungary, Poland) average above 80 percent in agreeing that individual credit is received, whereas Asians (e.g., Japan, India, Nepal) average below 45 percent. (The United States score is 72 percent.)

A third value dimension refers to the display of feelings in public. It identifies an **affective** versus **neutral** orientation. Cultures with high affective values tend to show emotions openly and to deal in emotional ways with problems. Loud laughter, anger, and intense passion may all be displayed in the course of a business negotiation, for example. Cultures with neutral values are more rational and stoic in their approach to problem solving. Instrumental, goal directed behaviors rather than emotions dominate interactions. For example, *if you became very upset at work or in class—say you feel slighted, offended, or angry—how likely would you be to display your feelings openly in public?* Managers in Japan, Ethiopia, and Hong Kong, for example, average 64 percent, 74 percent, and 81 percent respectively in refusing to show emotions publicly. On the other hand, 15 percent of Kuwait managers, 18 percent of Egyptian managers, and 19 percent of Spanish managers would refuse. (The United States score is 43 percent.)

A fourth dimension—**specific** versus **diffuse**—describes the difference between cultures that segregate the different roles in life so as to maintain privacy and personal autonomy compared to cultures that integrate and merge their roles. Cultures with specific values separate work relationships from family relationships, for example, whereas diffuse cultures entangle work and home relationships. People with specific values may seem hard to get to know because they keep a boundary between their personal lives and their work lives. People with diffuse values may seem too forward and too superficial because they seem to share personal information freely. Interestingly, diffuse cultures have lower turnover rates among employees and higher degrees of loyalty to an employer because work and personal relationships are more intertwined. To illustrate the difference, how would you respond to this question: *Your boss asks you to come to her home to help her paint her house. You don't want to do it since you hate painting. Would you refuse?* More than 90 percent of the Dutch and Swedes would refuse, whereas only 32 percent of the Chinese and 46 percent of Nigerians would refuse. (In the United States, 82 percent would refuse.)

A fifth value dimension differentiates cultures that emphasize an **achievement** orientation versus an **ascription** culture. People tend to acquire high status based on their personal accomplishments in some cultures, whereas in other cultures status and prestige are based more on ascribed characteristics such as age, gender, family heritage, or ethnic background. Who you know (ascription) versus what you can do (achievement) helps identify the difference on this value dimension. For example, the following statement helps highlight achievement versus ascription value differences: *It is important to act the way you are, to be consistent with your true self, even if you do not accomplish the task at hand.* Only 10 percent of managers from Uruguay, 12 percent from Argentina, and 13 percent from Spain disagree with the statement, whereas 77 percent of Norwegians and 75 percent of managers from the United States disagree.

A sixth value dimension relates to how people interpret and manage time. It distinguishes the emphasis placed on the past, present, or future in various cultures. Some cultures, for example, value past and tradition more than future; other cultures place more value on the future than the past. What you have achieved in the past matters more in some cultures than where you are headed in the future. Time differences also exist regarding short- versus long-time horizons. For example, some people are oriented toward very short time horizons where they think in terms of minutes and hours (a short-time horizon). Other people think in terms of months or years (a long-time horizon). Complete the following brief exercise, for example, to get a sense of your own time horizon. *Use the following scale and give a number to each of the following statements: My past started _____ ago, and ended _____ ago. My present started _____ ago and ended _____ from now. My future will start _____ from now and will end _____ from now. Use this rating scale: 7 = years, 6 = months, 5 = weeks, 4 = days, 3 = hours, 2 = minutes, 1 = seconds.*

By way of comparison, people in the Philippines averaged 3.40 on the scale, Irish managers averaged 3.82, and Brazilians averaged 3.85. On the other hand, managers in Hong Kong averaged 5.71, Portugal averaged 5.62, and Pakistan averaged 5.47. (People in the United States averaged 4.30.)

The seventh and final value dimension focuses on internal and external control. We will discuss this value dimension in more detail later in the chapter. It differentiates cultures that presume that individuals are in control of their own destinies from those that presume that nature or external forces control much of what happens. For example, some countries emphasize the value of individuals inventing or creating things themselves (internal control), whereas other countries emphasize the value of taking what already exists or has been created elsewhere and then refining or improving it (external control). Two statements that illustrate this difference are the following: *(1) What happens to me is my own doing. (2) Sometimes I feel that I do not have enough control over the directions my life is taking.* More than 80 percent of managers from Uruguay, Norway, Israel, and the United States agree with the first statement, whereas less than 40 percent of Venezuelans, Chinese, and Nepalese agree.

Throughout this book we will refer back to some of the differences that have been discovered among various cultures. We encourage you to begin using these dimensions to raise your awareness of individual differences around you. Because virtually every manager will be faced with the opportunity to interact with and manage individuals born in other cultures,

being aware of value differences, and being able to diagnose and manage those differences, is an important prerequisite for success in the twenty-first century. Of course, stereotyping people based on their national culture, or overgeneralizing based on trends such as those reported here, can be dangerous and misleading. None of us would like to be pigeonholed based on a general country profile. These dimensions, as you will see, are most useful for increasing sensitivity and helping with diagnosis rather than to place people in categories.

Like countries, organizations, too, have value systems, referred to as an **organizational culture**. Research has found that employees who hold values that are congruent with their organization's values are more productive and satisfied (Cable & Judge, 1996; Cameron & Quinn, 2006; Nwachukwu & Vitell, 1997; Posner & Kouzes, 1993). Holding values that are inconsistent with company values, on the other hand, is a major source of frustration, conflict, and nonproductivity. Being aware of your own priorities and values, the values of your organization, and the general value priorities of your country, are important if you expect to achieve compatibility at work and in a long-term career (Fisher, Macrosson, & Yusuff, 1996; Lobel, 1992). We will not spend time here discussing the various models available for assessing organizational culture. If you are interested in this topic, see Cameron and Quinn (2006).

Personal Values

Rokeach (1973) argued that the total number of values people possess is relatively small and that all individuals possess the same values, but in different degrees. For example, everyone values peace, but some make it a higher priority than others. Two general types of values were identified by Rokeach, and independent priority ratings have been found to exist for each type (that is, the two sets of values are largely unrelated). One general type of values is labeled instrumental, or means-oriented; the other type is terminal, or ends-oriented.

Instrumental values prescribe desirable standards of conduct or methods for attaining an end. Two types of instrumental values relate to morality and competence. Violating moral values (for example, behaving wrongly) causes feelings of guilt, while violating competence values (for example, behaving incapably) brings about feelings of shame.

Terminal values prescribe desirable ends or goals for the individual. There are fewer of them, according to Rokeach, than there are instrumental values, so the sum total for all individuals in all societies can be identified. Terminal values are either personal (for example, peace of mind) or social (for example, world peace). Rokeach has found that an increase in the priority of one personal value tends to increase the priority of other personal values and decrease the priority of social values. Conversely, an increase in the priority of one social value tends to increase the priority of other social values and decrease the value of personal values. Individuals who increase their priority for "a world at peace," for example, would also increase their priority for "equality" while decreasing their priority for "pleasure" or "self-respect." People tend to differ, in other words, in the extent to which they are self- versus others-orientated in their values.

In one study of 567 managers in 12 nations, the instrumental values "broadminded," "capable," and "courageous" were held in the highest esteem by managers from all 12 nations, but significant national differences were found on 75 percent of the values (Bigoness & Blakely, 1996). Another study of 658 Egyptians, 132 Americans, 43 Africans, and 101 Arabs found significant national differences on both instrumental and terminal values, with Egyptians being least like Americans (Elsayed-Elkhouly & Buda, 1997).

In a national study of 1,460 American managers, Schmidt and Posner (1982) assessed which of these values were most important in the workplace. Using Rokeach's instrumental values list, they asked managers to identify those that were most desired in the workplace. "Responsible" and "honest" were by far the most desired values in employees (over 85 percent of the managers selected them), followed by "capable" (65 percent), "imaginative" (55 percent), and "logical" (49 percent). "Obedient," "clean," "polite," and "forgiving" were the least important, being selected by fewer than 10 percent of the managers.

Different groups of people tend to differ in the values they hold. For example, in other studies, business school students and professors tend to rate "ambition," "capability," "responsibility," and "freedom" higher than people in general. They tend to place lower importance than people in general on concern and helpfulness to others, aesthetics and cultural values, and overcoming social injustice. In a study that compared highly successful, moderately successful, and unsuccessful managers, highly successful managers gave significantly higher scores to values relating to economic (for example, a comfortable life) and political values (for example, social recognition) than less successful managers.

Compared to the population in general, managers place substantially more value on "sense of accomplishment," "self-respect," "a comfortable life," and "independence." The instrumental value managers held highest for themselves, in fact, was "ambition"; their highest held terminal value was "sense of accomplishment." In other words, personal values (rather than social values) and those oriented toward achievement predominate among managers (Bilsky & Schwartz, 1994; Cable & Judge, 1996; Cavanaugh, 1980; Clare & Sanford, 1979). In the population in general, one study found that "openness to experience"—that is, a combination of a positive emphasis on broadmindedness, imagination, freedom, and self-direction coupled with a negative emphasis on recognition, obedience, and conformity—was the dominating value held by most people (Dollinger, Leong, & Ulicni, 1996). Interestingly, no gender differences have been found on the Rokeach instrument (Johnston, 1995).

These value preferences may explain why business students and even managers themselves have been criticized for being too self-centered and impatient for personal achievement and promotion (see Introduction). A balance of personal values and social values, such as justice and helpfulness, may characterize a more adaptable manager in the future.

Simply esteeming certain personal and achievement-oriented values does not mean, of course, that one will be a successful manager. On the other hand, it is clear that values do affect individual behavior. For example, sharing values among team members, as well as compatibility of instrumental and terminal values among team members, was found to be associated with significantly more effective teams (Fisher et al., 1996). More importantly, several authors have argued that the behavior displayed by individuals (that is, the means used to achieve their valued ends) is a product of their level of **values maturity** (e.g., Kohlberg, 1969; Kohlberg & Ryncarz, 1990). Individuals differ in their level of values development, according to these authors, so different sets of instrumental values are held by individuals at different stages of development. People progress from one level of maturity to another, and as they do, their value priorities change. Individuals who have progressed to more mature levels of values development possess a qualitatively different set of instrumental values than individuals who are at less mature levels. This theory of values maturity or moral development has received a great deal of attention from researchers, and research findings have some important implications for self-awareness and managerial effectiveness. Therefore, we shall discuss in some detail this notion of values maturity.

Values Maturity

Kohlberg's model is the best known and most widely researched approach to values maturity. It focuses on the kind of reasoning used to reach a decision about an issue that has value or moral connotations. The model consists of three major levels, each of which contains two stages. Table 1.2 summarizes the characteristics of each stage. In brief, the stages are sequential (for example, a person can't progress to stage 3 before passing through stage 2), and each stage represents a higher level of maturity. Kohlberg uses the terms *preconventional*, *conventional*, and *postconventional* to describe these three levels. In the following discussion, we have chosen to use different terms that capture the dominant characteristics of each stage.

The first level of maturity, the *self-centered level*, includes the first two stages of values development. Moral reasoning and instrumental values are based on personal needs or wants and on the consequences of an act. For example, something could be judged as right or good if it helped an individual obtain a reward or avoid punishment and if the consequences were not negative for someone else. Stealing $50,000 is worse than stealing $500 in the self-centered level because the consequences (that is, the losses) are more negative for someone else.

The second level, or *conformity level*, includes stages 3 and 4. Moral reasoning is based on conforming to and upholding the conventions and expectations of society. This level is sometimes referred to as the "law and order" level because the emphasis is on conformity to laws and norms. Right and wrong are judged on the basis of whether or not behaviors conform to the rules of those in authority. Respect from others based on obedience is a prized outcome. Stealing $50,000 and stealing $500 are equally wrong in this level because both violate the law. Most American adults function at this level of values maturity.

Third is the *principled level*. It includes the final two stages of maturity and represents the most mature level of moral reasoning and the most mature set of instrumental values. Right and wrong are

Table 1.2	Classification of Moral Judgment into Stages of Development
LEVEL BASIS OF MORAL JUDGMENT	**STAGE OF DEVELOPMENT**
A *PRECONVENTIONAL LEVEL (SELF-CENTERED)*	1. *Punishment and Obedience*
Moral value resides in external factors, and consequences, not persons or relationships.	Right is determined by avoiding punishment and not breaking an authority's rules.
	2. *Individual Instrumental Purpose and Exchange*
	Right is meeting one's own immediate interests, and what is fair or equal for others.
B *CONVENTIONAL LEVEL (CONFORMITY)*	3. *Mutual Interpersonal Expectations, Relationships, and Conformity*
Moral value resides in duty, maintaining social contracts, keeping commitments.	Right is being concerned about others' feelings and maintaining trust by keeping expectations and commitments. The Golden Rule is relevant.
	4. *Social System and Conscience Maintenance*
	Right is doing one's duty to society and upholding the social order.
C *POSTCONVENTIONAL (PRINCIPLED)*	5. *Prior Rights and Social Contract or Utility*
Moral value resides in commitment to freely selected standards, rights, and duties.	Right is upholding the rights, values, and contracts of others in society; moral behavior is freely chosen.
	6. *Universal Ethical Principles*
	Right is guided by internal, universal ethical principles. When laws violate principles, the laws are ignored.

SOURCE: *Adapted from Kohlberg (1981).*

judged on the basis of the internalized principles of the individual. That is, judgments are made on the basis of a set of principles or core values that have been developed from individual experience. In the highest stage of maturity, this set of principles is comprehensive (it covers all contingencies), consistent (it is never violated), and universal (it does not change with the situation or circumstance). Thus, stealing $50,000 and stealing $500 are still judged to be wrong, but the basis for the judgment is not the violation of laws or rules; rather, it is the violation of a set of comprehensive, consistent, universal principles developed by the individual. Few individuals, according to Kohlberg, reach this highest level of maturity on a consistent basis.

In short, self-centered individuals view rules and laws as outside themselves, but they obey because, by doing so, they may obtain rewards or avoid punishment. Conformist individuals view rules and laws as outside themselves, but they obey because they have learned and accepted those rules and laws, and they seek the respect of others. Principled individuals examine the rules and laws and develop a set of internal principles that they believe are morally right. If there is a choice to be made between obeying a law or obeying a principle, they choose the principle. Internalized principles supersede rules and laws in principled individuals.

To understand the different levels of values maturity, consider the following story used by Kohlberg (1969):

In Europe a woman was near death from a special kind of cancer. There was one drug that the doctors thought might save her. It was a form of radium that a druggist in the same town had recently discovered. The drug was expensive to make, but the druggist was charging ten times what the drug cost to make. He paid $200 for radium and charged $2,000 for a small dose of the drug. The sick woman's husband, Heinz, went to everyone he knew to borrow the money, but he could get together only about $1,000, which was half of what it cost. He told the druggist that his wife was dying and begged him to sell the drug at a lower price or let him pay later. But the druggist said, "No, I discovered the drug and I'm going to make money from it." So Heinz grew desperate and began to think about breaking into the store to steal the drug for his wife.

Now answer the following questions in reaction to the story:

YES   NO

____ ____ 1. Would it be wrong for Heinz to break into the store?

____ ____ 2. Did the druggist have the right to charge that much for the product?

____ ____ 3. Did Heinz have an obligation to steal the drug for his wife?

____ ____ 4. What if Heinz and his wife did not get along? Should Heinz steal the drug for her?

____ ____ 5. Suppose Heinz's best friend were dying of cancer, rather than Heinz's wife. Should Heinz steal the drug for his friend?

____ ____ 6. Suppose the person dying was not personally close to Heinz. Should Heinz steal the drug?

____ ____ 7. Suppose Heinz read in the paper about a woman dying of cancer. Should he steal the drug for her?

____ ____ 8. Would you steal the drug to save your own life?

____ ____ 9. Suppose Heinz was caught breaking in and brought before a judge. Should he be sentenced to jail?

For individuals in the self-centered level of maturity, stealing the drug might be justified because Heinz's wife had instrumental value: she could provide companionship, help rear the children, and so on. A stranger, however, would not have the same instrumental value for Heinz, so it would be wrong to steal the drug for a stranger. Individuals in the conformity level would base their judgments on the closeness of the relationship and on law and authority. Heinz has an obligation to steal for family members, according to this reasoning, but not for nonfamily members. A governing principle is whether or not an action is against the law (or society's expectations). Principled individuals base their judgments on a set of universal, comprehensive, and consistent principles. They may answer any question yes or no, but their reasoning will be based on their own internal principles, not on externally imposed standards or expectations. (For example, they might feel an obligation to steal the drug for anyone because they value human life more than property.)

Research on Kohlberg's model of values development reveals some interesting findings that have relevance to managerial behavior. For example, moral judgment stories were administered to college students who had earlier participated in Milgram's (1963) obedience study. Under the guise of a reinforcement-learning experiment, Milgram's subjects had been directed to give increasingly intense electric shocks to a person who was observed to be in great pain. Of the respondents at the principled level (stages 5 and 6), 75 percent refused to administer the shocks (i.e., to hurt someone), while only 12.5 percent of the respondents at the conformity level refused. Higher levels of values development were associated with more humane behavior toward other people.

It should also be noted that Kohlberg's model has been criticized by Carol Gilligan (1979, 1980, 1982, 1988) as containing a male bias. In her investigations of moral dilemmas among women, Gilligan indicated that women tend to value care, relationships, and commitment more highly than do males. The Kohlberg model, which tends to emphasize justice as the highest moral value, is more typical of males than females, she claimed. Whereas Gilligan's criticisms are somewhat controversial among researchers, they are less relevant to our discussion here because of our emphasis on the development of internalized principles for guiding behavior, whatever their basis. For our purposes in this chapter, the debate about whether justice is a male value and caring is a female value is largely beside the point.

Becoming more mature in values development requires that individuals develop a set of internalized principles by which they can govern their behavior. The development of those principles is enhanced and values maturity is increased as value-based issues are confronted, discussed, and thought about. Lickona (1976, p. 25) notes, "Simply increasing the amount of reciprocal communication that occurs among people is likely to enhance moral development."

To help you determine your own level of values maturity, an instrument developed by James Rest at the University of Minnesota's Moral Research Center was included in the Assessment section. It has been used extensively in research because it is easier to administer than Kohlberg's method for assessing maturity. According to Kohlberg (1976, p. 47), "Rest's approach does give a rough estimate of an individual's moral maturity level." Rather than placing a person on one single level of values maturity, it identifies the stage that the person relies on most. That is, it assumes that individuals use more than one level of maturity (or set of instrumental values), but that one level generally predominates. By completing this instrument, therefore, you will identify your predominant level of values maturity. To determine your maturity level, refer to the self-scoring instructions in the Appendix at the end of this chapter. An exercise in the Skill Practice section will help you develop or refine principles at the stage 5 and stage 6 level of maturity.

ETHICAL DECISION MAKING AND VALUES

In addition to its benefits for self-understanding, awareness of your own level of values maturity also has important practical implications for **ethical decision making.** By and large, the American public rates the honesty, integrity, and concern for moral values of American business executives as abysmal. A large majority of the public indicates that they think executives are dishonest, overly profit-oriented, and willing to step on other people to get what they want (Andrews, 1989; Harris & Sutton, 1995; Lozano, 1996). Although 9 out of 10 companies have a written code of ethics, evidence exists to support public perceptions that these documents are not influential in assuring high moral conduct.

In December 2001, Enron, the seventh largest U.S. corporation at the time, declared bankruptcy. Tragically, a once great company has become a synonym for managerial greed and corporate fraud. The Enron debacle spawned more than 30 major pieces of legislation designed to clamp down on financial loopholes exploited by Enron executives, as well as numerous books and articles criticizing Enron-like unethical business practices (Elliott & Schroth, 2002; Mitchell, 2002).

While Enron was arguably one of the largest corporate scandals in U.S. history, it is hardly the only lapse of ethical judgment staining the image of business. Martha Stewart's insider trading transaction, for example, netted her less than $50,000 in personal wealth but cost her firm billions of dollars in lost stock value. Ford Motor Company refused to alter the dangerous gas tank on the Pinto in order to save $11 per car. It cost Ford millions of dollars in lawsuits and cost many people their lives. Equity Funding tried to hide 64,000 phony insurance claims, but went bankrupt when the truth came out. Firestone denied that its 500-series tire was defective, but eventually took losses in the millions when the accident reports were publicized. A. H. Robins knew of problems with its Dalkon Shield for years before informing the public. The billion dollars set aside for lawsuits against the company was dwarfed by the actual claims, and the company filed Chapter 11. E. F. Hutton, General Dynamics, General Electric, Rockwell, Martin Marietta, Tyco, Lockheed, Bank of Boston, Dow Corning, and a host of other firms have also been in the news for violating ethical principles. One cartoon that seems to summarize these goings-on shows a group of executives sitting at a conference table. The leader remarks, "Of course, honesty is one of the better policies."

Corporate behavior that exemplifies unethical decision making is not our principal concern here. More to the point is a study by the American Management Association that included 3,000 managers in the United States. It reported that most individual managers felt they were under pressure to compromise personal standards to meet company goals (Harris & Sutton, 1995). Moreover, most individuals have encountered someone else violating ethical standards, but in a majority of cases, nothing is reported. For example, in a survey of federal employees asked whether they had observed any of the following activities in the last year, more than 50 percent answered yes to seeing: stealing funds, stealing property, accepting bribes, sexual harassment, ineligible people receiving funds, deficient goods or services, use of position for personal benefit, taking unfair advantage of a contractor, serious violation of the law. More than two thirds did not report what they saw. As an illustration, consider the following true incident (names have been changed). How would you respond? Why?

Dale Monson, a top manufacturing manager at Satellite Telecommunications, walked into the office of Al Lake, the head of quality control. Dale was carrying an assembled part that was to be shipped to a customer on the West Coast. Dale handed Al the part and said, "Look Al, this part is in perfect shape electronically, but the case has a gouge in it. I've seen engineering and they say that the mark doesn't affect form, fit, or function. Marketing says the customer won't mind because they are just going to bury the unit anyway. We can't rework it, and it would cost $75,000 to make new cases. We will only do 23 units, and they're already made. The parts are due to be shipped at the end of the week." Al responded, "Well, what do you want from me?" "Just sign off so we can move forward," said Dale. "Since you're the one who needs to certify acceptable quality, I thought I'd better get this straightened out now rather than waiting until the last minute before shipping."

Would you ship the part or not? Discuss this with your class members. Generate a recommendation for Al.

This case exemplifies the major values conflict faced over and over again by managers. It is a conflict between maximizing the economic performance of the organization (as indicated by revenues, costs, profits, and so forth) or the social performance of the organization (as indicated by obligations to customers, employees, suppliers, and so forth). Most ethical trade-offs are conflicts between these two desirable ends: economic versus social performance (Hosmer, 2003). Making these kinds of decisions effectively is not merely a matter of selecting between right and wrong alternatives or between good and bad choices. Most of these choices are between right and right or between one good and another. Individuals who effectively manage these kinds of ethical trade-offs are those who have a clear sense of their own values and who have developed a principled level of moral maturity. They have articulated and clarified their own internal set of universal, comprehensive, and consistent principles upon which to base their decisions. It is seldom the case, of course, that a manager could choose economic performance goals every time or that he or she could choose social performance goals every time. Trade-offs are inevitable.

It is not a simple matter, on the other hand, to generate a personal set of universal, comprehensive, and consistent principles that can guide decision making. According to Kohlberg's research, most adults have neither constructed, nor do they follow, a well-developed set of principles in making decisions. One reason is that they have no model or example of what such principles might be. We offer some standards against which to test your own principles for making moral or ethical choices. These standards are neither comprehensive nor absolute, nor are they independent of one another. They simply serve as reference against which to test the principles that you include in your personal values statement.

❏ *Front page test:* Would I be embarrassed if my decision became a headline in the local newspaper? Would I feel comfortable describing my actions or decision to a customer or stockholder?

❏ *Golden rule test:* Would I be willing to be treated in the same manner?

❏ *Dignity and liberty test:* Are the dignity and liberty of others preserved by this decision? Is the basic humanity of the affected parties enhanced? Are their opportunities expanded or curtailed?

- *Equal treatment test:* Are the rights, welfare, and betterment of minorities and lower status people given full consideration? Does this decision benefit those with privilege but without merit?

- *Personal gain test:* Is an opportunity for personal gain clouding my judgment? Would I make the same decision if the outcome did not benefit me in any way?

- *Congruence test:* Is this decision or action consistent with my espoused personal principles? Does it violate the spirit of any organizational policies or laws?

- *Procedural justice test:* Can the procedures used to make this decision stand up to scrutiny by those affected?

- *Cost-benefit test:* Does a benefit for some cause unacceptable harm to others? How critical is the benefit? Can the harmful effects be mitigated?

- *Good night's sleep test:* Whether or not anyone else knows about my action, will it produce a good night's sleep?

In the Skill Application section of this chapter, you may want to consider these alternatives when constructing your own set of comprehensive, consistent, and universalistic principles. You should be aware, however, that your set of personal principles will also be influenced by your orientation for acquiring and responding to the information you receive. This orientation is called cognitive style.

COGNITIVE STYLE

Each of us is constantly being exposed to an overwhelming amount of information, and only part of it can be given attention and acted upon at a time. For example, right now you have information entering your brain relating to the functioning of your physical body, the attributes of the room in which you are sitting, the words on this page, the ideas and memories that spring to mind as you read about self-awareness, long-held beliefs, recollections of recent events, and so on. Of course, not all of this information is conscious, otherwise your brain would become overloaded and you would go insane. Over time, we all develop strategies for suppressing some kinds of information and paying attention to other kinds. These strategies become habitual and ingrained, and they result in a particular kind of cognitive style for each of us.

Cognitive style refers to the inclination each of us has to perceive, interpret, and respond to information in a certain way. Cognitive style is based on two key dimensions: (1) the manner in which you gather information and (2) the way in which you evaluate and act on information. A large number of instruments are available to measure different dimensions of cognitive styles (see Eckstrom, French, & Harmon, 1979; Sternberg & Zhang, 2000; Cassidy, 2004), but here we focus on dimensions that have emerged in the most recent research on cognitive style. These dimensions are the ones that most researchers now identify as lying at the heart of cognitive style.

It is important to note that cognitive styles are not the same as personality types. They are not inherent attributes. Rather, they are inclinations toward information and learning that we have developed over time. Hence, cognitive styles can be altered and changed through practice and conscious development (Vance et al., 2007). No one is predestined to think in a particular way.

Based on an extensive literature review of models of cognitive style, we selected an instrument developed by Cools and Van den Broeck (2007) to assess your cognitive style. You completed this instrument in the Pre-Assessment section. This instrument assesses three dimensions of your cognitive style—knowing style, planning style, and creating style. These dimensions are independent in the sense that any person can score high or low on any of the three sections. They are not polar opposites from one another, but are just different ways that people process information. Each style emphasizes a different kind of information seeking and response, and the main attributes are summarized in Table 1.3.

Knowing Style

Individuals who score high on the knowing style tend to emphasize facts, details, and data. They seek clear and objective solutions to problems. They look for rationality, the validity of the data, and proof that the information being presented is accurate and credible. They focus on the underlying logic of the information and show a preference toward the data that creates legitimacy for their arguments. They are careful, slow to jump to conclusions, and precise in evaluating information, so decisions are usually not made quickly. They tend to prefer control in situations and to do things in the correct way, hence they tend to be critical of unexpected or aberrant behavior.

People with a knowing style are best at presenting a convincing argument based on evidence. They are

As pointed out earlier, both the half-life of knowledge and the amount of knowledge available to people are changing at incredible speeds. Even the half-life of most information technologies is now less than one year. (Consider how up-to-date your current computer is, regardless of how recently you purchased it.) It is estimated that in a decade, for example, personal computers will become anachronistic as etching on molecules replaces etching on silicon. It is predicted that computers as small as a pencil head will be implanted in the body to govern, for example, heart rate, or in eyeglasses to display the name of every person you pass by on the street.

Educated people who read the *Wall Street Journal*, *New York Times*, or *Herald Tribune* are now exposed to more information in one day than a person was exposed to in a lifetime in the eighteenth century. Most of the world's population has never known a world without a handheld computer, remote control, unlimited TV channels, and satellite transmission, yet the population group that is growing the fastest and that controls most of society's wealth is over 60 years old and have just encountered the information revolution in the last half of their lives. Alarmingly, a large majority of the world's population can only dream of having access to current information technology, and even a majority of the U.S. population cannot afford a computer. Hence, we face a real danger of perpetuating technological apartheid both in the United States and throughout the world.

In business organizations, no manager at the beginning of the twenty-first century would boast of being stable, constant, or maintaining the status quo. Even now, stability is interpreted more as stagnation than steadiness, and organizations not in the business of major transformation and revolution are generally viewed as recalcitrant. The frightening uncertainty that has always accompanied major change is now superseded by a fear of staying the same.

All this is to say that the environment of the twenty-first century will be characterized by turbulence, gigantic change, rapid-fire decisions, and chaos. No one will have time to read and analyze a case study. E-business has changed the rules of the game. For example, it is now possible for competitors in almost any business to emerge on the Internet within 24 hours. No one can predict the competitive environment anymore. Customers are no longer geographically constrained, and the standards for servicing them have changed completely. Speed to market and competing against time have begun to dominate the traditional competitive advantages learned in business schools. Rapid

decision making, mostly without the benefit of adequate information and careful analysis, is becoming the norm.

In the midst of this chaotic pace of change—what some refer to as "permanent white water"—being aware of your own orientation toward change is an important prerequisite for successfully coping with it. Two dimensions of change orientation particularly relevant for managers are discussed on the following pages.

Tolerance of Ambiguity

The first important dimension is **tolerance of ambiguity**, which refers to the extent to which individuals are threatened by or have difficulty coping with situations that are ambiguous, where change occurs rapidly or unpredictably, where information is inadequate or unclear, or where complexity exists. Stimulus-rich and information-overloaded environments (for example, air traffic control towers) are examples. Regardless of their cognitive style, people vary in their aptitude for operating in such circumstances.

People differ in the extent to which they are "cognitively complex" or in the extent to which they can cope with ambiguous, incomplete, unstructured, dynamic situations. Individuals who have a high tolerance of ambiguity also tend to be more cognitively complex. They tend to pay attention to more information, interpret more cues, and possess more sense-making categories than less complex individuals do. Research has found that cognitively complex and tolerant individuals are better transmitters of information, more sensitive to internal (nonsuperficial) characteristics of others when evaluating their performance at work, and more behaviorally adaptive and flexible under ambiguous and overloaded conditions than less tolerant and less cognitively complex individuals. Managers with higher tolerance-of-ambiguity scores are more likely to be entrepreneurial in their actions, to screen out less information in a complex environment, and to choose specialties in their occupations that possess less-structured tasks. They also cope more effectively with major organizational change, downsizing, and role stress and conflict (Armstrong-Stassen, 1998; Haase, Lee, & Banks, 1979; Teoh & Foo, 1997; Timothy, Thoresen, Pucik, and Welbourne, 1999).

It also should be pointed out, however, that individuals who are more tolerant of ambiguity have more difficulty focusing on a single important element of information—they are inclined to pay attention to a variety of items—and they may have somewhat less ability to concentrate without being distracted by interruptions. However, for the most part, in an information-rich environment, tolerance of ambiguity and cognitive complexity are more adaptive than the opposite characteristics.

In the Skill Assessment section of this chapter, a Tolerance of Ambiguity Scale (Budner, 1962) assesses the extent to which you have a tolerance for these kinds of complex situations. In scoring the Tolerance of Ambiguity Scale (see the scoring key at the end of the chapter), three different subscale scores are assessed. One is the *novelty* score, which indicates the extent to which you are tolerant of new, unfamiliar information or situations. The second subscale is the *complexity* score, which indicates the extent to which you are tolerant of multiple, distinctive, or unrelated information. The third subscale is the *insolubility* score, which indicates the extent to which you are tolerant of problems that are very difficult to solve because, for example, alternative solutions are not evident, information is unavailable, or the problem's components seem unrelated to each other. In general, the more tolerant people are of novelty, complexity, and insolubility, the more likely they are to succeed as managers in information-rich, ambiguous environments. They are less overwhelmed by ambiguous circumstances.

It is important to note that cognitive complexity and tolerance for ambiguity are not related to cognitive intelligence, and your score on the Tolerance of Ambiguity Scale is not an evaluation of how smart you are. Most important, individuals can learn to tolerate more complexity and more flexibility in their information-processing abilities. The first step toward increasing tolerance is becoming aware of where you are now by completing the Skill Assessment section. Then the Skill Analysis and Skill Practice sections of this chapter, along with discussions such as the one in the chapters on problem solving and creativity, provide ways to improve your tolerance for ambiguity and your cognitive complexity. It is also interesting to note that a positive correlation exists between tolerance of ambiguity and the second dimension of orientation toward change discussed here, internal locus of control.

Locus of Control

The second dimension of orientation toward change is **locus of control**. It is one of the most studied and written-about aspects of orientation toward change.

Locus of control refers to the attitude people develop regarding the extent to which they are in control of their own destinies. When individuals receive information about the success or failure of their own actions, or when something changes in the environment, they differ in how they interpret that information. People receive reinforcements, both positive or negative, as they attempt to make changes around them. If individuals interpret the reinforcement they receive to be contingent upon their own actions, it is called an **internal locus of control** (that is, "I was the cause of the success or failure of the change"). If they interpret the reinforcement as being a product of outside forces, it is called an **external locus of control** (that is, "Something or someone else caused the success or failure"). Over time, people develop a "generalized expectancy" about the dominant sources of the reinforcements they receive. Thus, they become largely internally focused or largely externally focused with regard to the source of control they perceive in a changing environment.

Over 10,000 studies have been done using the locus of control scale. In general, the research suggests that managers in North America have a far greater tendency to have an internal locus of control than, say, Middle Eastern and Far East managers (Trompenaars, 1996). In Japan, for example, an external locus of control has been associated with high levels of stress and violence among teenagers, presumably due to less emphasis on self-control (Tubbs, 1994). In American culture, internal locus of control is associated with the most successful managers (for reviews of the literature, see Hendricks, 1985; Spector, 1982). For example, people with an internal locus of control are more likely to (1) be attentive to aspects of the environment that provide useful information for the future, (2) engage in actions to improve their environment, (3) place greater emphasis on striving for achievement, (4) be more inclined to develop their own skills, (5) ask more questions, and (6) remember more information than people with an external locus of control.

In the management literature, individuals who have an internal locus of control are less alienated from the work environment, more satisfied with their work, and experience less job strain and more position mobility (promotions and job changes) than do individuals with an external locus of control (Bernardi, 1997; Coleman, Irving, & Cooper, 1999; Newton & Keenan, 1990; Seeman, 1982). A study of leadership and group performance found that internals were more likely to be leaders and that groups led by internals were more effective than those led by externals (Anderson &

Schneider, 1978; Blau, 1993). Internals also were found to outperform externals in stressful situations, to engage in more entrepreneurial activity, to be more active in managing their own careers, and to have higher levels of job involvement than externals (Bonnett & Furnham, 1991; Boone & Brabander, 1997; Cromie, Callahan, & Jansen, 1992; Hammer & Vardi, 1981; Kren, 1992). Differences have also been found regarding how power and authority are utilized by externals and internals (see Chapter 5: Gaining Power and Influence). External leaders tend to use coercive power and threat, whereas internal leaders rely more on persuasion and expertise as a source of power (Sweeney, McFarlin, & Cotton, 1991). Moreover, internals both demonstrate and are more satisfied with a participative management style than externals are (Judge, Erez, Bono, & Thoreson, 2002).

A study of locus of control among top executives found that the firms led by internals engaged in more innovation, more risky projects, more leadership in the marketplace, longer planning horizons, more scanning of the environment, and a more highly developed technology than external-led firms did (Miller, Kets de Vries, & Toulouse, 1982). In summarizing the results of this massive array of research on locus of control, the conclusion is consistent: in American culture, people are handicapped by an external locus of control.

On the other hand, research also has found that an internal locus of control is not a panacea for all management problems. Internal locus of control is not always a positive attribute. For example, individuals with an external locus of control have been found to be more inclined to initiate structure as leaders (to help clarify roles). Internals are less likely to comply with leader directions and are less accurate in processing feedback about successes and failures than are externals. Internals also have more difficulty arriving at decisions with serious consequences for someone else (Coleman et al., 1999; Rothenberg, 1980; Wheeler & Davis, 1979).

It is important to note that locus of control can shift over time, particularly as a function of the position held at work, and that external locus of control does not inhibit individuals from attaining positions of power and influence at the top of organizations. Therefore, no matter what your internal–external score, you can be a successful manager in the right setting, or you can alter your locus of control. Research has shown that people who interpret information about change as if they are in control of it, and who perceive themselves to be in charge of their own performance (and hence able to control outcomes related to that performance), are more likely to be effective managers in most circumstances in our culture.

The Locus of Control Scale in the Skill Assessment section helps you generate a score showing the extent to which you have an internal or external locus of control. The scoring key identifies your *External Locus of Control* score. Comparing your own score to the mean scores of several other groups at the end of this chapter can help you determine the extent to which you are internal (below the mean scores) or external (above the mean scores) in your orientation toward change.

In summary, two key attitudes toward change—tolerance of ambiguity and locus of control—have been found to be associated with success in management roles. Knowing your scores on these two factors can help you capitalize on your strengths and enhance your potential for management success. While substantial research exists associating some positive managerial behaviors with internal locus of control and tolerance of ambiguity, possessing these orientations is neither an assurance of success as a manager nor a solution to the problems that managers face. By knowing your scores, however, you will be able to choose situations in which you are more likely to feel comfortable, perform effectively, and understand the point of view of those whose perspectives differ from yours. Self-understanding is a prerequisite to self-improvement and change.

CORE SELF-EVALUATION

Every person has a distinct personality. This concept of *personality* refers to the relatively enduring combination of traits that makes an individual unique and at the same time produces consistencies in his or her thoughts and behaviors. We are all aware of the differences in personalities among the people around us. These differences are manifest in certain kinds of behaviors, attitudes, emotional reactions, and thought patterns. Collectively, we refer to these unique patterns as a person's personality. Usually, personality refers to a "trait" of individuals inasmuch as it is relatively enduring and stable, even though it may be changed and developed through conscious effort. There is much disagreement about how much of our personality is learned as opposed to being biologically or genetically determined. Some explanation for what makes us unique can certainly be attributed to the genetic predispositions we bring with us when we are born. Yet, a sizable portion of our behavioral makeup is learned and can be changed. We focus in this chapter on factors over which we have some control and can change if we determine to do so.

In the field of personality psychology, there has been a gradual convergence around a few major dimensions of personality. A review of the literature in 2001, for example, found that more than 50,000 studies had been conducted on just three attributes of personality—self-esteem, locus of control, and neuroticism or emotional stability (Bono & Judge, 2003). More than 100 studies a month are published on the topic of self-esteem alone! It has become popular in psychology to refer to the "Big Five" personality attributes as being the most important aspects of personality, although there is no scientific evidence that such a conclusion is merited. These Big Five attributes are the most researched, however, and they include *extroversion* (the extent to which people are inclined toward gregariousness and being outgoing instead of quiet and reserved), *agreeableness* (the extent to which people are friendly and affable as opposed to being disagreeable and aggressive), *conscientiousness* (the extent to which people are careful, task oriented, and orderly as opposed to being disorganized, flexible, and unreliable), *neuroticism* (the extent to which people are emotionally fragile, negative, and fearful as opposed to being optimistic, positive, and emotionally stable), and *openness* (the extent to which people are curious and open to new ideas as opposed to being rigid or dogmatic). Individuals tend to differ on these five attributes, and scores on these five factors have been used to predict a variety of outcomes including behavioral performance, life success, job satisfaction, interpersonal attraction, and intellectual achievement.

Timothy Judge and his colleagues have found, however, that differences in scores on these Big Five personality attributes can be explained by a more foundational personality factor. It is referred to as core self-evaluation, or the fundamental evaluation each person has developed about himself or herself. According to Judge and colleagues (2003), core evaluations influence people's appraisals of themselves, the world, and others, but these evaluations operate subconsciously. For the most part, people are not aware of their own core self-evaluations. Yet, when people respond to certain cues—including personality surveys, behavioral signals, or mental stimuli— their responses are determined to a nontrivial extent by this deeper and more fundamental self-appraisal. In fact, core self-evaluations have been found to predict individuals' scores on the Big Five personality attributes as well as a variety of other unique personal differences. Most people are not aware of the influence that their core self-evaluations have on their perceptions and behaviors, so the assessment instrument at the beginning of this chapter will be very useful in helping you identify your own core self-evaluation.

Core self-evaluation is sometimes referred to as overall positive self-regard—or the extent to which people value themselves and feel proficient as individuals. It is comprised of four components: (1) *self-esteem*, or the extent to which people see themselves as capable, successful, and worthy (Harter, 1990); (2) *generalized self-efficacy*, or the sense of one's ability to perform capably across a variety of circumstances (Locke, McClear, & Knight, 1996); (3) *neuroticism*, which is reversed-scored, or the tendency to have a negative outlook and pessimistic approach to life (Watson, 2000); and (4) *locus of control*, which has been discussed earlier, referring to a person's beliefs about the extent to which he or she can control his or her own experiences (Rotter, 1966). Whereas these four personality traits have been studied separately in psychology, it has been discovered that there is a great deal of overlap, and, in combination, they create a single, powerful factor that lies at the core of personality (Judge et al., 2002, 2003). This factor is called a "latent" attribute that lies at the foundation of personality manifestations.

The commonalties among the four factors that make up core self-evaluation are not difficult to understand. That is, when people view themselves in a positive way, or when they possess high self-esteem, they also tend to feel capable of performing effectively across a variety of situations (generalized self-efficacy), they feel in control of their circumstances (locus of control), and they feel emotionally stable (the opposite of neuroticism). Each of these factors by itself has a slightly different meaning, of course, but the overlap and shared meaning among them is the thing being measured by the Core Self-Evaluation Survey. In other words, core self-evaluation assesses the extent to which you possess positive self-regard, or that you feel valuable, capable, stable, and in control. The instrument you completed in the Pre-assessment section captures the commonality among these four factors rather than their unique meaning. That is, your scores reflect your own core self-evaluation rather than any one of the components by themselves.

Of course, we have all met people who are self-centered, braggarts, or narcissistic. They seem to possess an abundance of positive self-regard, and we

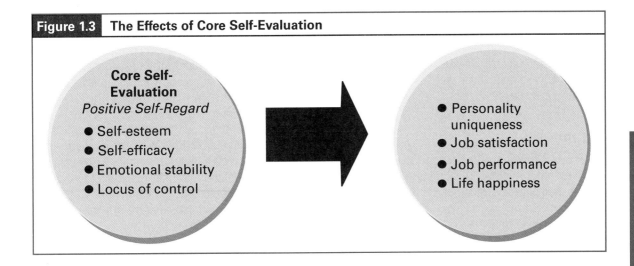

Figure 1.3 The Effects of Core Self-Evaluation

Core Self-Evaluation
Positive Self-Regard
- Self-esteem
- Self-efficacy
- Emotional stability
- Locus of control

- Personality uniqueness
- Job satisfaction
- Job performance
- Life happiness

might be tempted to think of them as having very high scores in core self-evaluation. However, these people also are likely to be insensitive to their abrasive impact on others. When threatened, they emphasize winning or getting their way. They tend to look in the mirror more often than others, spend more time thinking about themselves and the impressions they convey, and work to make themselves look good or be in the spotlight. They tend to be manipulative in their relationships with others. They are, in a word, selfish people. This is not the same as having a positive core self-evaluation. Rather, a positive core self-evaluation implies sensitivity to others and to the environment so that relationships with others are strengthened rather than weakened, developed rather than destroyed. As summarized in Figure 1.3, strong, confident people are better able to lead, to manage, and to form supportive relationships with others.

Evidence for this fact comes from the studies of the relationships between core self-evaluation and the effectiveness of individuals at work. A great deal of research has been conducted using this Core Self-Evaluation Survey, and its validity has been established in a variety of settings (Judge et al., 2003). Research findings indicate that individuals with high core self-evaluations tend to be more satisfied with their jobs. One explanation for this result is that people are more satisfied with their jobs when they are performing more rewarding work and when they have more complex and challenging work. As it turns out, people with higher core self-evaluation scores tend to select more challenging jobs and they tend to find the work in which they are engaged to be more intrinsically fulfilling. Their work is simply more rewarding and more stimulating to them.

In addition to job satisfaction, core self-evaluation is also strongly related to job performance. That is, people who score higher in core self-evaluation tend to perform more successfully at work as employees and as managers (Judge & Bono, 2001). One reason for this result is that high core self-evaluation scores are strongly associated with motivation, and motivated people (as you will see in Chapter 6) tend to perform better. Similarly, people with higher core self-evaluation scores tend to have higher levels of task motivation (a desire to accomplish a task), persistence (the inclination to spend the time needed to accomplish a task), productivity in the task itself (producing more output), goal setting (establishing goals for themselves), goal commitment (commitment to accomplishing a goal), and activity level (energized work behavior) (Erez & Judge, 2001). They tend also to be more effective at overcoming obstacles and challenges, in solving problems, and in adapting to organizational change. People with high core self-evaluation scores have also been found to have higher levels of life satisfaction and personal happiness and lower levels of personal stress on the job and experienced strain (headaches, backaches, and somatic symptoms). Higher salary levels, less career plateauing, and more organizational commitment have also been found to be associated with higher core self-evaluation scores.

In summary, core self-evaluation scores tend to be a very important predictor of personality differences, job satisfaction, job performance, and life happiness. When people have developed a positive self-regard—when they feel valuable, capable, stable, and in control—they tend to function better at work, in relationships, and in life. Developing management skills and acquiring the competency to perform effectively in work settings is one way to enhance feelings of positive self regard.

Summary

Corporate America increasingly has begun to discover the power of developing self-awareness among its managers. Each year, millions of executives complete instruments designed to increase self-awareness in companies such as Apple, AT&T, Citicorp, Exxon, General Electric, Honeywell, 3M, and the U.S. Army. An awareness of how individuals differ in their emotional maturity, values priorities and values maturity, cognitive style, orientation toward change, and personality has helped many companies cope better with interpersonal conflicts, botched communications, breakdowns in trust, and misunderstandings. For example, after requiring his top 100 managers to undergo self-awareness training, the president of the computer reservations company of Hilton Hotels and Budget Rent-a-Car stated:

We had some real morale problems. I realized I had a mixed bag of people reporting to me and that this training could help us better understand each other and also understand how we make decisions. We wouldn't have made it through [a recent company crisis] without self-awareness training (Moore, 1987).

Not only does self-awareness training assist individuals in their ability to understand, and thereby manage, themselves, but it also is important in helping individuals develop understanding of the differences in others. Most people will regularly encounter individuals who possess different styles, different sets of values, and different perspectives than they do. Most work forces are becoming more, not less, diverse. Self-awareness training as discussed in this chapter, therefore, can be a valuable tool in helping individuals develop empathy and understanding for the expanding diversity they will face in work and school settings. Self-awareness is a key component of and a prerequisite for successful management. The relationship between the five critical areas of self-awareness and these management outcomes is summarized in Figure 1.4.

Most of the following chapters relate to skills in interpersonal or group interaction, but successful skill development in those areas will occur only if individuals have a firm foundation in self-awareness. In fact, there is an interesting paradox in human behavior: we can know others only by knowing ourselves, but we can know ourselves only by knowing others. Our knowledge of others, and therefore our ability to manage or interact successfully with them, comes from relating what we see in them to our own experience. If we are not self-aware, we have no basis for knowing certain things about others. Self-recognition leads to recognition and understanding of others. As Harris (1981) puts it:

Nothing is really personal that is not first interpersonal, beginning with the infant's shock of separation from the umbilical cord. What we know about ourselves comes only from the outside, and is interpreted by the kind of experiences we have had; and what we know about others comes only from analogy with our own network of feelings.

Behavioral Guidelines

Following are the behavioral guidelines relating to the improvement of self-awareness. These guidelines will be helpful to you as you engage in practice and application activities designed to improve your self-awareness.

1. Identify your sensitive line. Determine what information about yourself you are most likely to defend against.
2. Use the seven dimensions of national culture to diagnose differences between your own values orientation and that of individuals from other cultures, age categories, or ethnic groups.
3. Identify a comprehensive, consistent, and universal set of principles on which you will base your behavior. Identify the most important terminal and instrumental values that guide your decisions.
4. Expand your cognitive style, your tolerance of ambiguity, and your internal locus of control by increasing your exposure to new information and engaging in different kinds of activities than you are used to. Seek ways to expand and broaden yourself.
5. Enhance your emotional intelligence by consciously monitoring your own emotional

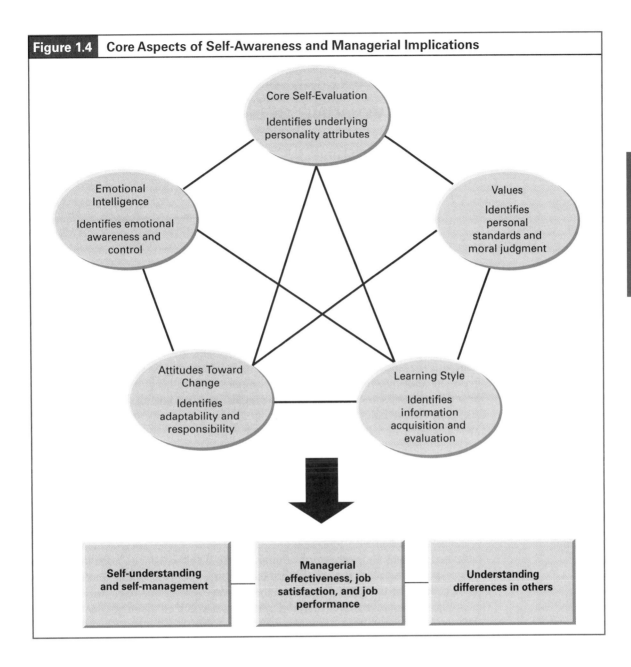

Figure 1.4 Core Aspects of Self-Awareness and Managerial Implications

Core Self-Evaluation

Identifies underlying personality attributes

Emotional Intelligence

Identifies emotional awareness and control

Values

Identifies personal standards and moral judgment

Attitudes Toward Change

Identifies adaptability and responsibility

Learning Style

Identifies information acquisition and evaluation

Self-understanding and self-management

Managerial effectiveness, job satisfaction, and job performance

Understanding differences in others

responses and by practicing the diagnosis of others' emotional cues.

6. Develop a healthy core self-evaluation and positive self-regard by consciously capitalizing on your personal strengths, and by highlighting and building on your successful accomplishments.

7. Engage in honest self-disclosure with someone who is close to you and accepting of you. Check out aspects of yourself that you are not sure of.

8. Keep a journal, and make time regularly to engage in self-analysis. Balance life's activities with some time for self-renewal.

CASES INVOLVING SELF-AWARENESS

Communist Prison Camp

To understand the development of increased self-awareness, it is helpful to consider the opposite process, that is, the destruction of self-awareness. Understanding the growth process is often enhanced by understanding the deterioration process. Hence, in the case below, a process of psychological self-destruction is described as it occurred among prisoners of war during the Korean War. Consider how these processes that destroy self-awareness can be reversed to create greater self-awareness. The setting is a prisoner-of-war camp managed by the Communist Chinese.

In such prisons the total regimen, consisting of physical privation, prolonged interrogation, total isolation from former relationships and sources of information, detailed regimentation of all daily activities, and deliberate humiliation and degradation, was geared to producing a confession of alleged crimes, the assumption of a penitent role, and the adoption of a Communist frame of reference. The prisoner was not informed what his crimes were, nor was he permitted to evade the issue by making up a false confession. Instead, what the prisoner learned he must do was reevaluate his past from the point of view of the Communists and recognize that most of his former attitudes and behavior were actually criminal from this point of view. For example, a priest who had dispensed food to needy peasants in his mission church had to "recognize" that he was actually a tool of imperialism and was using his missionary activities as cover for exploitation of the peasants. Even worse, he had used food as blackmail to accomplish his aims.

The key technique used by the Communists to produce social alienation to a degree sufficient to allow such redefinition and reevaluation to occur was to put the prisoner into a cell with four or more other prisoners who were somewhat more advanced in their "thought reform" than he. Such a cell usually had one leader who was responsible to the prison authorities, and the progress of the whole cell was made contingent upon the progress of the least "reformed" member. This condition meant in practice that four or more cell members devoted all their energies to getting their least "reformed" member to recognize "the truth" about himself and to confess. To accomplish this they typically swore at, harangued, beat, denounced, humiliated, reviled, and brutalized their victim 24 hours a day, sometimes for weeks or months on end. If the authorities felt that the prisoner was basically uncooperative, they manacled his hands behind his back and chained his ankles, which made him completely dependent on his cellmates for the fulfillment of his basic needs. It was this reduction to an animal-like existence in front of other humans which constituted the ultimate humiliation and led most reliably to the destruction of the prisoner's image of himself. Even in his own eyes he became something that was not worthy of the regard of his fellow man.

If, to avoid complete physical and personal destruction, the prisoner began to confess in the manner desired of him, he was usually forced to prove his sincerity by making irrevocable behavioral commitments, such as denouncing and implicating his friends and relatives in his own newly recognized crimes. Once he had done this he became further alienated from his former self, even in his own eyes, and could seek security only in a new identity and new social relationships. Aiding this process of confessing was the fact that the crimes gave the prisoner something concrete to which to attach the free-floating guilt that the accusing environment and his own humiliation usually stimulated.

A good example was the plight of the sick and wounded prisoners of war who, because of their physical confinement, were unable to escape from continual conflict with their interrogator or instructor, and who therefore often ended up forming a close relationship with him. Chinese Communist instructors often encouraged prisoners to take long walks or have informal talks with them and offered as incentives cigarettes, tea, and other rewards. If the prisoner was willing to cooperate and become a "progressive," he could join with other "progressives" in an active group life.

Within the political prison, the group cell not only provided the forces toward alienation but also offered the road to a "new self." Not only were there available among the fellow prisoners individuals with whom the prisoner could identify because of their shared plight, but once he showed any tendency to seek a new identity by truly trying to reevaluate his past, he received again a whole range of rewards, of which perhaps the most important was the interpersonal information that he was again a person worthy of respect and regard.

SOURCE: *Schein, 1960.*

Discussion Questions

1. What specific techniques were used to bring about the destruction of self-awareness among the prisoners?
2. What opposite processes could be used to create the reverse process, that is, a strengthening of the self-concept?
3. Assume that you are charged with the orientation of a cohort of new managers in your organization. How would you help them understand their own strengths and inclinations and how they could best contribute to the firm?
4. What mechanisms do people use, and what mechanisms could the prisoners of war have used, to resist a change in their self-concepts?
5. What could be done to reform or rebuild the self-awareness of these prisoners? What can be done to help individuals without self-awareness to improve that skill?

Computerized Exam

Graduate business school students were all required to take a one-credit-hour current events course. Like other courses in the business school, the final exam was administered on a computer. From a memory bank containing 350 questions, the computer was programmed to select 40 questions for each student, flashing them on the screen one at a time. Students could take the exam any time after the course began in January, whenever they felt ready.

Unfortunately, problems arose. When the test was computerized, a "skip feature" was added to the computer program. This feature was designed so that students could pass over a question they didn't want to answer immediately. The question, theoretically, would return to the screen at a later time, simulating the way in which students skip over and then return to questions on a written exam. However, the skip feature didn't work correctly. Instead of recycling skipped questions back to the student, the computer simply threw them out. Thus, the skip feature became a way for students to avoid any questions they couldn't answer.

Another snafu in the program was that when a certain number of questions were skipped during the exam—apparently between six and ten—the computer automatically ended the test. Scores were immediately flashed to the student and recorded in the computer memory. Scores were calculated on a percentage basis, only counting the questions that the student answered. Skipped questions were not counted as correct or incorrect. Therefore, a student who answered ten questions, nine of them correctly, and skipped enough other questions to trigger the automatic computer shutoff, received a score of 90 percent.

Knowledge of the skip command apparently was widely distributed well before the end of the term. One person estimated that at least half the students knew about it. Upon review, 77 out of 139 members of the graduating class answered fewer than the required 40 questions when they took the exam. When questioned, some students said that they didn't realize that a programming error had occurred and didn't keep track of how many questions were asked in total. Others argued that "it is like filling out an income tax form. People hire accountants all the time to find loopholes that they can use. That is not illegal, even if the government doesn't advertise the loopholes. The commuter program allowed for this loophole, and we did what we did."

1. *If you were one of the students in the class:*
   a. Would you tell the instructor about the programming error before the end of the term?
   b. Report the names of the other students you knew who cheated?
   c. Admit that you cheated?

2. *If you were the instructor for the course, which of the following would you do?*
   a. Flunk the 77 students who did not complete 40 questions.
   b. Require the 77 students to retake the exam, but let them graduate.
   c. Require all 139 students to retake the course since no student reported the problem, a violation of the student ethical code.
   d. Change the computer program, but do nothing to the students.
   e. Select another alternative.

3. *What is your rationale for the decisions you made in questions 1 and 2 above? Discuss your rationale with your colleagues.*

4. *What level of values maturity is displayed? What ethical principles are applied?*

Decision Dilemmas

For each of the five scenarios below, select the choice you would make if you were in the situation.

1. A young manager in a high-technology firm was offered a position by the firm's chief competitor for almost double her salary. Her firm sought to prevent her from changing jobs, arguing that her knowledge of certain specialized manufacturing processes would give the competitor unfair advantage. Since she had acquired that knowledge through special training and unique opportunities in her current position, the firm argued that it was unethical for her to accept the competitor's offer. What should the young manager do?

   _____ Accept the offer

   _____ Reject the offer

2. A consumer advocate organization conducted a survey to determine whether Wendy's hamburgers were really any more "hot and juicy" than any other hamburgers. After testing a Big Mac, a Whopper, a Teen Burger, and a Wendy's Hot and Juicy, each hamburger brand received approximately the same number of votes for being the juiciest. The consumer group advocated that Wendy's not advertise its hamburgers to be the juiciest. The company indicated that its own tests showed different results and that the image of the burger was the important thing, not the test results. Should the advertisements cease or not?

_____ Cease to advertise

_____ Continue to advertise

3. After several profitable years, the Bob Cummings Organic Vitamin Company was made available for sale. Bob's movie and TV appearances precluded him from keeping track of a large company, and it became apparent that, if present trends continued, the company would either have to expand substantially or lose a large share of the market. Several firms were interested in purchasing the company for the asking price, but one firm was particularly aggressive. It sponsored several parties and receptions in Bob's honor; a 35-foot yacht was made available for his use during the summer; and several gifts for family members arrived during the holidays. Bob's wife questioned the propriety of these activities. Was it appropriate for Bob to accept the gifts? Should he sell to that firm?

_____ Proper to accept

_____ Not proper

_____ Should not sell

_____ Should sell

4. John Waller was hired to coach football. After two seasons, he was so successful that he was named coach of the year by UPI, *Sporting News*, and ESPN. He was also very vocal about the need to clean up cheating in college athletics, especially among competitor schools in his own conference. He heard rumors about inappropriate alumni gifts to some of his own athletes, but after confronting those involved, he received assurances that the rumors weren't true. At the beginning of the next season, however, he received conclusive evidence that seven of the starters on his team, including an All-American, had received financial benefits from a wealthy booster. What should Waller do?

_____ Kick them off the team

_____ Suspend them for several games

_____ Warn them but do nothing

5. Roger's company had been battered by competition from Asian firms. Not only were Asian products selling for less money, but their quality was substantially higher. By investing in some high-technology equipment and fostering better union–management relations, Roger was relatively certain that the quality gap could be overcome. But his overhead rate was more than 40 percent above that of the competitor firms. He reasoned that the most efficient way to lower costs would be to close one of his older plants, lay off the employees, and increase production in the newer plants. He knew just which plant would be the one to close. The trouble was, the community was dependent on that plant as its major employer and had recently invested a great deal of money for highway repair and

streetlight construction around the plant. Most of the workforce were older people who had lived in the area most of their lives. It was improbable that they could obtain alternative employment in the same area. Should Roger close the plant or not?

_____ Close the plant

_____ Do not close

Discussion Questions

Form a small group and discuss the following questions regarding these five scenarios:

1. Why did you make the choices you did in each case? Justify each answer.
2. What principles or basic values for decision making did you use in each case?
3. What additional information would you need in order to be certain about your choices?
4. What circumstances might arise to make you change your mind about your decision? Could there be a different answer to each case in a different circumstance?
5. What do your answers tell you about your own emotional intelligence, values, cognitive style, attitude toward change, and core self-evaluation?

EXERCISES FOR IMPROVING SELF-AWARENESS THROUGH SELF-DISCLOSURE

Through the Looking Glass

In the nineteenth century, the concept of "looking-glass self" was developed to describe the process used by people to develop self-awareness. It means that other people serve as a looking glass for each of us. They mirror back our actions and behaviors. In turn, we form our opinions of ourselves as a result of observing and interpreting this mirroring. The best way to form accurate self-perceptions, therefore, is to share your thoughts, attitudes, feelings, actions, and plans with others. This exercise helps you do that by asking you to analyze your own styles and inclinations and then share and discuss them with others. This sharing exercise will provide insights that you haven't recognized before.

Assignment

In a group of three or four, share your scores on the Skill Assessment instruments. Determine what similarities and differences exist among you. Do systematic ethnic or gender differences exist? Now read aloud the 10 statements listed below. Each person should complete each statement, but take turns going first. The purpose of your completing the statements aloud is to help you articulate aspects of your self-awareness and to receive reactions to them from others.

1. In taking the assessment instruments, I was surprised by . . .

2. Some of my dominant characteristics captured by the instruments are . . .

3. Among my greatest strengths are . . .

4. Among my greatest weaknesses are . . .

5. The time I felt most successful was . . .

PRACTICE

6. The time I felt least competent was . . .

7. My three highest priorities in life are . . .

8. The way in which I differ most from other people is . . .

9. I get along best with people who . . .

10. From what the others in this group have shared, here is an impression I have formed about each:

Diagnosing Managerial Characteristics

This exercise is designed to give you practice in diagnosing differences in others' styles and inclinations. Being aware of the styles, values, and attitudes of others will help you manage them more effectively. Below are brief descriptions of four successful managers. They differ in values, learning styles, orientations toward change, and interpersonal orientation. After reading the scenarios, form small groups to discuss the questions that follow.

Michael Dell

Michael Dell is the kind of guy people either love or hate. He is worth more than $13 billion, loves to go to work each day, and is as likely to tear a computer apart and put it back together again as to read a financial report. More than 15 years after he started assembling computers in his dorm room, Michael is still fascinated with the hardware. Despite his billionaire status, "if anyone believes that he is not the chief technologist in this company, they are naive," says Robert McFarland, vice president of Dell's federal sales group. Although Dell Computer is the quintessential lean-and-mean company, Michael does not play the part of the whipcracker. After recently receiving an award from the Austin, Texas, Chamber of Commerce, for example, Michael and his wife stayed long after the program was over to chat with everyone who wanted to meet him. He has been described as shy and quiet and not inclined toward public hyperbole. "Michael has a genuine shyness . . . he is a genuinely mild-mannered, low-key person who was very focused on reaching his objectives," says Brian Fawkes, a former Dell employee. Admittedly, Dell has experienced several missteps and losses, but Michael has been unafraid to learn from missteps. "Michael makes mistakes. He just never makes the same mistake twice," says Mark Tebbe, president of a firm Dell recently acquired.

Source: *Adapted from Darrow, 1998.*

Patrick M. Byrne

As president and chairman of Overstock.com in Salt Lake City, Utah, Byrne was a Marshall Scholar who received his PhD in philosophy from Stanford University. His management style, personality, and core values are illustrated in his interview with *Fast Company*: "Learning philosophy has been useful in teaching me how to get to the heart of things—to be able to deconstruct what the real issues are. People think we're endless debaters, but what we're really doing is refining concepts in order to reach agreement. With negotiations, instead of trying to fight someone on every one of the issues, most of the time it turns out he cares about a whole bunch of things that you don't care about. Make those trade-offs, and he'll think you're being too generous when in fact you're just giving him the sleeves off your vest. Ultimately, philosophy is about values, and that definitely has its place in business. I consider myself a far outsider to Wall Street. There's a whole lot of obfuscation involved. In August, I spoke out on how the Wall Street system was corrupt and how the financial press was co-opted. Because of it I got called a buffoon and wacky; then a lot of lies came out about my being gay, taking cocaine, and hiring a stripper. That's sort of the fifth-grade level we're operating on. It doesn't bother me. When you decide to stand for things, you have to be prepared to face criticism, mockery, and derision."

SOURCE: *Adapted from* Fast Company, *2005.*

Maurice Blanks

When Maurice started architecture school, one of the professors said that only 25 percent of the students would make it. Sure enough, Maurice dropped out in his forties after operating his own office in Chicago. He moved to Minneapolis to devote himself full time to Blu Dot, a company he helped create. His discussion about architecture reveals a great deal about his personal attributes. "Architecture is about keeping track of thousands of pieces of information and making sure they're all covered in the design. The implications of failure are pretty high if you don't—people could get hurt. Therefore, you learn that you must be very efficient with information and organization, which naturally translates to running the day-to-day operations of a company. It's funny how the word 'sell' is never used in architecture school, but to me the critiques were kind of informal lessons in sales. For exams, you'd present your work to a jury—professors, peers, local architects, and so on. Their job was to shell you; your job was to defend yourself. It's pretty brutal. Tears are not uncommon. But it taught me how to communicate ideas quickly and tailor information to an audience."

SOURCE: *Adapted from* Fast Company, *2005.*

Gordon Bethune

Gordon Bethune has been described as the *other* earthy, exuberant, hard-drinking Texas CEO who turned around an airline that is now famous for good service, happy employees, and admirable profitability. Herb Kelleher at Southwest Airlines is the best known, but Gordon Bethune at Continental Airlines is the most successful. A high school dropout mechanic who spent years in the Navy, Gordon took over a twice-bankrupt airline in 1994 and led it from a $960 million loss to more than $600 million profit in five years. Even from his early years as a Navy mechanic, Gordon was known as superb motivator of people and a network builder. "He had a web of relationships that enabled him to get whatever he needed," said a former commanding officer. At Continental, Gordon turned around a culture where morale was in the pits, on-time performance was abysmal, and everything from the planes to the meals were a mess. Part of the turnaround was due to Gordon's personal attention to employees—for example, he attends the graduation ceremonies of every new class of flight attendants, hands out candy canes to employees during the Christmas season, shows up regularly at employee birthday parties, and holds a monthly open house in his office to encourage employee communication. "Anybody who's worked here longer than two months can recognize Gordon," says a baggage handler in Newark. When he walks through an airport, employees wave and call out his name. Whereas Gordon is known as an irreverent and wild guy, he demands precision and standardized levels of service in every place in the company. When he discovered slightly larger white coffee cups in a Houston airport lounge, for example, he was told that they were needed to fit the new coffee maker. He demanded that the coffee maker be changed so that the standard blue cups could be used. No exceptions."

SOURCE: *Adapted from O'Reilly, 1999.*

Discussion Questions

1. Rank these individuals from highest to lowest in terms of:
   - Emotional intelligence
   - Values maturity
   - Tolerance of ambiguity
   - Core self-evaluation

   Justify your evaluations in a discussion with your colleagues and compare your scores.

2. What is your prediction about the dominant learning styles of each of these individuals? What data do you use as evidence?

3. If you were assigned to hire a senior manager for your organization and this was your candidate pool, what questions would you ask to identify these individuals':
   - Cognitive styles
   - Values orientations
   - Orientation toward change
   - Core self-evaluation

   Which one of these people would you hire if you wanted a CEO for your company? Why?

4. Assume that each of these individuals were members of your team. What would be the greatest strengths and weaknesses of your team? What kinds of attributes would you want to add to your team to ensure that it was optimally heterogeneous?

An Exercise for Identifying Aspects of Personal Culture: A Learning Plan and Autobiography

The purpose of this exercise is to assist you in articulating your key goals and aspirations as well as identifying a personal learning plan to facilitate your success. Because continuous learning is so important for you to succeed throughout your life, we want to help you identify some specific ambitions and to develop a set of procedures to help you reach your potential.

This exercise is accomplished in three steps:

Step 1: (Aspirations): Write an autobiographical story that might appear in *Fortune Magazine, Fast Company*, or the *Wall Street Journal* on this date 15 years from now. This story should identify your notable accomplishments and your newsworthy successes. What will you have achieved that will fulfill your dreams? What outcomes would make you ecstatically happy? What legacy do you want to be known for?

Step 2: (Characteristics): Review your scores on the Pre-assessment instruments. Using Figure 1.5, identify the extent to which you are satisfied with your scores on these various

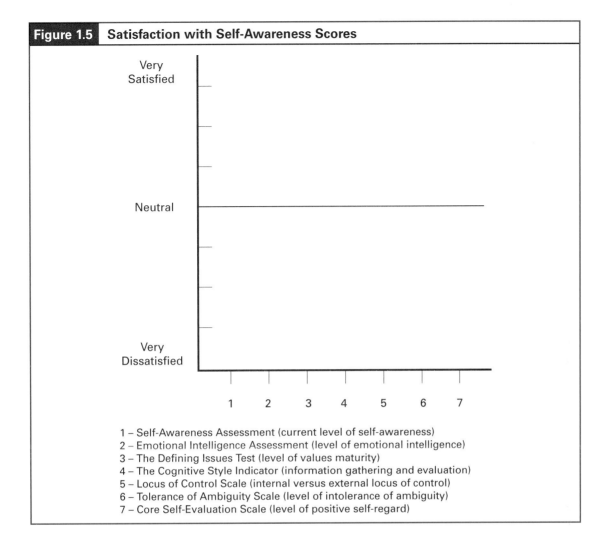

Figure 1.5   Satisfaction with Self-Awareness Scores

Very
Satisfied

Neutral

Very
Dissatisfied

1   2   3   4   5   6   7

1 – Self-Awareness Assessment (current level of self-awareness)
2 – Emotional Intelligence Assessment (level of emotional intelligence)
3 – The Defining Issues Test (level of values maturity)
4 – The Cognitive Style Indicator (information gathering and evaluation)
5 – Locus of Control Scale (internal versus external locus of control)
6 – Tolerance of Ambiguity Scale (level of intolerance of ambiguity)
7 – Core Self-Evaluation Scale (level of positive self-regard)

instruments. The vertical axis in the figure ranges from Very Satisfied to Very Dissatisfied. The horizontal axis identifies the five areas of self-awareness being assessed in this chapter. For each of the seven instruments, plot your satisfaction level with how you scored. By joining those points together, you will have created a Self-Awareness Satisfaction Profile. This will help you highlight areas in which you will want to improve.

Based on that plot, identify your distinctive competencies, your strengths, and your unique attributes. What are the values, styles, and attitudes that will assist you in achieving the aspirations you have identified in Step 1?

Step 3: (Feedback): Interview a member of your family or someone who knows you very well. Ask that person to describe what they see as your unique strengths and capabilities. What does he or she see for you in your future? Include the following questions in your interview:

- Who do you know that you admire a great deal because of their success in life? What capabilities and attributes do they possess?

- Who do you know that has failed to achieve their potential? What do you see as the most significant causes of their failure?

- What do you see as the distinctive and notable capabilities that I possess?

PRACTICE

- In what areas do you think I should focus my improvement and development efforts?
- What do you see me doing in 15 years?

Step 4: (Planning): Now identify the developmental activities in which you will engage if you are to achieve your aspirations. With the insight you have gained from steps 2 and 3, identify the things you must do to help you achieve what you hope to accomplish. Consider the following activities.

- What courses will you take?
- What people will you get to know?
- In what extracurricular or life-balance activities will you engage?
- What will you read?
- What spiritual activities will be most meaningful?

This written product should be handed in to your instructor, or it should be given to a family member for safekeeping. Open and reread this document in five years to determine the extent to which you are on track.

ACTIVITIES FOR DEVELOPING SELF-AWARENESS

Suggested Assignments

1. Keep a journal for at least the remainder of this course. Record significant discoveries, insights, learnings, and personal recollections, not daily activities. Write in your journal at least twice a week. Give yourself some feedback.

2. Ask someone you know well to complete the assessment instruments wherein that person rates you on each item. Compare your scores and those of this other person. Discuss differences, strengths, and areas of confusion. The goal is to help you increase your self-awareness by getting a picture of yourself from the standpoint of someone else.

3. Write down the comprehensive, consistent, and universal principles that guide your behavior under all circumstances. What core principles will you rarely violate?

4. After completing the personal assessment instruments and discussing their implications with someone else, write an essay responding to the following four questions: (1) Who am I? (2) What are my main strengths and weaknesses? (3) What do I want to achieve in my life? (4) What legacy do I want to leave?

5. Spend an evening with a close friend or relative discussing your emotional intelligence, values, cognitive style, attitude toward change, and core self-evaluation. You may want to have that person complete the instruments, giving his or her impressions of you, so you can compare and contrast your scores. Discuss implications for your future and for your relationship.

6. Teach someone else the value of self-awareness in managerial success and explain the relevance of emotional intelligence, values maturity, cognitive style, attitudes toward change, and core self-evaluation. Describe the experience in your journal.

Application Plan and Evaluation

The intent of this exercise is to help you apply this cluster of skills in a real-life, out-of-class setting. Now that you have become familiar with the behavioral guidelines that form the basis of effective skill performance, you will improve most by trying out those guidelines in an everyday context. Unlike a classroom activity, in which feedback is immediate and others can assist you with their evaluations, this skill application activity is one you must accomplish and evaluate on your own. There are two parts to this activity. Part 1 helps prepare you to apply the skill. Part 2 helps you evaluate and improve on your experience. Be sure to write down answers to each item. Don't short-circuit the process by skipping steps.

Part 1. Planning

1. Write down the two or three aspects of this skill that are most important to you. These may be areas of weakness, areas you most want to improve, or areas that are most salient to a problem you face right now. Identify the specific aspects of this skill that you want to apply.

2. Now identify the setting or the situation in which you will apply this skill. Establish a plan for performance by actually writing down a description of the situation. Who else will be involved? When will you do it? Where will it be done?
   Circumstances:
   Who else?
   When?
   Where?

3. Identify the specific behaviors in which you will engage to apply this skill. Operationalize your skill performance.

4. What are the indicators of successful performance? How will you know you have been effective? What will indicate you have performed competently?

Part 2. Evaluation

5. After you have completed your implementation, record the results. What happened? How successful were you? What was the effect on others?

6. How can you improve? What modifications can you make next time? What will you do differently in a similar situation in the future?

7. Looking back on your whole skill practice and application experience, what have you learned? What has been surprising? In what ways might this experience help you in the long term?

Emotional Response

4	a	0
	b	10
	c	0

EXPLANATION: Alternatives (a) and (c) may indicate that you are not sensitive to the emotional climate of the group, and your behavior may be inappropriate.

8	a	0
	b	5
	c	10

EXPLANATION: Alternative (b) may be appropriate if it isn't a sign of narcissism, but alternative (c) is clearly an indication of emotional control.

12	a	10
	b	0
	c	5

EXPLANATION: Alternative (b) implies losing emotional control, whereas (a) indicates remaining under control.

Total _____

Comparison Data (N = 5,000 students)

Mean score:	70
Top quartile:	86 or higher
Second quartile:	71–85
Third quartile:	55–70
Bottom quartile:	54 or lower

The Defining Issues Test

The possibility of misusing and misinterpreting this instrument is high enough that its author, James Rest, maintains control over the scoring procedure associated with its use. Some people may interpret the results of this instrument to be an indication of inherent morality, honesty, or personal worth, none of which the instrument is intended to assess. A scoring manual may be obtained from James Rest, Minnesota Moral Research Center, Burton Hall, University of Minnesota, Minneapolis, MN 55455.

Our purpose is to help you become aware of the stage of moral development you rely on most when facing moral dilemmas. To help determine that, the following lists present the stage of moral development each statement associated with each story reflects. By looking at the four statements you selected as most important in deciding what action to take in each situation, you can determine which stage of development you use most often.

After you have done this, you should discuss which action you would take in each situation and why, and why you selected the statements you did as the most important ones to consider.

The Escaped Prisoner

1. Hasn't Mr. Thompson been good enough for such a long time to prove he isn't a bad person? (Stage 3)

2. Every time someone escapes punishment for a crime, doesn't that just encourage more crime? (Stage 4)
3. Wouldn't we be better off without prisons and the oppression of our legal system? (Indicates antiauthoritarian attitudes.)
4. Has Mr. Thompson really paid his debt to society? (Stage 4)
5. Would society be failing what Mr. Thompson should fairly expect? (Stage 6)
6. What benefits would prison be apart from society, especially for a charitable man? (Nonsense alternative, designed to identify people picking high-sounding alternatives.)
7. How could anyone be so cruel and heartless as to send Mr. Thompson to prison? (Stage 3)
8. Would it be fair to all the prisoners who had to serve out their full sentences if Mr. Thompson was let off? (Stage 4)
9. Was Ms. Jones a good friend of Mr. Thompson? (Stage 3)
10. Wouldn't it be a citizen's duty to report an escaped criminal, regardless of circumstances? (Stage 4)
11. How would the will of the people and the public good best be served? (Stage 5)
12. Would going to prison do any good for Mr. Thompson or protect anybody? (Stage 5)

The Doctor's Dilemma

1. Whether the woman's family is in favor of giving her an overdose or not. (Stage 3)
2. Is the doctor obligated by the same laws as everybody else if giving her an overdose would be the same as killing her? (Stage 4)
3. Whether people would be much better off without society regimenting their lives and even their deaths. (Indicates antiauthoritarian attitudes.)
4. Whether the doctor could make it appear like an accident. (Stage 2)
5. Does the state have the right to force continued existence on those who don't want to live? (Stage 5)
6. What is the value of death prior to society's perspective on personal values? (Nonsense alternative, designed to identify people picking high-sounding alternatives.)
7. Whether the doctor has sympathy for the woman's suffering or cares more about what society might think. (Stage 3)
8. Is helping to end another's life ever a responsible act of cooperation? (Stage 6)
9. Whether only God should decide when a person's life should end. (Stage 4)
10. What values the doctor has set for himself in his own personal code of behavior. (Stage 5)
11. Can society afford to let everybody end their lives when they want to? (Stage 4)
12. Can society allow suicides or mercy killing and still protect the lives of individuals who want to live? (Stage 5)

The Newspaper

1. Is the principal more responsible to students or to the parents? (Stage 4)
2. Did the principal give his word that the newspaper could be published for a long time, or did he promise to approve the newspaper one issue at a time? (Stage 4)
3. Would the students start protesting even more if the principal stopped the newspaper? (Stage 2)
4. When the welfare of the school is threatened, does the principal have the right to give orders to students? (Stage 4)
5. Does the principal have the freedom of speech to say "no" in this case? (Nonsense alternative, designed to identify people picking high-sounding alternatives.)

6. If the principal stopped the newspaper, would he be preventing full discussion of important problems? (Stage 5)
7. Whether the principal's order would make Rami lose faith in the principal. (Stage 3)
8. Whether Rami was loyal to his school and patriotic to his country. (Stage 3)
9. What effect would stopping the paper have on the students' education in critical thinking and judgment? (Stage 5)
10. Whether Rami was in any way violating the rights of others in publishing his own opinions. (Stage 5)
11. Whether the principal should be influenced by some angry parents when it is the principal who knows best what is going on in the school. (Stage 4)
12. Whether Rami was using the newspaper to stir up hatred and discontent. (Stage 3)

Cognitive Style Indicator

Scoring and Comparison Data for the Cognitive Style Indicator

Scoring Key

Knowing Style: Items 5, 8, 11, 14   Add your scores and divide by 4: _____

Planning Style: Items 1, 3, 6, 9,
    12, 15, 17   Add your scores and divide by 7: _____

Creating Style: Items 2, 4, 7, 10, 13,
    16, 18   Add your scores and divide by 7: _____

Comparison Data

	YOUNG MANAGERS (N = 5,925)		YOUNG MANAGERS & MBA STUDENTS (N = 2,215)	
STYLE	MEAN	SD	MEAN	SD
Knowing	3.89	.65	4.06	.96
Planning	3.78	.77	3.81	1.16
Creating	4.01	.60	4.16	.80

Locus of Control Scale

Scoring Key

Count up the number of items you selected from the list below:

2a	5b	9a	12b	16a	20a	23a	28b
3b	6a	10a	13b	17a	21a	25a	29a
4b	7a	11b	15b	18a	22b	26b	

Total Score _____

Complete the online version of this new survey to see comparison data.

Comparison Data (N = 5,000 students)

Mean score:	5.19 (SD = 3.04)
Top quartile:	7 or above
Third quartile:	5–6
Second quartile:	3–4
Bottom quartile:	2 or below

ADDITIONAL COMPARISONS (FROM ROTTER, 1966, 1972, 1982)

SAMPLE	MEAN	SD	SOURCE
Ohio State psychology students (N=1,180)	8.29	3.97	1966
Connecticut psychology students (N=303)	9.22	3.88	1966
Peace Corps trainees (N=155)	5.95	3.96	1966
National high school students (N=1,000)	8.50	3.74	1966
Municipal administrators, Alberta, Canada (N=50)	6.24	3.31	1971
Business executives (N=71)	8.29	3.57	1980
Career military officers (N=261)	8.28	3.86	1980
Students using *Developing Management Skills*	5.19	3.04	2006

Tolerance of Ambiguity Scale

Scoring Key

High scores indicate an intolerance of ambiguity. Having high intolerance means that you tend to perceive situations as threatening rather than promising. Lack of information or uncertainty would tend to make you uncomfortable. Ambiguity arises from three primary sources: novelty, complexity, and insolubility. These three subscales are measured by the instrument.

In scoring the instrument, the *even-numbered* items must be reversed. That is, 7 becomes 1, 6 becomes 2, 5 becomes 3, 3 becomes 5, 2 becomes 6, and 1 becomes 7. After reversing the appropriate items, sum all 16 items to get your score.

ITEM	SUBSCALE	ITEM	SUBSCALE	ITEM	SUBSCALE	ITEM	SUBSCALE
1	I	5	C	9	N	13	N
2	N	6	C	10	C	14	C
3	I	7	C	11	N	15	C
4	C	8	C	12	I	16	C

N = Novelty Score (2, 9, 11, 13) _____

C = Complexity Score (4, 5, 6, 7, 8, 10, 14, 16) _____

I = Insolubility Score (1, 3, 12) _____

Total Score _____

Comparison Data (N = 5,000 students)

Mean score:	56.47
Top quartile:	63 or above
Third quartile:	57–62
Second quartile:	50–56
Bottom quartile:	49 or below

Core Self-Evaluation Scale

Scoring Key

Sum your scores for all 12 items, making certain that you reverse your scores for items 2, 4, 6, 8, 10, 12. That is, for these items, 1 becomes 5, 2 becomes 4, 4 becomes 2, and 5 becomes 1. Divide the sum by 12 to produce an average CSES score.

1. _____ I am confident I get the success I deserve in life.
2. _____ Sometimes I feel depressed. **(reverse)**
3. _____ When I try, I generally succeed.
4. _____ Sometimes when I fail I feel worthless. **(reverse)**
5. _____ I complete tasks successfully.
6. _____ Sometimes, I do not feel in control of my work. **(reverse)**
7. _____ Overall, I am satisfied with myself.
8. _____ I am filled with doubts about my competence. **(reverse)**
9. _____ I determine what will happen in my life.
10. _____ I do not feel in control of my success in my career. **(reverse)**
11. _____ I am capable of coping with most of my problems.
12. _____ There are times when things look pretty bleak and hopeless to me. **(reverse)**

Total _____
÷12 _____ (Average Score)

Comparison Data (N = 5,000 students)

(Compared to psychology students, business students, practicing managers)

Mean score: 3.88
Top quartile: 4.41 or above
Third quartile: 3.88 and 4.40
Second quartile: 3.35 and 3.87
Bottom quartile: 3.34 or below

Source: Cools and Van den Broeck, 2007.

SKILL *ASSESSMENT* ▶

- Stress Management Assessment
- Time Management Assessment
- Type A Personality Inventory
- Social Readjustment Rating Scale
- Sources of Personal Stress

SKILL *LEARNING* ■

- Improving the Management of Stress and Time
- Major Elements of Stress
- Managing Stress
- Eliminating Stressors
- Developing Resiliency
- Temporary Stress-Reduction Techniques
- Summary
- Behavioral Guidelines

SKILL *ANALYSIS* ▶

- The Turn of the Tide
- The Case of the Missing Time

SKILL *PRACTICE* ◆

- The Small-Wins Strategy
- Life-Balance Analysis
- Deep Relaxation
- Monitoring and Managing Time

SKILL *APPLICATION* ●

- Suggested Assignments
- Application Plan and Evaluation

SCORING KEYS AND *COMPARISON DATA* ■

2

Managing Personal Stress

SKILL DEVELOPMENT OBJECTIVES

- ELIMINATE STRESSORS
- DEVELOP RESILIENCY
- COPE WITH STRESS IN THE SHORT TERM

DIAGNOSTIC SURVEYS FOR MANAGING STRESS

STRESS MANAGEMENT ASSESSMENT

Step 1: Before you read the material in this chapter, please respond to the following statements by writing a number from the rating scale below in the left-hand column (Pre-assessment). Your answers should reflect your attitudes and behavior as they are now, not as you would like them to be. Be honest. This instrument is designed to help you discover your level of competency in stress management so you can tailor your learning to your specific needs. When you have completed the survey, use the scoring key at the end of the chapter to identify the skill areas discussed in this chapter that are most important for you to master.

Step 2: After you have completed the reading and the exercises in this chapter and, ideally, as many as you can of the Skill Application assignments at the end of this chapter, cover up your first set of answers. Then respond to the same statements again, this time in the right-hand column (Post-assessment). When you have completed the survey, use the scoring key at the end of the chapter to measure your progress. If your score remains low in specific skill areas, use the behavioral guidelines at the end of the Skill Learning section to guide further practice.

Rating Scale

1 Strongly disagree
2 Disagree
3 Slightly disagree
4 Slightly agree
5 Agree
6 Strongly agree

Assessment

Pre-   Post-

When faced with stressful or time-pressured situations:

_____   _____   1. I use effective time-management methods such as keeping track of my time, making to-do lists, and prioritizing tasks.

_____   _____   2. I maintain a program of regular exercise for fitness.

_____   _____   3. I maintain an open, trusting relationship with someone with whom I can share my frustrations.

_____   _____   4. I know and practice several temporary relaxation techniques such as deep breathing and muscle relaxation.

_____   _____   5. I frequently affirm my priorities so that less important things don't drive out more important things.

_____   _____   6. I maintain balance in my life by pursuing a variety of interests outside of work.

_____   _____   7. I have a close relationship with someone who serves as my mentor or advisor.

_____   _____   8. I effectively utilize others in accomplishing work assignments.

_____ _____ 9. I encourage others to generate recommended solutions, not just questions, when they come to me with problems or issues.

_____ _____ 10. I strive to redefine problems as opportunities for improvement.

TIME MANAGEMENT ASSESSMENT

In responding to the statements below, fill in each blank with the number from the rating scale that indicates the frequency with which you do each activity. Assess your behavior as it is, not as you would like it to be. How useful this instrument will be to you depends on your ability to accurately assess your own behavior.

Please note that the *first* section of the instrument can be completed by anyone. The *second* section applies primarily to individuals currently serving in a managerial position.

Turn to the end of the chapter to find the scoring key and an interpretation of your scores.

Rating Scale

0 Never
1 Seldom
2 Sometimes
3 Usually
4 Always

Section I

_____ 1. I read selectively, skimming the material until I find what is important, then high-lighting it.

_____ 2. I make a list of tasks to accomplish each day.

_____ 3. I keep everything in its proper place at work.

_____ 4. I prioritize the tasks I have to do according to their importance and urgency.

_____ 5. I concentrate on only one important task at a time, but I do multiple trivial tasks at once (such as signing letters while talking on the phone).

_____ 6. I make a list of short five- or ten-minute tasks to do.

_____ 7. I divide large projects into smaller, separate stages.

_____ 8. I identify which 20 percent of my tasks will produce 80 percent of the results.

_____ 9. I do the most important tasks at my best time during the day.

_____ 10. I have some time during each day when I can work uninterrupted.

_____ 11. I don't procrastinate. I do today what needs to be done.

_____ 12. I keep track of the use of my time with devices such as a time log.

_____ 13. I set deadlines for myself.

_____ 14. I do something productive whenever I am waiting.

_____ 15. I do redundant "busy work" at one set time during the day.

_____ 16. I finish at least one thing every day.

_____ 17. I schedule some time during the day for personal time alone (for planning, meditation, prayer, exercise).

_____ 18. I allow myself to worry about things only at one particular time during the day, not all the time.

_____ 19. I have clearly defined long-term objectives toward which I am working.

_____ 20. I continually try to find little ways to use my time more efficiently.

Section II

_____ 1. I hold routine meetings at the end of the day.

_____ 2. I hold all short meetings standing up.

_____ 3. I set a time limit at the outset of each meeting.

_____ 4. I cancel scheduled meetings that are not necessary.

_____ 5. I have a written agenda for every meeting.

_____ 6. I stick to the agenda and reach closure on each item.

_____ 7. I ensure that someone is assigned to take minutes and to watch the time in every meeting.

_____ 8. I start all meetings on time.

_____ 9. I have minutes of meetings prepared promptly after the meeting and see that follow-up occurs promptly.

_____ 10. When subordinates come to me with a problem, I ask them to suggest solutions.

_____ 11. I meet visitors to my office outside the office or in the doorway.

_____ 12. I go to subordinates' offices when feasible so that I can control when I leave.

_____ 13. I leave at least one-fourth of my day free from meetings and appointments I can't control.

_____ 14. I have someone else who can answer my calls and greet visitors at least some of the time.

_____ 15. I have one place where I can work uninterrupted.

_____ 16. I do something definite with every piece of paper I handle.

_____ 17. I keep my workplace clear of all materials except those I am working on.

_____ 18. I delegate tasks.

_____ 19. I specify the amount of personal initiative I want others to take when I assign them a task.

_____ 20. I am willing to let others get the credit for tasks they accomplish.

TYPE A PERSONALITY INVENTORY

Rate the extent to which each of the following statements is typical of you most of the time. Focus on your general way of behaving and feeling. There are no right or wrong answers. When you have finished, turn to the end of the chapter to find the scoring key and an interpretation of your scores.

Rating Scale

3 The statement is very typical of me.

2 The statement is somewhat typical of me.

1 The statement is not at all typical of me.

_____ 1. My greatest satisfaction comes from doing things better than others.

_____ 2. I tend to bring the theme of a conversation around to things I'm interested in.

_____ 3. In conversations, I frequently clench my fist, bang on the table, or pound one fist into the palm of another for emphasis.

_____ 4. I move, walk, and eat rapidly.

_____ 5. I feel as though I can accomplish more than others.

_____ 6. I feel guilty when I relax or do nothing for several hours or days.

_____ 7. It doesn't take much to get me to argue.

_____ 8. I feel impatient with the rate at which most events take place.

_____ 9. Having more than others is important to me.

_____ 10. One aspect of my life (e.g., work, family care, school) dominates all others.

_____ 11. I frequently regret not being able to control my temper.

_____ 12. I hurry the speech of others by saying "Uh huh," "Yes, yes," or by finishing their sentences for them.

_____ 13. People who avoid competition have low self-confidence.

_____ 14. To do something well, you have to concentrate on it alone and screen out all distractions.

_____ 15. I feel others' mistakes and errors cause me needless aggravation.

_____ 16. I find it intolerable to watch others perform tasks I know I can do faster.

_____ 17. Getting ahead in my job is a major personal goal.

_____ 18. I simply don't have enough time to lead a well-balanced life.

_____ 19. I take out my frustration with my own imperfections on others.

_____ 20. I frequently try to do two or more things simultaneously.

_____ 21. When I encounter a competitive person, I feel a need to challenge him or her.

_____ 22. I tend to fill up my spare time with thoughts and activities related to my work (or school or family care).

_____ 23. I am frequently upset by the unfairness of life.

_____ 24. I find it anguishing to wait in line.

SOURCE: _Tolerance of Ambiguity Scale, S. Budner (1962), "Intolerance of Ambiguity as a Personality Variable,"_ from Journal of Personality, _30: 29–50. Reprinted with the permission of Blackwell Publishing, Ltd._

SOCIAL READJUSTMENT RATING SCALE*

Circle any of the following you have experienced in the past year. Using the weightings at the left, total up your score.

Mean Value	Life Event
87	1. Death of spouse/mate
79	2. Death of a close family member
78	3. Major injury/illness to self
76	4. Detention in jail or other institution
72	5. Major injury/illness to a close family member
71	6. Foreclosure on loan/mortgage
71	7. Divorce
70	8. Being a victim of crime
69	9. Being a victim of police brutality

*This assessment is not available online.

69	10. Infidelity
69	11. Experiencing domestic violence/sexual abuse
66	12. Separation or reconciliation with spouse/mate
64	13. Being fired/laid-off/unemployed
62	14. Experiencing financial problems/difficulties
61	15. Death of a close friend
59	16. Surviving a disaster
59	17. Becoming a single parent
56	18. Assuming responsibility for sick or elderly loved one
56	19. Loss of or major reduction in health insurance/benefits
56	20. Self/close family member being arrested for violating the law
53	21. Major disagreement over child support/custody/visitation
53	22. Experiencing/involved in an auto accident
53	23. Being disciplined at work/demoted
51	24. Dealing with unwanted pregnancy
50	25. Adult child moving in with parent/parent moving in with adult child
49	26. Child develops behavior or learning problem
48	27. Experienced employment discrimination/sexual harassment
47	28. Attempting to modify addictive behavior of self
46	29. Discovering/attempting to modify addictive behavior of close family member
45	30. Employer reorganization/downsizing
44	31. Dealing with infertility/miscarriage
43	32. Getting married/remarried
43	33. Changing employers/careers
42	34. Failure to obtain/qualify for a mortgage
41	35. Pregnancy of self/spouse/mate
39	36. Experiencing discrimination/harassment outside the workplace
39	37. Release from jail
38	38. Spouse/mate begins/ceases work outside the home
37	39. Major disagreement with boss/coworker
35	40. Change in residence
34	41. Finding appropriate child care/day care
33	42. Experiencing a large unexpected monetary gain
33	43. Changing positions (transfer, promotion)
33	44. Gaining a new family member
32	45. Changing work responsibilities
30	46. Child leaving home
30	47. Obtaining a home mortgage
30	48. Obtaining a major loan other than home mortgage

28   49. Retirement

26   50. Beginning/ceasing formal education

22   51. Receiving a ticket for violating the law

Total of Circled Items: _____

SOURCE: *Social Readjustment Rating Scale, Hobson, Charles Jo, Joseph Kaen, Jane Szotek, Carol M. Nethercutt, James W. Tiedmann and Susan Wojnarowicz (1998), "Stressful Life Events: A Revision and Update of the Social Readjustment Rating Scale,"* International Journal of Stress Management, *5: 1–23.*

SOURCES OF PERSONAL STRESS

1 Identify the factors that produce the most stress for you right now. What is it that creates feelings of stress in your life?

Source of Stress   Rating

2 Now give each of those stressors above a rating from 1 to 100 on the basis of how powerful each is in producing stress. Refer to the Social Readjustment Rating Scale for relative weightings of stressors. A rating of 100, for example, might be associated with the death of a spouse or child, while a rating of 10 might be associated with the overly slow driver in front of you.

3 Use these specific sources of stress as targets as you discuss and practice the stress management principles presented in the rest of the chapter.

SKILL *LEARNING*

Improving the Management of Stress and Time

Managing stress and time is one of the most crucial, yet neglected, management skills in a competent manager's repertoire. Here is why: The National Institute for Occupational Safety and the American Psychological Association estimate that the growing problem of stress on the job siphons off more than $500 billion from the nation's economy. Almost half of all adults suffer adverse health effects due to stress; the percentage of workers feeling "highly stressed" more than doubled from 1985 to 1990 and doubled again in the 1990s. In one survey, 37 percent of workers reported that their stress level at work increased last year, while less than 10 percent say their stress level decreased. Between 75 and 90 percent of all visits to primary care physicians are for stress-related complaints or disorders. An estimated one million workers are absent on an average working day because of stress-related complaints, and approximately 550,000,000 workdays are lost each year due to stress. In one major corporation, more than 60 percent of absences were found to be stress related, and in the United States as a whole, about 40 percent of worker turnover is due to job stress. Between 60 and 80 percent of industrial accidents are attributable to stress, and worker compensation claims have skyrocketed in the last two decades, with more than 90 percent of the lawsuits successful. It is estimated that businesses in the United States alone will spend more than $12 billion on stress management training and products this year (American Institute of Stress, 2000). Name any other single factor that has such a devastating and costly effect on workers, managers, and organizations.

A review of the chapters in a recent medical book on stress illustrates the wide-ranging and devastating effects of stress: stress and the cardiovascular system, stress and the respiratory system, stress and the endocrine system, stress and the gastrointestinal tract, stress and the female reproductive system, stress and reproductive hormones, stress and male reproductive functioning, stress and immunodepression, stress and neurological disorders, stress and addiction, stress and malignancy, stress and immune functions with HIV-1, stress and dental pathology, stress and pain, and stress and anxiety disorders (Hubbard & Workman,

1998). Almost no part of life or health is immune from the effects of stress.

As an illustration of the debilitating effects of job-related stress, consider the following story reported by the Associated Press.

Baltimore (AP) The job was getting to the ambulance attendant. He felt disturbed by the recurring tragedy, isolated by the long shifts. His marriage was in trouble. He was drinking too much.

One night it all blew up.

He rode in back that night. His partner drove. Their first call was for a man whose leg had been cut off by a train. His screaming and agony were horrifying, but the second call was worse. It was a child-beating. As the attendant treated the youngster's bruised body and snapped bones, he thought of his own child. His fury grew.

Immediately after leaving the child at the hospital, the attendants were sent out to help a heart attack victim seen lying in a street. When they arrived, however, they found not a cardiac patient but a drunk—a wino passed out. As they lifted the man into the ambulance, their frustration and anger came to a head. They decided to give the wino a ride he would remember.

The ambulance vaulted over railroad tracks at high speed. The driver took the corners as fast as he could, flinging the wino from side to side in the back. To the attendants, it was a joke.

Suddenly, the wino began having a real heart attack. The attendant in back leaned over the wino and started shouting. "Die, you sucker!" he yelled. "Die!"

He watched as the wino shuddered. He watched as the wino died. By the time they reached the hospital, they had their stories straight. Dead on arrival, they said. Nothing they could do.

The attendant, who must remain anonymous, talked about that night at a recent counseling session on "professional burnout"— a growing problem in high-stress jobs.

As this story graphically illustrates, stress can produce devastating effects. Personal consequences can range from inability to concentrate, anxiety, and depression to stomach disorders, low resistance to illness, and heart disease. For organizations, consequences range from absenteeism and job dissatisfaction to high accident and turnover rates.

THE ROLE OF MANAGEMENT

Amazingly, a 25-year study of employee surveys revealed that incompetent management is the largest cause of workplace stress! Three out of four surveys listed employee relationships with immediate supervisors as the worst aspect of the job. Moreover, research in psychology has found that stress not only affects workers negatively, but it also produces less visible (though equally detrimental) consequences for managers themselves (Auerbach, 1998; Staw, Sandelands, & Dutton, 1981; Weick, 1993b). For example, when managers experience stress, they tend to:

- ❏ Selectively perceive information and see only that which confirms their previous biases
- ❏ Become very intolerant of ambiguity and demanding of right answers
- ❏ Fixate on a single approach to a problem
- ❏ Overestimate how fast time is passing (hence, they often feel rushed)
- ❏ Adopt a short-term perspective or crisis mentality and cease to consider long-term implications
- ❏ Have less ability to make fine distinctions in problems, so that complexity and nuances are missed
- ❏ Consult and listen to others less
- ❏ Rely on old habits to cope with current situations
- ❏ Have less ability to generate creative thoughts and unique solutions to problems

Thus, not only do the results of stress negatively affect employees in the workplace, but they also drastically impede effective management behaviors such as listening, making good decisions, solving problems effectively, planning, and generating new ideas. Developing the skill of managing stress, therefore, can have significant payoffs. The ability to deal appropriately with stress not only enhances individual self-development but can also have an enormous bottom-line impact on entire organizations.

Unfortunately, most of the scientific literature on stress focuses on its consequences. Too little examines how to cope effectively with stress, and even less addresses how to prevent stress (Hepburn, McLoughlin, & Barling, 1997). We begin our discussion by presenting a framework for understanding stress and learning how to cope with it. This model explains the major types of stressors faced by managers, the primary reactions to stress, and the reasons some people experience more negative reactions than others do. The last section presents principles for managing and adapting to stress, along with specific examples and behavioral guidelines.

Major Elements of Stress

One way to understand the dynamics of stress is to think of it as the product of a "force field" (Lewin, 1951). Kurt Lewin suggested that all individuals and organizations exist in an environment filled with reinforcing or opposing forces (i.e., stresses). These forces act to stimulate or inhibit the performance desired by the individual. As illustrated in Figure 2.1, a person's level of performance in an organization results from factors that may either complement or contradict one another. Certain forces drive or motivate changes in behavior, while other forces restrain or block those changes.

According to Lewin's theory, the forces affecting individuals are normally balanced in the force field. The strength of the driving forces is exactly matched by the strength of the restraining forces. (In the figure, longer arrows indicate stronger forces.) Performance changes when the forces become imbalanced. That is, if the driving forces become stronger than the restraining forces, or more numerous or enduring, change occurs. Conversely, if restraining forces become stronger or more numerous than driving forces, change occurs in the opposite direction.

Feelings of stress are a product of certain stressors inside or outside the individual. These stressors can be thought of as driving forces in the model. That is, they exert pressure on the individual to change present levels of performance physiologically, psychologically, and interpersonally. Unrestrained, those forces can lead to pathological results (e.g., anxiety, heart disease, and mental breakdown). However, most people have developed a certain amount of resiliency or restraining forces to counter stressors and inhibit pathological results. These restraining forces include behavior patterns, psychological characteristics, and supportive social relationships. Strong restraining forces lead to low heart rates, good interpersonal relationships, emotional stability, and

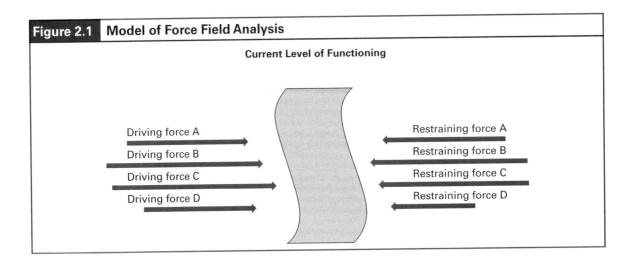

Figure 2.1 | **Model of Force Field Analysis**

Current Level of Functioning

Driving force A
Driving force B
Driving force C
Driving force D

Restraining force A
Restraining force B
Restraining force C
Restraining force D

effective stress management. An absence of restraining forces leads to the reverse.

Of course, stress produces positive as well as negative effects. In the absence of any stress, people feel completely bored and lack any inclination to act. Even when high levels of stress are experienced, equilibrium can be restored quickly if there is sufficient resiliency. In the case of the ambulance driver, for example, multiple stressors overpowered the available restraining forces and burnout occurred. Before reaching such an extreme state, however, individuals typically progress through three stages of reactions: an alarm stage, a resistance stage, and an exhaustion stage (Auerbach, 1998; Cooper, 1998; Selye, 1976).

REACTIONS TO STRESS

The **alarm stage** is characterized by acute increases in anxiety or fear if the stressor is a threat, or by increases in sorrow or depression if the stressor is a loss. A feeling of shock or confusion may result if the stressor is particularly acute. Physiologically, the individual's energy resources are mobilized and heart rate, blood pressure, and alertness increase. These reactions are largely self-correcting if the stressor is of brief duration. However, if it continues, the individual enters the **resistance stage**, in which defense mechanisms predominate and the body begins to store up excess energy.

Five types of defense mechanisms are typical of most people who experience extended levels of stress. The first is *aggression*, which involves attacking the stressor directly. It may also involve attacking oneself, other people, or even objects (e.g., whacking the computer). A second is *regression*, which is the adoption of a behavior pattern or response that was successful at some earlier

time (e.g., responding in childish ways). A third defense mechanism, *repression*, involves denial of the stressor, forgetting, or redefining the stressor (e.g., deciding that it isn't so scary after all). *Withdrawal* is a fourth defense mechanism, and it may take both psychological and physical forms. Individuals may engage in fantasy, inattention, or purposive forgetting, or they may actually escape from the situation itself. A fifth defense mechanism is *fixation*, which is persisting in a response regardless of its effectiveness (e.g., repeatedly and rapidly redialing a telephone number when it is busy).

If these defense mechanisms reduce a person's feeling of stress, negative effects such as high blood pressure, anxiety, or mental disorders are never experienced. The primary evidence that prolonged stress has occurred may simply be an increase in psychological defensiveness. However, when stress is so pronounced as to overwhelm defenses or so enduring as to outlast available energy for defensiveness, *exhaustion* may result, producing pathological consequences.

While each reaction stage may be experienced as temporarily uncomfortable, the exhaustion stage is the most dangerous one. When stressors overpower or outlast the resiliency capacities of individuals, or their ability to defend against them, chronic stress is experienced and negative personal and organizational consequences generally follow. Such pathological consequences may manifest physiologically (e.g., heart disease), psychologically (e.g., severe depression), or interpersonally (e.g., dissolution of relationships). These changes result from the damage done to an individual for which there was no defense (e.g., psychotic reactions among prisoners of war), from an inability to defend continuously against a stressor (e.g., becoming exhausted), from an overreaction (e.g., an ulcer produced by excessive secretion of

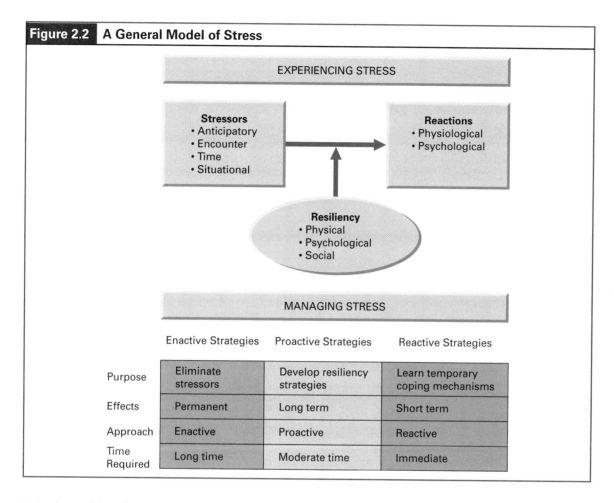

Figure 2.2 A General Model of Stress

EXPERIENCING STRESS

Stressors
- Anticipatory
- Encounter
- Time
- Situational

Reactions
- Physiological
- Psychological

Resiliency
- Physical
- Psychological
- Social

MANAGING STRESS

	Enactive Strategies	Proactive Strategies	Reactive Strategies
Purpose	Eliminate stressors	Develop resiliency strategies	Learn temporary coping mechanisms
Effects	Permanent	Long term	Short term
Approach	Enactive	Proactive	Reactive
Time Required	Long time	Moderate time	Immediate

body chemicals), or from lack of self-awareness so that stress is completely unacknowledged.

Figure 2.2 identifies the major categories of stressors (driving forces) that managers experience, as well as the major attributes of resiliency (restraining forces) that inhibit the negative effects of stress. Each of these forces is discussed in some detail in this chapter, so that it will become clear how to identify stressors, how to eliminate them, how to develop more resiliency, and how to cope with stress on a temporary basis.

COPING WITH STRESS

Individuals vary in the extent to which stressors lead to pathologies and dysfunctions. Some people are labeled "hot reactors," meaning they have a predisposition to experience extremely negative reactions to stress (Adler & Hillhouse, 1996; Eliot & Breo, 1984). For others, stress is experienced more favorably. Their physical condition, personality characteristics, and social support mechanisms mediate the effects of stress and produce resiliency, or the capacity to cope effectively with stress.

In effect, resiliency serves as a form of inoculation against the effects of stress. It eliminates exhaustion. This helps explain why some athletes do better in "the big game," while others do worse. Some managers appear to be brilliant strategists when the stakes are high; others fold under the pressure.

An elaboration of the differences in dispositions toward stress reactions comes from a set of studies in which hot reactors were more likely to be women (men reacted more quickly to stress, but more factors produced stress in women); individuals with low self-esteem and who viewed themselves as less attractive; and children who had been neglected, fearful, or in chaotic or broken homes (Adler, 1999). Physician Frank Trieber reported: "If you come from a family that's somehow chaotic, unstable, not cohesive, harboring grudges, very early on, it's associated later with greater blood pressure reactivity to various types of stress."

In managing stress, using a particular hierarchy of approaches has been found to be most effective (Kahn & Byosiere, 1992; Lehrer, 1996). First, the best way to manage stress is to eliminate or minimize stressors with

enactive strategies. These create, or enact, a new environment for the individual that does not contain the stressors. The second most effective approach is for individuals to enhance their overall capacity to handle stress by increasing their personal resiliency. These are called **proactive strategies** and are designed to initiate action that resists the negative effects of stress. Finally, developing short-term techniques for coping with stressors is necessary when an immediate response is required. These are **reactive strategies**; they are applied as on-the-spot remedies to reduce temporarily the effects of stress.

To understand why this hierarchy of stress management techniques is recommended, consider the physiological processes that occur when stress is encountered. Experiencing a stressor is like stepping on the accelerator pedal of an automobile: the engine "revs up." Within seconds, the body prepares for exertion by having blood pressure and heart rate rise substantially. The liver pours out glucose and calls up fat reserves to be processed into triglycerides for energy. The circulatory system diverts blood from nonessential functions, such as digestion, to the brain and muscles. The body's intent is to extinguish the stress by either "fight or flight." However, if the stressor is not eliminated as a result of these physiological responses, the elevated blood pressure begins to take its toll on arteries. Moreover, because the excess fat and glucose don't get metabolized right away, they stay in the blood vessels. Heart disease, stroke, and diabetes are common consequences. If the stress continues, minutes later a second, less severe physiological response occurs. The hypothalamus signals the pituitary to produce a substance called ACTH. This substance stimulates the adrenal cortex to produce a set of hormones known as glucocorticoids. The action of ACTH serves to stimulate a part of the brain vital to memory and learning, but an excess actually can be toxic. That's why impaired memory and lower levels of cognition occur under conditions of high stress. People actually get dumber! These same glucocorticoids also suppress parts of the immune system, so chronic stress leaves people more vulnerable to infections. Figure 2.3 summarizes these physiological consequences.

Individuals are better off if they can eliminate harmful stressors and the potentially negative effects of frequent, potent stress reactions. However, because most individuals do not have complete control over their environments or their circumstances, they can seldom eliminate all harmful stressors. Their next-best alternative, therefore, is to develop a greater capacity to withstand the negative effects of stress and to mobilize the energy generated by stressors. Developing personal resiliency that helps the body return to normal levels of activity more quickly—or that directs the "revved up engine" in a productive direction—is the next best strategy to eliminating the stressors altogether.

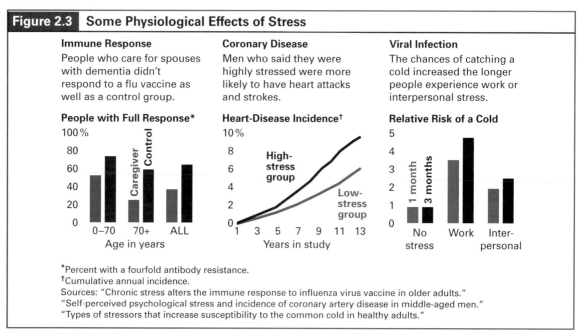

Figure 2.3 | **Some Physiological Effects of Stress**

Immune Response
People who care for spouses with dementia didn't respond to a flu vaccine as well as a control group.

Coronary Disease
Men who said they were highly stressed were more likely to have heart attacks and strokes.

Viral Infection
The chances of catching a cold increased the longer people experience work or interpersonal stress.

*Percent with a fourfold antibody resistance.
†Cumulative annual incidence.
Sources: "Chronic stress alters the immune response to influenza virus vaccine in older adults."
"Self-perceived psychological stress and incidence of coronary artery disease in middle-aged men."
"Types of stressors that increase susceptibility to the common cold in healthy adults."

Source: *American Institute of Stress (2000)*, **http://www.stress.org/problem.htm.**

Finally, on a temporary basis, individuals can respond to the revved-up state by using constructive strategies such as temporary relaxation techniques and mind control. Such techniques are designed to help the "engine" return to idle more quickly, at least for a short time.

Unfortunately, most people reverse the order of coping strategies presented previously—that is, they rely first on temporary reactive methods to cope with stress because these actions can be implemented immediately. But reactive strategies also have to be repeated whenever stressors are encountered because their effects are short-lived. Moreover, some common reactive strategies, such as drinking, taking sleeping pills, or letting off steam through anger, can become habit-forming and harmful in themselves. Without more long-term strategies, relying on repetitive reactive strategies can create a vicious circle.

It takes more effort to develop proactive resiliency strategies, but the effects are more long lasting. However, resiliency strategies can take time to implement; hence, the payoff, while substantial, is not immediate. The best and most permanent strategies are those that eliminate stressors altogether. They require the longest time to implement, and they may involve complex arrangements. But because stress is purged, the payoff is enduring.

Managing Stress

In the following sections, each of the three major strategies for managing stress is discussed in detail. Each section first describes the elements of the model in Figure 2.2 and then discusses specific techniques for effectively managing that aspect of stress. Because elimination of stress is the most important stress management tool, we cover it in the most detail.

STRESSORS

Table 2.1 lists the four main types of stressors illustrated in the story of the ambulance driver. The first, **time stressors**, generally result from having too much to do in too little time. These are the most common and most pervasive sources of stress faced by managers in corporations (Kahn & Byosiere, 1992; Mintzberg, 1973; Stalk & Hout, 1990; Vinton, 1992). One reason for time stressors is that Western culture is extremely time conscious and continues to be even more so year by year. Fifteen years ago, when asked for the time, a person might have responded, "It's about 2:30." Now the

response is more likely to be, "It's 2:28," or even, "It's 15 seconds before 2:28." The emphasis on time is also evidenced by the many ways we have of talking about time. We have time, keep time, buy time, save time, mark time, spend time, sell time, waste time, kill time, pass time, give time, take time, and make time.

This fascination with time makes it an important source of stress. A variety of researchers, for example, have studied the relationships between role overload and chronic time pressures, on the one hand, and psychological and physiological dysfunction on the other (Fisher & Gitelson, 1983; French & Caplan, 1972; Kahn et al., 1964; Singh, 1993, 1998). They found significant relationships between the presence of time stressors and job dissatisfaction, tension, perceived threat, heart rate, cholesterol levels, skin resistance, and other factors.

In the story of the ambulance drivers presented earlier, time stressors were evidenced by the drivers' work overload—that is, they felt compelled to accomplish a large number of tasks in a short time and were not in control of the time available. When experienced on a daily basis, time stressors can be highly detrimental. The presence of temporary time stressors may serve as motivators for getting work done, and some individuals accomplish much more when faced with an immediate deadline than when left to work at their own pace. However, a constant state of time pressure—having too much to do and not enough time to do it—is usually harmful.

Table 2.1	Four Key Sources of Stress
Time Stressors	
• Work overload	
• Lack of control	
Encounter Stressors	
• Role conflicts	
• Issue conflicts	
• Action conflicts	
Situational Stressors	
• Unfavorable working conditions	
• Rapid change	
Anticipatory Stressors	
• Unpleasant expectations	
• Fear	

As mentioned in the first chapter on self-awareness, time stressors are experienced differently in different national cultures (Trompenaars,1996; Trompenaars & Hampden-Turner, 1998). Some cultures, for example, have an orientation toward a short time horizon where time stressors are more prevalent (e.g., Philippines, the United States, Ireland, Brazil, India, Australia). In cultures with a longer time horizon (e.g., Hong Kong, Czech Republic, Austria, Sweden, Portugal), on the other hand, the immediacy of time demands is less prevalent. Long-term planning and extended time horizons make time stressors very different. Americans are more inclined to pack a day full of short-term activities, for example, each of which has a completion point. Japanese or Polynesian people, on the other hand, may have busy days, but their orientation is less toward immediate task completion than a long-term wholeness.

Encounter stressors are those that result from interpersonal interactions. Most people have experienced the debilitating effects of a quarrel with a friend, roommate, or spouse; of trying to work with an employee or supervisor with whom there has been an interpersonal conflict; or of trying to accomplish a task in a group that is divided by lack of trust and cohesion. Each of these stressors results from some kind of conflictual interpersonal encounter. Encounter stressors are especially common for managers. They generally arise from three types of conflicts: role conflicts, in which roles performed by group members are incompatible; issue conflicts, in which disagreement exists over how to define or solve a problem; and interaction conflicts, in which individuals fail to get along well because of mutual antagonism (Balzer, Doherty, & O'Connor, 1989; Cordes & Dougherty, 1993; Fisher & Gitelson, 1983; Singh, 1998).

Our own research has revealed that encounter stressors in organizations have significant negative effects on productivity and satisfaction (Cameron, 1994; Cameron, Whetten, & Kim, 1987), and encounter stressors have been found by other researchers to be at the very heart of most organizational dysfunction (Likert, 1967; Peters, 1988; Pfeffer, 1998; Thoits, 1995). Not surprisingly, encounter stressors more frequently affect managers with responsibility for people rather than equipment. The highest levels of encounter stress exist among managers who interact frequently with other people and have responsibility for individuals in the workplace (French & Caplan, 1972; Singh, 1998). Poor relationships with others cause particularly high levels of stress. Mishra (1992) reviewed literature on interpersonal trust, for example, and reported that lack of trust among

individuals not only blocks high quality communication, information sharing, decision competence, and problem-solving capabilities, but also results in high levels of personal stress.

Differences have also been discovered among national cultures with regard to encounter stressors (Trompenaars & Hampden-Turner, 1998). The cultures that are *egalitarian*, for example, and emphasize interpersonal relationships as a way to accomplish work (e.g., the United States, Norway, Ireland, and Finland) face more encounter stress as a general rule than countries with a *hierarchical* or position-based orientation (e.g., South Korea, India, Spain, and Israel). Similarly, country cultures emphasizing *affectivity* as opposed to *neutrality* (e.g., Iran and Mexico rather than China and Japan), also have a tendency toward more encounter stress due to the outward expression of emotions. Reacting personally or emotionally to issues tends to increase encounter stress in the workplace. The point to keep in mind in managing stress is that some people will experience certain kinds of stress more than others. National culture is one predictive factor. Thus, whereas encounter stress is a key for everyone, it will be more typical of some people than others.

In a national survey of workers in the United States by Northwestern National Life (1992), encounter stressors were cited as a major cause of burnout. Table 2.2 summarizes the results of that study. When workers reported not feeling free to interact socially, experienced workplace conflict, didn't talk openly to managers, felt unsupported by fellow employees, were stifled by red tape, and did not feel recognized, burnout was significantly higher than when those encounter stressors were not present. Of the 10 most significant stressors associated with burnout, 7 dealt with encounter stressors. The other 3 were situational stressors, to which we turn next.

The third category of stressors, **situational stressors**, arises from the environment in which a person lives or from an individual's circumstances. One of the most common forms of situational stress is unfavorable working conditions. For the ambulance drivers, these would include continual crises, long hours, and isolation from colleagues. In addition, wide-reaching and increasingly rapid change also creates an increase in stress. Cameron and his colleagues (1987, 1991, 1994), for example, reported that a large majority of organizations in industrialized nations have downsized or restructured since the beginning of the 1990s. Their research identified an almost universal

Table 2.2	Causes of Burnout
WORK SITE CHARACTERISTICS	**PERCENTAGE OF EMPLOYEES REPORTING BURNOUT**
Employees are not free to talk with one another.	48%
Employees are free to talk with one another.	28%
Personal conflicts on the job are common.	46%
Personal conflicts on the job are rare.	22%
Employees are given too little control.	46%
Employees are given enough control.	25%
Staffing or expense budgets are inadequate.	45%
Staffing or expense budgets are adequate.	21%
Management and employees do not talk openly.	44%
Management and employees talk openly.	20%
Management is unsupportive of employees.	44%
Management is supportive of employees.	20%
Sick and vacation benefits are below average.	44%
Sick and vacation benefits are average or better.	26%
Employee benefits have been reduced.	42%
Employee benefits have been maintained.	24%
Dealing with red tape is common.	40%
Dealing with red tape is rare.	22%
Employees are not recognized and rewarded.	39%
Employees are recognized and rewarded.	20%

Sample size: 1,299 private-sector employees in 37 organizations.

SOURCE: *"Employee Burnout: Causes and Cures."* Northwestern National Life Insurance Company, Minneapolis, MN, 1992, p. 6. Copyright © 1993 by Northwestern National Life Insurance Company. All rights reserved. No part of this information may be reproduced without the prior written permission of NWNL.

increase in situational stress as a result. The following quotation from one employee is illustrative:

> My husband and I both work for a huge conglomerate. We are carrying workloads that used to be handled by three or four employees. We come home exhausted after putting in 12-hour days, drag ourselves behind lawn mowers and vacuum cleaners at 9:00 at night, miss our children's soccer games and school plays, and barely see each other. Because of today's business climate, we feel totally helpless to make a move. Nobody dares quit a job these days. It's too risky. But the stress is killing us.

One of the most well-researched links between situational stressors and negative consequences involves rapid change, particularly the effects of changes in life events (Hobson et al., 1998; Holmes & Rahe, 1970; Wolff, Wolf, & Hare, 1950). The Social Readjustment Rating Scale (SRRS) was introduced in 1967 to track the number of changes individuals had experienced over the past 12 months. Since changes in some events were thought to be more stressful than others, a scaling method was used to assign weights to each life event. More than 3,100 studies have been published just since 1995 among a variety of cultures, age groups, and occupations using this SRRS instrument. More recently, Hobson and colleagues (1998) revised the SRRS so that the weightings of individual items have been updated. The instrument was expanded from the original 43 items in the Holmes and Rahe work to 51 items. Confirmation of the item weights was produced by 3,122 adults of various cultural, ethnic, socioeconomic, and gender backgrounds. The weightings are similar and consistent across each of these various groups. (Females have slightly higher stress scores than males, for example, but the differences are so small as to be nonmeaningful.) In other words, we can have some confidence that the revised instrument matches the situational stress experienced by most people in the twenty-first century (also see Adler & Hillhouse, 1996; Rahe, Ryman, & Ward, 1980). (You completed this revised instrument in the Assessment section.)

Statistical relationships between the amount of life-event change and physical illness and injury have been found consistently among managers, sports figures, naval personnel, and the general population. For example, on the original instrument, scores of 150 points or below resulted in a probability of less than 37 percent that a serious illness would occur in the next year, but the probability increased to about 50 percent with scores of 150–300. Those who scored over 300 on the SRRS had an 80 percent chance of serious illness (Holmes & Rahe, 1967; Kobasa, 1979). Evidence for the revised SRRS are the same. High scores are strongly associated with illness and/or injury, whereas low scores are much less likely to experience illness or injury.

Several studies have been conducted using college and high school football players to determine if life-event change is related to injury as well as to illness (Bramwell, Masuda, Wagner, & Holmes, 1975; Coddington & Troxell, 1980). Bramwell and colleagues found that college players with the lowest scores on the SRRS had a rate of injury (they missed three or more practices) of 35 percent. Those with medium scores had an injury rate of 44 percent, and those with high scores were injured at the amazing rate of 72 percent. Coddington and Troxell's results showed an injury rate five times as great for high scorers on the SRRS as for low scorers among high school athletes. Cordes and Dougherty (1993) reported findings about the extent to which daily health changes occurred as a result of life-event changes. Rather than focusing on major illness or injuries, they recorded minor symptoms such as headache, nausea, fever, backache, eyestrain, and so forth over 1,300 workdays. The results revealed high correlations between scores in life-event changes and the chronic presence of these symptoms.

We must caution, of course, that scoring high on the SRRS does not necessarily mean a person is going to become ill or be injured. A variety of coping skills and personal characteristics, to be discussed later, may counteract those tendencies. The point to be made here is that situational stressors are important factors to consider in learning to manage stress skillfully.

Anticipatory stressors, the fourth category, includes potentially disagreeable events that threaten to occur—unpleasant things that have not yet happened, but might happen. Stress results from the anticipation or fear of the event. In the case of the ambulance drivers, the constant threat of anticipating having to witness one more incident of human suffering or death served as an anticipatory stressor. In organizations that experience rapid change, restructuring, or downsizing, anticipatory stressors are also pervasive. People fear that they will lose their jobs, they fear that their friends will be ousted from the company, they become anxious about new reporting and interpersonal relationships that result from restructuring, and they worry that the future will be unpredictable and frightful. Brockner and Weisenfeld (1993) documented the negative effects of layoffs and plant closings on survivors (those who kept their jobs), and a paramount problem they identified is the presence of anticipatory stressors.

In other contexts, Schein (1960) reported that dramatic behavioral and psychological changes occurred in American prisoners in the Korean War. He identified anticipatory stressors (e.g., threat of severe punishment) as major contributors to psychological and physiological pathology among the prisoners (see the Skill Analysis section of Chapter 1, Communist Prison Camp). Stress levels in organizations that announce layoffs, mergers, or the introduction of new technologies skyrocket as employees anticipate potential job changes, layoffs, or new skills requirements (Cameron, 1998; Latack, Kinicki, & Prussia, 1995).

Anticipatory stressors need not be highly unpleasant or severe, however, to produce stress. Investigators have induced high levels of stress by telling individuals that they would experience a loud noise or a mild shock or that someone else might become uncomfortable because of their actions (Milgram, 1963). Fear of failure or fear of embarrassment in front of peers is a common anticipatory stressor. Anxieties about retirement and losing vitality during middle age have been identified by Levinson (1978), Hall (1976), and others as common stress producers as well.

Eliminating Stressors

Because eliminating **stressors** is a permanent stress reduction strategy, it is by far the most desirable. Although it is impossible, and even undesirable, for individuals to eliminate all the stressors they encounter, they can effectively eliminate those that are harmful. One way is to "enact" the environment rather than merely "react" to it. That is, individuals can actively work to create more favorable environmental circumstances in which to work and live. By so doing, they can rationally and systematically eliminate stressors.

Table 2.3	Management Strategies for Eliminating Stressors
Type of Stressor	**Elimination Strategy**
Time	Effective time management
	Efficient time management
	Delegating
Encounter	Collaboration and team building
	Emotional intelligence
Situational	Work redesign
Anticipatory	Goal setting
	Small wins

Table 2.3 outlines several ways to eliminate each of the four types of stressors.

ELIMINATING TIME STRESSORS THROUGH TIME MANAGEMENT

As pointed out earlier, time is usually the greatest source of stress for managers. With a literal explosion of time management books, organizers, consultants, efficiency enhancers, and technological time savers, you'd expect most of us to be pretty good at managing our time. We certainly have all the gadgets and advice we can use. The trouble is, most of us are getting worse. Just look around you. Whom do you know who is a terrific time manager, who isn't overloaded, or who doesn't complain about being stressed because of time? Which of your acquaintances is not increasingly stressed by a perceived absence of time? We're hard-pressed to name many. How about you?

It's no surprise that time stress is escalating because of the rapidity of change and the overwhelming amounts of information that people encounter in the twenty-first century. Most of us are moving pretty fast just to keep up, and most of us feel inadequate because we find it impossible to completely keep up. The Hilton Time Value Survey found that 77 percent of people identified their top goal in the coming decade as "spending more time with family and friends." Two thirds of the respondents indicated a desire to put more emphasis on "having free time" (Davidson, 1995). The trouble is, another study showed that the average manager was required to engage in between 237 and 1,073 separate incidents a day. More than a third of managers indicated that they don't accomplish what they set out to do each day. Time stress results. In this section we review some time management principles that can enable you to gain control over your time and organize your fragmented, chaotic environment.

Two sets of skills are important for effectively managing time and for eliminating time stressors. One set focuses on *efficiently* using time each day. The other set focuses on *effectively* using time over the long term. Because the effectiveness approach to time management serves as the foundation for the efficiency approach, we explain it first. Then we review the tools and techniques for achieving efficiency in time use.

Effective Time Management

Almost everyone suffers now and then from a pervasive feeling of time stress. Along with the information age has come an increasing sense that each of us is falling behind. For example, this week more books will be published in the United States alone than you could read in the remainder of your life. Consequently, we all have the feeling that we just can't quite keep up. Somehow, no matter how much time is available, it seems to get filled up and squeezed out. Currently, the most commonly prescribed solutions for attacking problems of time stress are to use calendars and planners, to generate to-do lists, and to learn to say "no." Although almost all of us have tried such tactics, however, almost all of us still claim to be under enormous time stress. This is not to say that calendars, lists, and saying "no" are never useful. They are, however, examples of an efficiency approach to time management rather than an effectiveness approach. In eliminating time stressors, efficiency without effectiveness is fruitless.

Managing time with an effectiveness approach means that (1) individuals spend their time on important matters, not just urgent matters; (2) people are able to distinguish clearly between what they view as important versus what they view as urgent; (3) results rather than methods are the focus of time management strategies; and (4) people have a reason not to feel guilty when they must say "no."

A number of time management experts have pointed out the usefulness of a "time management matrix" in which activities are categorized in terms of their relative importance and urgency (Covey, 1989; Lakein, 1989). *Important* activities are those that produce a desired result. They accomplish a valued end, or they achieve a meaningful purpose. *Urgent* activities are those that demand immediate attention.

They are associated with a need expressed by someone else, or they relate to an uncomfortable problem or situation that requires a solution as soon as possible. Figure 2.4 outlines this matrix and provides examples of types of activities that fit in each quadrant.

Activities such as handling employee crises or customer complaints are both urgent and important (Cell 1). A ringing telephone, the arrival of the mail, or unscheduled interruptions might be examples of urgent but potentially unimportant activities (Cell 2). Important but nonurgent activities include developmental opportunities, innovating, planning, and so on (Cell 3). Unimportant and nonurgent activities are escapes and routines that people may pursue but which produce little valuable payoff: for example, small talk, daydreaming, shuffling paper, or arguing (Cell 4).

Activities in the Important/Urgent quadrant (Cell 1) usually dominate the lives of managers. They are seen as "have to" activities that demand immediate attention. Attending a meeting, responding to a call or request, interacting with a customer, or completing a report might all legitimately be defined as Important/Urgent activities. The trouble with spending all one's time on activities in this quadrant, however, is that they all require the manager to react. They are usually controlled by someone else, and they may or may not lead to a result the manager wants to achieve.

The problem is even worse in the Unimportant/Urgent quadrant (Cell 2). Demands by others that may meet their needs but that serve only as deflections or interruptions to the manager's agenda only escalate a sense of time stress. Because they may not achieve results that are meaningful, purposeful, and valued—in other words, important—feelings of time stress will never be overcome. Experiencing overload and loss of control can be guaranteed. Managers are merely reactive. Moreover, when these time stressors are experienced over an extended period of time, people generally try to escape into Nonimportant/Nonurgent activities (Cell 4) to relieve the stress. They escape, shut out the world, or put everything on hold. However, although feelings of stress may be temporarily relieved, no long-term solutions are implemented, so time stress is never permanently reduced. That means lives are spent battling crises 95 percent of the time and escaping 5 percent of the time. A better alternative is to focus on activities in the Important/Nonurgent quadrant (Cell 3). Activities that are Important/Nonurgent might be labeled opportunities instead of problems. They are oriented toward accomplishing high-priority results. They prevent problems from occurring or build processes that eliminate problems rather than just reacting to them. Preparation, preventive maintenance, planning, building resiliency, and organizing are all "non-have-to" activities that are crucial for long-term success. Because they are not urgent, however, they often get driven out of managers' time schedules. Important/Nonurgent activities should be the top priority on the time management agenda. By ensuring that these kinds of activities get priority, the urgent problems being encountered can be reduced. Time stressors can be eliminated.

Figure 2.4	Types of Activities That Determine Time Use

Figure 2.4 Types of Activities That Determine Time Use

		URGENCY	
		High	**Low**
IMPORTANCE	**High**	1 Crises Customer complaints	3 Developmental opportunities Innovating Planning
	Low	2 Mail Ringing telephone Unscheduled interruptions	4 Escapes Routines Arguments

One of the most difficult yet crucially important decisions you must make in managing time effectively is determining what is important and what is urgent. There are no rules for dividing all activities, demands, or opportunities into those neat categories. Problems don't come with an "Important/Nonurgent" tag attached. In fact, every problem or time demand is important to someone. But if you let others determine what is and is not important, you will never effectively manage your time.

Barry Sullivan, CEO at First Chicago, for example, reorganized the way he manages his time. Instead of leaving his appointments calendar in the control of his secretary, he now decides what activities he wants to accomplish, then he allocates specific blocks of time to work on those activities. Only after he has made these determinations does he make his calendar available to his secretary to schedule other appointments. Jan Timmer, recent CEO of Philips Electronics, assigned an auditor to keep track of the way he used his time. He reported to the entire company quarterly the percent of his time he spent on key company objectives.

The question still remains, however: How can people make certain that they focus on activities that are important, not just urgent? The answer is to identify clear and specific personal priorities. In Chapter 1, Developing Self-Awareness, we pointed out how important it is for people to be aware of their own core values and to establish a set of basic principles to guide their behavior. In order to determine what is important in time management, those core values, basic principles, and personal priorities must be clearly identified. Otherwise, individuals are at the mercy of the unremitting demands that others place upon them.

In order to help you articulate clearly the basis for judging the importance of activities, consider the following questions:

1. What do I stand for? What am I willing to die (or live) for?
2. What do I care passionately about?
3. What legacy would I like to leave? What do I want to be remembered for?
4. What do I want to have accomplished 20 years from now?
5. If I could persuade everyone in the world to follow a few basic principles, what would they be?

Answering these questions can help you create a personal principles statement. A personal principles statement is an articulation of the criteria you use for evaluating what is important. Other people generally help determine what is urgent. But judging importance must be done in relation to a set of personal principles and values. Table 2.4 presents two different types of personal principles statements. They are provided as examples of the kinds of principles statements you can write for yourself. At the end of the Developing Self-Awareness chapter,

Table 2.4	Examples of Personal Principles Statements

From Mahatma Gandhi

Let then our first act every morning be to make the following resolve for the day:

- I shall not fear anyone on earth.
- I shall fear only God.
- I shall not bear ill will toward anyone.
- I shall not submit to injustice from anyone.
- I shall conquer untruth by truth.
- And in resisting untruth I shall put up with all suffering.

From William Rolfe Kerr

Prime Personal and Professional Principles:

- Succeed at home first.
- Seek and merit Divine help.
- Never compromise with honesty.
- Remember the people involved.
- Plan tomorrow today.
- Develop one new proficiency a year.
- Attain visibility by productivity.
- Hustle while I wait.
- Facilitate the success of my colleagues.
- Pursue excellence in all my endeavors.
- Be sincere and gentle yet decisive.
- Be a creative and innovative person.
- Don't fear mistakes.
- Concentrate all abilities on the task at hand.
- Obtain the counsel of others.
- Defend those who are absent.
- Listen twice as much as I speak.
- Be orderly in work and person.
- Maintain a positive attitude and sense of humor.

we urged you to take time to develop a statement of your own basic principles. These are the criteria upon which you judge activities to be important. Without such a statement, it is unlikely that you will be able to overcome the tyranny of urgent time demands.

Basing time management on core principles that serve to judge the importance of activities is also the key to being able to say "no" without feeling guilty. When you have decided what it is that you care about passionately, what it is you most want to accomplish, and what legacy you want to leave, you can more easily say "no" to activities that aren't congruent with those principles. We are always saying "no" to something anyway. But usually we are saying "no" to Important/Nonurgent activities (Cell 3) that are most congruent with our personal objectives or missions. People who experience the most time stress are those who allow others to generate their personal principles statement for them through their demands for time. Clarifying your core principles and making them public not only helps make them more powerful, but it also

provides a basis for saying "no" without feeling guilty. You can opt for prevention, planning, personal development, and continuous improvement, knowing that these Important/Nonurgent activities will help eliminate and prevent the problems that create time stress. Effectiveness in time management, then, means that you accomplish what you *want* to accomplish with your time. How you achieve those accomplishments relates to efficiency of time use, to which we now turn.

Efficient Time Management

In addition to approaching time management from the point of view of effectiveness (i.e., aligning time use with core personal principles), it is also important to adopt an efficiency point of view (i.e., accomplishing more by reducing wasted time). Many techniques are available to help managers utilize more efficiently the time they have each day.

One way to enhance efficient time use is to be alert to your own tendencies to use time inefficiently. The list of propositions in Table 2.5 shows general

Table 2.5	Typical Patterns of Time Use

- We do what we like to do before we do what we don't like to do.
- We do the things we know how to do faster than the things we do not know how to do.
- We do the things that are easiest before things that are difficult.
- We do things that require a little time before things that require a lot of time.
- We do things for which the resources are available.
- We do things that are scheduled (e.g., meetings) before nonscheduled things.
- We sometimes do things that are planned before things that are unplanned.
- We respond to demands from others before demands from ourselves.
- We do things that are urgent before things that are important.
- We readily respond to crises and to emergencies.
- We do interesting things before uninteresting things.
- We do things that advance our personal objectives or that are politically expedient.
- We wait until a deadline before we really get moving.
- We do things that provide the most immediate closure.
- We respond on the basis of who wants it.
- We respond on the basis of the consequences to us of doing or not doing something.
- We tackle small jobs before large jobs.
- We work on things in the order of arrival.
- We work on the basis of the squeaky-wheel principle (the squeaky wheel gets the grease).
- We work on the basis of consequences to the group.

patterns of behavior for most individuals in their use of time. In many situations, these tendencies may represent appropriate responses. In others, however, they can get in the way of efficient time management and increase time stressors unless individuals are aware of them and their possible consequences.

For example, if we do things that are planned before things that are unplanned, some important tasks may never get done unless consciously scheduled. Because many people have a tendency to do things that are urgent before things that are important, they may find themselves saying "no" to important things in order to attend to urgent things, thereby perpetuating feelings of overload. If we do the things that are easiest before the things that are difficult, our time may be taken up dealing with mundane and easy-to-resolve issues while difficult but important problems go unresolved.

To help you identify your own time management practices, and to help you determine the efficiency with which you use your time, we included in the Assessment section an instrument to help you diagnose your time management competency: The Time Management Survey. The first part of that survey applies to everyone in daily life. The second part is most applicable to individuals who have managed or worked in an organization. The scoring information at the end of the chapter will show you how well you manage your time compared to others. The rules set forth below correspond to the item numbers in the assessment survey.

The Time Management Survey lists guidelines or techniques that have been derived from research on the management of time. Whereas one kind of time stressor is having too much time available (i.e., boredom), that is not usually the one facing managers and students. The rules in this survey, therefore, relate to the opposite problem, that is, having too little time available due to an overloaded schedule.

Of course, no individual can or should implement all of these time management techniques at once. The amount of time spent trying to implement all the techniques would be so overwhelming that time stressors would only increase. Therefore, it is best to incorporate just a few of these techniques at a time into your everyday life. Implement those hints first that will lead to the most improvement in your use of time. Saving just 10 percent more time or using an extra 30 minutes a day more wisely can produce astounding results over months and years. Saving 30 minutes per day is the equivalent of one full year over a 48-year work life. That's one full year's time, nonstop, without sleep or eating! Effective time management, then, not only

helps a person accomplish more in a typical workday but also helps eliminate feelings of stress and overload that are so detrimental to personal accomplishment and satisfaction.

What follows is a brief discussion of these 40 techniques. The first 20 are applicable to anyone in all aspects of life; the remaining relate more directly to managers and the management role.

Rule 1 Read selectively. This applies mainly to individuals who find themselves with too much material they must read such as mail, magazines, newspapers, books, brochures, instructions, and so on. Except when you read for relaxation or pleasure, most reading should be done the way you read a newspaper, that is, skim most of it, but stop to read what seems most important. Even the most important articles don't need a thorough reading because important points are generally at the beginnings of paragraphs or sections. Furthermore, if you underline or highlight what you find important, you can review it quickly when you need to.

Rule 2 Make a list of things to accomplish today. Focus on what you want to achieve, not just on what you want to do. This is a commonsense rule that implies that you need to do some advance planning each day and not rely solely on your memory. (It also suggests that you should have only one list, not multiple lists on multiple scraps of paper.)

Rule 3 Have a place for everything and keep everything in its place. Letting things get out of place robs you of time in two ways: you need more time to find something when you need it, and you are tempted to interrupt the task you are doing to do something else. For example, if material for several projects is scattered on top of your desk, you will be continually tempted to switch from one project to another as you shift your eyes or move the papers.

Rule 4 Prioritize your tasks. Each day you should focus first on important tasks and then deal with urgent tasks. During World War II, with an overwhelming number of tasks to perform, General Dwight D. Eisenhower successfully managed his time by following rule 4 strictly. He focused his attention rigorously on important matters that only he could resolve, while leaving urgent, but less important matters to be dealt with by subordinates.

Rule 5 Do one important thing at a time but several trivial things simultaneously. You can accomplish a lot by doing more than one thing at a time when tasks are routine, trivial, or require little thought. This rule allows managers to get rid of multiple trivial tasks in less time (e.g., signing letters while talking on the phone). However, take a cue from great flight attendants, retail clerks, or food servers: give one important item, or person, all your attention.

Rule 6 Make a list of some 5- or 10-minute discretionary tasks. This helps use the small bits of time almost everyone has during his or her day (waiting for something to begin, between meetings or events, talking on the telephone, etc.). Beware, however, of spending all your time doing these small discretionary tasks while letting high-priority items go unattended.

Rule 7 Divide up large projects. This helps you avoid feeling overwhelmed by large, important, urgent tasks. Feeling that a task is too big to accomplish contributes to a feeling of overload and leads to procrastination.

Rule 8 Determine the critical 20 percent of your tasks. Pareto's law states that only 20 percent of the work produces 80 percent of the results. Therefore, it is important to analyze which tasks make up the most important 20 percent and spend the bulk of your time on those.

Rule 9 Save your best time for important matters. Time spent on trivial tasks should not be your "best time." Do routine work when your energy level is low, your mind is not sharp, or you aren't on top of things. Reserve your high-energy time for accomplishing the most important and urgent tasks. Many of us are often like puppets whose strings are being pulled by a crowd of unknown and unorganized people. Don't let others interrupt your best time with unwanted demands. You, not others, should control your best time.

Rule 10 Reserve some time during the day when others don't have access to you. Use this time to accomplish Important/Nonurgent tasks, or spend it just thinking. This might be the time before others in the household get up, after everyone else is in bed, or at a location where no one else comes. The point is to avoid being in the line of fire all day, every day, without personal control over your time.

Rule 11 Don't procrastinate. If you do certain tasks promptly, they will require less time and effort than if you put them off. Of course, you must guard against spending all your time on trivial, immediate concerns that crowd out more important tasks. The line between procrastination and time wasting is a fine one, but don't get in the habit of deciding that "I'll get to this later."

Rule 12 Keep track of your time. This is one of the best time management strategies. It is impossible to improve your management of time or decrease time stressors unless you know how you spend your time.

You should keep time logs in short enough intervals to capture the essential activities, but not so short that they create a recording burden. Try keeping track of what you do every 30 minutes or hour. Parts of the Skill Practice and Skill Application sections suggest that you keep a time log for at least two weeks. Eliminate activities that don't help you accomplish your desired outcomes, or your statement of personal principles.

Rule 13 Set deadlines. This helps improve your efficient use of time. Work always expands to fill the time available, so if you don't specify a termination time, tasks tend to continue longer than they need to.

Rule 14 Do something productive while waiting. It has been estimated that up to 20 percent of an average person's time is spent in waiting. During such time, try reading, planning, preparing, rehearsing, reviewing, outlining, or doing other things that help you accomplish your work.

Rule 15 Do busy work at one set time during the day. Because it is natural to let simple tasks drive out difficult tasks (see Table 2.5), specify a certain period of time to do busy work. Refusing to answer mail or read the newspaper until a specified time, for example, can help ensure that those activities don't supersede priority time.

Rule 16 Reach closure on at least one thing every day. Reaching the end of a day with nothing completely finished (even a 10-minute task) serves to increase a sense of overload and time stress. Finishing a task, on the other hand, produces a sense of relief and releases stress.

Rule 17 Schedule some personal time. You need some time when no interruptions will occur, when you can get off the "fast track" for awhile and be alone. This time should be used to plan, prioritize, take stock, pray, meditate, or just relax. Among other advantages, personal time also helps you maintain self-awareness.

Rule 18 Don't worry about anything on a continuing basis. Allow yourself to worry only at a specified time and avoid dwelling on a worrisome issue at other times. This keeps your mind free and your energy focused on the task at hand. It may seem difficult, but controlling your worry time will do wonders to make your time use more efficient and relieve your stress.

Rule 19 Write down long-term objectives. This helps you maintain consistency in activities and tasks. You can be efficient and organized but still accomplish nothing unless you have a clear direction in mind. Writing down your long-term objectives helps make them real and lets them constantly serve as reminders.

Rule 20 Be on the alert for ways to improve your management of time. Read a list of time management hints periodically. All of us need reminding, and it will help make continuous improvement in your time use a part of your lifestyle.

Efficient Time Management for Managers

The second list of rules encompasses the major activities in which managers engage at work. The first nine rules deal with conducting meetings, since managers report that approximately 70 percent of their time is spent in meetings (Cooper & Davidson, 1982; Mintzberg, 1973).

Rule 1 Hold routine meetings at the end of the day. Energy and creativity levels are highest early in the day and shouldn't be wasted on trivial matters. Furthermore, an automatic deadline—quitting time—will set a time limit on the meeting.

Rule 2 Hold short meetings standing up. This guarantees that meetings will be kept short. Getting comfortable helps prolong meetings.

Rule 3 Set a time limit. This establishes an expectation of when the meeting should end and creates pressure to conform to a time boundary. Set such limits at the beginning of every meeting and appointment.

Rule 4 Cancel meetings once in a while. Meetings should be held only if they are needed. If the agenda isn't full or isn't going to help you achieve your objectives, cancel it. This way, meetings that are held will be more productive and more time efficient. (Plus, people get the idea that the meeting really will accomplish something—a rare outcome.)

Rules 5, 6, and 7 Have agendas, stick to them, and keep track of time. These rules help people prepare for a meeting, stick to the subject, and remain work oriented. Many things will be handled outside of meetings if they have to appear on the agenda to be discussed. You can set a verbal agenda at the beginning of even impromptu meetings (i.e., "Here is what I want to cover in this meeting"). Keeping a record of the meeting ensures that assignments are not forgotten, that follow-up and accountability occur, and that everyone is clear about expectations. Keeping track of the time motivates people to be efficient and conscious of ending at the stated time.

Rule 8 Start meetings on time. This helps guarantee that people will arrive on time. (Some managers set meetings for odd times, such as 10:13 A.M., to make attendees

time conscious.) Starting on time rewards people who arrive on time rather than waiting for laggards.

Rule 9 Prepare minutes of the meeting and follow up. This practice keeps items from appearing again in a meeting without having been resolved. It also creates the expectation that accountability for accomplishments is expected and that some work should be done outside the meeting. Commitments and expectations made public through minutes are more likely to be fulfilled.

Rule 10 Insist that subordinates suggest solutions to problems. This rule is discussed in the Empowering and Delegating chapter (Chapter 8). The purpose of this rule is to eliminate the tendency toward upward delegation, that is, for your subordinates to delegate difficult problems back to you. They do this by sharing the problem and asking for your ideas and solutions rather than recommending solutions. It is more efficient to choose among alternatives devised by subordinates than to generate your own.

Rule 11 Meet visitors in the doorway. This practice helps you maintain control of your time by controlling the use of your office space. It is easier to keep a meeting short if you are standing in the doorway rather than sitting in your office.

Rule 12 Go to subordinates' offices for brief meetings. This is useful if it is practical. The advantage is that it helps you control the length of a meeting by being free to leave when you choose. Of course, if you spend a great deal of time traveling between subordinates' offices, the rule is not practical.

Rule 13 Don't overschedule the day. You should stay in control of at least some of your time each workday. Others' meetings and demands can undermine the control you have over your schedules unless you make an effort to maintain it. This doesn't mean that you can create large chunks of time when you're free. But good time managers take the initiative for, rather than responding to, schedule requirements.

Rule 14 Have someone else answer telephone calls and scan e-mail. Not being a slave to the telephone provides you with a buffer from interruptions for at least some part of the day. Having someone else scan e-mail helps eliminate the nonimportant items that can be eliminated or require perfunctory replies.

Rule 15 Have a place to work uninterrupted. This helps guarantee that when a deadline is near, you can concentrate on your task and concentrate uninterrupted. Trying to get your mind focused once more on a task or project after interruptions wastes a lot of time. "Mental gearing up" is wasteful if required repeatedly.

Rule 16   Do something definite with every piece of paperwork handled. This keeps you from shuffling the same items over and over. Not infrequently, "doing something definite" with a piece of paper means throwing it away.

Rule 17   Keep the workplace clean. This minimizes distractions and reduces the time it takes to find things.

Rules 18, 19, and 20   Delegate work, identify the amount of initiative recipients should take with the tasks they are assigned, and give others credit for their success. These rules all relate to effective delegation, a key time management technique. These last three rules are also discussed in the Empowering and Delegating chapter.

Remember that these techniques for managing time are a means to an end, not the end itself. If trying to implement techniques creates more rather than less stress, they should not be applied. However, research has indicated that managers who use these kinds of techniques have better control of their time, accomplish more, have better relations with subordinates, and eliminate many of the time stressors most managers ordinarily encounter (Davidson, 1995; Lehrer, 1996; Turkington, 1998). Remember that saving just 30 minutes a day amounts to one full year of free time during your working lifetime. That's 8,760 hours of free time! You will find that as you select a few of these hints to apply in your own life, the efficiency of your time use will improve and your time stress will decrease.

Most time management techniques involve single individuals changing their own work habits or behaviors by themselves. Greater effectiveness and efficiency in time use occurs because individuals decide to institute personal changes; the behavior of other people is not involved. However, effective time management must often take into account the behavior of others, because that behavior may tend to inhibit or enhance effective time use. For this reason, effective time management sometimes requires the application of other skills discussed in this book. The Empowering and Delegating chapter provides principles for efficient time management by involving other people in task accomplishment. The Motivating Employees chapter explains how to help others be more effective and efficient in their own work. The Communicating Supportively chapter identifies ways in which interpersonal relationships can be strengthened, thus relieving stressors resulting from interpersonal conflicts. It is to these encounter stressors that we now turn.

ELIMINATING ENCOUNTER STRESSORS THROUGH COLLABORATION AND EMOTIONAL INTELLIGENCE

We pointed out earlier that dissatisfying relationships with others, particularly with a direct manager or supervisor, are prime causes of job stress among workers. These encounter stressors result directly from abrasive, conflictual, nonfulfilling relationships. Even though work is going smoothly, when encounter stress is present, everything else seems wrong. It is difficult to maintain positive energy when you are fighting or at odds with someone, or when feelings of acceptance and amiability aren't typical of your important relationships at work.

Collaboration

One important factor that helps eliminate encounter stress is membership in a stable, closely-knit group or community. When people feel a part of a group, or accepted by someone else, stress is relieved. For example, it was discovered 35 years ago by Dr. Stewart Wolf that in the town of Roseto, Pennsylvania, residents were completely free from heart disease and other stress-related illnesses. He suspected that their protection sprang from the town's uncommon social cohesion and stability. The town's population consisted entirely of descendants of Italians who had moved there 100 years ago from Roseto, Italy. Few married outside the community, the firstborn was always named after a grandparent, conspicuous consumption and displays of superiority were avoided, and social support among community members was a way of life.

Wolf predicted that residents would begin to display the same level of stress-related illnesses as the rest of the country if the modern world intruded. It did, and they did. By the mid-1970s, residents in Roseto had Cadillacs, ranch-style homes, mixed marriages, new names, competition with one another, and a rate of coronary disease the same as any other town's (Farnham, 1991). They had ceased to be a cohesive, collaborative clan and instead had become a community of selfishness and exclusivity. Self-centeredness, it was discovered, was dangerous to health.

The most dramatic psychological discovery resulting from the Vietnam and the Persian Gulf wars related to the strength associated with small, primary work teams. In Vietnam, unlike the Persian Gulf, teams of soldiers did not stay together and did not form the strong bonds that occurred in the Persian Gulf War. The constant injection of new personnel into squadrons, and the constant transfer of soldiers from one location to another, made soldiers feel isolated, without loyalty, and vulnerable to stress-related illnesses. In the Persian Gulf War, by contrast, soldiers were kept in the same unit throughout the campaign, brought home together, and given lots of time to debrief together after the battle. Using a closely knit group to provide interpretation of, and social support for, behavior was found to be the most powerful deterrent to postbattle trauma. David Marlowe, chief of psychiatry at Walter Reed Army Institute of Research, indicated that "Squad members are encouraged to use travel time en route home from a war zone to talk about their battlefield experience. It helps them detoxify. That's why we brought them back in groups from Desert Storm. Epistemologically, we know it works" (Farnham, 1991).

Developing collaborative, clan-like relationships with others is a powerful deterrent to encounter stress. One way of developing this kind of relationship is by applying a concept described by Stephen Covey (1989)—an emotional bank account. Covey used this metaphor to describe the trust or feeling of security that one person develops for another. The more "deposits" made in an emotional bank account, the stronger and more resilient the relationship becomes. Conversely, too many "withdrawals" from the account weaken relationships by destroying trust, security, and confidence. "Deposits" are made through treating people with kindness, courtesy, honesty, and consistency. The emotional bank account grows when people feel they are receiving love, respect, and caring. "Withdrawals" are made by not keeping promises, not listening, not clarifying expectations, or not allowing choice. Because disrespect and autocratic rule devalue people and destroy a sense of self-worth, relationships are ruined because the account becomes overdrawn.

The more people interact, the more deposits must be made in the emotional bank account. When you see an old friend after years of absence, you can often pick up right where you left off, because the emotional bank account has not been touched. But when you interact with someone frequently, the relationship is constantly being fed or depleted. Cues from everyday interactions are interpreted as either deposits or withdrawals. When the emotional account is well stocked, mistakes, disappointments, and minor abrasions are easily forgiven and ignored. But when no reserve exists, those incidents may become creators of distrust and contention.

The commonsense prescription, therefore, is to base relationships with others on mutual trust, respect, honesty, and kindness. Make deposits into the emotional bank accounts of others. Collaborative, cohesive communities are, in the end, a product of the one-on-one relationships that people develop with each other. As Dag Hammarskjöld, former Secretary-General of the United Nations, stated: "It is more noble to give yourself completely to one individual than to labor diligently for the salvation of the masses." That is because building a strong, cohesive relationship with an individual is more powerful and can have more lasting impact than leading masses of people. Feeling trusted, respected, and loved is, in the end, what most people desire as individuals. We want to experience those feelings personally, not just as a member of a group. Therefore, because encounter stressors are almost always the products of abrasive individual relationships, they are best eliminated by building strong emotional bank accounts with others.

Social and Emotional Intelligence

As we discussed in the previous chapter, emotional intelligence is an important attribute of healthy and effective individuals. It is part of a repertoire of "intelligences" that have been identified by psychologists as predicting success in life, work, and managerial roles. As we mentioned before, emotional intelligence has become the catch-all phrase that incorporates multiple intelligences—for example, practical intelligence, abstract intelligence, moral intelligence, interpersonal intelligence, spiritual intelligence, and mechanical intelligence (Gardner, 1993; Sternberg, 1997). Therefore, it is convenient to use the term *emotional intelligence* to refer to a group of non-cognitive abilities and skills that people need to develop to be successful. It is clear from studies of various aspects of emotional intelligence that it is an important strategy for eliminating encounter stress. Most importantly, developing the social aspects of emotional intelligence—or *social intelligence*—helps people manage the stresses that arise from interpersonal encounters (Cantor & Kihlstrom, 1987; Goleman, 1998; Saarni, 1997).

Simply put, social intelligence refers to the ability to manage your relationships with other people. It consists of four main dimensions:

1. An accurate perception of others' emotional and behavioral responses.
2. The ability to cognitively and emotionally understand and relate to others' responses.
3. Social knowledge, or an awareness of what is appropriate social behavior.
4. Social problem solving, or the ability to manage interpersonal difficulties.

A large number of studies have confirmed that we all have multiple intelligences, the most common of which is IQ, or cognitive intelligence. By and large, cognitive intelligence is beyond our control, especially after the first few years of life. It is a product of the gifts with which we were born or our genetic code. Interestingly, above a certain threshold level, the correlation between IQ and success in life (e.g., achieving high occupational positions, accumulated wealth, luminary awards, satisfaction with life, performance ratings by peers and superiors) is essentially zero. Very smart people have no greater likelihood of achieving success in life or of achieving personal happiness than people with low IQ scores (Goleman, 1998; Spencer & Spencer, 1993; Sternberg, 1997). On the other hand, social and emotional intelligence have strong positive relationships to success in life and to a reduced degree of encounter stress.

For example, in a study at Stanford University, four-year-old children were involved in activities that tested aspects of their emotional intelligence. (In one study, a marshmallow was placed in front of them, and they were given two choices: eat it now, or wait until the adult supervisor returned from running an errand, then the child would get two marshmallows.) A follow-up study with these same children 14 years later, upon graduation from high school, found that students who demonstrated more emotional intelligence (i.e., postponed gratification in the marshmallow task) were less likely to fall apart under stress, became less irritated and less stressed by interpersonally abrasive people, were more likely to accomplish their goals, and scored an average of 210 points higher on the SAT college entrance exam (Shoda, Mischel, & Peake, 1990). The IQ scores of the students did not differ significantly, but the emotional intelligence scores were considerably different. Consistent with other studies, emotional intelligence predicted success in life as well as the ability to handle encounter stress for these students.

In another study, the social and emotional intelligence scores of retail store managers was assessed and found to be the largest factor in accounting for their abilities to handle personal stress and manage socially stressful events. These abilities, in turn, predicted profits, sales, and employee satisfaction in their stores (Lusch & Serpkenci, 1990). Social and emotional intelligence predicted managerial success. When managers were able to accurately identify others' emotions and respond to them, they were found to be more successful in their personal lives as well as in their work lives (Rosenthal, 1977), and were evaluated as the most desired and competent managers (Pilling & Eroglu, 1994).

If social and emotional intelligence are so important, how does one develop them? The answer is neither simple nor simplistic. Each of the chapters in this book contains answers to that question. The skills we hope to help you develop are among the most important competencies that comprise social and emotional intelligence. In other words, by improving your abilities in the management skills covered in this book—e.g., self-awareness, problem solving, supportive communication, motivating self and others, managing conflict, empowering others, and so on—your social and emotional competence scores will increase. This is important because a national survey of workers found that employees who rated their manager as supportive and interpersonally competent had lower rates of burnout, lower stress levels, lower incidence of stress-related illnesses, higher productivity, more loyalty to their organizations, and more efficiency in work than employees with nonsupportive and interpersonally incompetent managers (NNL, 1992). Socially and emotionally intelligent managers affect the success of their employees as much as they affect their own success.

The point we are making is a simple one: eliminating encounter stressors can be effectively achieved by developing social and emotional intelligence. Fewer conflicts arise, individuals with whom we interact are more collaborative, and more effective and satisfying interpersonal relationships are developed among those with whom we work. The remaining chapters in this book provide the guidelines and techniques to help you improve your interpersonal competence and your social and emotional intelligence. After completing the book, including engaging in the practice and application exercises, you will have improved your ability to eliminate many forms of encounter stress.

ELIMINATING SITUATIONAL STRESSORS THROUGH WORK REDESIGN

Most of us would never declare that we feel less stress now than a year ago, that we have less pressure, or that we are less overloaded. We all report feeling more stress than ever at least partly because it is the "in" thing to be stressed. "I'm busier than you are" is a common theme in social conversations. On the other hand, these feelings are not without substance for most people. A third of U.S. workers are thinking of quitting their jobs, repeated downsizings have introduced new threats to the workplace, highways are increasingly congested, financial pressures are escalating, crime is pervasive, and worker compensation claims for stress-related illness are ballooning. Unfortunately, in medical treatment and time lost, stress-related illnesses are almost twice as expensive as workplace injuries because of longer recovery times, the need for psychological therapy, and so on (Farnham, 1991). Situational stressors, in other words, are costly. And they are escalating.

For decades, researchers in the area of occupational health have examined the relationship between job strain and stress-related behavioral, psychological, and physiological outcomes. Studies have focused on various components of job strain, including level of task demand (e.g., the pressure to work quickly or excessively), the level of individual control (e.g., the freedom to vary the work pace), and the level of intellectual challenge (e.g., the extent to which work is interesting).

Research in this area has challenged the common myth that job strain occurs most frequently in the executive suite (Karasek et al., 1988). A federal government study of nearly 5,000 workers found that after controlling for age, sex, race, education, and health status (measured by blood pressure and serum cholesterol level), low-level workers tended to have a higher incidence of heart disease than their bosses who were in high-status, presumably success-oriented, managerial or professional occupations. This is true because certain characteristics of lower-level positions—high demand, low control, low discretion, and low interest—tend to produce higher levels of job strain.

A review of this research suggests that the single most important contributor to stress is lack of freedom (Adler, 1989; French & Caplan, 1972; Greenberger & Stasser, 1991). In a study of administrators, engineers, and scientists at the Goddard Space Flight Center, researchers found that individuals provided with more discretion in making decisions about assigned tasks experienced fewer time stressors (e.g., role overload), situational stressors (e.g., role ambiguity), encounter stressors (e.g., interpersonal conflict), and anticipatory stressors (e.g., job-related threats). Individuals without discretion and participation experienced significantly more stress.

In response to these dynamics, Hackman, Oldham, Janson, and Purdy (1975) proposed a model of job redesign that has proved effective in reducing stress and in increasing satisfaction and productivity. A detailed discussion of this job redesign model is provided in the chapter on Motivating Employees. It consists of five aspects of work—**skill variety** (the opportunity to use multiple skills in performing work), **task identity** (the opportunity to complete a whole task), **task significance** (the opportunity to see the impact of the work being performed), **autonomy** (the opportunity to choose how and when the work will be done), and **feedback** (the opportunity to receive information on

the success of task accomplishment). Here we briefly provide an overview of the applicability of this model to reducing stress-producing job strain. To eliminate situational stressors at work:

Combine Tasks   When individuals are able to work on a whole project and perform a variety of related tasks (e.g., programming all components of a computer software package), rather than being restricted to working on a single repetitive task or subcomponent of a larger task, they are more satisfied and committed. In such cases, they are able to use more skills and feel a pride of ownership in their job.

Form Identifiable Work Units   Building on the first step, when teams of individuals performing related tasks are formed, individuals feel more integrated, productivity improves, and the strain associated with repetitive work is diminished. When these groups combine and coordinate their tasks, and decide internally how to complete the work, stress decreases dramatically. This formation of natural work units has received a great deal of attention in Japanese auto plants in America as workers have combined in teams to assemble an entire car from start to finish, rather than do separate tasks on an assembly line. Workers learn one another's jobs, rotate assignments, and experience a sense of completion in their work.

Establish Customer Relationships   One of the most enjoyable parts of a job is seeing the consequences of one's labor. In most organizations, producers are buffered from consumers by intermediaries, such as customer relations departments and sales personnel. Eliminating those buffers allows workers to obtain first-hand information concerning customer satisfaction as well as the needs and expectations of potential customers. Stress resulting from filtered communication also is eliminated.

Increase Decision-Making Authority   Managers who increase the autonomy of their subordinates to make important work decisions eliminate a major source of job stress for them. Being able to influence the what, when, and how of work increases an individual's feelings of control. Cameron, Freeman, and Mishra (1991) found a significant decrease in experienced stress in firms that were downsizing when workers were given authority to make decisions about how and when they did the extra work required of them.

Open Feedback Channels   A major source of stress is not knowing what is expected and how task performance is being evaluated. As managers communicate their expectations more clearly and give timely and accurate feedback, subordinates' satisfaction and performance improve. A related form of feedback in production tasks is quality control. Firms that allow the individuals who assemble a product to test its quality, instead of shipping it off to a separate quality assurance group, find that quality increases substantially and that conflicts between production and quality control personnel are eliminated. The point is, providing more information to people on how they are doing always reduces stress.

These practices are used widely today in all types of organizations, from the Social Security Administration to General Motors. When Travelers Insurance Companies implemented a job redesign project, for example, productivity increased dramatically, absenteeism and errors fell sharply, and the amount of distractions and stresses experienced by managers decreased significantly (Hackman & Oldham, 1980; Singh 1998). In brief, work redesign can effectively eliminate situational stressors associated with the work itself.

ELIMINATING ANTICIPATORY STRESSORS THROUGH PRIORITIZING, GOAL SETTING, AND SMALL WINS

While redesigning work can help structure an environment where stressors are minimized, it is much more difficult to eliminate entirely the anticipatory stressors experienced by individuals. Stress associated with anticipating an event is more a product of psychological anxiety than current work circumstances. To eliminate that source of stress requires a change in thought processes, priorities, and plans. In the Developing Self-Awareness chapter, for example, we discussed the central place of learning style (thought processes), values (priorities), and moral maturity (personal principles) for effective management.

Earlier in this chapter, we discussed the central importance of establishing clear personal priorities, such as identifying what is to be accomplished in the long term, what cannot be compromised or sacrificed, and what lasting legacy one desires. Establishing this core value set or statement of basic personal principles helps eliminate not only time stressors but also eliminates anticipatory stress by providing clarity of direction. When traveling on an unknown road for the first time, having a road map reduces anticipatory stress. You don't have to figure out where to go or where you are by trying to identify the unknown landmarks along the roadside. In the same way, a personal principles statement acts as a map or guide. It makes clear where you will eventually end up. Fear of the unknown, or anticipatory stress, is thus eliminated.

Goal Setting

Similarly, establishing short-term plans also helps eliminate anticipatory stressors by focusing attention on immediate goal accomplishment instead of a fearful future. Short-term planning, however, implies more than just specifying a desired outcome. Several action steps are needed if short-term plans are to be achieved (Locke & Latham, 1990). The model in Figure 2.5 outlines the four-step process associated with successful short-term planning.

The first step is to identify the desired goal or objective. Most goal setting, performance appraisal, or management by objectives (MBO) programs begin with that step, but most also stop at that point. Unfortunately, this first step alone is not likely to lead to goal achievement or stress elimination. Merely establishing a goal, while helpful, is not sufficient. When people fail to achieve their goals, it is almost always because they have not followed through on steps 2, 3, and 4.

Step 2 is to identify, as specifically as possible, the activities and behaviors that will lead toward accomplishing the goal. The more difficult the goal is to accomplish, the more rigorous, numerous, and specific should be the behaviors and activities.

A friend once approached one of us with a problem. She was a wonderfully sensitive, caring, competent single woman of about 25 who was experiencing a high degree of anticipatory stress because of her size. She weighed well over 350 pounds, but she had experienced great difficulty losing weight over the last several years. She was afraid of both the health consequences and the social consequences of not being able to reduce her weight. With the monitoring of a physician, she set a goal, or short-term plan, to lose 100 pounds in the next 12 months. Because it was to be such a difficult goal to reach, however, she asked us for help in achieving her ambitious objective. We first identified a dozen or so specific actions and guidelines that would facilitate the attainment of the goal: for example, never shop alone nor without a menu, never carry more than 50 cents in change (in order to avoid the temptation to buy a doughnut), exercise with friends each day at 5:30 P.M., arise each morning at 7:00 A.M. and eat a specified breakfast with a friend, forgo watching TV to reduce the temptation to snack, and go to bed by 10:30 P.M. The behaviors were rigid, but the goal was so difficult that they were

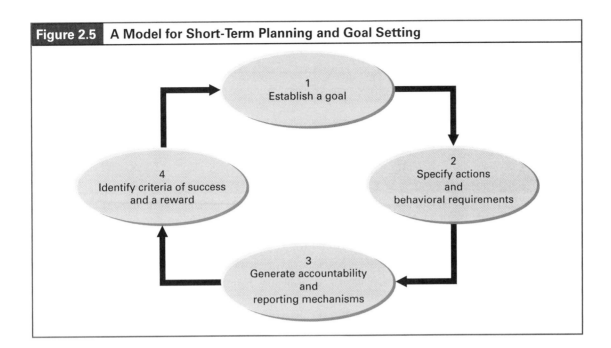

Figure 2.5 **A Model for Short-Term Planning and Goal Setting**

1
Establish a goal

2
Specify actions
and
behavioral requirements

3
Generate accountability
and
reporting mechanisms

4
Identify criteria of success
and a reward

necessary to ensure progress. In each case, these specific behaviors could be seen as having a direct effect on the ultimate goal of losing 100 pounds.

Step 3 involves establishing accountability and reporting mechanisms. If no one else will ever know if the goal was achieved, chances are it will not be. The principle at the foundation of this step is: "Make it more difficult to stay the same than to change." This is done by involving others in ensuring adherence to the plan, establishing a social support network to obtain encouragement from others, and instituting penalties for nonconformance. In addition to announcing to coworkers, friends, and a church group that she would lose the 100 pounds, for example, our friend had her doctor register her for a hospital stay at the end of the 12-month period. If she did not achieve the goal on her own, she was to go on an intravenous feeding schedule in the hospital to lose the weight, at a cost of over $250 per day. Because of her public commitments, her self-imposed penalties, and the potential high medical expenses, it became more uncomfortable and costly not to succeed than to accomplish the goal.

Step 4 involves establishing an evaluation and reward system. This means identifying the evidence that the goal has been accomplished. In the case of losing weight, it's a matter of simply getting on the scales. But for improving management skills, becoming a better friend, developing more patience, establishing more effective leadership, and so on, the criteria of success are not so easily identified. That is why this step is crucial. "I'll know it when I see it" isn't good enough. Specific indicators of success, or specific changes that will have been produced when the goal is achieved, must be identified. (For example, I'll know I have become more patient when I reinterpret the situation and refuse to get upset when my spouse, or friend, is late for an appointment.) Carefully outlining these criteria serves as a motivation toward goal accomplishment by making the goal more observable and measurable.

The purpose of this short-term planning model is to eliminate anticipatory stress by establishing a focus and direction for activity. The anxiety associated with uncertainty and potentially negative events is dissipated when mental and physical energy are concentrated on purposeful activity. (By the way, the last time we saw our friend, her weight was below 200 pounds.)

Small Wins

Another principle related to eliminating anticipatory stressors is the small-wins strategy (Weick, 1984). By "small win," we mean a tiny but definite change made in a desired direction. We begin by changing something that is relatively easy to change. Then we change a second thing that is easy to change, and so on. Although each individual success may be relatively modest when considered alone, the multiple small gains eventually mount up, generating a sense of momentum that creates the impression of substantial movement toward a desired goal. This momentum helps convince ourselves, as well as others, of our ability to accomplish our objective. The fear associated with anticipatory change is eliminated as we build self-confidence through small wins. We also gain the support of others as they see progress being made.

In the case of our overweight friend, one key was to begin changing what she could change, a little at a time. Tackling the loss of 100 pounds all at once would have been too overwhelming a task. But she could change the time she shopped, the time she went to bed, and the menu she ate for breakfast. Each successful change generated more and more momentum that, when combined, led to the larger change that she desired. Her ultimate success was a product of multiple small wins.

Similarly, Weick (1993b) has described Poland's peaceful transition from a communistic command-type economy to a capitalistic free-enterprise economy as a product of small wins. Not only is Poland now one of the most thriving economies in eastern Europe, but it made the change to free enterprise without a single shot being fired, a single strike being called, or a single political upheaval. One reason for this is that long before the Berlin Wall fell, small groups of volunteers in Poland began to change the way they lived. They adopted a theme that went something like this: "If you value freedom, then behave freely; if you value honesty, then speak honestly; if you desire change, then change what you can."

Polish citizens organized volunteer groups to help at local hospitals, assist the less fortunate, and clean up parks. They behaved in a way that was outside the control of the central government but reflected their free choice. Their changes were not on a large enough scale to attract attention and official opposition from the central government. But their actions nevertheless reflected their determination to behave in a free, self-determining way. They controlled what they could control, namely, their own voluntary service. These voluntary service groups spread throughout Poland, so when the transition from communism to capitalism occurred, a large number of people in Poland had already gotten used to behaving in a way consistent with self-determination. Many of these people simply stepped into positions where independent-minded managers were needed. The transition was smooth because of the multiple small wins that had previously spread throughout the country relatively unnoticed.

In summary, the rules for instituting small wins are simple: (1) identify something that is under your control; (2) change it in a way that leads toward your desired goal; (3) find another small thing to change, and change it; (4) keep track of the changes you are making; and (5) maintain the small gains you have made. Anticipatory stressors are eliminated because the fearful unknown is replaced by a focus on immediate successes.

Developing Resiliency

Now that we have examined various causes of stress and outlined a series of preventive measures, we turn our attention to a second major strategy for managing stress as shown in Figure 2.2, the development of **resiliency** to handle stress that cannot be eliminated. When stressors are long lasting or are impossible to remove, coping requires the development of personal resiliency. This is the capacity to withstand or manage the negative effects of stress, to bounce back from adversity, and to endure difficult situations (Masten & Reed, 2002). The first studies of resiliency emerged from investigations of children in abusive, alcoholic, poverty, or mentally ill parent circumstances. Some of these children surprised researchers by rising above their circumstances and developing into healthy, well-functioning adolescents and adults. They were referred to as highly resilient individuals (Masten & Reed, 2002).

We all differ widely in our ability to cope with stress. Some individuals seem to crumble under pressure, while others appear to thrive. A major predictor of which individuals cope well with stress and which do not is the amount of resiliency that they have developed. Two categories of factors explain differences in resiliency. One is personal factors—such as positive self-regard and core self-evaluation, good cognitive abilities, and talents valued by society—and the second is personal coping strategies—such as improving relationships and social capital, and a reduction in risk factors such as abuse, neglect, homelessness, and crime (Masten & Reed, 2002). Several of the first set of factors were measured in Chapter 1, including aspects of personality, self-efficacy, values maturity, and so on. The second set of factors is more behavioral and can be summarized by Figure 2.6. The figure illustrates that resiliency is fostered by achieving balance in the various aspects of life.

The wheel in Figure 2.6 represents the key activities that characterize most people's lives. Each segment in the figure identifies an important aspect of life that must be developed in order to achieve resiliency. The most resilient individuals are those who have achieved a certain degree of **life balance**. They

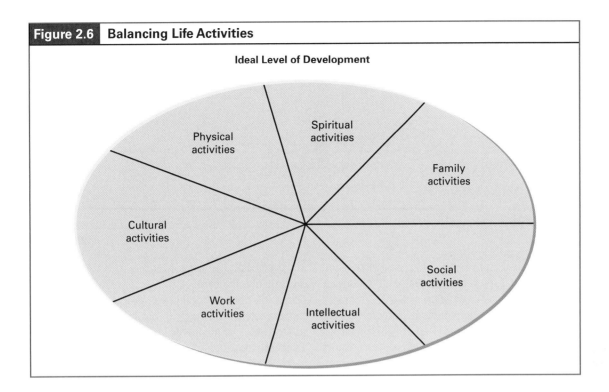

Figure 2.6 Balancing Life Activities

Ideal Level of Development

Physical activities

Spiritual activities

Family activities

Cultural activities

Social activities

Work activities

Intellectual activities

actively engage in activities in each segment of the circle so that they achieve a degree of balance in their lives. For example, assume that the center of the figure represents the zero point of involvement and the outside edge of the figure represents maximum involvement. Shading in a portion of the area in each of the seven segments would represent the amount of attention paid to each area. (This exercise is included in the Skill Practice section.) Individuals who are best able to cope with stress would shade in a substantial portion of each segment, indicating they have spent time developing a variety of dimensions of their lives. The pattern of shading in this exercise, however, should also be relatively balanced. A lopsided pattern is as much an indicator of nonresiliency as not having some segments shaded at all. Overemphasizing one or two areas to the exclusion of others often creates more stress than it eliminates. Life balance is key (Lehrer, 1996; Murphy, 1996; Rostad & Long, 1996).

This prescription, of course, is counterintuitive. Generally, when we are feeling stress in one area of life, such as an overloaded work schedule, we respond by devoting more time and attention to it. While this is a natural reaction, it is counterproductive for several reasons. First, the more we concentrate exclusively on work, the more restricted and less creative we become. We lose perspective, cease to take fresh points of view,

and become overwhelmed more easily. As we shall see in the discussion of creativity in Chapter 3, many breakthroughs in problem solving come from the thought processes stimulated by unrelated activities. That is why several major corporations send senior managers on high-adventure wilderness retreats, invite thespian troupes to perform plays before the executive committee, require volunteer community service, or encourage their managers to engage in completely unrelated activities outside of work.

Second, refreshed and relaxed minds think better. A bank executive commented recently during an executive development workshop that he gradually has become convinced of the merits of taking the weekend off from work. He finds that he gets twice as much accomplished on Monday as his colleagues who have been in their offices all weekend. He encourages members of his unit to take breaks, get out of the office periodically, and make sure to use their vacation days.

Third, the cost of stress-related illness decreases markedly when employees participate in well-rounded wellness programs. A study by the Association for Fitness in Business concluded that companies receive an average return of $3 to $4 on each dollar invested in health and wellness promotion. AT&T, for example, expects to save $72 million in the next 10 years as a result of investment in wellness programs for employees.

Table 2.6 Resiliency: Moderating the Effects of Stress

PHYSIOLOGICAL RESILIENCY	PSYCHOLOGICAL RESILIENCY	SOCIAL RESILIENCY
Cardiovascular conditioning	Balanced lifestyle	Supportive social relations
Proper diet	Hardy personality	Mentors
	• High internal control	Teamwork
	• Strong personal commitment	
	• Love of challenge	
	Small-wins strategy	
	Deep-relaxation techniques	

Well-developed individuals, who give time and attention to cultural, physical, spiritual, family, social, and intellectual activities in addition to work, are more productive and less stressed than those who are workaholics (Adler & Hillhouse, 1996; Hepburn, McLoughlin, & Barling, 1997). In this section, therefore, we concentrate on three common areas of resiliency development for managers: physical resiliency, psychological resiliency, and social resiliency. Development in each of these areas requires initiative on the part of the individual and takes a moderate amount of time to achieve. These are not activities that can be accomplished by lunchtime or by the weekend. Rather, achieving life balance and resiliency requires ongoing initiative and continuous effort. Components of resiliency are summarized in Table 2.6.

PHYSIOLOGICAL RESILIENCY

One of the most crucial aspects of resiliency development involves one's physical condition because physical condition significantly affects the ability to cope with stress. Two aspects of physical condition combine to determine physical resiliency: cardiovascular conditioning and dietary control.

Cardiovascular Conditioning

Henry Ford is reputed to have stated, "Exercise is bunk. If you are healthy, you don't need it. If you are sick, you shouldn't take it." Fortunately, American business has not taken Ford's advice; thousands of major corporations now have in-house fitness facilities. An emphasis on physical conditioning in business has resulted partly from overwhelming evidence that individuals in good physical condition are better able to cope with stressors than those in poor physical condition. Table 2.7 shows the benefits of regular physical exercise.

Mesa Petroleum experienced an annual saving of $1.6 million in health care costs for its 650 employees as a result of its physical fitness program. As a result of its Live for Life program, Johnson & Johnson lowered absenteeism and slowed the rate of health care expenses, resulting in savings of $378 per employee. Exercisers at General Electric Aircraft in Cincinnati were absent from work 45 percent fewer days than nonexercisers. Prudential Life Insurance found a 46 percent reduction in major medical expenses over five years resulting from a workplace fitness program. The Scoular Grain Company opened a fitness center for its 600 employees and reaped an annual saving in health care costs of a million dollars—$1,500 per employee. The advantages of physical conditioning, both for individuals and for companies, are irrefutable (Rostad & Long, 1996).

Three primary purposes exist for a regular exercise program: maintaining optimal weight, increasing psychological well-being, and improving the cardiovascular system.

We mentioned earlier that ongoing stress tends to make us fat. Recall that excess fat is released by the body when we encounter a stressor, and when it is not expended, that fat tends to settle around our middles. The rest of our bodies may be trim, but stress creates potbellies and pear-shapes. Couple that with the sedentary life style that many people live, and we face significant health concerns. For example, an office worker burns up only about 1,200 calories during an eight-hour day. That is fewer calories than are contained in the typical lunch of a hamburger, french fries, and a milkshake. More than 90 million adults watch at least two hours of television per day (and, parenthetically, by the age of 6 children have spent more time watching television than they will spend speaking to their fathers over their entire lifetimes), so it is easy to predict the

Table 2.7	Confirmed Benefits of Regular Vigorous Exercise

- Blood pressure is lowered.
- Resting heart rate is lowered; the heart is better able to distribute blood where needed under stress.
- Cardiac output is increased; the heart is better able to distribute blood where needed under stress.
- Number of red blood cells is increased; more oxygen can be carried per quart of blood.
- Elasticity of arteries is increased.
- Triglyceride level is lowered.
- Blood cholesterol level is decreased. High-density cholesterol, which is more protective of blood vessels than low-density cholesterol, is proportionately increased.
- Adrenal secretions in response to emotional stress are lowered.
- Lactic acid is more efficiently eliminated from the muscles. (This has been associated with decreased fatigue and tension.)
- Fibrin, a protein that aids in the formation of blood clots, is decreased.
- Additional routes of blood supply are built up in the heart.

SOURCE: *Rostad & Long, 1996. Courtesy of Edizione Posse.*

LEARNING

long-term physical and psychological effects. It is little wonder that almost half of adult Americans are at least 10 percent overweight and more than half report excessive levels of stress. The resulting strain on both the heart and the self-image makes overweight individuals more vulnerable to stressors.

An advantage of regular physical exercise as a resiliency development strategy is that it improves mental as well as physical outlook. It increases self-esteem. It gives individuals the energy to be more alert and attentive throughout the day. Episodes of depression are far less frequent. Exercise fosters the necessary energy to cope with the stresses of both unexpected events and dull routine. Physically active individuals are less prone to anxiety, have less illness, and miss fewer days of work (Griest et al., 1979; Murphy, 1996). Researchers have found a chemical basis for the psychological benefit of exercise: the brain releases endorphins (similar to morphine) during periods of intense physical activity. This substance numbs pain and produces a feeling of well-being, sometimes referred to as "jogger's high," which is a euphoric, relaxed feeling reported by long-distance runners (Rostad & Long, 1996).

Another vital benefit of exercise is a strengthened cardiovascular system (Greenberg, 1987). The best results come from aerobic exercises that do not require more oxygen than a person can take in comfortably (as compared with all-out sprinting or long-distance swimming). This type of exercise includes brisk walking, jogging, riding a bicycle, or climbing stairs. However, the cardiovascular system is improved by exercise only when the following two conditions are met:

1. The target heart rate is sustained throughout the exercise. This rate is 60–80 percent of the heart's maximum. To figure your target rate, subtract your age in years from 220, then take 60–80 percent of that number. You should begin your exercise program at the 60-percent level and gradually increase to the 80-percent rate. To check your heart rate during your exercise, periodically monitor your heartbeat for 6 seconds and multiply by 10.
2. The exercise occurs for 20 to 30 minutes, three or four days each week. Since cardiovascular endurance decreases after 48 hours, it is important to exercise at least every other day.

Dietary Control

The adage that "You are what you eat" is sobering, especially given the fact that Americans annually consume an average of 100 pounds of refined sugar, 125 pounds of fat, 36 gallons of carbonated beverages, and 25 times more salt than the human body requires (Adler & Hillhouse, 1996). Since diet has received a great deal of attention among Americans in the past decade or so, most people are well informed about healthy foods and eating habits, but the key principles can't be repeated too often. Here are some of the key prescriptions agreed upon by most medical professionals (see Adler, 2005; Adler & Hillhouse, 1996; Hubbard & Workman, 1998).

Eat a Variety of Foods   There are approximately 40–60 nutrients you need to stay healthy. Nutritionists recommend the following balanced diet for adults each day: five or six servings of fruits and vegetables; four servings of bread or cereal; two servings of milk, cheese, or yogurt; and two servings of meat, poultry, fish, eggs, beans, or peas.

Maintain Optimal Weight   Optimal weight is best maintained through a combination of proper diet and exercise. To lose a pound in a week, you need to burn 500 more calories a day than you consume. Although there are a number of fad diets, sound and simple practices that can help individuals avoid overeating include:

- ❏ Start each meal with a filling, low-calorie appetizer, such as a clear broth or salad.
- ❏ Curb between-meal hunger pangs with large glasses of water or fruit juices.
- ❏ A half-hour before mealtime, eat a carbohydrate food such as two soda crackers or half a wheat bagel.
- ❏ Use vegetables to provide low-calorie bulk in a meal.
- ❏ Eat slowly. (It takes approximately 20 minutes after you begin eating for your brain to get the message that you are doing so.)
- ❏ Eat regularly (every three to five hours) to avoid binge eating.
- ❏ Eat smaller portions. Concentrate on your eating (rather than, for example, on watching TV) so you are aware of how much you've eaten.
- ❏ Don't eat to cope with being bored, angry, tired, or anxious. Try exercise instead.

Reduce Fat Intake   Fat is an essential nutrient, but Americans tend to eat too much of it. They get approximately 45 percent of their calories from fat, whereas a healthy diet should contain no more than about 30 percent fat. Current medical research indicates that saturated fats (those that are solid at room temperature, such as meat fat, butter, and heavy cream) tend to elevate the level of "bad" cholesterol in the blood, contributing to heart disease.

Eat More Whole Foods   These include raw or lightly steamed vegetables, fruits, whole grains and cereals, brown rice, beans, dried peas, nuts, and seeds. These are complex-carbohydrate foods that contain a mix of starch, fiber, sugar, vitamins, and minerals. Simple-carbohydrate foods to avoid are white flour, white rice, refined sugar, processed fruit products, and overcooked vegetables.

Reduce Sugar Intake   Americans get 25 percent of their calories from sugar in various forms, consuming an average of 160 pounds of sugar a year per adult. Sugar gives people a boost of energy and a feeling of restlessness. However, it also stimulates the pancreas to produce insulin, which counteracts the sugar in the blood. Sixty percent of the population have pancreases that overreact, creating feelings of irritability, depression, nausea, anxiety, and, potentially, diabetes.

Reduce Sodium Intake   Sodium is an important mineral, but Americans, on the average, consume approximately 10 times more than they need. Sodium is found in table salt (40 percent sodium), as well as many condiments, processed foods, soft drinks, and salty snacks. Consuming more than five grams a day is unwise, especially for individuals with high blood pressure.

Avoid Alcohol   Alcohol is high in calories and low in other nutrients. It also depletes the body of Vitamin B, which is important for coping with stress.

Restrict Caffeine Intake   Caffeine is a stimulant that chemically induces the fight or flight reaction. In addition, it also depletes the body's supply of Vitamin B. Although many people seek a cup of coffee or a cola drink when they are under stress, caffeine actually makes stress worse. Moreover, recent medical research links caffeine to health risks such as heart disease, hypertension, and various kinds of cancer.

Take Vitamin and Mineral Supplements   Although there is disagreement among nutritionists regarding the need for supplemental vitamins and minerals, most people don't eat a well-balanced diet on a regular basis. It is a good idea, therefore, to make sure you are getting an adequate supply of supplemental nutrients during periods of high stress. Deficiencies in the B vitamins, Vitamin C, and calcium/magnesium have been linked to stress-related symptoms such as insomnia, irritability, depression, and fatigue.

Make Eating a Relaxing Time   Take time to enjoy nutritious meals eaten in peaceful surroundings. Frequent, small meals, associated with periods of relaxation, are more beneficial than two or three large, frantic meals.

PSYCHOLOGICAL RESILIENCY

Another important moderator of the effects of stress is an individual's psychological resiliency. Individuals with certain psychological characteristics, sometimes referred to as "resilient personality types," tend to handle stress better than others. We will focus on two examples that show best the relationship between personality and vulnerability to stress: the hardy personality and the Type A personality. First we will introduce the concept of "hardiness" and use it to discuss general psychological attributes that foster resiliency. Then we will focus on three stress-prone elements of the Type A personality and outline techniques for eliminating them.

Hardiness

Psychological resiliency has recently begun to be studied much more than in the past (for example, see Gittell, Cameron, & Lim, 2006; Sutcliffe & Vogus, 2003), but one of the best sources for learning how to develop psychological resiliency remains a book that is more than two decades old. In *The Hardy Executive*, Maddi and Kobasa (1984) described three elements that characterize a hardy, or highly stress-resistant, personality. **Hardiness** results from (1) feeling in control of one's life, rather than powerless to shape external events; (2) feeling committed to and involved in what one is doing, rather than alienated from one's work and other individuals; and (3) feeling challenged by new experiences rather than viewing change as a threat to security and comfort. According to these authors, hardy individuals tend to interpret stressful situations positively and optimistically, and they respond to stress constructively. As a result, their incidence of illness and emotional dysfunction under stressful conditions is considerably below the norm.

These three concepts—control, commitment, and challenge—are central to the development of a variety of management skills, and are crucial for mitigating the harmful effects of stress (Cowley, 2000; Kobasa, 1979, 1982). As we discussed in the Developing Self-Awareness chapter, individuals who score high on internal locus of control feel that they are in charge of their own destinies. They take responsibility for their actions and feel they can neutralize negative external forces. They generally believe that stressors are the result of their personal choices rather than uncontrollable, capricious, or even malicious external forces. The belief that one can influence the course of events is central to developing high self-esteem. Self-esteem, in turn, engenders self-confidence and the optimistic view that bad situations can be improved and that problems can be overcome. Confidence in one's own efficacy produces low fear of failure, high expectations, willingness to take risks, and persistence under adversity (Anderson, 1977; Bandura 1997; Ivancevich & Matteson, 1980; Mednick, 1982; Sorenson, 1998), all of which contribute to resiliency under stress. Holding a positive self-regard or having a high core self-evaluation score is strongly related to psychological resiliency (Judge & Bono, 2001).

Commitment implies both selection and dedication. Hardy individuals not only feel that they choose what they do, but they also strongly believe in the importance of what they do. This commitment is both internal (that is, applied to one's own activities) and external (that is, applied to a larger community). The feeling of being responsible to others is an important buffer against stress. Whereas self-esteem and a sense of purpose help provide a psychological support system for coping with stressful events, an individual's belief that others are counting on him or her to succeed and that he or she belongs to a larger community fosters psychological resiliency during stressful periods. Feeling part of a group, feeling cared about, and feeling trusted by others engender norms of cooperation and commitment and encourage constructive responses to stress (Bandura, 1997).

Hardy people also welcome challenge. They believe that change, rather than stability, is the normal and preferred mode of life. Therefore, much of the disruption associated with a stressful life event is interpreted as an opportunity for personal growth rather than as a threat to security. This mode of thinking is consistent with the Chinese word for crisis, which has two meanings: "threat" and "opportunity." Individuals who seek challenges search for new and interesting experiences and accept stress as a necessary step toward learning. Because these individuals prefer change to stability, they tend to have high tolerance for ambiguity and high resiliency under stress (Ivancevich & Ganster, 1987; Maddi & Kobasa, 1984). The three characteristics of hardy personalities—control, commitment, and challenge—have been found to be among the most powerful mitigators of the adverse consequences of stress. By contrast, a different complex of personality attributes, the so-called Type A Syndrome, is associated with reduced hardiness and higher levels of psychological stress.

The Type A Personality

A second important aspect of psychological resiliency relates to a personality pattern many individuals develop as they enter the competitive worlds of advanced education and of management. By far, the most well-known connection between personality and resiliency relates to a combination of attributes known as the **Type A personality**. For more than four decades, scientists have been aware of a link between certain personality attributes and stress-related behavioral, psychological, and physiological problems such as anxiety, deteriorating relationships, and heart disease (Friedman & Rosenman, 1974). Table 2.8 summarizes the primary attributes of Type A personalities that have emerged from the research.

The manner in which Friedman and Rosenman (both cardiologists) discovered the link between personality and heart disease is intriguing. Observing that their waiting room was becoming a bit shabby, they decided to have their chairs reupholstered. The decorator pointed out that only the front edges of the chairs were worn. The doctors suddenly realized that their patients seemed to be "on edge," literally sitting on the edges of their seats, prepared for action.

Following up their observations with intensive interviews, they noted that during interviews, many of their patients showed signs of impatience and hostility such as fidgeting, eye blinking, grimaces, rapid or explosive speech, interrupting, and filling in incomplete sentences during a pause. The opposite personality types, which they labeled Type B, appeared more relaxed, patient, and able to listen without interrupting. Over 15 percent of Friedman and Rosenman's Type A's had had heart attacks, compared to 7 percent of Type B's.

Subsequent research has found that in America about 70 percent of men and 50 percent of women exhibit Type A personality traits, such as extreme competitiveness, strong desires for achievement, haste, impatience, restlessness, hyperalertness, explosiveness of speech, tenseness of facial muscles, free-floating hostility, and so on. Rosenman suggested that anger, impatience, and competitiveness were the most debilitating factors in the Type A personality although other factors such as hostility, blaming, and feelings of urgency also have been identified as causes of continuous adrenaline secretions in the body. Regardless of the key ingredient, the Type A personality is certainly a high risk factor in maintaining personal well-being (Friedman, 1996; Siegman & Smith, 1994; William & Williams, 1998).

In one of the most extensive studies of personality effects on heart disease ever conducted, an eight-year survey of 3,400 men found that Type A individuals in the

Table 2.8	**Characteristics of the Type A Personality**

- Signs of personal tension, such as a clenched jaw, tight muscles, tics.
- Personal commitment to having, rather than being.
- Unawareness of the broader environment.
- Ignorance of elements outside the immediate task.
- Strong need to be an expert on a subject; otherwise, lack of involvement.
- Compulsion to compete with other Type A's rather than understand and cooperate with them.
- Speech characterized by explosive accentuation, acceleration of the last few words of a sentence, impatience when interrupted.
- Chronic sense of being in a hurry.
- Polyphasic thoughts and actions, that is, a tendency to do several things simultaneously.
- Impatience with the normal pace of events. Tendency to finish others' sentences.
- Doing everything rapidly.
- Feelings of guilt when relaxing.
- Tendency to evaluate all activities in terms of measurable results.
- Belief that Type A attributes are what lead to success.
- Frequent knee-jiggling or finger-tapping.
- Determination to win every game, even when playing with those who are less skilled or experienced.

39- to 49-year age group had approximately 6.5 times the likelihood of heart disease as Type B's. Even when factors such as cigarette smoking, parental medical history, blood pressure, and cholesterol levels were factored out, the Type A personality still accounted for a two to three times greater likelihood of heart disease. This research concluded that personality is a better predictor than physiology of cardiovascular illness (Friedman, 1996; Friedman & Rosenman, 1974). Ironically, subsequent research has also found that whereas Type A personalities are more prone to experience heart attacks, they are also more likely to recover from them.

Most Type A individuals believe it is their Type A personality that has led to their success. Many are unwilling to give up that orientation because hard-driving, intense, persistent action is generally admired and valued among managers. This has often been associated with the traditional male management role, but it has also been connected to the disproportionately high incidence of heart disease among men. In fact, several researchers initially linked Type A personality characteristics to certain sex-linked behavior patterns (Friedman, 1996; Goldberg, 1976; Jourard, 1964; Siegman & Smith, 1994).

Specifically, males or females who followed stereotypic views of appropriate male behavior were found to be more likely to experience stress-related illness. They tended to equate low self-disclosure, low emotional involvement, low display of feelings, high defensiveness, and high insensitivity to the acquisition of power and control—the presumed prerequisites for success. These were so typical of male behavior in the workplace that they became known as "the lethal aspects of the male role." As more women began to enter the workforce, this same pattern became less and less gender-linked. Many women also behaved as if acceptance in the workplace required "acting as masculine" as their male counterparts. As a result, the gap between stress-related illness among professional men and women has narrowed. In recent years, female stress-related illnesses (e.g., heart attacks, suicides, migraine headaches) actually have surpassed those of males in some professions. This trend is not only tragic but ironic, because corporations are spending millions of dollars each year on training workshops designed to encourage their managers to become more sensitive, understanding, and supportive. The folly of the Type A approach to management, and to life, is illustrated in the following story from the lore of Zen Buddhism.

Matajura wanted to become a great swordsman, but his father said he wasn't quick enough and could never learn. So Matajura went to the famous dueler, Banzo, and asked to become his pupil. "How long will it take me to become a master?" he asked. "Suppose I become your servant, and spend every minute with you; how long?"

"Ten years," said Banzo.

"My father is getting old. Before 10 years have passed, I will have to return home to take care of him. Suppose I work twice as hard; how long will it take me?"

"Thirty years," said Banzo.

"How is that?" asked Matajura. "First you say 10 years. Then when I offer to work twice as hard, you say it will take three times as long. Let me make myself clear: I will work unceasingly; no hardship will be too much. How long will it take?"

"Seventy years," said Banzo. "A pupil in such a hurry learns slowly."

This Type A sense of urgency, of being able to overcome any obstacle by working harder and longer, works against the ability to develop psychological hardiness. When stressors are encountered, arousal levels increase, and the tendency is to combat them by increasing arousal levels, or effort, even further. But at high arousal levels, coping responses become more primitive (Staw, Sandelands, & Dutton, 1981; Weick, 1995). Patterns of response that were learned most recently are the first ones to disappear, which means that the responses that are most finely tuned to the current stressful situation are the first ones to go. The ability to distinguish among fine-grained stimuli actually deteriorates, so the extra energy expended by individuals trying to cope becomes less and less effective. Weick (1984, 1995) pointed out that highly stressed people consequently find it difficult to learn new responses, to brainstorm, to concentrate, to resist relying on old nonadaptive behavior patterns, to perform complex responses, to delegate, and to avoid the vicious spiral of escalating arousal. Resiliency deteriorates.

You completed the Type A Personality Inventory in the Pre-Assessment section of this chapter. It assesses four behavioral tendencies that comprise a Type A personality: a sense of extreme competitiveness; significant life imbalance, usually indicated by high work involvement and an overemphasis on instrumental tasks; strong feelings of hostility and anger; and an extreme sense of urgency and impatience. Scores above 12 in each area suggest that you have a pronounced tendency toward being Type A. Research suggests that the hostility tendency is the most damaging to personal health.

The Small-Wins Strategy

An effective antidote to this Type A escalation problem is working for "small wins," discussed earlier in this chapter. When individuals work for incremental accomplishments rather than trying to achieve a major milestone or "hit a home run," they consciously remain sensitive to the progress they are making, they can celebrate victories, and they can develop a sense of making progress, all the while coping with a major stressor.

A hypothetical example introduced by Kuhn and Beam (1982, pp. 249–250) illustrates the power of small wins.

> *Your task is to count out a thousand sheets of paper while you are subject to periodic interruptions. Each interruption causes you to lose track of the count and forces you to start over. If you count the thousand as a single sequence, then an interruption could cause you to lose count of as many as 999. If the sheets are put into stacks of 100, however, and each stack remains undisturbed by interruptions, then the worst possible count loss from interruption is 108. That number represents the recounting of nine stacks of 100 each plus 99 single sheets. Further, if sheets are first put into stacks of 10, which are then joined into stacks of 100, the worst possible loss from interruption would be 27. That number represents nine stacks of 100 plus nine stacks of 10 plus nine single sheets. Not only is far less recounting time lost by putting the paper into "subsystems" of tens and hundreds, but the chances of completing the count are vastly higher.*

When individuals work for a small, concrete outcome, giving them a chance to enjoy visible success, they develop heightened confidence, excitement, and optimism, which motivate an attempt to accomplish another small win. By itself, a small win may seem unimportant. A series of wins at seemingly insignificant tasks, however, reveals a pattern that tends to attract allies, deter opponents, and lower resistance to further action. Once a small win has been accomplished, forces are set in motion that favor another small win. When one solution has been identified, the next solvable problem often becomes more visible. Additional resources also tend to flow toward winners, so the probability of additional successes increases.

Research clearly demonstrates that a small-wins strategy is superior to a strategy of trying to cope with stressors in large chunks (Weick, 1984, 1995). For example, successive small requests are more likely to be approved and achieve compliance than one large request. Positions advocated within the latitude of acceptance (i.e., that are only slightly different from current positions) modify opinions more than does advocacy of a position that exceeds those limits (i.e., large differences exist between current and proposed positions). People whose positions are close to one's own tend to be the targets of the most intensive persuasion attempts, while those whose positions are farther away are dismissed, isolated, or derogated. Cognitive therapy is most successful when the patient is persuaded to do just one thing differently that changes his or her pattern of coping up to that point. Learning tends to occur in small increments rather than in large, all-or-nothing chunks. Retention of learning is better when individuals are in an emotional state similar to the one in which they learned the original material. Over 75 percent of the changes and improvements in both individuals and organizations over time can be accounted for by minor improvements, not major alterations. The point is that the incremental approach used in a small-wins strategy is the most basic and the one most compatible with human preferences for learning, perception, motivation, and change.

What does this have to do with hardiness and resiliency? A small-wins strategy both engenders hardiness and helps overcome the Type A personality syndrome, which is basically a large-win, winner-takes-all approach to stress. Recall that hardiness is composed of control, commitment, and challenge. The deliberate cultivation of a strategy of small wins helps produce precisely those psychological states. Small wins reinforce the perception that individuals can influence what happens to them (being in control); it helps motivate further action by building on the confidence of past successes (which creates commitment); and it produces changes of manageable size that serve as incentives to broaden, learn, and seek new opportunities or challenges. "Continuing pursuit of small wins can build increasing resistance to stress in people not originally predisposed toward hardiness" (Weick, 1984, p. 46).

Deep-Relaxation Strategies

In addition to a small-wins strategy, a second approach to building psychological resiliency is to learn and practice a deep-relaxation technique. Research demonstrates a marked decrease in Type A personality characteristics for regular users of meditation and deep-relaxation techniques. Using the automotive analogy, individuals who use deep-relaxation exercises find that when stress occurs, their "engines" don't rev up as high, and they return to idle faster (Curtis & Detert, 1981; Davis, Eshelman, & McKay, 1980; Greenberg, 1987). Deep-relaxation techniques differ from temporary, short-term relaxation techniques, which we will discuss later.

Deep-relaxation techniques include meditation, yoga, autogenic training or self-hypnosis, biofeedback, and so on. Considerable evidence exists that individuals who practice such techniques regularly are able to condition their bodies to inhibit the negative effects of stress (Beary & Benson, 1977; Cooper & Aygen, 1979; Deepak, 1995; Dellbeck & Shatkin, 1991; Orme-Johnson, 1973; Stone & Deleo, 1976; Yogi, 1994). Most of these deep-relaxation techniques must be practiced over a period of time to develop fully, but they are not difficult to learn. Most deep-relaxation techniques require the following conditions:

1. A quiet environment in which external distractions are minimized.

2. A comfortable position so that muscular effort is minimized.

3. A mental focus. Transcendental meditation (TM) advocates recommend concentrating on one word, phrase, or object. Benson (1975) suggests the word "one." Others suggest picturing a plain vase. The ancient Chinese used a carved jade object that resembled a mountain and sat on a desktop. The purpose of focusing on a word or object is to rid the mind of all other thoughts.

4. Controlled breathing (i.e., deliberate breathing) with pauses between breaths. Thoughts are focused on rhythmic breathing, which helps clear the mind and aids concentration.

5. A passive attitude, so that if other thoughts enter the mind, they are ignored.

6. Focused bodily changes. While meditation uses the mind to relax the body, autogenic training uses bodily sensations of heaviness and warmth to change the psychological state. Feelings of warmth and heaviness are induced in different parts of the body, which, in turn, create deep relaxation.

7. Repetition. Because physiological and psychological results depend on consistent practice, the best results occur when such techniques are practiced from 20 to 30 minutes each day.

The Skill Practice section contains an example of a deep-relaxation exercise.

SOCIAL RESILIENCY

The third factor moderating the harmful effects of stress and contributing to resiliency involves developing close social relationships. Individuals who are embedded in supportive social networks are less likely to experience stress and are better equipped to cope with its consequences (Cordes & Dougherty, 1993; Lehrer, 1996; Singh, 1993). Supportive social relations provide opportunities to share one's frustrations and disappointments, to receive suggestions and encouragement, and to experience emotional bonding. Such supportive interactions provide the empathy and bolstering required to cope with stressful events. They are formed most easily among individuals who share close emotional ties (e.g., family members) or common experiences (e.g., coworkers).

Poignant testimony to the value of social support systems during periods of high stress comes from the experiences of soldiers captured during World War II and the Korean and Vietnam wars. When it was possible for prisoners to form permanent, interacting groups, they maintained better health and morale and were able to resist their captors more effectively than when they were isolated or when groups were unstable. Indeed, the well-documented technique used by the Chinese during the Korean War for breaking down soldiers' resistance to their indoctrination efforts involved weakening group solidarity through planting seeds of mistrust and doubt about members' loyalty.

Aside from personal friendships or family relations, two types of social support systems can be formed as part of a manager's job. One is a mentor relationship; the other is a task team. Most individuals, with the possible exception of the most senior managers, can profit from a mentoring relationship. The research is clear, in fact, that career success, work satisfaction, and resiliency to stress are enhanced by a mentoring relationship (Bell, 1998; Hendricks, 1996; Kram, 1985). Individuals need someone else in the organization that can provide a role model, from whom they can learn, and from whom they can receive personal attention and a reinforcement of self-worth, especially under uncertain, crucial, and stressful situations.

Many organizations formally prescribe a mentoring system by assigning a senior manager to shepherd a younger manager when he or she enters the organization. With rare exceptions, when the contact is one-way, from the top down, these relationships don't work out (Kram, 1985). The junior manager must actively seek and foster the mentoring relationship as well. The junior manager can do this, not by demonstrating overdependence or overingratiation, but by expressing a desire to use the senior person as a mentor and then by making certain that the relationship does not become a one-way street. The subordinate can pass along important information and resources to the potential mentor, while both will share in working out solutions to problems. That way, the mentoring relationship becomes mutually satisfying and mutually beneficial for both parties, and resiliency to stress is enhanced because of the commitment, trust, and cooperation that begin to characterize the relationship. A mentor's guidance can both help avoid stressful situations and provide support for coping with them.

Smoothly functioning work teams also enhance social resiliency. The social value of working on a team has been well documented in research, and Chapter 9 in this book reviews some of that evidence (also see Dyer, 1987; Katzenbach & Smith, 1993). The more cohesive the team, the more support it provides its members. Members of highly cohesive teams communicate with one another more frequently and more positively and report higher satisfaction, lower stress, and higher commitment levels than do individuals who do not feel as though they are part of a work team (Lawler, Mohrman, and Ledford, 1992).

The value of work teams has been amply demonstrated in practice as well. In the Introductory chapter, for example, we recounted a dramatic change that occurred in the Fremont, California, plant of General Motors when U.S. workers came under Japanese management. In just one year, marked improvements in productivity, morale, and quality occurred, due in large part to the use of effective work teams. Relationships were formed based not only on friendship but on a common commitment to solving work-related problems and to generating ideas for improvement. Teams met regularly during work hours to discuss ideas for improvement and to coordinate and resolve issues.

Similar dynamics have been fostered in most of the successful companies in the United States and abroad. The productivity and success of the East Asian economies, for example, has been attributed largely to the effective use of work teams. Almost every company that has won the Malcolm Baldrige National Quality Award (e.g., Motorola, Ritz-Carlton, Westinghouse, Xerox, Millikin) has fostered teamwork among employees as a crucial part of its improvement efforts. The marked improvements that occur in individual satisfaction and lowered stress levels suggest that each person should likewise help facilitate similar teamwork in his or her work setting as part of a social resiliency repertoire.

To foster teamwork in your own work settings, you might consider involving others in defining the challenges (stressors), tasks, or issues you encounter, encourage broad participation and two-way feedback with every person involved, share information and resources broadly so that knowledge sharing occurs, and cultivate a feeling of cohesion and commitment among team members by identifying team rewards or positive outcomes rather than focusing on individual accomplishment. A detailed discussion of these and other team dynamics is found in Chapter 9 on Building Effective Teams.

Temporary Stress-Reduction Techniques

Thus far, we have emphasized eliminating sources of stress and developing resiliency to stress. These are the most desirable stress-management strategies because they have a permanent or long-term effect on your well-being. However, the occurrence of stressors is sometimes beyond our control so it may be impossible to eliminate them. Moreover, developing resiliency takes time, so sometimes we must use temporary reactive mechanisms in order to maintain equilibrium. Although increased resilience can buffer the harmful effects of stress, we must sometimes take immediate action in the short term to cope with the stress we encounter.

Implementing short-term strategies reduces stress temporarily so that longer-term stress-elimination or resiliency strategies can operate. Short-term strategies are largely reactive and must be repeated whenever stressors are encountered because, unlike other strategies, their effects are only temporary. On the other hand, they are especially useful for immediately calming feelings of anxiety or apprehension. You can use them when you are asked a question you can't answer, when you become embarrassed by an unexpected event, when you are faced with a presentation or an important meeting, or almost any time you are suddenly stressed and must respond in a short period of time. Although more than 5,000 books have been published on temporary stress-reduction techniques since 1990, we review only five of the best-known and easiest to learn techniques here. The first two are physiological; the last three are psychological.

Muscle relaxation involves easing the tension in successive muscle groups. Each muscle group is tightened for five or ten seconds and then completely relaxed. Starting with the feet and progressing to the calves, thighs, stomach, and on to the neck and face, one can relieve tension throughout the entire body. All parts of the body can be included in the exercise. One variation is to roll the head around on the neck several times, shrug the shoulders, or stretch the arms up toward the ceiling for five to ten seconds, then release the position and relax the muscles. The result is a state of temporary relaxation that helps eliminate tension and refocus energy.

A variation of muscle relaxation involves **deep breathing**. This is done by taking several successive, slow, deep breaths, holding them for five seconds, and exhaling completely. You should focus on the act of breathing itself, so that your mind becomes cleared for a brief time while your body relaxes. After each deep breath, muscles in the body should consciously be relaxed.

A third technique uses **imagery and fantasy** to eliminate stress temporarily by changing the focus of your thoughts. Imagery involves visualizing an event, using "mind pictures." An increasingly common practice for athletes is to visualize successful performance or to imagine themselves achieving their goal. Research has confirmed both the stress-reduction advantages of this technique as well as the performance enhancement benefits (e.g., Deepak, 1995).

In addition to visualization, imagery also can include recollections of sounds, smells, and textures. Your mind focuses on pleasant experiences from the past (e.g., a fishing trip, family vacation, visit with relatives, day at the beach) that can be recalled vividly. Fantasies, on the other hand, are not past memories but make-believe events or images. It is especially well known, for example, that children often construct imaginary friends, make-believe occurrences, or special wishes that are comforting to them when they encounter stress. Adults also use daydreams or other fantasy experiences to get them through stressful situations. The purpose of this technique is to relieve anxiety or pressure temporarily by focusing on something pleasant so that other, more productive stress-reducing strategies can be developed for the longer term.

The fourth technique is called **rehearsal**. Using this technique, people work themselves through potentially stressful situations, trying out different scenarios and alternative reactions. Appropriate reactions are rehearsed, either in a safe environment before stress occurs, or "off-line," in private, in the midst of a stressful situation. Removing oneself temporarily from a stressful circumstance and working through dialogue or reactions, as though rehearsing for a play, can help one regain control and reduce the immediacy of the stressor.

A final strategy, **reframing**, involves temporarily reducing stress by optimistically redefining a situation as manageable. Reframing serves as a key to developing "hardiness" and "emotional intelligence" discussed earlier. Although reframing is difficult in the midst of a stressful situation, it can be facilitated by using the following cues:

❑ "I understand this situation."
❑ "I've solved similar problems before."
❑ "Other people are available to help me get through this situation."
❑ "Others have faced similar situations and made it through."
❑ "In the long run, this really isn't so critical."
❑ "I can learn something from this situation."
❑ "There are several good alternatives available to me."

Each of these statements can assist you in reframing a situation in order to develop long-term proactive or enactive strategies.

Summary

We began this chapter by explaining stress in terms of a relatively simple model. Four kinds of stressors—time, encounter, situational, and anticipatory—cause negative physiological, psychological, and social reactions in individuals. These reactions are moderated by the resiliency that individuals have developed for coping with stress. The best way to manage stress is to eliminate it through time management, delegation, collaboration, interpersonal competence, work redesign, prioritizing, goal setting, and small wins. This strategy has permanent consequences, but it often takes an extended period of time to implement.

The next most effective stress management strategy is improving one's resiliency. Physiological resiliency is strengthened through increased cardiovascular conditioning and improved diet. Psychological resiliency and hardiness are improved by practicing small-wins strategies and deep relaxation. Social resiliency is increased by fostering mentoring relationships and teamwork among coworkers. These strategies produce long-term benefits, but they also take quite a long time to implement.

When circumstances make it impossible to apply longer-term strategies for reducing stress, short-term relaxation techniques can temporarily alleviate the symptoms of stress. These strategies have short-term consequences, but they can be applied immediately and repeated over and over again.

Behavioral Guidelines

Following are specific behavioral guidelines for improving one's stress management skills.

1. Use effective time management practices. Make sure that you use time effectively as well as efficiently by generating your own personal mission statement. Make sure that low-priority tasks do not drive out time to work on high-priority activities. Make better use of your time by using the guidelines in the Time Management Survey in the Assessment Section.

2. Build collaborative relationships with individuals based on mutual trust, respect, honesty, and kindness. Make "deposits" into the "emotional bank accounts" of other people. Form close, stable relationships among those with whom you work.

3. Consciously work to improve your emotional intelligence by learning and practicing the principles discussed in other chapters of this book.

4. Try redesigning your work to increase its skill variety, importance, task identity (comprehensiveness), autonomy, and feedback. Make the work itself stress reducing, rather than stress inducing.

5. Reaffirm priorities and short-term plans that provide direction and focus to activities. Give important activities priority over urgent ones.

6. Increase your general resiliency by leading a balanced life and consciously developing yourself in physical, intellectual, cultural, social, family, and spiritual areas, as well as in your work.

7. Increase your physical resiliency by engaging in a regular program of exercise and proper eating.

8. Increase your psychological resiliency and hardiness by implementing a small-wins strategy. Identify and celebrate the small successes that you and others achieve.

9. Learn at least one deep-relaxation technique and practice it regularly.

10. Increase social resiliency by forming an open, trusting, sharing relationship with at least one other person. Facilitate a mentoring relationship with someone who can affirm your worth as a person and provide support during periods of stress.

11. Establish a teamwork relationship with those with whom you work or study by identifying shared tasks and structuring coordinated action among team members.

12. Learn at least two short-term relaxation techniques and practice them consistently.

CASES INVOLVING STRESS MANAGEMENT

The Turn of the Tide

Not long ago I came to one of those bleak periods that many of us encounter from time to time, a sudden drastic dip in the graph of living when everything goes stale and flat, energy wanes, enthusiasm dies. The effect on my work was frightening. Every morning I would clench my teeth and mutter: "Today life will take on some of its old meaning. You've got to break through this thing. You've got to!"

But the barren days went by, and the paralysis grew worse. The time came when I knew I had to have help. The man I turned to was a doctor. Not a psychiatrist, just a doctor. He was older than I, and under his surface gruffness lay great wisdom and compassion. "I don't know what's wrong," I told him miserably, "but I just seem to have come to a dead end. Can you help me?"

"I don't know," he said slowly. He made a tent of his fingers and gazed at me thoughtfully for a long while. Then, abruptly, he asked, "Where were you happiest as a child?"

"As a child?" I echoed. "Why, at the beach, I suppose. We had a summer cottage there. We all loved it."

He looked out the window and watched the October leaves sifting down. "Are you capable of following instructions for a single day?"

"I think so," I said, ready to try anything.

"All right. Here's what I want you to do."

He told me to drive to the beach alone the following morning, arriving not later than nine o'clock. I could take some lunch; but I was not to read, write, listen to the radio, or talk to anyone. "In addition," he said, "I'll give you a prescription to be taken every three hours."

He then tore off four prescription blanks, wrote a few words on each, folded them, numbered them, and handed them to me. "Take these at nine, twelve, three, and six."

"Are you serious?" I asked.

He gave a short bark of laughter. "You won't think I'm joking when you get my bill!"

The next morning, with little faith, I drove to the beach. It was lonely, all right. A northeaster was blowing; the sea looked gray and angry. I sat in the car, the whole day stretching emptily before me. Then I took out the first of the folded slips of paper. On it was written: LISTEN CAREFULLY.

I stared at the two words. "Why," I thought, "the man must be mad." He had ruled out music and newscasts and human conversation. What else was there? I raised my head and I did listen. There were no sounds but the steady roar of the sea, the creaking cry of a gull, the drone of some aircraft high overhead. All these sounds were familiar. I got out of the car. A gust of wind slammed the door with a sudden clap of sound. "Am I supposed to listen carefully to things like that?" I asked myself.

I climbed a dune and looked out over the deserted beach. Here the sea bellowed so loudly that all other sounds were lost. And yet, I thought suddenly, there must be sounds beneath sounds—the soft rasp of drifting sand, the tiny wind-whisperings in the dune grasses—if the listener got close enough to hear them.

On an impulse I ducked down and, feeling fairly ridiculous, thrust my head into a clump of sea-oats. Here I made a discovery: If you listen intently, there is a fractional moment in which everything seems to pause, wait. In that instant of stillness, the racing thoughts halt. For a moment, when you truly listen for something outside yourself, you have to silence the clamorous voices within. The mind rests.

I went back to the car and slid behind the wheel. LISTEN CAREFULLY. As I listened again to the deep growl of the sea, I found myself thinking about the white-fanged fury of its storms.

I thought of the lessons it had taught us as children. A certain amount of patience: you can't hurry the tides. A great deal of respect: the sea does not suffer fools gladly. An awareness of the vast and mysterious interdependence of things: wind and tide and current, calm and squall and hurricane, all combining to determine the paths of the birds above and the fish below. And the cleanness of it all, with every beach swept twice a day by the great broom of the sea.

Sitting there, I realized I was thinking of things bigger than myself—and there was relief in that.

Even so, the morning passed slowly. The habit of hurling myself at a problem was so strong that I felt lost without it. Once, when I was wistfully eyeing the car radio, a phrase from Carlyle jumped into my head: "Silence is the element in which great things fashion themselves."

By noon the wind had polished the clouds out of the sky, and the sea had merry sparkle. I unfolded the second "prescription." And again I sat there, half amused and half exasperated. Three words this time: TRY REACHING BACK.

Back to what? To the past, obviously. But why, when all my worries concerned the present or the future?

I left the car and started tramping reflectively along the dunes. The doctor had sent me to the beach because it was a place of happy memories. Maybe that was what I was supposed to reach for: the wealth of happiness that lay half-forgotten behind me.

I decided to experiment: to work on these vague impressions as a painter would, retouching the colors, strengthening the outlines. I would choose specific incidents and recapture as many details as possible. I would visualize people complete with dress and gestures. I would listen (carefully) for the exact sound of their voices, the echo of their laughter.

The tide was going out now, but there was still thunder in the surf. So I chose to go back 20 years to the last fishing trip I made with my younger brother. (He died in the Pacific during World War II and was buried in the Philippines.) I found that if I closed my eyes and really tried, I could see him with amazing vividness, even the humor and eagerness in his eyes that far-off morning.

In fact, I could see it all: the ivory scimitar of beach where we were fishing; the eastern sky smeared with sunrise; the great rollers creaming in, stately and slow. I could feel the backwash swirl warm around my knees, see the sudden arc of my brother's rod as he struck a fish, hear his exultant yell. Piece by piece I rebuilt it, clear and unchanged under the transparent varnish of time. Then it was gone.

I sat up slowly. TRY REACHING BACK. Happy people were usually assured, confident people. If, then, you deliberately reached back and touched happiness, might there not be released little flashes of power, tiny sources of strength?

This second period of the day went more quickly. As the sun began its long slant down the sky, my mind ranged eagerly through the past, reliving some episodes, uncovering others that had been completely forgotten. For example, when I was around 13 and my brother 10, Father had promised to take us to the circus. But at lunch there was a phone call: Some urgent business required his attention downtown.

We braced ourselves for disappointment. Then we heard him say, "No, I won't be down. It'll have to wait."

When he came back to the table, Mother smiled. "The circus keeps coming back, you know."

"I know," said Father. "But childhood doesn't."

Across all the years I remembered this and knew from the sudden glow of warmth that no kindness is ever wasted or ever completely lost.

By three o'clock the tide was out and the sound of the waves was only a rhythmic whisper, like a giant breathing. I stayed in my sandy nest, feeling relaxed and content—and a little complacent. The doctor's prescriptions, I thought, were easy to take.

But I was not prepared for the next one. This time the three words were not a gentle suggestion. They sounded more like a command. REEXAMINE YOUR MOTIVES.

My first reaction was purely defensive. "There's nothing wrong with my motives," I said to myself. "I want to be successful—who doesn't? I want to have a certain amount of recognition—but so does everybody. I want more security than I've got—and why not?"

"Maybe," said a small voice somewhere inside my head, "those motives aren't good enough. Maybe that's the reason the wheels have stopped going around."

I picked up a handful of sand and let it stream between my fingers. In the past, whenever my work went well, there had always been something spontaneous about it, something uncontrived, something free. Lately it had been calculated, competent—and dead. Why? Because I had been looking past the job itself to the rewards I hoped it would bring. The work had ceased to be an end in itself, it had been merely a means to make money, pay bills. The sense of giving something, of helping people, of making a contribution, had been lost in a frantic clutch at security.

In a flash of certainty, I saw that if one's motives are wrong, nothing can be right. It makes no difference whether you are a mailman, a hairdresser, an insurance salesman, a housewife—whatever. As long as you feel you are serving others, you do the job well. When you are concerned only with helping yourself, you do it less well. This is a law as inexorable as gravity.

For a long time I sat there. Far out on the bar I heard the murmur of the surf change to a hollow roar as the tide turned. Behind me the spears of light were almost horizontal. My time at the beach had almost run out, and I felt a grudging admiration for the doctor and the "prescriptions" he had so casually and cunningly devised. I saw, now, that in them was a therapeutic progression that might well be of value to anyone facing any difficulty.

LISTEN CAREFULLY: To calm a frantic mind, slow it down, shift the focus from inner problems to outer things.

TRY REACHING BACK: Since the human mind can hold but one idea at a time, you blot out present worry when you touch the happiness of the past.

REEXAMINE YOUR MOTIVES: This was the hard core of the "treatment," this challenge to reappraise, to bring one's motives into alignment with one's capabilities and conscience. But the mind must be clear and receptive to do this—hence the six hours of quiet that went before.

The western sky was a blaze of crimson as I took out the last slip of paper. Six words this time. I walked slowly out on the beach. A few yards below the high water mark I stopped and read the words again: WRITE YOUR TROUBLES ON THE SAND.

I let the paper blow away, reached down and picked up a fragment of shell. Kneeling there under the vault of the sky, I wrote several words on the sand, one above the other. Then I walked away, and I did not look back. I had written my troubles on the sand. And the tide was coming in.

SOURCE: *"The Day at the Beach" Copyright by Arthur Gordon, 1959. Reprinted with permission from the January 1960* Reader's Digest.

Discussion Questions

1. What is effective about these strategies for coping with stress, and why did they work?
2. What troubles, challenges, or stressors do you face right now to which these prescriptions might apply?
3. Are these prescriptions effective coping strategies or merely escapes?
4. What other prescriptions could the author take besides the four mentioned here? Generate your own list based on your own experiences with stress.

The Case of the Missing Time

At approximately 7:30 A.M. on Tuesday, June 23, 1959, Chet Craig, manager of the Norris Company's Central Plant, swung his car out of the driveway of his suburban home and headed toward the plant located some six miles away, just inside the Midvale city limits. It was a beautiful day. The sun was shining brightly and a cool, fresh breeze was blowing. The trip to the plant took about 20 minutes and sometimes gave Chet an opportunity to think about plant problems without interruption.

The Norris Company owned and operated three printing plants. Norris enjoyed a nationwide commercial business, specializing in quality color work. It was a closely held company with some 350 employees, nearly half of whom were employed at the Central Plant, the largest of the three Norris production operations. The company's main offices were also located in the Central Plant building.

Chet had started with the Norris Company as an expediter in its Eastern Plant in 1948, just after he graduated from Ohio State. After three years Chet was promoted to production supervisor, and two years later he was made assistant to the manager of the Eastern Plant. Early in 1957 he was transferred to the Central Plant as assistant to the plant manager and one month later was promoted to plant manager when the former manager retired (see Figure 2.7).

Chet was in fine spirits as he relaxed behind the wheel. As his car picked up speed, the hum of the tires on the newly paved highway faded into the background. Various thoughts occurred to him, and he said to himself, "This is going to be the day to really get things done."

He began to run through the day's work, first one project, then another, trying to establish priorities. After a few minutes he decided that the open-end unit scheduling was probably the most important, certainly the most urgent. He frowned for a moment as he recalled that on Friday the vice president and general manager had casually asked him if he had given the project any further thought. Chet realized that he had not been giving it much thought lately. He had been meaning to get to work on this idea for over three months, but something else always seemed to crop up. "I haven't had much time to sit down and really work it out," he said to himself. "I'd better get going and hit this one today for sure." With that he began to break down the objectives, procedures, and installation steps of the project. He grinned as he reviewed the principles involved and calculated roughly the anticipated savings. "It's about time," he told himself. "This idea should have been followed up long ago." Chet remembered that he had first conceived of the open-end unit scheduling idea nearly a year and a half ago, just prior to his leaving Norris's Eastern Plant. He had spoken to his boss, Jim Quince, manager of the Eastern Plant, about it then, and both agreed that it was worth looking into. The idea was temporarily shelved when he was transferred to the Central Plant a month later.

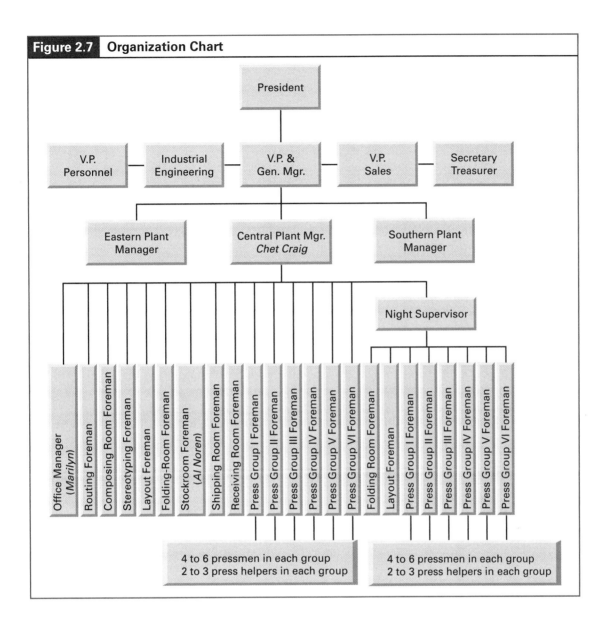

Figure 2.7   Organization Chart

A blast from a passing horn startled him, but his thoughts quickly returned to other plant projects he was determined to get underway. He started to think through a procedure for simpler transport of dies to and from the Eastern Plant. Visualizing the notes on his desk, he thought about the inventory analysis he needed to identify and eliminate some of the slow-moving stock items, the packing controls that needed revision, and the need to design a new special-order form. He also decided that this was the day to settle on a job printer to do the simple outside printing of office forms. There were a few other projects he couldn't recall offhand, but he could tend to them after lunch, if not before. "Yes, sir," he said to himself, "this is the day to really get rolling."

Chet's thoughts were interrupted as he pulled into the company parking lot. When he entered the plant Chet knew something was wrong as he met Al Noren, the stockroom foreman, who appeared troubled. "A great morning, Al," Chet greeted him cheerfully.

"Not so good, Chet; my new man isn't in this morning," Noren growled.

"Have you heard from him?" asked Chet.

"No, I haven't," replied Al.

Chet frowned as he commented, "These stock handlers assume you take it for granted that if they're not here, they're not here, and they don't have to call in and verify it. Better ask Personnel to call him."

Al hesitated for a moment before replying, "Okay, Chet, but can you find me a man? I have two cars to unload today."

As Chet turned to leave he said, "I'll call you in half an hour, Al, and let you know."

Making a mental note of the situation, Chet headed for his office. He greeted the group of workers huddled around Marilyn, the office manager, who was discussing the day's work schedule with them. As the meeting broke up, Marilyn picked up a few samples from the clasper, showed them to Chet, and asked if they should be shipped that way or if it would be necessary to inspect them. Before he could answer, Marilyn went on to ask if he could suggest another clerical operator for the sealing machine to replace the regular operator, who was home ill. She also told him that Gene, the industrial engineer, had called and was waiting to hear from Chet.

After telling Marilyn to go ahead and ship the samples, he made a note of the need for a sealer operator for the office and then called Gene. He agreed to stop by Gene's office before lunch and started on his routine morning tour of the plant. He asked each foreman the types and volumes of orders they were running, the number of people present, how the schedules were coming along, and the orders to be run next; helped the folding-room foreman find temporary storage space for consolidating a carload shipment; discussed quality control with a pressman who had been running poor work; arranged to transfer four people temporarily to different departments, including two for Al in the stockroom; and talked to the shipping foreman about pickups and special orders to be delivered that day. As he continued through the plant, he saw to it that reserve stock was moved out of the forward stock area, talked to another pressman about his requested change of vacation schedule, had a "heart-to-heart" talk with a press helper who seemed to need frequent reassurance, and approved two type and one color-order okays for different pressmen.

Returning to his office, Chet reviewed the production reports on the larger orders against his initial productions and found that the plant was running behind schedule. He called in the folding-room foreman and together they went over the lineup of machines and made several necessary changes.

During this discussion, the composing-room foreman stopped in to cover several type changes, and the routing foreman telephoned for approval of a revised printing schedule. The stockroom foreman called twice, first to inform him that two standard, fast-moving stock items were dangerously low, later to advise him that the paper stock for the urgent Dillion job had finally arrived. Chet made the necessary subsequent calls to inform those concerned.

He then began to put delivery dates on important and difficult inquiries received from customers and salesmen. (The routine inquiries were handled by Marilyn.) While he was doing this he was interrupted twice, once by a sales correspondent calling from the West Coast to ask for a better delivery date than originally scheduled, once by the personnel vice president asking him to set a time when he could hold an initial training and induction interview with a new employee.

After dating the customer and salesmen inquiries, Chet headed for his morning conference in the executive offices. At this meeting he answered the sales vice president's questions in connection with "hot" orders, complaints, and the status of large-volume orders and potential new orders. He then met with the general manager to discuss a few ticklish policy matters and to answer "the old man's" questions on several specific production and personnel problems. Before leaving the executive offices, he stopped at the office of the secretary-treasurer to inquire about delivery of cartons, paper, and boxes and to place a new order for paper.

On the way back to his own office, Chet conferred with Gene about two current engineering projects concerning which he had called earlier. When he reached his desk, he looked at his watch. It was 10 minutes before lunch, just time enough to make a few notes of the details he needed to check in order to answer the knotty questions raised by the sales manager that morning.

After lunch Chet started again. He began by checking the previous day's production reports, did some rescheduling to get out urgent orders, placed appropriate delivery dates on new orders and inquiries received that morning, and consulted with a foreman on a personal problem. He spent some 20 minutes at the TWX going over mutual problems with the Eastern Plant.

By midafternoon Chet had made another tour of the plant, after which he met with the personnel director to review with him a touchy personal problem raised by one of the clerical employees, the vacation schedules submitted by his foremen, and the pending job-evaluation program. Following this conference, Chet hurried back to his office to complete the special statistical report for Universal Waxing Corporation, one of Norris' best customers. As he finished the report, he discovered that it was 10 minutes after six and he was the only one left in the office. Chet was tired. He put on his coat and headed through the plant toward the parking lot; on the way he was stopped by both the night supervisor and night layout foremen for approval of type and layout changes.

With both eyes on the traffic, Chet reviewed the day he had just completed. "Busy?" he asked himself. "Too much so—but did I accomplish anything?" His mind raced over the day's activities. "Yes and no" seemed to be the answer. "There was the usual routine, the same as any other day. The plant kept going and I think it must have been a good production day. Any creative or special-project work done?" Chet grimaced as he reluctantly answered, "No."

With a feeling of guilt, he probed further. "Am I an executive? I'm paid like one, respected like one, and have a responsible assignment with the necessary authority to carry it out. Yet one of the greatest values a company derives from an executive is his creative thinking and accomplishments. What have I done about it? An executive needs some time for thinking. Today was a typical day, just like most other days, and I did little, if any, creative work. The projects that I so enthusiastically planned to work on this morning are exactly as they were yesterday. What's more, I have no guarantee that tomorrow night or the next night will bring me any closer to their completion. This is the real problem and there must be an answer."

Chet continued, "Night work? Yes, occasionally. This is understood. But I've been doing too much of this lately. I owe my wife and family some of my time. When you come down to it, they are the people for whom I'm really working. If I am forced to spend much more time away from them, I'm not meeting my own personal objectives. What about church work? Should I eliminate that? I spend a lot of time on this, but I feel I owe God some time, too. Besides, I believe I'm making a worthwhile contribution in this work. Perhaps I can squeeze a little time from my fraternal activities. But where does recreation fit in?"

Chet groped for the solution. "Maybe I'm just rationalizing because I schedule my own work poorly. But I don't think so. I've studied my work habits carefully and I think I plan intelligently and delegate authority. Do I need an assistant? Possibly, but that's a long-term project and I don't believe I could justify the additional overhead expenditure. Anyway, I doubt whether it would solve the problem."

By this time Chet had turned off the highway onto the side street leading to his home—the problem still uppermost in his mind. "I guess I really don't know the answer," he told himself as he pulled into his driveway. "This morning everything seemed so simple, but now . . . " His thoughts were interrupted as he saw his son running toward the car calling out, "Mommy, Daddy's home."

SOURCE: © *Kellogg School of Management, 1973, 2004. Used with permission.*

Discussion Questions

1. What principles of time and stress management are violated in this case?
2. What are the organizational problems in the case?
3. Which of Chet's personal characteristics inhibit his effective management of time?
4. If you were hired as a consultant to Chet, what would you advise him?

EXERCISES FOR LONG-TERM AND SHORT-RUN STRESS MANAGEMENT

In this section, we provide four relatively short exercises to help you practice good stress management. We strongly urge you to complete the exercises with a partner who can give you feedback and who will monitor your progress in improving your skill. Because managing stress is a personal skill, most of your practice will be done in private. But having a partner who is aware of your commitment will help foster substantial improvement.

The Small-Wins Strategy

An ancient Chinese proverb states that long journeys are always made up of small steps. In Japan, the feeling of obligation to make small, incremental improvements in one's work is known as kaizen. In this chapter the notion of small wins was explained as a way to break apart large problems and identify small successes in coping with them. Each of these approaches represents the same basic philosophy—to recognize incremental successes—and each helps an individual build up psychological resiliency to stress.

Assignment

Answer the following questions. An example is given to help clarify each question, but your response need not relate to the example.

1. What major stressor do you currently face? What creates anxiety or discomfort for you? (For example, "I have too much to do.")

2. What are the major attributes or components of the situation? Divide the major problem into smaller parts or subproblems. (For example, "I have said 'yes' to too many things. I have deadlines approaching. I don't have all the resources I need to complete all my commitments right now.")

3. What are the subcomponents of each of those subproblems? Divide them into yet smaller parts. (For example, "I have the following deadlines approaching: a report due, a large amount of reading to do, a family obligation, an important presentation, a need to spend some personal time with someone I care about, a committee meeting that requires preparation.")

Attribute 1:

Attribute 2:

Attribute 3:

And so on:

4. What actions can I take that will affect any of these subcomponents? (For example, "I can engage the person I care about in helping me prepare for the presentation. I can write a shorter report than I originally intended. I can carry the reading material with me wherever I go.")

5. What actions have I taken in the past that have helped me cope successfully with similar stressful circumstances? (For example, "I have found someone else to share some of my tasks. I have gotten some reading done while waiting, riding, and eating. I have prepared only key elements for the committee meeting.")

6. What small thing should I feel good about as I think about how I have coped or will cope with this major stressor? (For example, "I have accomplished a lot when the pressure has been on in the past. I have been able to use what I had time to prepare to its best advantage.")

Repeat this process when you face major stressors. The six specific questions may not be as important to you as (1) breaking the problem down into incremental parts and then breaking those parts down again, and (2) identifying actions that can be done that will be successful in coping with components of the stressor.

Life-Balance Analysis

The prescription to maintain a balanced life seems both intuitive and counterintuitive. On the one hand, it makes sense that life should have variety and that each of us should develop multiple aspects of ourselves. Narrowness and rigidity are not highly valued by anyone. On the other hand, the demands of work, school, or family, for example, can be so overwhelming that we don't have time to do much except respond to those demands. Work could take all of our time. So could school. So could family. The temptation for most of us, then, is to focus on only a few areas of our lives that demand our attention and leave the other areas undeveloped. This exercise helps you discover which areas those might be and which areas need more attention.

Assignment

Use Figure 2.8 below to complete this exercise. In responding to the four items in the exercise, think of the amount of time you spend in each area, the amount of experience and development you have had in the past in each area, and the extent to which development in each area is important to you.

1. In Figure 2.8, shade in the portion of each section that represents the extent to which that aspect of your life has been well developed. In other words, rate how satisfied you are that each aspect is adequately cultivated.

2. Now write down at least one thing you can start doing to improve your development in the areas that need it. For example, you might do more outside reading to develop culturally, invite a foreign visitor to your home to develop socially, engage in regular prayer or meditation to develop spiritually, begin a regular exercise program to develop physically, and so on.

Figure 2.8   Life-Balance Analysis Form

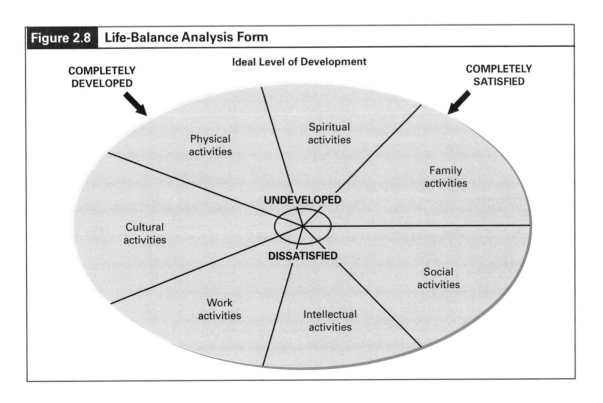

3. Because the intent of this exercise is not to add more pressure and stress to your life but to increase your resiliency through life balance, identify the things you will *stop* doing in various areas that will make it possible to achieve better life balance.

4. To make this a practice exercise and not just a planning exercise, do something today that you have on your list for items 2 and 3 above. Write down specifically what you'll do and when. Don't let the rest of the week go by without implementing something you've written.

Deep Relaxation

To engage in deep relaxation, you need to reserve time that can be spent concentrating on relaxation. Cognitive control and physiological control are involved. By focusing your mind, you can positively affect both your mental and physical states (Davis, Eshelman, & McKay, 1980). This exercise describes one technique that is easily learned and practiced.

The deep-relaxation technique presented below combines key elements of several well-known formulas. It is recommended that this technique be practiced for 20 minutes a day, three times a week. Reserve at least 30 minutes to engage in this exercise for the first time.

Find a quiet spot with a partner. You may want to do this in the classroom itself the first time. Have that person read the instructions below. Do not rush through the instructions. Allow time between each step to complete it unrushed. When you have finished, switch roles. (Since you will be practicing this exercise later in a different setting, you may want to make a tape recording of these instructions. Alternatively, agree to do the exercise regularly with a friend or a spouse.)

Assignment

Step 1: Assume a comfortable position. You may lie down. Loosen any tight clothing. Close your eyes and be quiet. Slow down and let go.

Step 2: Focus on your body and on relaxing specific muscles. Tune out all other thoughts. Assume a passive attitude.

Step 3: Now tense and relax each of your muscle groups for five to ten seconds each. Do it in the following order:

> *Forehead.* Wrinkle your forehead. Try to make your eyebrows touch your hairline for five seconds, then relax.
>
> *Eyes and nose.* Close your eyes as tightly as you can for five seconds, then relax.
>
> *Lips, cheeks, and jaw.* Draw the corners of your mouth back and grimace for five seconds, then relax.
>
> *Hands.* Extend your arms in front of you. Clench your fists tightly for five seconds, then relax.
>
> *Forearms.* Extend your arms out against an invisible wall and push forward for five seconds, then relax.

Upper arms. Bend your elbows and tense your biceps for five seconds, then relax.

Shoulders. Shrug your shoulders up to your ears for five seconds, then relax.

Back. Arch your back off the floor for five seconds, then relax.

Stomach. Tighten your stomach muscles by lifting your legs off the ground about two inches for five seconds, then relax.

Hips and buttocks. Tighten your hip and buttock muscles for five seconds, then relax.

Thighs. Tighten your thigh muscles by pressing your legs together as tightly as you can for five seconds, then relax.

Feet. Bend your ankles toward your body as far as you can for five seconds, then point your toes for five seconds, then relax.

Toes. Curl your toes as tightly as you can for five seconds, then relax.

Step 4: Focus on any muscles that are still tense. Repeat the exercise for that muscle group three or four times until it relaxes.

Step 5: Now focus on your breathing. Do not alter it artificially, but focus on taking long, slow, deep breaths. Breathe through your nose and exhale through your mouth. Concentrate exclusively on the rhythm of your breathing until you have taken at least 45 breaths.

Step 6: Now focus on the heaviness and warmth of your body. Let all the energy in your body seep away. Let go of your normal tendency to control your body and mobilize it toward activity.

Step 7: With your body completely relaxed, relax your mind. Picture a plain object such as a glass ball, an empty white vase, the moon, or some favorite thing. Don't analyze it; don't examine it; just picture it. Concentrate fully on the object for at least three minutes without letting any other thoughts enter your mind. Begin now.

Step 8: Now open your eyes, slowly get up, and return to your hectic, stressful, anxiety-ridden, Type-A environment better prepared to cope with it effectively.

Monitoring and Managing Time

Time management is the most often identified problem faced by managers and business school students. Most people feel overwhelmed at least part of the time with having too much to accomplish in too little time. It is interesting, however, that even though people may be extremely busy, if they feel that their time is *discretionary*—that is, it can be used in any way that they choose, such as in recreation, playing with friends or family, or by themselves—they feel less stress. Increasing discretionary time, therefore, is a key to effective time management.

This exercise helps you identify and better manage your discretionary time. It takes one full week to complete. It requires that you record how you spend your time for the next seven days. Virtually every executive who is a good time manager has completed this exercise and, in fact, regularly repeats this exercise.

Assignment

Complete the following five steps, then use a partner to get feedback and ideas for improving and refining your plans.

Step 1: Beginning today, keep a time log for one full week. Record how you spend each 30-minute block in the next seven 24-hour periods. Using the following format, record the log in your own notebook, diary, or journal. Simply write down what you did during the 30-minute period. If you did multiple things, record them one above the other.

TIME	ACTIVITY	REQUIRED/ DISCRETIONARY	PRODUCTIVE/ UNPRODUCTIVE
12:00–1:00			
1:00–1:30			
1:30–2:00			
2:00–3:00			
.			
.			
.			
23:00–23:30			
23:30–24:00			

Step 2: Beneath the heading "Required/Discretionary," write whether the time spent in each 30-minute block was required by someone or something else (R) or was discretionary (D). That is, to what extent did you have a choice about whether or not you would engage in this activity? You don't have a choice about a certain amount of sleep, for example, or attending class. But you do have a choice about watching TV or spending time socializing.

Step 3: Beneath the heading "Productive/Unproductive," rate the extent to which each activity was productive. That is, identify the extent to which the activity achieved what it was intended to achieve. To what extent did the activity accomplish your own goals or lead to improvements of some kind ? Use the following scale for your rating:

    4 Time was used productively
    3 Time was used somewhat productively
    2 Time was used somewhat unproductively
    1 Time was used unproductively

Step 4: Draw up a plan for increasing the amount of discretionary time you have during the week. Refer to the Time Management Survey in the Assessment Section for suggestions. Write down the things you will *stop* doing and *start* doing.

Step 5: Identify ways in which you can use your discretionary time more productively, especially any blocks of time you rated 1 or 2 in step 3. What will you do to make sure the time you control is used for more long-term benefit? What will you stop doing that impedes your effective use of time?

ACTIVITIES FOR MANAGING STRESS

Suggested Assignments

1. Do a systematic analysis of the stressors you face in your job, family, school, and social life. List the types of stressors you face, and identify strategies to eliminate or sharply reduce them. Record this analysis in your journal.

2. Find someone you know well who is experiencing a great deal of stress. Teach him or her how to manage that stress better by applying the concepts, principles, techniques, and exercises in this chapter. Describe what you taught and record the results in your journal.

3. Implement at least three of the time management techniques suggested in the Time Management Survey or elsewhere that you are not currently using but think you might find helpful. In your time log, keep track of the amount of time these techniques save you over a one-month period. Be sure to use that extra time productively.

4. With a coworker or colleague, identify ways in which your work at school, job, or home can be redesigned to reduce stress and increase productivity. Use the hints provided in the chapter to guide your redesign.

5. Write a personal principles statement. Specify precisely your core principles; those things you consider to be central to your life and your sense of self-worth; and the legacy you want to leave. Identify at least one thing that you want to accomplish in your life that you would like to be known for. Begin working on it today.

6. Establish a short-term goal or plan that you wish to accomplish this year. Make it compatible with the top priorities in your life. Specify the behavioral action steps, the reporting and accounting mechanisms, and the criteria of success and rewards as outlined in Figure 2.5. Share this plan with others you know so that you have an incentive to pursue it even after you finish this class.

7. Get a physical examination, then outline and implement a regular physical fitness and diet program. Even if it is just regular walking, do some kind of physical exercise at least three times a week. Preferably, institute a regular, vigorous cardiovascular fitness program. Record your progress in your journal.

8. Pick at least one long-term deep-relaxation technique. Learn it and practice it on a regular basis. Record your progress in your journal.

9. Establish a mentoring relationship with someone with whom you work or go to school. Your mentor may be a professor, a senior manager, or someone who has been around longer than you have. Make certain that the relationship is reciprocal and that it will help you cope with the stresses you face at work or school.

Application Plan and Evaluation

The intent of this exercise is to help you apply this cluster of skills in a real-life, out-of-class setting. Now that you have become familiar with the behavioral guidelines that form the basis of effective skill performance, you will improve most by trying out those guidelines in an everyday context. Unlike a classroom activity, in which feedback is immediate and others can assist you with their evaluations, this skill application activity is one you must accomplish and evaluate on your own. There are two parts to this activity. Part 1 helps prepare you to apply the skill. Part 2 helps you evaluate and improve on your experience. Be sure to write down answers to each item. Don't short-circuit the process by skipping steps.

Part 1. Planning

1. Write down the two or three aspects of this skill that are most important to you. These may be areas of weakness, areas you most want to improve, or areas that are most salient to a problem you face right now. Identify the specific aspects of this skill that you want to apply.

2. Now identify the setting or the situation in which you will apply this skill. Establish a plan for performance by actually writing down a description of the situation. Who else will be involved? When will you do it? Where will it be done?
   Circumstances:
   Who else?
   When?
   Where?

3. Identify the specific behaviors in which you will engage to apply this skill. Operationalize your skill performance.

4. What are the indicators of successful performance? How will you know you have been effective? What will indicate you have performed competently?

Part 2. Evaluation

5. After you have completed your implementation, record the results. What happened? How successful were you? What was the effect on others?

6. How can you improve? What modifications can you make next time? What will you do differently in a similar situation in the future?

7. Looking back on your whole skill practice and application experience, what have you learned? What has been surprising? In what ways might this experience help you in the long term?

APPLICATION

SCORING KEYS AND COMPARISON DATA

Stress Management Assessment

Scoring Key

SKILL AREA	ITEMS	ASSESSMENT	
		PRE-	POST-
Eliminating stressors	1, 5, 8, 9	_____	_____
Developing resiliency	2, 3, 6, 7	_____	_____
Short-term coping	4, 10	_____	_____
	Total Score	_____	_____

Comparison Data (N = 5,000 students)

Compare your scores to three standards:
1. The maximum possible score = 60.
2. The scores of other students in the class.
3. Norm data from more than 5,000 business school students.

Pre-Test				Post-Test
41.11	=	mean	=	47.84
48 or above	=	top quartile	=	53 or above
44–47	=	third quartile	=	48–52
39–43	=	second quartile	=	44–47
38 or below	=	bottom quartile	=	43 or below

Time Management Assessment

Scoring Key

To see how effective you are as a manager of your time, give yourself the following number of points for the boxes you checked:

POINTS	FREQUENCY
0	Never
1	Seldom
2	Sometimes
3	Usually
4	Always

If you completed only Section 1 of the assessment, double the scores for each category. Add up your total points for the 40 items.

First half score   _____

Second half score _____

Total score   _____

Comparison Data (N = 5,000 students)

Mean score:	92
Top quartile:	108 or above
Second quartile:	93–107
Third quartile:	78–92
Bottom quartile:	77 or below

Note: Sometimes people have markedly different scores in the two sections of this instrument. That is, they are better time managers at the office than in their personal lives, or vice versa. Compare your scores for each half of the instrument separately, and discuss with your colleagues how you interpret those scores.

Type A Personality Inventory

Scoring Key

The Type A Personality Inventory consists of four behavioral tendencies: extreme competitiveness, significant life imbalance (typically coupled with high work involvement), strong feelings of hostility and anger, and an extreme sense of urgency and impatience. Scores above 12 in each area suggest that you have a pronounced tendency toward Type A behavior.

COMPETITIVENESS		WORK INVOLVEMENT		HOSTILITY/ANGER		IMPATIENCE/URGENCY	
ITEM	SCORE	ITEM	SCORE	ITEM	SCORE	ITEM	SCORE
1	_____	2	_____	3	_____	4	_____
5	_____	6	_____	7	_____	8	_____
9	_____	10	_____	11	_____	12	_____
13	_____	14	_____	15	_____	16	_____
17	_____	18	_____	19	_____	20	_____
21	_____	22	_____	23	_____	24	_____
Total	_____	Total	_____	Total	_____	Total	_____

Total Score _____

Comparison Data (N = 5,000 students)

Scores above 12 in each of the four areas indicate a pronounced tendency toward that factor and, consequently, a detrimental effect on physiological, psychological, and social health.

Mean score:	45.83
Top quartile:	51 or above
Third quartile:	45–50

| Second quartile: | 40–44 |
| Bottom quartile: | 39 or below |

Social Readjustment Rating Scale

Scores of 150 points or below resulted in a probability of less than 37 percent that a serious illness would occur in the next year, but the probability increased to about 50 percent with scores of 150–300. Those who scored over 300 on the SRRS had an 80 percent chance of serious illness. Research results also show an injury rate among athletes five times as great for high scorers on the SRRS as for low scorers.

Comparison Data (N = 5,000 students)

Mean score:	257.76
Top quartile:	347 or above
Third quartile:	222–346
Second quartile:	123–221
Bottom quartile:	122 or below

Source of Personal Stress

This exercise does not have a solution or scoring data. Answers will vary among students. Solutions for this exercise are not available online.

SKILL *ASSESSMENT*

- Problem Solving, Creativity, and Innovation
- How Creative Are You?
- Innovative Attitude Scale
- Creative Style Assessment

SKILL *LEARNING*

- Problem Solving, Creativity, and Innovation
- Steps in Analytical Problem Solving
- Limitations of the Analytical Problem-Solving Model
- Impediments to Creative Problem Solving
- Multiple Approaches to Creativity
- Conceptual Blocks
- Conceptual Blockbusting
- International Caveats
- Hints for Applying Problem-Solving Techniques
- Fostering Creativity in Others
- Summary
- Behavioral Guidelines

SKILL *ANALYSIS*

- Chip and Bin
- Creativity at Apple

SKILL *PRACTICE*

- Individual Assignment—Analytical Problem Solving
- Team Assignment—Creative Problem Solving
- Moving Up in the Rankings
- Keith Dunn and McGuffey's Restaurant
- Creative Problem-Solving Practice

SKILL *APPLICATION*

- Suggested Assignments
- Application Plan and Evaluation

SCORING KEYS AND *COMPARISON DATA*

Solving Problems Analytically and Creatively

SKILL DEVELOPMENT OBJECTIVES

- INCREASE PROFICIENCY IN ANALYTICAL PROBLEM SOLVING

- RECOGNIZE PERSONAL CONCEPTUAL BLOCKS

- ENHANCE CREATIVITY BY OVERCOMING CONCEPTUAL BLOCKS

- FOSTER INNOVATION AMONG OTHERS

DIAGNOSTIC SURVEYS FOR CREATIVE PROBLEM SOLVING

PROBLEM SOLVING, CREATIVITY, AND INNOVATION

Step 1: Before you read the material in this chapter, please respond to the following statements by writing a number from the rating scale below in the left-hand column (Pre-assessment). Your answers should reflect your attitudes and behavior as they are now, not as you would like them to be. Be honest. This instrument is designed to help you discover your level of competency in problem solving and creativity so you can tailor your learning to your specific needs. When you have completed the survey, use the scoring key at the end of the chapter to identify the skill areas discussed in this chapter that are most important for you to master.

Step 2: After you have completed the reading and the exercises in this chapter and, ideally, as many as you can of the Skill Application assignments at the end of this chapter, cover up your first set of answers. Then respond to the same statements again, this time in the right-hand column (Post-assessment). When you have completed the survey, use the scoring key at the end of the chapter to measure your progress. If your score remains low in specific skill areas, use the behavioral guidelines at the end of the Skill Learning section to guide further practice.

Rating Scale

1 Strongly disagree
2 Disagree
3 Slightly disagree
4 Slightly agree
5 Agree
6 Strongly agree

Assessment

Pre-   Post-

When I encounter a routine problem:

_____   _____   1. I state clearly and explicitly what the problem is. I avoid trying to solve it until I have defined it.

_____   _____   2. I always generate more than one alternative solution to the problem, instead of identifying only one obvious solution.

_____   _____   3. I keep in mind both long-term and short-term consequences as I evaluate various alternative solutions.

_____   _____   4. I gather as much information as I can about what the problem is before trying to solve it.

_____   _____   5. I keep steps in the problem-solving process distinct; that is, I define the problem before proposing alternative solutions, and I generate alternatives before selecting a single solution.

When faced with an ambiguous or difficult problem that does not have an easy solution:

_____ _____ 6. I try out several definitions of the problem. I don't limit myself to just one way to define it.

_____ _____ 7. I try to be flexible in the way I approach the problem by trying out several different alternative methods rather than relying on the same approach every time.

_____ _____ 8. I try to find underlying patterns among elements in the problem so that I can uncover underlying dimensions or principles that help me understand the problem.

_____ _____ 9. I try to unfreeze my thinking by asking lots of questions about the nature of the problem before considering ways to solve it.

_____ _____ 10. I try to think about the problem from both the left (logical) side of my brain and the right (intuitive) side of my brain.

_____ _____ 11. To help me understand the problem and generate alternative solutions, I use analogies and metaphors that help me identify what else this problem is like.

_____ _____ 12. I sometimes reverse my initial definition of the problem to consider whether or not the exact opposite is also true.

_____ _____ 13. I do not evaluate the merits of an alternative solution to the problem before I have generated a list of alternatives. That is, I avoid selecting one solution until I have developed several possible solutions.

_____ _____ 14. I often break down the problem into smaller components and analyze each one separately.

_____ _____ 15. I have some specific techniques that I use to help develop creative and innovative solutions to problems.

When trying to foster more creativity and innovation among those with whom I work:

_____ _____ 16. I help arrange opportunities for individuals to work on their ideas outside the constraints of their normal job assignments.

_____ _____ 17. I make sure there are divergent points of view represented or expressed in every complex problem-solving situation.

_____ _____ 18. I sometimes make outrageous suggestions to stimulate people to find new ways of approaching problems.

_____ _____ 19. I try to acquire information from individuals outside the problem-solving group who will be affected by the decision, mainly to determine their preferences and expectations.

_____ _____ 20. I sometimes involve outsiders (e.g., customers or recognized experts) in problem-solving discussions.

_____ _____ 21. I try to provide recognition not only to those who come up with creative ideas (the idea champions) but also to those who support others' ideas (supporters) and who provide resources to implement them (orchestrators).

_____ _____ 22. I encourage informed rule-breaking in pursuit of creative solutions.

HOW CREATIVE ARE YOU?©

How creative are you? The following test helps you determine if you have the personality traits, attitudes, values, motivations, and interests that characterize creativity. It is based on several years' study of attributes possessed by men and women in a variety of fields and occupations who think and act creatively.

For each statement, write in the appropriate letter:

A Agree

B Undecided or Don't Know

C Disagree

Be as frank as possible. Try not to second-guess how a creative person might respond. Turn to the end of the chapter to find the answer key and an interpretation of your scores.

_____ 1. I always work with a great deal of certainty that I am following the correct procedure for solving a particular problem.

_____ 2. It would be a waste of time for me to ask questions if I had no hope of obtaining answers.

_____ 3. I concentrate harder on whatever interests me than do most people.

_____ 4. I feel that a logical step-by-step method is best for solving problems.

_____ 5. In groups I occasionally voice opinions that seem to turn some people off.

_____ 6. I spend a great deal of time thinking about what others think of me.

_____ 7. It is more important for me to do what I believe to be right than to try to win the approval of others.

_____ 8. People who seem uncertain about things lose my respect.

_____ 9. More than other people, I need to have things interesting and exciting.

_____ 10. I know how to keep my inner impulses in check.

_____ 11. I am able to stick with difficult problems over extended periods of time.

_____ 12. On occasion I get overly enthusiastic.

_____ 13. I often get my best ideas when doing nothing in particular.

_____ 14. I rely on intuitive hunches and the feeling of "rightness" or "wrongness" when moving toward the solution of a problem.

_____ 15. When problem solving, I work faster when analyzing the problem and slower when synthesizing the information I have gathered.

_____ 16. I sometimes get a kick out of breaking the rules and doing things I am not supposed to do.

_____ 17. I like hobbies that involve collecting things.

_____ 18. Daydreaming has provided the impetus for many of my more important projects.

_____ 19. I like people who are objective and rational.

_____ 20. If I had to choose from two occupations other than the one I now have, I would rather be a physician than an explorer.

_____ 21. I can get along more easily with people if they belong to about the same social and business class as myself.

_____ 22. I have a high degree of aesthetic sensitivity.

_____ 23. I am driven to achieve high status and power in life.

_____ 24. I like people who are sure of their conclusions.

_____ 25. Inspiration has nothing to do with the successful solution of problems.

_____ 26. When I am in an argument, my greatest pleasure would be for the person who disagrees with me to become a friend, even at the price of sacrificing my point of view.

_____ 27. I am much more interested in coming up with new ideas than in trying to sell them to others.

_____ 28. I would enjoy spending an entire day alone, just "chewing the mental cud."

_____ 29. I tend to avoid situations in which I might feel inferior.

_____ 30. In evaluating information, the source is more important to me than the content.

_____ 31. I resent things being uncertain and unpredictable.

_____ 32. I like people who follow the rule "business before pleasure."

_____ 33. Self-respect is much more important than the respect of others.

_____ 34. I feel that people who strive for perfection are unwise.

_____ 35. I prefer to work with others in a team effort rather than solo.

36. I like work in which I must influence others.
37. Many problems that I encounter in life cannot be resolved in terms of right or wrong solutions.
38. It is important for me to have a place for everything and everything in its place.
39. Writers who use strange and unusual words merely want to show off.
40. Below is a list of terms that describe people. Choose 10 words that best characterize you.

energetic	persuasive	observant
fashionable	self-confident	persevering
original	cautious	habit-bound
resourceful	egotistical	independent
stern	predictable	formal
informal	dedicated	forward-looking
factual	open-minded	tactful
inhibited	enthusiastic	innovative
poised	acquisitive	practical
alert	curious	organized
unemotional	clear-thinking	understanding
dynamic	self-demanding	polished
courageous	efficient	helpful
perceptive	quick	good-natured
thorough	impulsive	determined
realistic	modest	involved
absent-minded	flexible	sociable
well-liked	restless	retiring

SOURCE: *Excerpted from* How Creative Are You? *By Eugene Raudsepp.*
Copyright ©1981 by Eugene Raudsepp. Used by permission. Published by
Perigee Books/G.P. Putnam's Sons, Inc.

INNOVATIVE ATTITUDE SCALE

Indicate the extent to which each of the following statements is true of either your actual behavior or your intentions at work. That is, describe the way you are or the way you intend to be on the job. Use the scale for your responses.

Rating Scale

5 Almost always true
4 Often true
3 Not applicable
2 Seldom true
1 Almost never true

1. I openly discuss with my fellow students and colleagues how to get ahead.
2. I try new ideas and approaches to problems.
3. I take things or situations apart to find out how they work.
4. I welcome uncertainty and unusual circumstances related to my tasks.
5. I maintain an open dialogue with others who disagree with me.
6. I can be counted on to find a new use for existing methods or equipment.
7. I will usually be the first to try out a new idea or method among my colleagues or fellow students.

_____ 8. I take the opportunity to incorporate ideas from other fields or disciplines in my work.
_____ 9. I demonstrate originality in my work.
_____ 10. I will willingly work on a problem that has caused others great difficulty.
_____ 11. I provide important input regarding new solutions when working in a group.
_____ 12. I avoid jumping to conclusions about others' proposed ideas.
_____ 13. I develop contacts with experts outside my area of interest or specialty.
_____ 14. I use personal contacts to expand my options for new jobs or assignments.
_____ 15. I make time to pursue my own pet ideas or projects.
_____ 16. I set aside resources for pursuing a risky project that interests me.
_____ 17. I tolerate people who depart from organizational routine.
_____ 18. I speak out in class and in meetings.
_____ 19. I am good at working in teams to solve complex problems.
_____ 20. If my fellow students or colleagues are asked, they will say I am a wit.

SOURCE: *Innovative Attitude Scale, John E. Ettlie & Robert D. O'Keefe (1982), "Innovative Attitudes, Values, and Intentions in Organizations,"* Journal of Management Studies, *19: 163–182.*

CREATIVE STYLE ASSESSMENT

Four alternatives exist in each of the items below. You should divide 100 points among each of the four alternatives depending on which alternative is most similar to you. Rate yourself as you are right now, not as you would like to be or as you think you should be. No correct answers exist, so be as accurate as you can. For example, in question 1, if you think alternative "A" is very similar to you, "B" is somewhat similar, and "C" and "D" are hardly similar at all, you might give 50 points to A, 30 points to B, and 10 points each to C and D. Any combination of numbers is acceptable, including 100, 0, 0, 0, or 25, 25, 25, 25. **Just be sure that for each question, the total points add up to 100.**

1. I usually approach difficult problems by:

_____ a. Brainstorming solutions

_____ b. Carefully evaluating alternatives

_____ c. Engaging other people

_____ d. Responding quickly

100

2. My friends and colleagues usually think of me as:

_____ a. Creative

_____ b. Systematic

_____ c. Collaborative

_____ d. Competitive

100

3. I am good at:

_____ a. Experimenting

_____ b. Administering

_____ c. Empowering people

_____ d. Meeting challenges

100

4. When I complete a project or an assignment, I am likely to:

_____ a. Come up with a new project

_____ b. Review the results to see how I might be able to improve them

_____ c. Share what I have learned with others

_____ d. Determine the grade or the evaluation of the results

100

5. I would describe myself as:

_____ a. Flexible

_____ b. Organized

_____ c. Supportive

_____ d. Driven

100

6. I like to work on projects that:

_____ a. Let me invent something new

_____ b. Create practical improvements

_____ c. Get other people involved

_____ d. Can be completed quickly

100

7. When solving a problem, I:

_____ a. Enjoy exploring a lot of options

_____ b. Collect a lot of data

_____ c. Communicate a lot with others

_____ d. Emphasize getting the job done

100

SOURCE: *Adapted from "Creative Style Assessment," J. DeGraff and K.A. Lawerence, (2002).*
Creativity at Work. *San Francisco: Jossey-Bass, pp. 46–49.* © *by John Wiley and Sons.*

Problem Solving, Creativity, and Innovation

Problem solving is a skill that is required of every person in almost every aspect of life. Seldom does an hour go by without an individual's being faced with the need to solve some kind of problem. The manager's job, in particular, is inherently a problem-solving job. If there were no problems in organizations, there would be no need for managers. Therefore, it is hard to conceive of an incompetent problem solver succeeding as a manager.

In this chapter we offer specific guidelines and techniques for improving problem-solving skills. Two kinds of problem solving—analytical and creative—are addressed. Effective managers are able to solve problems both analytically and creatively, even though different skills are required for each type of problem. First we discuss analytical problem solving—the kind of problem solving that managers use many times each day. Then we turn to creative problem solving, a kind of problem solving that occurs less frequently. Yet this creative problem-solving ability often separates career successes from career failures, heroes from goats, and achievers from derailed executives. It can also produce a dramatic impact on organizational effectiveness. A great deal of research has highlighted the positive relationship between creative problem solving and successful organizations (Sternberg, 1999). This chapter provides guidelines for how you can become a more effective problem solver, both analytical and creative, and concludes with a brief discussion of how managers can foster creative problem solving and innovation among the people with whom they work.

Steps in Analytical Problem Solving

Most people, including managers, don't particularly like problems. Problems are time consuming, they create stress, and they never seem to go away. In fact, most people try to get rid of problems as soon as they can. Their natural tendency is to select the first reasonable solution that comes to mind (Koopman, Broekhuijsen, & Weirdsma, 1998; March, 1994; March & Simon, 1958). Unfortunately, that first solution is often not the best one. In typical problem solving, most people implement a marginally acceptable or merely satisfactory solution instead of the optimal or ideal solution. In fact, many observers have attributed the extensive failures of Internet and dot.com firms—as well as more established companies—to the abandonment of correct problem-solving principles by managers. Shortcuts in analytical problem solving by managers and entrepreneurs, they argue, have had a major negative effect on company survival (Goll & Rasheed, 1997). Malcolm Gladwell, in his intriguing book entitled *Blink* (2005), argued that people are able to make decisions and reach conclusions on very, very little data—thin slices of behavior—because of their intuitive sense. In one or two seconds people can reach a conclusion that is as valid as the one made after studying a problem for a long time. First impressions count, he argued, and are valid a lot of the time. These first impressions and instantaneous judgments are valid, however, mainly when problems are not complex, when people have experience with the issue they are judging, and when they have developed an attunement to their own internal cues (that is, they have developed adequate self-awareness and emotional intelligence). Most of the time, the problems we face are complicated, multifaceted, and ambiguous. In such instances, effective problem-solving techniques are required, and they rely on a systematic and logical approach. This approach involves at least four steps, which are explained next.

DEFINING THE PROBLEM

The most widely accepted model of analytical problem solving is summarized in Table 3.1. This method is well known and widely utilized in firms, and it lies at the heart of the quality improvement movement. It is widely asserted that to improve effectiveness of individuals and organizations, an essential step is to learn and apply this analytical method of problem solving (see, for example, Juran, 1988; Riley, 1998). Many large organizations (e.g., Ford Motor Company, General Electric, Hewlett-Packard), for example, spend millions of dollars to teach their managers this type of problem solving as part of their productivity and improvement process. Variations on this four-step approach have been implemented in various firms (e.g., Ford uses an eight-step approach), but all the steps are merely derivations of the standard model we discuss here.

Table 3.1 A Model of Problem Solving

Step	Characteristics
1. Define the problem.	• Differentiate fact from opinion. • Specify underlying causes. • Tap everyone involved for information. • State the problem explicitly. • Identify what standard is violated. • Determine whose problem it is. • Avoid stating the problem as a disguised solution.
2. Generate alternative solutions.	• Postpone evaluating alternatives. • Be sure all involved individuals generate alternatives. • Specify alternatives that are consistent with goals. • Specify both short-term and long-term alternatives. • Build on others' ideas. • Specify alternatives that solve the problem.
3. Evaluate and select an alternative.	• Evaluate relative to an optimal standard. • Evaluate systematically. • Evaluate relative to goals. • Evaluate main effects and side effects. • State the selected alternative explicitly.
4. Implement and follow up on the solution.	• Implement at the proper time and in the right sequence. • Provide opportunities for feedback. • Engender acceptance of those who are affected. • Establish an ongoing monitoring system. • Evaluate based on problem solution.

LEARNING

The first step is to *define* a problem. This involves diagnosing a situation so that the focus is on the real problem, not just its symptoms. For example, suppose you must deal with an employee who consistently fails to get work done on time. Slow work might be the problem, or it might be only a symptom of another underlying problem such as bad health, low morale, lack of training, or inadequate rewards. Defining the problem, therefore, requires a wide search for information. The more relevant information that is acquired, the more likely it is that the problem will be defined accurately. As Charles Kettering put it, "It ain't the things you don't know that'll get you in trouble, but the things you know for sure that ain't so."

Following are some attributes of good problem definition:

1. Factual information is differentiated from opinion or speculation. Objective data are separated from perceptions and suppositions.
2. All individuals involved are tapped as information sources. Broad participation is encouraged.
3. The problem is stated explicitly. This often helps point out ambiguities in the definition.
4. The problem definition clearly identifies what standard or expectation has been violated. Problems, by their very nature, involve the violation of some standard or expectation.

5. The problem definition must address the question "Whose problem is this?" No problems are completely independent of people. Identify for whom this is a problem.

6. The definition is not simply a disguised solution. Saying "The problem is that we need to motivate slow employees" is inappropriate because the problem is stated as a solution. The problem should be described, not resolved.

Managers often propose a solution before an adequate definition of a problem has been given. This may lead to solving the wrong problem or to reaching conclusions that are misleading or inadequate. Effectively identifying the problem in Iraq, for example, or in the merger of Daimler and Chrysler into one company, required careful analysis. Premature problem definition can become problematic. The definition step in problem solving, therefore, is extremely important.

GENERATING ALTERNATIVES

The second step is to generate alternative solutions. This requires postponing the selection of any one solution until several alternatives have been proposed. Much research on problem solving (e.g., March, 1999) supports the prescription that the quality of solutions can be significantly enhanced by considering multiple alternatives. Judgment and evaluation, therefore, must be postponed so the first acceptable solution suggested isn't the one immediately selected. The problem with evaluating and selecting an alternative too early is that we may rule out some good ideas by just not getting around to thinking about them. We hit on an idea that sounds good and we go with it, thereby never even thinking of alternatives that may be better in the long run.

Many alternative solutions should be produced before any of them are evaluated. A common problem in managerial decision making is that alternatives are evaluated as they are proposed, so the first acceptable (although frequently not optimal) one is chosen.

Some attributes of good alternative generation follow:

1. The evaluation of each proposed alternative is postponed. All relevant alternatives should be proposed before evaluation is allowed.

2. Alternatives are proposed by all individuals involved in the problem. Broad participation in proposing alternatives improves solution quality and group acceptance.

3. Alternative solutions are consistent with organizational goals or policies. Subversion and criticism are detrimental to both the organization and the alternative generation process.

4. Alternatives take into consideration both short-term and long-term consequences.

5. Alternatives build on one another. Bad ideas may become good ones if they are combined with or modified by other ideas.

6. Alternatives solve the problem that has been defined. Another problem may also be important, but it should be ignored if it does not directly affect the problem being considered.

EVALUATING ALTERNATIVES

The third problem-solving step is to evaluate and select an alternative. This step involves careful weighing of the advantages and disadvantages of the proposed alternatives before making a final selection. In selecting the best alternative, skilled problem solvers make sure that alternatives are judged in terms of the extent to which they will solve the problem without causing other unanticipated problems; the extent to which all individuals involved will accept the alternative; the extent to which implementation of the alternative is likely; and the extent to which the alternative fits within organizational constraints (e.g., is consistent with policies, norms, and budget limitations). Care is taken not to short-circuit these considerations by choosing the most conspicuous alternative without considering others. The classic description of the difficulty with problem solving—made almost 50 years ago—still remains as a core principle in problem solving (March & Simon, 1958):

> Most human decision making, whether individual or organizational, is concerned with the discovery and selection of satisfactory alternatives; only in exceptional cases is it concerned with the discovery and selection of optimal alternatives. To optimize requires processes several orders of magnitude more complex than those required to satisfy. An example is the difference between searching a haystack to find the sharpest needle in it and searching the haystack to find a needle sharp enough to sew with.

Given the natural tendency to select the first satisfactory solution proposed, this step deserves particular attention in problem solving. Some attributes of good evaluation are:

1. Alternatives are evaluated relative to an optimal, rather than a satisfactory standard. Determine what is best rather than just what will work.
2. Evaluation of alternatives occurs systematically so each alternative is given due consideration. Short-circuiting evaluation inhibits selection of optimal alternatives, so adequate time for evaluation and consideration should be allowed.
3. Alternatives are evaluated in terms of the goals of the organization and the needs and expectations of the individuals involved. Organizational goals should be met, but individual preferences should also be considered.
4. Alternatives are evaluated in terms of their probable effects. Both side effects and direct effects on the problem are considered, as well as long-term and short-term effects.
5. The alternative ultimately selected is stated explicitly. This can help ensure that everyone involved understands and agrees with the same solution, and it uncovers ambiguities.

IMPLEMENTING THE SOLUTION

The final step is to implement and follow up on the solution. A surprising amount of the time, people faced with a problem will try to jump to step 4 before having gone through steps 1 through 3. That is, they react to a problem by trying to implement a solution before they have defined it, analyzed it, or generated and evaluated alternative solutions. It is important to remember, therefore, that "getting rid of the problem" by solving it will not occur successfully without the first three steps in the process.

Implementing any problem solution requires sensitivity to possible resistance from those who will be affected by it. Almost any change engenders some resistance. Therefore, the best problem solvers are careful to select a strategy that maximizes the probability that the solution will be accepted and fully implemented. This may involve ordering that the solution be implemented by others, "selling" the solution to others, or involving others in the implementation. Several authors (e.g., Dutton & Ashford, 1993; Miller, Hickson, & Wilson, 1996; Vroom & Yetton, 1973) have provided guidelines for managers to determine which of these implementation behaviors is most appropriate under which circumstances. Generally speaking, participation by others in

the implementation of a solution will increase its acceptance and decrease resistance (Black & Gregersen, 1997).

Effective implementation is usually most effective when it is accomplished in small steps or increments. Weick (1984) introduced the idea of "small wins" in which solutions to problems are implemented little by little. The idea is, implement a part of the solution that is easy to accomplish, then make the successful implementation public. Follow that up by implementing another part of the solution that is easy to accomplish, and publicize it again. Continue implementing incrementally to achieve small wins. This strategy decreases resistance (small changes are usually not worth fighting over), creates support as others observe progress (a bandwagon effect occurs), and reduces costs (failure is not career-ending, and large allocations of resources are not required before success is assured). It also helps ensure persistence and perseverance in implementation. Calvin Coolidge's well-known quotation is apropos:

Nothing in the world can take the place of perseverance. Talent will not; nothing is more common than unsuccessful people with talent. Genius will not; unrewarded genius is almost a proverb. Education will not; the world is full of educated derelicts. Persistence and determination alone are omnipotent.

Of course, any implementation requires follow-up to prevent negative side effects and ensure solution of the problem. Follow-up not only helps ensure effective implementation, but it also serves a feedback function by providing information that can be used to improve future problem solving.

Some attributes of effective implementation and follow-up are:

1. Implementation occurs at the right time and in the proper sequence. It does not ignore constraining factors, and it does not come before steps 1, 2, and 3 in the problem-solving process.
2. Implementation occurs using a "small wins" strategy in order to discourage resistance and engender support.
3. The implementation process includes opportunities for feedback. How well the solution works is communicated and recurring information exchange occurs.
4. Participation by individuals affected by the problem solution is facilitated in order to create support and commitment.

5. An ongoing measurement and monitoring system is set up for the implemented solution. Long-term as well as short-term effects are assessed.

6. Evaluation of success is based on problem solution, not on side benefits. Although the solution may provide some positive outcomes, it is unsuccessful unless it solves the problem being considered.

Limitations of the Analytical Problem-Solving Model

Most experienced problem solvers are familiar with the preceding steps in analytical problem solving, which are based on empirical research results and sound rationale (March, 1994; Miller, Hickson, & Wilson, 1996; Mitroff, 1998; Zeitz, 1999). Unfortunately, managers do not always practice these steps. The demands of their jobs often pressure managers into circumventing some steps, and problem solving suffers as a result. When these four steps are followed, however, effective problem solving is markedly enhanced.

On the other hand, simply learning about and practicing these four steps does not guarantee that an individual will effectively solve all types of problems. These problem-solving steps are most effective mainly when the problems faced are straightforward, when alternatives are readily definable, when relevant information is available, and when a clear standard exists against which to judge the correctness of a solution. The main tasks are to agree upon a single definition, gather the accessible information, generate alternatives, and make an informed choice. But many managerial problems are not of this type. Definitions, information, alternatives, and standards are seldom unambiguous or readily available. In a complex, fast-paced, digital world, these conditions appear less and less frequently. Hence, knowing the steps in problem solving and being able to implement them are not necessarily the same thing.

For example, problems such as discovering why morale is so low, determining how to implement downsizing without antagonizing employees, developing a new process that will double productivity and improve customer satisfaction, or identifying ways to overcome resistance to change are common—and often very complicated—problems faced by most managers. Such problems may not always have an easily identifiable definition or set of alternative solutions available. It may not be clear how much information is needed, what the complete set of alternatives is, or how one knows if the information being obtained is accurate. Analytical problem solving may help, but

something more is needed to address these problems successfully. Tom Peters said, in characterizing the modern world faced by managers: "If you're not confused, you're not paying attention."

Table 3.2 summarizes some reasons why analytical problem solving is not always effective in day-to-day managerial situations. Constraints exist on each of these four steps and stem from other individuals, from organizational processes, or from the external environment that make it difficult to follow the prescribed model. Moreover, some problems are simply not amenable to systematic or rational analysis. Sufficient and accurate information may not be available, outcomes may not be predictable, or means-ends connections may not be evident. In order to solve such problems, a new way of thinking may be required, multiple or conflicting definitions may be needed, and unprecedented alternatives may have to be generated. In short, creative problem solving must be used.

Impediments to Creative Problem Solving

As mentioned in the beginning of the chapter, analytical problem solving is focused on getting rid of problems. Creative problem solving is focused on generating something new (DeGraff & Lawrence, 2002). The trouble is, most people have trouble solving problems creatively. There are two reasons why. First, most of us misinterpret creativity as being one-dimensional—that is, creativity is limited to generating new ideas. We are not aware of the multiple strategies available for being creative, so our repertoire is restricted. Second, all of us have developed certain conceptual blocks in our problem-solving activities, of which we are mostly not aware. These blocks inhibit us from solving certain problems effectively. These blocks are largely personal, as opposed to interpersonal or organizational, so skill development is required to overcome them.

In this chapter, we focus primarily on the individual skills involved in becoming a better creative problem solver. A large literature exists on how managers and leaders can foster creativity in organizations, but this is not our focus (Zhou & Shalley, 2003). Rather, we are interested in helping you strengthen and develop your personal skills and expand your repertoire of creative problem-solving alternatives. We spend most of our time in this chapter on the problem of conceptual blocks inasmuch as it is the obstacle people have the most difficulty addressing. However, the first problem—the need to develop multiple approaches to creativity—is also important and is addressed in the section that follows.

Table 3.2	Some Constraints on the Analytical Problem-Solving Model
STEP	**CONSTRAINTS**
1. Define the problem.	• There is seldom consensus as to the definition of the problem.
	• There is often uncertainty as to whose definition will be accepted.
	• Problems are usually defined in terms of the solutions already possessed.
	• Symptoms get confused with the real problem.
	• Confusing information inhibits problem identification.
2. Generate alternative solutions.	• Solution alternatives are usually evaluated one at a time as they are proposed.
	• Few of the possible alternatives are usually known.
	• The first acceptable solution is usually accepted.
	• Alternatives are based on what was successful in the past.
3. Evaluate and select an alternative.	• Limited information about each alternative is usually available.
	• Search for information occurs close to home—in easily accessible places.
	• The type of information available is constrained by factors such as primacy versus recency, extremity versus centrality, expected versus surprising, and correlation versus causation.
	• Gathering information on each alternative is costly.
	• Preferences of which is the best alternative are not always known.
	• Satisfactory solutions, not optimal ones, are usually accepted.
	• Solutions are often selected by oversight or default.
	• Solutions often are implemented before the problem is defined.
4. Implement and follow up on the solution.	• Acceptance by others of the solution is not always forthcoming.
	• Resistance to change is a universal phenomenon.
	• It is not always clear what part of the solution should be monitored or measured in follow-up.
	• Political and organizational processes must be managed in any implementation effort.
	• It may take a long time to implement a solution.

Multiple Approaches to Creativity

One of the most sophisticated approaches to creativity identifies four distinct methods for achieving it. This approach is based on the Competing Values Framework (Cameron, Quinn, DeGraff, & Thakor, 2006), which identifies competing or conflicting dimensions that describe people's attitudes, values, and behaviors. Figure 3.1 describes the four different types of creativity and the relationships. These four types were developed by our colleague Jeff DeGraff (DeGraff & Lawrence, 2002).

For example, achieving creativity through **imagination** refers to the *creation* of new ideas, breakthroughs, and radical approaches to problem solving. People who pursue creativity in this way tend to be experimenters, speculators, and entrepreneurs,

Figure 3.1 | Four Types of Creativity

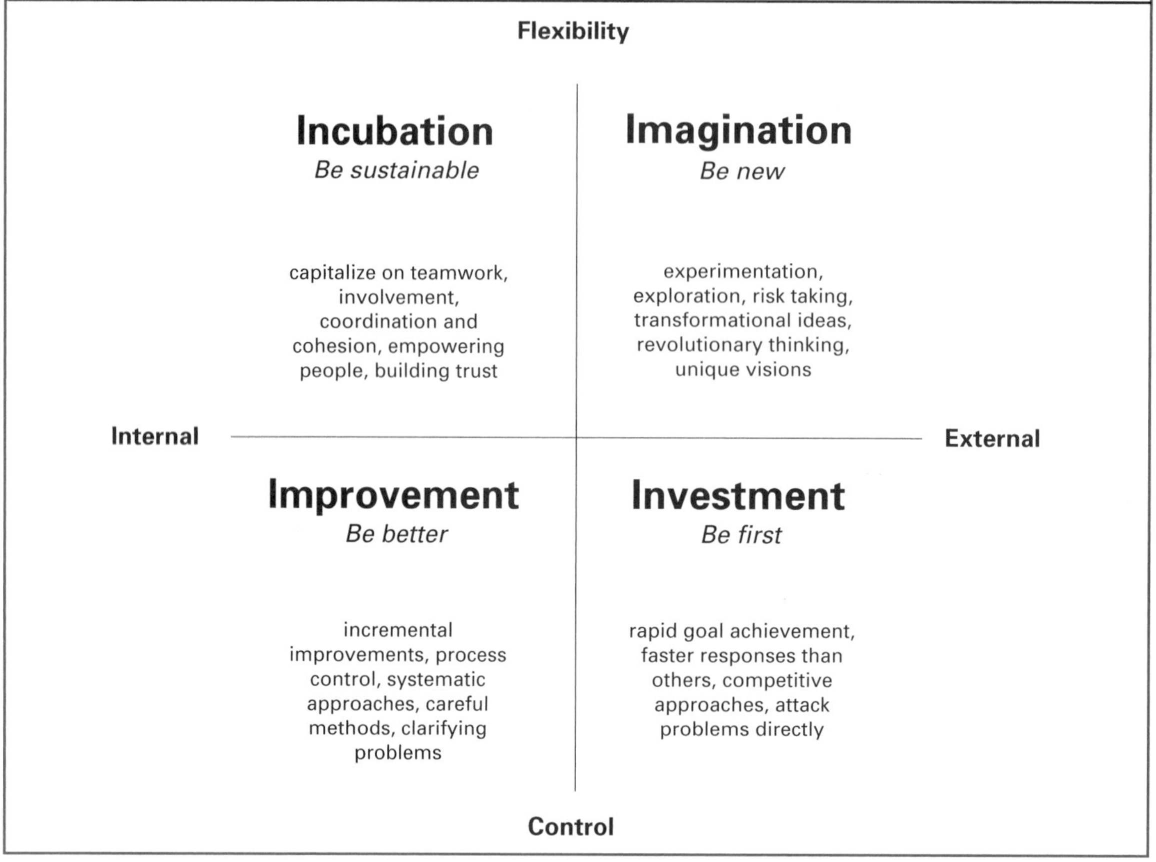

Flexibility

Incubation
Be sustainable

capitalize on teamwork,
involvement,
coordination and
cohesion, empowering
people, building trust

Imagination
Be new

experimentation,
exploration, risk taking,
transformational ideas,
revolutionary thinking,
unique visions

Internal ———————————————— **External**

Improvement
Be better

incremental
improvements, process
control, systematic
approaches, careful
methods, clarifying
problems

Investment
Be first

rapid goal achievement,
faster responses than
others, competitive
approaches, attack
problems directly

Control

SOURCE: *Adapted from DeGraff & Lawrence, 2002.*

and they define creativity as exploration, new product innovation, or developing unique visions of possibilities. When facing difficult problems in need of problem solving, their approach is focused on coming up with revolutionary possibilities and unique solutions. Well-known examples include Steve Jobs at Apple, the developer of the iPod and the Macintosh computer, and Walt Disney, the creator of animated movies and theme parks. Both of these people approached problem solving by generating radically new ideas and products that created entirely new industries. The most famous design firm in the world—*Ideo* in Palo Alto, California—produces more than 90 new products a year and has become renowned for creating product designs that no one had ever thought of before—neat-squeeze toothpaste containers, computer mouses, flat-screen monitors, Nerf footballs. They hire radical thinkers, rule breakers, and risk takers to think "outside the box."

People may also achieve creativity, however, through opposite means—that is, by developing incrementally better alternatives, *improving* on what already exists, or clarifying the ambiguity that is associated with the problem. Rather than being revolutionaries and risk takers, they are systematic, careful, and thorough. Creativity comes by finding ways to improve processes or functions. An example is Ray Kroc, the magician behind McDonald's remarkable success. As a salesman in the 1950s, Kroc bought out a restaurant in San Bernardino, California, from the McDonald brothers and, by creatively changing the way hamburgers were made and served, he created the largest food service company in the world. He didn't invent fast food— White Castle and Dairy Queen had long been established—but he changed the processes. Creating a limited, standardized menu, uniform cooking procedures, consistent service quality, cleanliness of facilities, and inexpensive food—no matter where in the country (and now, in the world) you eat—demonstrated a very different approach to creativity. Instead of breakthrough ideas, Kroc's secret was incremental improvements on existing ideas. This type of creativity is referred to as **improvement**.

A third type of creativity is called **investment**, or the pursuit of rapid goal achievement and *competitiveness*. People who approach creativity in this way meet challenges head on, adopt a competitive posture, and focus on achieving results faster than others. People achieve creativity by working harder than the competition, exploiting others' weaknesses, and being first to offer a product, service, or idea. The advantages of being a "first mover" company are well-known. This kind of creativity can be illustrated by Honda President Kawashima in the "Honda-Yamaha Motorcycle War." Honda became the industry leader in motorcycles in Japan in the 1960s but decided to enter the automobile market in the 1970s. Yamaha saw this as an opportunity to overtake Honda in motorcycle market share in Japan. In public speeches at the beginning of the 1980s, Yamaha's President Koike promised that Yamaha would soon overtake Honda in motorcycle production because of Honda's new focus on automobiles. "In a year we will be the domestic leader, and in two years we will be number one in the world," touted Koike in his 1982 shareholders' meeting. At the beginning of 1983, Honda's president replied: "As long as I am president of this company, we will surrender our number one spot to no one . . . *Yamaha wo tubusu*!"—meaning, we will smash, break, annihilate, destroy Yamaha. In the next year, Honda introduced 81 new models of motorcycles and discontinued 32 models for a total of 113 changes to its product line. In the following year, Honda introduced 39 additional models and added 18 changes to the 50cc line. Yamaha's sales plummeted 50 percent and the firm endured a loss of 24 billion yen for the year. Yamaha's president conceded: "I would like to end the Honda-Yamaha war . . . From now on we will move cautiously and ensure Yamaha's relative position as second to Honda." Approaching creativity through investment—rapid response, competitive maneuvering, and being the first mover—characterized Honda president Kawashima's approach to creativity.

The fourth type of creativity is **incubation**. This refers to an approach to creative activity through teamwork, involvement, and coordination among individuals. Creativity occurs by unlocking the potential that exists in interactions among networks of people. Individuals who approach creativity through incubation encourage people to work together, foster trust and cohesion, and empower others. Creativity arises from a collective mind-set and shared values. For example, Mahatma Gandhi was probably the only person in modern history who has single-handedly stopped a war. Lone individuals have started wars, but Gandhi was creative enough to stop one. He did so by mobilizing networks of people to pursue a clear vision and set of values. Gandhi would probably have been completely noncreative and ineffective had he not been adept at capitalizing on incubation dynamics. By mobilizing people to march to the sea to make salt, or to burn passes that demarcated ethnic group status, Gandhi was able to engender creative outcomes that had not been considered possible. He was a master at incubation by connecting, involving, and coordinating people. The same could be said for Bill Wilson, the founder of Alcoholics Anonymous, whose 12-step program is the foundation for almost all addiction treatment organizations around the world—gambling addiction, drug addiction, eating disorders, and so on. To cure his own alcoholism, Wilson began meeting with others with the same problem and, over time, developed a very creative way to help himself as well as other people overcome their dependencies. The genius behind Alcoholics Anonymous is the creativity that emerges when human interactions are facilitated and encouraged.

Figure 3.2 helps place these four types of creativity into perspective. You will note that imagination and improvement emphasize opposite approaches to creativity. They differ in the *magnitude* of the creative ideas being pursued. Imagination focuses on new, revolutionary solutions to problems. Improvement focuses on incremental, controlled solutions. Investment and incubation are also contradictory and opposing in their approach to creativity. They differ in *speed* of response. Investment focuses on fast, competitive responses to problems, whereas incubation emphasizes more developmental and deliberate responses.

It is important to point out that no one approach to creativity is best. Different circumstances call for different approaches. For example, Ray Kroc and McDonald's would not have been successful with an imagination strategy (revolutionary change), and Walt Disney would not have been effective with an incubation strategy (group consensus). Kawashima at Honda could not afford to wait for an incubation strategy (slow, developmental change), whereas it would have made no sense for Gandhi to approach creativity using investment (a competitive approach). Different circumstances require different approaches. Circumstances in which each of these four approaches to creativity are most effective are listed in Figure 3.3.

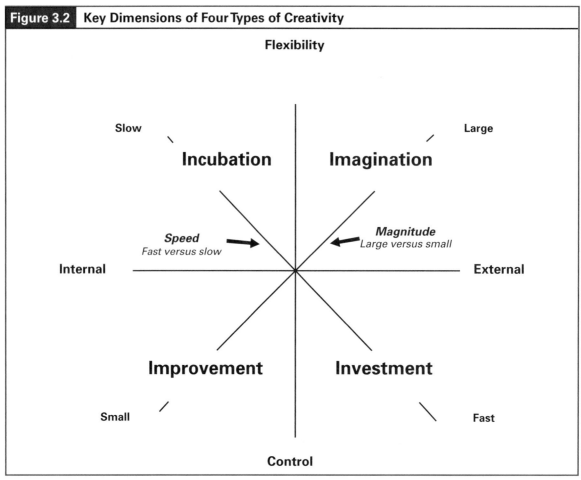

Figure 3.2   Key Dimensions of Four Types of Creativity

Flexibility

Slow   Large

Incubation   ### Imagination

Speed   *Magnitude*
Fast versus slow   Large versus small

Internal ————————————————————————— External

Improvement   ### Investment

Small   Fast

Control

SOURCE: *Adapted from DeGraff & Lawrence, 2002.*

This figure shows that imagination is the most appropriate approach to creativity when breakthroughs are needed and when original ideas are necessary—being new. The improvement approach is most appropriate when incremental changes or tightening up processes are necessary—being better. The investment approach is most appropriate when quick responses and goal achievement takes priority—being first. And, the incubation approach is most appropriate when collective effort and involvement of others is important—being sustainable.

The Creativity Assessment survey that you completed in the Pre-assessment section helps identify your own preferences regarding these different approaches to creativity. You were able to create a profile showing the extent to which you are inclined toward imagination, improvement, investment, or incubation as you approach problems calling for creativity. Your profile

will help you determine which kinds of problems you are inclined to solve when creativity is required. Of course, having a preference is not the same as having ability or possessing competence in a certain approach, but the remainder of this chapter as well as several additional chapters in this book will help with your creative competence development.

Your profile is in the shape of a kite, and it identifies your most preferred style of creativity. The quadrant in which you score highest is your preferred approach but you will notice that you do not have a single approach. No one gives all of their points to a single alternative. Just as you have points in each of the four quadrants on the creativity profile, you also have an inclination to approach creativity in multiple ways. However, most people have certain dominant inclinations toward creativity, and those inclinations are helpful guides to you as you approach problems.

Figure 3.3 | Examples of Situations in Which Each Approach Is Effective

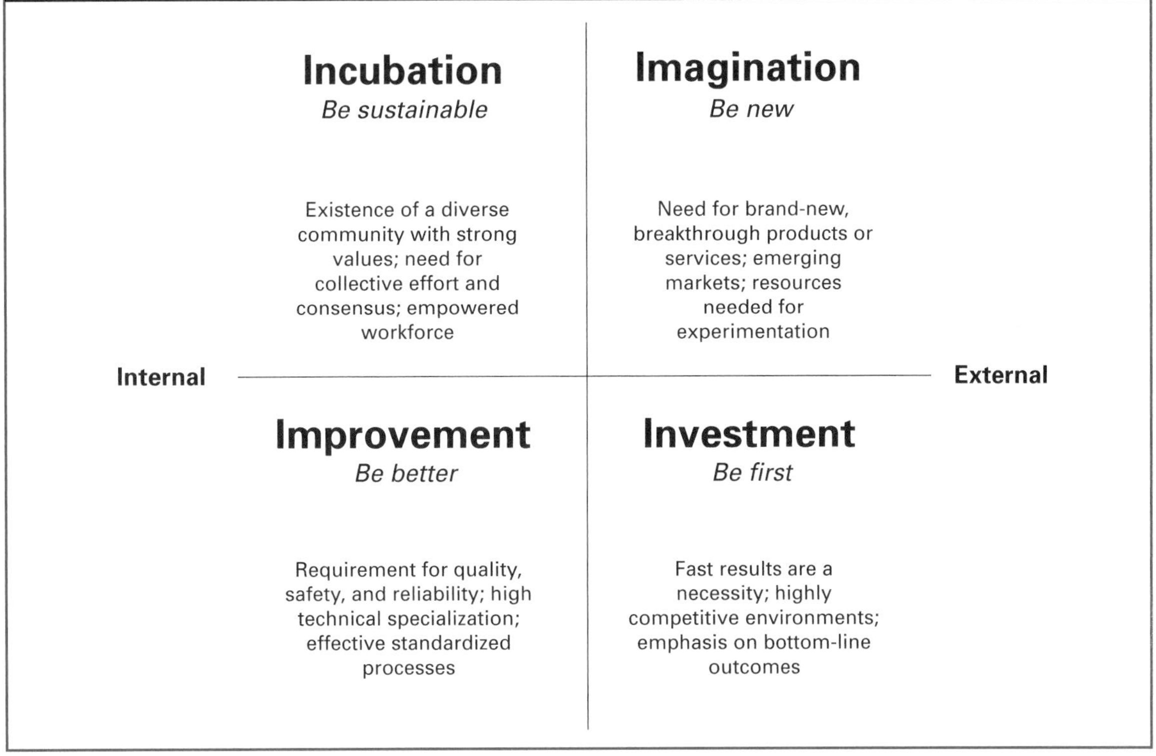

Incubation
Be sustainable

Existence of a diverse community with strong values; need for collective effort and consensus; empowered workforce

Imagination
Be new

Need for brand-new, breakthrough products or services; emerging markets; resources needed for experimentation

Internal —————————————————— External

Improvement
Be better

Requirement for quality, safety, and reliability; high technical specialization; effective standardized processes

Investment
Be first

Fast results are a necessity; highly competitive environments; emphasis on bottom-line outcomes

SOURCE: *Adapted from DeGraff & Lawrence, 2002.*

LEARNING

Most of us are not aware that we can be creative in multiple ways, yet anyone can be creative and add value to problem solving. Just because you are not a clever producer of unique ideas, for example, does not mean that you are not creative and cannot add value to the creative process.

Conceptual Blocks

The trouble is, each of these different approaches to creativity can be inhibited. That is, in addition to being unaware of the multiple ways in which we can be creative, most of us have difficulty in solving problems creatively because of the presence of **conceptual blocks.** Conceptual blocks are mental obstacles that constrain the way problems are defined, and they can inhibit us from being effective in any of the four types of creativity. Conceptual blocks limit the number of alternative solutions that people think about (Adams, 2001). Every individual has conceptual blocks, but some people have more numerous and more intense ones than others. These blocks are largely unrecognized or unconscious, so the only way individuals can

be made aware of them is to be confronted with problems that are unsolvable because of them. Conceptual blocks result largely from the thinking processes that problem solvers use when facing problems. Everyone develops some conceptual blocks over time. In fact, we need some of them to cope with everyday life. Here's why.

At every moment, each of us is bombarded with far more information than we can possibly absorb. For example, you are probably not conscious right now of the temperature of the room, the color of your skin, the level of illumination overhead, or how your toes feel in your shoes. All of this information is available to you and is being processed by your brain, but you have tuned out some things and focused on others. Over time, you must develop the habit of mentally filtering out some of the information to which you are exposed; otherwise, information overload would drive you crazy. These filtering habits eventually become conceptual habits or blocks. Though you are not conscious of them, they inhibit you from registering some kinds of information and, therefore, from solving certain kinds of problems.

Paradoxically, the more formal education individuals have, and the more experience they have in a job, the less able they are to solve problems in creative ways. It has been estimated that most adults over 40 display less than two percent of the creative problem-solving ability of a child under five years old. That's because formal education often prescribes "right" answers, analytic rules, or thinking boundaries. Experience in a job often leads to "proper" ways of doing things, specialized knowledge, and rigid expectation of appropriate actions. Individuals lose the ability to experiment, improvise, or take mental detours. Consider the following example:

If you place in a bottle half a dozen bees and the same number of flies, and lay the bottle down horizontally, with its base to the window, you will find that the bees will persist, till they die of exhaustion or hunger, in their endeavor to discover an issue through the glass; while the flies, in less than two minutes, will all have sallied forth through the neck on the opposite side. . . . It is [the bees'] love of light, it is their very intelligence, that is their undoing in this experiment. They evidently imagine that the issue from every prison must be there when the light shines clearest; and they act in accordance, and persist in too logical an action. To them glass is a supernatural mystery they never have met in nature; they have had no experience of this suddenly impenetrable atmosphere; and the greater their intelligence, the more inadmissible, more incomprehensible, will the strange obstacle appear. Whereas the feather-brained flies, careless of logic as of the enigma of crystal, disregarding the call of the light, flutter wildly, hither and thither, meeting here the good fortune that often waits on the simple, who find salvation where the wiser will perish, necessarily end by discovering the friendly opening that restores their liberty to them (Weick, 1995, p. 59).

This illustration identifies a paradox inherent in learning to solve problems creatively. On the one hand, more education and experience may inhibit creative problem solving and reinforce conceptual blocks. Like the bees in the story, individuals may not find solutions because the problem requires less "educated," more "playful" approaches. On the other hand, as several researchers have found, training focused on improving thinking significantly enhances creative problem-solving abilities and managerial effectiveness (Albert & Runco,

1999; Mumford, Baughman, Maher, Costanza, & Supinski, 1997; Nickerson, 1999; Smith, 1998).

For example, research has found that training in thinking increased the number of good ideas produced in problem solving by more than 125 percent (Scope, 1999). Creativity in art, music composition, problem finding, problem construction, and idea generation have been found to improve substantially when training in creative problem solving and thinking skills is received (de Bono, 1973, 1992; Finke, Ward, & Smith, 1992; Getzels & Csikszentmihalyi, 1976; Nickerson, 1999; Starko, 2001). Moreover, substantial data also exists that such training can enhance the profitability and efficiency of organizations (Williams & Yang, 1999). Many organizations—such as Microsoft, General Electric, and AT&T—now send their executives to creativity workshops in order to improve their creative-thinking abilities. Creative problem-solving experts are currently hot properties on the consulting circuit, and about a million copies of books on creativity are sold each year in North America. Several well-known products have been produced as a direct result of this kind of training: for example, NASA's Velcro snaps, G.E.'s self-diagnostic dishwashers, Mead's carbonless copy paper, and Kodak's Trimprint film.

Resolving this paradox is not just a matter of more exposure to information or education. Rather, people must master the process of thinking about certain problems in a creative way. As Csikszentmihalyi (1996, p. 11) observed:

Each of us is born with two contradictory sets of instructions: a conservative tendency, made up of instincts for self-preservation, self-aggrandizement, and saving energy, and an expansive tendency made up of instincts for exploring, for enjoying novelty and risk—the curiosity that leads to creativity belongs to this set. We need both of these programs. But whereas the first tendency requires little encouragement or support from the outside to motivate behavior, the second can wilt if it is not cultivated. If too few opportunities for curiosity are available, if too many obstacles are placed in the way of risk and exploration, the motivation to engage in creative behavior is easily extinguished.

In the next section, we focus on problems that require creative rather than analytical solutions. These are problems for which no acceptable alternative seems to be available, all reasonable solutions seem to be blocked, or no obvious best answer is accessible. Analytical problem solving just doesn't seem to apply. This situation often exists because conceptual blocks inhibit the range of solutions thought possible. We introduce some tools and techniques that help overcome conceptual blocks and unlock problem-solving creativity. First consider these two examples that illustrate creative problem solving and breaking through conceptual blocks.

PERCY SPENCER'S MAGNETRON

During World War II, the British developed one of the best-kept military secrets of the war, a special radar detector based on a device called the magnetron. This radar was credited with turning the tide of battle in the war between Britain and Germany and helping the British withstand Hitler's Blitzkrieg. In 1940, Raytheon was one of several U.S. firms invited to produce magnetrons for the war effort.

The workings of magnetrons were not well understood, even by sophisticated physicists. Even among the firms that made magnetrons, few understood what made them work. A magnetron was tested, in those early days, by holding a neon tube next to it. If the neon tube got bright enough, the magnetron tube passed the test. In the process of conducting the test, the hands of the scientist holding the neon tube got warm. It was this phenomenon that led to a major creative breakthrough that eventually transformed lifestyles throughout the world.

At the end of the war, the market for radar essentially dried up, and most firms stopped producing magnetrons. At Raytheon, however, a scientist named Percy Spencer had been fooling around with magnetrons, trying to think of alternative uses for the devices. He was convinced that magnetrons could be used to cook food by using the heat produced in the neon tube. But Raytheon was in the defense business. Next to its two prize products—the Hawk and Sparrow missiles—cooking devices seemed odd and out of place. Percy Spencer was convinced that Raytheon should continue to produce magnetrons, even though production costs were prohibitively high. But Raytheon had lost money on the devices, and now there was no available market for magnetrons. The consumer product Spencer had in mind did not fit within the bounds of Raytheon's business.

As it turned out, Percy Spencer's solution to Raytheon's problem produced the microwave oven and a revolution in cooking methods throughout the world. Later, we will analyze several problem-solving techniques illustrated by Spencer's creative triumph.

SPENCE SILVER'S GLUE

A second example of creative problem solving began with Spence Silver's assignment to work on a temporary project team within the 3M company. The team was searching for new adhesives, so Silver obtained some material from AMD, Inc., which had potential for a new polymer-based adhesive. He described one of his experiments in this way: "In the course of this exploration, I tried an experiment with one of the monomers in which I wanted to see what would happen if I put a lot of it into the reaction mixture. Before, we had used amounts that would correspond to conventional wisdom" (Nayak & Ketteringham, 1986). The result was a substance that failed all the conventional 3M tests for adhesives. It didn't stick. It preferred its own molecules to the molecules of any other substance. It was more cohesive than adhesive. It sort of "hung around without making a commitment." It was a "now-it-works, now-it-doesn't" kind of glue.

For five years, Silver went from department to department within the company trying to find someone interested in using his newly found substance in a product. Silver had found a solution; he just couldn't find a problem to solve with it. Predictably, 3M showed little interest. The company's mission was to make adhesives that adhered ever more tightly. The ultimate adhesive was one that formed an unbreakable bond, not one that formed a temporary bond.

After four years the task force was disbanded, and team members were assigned to other projects. But Silver was still convinced that his substance was good for something. He just didn't know what. As it turned out, Silver's solution has become the prototype for innovation in American firms, and it has spawned a multibillion-dollar business for 3M—in a unique product called Post-it Notes.

These two examples are positive illustrations of how solving a problem in a unique way can lead to phenomenal business success. Creative problem solving can have remarkable effects on individuals' careers and on business success. To understand how to solve problems creatively, however, we must first consider the blocks that inhibit creativity.

THE FOUR TYPES OF CONCEPTUAL BLOCKS

Table 3.3 summarizes four types of conceptual blocks that inhibit creative problem solving. Each is discussed and illustrated next with problems or exercises. We encourage you to complete the exercises and solve the

Table 3.3	Conceptual Blocks That Inhibit Creative Problem Solving

1. Constancy

• Vertical thinking	Defining a problem in only one way without considering alternative views.
• One thinking language	Not using more than one language to define and assess the problem.

2. Commitment

• Stereotyping based on past experience	Present problems are seen only as the variations of past problems.
• Ignoring commonalities	Failing to perceive commonalities among elements that initially appear to be different.

3. Compression

• Distinguishing figure from ground	Not filtering out irrelevant information or finding needed information.
• Artificial constraints	Defining the boundaries of a problem too narrowly.

4. Complacency

• Noninquisitiveness	Not asking questions.
• Nonthinking	A bias toward activity in place of mental work.

problems as you read the chapter, because doing so will help you become aware of your own conceptual blocks. Later, we shall discuss in more detail how you can overcome those blocks.

Constancy

One type of conceptual block occurs because individuals become wedded to one way of looking at a problem or using one approach to define, describe, or solve it. It is easy to see why **constancy** is common in problem solving. Being constant, or consistent, is a highly valued attribute for most of us. We like to appear at least moderately consistent in our approach to life, and constancy is often associated with maturity, honesty, and even intelligence. We judge lack of constancy as untrustworthy, peculiar, or airheaded. Some prominent psychologists theorize, in fact, that a need for constancy is the primary motivator of human behavior (Festinger, 1957; Heider, 1946; Newcomb, 1954). Many psychological studies have shown that once individuals take a stand or employ a particular approach to a problem, they are highly likely to pursue that same course without deviation in the future (see Cialdini, 2001, for multiple examples).

On the other hand, constancy can inhibit the solution of some kinds of problems. Consistency sometimes drives out creativity. Two illustrations of the constancy block are vertical thinking and using only one thinking language.

Vertical Thinking   The term **vertical thinking** was coined by Edward de Bono (1968, 2000). It refers to defining a problem in a single way and then pursuing that definition without deviation until a solution is reached. No alternative definitions are considered. All information gathered and all alternatives generated are consistent with the original definition. De Bono contrasted lateral thinking to vertical thinking in the following ways: vertical thinking focuses on continuity, lateral thinking focuses on discontinuity; vertical thinking chooses, lateral thinking changes; vertical thinking is concerned with stability, lateral thinking is concerned with instability; vertical thinking searches for what is right, lateral thinking searches for what is different; vertical thinking is analytical, lateral thinking is provocative; vertical thinking is concerned with where an idea came from, lateral thinking is concerned with where the idea is going; vertical thinking moves in the most likely directions, lateral thinking moves in the least likely directions; vertical thinking develops an idea, lateral thinking discovers the idea.

In a search for oil, for example, vertical thinkers determine a spot for the hole and drill the hole deeper and deeper until they strike oil. Lateral thinkers, on the other hand, drill a number of holes in different places in search of oil. The vertical-thinking conceptual block arises from not being able to view the problem from multiple perspectives—to drill several holes—or to think laterally as well as vertically in problem solving.

Plenty of examples exist of creative solutions that occurred because an individual refused to get stuck with a single problem definition. Alexander Graham Bell was trying to devise a hearing aid when he shifted definitions and invented the telephone. Harland Sanders was trying to sell his recipe to restaurants when he shifted definitions and developed his Kentucky Fried Chicken business. Karl Jansky was studying telephone static when he shifted definitions, discovered radio waves from the Milky Way galaxy, and developed the science of radio astronomy.

In developing the microwave industry described earlier, Percy Spencer shifted the definition of the problem from "How can we save our military radar business at the end of the war?" to "What other applications can be made for the magnetron?" Other problem definitions followed, such as: "How can we make magnetrons cheaper?" "How can we mass-produce magnetrons?" "How can we convince someone besides the military to buy magnetrons?" "How can we enter a consumer products market?" "How can we make microwave ovens practical and safe?" And so on. Each new problem definition led to new ways of thinking about the problem, new alternative approaches, and, eventually, to a new microwave oven industry.

Spence Silver at 3M is another example of someone who changed problem definitions. He began with "How can I get an adhesive that has a stronger bond?" but switched to "How can I find an application for an adhesive that doesn't stick firmly?" Eventually, other problem definitions followed: "How can we get this new glue to stick to one surface but not another (e.g., to notepaper but not normal paper)?" "How can we replace staples, thumbtacks, and paper clips in the workplace?" "How can we manufacture and package a product that uses nonadhesive glue?" "How can we get anyone to pay $1.00 a pad for scratch paper?" And so on.

Shifting definitions is not easy, of course, because it is not natural. It requires individuals to deflect their tendency toward constancy. Later, we will discuss some hints and tools that can help overcome the constancy block while avoiding the negative consequences of inconsistency.

A Single Thinking Language
A second manifestation of the constancy block is the use of only one **thinking language**. Most people think in words—that is, they think about a problem and its solution in terms of verbal language. **Analytical problem solving** reinforces this approach. Some writers, in fact, have argued that thinking cannot even occur without words (Feldman, 1999; Vygotsky, 1962). Other thought languages are available, however, such as nonverbal or symbolic languages (e.g., mathematics), sensory imagery (e.g., smelling or tactile sensation), feelings and emotions (e.g., happiness, fear, or anger), and visual imagery (e.g., mental pictures). The more languages available to problem solvers, the better and more creative will be their solutions. As Koestler (1964, p. 177) puts it, "[Verbal] language can become a screen which stands between the thinker and reality. This is the reason that true creativity often starts where [verbal] language ends."

Percy Spencer at Raytheon is a prime example of a visual thinker:

> One day, while Spencer was lunching with Dr. Ivan Getting and several other Raytheon scientists, a mathematical question arose. Several men, in a familiar reflex, pulled out their slide rules, but before any could complete the equation, Spencer gave the answer. Dr. Getting was astonished. "How did you do that?" he asked. "The root," said Spencer shortly. "I learned cube roots and squares by using blocks as a boy. Since then, all I have to do is visualize them placed together." (Scott, 1974, p. 287)

The microwave oven depended on Spencer's command of multiple thinking languages. Furthermore, the new oven would never have gotten off the ground without a critical incident that illustrates the power of visual thinking. By 1965, Raytheon was just about to give up on any consumer application of the magnetron when a meeting was held with George Foerstner, president of the recently acquired Amana Refrigeration Company. In the meeting, costs, applications, manufacturing obstacles, and production issues were discussed. Foerstner galvanized the entire microwave oven effort with the following statement, as reported by a Raytheon vice president.

> George says, "It's no problem. It's about the same size as an air conditioner. It weighs about the same. It should sell for the same. So we'll price it at $499." Now you think that's silly, but you stop and think about it. Here's a man who really didn't understand the technologies. But there is about the same amount of copper involved, the same amount of steel as an air conditioner. And these are basic raw

LEARNING

materials. It didn't make a lot of difference how you fit them together to make them work. They're both boxes; they're both made out of sheet metal; and they both require some sort of trim. (Nayak & Ketteringham, 1986, p. 181)

In several short sentences, Foerstner had taken one of the most complicated military secrets of World War II and translated it into something no more complex than a room air conditioner. He had painted a picture of an application that no one else had been able to capture by describing a magnetron visually, as a familiar object, not as a set of calculations, formulas, or blueprints.

A similar occurrence in the Post-it Note chronology also led to a breakthrough. Spence Silver had been trying for years to get someone in 3M to adopt his unsticky glue. Art Fry, another scientist with 3M, had heard Silver's presentations before. One day while singing in North Presbyterian Church in St. Paul, Minnesota, Fry was fumbling around with the slips of paper that marked the various hymns in his book. Suddenly, a visual image popped into his mind.

> I thought, "Gee, if I had a little adhesive on these bookmarks, that would be just the ticket." So I decided to check into that idea the next week at work. What I had in mind was Silver's adhesive. . . . I knew I had a much bigger discovery than that. I also now realized that the primary application for Silver's adhesive was not to put it on a fixed surface like bulletin boards. That was a secondary application. The primary application concerned paper to paper. I realized that immediately." (Nayak & Ketteringham, 1986, pp. 63–64)

Years of verbal descriptions had not led to any applications for Silver's glue. Tactile thinking (handling the glue) also had not produced many ideas. However, thinking about the product in visual terms, as applied

to what Fry initially called "a better bookmark," led to the breakthrough that was needed.

This emphasis on using alternative thinking languages, especially visual thinking, has become a new frontier in scientific research (McKim, 1997). With the advent of the digital revolution, scientists are more and more working with pictures and simulated images rather than with numerical data. "Scientists who are using the new computer graphics say that by viewing images instead of numbers, a fundamental change in the way researchers think and work is occurring. People have a lot easier time getting an intuition from pictures than they do from numbers and tables or formulas. In most physics experiments, the answer used to be a number or a string of numbers. In the last few years the answer has increasingly become a picture" (Markoff, 1988, p. D3).

To illustrate the differences among thinking languages, consider the following simple problem:

> Figure 3.4 shows seven matchsticks. By moving only one matchstick, make the figure into a true equality (i.e., the value on one side equals the value on the other side). Before looking up the answers in the section at the end of the chapter with scoring keys and comparison data, try defining the problem by using different thinking languages. What thinking language is most effective?

Commitment

Commitment can also serve as a conceptual block to creative problem solving. Once individuals become committed to a particular point of view, definition, or solution, it is likely that they will follow through on that commitment. Cialdini (2001) reported a study, for example, in which investigators asked Californians to put a large, poorly lettered sign on their front lawns saying DRIVE CAREFULLY. Only 17 percent agreed to do so. However,

| Figure 3.4 | The Matchstick Configuration |

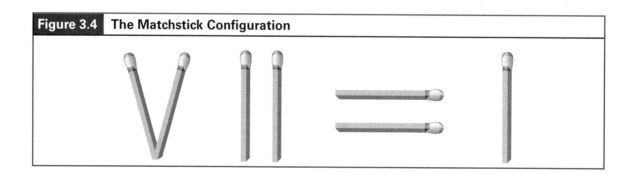

after signing a petition favoring "keep California beautiful," the people were again asked to put the DRIVE CAREFULLY sign on their lawns, and 76 percent agreed to do so. Once they had committed to being active and involved citizens (i.e., to keeping California beautiful), it was consistent for these people to agree to the large unsightly sign as visible evidence of their commitment. Most people have the same inclination toward being consistent and maintaining commitments.

Two forms of commitment that produce conceptual blocks are stereotyping based on past experiences and ignoring commonalities.

Stereotyping Based on Past Experiences March (1999) pointed out that a major obstacle to innovative problem solving is that individuals tend to define present problems in terms of problems they have faced in the past. Current problems are usually seen as variations on some past situation, so the alternatives proposed to solve the current problem are ones that have proven successful in the past. Both problem definitions and proposed solutions are therefore restricted by past experience. This restriction is referred to as **perceptual stereotyping** (Adams, 2001). That is, certain preconceptions formed on the basis of past experience determine how an individual defines a situation.

When individuals receive an initial cue regarding the definition of a problem, all subsequent problems are frequently framed in terms of the initial cue. Of course, this is not all bad, because perceptual stereotyping helps organize problems on the basis of a limited amount of data, and the need to consciously analyze every problem encountered is eliminated. On the other hand, perceptual stereotyping prevents individuals from viewing a problem in novel ways.

The creation of microwave ovens and of Post-it Notes provide examples of overcoming stereotyping based on past experiences. Scott (1974) described the first meeting of John D. Cockcroft, technical leader of the British radar system that invented magnetrons, and Percy Spencer of Raytheon.

> *Cockcroft liked Spencer at once. He showed him the magnetron, and the American regarded it thoughtfully. He asked questions—very intelligent ones—about how it was produced, and the Britisher answered at length. Later Spencer wrote, "The technique of making these tubes, as described to us, was awkward and impractical." Awkward and impractical! Nobody else dared draw such a judgment about a product of undoubted scientific brilliance, produced and displayed by the leaders of British science.*

Despite his admiration for Cockcroft and the magnificent magnetron, Spencer refused to abandon his curious and inquisitive stance. Rather than adopting the position of other scientists and assuming that since the British invented it and were using it, they surely knew how to produce a magnetron, Spencer broke out of the stereotypes and pushed for improvements.

Similarly, Spence Silver at 3M described his invention in terms of breaking stereotypes based on past experience.

> *The key to the Post-It adhesive was doing the experiment. If I had sat down and factored it out beforehand, and thought about it, I wouldn't have done the experiment. If I had really seriously cracked the books and gone through the literature, I would have stopped. The literature was full of examples that said you can't do this. (Nayak & Ketteringham, 1986, p. 57)*

This is not to say that one should avoid learning from past experience or that failing to learn the mistakes of history does not doom us to repeat them. Rather, it is to say that commitment to a course of action based on past experience can sometimes inhibit viewing problems in new ways, and can even prevent us from solving some problems at all. Consider the following problem as an example.

Assume that there are four volumes of Shakespeare on the shelf (see Figure 3.5). Assume that the pages of each volume are exactly two inches thick, and that the covers of each volume are each one-sixth of an inch thick. Assume that a bookworm began eating at page 1 of Volume 1, and it ate straight through to the last page of Volume IV. What distance did the worm cover? Solving this problem is relatively simple, but it requires that you overcome a stereotyping block to get the correct answer. (See the end of the chapter for the correct answer.)

Ignoring Commonalities A second manifestation of the commitment block is failure to identify similarities among seemingly disparate pieces of data. This is among the most commonly identified blocks to creativity. It means that a person becomes committed to a particular point of view, to the fact that elements are different, and, consequently, becomes unable to make connections, identify themes, or perceive commonalities.

The ability to find one definition or solution for two seemingly dissimilar problems is a characteristic of creative individuals (see Sternberg, 1999). The inability to do this can overload a problem solver by requiring

Figure 3.5 Shakespeare Riddle

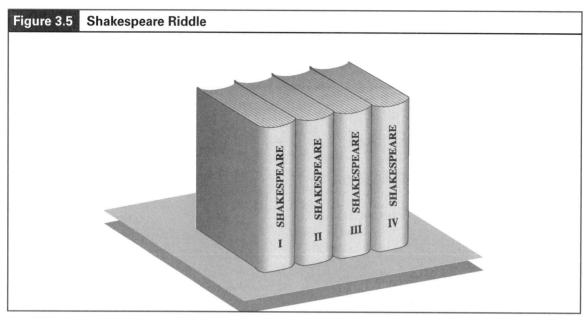

SOURCE: "Shakespeare Riddle" from CREATIVE GROWTH GAMES by Eugene Raudsepp and George P. Haugh, Copyright © 1977 by Eugene Raudsepp & George P. Haugh, Jr. Used with permission of Berkley Publishing Group, a division of Penguin Group (USA) Inc.

that every problem encountered be solved individually. The discovery of penicillin by Sir Alexander Fleming resulted from his seeing a common theme among seemingly unrelated events. Fleming was working with some cultures of staphylococci that had accidentally become contaminated. The contamination, a growth of fungi, and isolated clusters of dead staphylococci led Fleming to see a relationship no one else had ever seen previously and thus to discover a wonder drug. The famous chemist Friedrich Kekule saw a relationship between his dream of a snake swallowing its own tail and the chemical structure of organic compounds. This creative insight led him to the discovery that organic compounds such as benzene have closed rings rather than open structures (Koestler, 1964).

For Percy Spencer at Raytheon, seeing a connection between the heat of a neon tube and the heat required to cook food was the creative connection that led to his breakthrough in the microwave industry. One of Spencer's colleagues recalled: "In the process of testing a bulb [with a magnetron], your hands got hot. I don't know when Percy really came up with the thought of microwave ovens, but he knew at that time—and that was 1942. He [remarked] frequently that this would be a good device for cooking food." Another colleague described Spencer this way: "The way Percy Spencer's mind worked is an interesting thing. He had a mind that allowed him to hold an extraordinary array of associations on phenomena and relate them to one another"

(Nayak & Ketteringham, 1986, pp. 184, 205). Similarly, the connection Art Fry made between a glue that wouldn't stick tightly and marking hymns in a choir book was the final breakthrough that led to the development of the revolutionary Post-it Note business.

To test your own ability to see commonalities, answer the following two questions: (1) What are some common terms that apply to both the substance water and the field of finance? (For example, "financial float.") (2) In Figure 3.6, using the code letters for the smaller ships as a guide, what is the name of the larger ship? (Some of the answers are at the end of the chapter.)

Compression

Conceptual blocks also occur as a result of **compression** of ideas. Looking too narrowly at a problem, screening out too much relevant data, and making assumptions that inhibit problem solution are common examples. Two especially cogent examples of compression are artificially constraining problems and not distinguishing figure from ground.

Artificial Constraints   Sometimes people place boundaries around problems, or constrain their approach to them, in such a way that the problems become impossible to solve. Such constraints arise from hidden assumptions people make about problems they encounter. People assume that some problem definitions or alternative solutions are off limits, so

Figure 3.6 | Name That Ship!

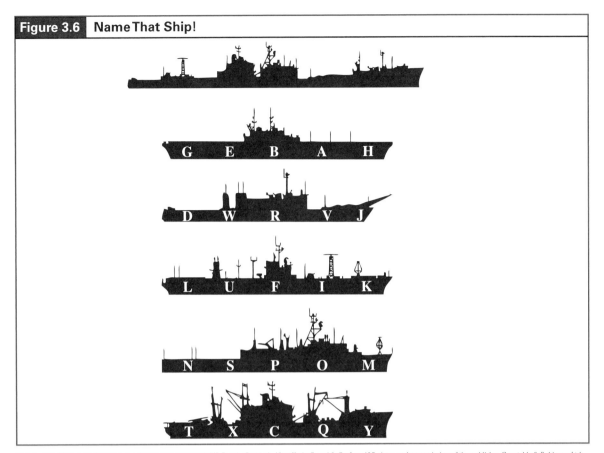

G E B A H

D W R V J

L U F I K

N S P O M

T X C Q Y

SOURCE: *Ship Shapes;* Bodycombe, D.J. (1997). The Mammoth NB Puzzle Carnival. *New York: Carrol & Graf, p. 405. Appears by permission of the publisher Constable & Robinson Ltd., London.*

they ignore them. For an illustration of this conceptual block, look at Figure 3.7. This is a problem you have probably seen before. Without lifting your pencil from the paper, draw four straight lines that pass through all nine dots. Complete the task before reading further.

By thinking of the figure as more constrained than it actually is, the problem becomes impossible to solve. It is easy if you break out of your own limiting assumptions on the problem. Now that you have been cued, can you do the same task with only three lines? What limiting constraints are you placing on yourself?

If you are successful, now try to do the task with only one line. Can you determine how to put a single straight line through all nine dots without lifting your pencil from the paper? Both the three-line solution and some one-line solutions are provided at the end of the chapter.

Artificially constraining problems means that the problem definition and the possible alternatives are limited more than the problem requires. Creative problem solving requires that individuals become adept at

recognizing their hidden assumptions and expanding the alternatives they consider—whether they imagine, improve, invest, or incubate.

Figure 3.7 | The Nine-Dot Problem

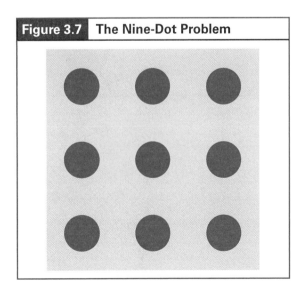

Separating Figure from Ground Another illustration of the compression block is the reverse of artificial constraints. It is the inability to constrain problems sufficiently so that they can be solved. Problems almost never come clearly specified, so problem solvers must determine what the real problem is. They must filter out inaccurate, misleading, or irrelevant information in order to define the problem correctly and generate appropriate alternative solutions. The inability to separate the important from the unimportant, and to compress problems appropriately, serves as a conceptual block because it exaggerates the complexity of a problem and inhibits a simple definition.

How well do you filter out irrelevant information and focus on the truly important part of a problem? Can you ask questions that get to the heart of the matter? Consider Figure 3.8. For each pair, find the pattern on the left that is embedded in the more complex pattern on the right. On the complex pattern, outline the embedded pattern. Now try to find at least two figures in each pattern. (See the end of the chapter for some solutions.)

Overcoming this compression block—separating figure from ground and artificially constraining problems—was an important explanation for the microwave oven and Post-it Note breakthroughs. George Foerstner's contribution to the development and manufacture of the microwave oven was to compress the problem, that is, to separate out all the irrelevant complexity that constrained others. Whereas the magnetron was a device so complicated that few people understood it, Foerstner focused on its basic raw materials, its size, and its functionality. By comparing it to an air conditioner, he eliminated much of the complexity and mystery, and, as described by two analysts, "He had seen what all the researchers had failed to see, and they knew he was right" (Nayak & Ketteringham, 1986, p. 181).

On the other hand, Spence Silver had to add complexity, to overcome compression, in order to find an application for his product. Because the glue had failed every traditional 3M test for adhesives, it was categorized as a useless configuration of chemicals. The potential for the product was artificially constrained by traditional assumptions about adhesives—more stickiness, stronger bonding is best—until Art Fry visualized some unconventional applications—a better bookmark, a bulletin board, scratch paper, and, paradoxically, a replacement for 3M's main product, tape.

Complacency

Some conceptual blocks occur not because of poor thinking habits or inappropriate assumptions but because of fear, ignorance, insecurity, or just plain mental laziness. Two especially prevalent examples of the **complacency** block are a lack of questioning and a bias against thinking.

Noninquisitiveness Sometimes the inability to solve problems results from an unwillingness to ask questions, obtain information, or search for data. Individuals may think they will appear naive or ignorant if they question something or attempt to redefine a problem. Asking questions puts them at risk of exposing their ignorance. It also may be threatening to others because it implies that what they accept may not be correct. This may create resistance, conflict, or even ridicule by others.

Creative problem solving is inherently risky because it potentially involves interpersonal conflict. It is risky also because it is fraught with mistakes. As Linus Pauling, the Nobel laureate, said, "If you want to have a good idea, have a lot of them, because most of them will be bad ones." Years of nonsupportive socialization, however, block the adventuresome and

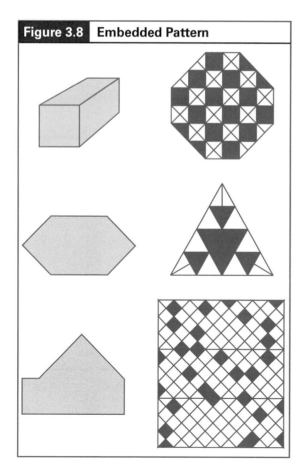

Figure 3.8	Embedded Pattern

inquisitive stance in most people. Most of us are not rewarded for bad ideas. To illustrate, answer the following questions for yourself:

1. When would it be easier to learn a new language, when you were five years old or now? Why?
2. How many times in the last month have you tried something for which the probability of success was less than 50 percent?
3. When was the last time you asked three "why" questions in a row?

To illustrate the extent of our lack of inquisitiveness, how many of the following commonly experienced questions can you answer?

❏ Why are people immune to their own body odor?
❏ What happens to the tread that wears off tires?
❏ Why doesn't sugar spoil or get moldy?
❏ Why doesn't a two-by-four measure two inches by four inches?
❏ Why is a telephone keypad arranged differently from that of a calculator?
❏ Why do hot dogs come 10 in a package while buns come 8 in a package?
❏ How do military cadets find their caps after throwing them in the air at football games and graduation?
❏ Why is Jack the nickname for John?

Most of us adopt a habit of being a bit complacent in asking such questions, let alone finding out the answers. We often stop being inquisitive as we get older because we learn that it is good to be intelligent, and being intelligent is interpreted as already knowing the answers, instead of asking good questions. Consequently, we learn less well at 25 than at 5, take fewer risks, avoid asking why, and function in the world without really trying to understand it. Creative problem solvers, on the other hand, are frequently engaged in inquisitive and experimental behavior. Spence Silver at 3M described his attitude about the complacency block this way:

People like myself get excited about looking for new properties in materials. I find that very satisfying, to perturb the structure slightly and just see what happens. I have a hard time talking people into doing that—people who are more highly trained. It's been my experience that people are reluctant just to try, to experiment—just to see what will happen. (Nayak & Ketteringham, 1986, p. 58)

Bias Against Thinking A second manifestation of the complacency block is in an inclination to avoid doing mental work. This block, like most of the others, is partly a cultural bias as well as a personal one. For example, assume that you passed by your roommate's or colleague's office one day and noticed him leaning back in his chair, staring out the window. A half-hour later, as you passed by again, he had his feet up on the desk, still staring out the window. And 20 minutes later, you noticed that his demeanor hadn't changed much. What would be your conclusion? Most of us would assume that the fellow was not doing any work. We would assume that unless we saw action, he wasn't being productive.

When was the last time you heard someone say, "I'm sorry. I can't go to the ball game (or concert, dance, party, or movie) because I have to think?" Or, "I'll do the dishes tonight. I know you need to catch up on your thinking"? That these statements sound silly illustrates the bias most people develop toward action rather than thought, or against putting their feet up, rocking back in their chair, looking off into space, and engaging in solitary cognitive activity. This does not mean daydreaming or fantasizing, just thinking.

A particular conceptual block exists in Western cultures against the kind of thinking that uses the right hemisphere of the brain. **Left-hemisphere thinking**, for most people, is concerned with logical, analytical, linear, or sequential tasks. Thinking using the left hemisphere is apt to be organized, planned, and precise. Language and mathematics are left-hemisphere activities. **Right-hemisphere thinking**, on the other hand, is concerned with intuition, synthesis, playfulness, and qualitative judgment. It tends to be more spontaneous, imaginative, and emotional than left-hemisphere thinking. The emphasis in most formal education is toward left-hemisphere thought development even more in Eastern cultures than in Western cultures. Problem solving on the basis of reason, logic, and utility is generally rewarded, while problem solving based on sentiment, intuition, or pleasure is frequently considered tenuous and inferior.

A number of researchers have found that the most creative problem solvers are **ambidextrous** in their thinking. That is, they use both left- and right-hemisphere thinking and easily switch from one to the other (Hermann, 1981; Hudspith, 1985; Martindale, 1999). Creative ideas arise most frequently in the right

Table 3.4	Exercise to Test Ambidextrous Thinking	
List 1	**List 2**	
sunset	decline	
perfume	very	
brick	ambiguous	
monkey	resources	
castle	term	
guitar	conceptual	
pencil	about	
computer	appendix	
umbrella	determine	
radar	forget	
blister	quantity	
chessboard	survey	

hemisphere but must be processed and interpreted by the left, so creative problem solvers use both hemispheres equally well.

Try the exercise in Table 3.4. It illustrates this ambidextrous principle. There are two lists of words. Take about two minutes to memorize the first list. Then, on a piece of paper, write down as many words as you can remember. Now take about two minutes and memorize the words in the second list. Repeat the process of writing down as many words as you can remember.

Most people remember more words from the first list than from the second. This is because the first list contains words that relate to visual perceptions. They connect with right-brain activity as well as left-brain activity. People can draw mental pictures or fantasize about them. The same is true for creative ideas. The more both sides of the brain are used, the more creative the ideas.

REVIEW OF CONCEPTUAL BLOCKS

So far, we have suggested that certain conceptual blocks prevent individuals from solving problems creatively and from engaging in the four different types of creativity. These blocks narrow the scope of problem definition, limit the consideration of alternative solutions, and constrain the selection of an optimal solution. Unfortunately, many of these conceptual blocks are unconscious, and it is only by being confronted with problems that are

unsolvable because of conceptual blocks that individuals become aware that they exist. We have attempted to make you aware of your own conceptual blocks by asking you to solve some simple problems that require you to overcome these mental barriers. These conceptual blocks are not all bad, of course; not all problems should be addressed by creative problem solving. But research has shown that individuals who have developed creative problem-solving skills are far more effective with complex problems that require a search for alternative solutions than others who are conceptually blocked (Basadur, 1979; Collins & Amabile, 1999; Sternberg, 1999; Williams & Yang, 1999).

In the next section, we provide some techniques and tools that help overcome these blocks and improve creative problem-solving skills.

Conceptual Blockbusting

Conceptual blocks cannot be overcome all at once because most blocks are a product of years of habit-forming thought processes. Overcoming them requires practice in thinking in different ways over a long period of time. You will not become a skilled creative problem solver just by reading this chapter. On the other hand, by becoming aware of your conceptual blocks and practicing the following techniques, research has demonstrated that you can enhance your **creative problem-solving** skills.

STAGES IN CREATIVE THOUGHT

A first step in overcoming conceptual blocks is recognizing that creative problem solving is a skill that can be developed. Being a creative problem solver is not an inherent ability that some people naturally have and others do not have. Jacob Rainbow, an employee of the U.S. Patent Office who has more than 200 patents by himself, described the creative process as follows:

So you need three things to be an original thinker. First, you have to have a tremendous amount of information—a big data base if you like to be fancy. Then you have to be willing to pull the ideas, because you're interested. Now, some people could do it, but they don't bother. They're interested in doing something else. It's fun to come up with an idea, and if nobody wants it, I don't give a damn. It's just fun to come up with something strange and different. And then you must have the ability to get rid of the trash which you think of. You cannot only think of good ideas. And by the way, if you're not well-trained, but you've got good ideas, and you don't know if they're good or bad, then you send them to the Bureau of Standards, National Institute of Standards, where I work, and we evaluate them. And we throw them out. (Csikszentmihalyi, 1996, p. 48)

In other words, gather a lot of information, use it to generate a lot of ideas, and sift through your ideas and get rid of the bad ones. Researchers generally agree that creative problem solving involves four stages: *preparation, incubation, illumination,* and *verification* (see Albert & Runco, 1999; Nickerson, 1999; Poincare, 1921; Ribot, 1906; Wallas, 1926). The **preparation stage** includes gathering data, defining the problem, generating alternatives, and consciously examining all available information. The primary difference between skillful creative problem solving and analytical problem solving is in how this first step is approached. Creative problem solvers are more flexible and fluent in data gathering, problem definition, alternative generation, and examination of options. In fact, it is in this stage that training in creative problem solving can significantly improve effectiveness because the other three steps are not amenable to conscious mental work (Adams, 2001; Ward, Smith, & Finke, 1999). The following discussion, therefore, is limited primarily to improving functioning in this first stage. The **incubation stage** involves mostly unconscious mental activity in which the mind combines unrelated thoughts in pursuit of a solution. Conscious effort is not involved. **Illumination**, the third stage, occurs when an insight is recognized and a creative solution is articulated. **Verification** is the final stage, which involves evaluating the creative solution relative to some standard of acceptability.

In the preparation stage, two types of techniques are available for improving creative problem-solving abilities. One technique helps individuals think about and *define problems more creatively;* the other helps individuals gather information and *generate more alternative solutions* to problems.

One major difference between effective, creative problem solvers and other people is that creative problem solvers are less constrained. They allow themselves to be more flexible in the definitions they impose on problems and the number of solutions they identify. They develop a large repertoire of approaches to problem solving. In short, they engage in what Csikszentmihalyi (1996) described as "playfulness and childishness." They try more things and worry less about their false

starts or failures. As Interaction Associates (1971, p. 15) explained:

Flexibility in thinking is critical to good problem solving. A problem solver should be able to conceptually dance around the problem like a good boxer, jabbing and poking, without getting caught in one place or "fixated." At any given moment, a good problem solver should be able to apply a large number of strategies [for generating alternative definitions and solutions]. Moreover, a good problem solver is a person who has developed, through his understanding of strategies and experiences in problem solving, a sense of appropriateness of what is likely to be the most useful strategy at any particular time.

As a perusal through any bookstore will show, the number of books suggesting ways to enhance creative problem solving is enormous. We now present a few tools and hints that we have found to be especially effective and relatively simple for business executives and students to apply. Although some of them may seem game-like or playful, a sober pedagogical rationale underlies all of them. Our purpose is to address your own personal skills as a creative problem solver, not to discuss how creativity can be fostered in an organizational setting. These tools, therefore, will help to unfreeze you from your normal skeptical, analytical approach to problems and increase your playfulness. They relate to (1) defining problems and (2) generating alternative solutions.

METHODS FOR IMPROVING PROBLEM DEFINITION

Problem definition is probably the most critical step in creative problem solving. Once a problem is defined, solving it is often relatively simple. However, as explained in Table 3.2, individuals tend to define problems in terms with which they are familiar. Even well-trained scientists suffer from this problem: "Good scientists study the most important problems they think they can solve" (Medawar, 1967). When a problem is faced that is new or complex or does not appear to have an easily identified solution, the problem either remains undefined or is redefined in terms of something familiar. Unfortunately, new problems may not be the same as old problems, so relying on past definitions may impede the process of solving current problems, or lead to solving the wrong problem. Applying techniques for creative problem definition can help individuals see problems in alternative ways so their definitions are less narrowly constrained. Three such techniques for improving and expanding the definition process are discussed below.

Make the Strange Familiar and the Familiar Strange

One well-known, well-tested technique for improving creative problem solving is called **synectics** (Gordon, 1961; Roukes, 1988). The goal of synectics is to help you put something you don't know in terms of something you do know, then reverse the process back again. The point is, by analyzing what you know and applying it to what you don't know, you can develop new insights and perspectives. The process of synectics relies on the use of analogies and metaphors, and it works this way.

First you form a definition of a problem (make the strange familiar). Then you try to transform that definition so it is made similar to something completely different that you know more about (make the familiar strange). That is, you use analogies and metaphors (synectics) to create this distortion. Postpone the original definition of the problem while you examine the analogy or the metaphor. Then impose this same analysis on the original problem to see what new insights you can uncover.

For example, suppose you have defined a problem as low morale among members of your team. You may form an analogy or metaphor by answering questions such as the following about the problem:

❏ What does this remind me of?
❏ What does this make me feel like?
❏ What is this similar to?
❏ What is this opposite of?

Your answers, for example, might be: This problem reminds me of trying to get warm on a cold day (I need more activity). It makes me feel like I do when visiting a hospital ward (I need to smile and go out of my way to empathize with people). It is similar to the loser's locker room after an athletic contest (I need to find an alternative purpose or goal). This isn't like a well-tuned automobile (I need to do a careful diagnosis). And so on. Metaphors and analogies should connect what you are less sure about (the original problem) to what you are more sure about (the metaphor). By analyzing the metaphor or analogy, you may identify attributes of the problem that were not evident before. New insights can occur and new ideas can come to mind.

Many creative solutions have been generated by such a technique. For example, William Harvey was the first to apply the "pump" analogy to the heart, which led to the discovery of the body's circulatory system. Niels Bohr compared the atom to the solar system and supplanted Rutherford's prevailing "raisin pudding" model of matter's building blocks. Consultant Roger von Oech (1986) helped turn around a struggling computer company by applying a restaurant analogy to the company's operations. The real problems emerged when the restaurant, rather than the company, was analyzed. Major contributions in the field of organizational behavior have occurred by applying analogies to other types of organization, such as machines, cybernetic or open systems, force fields, clans, and so on. Probably the most effective analogies (called parables) were used by Jesus to teach principles that otherwise were difficult for individuals to grasp (for example, the prodigal son, the good Samaritan, a shepherd and his flock).

Some hints to keep in mind when constructing analogies include:

❏ Include action or motion in the analogy (e.g., driving a car, cooking a meal, attending a funeral).
❏ Include things that can be visualized or pictured in the analogy (e.g., circuses, football games, crowded shopping malls).
❏ Pick familiar events or situations (e.g., families, kissing, bedtime).
❏ Try to relate things that are not obviously similar (e.g., saying an organization is like a big group is not nearly as rich a simile as saying that an organization is like, say, a psychic prison or a poker game).

Four types of analogies are recommended as part of synectics: *personal analogies*, in which individuals try to identify themselves as the problem ("If I were the problem, how would I feel, what would I like, what could satisfy me?"); *direct analogies*, in which individuals apply facts, technology, and common experience to the problem (e.g., Brunel solved the problem of underwater construction by watching a shipworm tunneling into a tube); *symbolic analogies*, in which symbols or images are imposed on the problem (e.g., modeling the problem mathematically or diagramming the process flow); and *fantasy analogies*, in which individuals ask the question "In my wildest dreams, how would I wish the problem to be resolved?" (e.g., "I wish all employees would work with no supervision.").

Elaborate on the Definition

There are a variety of ways to enlarge, alter, or replace a problem definition once it has been specified. One way is to force yourself to generate at least two alternative hypotheses for every problem definition. That is, specify at least two plausible definitions of the problem in addition to the one originally accepted. Think in plural rather than singular terms. Instead of asking, "What is the problem?" "What is the meaning of this?" "What will be the result?" ask instead questions such as: "What are the problems?" "What are the meanings of this?" "What will be the results?"

As an example, look at Figure 3.9. Select the figure that is different from all the others.

A majority of people select B first. If you did, you're right. It is the only figure that has all straight lines. On the other hand, quite a few people pick A. If you are one of them, you're also right. It is the only figure with a continuous line and no points of discontinuity. Alternatively, C can also be right, with the rationale that it is the only figure with two straight and two curved lines. Similarly, D is the only one with one curved and one straight line, and E is the only figure that is nonsymmetrical or partial. The point is, there can often be more than one problem definition, more than one right answer, and more than one perspective from which to view a problem.

Another way to elaborate definitions is to use a question checklist. This is a series of questions designed to help you think of alternatives to your accepted definitions. Several creative managers have shared with us some of their most fruitful questions, such as:

❏ Is there anything else?
❏ Is the reverse true?
❏ Is this a symptom of a more general problem?
❏ Who sees it differently?

Nickerson (1999) reported an oft-used acronym—SCAMPER—designed to bring to mind questions having to do with **S**ubstitution, **C**ombination, **A**daptation, **M**odification (Magnification–Minimization), **P**utting to other uses, **E**limination, and **R**earrangement.

As an exercise, take a minute now to think of a problem you are currently experiencing. Write it down so it is formally defined. Now manipulate that definition by answering the four questions in the checklist. If you can't think of a problem, try the exercise with this one. "I am not as attractive/intelligent/creative as I would like to be." How would you answer the four questions?

Reverse the Definition

A third tool for improving and expanding problem definition is to reverse the definition of the problem. That is, turn the problem upside down, inside out, or back to front. Reverse the way in which you think of the problem. For example, consider the following problem:

A tradition in Sandusky, Ohio, for as long as anyone could remember was the Fourth of July Parade. It was one of the largest and most popular events on the city's annual calendar. Now, in 1988, the city mayor was hit with some startling and potentially disastrous news. The State of Ohio was mandating that liability insurance be carried on every attraction—floats, bands, majorettes—that participated in the parade. To protect against the possibility of injury or accident of any parade participant, each had to be covered by liability insurance.

The trouble, of course, was that taking out a liability insurance policy for all parade participants would require far more expense than the city could afford. The amount of insurance required for that large a number of participants and equipment made it impossible for the city to carry the cost. On the one hand, the mayor hated to cancel an important tradition that everyone in town looked forward to. On the

---

Figure 3.9	The Five-Figure Problem

Of the five figures below, select the one that is different from all of the others.

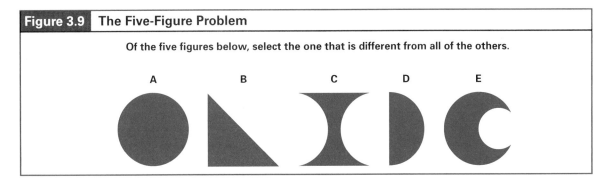

A   B   C   D   E

other hand, to hold the event would break the city budget. If you were a consultant to the mayor, what would you suggest?

Commonly suggested alternatives in this problem include the following:

1. Try to negotiate with an insurance company for a lower rate. (However, the risk is merely being transferred to the insurance company.)

2. Hold fund-raising events to generate enough money to purchase the insurance policy, or find a wealthy donor to sponsor the parade. (However, this may deflect potential donations away from, or may compete with, other community service agencies such as United Way, Red Cross, or local churches that also sponsor fund-raisers and require donations.)

3. Charge a "participation fee" to parade participants to cover the insurance expense. (However, this would likely eliminate most high school, middle school, and elementary school bands and floats. It would also reduce the amount of money float builders and sponsoring organizations could spend on the actual float. Such a requirement would likely be a parade killer.)

4. Charge a fee to spectators of the parade. (However, this would require restricted access to the parade, an administrative structure to coordinate fee collection and ticketing, and the destruction of the sense of community participation that characterized this traditional event.)

Each of these suggestions is good, but each maintains a single definition of the problem. Each assumes that the solution to the problem is associated with solving the financial problem associated with the liability insurance requirement. Each suggestion, therefore, brings with it some danger of damaging the traditional nature of the parade or eliminating it altogether. If the problem is reversed, other answers normally not considered become evident. That is, the need for liability insurance at all could be addressed.

Here is an excerpt from a newspaper report of how the problem was addressed:

Sandusky, Ohio (AP) *The Fourth of July parade here wasn't canceled, but it was immobilized by liability insurance worries. The band marched in place to the beat of a drum, and a country fair queen waved to her subjects from a float moored to the curb.*

The Reverse Community Parade began at 10:00 A.M. Friday along Washington Row at the north end of the city and stayed there until dusk. "Very honestly, it was the issue of liability," said Gene Kleindienst, superintendent of city schools and one of the celebration's organizers. "By not having a mobile parade, we significantly reduced the issue of liability," he said.

The immobile parade included about 20 floats and displays made by community groups. Games, displays, and food booths were in an adjacent park. Parade chairman Judee Hill said some folks didn't understand, however. "Someone asked me if she was too late for the parade, and she had a hard time understanding the parade is here all day," she said.

Those who weren't puzzled seemed to appreciate the parade for its stationary qualities. "I like this. I can see more," said 67-year-old William A. Sibley. "I'm 80 percent blind. Now I know there's something there," he said pointing to a float.

Spectator Emmy Platte preferred the immobile parade because it didn't go on for "what seemed like miles," exhausting participants. "You don't have those little drum majorettes passing out on the street," she commented.

Baton twirler Tammy Ross said her performance was better standing still. "You can throw better. You don't have to worry about dropping it as much," she explained.

Mr. Kleindienst said community responses were favorable. "I think we've started a new tradition," he said.

By reversing the definition, Sandusky not only eliminated the problem without damaging the tradition and without shifting the risk to insurance companies or other community groups, it added a new dimension that allowed at least some people to enjoy the event more than ever.

This reversal is similar to what Rothenberg (1979, 1991) referred to as **Janusian thinking**. Janus was the Roman god with two faces that looked in opposite directions. Janusian thinking means thinking contradictory thoughts at the same time: that is, conceiving two opposing ideas to be true concurrently. Rothenberg claimed, after studying 54 highly creative artists and scientists (e.g., Nobel Prize winners), that most major scientific breakthroughs and artistic masterpieces are products of Janusian thinking. Creative people who actively formulate antithetical ideas and then resolve them produce the most valuable contributions to the scientific and artistic worlds. Quantum leaps in knowledge often occur.

An example is Einstein's account (1919, p. 1) of having "the happiest thought of my life." He developed the concept that, "for an observer in free fall from the roof of a house, there exists, during his fall, no gravitational field. . . in his immediate vicinity. If the observer releases any objects, they will remain, relative to him, in a state of rest. The [falling] observer is therefore justified in considering his state as one of rest." Einstein concluded, in other words, that two seemingly contradictory states could be present simultaneously: motion and rest. This realization led to the development of his revolutionary general theory of relativity.

In another study of creative potential, Rothenberg and Hausman (2000) found that when individuals were presented with a stimulus word and asked to respond with the word that first came to mind, highly creative students, Nobel scientists, and prize-winning artists responded with antonyms significantly more often than did individuals with average creativity. Rothenberg argued, based on these results, that creative people think in terms of opposites more often than do other people (also see research by Blasko & Mokwa, 1986).

For our purposes, the whole point is to reverse or contradict the currently accepted definition in order to expand the number of perspectives considered. For instance, a problem might be that morale is too high instead of (or in addition to) too low in our team (we may need more discipline), or maybe employees need less motivation (more direction) instead of more motivation to increase productivity. Opposites and backward looks often enhance creativity.

These three techniques for improving creative problem definition are summarized in Table 3.5. Their purpose is not to help you generate alternative definitions just for the sake of alternatives but to broaden your perspectives, to help you overcome conceptual blocks, and to produce more elegant (i.e., high-quality and parsimonious) solutions. They are tools or techniques that you can easily use when you are faced with the need to solve problems creatively.

WAYS TO GENERATE MORE ALTERNATIVES

Because a common tendency is to define problems in terms of available solutions (i.e., the problem is defined as already possessing a certain set of possible solutions, e.g., March & Simon, 1958; March 1999), most of us consider a minimal number and a narrow range of alternatives in problem solving. Most experts agree, however, that the primary characteristics of effective creative problem solvers are their **fluency** and their **flexibility of thought** (Sternberg, 1999). Fluency refers to the number of ideas or concepts produced in a given length of time. Flexibility refers to the diversity of ideas or concepts generated. While most problem solvers consider a few homogeneous alternatives, creative problem solvers consider many heterogeneous alternatives.

The following techniques are designed to help you improve your ability to generate a large number and a wide variety of alternatives when faced with problems, whether they be imagination, improvement, investment, or incubation. They are summarized in Table 3.6.

Defer Judgment

Probably the most common method of generating alternatives is the technique of ***brainstorming*** developed by Osborn (1953). This tool is powerful because most people make quick judgments about each piece of information or each alternative solution they encounter. Brainstorming is designed to help people generate alternatives for problem solving without prematurely evaluating, and hence discarding, them. It is practiced by having a group of people get together and simply begin sharing ideas about a problem—one at a time, with

Table 3.5	Techniques for Improving Problem Definition

1. **Make the strange familiar and the familiar strange** (for example, analogies and metaphors).

2. **Elaborate on the definition** (for example, question checklists and SCAMPER).

3. **Reverse the definition** (for example, Janusian thinking and opposition).

Table 3.6	Techniques for Generating More Alternatives

1. **Defer judgment** (for example, brainstorming).

2. **Expand current alternatives** (for example, subdivision).

3. **Combine unrelated attributes** (for example, morphological synthesis and relational algorithm).

someone recording the ideas that are suggested. Four main rules govern brainstorming:

1. No evaluation of any kind is permitted as alternatives are being generated. Individual energy is spent on generating ideas, not on defending them.
2. The wildest and most divergent ideas are encouraged. It is easier to tighten alternatives than to loosen them up.
3. The quantity of ideas takes precedence over the quality. Emphasizing quality engenders judgment and evaluation.
4. Participants should build on or modify the ideas of others. Poor ideas that are added to or altered often become good ideas.

The idea of brainstorming is to use it in a group setting so individuals can stimulate ideas in one another. Often, after a rush of alternatives is produced at the outset of a brainstorming session, the quantity of ideas often rapidly subsides. But to stop at that point is an ineffective use of brainstorming. When easily identifiable solutions have been exhausted, that's when the truly creative alternatives are often produced in brainstorming groups. So keep working. Apply some of the tools described in this chapter for expanding definitions and alternatives. Brainstorming often begins with a flurry of ideas that then diminish. If brainstorming continues and members are encouraged to think past that point, breakthrough ideas often emerge as less common or less familiar alternatives are suggested. After that phase has unfolded in brainstorming, it is usually best to terminate the process and begin refining and consolidating ideas.

Recent research has found that brainstorming in a group may be less efficient and more time consuming than alternative forms of brainstorming due to free riders, unwitting evaluations, production blocking, and so on. One widely used alternative brainstorming technique is to have individual group members generate ideas on their own then submit them to the group for exploration and evaluation (Finke, Ward, & Smith, 1992). Alternatively, electronic brainstorming in which individuals use chat rooms or their own computer to generate ideas has shown positive results as well (Siau, 1995). What is clear from the research is that generating alternatives in the presence of others produces more and better ideas than can be produced alone.

The best way to get a feel for the power of brainstorming groups is to participate in one. Try the following exercise based on an actual problem faced by a group of students and university professors. Spend at least 10 minutes in a small group, brainstorming your ideas.

The business school faculty has become increasingly concerned about the ethics associated with modern business practice. The general reputation of business executives is in the tank. They are seen as greedy, dishonest, and untrustworthy. What could the faculty or the school do to affect this problem?

How do you define the problem? What ideas can you come up with? Generate as many ideas as you can following the rules of brainstorming. After at least 10 minutes, assess the fluency (the number) and flexibility (the variety) of the ideas you generated as a team.

Expand Current Alternatives

Sometimes, brainstorming in a group is not possible or is too costly in terms of the number of people involved and hours required. Managers facing a fast-paced twenty-first-century environment may find brainstorming to be too inefficient. Moreover, people sometimes need an external stimulus or way to break through conceptual blocks to help them generate new ideas. One useful and readily available technique for expanding alternatives is **subdivision**, or dividing a problem into smaller parts. This is a well-used and proven technique for enlarging the alternative set.

For example, March and Simon (1958, p. 193) suggested that subdivision improves problem solving by increasing the speed with which alternatives can be generated and selected.

The mode of subdivision has an influence on the extent to which planning can proceed simultaneously on the several aspects of the problem. The more detailed the factorization of the problem, the more simultaneous activity is possible, hence, the greater the speed of problem solving.

To see how subdivision helps develop more alternatives and speeds the process of problem solving, consider the problem, common in the creativity literature, of listing alternative uses for a familiar object. For example, in one minute, how many uses can you list for a Ping-Pong ball? Ready . . . go.

The more uses you identify, the greater is your fluency in thinking. The more variety in your list, the greater is your flexibility in thinking. You may have included the following in your list: bob for a fishing line, Christmas ornament, toy for a cat, gearshift knob, model for a molecular structure, wind gauge when hung from a string, head for a finger puppet, miniature basketball. Your list will be much longer.

Now that you have produced your list, apply the technique of subdivision by identifying the specific characteristics of a Ping-Pong ball. That is, divide it into its component attributes. For example, weight, color, texture, shape, porosity, strength, hardness, chemical properties, and conduction potential are all attributes of Ping-Pong balls that help expand the uses you might think of. By dividing an object mentally into more specific attributes, you can arrive at many more alternative uses (e.g., reflector, holder when cut in half, bug bed, ball for lottery drawing, inhibitor of an electrical current, and so on).

One exercise we have used with students and executives to illustrate this technique is to have them write down as many of their leadership or managerial strengths as they can think of. Most people list 10 or 12 attributes relatively easily. Then we analyze the various aspects of the manager's role, the activities in which managers engage, the challenges that most managers face from inside and outside the organization, and so on. We then ask these same people to write down another list of their strengths as managers. The list is almost always more than twice as long as the first list. By identifying the subcomponents of any problem, far more alternatives can be generated than by considering the problem as a whole. Try this by yourself. Divide your life into the multiple roles you play—student, friend, neighbor, leader, brother or sister, and so on. If you list your strengths associated with each role, your list will be much longer than if you just create a general list of personal strengths.

Combine Unrelated Attributes

A third technique focuses on helping problem solvers expand alternatives by forcing the integration of seemingly unrelated elements. Research in creative problem solving has shown that an ability to see common relationships among disparate factors is a major factor differentiating creative from noncreative individuals (Feldman, 1999). Two ways to do this are through morphological synthesis (Koberg & Bagnall, 2003) and the relational algorithm (Crovitz, 1970). (For literature reviews, see Finke, Ward, & Smith, 1992; and Starko, 2001.)

With **morphological synthesis**, a four-step procedure is involved. First, the problem is written down. Second, attributes of the problem are listed. Third, alternatives to each attribute are listed. Fourth, different alternatives from the attributes list are combined together.

This seems a bit complicated so let us illustrate the procedure. Suppose you are faced with the problem of an employee who takes an extended lunch break almost every day despite your reminders to be on time. Think of alternative ways to solve this problem. The first solution that comes to mind for most people is to sit down and have a talk with (or threaten) the employee. If that doesn't work, most of us would reduce the person's pay, demote or transfer him or her, or just fire the person. However, look at what other alternatives can be generated by using morphological synthesis (see Table 3.7).

You can see how many more alternatives come to mind when you force together attributes that aren't obviously connected. The matrix of attributes can create a very long list of possible solutions. In more complicated problems—for example, how to improve quality, how to better serve customers, how to improve the reward system, how to land a great job—the potential number of alternatives is even greater, and, hence, more creativity is required to analyze them.

The second technique for combining unrelated attributes in problem solving, the **relational algorithm**, involves applying connecting words that force a relationship between two elements in a problem. For example, the following is a list of some words that connect other words together. They are called "relational" words.

about	across	after
against	opposite	or
out	among	and
as	at	over
round	still	because
before	between	but
so	then	though
by	down	for
from	through	till
to	if	in
near	not	under
up	when	now
of	off	on
where	while	with

To illustrate the use of this technique, suppose you are faced with the following problem: *Our customers are dissatisfied with our service.* The two major subjects in this problem are *customers* and *service.* They are connected by the phrase *are dissatisfied with.* With the relational algorithm technique, the relational words in the problem statement are removed and replaced with other relational words to see if new ideas for alternative solutions can be

LEARNING

Table 3.7	**Morphological Synthesis**			

Step 1. Problem statement: The employee takes extended lunch breaks every day with friends in the cafeteria.

Step 2. Major attributes of the problem:

AMOUNT OF TIME	**START TIME**	**PLACE**	**WITH WHOM**	**FREQUENCY**
More than 1 hour	12 noon	Cafeteria	Friends	Daily

Step 3. Alternative attributes:

AMOUNT OF TIME	**START TIME**	**PLACE**	**WITH WHOM**	**FREQUENCY**
30 minutes	11:00	Office	Coworkers	Weekly
90 minutes	11:30	Conference Room	Boss	Twice a Week
45 minutes	12:30	Restaurant	Management Team	Alternate Days

Step 4. Combining attributes:

1. A 30-minute lunch beginning at 12:30 in the conference room with the boss once a week.

2. A 90-minute lunch beginning at 11:30 in the conference room with coworkers twice a week.

3. A 45-minute lunch beginning at 11:00 in the cafeteria with the management team every other day.

4. A 30-minute lunch beginning at 12:00 alone in the office on alternate days.

identified. For example, consider the following connections where new relational words are used:

- ❑ Customers *among* service (e.g., customers interact with service personnel).
- ❑ Customers *as* service (e.g., customers deliver service to other customers).
- ❑ Customers *and* service (e.g., customers and service personnel work collaboratively together).
- ❑ Customers *for* service (e.g., customer focus groups can help improve service).
- ❑ Service *near* customers (e.g., change the location of the service to be nearer customers).
- ❑ Service *before* customers (e.g., prepare personalized service before the customer arrives).
- ❑ Service *through* customers (e.g., use customers to provide additional service).
- ❑ Service *when* customers (e.g., provide timely service when customers want it).

By connecting the two elements of the problem in different ways, new possibilities for problem solution can be formulated.

International Caveats

The perspective taken in this chapter has a clear bias toward Western culture. It focuses on analytical and creative problem solving as methods for addressing specific issues. Enhancing creativity has a specific purpose, and that is to solve certain kinds of problems better. Creativity in Eastern cultures, on the other hand, is often defined differently. Creativity is focused less on creating solutions than on uncovering enlightenment, one's true self, or the achievement of wholeness or self-actualization (Chu, 1970; Kuo, 1996). It is aimed at getting in touch with the unconscious (Maduro, 1976). In both the East and the West, however, creativity is viewed positively. Gods of creativity are worshipped in West African cultures (Olokun) and among Hindus (Vishvakarma), for example (Ben-Amos, 1986; Wonder & Blake, 1992), and creativity is often viewed in mystical or religious terms rather than managerial or practical terms.

In fostering creative problem solving in international settings or with individuals from different countries, Trompenaars and Hampden-Turner's (1987, 2004) model is useful for understanding the caveats that must be kept in mind. Countries differ, for example, in their orientation toward *internal control* (Canada, United States, United Kingdom) versus *external control* (Japan, China, Czech Republic). In internal cultures, the environment is assumed to be changeable, so creativity focuses on attacking problems directly. In external cultures, because individuals assume less control of the environment, creativity focuses less on problem resolution and more on achieving insight or oneness with nature. Changing the environment is not the usual objective.

Similarly, cultures emphasizing a *specific orientation* (Sweden, Denmark, United Kingdom, France) are more likely to challenge the status quo and seek new ways to address problems than cultures emphasizing a *diffuse culture* (China, Nigeria, India, Singapore) in which loyalty, wholeness, and long-term relationships are more likely to inhibit individual creative effort. This is similar to the differences that are likely in countries emphasizing *universalism* (Korea, Venezuela, China, India) as opposed to *particularism* (Switzerland, United States, Sweden, United Kingdom, Germany). Cultures emphasizing universalism tend to focus on generalizable outcomes and consistent rules or procedures. Particularistic cultures are more inclined to search for unique aberrations from the norm, thus having more of a tendency toward creative solution finding. Managers encouraging conceptual blockbusting and creative problem solving, in other words, will find some individuals more inclined toward the rule-oriented procedures of analytical problem solving and less inclined toward the playfulness and experimentation associated with creative problem solving than others.

Hints for Applying Problem-Solving Techniques

Not every problem is amenable to these techniques and tools for conceptual blockbusting, of course, nor is every individual equally inclined or skilled. Our intent in presenting these six suggestions is to help you expand the number of options available to you for defining problems and generating additional alternatives. They are most useful with problems that are not straightforward, are complex or ambiguous, or are imprecise in their definitions. All of us have enormous creative potential, but the stresses and pressures of daily life, coupled with the inertia of conceptual habits, tend to submerge that potential. These hints are ways to help unlock it again.

Reading about techniques or having a desire to be creative is not, alone, enough to make you a skillful creative problem solver, of course. Although research has confirmed the effectiveness of these techniques for improving creative problem solving, they depend on application and practice as well as an environment that is conducive to creativity. Here are six practical hints that will help facilitate your own ability to apply these techniques effectively and improve your creative problem solving ability.

1. *Give yourself some relaxation time.* The more intense your work, the more your need for complete breaks. Break out of your routine sometimes. This frees up your mind and gives room for new thoughts.

2. *Find a place (physical space) where you can think.* It should be a place where interruptions are eliminated, at least for a time. Reserve your best time for thinking.

3. *Talk to other people about ideas.* Isolation produces far fewer ideas than does conversation. Make a list of people who stimulate you to think. Spend some time with them.

4. *Ask other people for their suggestions about your problems.* Find out what others think about them. Don't be embarrassed to share your problems, but don't become dependent on others to solve them for you.

5. *Read a lot.* Read at least one thing regularly that is outside your field of expertise. Keep track of new thoughts from your reading.

6. *Protect yourself from idea-killers.* Don't spend time with "black holes"—that is, people who absorb all of your energy and light but give nothing in return. Don't let yourself or others negatively evaluate your ideas too soon.

You'll find these hints useful not only for enhancing creative problem solving but for analytical problem solving as well. Figure 3.10 summarizes the two problem-solving processes—analytical and creative—and the factors you should consider when determining how to approach each type of problem. In brief, when you encounter a problem that is straightforward—that is, outcomes are predictable, sufficient information is available, and means-ends connections are clear—analytical problem-solving techniques are most appropriate. You should apply the four distinct, sequential steps. On the other hand, when the problem is not straightforward—that is, information is ambiguous or unavailable and alternative solutions are not apparent —you should apply creative problem-solving techniques in order to improve problem definition and alternative generation.

Fostering Creativity in Others

Unlocking your own creative potential is important but insufficient, of course, to make you a successful manager. A major challenge is to help unlock it in other people as well. Fostering creativity among those with whom you work is at least as great a challenge as increasing your own creativity. In this last section of the

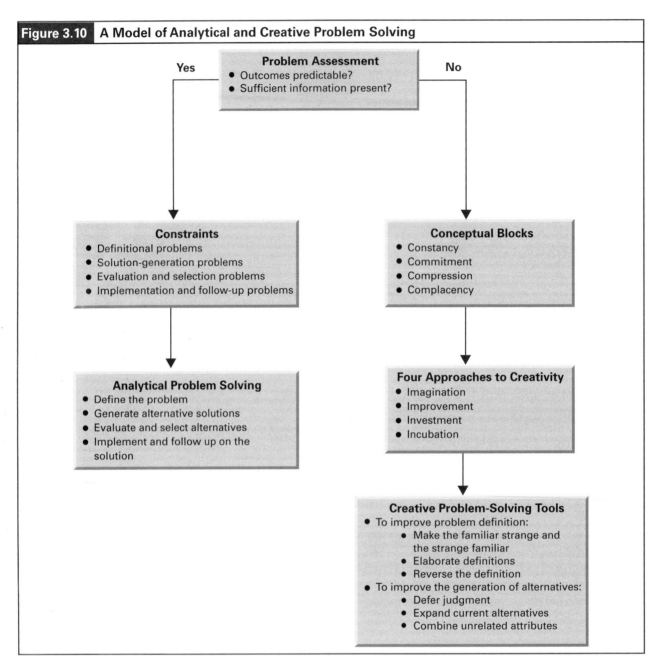

Figure 3.10 | **A Model of Analytical and Creative Problem Solving**

Problem Assessment
- Outcomes predictable?
- Sufficient information present?

Yes / No

Constraints
- Definitional problems
- Solution-generation problems
- Evaluation and selection problems
- Implementation and follow-up problems

Conceptual Blocks
- Constancy
- Commitment
- Compression
- Complacency

Analytical Problem Solving
- Define the problem
- Generate alternative solutions
- Evaluate and select alternatives
- Implement and follow up on the solution

Four Approaches to Creativity
- Imagination
- Improvement
- Investment
- Incubation

Creative Problem-Solving Tools
- To improve problem definition:
  - Make the familiar strange and the strange familiar
  - Elaborate definitions
  - Reverse the definition
- To improve the generation of alternatives:
  - Defer judgment
  - Expand current alternatives
  - Combine unrelated attributes

chapter, we briefly discuss some principles that will help you better accomplish the task of fostering creativity.

MANAGEMENT PRINCIPLES

Neither Percy Spencer nor Spence Silver could have succeeded in his creative ideas had there not been a support system present that fostered creative problem solving. In each case, certain characteristics were present in their organizations, fostered by managers around them, which made their innovations possible. In this section we will not discuss the macro-organizational issues associated with innovation (e.g., organization design, strategic orientation, and human resource systems). Excellent discussions of those factors are reviewed in sources such as Amabile (1988), DeGraff and Lawrence (2002), McMillan (1985), Tichy (1983), Tushman and Anderson (1997), and Van de Ven (1997). Instead, we'll focus on activities in which individual managers can engage that foster creativity. Table 3.8 summarizes three management principles that help engender creative problem solving among others.

Table 3.8	Three Principles for Fostering Creativity
PRINCIPLE	**EXAMPLES**
1. Pull people apart; put people together.	• Let individuals work alone as well as with teams and task forces. • Encourage minority reports and legitimize "devil's advocate" roles. • Encourage heterogeneous membership in teams. • Separate competing groups or subgroups.
2. Monitor and prod.	• Talk to customers. • Identify customer expectations both in advance and after the sale. • Hold people accountable. • Use "sharp-pointed" prods.
3. Reward multiple roles.	• Idea champion • Sponsor and mentor • Orchestrator and facilitator • Rule breaker

Pull People Apart; Put People Together

Percy Spencer's magnetron project involved a consumer product closeted away from Raytheon's main-line business of missiles and other defense contract work. Spence Silver's new glue resulted when a polymer adhesive task force was separated from 3M's normal activities. The Macintosh computer was developed by a task force taken outside the company and given space and time to work on an innovative computer. Many new ideas come from individuals being given time and resources and allowed to work apart from the normal activities of the organization. Establishing bullpens, practice fields, or sandlots is as good a way to develop new skills in business as it has proven to be in athletics. Because most businesses are designed to produce the 10,000th part correctly or to service the 10,000th customer efficiently, they do not function well at producing the first part. That is why pulling people apart is often necessary to foster innovation and creativity. This principle is the same as providing autonomy and discretion for other people to pursue their own ideas.

On the other hand, forming teams (putting people together) is almost always more productive than having people work by themselves. Such teams should be characterized by certain attributes, though. For example, Nemeth (1986) found that creativity increased markedly when minority influences were present in the team, for example, when "devil's advocate" roles were legitimized, when a formal minority report was always included in

final recommendations, and when individuals assigned to work on a team had divergent backgrounds or views. "Those exposed to minority views are stimulated to attend to more aspects of the situation, they think in more divergent ways, and they are more likely to detect novel solutions or come to new decisions" (Nemeth, 1986, p. 25). Nemeth found that those positive benefits occur in groups even when the divergent or minority views are wrong. Similarly, Janis (1971) found that narrow-mindedness in groups (dubbed **groupthink**) was best overcome by establishing competing groups working on the same problem, participation in groups by outsiders, assigning a role of critical evaluator in the group, and having groups made up of cross-functional participants. The most productive groups are those characterized by fluid roles, lots of interaction among members, and flat power structures. On the other hand, too much diversity, too much disagreement, and too much fluidity can sidetrack groups, so devil's advocates must be aware of when to line up and support the decision of the group. Their role is to help groups rethink quick decisions or solutions that have not been considered carefully enough, not to avoid making group decisions or solving problems.

You can help foster creativity among people you manage, therefore, by pulling people apart (e.g., giving them a bullpen, providing them with autonomy, encouraging individual initiative) as well as putting people together (e.g., putting them in teams, enabling minority influence, and fostering heterogeneity).

Monitor and Prod

Neither Percy Spencer nor Spence Silver was allowed to work on their projects without accountability. Both men eventually had to report on the results they accomplished with their experimentation and imagination. At 3M, for example, people are expected to allocate 15 percent of their time away from company business to work on new, creative ideas. They can even appropriate company materials and resources to work on them. However, individuals are always held accountable for their decisions. They need to show results for their "play time."

Holding people accountable for outcomes, in fact, is an important motivator for improved performance. Two innovators in the entertainment industry captured this principle with these remarks: "The ultimate inspiration is the deadline. That's when you have to do what needs to be done. The fact that twice a year the creative talent of this country is working until midnight to get something ready for a trade show is very good for the economy. Without this kind of pressure, things would turn to mashed potatoes" (von Oech, 1986, p. 119). One way Woody Morcott, former CEO at Dana Corporation, held people accountable for creativity was to require that each person in the company submit at least two suggestions for improvement each month. At least 70 percent of the new ideas had to be implemented. Woody admitted that he stole the idea during a visit to a Japanese company where he noticed workers huddled around a table scribbling notes on how some ideas for improvement might work. At Dana, this requirement is part of every person's job assignment. Rewards are associated with such ideas as well. A plant in Chihuahua, Mexico, for example, rewards employees with $1.89 for every idea submitted and another $1.89 if the idea is used. "We drill into people that they are responsible for keeping the plant competitive through innovation," Morcott said (personal communication).

In addition to accountability, creativity is stimulated by what Gene Goodson at Johnson Controls called "sharp-pointed prods." After taking over the automotive group at that company, Goodson found that he could stimulate creative problem solving by issuing certain mandates that demanded new approaches to old tasks. One such mandate was, "There will be no more forklift trucks allowed in any of our plants." At first hearing, that mandate sounded absolutely outrageous. Think about it. You have a plant with tens of thousands of square feet of floor space. The loading docks are on one side of the building, and many tons of heavy raw materials are unloaded weekly and moved from the loading docks to work stations throughout the entire facility. The only way it can be done is with forklifts. Eliminating forklift trucks would ruin the plant, right?

Wrong. This sharp-pointed prod demanded that individuals working in the plant find ways to move the work stations closer to the raw materials, to move the unloading of the raw materials closer to the work stations, or to change the size and amounts of material being unloaded. The innovations that resulted from eliminating forklifts saved the company millions of dollars in materials handling and wasted time; dramatically improved quality, productivity, and efficiency; and made it possible for Johnson Controls to capture some business from their Japanese competitors.

One of the best methods for generating useful prods is to regularly monitor customer preferences, expectations, and evaluations. Many of the most creative ideas have come from customers, the recipients of goods and services. Identifying their preferences in advance and monitoring their evaluations of products or services later are good ways to get creative ideas and to foster imagination, improvement, investment, and incubation. All employees should be in regular contact with their own customers, asking questions and monitoring performance.

By customers, we don't mean just the end users of a business product or service. In fact, all of us have customers, whether we are students in school, members of a family, players on a basketball team, or neighbors in an apartment complex. Customers are simply those we serve or for whom we are trying to produce something. Students, for example, can count their instructors, class members, and potential employers as customers whom they serve. A priori and post hoc monitoring of their expectations and evaluations is an important way to help foster new ideas for problem solving. This monitoring is best done through one-on-one meetings, but it can also be done through follow-up calls, surveys, customer complaint cards, suggestion systems, and so on.

In summary, you can foster creativity by holding people accountable for new ideas and by stimulating them with periodic prods. The most useful prods generally come from customers.

Reward Multiple Roles

The success of Post-it Notes at 3M is more than a story of the creativity of Spence Silver. It also illustrates the necessity of people playing multiple roles in enabling creativity and the importance of recognizing and rewarding those who play such roles. Without a number of people playing multiple roles, Spence Silver's glue would probably still be on a shelf somewhere.

Four crucial roles for enabling creativity in others include the **idea champion** (the person who comes up with creative problem solutions), the **sponsor** or mentor (the person who helps provide the resources, environment, and encouragement for the idea champion to work on his idea), the **orchestrator** or facilitator (the person who brings together cross-functional groups and necessary political support to facilitate implementation of creative ideas), and the **rule breaker** (the person who goes beyond organizational boundaries and barriers to ensure success of the creative solution). Each of these roles is present in most important innovations in organizations, and all are illustrated by the Post-it Note example.

This story has four major parts.

1. Spence Silver, while fooling around with chemical configurations that the academic literature indicated wouldn't work, invented a glue that wouldn't stick. Silver spent years giving presentations to any audience at 3M that would listen, trying to pawn off his glue on some division that could find a practical application for it. But nobody was interested.

2. Henry Courtney and Roger Merrill developed a coating substance that allowed the glue to stick to one surface but not to others. This made it possible to produce a permanently temporary glue, that is, one that would peel off easily when pulled but would otherwise hang on forever.

3. Art Fry found a problem that fit Spence Silver's solution. He found an application for the glue as a "better bookmark" and as a note pad. No equipment existed at 3M to coat only a part of a piece of paper with the glue. Fry therefore carried 3M equipment and tools home to his own basement, where he designed and made his own machine to manufacture the forerunner of Post-it Notes. Because the working machine became too large to get out of his basement, he blasted a hole in the wall to get the equipment back to 3M. He then brought together engineers, designers, production managers, and machinists to demonstrate the prototype machine and generate enthusiasm for manufacturing the product.

4. Geoffrey Nicholson and Joseph Ramsey began marketing the product inside 3M. They also submitted the product to the standard 3M market tests. The product failed miserably. No one wanted to pay $1.00 for a pad of scratch paper. But when Nicholson and Ramsey broke 3M rules by personally visiting test market sites and giving away free samples, the consuming public became addicted to the product.

In this scenario, Spence Silver was both a rule breaker and an idea champion. Art Fry was also an idea champion, but more importantly, he orchestrated the coming together of the various groups needed to get the innovation off the ground. Henry Courtney and Roger Merrill helped sponsor Silver's innovation by providing him with the coating substance that would allow his idea to work. Geoff Nicholson and Joe Ramsey were both rule breakers and sponsors in their bid to get the product accepted by the public. In each case, not only did all these people play unique roles, but they did so with tremendous enthusiasm and zeal. They were confident of their ideas and willing to put their time and resources on the line as advocates. They fostered support among a variety of constituencies, both within their own areas of expertise as well as among outside groups. Most organizations are inclined to give in to those who are sure of themselves, persistent in their efforts, and savvy enough to make converts of others.

Not everyone can be an idea champion. But when managers reward and recognize those who sponsor and orchestrate the ideas of others, creativity increases in organizations. Teams form, supporters replace competitors, and innovation thrives. Facilitating multiple role development is the job of the managers who want to foster creativity. Figure 3.11 summarizes this process.

Summary

In the twenty-first century, almost no manager or organization can afford to stand still, to rely on past practices, and to avoid innovation. In a fast-paced environment in which the half-life of knowledge is about three years and the half-life of almost any technology is counted in weeks and months instead of years, creative problem solving is increasingly a prerequisite for success. The digital revolution makes the rapid production of new ideas almost mandatory. This is not to negate the importance of analytical problem solving, of course. The quality revolution of the 1980s and 1990s taught us important lessons about carefully proscribed, sequential, and analytic problem-solving processes. Error rates, response times, and missed deadlines dropped dramatically when analytical problem solving was institutionalized in manufacturing and service companies.

In this chapter we have discussed a well-developed model for solving problems. It consists of four separate

Figure 3.11 | Enabling Creativity in Others

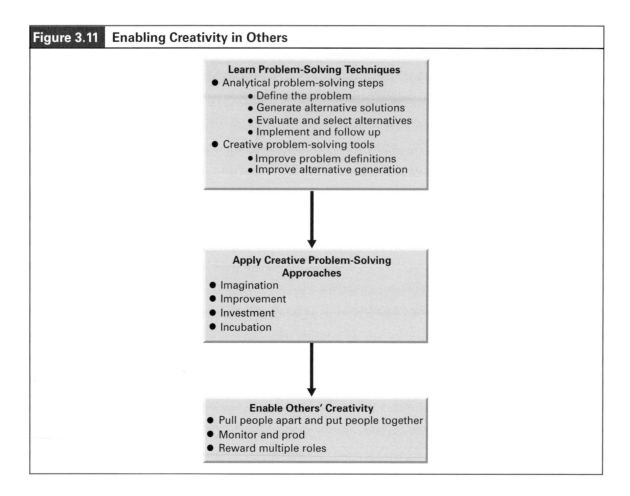

Learn Problem-Solving Techniques
- Analytical problem-solving steps
  - Define the problem
  - Generate alternative solutions
  - Evaluate and select alternatives
  - Implement and follow up
- Creative problem-solving tools
  - Improve problem definitions
  - Improve alternative generation

Apply Creative Problem-Solving Approaches
- Imagination
- Improvement
- Investment
- Incubation

Enable Others' Creativity
- Pull people apart and put people together
- Monitor and prod
- Reward multiple roles

and sequential stages: defining a problem; generating alternative solutions; evaluating and selecting the best solution; and implementing the chosen solution. This model, however, is mainly useful for solving straightforward problems. Many problems faced by managers are not of this type, and frequently managers are called on to exercise creative problem-solving skills. That is, they must broaden their perspective of the problem and develop alternative solutions that are not immediately obvious.

We have discussed four different types of creativity and encouraged you to consider all four when faced with the need to be creative. However, we have also illustrated eight major conceptual blocks that inhibit most people's creative problem-solving abilities. Conceptual blocks are mental obstacles that artificially constrain problem definition and solution and that keep most people from being effective creative problem solvers.

Overcoming these conceptual blocks is a matter of skill development and practice in thinking, not a matter of innate ability. Everyone can become a skilled creative

problem solver with practice. Becoming aware of these thinking inhibitors helps individuals overcome them. We also discussed three major techniques for improving creative problem definition and three major techniques for improving the creative generation of alternative solutions. Specific suggestions were offered that can help implement these six techniques.

We concluded by offering some hints about how to foster creativity among other people. Becoming an effective problem solver yourself is important, but effective managers can also enhance this activity among those with whom they work.

Behavioral Guidelines

Below are specific behavioral action guidelines to help guide your skill practice in analytical and creative problem solving.

1. Follow the four-step procedure outlined in Table 3.1 when solving straightforward problems. Keep the steps separate, and do not take

shortcuts—define the problem, generate alternative solutions, evaluate the alternatives, select and implement the optimal solution.

2. When approaching a difficult or complex problem, remember that creative solutions need not be a product of revolutionary and brand-new ideas. Four different types of creativity are available to you—imagination, improvement, investment, and incubation.

3. Try to overcome your conceptual blocks by consciously doing the following:
   - ❏ Use lateral thinking in addition to vertical thinking
   - ❏ Use several thought languages instead of just one
   - ❏ Challenge stereotypes based on past experiences
   - ❏ Identify underlying themes and commonalities in seemingly unrelated factors
   - ❏ Delete superfluous information and fill in important missing information when studying the problem
   - ❏ Avoid artificially constraining problem boundaries
   - ❏ Overcome any unwillingness to be inquisitive
   - ❏ Use both right- and left-brain thinking

4. To enhance creativity, use techniques that elaborate problem definition such as:
   - ❏ Making the strange familiar and the familiar strange by using metaphors and analogies
   - ❏ Developing alternative (opposite) definitions and applying a question checklist
   - ❏ Reversing the definition

5. To enhance creativity, use techniques that elaborate possible alternative solutions such as:
   - ❏ Deferring judgment
   - ❏ Subdividing the problem into its attributes
   - ❏ Combining unrelated problem attributes

6. Foster creativity among those with whom you work by doing the following:
   - ❏ Providing autonomy, allowing individuals to experiment and try out ideas
   - ❏ Putting people together who hold different perspectives into teams to work on problems
   - ❏ Holding people accountable for innovation
   - ❏ Using sharp-pointed prods to stimulate new thinking
   - ❏ Recognizing, rewarding, and encouraging multiple roles including idea champions, sponsors, orchestrators, and rule breakers

LEARNING

CASES INVOLVING PROBLEM SOLVING

Chip and Bin

Steven Henderson has some serious concerns over the new "chip and bin" system that Southeast Norfolk District Council has agreed to trial.

As part of the UK's attempts to reduce household waste consigned to landfills, a number of trials were carried out. Steven Henderson, leader of the Southeast Norfolk District Council, found that his council had been chosen to trial microchips on household bins. The trial would include over 50,000 households. Each of the council's 12 refuse trucks was fitted with $40,000 of scanning technology. The idea was that the refuse collectors would be able to identify a household's bin and weigh it. The information captured would be transferred to the truck's onboard computer. Each bin was weighed six times as it was lifted and six times on its way down to ensure accuracy. The council could then accurately bill each address, charging those responsible for excess waste and reducing bills for those not submitting the maximum amount of waste.

This initiative became known as "chip and bin," or "pay as you throw." Many residents, together with environmentalists and the news media, viewed it as a way for the government to collect additional taxes. However, the system was fatally flawed; the technology did not work. Henderson realized that the technology had to be trusted by households; it had to work for every bin on every street on every day of the year. Henderson was also uncomfortable that his refuse collectors were becoming government tax collectors.

The system had electrical, mechanical, hydraulic, and data faults. Numerous times the equipment broke down, and the collectors had to carry out repairs or try to override the system. Two weeks into the trial, Henderson attended a meeting with his recycling and refuse collection department, plus representatives from central government. The first devastating news was that there had been a 250 percent increase in "fly tipping." Rubbish was being abandoned at waste sites and along roadsides across the council's area. Residents were choosing to avoid paying higher costs by abandoning their refuse in the countryside. Second, the council's two recycling centers reported a 300 percent increase in the amount of waste material being brought to the sites. There was no charge for items taken to the recycling centers, and residents were choosing this option as an alternative to paying waste fees. Congestion around the recycling centers was becoming a major issue, and the recycling center managers reported that their employees were becoming overwhelmed.

Henderson listened to the problems and complaints his managers and staff were reporting. He considered the additional pressure and stress being placed on his departments. His public relations officer, Beatrice Watkins, summed up Henderson's feelings:

This is a PR disaster. It is bringing the council into disrepute. If the residents are losing faith with the council and view our carefully considered recycling policies as being a way to tax them more heavily, then we will lose support. We have already seen more rubbish being abandoned in the past few weeks than we did for the whole of the last quarter. I have heard that people in other parts of the country that are to be in stage 2 of the trial are peeling off the bar codes and the chip and pin details from their bins in protest.

I don't think we've told people enough about this. We are losing their trust. I would recommend terminating the trial as soon as possible.

Henderson agreed with her, but he could not say so. He had accepted nearly $1 million in grants and other payments from the central government to run the trial for a year. It was legally binding, and Henderson feared the consequences if he were to terminate the program. Before Henderson could comment, the representative from central government raised his hand, and Henderson asked him to speak:

This is not about pay as you throw, more save as you throw. There should be no increase in council taxes. It has public support, and the council has laws to prevent fly tipping. According to the European Union, Britain only recycles 18 percent of its rubbish, compared to 58 percent in Germany. Only Greece and Portugal have worse recycling rates. From 2010 the UK will face stiff EU penalties for landfill waste, so these tougher targets for everyone are unavoidable.

Henderson sensed the veiled threats. He determined not to make a decision but to reconvene the meeting in a week, after he had talked to his advisors. He needed a way to increase recycling rates, divert waste from the landfills, make the best use of the government-funded technology and, as a politician, regain the trust of the people in southeast Norfolk. "What we need is an incentive scheme and not a payment scheme. I want a more innovative way to encourage people to recycle rather than charging them money if they don't," he thought to himself.

Before Henderson could meet with his advisors he received a telephone call from the Department for the Environment, Food and Rural Affairs. It was a senior advisor to the minister:

Mr. Henderson, in good faith the government has awarded your council a grant to run this trial on our behalf. We fail to see why you have not acted decisively. You have barely given the trial a chance. There will inevitably be problems in the first few weeks; that is to be expected. Added to this you should be enforcing fly tipping legislation and prosecuting those dumping rubbish and limit the number of visits that residents can make to recycling centers. By taking their refuse there, they are undermining the whole trial. You are contractually obliged to run this trial, and the department expects you to give it your unreserved support and attention.

Henderson simply replied, "I will."

An hour later, Henderson called an emergency meeting with his most trusted advisors. He was deeply concerned about putting the council in this position and that the residents were blaming them for the problems. He listened to various points of view and the fact that the council would have to repay half of the government grant within 30 days if they broke the terms of the contract.

"How much money have we got?" he asked the finance director.

"Enough, but there will be nothing left in the contingency fund," was the reply.

"Do it, terminate the contract," Henderson decided. "But we need an upside to this. There's a new business working alongside councils, providing rewards for recycling. Their trials show boosts in recycling rates, and households get redeemable reward points based on how much they recycle. I want to see those people tomorrow and have something to say before we make this public."

At 9:30 the next morning, Henderson and Beatrice worked out a deal with Envirobank to set up a pilot scheme to reward residents for the amount of weekly recycling material collected. It was exactly what Henderson wanted—a reward and not a tax. But it would cost the council $250,000 per year to subsidize. Henderson made the decision without speaking to the finance director.

Afterwards, Henderson and Beatrice prepared a press release focusing on the positives. For Henderson, the most important thing was that instead of residents paying extra money using the chip and bin system, they would now be rewarded for recycling. The trial scheme would give residents redeemable reward points based on how much they recycled. Like a loyalty program, residents would receive reward points that they could spend at a range of participating retailers in the vicinity. Similar schemes had worked well in the United States and other countries.

Henderson knew that his next telephone call would be difficult. But to stop himself from being persuaded otherwise he had e-mailed all concerned, stating that at the end of the week the chip and bin trial would be terminated. There was no going back now.

Henderson's contact at the Department of the Environment took the news with calm resignation, but there was something else:

> *I hope you understand the implications of your decision. In rejecting chip and pin, you will add at least $160 to every household council tax bill. The country will be fined by the European Union every time it buries waste in a landfill site. That money has to come from somewhere; it will be your residents who cover the costs. I don't want you to have to decide between increasing council tax bills or closing day centers for the elderly, shutting swimming pools, or not having sufficient money to mend roads, but I suppose that is your decision.*

Discussion Questions

1. Identify the conceptual blocks illustrated in this case.
2. Outline the problem-solving steps followed by Henderson and the council. What steps in analytical problem solving were skipped or short-circuited?
3. If you were Henderson's advisor, knowing what you know about problem solving, what would you have suggested to help his problem-solving processes? What kinds of conceptual blockbusters could have been useful to Henderson?
4. What did you learn from this case that would help you advise Microsoft in its anticompetitive behavior case with the European Commission or the British Airports Authority being told to sell two of its London airports by the Competition Commission? What practical hints, in other words, do you derive from this case of analytical problem solving gone awry?

Creativity at Apple

> *In his annual speech in Paris in 2003, Steven Jobs, the lionized CEO of Apple Computer, Inc., proudly described Apple in these terms: "Innovate. That's what we do." And innovate they have. Jobs and his colleagues, Steve Wozniak and Mike Markkula, invented the personal computer market in 1977 with the introduction of the Apple II. In 1980, Apple was the number one vendor of personal computers in the world. Apple's success, in fact, helped spawn what became known as Silicon Valley in California, the mother lode of high technology invention and production for the next three decades.*

Apple has always been a trailblazing company whose innovative products are almost universally acknowledged as easier to use, more powerful, and more elegant than those of its rivals. In the last ten years, Apple has been granted 1,300 patents, half as many as Microsoft, a company 145 times the size of Apple. Dell Computer, by contrast, has been granted half as many patents as Apple. Apple has invented, moreover, more businesses than just the personal computer. In 1984, Apple created the first computer network with its Macintosh machines, whereas Windows-based PC's didn't network until the mid-1990s. A decade ago, Apple introduced the first handheld, pen-based computing device known as the Newton and followed that up with a wireless mouse, ambient-lit keyboards for working in the dark, and the fastest computer on the market in 2003. In 2003, Apple also introduced the first legal, digital music store for downloading songs—iTunes—along with its compatible technology, iPods. In other words, Apple has been at the forefront of product and technological innovation for almost 30 years. Apple has been, hands down, the most innovative company in its industry and one of the most innovative companies on the planet.

Here's the problem. Today, Apple commands just two percent of the $180 billion worldwide market for PCs. Apple's rivals have followed its creative leads and snatched profits and market share from Apple with astonishing effectiveness. From its number one position two decades ago, Apple currently ranks as the ninth largest PC firm—behind name-brand firms such as Dell, Hewlett-Packard, and IBM, but embarrassingly, also behind no-name firms such as Acer and Legend. These clone-makers, from Taiwan and China respectively, have invented no new products.

Moreover, whereas Apple was once among the most profitable companies in the PC industry, its operating profits have shrunk from 20 percent in 1981 to 0.4 percent in 2004, one-tenth the industry average. Its chief competitor in software—Microsoft—sold $2.6 billion in software in the most recent quarter compared to $177 million for Apple.

What could possibly be wrong? If one takes seriously the messages being declared loudly and prominently in the business press and in the broader global society today, innovation and creativity are the keys to success. "Change or die." "Innovate or get passed over." "Be creative to be successful." A key tenet upon which progressive, market-based, capitalistic societies are based is the idea of creative destruction. That is, without creativity and innovation, individuals and organizations become casualties of the second law of thermodynamics—they disintegrate, wither, disorganize, and die. New products are needed to keep consumers happy. Obsolescence is ubiquitous. Innovation and creativity, consequently, are touted as being at the very heart of success. For more evidence, just skim over the more than 49,000 book titles when you log onto Amazon and search using the key word "innovation."

On the other hand, consider some of the most innovative companies in recent American history. Xerox Corporation's famed Palo Alto Research Center gave the world laser printing, the Ethernet, Windows-type software, graphical user interfacing, and the mouse, yet it is notorious for not having made any money at all. Polaroid introduced the idea of instant images, yet it filed for bankruptcy in 2001. The Internet boom in the late 1990s was an explosion of what is now considered to be worthless innovation. And, Enron may have been the most innovative financial company ever.

On the other hand, Amazon, Southwest Airlines, eBay, Wal-Mart, and Dell are examples of incredibly successful companies, but did not invent any new products or technologies. They are acknowledged as innovative and creative companies, but they don't hold a candle to Apple. Instead of new products, they have invented new processes, new ways to deliver products, new distribution channels, new marketing approaches. It is well known that Henry Ford didn't invent the automobile. He simply invented a new way to assemble a car at a cost affordable to his own workers. The guy who invented the automobile hardly made a dime.

The trouble is, creativity as applied to business processes—manufacturing methods, sales and marketing, employee incentive systems, or leadership development—are usually seen as humdrum, nitty gritty, uncool, plodding, unimaginative, and boring. Creative people and creative companies that capture headlines are usually those that come up with great new product ideas or splashy features. But, look at the list of *Fortune* 500 companies and judge how many are product champions versus process champions. Decide for yourself which is the driver of economic growth: good innovation or good management.

SOURCE: Adapted from Hawn, 2004.

Discussion Questions

1. Consider the four approaches to creativity. What approach(es) has Apple relied upon? What alternatives have other firms in the industry pursued? What other alternatives could Apple implement?

2. Assume you were a consultant to the CEO at Apple. What advice would you give on how Apple could capitalize on its creativity? How can Apple make money based on its own inclination to pursue creativity in certain ways?

3. What are the major obstacles and conceptual blocks that face Apple right now? What do employees need to watch out for?

4. What tools for fostering creative problem solving are applicable to Apple, and which would not be workable? Which ones do you think are used the most there?

EXERCISES FOR APPLYING
CONCEPTUAL BLOCKBUSTING

The purpose of this exercise is to have you practice problem solving—both analytical and creative. Two actual scenarios are provided below. Both present real problems faced by real managers. They are very likely the same kinds of problems faced by your own business school and by many of your local businesses. Your assignment in each case is to identify a solution to the problem. You will approach the problem in two ways: first using analytical problem solving techniques; second, using creative problem-solving techniques. The first approach—analytical problem solving—you should accomplish by yourself. The second approach—creative problem solving—you should accomplish in a team. Your task is to apply the principles of problem solving to come up with realistic, cost-efficient, and effective solutions to these problems. Consider each scenario separately. You should take no more than ten minutes to complete the analytical problem-solving assignment. Then take twenty minutes to complete the creative problem-solving assignment.

Individual Assignment—Analytical Problem Solving (10 minutes)

1. After reading the first case, write down a specific problem definition. What precisely worded problem are you going to solve? Complete the sentence: The problem I am going to solve is . . .

2. Now identify at least four or five alternative solutions. What ideas do you have for resolving this problem? Complete this sentence: Possible ways to resolve this problem are . . .

3. Next, evaluate the alternatives you have proposed. Make sure you don't evaluate each alternative before proposing your complete set. Evaluate your set of alternatives on the basis of these criteria: Will this alternative solve the problem you have defined? Is this alternative realistic in terms of being cost-effective? Can this solution be implemented in a short time frame?

4. Now write down your proposed solution to the problem. Be specific about what should be done and when. Be prepared to share that solution with other team members.

Team Assignment—Creative Problem Solving (20 minutes)

1. Now form a team of four or five people. Each team member should share his or her own definition of the problem. It is unlikely that they will all be the same, so make sure you keep track of them. Now add at least three more plausible definitions of the problem. In doing so, use at least two techniques for expanding problem definition discussed in the text. Each problem definition should differ from the others in what the problem is, not just a statement of different causes of the problem.

2. Now examine each of the definitions you have proposed. Select one that the entire team can agree upon. Since it is unlikely that you can solve multiple problems at once, select just one problem definition that you will work on.

3. Share the four or five proposed solutions that you generated on your own, even if they don't relate to the specific problem your team has defined. Keep track of all the different alternatives proposed by team members. After all team members have shared their alternatives, generate at least five additional alternative solutions to the problem you have agreed upon. Use at least two of the techniques for expanding alternatives discussed in the text.

4. Of all the alternatives your team proposed, select the five that you consider to be the most creative and having the highest probability of success.

5. Select one team member from each team to serve as a judging panel. This panel is charged with selecting the team with the most creative and potentially successful alternatives to the problem. Team members cannot vote for their own team.

6. Each team now shares their five alternatives with the class. The judging panel selects the winner.

Moving Up in the Rankings

Business schools seem to have lost the ability to evaluate their own quality and effectiveness. With the emergence of rankings of business schools in the popular press, the role of judging quality seems to have been captured by publications such as *Business Week*, *U.S. News and World Report*, and the *Financial Times*. The accreditation association for business schools, AACSB, mainly assesses the extent to which a school is accreditable or not, a 0–1 distinction, so a wide range in quality exists among accredited business schools. More refined distinctions have been made in the popular press by identifying the highest rated 50, the first, second, or third tiers, or the top 20. Each publication relies on slightly different criteria in their rankings, but a substantial portion of each ranking rests on name recognition, visibility, or public acclaim. In some of the polls, more than 50 percent of the weighting is placed on the reputation or notoriety of the school. This is problematic, of

spend $300,000 on renovations, including the addition of a patio and upgraded equipment. The agent agreed. With almost no market research, they opened the second McGuffey's 18 months later. The first, in Asheville, was still roaring, having broken the $2 million mark in sales its first year, with a marginal loss of just over $16,000.

By midsummer, the 200-seat Hendersonville restaurant was hauling in $35,000 a week. "Gee, you guys must be getting rich," the partners heard all around town. "When are you going to buy your own jets?" "Everyone was telling us we could do no wrong," says Dunn. The Asheville restaurant, though, was developing some problems. Right after the Hendersonville McGuffey's opened, sales at Asheville fell 15 percent. But the partners shrugged it off; some Asheville customers lived closer to Hendersonville, so one restaurant was probably pulling some of the other's customers. Either way, the customers were still there. "We're just spreading our market a little thinner," Dunn told his partners. When Asheville had lost another 10 percent and Hendersonville 5 percent, Dunn blamed the fact that the drinking age had been raised to 21 in Asheville, cutting into liquor sales.

By the end of that year, the company recorded nearly $3.5 million in sales, with nominal losses of about $95,000. But the adulation and the expectation of big money and fancy cars were beginning to cloud the real reason they had started the business. "McGuffey's was born purely out of frustration," says Dunn. Now, the frustration was gone. "You get pulled in so many directions that you just lose touch," says Laibson. "There are things that you simply forget."

What the partners forgot, in the warm flush of success, were their roots.

"Success breeds ego," says Dunn, "and ego breeds contempt." He would come back from trade shows or real-estate meetings all pumped up. "Isn't this exciting?" he'd ask an employee. "We're going to open a new restaurant next year." When the employee stared back blankly, Dunn felt resentful. "I didn't understand why they weren't thrilled," he says. He didn't see that while his world was constantly growing and expanding, his employees' world was sliding downhill. They were still busing tables or cooking burgers and thinking, "Forget the new restaurant; you haven't said hello to me in months; and by the way, why don't you fix the tea machine?"

"I just got too good, and too busy, to do orientation," he says. So he decided to tape orientation sessions for new employees, to make a film just like the one he had been subjected to when he worked at Bennigan's. On tape, Dunn told new employees one of his favorite stories, the one about the customer who walks into a chain restaurant and finds himself asking questions of a hostess sign because he can't find a human. The moral: "McGuffey's will never be so impersonal as to make people talk to a sign." A film maybe, but never a sign.

Since Dunn wasn't around the restaurants all that much, he didn't notice that employees were leaving in droves. Even the departure of Tom Valdez, the kitchen manager in Asheville, wasn't enough to take the shine off his "glowing ego," as he calls it.

Valdez had worked as Dunn's kitchen manager at TGI Friday's. When the Hendersonville McGuffey's was opening up, Dunn recruited him as kitchen manager. A few months later, Valdez marched into Dunn's office and announced that he was heading back to Indianapolis. "There's too much b.s. around here," he blurted out. "You don't care about your people." Dunn was shocked. "As soon as we get this next restaurant opened, we'll make things the way they used to be," he replied. But Valdez wouldn't budge. "Keith," he said bitterly, "you are turning out to be like all the other companies." Dunn shrugged. "We're a big company, and we've got to do big-company things," he replied.

Valdez walked out, slamming the door. Dunn still didn't understand that he had begun imitating the very companies that he had so loathed. He stopped wanting to rebel against them; under the intense pressure of growing a company, he just wanted to master their tried-and-true methods. "I was allowing the company to become like the companies we hated because I thought it was inevitable," he says.

PRACTICE

Three months later, McGuffey's two top managers announced that they were moving to the West Coast to start their own company. Dunn beamed, "Our employees learn so much," he would boast, "that they are ready to start their own restaurants."

Before they left, Dunn sat down with them in the classroom at Hendersonville. "So," he asked casually, "how do you think we could run the place better?" Three hours later, he was still listening. "The McGuffey's we fell in love with just doesn't exist anymore," one of them concluded sadly.

Dunn was outraged. How could his employees be so ungrateful? Couldn't they see how everybody was sharing the success? Who had given them health insurance as soon as the partners could afford it? Who had given them dental insurance this year? And who—not that anyone would appreciate it—planned to set up profit sharing next year?

Sales at both restaurants were still dwindling. This time, there were no changes in the liquor laws or new restaurants to blame. With employees feeling ignored, resentful, and abandoned, the rest rooms didn't get scrubbed as thoroughly, the food didn't arrive quite as piping hot, the servers didn't smile so often. But the owners, wrapped up in themselves, couldn't see it. They were mystified. "It began to seem like what made our company great had somehow gotten lost," says Laibson.

Shaken by all the recent defections, Dunn needed a boost of confidence. So he sent out the one-page survey, which asked employees to rate the owners' performance. He was crushed by the results. Out of curiosity, Dunn later turned to an assistant and asked a favor. Can you calculate our turnover rate? Came the reply: "220 percent, sir."

Keith Dunn figured he would consult the management gurus through their books, tapes, and speeches. "You want people-oriented management?" he thought. "Fine. I'll give it to you."

Dunn and Laibson had spent a few months visiting 23 of the best restaurants in the Southeast. Driving for hours, they'd listen to tapes on management, stop them at key points, and ask, "Why don't we do something like this?" At night, they read management books, underlining significant passages, looking for answers.

"They were all saying that people is where it's at," says Dunn. "We've got to start thinking of our people as an asset," they decided. "And we've got to increase the value of that asset." Dunn was excited by the prospect of forming McGuffey's into the shape of a reverse pyramid, with employees on top. Keeping employees, he now knew, meant keeping employees involved.

He heard one consultant suggest that smart companies keep managers involved by tying their compensation to their performance. McGuffey's had been handing managers goals every quarter; if they hit half the goals, they pocketed half their bonus. Sound reasonable? No, preached the consultant, you can't reward managers for a halfhearted job. It has to be all or nothing. "From now on," Dunn told his managers firmly, "there's no halfway."

Dunn also launched a contest for employees. Competition, he had read, was a good way of keeping employees motivated.

So the CUDA (Customer Undeniably Deserves Attention) contest was born. At Hendersonville and Asheville, he divided the employees into six teams. The winning team would win $1,000, based on talking to customers, keeping the restaurant clean, and collecting special tokens for extra work beyond the call of duty.

Employees came in every morning, donned their colors, and dug in for battle. Within a few weeks, two teams pulled out in front. Managers also seemed revitalized. To Dunn, it seemed like they would do anything, anything, to keep their food costs down, their sales up, their profit margins in line. This was just what all the high-priced consultants had promised.

But after about six months, only one store's managers seemed capable of winning those all-or-nothing bonuses. At managers' meetings and reviews, Dunn started hearing grumblings. "How come your labor costs are so out of whack?" he'd ask. "Heck, I can't win the bonus any-way," a manager would answer, "so why try?" "Look, Keith," another would say, "I haven't seen a bonus in so long, I've forgotten what they look like." Some managers wanted the bonus so badly that they worked understaffed, didn't fix equipment, and ran short on supplies.

The CUDA contest deteriorated into jealousy and malaise. Three teams lagged far behind after the first month or so. Within those teams people were bickering and complaining all the time: "We can't win, so what's the use?" The contest, Dunn couldn't help but notice, seemed to be having a reverse effect than the one he had intended. "Some people were really killing themselves," he says. About 12, to be exact. The other 100-plus were utterly demoralized.

Dunn was angry. These were the same employees who, after all, had claimed he wasn't doing enough for them. But OK, he wanted to hear what they had to say. "Get feedback," the management gurus preached; "find out what your employees think." Dunn announced that the owners would hold informal rap sessions once a month.

"This is your time to talk," Dunn told the employees who showed up—all three of them. That's how it was most times, with three to five employees in attendance, and the owners dragging others away from their jobs in the kitchen. Nothing was sinking in, and Dunn knew it. He now was clear about what didn't work. He just needed to become clear about what would work.

SOURCE: Inc: *The Magazine for Growing Companies by J. Hyatt. Copyright 1989 by Mansueto Ventures LLC. Reproduced with permission of Mansueto Ventures LLC in the format CD-ROM via Copyright Clearance Center.*

Creative Problem-Solving Practice

In a team of colleagues, apply as many of the creative problem-solving tools as you can in developing alternative solutions to any of the following problems. Different teams may take different problems and then report their solutions to the entire class. You may substitute a current pressing issue you are facing instead of one of these problems if you choose. Try consciously to break through your conceptual blocks and apply the hints that can help you expand your problem definition and the alternatives you consider to be relevant. Keep in mind the four different approaches to creativity.

Problem 1:   Consumers now have access to hundreds of television channels and thousands of shows on demand. The average person is lost. Without major advertising dollars, many networks, not to mention many programs, simply get ignored. How could you address this problem?

Problem 2:   At least 20 different rankings of schools appear periodically in the modern press. Students are attracted to schools that receive high rankings, and resources tend to flow to the top schools more than to the bottom schools. What could be done to affect the rankings of your own school?

Problem 3:   In the last five years, Virgin Atlantic Airlines has been growing at double digit rates while most U.S.-based airlines have struggled to make any money at all. What could the U.S. airline industry do to turn itself around?

Problem 4:   The newspaper industry has been slowly declining over the past several decades. People rely less and less on newspapers to obtain the news. What could be done to reverse this trend?

Have a team of observers watch the analytical and creative problem-solving process as it unfolds. Use the Observers' forms at the end of the chapter to provide feedback to the individuals and the teams on the basis of how well they applied the analytical and creative problem-solving techniques.

ACTIVITIES FOR SOLVING PROBLEMS CREATIVELY

Suggested Assignments

1. Teach someone else how to solve problems creatively. Explain the guidelines and give examples from your own experience. Record your experience in your journal.

2. Think of a problem that is important to you right now for which there is not an obvious solution. It may relate to your family, your classroom experiences, your work situation, or some interpersonal relationship. Use the principles and techniques discussed in the chapter to work out a creative solution to that problem. Spend the time it takes to do a good job, even if several days are required. Describe the experience in your journal.

3. Help direct a group (your family, roommates, social club, church, etc.) in a carefully crafted analytical problem-solving process—or a creative problem-solving exercise—using techniques discussed in the chapter. Record your experience in your journal.

4. Write a letter to your dean or a CEO of a firm identifying solutions to some perplexing problem facing his or her organization right now. Write about an issue that you care about. Be sure to offer suggested solutions. This will require that you apply in advance the principles of problem solving discussed in the chapter.

Application Plan and Evaluation

The intent of this exercise is to help you apply this cluster of skills in a real-life, out-of-class setting. Now that you have become familiar with the behavioral guidelines that form the basis of effective skill performance, you will improve most by trying out those guidelines in an everyday context. Unlike a classroom activity, in which feedback is immediate and others can assist you with their evaluations, this skill application activity is one you must accomplish and evaluate on your own. There are two parts to this activity. Part 1 helps prepare you to apply the skill. Part 2 helps you evaluate and improve on your experience. Be sure to write down answers to each item. Don't short-circuit the process by skipping steps.

Part 1. Planning

1. Write down the two or three aspects of this skill that are most important to you. These may be areas of weakness, areas you most want to improve, or areas that are most salient to a problem you face right now. Identify the specific aspects of this skill that you want to apply.

2. Now identify the setting or the situation in which you will apply this skill. Establish a plan for performance by actually writing down a description of the situation. Who else will be involved? When will you do it? Where will it be done?

> Circumstances:
> Who else?
> When?
> Where?

3. Identify the specific behaviors in which you will engage to apply this skill. Operationalize your skill performance.

4. What are the indicators of successful performance? How will you know you have been effective? What will indicate you have performed competently?

Part 2. Evaluation

5. After you have completed your implementation, record the results. What happened? How successful were you? What was the effect on others?

6. How can you improve? What modifications can you make next time? What will you do differently in a similar situation in the future?

7. Looking back on your whole skill practice and application experience, what have you learned? What has been surprising? In what ways might this experience help you in the long term?

APPLICATION

SCORING KEYS AND COMPARISON DATA

Problem Solving, Creativity, and Innovation

Scoring Key

SKILL AREA	ITEMS	ASSESSMENT	
		PRE-	POST-
Analytical Problem Solving	1, 2, 3, 4, 5	_____	_____
Creative Problem Solving	6, 7, 8, 9, 10, 11, 12, 13, 14, 15	_____	_____
Fostering Creativity	16, 17, 18, 19, 20, 21, 22	_____	_____
	Total Score	_____	_____

Comparison Data (N = 5,000 students)

Compare your scores to three standards:
1. The maximum possible score = 132.
2. The scores of other students in the class.
3. Norm data from more than 5,000 business school students.

Pre-Test				Post-Test
98.59	=	mean	=	107.47
114 or above	=	top quartile	=	118 or above
106–113	=	second quartile	=	109–117
102–105	=	third quartile	=	98–108
101 or below	=	bottom quartile	=	97 or below

How Creative Are You?©

Scoring Key

Circle and add up the values assigned to each item below.

ITEM	A AGREE	B UNDECIDED/ DON'T KNOW	C DISAGREE	ITEM	A AGREE	B UNDECIDED/ DON'T KNOW	C DISAGREE
1	0	1	2	21	0	1	2
2	0	1	2	22	3	0	−1
3	4	1	0	23	0	1	2
4	−2	0	3	24	−1	0	2
5	2	1	0	25	0	1	3
6	−1	0	3	26	−1	0	2

ITEM	A AGREE	B UNDECIDED/ DON'T KNOW	C DISAGREE	ITEM	A AGREE	B UNDECIDED/ DON'T KNOW	C DISAGREE
7	3	0	−1	27	2	1	0
8	0	1	2	28	2	0	−1
9	3	0	−1	29	0	1	2
10	1	0	3	30	−2	0	3
11	4	1	0	31	0	1	2
12	3	0	−1	32	0	1	2
13	2	1	0	33	3	0	−1
14	4	0	−2	34	−1	0	2
15	−1	0	2	35	0	1	2
16	2	1	0	36	1	2	3
17	0	1	2	37	2	1	0
18	3	0	−1	38	0	1	2
19	0	1	2	39	−1	0	2
20	0	1	2				

40. These words have values of 2:

energetic	perceptive
resourceful	innovative
original	self-demanding
enthusiastic	persevering
dynamic	dedicated
flexible	courageous
observant	curious
independent	involved

These words have values of 1:

self-confident	informal
thorough	alert
	forward-looking
restless	open-minded

The remaining words have a value of 0.

Total Score_____

Comparison Data (N = 5,000 students)

Mean score:	55.99
Top quartile:	65 or above
Second quartile:	55–64
Third quartile:	47–54
Bottom quartile:	46 or below

Innovative Attitude Scale

Scoring Key

Add up the numbers associated with your responses to the 20 items. When you have done so, compare your scores to the norm group of approximately 5,000 graduate and undergraduate business school students.

Mean score:	72.41
Top quartile:	79 or above

Second quartile: 73–78
Third quartile: 66–72
Bottom quartile: 65 or below

Creative Style Assessment

Scoring Key

Add up the points you gave to all of the "A" alternatives, the "B" alternatives, the "C" alternatives, and the "D" alternatives. Then divide by 7 to get an average score for each of the alternatives. Plot your score on the profile below, connecting the lines so that you produce some kind of kite-like shape.

Total of As: _____ / 7   Average score for A: _____ Imagine
Total of Bs: _____ / 7   Average score for B: _____ Incubate
Total of Cs: _____ / 7   Average score for C: _____ Invest
Total of Ds: _____ / 7   Average score for D: _____ Improve

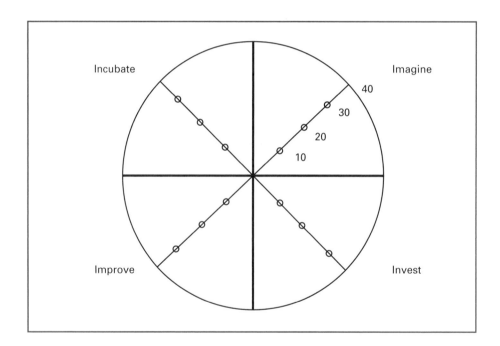

Comparison Data (N = 2500 students)

	MEAN SCORE	*TOP QUARTILE*	*THIRD QUARTILE*	*SECOND QUARTILE*	*BOTTOM QUARTILE*
A. Imagine	24.70	29 or above	25–28	20–24	19 or below
B. Incubate	25.92	30 or above	26–29	21–25	20 or below
C. Invest	25.47	30 or above	26–29	21–25	20 or below
D. Improve	24.04	27 or above	24–26	19–23	18 or below

The following Observer's Feedback Form can be used for each of the cases within the Skill Practice section (Moving Up in the Rankings, Keith Dunn and McGuffey's Restaurant).

Observer's Feedback Form

After the group has completed its problem-solving task, take the time to give the group feedback on its performance. Also provide feedback to each individual group member, either by means of written notes or verbal comments.

Group Observation

1. Was the problem defined explicitly?
   a. To what extent was information sought from all group members?
   b. Did the group avoid defining the problem as a disguised solution?
   c. What techniques were used to expand or alter the definitions of the problem?

2. Were alternatives proposed before any solution was evaluated?
   a. Did all group members help generate alternative solutions without judging them one at a time?
   b. Did people build on the alternatives proposed by others?
   c. What techniques were used to generate more creative alternatives for solving the problem?

3. Was the optimal solution selected?
   a. Were alternatives evaluated systematically?
   b. Was consideration given to the realistic long-term effects of each alternative?

4. Was consideration given to how and when the solution could be implemented?
   a. Were obstacles to implementation discussed?
   b. Was the solution accepted because it solved the problem under consideration, or for some other reason?

5. How creative was the group in defining and solving the problem?

6. What techniques of conceptual blockbusting did the group use?

Individual Observation

1. What violations of the rational problem-solving process did you observe in this person?

2. What conceptual blocks were evident in this person?

3. What conceptual blockbusting efforts did this person make?

4. What was especially effective about the problem-solving attempts of this person?

5. What could this individual do to improve problem-solving skills?

Answer to Matchstick Problem in Figure 3.4

Placing the match at the top turns the figure into a square root sign. The square root of 1 equals 1. ($\sqrt{1} = 1$).

Answer to Shakespeare Riddle in Figure 3.5

The answer is 5 inches. Be careful to note where page 1 of Volume I is and where the last page of Volume IV is.

Some Common Themes Applying to Water and Finance (page 212)

banks	capital drain
currency	sinking funds
cash flow	liquid assets
washed up	slush fund
deposits	financial float
frozen assets	underwater pricing
float a loan	

Answer to Name That Ship Problem in Figure 3.6

Comparing each part of the ship with the parts from the smaller ships, we find that the ship's name is DISCOVERY:

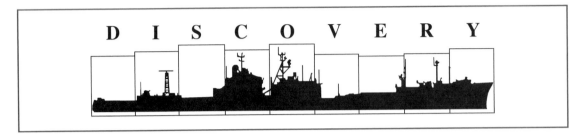

Answer to Nine-Dot Problem in Figure 3.7

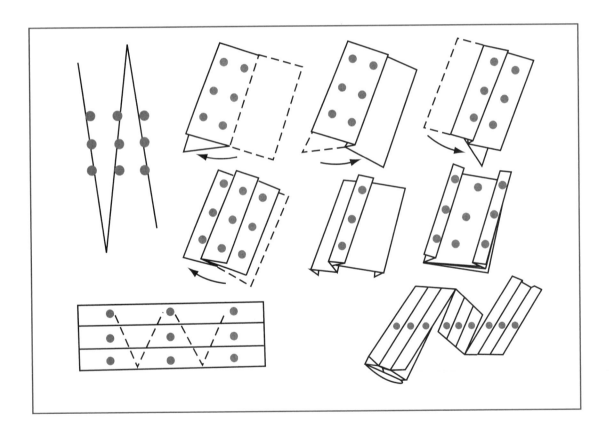

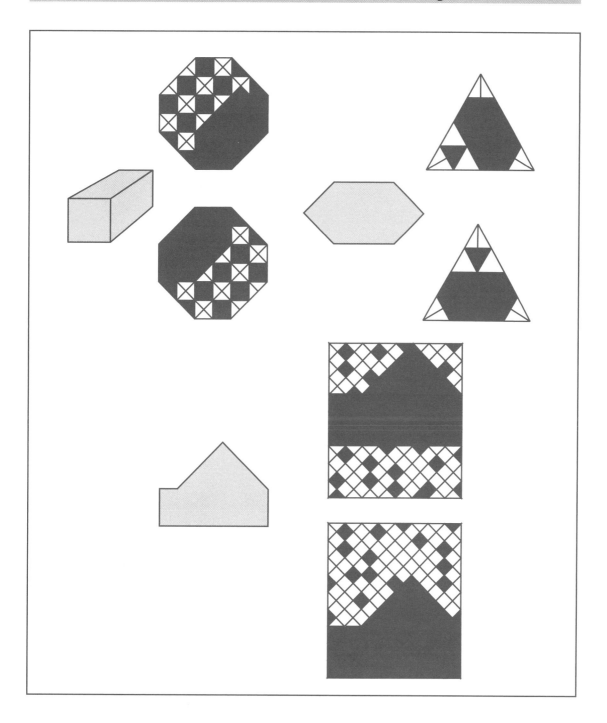

Part II

Interpersonal Skills

CHAPTERS

SKILL ASSESSMENT ▶

- Communicating Supportively
- Communication Styles

SKILL *LEARNING* ■

- Building Positive Interpersonal Relationships
- The Importance of Effective Communication
- What Is Supportive Communication?
- Coaching and Counseling
- Principles of Supportive Communication
- The Personal Management Interview
- International Caveats
- Summary
- Behavioral Guidelines

SKILL *ANALYSIS* ▶

- When the Cat's Away, the Mice Will Play
- Rejected Plans

SKILL *PRACTICE* ◆

- United Chemical Company
- Byron vs. Thomas
- Active Listening Exercise

SKILL *APPLICATION* ●

- Suggested Assignments
- Application Plan and Evaluation

SCORING KEYS AND *COMPARISON DATA* ■

4

Building Relationships by Communicating Supportively

SKILL DEVELOPMENT OBJECTIVES

- BUILD SUPPORTIVE RELATIONSHIPS EVEN WHEN DELIVERING NEGATIVE FEEDBACK

- AVOID DEFENSIVENESS AND DISCONFIRMATION IN INTERPERSONAL COMMUNICATION

- IMPROVE ABILITY TO APPLY PRINCIPLES OF SUPPORTIVE COMMUNICATION

- IMPROVE RELATIONSHIPS BY USING PERSONAL MANAGEMENT INTERVIEWS

255

DIAGNOSTIC SURVEYS FOR SUPPORTIVE COMMUNICATION

COMMUNICATING SUPPORTIVELY

Step 1: Before you read the material in this chapter, please respond to the following statements by writing a number from the rating scale below in the left-hand column (Pre-assessment). Your answers should reflect your attitudes and behavior as they are now, not as you would like them to be. Be honest. This instrument is designed to help you discover your level of competency in communicating supportively so you can tailor your learning to your specific needs. When you have completed the survey, use the scoring key at the end of the chapter to identify the skill areas discussed in this chapter that are most important for you to master.

Step 2: After you have completed the reading and the exercises in this chapter and, ideally, as many as you can of the Skill Application assignments at the end of this chapter, cover up your first set of answers. Then respond to the same statements again, this time in the right-hand column (Post-assessment). When you have completed the survey, use the scoring key at the end of the chapter to measure your progress. If your score remains low in specific skill areas, use the behavioral guidelines at the end of the Skill Learning section to guide further practice.

Rating Scale

1 Strongly disagree
2 Disagree
3 Slightly disagree
4 Slightly agree
5 Agree
6 Strongly agree

Assessment

Pre-   Post-

In situations where I have to provide negative feedback or offer corrective advice:

_____ _____ 1. I am clear about when I should coach someone and when I should provide counseling instead.

_____ _____ 2. I am able to help others recognize and define their own problems when I counsel them.

_____ _____ 3. I am able to be completely honest in the feedback that I give to others, even when it is negative.

_____ _____ 4. When I give feedback to others, I avoid referring to personal characteristics and focus on problems or solutions instead.

_____ _____ 5. I always link negative feedback to a standard or expectation that has been violated.

_____ _____ 6. When I try to correct someone's behavior, our relationship is almost always strengthened.

_____ _____ 7. I am descriptive in giving negative feedback to others. That is, I objectively describe events, their consequences, and my feelings about them.

_____ _____ 8. I always suggest specific alternatives to individuals whose behavior I'm trying to correct.

_____ _____ 9. I reinforce other people's sense of self-worth and self-esteem in my communication with them.

_____ _____ 10. I convey genuine interest in the other person's point of view, even when I disagree with it.

_____ _____ 11. I don't talk down to those who have less power or less information than I.

_____ _____ 12. Even when I feel strongly about my point of view, I convey to others that I am flexible and open to new information.

_____ _____ 13. I strive to identify some area of agreement in a discussion with someone who has a different point of view.

_____ _____ 14. My feedback is always specific and to the point, rather than general or vague.

_____ _____ 15. I don't dominate conversations with others.

_____ _____ 16. I take ownership of my statements and point of view by using personal words such as, "I think" instead of impersonal words such as "they think."

_____ _____ 17. When discussing someone's problem, I usually respond with a reply that indicates understanding rather than advice.

_____ _____ 18. When asking questions of others in order to understand their viewpoints better, I generally ask "what" questions instead of "why" questions.

_____ _____ 19. I hold regular, private meetings with people with whom I work and with whom I live.

_____ _____ 20. I understand clearly when it is appropriate to offer advice and direction to others and when it is not.

COMMUNICATION STYLES

This assessment instrument is divided into two parts.

In Part 1, four people complain about problems they face in their jobs. Following each complaint are five possible responses. Rank three of the responses you would be most likely to make, with 3 being your first choice, 2 being your second choice, and 1 being your third choice.

Part 2 of the assessment describes a particular situation. Several pairs of statements follow. Place a check mark next to the statement in each pair that you would most likely use in responding to that situation. Don't identify your preference. Rather, mark the alternatives that are most like your current behavior.

To score the Communication Styles instrument, turn to the end of the chapter to find the answer key and an interpretation of your scores.

Part 1

1. I've been in this job now for six months, and I hardly know anyone at all in the organization. I just can't seem to make friends or to be accepted by other people. Most people are extremely busy and don't take time to socialize. I feel isolated and excluded from what's going on.

_____ a. Don't be concerned about not making friends so soon. Things will get better the longer you're with the organization, you'll see.

_____ b. When you first meet people, what do you say? Are you the one to be friendly first?

_____ c. Because organization members are so busy, probably no one has time to get close socially. You shouldn't expect too much.

_____ d. So you're feeling that people haven't accepted you in the organization?

_____ e. When I first joined the organization it took me more than six months to get adjusted. I still don't know some of the people in several departments.

2. I can't stand my boss. He is the most autocratic, demanding person you can imagine. I've never worked around anyone who cared less for his employees than he does. His complete insensitivity and lack of humanity have made this a miserable place to work.

_____ a. You sound as if you're having difficulty dealing with rigid control and authority.

_____ b. I know how you feel because last year we had a woman in our department who would drive anybody crazy. She was the ultimate domineering boss.

_____ c. You're going to have problems unless you work this out. I think you should go to him and tell him how you feel.

_____ d. You really are having a hard time adjusting to your boss, aren't you?

_____ e. Why is it you feel so strongly about him?

3. What I want to know is, what happened on that last promotion decision? I thought I was in line for it. I'm sure no else in the department has my experience, and the scuttlebutt I heard indicated the job was mine for the asking. I'm really disappointed that you brought in someone from the outside over me. I don't think it's fair. What does it take to get promoted around here anyway?

_____ a. What was it that made you think this promotion was yours? Are you aware of the requirements of the job and what kind of person we were looking for?

_____ b. Don't be discouraged. Your work is good, and if you're patient I'm sure other chances will come along. I'll try to help you be ready the next time around.

_____ c. I think you have the wrong impression about this. The criteria were very clear for the new position, and the other person was just a better fit.

_____ d. In other words, you feel kind of puzzled about where you stand with the company.

_____ e. Are you interpreting this promotion decision as a challenge to your technical competence?

4. Hey, what's the idea of not approving my request for a new personal computer? I really need it in the office. We've got far more work to do than one machine can handle, and we're doing things manually that ought to be done on a spreadsheet. And don't give me that old story about tight company resources again. I've been in line for new equipment for a long time now.

_____ a. I understand that you are really upset about not getting your request approved.

_____ b. Why do you need a new computer? Can you borrow one during the times you really feel the crunch?

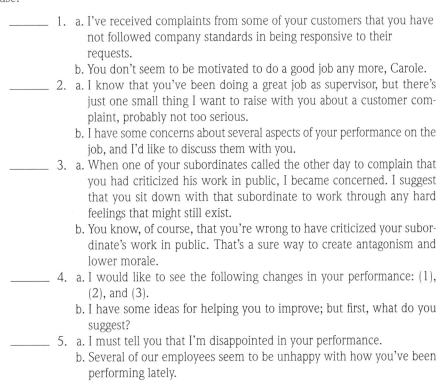

_____ c. You know, others are facing the same problem. We're having a terrible time trying to get the necessary work accomplished with the existing machines.

_____ d. If you'll be patient, I'm sure I can work out a solution to your problem.

_____ e. We turned you down because resources are really tight. You'll just have to make do.

Part 2

You are the manager of Carole Schulte, a 58-year-old supervisor who has been with the company for 21 years. She will retire at age 62, the first year she's eligible for a full pension. The trouble is, her performance is sliding, she is not inclined to go the extra mile by putting in extra time when required, and occasionally her work is even a little slipshod. Several line workers and customers have complained that she's treated them rather abruptly and without much sensitivity, even though superior customer service is a hallmark of your organization. She doesn't do anything bad enough to be fired, but she's just not performing up to levels you expect. Assume that you are having your monthly one-on-one meeting with her in your office. Which of the statements in each pair would you be most likely to use?

_____ 1. a. I've received complaints from some of your customers that you have not followed company standards in being responsive to their requests.

   b. You don't seem to be motivated to do a good job any more, Carole.

_____ 2. a. I know that you've been doing a great job as supervisor, but there's just one small thing I want to raise with you about a customer complaint, probably not too serious.

   b. I have some concerns about several aspects of your performance on the job, and I'd like to discuss them with you.

_____ 3. a. When one of your subordinates called the other day to complain that you had criticized his work in public, I became concerned. I suggest that you sit down with that subordinate to work through any hard feelings that might still exist.

   b. You know, of course, that you're wrong to have criticized your subordinate's work in public. That's a sure way to create antagonism and lower morale.

_____ 4. a. I would like to see the following changes in your performance: (1), (2), and (3).

   b. I have some ideas for helping you to improve; but first, what do you suggest?

_____ 5. a. I must tell you that I'm disappointed in your performance.

   b. Several of our employees seem to be unhappy with how you've been performing lately.

Building Positive Interpersonal Relationships

A great deal of research supports the idea that **positive interpersonal relationships** are a key to creating positive energy in people's lives (Baker, 2000; Dutton, 2003). When people experience positive interactions—even if they are just temporary encounters—they are elevated, revitalized, and enlivened. Positive relationships create positive energy. All of us have experienced people who give us energy—they are pleasant to be around, they lift us, and they help us flourish. We also have encountered people who have the reverse effect—we feel depleted, less alive, and emotionally exhausted when we interact with them. Such encounters are personally de-energizing.

The effects of positive relationships are much stronger and more long-lasting than just making people feel happy or uplifted, however. When individuals are able to build relationships that are positive and that create energy, important physiological, emotional, intellectual, and social consequences result. For example, people's physical well-being is significantly affected by their interpersonal relationships. Individuals in positive relationships recover from surgery twice as fast as those in conflicting or negative relationships. They have fewer incidences of cancer and fewer heart attacks, and they recover faster if they experience them. They contract fewer minor illnesses such as colds, flu, or headaches; they cope better with stress; and they actually have fewer accidents (i.e., being in the wrong place at the wrong time). As might be expected, they also have a longer life expectancy. These benefits occur because positive relationships actually strengthen the immune system, the cardiovascular system, and the hormonal system (Dutton, 2003; Heaphy & Dutton, 2006; Reis & Gable, 2003).

Positive relationships also help people perform better in tasks and at work, and learn more effectively. That is, positive relationships help people feel safe and secure, so individuals are more able to concentrate on the tasks at hand. They are less distracted by feelings of anxiety, frustration, or uncertainty that accompany almost all relationships that are nonpositive. People are more inclined to seek information and resources from people who are positively energizing, and they are less likely to obtain what they need to succeed if it means interacting with energy-depleting people. The amount of information exchange, participation, and commitment with other people is significantly higher when relationships are positive, so productivity and success at work are also markedly higher (see Dutton, 2003, for a review of studies).

Positive emotions—such as joy, excitement, and interest—are a product of positive relationships, and these emotions actually expand people's mental capacities. Feelings of joy and excitement, for example, create a desire to act, to learn, and to contribute to others. Moreover, the amount of information people pay attention to, the breadth of data they can process, and the quality of the decisions and judgments they make are all enhanced in conditions in which positive relationships are present. People's intellectual capacities are actually broadened (mental acuity expands), they learn more and more efficiently, and they make fewer mental errors when experiencing positive relationships (Fredrickson, 2001).

Not surprisingly, the performance of organizations is also enhanced by the presence of positive relationships among employees. Positive relationships foster cooperation among people, so the things that get in the way of highly successful performance—such as conflict, disagreements, confusion and ambiguity, unproductive competition, anger, or personal offense—are minimized. Employees are more loyal and committed to their work and to the organization when positive relationships exist, and information exchange, dialogue, and knowledge transfer are significantly enhanced. Creativity and innovation, as well as the ability of the system to adapt to change, are substantially higher when positive relationships characterize the workforce (Gittell, 2003; Gittell, Cameron, & Lim, 2006).

It is hard to find a reason why people would *not* want to build and enhance positive relationships with other human beings. Many advantages and very few liabilities are associated with positive interpersonal relationships. Creating such relationships sounds like a simple prescription, of course, but it is much easier said than done. It is not difficult to build positive relationships with people who are like us, to whom we are attracted, or who behave according to our expectations. But when we encounter people who are abrasive, who are not easy to like, or who make a lot of errors or blunders, building relationships is more difficult. In other words, building positive relationships in negative circumstances or with negative people requires special skill.

Arguably the most important skill in building and strengthening positive relationships is the ability to communicate with people in a way that enhances feelings of trust, openness, and support. In this chapter we focus on helping you develop and improve this skill. Of course, all of us communicate constantly, and we all feel that we do a reasonably good job of it. We haven't gotten this far in life without being able to communicate effectively. On the other hand, in study after study, communication problems are identified as the single biggest impediment to positive relationships and positive performance in organizations (Carrell & Willmington, 1996; Thorton, 1966). We focus in this chapter on this most important skill that effective managers must possess: the ability to communicate supportively.

The Importance of Effective Communication

In an age of electronic communication, the most frequently used means of passing messages to other people is via electronic technology (Gackenbach, 1998). E-mail now dominates communication channels in organizations, and it is purported to enhance information flow, the sharing of knowledge, consistency of communication, quality of feedback, and speed or cycle time (Council of Communication Management, 1996; Synopsis Communication Consulting of London, 1998). However, international surveys indicate that face-to-face communication is still the second most frequent form of communication, but it remains the most problematic (Rosen, 1998). One report concluded: "Technology is ahead of people's ability to cope and use it; it's becoming part of the problem, not part of the solution" (Synopsis Communication Consulting of London, 1998).

The problems with electronic communication are that: (1) people are bombarded with an overabundance of information, often poorly presented, so they are less willing to consume all the messages aimed at them; (2) no one puts all these rapid-fire messages in context, so much of the information lacks significance or meaning; and (3) effective interpretation and use of the information still depends on the relationship the recipient has with the sender. Accurate interpretation and effective message delivery depends on relationships of trust and shared context. Technology doesn't make messages more useful unless good interpersonal

relationships are in place first. Simply put, relationships determine meaning.

Of course, some relationships can be created electronically, but meaningful relationships based on trust are the exceptions rather than the rule. In a study of problems in marital relationships, for example, 87 percent said that communication problems were the root, double that of any other kind of problem (Beebe, Beebe, & Redmond, 1996). For the most part, the conclusion of an international study of communications in the workplace summarizes the key to effective communication: "To make the most of electronic communication requires learning to communicate better face to face" (Rosen, 1998).

Surveys have consistently shown that the ability to effectively communicate face to face is the characteristic judged by managers to be most critical in determining promotability (see surveys reported by Bowman, 1964; Brownell, 1986, 1990; Hargie, 1997; Randle, 1956; Steil, Barker, & Watson, 1983). Frequently, the quality of communication between managers and their employees is fairly low (Schnake, Dumler, Cochran, & Barnett, 1990). This ability may involve a broad array of activities, from writing to speech-making to body language. Whereas skill in each of these activities is important, for most managers it is face-to-face, one-on-one communication that dominates all the other types in predicting managerial success. In a study of 88 organizations, both profit and nonprofit, Crocker (1978) found that, of 31 skills assessed, interpersonal communication skills, including listening, were rated as the most important. Spitzberg (1994) conducted a comprehensive review of the interpersonal competence literature and found convincing and unequivocal evidence that incompetence in interpersonal communication is "very damaging personally, relationally, and socially." Thorton (1966, p. 237) summarized a variety of survey results by stating, "A manager's number-one problem can be summed up in one word: communication."

At least 80 percent of a manager's waking hours are spent in verbal communication, so it is not surprising that serious attention has been given to a plethora of procedures to improve interpersonal communication. Scholars and researchers have written extensively on communicology, semantics, rhetoric, linguistics, cybernetics, syntactics, pragmatics, proxemics, and canalization; and library shelves are filled with books on the physics of the communication process—encoding, decoding, transmission, media, perception, reception, and noise. Similarly, volumes are available on effective public-speaking techniques, making formal presentations, and the processes of organizational communication. Most colleges and universities have academic departments dedicated to the field of speech communication; most business schools provide a business communication curriculum; and many organizations have public communication departments and intraorganizational communication specialists such as newsletter editors and speech writers.

Even with all this available information about the communication process and the dedicated resources in many organizations for fostering better communication, most managers still indicate that poor communication is their biggest problem (Schnake et al., 1990). In a study of major manufacturing organizations undergoing large-scale changes, Cameron (1994) asked two key questions: (1) What is your major problem in trying to get organizational changes implemented? and (2) What is the key factor that explains your past success in effectively managing organizational change? To both questions, a large majority of managers gave the same answer: communication. All of them agreed that more communication is better than less communication. Most thought that over-communicating with employees was more a virtue than a vice. It would seem surprising, then, that in light of this agreement by managers about the importance of communication, communication remains a major problem for managers. Why might this be?

One reason is that most individuals feel that they are very effective communicators. They feel that communication problems are a product of others' weaknesses, not their own (Brownell, 1990; Carrell & Willmington, 1996; Golen, 1990). Haney (1992) reported on a survey of over 8,000 people in universities, businesses, military units, government agencies, and hospitals in which "virtually everyone felt that he or she was communicating at least as well as and, in many cases, better than almost everyone else in the organization. Most people readily admit that their organization is fraught with faulty communication, but it is almost always 'those other people' who are responsible" (p. 219). Thus, while most agree that proficiency in interpersonal communication is critical to managerial success, most individuals don't seem to feel a strong need to improve their own skill level (Spitzberg, 1994).

THE FOCUS ON ACCURACY

Much of the writing on interpersonal communication focuses on the *accuracy* of the information being communicated. The emphasis is generally on making certain that messages are transmitted and received with little alteration or variation from original intent. The communication skill of most concern is the ability to transmit clear, precise messages. The following incidents illustrate problems that result from inaccurate communication:

A motorist was driving on the Merritt Parkway outside New York City when his engine stalled. He quickly determined that his battery was dead and managed to stop another driver who consented to push his car to get it started.

"My car has an automatic transmission," he explained, "so you'll have to get up to 30 or 35 miles an hour to get me started."

The second motorist nodded and walked back to his own car. The first motorist climbed back into his car and waited for the good Samaritan to pull up behind him. He waited—and waited. Finally, he turned around to see what was wrong.

There was the good Samaritan—coming up behind his car at about 35 miles an hour!

The damage amounted to $3,800. (Haney, 1992, p. 285)

A woman of 35 came in one day to tell me that she wanted a baby but had been told that she had a certain type of heart disease that, while it might not interfere with a normal life, would be dangerous if she ever had a baby. From her description, I thought at once of mitral stenosis. This condition is characterized by a rather distinctive rumbling murmur near the apex of the heart and especially by a peculiar vibration felt by the examining finger on the patient's chest. The vibration is known as the "thrill" of mitral stenosis.

When this woman had undressed and was lying on my table in her white kimono, my stethoscope quickly found the heart sounds I had expected. Dictating to my nurse, I described them carefully. I put my stethoscope aside and felt intently for the typical vibration which may be found in a small and variable area of the left chest.

I closed my eyes for better concentration and felt long and carefully for the tremor. I did not find it, and with my hand still on the woman's bare breast, lifting it upward and out of the way, I finally turned to the nurse and said: "No thrill."

The patient's black eyes snapped, and with venom in her voice, she said, "Well, isn't that just too bad! Perhaps it's just as well you don't get one. That isn't what I came for."

My nurse almost choked, and my explanation still seems a nightmare of futile words. (Loomis, 1939, p. 47)

*In a Detroit suburb, a man walked onto a private plane and greeted the co-pilot with, "Hi, Jack!" The salutation, picked up by a microphone in the cockpit and interpreted as "hijack" by control tower personnel, caused police, the county sheriff's SWAT team, and the FBI all to arrive on the scene with sirens blaring. (*Time, *2000, p. 31)*

In the English language, in particular, we face the danger of miscommunicating with one another merely because of the nature of our language. For example, Table 4.1 lists 22 examples of the same word whose meaning and pronunciation are completely different, depending on the circumstances. No wonder individuals from other cultures and languages have trouble communicating accurately in the United States.

This doesn't account, of course, for the large number of variations in English-language meaning throughout the world. For example, because in England a billion is a million million, whereas in the United States and Canada a billion is a thousand million, it is easy to see how misunderstanding can occur regarding financial performance. Similarly, in an American meeting, if you "table" a subject, you postpone its discussion. In a British meeting, to "table" a topic means to discuss it now.

A Confucian proverb states: "Those who speak do not know. Those who know do not speak." It is not difficult to understand why Americans are often viewed as brash and unsophisticated in Asian cultures. A common problem for American business executives has been to announce, upon their return home, that a business deal has been struck, only to discover that no agreement was made at all. Usually it is because Americans assume that when their Japanese colleagues say "hai," the Japanese word for "yes," it means agreement. To the Japanese, it often means "Yes, I am trying to understand you (but I may not necessarily agree with you)."

When accuracy is the primary consideration, attempts to improve communication generally center on improving the mechanics: transmitters and receivers, encoding and decoding, sources and destinations, and noise. Improvements in voice recognition software have made accuracy a key factor in electronic communication. One cardiologist friend, who always records his diagnoses via voice recognition software, completed a procedure to clear a patient's artery by installing a shunt (a small tube in the artery). He then reported in the patient's record: "The patient was shunted and is recovering nicely." The next time he checked the record, the software had recorded: "The patient was shot dead and is recovering nicely."

Fortunately, much progress has been made recently in improving the transmission of accurate messages—that is, in improving their clarity and precision. Primarily through the development of a sophisticated information-based technology, major strides have been taken to enhance communication speed and accuracy in organizations. Computer networks with multimedia

Table 4.1	Inconsistent Pronunciations in the English Language

- We polish Polish furniture.
- He could lead if he would get the lead out.
- A farm can produce produce.
- The dump was so full it had to refuse refuse.
- The Iraqi soldiers decided to desert in the desert.
- The present is a good time to present the present.
- In the college band, a bass was painted on the head of a bass drum.
- The dove dove into the bushes.
- I did not object to that object.
- The insurance for the invalid was invalid.
- The bandage was wound around the wound.
- There was a row among the oarsmen about how to row.
- They were too close to the door to close it.
- The buck does funny things when the does are present.
- They sent a sewer down to stitch the tear in the sewer line.
- She shed a tear because of the tear in her skirt.
- To help with planting, the farmer taught his sow to sow.
- The wind was too strong to be able to wind the sail.
- After a number of Novocaine injections, my jaw got number.
- I had to subject the subject to a series of tests.
- How can I intimate this to my most intimate friend?
- I spent last evening evening out a pile of dirt.

capabilities now enable members of an organization to transmit messages, documents, video images, and sound almost anywhere in the world. The technology that enables modern companies to share, store, and retrieve information has dramatically changed the nature of business in just a decade. Customers and employees routinely expect information technology to function smoothly and the information it manages to be reliable. Sound decisions and competitive advantage depend on such accuracy.

However, comparable progress has not occurred in the interpersonal aspects of communication. People still become offended at one another, make insulting statements, and communicate clumsily. The interpersonal aspects of communication involve the nature of the relationship between the communicators. Who says what to whom, what is said, why it is said, and how it is said all have an effect on the relationships between people. This has important implications for the effectiveness of the communication, aside from the accuracy of the statement.

Similarly, irrespective of the availability of sophisticated information technologies and elaborately developed models of communication processes, individuals still frequently communicate in abrasive, insensitive, and unproductive ways. Rather than building and enhancing positive relationships, they damage relationships. More often than not, it is the interpersonal aspect of communication that stands in the way of effective message delivery rather than the inability to deliver accurate information (Golen, 1990).

Ineffective communication may lead individuals to dislike each other, be offended by each other, lose confidence in each other, refuse to listen to each other, and disagree with each other, as well as cause a host of other interpersonal problems. These interpersonal problems, in turn, generally lead to restricted communication flow, inaccurate messages, and misinterpretations of meanings. Figure 4.1 summarizes this process.

To illustrate, consider the following situation. Latisha is introducing a new goal-setting program to the organization as a way to overcome some productivity problems. After Latisha's carefully prepared presentation in the management council meeting, Jose raises his hand. "In my opinion, this is a naive approach to solving our productivity issues. The considerations are much more complex than Latisha seems to realize. I don't think we should waste our time by pursuing this plan any further." Jose's opinion may be justified, but the manner in which he delivers the message will probably eliminate any hope of its being dealt with objectively. Instead, Latisha will probably hear a message such as, "You're naive," "You're stupid," or "You're incompetent." Therefore, we wouldn't be surprised if Latisha's response was defensive or even hostile. Any good feelings between the two have probably been jeopardized, and their communication will probably be reduced to self-image protection. The merits of the proposal will be smothered by personal defensiveness. Future communication between the two will probably be minimal and superficial.

What Is Supportive Communication?

In this chapter, we focus on a kind of interpersonal communication that helps you communicate accurately and honestly, especially in difficult circumstances, without jeopardizing interpersonal relationships. It is not hard to communicate supportively—to express confidence, trust, and openness—when things are going well and when people are doing what you like. But when you have to correct someone else's behavior, when you have to deliver negative feedback, or when you have to point out shortcomings of another person, communicating in a way that builds and strengthens the relationship is more difficult. This type of communication is called **supportive communication**. Supportive communication seeks to preserve or enhance a positive relationship

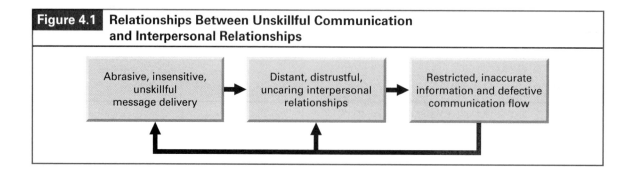

Figure 4.1 **Relationships Between Unskillful Communication and Interpersonal Relationships**

Abrasive, insensitive, unskillful message delivery → Distant, distrustful, uncaring interpersonal relationships → Restricted, inaccurate information and defective communication flow

between you and another person while still addressing a problem, giving negative feedback, or tackling a difficult issue. It allows you to communicate information to others that is not complimentary, or to resolve an uncomfortable issue with another person but, in the process, strengthen your relationship.

Supportive communication has eight attributes, which are summarized in Table 4.2. Later in the chapter we expand on each attribute. When supportive communication is used, not only is a message delivered accurately, but the relationship between the two communicating parties is supported, even enhanced, by the interchange. Positive interpersonal relationships result. People feel energized and uplifted, even when the information being communicated is negative.

The goal of supportive communication is not merely to be liked by other people or to be judged to be a nice person. Nor is it used merely to produce social

Table 4.2	The Eight Attributes of Supportive Communication		
• Congruent, Not Incongruent			
A focus on honest messages where verbal statements match thoughts and feelings.			
Example: "Your behavior really upset me."		*Not*	*"Do I seem upset? No, everything's fine."*
• Descriptive, Not Evaluative			
A focus on describing an objective occurrence, describing your reaction to it, and offering a suggested alternative.			
Example: "Here is what happened; here is my reaction; here is a suggestion that would be more acceptable."		*Not*	*"You are wrong for doing what you did."*
• Problem-Oriented, Not Person-Oriented			
A focus on problems and issues that can be changed rather than people and their characteristics.			
Example: "How can we solve this problem?"		*Not*	*"Because of you a problem exists."*
• Validating, Not Invalidating			
A focus on statements that communicate respect, flexibility, collaboration, and areas of agreement.			
Example: "I have some ideas, but do you have any suggestions?"		*Not*	*"You wouldn't understand, so we'll do it my way."*
• Specific, Not Global			
A focus on specific events or behaviors and avoid general, extreme, or either-or statements.			
Example: "You interrupted me three times during the meeting."		*Not*	*"You're always trying to get attention."*
• Conjunctive, Not Disjunctive			
A focus on statements that flow from what has been said previously and facilitate interaction.			
Example: "Relating to what you just said, I'd like to raise another point."		*Not*	*"I want to say something (regardless of what you just said)."*
• Owned, Not Disowned			
A focus on taking responsibility for your own statements by using personal ("I") words.			
Example: "I have decided to turn down your request because . . . "		*Not*	*"You have a pretty good idea, but it wouldn't get approved."*
• Supportive Listening, Not One-Way Listening			
A focus on using a variety of appropriate responses, with a bias toward reflective responses.			
Example: "What do you think are the obstacles standing in the way of improvement?"		*Not*	*"As I said before, you make too many mistakes. You're just not performing."*

acceptance. As pointed out previously, positive interpersonal relationships have practical, instrumental value in organizations. Researchers have found, for example, that organizations fostering supportive interpersonal relationships enjoy higher productivity, faster problem solving, higher-quality outputs, and fewer conflicts and subversive activities than do groups and organizations in which relationships are less positive. Moreover, delivering outstanding customer service is almost impossible without supportive communication. Customer complaints and misunderstandings frequently require supportive communication skills to resolve. Not only must managers be competent in using this kind of communication, therefore, but they must help their subordinates develop this competency as well.

One important lesson that American managers have been taught by foreign competitors is that good relationships among employees, and between managers and employees, produce bottom-line advantages (Ouchi, 1981; Peters, 1988; Pfeffer, 1998). Hanson (1986) found, for example, that the presence of good interpersonal relationships between managers and subordinates was three times more powerful in predicting profitability in 40 major corporations over a five-year period than the four next most powerful variables—market share, capital intensity, firm size, and sales growth rate—combined. Supportive communication, therefore, isn't just a "nice-person technique," but a proven competitive advantage for both managers and organizations.

Coaching and Counseling

One of the ways to illustrate the principles of supportive communication is to discuss two common roles performed by managers (and parents, friends, and coworkers): coaching and counseling others. In coaching, managers pass along advice and information, or they set standards to help others improve their work skills. In counseling, managers help others recognize and address problems involving their level of understanding, emotions, or personalities. Thus, coaching focuses on abilities, counseling on attitudes.

The skills of coaching and counseling also apply to a broad array of activities, of course, such as motivating others, handling customer complaints, passing critical or negative information upward, handling conflicts between other parties, negotiating for a certain position, and so on. Because most managers—and most people—are involved in coaching and counseling at some time, however, we will use them to illustrate and explain the behavioral principles involved.

Skillful coaching and counseling are especially important in (1) rewarding positive performance and (2) correcting problem behaviors or attitudes. Both of these activities are discussed in more detail in the chapter on Motivating Others. In that chapter, we discuss the *content* of rewarding and correcting behavior (i.e., *what* to do), whereas in our present discussion we focus on the *processes* of rewarding and correcting behavior (i.e., *how* to do it).

Coaching and counseling are more difficult to perform effectively when individuals are not performing up to expectations, when their attitudes are negative, when their behavior is disruptive, or when their personalities clash with others in the organization. Whenever managers have to help people change their attitudes or behaviors, coaching or counseling is required. In these situations, managers face the responsibility of providing negative feedback to others or getting them to recognize problems that they don't want to acknowledge. Managers must reprimand or correct employees, but in a way that facilitates positive work outcomes, positive feelings, and positive relationships.

What makes coaching and counseling so challenging is the risk of offending or alienating other people. That risk is so high that many managers ignore completely the feelings and reactions of others by taking a directive, hard-nosed, "shape up or ship out" approach. Alternatively, they soft-pedal, avoid confrontations, or drop hints for fear of hurting feelings and destroying relationships—the "don't worry be happy" approach. The principles we describe in this chapter not only facilitate accurate message delivery in sensitive situations, but their effective use can produce higher levels of motivation, increased productivity, and better interpersonal relationships.

Of course, coaching and counseling skills are also required when negative feedback is not involved, such as when other people ask for advice, need someone to listen to their problems, or want to register complaints. Sometimes just listening is the most effective form of coaching or counseling. Although the risk of damaged relationships, defensiveness, or hurt feelings is not as likely as when negative feedback is given, these situations still require competent supportive communication skills. Guidelines for how to implement supportive communication effectively in both negative and positive coaching and counseling situations are discussed in the rest of this chapter.

To illustrate, consider the following two scenarios:

Jagdip Ahwal is the manager of the division sales force in your firm, which makes and sells components for the aerospace industry. He reports directly to you. Jagdip's division consistently misses its sales projections, its revenues per salesperson are below the firm average, and Jagdip's monthly reports are almost always late. You make another appointment to visit with Jagdip after getting the latest sales figures, but he isn't in his office when you arrive. His secretary tells you that one of Jagdip's sales managers dropped by a few minutes ago to complain that some employees are coming in late for work in the morning and taking extra-long coffee breaks. Jagdip had immediately gone with the manager to his sales department to give the salespeople a "pep talk" and to remind them of performance expectations. You wait for 15 minutes until he returns.

Betsy Christensen has an MBA from a prestigious Big Ten school and has recently joined your firm in the financial planning group. She came with great recommendations and credentials. However, she seems to be trying to enhance her own reputation at the expense of others in her group. You have heard increasing complaints lately that Betsy acts arrogantly, is self-promotional, and is openly critical of other group members' work. In your first conversation with her about her performance in the group, she denied that there is a problem. She said that, if anything, she was having a positive impact on the group by raising its standards. You schedule another meeting with Betsy after this latest set of complaints from her coworkers.

What are the basic problems in these two cases? Which one is primarily a coaching problem and which is primarily a counseling problem? How would you approach them so that the problems got solved and, at the same time, your relationships with Jagdip and Betsy are strengthened? What would you say, and how would you say it, so that the best possible outcomes result? This chapter can help you improve your skill in handling such situations effectively.

COACHING AND COUNSELING PROBLEMS

The two cases above help identify the two basic kinds of interpersonal communication problems faced by managers. Although no situation is completely one

thing versus the other, in the case with Jagdip Ahwal, the basic need is primarily for **coaching**. Coaching situations are those in which managers must pass along advice and information or set standards for others. People must be advised on how to do their jobs better and to be coached to better performance. Coaching problems are usually caused by lack of ability, insufficient information or understanding, or incompetence on the part of individuals. In these cases, the accuracy of the information passed along by managers is important. The other person must understand clearly what the problem is and how to overcome it.

In the Jagdip Ahwal case, Jagdip was accepting upward delegation from his subordinates, and he was not allowing them to solve their own problems. In the chapter on Managing Personal Stress, we learned that upward delegation is one of the major causes of ineffective time management. By not insisting that his subordinates bring recommendations for solutions to him instead of problems, and by intervening directly in the problems of his subordinate's subordinates, Jagdip became overloaded himself. He didn't allow his subordinates to do their jobs. Productivity almost always suffers in cases in which one person is trying to resolve all the problems and run the whole show. Jagdip needs to be coached regarding how to avoid upward delegation and how to delegate responsibility as well as authority effectively. The chapter on Motivating Employees gives some guidelines for diagnosing the reasons for poor performance, and these guidelines could help guide the coaching suggestions.

The Betsy Christensen case illustrates primarily a **counseling** problem. Managers need to counsel others instead of coach them when the problem stems from attitudes, personality clashes, defensiveness, or other factors tied to emotions. Betsy's competency or skill is not a problem, but her unwillingness to recognize that a problem exists or that a change is needed on her part requires counseling by the manager. Betsy is highly qualified for her position, so coaching or giving advice would not be a useful approach. Instead, an important goal of counseling is to help Betsy recognize that a problem exists, that her attitude is of critical importance, and to identify ways in which that problem might be addressed.

Coaching applies to ability problems, and the manager's approach is, "I can help you do this better." Counseling applies to attitude problems, and the manager's approach is, "I can help you recognize that a problem exists."

Although many problems involve both coaching and counseling, it is important to recognize the difference between these two types of problems because a mismatch of problem with communication approach can aggravate, rather than resolve, a problem. Giving direction or advice (coaching) in a counseling situation often increases defensiveness or resistance to change. For example, advising Betsy Christensen about how to do her job or about the things she should not be doing (such as criticizing others' work) will probably only magnify her defensiveness because she doesn't perceive that she has a problem. Similarly, counseling in a situation that calls for coaching simply side-steps the problem and doesn't resolve it. Jagdip Ahwal knows that a problem exists, for example, but he doesn't know how to resolve it. Coaching, not problem recognition, is needed.

The question that remains, however, is, "How do I effectively coach or counsel another person? What behavioral guidelines help me perform effectively in these situations?" Both coaching and counseling rely on the same set of key supportive communication principles summarized in Table 4.1, which we'll now examine more closely.

DEFENSIVENESS AND DISCONFIRMATION

If principles of supportive communication are not followed when coaching or counseling subordinates, two major obstacles result that lead to a variety of negative outcomes (Brownell, 1986; Cupach & Spitzberg, 1994; Gibb, 1961; Sieburg, 1978; Steil et al., 1983). These two obstacles are defensiveness and disconfirmation (see Table 4.3).

Defensiveness is an emotional and physical state in which one is agitated, estranged, confused, and inclined to strike out (Gordon, 1988). Defensiveness arises when one of the parties feels threatened or punished by the communication. For that person, self-protection becomes more important than listening, so defensiveness blocks both the message and the interpersonal relationship. Clearly a manager's coaching or counseling will not be effective if it creates defensiveness in the other party. But defensive thinking may be pervasive and entrenched within an organization. Overcoming it calls for awareness by managers of their own defensiveness and vigorous efforts to apply the principles of supportive communication described in this chapter (Argyris, 1991).

The second obstacle, **disconfirmation**, occurs when one of the communicating parties feels put down, ineffectual, or insignificant because of the communication. Recipients of the communication feel that their self-worth is being questioned, so they focus more on building themselves up rather than listening. Reactions are often self-aggrandizing or show-off behaviors, loss of motivation, withdrawal, and loss of respect for the offending communicator.

The eight attributes of supportive communication, which we'll explain and illustrate in the following pages, serve as behavioral guidelines for overcoming defensiveness and disconfirmation. Competent coaching and counseling depend on knowing and practicing these guidelines. They also depend on maintaining a balance among the guidelines, as we will illustrate.

Table 4.3	Two Major Obstacles to Effective Interpersonal Communication

Supportive communication engenders feelings of support, understanding, and helpfulness. It helps overcome the two main obstacles resulting from poor interpersonal communication:

Defensiveness

• One individual feels threatened or attacked as a result of the communication.

• Self-protection becomes paramount.

• Energy is spent on constructing a defense rather than on listening.

• Aggression, anger, competitiveness, and avoidance are common reactions.

Disconfirmation

• One individual feels incompetent, unworthy, or insignificant as a result of the communication.

• Attempts to reestablish self-worth take precedence.

• Energy is spent trying to portray self-importance rather than on listening.

• Showing off, self-centered behavior, withdrawal, and loss of motivation are common reactions.

1. SUPPORTIVE COMMUNICATION IS BASED ON CONGRUENCE, NOT INCONGRUENCE

Most researchers and observers agree that the best interpersonal communications, and the best relationships, are based on **congruence**. That is, what is communicated, verbally and nonverbally, matches exactly what the individual is thinking and feeling (Dyer, 1972; Hyman, 1989; Knapp & Vangelisti, 1996; Rogers, 1961; Schnake et al.,1990). Congruence simply means being honest. It means communicating what you intend.

Two kinds of **incongruence** are possible: One is a mismatch between what one is experiencing and what one is aware of. For example, an individual may not even be aware that he or she is experiencing anger or hostility toward another person, even though the anger or hostility is really present. In severe cases, therapists must help individuals reach greater congruence between experience and awareness. A second kind of incongruence, and the one more closely related to supportive communication, is a mismatch between what one thinks or feels and what one communicates. For example, an individual may be aware of a feeling of anger but deny saying that the feeling exists.

When building interpersonal relationships, and when coaching and counseling others, genuine, honest statements are always better than artificial or dishonest statements. Managers who hold back their true feelings or opinions, or who don't express what's really on their minds, create the impression that a hidden agenda exists. Other people sense that there is something else not being said, or that an opinion or thought is not being expressed. Therefore, they trust the communicator less and focus on trying to figure out what the hidden message is, not on listening or trying to improve. The relationship between the two communicators stays superficial and distrusting.

The chapter on Managing Personal Stress discussed Covey's (1989) "emotional bank account" in which individuals make deposits in an account that builds the relationship with another person. These deposits help establish mutual trust and respect in the relationship. Similarly, communication cannot be genuinely supportive unless it is based on trust and respect and is also *perceived* as trusting and respectful. Otherwise, false impressions and miscommunication result. Congruence

is a prerequisite of trust. Genuineness and authenticity lie at the heart of positive relationships.

Rogers (1961) suggested that congruence in communication lies at the heart of "a general law of interpersonal relationships." After 40 years of clinical treatment of psychological problems in patients, Rogers concluded that this one law was the fundamental key to positive interpersonal relationships.

The greater the congruence of experience, awareness, and communication on the part of one individual, the more the ensuing relationship will involve a tendency toward reciprocal communication with increasing congruence; a tendency toward more mutually accurate understanding of the communications; improved psychological adjustment and functioning in both parties; mutual satisfaction in the relationship.

Conversely, the greater the communicated incongruence of experience and awareness, the more the ensuing relationship will involve further communication with the same quality; disintegration of accurate understanding; less adequate psychological adjustment and functioning in both parties; mutual dissatisfaction in the relationship. (pp. 344–345)

Congruence also relates to matching the content of the words spoken to the communicator's manner and tone of voice. "What a nice day" can mean the opposite if muttered sarcastically. "I'm just here to help" can mean the opposite if said without sincerity, especially if the history of the relationship suggests otherwise.

Striving for congruence, being honest and open, or demonstrating authenticity does not mean, of course, that we should blow off steam immediately upon getting upset, nor does it mean that we cannot repress certain inappropriate feelings (e.g., keeping anger, disappointment, or aggression under wraps). Other principles of supportive communication must also be practiced, and achieving congruence at the expense of all other consideration is not productive. On the other hand, in problematic interactions, when reactive feedback must be given, or when correcting someone else's behavior, individuals are more likely to express too little congruence than too much. This is because many people are afraid to respond in a completely honest way or are not sure how to communicate congruently without being offensive. It is often a matter of not knowing *how* to be congruent. Saying exactly what we feel, of course, can sometimes offend the other person.

Consider the problem of a person who is not performing up to expectations and displays a nonchalant attitude even after having been given hints that the organization's rating is being negatively affected. What could you say that would strengthen the relationship with this person and still resolve the problem? How could you express honest feelings and opinions and still remain nonjudgmental? How can you ever be completely honest without offending another person? This is even more difficult when you consider how to respond supportively to someone who constantly has bad breath or displays poor manners while eating. The more personal the feedback, the more difficult it is to be completely congruent. This is where skillful communication is important. Other principles of supportive communication provide some guidelines.

2. SUPPORTIVE COMMUNICATION IS DESCRIPTIVE, NOT EVALUATIVE

It is difficult to be congruent in isolation—that is, without using other rules of thumb for supportive communication. If your friend asks you, "How did I do?" and he or she didn't do so well, it is difficult to know how to respond honestly without being offensive. **Evaluative communication** makes a judgment or places a label on other individuals or on their behavior: "You are doing it wrong," or "You are incompetent." Such evaluation generally makes other people feel under attack and, consequently, respond defensively. They see the communicator as judgmental. Examples of probable responses are, "I am *not* doing it wrong," or "I am more capable than *you* are." Arguments, bad feelings, and a deterioration in the interpersonal relationship result—"No, I'm not." "Yes, you are." "No, I'm not." "Yes, you are." And so on.

The tendency to evaluate others is strongest when the issue is emotionally charged or when a person feels personally attacked. For example, it is more threatening to provide negative messages when others may be emotionally wounded. Sometimes people try to resolve their own bad feelings or anxieties by placing a label on others: "You are dumb" implies "Therefore, I am smart," and it makes me feel better. They may have such strong feelings that they want to punish the other person for violating their expectations or standards: "What you have done deserves to be punished. You have it coming." Most often, evaluations occur merely because people don't have any other alternatives in mind. They don't know how to be congruent without being judgmental or evaluating the other person.

The problem with evaluative communication is that it is likely to be self-perpetuating. Placing a label on someone else generally leads that person to place a label on you, which makes you defensive in return. When you are defensive and the other person is defensive, it's not hard to see why effective communication does not occur. Both the accuracy of the communication and quality of the relationship weaken. Arguments ensue.

An alternative to evaluation is **descriptive communication**. It is difficult to avoid evaluating other people without having an alternative strategy, so descriptive communication is designed to reduce the tendency to evaluate and to perpetuate a defensive interaction. It allows a person to be congruent and authentic as well as being helpful. Descriptive communication involves three steps, summarized in Table 4.4.

First, *describe objectively your observation of the event that occurred or the behavior that you think needs to be modified.* As objectively and dispassionately as possible, talk about *what* happened instead of about the person involved. This description should identify elements of the behavior that can be confirmed by someone else. Behavior should be compared to accepted standards rather than to personal opinions or preferences. Subjective impressions or attributions to the motives of another person should be avoided. The description "You have finished fewer projects this month than anyone else in the division" can be confirmed by an objective record. It relates strictly to the behavior and to an objective standard, not to the motives or personal characteristics of the subordinate. There is less likelihood of the other person feeling unfairly treated, since no evaluative label is placed on the behavior or the person. Describing a behavior, as opposed to evaluating a behavior, is relatively neutral, as long as the manager's manner is congruent with the message.

Second, *describe your (or others') reactions to the behavior or describe the consequences of the behavior.* Rather than projecting onto another person the cause of the problem, focus on the reactions or consequences the behavior has produced. This requires that communicators are aware of their own reactions and are able to describe them. Using one-word descriptions for feelings is often the best method: "I'm concerned about our productivity." "Your level of accomplishment frustrates me." Similarly, the consequences of the behavior can be pointed out: "Profits are off this month," "Department quality ratings are down," or "Two customers have called in to express dissatisfaction." Describing feelings or consequences also lessens the likelihood of defensiveness since the problem is

Table 4.4	Descriptive Communication

Step 1: Describe objectively the event, behavior, or circumstance.

- Avoid accusations.
- Present data or evidence.

Example: Three clients have complained to me this month that you have not responded to their requests.

Step 2: Focus on the behavior and your reaction, not on the other person's attributes.

- Describe your reactions and feelings.
- Describe the objective consequences that have resulted or will result.

Example: I'm worried because each client has threatened to go elsewhere if we aren't more responsive.

Step 3: Focus on solutions.

- Avoid discussing who's right or wrong.
- Suggest an acceptable alternative.
- Be open to other alternatives.

Example: We need both to win back their confidence and to show them you are responsive. I suggest you offer to do a free analysis of their systems.

LEARNING

framed in the context of the communicator's feelings or objective consequences, not the attributes of the subordinate. If those feelings or consequences are described in a nonaccusing way, the major energies of the communicators can be focused on problem solving rather than on defending against evaluations. That is, if *I* am concerned, *you* have less of a reason to feel defensive.

Third, *suggest a more acceptable alternative.* This focuses the discussion on the suggested alternative, not on the person. It also helps the other person save face and avoid feeling personally criticized because the individual is separated from the behavior. Self-esteem is preserved because it is the behavior— something controllable—not the person, that should be modified. Of course, care should be taken not to give the message, "I don't like the way things are, so what are *you* going to do about it?" The change need not be the responsibility of only one of the communicating parties. Instead, the emphasis should be on finding a solution that is acceptable to both people, not on deciding who is right and who is wrong or who should change and who shouldn't. For example, "I suggest that you identify what it would take to complete six more projects than you did last month," or "I would like to help you identify the things that are standing in the way of higher performance."

One concern that is sometimes expressed regarding descriptive communication is that these steps may not work unless the other person knows the rules, too. We have heard people say that if both people know about supportive communication, it works; otherwise the person who doesn't want to be supportive can subvert any positive result. For example, the other person might say, "I don't care how you feel," or "I have an excuse for what happened, so it's not my fault," or "It's too bad if this annoys you. I'm not going to change." How might you respond to these responses? Do you abandon principles of descriptive communication and become evaluative and defensive in return? Do you engage in the "Yes, you are"; "No, I'm not"; "Yes, you are"; "No, I'm not" kind of argument?

There is an alternative. This display of lack of concern, or a defensive reaction, now becomes the priority problem. The problem of low performance will be very difficult to address as long as the more important interpersonal problem between these two people is blocking progress. In effect, the focus must shift from coaching to counseling, from focusing on ability to focusing on attitude. If two people cannot work on the problem together, no amount of communication about the consequences of poor performance will be productive. Instead, the focus of the communication should be shifted to the lack of concern in the relationship, or the obstacles that inhibit working together to improve performance. Staying focused on the problem, remaining congruent, and using descriptive language become critical.

Effective supportive communicators do not abandon the three steps. They simply switch the focus. They might respond, "I'm surprised to hear you say that you don't care how I feel about this problem (step 1). Your response concerns me, and I think it might have important implications for the productivity of our team (step 2). I suggest we spend some time trying to identify the obstacles you feel might be inhibiting our ability to work together on this problem (step 3)."

It has been our experience that few individuals are completely recalcitrant about wanting to improve, and few are completely unwilling to work on problem solving when they believe that the communicator has their interests at heart. A common criticism of American managers, however, is that compared to their Asian counterparts, many do not believe in these assumptions. They do not accept the fact that employees are "doing the best that they can," that "people want to get along with one another," and that "people are motivated by opportunities for improvement." In Trompenaars' (1996, 1998) terms, national cultures differ in the extent to which they focus on individual achievement ("I'll do what's best for me") versus the collective good ("I'm concerned about what is best for the group"). These are also similar to McGregor's (1960) Theory Y assumptions (e.g., individuals can be trusted to do what is right) as opposed to Theory X assumptions (e.g., individuals should be mistrusted since it takes threats of punishment to motivate change). In our experience, regardless of the national culture, most people want to perform successfully, to be a part of a productive and satisfying team, and to be contributors. When managers use supportive communication principles, not as manipulative devices but as genuine techniques to foster development and improvement, we have seldom found that people will not accept these genuine, authentic, congruent expressions. This applies to cultures all over the globe.

It is important to keep in mind, however, that the steps of descriptive communication do not imply that one person should do all the changing. Frequently a middle ground must be reached on which both individuals are satisfied (e.g., one person becomes more tolerant of deliberate work, and the other person becomes more conscious of trying to work faster). It is important to follow up these kinds of interaction sessions with discussions to monitor and clarify what was heard, what the reactions were, and whether progress is being made. A person's performance problems, for example, may stem from poor work habits developed over time. Such habits are not likely to change abruptly even if a coaching sessions goes especially well. Moreover, it is important to ensure that misinterpretation of the message or its intent did not occur after the fact.

Reinforcing a sense of caring and genuine concern is an important follow-up step.

When it is necessary to make evaluative statements, the evaluations should be made in terms of some established criteria (e.g., "Your behavior does not meet the prescribed standard"), some probable outcomes (e.g., "Continuation of your behavior will lead to worse consequences"), or some past successes by the same individual (e.g., "This behavior is not as good as your past behavior"). The important point is to avoid disconfirming the other person or arousing defensiveness.

3. SUPPORTIVE COMMUNICATION IS PROBLEM-ORIENTED, NOT PERSON-ORIENTED

Problem-oriented communication focuses on problems and solutions rather than on personal traits. Person-oriented communication focuses on the characteristics of the individual, not the event. "This is the problem" rather than "You are the problem" illustrates the difference between problem and person orientation. Problem-oriented communication is useful even when personal appraisals are called for because it focuses on behaviors and events. Person-oriented communication, on the other hand, often focuses on things that cannot be changed or controlled, and it can send the message that the individual is inadequate.

Statements such as "You are dictatorial" and "You are insensitive" describe the person, while "I am being left out of decision making" and "We don't seem to see things the same way" describe problems. Imputing motives is person-oriented ("It's because you want to control other people"), whereas describing overt behaviors is problem-oriented ("You made several sarcastic comments in the meeting today").

One problem with person-oriented communication is that, while most people can change their behavior, few can change their basic personalities. Because nothing can generally be done to accommodate person-oriented communication, it leads to a deterioration in the relationship rather than to problem solving. Person-oriented messages often try to persuade the other individual that "this is how you should feel" or "this is what kind of person you are" (e.g., "You are an incompetent manager, a lazy worker, or an insensitive office mate"). But since most individuals accept themselves pretty much as they are, their common reaction to person-oriented communication is to defend themselves against it or reject it outright. Even when communication is positive (e.g., "You are a wonderful person"), it may not be viewed as trustworthy if it is not tied to a behavior or an accomplishment (e.g., "I think you are a terrific person because of the extra-mile service you rendered to our organization"). The absence of a meaningful referent is the key weakness in person-oriented communication.

In building positive, supportive relationships, problem-oriented communication should also be linked to accepted standards or expectations rather than to personal opinions. Personal opinions are more likely to be interpreted as person-oriented and arouse defensiveness than statements in which the behavior is compared to an accepted standard or performance. For example, the statement, "I don't like the way you dress" is an expression of a personal opinion and will probably create resistance, especially if the listener does not feel that the communicator's opinions are any more legitimate than his or her own. On the other hand, "Your dress is not in keeping with the company dress code," or "In this firm, everyone is expected to wear a tie to work," are comparisons to external standards that have some legitimacy. Feelings of defensiveness are less likely to arise since the problem, not the person, is being addressed. In addition, other people are more likely to support a statement based on a commonly accepted standard.

Supportive communicators need not avoid expressing personal opinions or feelings about the behavior or attitudes of others. When doing so, however, they should keep in mind the following additional principles.

4. SUPPORTIVE COMMUNICATION VALIDATES RATHER THAN INVALIDATES INDIVIDUALS

Validating communication helps people feel recognized, understood, accepted, and valued. Communication that is **invalidating** arouses negative feelings about self-worth, identity, and relatedness to others. It denies the presence, uniqueness, or importance of other individuals. Especially important are communications that invalidate people by conveying superiority, rigidity, indifference, and imperviousness (Brownell, 1986; Cupach & Spitzberg, 1994; Sieburg, 1978; Steil et al., 1983). Barnlund's (1968) observation more than a quarter century ago is even more true today:

> *People often do not take time, do not listen, do not try to understand, but interrupt, anticipate, criticize, or disregard what is said; in their own remarks they are frequently vague,*

> *inconsistent, verbose, insincere, or dogmatic. As a result, people often conclude conversations feeling more inadequate, more misunderstood, and more alienated than when they started. (p. 618)*

Communication that is superiority oriented gives the impression that the communicator is informed while others are ignorant, adequate while others are inadequate, competent while others are incompetent, or powerful while others are impotent. It creates a barrier between the communicator and those to whom the message is sent.

Superiority-oriented communication can take the form of put-downs, in which others are made to look bad so that the communicator looks good. Or it can take the form of "one-upmanship," in which the communicator tries to elevate himself or herself in the esteem of others. One form of one-upmanship is withholding information, either boastfully ("If you knew what I knew, you would feel differently") or coyly to trip people up ("If you had asked me, I could have told you the executive committee would disapprove of your proposal"). Boasting almost always makes others uncomfortable, mainly because it is designed to convey superiority.

Another common form of superiority-oriented communication is the use of jargon, acronyms, or words in such a way as to exclude others or to create barriers in a relationship. Doctors, lawyers, government employees, and many professionals are well known for their use of jargon or acronyms, designed to exclude others or to elevate themselves rather than to clarify a message. Speaking a foreign language in the presence of individuals who don't understand it may also be done to create the impression of exclusiveness or superiority. In most circumstances, using words or language that a listener can't understand is bad manners because it invalidates the other person.

Rigidity in communication is the second major type of invalidation: The communication is portrayed as absolute, unequivocal, or unquestionable. No other opinion or point of view could possibly be considered. Individuals who communicate in dogmatic, "know-it-all" ways often do so in order to minimize others' contributions or to invalidate others' perspectives. It is possible to communicate rigidity, however, in ways other than just being dogmatic. Rigidity is also communicated by:

- ❏ Reinterpreting all other viewpoints to conform to one's own.
- ❏ Never saying, "I don't know," but having an answer for everything.

- Appearing unwilling to tolerate criticisms or alternative points of view.
- Reducing complex issues to simplistic definitions or generalizations.
- Placing exclamation points after statements so the impression is created that the statement is final, complete, or unqualified.
- Resistance to receiving personal feedback.

Indifference is communicated when the other person's existence or importance is not acknowledged. A person may do this by using silence, by making no verbal response to the other's statements, by avoiding eye contact or any facial expression, by interrupting the other person frequently, by using impersonal words ("one should not" instead of "you should not"), or by engaging in unrelated activity during a conversation. The communicator appears not to care about the other person and gives the impression of being impervious to the other person's feelings or perspectives. To be indifferent is to exclude others, to treat them as if they are not even present.

Imperviousness means that the communicator does not acknowledge the feelings or opinions of the other person. They are either labeled illegitimate— "You shouldn't feel that way" or "Your opinion is incorrect"—or they are labeled as ignorant—"You don't understand," "You've been misinformed," or (worse yet) "Your opinion is naive." Being impervious means to ignore or make unimportant the personal feelings or thoughts of another. It serves to exclude the other person's contribution to the conversation or the relationship, and it makes the other person feel illegitimate or unimportant.

Communication is invalidating when it denies the other person an opportunity to establish a mutually satisfying relationship or when contributions cannot be made by both parties. When one person doesn't allow the other to finish a sentence, adopts a competitive, win-or-lose stance, sends confusing messages, or disqualifies the other person from making a contribution, communication is invalidating and, therefore, dysfunctional for effective problem solving.

Invalidation is even more destructive in interpersonal relationships than criticism or disagreement because criticism and disagreement do, in fact, validate the other person by recognizing that what was said or done is worthy of correction, response, or notice. As William James (1965) stated, "No more fiendish punishment could be devised, even were such a thing physically possible, than that one could be turned loose in a society and remain absolutely unnoticed by all the members thereof."

Validating communication, on the other hand, helps people feel recognized, understood, accepted, and valued (see also the chapter on Empowering and Delegating). It has four attributes: It is *egalitarian, flexible, two-way,* and *based on agreement.*

Respectful, egalitarian communication (the opposite of superiority-oriented communication) is especially important when a person with a higher status interacts with a person of a lower status. When a hierarchical distinction exists between individuals, for example, it is easy for subordinates to feel invalidated since they have access to less power and information than their managers. Supportive communicators, however, help subordinates feel that they have a stake in identifying problems and resolving them by communicating an egalitarian stance. They treat subordinates as worthwhile, competent, and insightful and emphasize joint problem solving rather than projecting a superior position. They can do this merely by asking for opinions, suggestions, and ideas. Another way they do this is by using flexible (rather than rigid) statements.

Even without hierarchical differences, however, communicating respectfully and in an egalitarian way is important. When people of different nationalities, ethnic groups, or genders are communicating, for example, some people are almost always vulnerable to feeling excluded or inferior. In those circumstances, egalitarian and inclusive statements are especially important in order to foster supportive relationships.

Flexibility in communication is the willingness of a person to communicate an understanding that the other party may possess additional data and other alternatives that may make significant contributions both to the problem solution and to the relationship. It simply implies being receptive to other people. It means communicating genuine humility—not self-abasement or weakness— and a willingness to learn and to be open to new experience. It means remaining open to new insights. As Benjamin Disraeli noted, "To be conscious that you are ignorant is a first great step toward knowledge."

Perceptions and opinions are not presented as facts in flexible communication, but are stated provisionally. No claim is made for the absolute truthfulness of opinions or assumptions. Rather, they are identified as being changeable if more data should become available. Flexible communication conveys a willingness to enter into joint problem solving rather than to control the other person or to assume a master–teacher role. However, being flexible is not synonymous with being wishy-washy. "Gee, I can't make up my mind" is wishy-washy, whereas "I have my own opinions, but what do you think?" suggests flexibility.

Two-way communication is an implied result of respectfulness and flexibility. Individuals feel validated when they are asked questions, given "air time" to express their opinions, and encouraged to participate actively in the interpersonal interaction. Two-way interchange communicates the message that the other person is valued, which is a prerequisite for building collaboration and teamwork (see the chapter on Building Effective Teams and Teamwork).

Finally, one person's communication validates another when it *identifies areas of agreement* and joint commitment. One way to express validation based on agreement is to identify positive behaviors, positive attitudes, and positive consequences. Almost all models of negotiation, teambuilding, and conflict resolution prescribe finding areas of agreement upon which everyone can concur. Agreement makes progress possible. Similarly, highlighting positive factors also provides positive energy and a willingness to invest in conversation. Some examples include pointing out important points made by the other person before pointing out trivial ones, areas of agreement before areas of disagreement, advantages of the other person's statements before disadvantages, compliments before criticisms, and positive next steps before past mistakes. The point is, validating other people helps create feelings of self-worth and self-confidence that can translate into self-motivation and improved performance. Positive relationships result. Invalidation, on the other hand, seldom produces such positive outcomes, yet it is a common form of response when people encounter something that they feel a need to criticize or correct.

5. SUPPORTIVE COMMUNICATION IS SPECIFIC (USEFUL), NOT GLOBAL (NONUSEFUL)

Specific statements are supportive because they identify something that can be easily understood and acted upon. In general, the more specific a statement is, the more effective it is in motivating improvement. For example, the statement "You have trouble managing your time" is too general to be useful, whereas "You spent an hour scheduling meetings today when that could have been done by your assistant" provides specific information that can serve as a basis for behavioral change. "Your communication needs to improve" is not nearly as useful

as a more specific "In this role play exercise, you used evaluative statements 60 percent of the time and descriptive statements 10 percent of the time."

Specific statements avoid extremes and absolutes. The following are extreme or global (and nonuseful) statements that lead to defensiveness or disconfirmation:

> A: "You never ask for my advice."
> B: "Yes, I do. I always consult you before making a decision."
>
> A: "You have no consideration for others' feelings."
> B: "I do so. I am always considerate."
>
> A: "This job stinks."
> B: "You're wrong. It's a great job."

Another common type of global communication is the either–or statement, such as "You either do what I say or I'll fire you," "Life is either a daring adventure or nothing" (Helen Keller), and "If America doesn't reduce its national debt, our children will never achieve the standard of living we enjoy today."

The problem with extreme and either–or statements is that they deny any alternatives. The possible responses of the recipient of the communication are severely constrained. To contradict or deny the statement generally leads to defensiveness and arguments. A statement by Adolf Hitler in 1933 illustrates the point: "Everyone in Germany is a National Socialist; the few outside the party are either lunatics or idiots." On the other hand, a friend of ours was asked to serve as a consultant to a labor and management committee. As he entered the room and was introduced as a professor, the union president declared: "Either he goes or I go."

What would you do? How would you use supportive communication when the union president has made a global statement that either excludes you or cancels the negotiations? Our friend's reply was, "I hope there are more alternatives than that. Why don't we explore them?" This response provided a way for communication to continue and for the possibility of a supportive relationship to be formed.

Specific statements are more useful in interpersonal relationships because they focus on behavioral events and indicate gradations in positions. More useful forms of the examples above are the following:

> A: "You made that decision yesterday without asking for my advice."
> B: "Yes, I did. While I generally like to get your opinion, I didn't think it was necessary in this case."

LEARNING

A: *"By using sarcasm in your response to my request, you gave me the impression you don't care about my feelings."*

B: *"I'm sorry. I know I am often sarcastic without thinking how it affects others."*

A: *"The pressure to meet deadlines affects the quality of my work."*

B: *"Since deadlines are part of our work, let's discuss ways to manage the pressure."*

Specific statements may not be useful if they focus on things over which another person has no control. "I hate it when it rains," for example, may relieve some personal frustration, but nothing can be done to change the weather. Similarly, communicating the message (even implicitly) "The sound of your voice (or your personality, your weight, your tastes, the way you are, etc.) bothers me" only proves frustrating for the interacting individuals. Such a statement is usually interpreted as a personal attack. The reaction is likely to be, "What can I do about that?" or "I don't even understand what you mean." Specific communication is useful to the extent that it focuses on an identifiable problem or behavior about which something can be done (e.g., "It bothers me when you talk so loudly in the library that it disturbs others' concentration").

Even when offering compliments to another person, being specific is better than being global or general. For example, providing positive feedback to someone by saying "You are a nice person" is not nearly as helpful as describing an incident or a behavior that created that impression; for example, "You seem to always smile when I see you, and you express interest in my work." Whereas both statements are pleasant to hear, the specific comment is much more helpful than the general comment.

6. SUPPORTIVE COMMUNICATION IS CONJUNCTIVE, NOT DISJUNCTIVE

Conjunctive communication is joined to previous messages in some way. It flows smoothly. **Disjunctive communication** is disconnected from what was stated before.

Communication can become disjunctive in at least three ways. First, there can be a lack of equal opportunity to speak. When one person interrupts another, when someone dominates by controlling "air time," or when two or more people try to speak at the same time, the communication is disjunctive. The transitions between exchanges do not flow smoothly. A smooth transition does not occur between one statement and the next. Second, extended pauses are disjunctive. When speakers pause for long periods in the middle of their speeches or when there are long pauses before responses, the communication is disjunctive. Pauses need not be total silence; the space may be filled with "umm," "aaah," or a repetition of something stated earlier, but the communication does not progress. Third, topic control can be disjointed. When one person decides unilaterally what the next topic of conversation will be (as opposed to having it decided bilaterally), the communication is disjunctive. Individuals may switch topics, for example, with no reference to what was just said, or they may control the other person's communication topic by directing what should be responded to. Sieburg (1969) found that more than 25 percent of the statements made in small-group discussions failed to refer to or even acknowledge prior speakers or their statements.

These three factors—taking turns speaking, management of timing, and topic control—contribute to what Wiemann (1977) called "interaction management." They have been found to be crucial in supportive communication. In an empirical study of perceived communication competence, Wiemann (1977, p. 104) found that "the smoother the management of the interaction, the more competent the communicator was perceived to be." People who took turns, who did not dominate with pauses or excessive air time, and who connected what they said to what others had said in the past were judged as competent communicators. In fact, interaction management was concluded to be the most powerful determinant of perceived communication competence in his experimental study. Individuals who used conjunctive communication were rated as being significantly more competent in interpersonal communication than were those whose communication was disjunctive.

This suggests that people who are good at building positive relationships use several kinds of behaviors in managing communication situations so they are conjunctive rather than disjunctive. For example, they foster conjunctive communication in an interaction by asking questions that are based directly on the subordinate's previous statement, by waiting for a sentence to be completed before beginning a response (e.g., not finishing a sentence for someone else), and by saying only three or four sentences at a time before pausing to give the other person a chance to add input. All of us have been in interactions in which one person goes on and on and on without allowing others to comment

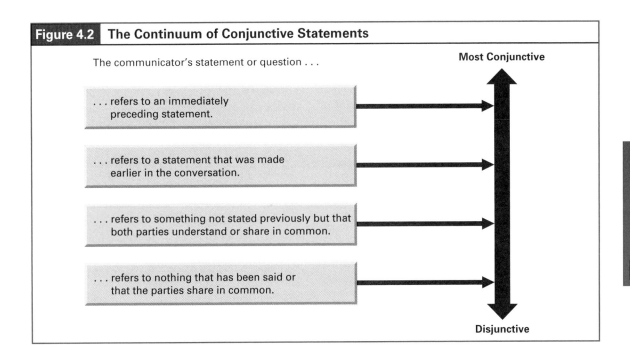

Figure 4.2   The Continuum of Conjunctive Statements

The communicator's statement or question . . .

Most Conjunctive

. . . refers to an immediately preceding statement.

. . . refers to a statement that was made earlier in the conversation.

. . . refers to something not stated previously but that both parties understand or share in common.

. . . refers to nothing that has been said or that the parties share in common.

Disjunctive

or contribute. Almost always it produces discomfort because it is disjunctive. Interaction, exchange, and give-and-take are necessary for supportive communication to occur. In other words, supportive communicators avoid long pauses, their statements refer to what has been said before, and they take turns speaking. Figure 4.2 illustrates the continuum of conjunctive and disjunctive statements.

By using conjunctive communication, managers confirm the worth of the other person's statements, thereby helping to foster joint problem solving and teamwork.

7. SUPPORTIVE COMMUNICATION IS OWNED, NOT DISOWNED

Taking responsibility for one's statements and acknowledging that the source of the ideas is oneself and not another person or group is **owning communication**. Using first-person words, such as "I," "me," "mine," indicates owning communication. **Disowning communication** is suggested by use of third-person or first-person-plural words: "We think," "They said," or "One might say." Disowned communication is attributed to an unknown person, group, or to some external source (e.g., "Lots of people think"). The communicator avoids taking responsibility for the message and therefore avoids investing in the interaction. This may convey the

message that the communicator is aloof or uncaring about the receiver or is not confident enough in the ideas expressed to take responsibility for them.

Glasser (1965, 2000) based his approach to mental health—reality therapy—on the concept of taking responsibility for, or owning, communication and behavior. According to Glasser, people's mental health depends on their accepting responsibility for their statements and behaviors. The basic assumption of reality therapy is that taking responsibility for your own communication builds self-confidence and a sense of self-worth. The opposite, attributing what one feels or says to someone or something else (e.g., "My being cranky isn't my fault because my roommate stayed up all night playing loud music") leads to poor mental health and loss of self-control. Ownership and responsibility are keys to personal growth and to trusting and effective interpersonal relationships. You will trust me more if you know that I take responsibility for my statements.

One result of disowned communication is that the listener is never sure whose point of view the message represents: "How can I respond if I don't know to whom I am responding?" "If I don't understand the message, whom can I ask since the message represents someone else's point of view?" Moreover, an implicit message associated with disowned communication is, "I want to keep distance between you and me." The speaker communicates as a representative rather than as a person, as a message-conveyer rather than an interested individual. Owned communication, on the other hand, indicates a willingness to invest oneself in a relationship and to act as a colleague or helper.

This last point suggests that coaches or counselors should encourage others to own their own statements. This can be done by example but also by asking the other person to restate disowning statements, as in this exchange:

> SUBORDINATE: Everyone else says my work is fine.
> MANAGER: So no one besides me has ever expressed dissatisfaction with your work or suggested how to improve it?
> SUBORDINATE: Well . . . Mark complained that I took shortcuts and left him to clean up after me.
> MANAGER: Was his complaint fair?
> SUBORDINATE: Yeah, I guess so.
> MANAGER: What led you to take shortcuts?
> SUBORDINATE: My work was piling up, and I felt I had too much to do.
> MANAGER: Does this happen often, that your work builds up and you look for shortcuts?
> SUBORDINATE: More than I'd like.

Here the manager has used conjunctive questions to guide the subordinate away from disowning responsibility toward acknowledging a behavior that may be affecting others' performance.

8. SUPPORTIVE COMMUNICATION REQUIRES SUPPORTIVE LISTENING, NOT ONE-WAY MESSAGE DELIVERY

The previous seven attributes of supportive communication all focus on message delivery, where a message is initiated by the coach or counselor. But another aspect of supportive communication—that is, *listening and responding* effectively to someone else's statements—is at least as important as delivering supportive messages. As Maier, Solem, and Maier (1973, p. 311) stated: "In any conversation, the person who talks the most is the one who learns the least about the other person. The good supervisor therefore must become a good listener."

Haas and Arnold (1995) found that in the workplace, about one-third of the characteristics people use to judge communication competence have to do with listening. Kramer (1997) found that good listening skills accounted for 40 percent of the variance in effective leadership. In short, good listeners are more likely to be perceived to be skillful communicators. In fact, people who are judged to be the most "wise," or to possess the attribute of wisdom—and, therefore, are the most sought-after people with whom to interact—are also the best listeners (Kramer, 2000; Sternberg, 1990).

In a survey of personnel directors in 300 businesses and industries conducted to determine what skills are most important in becoming a manager, Crocker (1978) reported that effective listening was ranked highest. Despite its importance in managerial success, however, and despite the fact that most people spend at least 45 percent of their communication time listening, most people have underdeveloped listening skills. Tests have shown, for example, that individuals are usually about 25 percent effective in listening; that is, they listen to and understand only about a fourth of what is being communicated (Bostrom, 1997; Huseman, Lahiff, & Hatfield, 1976). Geddie (1999) reported that in a survey across 15 countries, listening was found to be the poorest communication skill. When asked to rate the extent to which they are skilled listeners, 85 percent of all individuals rate themselves as average or worse. Only 5 percent rate themselves as highly skilled (Steil, 1980). It is particularly unfortunate that listening skills are often poorest when people interact with those closest to them, such as family members and coworkers. They interrupt and jump to conclusions more frequently (i.e., they stop listening) with people close to them than with others.

When individuals are preoccupied with meeting their own needs (e.g., saving face, persuading someone else, winning a point, avoiding getting involved), when they have already made a prior judgment, or when they hold negative attitudes toward the communicator or the message, they don't listen effectively. Because a person listens at the rate of 500 words a minute but speaks at a normal rate of only 125 to 250 words a minute, the listener's mind can dwell on other things half the time. Therefore, being a good listener is neither easy nor automatic. It requires developing the ability to hear and understand the message sent by another person, while at the same time helping to strengthen the relationship between the interacting parties.

Rogers and Farson (1976) suggest that this kind of listening conveys the idea that:

> I'm interested in you as a person, and I think what you feel is important. I respect your thoughts, and even if I don't agree with them, I know they are valid for you. I feel sure you

have a contribution to make. I think you're worth listening to, and I want you to know that I'm the kind of person you can talk to. (p. 99)

People do not know they are being listened to unless the listener makes some type of response. This can be simple eye contact and nonverbal responsiveness such as smiles, nods, and focused attention. However, competent managers who must coach and counsel also select carefully from a repertoire of verbal response alternatives that clarify the communication as well as strengthen the interpersonal relationship. The mark of a supportive listener is the competence to select appropriate responses to others' statements (Bostrom, 1997).

The appropriateness of a response depends to some degree on whether the focus of the interaction is primarily coaching or counseling. Of course, seldom can these two activities be separated from one another completely—effective coaching often involves counseling and effective counseling sometimes involves coaching—and attentive listening involves the use of a variety of responses. Some responses, however, are more appropriate under certain circumstances than others.

Figure 4.3 lists four major response types and arranges them on a continuum from most directive and closed to most nondirective and open. Closed responses eliminate discussion of topics and provide direction to individuals. They represent methods by which the listener can control the topic of conversation. Open responses, on the other hand, allow the communicator, not the listener, to control the topic of conversation. Each of these response types has certain advantages and disadvantages, and none is appropriate all the time under all circumstances.

Most people get in the habit of relying heavily on one or two response types, and they use them regardless of the circumstances. Moreover, most people have been found to rely first and foremost on evaluative or judgmental responses (Bostrom, 1997; Rogers, 1961). That is, when they encounter another person's statements, most people tend to agree or disagree, to pass judgment, or to immediately form a personal opinion about the legitimacy or veracity of the statement. On the average, about 80 percent of most people's responses have been found to be evaluative. Supportive listening, however, avoids evaluation and judgment as a first response. Instead, it relies on flexibility in response types and the appropriate match of responses to circumstances. The four major types of responses are discussed below.

Advising

An **advising response** provides direction, evaluation, personal opinion, or instructions. Such a response imposes on the communicator the point of view of the listener, and it creates listener control over the topic of conversation. The advantages of an advising response are that it helps the communicator understand something that may have been unclear before, it helps identify a problem solution, and it can provide clarity about how the communicator should act or interpret the problem. It is most appropriate when the listener has expertise that the communicator doesn't possess or when the communicator is in need of direction. Supportive listening sometimes means that the listener does the talking, but this is usually appropriate only

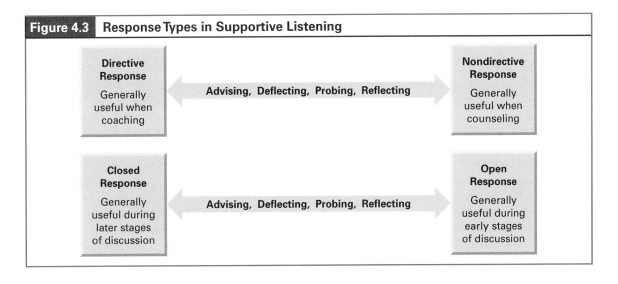

| **Figure 4.3** | **Response Types in Supportive Listening** |

Directive Response
Generally useful when coaching

← Advising, Deflecting, Probing, Reflecting →

Nondirective Response
Generally useful when counseling

Closed Response
Generally useful during later stages of discussion

← Advising, Deflecting, Probing, Reflecting →

Open Response
Generally useful during early stages of discussion

when advice or direction is specifically requested. Most listeners have a tendency to offer much more advice and direction than is appropriate.

One problem with advising is that it can produce dependence. Individuals get used to having someone else generate answers, directions, or clarifications. They are not permitted to figure out issues and solutions for themselves. A second problem is that advising also creates the impression that the communicator is not being understood by the listener. Rogers (1961) found that most people, even when they seem to be asking for advice, mainly desire understanding and acceptance, not advice. They want the listener to share in the communication but not take charge of it. The problem with advising is that it removes from the communicator the opportunity to stay focused on the issue that is on the communicator's mind. Advice shifts the control of the conversation away from the communicator. A third problem with advising is that it shifts focus from the communicator's issue to the listener's advice. When listeners feel advising is appropriate, they concentrate more on the legitimacy of the advice or on the generation of alternatives and solutions than on simply listening attentively. When listeners are expected to generate advice and direction, they may focus more on their own experience than on the communicator's experience, or on formulating their advice more than on the nuances of the communicator's message. It is difficult to simultaneously be a good listener and a good adviser. A fourth potential problem with advising is that it can imply that communicators don't have the necessary understanding, expertise, insight, or maturity, so they need help because of their incompetence.

One way to overcome the disadvantages of advising is to avoid giving advice as a first response. Almost always advising should follow other responses that allow communicators to have control over the topics of conversation, that show understanding and acceptance, and that encourage analysis and self-reliance on the part of communicators. First communicating concern and personal interest, for example, makes much more likely that any advice being offered will be heard and accepted.

In addition, advice should either be connected to an accepted standard or should be tentative. An accepted standard means that communicators and listeners both acknowledge that the advice will lead to a desired outcome and that it is inherently good, right, or appropriate. When this is impossible, the advice should be communicated as the listener's opinion or feeling, and as only one option (i.e., with flexibility), not as the only option. This permits communicators to accept or reject the advice without feeling that the adviser is being invalidated or rejected if the advice is not accepted.

Deflecting

A **deflecting response** switches the focus from the communicator's problem to one selected by the listener. Listeners deflect attention away from the original problem or the original statement. The listener essentially changes the subject. Listeners may substitute their own experience for that of the communicator (e.g., "Let me tell you something similar that happened to me") or introduce an entirely new topic (e.g., "That reminds me of [something else]"). The listener may think the current problem is unclear to the communicator and that the use of examples or analogies will help. Or, the listener may feel that the communicator needs to be reassured that others have experienced the same problem and that support and understanding are available.

Deflecting responses are most appropriate when a comparison or some reassurance is needed. They can provide empathy and support by communicating the message "I understand because of what happened to me (or someone else)." They can also convey the assurance "Things will be fine. Others have also had this experience." Deflection is also often used to avoid embarrassing either the communicator or the listener. Changing the subject when either party becomes uncomfortable or answering a question other than the one asked are common examples.

The disadvantages of deflecting responses, however, are that they can imply that the communicator's message is not important or that the experience of the listener is more significant than that of the communicator. They may produce competitiveness or feelings of being one-upped by the listener. Deflection can be interpreted as, "My experience is more worthy of discussion than yours." Or it may simply change the subject from something that is important and central to the communicator to a topic that is not as important. ("I want to talk about something important to me, but you changed the subject to your own experience.")

Deflecting responses are most effective when they are conjunctive—that is, when they are clearly connected to what the communicator just said, when the listener's response leads directly back to the communicator's concerns, and when the reason for the deflection is made clear. That is, deflecting can produce desirable outcomes if the communicator feels supported and understood, not invalidated, by the change in topic focus.

Probing

A **probing response** asks a question about what the communicator just said or about a topic selected by the listener. The intent of a probe is to acquire additional information, to help the communicator say more about the topic, or to help the listener foster more appropriate responses. For example, an effective way to avoid being evaluative and judgmental and to avoid triggering defensive reactions is to continue to ask questions. Questioning helps the listener adopt the communicator's frame of reference so that in coaching situations suggestions can be specific (not global) and in counseling situations statements can be descriptive (not evaluative). Questions tend to be more neutral in tone than direct statements. A study of top management team communication, for example, found that high-performing teams had a balance between inquiry (asking questions or probing) and advocacy (declaring or advocating a perspective), so that questions and probes received equal time. Low-performing teams were heavily oriented toward advocacy and away from inquiry and probing (Losada & Heaphy, 2004).

Questioning, however, can sometimes have the unwelcome effect of switching the focus of attention from the communicator's statement to the reasons behind it. The question "Why do you think that way?" for example, might pressure the communicator to justify a feeling or a perception rather than just report it. Similarly, probing responses can serve as a mechanism for escaping discussion of a topic or for maneuvering the topic around to one the listener wants to discuss (e.g., "Instead of discussing your feelings about your job, tell me why you didn't respond to my memo"). Probing responses can also allow the communicator to lose control of the conversation, especially when difficult subjects need to be addressed (e.g., "Why aren't you performing up to your potential?" allows all kinds of other issues to be raised that may or may not be apropos.)

Two important hints should be kept in mind to make probing responses more effective. One is that "why" questions are seldom as effective as "what" questions. "Why" questions lead to topic changes, escapes, and speculations more often than to valid information. For example, the question "Why do you feel that way?" can lead to off-the-wall statements such as "Because I am a redhead," or "Because my father was an alcoholic and my mother beat me," or "Because Dr. Laura said so." These are silly examples, but they illustrate how ineffective "why" questions can be. "What do you mean by that?" is likely to be more fruitful.

A second hint is to tailor the probes to fit the situation. Four types of probes are useful in interviewing. When the communicator's statement does not contain enough information, or part of the message is not understood, an **elaboration probe** should be used (e.g., "Can you tell me more about that?"). When the message is not clear or is ambiguous, a **clarification probe** is best (e.g., "What do you mean by that?"). A **repetition probe** works best when the communicator is avoiding a topic, hasn't answered a previous question, or a previous statement is unclear (e.g., "Once again, what do you think about this?"). A **reflection probe** is most effective when the communicator is being encouraged to keep pursuing the same topic in greater depth (e.g., "You say you are discouraged?"). Table 4.5 summarizes these four kinds of questions or probes.

Probing responses are especially effective in turning hostile or conflictive conversations into supportive conversations. Asking questions can often turn attacks into consensus, evaluations into descriptions, general statements into specific statements, disowning statements into owning statements, or person-focused declarations

Table 4.5	Four Types of Probing Responses
TYPE OF PROBE	**EXPLANATION**
Elaboration Probe	Use when more information is needed. ("Can you tell me more about that?")
Clarification Probe	Use when the message is unclear or ambiguous. ("What do you mean by that?")
Repetition Probe	Use when topic drift occurs or statements are unclear. ("Once again, what do you think about this?")
Reflection Probe	Use to encourage more in-depth pursuit of the same topic. ("You say you are having difficulty?")

into problem-focused declarations. In other words, probes can often be used to help others use supportive communication when they have not been trained in advance to do so.

Reflecting

The primary purpose of the **reflecting response** is to mirror back to the communicator the message that was heard and to communicate understanding and acceptance of the person. Reflecting the message *in different words* allows the speaker to feel listened to, understood, and free to explore the topic in more depth. Reflective responding involves paraphrasing and clarifying the message. Instead of simply mimicking the communication, supportive listeners also contribute meaning, understanding, and acceptance to the conversation while still allowing communicators to pursue topics of their choosing. Athos and Gabarro (1978); Brownell (1986); Steil, Barker, and Watson (1983); Wolvin and Coakley (1988); and others argue that this response should be most typical in supportive communication and should dominate coaching and counseling situations. It leads to the clearest communication, the most two-way exchanges, and the most supportive relationships. For example:

> SUPERVISOR: Jerry, I'd like to hear about any problems you've been having with your job over the last several weeks.
> SUBORDINATE: Don't you think they ought to do something about the air conditioning in the office? It gets to be like an oven in here every afternoon! They said they were going to fix the system weeks ago!
> SUPERVISOR: It sounds like the delay is really beginning to make you angry.
> SUBORDINATE: It sure is! It's just terrible the way maintenance seems to being goofing off instead of being responsive.
> SUPERVISOR: So it's frustrating . . . and discouraging.
> SUBORDINATE: Amen. And by the way, there's something else I want to mention. . . .

A potential disadvantage of reflective responses is that communicators can get an impression opposite from the one intended. That is, they can get the feeling that they are not being understood or listened to carefully. If they keep hearing reflections of what they just said, their response might be, "I just said that. Aren't you listening to me?" Reflective responses, in other words, can be perceived as an artificial "technique" or as a superficial response to a message.

The most effective listeners keep the following rules in mind when using reflective responses.

1. Avoid repeating the same response over and over, such as "You feel that . . . ," "Are you saying that . . . ?" or "What I heard you say was. . . ."
2. Avoid mimicking the communicator's words. Instead, restate what you just heard in a way that helps ensure that you understand the message and the communicator knows that you understand.
3. Avoid an exchange in which listeners do not contribute equally to the conversation, but serve only as mimics. (One can use understanding or reflective responses while still taking equal responsibility for the depth and meaning of the communication.)
4. Respond to the personal rather than the impersonal. For example, to a complaint by a subordinate about close supervision and feelings of incompetence and annoyance, a reflective response would focus on personal feelings before supervision style.
5. Respond to expressed feelings before responding to content. When a person expresses feelings, they are the most important part of the message. They may stand in the way of the ability to communicate clearly unless acknowledged.
6. Respond with empathy and acceptance. Avoid the extremes of complete objectivity, detachment, or distance on the one hand, or over-identification (accepting the feelings as one's own) on the other.
7. Avoid expressing agreement or disagreement with the statements. Use reflective listening and other listening responses to help the communicator explore and analyze the problem. Later you can draw on this information to help fashion a solution.

The Personal Management Interview

Not only are the eight attributes of supportive communication effective in normal discourse and problem-solving situations, but they can be most effectively applied when specific interactions with subordinates are planned and conducted frequently. One important difference between effective and ineffective managers is the extent to which they provide their subordinates with opportunities to receive regular feedback, to feel supported and bolstered, and to be coached and counseled. Providing these opportunities is difficult, however, because of the tremendous time demands most managers face. Many managers want to coach, counsel, train, and develop subordinates, but they simply never find the time. Therefore, one important mechanism for applying supportive communication and for providing subordinates with development and feedback opportunities is to implement a **personal management interview (PMI) program**. This program is probably the most frequently adopted tool that managers employ in the executive education programs we teach when they commit themselves to improving relationships with their subordinates and team members. We have received more feedback about the success of the PMI program than almost any other management improvement technique we have shared. It is a very simple and straightforward technique for implementing supportive communication and building positive relationships in a manager's role. Most importantly, however, it has also been proven to be equally effective in family settings, community groups, church

service, or peer teams. Many people have implemented the PMI system in their own families with their children, for instance.

A PMI program is a regularly scheduled, one-on-one meeting between a manager and his or her subordinates. In a study of the performance of working departments and intact teams in a variety of organizations, Boss (1983) found that effectiveness increased significantly when managers conducted regular, private meetings with subordinates on a biweekly or monthly basis. In a study of health care organizations holding these regular personal management interviews compared to those that did not, significant differences were found in organizational performance, employee performance and satisfaction, and personal stress management scores. The facilities that had instituted a PMI program were significantly higher performers on all the personal and organizational performance dimensions. Figure 4.4 compares the performance effectiveness of teams and departments that implemented the program versus those that did not.

Our own personal experience is also consistent with the empirical findings. We have conducted personal management interviews with individuals for whom we have responsibility in a variety of professional,

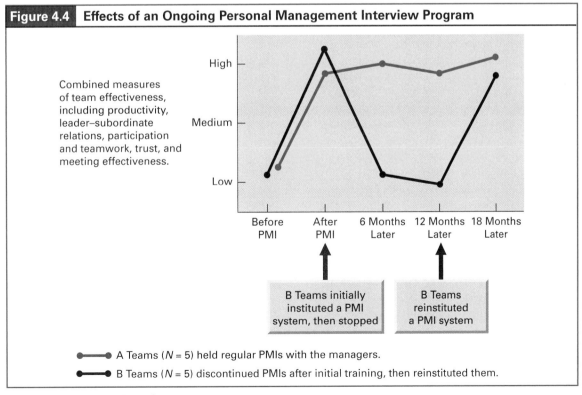

Figure 4.4   Effects of an Ongoing Personal Management Interview Program

Combined measures of team effectiveness, including productivity, leader–subordinate relations, participation and teamwork, trust, and meeting effectiveness.

B Teams initially instituted a PMI system, then stopped

B Teams reinstituted a PMI system

A Teams (N = 5) held regular PMIs with the managers.

B Teams (N = 5) discontinued PMIs after initial training, then reinstituted them.

SOURCE: Journal of Applied Behavioral Science, *Online*.

LEARNING

community, and church organization settings. We also have conducted these sessions with our individual family members. Rather than being an imposition and an artificial means of communication, these sessions—held one-on-one with each child or each member of the unit—have been incredibly productive. Close bonds have resulted, open sharing of information and feelings has emerged, and the meetings themselves are eagerly anticipated by both us and those with whom we have conducted the PMI.

Instituting a PMI program consists of two steps. First, a role-negotiation session is held in which expectations, responsibilities, standards of evaluation, reporting relationships, and so on, are clarified. If possible, this meeting is held at the outset of the relationship. Unless such a meeting is held, most subordinates do not have a clear idea of exactly what is expected of them or on what basis they will be evaluated. In our own experiences with managers and executives, few have expressed confidence that they know precisely what is expected of them or how they are being evaluated in their jobs. In a role-negotiation session, that uncertainty is addressed. The manager and subordinate negotiate all job-related issues that are not prescribed by policy or by mandate. A written record is made of the agreements and responsibilities that result from the meeting that can serve as an informal contract between the manager and the subordinate. The goal of a role-negotiation session is to obtain clarity between both parties regarding what each expects from the other, what the goals and standards are, and what the ground rules for the relationship are. Because this role negotiation is not adversarial but rather focuses on supportiveness and building a positive relationship, the eight supportive communication principles should characterize the interaction. When we hold PMIs in our families, these agreements have centered on household chores, planned vacations, father–daughter or father–son activities, and so on. This role-negotiation session, to repeat, is simply a meeting to establish ground rules, spell out expectations, and clarify standards. It provides a foundation upon which the relationship can be built and helps foster better performance on the part of the manager as well as the subordinate.

The second, and most important, step in a PMI program is a set of ongoing, one-on-one meetings between the manager and each subordinate. These meetings are regular (not just when a mistake is made or a crisis arises) and private (not overheard by others). It is not a department staff meeting, a family gathering, or an end-of-the-day check-up. The meeting occurs one-on-one. We have never seen this program work when these meetings have been less frequent than once per month—both in

organizations and in families. Many times managers choose to hold them more frequently than that, depending on the life cycle of their work and the time pressures they face. This meeting provides the two parties with a chance to communicate freely, openly, and collaboratively. It also provides managers with the opportunity to coach and counsel subordinates and to help them improve their own skills or job performance. Therefore, each meeting lasts from 45 to 60 minutes and focuses on items such as the following: (1) managerial and organizational problems, (2) information sharing, (3) interpersonal issues, (4) obstacles to improvement, (5) training in management skills, (6) individual needs, (7) feedback on job performance and personal capabilities, and (8) personal concerns or problems.

This meeting is not just a time to sit and chat. It has two overarching—and crucial—objectives: to foster improvement and to strengthen relationships. If improvement does not occur as a result of the meeting, it is not being held correctly. If relationships are not strengthened over time, something is not working as it should. The meeting always leads toward action items to be accomplished before the next meeting, some by the subordinate and others by the manager. Those action items are reviewed at the end of the meeting and reviewed again at the beginning of the next meeting. Accountability is maintained for improvement. This is not a meeting just to hold a meeting. Without agreements as to specific actions that will be taken, and the accountability that will be maintained, it can be a waste of both people's time. This means both parties prepare for the meeting, and both bring agenda items to be discussed. It is not a formal appraisal session called by the manager, but a development and improvement session in which both the manager and subordinate have a stake. It does not replace formal performance appraisal sessions, but it supplements them. The purposes of PMIs are not to conduct evaluation or performance appraisals. Rather, they provide a chance for subordinates to have personal time with the manager to work out issues, report information, receive coaching and counseling, and improve performance. Consequently, they help eliminate unscheduled interruptions and long, inefficient group meetings. At each subsequent meeting, action items are reviewed from previous meetings, so that continuous improvement is encouraged. The meetings, in other words, become an institutionalized continuous improvement activity. They are also a key to building the collaboration and teamwork needed in organizations. Table 4.6 summarizes the characteristics of the personal management interview program.

Table 4.6	Characteristics of a Personal Management Interview Program

- The interview is regular and private.
- The major intent of the meeting is continuous improvement in personal, interpersonal, and organizational performance, so the meeting is action oriented.
- Both the manager and the subordinate prepare agenda items for the meeting. It is a meeting for improving both of them, not just for the manager's appraisal.
- Sufficient time is allowed for the interaction, usually about an hour.
- Supportive communication is used so that joint problem solving and continuous improvement result (in both task accomplishment and interpersonal relationships).
- The first agenda item is a follow-up on the action items generated by the previous meeting.
- Major agenda items for the meeting might include:
  - Managerial and organizational problems
  - Organizational values and vision
  - Information sharing
  - Interpersonal issues
  - Obstacles to improvement
  - Training in management skills
  - Individual needs
  - Feedback on job performance
  - Personal concerns and problems
- Praise and encouragement are intermingled with problem solving but are more frequently communicated.
- A review of action items generated by the meeting occurs at the end of the interview.

The major objection to holding these PMI sessions, of course, is lack of time. Most people think that they simply cannot impose on their schedules a group of one-on-one meetings with each of their team members, subordinates, or children. Boss' research (1983) found, however, that a variety of benefits resulted in teams that instituted this program. It not only increased their effectiveness, but it improved individual accountability, department meeting efficiency, and communication flows. Managers actually found that more discretionary time became available because the program reduced interruptions, unscheduled meetings, mistakes, and problem-solving time. Furthermore, participants defined it as a success experience in itself. When correction or negative feedback had to be communicated, and when coaching or counseling was called for (which is typical of almost every manager–subordinate relationship at some point), supportive communication helped strengthen the interpersonal relationship at the same time that problems were solved and performance improved. In summary, setting aside time for formal, structured interaction between managers and their subordinates in which supportive communication played a part produced markedly improved bottom-line results in those organizations that implemented the program.

International Caveats

We point out in other chapters that it is important to keep in mind that cultural differences sometimes call for a modification of the skills discussed in this book. We noted, for example, that Asian managers are often less inclined to be open in initial stages of a conversation, and they consider managers from the United States or Latin America to be a bit brash and aggressive because they may be too personal too soon. Similarly, certain types of response patterns may differ among cultures—for example, deflecting responses are more typical of Eastern cultures than Western cultures. The language patterns and language structures across cultures can be dramatically different, and remember that considerable evidence exists that individuals are most effective interpersonally, and they display the greatest amount of emotional intelligence, when they recognize, appreciate, and capitalize on these differences among others.

On the other hand, whereas stylistic differences may exist among individuals and among various cultures, certain core principles of effective communication are, nevertheless, critical to effective communication. The research on interpersonal communication among various cultures and nationalities confirms that the eight attributes of supportive communication are effective in all cultures and nationalities (Gudykunst, Ting-Toomey, & Nishida, 1996; Triandis, 1994). These eight factors have almost universal applicability in solving interpersonal problems.

We have used Trompenaars' (1996, 1998) model of cultural diversity to identify key differences among people raised in different cultural contexts. (Chapter 1 in this book provides a more detailed explanation of these value dimensions.) Differences exist, for example, on an *affectivity orientation* versus a *neutral orientation*. Affective cultures (e.g., the Middle East, Southern Europe, South Pacific) are more inclined to be expressive and personal in their responses than neutral cultures (e.g., East Asia, Scandinavia). Sharing personal data and engaging quickly in sensitive topics may be comfortable for people in some cultures, for example, but very uncomfortable in others. The timing and pace of communication will vary, therefore, among different cultures. Similarly, *particularistic* cultures (e.g., Korea, China, Indonesia) are more likely to allow individuals to work out issues in their own way compared to *universalistic* cultures (e.g., Norway, Sweden, United States) where a common pattern or approach is preferred. This implies that reflective responses may be more common in particularistic cultures and advising responses more typical of universalistic cultures. When individuals are assumed to have a great deal of individual autonomy, for example, coaching responses (directing, advising, correcting) are less common than counseling responses (empathizing, probing, reflecting) in interpersonal problem solving.

Trompenaars (1996), Gudykunst and Ting-Toomey (1988), and others' research clearly points out, however, that the differences among cultures are not great enough to negate or dramatically modify the principles outlined in this chapter. Regardless of the differences in cultural background of those with whom you interact, being problem centered, congruent, descriptive, validating, specific, conjunctive, owned, and supportive in listening are all judged to indicate managerial competence and serve to build strong interpersonal relationships.

Sensitivity to individual differences and styles is an important prerequisite to effective communication.

Summary

The most important barriers to effective communication in organizations are interpersonal. Much technological progress has been made in the last two decades in improving the accuracy of message delivery in organizations, but communication problems still persist among people, regardless of their relationships or roles. A major reason for these problems is that a great deal of communication does not support a positive interpersonal relationship. Instead, it frequently engenders distrust, hostility, defensiveness, and feelings of incompetence and low self-esteem. Ask any manager about the major problems being faced in their organizations, and communication problems will most assuredly appear near the top of the list.

Dysfunctional communication is seldom associated with situations in which compliments are given, congratulations are made, a bonus is awarded, or other positive interactions occur. Most people have little trouble communicating effectively in positive or complimentary situations. The most difficult, and potentially harmful, communication patterns are most likely to emerge when you are giving feedback on poor performance, saying "no" to a proposal or request, resolving a difference of opinion between two subordinates, correcting problem behaviors, receiving criticism from others, providing feedback that could hurt another person's feelings, or encountering other negative interactions. Handling these situations in a way that fosters interpersonal growth and engenders stronger positive relationships is one mark of an effective manager. Rather than harming a relationship, using supportive communication builds and strengthens the relationship even when delivering negative news.

In this chapter, we pointed out that effective managers adhere to the principles of supportive communication. Thus, they ensure greater clarity and understanding of messages while making other persons feel accepted, valued, and supported. Of course, it is possible to become overly concerned with technique in trying to incorporate these principles and thereby to defeat the goal of being supportive. One can become artificial, inauthentic, or incongruent by focusing on technique alone, rather than on honest, caring communication. But if the principles are practiced and consciously implemented in everyday interactions, they can be important tools for improving your communication competence.

Behavioral Guidelines

The following behavioral guidelines will help you practice supportive communication:

1. Differentiate between coaching situations, which require giving advice and direction to help foster behavior change, and counseling situations, in which understanding and problem recognition are the desired outcomes.

2. Communicate congruently by acknowledging your true feelings without acting them out in destructive ways. Make certain that your statements match your feelings and thoughts and that you communicate authentically.

3. Use descriptive, not evaluative, statements. Describe objectively what occurred, describe your reactions to events and their objective consequences, and suggest acceptable alternatives.

4. Use problem-oriented statements rather than person-oriented statements; that is, focus on behavioral referents or characteristics of events, not attributes of the person.

5. Use validating statements that acknowledge the other person's importance and uniqueness. Communicate your investment in the relationship by demonstrating your respect of the other person and your flexibility and humility is being open to new ideas or new data. Foster two-way interchanges rather than dominating or interrupting the other person. Identify areas of agreement or positive characteristics of the other person before pointing out areas of disagreement or negative characteristics.

6. Use specific rather than global (either–or, black-or-white) statements, and, when trying to correct behavior, focus on things that are under the control of the other person rather than factors that cannot be changed.

7. Use conjunctive statements that flow smoothly from what was said previously. Ensure equal speaking opportunities for others participating in the interaction. Do not cause long pauses that dominate the time. Be careful not to completely control the topic being discussed. Acknowledge what was said before by others.

8. Own your statements, and encourage the other person to do likewise. Use personal words ("I") rather than impersonal words ("management").

9. Demonstrate supportive listening. Make eye contact and be responsive nonverbally. Use a variety of responses to others' statements, depending on whether you are coaching or counseling someone else. Have a bias toward the use of reflective responses.

10. Implement a personal management interview program with people for whom you have responsibility, and use supportive communication to coach, counsel, foster personal development, and build strong positive relationships.

CASES INVOLVING BUILDING POSITIVE RELATIONSHIPS

When the Cat's Away, the Mice Will Play

Tarek Abdo was away from the office on a business trip. Upon his return, he discovered that there had been problems among the staff members, and top management was not happy.

Tarek Abdo, the director of the Research and Development Department, was invited to be the keynote speaker at a conference in Paris. His talk centered on the latest methods to enhance creativity and innovation.

Being the flexible person that he was, he encouraged open communication in the office and wanted his staff to demonstrate a positive attitude. "We are in research; it can be dull or exciting," he explained at a staff meeting, "we can choose the attitude we bring to work." He hoped that through persistent interaction with one another the employees would realize that they needed to build on synergy in the office. Tarek had only been head of R&D for 8 months, and he had inherited an office that housed individuals who were only energized to practice resistance.

After much contemplation, Tarek called for a staff meeting. Bassam, Nuha, Ibtisam, Hafez, and Mario sat at the round table and eyed one another. He started with a positive note of recognition for their efforts during his absence. Tarek then brought up the subject of the conflicts that existed and how top management had not hesitated to make them known to him upon his return from Paris. Hafez immediately became defensive and started pointing the finger at each of his coworkers. Consequently, the others started interjecting, until all that could be heard was a chorus of complaints.

Tarek allowed the emotions to come out in hopes of clearing the air. This confrontation was healthy, so he sat and listened for a while. Then he abruptly banged on the table for a ceasefire. All anxious eyes were fixed on their director, as they remembered that he was sitting there with them. He, in turn, eyed each of them and said, "Talking does not mean someone is hearing. Hearing does not mean someone is listening. Listening does not mean someone understands. I want each one of you to give me an interpretation of what happened in my absence."

After a very long session, Tarek found that everyone had had an encounter with Hafez, who of course blamed the opposite parties. Hafez was the company vice president's nephew. All of the staff were aware of this fact, and Hafez made no effort to hide it.

Tarek was trying to be as patient as he could. He explained to them that poor communication was the reason for these interpersonal conflicts and noted that it was negatively affecting their productivity. Tarek told them, "We need to be professionals and leave our personal lives at home. We must fight 'back noise' in the workplace, because it will only result in gossip, disloyal behavior, lack of team spirit, and general employee unrest."

Tarek felt that the meeting had helped to clear the air. Tarek then reminded his employees of their duties and responsibility to the office and to the company. After a revision of the department's goals, objectives, and strategies, Tarek concluded the meeting by telling them about a book he had just read entitled *FISH*.

"Yes," Tarek continued, "the book by Lundin, Paul, and Christensen is entitled *FISH*. It's about building relationships and boosting morale. An office manager, Jane, had the challenge of motivating a group of extremely disheartened employees." Tarek was glad to notice that he had their attention. "Nothing seemed to work but one day as she was walking near the markets during her lunch break, Jane witnessed an intriguing game at a fish market. She approached the head of the team and explained her problem. He told Jane to observe their interactions and she will learn why they were successful. The men at the market had discovered four pillars to motivating people."

The employees were really interested and wanted to know the secrets. Tarek went on to explain that after Jane witnessed the game, she took her employees to the market and told them to watch and learn. The four tips that the men had given Jane worked wonders with her staff and turned their personal and professional lives around. The four pillars are: (1) choose your attitude, (2) play and have fun, (3) make each other's day, and (4) be present.

Finally, Tarek reminded them that it was their choice; they could either be depressed or liven up the atmosphere at work. He told them, "We can make our day exciting and share and help one another or just hold grudges. It's only with trust and support and acknowledgment that we can work together, and, most important, we need to listen to one another. Now, I want you all to meditate on what we achieved and learned today and I will see you all tomorrow."

Discussion Questions

1. Did Tarek demonstrate supportive communication and listening? Explain.
2. What was the most dominant blocking role of this case? Discuss it and give the reasons for this.
3. The eight relationship-building roles discussed in this chapter are evident in this case. Identify each as it appears in this case.
4. How does synergy contribute to positive relationships?

Rejected Plans

The following dialogue occurred between two employees in a large firm. The conversation illustrates several characteristics of supportive communication.

SUSETTE: How did your meeting go with Mr. Schmidt yesterday?

LEONARDO: Well, uh, it went . . . aaah . . . it was no big deal.

SUSETTE: It looks as if you're pretty upset about it.

LEONARDO: Yeah, I am. It was a totally frustrating experience. I, uh, well, let's just say I would like to forget the whole thing.

SUSETTE: Things must not have gone as well as you had hoped they would.

LEONARDO: I'll say! That guy was impossible. I thought the plans I submitted were very clear and well thought out. Then he rejected the entire package.

SUSETTE: You mean he didn't accept any of them?

LEONARDO: You got it.

SUSETTE: I've seen your work before, Leonardo. You've always done a first-rate job. It's hard for me to figure out why your plans were rejected by Schmidt. What did he say about them?

LEONARDO: He said they were unrealistic and too difficult to implement, and . . .

SUSETTE: Really?

LEONARDO: Yeah, and when he said that I felt he was attacking me personally. But, on the other hand, I was also angry because I thought my plans were very good, and, you know, I paid close attention to every detail in those plans.

SUSETTE: I'm certain that you did.

LEONARDO: It just really ticks me off.

SUSETTE: I'll bet it does. I would be upset, too.

LEONARDO: Schmidt has something against me.

SUSETTE: After all the effort you put into those plans, you still couldn't figure out whether Schmidt was rejecting you or your plans, right?

LEONARDO: Yeah. Right. How could you tell?

SUSETTE: I can really understand your confusion and uncertainty when you felt Schmidt's actions were unreasonable.

LEONARDO: I just don't understand why he did what he did.

SUSETTE: Sure. If he said your plans were unrealistic, what does that mean? I mean, how can you deal with a rationale like that? It's just too general—meaningless, even. Did he mention anything specific? Did you ask him to point out some problems or explain the reasons for his rejection more clearly?

LEONARDO: Good point, but, uh, you know . . . I was so disappointed at the rejection that I was kinda like in outer space. You know what I mean?

SUSETTE: Yeah. It's an incapacitating experience. You have so much invested personally that you try to divest as fast as you can to save what little self-respect is left.

LEONARDO: That's it all right. I just wanted to get out of there before I said something I would be sorry for.

SUSETTE: Yet, in the back of your mind, you probably figured that Schmidt wouldn't risk the company's future just because he didn't like you personally. But then, well . . . the plans were good! It's hard to deal with that contradiction on the spot, isn't it?

LEONARDO: Exactly. I knew I should have pushed him for more information, but, uh, I just stood there like a dummy. But what can you do about it now? It's spilled milk.

SUSETTE: I don't think it's a total loss, Leonardo. I mean, from what you have told me—what he said and what you said—I don't think that a conclusion can be reached. Maybe he doesn't understand the plans, or maybe it was just his off day. Who knows? It could be a lot of things. What would you think about pinning Schmidt down by asking for his objections, point by point? Do you think it would help to talk to him again?

LEONARDO: Well, I would sure know a lot more than I know now. As it is, I wouldn't know where to begin revising or modifying the plans. And you're right, I really don't know what Schmidt thinks about me or my work. Sometimes I just react and interpret with little or no evidence.

SUSETTE: Maybe, uh . . . maybe another meeting would be a good thing, then.

LEONARDO: Well, I guess I should get off my duff and schedule an appointment with him for next week. I am curious to find out what the problem is, with the plans, or me. (Pause) Thanks, Susette, for helping me work through this thing.

Discussion Questions

1. Categorize each statement in the case according to the supportive communication characteristic or type of response it represents. For example, the first statement by Leonardo obviously is not very congruent, but the second one is much more so.

2. Which statements in the conversation were most helpful? Which were least helpful, or could have produced defensiveness or closed off the conversation?

3. If you were the coach of Susette, how would you assist her in being more competent as a supportive communicator? How would you coach Leonardo to be more supportive even though it is he who faces the problem?

EXERCISES FOR DIAGNOSING COMMUNICATION PROBLEMS AND FOSTERING UNDERSTANDING

United Chemical Company

The role of manager encompasses not only one-on-one coaching and counseling with an employee but also frequently entails helping other people understand coaching and counseling principles for themselves. Sometimes it means refereeing interactions and, by example, helping other people learn about correct principles of supportive communication. This is part of the task in this exercise. In a group setting, coaching and counseling become more difficult because multiple messages, driven by multiple motives, interact. Skilled supportive communicators, however, help each group member feel supported and understood in the interaction, even though the solution to an issue may not always be the one he or she would have preferred.

Assignment

In this exercise you should apply the principles of supportive communication you have read about in the chapter. First, you will need to form groups of four people each. Next, read the case and assign the following roles in your group: Max, Marquita, Keeshaun, and an observer. Assume that a meeting is being held with Max, Marquita, and Keeshaun immediately after the end of the incidents in the following case. Play the roles you have been assigned and try to resolve the problems. The observer should provide feedback to the three players at the end of the exercise. An Observer's Feedback Form can be found at the end of the chapter.

The Case

The United Chemical Company is a large producer and distributor of commodity chemicals, with five production plants in the United States. The main plant in Baytown, Texas, is not only a production plant but also the company's research and engineering center.

The process design group consists of eight male engineers and their supervisor, Max Kane. The group has worked together steadily for a number of years, and good relationships have developed among all the members. When the workload began to increase, Max hired a new design engineer, Marquita Davis, a recent master's degree graduate from one of the foremost engineering schools in the country. Marquita was assigned to a project that would expand the capacity of one of the existing plant facilities. Three other design engineers were assigned to the project along with Marquita: Keeshaun Keller (age 38, 15 years with the company), Sam Sims (age 40, 10 years with the company), and Lance Madison (age 32, 8 years with the company).

As a new employee, Marquita was very enthusiastic about the opportunity to work at United. She liked her work very much because it was challenging and it offered her a chance to apply much of the knowledge she had gained in her university studies. On the job, Marquita kept mostly to herself and her design work. Her relations with her fellow

PRACTICE

project members were friendly, but she did not go out of her way to have informal conversations with them during or after working hours.

Marquita was a diligent employee who took her work seriously. On occasions when a difficult problem arose, she would stay after hours in order to come up with a solution. Because of her persistence, coupled with her more current education, Marquita usually completed her portion of the various project stages several days ahead of her colleagues. This was somewhat irritating to her because on these occasions she had to go to Max to ask for additional work to keep her busy until her coworkers caught up to her. Initially, she had offered to help Keeshaun, Sam, and Lance with their assignments, but each time she was abruptly turned down.

About five months after Marquita had joined the design group, Keeshaun asked to see Max about a problem the group was having. The conversation between Max and Keeshaun went as follows:

MAX: Keeshaun, I understand you want to discuss a problem with me.

KEESHAUN: Yes, Max, I don't want to waste your time, but some of the other design engineers want me to discuss Marquita with you. She is irritating everyone with her know-it-all, pompous attitude. She's just not the kind of person we want to work with.

MAX: I can't understand that, Keeshaun. She's an excellent worker, and her design work is always well done and usually flawless. She's doing everything the company wants her to do.

KEESHAUN: The company never asked her to disrupt the morale of the group or to tell us how to do our work. The animosity in our group could eventually result in lower-quality work for the whole unit.

MAX: I'll tell you what I'll do. Marquita has a meeting with me next week to discuss her six-month performance. I'll keep your thoughts in mind, but I can't promise an improvement in what you and the others believe is a pompous attitude.

KEESHAUN: Immediate improvement in her behavior is not the problem; it's her coaching others when she has no right to. She publicly shows others what to do. You'd think she was lecturing an advance class in design with all her high-powered, useless equations and formulas. She'd better back off soon, or some of us will quit or transfer.

During the next week, Max thought carefully about his meeting with Keeshaun. He knew that Keeshaun was the informal leader of the design engineers and generally spoke for the other group members. On Thursday of the following week, Max called Marquita into his office for her mid-year review. One portion of the conversation went as follows:

MAX: There is one other aspect I'd like to discuss with you about your performance. As I just related to you, your technical performance has been excellent; however, there are some questions about your relationships with the other workers.

MARQUITA: I don't understand. What questions are you talking about?

MAX: Well, to be specific, certain members of the design group have complained about your apparent "know-it-all attitude" and the manner in which you try to tell them how to do their job. You're going to have to be patient with them and not publicly call them out about their performance. This is a good group of engineers, and their work over the years has been more than acceptable. I don't want any problems that will cause the group to produce less effectively.

MARQUITA: Let me make a few comments. First of all, I have never publicly criticized their performance to them or to you. Initially, when I finished ahead of them, I offered to help them with their work but was bluntly told to mind my own business. I took the hint and concentrated only on my part of the work. What you don't understand is that after five months of working in this group I have come to the conclusion that what is going on is a rip-off of the company. The other engineers are goldbricking; they're setting a work pace much slower than they're capable of. They're more interested in the music from Sam's radio, the local football team, and the bar they're going to go to for TGIF. I'm sorry, but this is just not the way I was raised or trained. And finally, they've never looked on me as a qualified engineer, but as a woman who has broken their professional barrier.

SOURCE: *United Chemical Company. Szilagyi, A. D. and M. J. Wallace,* Organizational Behavior and Performance, Third Edition, *pp. 204–205. © 1983.* *Glenview, IL: Scott Foresman*

Byron vs. Thomas

Effective one-on-one coaching and counseling are skills that are required in many settings in life, not just in management. It is hard to imagine a parent, roommate, Little League coach, room mother, or good friend who would not benefit from training in supportive communication. Because there are so many aspects of supportive communication, however, it is sometimes difficult to remember all of them. That is why practice, with observation and feedback, is so important. These attributes of supportive communication can become a natural part of your interaction approach as you conscientiously practice and receive feedback from a colleague.

Assignment

In the following exercise, one individual should take the role of Hal Byron, and another should take the role of Judy Thomas. To make the role-play realistic, do not read each other's role descriptions. When you have finished reading, hold a meeting between Hal Byron and Judy Thomas. A third person should serve as the observer. An Observer's Feedback Form to assist in providing feedback is at the end of the chapter.

Hal Byron, Department Head

You are Hal Byron, head of the operations group—the "back room"—in a large bank corporation. This is your second year on the job, and you have moved up rather quickly in the bank. You enjoy working for this firm, which has a reputation for being one of the finest in the region. One reason is that outside opportunities for management development and training are funded by the bank. In addition, each employee is given an opportunity for a personal management interview each month, and these sessions are usually both productive and developmental.

One of the department members, Judy Thomas, has been in this department for 19 years, 15 of them in the same job. She is reasonably good at what she does, and she is always punctual and efficient. She tends to get to work earlier than most employees in order to peruse the *American Banker* and *USA Today*. You can almost set your watch by the time Judy visits the restroom during the day and by the time she makes her phone call to her daughter every afternoon.

Your feeling about Judy is that although she is a good worker, she lacks imagination and initiative. This has been indicated by her lack of merit increases over the last five years and by the fact that she has had the same job for 15 years. She's content to do just what is assigned, nothing more. Your predecessor must have given hints to Judy that she might be in line for a promotion, however, because Judy has raised this with you more than once. Because she has been in her job so long, she is at the top of her pay range, and without a promotion, she cannot receive a salary adjustment above the basic cost-of-living increase.

The one thing Judy does beyond the basic minimum job requirements is to help train young people who come into the department. She is very patient and methodical with them, and she seems to take pride in helping them learn the ropes. She has not been hesitant to point out this contribution to you. Unfortunately, this activity does not qualify Judy for a promotion, nor could she be transferred into the training and development department. Once you suggested that she take a few courses at the local college, paid for by the bank, but she matter-of-factly stated that she was too old to go to school. You surmise that she might be intimidated because she doesn't have a college degree.

As much as you would like to promote Judy, there just doesn't seem to be any way to do that in good conscience. You have tried putting additional work under her control, but she seems to be slowing down in her productivity rather than speeding up. The work needs to get done, and expanding her role just puts you behind schedule.

This interview coming up is probably the time to level with Judy about her performance and her potential. You certainly don't want to lose her as an employee, but there is not going to be a change in job assignment for a long time unless she changes her performance dramatically.

Judy Thomas, Department Member

You are a member of the operations group in a large bank corporation. You have been with the bank now for 19 years, 15 of them in the same job. You enjoy the company because of its friendly climate and because of its prestigious image in the region. It's nice to be known as an employee of this firm. However, lately you have become more dissatisfied as you've seen person after person come into the bank and get promoted ahead of you. Your own boss, Hal Byron, is almost 20 years your junior. Another woman who joined the bank the same time you did is now a senior vice president. You can't understand why you've been neglected. You are efficient and accurate in your work, you have a near-perfect attendance record, and you consider yourself to be a good employee. You have gone out of your way on many occasions to help train and orient young people who are just joining the bank. Several of them have written letters later telling you how important your help was in getting them promoted. A lot of good that does you!

The only thing you can figure out is that there is a bias against you because you haven't graduated from college. On the other hand, others have moved up without a diploma. You haven't taken advantage of any college courses paid for by the bank, but after a long day at work, you're not inclined to go to class for another three hours. Besides, you only see your family in the evenings, and you don't want to take time away from them. It doesn't take a college degree to do your job, anyway.

Your monthly personal management interview is coming up with your department head, Hal Byron, and you've decided the time has come to get a few answers. Several things need explaining. Not only haven't you been promoted, but you haven't even received a merit increase for five years. You're not getting any credit for the extra contributions you make with new employees, nor for your steady, reliable work. Could anyone blame you for being a little bitter?

Active Listening Exercise

Form a trio of colleagues who hold differing opinions about any of the following topics. Hold a 10- or 15-minute conversation about any of the topics. Take a position on the issue. Make a case for your point of view. Convince your partners that you are right. When you are finished, complete the short questionnaire below, and discuss the results together. Offer any helpful feedback to your colleagues that you think may be appropriate.

1. Should the United States have invaded Iraq in 2003?
2. Should late-term abortions be performed?
3. Is global warming a critical issue?
4. Should the United States prosecute and deport illegal aliens?
5. Should English become the national language in the United States?

6. Does the international media have a liberal bias, and does it matter either way?
7. Are business school rankings helpful or harmful?
8. Who is the world's most dangerous person?
9. Should professional athletes be allowed to compete in the Olympics?
10. Should the United Nations exist?

Rate your two colleagues on the following items using this response scale:

1 = *Strongly disagree*
2 = *Disagree*
3 = *Neither*
4 = *Agree*
5 = *Strongly agree*

ITEM	COLLEAGUE 1	COLLEAGUE 2
My colleague . . .		
1. Maintained eye contact and interest	1 2 3 4 5	1 2 3 4 5
2. Used inquiry more than advocacy	1 2 3 4 5	1 2 3 4 5
3. Interrupted	1 2 3 4 5	1 2 3 4 5
4. Displayed appropriate emotional engagement	1 2 3 4 5	1 2 3 4 5
5. Used a variety of response types	1 2 3 4 5	1 2 3 4 5
6. Used reflective responses	1 2 3 4 5	1 2 3 4 5

Reverse the scoring for item 3, and add up the scores for each colleague. Provide those scores to one another and discuss the results. Provide helpful feedback to one another.

PRACTICE

SKILL *APPLICATION*

ACTIVITIES FOR COMMUNICATING SUPPORTIVELY

Suggested Assignments

1. Tape record an interview with someone such as a coworker, friend, or spouse. Focus on an issue or challenge faced right now by that person. Diagnose the situation to determine if you should be a coach or a counselor. (Our bet is that it will be the latter.) Conduct a conversation in which you apply the principles of supportive communication discussed in the chapter. (The Rejected Plans case provides an example of such an interview.) Use the tape to determine how you could improve your own supportive communication skill.

2. Teach someone you know the concepts of supportive communication and supportive listening. Provide your own explanations and illustrations so the person understands what you are talking about. Describe your experience in your journal.

3. Identify a person with whom you have had a disagreement, some difficulty in the past, or some discomfort in your relationship. This could be a roommate, parent, friend, or instructor. Approach that person and ask to hold a conversation in which you discuss the interpersonal problem. To be successful, you'll discover how crucial supportive communication is in the conversation. When you have finished, write up the experience in as much detail as possible. What did you say and what did the other person say? What was especially effective and what didn't work so well? Identify areas in which you need to improve.

4. Write two mini–case studies. One should recount an effective coaching or counseling situation. The other should recount an ineffective coaching or counseling situation. The cases should be based on a real event, either from your own personal experience or from the experience of someone you know well. Use principles of supportive communication and listening in your cases.

Application Plan and Evaluation

The intent of this exercise is to help you apply this cluster of skills in a real-life, out-of-class setting. Now that you have become familiar with the behavioral guidelines that form the basis of effective skill performance, you will improve most by trying out those guidelines in an everyday context. Unlike a classroom activity, in which feedback is immediate and others can assist you with their evaluations, this skill application activity is one you must accomplish and evaluate on your own. There are two parts to this activity. Part 1 helps prepare you to apply the skill. Part 2 helps you evaluate and improve on your experience. Be sure to write down answers to each item. Don't short-circuit the process by skipping steps.

Part 1. Planning

1. Write down the two or three aspects of this skill that are most important to you. These may be areas of weakness, areas you most want to improve, or areas that are most salient to a problem you face right now. Identify the specific aspects of this skill that you want to apply.

2. Now identify the setting or the situation in which you will apply this skill. Establish a plan for performance by actually writing down a description of the situation. Who else will be involved? When will you do it? Where will it be done?
   Circumstances:
   Who else?
   When?
   Where?

3. Identify the specific behaviors in which you will engage to apply this skill. Operationalize your skill performance.

4. What are the indicators of successful performance? How will you know you have been effective? What will indicate you have performed competently?

Part 2. Evaluation

5. After you have completed your implementation, record the results. What happened? How successful were you? What was the effect on others?

6. How can you improve? What modifications can you make next time? What will you do differently in a similar situation in the future?

7. Looking back on your whole skill practice and application experience, what have you learned? What has been surprising? In what ways might this experience help you in the long term?

APPLICATION

Communicating Supportively

Scoring Key

SKILL AREA	ITEMS	ASSESSMENT	
		PRE-	POST-
Knowledge of Coaching and Counseling	1, 2, 20	_____	_____
Providing Effective Negative Feedback	3, 4, 5, 6, 7, 8	_____	_____
Communicating Supportively	9, 10, 11, 12, 13, 14, 15, 16, 17, 18, 19	_____	_____
	Total Score	_____	_____

Comparison Data (N = 5,000 Students)

Compare your scores to three standards:
1. The maximum possible score = 120.
2. The scores of other students in the class.
3. Norm data from more than 5,000 business school students.

Pre-Test				Post-Test
90.91	=	mean	=	99.75
99 or above	=	top quartile	=	108–120
92–98	=	second quartile	=	100–107
84–91	=	third quartile	=	93–99
83 or below	=	bottom quartile	=	92 or below

Communication Styles

Comparison Data

Identify the type of response pattern that you rely on the most by adding the numbers you gave to each response alternative in Part I. The chapter discusses the advantages and disadvantages of each of these response types. The most skilled supportive communicators score 9 or above on Reflecting responses and 6 or above on Probing responses. They score 2 or less on Advising responses and 4 or less on Deflecting responses.

In Part II, circle the alternative that you chose. The most skilled supportive communicators select alternatives 1a, 2b, 3a, 4b, and 5a.

Part I
1. a. Deflecting response
    b. Probing response
    c. Advising response
    d. Reflecting response
    e. Deflecting response

2. a. Reflecting response
   b. Deflecting response
   c. Advising response
   d. Reflecting response
   e. Probing response
3. a. Probing response
   b. Deflecting response
   c. Advising response
   d. Reflecting response
   e. Probing response
4. a. Reflecting response
   b. Probing response
   c. Deflecting response
   d. Deflecting response
   e. Advising response

Part II
1. a. Problem-oriented statement
   b. Person-oriented statement
2. a. Incongruent–minimizing statement
   b. Congruent statement
3. a. Descriptive statement
   b. Evaluative statement
4. a. Invalidating statement
   b. Validating statement
5. a. Owned statement
   b. Disowned statement

Observer's Feedback Form

As the observer, rate the extent to which each of the role players displayed the following behaviors effectively. Use the following numerical rating scale for each person. Identify specific things that each person can do to improve his or her performance.

1 = Strongly disagree
2 = Disagree
3 = Neither
4 = Agree
5 = Strongly agree

COMMUNICATION ATTRIBUTE	ROLE 1	ROLE 2	ROLE 3
1. Communicated congruently.	_____	_____	_____
2. Used descriptive communication.	_____	_____	_____
3. Used problem-oriented communication.	_____	_____	_____
4. Used validating communication.	_____	_____	_____
5. Used specific and qualified communication.	_____	_____	_____
6. Used conjunctive communication.	_____	_____	_____

COMMUNICATION ATTRIBUTE	ROLE 1	ROLE 2	ROLE 3
7. Owned statements and used personal words.	_____	_____	_____
8. Listened inventively.	_____	_____	_____
9. Used a variety of response alternatives appropriately.	_____	_____	_____

Comments:

SKILL ASSESSMENT ▶

- Gaining Power and Influence
- Using Influence Strategies

SKILL LEARNING ■

- Building a Strong Power Base and Using Influence Wisely
- A Balanced View of Power
- Strategies for Gaining Organizational Power
- Transforming Power into Influence
- Summary
- Behavioral Guidelines

SKILL ANALYSIS ▶

- Banning Foreign Recruitment

SKILL PRACTICE ◆

- Repairing Power Failures in Management Circuits
- Ann Lyman's Proposal
- Cindy's Fast Foods
- 9:00 to 7:30

SKILL APPLICATION ●

- Suggested Assignments
- Application Plan and Evaluation

SCORING KEYS AND COMPARISON DATA ■

5

Gaining Power and Influence

SKILL DEVELOPMENT OBJECTIVES

- ENHANCE PERSONAL AND POSITIONAL POWER
- USE INFLUENCE APPROPRIATELY TO ACCOMPLISH EXCEPTIONAL WORK
- NEUTRALIZE INAPPROPRIATE INFLUENCE ATTEMPTS

DIAGNOSTIC SURVEYS FOR GAINING POWER AND INFLUENCE

GAINING POWER AND INFLUENCE

Step 1: Before you read this chapter, respond to the following statements by writing a number from the rating scale that follows in the left-hand column (Pre-Assessment). Your answers should reflect your attitudes and behavior as they are now, not as you would like them to be. Be honest. This instrument is designed to help you discover your level of competency in gaining power and influence so you can tailor your learning to your specific needs. When you have completed the survey, use the scoring key at the end of the chapter to identify the skill areas discussed in this chapter that are most important for you to master.

Step 2: After you have completed the reading and the exercises in this chapter and, ideally, as many of the Skill Application assignments at the end of this chapter as you can, cover up your first set of answers. Then respond to the same statements again, this time in the right-hand column (Post-Assessment). When you have completed the survey, use the scoring key at the end of the chapter to measure your progress. If your score remains low in specific skill areas, use the behavioral guidelines at the end of the Skill Learning section to guide your further practice.

Rating Scale

1 Strongly disagree
2 Disagree
3 Slightly disagree
4 Slightly agree
5 Agree
6 Strongly agree

Assessment

Pre-   Post-

In a situation in which it is important to obtain more power:

_____ _____ 1. I strive to become highly proficient in my line of work.

_____ _____ 2. I express friendliness, honesty, and sincerity toward those with whom I work.

_____ _____ 3. I put forth more effort and take more initiative than expected in my work.

_____ _____ 4. I support organizational ceremonial events and activities.

_____ _____ 5. I form a broad network of relationships with people throughout the organization at all levels.

_____ _____ 6. I send personal notes to others when they accomplish something significant or when I pass along important information to them.

_____ _____ 7. In my work I strive to generate new ideas, initiate new activities, and minimize routine tasks.

_____ _____ 8. I try to find ways to be an external representative for my unit or organization.

_____ _____ 9. I am continually upgrading my skills and knowledge.

_____ _____ 10. I strive to enhance my personal appearance.

_____ _____ 11. I work harder than most coworkers.

_____ _____ 12. I encourage new members to support important organizational values by both their words and their actions.

_____ _____ 13. I gain access to important information by becoming central in communication networks.

_____ _____ 14. I strive to find opportunities to make reports about my work, especially to senior people.

_____ _____ 15. I maintain variety in the tasks that I do.

_____ _____ 16. I keep my work connected to the central mission of the organization.

When trying to influence someone for a specific purpose:

_____ _____ 17. I emphasize reason and factual information.

_____ _____ 18. I feel comfortable using a variety of different influence techniques, matching them to specific circumstances.

_____ _____ 19. I reward others for agreeing with me, thereby establishing a condition of reciprocity.

_____ _____ 20. I use a direct, straightforward approach rather than an indirect or manipulative one.

_____ _____ 21. I avoid using threats or demands to impose my will on others.

When resisting an inappropriate influence attempt directed at me:

_____ _____ 22. I use resources and information I control to equalize demands and threats.

_____ _____ 23. I refuse to bargain with individuals who use high-pressure negotiation tactics.

_____ _____ 24. I explain why I can't comply with reasonable-sounding requests by pointing out how the consequences would affect my responsibilities and obligations.

When trying to influence those above me in the organization:

_____ _____ 25. I help determine the issues to which they pay attention by effectively selling the importance of those issues.

_____ _____ 26. I convince them that the issues on which I want to focus are compatible with the goals and future success of the organization.

_____ _____ 27. I help them solve problems that they didn't expect me to help them solve.

_____ _____ 28. I work as hard to make them look good and be successful as I do for my own success.

USING INFLUENCE STRATEGIES

Indicate, by writing the appropriate number in the blank, how often you use each of the following strategies for getting others to comply with your wishes. Choose from a scale of 1 to 5, with 1 being "rarely," 3 being "sometimes," and 5 being "always." After you have completed the survey, use the scoring key at the end of the chapter to tabulate your results.

_____ 1. "If you don't comply, I'll make you regret it."

_____ 2. "If you comply, I will reward you."

_____ 3. "These facts demonstrate the merit of my position."

_____ 4. "Others in the group have agreed; what is your decision?"

_____ 5. "People you value will think better (worse) of you if you do (do not) comply."

_____ 6. "The group needs your help, so do it for the good of us all."

_____ 7. "I will stop nagging you if you comply."

_____ 8. "You owe me compliance because of past favors."

_____ 9. "This is what I need; will you help out?"

_____ 10. "If you don't act now, you'll lose this opportunity."

_____ 11. "I have moderated my initial position; now I expect you to be equally reasonable."

_____ 12. "This request is consistent with other decisions you've made."

_____ 13. "If you don't agree to help out, the consequences will be harmful to others."

_____ 14. "I'm only requesting a small commitment [now]."

_____ 15. "Compliance will enable you to reach a personally important objective."

Building a Strong Power Base and Using Influence Wisely

"The difference between someone who can get an idea off the ground and accepted in an organization and someone who can't isn't a question of who has the better idea. It's a question of who has political competence. Political competence isn't something you're born with, but a skill you learn. It's an out-in-the-open process of methodically mapping the political terrain, building coalitions, and leading them to get your idea adopted." So says Samuel Bacharach, a Cornell University professor who has spent his career negotiating the halls of powerful New York businesses and labor unions (Bacharach, 2005, p. 93).

The skill of political competence is particularly relevant for today's workforce, which, according to a recent *Fortune* magazine report, includes large numbers of "fearless and ambitious unseasoned twenty-somethings flooding the managerial job market." These new managers are taking positions traditionally reserved for battle-tested pros who understand from experience the ins and outs of gaining power and influence. Nearly 12 percent of employed 20- to 34-year-olds held management positions in 1998. These young, inexperienced managers report difficulties managing "up"—getting their bosses to respect them—as well as managing "down"—getting their older subordinates to respect their position (Leger, 2000).

Professor John Kotter of Harvard University, an authority on managerial power, agrees with this assessment. "It makes me sick to hear economists tell students that their job is to maximize shareholder profits," he says. "Their job is going to be managing a whole host of constituencies: bosses, underlings, customers, suppliers, unions, you name it. Trying to get cooperation from different constituencies is an infinitely more difficult task than milking your business for money" (Gelman, 1985).

While serving as a young senior systems analyst at General Motors, Bogdan J. Dawidowicz, commented on the benefits of taking Professor Kotter's course on power in the Harvard MBA program. He credited it with his ability to handle extremely delicate assignments. For example, when he was told to evaluate product scheduling at a GM plant, he knew that plant management would not take kindly to an outsider's disrupting their routine, demanding information, and critiquing their performance. So he called the plant superintendent and enlisted his support. Following an extended discussion, the superintendent took the lead in scheduling appointments with his staff and compiling all the necessary information prior to the visit (Buell & Cowan, 1985).

A Balanced View of Power

It should come as no surprise that many authorities argue the effective use of power is the most critical element of management. One such authority, Warren Bennis, seeking the quintessential ingredients of effective leaders, interviewed 90 individuals who had been nominated by peers as the most influential leaders in all walks of our society. Bennis found these individuals shared one significant characteristic: They made others feel powerful. These leaders were powerful because they had learned how to build a strong power base in their organizations or institutions. They were influential because they used their power to help peers and subordinates accomplish exceptional tasks. It requires no particular power, skill, or genius to accomplish the ordinary. But it is difficult to do the truly unusual without political clout (Bennis & Nanus, 2003).

LACK OF POWER

John Gardner has observed, "In this country—and in most democracies—power has such a bad name that many people persuade themselves they want nothing to do with it" (1990). For these people, power is a "four-letter word," conjuring up images of vindictive, domineering bosses and manipulative, cunning subordinates. It is associated with dirty office politics engaged in by ruthless individuals who use as their handbooks for corporate guerrilla warfare books such as *Winning Through Intimidation*, and who subscribe to the philosophy of Heinrich von Treitschke: "Your neighbor, even though he may look upon you as a natural ally against another power which is feared by you both, is always ready, at the first opportunity, as soon as it can be done with safety, to better himself at your expense. . . . Whoever fails to increase his power, must decrease it, if others increase theirs" (Mulgan, 1998, p. 68).

Those with a distaste for power argue that teaching managers and prospective managers how to increase their power is tantamount to sanctioning the use of primitive forms of domination. They support this argument by noting the nasty political fight between Lewis Glucksman and Peter Peterson for control of Lehman Brothers that cost Lehman its independence; the conflict between cofounders Steven Jobs and John Sculley that turned Apple Computer into a battleground; and the firing of Frank Biondi, the president of Viacom, by its power-hungry chairperson Sumner Redstone (Korda, 1991; Pfeffe 1994).

This negative view of "personal power" is especially common in cultures that place a high value on ascription, rather than achievement, and on collectivism, rather than individualism (Triandis, 1994; Trompenaars, 1996). People who view interpersonal relations through the lens of ascription believe power resides in stable, personal characteristics, such as age, gender, level of education, ethnic background, or social class. Hence, focusing the attention of organizational members on "getting ahead," "taking charge," and "making things happen" seems contrary to the natural social order. Those who place a high value on collectivism are also likely to feel uncomfortable with our approach, but for a different reason. Their concern would be that placing too much emphasis on increasing a single individual's power might not be in the best interests of the larger group.

We acknowledge this chapter has a very "American" orientation. Consequently, it might not be an appropriate skill development framework for all readers. For those who feel uncomfortable modeling their own behavior after the principles and guidelines in this chapter, we suggest you think of this as a useful "translation guide" for helping you understand how American business managers view power and how American corporations treat power. In addition, we hope readers who might be tempted to assume our approach is the only reasonable approach will understand they are likely to interact with individuals from different cultures who will probably believe some of these strategies are ineffective and/or inappropriate.

There are many American business leaders and scholars who make a persuasive case for operating from a position of power in an organization. Robert Dilenschneider, president and chief executive officer (CEO) of a leading public relations firm, states: "The use of influence is itself not negative. It can often lead to a great good. Like any powerful force—from potent medicine to nuclear power—it is the morality with which influence is used that makes all the difference" (Dilenschneider, 1990, p. xviii; see also Dilenschneider, 2007). Power need not be associated with aggression, brute force, craftiness, or deceit. Power can also be viewed as a sign of personal efficacy. It is the ability to mobilize resources to accomplish productive work. People with power shape their environment, whereas the powerless are molded by theirs. Rollo May, in *Power and Innocence* (1998), suggests those who are unwilling to exercise power and influence are condemned to experience unhappiness throughout their lives.

There is nothing more demoralizing than feeling you have a creative new idea or a unique insight into a significant organizational problem and then coming face-to-face with your organizational impotence. This face of power is seen by many young college graduates, who annually flood the corporate job market. They are energetic, optimistic, and supremely confident that their "awesome" ability, state-of-the-art training, and indefatigable energy will rocket them up the corporate ladder. However, many soon become discouraged and embittered. They blame "the old guard" for protecting their turf and not being open to new ideas. Their feelings of frustration prompt many to look for greener pastures of opportunity in other companies—only to be confronted anew with rejection and failure. One such "victim" stated dejectedly, "Hell is knowing you have a better solution than someone else but not being able to get the votes."

These individuals learn quickly that only the naive believe the best recommendation always gets selected, the most capable individual always gets the promotion, and the deserving unit gets its fair share of the budget. These are political decisions heavily influenced by the interests of the powerful.

Astute managers understand in the long run no one benefits from lopsided distributions of power. One seasoned veteran of organizational power games summarized his experience: "Powerless members of an organization either get angry and try to tear down the system, or they become apathetic and withdraw. Either way, everyone loses."

Rosabeth Kanter (1979) has pointed out that powerful managers not only can accomplish more personally, but can also pass on more information and make more resources available to subordinates. For this reason, people tend to prefer bosses with "clout." Subordinates tend to feel they have higher status in an organization and their morale is higher when they perceive that their boss has considerable upward influence. In contrast, Kanter argues, powerlessness tends to foster bossiness, rather than true leadership. "In large organizations, at

Table 5.1	Indicators of a Manager's Upward and Outward Power

Powerful managers can:

- Intercede favorably on behalf of someone in trouble.
- Get a desirable placement for a talented subordinate.
- Get approval for expenditures beyond the budget.
- Get items on and off the agenda at policy meetings.
- Get fast access to top decision makers.
- Maintain regular, frequent contact with top decision makers.
- Acquire early information about decisions and policy shifts.

SOURCE: *Reprinted by permission of* Harvard Business Review. *Indicators of a Manager's Upward and Outward Power. From "Power Failures in Management Circuits" by R. Kanter, 57. Copyright © 1979 by the Harvard Business School Publishing Corporation; all rights reserved.*

least," she notes, "it is powerlessness that often creates ineffective, desultory management and petty, dictatorial, rules-minded managerial styles" (p. 65).

Kanter (1979) has identified several indicators of a manager's upward and outward power in an organization. These are shown in Table 5.1. In some respects, these serve as a set of behavioral objectives for our discussion of power and influence.

ABUSE OF POWER

But what about Lord Acton's well-known dictum, "Power corrupts, and absolute power corrupts absolutely"? Hardly a week goes by that new evidence of this seemingly ageless observation isn't reflected in news headlines. Doesn't that suggest effective managers should avoid power because "abuse of office," with a likely fall from power, will inevitably follow?

This certainly appears to be an ageless lesson of history. In the Greek plays of Sophocles, for instance, the viewer is confronted with the image of great and powerful rulers transformed by their prior success so that they are filled with a sense of their own worth and importance—with hubris—which causes them to be impatient of the advice of others and unwilling to listen to opinions different from their own. Yet in the end they are destroyed by events that they discover, to their anguish, they cannot control. Oedipus is destroyed soon after the crowds say (and he believes) "he is almost like a God"; King Creon, at the zenith of his political and military power, is brought down as a result of his unjust and unfeeling belief in the infallibility of his judgments.

Headlines of business trade periodicals regularly trumpet claims of modern-day hubris among business elites (Bunker, Kram, & Ting, 2002). One of the most frequently mentioned examples is the "slash and burn" management style of Al Dunlap at Scott Paper and Sunbeam Electric. He takes pride in being responsible for thousands of employees losing their jobs while he takes home multimillion-dollar bonuses (DeGeorge, 1999).

Sophocles warns us never to be envious of the powerful until we see the nature of their endings. Support for the modern-day relevance of this timeless warning that arrogance tends to be self-checking is reflected in the results of studies of both successful and failed corporate executives (McCall & Lombardo, 1983; Shipper & Dillard, 2000). In the first study of its kind, scholars at the Center for Creative Leadership identified approximately 20 executives who had risen to the top of their firms and matched them with a similar group of 20 executives who had failed to reach their career aspirations. Earlier, both groups had entered their respective organizations with equal promise. There were no noticeable differences in their preparation, expertise, education, and so forth. However, over time, the second group's careers had become "derailed" by the personal inadequacies shown in Table 5.2.

It is sobering to note how many of these problems relate to the ineffective use of power in interpersonal relationships. In general, this group tends to support Lord Acton's dictum as well as the warnings of Sophocles. They were given a little authority, and they failed the test of worthy stewardship.

This observation is consistent with the research findings of David McClelland, who has spent many years studying what he considers to be one of the fundamental human needs, the "need for power" (McClelland & Burnham, 2003). According to McClelland, managers

Table 5.2	Characteristics That Derail Managers' Careers

- Insensitive to others; abrasive and intimidating
- Cold, aloof, and arrogant
- Betraying others' trust
- Overly ambitious; playing politics and always trying to move up
- Unable to delegate to others or to build a team
- Overdependent on others (e.g., a mentor)

SOURCE: *Reproduced with permission from* Psychology Today, *Copyright © 2006 www.psychologytoday.com.*

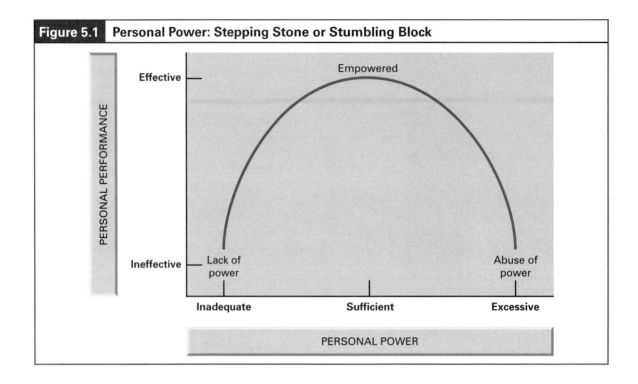

Figure 5.1 Personal Power: Stepping Stone or Stumbling Block

with an *institutional power* orientation use their power to advance the goals of the organization, whereas those with a *personal power* view of power tend to use their power for personal gain. For example, he found that although leaders with both orientations are likely to exhort their subordinates to engage in heroic endeavors, the "institutional power" leaders tend to link those efforts to organizational objectives, whereas the "personal power" leaders are more likely to use their subordinates' accomplishments to further enhance their own power base.

The relationship between power and personal effectiveness that we have described is depicted in Figure 5.1. Both a lack of power and the abuse of power are equally debilitating and counterproductive. In contrast, empowerment uses sufficient amounts of personal power to achieve high levels of effectiveness.

The purpose of this chapter is to help managers "stay on top of the power curve," as represented by the indicators of organizational power reported by Kanter in Table 5.1. This is accomplished with the aid of two specific management skills:

1. Gaining power (overcoming feelings of powerlessness); and
2. Converting power effectively into interpersonal influence in ways that avoid the abuse of power.

Strategies for Gaining Organizational Power

We will define power as the potential to influence behavior. This is an important departure from a more traditional definition that focuses on authority-based control of behavior, as in "powerful" bosses having authority over their subordinates or "powerful" parents having control over their children. We believe there are several trends in organizations that warrant this shift in the definition of power from "having authority over others" to "being able to get things done."

THE NECESSITY OF POWER AND EMPOWERMENT

Our discussion to this point should be viewed as a cautionary warning, reminiscent of similar concerns expressed about the potential harm resulting from the unintentional, improper use of medicine or the deliberate, harmful misapplication of powerful information technologies. Despite these legitimate concerns, people generally believe in and benefit from medicine and information technologies. The implication for our current discussion is not that we need to avoid the use of power, but we need to learn how to use it wisely.

1. Organizations are becoming less hierarchical, or flatter, as they downsize layers of management (especially middle managers) and as they outsource work that can be done more cheaply by someone else. Rather than adding to their full-time employment ranks, many organizations are choosing to grow through the use of temporary and part-time workers who can more easily be let go during tough economic times. These leaner organizations are staffed by fewer managers who must learn to yield influence to lower-level employees in order to get the work of the organization done (Stewart, 1992).

2. Information technology, such as computers, is helping to decentralize the flow of information to lower levels of the organizational hierarchy. This not only gives lower-level employees more influence, but also increases their flexibility. Today, more and more workers are telecommuting or working out of their homes but staying linked to the organization through the use of computers, faxes, and phones. When employees are off-site, managers must cede more decision-making control and discretion to them.

3. Traditional boundaries within and between organizations are becoming blurred. The "boundaryless" organization is becoming in vogue as we see evidence of the virtual organization composed of a network of different entities (Tully, 1993). Such an organization will exist only for the life of a project (say, a motion picture) and then disband upon its completion. These structural changes shift the nature of authority relationships as well.

4. The percentage of the workforce working in companies with fewer than 100 employees is increasing. In a small business where the organization's survival depends on good customer relations, imaginative ideas for new products, and favorable financial agreements with banks, personal characteristics are often the predominant source of power. The work of each employee is highly visible and the unique contribution of the aggressive salesperson or the problem-solving engineer will likely be recognized and rewarded. This may be why we see more and more MBAs choosing to forgo employment with blue-chip firms for smaller, entrepreneurial ventures (Labich, 1995).

Each of these changes is contributing to the evolution of the role of the typical manager from director to coach and mentor. Under these conditions, power is likely to come less from someone's formal position in the organization than from one's ability to perform. These conditions make the notion of empowerment particularly important for your effectiveness in today's organizations.

Two basic factors determine a person's power in an organization: personal attributes and position characteristics. Naturally, the importance of each factor varies depending on the organizational context. For example, position title is extremely important in a strong hierarchical system, such as the military or civil service. The saying "Rank has its privileges" illustrates the fact that in these organizations many rewards are allocated more on the basis of position title than personal performance. However, given the trends noted above, you will notice that our discussion of position power is very nonhierarchical. By this we mean rather than focusing on the level of authority attached to a position, we focus on the opportunities embedded in a position or a job.

Although the trend in American firms is toward person-based views of power, there are cultural reasons why individuals might prefer a position-based orientation regarding power. Research has shown people who have been raised in different cultures are likely to hold different views regarding the determinants of success (Chiu, 2001; Choi, Nisbett, & Norenzayan, 1999). Specifically, it has been shown that Eastern cultures encourage contextual, or situational, logic ("He was promoted because he got to know lots of people while working in headquarters"), whereas Western cultures foster personal, or dispositional, explanations ("He was promoted because he is the smartest engineer in the company"). This comparison was summarized by Chiu (1972) as follows: "Chinese are situation-centered. They are obliged to be sensitive to their environment. Americans are individual-centered. They expect their environment to be sensitive to them" (p. 236).

The strength of this "dispositional bias" in Western thought is reflected in research showing that Americans are willing to make very confident predictions about future behavior on the basis of a very small sample of past behavior and they consistently overestimate the predictive power of personality traits (Choi et al., 1999, p. 55). Psychologists have also observed that Japanese and American college students describe themselves in very different ways. For example, phrases like "I am curious" and "I am sincere" appeared three times more often in the Americans' descriptions. In contrast, Japanese students were far more likely to describe themselves in terms of their social identities (e.g., "I am a Keiyo student") or in terms of a specific context (e.g., "One who plays Majong on Friday nights") (Choi et al., 1999, p. 49).

It is worth noting there are differences of opinion among organizational scholars regarding the relative importance of these two sources of power: who you are versus where you are (Bolman & Deal, 1997; Kanter, 1979; Kotter, 1977; Pfeffer, 1981, 1994). We have found the distinction between human capital and social capital useful in sorting out these competing claims (Adler & Kwon, 2002; Burt, 1997). **Human capital** refers to an individual's abilities and competencies, whereas **social capital** refers to a person's social connections within and outside an organization. In a sense, this is the difference between saying "I know the answer to that question" versus "I know someone who does." Burt's underlying argument is managers with high social capital (what we are calling high position power) are in a better position to capitalize on their human capital (personal power) because their social connections allow them to leverage their personal knowledge and abilities. Hence, it makes sense for managers seeking to increase their influence in an organization to increase both sources of power.

SOURCES OF PERSONAL POWER

Four personal characteristics are important sources of power. As Table 5.3 shows, these are *expertise, personal attraction, effort,* and *legitimacy.* Expertise reflects knowledge and capabilities; personal attraction involves affective appeal; effort suggests personal commitment and motivation; and legitimacy conveys credibility.

Expertise

It is self-evident that in an era of technological sophistication, expertise is an important source of power. In an e-commerce business environment, in which the most highly sought-after skills are more likely possessed by teenagers who have never had a real job than by their parents who have been working for 20 years, and in which the median age of millionaires will soon be closer to 30 than to 60, it is hard to dispute the claim that

expertise is the ascending "coin of the realm" in business. Increasingly, what you know is more important than who you know in getting a job and what you can do technically is the key to what you can become organizationally. **Expertise**, or work-related knowledge, is the great organizational equalizer because it can come from formal education, self-directed learning, or on-the-job experience. In addition, the universally understood and accessible standard of competence is the basis for evaluation and the antecedent of accomplishment.

Because the preponderance of management positions are not in small "dot.com" companies, but in larger, more diversified businesses, our focus will be on expertise as a source of personal power in that organizational setting. Expertise is especially salient in established business organizations because of their preference for a highly rationalized decision-making process (Bunderson, 2003; Pfeffer, 1977). In an environment in which choices are supposed to be made by objectively considering information supporting each alternative, a person possessing knowledge readily accrues power. This can become problematic when subordinates have more expertise than their bosses. The skillful subordinate makes knowledge available to the superior in a manner that does not threaten the boss's right to make the final decision but at the same time reinforces the subordinate's position as an expert. In essence, expert knowledge is deemed to be reliable information—something decision makers can bank on because it comes from someone whose expertise inspires trust.

That staff specialists gain power by virtue of their expertise points out the importance of examining both position and personal sources of power. If you examined only the position-power of staff specialists, you might conclude they have very little power. Their role in the organization is not very visible, compared to line management; their jobs are often routine; and their tasks, by themselves, are generally not linked to the most central objectives and concerns of the firm. However, a staff specialist can compensate for weak position-power by developing expertise in a particular

Table 5.3	Determinants of Personal Power
Characteristic	**Description**
Expertise	Task-relevant knowledge or experience
Personal attraction	Desirable characteristics associated with friendship
Effort	Higher-than-expected commitment of time
Legitimacy	Behavior consistent with key organizational values

aspect of organizational life. This might involve a new accounting system, tax loopholes, safety and pollution regulations, or recent legal precedents in acquisitions.

There is, however, a catch-22 associated with expert power. Becoming an expert on a subject typically requires considerable time and effort, and in organizations using rapidly changing technologies, individuals must continually upgrade their expertise to avoid the "sell-by date" of their knowledge (Grove, 1983). Given the investment required to stay up to date in a particular area of specialization, it is easy to become typecast as a specialist. If you are interested in moving into general management positions, this perception can be a hindrance. The increasing boundarylessness of today's organizations may especially devalue overspecialization. Given the dynamic environment facing today's organizations, overspecialization may be a recipe for obsolescence. Aspiring young managers must be careful not to limit advancement opportunities by focusing their attention on very narrow aspects of a business's activities. This is tempting for individuals who are overly anxious to establish a power base. There are always small niches in an organization to which power-hungry novices can quickly lay claim. Only when they have fallen into the specialist trap do they recognize the value of building a broad base of knowledge about a wide variety of organizational activities to enhance their long-term attractiveness for promotion.

Attraction

We will consider three ways in which interpersonal **attraction** is a source of personal power: charisma, agreeable behavior, and physical characteristics. The charismatic leader has been the subject of extensive scholarly study (Yukl, 2002). The three definitions of *charisma* in the Oxford dictionary are instructive: (1) the ability to inspire followers with devotion and enthusiasm; (2) an attractive aura, great charm; (3) a divinely conferred power or talent. These definitions reflect the Greek origin of the word, which meant favor or grace from God.

The notion that charismatic leaders are favored by God stems from the common observation that their uncommon ability to engender devotion and enthusiasm stems from an innate gift—a seemingly mystical quality that cannot be acquired in a skill development workshop. This quality is reflected in comments like the following: "When she makes a presentation in a management meeting, her presence is so powerful any message sounds good"; "His magnetic personality enables him to attract the most qualified and dedicated people to his department—everyone wants to work for him."

These anecdotal comments are consistent with research showing that a leader's charisma is associated with higher positivity among followers (Erez et al., 2008).

Given that charisma is an attribution made by others, it is natural to wonder what characteristics of leaders tend to be associated with this label. Research on this topic (Conger & Kanungo, 1998) has found leaders are more likely to be considered charismatic if they (1) express a vision that is inspiring; (2) incur personal sacrifice and even risk their personal well-being in pursuing their vision; (3) recommend the use of unconventional, nontraditional approaches to achieving shared goals; (4) have a seemingly uncanny feel for what is possible, including an acute sense of timing; and (5) demonstrate sensitivity to members' needs and concerns. It has also been shown that leaders of high-performing organizations are more likely to be characterized as charismatic (Agle et al., 2006).

The implication of this research is it is a mistake to treat charisma as a personal, innate trait. Although it is uncommon to refer to a leader as charismatic (and one is not likely to receive flyers advertising weekend workshops for "aspiring charismatic leaders"), the behaviors and characteristics associated with this type of leader are far from mystical or even mysterious.

A related source of interpersonal attraction is much more mundane, but equally powerful. Social psychologists who have done research on interpersonal attraction have isolated several critical behaviors that determine what they call *agreeable behavior*. These behaviors are the kinds one would normally associate with friendship. Indeed, much of this research has been motivated by a desire to understand the essential ingredients of friendships. Studies of this type have identified several major factors that foster interpersonal attraction. Some of these are shown in Table 5.4 (Anderson, John, Keltner, & Kring, 2001; Canfield & LaGaipa, 1970; Furman, 2001).

How can we relate this information on friendship to the supposedly hard-nosed world of management? Does this imply you must become good friends with your coworkers, subordinates, or boss? Not necessarily. Very often, people choose to work with others because of their demonstrated expertise, even when they know they will have difficulty getting along with them. Furthermore, it is often inappropriate to establish a close friendship with someone in your office. Thus, one need not become friends with everyone at work, but people who possess personality characteristics that are attractive to their coworkers (the kind that, if circumstances permitted, would likely lead to a strong friendship) will likely feel empowered (Hogg, 2001; Mechanic, 1962).

Table 5.4	Characteristics of Likable People

We like people when we have reason to believe they will:

- Support an open, honest, and loyal relationship.
- Foster intimacy by being emotionally accessible.
- Provide unconditional, positive regard and acceptance.
- Endure some sacrifices if the relationship should demand them.
- Provide social reinforcement in the form of sympathy or empathy.
- Engage in the social exchanges necessary to sustain a relationship.

SOURCE: *Adapted from Canfield and LaGaipa, 1970.*

This proposition has been corroborated by an impressive amount of evidence. For example, individuals making persuasive arguments are more likely to be effective if they are liked by their audience. This stems from the fact that likable individuals are viewed as more trustworthy and impartial than disliked individuals. Subordinates who are liked by their supervisor also tend to be given the benefit of the doubt in performance appraisals. This benevolent orientation is also manifest in the fact that bosses use rewards rather than coercion to influence subordinates they like (Allinson, Armstrong, & Hayes, 2001; Tedeschi, 1974).

We don't want to overemphasize this point, nor do we mean to suggest "good guys" always win, but there is an impressive amount of evidence that individuals with agreeable personalities become more influential than those with disagreeable personalities. Their arguments are given more credence, their influence attempts are less likely to evoke resistance, and coworkers seem less threatened if they are promoted.

In general, given a strong cultural distrust of individuals with power, leaders with likable personalities tend to put others at ease and, in so doing, gain greater trust and influence. This pattern is consistent with the explanations for promising management candidates ending up as "derailed executives" (Table 5.2) because they were perceived to be insensitive to others, abrasive and intimidating, as well as cold, aloof, and arrogant.

The third basis for interpersonal attraction, *physical appearance,* operates independently of personality or even behavior (Hosoda, Stone-Romero, & Coats, 2003; Langlois et al., 2000). Studies have shown that people judged to have an attractive appearance are judged to have socially desirable personality characteristics and to lead highly successful lives. It is further assumed that they hold prestigious jobs and are highly successful marriage partners and parents. In addition, attractive individuals are judged to be masters of their own fate—pursuing their own goals, imbued with a sense of mission—rather than being buffeted by environmental forces. In general, it appears that people assume attractive individuals are also virtuous and efficacious.

There is considerable evidence that these are not merely fanciful attributions. In some respects, attractive people are more successful. Research has found on average, physically attractive people are paid more than their counterparts in organizations. Attractive students are assumed by teachers to be intelligent and disinclined to get into mischief. In a work setting, the written work of attractive people is more likely to be judged of high quality, and attractive people are more likely to receive high performance appraisals from their supervisors than are other people (Hosoda et al., 2003; Langlois et al., 2000).

Findings on personal attraction are obviously the most difficult to transform into concrete suggestions for personal development. There is not much one can do as an adult to radically transform one's basic appearance. However, this information is still highly relevant for managers for two reasons. First, in many of these studies, attractiveness was achieved through dress and grooming (Thompson, 2001, p. 141). Hence, it appears unnecessary for most people to resort to plastic surgery and other artificial forms of physical enhancement to boost their self-confidence. Second, one can become more sensitive to the way others form impressions and make evaluations. If you suspect you do not measure up very well in this category, despite your best efforts at "accentuating the positive," it is a good idea to compensate by emphasizing other sources of power. If, indeed, self-confidence is the primary mechanism for transforming personal attractiveness into organizational power, then other personal and positional characteristics can contribute in a similar manner to one's self-confidence.

Effort

A high level of personal **effort** is one of the most highly prized characteristics of employees because it means they are dependable, reliable human resources. If individuals can be counted on to stay late to get out a delivery following a technological breakdown, to catch an early-morning flight to visit a promising new customer, or to take a night class to learn a new software program, they earn the trust of their coworkers and their supervisors. Being known as a person who will do "whatever it takes" to get the job done is a valuable personal asset, especially in today's highly uncertain and rapidly changing business climate.

There are a variety of other ways by which effort fosters personal power. In a seminal article entitled "Sources of Power of Lower Participants," David Mechanic (1962) described a particular process whereby members of organizations often obtain more power than is warranted by their position in the hierarchy. His observation is based on the premise that because senior members of an organization are unable to attend to all their important business, they are forced to rely on junior members to perform many tasks critical to the goals of the organization. The senior officers thus become highly dependent on their subordinates. If subordinates do not perform well, it reflects poorly on their bosses' judgment and ability to supervise. As a result, subordinates are in a position to increase their power by working hard on these vital assignments, thereby gaining favor with their supervisors.

In addition to creating a sense of indebtedness, or obligation, a high level of effort can enhance other personal characteristics. For example, individuals who work hard at a task tend to increase their knowledge of the subject. Therefore, they are more likely to be sought out for their advice on that topic. They are also more apt to gather information that is relevant to other members of the organization. This information often can be the key to reducing another person's uncertainty.

The efficacy of personal effort is borne out in the career of Gordon McGovern, CEO of Campbell Soup and erstwhile president of Pepperidge Farms. During the 1960s, when he was a young executive rising through the ranks at Pepperidge Farms, McGovern liked to get up before dawn and hop aboard one of the company's bread delivery trucks. "I'd talk to the distributors and to the store managers to see what people were buying," he recalls. In addition, as a trainee, he learned how to mix bread in 10-quart bowls and knead it by hand. This extra effort gave McGovern personal knowledge of the production process, the distribution system, and customers' preferences (Miller, 1985). Similarly, Herb Kelleher, CEO of Southwest Airlines, is known for his "management by walking around." He frequently serves customers on flights and visits baggage handlers and gate agents to listen to their concerns.

An extraordinary level of personal effort can also result in increased responsibility and opportunity through a process known as cognitive dissonance reduction. A fundamental principle of psychology is that individuals strive to reduce inconsistencies between their own personal beliefs and personal behavior and between their expectations of others and the behavior of others. Applied to our discussion of effort, this principle has an important implication. When individuals exert more effort to perform their jobs than is expected,

according to organizational policy or office norms, an inconsistency exists. Because the person's rewards are based on completion of the amount of work normally expected, the inconsistency can be eliminated only by reduced effort or increased responsibility. While it is quite common for "rate-busters" in blue-collar jobs to be informed by their coworkers that their extra effort is unacceptable because it makes the rest of the group look bad, this approach to dissonance reduction is less common in managerial ranks. At that level, extraordinary effort is viewed as a sign of commitment and dedication that should be encouraged and rewarded.

Before leaving this topic, we want to make a distinction between extraordinary effort and extraordinary image. The former focuses on enhanced performance, the latter on enhanced regard (without performance). The objective of the first is enhancing the boss; the objective of the second is impressing the boss. Based on their intensive examination of effective boss–subordinate relationships in major corporations, Jack Gabarro and John Kotter (Gabarro & Kotter, 2007) suggest several highly relevant guidelines for directing your efforts to the benefit of your boss. As shown in Table 5.5, these include understanding your boss's

Table 5.5	Managing the Relationship with Your Boss

Make sure you understand your boss, including:

• Your boss's goals and objectives.

• The pressures on him or her.

• Your boss's strengths, weaknesses, blind spots.

• His or her preferred work style.

Assess yourself, including:

• Your own strengths and weaknesses.

• Your personal style.

• Your predisposition toward dependence on authority figures.

Develop and maintain a relationship that:

• Fits the needs and styles of you both.

• Is characterized by mutual expectations.

• Keeps your boss informed.

• Is based on dependability and honesty.

• Selectively uses your boss's time and resources.

pressures and priorities as well as assessing your own needs and strengths. This knowledge helps you improve your performance by targeting your efforts to maximize their impact.

Legitimacy

Actions congruent with the prevailing value system are deemed credible, or legitimate, by other organizational members. They are taken for granted, rather than challenged or scrutinized. Therefore, **legitimacy** increases acceptance, and acceptance is a key to personal influence. Organizational leaders are vigilant in defending core organizational values and in socializing newcomers to proper modes of thinking and acting. Often, new members or outsiders fail to understand the critical role an organization's culture plays in articulating, and defending, its raison d'être. Conventional thinking may appear peculiar or arbitrary until it is examined from both a historical and a strategic perspective.

Managers understand a precondition for their organization's becoming a market leader is to be perceived as a unique player in the market (e.g., not just another computer company). They strive to create a distinctiveness that merits attention from the financial community, potential employees, and customers. This may involve placing a premium on quality, economy, value, service, loyalty to employees, or civic involvement. This uniqueness is the basis for internal organizational pride and external projections of excellence.

This perspective is initially articulated as the vision of a dominant leader (often the founder) and institutionalized as the organization's culture (Deal & Kennedy, 1982; Peters, 1978; Schein, 1999). It typically focuses on the "hows" and "whys" of doing business the "right" way. Values are proclaimed via the insistent message of a strong leader. For example, Harold Geneen at ITT stressed, "Search for the unshakable facts"; Tom Jones at Northrop emphasized, "Everybody at Northrop is in marketing"; John DeButts at AT&T drummed into employees, "The system is the solution"; and Ed Rust at State Farm frequently asked colleagues, "How would a good neighbor handle this?"

New members of an organization are taught what is acceptable behavior through stories (the engineer who worked for 72 hours straight to save a project), rites (graduation or promotion ceremonies), and symbols (uniforms, no private offices for managers). The savvy newcomer looks beyond formal position statements, probing for answers to questions such as: "What are the organization's 'sacred cows'?" "What's the quickest way to get into trouble?" "What is the source of organizational pride?" "Who are the corporate heroes?" "What are the revered traditions?"

Many required organizational practices make sense only when viewed as symbolic support for fundamental values. For example, a large insurance firm stipulates that no one can be promoted above a certain level in any department unless he or she has completed the requirements for insurance industry professional certification (i.e., Certified Life Underwriter). Young employees in data processing, accounting, or personnel who chafe under the edict to take classes on the details of the insurance business miss the symbolic meaning of this requirement. The founders of the firm felt that the organization's key to success was a workforce deeply committed to delivering the best product and backing it with the best service. They further believed that the natural tendency for some individuals to identify more closely with their department's interests than with the insurance business undermined this corporate objective. They feared organizational factions would lose sight of the overarching goal. Therefore, commitment to taking insurance courses has become synonymous with commitment to the organization's mission, and organizational commitment is a litmus test for organizational advancement.

This does not mean a nonconformist can't get ahead in the corporate world. It simply suggests he or she will be held to a higher standard in terms of other sources of personal power, such as expertise and effort. A conversation during a promotion review meeting in a major corporation reflects this attitude: "Sometimes I don't know where he's coming from, but he is so blasted smart and he works so darn hard, we have no choice but to promote him."

Such an outcome appears less sinister and more rational when one considers that organizations abhor uncertainty, both in their environment and internally. Espoused values and beliefs help reduce uncertainty. They provide a framework for interpreting the behavior of others, communicate a consistent set of priorities, and increase the efficiency of the interpersonal transactions. Individuals who fail to conform to these organizational expectations create "noise" in the system. Their inconsistency makes communication and interaction problematic, because, in common parlance, colleagues "don't know where they're coming from." Consequently, these individuals tend to become bypassed and isolated. In fact, Jack Welch, recent CEO of General Electric, proclaimed that managers at GE who "make their numbers" but who do not espouse the value system of GE will not be promoted as they have been in the past.

Before leaving the subject of organizational culture and personal legitimacy, it is important to note the discussion so far has been descriptive rather than normative. That is, we have described what it takes to become empowered in an organization, especially one with strong cultural values. That doesn't mean strict conformity is morally right or that it is necessarily in the best long-term interests of the firm. In fact, evidence suggests that successful organizations have members who are capable of both gaining power by fitting in and using that power to challenge the prevailing belief system that, in some sense, has been responsible for their gaining power (Pascale, 1985). Unchallenged organizational beliefs often interfere with a company's necessary adaptation to changing competitive and regulatory conditions. However, challenges are most successful when mounted by members whose commitment to the organization has been the most loyal. "Paying your dues" creates legitimacy, and legitimacy is a prerequisite for effective criticism.

In summary, we have highlighted four sources of personal power, in the sense that they are organizational-valued assets attributed to individuals, not to the positions they occupy or the titles they carry. These personal characteristics have one thing in common—they are the antecedents of trust (Dirks & Ferrin, 2001; Hosmer, 1995). The relationship between trust and power is central to the overall view of power and influence espoused in this chapter. One meaning of the term *trustworthy* is "being above suspicion." Hence, individuals who are deemed trustworthy by their peers are likely candidates for positions of power and influence in organizations because organizational authority in their hands is less threatening. As shown in Table 5.6, there is a direct relationship between the four bases of personal power we've discussed and the requirements for personal trust. Basically, the trustworthiness of an individual's claims, promises, or commitments is a function of two factors: (1) How likely is it that the person *can* do what he or she says? and (2) How likely is it the person *will* do what he or she says? In other words, questions of trust devolve into assessments of probable performance informed by judgments regarding ability and motivation. This is why organizations place a great deal of emphasis on placing proven performers in positions of high trust (read: power).

SOURCES OF POSITIONAL POWER

Not all power stems from personal characteristics. In addition, the nature of one's position and task assignments play an important role. This is illustrated by the standard practice in most organizations of placing limits on how much position holders at different hierarchical levels can spend, or on the size of the exception they can authorize. Four important characteristics of a position account for its power potential in an organization: *centrality, flexibility, visibility,* and *relevance* (Fiol, O'Connor, & Aguinis, 2001; Kanter, 1979; Pfeffer, 1994). These are shown in Table 5.7.

Centrality

Based on data collected since 1993, Right Management Consultants reports that, "Failure to build strong relationships and teamwork with peers and subordinates is the chief culprit in 61% of new hires and promotions that don't work out" (Fisher, 2005). As suggested by this study, one of the most important ways of gaining power in an organization is by occupying a position of **centrality** in a broad network of task and interpersonal relationships. Networks are critical to effective performance for one compelling reason: except for routine jobs, no one has all the necessary information and resources to accomplish what's expected of him or her. Indeed, one investigation of the determinants of effective management performance concluded that a key factor distinguishing high and low performers was the ability to establish informal relationships via networks.

Table 5.6	The Relationship Between the Sources of Personal Power and Personal Trustworthiness	
SOURCES OF PERSONAL POWER	**RELATED PERSONAL CHARACTERISTIC**	**REQUIREMENTS FOR PERSONAL TRUSTWORTHINESS**
Expertise	Reliable	Ability: *Can* they make good on their commitments?
Effort	Dependable	
Attraction	Likable	Motivation: *Will* they make good on their commitments?
Legitimacy	Acceptable	

Table 5.7	Determinants of Position-Power
CHARACTERISTIC	**DESCRIPTION**
Centrality	Access to information in a communication network
Flexibility	Amount of discretion vested in a position
Visibility	Degree to which task performance is seen by influential people in the organization
Relevance	Alignment of assigned tasks and organizational priorities

Isolates in informal networks were unable to gather the information, resource commitments, and personal support necessary to accomplish unusual, important tasks (Kaplan & Mazique, 1983; Sparrowe, Liden, & Kraimer, 2001). On the other hand, those who have extensive diverse social networks in their work earn higher salaries and are more successful than those with extensive but narrow contact with others (Pfeffer & Konrad, 1991; Sparrowe et al., 2001).

Power is accrued via horizontal and vertical network relationships by virtue of one's location and function in the network. Horizontal networks link positions with similar levels of authority, whereas vertical networks include positions with different levels of authority. The more central a position is to the flow of information throughout a network, and the more critical the function is to the performance of others in a network, the more power will be accrued. This view of organizational power is referred to as *strategic contingencies* (Pfeffer, 1994). It argues the reason for the uneven distribution of power in organizations is that units and positions differ in their ability to control strategic contingencies (e.g., the securing of information, expertise, financing) critical to the effective performance of others. Few important activities occur in isolation; what happens in one unit affects another. It follows that the more pervasive the effect of a position's activities throughout the organization, the greater is its power base.

Increasing the power of a position by increasing its centrality in a communication or work-flow network represents a very different approach from conventional strategies. Typically, young aspiring members of an organization think only in terms of increasing their power by moving up the organizational career ladder. They mistakenly assume that power is the exclusive right of hierarchical position. If they are not promoted as quickly as they would like, they assume their ability to accomplish the unusual is thereby curtailed. Inexperienced, ineffective organizational members grumble about not having enough formal power to get

work done, and they covet the influence wielded on higher levels. In contrast, savvy organizational members realize informal network power is available to individuals at all levels. Furthermore, they understand that informal personal power generally precedes, rather than follows from, formal organizational power. A promotion is simply a formal recognition by senior management that an individual has demonstrated the ability to get work done using informal networks.

The merits of building a horizontal power base became clear to Alan Brewer, a business manager in the medical supplies division of Hewlett-Packard (HP), when his initiatives were blocked by senior managers. He suggested to a manager in the medical instruments division that the reusable electrodes on HP electrocardiograph machines be replaced with disposable electrodes, which were becoming much more popular. The reply was, "It's too expensive to make the switch." Alan had done enough research to know this wasn't true. Further investigation revealed the real problem. The man who had helped develop the disposable electrodes was abrasive, and he had alienated members of the instruments division. Now, members were unwilling to take any action that would make this person look good.

Alan overcame this problem by asking people in his division to develop a new electrode—one that would not be burdened by association with an unpopular executive. During the development stage, he actively served as a mediator, keeping colleagues in other divisions abreast of his progress. Several suggestions for enhancements were incorporated during this phase. After building a broad base of support for the new product throughout the organization, he had no difficulty getting the second request approved (Gelman, 1985).

This example illustrates the merits of establishing broad networks of organizational contacts. One of the biggest mistakes individuals make at the outset of their management careers is to become isolated. Such people assume that getting ahead in their department is sufficient for getting ahead in the organization. As a result, they concentrate all their attention on building strong relations with their immediate coworkers. If you reconsider organizations in terms of horizontal structures, you will see how isolated a communication network in a single department is. It is important to become a central actor in the organization's communication network, not just the department's. This can be done by going to lunch with people in other departments, reading the annual reports of all the divisions, volunteering for interdepartmental task forces, and seeking out boundary-spanning positions that require you to work with other departments.

It is important that managers seeking to form wide-reaching social networks understand that social relations look very different in different cultural settings. Specifically, research has shown that members of different cultures differ in terms of how many friendships they are likely to form at work, the extent to which they are likely to mix socioemotional and instrumental social ties, the strength and longevity of their social relations, and the likelihood of their forming social networks that are upward, lateral, or downward directed (Morris, Podolny, & Ariel, 2000). For example, American business relationships are characterized by the norms of the marketplace (they must be profitable). In contrast, Chinese business relationships are characterized by a familial orientation (doing whatever is good for the organization), German relationships are characterized by a legal-bureaucratic orientation (play by the rules), and Spanish relationships are characterized by an affiliative orientation (sociability and friendship) (Morris et al., 2000).

Flexibility

A critical requirement for building a power base is **flexibility**, or discretion—that is, freedom to exercise one's judgment. A person who has little latitude to improvise, to innovate, or to demonstrate initiative will find it extremely difficult to become powerful (except in unusual situations in which meticulous obedience to rules disrupts the system, as in the case of air traffic controllers' slowdowns). Power can be lost because circumstances often change more readily than people or their jobs can change to keep up with the new times (Pfeffer, 1994). A flexible position has few rules or established routines governing how work should be done. In addition, when a manager needs to make a nonroutine decision, it is not necessary to seek a senior manager's approval. Flexibility tends to be associated with certain types of work assignments, particularly tasks that are high in variety and novelty

(Hinings, Hickson, Pennings, & Schneck, 1974). People in such positions are assigned several types of activities, each of which requires the use of considerable judgment. The more routine the work and the fewer the tasks assigned a person, the easier it is to pre-program the job to eliminate the need for discretion.

Flexibility is also correlated with the life cycle of a position. New tasks are much more difficult to routinize than old ones. Similarly, the number of rules governing a position tends to be positively correlated with the number of individuals who have previously occupied it. Because the intention of rules is to expose exceptions, the longer a position has been in existence, the more likely it is that exceptions have been discovered.

The same logic applies to the life cycle of a decision-making process. The longer a group has been meeting to discuss an issue, the more difficult it is to have any significant amount of influence over its deliberations, unless the decision-making process becomes hopelessly stalemated. The critical decisions about how discussions will be conducted, what evidence should be examined, and which alternatives are germane are all made early in a group's history. To make a difference, therefore, it is important to be a participant from the beginning.

One indication of the amount of flexibility inherent in a position is the reward system governing it. If people occupying a position are rewarded for being reliable and predictable, that suggests the organization will penalize people who use discretion. On the other hand, if people are rewarded for unusual performance and innovation, discretion is encouraged. A "reliable performance" reward system uses as its performance criterion conformity to a set of prescribed means for performing a task, such as a detailed procedure for assembling an electronic circuit. In contrast, an "unusual performance" reward system eschews consistency in favor of initiative. For example, a company may teach salespeople how to close a deal but at the same time encourage them to figure out better ways to do the task. Individuals with a high need for power should avoid a job that is governed by the reliable performance criterion, no matter how attractive it might appear in other aspects, because it will strip them of a necessary prerequisite of power.

Visibility

A sage corporate executive once counseled a young, aspiring MBA, "The key formula for promotion is excellent performance multiplied by visibility." Obviously, a highly visible, poor performance will not lead to promotion, but the real message of this advice is that an excellent, but obscure, performance won't either. This advice is supported by a Chicago consultant, Karolus Smejda, who is frequently brought into organizations to coach "competent but invisible" young managers. "The boss will say to me, 'Karolus, this guy is a wonderful worker, but he's just not visible enough.' My job is to make that person aware of the need to become well connected," he says (Gelman, 1985).

One measure of **visibility** is the number of influential people with whom you normally interact in your organization. This helps explain why people-oriented positions are often more powerful than task-oriented positions. Of course, contacts with some members of an organization are more important than with others. It is critical that a position foster frequent contact with senior officials, decision makers, and informal leaders. This can be accomplished through participation in company or outside programs, meetings, and conferences. Many a young career has been secured by a strong presentation at a trade association convention or board meeting.

Recognizing this point, an enterprising junior executive in a large Chicago conglomerate seized on a chance occurrence to impress the chairman of the board. By a strange set of circumstances, the young executive was asked to fill in for the secretary of the board of directors and take notes at a stockholders' meeting. Making sure he arrived early, he greeted every person who entered the boardroom and then introduced that person to every other member in the room. The fact that this young man was able to put everyone at ease (not to mention remember the names of a large number of strangers) so impressed the chairman, he subsequently provided several opportunities for him to advance rapidly in the organization.

This example points out an important distinction between centrality and visibility. The purpose of becoming central in a broad communication network is to tap into a rich flow of information so you can satisfy the information needs of others. In contrast, from the point of view of visibility, being in a position that allows you to interact with a large number of influential people increases your power by making your accomplishments more evident to the people who allocate resources, such as desirable assignments and promotions.

The value of visibility is clearly demonstrated in the position of an executive secretary. For example, Jean C. Jones, while serving as executive secretary to the chairman of Intel Corporation, decided each day how many of the 125 telephone calls would gain Gordon Moore's

ear and how much of the 30-inch stack of mail he would see. The power inherent in this gatekeeping role is also reflected in the fact that Kathleen Kallmer parlayed her job as executive secretary to Beatrice Company's chairman James L. Dutt into an assistant vice presidency in four years (Baum & Byre, 1986).

By far, the best way to gain visibility is by means of direct contact, and face-to-face communication is the most influential means to accomplish this. Inexperienced managers often assume that credit for writing an excellent report automatically goes to the author. Unfortunately for good writers, this is not always the case. If one member of a group composes a very good report and another member gives a very good presentation of the report to an executive committee, the presenter will likely receive a disproportionately large share of the credit for the work. Busy executives tend to be more impressed by what they see in a meeting than by what they read in their offices. They have fewer distractions in meetings (no stacks of other reading material or interruptions by phone calls), and a slightly positive personal evaluation of a presentation can be transformed into a very strong positive evaluation by the approving nods and smiles of other executives in the meeting.

Another important opportunity for gaining visibility is participation in problem-solving task forces. Being asked to serve in this capacity conveys to others that you have valuable expertise. More importantly, if the task force's report is received well by senior officials, your name will be associated with the group responsible for the "breakthrough." Using the language of the strategic contingencies model, problem solvers gain power by helping others cope with uncertainty. For example, those heads of government whose accomplishments stand out dramatically in a historical perspective are those who proposed remedies during major crises. Consider that Winston Churchill is credited with helping Britain survive World War II. On the smaller scale of a business firm, this truism is equally reliable. The visibility of a person's performance is directly proportional to the significance of the tasks performed and the popularity of the causes championed.

An additional source of visibility is name recognition. Elected officials recognize the value of keeping their names before the electorate, so they place signs at state and city boundaries and entrances to public transportation terminals welcoming travelers. In organizations there are analogous opportunities for enhancing your visibility. For example, if your office regularly sends information to the public or other departments, try enclosing a signed cover note. If you are new to an organization, introduce yourself to other members. If you have a good idea, formally communicate it to the appropriate parties in person, as well as in a follow-up memo. If someone has recently accomplished something significant, send a note expressing congratulations and appreciation.

Relevance

This leads us to the fourth critical characteristic of powerful positions, **relevance**, which means being associated with activities that are directly related to the central objectives and issues in an organization. As one manager put it, "My peers are responsive to me because the functions that I manage are the lifeblood of the organization. I manage the people who provide readings on their vital signs; consequently, my presence in their office implies that there's a vital concern of one sort or another that needs to be dealt with" (Kaplan & Mazique, 1983, p. 10).

A noted organizational sociologist, Charles Perrow (1970), argues in an advanced consumer products-oriented economy, sales and marketing represent the central concerns of most businesses. Because other activities in the organization are dependent on revenues from sales, the work performed by sales personnel is most relevant to the central concern of organizational survival.

Refining this general proposition, Paul Lawrence and Jay Lorsch (1986) identified the "dominant competitive issue" for companies using different types of technology. The dominant competitive issue is the organizational activity that most accounts for the firm's ability to compete effectively with other members of its industry. Companies using a flow-process form of technology, such as oil refineries and chemical plants, were found to be most dependent on effective marketing because of their sizable capital investment and small range of product alternatives. In contrast, companies using a standard mass-production (assembly-line) form of technology, with a stable line of products and established customers, were most dependent on the efficiency of their production processes. Finally, high-tech firms, or companies producing custom-designed products, were most successful when they had strong research and development departments.

This general principle accounts for a significant recent shift in the power of the human resources department in large corporations. In the past, human resource executives occupied the outer circle in the corporate power structure. They ran a staff of personnel specialists, occupying the lower floors of the headquarters building. Today, a great many report directly to the CEO and play a key role in strategic decisions. The reason for this dramatic change is that with the increase in acquisitions, mergers, and divestments, corporations must base strategic decisions on human resource considerations. These include matching high-priced skills with critical jobs, keeping key personnel after a merger, solving human resource problems that arise from introducing new technology or closing a plant, and formulating agreements with the unions of an acquired firm (Conner & Ulrich, 1996).

According to business authorities, "The rise of the human resources function is the most dramatic change in managerial function since financial executives rose to power in the 1960s during the 'conglomerate era,' when asset management was the pressing problem in corporations" (Hoerr, 1985).

These results have significant implications for task relevance. An individual who seeks influential positions must be sensitive to the relevance of his or her department's activities for the company. For example, a design engineer who works for an oil company is less likely to become influential than one who works for an electronics firm, and operations researchers will have more influence in companies with established product lines and an assembly-line production process. Computer scientists are more likely to feel empowered in a software development firm than if they are working for an insurance company or a public utility. In the latter organization, computer programming is viewed as a support function, with only an indirect effect on profitability.

There are other indications of the relevance of assigned activities besides their relationship to the firm's dominant competitive issue. For example, the role of representative or advocate is powerful because it enables a person to become identified with important causes. Another key role is that of evaluator. Positions designated by the organization as checkpoints become powerful by virtue of the fact that they create dependence. The approval controlled by people in these positions is highly relevant to those individuals who must receive it to obtain organizational rewards.

The role of trainer or mentor to new members of a work unit is another powerful position. It places you in a critical position to reduce uncertainty for newcomers and substantially enhance their performance. Newcomers are generally apprehensive, and they will appreciate your showing them the ropes. Also, successful performance in this developmental role earns you the respect and admiration of those colleagues who stand to benefit from your effective training.

To summarize, we have discussed four aspects of organizational positions that are critical to the achievement of power. As Table 5.7 shows, centrality and relevance encourage the gaining of power through horizontal relationships. That is, a position's potential for power is based on its relationship to other lateral positions and activities in the organization. However, visibility and flexibility are linked to hierarchical power. Flexibility reflects the amount of discretion vested in a position by superiors. Positions that are closely supervised provide a poor vantage point for establishing a power base. A highly visible position has close ties with higher levels of authority, so a noteworthy performance in a visible position receives more recognition, which is an important prerequisite for an individual's upward mobility in an organization.

Transforming Power into Influence

Having discussed the skill of gaining power, we now turn our attention to converting power into influence. This concept requires an understanding of the difference between power and influence. As indicated at the beginning of this chapter, many popular books on this subject suggest power is an end in itself. They bring to mind the old commercials about "98-pound weaklings" who take up body building to punish bullies for stealing their girlfriends.

Our goal here is not to help people gain power for its own sake. When the weak seek power simply because they are tired of being pushed around, tyranny generally follows their ascension. Our interest, instead, is in helping people accomplish the exceptional in organizations, recognizing that this generally requires political clout. The well-meaning but politically naive seldom make major contributions to organizations. Consequently, our focus is on how you can become influential as well as powerful.

However, we cannot talk about influence without first understanding power, because power is a necessary precondition for influence. Influential people have power, but not all powerful people have influence. Influence entails actually securing the consent of others to work with you in accomplishing an objective. Many powerful people cannot do that, as evidenced by the chronic inability of American presidents to convince Congress to pass what the president considers to be essential legislation. The skill of transforming power into influence hinges on securing the consent of others in ways that engender support and commitment, instead of resistance and resentment.

INFLUENCE STRATEGIES: THE THREE Rs

Power is converted into influence when the target individual consents to behave according to the desires of the power holder. The influence strategies used by managers to obtain compliance fall into three broad categories: *retribution, reciprocity,* and *reason* (Allen, Madison, Porter, Renwick, & Mayer, 1979; Kipnis, 1987; Kipnis, Schmidt, & Wilkinson, 1980). Table 5.8 lists these strategies and the corresponding direct and indirect approaches. Specific examples of these strategies are shown in Table 5.9 (Cialdini, 2001; Marwell & Schmitt, 1967).

You may have mixed reactions to these lists. Some strategies will probably strike you as particularly effective; others may seem inappropriate or even manipulative or dishonest. Our purpose in listing these is not to imply all strategies within a category ought to be used. Rather, the full arsenal of influence strategies is presented so that you can informatively choose those with which you feel most comfortable, and so that you can be aware when others are attempting to influence you.

These three influence strategies rely on different mechanisms for obtaining compliance. Fear of **retribution** is based on personal threat, which typically stems from formal authority. The direct form of this approach, *coercion*, involves an explicit threat to impose sanctions if the manager's will is not obeyed.

Table 5.8	Influence Strategies		
STRATEGIES	**DIRECT APPROACH**	**INDIRECT APPROACH**
Retribution: Force others to do what you say	1. Coercion (threaten)	2. Intimidation (pressure)
Reciprocity: Help others want to do what you say	3. Bargaining (exchange)	4. Ingratiation (obligate)
Reason: Show others that it makes sense to do what you say	5. Present facts (or needs)	6. Appeal to personal values (or goals)

Table 5.9 | Examples of Influence Strategies

RETRIBUTION (COERCION AND INTIMIDATION)

General form:	"If you don't do X, you will regret it!"
Threat:	"If you do not comply, I will punish you."
Social pressure:	"Others in your group have agreed; what's your decision?"
Had enough?:	"I will stop nagging you if you comply."
Perceived scarcity and time pressure:	"If you don't act now, you'll lose this opportunity/cause problems for others."
Avoid causing pain to others:	"If you don't agree, others will be hurt/disadvantaged."

RECIPROCITY (EXCHANGE AND INGRATIATION)

General form:	"If you do X, you'll receive Y."
Promise:	"If you comply, I will reward you."
Esteem:	"People you value will think better (worse) of you if you do (do not) comply."
Pregiving:	"I will do something you like for you; then will you do this for me?"
Obligation:	"You owe me compliance because of past favors." (Even though I implied there would be no future obligation.)
Reciprocal compromise:	"I have lowered my initial offer/price, and now I expect you to reciprocate" (no matter how unreasonable my initial position was).
Escalation of commitment:	"I'm only interested in a small commitment." (But I'll be back later for more.)

REASON (PERSUASION BASED ON FACTS, NEEDS, OR PERSONAL VALUES)

General form:	"I want you to do X, because it's consistent with/good for/necessary to . . ."
Evidence:	"These facts/experts' opinions demonstrate the merits of my position/request."
Need:	"This is what I need; will you help me out?"
Goal attainment:	"Compliance will enable you to reach a personally important objective."
Value congruence:	"This action is consistent with your commitment to X."
Ability:	"This endeavor would be enhanced if we could count on your ability/experience."
Loyalty:	"Because we are friends/minorities, will you do this?"
Altruism:	"The group needs your support, so do it for the good of us all."

Recognizing their vulnerability to sanctions controlled by the boss, subordinates generally comply, reluctantly. The threat usually involves either the denial of expected rewards or the imposition of punishment.

Intimidation is an indirect form of retribution because the threat is only implied. Behind the manager's forceful request is the possibility of organizationally based sanctions for noncompliance, but the dominant feature of the demand is an intimidating interpersonal style. Intimidation can take many forms: a manager publicly criticizes a subordinate's report, a member of a management committee is systematically ignored during meetings, or junior executives are given impossible tasks by insecure senior executives.

Acts of intimidation are generally accompanied by special emphasis on the authority of the power holder. Assignments are typically given in the boss's office, in a highly formal manner, with reference to the vulnerability of the target (e.g., mentioning his junior grade or short tenure with the organization). This sets the stage for an implicit threat (e.g., "If people aren't willing to work overtime on this project, corporate headquarters is going to pull the plug on our budget and a number of younger employees will get hurt").

Intimidation can also occur through peer pressure. Managers who know a majority of their subordinates support a controversial action can use group dynamics to secure the compliance of the minority. This is done by telling the majority that a decision must be unanimous and it's their responsibility to demonstrate leadership by securing the commitment of all members. Or, the manager can apply pressure directly to the holdout members of the group by stressing the need for harmony, mutual support, and working for the common good.

The second strategy extracts compliance from others by invoking the norm of **reciprocity**. Reciprocity operates on the principle of satisfying the self-interest of both parties. The direct form of this approach involves straightforward *bargaining* in which each party gains something from the exchange. In bargaining, both parties are aware of the costs and benefits associated with striking a deal, and their negotiations focus on reaching an agreement that is satisfactory to both. *Ingratiation*, however, is more subtle. It involves using friendliness and favors to incur social obligations. When compliance is required or support is needed, previous benefactors are then reminded of their debts.

Reciprocity is used in many ways in organizations. These include striking deals with influential opinion leaders to support a new program, asking subordinates to work overtime in exchange for an extended weekend, doing small favors for the boss so one can occasionally take longer lunch hours, and formally negotiating with staff members to get them to accept undesirable assignments (Cohen & Bradford, 2003).

Although the retribution and reciprocity strategies are both grounded in the manager's control of outcomes valued by others, the dynamics of these strategies are different. Retribution strategies exploit a subordinate's natural desire to avoid pain or unpleasantness, while strategies of reciprocity are used to make the outcomes desired by the manager seem desirable and attractive to the subordinate. Retribution strategy ignores the rights of

others and the norm of fairness, whereas reciprocity strategy honors both. An emphasis on retribution leads to ignoring the quality of the ongoing relationship between the parties, while reciprocity implies a recognition of the value of strengthening their interdependence.

The third approach is based on the manager's persuasive ability. Instead of seeking compliance by making the instrumental nature of their relationship salient to the target person, this approach appeals to **reason**. The manager argues compliance is warranted because of the inherent merits of the request. Here, the focus is on helping others to see why your ideas make sense. This is most likely to occur if the manager is perceived as knowledgeable on the subject and if his or her personal characteristics are attractive to the target person. The direct approach to persuasion relies on the compelling nature of the *facts or needs* supporting the case. A convincing statement is made, coupled with a specific request. For example, "If your shift doesn't work overtime tonight, we will lose $5,000 worth of product. Will you pitch in and help us solve this problem?" In the indirect form, the manager appeals to the other person's *personal values or goals*. These might include being altruistic, a loyal team member, respected as an expert; and helping to keep the plant nonunion or keeping customers satisfied.

Because persuasion is sometimes confused with manipulation, it is important here to distinguish between the two. A persuasive appeal is explicit and direct, while a manipulative act is implicit and deceptive. The persuader respects the autonomy of decision makers and trusts their ability to judge evidence effectively. In contrast, a manipulator has low regard for the abilities of decision makers and doesn't trust them to make good decisions. Manipulators have the same objectives as authoritarian leaders—they simply use more subtle tactics. Manipulative managers, therefore, often appear to the casual observer to be using a democratic leadership style. In fact, they are actually "illusory democrats" because, while their actions may appear democratic, they have no inclination to share power. They use a democratic style only because it makes others less defensive and therefore more vulnerable to their power initiatives (Dyer, 1972).

THE PROS AND CONS OF EACH STRATEGY

As Table 5.10 notes, each approach has advantages and limitations (Cuming, 1984; Mulder, Koppelaar, de Jong, & Verhage, 1986). The retribution strategy produces immediate action, and work is performed exactly

Table 5.10	Comparisons Among Influence Strategies			
INFLUENCE STRATEGY	**WHEN TO USE IT**	**POSSIBLE ADVANTAGES**	**POSSIBLE DISADVANTAGES**	**POSSIBLE COMPLAINTS**
Retribution	• Unequal power, in influencer's favor • Commitment and quality not important • Tight time constraints • Serious violation • Issue not important to target • If issue is important, retribution not likely • Specific, unambiguous request • Resistance to request is likely	• Quick, direct action	• Stifles commitment, creativity • Insecurity of boss • Engenders resentment • Must increase seriousness of threats to maintain pressure	• Violation of rights • Ethical violations
Reciprocity	• Parties mutually dependent • Each party has resources valued by other • Adequate time for negotiating • Established exchange norms exist • Parties viewed as trustworthy • Commitment to broad goals and values not critical • Needs are specific and short-term	• Low incidence of resentment • Justification for request not required	• Engenders instrumental view of work (expectation of specific rewards for specific actions) • Encourages people to feel that the terms of assignments are open for negotiation	• Unfairness, dashed expectations, manipulation
Reason	• Adequate time for extensive discussion • Common goals/values • Parties share mutual respect/credibility • Parties share ongoing relationship	• Need for surveillance reduced	• Considerable time required to build trust (time increases as number of people increases) • Requires common goals and values	• Difference of opinions, conflicting perceptions of priorities

according to the manager's specifications. But the retribution strategy comes with high costs. Of the three strategies, it is the most likely to engender resistance. Most people do not like to be forced to do something. Effective managers use this approach sparingly, generally reserving it for crises or as a last resort when the other strategies have failed. It is best suited to situations in which the goals of the parties are competing or independent. This approach is effective only when the target person perceives that the manager has both the power and the will to follow through on his or her threat. Otherwise, the person being influenced may be tempted to call the manager's bluff. Also, the threatened sanctions must be sufficiently severe that disobedience is unthinkable.

When used repeatedly, the retribution approach produces resentment and alienation, which frequently generates overt or covert opposition. Consequently, it should be used extensively only when the ongoing commitment of the target person is not critical, when opposition is acceptable (the target person can be replaced if necessary), and when extensive surveillance is possible. Because these conditions tend to stifle initiative and innovative behavior—even when individual compliance is obtained—organizational performance is likely to suffer because affected individuals have little incentive to bring emerging problems resulting from changing conditions to their supervisor's attention.

The reciprocity strategy allows the manager to obtain compliance without causing resentment, since both parties benefit from the agreement. Also, because of the instrumental nature of the exchange, it is not necessary to take time to justify the manager's actions. It is most appropriate when each party controls some outcomes valued by the other party and established rules govern the transaction, including provisions for adjudication of grievances. Even under these conditions, such exchanges—especially agreements that are not formally documented—require some degree of trust. If individuals have reneged on past agreements, their credibility as negotiating partners becomes suspect. Reciprocity is also best suited to situations in which the power holder needs the target person to perform specific unambiguous assignments. Consequently, neither a long-term commitment to general goals and values nor the extensive use of personal judgment is required. An agreement to perform certain tasks according to specified terms is sufficient.

The chief disadvantage of this approach, when used frequently, is that it engenders a highly instrumental view of work. The other person begins to expect that every request is open for negotiation and that every completed assignment will generate a reward of equal value. As a result, the reciprocal approach tends to undercut internalized commitment as members take on a highly calculative orientation and downplay the value of working hard to achieve organizational goals, regardless of personal gain.

The assets and liabilities of the third approach—reason—are more complicated. The objective of the rational strategy is a higher form of compliance, that is, internalized commitment. While the focus of compliance is acceptable behavior, commitment requires shared understanding. Commitment relies on teaching correct principles and explaining legitimate needs and then trusting the good intent and sound judgment of subordinates to act appropriately. In its ideal form, commitment decreases the need for surveillance based on accountability and enhances the subordinate's initiative, commitment, and creativity. This approach works best when the worst thing the other person can do is turn down the request, since he or she has little incentive to hurt the manager. Also, the target person should feel there is little potential for the manager to cause harm, as is typically the case when the target person is the manager's coworker or superior. However, when the target person is a subordinate, the manager must demonstrate his or her unwillingness to rely on coercion and intimidation in seeking compliance.

The principal disadvantage of the rational, or reason, approach is the amount of time required to build the trust and mutual understanding required to make it operate effectively. This time increases as the number of involved individuals expands. Also, because the success of this strategy requires congruence of goals and values (rather than the rewards or sanctions a person controls), this approach is difficult to implement when the parties have dissimilar backgrounds, subscribe to competing philosophies, or are assigned conflicting responsibilities, such as maintaining quality versus meeting deadlines.

In their classic studies on influence strategies, Schmidt and Kipnis (1987; Kipnis & Schmidt, 1988) provided compelling evidence supporting the superior benefits of the approach based on reason. Individuals who rely primarily on reason and logic to influence others are rated as highly effective by their bosses, and they report low levels of job-related stress and high levels of job satisfaction. In contrast, individuals who persistently use any other approach to get their way tend to receive lower performance ratings and experience higher levels of personal stress and job dissatisfaction.

Although the evidence is not clear-cut, it does appear that a more general rule can be proposed.

Higher-numbered strategies in Table 5.8 are more effective than lower-numbered strategies. This ordering reflects the overall value system portrayed here: direct is better than indirect; open is better than closed; exchange is better than intimidation; and sincere requests are better than guile.

One justification for this conclusion is that the higher-numbered strategies are more likely to be perceived as fair and just, because they are more likely to be accompanied by an explanation. Research on organizational change has consistently shown that people are more willing to change when they understand why. For example, in a study of 187 employees in seven business firms that had just been relocated, they rated the process as fair, even though they felt the move was unfavorable, when they understood the reasons behind the action (Daly, 1995).

It is important to point out how cultural preferences need to be factored into your choice of influence strategy. First, your influence strategy needs to be congruent with your personal cultural values. Second, it needs to be congruent with the cultural values of the influence "target." Third, it needs to be congruent with the general context in which your relationship is embedded. As an extreme case of these three situational factors, one can imagine a Japanese manager trying to influence an African employee in an auto plant in Germany. To illustrate the importance of cultural congruence, our claims regarding the merits and liabilities of these influence attempts are clearly bounded by traditional American cultural norms, including egalitarian relations, direct communication, and individualism. In contrast, members of cultures that place a high value on social obligation would be more prone to favor the reciprocity influence strategies. In addition, cultures that emphasize indirect communication methods, such as storytelling and inference making, would likely prefer the indirect over the direct strategies. Similarly, individuals who place particular importance on hierarchical relationships may feel more comfortable with the forcing strategies (Thompson, 2001).

Exercising Upward Influence—A Special Case of the Reason Strategy

There is a particular form of influence that warrants special attention. Our discussion of the "Three Rs" has largely assumed that the influence attempt involved a peer or a subordinate. The role that is obviously missing from this set of influence targets is "the boss." Given Kanter's (1979) notion discussed earlier in this chapter that organizational power can be measured in terms of

one's control over making "exceptions to the rule," it is important that we examine strategies for getting exceptional requests granted by exerting upward influence. As you recall, Table 5.1 listed a number of exceptions that subordinates believed were the result of having a "boss with clout," including actions like interceding favorably on behalf of someone in trouble, getting a desirable placement for a talented subordinate, and getting approval for expenditures beyond the budget. Given the stress we've placed on using power to have a positive, constructive influence in an organization, it is important to underscore the merits of managers using their power to benefit their subordinates by exerting upward and outward influence. If subordinates perceive that their unit leader's clout will shield them from outside, disruptive pressures and help them break down artificial organizational barriers to getting the job done right, then they are naturally inclined to strengthen their boss's power base.

The synergy in this "win–win" process should be obvious. Unfortunately, the means whereby bosses can effectively influence their superiors is far from obvious. One approach that has received a great deal of attention is called **issue selling** (Dutton & Ashford, 1993). Effective issue selling draws attention to those issues or problems that concern you, notwithstanding the numerous other issues that compete for your superior's time and attention. The issues busy leaders believe warrant their attention are those that they perceive are most consequential. Effectively influencing upward, therefore, means that you need to convince your boss that a particular issue you espouse is so important that it requires his or her attention. Table 5.11 contains a summary of the key strategies that can be used to exercise upward influence through effective issue selling (Dutton & Ashford, 1993; Dutton & Duncan, 1987).

There is another important reason to exercise upward influence. In today's decentralized and exceptionally complex corporate environment, uninformed bosses are prone to make bad decisions. As a consequence, the organization as a whole suffers and subordinates and their units may become demoralized and discouraged. According to Michael Useem, Director of the Center for Leadership and Change Management, too often subordinates could prevent or reverse bad decisions, but they remain silent. In an interview regarding his book, *Leading Up: How to Lead Your Boss So You Both Win*, Useem says, bluntly, "If people are afraid to help their leaders lead, their leaders will fail" (Breen, 2001). He offers several tips for what he calls "trickle-up leadership." First, you've got to speak up to lead up. Too often people with good ideas or with

Table 5.11	Ways to Sell Issues Upward
PRINCIPLE	**EXPLANATION**
Congruence	The issue must be congruent with your position and role. A person in the marketing department trying to sell an issue relating to computers would be less effective than would an information specialist.
Credibility	Maintain credibility by being honest, open, non-self-serving, and straightforward. Demonstrate that your interest in the issue is not mere personal gain. Issues that seem self-serving are more difficult to sell.
Communication	Gain or maintain access to a broad communication network. Use multiple communication channels, including face-to-face conversations, written memos, e-mail, conferences, news clippings, and so on.
Compatibility	Select issues that are compatible and in harmony with the organization. Avoid issues that contradict the company culture.
Solvability	The issue must be solvable. Make it clear that the issue can be solved. Show that solution alternatives are available. Unresolvable issues don't capture attention.
Payoff	Clearly point out the long-term payoff, for the organization or the manager, of addressing the issue. The higher the potential payoff appears to be, the more likely the issue will receive attention.
Expertise	Identify the expertise needed to solve the problem. Issues are more likely to capture attention if it is clear that the expertise necessary to resolve them resides in the organization, or better still, under the purview of the top manager or boss.
Responsibility	Point out the responsibility that top managers have to address the issue. Emphasize the negative consequences associated with ignoring the issue or leaving it unresolved.
Presentation	Ensure that the issue is presented succinctly, in emotionally positive terms, with supporting data and novel information. Complex and convoluted information does not capture attention, so the issue must be explained in precise, simple terms.
Bundling	Bundle similar issues together with other important issues that interest top managers. Point out the relationship between your issue and other issues already being addressed.
Coalitions	The issue must be sponsored by other people who will help see the issue. Building coalitions of supporters makes the issue hard to ignore.
Visibility	Present and sell the issue in a public forum rather than in a private meeting. The more individuals who hear about the issue, the more likely it is to reach the boss's agenda.

SOURCE: *Adapted from Dutton and Ashford, 1993.*

knowledge regarding a misinformed decision or misinterpreted report elect to remain silent. He notes that even in the Marine Corps officers are expected to speak up if their superior issues a flawed order. Second, before you lead up, you've got to team up. When the implications of your message will require a major change of course, it is particularly important to work with allies, especially those who add credibility to your argument. Third, lead up, don't argue up. When offering a contrary perspective, disagree without being disagreeable. By modeling open-mindedness, support, and trustworthiness, your example of how you disagree may be your most important message, especially during times of high stress and conflict. Fourth, try to be all things to

everyone, and you'll be nothing to anybody. Superiors are more willing to hear bad news from subordinates whose judgment they can trust and whose loyalty is unquestioned. Trying to keep everyone happy or working on too many agendas can cloud one's judgment and lead others to question your loyalty.

ACTING ASSERTIVELY: NEUTRALIZING INFLUENCE ATTEMPTS

In general, managers are more effective when they assume that others are reasonable, well meaning, and motivated. Unfortunately, in some cases, these assumptions are proven false. When this happens, it is important to be prepared to protect ourselves from unwanted, inappropriate efforts by others to influence our actions. Therefore, it is not only important to learn how to influence others effectively, but we must also understand how to protect ourselves against the undesirable attempts of others to influence us. As we discussed earlier, one-sided dependence is the antithesis of empowerment. Recalling Figure 5.1, feelings of lack of power are just as harmful to personal performance as flagrant, excessive use of power. Therefore, it is just as important to be skillful at resisting unwanted influence attempts as it is to influence the behavior of others effectively and appropriately. This skill is particularly relevant in work situations in which maintaining personal initiative is difficult in the face of strong countervailing pressures.

Tables 5.8 and 5.9 contain an impressive arsenal of influence strategies. Is it possible to neutralize the impact of such a highly developed, well-conceived set of tools? Many people succumb to these influence attempts, either because they are unaware of the social dynamics affecting their decisions or because they feel compelled to give in without offering any resistance. To avoid this plight, it is important to develop the skill of resisting inappropriate efforts to control your behavior. Assertiveness increases self-determination by thwarting exploitation at the hands of overpowering bosses, manipulative sales personnel, and high-pressured negotiators (Cialdini, 2001). This is consistent with the time-honored sociological theory that power is the opposite of dependence, and hence the pathway to empowerment involves throwing off the choice-limiting constraints imposed by dependence (Emerson, 1962).

The importance of avoiding relationships in which individuals in power positions attempt to foster dependency in others has been the subject of research on the "toxic effects of tyranny in organizations" (Bies & Tripp, 1998). A summary of the characteristics of abusive bosses, from this study, is shown in Table 5.12. Given the tendency for most leaders to occasionally take advantage of their position of power, we include this as a tool for identifying situations in which excess has become the norm. As you examine the following strategies for neutralizing inappropriate influence attempts, you might find it useful to use these characteristics of abusive relationships as a frame of reference.

Neutralizing Retribution Strategies Used by Others

Coercive and intimidating actions are intended to create a power imbalance by substituting dependence for interdependence. This is the most detrimental form of influence, and therefore it should be resisted most vigorously and directly. You can use several approaches. The following can be thought of as a hierarchy of preferred responses (begin with the first and progress to the next responses, if necessary).

1. **Use countervailing power to shift dependence to interdependence.** The primary reason individuals (particularly bosses) rely heavily on the threat of retribution as an influence strategy is because they perceive an inequality in power. Obviously, the boss in an organization has the final say, but the larger the perceived discrepancy in power, the greater the temptation to exploit the powerless. The first half of this chapter outlined several techniques for increasing your power base. However, when exploitation occurs, the time for planning how to increase your power base has passed. Ideally, you are in a position to focus your boss's attention on your mutual

Table 5.12	Characteristics of Abusive Bosses

- Micromanager—obsessed with details and perfection.
- Inexplicit direction with decisive delivery—treats everything as a priority, requiring immediate, careful attention.
- Mercurial mood swings—responses are very unpredictable.
- Obsession with loyalty and obedience—believes, "You are either for me or against me."
- Status derogation—criticizes subordinates in public, to the point of ridicule.
- Capricious actions—known for arbitrariness and hypocrisy.
- Exercises raw power for personal gain—feels entitled to the "spoils of victory."

Source: *Adapted from Bies and Tripp, 1988.*

dependence, that is, your interdependence. Point out the negative consequences of failing to respect your rights and acting cooperatively. As part of this discussion, it may be appropriate to discuss more acceptable means of satisfying the boss's demands.

2. **Confront the exploiting individual directly.** All individuals, no matter what their job or organizational status, must protect their personal rights. One of those rights is to be treated as an intelligent, mature, responsible adult. To initiate a complaint effectively, key elements include describing the problem in terms of behaviors, consequences, and feelings, persisting until understood, and making specific suggestions. These techniques can be used in this situation to stress the seriousness of your concerns. If necessary, you should specify actions you are willing to take to stop coercive behavior. For example, whistle-blowing involves registering a complaint with an external governing body.

3. **Actively resist.** As a last resort, you should consider "fighting fire with fire." This is obviously a sensitive matter, but there are some individuals who will keep pushing others until they meet resistance. A work slowdown, deliberate disobedience to orders, or reporting the problem to a senior manager might be necessary. Again, this step should be pursued only after all other efforts to counter unwanted threats and demands have failed.

Neutralizing Reciprocity Strategies by Others

Many of the persuasion strategies used in sales and advertising fall into this category. In the marketplace, your concern is to avoid being duped. In the workplace, your concern is to avoid being manipulated. The following hierarchically arranged actions should be helpful in either situation. Once again, begin with the first response and follow with others if necessary.

1. **Examine the intent of any gift or favor-giving activity.** When a favor or gift is offered, you should consider the motives of the person, the appropriateness of the behavior, and the probable consequences. You should ask yourself questions such as "Is the giver likely to profit from this?" "Is this transaction inappropriate, unethical, or illegal?" "Is there a stated or implied expectation of reciprocation, and

would I feel good about complying if the gift or favor were not offered?" In brief, when in doubt about a benefactor's motives, ask questions or decline the gift.

2. **Confront individuals who are using manipulative bargaining tactics.** Common ploys used in these situations are escalating commitments ("I'm only interested in a small commitment [now]") and reciprocal compromises ("I've lowered my [extreme] initial position; now I expect you [in the spirit of fair play] to also offer a compromise"). Simply drawing attention to these attempts at manipulation will enhance your power in the relationship. State that you do not approve of the manipulative strategy; then propose an alternative exchange, with emphasis on the merits of the case or the true value of the product rather than on the craftiness of the negotiators. You will thus be able to reshape the exchange process and avoid being manipulated.

3. **Refuse to bargain with individuals who use high-pressure tactics.** If steps 1 and 2 have failed, refuse to continue the discussion unless high-pressure tactics, such as imposing unrealistic time constraints or emphasizing the limited supply of the commodity or service, are dropped. If you suspect the dynamics of the negotiation process may be clouding your judgment about the value of the object or the importance of the issue, ask yourself, "Would I be interested in this item if there were an unlimited supply and no decision-making deadline?" If the answer is negative, either disengage from the negotiation process or focus your attention on its inequality. By shifting attention from content to process, you neutralize the advantage of a more experienced or powerful bargainer. By refusing to continue unless artificial constraints of time and supply are removed, you can establish fairer terms of trade.

Neutralizing Reason Strategies by Others

Although strategies based on reason are the most egalitarian of influence attempts, they can still create or exacerbate conditions of inequity. The following ordered guidelines should help you avoid these situations:

1. **Explain the adverse effects of compliance on performance.** Often, others' pressing priorities are your incidentals. The fact that someone

can present a legitimate, convincing case does not mean you should comply with the request. For example, a request may be reasonable, but its timing bad; compliance would mean your having to miss important personal deadlines or neglect your customers. You should discuss these concerns with the influencer. By acknowledging the other person's need, explaining your concerns about personal compliance, and then, helping to find alternatives, you avoid becoming overcommitted without giving offense.

2. **Defend your personal rights.** If you have used step 1 and your petitioner persists, focus the discussion on your personal rights. If individuals frequently come to you for help because they mismanage their time or resources, appeal to their sense of fairness. Ask if it is right to ask you to get behind in your own work in order to bail them out of their predicaments. Coworkers have the right to request your help in a pinch, but you also have the right to say no when even reasonable requests place you at a serious disadvantage or when they stem from the negligence or overdependence of others.

3. **Firmly refuse to comply with the request.** If your efforts to explain why you are unable to comply have not worked, you should firmly restate your refusal and terminate the discussion. Some people believe that their case is so compelling, they have difficulty believing others won't comply. If your coworker still "won't take no for an answer," it's probably because your "no" was not firm enough. As a last resort, you may have to seek the support of a higher authority.

Summary

In Figure 5.2, the two skills discussed in this chapter—gaining power and translating power into influence—are highlighted. We began by discussing sources of power, such as personal attributes and position characteristics. Both of these must be developed if one is to maximize one's potential as a power holder. A strong person in a weak position and a weak person in a

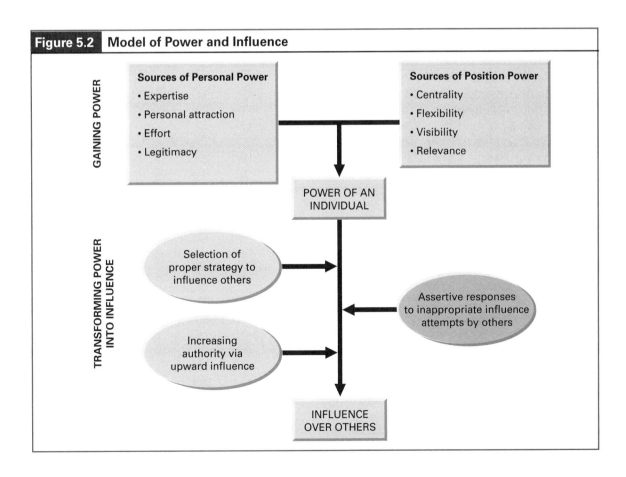

Figure 5.2 Model of Power and Influence

GAINING POWER

Sources of Personal Power
- Expertise
- Personal attraction
- Effort
- Legitimacy

Sources of Position Power
- Centrality
- Flexibility
- Visibility
- Relevance

POWER OF AN INDIVIDUAL

TRANSFORMING POWER INTO INFLUENCE

Selection of proper strategy to influence others

Increasing authority via upward influence

Assertive responses to inappropriate influence attempts by others

INFLUENCE OVER OTHERS

LEARNING

GAINING POWER AND INFLUENCE CHAPTER 5 **329**

strong position are both at a disadvantage. Ideally, one should become a strong person in a strong position.

A manager must establish a power base in order to get work accomplished and obtain commitments to important objectives. But power without influence is not sufficient. Consequently, we discussed how to translate power into influence by selecting an appropriate influence strategy and implementing it in such a way that resistance is minimized. In general, this is most likely to occur when managers use the higher-numbered strategies in Table 5.8. Persuasion tends to build trust and encourage internalized commitment, while coercion and intimidation erode trust, produce only superficial compliance, and encourage servility.

The unbridled use of power tends to increase resistance among subordinates, which in turn erodes the manager's power base. It also transforms the nature of the manager's stewardship over subordinates. The more a manager dominates subordinates, the more dependent they become on management's initiatives. As a result, managers tend to overvalue their contribution to their workers' job-performance activities ("Without me, they would be lost"). This inflated sense of self-importance encourages abuse of power that weakens the manager's influence and may even lead others to demand the manager's resignation. Thus, the abuse of power is both organizationally and personally destructive.

Power need not be abused, however. Managers, by definition, are located somewhere above the mid-point in the range of organizational levels (from the CEO at the top to hourly employees at the bottom). Managers who shun initiative and refuse to take responsibility for their actions see themselves as the "janitors" for the management pyramid above them. Their job, as they see it, is to clean up messes and carry out orders. Their attitude and demeanor reflect that of their bosses. In contrast, managers characterized by high initiative, personal responsibility, and influence see themselves as presidents of the organizational pyramid below them. They work within acknowledged constraints, but they figure out ways to do things right. They take full responsibility for their subordinates' performance, as well as for their commitment to their work and their membership in the organization.

Translating power into influence should not only be directed downward (i.e., toward organizational subordinates) but also upward (i.e., toward organizational superiors). Incompetent attempts to influence upward can quickly derail a manager's career, while competent upward influence can markedly enhance it. By helping to set the agenda of senior managers (issue selling) and by working for senior management's success (benefiting the boss), a manager's influence can increase significantly. When applying these two principles, however, managers should be motivated not by a thirst for mere self-aggrandizement, but by an honest desire to benefit their companies and strengthen their bosses' position.

The counsel of the late A. Bartlett Giamatti, former president of Yale University and commissioner of Major League Baseball, serves as a particularly fitting conclusion to this discussion: "Far better to conceive of power as consisting in part of the knowledge of when not to use all the power you have . . . Whoever knows how to restrain and effectively release power finds . . . that power flows back to him" (1981, p. 169).

Behavioral Guidelines

Effective management within an organization includes both gaining power and exercising influence wisely. Key guidelines for gaining power include:

1. Enhance your personal power in the organization by:
   - ❑ Developing your knowledge and skills to the point of becoming an acknowledged expert.
   - ❑ Enhancing your attractiveness to others, for example, by fostering the attributes of friendship (genuineness, intimacy, acceptance, validation of self-worth, tolerance, and social exchange).
   - ❑ Being extremely dependable and, when appropriate, putting forth more effort than expected.
   - ❑ Increase your legitimacy by aligning your behaviors and decisions with core organizational values.

2. Increase the centrality of your position by:
   - ❑ Expanding your network of communication contacts.
   - ❑ Staying abreast of relevant information.
   - ❑ Serving as the source of information for others.

3. Increase the latitude and flexibility of your job by:
   - ❑ Reducing the percentage of routine activities.
   - ❑ Expanding task variety and novelty.
   - ❑ Initiating new ideas.
   - ❑ Getting involved in new projects.
   - ❑ Participating in the early stages of decision-making processes.
   - ❑ Seeking unusual and design-oriented jobs, rather than those that are repetitive and maintenance oriented.

4. Increase the visibility of your job performance by:
   - ❏ Expanding the number of contacts you have with senior people.
   - ❏ Making oral presentations of written work.
   - ❏ Participating in problem-solving task forces.
   - ❏ Inviting senior managers to help you recognize important accomplishments within your work group.
   - ❏ Sending personal notes of congratulations or cover notes accompanying reports or useful information.

5. Increase the relevance of your tasks to the organization by:
   - ❏ Becoming an internal coordinator or external representative.
   - ❏ Providing services and information to other units.
   - ❏ Monitoring and evaluating activities within your own unit.
   - ❏ Expanding the domain of your work activities.
   - ❏ Becoming involved in activities central to the organization's top priorities.
   - ❏ Becoming a trainer or mentor for new members.

   The general guidelines for influencing others effectively involve matching your influence strategy to specific situations, acting assertively when others attempt to influence you inappropriately, and empowering others. In general, use reason strategies more often than reciprocity strategies, and reciprocity more than threats of retribution. Use open, direct approaches in preference to indirect, manipulative approaches.

6. Use reason strategies when:
   - ❏ There are few time constraints.
   - ❏ Initiative and innovation are vital.
   - ❏ Interpersonal trust is high.
   - ❏ The relationship is long term.
   - ❏ Interpersonal conflict is not high.
   - ❏ Personal goals are congruent and/or respected by both parties.
   - ❏ It is important for the other person to understand why the request is being made.

7. Use reciprocity strategies when:
   - ❏ The parties are mutually dependent.
   - ❏ There are clearly specified rules governing interpersonal transactions.
   - ❏ Long-term commitment to common goals and values is not important.

- ❏ There is sufficient time to reach satisfactory agreements.

8. Use retribution strategies when:
   - ❏ There is a substantial imbalance of power between the parties.
   - ❏ The ongoing commitment of the other person is not critical.
   - ❏ Quality and innovation are not important.
   - ❏ Opposition is acceptable (e.g., when personnel replacement is possible, if necessary).
   - ❏ Extensive surveillance is possible.
   - ❏ No other alternatives exist.

9. To neutralize reason influence strategies of others:
   - ❏ Explain the negative consequences of compliance.
   - ❏ Defend your rights.
   - ❏ Firmly refuse to comply with request.

10. To neutralize reciprocity, influence strategies of others:
    - ❏ Examine the context of any gift- or favor-giving activity.
    - ❏ Confront individuals using escalating or compromising tactics.
    - ❏ Refuse to bargain with individuals using high-pressure tactics.

11. To neutralize retribution influence strategies of others:
    - ❏ Use countervailing power to shift dependence to interdependence.
    - ❏ Confront the exploitative individual directly.
    - ❏ Actively resist.

12. To sell issues to your superiors:
    - ❏ Select issues that are congruent with your position or role.
    - ❏ Present the issue honestly and without being self-serving.
    - ❏ Communicate the issue broadly.
    - ❏ Select an issue that is compatible with the culture.
    - ❏ Select a solvable issue.
    - ❏ Clarify the payoff to be achieved.
    - ❏ Identify the needed expertise.
    - ❏ Point out senior managers' responsibility for the issue.
    - ❏ Be succinct, use emotional imagery, and provide supporting data and novel information.
    - ❏ Bundle the issue with other similar important issues.
    - ❏ Find like-minded supporters.
    - ❏ Use public forums.

LEARNING

CASE INVOLVING POWER AND INFLUENCE

Banning Foreign Recruitment

In January 2009, Malaysia banned the hiring of foreign workers for factories, shops, and other services. For many years, Malaysia had been a leading importer of labor, with more than 2 million foreign workers, primarily from Southeast Asian countries. Exemptions were available for those working in highly skilled industries. The goal of the move was to protect Malaysian citizens during the economic downturn.

The Home Minister, Syed Hamid Albar, explained that the decision was made following a report showing that 45,000 people would lose their jobs by the end of January 2009. In the last quarter of 2008, 13,000 had lost their jobs, and 75 percent of these were Malaysian.

A major Malaysian limited company decided to react to the possible downturn and change in law by decentralizing its management structure. Previously, all major decisions, including operations, marketing, sales, and personnel had been undertaken by the head office. This had meant that none of the four major sites in Malaysia had a general manager, but each department on the site reported to its senior counterpart in the head office. The new structure would give the site manager responsibility for all management decisions, with the exception of sales and marketing.

The company felt that this new initiative would make it more competitive, better placed to make decisions and exploit new opportunities once the economic downturn had passed. However, there would be new difficulties for the general managers at each site; personnel would need skills upgrades and lines of reporting and communication would need attention.

The company also made the decision that these new general managers would be Malaysian. For many years, the company had been over-reliant on predominantly U.S. and European senior management, but now there were adequately educated and experienced potential Malaysian candidates for each new job role. This would protect the business in the longer term if the government decided to make the ban on foreign workers permanent or extended it to senior positions.

The company would have to transform itself from a centralized organization where the bulk of power and influence was held by a handful of individuals at the head office to a more decentralized and autonomous management system.

Discussion Questions

1. If you were part of the selection committee for the new site managers, based on what you have learned about the sources of personnel power in this chapter, describe what you consider to be the ideal candidate's qualifications.

2. If you were offered one of the new managerial positions, based on what you have learned about the sources of position power, what actions would you take to ensure that as a general manager you had the necessary power to accomplish your assigned duties?

3. Using the information on influence strategies in the second half of this chapter as your guide, strategize how you would address the challenges you are likely to encounter if you accepted one of the new positions.

SKILL *PRACTICE*

EXERCISE FOR GAINING POWER

Repairing Power Failures in Management Circuits

Rosabeth Kanter (1979) argues that much of what is labeled "poor management" in organizations is simply individuals protecting their diminished power bases. Instead of criticizing these managers as incompetent, she proposes we bolster their feelings of personal power. If we solve the real problem of perceived lack of power, the undesirable symptoms of poor leadership often evaporate. This point of view is consistent with the principles discussed in this chapter.

Assignment

In this exercise, you are asked to give advice to individuals who feel powerless. For each of the situations below, form groups to explore opportunities for enhancing the power base of these three individuals. Prepare to report your recommendations.

Situation 1: First-Line Supervisor

Kate Shalene has been a first-line supervisor for six months. She was proud of her new promotion, but surprised to discover she felt increasingly powerless. Instead of being a stepping stone, this position was feeling more and more like a dead end. Managers above her were about her age and the hoped-for company expansion never materialized. She was not a central part of the organization, and she felt no one ever noticed her unless she messed up. She was expected to be supportive of her subordinates, but they never returned the favor. She was expected to absorb their flack without support from above. In general, she felt as though she was constantly "getting it from both ends." Her job was extremely rule-bound, so she had little discretion in what she did or how she did it. She had only modest control over the pay or benefits of her subordinates, because their union agreement left very little flexibility. So she felt powerless to reward them or punish them in ways that really mattered.

As a result, she found she was more and more apt to impose rules to get subordinates to do what she wanted. She became increasingly jealous of any successes and recognition achieved by her subordinates, so she tended to isolate them from people higher up in the organization and from complete information. She lost her penchant for informality and became increasingly rigid in following standard operating procedures. Predictably, her subordinates were becoming more resentful and less productive.

Situation 2: Staff Professional

Shawn Quinn came to the organization a year ago as a staff professional. He believed it might be a way for him to achieve considerable visibility with the top brass, but instead he felt isolated and forgotten. As a staff officer, he had almost no decision-making authority except in his narrow area of expertise. Most of what went on in the organization occurred without his involvement. Innovation and entrepreneurial activity were completely out of his realm. While some of the line officers were given opportunities for professional development, no one seemed to care about his becoming more experienced and capable. They saw him only as a specialist. Because his job didn't require that he work with others, he had little opportunity to cultivate relationships that might lead to contacts with someone near the top.

PRACTICE

What hurt was that a consultant had been hired a few times to work on projects that were part of his area. If consultants could be brought in to do his work, he thought, he must not be very important to the organization.

Shawn found himself being more and more turf conscious. He didn't want others encroaching on his area of expertise. He tried to demonstrate his competence to others, but the more he did so, the more he became defined as a specialist, outside the mainstream of the organization. Overall, he felt he was losing ground in his career.

Situation 3: Top Executive

May Phelps has been a top executive for three years now. When she obtained the position, she felt that her ultimate career goal had been achieved. Now she was not so sure. Surprisingly, she discovered myriad constraints limiting her discretion and initiative. For example, the job had so many demands and details associated with it that she never had time to engage in any long-term planning. There always seemed to be one more crisis that demanded her attention. Unfortunately, most of the constraints were from sources she couldn't control, such as government regulations, demands for greater accountability made by the board of directors and by stockholders, union relationships, equal opportunity statutes, and so on. She had built her reputation as a successful manager by being entrepreneurial, creative, and innovative, but none of those qualities seemed appropriate for the demands of her current work. Furthermore, because she was so mired in operations, she had become more and more out of touch with the information flow in the organization. Some things had to remain confidential with her, but her secrecy made others unwilling to share information with her. She had assistants who were supposed to be monitoring the organization and providing her with information, but she often felt they only told her what she wanted to hear.

May had begun to hear rumors that certain special-interest groups were demanding her removal from the top job. She responded by becoming more dictatorial and defensive, with the result that the organization was becoming more control-oriented and conservative. She felt that she was on a downward spiral, but she couldn't find a way to reverse the trend. "I always thought the saying 'It's lonely at the top' was just a metaphor," she mused.

EXERCISE FOR USING INFLUENCE EFFECTIVELY

Managers are given formal power in an organization by virtue of their position of authority. However, they often find this authority does not readily translate into actual influence. Particularly when they are working with peers, they find it necessary to develop informal relationships through making deals, persuasive arguments, and so forth. These relationships form the basis of real influence in an organization.

Assignment

After reading the following case, assume the roles of Ann's staff members. Divide into small groups and conduct an informal staff discussion in which you design a plan for influencing

Ann's colleagues and superiors to support her proposal. First, decide which general influence strategy (or combination of strategies) is most appropriate for this situation. Second, using Table 5.7, recommend specific actions for implementing your general strategy. Prepare to present your suggestions, including justifications.

Ann Lyman's Proposal

Ann Lyman was recently hired by the Challenge Products Corporation (CPC) as a senior marketing executive for the electronic housewares division. Her previous experience at Pearces, a major competitor, had earned her a reputation for being a creative and hard-working manager. Her department at Pearces had increased its sales at least 15 percent per year over the past five years, and she had been featured in a lead article in *Contemporary Management.* This combination of competence and visibility was what attracted the attention of John Dilworth, the CEO of Challenge. John was troubled about the two-quarter decline in electronic sales. This was the core of CPC's business, and he could not risk losing market share.

In the past, CPC's products had dominated such a large market share that, ironically, marketing wasn't considered very important. Production touted its high quality and low costs, purchasing emphasized its contribution to keeping costs low, and engineering stressed the durability of its designs. CPC products, it was argued by many, "sold themselves."

But that was before the cheaper, "look-alike" products from Asia flooded the discount stores. No longer could CPC expect high customer loyalty simply because it was the oldest, best-known, most reliable name brand on the shelf. Ann was convinced that in order for CPC to stay competitive, the company needed to expand its product line, offering more options at different price levels. She felt it also needed to branch out into "trend designs" that appealed to the contemporary lifestyles of young adults. These options would require the company to find new channels of distribution, such as specialty mail-order catalogs, as well as to manufacture generic products for department stores' private labels.

These changes had far-reaching ramifications for other departments at CPC. For one thing, they meant engineering would have to shorten its design cycle, provide support for a broader range of products, and emphasize customer-oriented, rather than functional, features. These changes would obviously not sit well with the production department, which jealously protected its long production runs based on standard orders and relatively few model changes. It also stressed ease of fabrication and assembly. In addition, purchasing would be required to find new sourcing alternatives for nonstandard parts, which would make it more difficult to get volume discounts and ensure quality.

After three months on the job, Ann felt she was ready to make her proposal to John. She pushed her staff hard to add the finishing touches before John left on his two-week vacation to Lake Tahoe. She wasn't disappointed—he thought it was a winner. He was excited and ready to "sign on." But he was also realistic about the difficulty they faced convincing others that these changes were necessary. Ann's counterparts in production, purchasing, and engineering would certainly object. "It'll be a hard sell, but I think you have some good ideas," he concluded. "While I'm away, I'd like you to design a plan for getting the cooperation of the other departments. You can count on me for general support, but the culture in this organization isn't consistent with sending out an edict. You'll have to figure out how to get their support some other way."

PRACTICE

EXERCISES FOR NEUTRALIZING UNWANTED INFLUENCE ATTEMPTS

An important aspect of becoming empowered and influential is reducing inappropriate dependence. Obviously, social and work interdependence are integral parts of organizational life. Most forms of interdependence are natural and healthy. However, sometimes individuals attempt to turn interdependence into dependence by exercising inappropriate influence. Their objective is to increase their power over others by creating a significant imbalance of power.

Assignment

In each of the following role plays, assume the role of the person who needs to resist unwanted influence (Betty or Pat). Prior to the beginning of the role play, review the relevant behavioral guidelines, determine which combination is most appropriate, and plan your strategy for dealing with this problem. Do not read the other role descriptions (Bill or Lynn). Following the role play, an assigned observer will give you feedback using the Observer's Feedback Form (found at the end of the chapter) as a guide.

Cindy's Fast Foods

Betty, Assistant Manager

You are the assistant manager of Cindy's, a fast-food franchise in a college town. You are one of the few student employees who has stayed on after graduation. You weren't ready to move on, and there weren't that many good jobs in elementary education, anyway. The spring before graduation, the owner offered you the job of assistant manager. The timing was perfect because the offer would relieve the pressure on you to pursue teaching jobs in which you really weren't interested. Your work at Cindy's had sparked your interest in business, and your student-teaching experience had not been very successful. Even though your parents weren't too pleased about paying four years' tuition at an expensive private liberal arts college to have you end up "cooking hamburgers" for a career, their feelings mellowed when you explained the opportunities you would have to advance and possibly purchase a franchise. "Besides," you told them, "I'll only be in this position for three years, and then I can decide whether I want to apply for a manager's position or try again for a teaching job."

It's hard to believe it's been two years since graduation. Your manager, Bill, has done a conscientious job helping you learn the ropes as a manager. He has worked you hard, but trained you well. You feel indebted to him for his help. You have become quite close friends, although his occasional dirty jokes and sexist comments with the guys on break in the back room make you feel uncomfortable.

One night after the rest of the crew has gone home, you are finishing your book work for the day. These late nights are the one really bad feature of your job. Just as you are about to turn out the lights, Bill comes in. It is not unusual for him to stop by at closing. He is single, likes to bowl after work, and sometimes drops by later on his way home. You are just putting on your coat when he asks you to come into his office. He shuts the door, and pulls up a chair next to you. "Betty, I've been watching your performance very closely. You're a hard worker. The employees enjoy your management style. And I've taken a liking to you as well. I think I have a good shot at transferring to a much larger store in Cincinnati. I'll be glad to get out of this one-horse town and gain more visibility closer to corporate headquarters."

You start getting a little nervous as he moves his chair closer to yours. "I think you would be a really good replacement for me, but you haven't completed your full term as assistant. So I'll need to ask for a special exception to the corporate policy. And I'll have to put in a good word for you with the owner. However, there's some risk involved for me, because the regional manager is a real stickler on rules, and I've asked him to recommend me for the Cincinnati job. But I'd be willing to take that risk under certain conditions." As he waits for a response, you know very well where this conversation is headed.

Bill, Manager

You have been attracted to Betty for some time. You find her very attractive, and you enjoy her company. You have several times manufactured excuses to have personal chats with her or to be alone with her. You think Betty finds you attractive, also. It seems that she has been extra friendly lately. You figure she's either bucking for your job or sending you signals that she'd like to expand your relationship beyond strictly business—or both.

Besides, you feel she owes you something. You have worked extra hard to train her, and you've been dropping hints to the owner that you think Betty might be ready to move up.

9:00 to 7:30

Pat Simpson, Loan Officer

You are a member of a small consumer loan company. The staff consists of you, another loan officer, and a secretary. Last month, a larger financial institution acquired your firm and made some personnel changes. The other loan officer, with whom you had worked for four years, was replaced by Lynn Johnson. Having entered the company at about the same time, you and Lynn have known each other for years. In fact, you worked in the Ann Arbor office together for a year. During that time, you were both single, and together you enjoyed the night life of Detroit. You learn Lynn is still single and "living it up." In contrast, you have been married for about three years. You looked forward to working with Lynn again but wondered if your lack of interest in the local night scene would affect your relationship. Lynn has the reputation of being capable but lazy. She's known for taking in lots of loan applications and then striking bargains with or cajoling coworkers into helping out with the dreaded credit-checking process. You wonder if this practice has anything to do with the fact that her uncle was a founding partner in the bank.

After Lynn arrives, you are shocked at the difference in your work attitudes and lifestyles. "Boy, what a difference three years makes!" you think to yourself. You and your previous office mate, Jim, were both married, and both of you favored a vigorous working tempo from 9:00 to 5:15, taking lunch when convenient. You and Jim had a great working relationship, and the loan volume in your office increased steadily. There was even some discussion of expanding the size of the staff. In contrast, Lynn prefers leisurely mornings that begin around 10:30, luncheons as long as Mexican siestas, and a flurry of activity between 4:00 and 7:30 P.M.

You and your spouse are experiencing some marital turbulence, and you feel it is very important to be home in the evenings. Your spouse has begun attending night classes and leaves for school at 8:00 P.M. The educational program is an extremely intense three-year ordeal. Unfortunately, the stress level already seems unbearable. When you stay at the office late, you not only miss dinner together but you don't even see each other until after class, when you are both so tired there is no opportunity for quality time. It seems as though most weekends are devoted to homework.

Because the office staff is so small, the difference in workday rhythms is creating a serious hardship on you. Lynn doesn't function very well in the morning and has begun expressing irritation when you rush out the door at closing time. Lately, your relationship

PRACTICE

has become strained. You handle most of the walk-in business early in the morning, eat lunch at your desk, and have your paperwork done by 5:30 at the latest. In contrast, Lynn is just getting into high gear about 4:00. Because company rules require checking each other's loan approvals, Lynn becomes testy when you say you can't stay after 5:30 to check her work. Some evenings you have relented and stayed until 7:00 or 8:00, but your spouse got very upset. When you don't stay late, you are greeted by a stack of paperwork on your desk in the morning, which makes it difficult for you to meet with new customers. Several times Lynn has tried to get you to do the credit checks on her loan applications, saying that the press of new business was too great.

Something has got to change! You decide to go to lunch with Lynn today and tell her how you feel.

Lynn Johnson, Loan Officer

You have worked for this firm for 10 years, and you are very good at your work. During that time, you have passed up offers from larger financial institutions because you like the flexibility of working in a small office. Besides, your family is financially well off, so you aren't concerned about making a lot of money.

In every other office, your coworkers have been willing to accommodate your work style. They recognize you are one of the top loan officers in the company—and having the right last name doesn't hurt any—so they make allowances for your idiosyncrasies.

But your new office mate (and, you thought, old friend) is an exception. Since you arrived, the relationship has been testy because of your different schedules. You don't understand why there can't be more tolerance for your work style. After all, you get the job done, and that's what counts. Besides, your requests for assistance are not that unreasonable; other coworkers have always been willing to comply.

Thinking about the impending discussion, you realize how important it is for you to get Pat to change her work habits to conform with yours. You certainly hope you can convince Pat to pitch in and help you when you get behind. "I mean, that's what coworkers (and old friends) are for, right?" you muse on the way to work. During the discussion, you plan to stress the reasonableness of your requests. Others have never objected strenuously; why should Pat? If that doesn't work, you plan to try and work out a bargain. Maybe you could put in a good word for Pat with your uncle, a founder of the company. Pat's career hasn't exactly skyrocketed, and she is probably itching to move to a larger office in a metropolitan city. Possibly, her title could be upgraded to Senior Loan Officer.

ACTIVITIES FOR GAINING POWER
AND INFLUENCE

Suggested Assignments

1. Select a friend or associate who has complained to you about feeling powerless in an organizational position. This might be a person who holds a relatively insignificant leadership position in a campus organization or a low-level position in a work organization. Perhaps the individual feels his or her personal abilities do not command respect in that position. Sit down with this person and teach him or her the guidelines for gaining power in an organization. (You might use the Assessment Survey at the beginning of this chapter as a diagnostic instrument.) As part of this conversation, design a specific plan of action for increasing both the position and personal bases of power. Discuss the outcomes of this plan with your friend and report on his or her success.

2. Using the guidelines for gaining power, develop a plan for increasing your power in an organizational setting. Describe the setting, including the factors you feel account for your feelings of powerlessness. Use your score on the Assessment Survey as a diagnostic aid. Formulate a detailed strategy for increasing your positional and personal power. Report on your results and describe the benefits of becoming more empowered.

3. Over time, analyze your efforts to influence other people. Use the "Three Rs" model to catalog your strategies. Consider why you used each strategy. Did you repeatedly rely on one or two strategies, or did you vary your approach according to circumstances? Keep track of the outcome of each attempt. Did you seem to have more success with one of the strategies? Next, select a person you have attempted to influence, one with whom you have a close, ongoing relationship. Discuss the alternative influence strategies with that person and ask him or her what effect the frequent use of each approach might have on your relationship.

4. Watch at least two realistic dramas (movies, plays, TV). Observe the influence strategies used by various characters. Which form of influence did they use most frequently, and why? Did certain people demonstrate a preference for a particular strategy? If so, was this based on personality traits, gender roles, authority relationships, or other situational factors? How successful were these influence attempts, and what impact did they have on ongoing relationships?

5. Identify a specific relationship in which you are regularly asked to do things that you feel are inappropriate. Using the relevant guidelines for resisting unwanted influence, formulate a strategy for assertively responding to the next attempt. Role-play this approach with a friend or coworker and incorporate his or her suggestions. After you implement your plan, report on the outcome. What was the reaction? Were you successful in communicating your position? Was an understanding reached regarding future interactions that is more fair? Based on this experience, examine other relationships for which this approach might be appropriate.

Application Plan and Evaluation

The intent of this exercise is to help you apply this cluster of skills in a real-life, out-of-class setting. Now that you have become familiar with the behavioral guidelines that form the basis of effective skill performance, you will improve most by trying out those guidelines in an everyday context. Unlike a classroom activity, in which feedback is immediate and others can assist you with their evaluations, this skill application activity is one you must accomplish and evaluate on your own. There are two parts to this activity. Part 1 helps prepare you to apply the skill. Part 2 helps you evaluate and improve on your experience. Be sure to write down answers to each item. Don't short-circuit the process by skipping steps.

Part 1. Planning

1. Write down the two or three aspects of this skill that are most important to you. These may be areas of weakness, areas you most want to improve, or areas that are most salient to a problem you face right now. Identify the specific aspects of this skill that you want to apply.

2. Now identify the setting or the situation in which you will apply this skill. Establish a plan for performance by actually writing down a description of the situation. Who else will be involved? When will you do it? Where will it be done?

    Circumstances:
    Who else?
    When?
    Where?

3. Identify the specific behaviors you will engage in to apply this skill. Operationalize your skill performance.

4. What are the indicators of successful performance? How will you know you have been effective? What will indicate you have performed competently?

Part 2. Evaluation

5. After you have completed your implementation, record the results. What happened? How successful were you? What was the effect on others?

6. How can you improve? What modifications can you make next time? What will you do differently in a similar situation in the future?

7. Looking back on your whole skill practice and application experience, what have you learned? What has been surprising? In what ways might this experience help you in the long term?

Gaining Power and Influence

Scoring Key

SKILL AREA	ITEM	ASSESSMENT	
		PRE-	POST-
Gaining power			
Expertise (Personal Characteristics)	1	_____	_____
	9	_____	_____
Interpersonal attraction	2	_____	_____
	10	_____	_____
Effort	3	_____	_____
	11	_____	_____
Legitimacy	4	_____	_____
	12	_____	_____
Centrality (Position Characteristics)	5	_____	_____
	13	_____	_____
Visibility	6	_____	_____
	14	_____	_____
Flexibility	7	_____	_____
	15	_____	_____
Relevance	8	_____	_____
	16	_____	_____
Using influence	17	_____	_____
	18	_____	_____
	19	_____	_____
	20	_____	_____
	21	_____	_____
Resisting influence	22	_____	_____
	23	_____	_____
	24	_____	_____
Increasing authority	25	_____	_____
	26	_____	_____
	27	_____	_____
	28	_____	_____
Total Score		_____	_____

Comparison Data (N = 5,000 Students)

Compare your scores to three comparison standards:
1. The maximum possible score = 168.
2. The scores of other students in your class.
3. Norm data from more than 5,000 business school students.

Pre-Test				Post-Test
134.93	=	mean	=	142.95
145 or above	=	top quartile	=	154 or above
136–144	=	second quartile	=	144–153
126–135	=	third quartile	=	134–143
125 or below	=	bottom quartile	=	133 or below

Using Influence Strategies

Scoring Key

RETRIBUTION		RECIPROCITY		REASON	
ITEM	*SCORE*	*ITEM*	*SCORE*	*ITEM*	*SCORE*
1	_____	2	_____	3	_____
4	_____	5	_____	6	_____
7	_____	8	_____	9	_____
10	_____	11	_____	12	_____
13	_____	14	_____	15	_____
Total	_____	Total	_____	Total	_____

Primary influence strategy (highest score): _____

Secondary influence strategy (second highest score): _____

Observer's Feedback Form

Rating

1 = Low
5 = High

Neutralizing Retribution Strategies

_____ 1. Used countervailing power to shift dependence to interdependence. (Focused on the value of mutual respect and cooperation. Pointed out the negative consequences to both parties of exploitation. If appropriate, suggested alternatives.)

_____ 2. Confronted exploitative individuals directly. (Challenged the right to intimidate and threaten. Stated what he/she was willing to do to stop actions.)

_____ 3. If necessary, actively resisted. (If 1 and 2 failed, did what was necessary to stop retribution attempts. Minimized consequences of resistance on others.)

Neutralizing Reciprocity Strategies

_____ 4. Examined the intent of any gift-or favor-giving activity. (Asked questions to determine the motivation behind favors.)

_____ 5. Confronted unfair bargaining practices, for example, escalating or reciprocally compromising tactics. (Questioned unfair bargaining tactics. Explored alternative ground rules.)

_____ 6. If necessary, refused to bargain with individuals who used high-pressure tactics. (If 4 and 5 failed, terminated the negotiation process.)

Neutralizing Reason Strategies

_____ 7. Explained the negative effect of compliance on performance. (Described effects on personal responsibilities of complying with request. If appropriate, suggested options.)

_____ 8. Defended personal rights. (Assertively restated position, emphasizing personal rights.)

_____ 9. If necessary, refused to comply with request. (If 7 and 8 failed, politely but firmly terminated discussion.)

Comments:

SCORING KEYS AND COMPARISON DATA

SKILL *ASSESSMENT*

- Diagnosing Poor Performance and Enhancing Motivation
- Work Performance Assessment

SKILL *LEARNING*

- Increasing Motivation and Performance
- Diagnosing Work Performance Problems
- Enhancing Individuals' Abilities
- Fostering a Motivating Work Environment
- Elements of an Effective Motivation Program
- Summary
- Behavioral Guidelines

SKILL *ANALYSIS*

- Electro Logic

SKILL *PRACTICE*

- Joe Chaney
- Work Performance Assessment
- Shaheen Matombo

SKILL *APPLICATION*

- Suggested Assignments
- Application Plan and Evaluation

SCORING KEYS AND *COMPARISON DATA*

6

Motivating Others

SKILL DEVELOPMENT OBJECTIVES

- DIAGNOSE WORK PERFORMANCE PROBLEMS
- ENHANCE THE WORK-RELATED ABILITIES OF OTHERS
- FOSTER A MOTIVATING WORK ENVIRONMENT

DIAGNOSTIC SURVEYS FOR MOTIVATING OTHERS

DIAGNOSING POOR PERFORMANCE AND ENHANCING MOTIVATION

Step 1: Before you read the material in this chapter, respond to the following statements by writing a number from the rating scale that follows in the left-hand column (Pre-Assessment). Your answers should reflect your attitudes and behaviors as they are now, not as you would like them to be. Be honest. This instrument is designed to help you discover your level of competency in motivating others so you can tailor your learning to your specific needs. When you have completed the survey, use the scoring key at the end of the chapter to identify the skill areas discussed in this chapter that are most important for you to master.

Step 2: After you have completed the reading and the exercises in this chapter and, ideally, as many as you can of the Skill Application assignments at the end of the chapter, cover up your first set of answers. Then respond to the same statements again, this time in the right-hand column (Post-Assessment). When you have completed the survey, use the scoring key at the end of the chapter to measure your progress. If your score remains low in specific skill areas, use the behavioral guidelines at the end of the Skill Learning section to guide your further practice.

Rating Scale

1 Strongly disagree
2 Disagree
3 Slightly disagree
4 Slightly agree
5 Agree
6 Strongly agree

Assessment

Pre-   Post-

When another person needs to be motivated:

_____ _____   1. I approach a performance problem by first establishing whether it is caused by a lack of motivation or ability.

_____ _____   2. I establish a clear standard of expected performance.

_____ _____   3. I offer to provide training and information, without offering to do tasks myself.

_____ _____   4. I am honest and straightforward in providing feedback on performance and assessing advancement opportunities.

_____ _____   5. I use a variety of rewards to reinforce exceptional performances.

_____ _____   6. When discipline is required, I give specific suggestions for improvement.

_____ _____   7. I design task assignments to make them interesting and challenging.

_____ _____   8. I provide the rewards that each person values.

_____ _____ 9. I make sure that people feel fairly and equitably treated.

_____ _____ 10. I make sure that people get timely feedback from those affected by task performance.

_____ _____ 11. I carefully diagnose the causes of poor performance before taking any remedial or disciplinary action.

_____ _____ 12. I help people establish performance goals that are challenging, specific, and time bound.

_____ _____ 13. Only as a last resort do I attempt to reassign or release a poorly performing individual.

_____ _____ 14. Whenever possible, I make sure valued rewards are linked to high performance.

_____ _____ 15. I discipline when effort is below expectations and below capabilities.

_____ _____ 16. I combine or rotate assignments so that people can use a variety of skills.

_____ _____ 17. I arrange for an individual to work with others in a team, for the mutual support of all.

_____ _____ 18. I make sure that people use realistic standards for measuring fairness.

_____ _____ 19. I provide immediate compliments and other forms of recognition for meaningful accomplishments.

_____ _____ 20. I determine if a person has the necessary resources and support to succeed in a task.

WORK PERFORMANCE ASSESSMENT

Respond to the following statements, based on your current (or recent) work situation. Then turn to the scoring key at the end of this chapter.

Rating Scale

1 Strongly disagree
2 Disagree
3 Neutral
4 Agree
5 Strongly agree

_____ 1. My supervisor and I agree on the quality of my performance.

_____ 2. I feel I have adequate training to perform my current job assignments.

_____ 3. I believe that my native skills and abilities are matched very well with my job responsibilities.

_____ 4. I believe that I have adequate resources and supplies to do my job well.

_____ 5. I understand my boss's expectations and generally feel they are realistic.

_____ 6. I believe that rewards are distributed fairly, on the basis of performance.

_____ 7. The rewards and opportunities available to me if I perform well are attractive to me personally.

_____ 8. My supervisor indicates that I am not performing as well as I should, but I disagree.

_____ 9. I could do a much better job if I had more training.

_____ 10. I believe that my job is too difficult for my ability level.

_____ 11. I believe that my job performance is hindered by a lack of supplies and resources.

_____ 12. I believe my boss's expectations are unclear and unrealistic.

_____ 13. I believe my boss plays favorites in allocating rewards.

_____ 14. I do not find the rewards and opportunities available to high performers very appealing.

Increasing Motivation and Performance

Focus groups at Intermountain Health Care (IHC), a Utah-based health care organization with more than 23,000 employees, revealed that a majority of front-line workers would not leave their jobs unless another employer offered them a 20 percent increase in pay and a 30 percent increase in benefits. Such commitment and motivation toward employed work is an extremely valued commodity in our current economy. Most organizations struggle to retain their best employees and to motivate them to high performance. The comments from three front-line workers at IHC reveal that their commitment has been won through the motivating and rewarding work environment they experience and the values IHC reinforces (Interview with Alison Mackey).

"I have never worked at a place where people have been so concerned about their employees. And because of that we can turn around and give the same to our customers."

"I think [IHC] is a system that's concerned about its employees and as a result it can attract employees with strong technical and people-based knowledge and experience."

"The values that IHC stands for make me never want to leave" (IHC Employee Opinion Survey Database).

The efforts IHC has taken to create such a motivating work environment have improved its clinical care and its bottom line. *Modern Healthcare* honored IHC in January 2000 as the number-one integrated health care system in America. President and Chief Executive Officer (CEO) William H. Nelson attributes its clinical success and national recognition to its employees (IHC Annual Report, 1999).

Organizations like IHC that have highly motivated and committed employees are well equipped to compete in any market, be it health care or heavy industry. But like any distinctive competence, employee commitment is difficult to achieve—if it were otherwise it would have no competitive value. The focus of this chapter is on creating work environments where employees are highly productive and highly motivated.

After winning an unprecedented seventh NBA title as a coach, Phil Jackson was asked what his method was for motivating professional basketball players. "I don't motivate my players. You cannot motivate someone, all you can do is provide a motivating environment and the players will motivate themselves" (Jackson, 2000). We believe the imagery of "manager-as-coach" and "motivation-as-facilitation" suggested by this interview with one of the most successful coaches of our time provides the appropriate backdrop for our discussion. Whether managers are working with a group of steel workers, computer programmers, artists, or basketball players, they face a common challenge of fostering a motivating work environment.

The core of this chapter outlines a six-step process for accomplishing this goal. But first, to set the stage for this discussion, we begin with one of the most nettlesome problems facing managers—how to correctly identify the underlying causes of a specific employee's poor performance.

Diagnosing Work Performance Problems

Let's begin by examining the case for managers sharpening their skills for diagnosing work performance problems. There is a tendency for supervisors to attribute the cause of poor performance to low motivation (Bitter & Gardner, 1995). That is, when employees fail to meet performance expectations, supervisors tend to blame this outcome on insufficient effort—often expressed in terms of a lack of interest or commitment. The tendency to make assumptions about why things happen, without the benefit of scrutiny, is an example of what psychologists call an attribution (Ross, 1977; Choi, Nisbett, & Norenzayan, 1999). Because supervisors generally believe that if they work harder they will perform better, they assume their own experience applies to other organizational positions and work environments. The problem with this approach to problem diagnosis is that it lends itself to simplistic solutions, reminiscent of the Chinese proverb, "For every hundred men hacking away at the leaves of a diseased tree, only one man stoops to inspect the roots."

Let's consider one increasingly common set of work conditions that illustrates the need to "stoop and inspect the roots" of observed poor worker performance. It is estimated that one-third of American workers are assigned to irregular schedules (often involving night work), commonly known as shift work. In a recent article on the challenges facing shift workers, the story was told of a supervisor who sought permission from the human resources department to fire a worker because he didn't "stay on task," often walked around talking to others, and occasionally fell asleep on the job. Research on shift workers suggests the need to look beyond a simplistic "poor performance equals low motivation and commitment" explanation for this worker's unacceptable behavior. For example, shift workers sleep two to three hours less per night than day workers, they are four to five times more likely to experience digestive disorders due to eating the wrong foods at the wrong times, chronic fatigue is reported by 80 percent of shift workers, 75 percent of shift workers report feeling isolated on the job, and drug and alcohol abuse are three times greater among permanent shift workers (Perry, 2000).

To avoid falling prey to simplistic, ill-informed diagnoses of work performance problems, managers need a model, or framework, to guide their inquiry process. Various organizational scholars (e.g., Gerhart, 2003; Steers, Porter, & Bigley, 1996; Vroom, 1964) have summarized the determinants of task performance as follows:

$$Performance = Ability \times Motivation\ (Effort)$$

where

$$Ability = Aptitude \times Training \times Resources$$

$$Motivation = Desire \times Commitment$$

According to these formulas, **performance** is the product of ability multiplied by motivation, **ability** is the product of aptitude multiplied by training and resources, and **motivation** is the product of desire and commitment. The multiplicative function in these formulas suggests that all elements are essential. For example, workers who have 100 percent of the motivation and 75 percent of the ability required to perform a task can perform at an above-average rate. However, if these individuals have only 10 percent of the ability required, no amount of motivation will enable them to perform satisfactorily.

Aptitude refers to the native skills and abilities a person brings to a job. These involve physical and mental capabilities; but for many people-oriented jobs, they also include personality characteristics. Most of our inherent abilities can be enhanced by education and *training*. Indeed, much of what we call native ability in adults can be traced to previous skill-enhancement

experiences, such as modeling the social skills of parents or older siblings. Nevertheless, it is useful to consider training as a separate component of ability, since it represents an important mechanism for improving employee performance. Ability should be assessed during the job-matching process by screening applicants against the skill requirements of the job. If an applicant has minor deficiencies in skill aptitude but many other desirable characteristics, an intensive training program can be used to increase the applicant's qualifications to perform the job.

Our definition of ability is broader than most. We are focusing on the ability to perform, rather than the performer's ability. Therefore, our definition includes a third, situational component: adequate *resources*. Frequently, highly capable and well-trained individuals are placed in situations that inhibit job performance. Specifically, they aren't given the resources (technical, personnel, political) to perform assigned tasks effectively.

Motivation represents an employee's *desire* and *commitment* to perform and is manifested in job-related effort. Some people want to complete a task but are easily distracted or discouraged. They have high desire but low commitment. Others plod along with impressive persistence, but their work is uninspired. These people have high commitment but low desire.

The first diagnostic question that must be asked by the supervisor of a poor performer is whether the person's performance deficiencies stem from lack of ability or lack of motivation. Managers need four pieces of information in order to answer this question (Michener, Fleishman, & Vaske, 1976):

1. How difficult are the tasks being assigned to the individual?
2. How capable is the individual?
3. How hard is the individual trying to succeed at the job?
4. How much improvement is the individual making?

In terms of these four questions, low ability is generally associated with very difficult tasks, overall low individual ability, evidence of strong effort, and lack of improvement over time.

The answer to the question "Is this an ability or motivation problem?" has far-reaching ramifications for manager-subordinate relations. Research on this topic has shown that managers tend to apply more pressure to a person if they feel that the person is deliberately not performing up to expectations, rather than not performing effectively due to external, uncontrollable forces. Managers sometimes justify their choice of a forceful influence strategy on the grounds that the subordinate has a poor attitude, is hostile to authority, or lacks dedication.

Unfortunately, if the manager's assessment is incorrect and poor performance is related to ability rather than motivation, the response to increased pressure will worsen the problem. If poor performers feel that management is insensitive to their problems—that they lack resources, adequate training, or realistic time schedules—they may respond counterproductively to any tactics aimed at increasing their effort. Quite likely they will develop a motivational problem—that is, their desire and commitment will decrease—in response to management's insensitive, "iron-fisted" actions. Seeing this response, management will feel that their original diagnosis is confirmed, and they will use even stronger forms of influence to force compliance. The resulting vicious cycle is extremely difficult to break and underscores the high stakes involved in accurately diagnosing poor performance problems.

In this chapter, we will examine the two components of performance in more detail, beginning with ability. We'll discuss manifestations of low ability and poor motivation, their causes, and some proposed remedies. We'll devote more attention to motivation, since motivation is more central to day-to-day manager-subordinate interactions. While ability tends to remain stable over long periods of time, motivation fluctuates; therefore, it requires closer monitoring and frequent recharging.

Enhancing Individuals' Abilities

A person's lack of ability might inhibit good performance for several reasons. Ability may have been assessed improperly during the screening process prior to employment, the technical requirements of a job may have been radically upgraded, or a person who performed very well in one position may have been promoted into a higher-level position that is too demanding. (The Peter Principle states that people are typically promoted one position above their level of competence.) In addition, human and material resource support may have been reduced because of organizational budget cutbacks.

As noted by Quick (1977, 1991), managers should be alert for individuals who show signs of ability deterioration. Following are three danger signals for management positions:

1. **Taking refuge in a specialty.** Managers show signs of insufficient ability when they respond to situations not by managing, but by retreating to their technical specialty. This often occurs when general managers who feel insecure address problems outside their area of expertise and experience. Anthony Jay, in *Management and Machiavelli* (1967), dubs this type of manager "George I," after the King of England who, after assuming the throne, continued to be preoccupied with the affairs of Hanover, Germany, whence he had come.

2. **Focusing on past performance.** Another danger sign is measuring one's value to the organization in terms of past performance or on the basis of former standards. Some cavalry commanders in World War I relied on their outmoded knowledge of how to conduct successful military campaigns and, as a result, failed miserably in mechanized combat. This form of obsolescence is common in organizations that fail to shift their mission in response to changing market conditions.

3. **Exaggerating aspects of the leadership role.** Managers who have lost confidence in their ability tend to be very defensive. This often leads them to exaggerate one aspect of their managerial role. Such managers might delegate most of their responsibilities because they no longer feel competent to perform them well. Or they might become nuts-and-bolts administrators who scrutinize every detail to an extent far beyond its practical value. Still others become "devil's advocates," but rather than stimulating creativity, their negativism thwarts efforts to change the familiar.

There are five principal tools available for overcoming poor performance problems due to lack of ability: *resupply, retrain, refit, reassign,* and *release.* We will discuss these in the order in which a manager should consider them.

Once a manager has ascertained that lack of ability is the primary cause of someone's poor performance, a performance review interview should be scheduled to explore these options, beginning with resupplying and retraining. Unless the manager has overwhelming evidence that the problem stems from low aptitude, it is wise to assume initially that it is due to a lack of resources or training. This gives the subordinate the benefit of the doubt and reduces the likely defensive reaction to an assessment of inadequate aptitude.

The **resupply** option focuses on the support needs of the job, including personnel, budget, and political clout. Asking "Do you have what you need to perform this job satisfactorily?" allows the subordinate to express his or her frustration related to inadequate support. Given the natural tendency for individuals to blame external causes for their mistakes, managers should explore their subordinates' complaints about lack of support in detail to determine their validity. Even if employees exaggerate their claims, starting your discussion of poor performance in this manner signals your willingness to help them solve the problem from their perspective rather than to find fault from your perspective.

The next least threatening option is to **retrain**. American companies with more than 100 employees budgeted in excess of $60 billion for formal training. To deliver this training, these firms spent $42 billion on corporate trainers and an additional $14.3 billion on commercial trainers (Reese, 1999; Tomlinson, 2002). This is a sizeable expenditure for American corporations, but the reasons for these expenditures are clear. First of all, technology is changing so quickly that employees' skills can soon become obsolete. It has been estimated that 50 percent of employees' skills become outdated within three to five years (Moe & Blodget, 2000). Second, employees will typically fill a number of different positions throughout their careers, each demanding different proficiencies. Finally, demographic changes in our society will lead to an increasingly older workforce. In order for companies to remain competitive, more and more of them must retrain their older employees.

Training programs can take a variety of forms. For example, many firms are using computer technology more in education. This can involve interactive technical instruction and business games that simulate problems likely to be experienced by managers in the organization. More traditional forms of training include subsidized university courses and in-house technical or management seminars. Some companies have experimented with company sabbaticals to release managers or senior technical specialists from the pressures of work so they can concentrate on retooling. The most rapidly increasing form of training is "distance learning," in which formal courses are offered over the Internet. Web-based corporate learning is expected to soon top $11 billion (Moe & Blodget, 2000). In a recent report, the U.S. Department of Education stated that 1,680 academic institutions offered 54,000 online courses in 1998—for which 1.6 million students enrolled. That marked a 70 percent increase since 1995 (Boehle, Dobbs, & Stamps, 2000).

In many cases, resupplying and retraining are insufficient remedies for poor performance. When this happens, the next step should be to explore **refitting** poor performers to their task assignments. While the subordinates remain on the job, the components of their work are analyzed, and different combinations of tasks and abilities that accomplish organizational objectives and provide meaningful and rewarding work are explored. For example, an assistant may be brought in to handle many of the technical details of a first-line supervisor's position, freeing up more time for the supervisor to focus on people development or to develop a long-term plan to present to upper management.

If a revised job description is unworkable or inadequate, the fourth alternative is to **reassign** the poor performer, either to a position of less responsibility or to one requiring less technical knowledge or interpersonal skills. For example, a medical specialist in a hospital who finds it increasingly difficult to keep abreast of new medical procedures but has demonstrated management skills might be shifted to a full-time administrative position.

The last option is to **release**. If retraining and creative redefinition of task assignments have not worked and if there are no opportunities for reassignment in the organization, the manager should consider releasing the employee from the organization. This option is generally constrained by union agreements, company policies, seniority considerations, and government regulations. Frequently, however, chronic poor performers who could be released are not because management chooses to sidestep a potentially unpleasant task. Instead, the decision is made to set these individuals "on the shelf," out of the mainstream of activities, where they can't cause any problems. Even when this action is motivated by humanitarian concerns ("I don't think he could cope with being terminated"), it often produces the opposite effect. Actions taken to protect an unproductive employee from the embarrassment of termination just substitute the humiliation of being ignored. Obviously, termination is a drastic action that should not be taken lightly. However, the consequences for the unproductive individuals and their coworkers of allowing them to remain after the previous four actions have proven unsuccessful should be weighed carefully in considering this option.

This approach to managing ability problems is reflected in the philosophy of Wendell Parsons, CEO of Stamp-Rite. He argues that one of the most challenging aspects of management is helping employees recognize that job enhancements and advancements are not always possible. Therefore, he says, "If a long-term employee slows down, I try to turn him around by saying how much I value his knowledge and experience, but pointing out that his production has slipped too much. If boredom has set in and I can't offer the employee a change, I encourage him to face the fact and consider doing something else with his life" (Nelton, 1988).

Fostering a Motivating Work Environment

The second component of employee performance is motivation. While it is important to see to the training and the support needs of subordinates and to be actively involved in the hiring and the job-matching processes to ensure adequate aptitude, the influence of a manager's actions on the day-to-day motivation of subordinates is equally vital. Effective managers devote considerable time to gauging and strengthening their subordinates' motivation, as reflected in their effort and concern.

In one of the seminal contributions to management thought, Douglas McGregor (1960) introduced the term *Theory X* to refer to a management style characterized by close supervision. The basic assumption of this theory is that people really do not want to work hard or assume responsibility. Therefore, in order to get the job done, managers must coerce, intimidate, manipulate, and closely supervise their employees. In contrast, McGregor espouses a *Theory Y* view of workers. He argues workers basically want to do a good job and assume more responsibility; therefore, management's role is to assist workers to reach their potential by productively channeling their motivation to succeed. Unfortunately, McGregor believes most managers subscribe to *Theory X* assumptions about workers' motives.

The alleged prevalence of the *Theory X* view brings up an interesting series of questions about motivation. What is the purpose of teaching motivation skills to managers? Should managers learn these skills so they can help employees reach their potential? Or are we teaching these skills to managers so they can more effectively manipulate their employees' behavior? These questions naturally lead to a broader set of issues regarding employee-management relations. Assuming a manager feels responsible for maintaining a given level of productivity, is it also possible to be concerned about the needs and desires of employees? In other words, are concerns about employee morale and company productivity compatible, or are they mutually exclusive?

Contemporary research, as well as the experience of highly acclaimed organizational motivation programs (Harter, Schmidt, & Hayes, 2002), supports the position that concerns about morale and performance can coexist. As Figure 6.1 shows, effective motivational programs not only can, but must focus on increasing both satisfaction and productivity. A high emphasis on satisfaction with a low emphasis on performance represents an irresponsible view of the role of management. Managers are hired by owners to look after the owners' interests. This entails holding employees accountable for producing satisfactory results. Managers who emphasize satisfaction to the exclusion of performance will be seen as nice people, but their **indulging** management style undermines the performance of their subordinates.

Bob Knowling, former head of a group of internal change agents at Ameritech that reported directly to the CEO, joined US West in February 1996 as vice president of network operations and technology. His new job was to lead more than 20,000 employees in a large-scale change effort to improve service to US West's more than 25 million customers.

When asked what the biggest challenge facing companies is, even successful ones, he responded: "For me, it begins with changing a culture of entitlement into

| Figure 6.1 | Relationship Between Satisfaction and Performance |

a culture of accountability. My first week on the job [at US West], it was immediately apparent that nobody had been accountable for the reengineering effort. Beyond that, no one had been accountable for meeting customer expectations or for adhering to a cost structure. It was acceptable to miss budgets. Service was in the tank, we were overspending our budgets by more than $100 million—yet people weren't losing their jobs and they still got all or some of their bonuses. That's very much like Ameritech had been. When people failed, we moved them to human resources or sent them to international. When I got to US West, I felt like I was walking into the same bad movie" (Tichy, 1997).

A strong emphasis on performance to the exclusion of satisfaction is equally ineffective. This time, instead of indulging, the manager is **imposing**. In this situation, managers have little concern for how employees feel about their jobs. The boss issues orders, and the employees must follow them. Exploited employees are unhappy employees, and unhappy employees may seek employment with the competition. Thus, while exploitation may increase productivity in the short run, its long-term effects generally decrease productivity through increased absenteeism, employee turnover, and in some cases, even sabotage and violence.

Jim Stuart, who ran several companies before accepting the position of executive director of the Florida Aquarium in 1995, reflected on how life's experiences convinced him to alter his authoritarian leadership style:

My classmates at Harvard Business School used to call me the Prussian General: For many years, that was my approach to leadership. Then I was hit by a series of personal tragedies and professional setbacks. My wife died. A mail-order venture that I had started went bankrupt. The universe was working hard to bring a little humility into my life. Rather than launch another business, I accepted a friend's offer to head an aquarium project in Tampa. I spent the next six years in a job that gave me no power, no money, and no knowledge. That situation forced me to draw on a deeper part of myself. We ended up with a team of people who were so high-performing that they could almost walk through walls. Why, I wondered, was I suddenly able to lead a team that was so much more resilient and creative than any team that I had run before? The answer: Somewhere, amid all of my trials, I had begun to trust my colleagues as much as I trusted myself. (McCauley, 1999)

When managers emphasize neither satisfaction nor performance, they are **ignoring** their responsibilities and the facts at hand. The resulting neglect reflects a lack of management. There is no real leadership, in the sense that employees receive neither priorities nor direction. Paralyzed between what they consider to be mutually exclusive options of emphasizing performance or satisfaction, managers choose neither. The resulting neglect, if allowed to continue, may ultimately lead to the failure of the work unit.

The **integrating** motivation strategy emphasizes performance and satisfaction equally. Effective managers are able to combine what appear to be competing forces into integrative, synergistic programs. Instead of accepting the conventional wisdom that says competing forces cancel each other out, they capitalize on the tension between the combined elements to forge new approaches creatively. However, this does not mean that both objectives can be fully satisfied in every specific case. Some trade-offs occur naturally in ongoing work situations. However, in the long run, both objectives should be given equal consideration.

The integrative view of motivation proposes that while the importance of employees' feeling good about what they are doing and how they are being treated cannot be downplayed, this concern should not overshadow management's responsibility to hold people accountable for results. Managers should avoid the twin traps of working to engender high employee morale for its own sake or pushing for short-term results at the expense of long-term commitment. The best managers have productive people who are also satisfied with their work environment (Kotter, 1996).

Elements of an Effective Motivation Program

We now turn to the core of this discussion: a step-by-step program for creating an integrative, synergistic motivational program grounded in the belief that employees can simultaneously be high performers and personally satisfied. The key assumptions underlying our framework are summarized in Table 6.1.

It is useful to note the prevailing wisdom among organizational scholars regarding the relationships between motivation, satisfaction, and performance has changed dramatically over the past several decades. When the authors took their first academic courses on this subject, they were taught the following model:

Satisfaction → Motivation → Performance

Table 6.1	Key Assumptions Underlying Our Framework

1. Employees typically start out motivated. Therefore, a lack of motivation is a learned response, often fostered by misunderstood or unrealistic expectations.

2. The role of management is to create a supportive, problem-solving work environment in which facilitation, not control, is the prevailing value.

3. Rewards should encourage high personal performance that is consistent with management objectives.

4. Motivation works best when it is based on self-governance.

5. Individuals should be treated fairly.

6. Individuals deserve timely, honest feedback on work performance.

However, over the course of our careers we have observed the following criticisms of this "contented cows give more milk" view of employee performance.

First, as researchers began collecting longitudinal data on the predictors of performance, they discovered that the satisfaction, motivation, performance causal logic was wrong. For reasons we will discuss later in this chapter, it is now believed that:

Motivation → Performance → Satisfaction

Second, the correlations among these three variables was very low, suggesting there were a large number of additional factors that needed to be added to this basic model. For example, we now know high performance leads to high satisfaction if workers believe that their organization reinforces high performance by contingently linking it to valued rewards. ("I want X and I am more likely to get X if I perform well.") In other words, performance leads to satisfaction when it is clear rewards are based on performance, as compared with seniority or membership. The addition of this intermediate link between performance and rewards (more generally referred to as outcomes) has so dramatically improved our understanding of the organizational dynamics associated with work performance that it has been incorporated into a revised model:

*Motivation → Performance →
Outcomes → Satisfaction*

The remainder of this chapter is basically an account of the improvements that have been made over the past few decades in this basic "four factors" model of work motivation. We will not only discuss in more detail the causal logic linking these core variables, but we will also introduce several additional factors that we now know must also be included in a comprehensive motivation program. For example, earlier in this chapter we introduced the notion that people's performance is a function of *both* their motivation and their ability. This suggests we need to add ability to the basic model as a second factor (besides motivation) contributing to performance. Each of the following sections of this chapter introduce additional variables that, like ability, need to be added to the basic, four-factor model. Table 6.2 shows the key building blocks of the complete model, in the form of six diagnostic questions, organized with reference to the "four-factor" model of motivation. A model encapsulating these questions will be used to summarize our presentation at the end of the chapter (Figure 6.5), and a diagnostic tool based on these questions will be described in the Skill Practice section (Figure 6.7).

ESTABLISH CLEAR PERFORMANCE EXPECTATIONS

As shown in Table 6.2, the first two elements of our comprehensive motivational program focus on the Motivation → Performance link. We begin by focusing on the manager's role in establishing clear expectations and then shift to the manager's role in enabling members of a work group to satisfy those expectations.

It is important to point out we're not just talking about hourly employees. Based on data collected since 1993, Right Management Consultants reported that one-third of all managers who change jobs fail in their new positions within 18 months (Fisher, 2005). According to this study, the number-one tip for getting off to a good start is asking your boss exactly what's expected of you and how soon you're supposed to deliver it. In fact, there tends to be a negative correlation between the level of one's position in an organization and the likelihood of receiving a job description or detailed performance expectations. Too often the boss's attitude is, "I pay people to know without being told."

Discussions of goal setting often make reference to an insightful conversation between Alice in Wonderland and the Cheshire Cat. When confronted with a choice among crossing routes, Alice asked the Cat which one she should choose. In response, the Cat asked Alice where she was heading. Discovering Alice had no real destination in mind, the Cat appropriately advised her any choice would do. It is surprising how often

Table 6.2	Six Elements of an Integrative Motivation Program

MOTIVATION → PERFORMANCE

1. Establish moderately difficult goals that are understood and accepted.

   Ask: "Do subordinates understand and accept my performance expectations?"

2. Remove personal and organizational obstacles to performance.

   Ask: "Do subordinates feel it is possible to achieve this goal or expectation?"

PERFORMANCE → OUTCOMES

3. Use rewards and discipline appropriately to extinguish unacceptable behavior and encourage exceptional performance.

   Ask: "Do subordinates feel that being a high performer is more rewarding than being a low or average performer?"

OUTCOMES → SATISFACTION

4. Provide salient internal and external incentives.

   Ask: "Do subordinates feel the rewards used to encourage high performance are worth the effort?"

5. Distribute rewards equitably.

   Ask: "Do subordinates feel that work-related benefits are being distributed fairly?"

6. Provide timely rewards and specific, accurate, and honest feedback on performance.

   Ask: "Are we getting the most out of our rewards by administering them on a timely basis as part of the feedback process?"

   Ask: "Do subordinates know where they stand in terms of current performance and long-term opportunities?"

supervisors violate the commonsense notion that they need to make sure individuals under their charge not only understand which road they should take but what constitutes an acceptable pace for the journey.

With this parable in mind, managers should begin assessing the motivational climate of their work environment by asking, "Is there agreement on, and acceptance of, performance expectations?" The foundation of an effective motivation program is proper **goal setting** (Locke & Latham, 2002). Across many studies of group performance it was shown that the average performance of groups that set goals is significantly higher than that of groups that didn't set goals. Goal-setting theory suggests goals are associated with enhanced performance because they mobilize effort, direct attention, and encourage persistence and strategy development (Sue-Chan & Ong, 2002). The salience of goal setting is so well recognized that it has been incorporated in several formal management tools, such as management by objectives (MBO). Effective goal setting has three critical components: *goal-setting process, goal characteristics*, and *feedback*.

A common theme in this book is, "The way you do things is very often as important as what you do." Applied to the **goal-setting process**, this means the manner by which goals are established must be considered carefully. The basic maxim is goals must be both understood and accepted if they are to be effective. To that end, research has shown subordinates are more likely to "buy into" goals if they feel they are part of the goal-setting process. It has been well documented that the performance of work groups is higher when groups choose their goals rather than have them assigned (Sue-Chan & Ong, 2002).

The motivating potential of chosen goals is especially important if the work environment is unfavorable for goal accomplishment (Latham, Erez, & Locke, 1988). For example, a goal might be inconsistent with accepted practice, require new skills, or exacerbate poor management-employee relations. To be sure, if working conditions are highly conducive to goal accomplishment, subordinates may be willing to commit themselves to the achievement of goals in whose formulation they did not participate. However, such acceptance usually occurs only when management demonstrates an overall attitude of understanding and support. When management does not exhibit a supportive attitude, the imposed goals or task assignments are likely to be viewed as unwelcome demands. As a result, subordinates will question the premises underlying the goals or assignments and will comply only reluctantly with the demands.

Sometimes it is difficult to allow for extensive participation in the establishment of work goals. For example, a manager frequently is given directions regarding new tasks or assignment deadlines that must be passed on. However, if subordinates believe management is committed to involving them in all discretionary aspects of the governance of their work unit, they are more willing to accept top-down directions regarding the nondiscretionary aspects of work assignments. For example, a computer programming unit may not have any say about which application programs are assigned to the group or what priority is assigned each incoming assignment. However, the manager can still involve unit members in deciding how much time to allocate to each assignment ("What is a realistic goal for completing this task?") or who should receive which job assignment ("Which type of programs would you find challenging?").

Shifting from process to content, research has shown that **goal characteristics** significantly affect the likelihood that the goal will be accomplished (Locke & Latham, 2002). Effective goals are *specific, consistent*, and *appropriately challenging*.

Goals that are **specific** are measurable, unambiguous, and behavioral. Specific goals reduce misunderstanding about what behaviors will be rewarded. Admonitions such as "be dependable," "work hard," "take initiative," or "do your best" are too general and too difficult to measure and are therefore of limited motivational value. In contrast, when a new vice president of operations was appointed at a major midwestern steel factory, he targeted three goals: Reduce finished product rejection by 15 percent (quality); reduce average shipment period by two days (customer satisfaction); and respond to all employee suggestions within 48 hours (employee involvement).

Goals should also be **consistent**. An already hardworking assistant vice president in a large metropolitan bank complains she cannot increase both the number of reports she writes in a week and the amount of time she spends "on the floor," visiting with employees and customers. Goals that are inconsistent—in the sense that they are logically impossible to accomplish simultaneously—or incompatible—in the sense that they both require so much effort they can't be accomplished at the same time—create frustration and alienation. When subordinates complain goals are incompatible or inconsistent, managers should be flexible enough to reconsider their expectations.

One of the most important characteristics of goals is that they are **appropriately challenging** (Knight, Durham, & Locke, 2001). Simply stated, hard goals are

more motivating than easy goals. One explanation for this is called "achievement motivation" (Atkinson, 1992; Weiner, 2000). According to this perspective, workers size up new tasks in terms of their chances for success and the significance of the anticipated accomplishment.

Based only on perceived likelihood of success, one would predict that those who seek success would choose an easy task to perform because the probability for success is the highest. However, these individuals also factor into their decisions the significance of completing the task. To complete a goal anyone can reach is not rewarding enough for highly motivated individuals. In order for them to feel successful, they must believe an accomplishment represents a meaningful achievement. Given their desire for success and achievement, it is clear these workers will be most motivated by challenging, but reachable, goals.

Although there is no single standard of difficulty that fits all people, it is important to keep in mind high expectations generally foster high performance and low expectations decrease performance (Davidson & Eden, 2000). As one experienced manager said, "We get about what we expect." Warren Bennis, author of *The Unconscious Conspiracy: Why Leaders Can't Lead*, agrees. "In a study of schoolteachers, it turned out that when they held high expectations of their students, that alone was enough to cause an increase of 25 points in the students' IQ scores" (Bennis, 1984, 2003).

In addition to selecting the right type of goal, an effective goal program must also include **feedback**. Feedback provides opportunities for clarifying expectations, adjusting goal difficulty, and gaining recognition. Therefore, it is important to provide benchmark opportunities for individuals to determine how they are doing. These along-the-way progress reports are particularly critical when the time required to complete an assignment or reach a goal is very long. For example, feedback is very useful for projects such as writing a large computer program or raising a million dollars for a local charity. In these cases, feedback should be linked to accomplishing intermediate stages or completing specific components.

REMOVE OBSTACLES TO PERFORMANCE

One of the key ingredients of an effective goal program is a supportive work environment. After setting goals, managers should shift their focus to facilitating successful accomplishment by focusing on the ability part of the performance formula. From a diagnostic perspective, this can be done by asking, "Do subordinates feel it is possible to achieve this goal?" Help from management must come in many forms, including making sure the worker has the aptitude required for the job, providing the necessary training, securing needed resources, and encouraging cooperation and support from other work units. It is the manager's job to make the paths leading toward the targeted goals easier for the subordinate to travel.

This management philosophy can be illustrated readily with examples from sports. Instead of assuming the role of the star quarterback who expects the rest of the team to make him look good, the facilitative manager is more like the blocking fullback or the pulling guard who specializes in downfield blocking and punching holes in the opposition's defenses. In a basketball example, this type of leader is like the player who takes more pride in his number of assists than in the number of points he has scored.

However, as with all general management guidelines, effective results follow from sensitive, informed implementation tailored to specific circumstances. In this case, the manner in which this enabling, facilitative role should be implemented varies considerably among individuals, organizational settings, and tasks. When subordinates believe strong management support is needed, leaders who are not aware of the obstacles to performance, or not assertive enough to remove them, probably will be perceived as part of the employee's problem, rather than the source of solutions. By the same token, when management intervention is not

needed or expected, managers who are constantly involved in the details of subordinates' job performance will be viewed as meddling and unwilling to trust. This view of management is incorporated in the "path goal" theory of leadership (House & Mitchell, 1974; see also, Schriesheim & Neider, 1996; Shamir, House, & Arthur, 1993), shown in Figure 6.2. The key question it addresses is, "How much help should a manager provide?" In response, the model proposes that the level of involvement should vary according to how much subordinates need to perform a specific task; how much they expect, in general; and how much support is available to them from other organizational sources.

The key task characteristics of the path-goal model are structure and difficulty. A task that is highly structured, as reflected in the degree of built-in order and direction, and relatively easy to perform does not require extensive management direction. If managers offer too much advice, they will come across as controlling, bossy, or nagging, because from the nature of the task itself, it is already clear to the subordinates what they should do. On the other hand, for an unstructured and difficult task, management's direction and strong involvement in problem-solving activities will be seen as constructive and satisfying.

The second factor that influences the appropriate degree of management involvement is the expectations of the subordinates. Three distinct characteristics influence expectations: desire for autonomy, experience, and ability. Individuals who prize their autonomy and

Figure 6.2 | Leader Involvement and Subordinate Performance

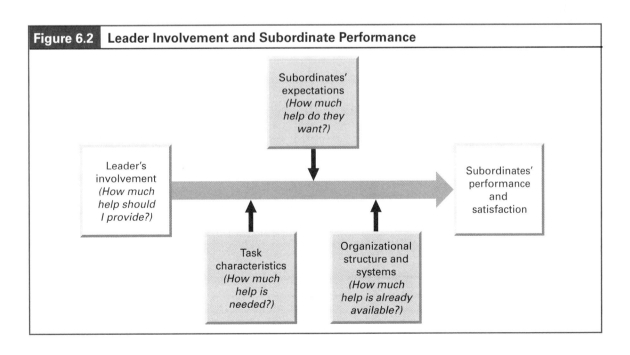

independence prefer managers with a highly participative leadership style because it gives them more latitude for controlling what they do. In contrast, people who prefer the assistance of others in making decisions, establishing priorities, and solving problems prefer greater management involvement.

The connection between a worker's ability and experience levels and preferred management style is straightforward. Capable and experienced employees feel they need less assistance from their managers because they are adequately trained, know how to obtain the necessary resources, and can handle political entanglements with their counterparts in other units. They appreciate managers who "give them their head" but periodically check to see if further assistance is required. On the other hand, it is frustrating for relatively new employees, or those with marginal skills, to feel that their manager has neither the time nor interest to listen to basic questions.

An important concept in the path-goal approach to leadership is management involvement should complement, rather than duplicate, organizational sources of support. Specifically, managers should provide more "downfield blocking" in situations wherein work-group norms governing performance are not clear, organizational rewards for performance are insufficient, and organizational controls governing performance are inadequate.

One of the important lessons from this discussion of the path-goal model is managers must tailor their management style to specific conditions, such as those shown in Table 6.3. Although managers should focus on facilitating task accomplishment, their level of direct involvement should be calibrated to the nature of the work and the availability of organizational support, as well as the ability and experience of the individuals. If managers are insensitive to these contingencies, they probably will be perceived by some subordinates as interfering with their desires to explore their own way, while others will feel lost.

This conclusion underscores how important it is that managers understand the needs and expectations of their subordinates. Bill Dyer, a leading business consultant, observed that effective managers regularly ask their subordinates three simple questions: "How is your work going?" "What do you enjoy the most/least?" "How can I help you succeed?" Asking these questions communicates a supportive style; hearing the answers allows managers to fine-tune their facilitative actions.

REINFORCE PERFORMANCE-ENHANCING BEHAVIOR

Referring back to the basic "four-factor" model of motivation, we now shift our focus from the antecedents of work performance (the Motivation → Performance link) to its consequences (the Performance → Outcomes link). Once clear goals have been established and the paths to goal completion have been cleared by management, the next step in an effective motivational program is to encourage goal accomplishment by contingently linking performance to extrinsic outcomes (rewards and discipline) and fostering intrinsic outcomes. Given our overall emphasis in this book on improving management skills that are used day in and day out, the majority of this section will focus on linking performance to extrinsic outcomes.

Table 6.3	Factors Influencing Management Involvement		
CONTINGENCIES	CONDITIONS APPROPRIATE FOR HIGH MANAGEMENT INVOLVEMENT	CONDITIONS APPROPRIATE FOR LOW MANAGEMENT INVOLVEMENT
Task structure	Low	High
Task mastery	Low	High
Subordinate's desire for autonomy	Low	High
Subordinate's experience	Low	High
Subordinate's ability	Low	High
Strength of group norms	Low	High
Effectiveness of organization's controls and rewards	Low	High

The relevant diagnostic question here is, "Do subordinates feel being a high performer is more rewarding than being a low or average performer?" Our discussion of this important element of an effective motivational program is based on two related principles: (1) in general, managers should link rewards to performance, rather than seniority or membership; and (2) managers should use discipline to extinguish counterproductive behaviors and use rewards to reinforce productive behaviors.

Use Rewards as Reinforcers

Here is the key to encouraging high performance: behaviors that positively affect performance should be contingently reinforced, using highly desirable rewards. When rewards are linked to desired behaviors, they reinforce (strengthen; increase the frequency of) that behavior (Luthans & Stajkovic, 1999; Stajkovic & Luthans, 2001). If an organization rewards all people identically, or on some basis other than performance, then high performers are likely to feel they are receiving fewer "rewards" than they deserve. Obviously, high performers are the key to the success of any organization. Therefore, motivational schemes should be geared to keeping this employee group satisfied. This observation has led some organizational consultants to use the performance ratings of individuals leaving an organization as an index of the organization's motivational climate.

Ed Lawler, one of the foremost authorities on reward systems, underscored this point when he said, "Often the early reward systems of an organization are particularly important in shaping its culture. They reinforce certain behavior patterns and signal how highly valued different individuals are by the organization. They also attract a certain type of employee and in a host of little ways indicate what the organization stands for and values" (Lawler, 2000a, p. 39).

The principle that rewards should be linked to performance points to a need for caution regarding the practice in some organizations of minimizing distinctions between workers. Some "progressive" organizations have received considerable publicity for motivational programs that include providing recreational facilities, library services, day care, and attractive stock option programs for all employees. These organizations work hard to reduce status distinctions by calling everyone "associates" or "partners," eliminating reserved parking places, and instituting a company uniform. Although there are obvious motivational benefits from employees feeling they are receiving basically the same benefits ("perks") regardless of seniority or level of authority, this

motivational philosophy, when carried to an extreme or implemented indiscriminately, runs the risk of undermining the motivation of high performers. In an era of egalitarianism, managers often overlook the vital link between performance and rewards and as a consequence find it difficult to attract and retain strong performers (Pfeffer, 1995).

Fortunately, many firms recognize this pitfall. In a survey, 42 percent of 125 organizations contacted indicated they had made changes in their compensation plan during the previous three years to achieve a better link between pay and performance (Murlis & Wright, 1985). These respondents reported an interesting set of pressures were prompting them to move in this direction. Hard-charging, typically younger managers were insisting on tighter control over employee performance; executives were determined to "get more bang for the buck" during periods of shrinking resources; personnel managers were trying to reduce the number of grievances focusing on "unfair" pay decisions; and employees were trying to eliminate what they considered to be discrimination in the workplace.

A sampling of the creative methods firms are using to establish closer connections between individual performance and pay includes sales commissions that include follow-up customer satisfaction ratings; pay increases linked to the acquisition of new knowledge, skills, and/or demonstrated competencies; compensating managers based on their ability to mentor new group members and resolve difficult intergroup relationships; and linking the pay of key employees to the accomplishment of new organizational goals or strategic initiatives (Zingheim & Schuster, 1995).

In an attempt to examine the impact of one of these innovative compensation programs, a study was conducted in which the productivity, quality, and labor costs of companies using skill-based pay were compared with comparable firms. The results indicated that firms using this type of pay plan benefited from 58 percent greater productivity, 16 percent lower labor costs per part produced, and an 82 percent better level of quality (Murray & Gerhart, 1998).

Technological constraints sometimes make it difficult to perfectly link individual performance with individual rewards. For example, people working on an automobile assembly line or chemists working on a group research project have little control over their personal productivity. In these situations, rewards linked to the performance of the work group will foster group cohesion and collaboration and partially satisfy the individual members' concerns about fairness (Lawler, 1988, 2000b). When it is not possible to assess the performance of a work group (work shift, organizational department), it is advisable to consider an organization-wide performance bonus. While the merits and technical details of various group and organizational reward systems are beyond the scope of this chapter, managers should link valued rewards and good performance at the most appropriate level of aggregation (Steers et al., 1996).

This discussion of the appropriate unit for measuring and rewarding performance reminds us of the need to take into consideration cultural values and expectations. For example, individuals from collectivist cultures tend to see the group as the appropriate target for improving performance (Graham & Trevor, 2000; Parker, 2001; Triandis, 1994). This implies that in addition to examining contextual factors that might make it difficult to reward individual workers, it is also important to take into consideration different culturally based assumptions about what is the appropriate unit of analysis (group or individual) for measuring and rewarding performance. If a manager of a sales department is concerned about heading off a slump in new orders that has traditionally occurred in the organization during the coming eight-week period, and if she has reason to believe department members would respond positively to a bonus program targeting that time period, she still has to decide if the bonus should be linked to group performance or individual performance. If this particular work unit consists of a mixture of individuals holding collectivist and individualist value perspectives, the manager should look for ways to factor these conflicting perspectives into the design of the bonus program.

It is also important to point out that nonfinancial rewards (often treated as awards) need to be included in an effective performance-reinforcing program. Lawler argues firms will get the greatest motivational impact from awards programs if they follow these guidelines: (1) give the awards publicly, (2) use awards infrequently, (3) embed them in a credible reward process, (4) use the awards presentation to acknowledge past recipients, and (5) make sure the award is meaningful within the organization's culture (Lawler, 2000a, p. 72–73).

The Role of Managers' Actions as Reinforcers

An effective motivational program goes beyond the design of the formal organizational reward system, including such things as pay, promotions, and the like. Managers must also recognize that their daily interactions with subordinates constitute an important source of motivation. It is difficult for even highly sensitive and aware managers to understand fully the impact of their actions on the behavior and attitudes of subordinates. Unfortunately, some managers don't even try to monitor these effects. The danger of this lack of awareness is it may lead to managerial actions that actually reinforce undesirable behaviors in their subordinates. This has been called "the folly of rewarding A while hoping for B" (Kerr, 1995). For example, a vice president of research and development with a low tolerance for conflict and uncertainty may unwittingly undermine the company's avowed objective of developing highly creative products by punishing work groups that do not exhibit unity or a clear, consistent set of priorities. Further, while avowing the virtue of risk, the manager may punish failure; while stressing creativity, he or she may kill the spirit of the idea champion. These actions will encourage a work group to avoid challenging projects, suppress debate, and routinize task performance.

The dos and don'ts for encouraging subordinates to assume more initiative, shown in Table 6.4, demonstrate the power of managers' actions in shaping behavior. Actions and reactions that might appear insignificant to the boss often have strong reinforcing or extinguishing effects on subordinates. Hence the truism, "Managers get what they reinforce, not what they want," and its companion, "People do what is inspected, not what is expected." Indeed, the reinforcing potential of managers' reactions to subordinates' behaviors is so strong that it has been argued, "The best way to change an individual's behavior in a work setting is to change his or her manager's behavior" (Thompson, 1978, p. 52). Given the considerable leverage managers have over their subordinates' motivation to reach optimal performance, it is important that they learn how to use rewards and punishments effectively to produce positive, intended results consistently.

Use Rewards and Discipline Appropriately

Psychologists call the process of linking rewards and punishments with behaviors in such a manner that the behaviors are more or less likely to persist "operant conditioning" (Komaki, Coombs, & Schepman, 1996). This approach uses a wide variety of motivational strategies that involve the presentation or withdrawal of positive or negative reinforcers or the use of no reinforcement whatsoever. Although there are important theoretical and experimental differences in these strategies, such as between negative reinforcement and punishment, for

Table 6.4	Guidelines for Fostering Subordinate Initiative
Do	**Don't**
Ask "How are we going to do this? What can I contribute to this effort? How will we use this result?," thus implying your joint stake in the work and results.	Imply that the task is the employee's total responsibility, that they hang alone if they fail. Individual failure means organizational failure.
Use an interested, exploring manner, asking questions designed to bring out factual information.	Play the part of an interrogator, firing questions as rapidly as they can be answered. Also, avoid asking questions that require only "yes" or "no" replies.
Keep the analysis and evaluation as much in the employees' hands as possible by asking for their best judgment on various issues.	React to their presentations on an emotional basis.
Present facts about organization needs, commitments, strategy, and so on, which permit them to improve, and interest them in improving what they propose to do.	Demand a change or improvement in a preemptory tone of voice or on what appears to be an arbitrary basis.
Ask them to investigate or analyze further if you feel that they have overlooked some points or overemphasized others.	Take their planning papers and cross out, change dates, or mark "no good" next to certain activities.
Ask them to return with their plans after factoring these items in.	Redo their plans for them unless their repeated efforts show no improvement.

the purposes of our discussion we will focus on three types of management responses to employee behavior: no response (ignoring), negative response (disciplining), and positive response (rewarding).

The trickiest strategy to transfer from the psychologist's laboratory to the manager's work environment is "no response." Technically, what psychologists refer to as "extinction" is defined as a behavior followed by no response whatsoever. However, in most managerial situations, people develop expectations about what is likely to follow their actions based on their past experience, office stories, and so forth. Consequently, what is intended as a nonresponse, or a neutral response, generally is interpreted as either a positive or negative response. For example, if a subordinate comes into your office complaining bitterly about a coworker, and you attempt to discourage this type of behavior by changing the subject or responding in a low, unresponsive monotone voice, the subordinate may view this as a form of rejection. If your secretary sheepishly slips a delinquent report on your desk, and you ignore her behavior because you are busy with other business, she may be so relieved at not being reprimanded for her tardiness that she actually feels reinforced.

These simple examples underscore an important point: any behavior repeatedly exhibited in front of a boss is being rewarded, regardless of the boss's intention ("I don't want to encourage that type of behavior, so

I'm purposely ignoring it"). By definition, if a behavior persists, it is being reinforced. Thus, if an employee is chronically late or continually submits sloppy work, the manager must ask where the reinforcement for this behavior is coming from. Consequently, while extinction plays an important role in the learning process when conducted in strictly controlled laboratory conditions, it is a less useful technique in organizational settings because the interpretation of a supposedly neutral response is impossible to control. Thus, the focus of our discussion will be on the proper use of disciplining and rewarding strategies, as shown in Figure 6.3.

The **disciplining** approach involves responding negatively to an employee's behavior with the intention of discouraging future occurrences of that behavior. For example, if an employee is consistently late, a supervisor may reprimand him with the hope that this action will decrease the employee's tardiness. Nagging subordinates for their failure to obey safety regulations is another example.

The **rewarding** approach consists of linking desired behaviors with employee-valued outcomes. When a management trainee completes a report in a timely manner, the supervisor should praise his promptness. If a senior executive takes the initiative to solve a thorny, time-consuming problem on her own, she could be given some extra time to enjoy a scenic location at the conclusion of a business trip. Unfortunately,

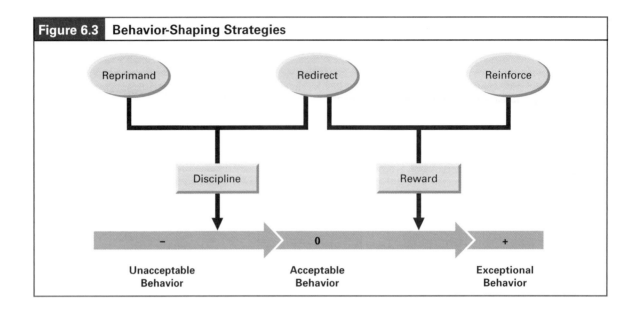

Figure 6.3   Behavior-Shaping Strategies

even simple rewards like these appear to be the exception, not the rule. Dr. Noelle Nelson, the author of a book on the power of appreciation in the workplace (2005), points out that according to U.S. Department of Labor data, the number-one reason people leave their job is that they do not feel appreciated. She also points to a Gallup poll report that 65 percent of workers said they didn't receive a single word of praise or recognition during the past year. Elaborating on these data, Nelson argues even the most energetic and effective employees get worn down when they are rarely acknowledged for their good work and only singled out when they make mistakes.

Disciplining and rewarding are both viable and useful techniques and each has its place in the effective manager's motivational repertoire. However, as Figure 6.3 shows, each technique is associated with different behavior-shaping goals. Discipline should be used to extinguish unacceptable behaviors. However, once an individual's behavior has reached an acceptable level, negative responses will not push the behavior up to the exceptional level. It is difficult to encourage employees to perform exceptional behaviors through nagging, threatening, or related forms of discipline. The left-hand side of Figure 6.3 shows that subordinates work to remove an aversive response rather than to gain a desired reward. Only through positive reinforcement do employees have control over achieving what they want and, therefore, the incentive to reach a level of exceptional performance.

The emphasis in Figure 6.3 on matching discipline and rewards with unacceptable and acceptable behaviors, respectively, highlights two common misapplications

of reinforcement principles. First, it helps us better understand why top performers frequently get upset because they feel "management is too soft on those guys who are always screwing things up." Thinking it is good management practice always to be upbeat and optimistic and to discourage negative interactions, some managers try to downplay the seriousness of mistakes by ignoring them, by trying to temper the consequences by personally fixing errors, or by encouraging the high performers to be more tolerant and patient. Other managers feel so uncomfortable with confronting personal performance problems they are willing to overlook all but the most egregious mistakes.

Although there is a lot to be said for managers having a positive attitude and giving poor performers the benefit of the doubt, their failure to reprimand and redirect inappropriate behaviors leads to two undesirable outcomes: the work unit's morale is seriously threatened, and the poor performers' behaviors are not improved.

Just as some managers find it unpleasant to issue reprimands for poor performance, other managers have difficulty praising exceptional performance. As a result, subordinates complain, "Nothing ever satisfies him." This second misapplication of the negative-response behavior-shaping strategy is just as dysfunctional as the indiscriminate use of praise. These managers mistakenly believe the best way to motivate people is by always keeping expectations a little higher than their subordinates' best performance and then chiding them for their imperfection. In the process, they run the risk of burning out their staff or inadvertently encouraging lower performance ("We'll get chewed out anyway, so why try so hard?"). Furthermore, the irony is that this method creates a competitive, self-defeating situation in which subordinates look forward to the boss's making mistakes—the bigger the better!

Unfortunately, many managers genuinely believe this is the best way to manage in all situations. They define their role as that of a "sheepdog," circling the perimeter of the group, nipping at the heels of those who begin to stray. They establish a fairly broad range of acceptable behaviors and then limit their interactions with employees to barking at those who exceed the boundaries. This negative, desultory style of management creates a demoralizing work environment and does not foster exceptional performance. Instead, workers are motivated to stay out of the boss's way and to avoid doing anything unusual or untried. Innovation and involvement are extinguished, and mundane performance becomes not only acceptable but desirable.

Having looked at the consequences of misapplying rewards and discipline, we will now turn our attention to the proper use of behavior-shaping techniques. The mark of exceptional managers is their ability to foster exceptional behavior in their subordinates. This is best accomplished by using a nine-step behavior-shaping process, which can be applied to the full range of subordinates' behaviors. They can be used either to make unacceptable behaviors acceptable or to transform acceptable behaviors into exceptional ones. They are designed to avoid the harmful effects typically associated with the improper use of discipline discussed in the previous section (Wood & Bandura, 1989). They also ensure the appropriate use of rewards.

Strategies for Shaping Behavior

Table 6.5 shows the nine steps for improving behaviors. These are organized into three broad initiatives: *reprimand, redirect*, and *reinforce*. As shown in Figure 6.3, steps 1 through 6 (reprimand and redirect) are used to extinguish unacceptable behaviors and replace them with acceptable ones. Steps 4 through 9 (redirect and reinforce) are used to transform acceptable behaviors into exceptional behaviors.

An important principle to keep in mind when issuing a **reprimand** is discipline should immediately follow the offensive behavior and focus exclusively on the specific problem. This is not an appropriate time to dredge up old concerns or make general, unsubstantiated accusations. The focus of the discussion should be on eliminating a problem behavior, not on making the subordinate feel bad. This approach increases the likelihood the employee will associate the negative response with a specific act rather than viewing it as a generalized negative evaluation, which will reduce the hostility typically engendered by being reprimanded.

Second, it is important to **redirect** inappropriate behaviors into appropriate channels. It is important that people being reprimanded understand how they

Table 6.5	Guidelines for Improving Behaviors

Reprimand

1. Identify the specific inappropriate behavior. Give examples. Indicate that the action must stop.

2. Point out the impact of the problem on the performance of others, on the unit's mission, and so forth.

3. Ask questions about causes and explore remedies.

Redirect

4. Describe the behaviors or standards you expect. Make sure the individual understands and agrees that these are reasonable.

5. Ask if the individual will comply.

6. Be appropriately supportive. For example, praise other aspects of their work, identify personal and group benefits of compliance; make sure there are no work-related problems standing in the way of meeting your expectations.

Reinforce

7. Identify rewards that are salient to the individual.

8. Link the attainment of desirable outcomes with incremental, continuous improvement.

9. Reward (including using praise) all improvements in performance in a timely and honest manner.

can receive rewards in the future. The process of redirection reduces the despair that occurs when people feel they are likely to be punished no matter what they do. If expected behaviors are not made clear, then workers may stop the inappropriate behavior but feel lost, not knowing how to improve. Keep in mind the ultimate goal of any negative feedback should be to transform inappropriate behaviors into appropriate behaviors, in contrast to simply punishing a person for causing a problem or making the boss look bad. The lingering negative effects of a reprimand will quickly wear off if the manager begins using rewards to **reinforce** desirable behaviors shortly thereafter. This goal can be achieved only if workers know how they can receive positive outcomes and perceive that the available rewards are personally salient (a subject we'll discuss in detail shortly).

Experienced managers know it is just as difficult to transform acceptable behaviors into exceptional ones. Helping an "OK, but uninspired" subordinate catch the vision of moving up to a higher level of desire and commitment can be very challenging. This process begins at step 4 (redirect) by first clearly describing the goal or target behavior. The goal of skilled managers is to avoid having to administer any negative responses and especially to avoid trial-and-error learning among new subordinates. This is done by clearly laying out their expectations and collaboratively establishing work objectives. In addition, it is a good idea to provide an experienced mentor, known for exceptional performance, as a sounding board and role model.

Foster Intrinsic Outcomes

So far our discussion of the Performance → Outcomes link has focused on **extrinsic outcomes**. These are things like pay and promotions and praise that are controlled by someone other than the individual performer. In addition, the motivating potential of a task is affected by its associated **intrinsic outcomes**, which are experienced directly by an individual as a result of successful task performance. They include feelings of accomplishment, self-esteem, and the development of new skills. Although our emphasis has been on the former, a complete motivational program must take into account both types of outcomes.

Effective managers understand that the person-job interface has a strong impact on work performance. No matter how many externally controlled rewards managers use, if individuals find their jobs uninteresting and unfulfilling, performance will suffer. This is particularly true for certain individuals. For example, researchers have discovered that the level of job satisfaction reported by highly intelligent people is closely linked to the degree of difficulty they encounter in performing their work (Ganzach, 1998). In addition, attention to intrinsic outcomes is particularly important in situations in which organizational policies do not permit a close link between performance and rewards; for example, in a strong seniority personnel system. In these cases, it is often possible to compensate for lack of control over extrinsic outcomes by fine-tuning the person-job fit.

Motivating Workers by Redesigning Work

Work design is the process of matching job characteristics and workers' skills and interests. One popular work-design model proposes that particular job dimensions cause workers to experience specific psychological reactions called "states." In turn, these psychological reactions produce specific personal and work outcomes. Figure 6.4 shows the relationship between the core job dimensions, the critical psychological states they produce, and the resulting personal and work outcomes (Hackman & Oldham, 1980). A variety of empirical research has found the five core job dimensions—skill variety, task identity, task significance, autonomy, and feedback—are positively related to job satisfaction.

The more variety in the skills a person can use in performing work, the more the person perceives the task as meaningful or worthwhile. Similarly, the more an individual can perform a complete job from beginning to end (task identity) and the more the work has a direct effect on the work or lives of other people (task significance), the more the employee will view the job as meaningful. On the other hand, when the work requires few skills, only part of a task is performed, or there seems to be little effect on others' jobs, experienced meaningfulness is low.

The more autonomy in the work (freedom to choose how and when to do particular jobs), the more responsibility workers feel for their successes and failures. Increased responsibility results in increased commitment to one's work. Autonomy can be increased by instituting flexible work schedules, decentralizing decision making, or selectively removing formalized controls, such as the ringing of a bell to indicate the beginning and end of a workday.

Finally, the more feedback individuals receive about how well their jobs are being performed, the more knowledge of results they have. Knowledge of results

Figure 6.4 Designing Highly Motivating Jobs

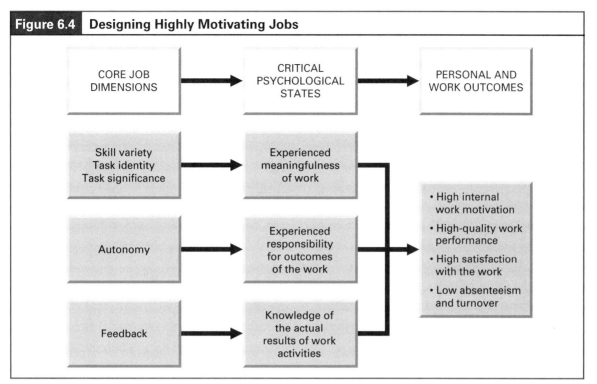

SOURCE: *Hackman/Oldham*, Work Redesign, © 1980. Reprinted by permission of Pearson Education, Inc. Upper Saddle River, NJ.

permits workers to understand the benefits of the jobs they perform. Employees' knowledge of results may be enhanced by increasing their direct contact with clients or by giving them feedback on how their jobs fit in and contribute to the overall operation of the organization.

By enhancing the core job dimensions and increasing critical psychological stages, employees' job fulfillment is increased. Job fulfillment (high internal work motivation) is associated with other outcomes valued by management. These include high-quality work performance, high employee satisfaction with their jobs, and low absenteeism and turnover. Employees who have well-designed jobs enjoy doing them because they are intrinsically satisfying.

This discussion of work design suggests five managerial action guidelines that can help increase desirable personal and work outcomes. These are summarized in Table 6.6. The first one is to *combine tasks*. A combination of tasks is by definition a more challenging and complex work assignment. It requires workers to use a wider variety of skills, which makes the work seem more challenging and meaningful. Telephone directories at the former Indiana Bell Telephone company used to be compiled in 21 steps along an assembly line.

Through job redesign, each worker was given responsibility for compiling an entire directory.

A related managerial principle is to *form identifiable work units* so task identity and task significance can be increased. Clerical work in a large insurance firm was handled by 80 employees organized by functional task (e.g., opening the mail, entering information into the computer, sending out statements). Work was assigned, based on current workload, by a supervisor over each functional area. To create higher levels of task identity and task significance, the firm reorganized the clerical staff into eight self-contained groups. Each group handled all business associated with specific clients.

The third guideline for enhancing jobs is to *establish client relationships*. A client relationship involves an ongoing personal relationship between an employee (the producer) and the client (the consumer). The establishment of this relationship can increase autonomy, task identity, and feedback. Take, for example, research and development (R&D) employees. While they may be the ones who design a product, feedback on customer satisfaction generally is routed through their managers or a separate customer relations unit. At Caterpillar, Inc., members of each

Table 6.6	Strategies for Increasing the Motivational Potential of Assigned Work		
Combine tasks	→	Increase skill variety and task significance	
Form identifiable work units	→	Increase task identity and significance	
Establish client relationships	→	Increase autonomy, task identity, and feedback	
Increase authority	→	Increase autonomy, task significance, and task identity	
Open feedback channels	→	Increase autonomy and feedback	

division's R&D group are assigned to make regular contacts with their major clients.

The fourth suggestion, *increase authority,* refers to granting more authority for making job-related decisions to workers. When we speak here of "vertical," we refer to the distribution of power between a subordinate and a boss. As supervisors delegate more authority and responsibility, their subordinates' perceived autonomy, task significance, and task identity increase. Historically, workers on auto assembly lines have had little decision-making authority. However, in conjunction with increased emphasis on quality, many plants now allow workers to adjust their equipment, reject faulty materials, and even shut down the line if a major problem is evident.

The final managerial suggestion is to *open feedback channels.* Workers need to know how well or how poorly they are performing their jobs if any kind of improvement is expected. Thus, it is imperative they receive timely and consistent feedback, which allows them to make appropriate adjustments in their behavior so they can receive desired rewards. The traditional approach to quality assurance in American industry is to "inspect it in." A separate quality assurance group is assigned to check the production team's quality. The emerging trend is to give producers responsibility for checking their own work. If it doesn't meet quality standards, they immediately fix the defect. Following this procedure, workers receive immediate feedback on their performance.

A different approach to job design focuses on matching individuals' "deeply embedded life interests" with the task characteristics of their work (Butler & Waldroop, 1999). The proponents of this approach argue that for too long people have been advised to select careers based on what they are good at, rather than what they enjoy. The assumption behind this advice is that individuals who excel at their work are satisfied with their jobs. However, critics of this perspective argue many professionals are so well educated and achievement oriented they could succeed in virtually any job. This suggests people stay in jobs because they become involved in activities consistent with their long-held, emotionally driven passions, intricately entwined with their personality.

Setting aside the differences among the various approaches to matching workers and their work, the overall record of job redesign interventions is impressive. In general, firms typically report a substantial increase in productivity, work quality, and worker satisfaction (reflected in lower rates of absenteeism). For example, the Social Security Administration increased productivity 23.5 percent among a group of 50 employees; General Electric realized a 50 percent increase in product quality as a result of a job redesign program; and the absenteeism rate among data-processing operators at Travelers Insurance decreased 24 percent (Kopelman, 1985).

In summary, managers should recognize both extrinsic and intrinsic outcomes are necessary ingredients of effective motivational programs. For example, because most people desire interesting and challenging work activities, good wages and job security will do little to overcome the negative effects of individuals' feeling that their abilities are being underutilized. In addition, recognizing individual preferences for outcomes vary, managers should not assume a narrow-gauged, outcomes-contingent, performance-reinforcing motivation program will satisfy the needs and interests of a broad group of individuals. This brings us to the subject of reward salience.

PROVIDE SALIENT REWARDS

Having established a link between performance and outcomes (rewards and discipline) as part of an integrative motivational program, we now move to the final link in the four-factor model of motivation: Outcomes → Satisfaction. In the following sections we will discuss the three remaining elements of our motivational program, as shown in Table 6.2. Each of these elements has been shown to affect how satisfied individuals are with their work-related outcomes, and as a set they help us understand the key distinction between a reward and a reinforcer. The likelihood a "reward" (so labeled by the reward giver) will actually reinforce a specific performance-enhancing behavior depends on the extent to which the reward recipient: (1) actually values the specific outcome, (2) believes that the reward allocation process was handled fairly, and (3) receives the reward in a timely manner.

We begin this discussion, with diagnostic question 4, "Do subordinates feel the rewards used to encourage high performance are worth the effort?" One of the biggest mistakes that can be made in implementing a "reward program" is assuming managers understand their subordinates' preferences. For example, while it is assumed most people prefer cash incentives, according to a 2004 study conducted by the University of Chicago, performance increases much faster when it is linked to noncash rewards (14.6 percent increase for cash vs. 38.6 percent increase for noncash) (Cook, 2005, p. 6). On an individual level, the manager's lament "What does Joe expect, anyway? I gave him a bonus, and he's still complaining to other members of the accounting department that I don't appreciate his superior performance," indicates an apparent miscalculation of what Joe really values. This miscalculation also suggests the manager needs a better understanding of the relationship between personal needs and personal motivation.

Personal Needs and Personal Motivation

One of the most enduring theories of motivation is based on our scientific understanding of human needs. One way to categorize the various theories of human needs is by whether the theories assume that needs are arranged in a hierarchical fashion. The logic of a **hierarchical needs model** is people are motivated to satisfy their most basic unfulfilled need. That is, until a lower-level need has been satisfied, a higher-level need won't become activated. Probably the best-known example of a hierarchical needs model was proposed by Abraham Maslow (1970). He posited five levels of needs, beginning with *physiological,* followed by *safety, belongingness, esteem,* and *self-actualization.* Clay Alderfer proposed a more parsimonious hierarchical model (1977) that contained only three levels, or categories: *existence, relatedness,* and *growth.* Like Maslow, Alderfer proposed satisfied needs become dormant unless a dramatic shift in circumstances increases their salience. For example, a middle-level executive who is fired during a hostile takeover may suddenly find her interest in personal growth is overwhelmed by a pressing need for security. The problem with hierarchical needs theories is although they help us understand general developmental processes, from child to adult, they aren't very useful for understanding the day-to-day motivation levels of adult employees. A comparison of these hierarchical needs models is shown in Table 6.7.

An alternative perspective can be found in Murray's **manifest needs model** (McClelland, 1971, p. 13). Murray proposes individuals can be classified according to the strengths of their various needs. In contrast to hierarchical models, in which needs are categorized based on their inherent strength (hunger is a stronger need than self-actualization), Murray poses people have divergent and often conflicting needs. Murray proposes about two dozen needs, but later studies have suggested only three or four of them are relevant to the workplace, including the needs for *achievement, affiliation,* and *power.* Another important distinction of Murray's conception is his belief these needs are primarily learned, rather than inherited, and they are activated by cues from the environment. That is, if a person has a high need for achievement it will become manifest, or an active motivational force, only if the environment cues achievement-oriented behavior.

The **need for achievement** is defined as "behavior toward competition with a standard of excellence" (McClelland, Arkinson, Clark, & Lowell, 1953, p. 111). This suggests individuals with a high need for achievement would be characterized by: (1) a tendency to set moderately difficult goals, (2) a strong desire to assume personal responsibility for work activities, (3) a single-minded focus on accomplishing a task, and (4) a strong desire for detailed feedback on task performance. The level of a person's need for achievement (high to low) has been shown to be a good predictor of job performance. In addition, it is highly correlated with a person's preference for an enriched job with greater responsibility and autonomy.

Table 6.7	Comparison of Hierarchical Needs Theories	
MASLOW	**ALDERFER**
Self-actualization	Growth
Esteem	
Belongingness	Relatedness
Safety	
Physiological	Existence

LEARNING

The second of Murray's needs, **need for affiliation**, involves attractions to other individuals in order to feel reassured and acceptable (Birch & Veroff, 1966, p. 65). It has been suggested that people with a high need for affiliation are characterized by: (1) a sincere interest in the feelings of others; (2) a tendency to conform to the expectations of others, especially those whose affiliation they value; and (3) a strong desire for reassurance and approval from others. One would expect individuals with a high need for affiliation to gravitate toward jobs that provide a high degree of interpersonal contact. It is useful to point out in contrast to the need for achievement, the need for affiliation does not seem to be correlated with job performance.

Rounding out Murray's model is the **need for power**, which represents a desire to influence others and to control one's environment. Individuals with a high need for power seek leadership positions and tend to influence others in a fairly open, direct manner. McClelland and Burnham (2003) suggest there are two manifestations of the general need for power. Individuals with a high need for *personal power* tend to seek power and influence for its own sake. To them, control and dominance and conquest are important indicators of personal efficacy. These leaders inspire their subordinates to perform heroic feats, but for the sake of the leader, not the organization. In contrast, individuals with high *institutional power* needs are more oriented toward using their influence to advance the goals of the group or organization. These individuals are described by McClelland as follows: (1) they are organization minded, feeling personally responsible for advancing the purposes of the organization; (2) they enjoy work and accomplishing tasks in an orderly fashion; (3) they are often willing to sacrifice their own self-interests for the good of the organization; (4) they have a strong sense of justice and equity; and (5) they seek expert advice and are not defensive when their ideas are criticized.

Using Need Theory to Identify Personally Salient Outcomes

An understanding of need theory helps managers understand whether organizational rewards are salient reinforcers for specific individuals. Simply put, if a reward satisfies an activated personal need, it can be used to reinforce desired individual behaviors. In practice, this means managers need to understand what motivates each of their subordinates. Table 6.8 demonstrates the difficulty of this task. These research results highlight differences in what various types of organizational members tend to see as highly motivating aspects of their work. For example, while on average the employees in this study placed the highest value on "interesting work" and the lowest value on "sympathetic help with personal problems," we see significant differences in the ratings for these two outcomes across gender, age, and income categories. It is easy to spot equally disparate outcome preferences expressed by different groups of workers for many of the other benefits and rewards, in the left-hand column, commonly used by business firms to attract, retain, and motivate employees.

In the abstract it is not surprising to learn individuals with different demographic and economic profiles have different needs and, thus, bring different expectations to the workplace. The relevance of this data for effective motivational practices is underscored by a parallel research study suggesting that managers are not particularly good at predicting how their subordinates would rank the outcomes shown in Table 6.8 (LeDue, 1980). More particularly, this research suggests that managers tend to base their answers to the question, "What motivates your subordinates?" on two faulty assumptions. First, they assume the outcome preferences among their subordinates are fairly homogenous, and second, they assume their personal outcome preferences are similar to those held by their subordinates. Knowing this, the data shown in Table 6.8 illustrates how easy it is for managers with a certain gender, age, and income profile to systematically misread the salient needs of subordinates characterized by a different profile. Furthermore, it is not difficult to imagine individual circumstances that would result in a person's preferences being significantly different from those of others with a similar demographic and economic profile. In summary, this data underscores the importance of managers getting to know their subordinates well enough that they can effectively match individual and group performance expectations with personally salient outcomes.

The importance of gaining this person-specific information is illustrated in the case of a stockbroker who was promoted to office manager because upper management in the home office felt he was "the most qualified and most deserving." Unfortunately, they failed to ask him if he wanted to be promoted. They assumed that because they had worked hard to qualify for their management positions, all hard workers were similarly motivated. Two weeks after receiving his "reward" for outstanding performance, the supersalesman-turned-manager was in the hospital with a stress-related illness.

Effective managers gain information about active needs and personal values through frequent, supportive,

Table 6.8 — What Workers Want, Ranked by Subgroups*

	All Employees	Men	Women	Under 30	31–40	41–50	Over 50	Under $25,000	$25,001–$40,000	$40,001–$50,000	Over $50,000	Blue-Collar Unskilled	Blue-Collar Skilled	White-Collar Unskilled	White-Collar Skilled	Lower Nonsupervisory	Middle Nonsupervisory	Higher Nonsupervisory
Interesting work	1	1	2	4	2	3	1	5	2	1	1	2	1	1	2	3	1	1
Full appreciation of work done	2	2	1	5	3	2	2	4	3	3	2	1	6	3	1	4	2	2
Feeling of being in on things	3	3	3	6	4	1	3	6	1	2	4	5	2	5	4	5	3	3
Job security	4	5	4	2	1	4	7	2	4	4	3	4	3	7	5	2	4	6
Good wages	5	4	5	1	5	5	8	1	5	6	8	3	4	6	6	1	6	8
Promotion and growth in organization	6	6	6	3	6	8	9	3	6	5	7	6	5	4	3	6	5	5
Good working conditions	7	7	10	7	7	7	4	8	7	7	6	9	7	2	7	7	7	4
Personal loyalty to employees	8	8	8	9	9	6	5	7	8	8	5	8	9	9	8	8	8	7
Tactful discipline	9	9	9	8	10	9	10	10	9	9	10	7	10	10	9	9	9	10
Sympathetic help with personal problems	10	10	7	10	8	10	6	9	10	10	9	10	8	8	10	10	10	9

*Ranked from 1 (highest) to 10 (lowest).

Source: Courtesy of George Mason University. Results are from a study of 1,000 employees conducted in 1995.

generally informal, discussions with their subordinates. One approach used by some managers is to discuss with subordinates recent significant changes in the roles or work assignments of common acquaintances, possibly involving a promotion, a change of work assignment, or a transfer to a new location or work unit. Subordinates' responses to the consequences of these changes, including level of pay, type of pay (e.g., sales commissions vs. salary), travel expectations, responsibilities for coordinating the work of others, level of pressure to produce, capitalizing on old skills vs. learning new ones, an individual vs. team-oriented work environment, opportunities for promotion, and so forth, often provide insights into their own personal preferences. When engaging in discussions such as these, keep in mind information regarding preferred trade-offs is particularly useful. In the abstract, everyone values everything. In reality, we have to make choices and those choices reflect our underlying needs and values. Thus, it is particularly instructive to see how someone responds to the prospect that a colleague's new job provides opportunities for more pay, but at the expense of being away from home three nights a week. Or, the opportunity to be involved with the design of a new product line also means longer hours at work, higher levels of personal stress, and the possibility that the failure

to meet high expectations may reflect negatively on the team members.

The data reported in Table 6.8 is also relevant for individuals in a position to shape the pay and benefits package for an entire organization. Scanning these results, it is easy to pick out differences between the ratings of blue-collar vs. white-collar, unskilled and skilled, lower and higher level employees. Recognizing the wide diversity in outcome preferences within the employee ranks of most large businesses, many firms, ranging from investment banks, like Morgan Stanley, to manufacturing firms, like American Can, have experimented with "cafeteria-style" incentive systems (Abbott, 1997; Lawler, 1987). This approach takes much of the guesswork out of linking an individual's organizational membership and work performance with personally salient outcomes, by allowing employees some say in the matching process. Using this approach, employees receive a certain number of work credits based on performance, seniority, or task difficulty, and they are allowed to trade those in for a variety of benefits, including upgraded insurance packages, financial planning services, disability income plans, extended vacation benefits, tuition reimbursement for educational programs, and so forth.

BE FAIR AND EQUITABLE

Once appropriate rewards have been determined for each employee, managers must then consider how to distribute those rewards (Cropanzano & Folger, 1996). This brings us to concerns about equity. Any positive benefits of salient rewards will be negated if workers feel they are not receiving their fair share. The relevant diagnostic question here is, "Do subordinates feel that work-related benefits are distributed fairly?" (As in the previous section, we will focus here only on rewards. However, the same principles also apply to the equitable use of discipline.)

Equity refers to workers' perceptions of the fairness of rewards. Evaluations of equity are based on a social comparison process in which workers individually compare what they are getting out of the work relationship (outcomes) to what they are putting into the work relationship (inputs). Outcomes include such items as pay, fringe benefits, increased responsibility, and prestige, while inputs may include hours worked and work quality, as well as education and experience. The ratio of outcomes to inputs is then compared to corresponding ratios of other individuals, judged to be an appropriate comparison group. The outcome of this comparison is the basis for beliefs about fairness.

If workers experience feelings of inequity, they will behaviorally or cognitively adjust their own or fellow workers' inputs and/or outputs. In some cases, this may lead to a decrease in motivation and performance. For example, if employees believe they are underpaid, they have a number of options. Cognitively, they may rationalize they really are not working as hard as they thought they were; thus, they reduce the perceived value of their own inputs. Alternatively, they might convince themselves coworkers are actually working harder than they thought they were. Behaviorally, workers can request a pay raise (increase their outcomes), or they can decrease their inputs by leaving a few minutes early each day, decreasing their effort, deciding not to complete an optional training program, or finding excuses not to accept difficult assignments.

The significance of this aspect of motivation underscores the need for managers to closely monitor subordinates' perceptions of equity (Janssen, 2001). In some cases, these conversations may uncover faulty comparison processes. For example, employees might misunderstand the value placed on various inputs, such as experience versus expertise or quantity versus quality; or they might have unrealistic views of their own or others' performance. It has been noted most people believe their leadership skills are better than those of most of the population.

However, just as often these discussions uncover real inequities. For example, the hourly rate of a worker may not be keeping up with recent skill upgrades or increased job responsibilities. The act of identifying and correcting legitimate inequities generates enormous commitment and loyalty. For example, a manager in the computer industry felt he had been unfairly passed over for promotion by a rival. Utilizing the company's open-door policy, he took his case to a higher level in the firm. After a thorough investigation, the decision was reversed and the rival reprimanded. The individual's response was, "After they went to bat for me, I could never leave the company."

The important thing to keep in mind about equity and fairness is we are dealing with perceptions. Consequently, whether they are accurate or distorted, legitimate or ill-founded, they are both accurate and legitimate in the mind of the perceiver until proven otherwise. A basic principle of social psychology states: "That which is perceived as being real is real in its consequences." Therefore, effective managers should constantly perform "reality checks" on their subordinates' perceptions of equity, using questions such as: "What criteria for promotions, pay raises, and so on do you feel management should be placing more/less emphasis on?" "Relative to others similar to you in this organization, do you feel your job assignments, promotions, and so on are appropriate?" "Why do you think Alice was recently promoted over Jack?"

PROVIDE TIMELY REWARDS AND ACCURATE FEEDBACK

Up to this point, we have emphasized employees need to understand and accept performance standards; they should feel that management is working hard to help them reach their performance goals; they should feel that available internal and external rewards are personally attractive; they should believe rewards and reprimands are distributed fairly; and they should feel these outcomes are administered primarily on the basis of performance.

All these elements are necessary for an effective motivational program, but they are not sufficient. As we noted earlier, a common mistake is to assume all rewards are reinforcers. In fact, the reinforcing potential of a "reward" depends on its being linked in the mind of the reward recipient to the specific behaviors the reward giver desires to strengthen. ("When I did behavior X, I received outcome Y. And, because I value Y, I am going to repeat X.") The ability of reward recipients to make this reinforcing (X behavior–Y outcome) mental connection is related to two specific aspects of how the reward is administered: (1) the length of time between the occurrence of the desirable behavior and the receipt of the reward, and (2) the specificity of the explanation for the reward. These are the two final components of our motivational program. Hence, the sixth and final diagnostic question contains two parts. The first is, "Are we getting the most out of our rewards by administering them on a timely basis as part of the feedback process?"

As a general rule, the longer the delay in the administration of rewards the less reinforcement value they have. Even if the recipient greatly values the recognition and the reward giver clearly identifies the behaviors being rewarded, unless the reward is received soon after the behavior has been exhibited (or the goal accomplished), the intended reinforcement value of the reward is diminished.

Ironically, in a worst-case situation, the mistiming of a reward may actually reinforce undesirable behaviors. Giving a long overdue, fully warranted raise to a subordinate during an interview in which she or he is complaining about the unfairness of the reward system may reinforce complaining rather than good work performance. Moreover, failure to give a reward when a desired behavior occurs will make it even more difficult to sustain that behavior in the future. If the owners of a new business have delayed the implementation of a promise to grant stock options for the core start-up cadre as compensation for their low wages and 70- to 80-hour workweeks, the workers' willingness to sustain such a pace on promises and dreams alone may begin to wane.

The importance of timing becomes obvious when one considers all the research findings supporting the value of operant conditioning as a motivational system assume outcomes immediately follow behaviors. Imagine how little we would know about behavior-shaping processes if, in the experiments with birds and rats described in psychology textbooks, the food pellets were dropped into the cage several minutes after the desired behavior occurred.

Today's managers have a number of technological tools that can be used to speed up feedback. Hatim Tyabji, while serving as CEO of Verifone, used e-mail to reinforce important contributions. "We recently had a major win in a market where we hadn't been having much success. Against all odds, we went after a big customer and won. When I got word that we had won—and I'm so enmeshed in the organization that people just ignore the hierarchy and e-mail me that kind of news—my first reaction, apart from pure joy,

was: Why did we win? My next question was: Who are the key people who made the difference? Then I immediately sent out a message of congratulations. The e-mails and phone calls I got back were enough to make my eyes moist. That to me is what makes us tick" (Adria, 2000; Nelson, 2000; Taylor, 1995).

Unfortunately, although timing is a critical contributor to the reinforcement potential of a reward, it is frequently ignored in everyday management practice. The formal administrative apparatus of many organizations often delays for months the feedback on the consequences of employee performance. It is customary practice to restrict in-depth discussions of job performance to formally designated appraisal interviews, which generally take place every six or twelve months. ("I'll have to review this matter officially later, so why do it twice?") The problem with this common practice is the resulting delay between performance and outcomes dilutes the effectiveness of any rewards or discipline dispensed as a result of the evaluation process.

In contrast, effective managers understand the importance of immediate, spontaneous rewards. They use the formal performance evaluation process to discuss long-term trends in performance, solve problems inhibiting performance, and set performance goals. But they don't expect these infrequent general discussions to significantly alter an employee's motivation. For this, they rely on brief, frequent, highly visible performance feedback. At least once a week they seek some opportunity to praise desirable work habits among their subordinates.

Peters and Waterman, in their classic book *In Search of Excellence* (1988), stress the importance of immediacy by relating the following amusing anecdote:

> *At Foxboro, a technical advance was desperately needed for survival in the company's early days. Late one evening, a scientist rushed into the president's office with a working prototype. Dumbfounded at the elegance of the solution and bemused about how to reward it, the president bent forward in his chair, rummaged through most of the drawers in his desk, found something, leaned over the desk to the scientist, and said, "Here!" In his hand was a banana, the only reward he could immediately put his hands on. From that point on, the small "gold banana" pin has been the highest accolade for scientific achievement at Foxboro. (pp. 70–71)*

The implication for effective management is clear: effective rewards are spontaneous rewards. Reward programs that become highly routinized, especially those linked to formal performance appraisal systems, lose their immediacy.

There is a second critical aspect of reinforcement timing: the consistency of reward administration. Administering a reward every time a behavior occurs is called continuous reinforcement. Administering rewards on an intermittent basis (the same reward is always used but is not given every time it is warranted) is referred to as partial, or intermittent, reinforcement. Neither approach is clearly superior; both approaches have trade-offs. Continuous reinforcement represents the fastest way to establish new behavior. For example, if a boss consistently praises a subordinate for writing reports using the manager's preferred format, the subordinate will readily adopt that style in order to receive more and more contingent rewards. However, if the boss suddenly takes an extended leave of absence, the learned behavior will be highly vulnerable to extinction because the reinforcement pattern is broken. In contrast, while partial reinforcement results in very slow learning, it is very resistant to extinction. The persistence associated with gambling behavior illustrates the addictive nature of a partial reinforcement schedule. Not knowing when the next payoff may come preserves the myth that the jackpot is only one more try away.

This information about reinforcement timing derived from experimental research has important implications for effective management. First, it is important to realize continuous reinforcement systems are very rare in organizations unless they are mechanically built into the job, as in the case of the piece-rate pay plan. Seldom are individuals rewarded every time they make a good presentation or effectively handle a customer's complaint. When we recognize most non-assembly-line work in an organization is typically governed by a partial reinforcement schedule, we gain new insights into some of the more frustrating aspects of a manager's role. For example, it helps explain why new employees seem to take forever to catch on to how the boss wants things done. It also suggests why it is so difficult to extinguish outdated behaviors, particularly in older employees.

Second, given how difficult it is for one manager to reinforce consistently the desired behaviors in a new employee (or an employee who is going through a reprimand, redirect, reward cycle), it is generally a good idea to use a team effort. By sharing your developmental objectives with other individuals who interact with the target employee, you increase the likelihood of the desired behaviors being reinforced

during the critical early stages of improvement. For example, if a division head is trying to encourage a new member of her staff to become more assertive, she might encourage other staff members to respond positively to the newcomer's halting efforts in meetings or private conversations.

This brings us to the second half of the sixth diagnostic question, related to the accuracy of feedback, "Do subordinates know where they stand in terms of current performance and long-term opportunities?" In addition to the timing of feedback, the content of feedback significantly affects its reinforcement potential. As a rule of thumb, to increase the motivational potential of performance feedback, be very specific—including examples whenever possible. Keep in mind feedback, whether positive or negative, is itself an outcome. The main purpose for giving people feedback on their performance is to reinforce productive behaviors and extinguish counterproductive behaviors. But this can only occur if the feedback focuses on specific behaviors. To illustrate this point, compare the reinforcement value of the following, equally positive, messages: "You are a great member of this team—we couldn't get along without you." "You are a great member of this team. In particular, you are willing to do whatever is required to meet a deadline."

It is especially important managers provide accurate and honest feedback when a person's performance is marginal or substandard. There are many reasons why managers are reluctant to "tell it like it is" when dealing with poor performers. It is unpleasant to deliver bad news of any kind. It is especially painful to give negative feedback regarding a person's performance. Therefore, it is easy to justify sugarcoating negative information, especially when it is unexpected, on the basis that you are doing the recipient a favor. In practice, it is rarely the case that a poor performer is better off not receiving detailed, honest, accurate feedback. If the feedback is very general, or if it contains mixed signals, improvement is frustratingly difficult. And if a person truly is not well suited for a particular job, then no one benefits from delaying a shift in responsibilities or encouragement to seek other work opportunities.

When managers are reluctant to share unflattering or unhopeful feedback, it is often because they are unwilling to spend sufficient time with individuals receiving negative feedback to help them thoroughly understand their shortcomings, put them in perspective, consider options, and explore possible remedies. It is sometimes easier to pass on an employee with a poor performance record or unrealistic expectations to the next supervisor than it is to confront the problem directly, provide honest and constructive feedback, and help the individual respond appropriately. Therefore, many individuals feel that supportive communication of negative performance information is the management skill which is most difficult to master—and therefore the one most highly prized. If you are particularly interested in polishing this skill, we recommend you review the specific techniques described under the heading "Use Rewards and Discipline Appropriately."

Summary

Our discussion of enhancing work performance has focused on specific analytical and behavioral management skills. We first introduced the fundamental distinction between ability and motivation. Then we discussed several diagnostic questions for determining whether inadequate performance was due to insufficient ability. A five-step process for handling ability problems (resupply, retrain, refit, reassign, and release) was outlined. We introduced the topic of motivation by stressing the need for placing equal emphasis on

concerns for satisfaction and performance. The remainder of this chapter focused on the second skill by presenting six elements of an integrative approach to motivation.

The summary model shown in Figure 6.5 (and its "diagnostic" version discussed in the Skill Practice section as Figure 6.7) highlights our discussion of an expanded version of the basic "four factors" model of motivation. The resulting comprehensive model underscores the necessary role of, as well as the interdependence among, the various components. Skilled managers incorporate all components of this model into their motivational efforts rather than concentrating only on a favorite subset. There are no shortcuts to effective management. All elements of the motivation process must be included in a total, integrated program for improving performance and satisfaction.

The fact the flowchart begins with motivation is important, because it makes explicit our assumption individuals are initially motivated to work hard and do a good job. Recall motivation is manifested as work effort and effort consists of desire and commitment. This means that motivated employees have the desire to initiate a task and the commitment to do their best.

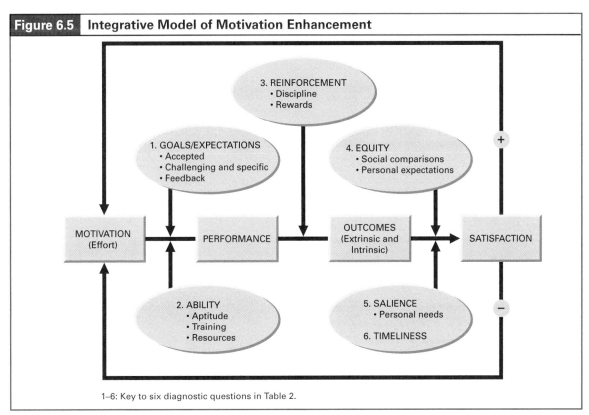

Figure 6.5   Integrative Model of Motivation Enhancement

Note: 1–6: Key to six diagnostic questions in Table 6.2.

Whether their motivation is sustained over time depends on the remaining elements of the model, which are actually amplifications of the Motivation → Performance link, the Performance → Outcomes link, and the Outcomes → Satisfaction link. These crucial links in the motivational process can best be summarized as questions pondered by individuals asked to work harder, change their work routine, or strive for a higher level of quality: First, "If I put forth more effort, am I likely to be able to perform up to performance expectations?" Second, "Will my level of performance matter in this organization?" Third, "Will the experience of being a high performer likely be personally rewarding?"

Beginning on the left side of the model, we see that the combination of goals and ability determines the extent to which effort is successfully transformed into performance. In the path-goal theory of leadership, the importance of fitting the right job to the right person and providing necessary resources and training is emphasized. These factors must be combined with effective goal setting (understanding and accepting moderately difficult goals) if increased effort is to result in increased performance.

The next section of the model focuses on reinforcing good performance, in terms of both increasing the frequency of performance-enhancing behaviors and linking outcomes to successful goal accomplishment. It is important to keep in mind people are, in general, motivated by both extrinsic and intrinsic outcomes. In addition, the effective manager is adept at using the full range of behavior-shaping tools, spanning the spectrum from discipline to rewards. Although our discussion focused more on rewards than discipline, when faced with the challenge of providing constructive but negative performance feedback, and developing an accompanying plan for remediation, Table 6.5 provides a useful set of guidelines.

Proceeding to the Outcomes → Satisfaction segment of the model, the importance of perceived equity and reward salience stands out. Individuals must believe the rewards offered are appropriate, not only for their personal performance level but also in comparison to the rewards achieved by "similar" others. The subjective value that individuals attach to incentives for performance reflects their personal relevance, or salience. Rewards with little personal value have low motivational potential. These subjective factors combine with the timeliness and accuracy of feedback to determine the overall motivational potential of rewards.

Based on their perceptions of outcomes, workers will experience varying degrees of satisfaction or dissatisfaction. Satisfaction creates a positive feedback loop, increasing the individual's motivation, as manifested by increased effort. Dissatisfaction, on the other hand, results in decreased effort and, therefore, lower performance and rewards. If uncorrected, this pattern may ultimately result in absenteeism or turnover.

Behavioral Guidelines

This discussion is organized around key diagnostic models and questions that serve as the basis for enhancing the following skills: (1) properly diagnosing performance problems; (2) initiating actions to enhance individuals' abilities; and (3) strengthening the motivational aspects of the work environment.

Table 6.2 summarizes the process for properly diagnosing the causes of poor work performance in the form of six diagnostic questions. (A "decision tree" version of these questions is included in the Skill Practice section as Figure 6.7.)

The key guidelines for creating a highly motivating work environment are:

1. Clearly define an acceptable level of overall performance or specific behavioral objective.
   - ❏ Make sure the individual understands what is necessary to satisfy expectations.
   - ❏ Formulate goals and expectations collaboratively, if possible.
   - ❏ Make goals as challenging and specific as possible.

2. Help remove all obstacles to reaching performance objectives.
   - ❏ Make sure the individual has adequate technical information, financial resources, personnel, and political support.
   - ❏ If a lack of ability appears to be hindering performance, use the resupply, retrain, refit, reassign, or release series of remedies.
   - ❏ Gear your level of involvement as a leader to how much help a person expects, needs, and how much help is otherwise available.

3. Make rewards and discipline contingent on high performance or drawing nearer to the performance objective.
   - ❏ Carefully examine the behavioral consequences of your nonresponses. (Ignoring a behavior is rarely interpreted as a neutral response.)
   - ❏ Use discipline to extinguish counterproductive behavior and rewards to reinforce productive behaviors.

4. When discipline is required, treat it as a learning experience for the individual.
   - ❏ Specifically identify the problem and explain how it should be corrected.
   - ❏ Use the reprimand and redirect guidelines in Table 6.5.
5. Transform acceptable into exceptional behaviors.
   - ❏ Reward each level of improvement.
   - ❏ Use the redirect and reward guidelines in Table 6.5.
6. Use reinforcing rewards that appeal to the individual.
   - ❏ Allow flexibility in individual selection of rewards.
   - ❏ Provide salient external rewards as well as satisfying and rewarding work (intrinsic satisfaction).
   - ❏ To maintain salience, do not overuse rewards.

7. Periodically check subordinates' perceptions regarding the equity of reward allocations.
   - ❏ Correct misperceptions related to equity comparisons.
8. Provide timely rewards and accurate feedback.
   - ❏ Minimize the time lag between behaviors and feedback on performance, including the administration of rewards or reprimands. (Spontaneous feedback shapes behavior best.)
   - ❏ Provide specific, honest, and accurate assessments of current performance and long-range opportunities.

CASE INVOLVING MOTIVATION PROBLEMS

Electro Logic

Electro Logic (EL) is a small R&D firm located in a midwestern college town adjacent to a major university. Its primary mission is to perform basic research on, and development of, a new technology called "Very Fast, Very Accurate" (VFVA). Founded four years ago by Steve Morgan, an electrical engineering professor and inventor of the technology, EL is primarily funded by government contracts, although it plans to market VFVA technology and devices to nongovernmental organizations within the year.

The government is very interested in VFVA, as it will enhance radar technology, robotics, and a number of other important defense applications. EL recently received the largest small-business contract ever awarded by the government to research and develop this or any other technology. Phase I of the contract has just been completed, and the government has agreed to Phase II contracting as well.

The organizational chart of EL is shown in Figure 6.6. Current membership is 75, with roughly 88 percent in engineering. The hierarchy of engineering titles and requirements for each are listed in Table 6.9. Heads of staff are supposedly appointed based on their knowledge of VFVA technology and their ability to manage people. In practice, the president of EL hand-picks these people based on what some might call arbitrary guidelines: most of the staff leaders were or are the president's graduate students. There is no predetermined time frame for advancement up the hierarchy. Raises are, however, directly related to performance appraisal evaluations.

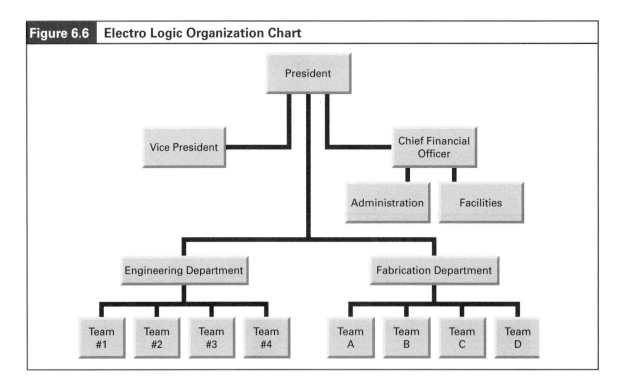

Figure 6.6 | **Electro Logic Organization Chart**

Table 6.9	Engineering Titles and Requirements
TITLE	**REQUIREMENT**
Member of Technical Staff	BSEE, MSEE
Senior Member of Technical Staff	PhD, MSEE with 2 years of industrial experience; BSEE with 5 years of industrial experience
Research Engineer	PhD with 2 years of industrial experience
	BSEE or MSEE with 7 years of industrial experience
Research Scientist	PhD with appropriate experience in research
Senior Research Scientist	PhD with appropriate industrial and research experience

ANALYSIS

Working directly with the engineers are the technicians. These people generally have a high school degree, although some also have college degrees. They are trained on the job, although some have gone through a local community college's program on microtechnology fabrication. The technicians perform the mundane tasks of the engineering department: running tests, building circuit boards, manufacturing VFVA chips, and so on. Most are full-time, hourly employees.

The administrative staff is composed of the staff head (with an MBA from a major university), accountants, personnel director, graphic artists, purchasing agent, project controller, technical writers/editors, and secretaries. Most of the people in the administrative staff are women. All are hourly employees except the staff head, personnel director, and project controller. The graphic artists and technical writer/editor are part-time employees.

The facilities staff is composed of the staff head and maintenance personnel. EL is housed in three different buildings, and the primary responsibility of the facilities staff is to ensure that the facilities of each building are in good working order. Additionally, the facilities staff is often called upon to remodel parts of the buildings as the staff continues to grow.

EL anticipates a major recruiting campaign to enhance the overall staff. In particular, it is looking for more technicians and engineers. Prior to this recruiting campaign, however, the president of EL hired an outside consultant to assess employee needs as well as the morale and overall effectiveness of the firm. The consultant has been observing EL for about three weeks and has written up some notes of her impressions and observations of the company.

Consultant's Notes from Observations of Electro Logic

Facilities: Electro Logic (EL) is housed in three different buildings. Two are converted houses, and one is an old school building. Senior managers and engineers are in the school, and others are scattered between the houses.

Meetings: Weekly staff meetings are held in the main building to discuss objectives and to formulate and review milestone charts.

Social interaction: A core group of employees interact frequently on a social basis; for example, sports teams, parties. The administrative staff celebrates birthdays at work. The president occasionally attends.

Work allocation: Engineers request various tasks from the support staff, which consists of technicians and administrative unit personnel. There is obviously some discretion used by the staff in assigning priorities to the work requests, based on rapport and desirability of the work.

Turnover: The highest turnover is among administrative personnel and technicians. Exit interviews with engineers indicate they leave because of the company's crisis-management style, better opportunities for career advancement and security in larger organizations, and overall frustration with EL's "pecking order." Engineers with the most responsibility and authority tend to leave.

Salary and benefits: In general, wages at EL are marginal by national and local standards. A small group of scientists and engineers do make substantial salaries and have a very attractive benefits package, including stock options. Salaries and benefits for new engineers tend to be linked to the perceived level of their expertise.

Offices and facilities: Only EL's president, vice president, and chief financial officer have their own offices. Engineers are grouped together in "pods" by project assignment. There is very little privacy in these work areas, and the noise from the shared printer is distracting. The head of administration shares a pod with the personnel director, facilities head, and the project controller. One to three secretaries per building are located in or near the reception areas. The large building has an employee lounge with three vending machines. There is also a coffee-and-tea station. The smaller buildings have only a soft-drink machine in the reception area.

Consultant's Interviews with Employees

After making these observations, the consultant requested interviews with a cross-section of the staff for the purpose of developing a survey to be taken of all employees. Presented below are excerpts from those interviews.

Pat Klausen, Senior Member of the Technical Staff

CONSULTANT: What is it about Electro Logic (EL) that gives you the most satisfaction?

PAT: I really enjoy the work. I mean, I've always liked to do research, and working on VFVA is an incredible opportunity. Just getting to work with Steve (EL's president and VFVA's inventor) again is exciting. I was his graduate student about six years ago, you know. He really likes to work closely with his people—perhaps sometimes too closely. There have been times when I could have done with a little less supervision.

CONSULTANT: What's the least satisfying aspect of your work?

PAT: Probably the fact that I'm never quite sure we'll be funded next month, given the defense budget problems and the tentativeness of our research. I've got a family to consider, and this place isn't the most stable in terms of its financial situation. Maybe it'll change once we get more into commercial production. Who knows?

CONSULTANT: You've offered some general positives and negatives about EL. Can you be more specific about day-to-day dealings? What's good and bad about working here on a daily basis?

PAT: You're sure this isn't going to get back to anyone? Okay. Well, in general I'm not satisfied with the fact that too often we end up changing horses in the middle of the stream, if you know what I mean. In the past seven months, three of my engineers and four of my techs have been pulled off my project onto projects whose deadlines were nearer than mine. Now I'm faced with a deadline, and I'm supposed to be getting more staff. But I'll have to spend so much time briefing them that it might make more sense for me to just finish the project myself. On the other hand, Steve keeps telling me that we have to be concerned with EL's overall goals, not just our individual concerns—you know, we have to be "team players," "good members of the family." It's kind of hard to deal with that, though, when deadlines are bearing down and you know your butt's on the line, team player or not. But if you go along with this kind of stuff and don't complain, the higher-ups treat you well. Still, it seems to me there's got to be a better way to manage these projects.

CONSULTANT: What are the positive aspects of your daily work?

PAT: Well, the people here are all great to work with. They know their stuff or can learn quickly. I tend to be a social person and I really like socializing with these people. We play softball and basketball together and do happy hours and stuff. I like that. I've got some good friends here, which helps get my work orders filled quickly, if you know what I mean.

Bob Christensen, Member of the Technical Staff

CONSULTANT: You said earlier that Steve was your adviser for your M.S. So you've known him a long time.

BOB: Yes, that's right. I've known Professor Morgan—Steve—for about eight years. I had him for a few undergraduate classes; then, of course, he was my adviser for my two-year master's program, and now I've worked at Electro Logic (EL) for two years.

CONSULTANT: It seems as if you enjoy working with Steve.

BOB: Oh, yeah. But I really don't get to work directly with him anymore. I'll see him at meetings and such, but that's about it.

CONSULTANT: So he's not your immediate supervisor?

BOB: No, but for the amount of time I spend with my supervisor, Steve might as well be. My boss and I meet maybe once every three weeks for about an hour to see if all is well. And that's it. The rest of the time, I'm on my own. I used to talk to Steve when I had questions, but he's gotten so busy now that it's hard to see him—you need to make an appointment a few days in advance.

CONSULTANT: Do you think your supervisor treats all his staff this way?

BOB: To be honest, I have heard some complaints. In fact, about six months ago, the situation was so bad, some other people and I had a meeting with him. He promised that he would be more available to us and was, for about a month. Then we got involved in a new proposal, so he made himself scarce again. So nothing's really changed. We're coming up on finalizing the proposal now, and it's important that I see him, ask him questions. The last few drafts I've submitted to him, he's returned, rewritten in his own way, and with no explanation of the changes. Sometimes I think he treats me like somebody who doesn't know anything, as if I had no training what-soever. I realize his neck is on the line with this project, but sometimes it seems that he uses being busy to avoid talking to me.

Chris Chen, Research Scientist

CONSULTANT: What kind of characteristics should a person have if he/she wants to work as a research scientist at Electro Logic (EL)?

CHRIS: Well, certainly technical knowledge is important. When I've interviewed recent college grads for entry-level positions, I am always concerned with their GPA. I like to see straight-A averages, if possible. But for experienced research scientists, technical knowledge shows up in their publication records, mostly. So I'll read their papers. I also think a research scientist has to be highly self-motivated, not look to others for praise and such. Particularly here. If you want someone to tell you you've done a good job, you'll be waiting a long time. It's not clear to me that research scientists really get the support we need from the rest of the staff here. Work orders are often lost or put off for one reason or another. Senior members seem to get more techs than scientists do, and they certainly get more attention from Steve. The rumor is that these guys also get higher raises than the scientists; allegedly, this is to keep pay at an equitable rate—you know, they're supposedly more valuable to the company. Of course, everybody knows that most of the senior members are Steve's old graduate students, and so he takes care of them really well. One of the things that really galls me is that I need to keep up my publication record to maintain my career options. But publishing is frowned on because it takes time away from your work. I've even been told that my work can't be published because of proprietary rights or that the defense department considers the information classified. However, if somebody important is working with me and needs the publication, then it's full steam ahead.

CONSULTANT: You sound pretty disgruntled with your work.

CHRIS: It's not my work so much. I'm really very happy doing this work—it's cutting-edge, after all. The problem is I'm never quite sure where the work is going. I do my part of a project, and unless I go out of my way to talk to other people, I never find out the final results of the total project. That's just something you learn to live with around here—being part of a system that's not particularly open.

Meg Conroy, Assistant to the Head of Administration

CONSULTANT: You've only been here a short time, is that correct?

MEG: That's right—just a little over a year.

CONSULTANT: Why did you take the job?

MEG: Well, I was in my last semester of college and was looking for a job, like most college seniors. My fiancé at the time—now he's my husband—was already working for Electro Logic (EL) and found out that there was an opening. So I applied.

CONSULTANT: So you were a business major in school?

MEG: Oh, no. I was a history major.

CONSULTANT: Do you like your job?

MEG: It has a lot to offer. I get paid pretty well for what I'm doing. And I'm learning a lot. I just wish the company would let me take some classes in administration, like accounting. The auditors ask some pretty tough questions. Steve says we should hire that expertise, but I'd still be responsible for supervising the people.

CONSULTANT: Is there any particular aspect about your job that you really find satisfying?

MEG: Well, let me think. I guess I like the fact that I get to do a lot of different tasks so that things don't get so boring. I would hate to have to do the same thing, day in and day out. A lot of times, I go to the library to do research on different things, and that's nice because it gets me out of the office.

CONSULTANT: What don't you like about your job?

MEG: Well, I often get the feeling that administration isn't taken seriously. You know, the engineers could get along without us quite nicely, or so they seem to think. The whole structure of the department shows that we're the catch-all department: if you don't fit anywhere else, they put you in here. Perhaps some of that is because our department is primarily women—in fact, I've been told that 95 percent of all the female employees are in administration. Sometimes it's hard to work with the engineers because they treat you like you don't know anything, and they always want things to be done their way. Clearly, the engineers get the money and consideration and yet, well, we do contribute quite a lot to the whole team, as Steve would say. But words of praise just aren't as impressive as actions. Sure, we get our birthday parties, but that still seems to be a little patronizing. We rarely get to see what's going on in the research area. I've asked a number of engineers specific questions, and they just kind of look at me with a blank stare and give me some really simplified answer. It seems to me if you want to build a family, like the president says, you can't treat administration like a bad relation.

P. J. Ginelli, Technician

CONSULTANT: I gather you've just been through your semiannual performance appraisal. How did it go?

P. J.: Like I expected. No surprises.

CONSULTANT: Do you find these appraisals useful?

P. J.: Sure. I get to find out what he thinks of my work.

CONSULTANT: Is that all?

P. J.: Well, I suppose it's a nice opportunity to understand what my supervisor wants. Sometimes he's not so clear during the rest of the year. I suppose he's been given specific goals from higher-ups before he talks with me, so he's clear and then I'm clear.

CONSULTANT: Do you like what you're doing?

P. J.: Oh yeah. The best part is that I'm not at the main building and so I don't have to put up with the "important" people, you know? I've heard from other techs that those guys can be a real pain—trying to be nice and all, but really just being a bother. I mean, how can you get your stuff done when the president's looking over your shoulder all the time? On the other hand, if the president knows your name, I suppose that's a good thing when it comes to raises and promotions. But my boss sticks up for his techs; we get a fair deal from him.

CONSULTANT: Do you think you'll be able to get ahead at Electro Logic (EL)?

P. J.: Get ahead? You mean become an engineer or something? No, and I really don't want to do that. Everyone around here keeps pushing me to move up. I'm afraid to tell people how I really feel for fear they'll decide I don't fit into this high-tech environment. I don't want to be the "black sheep of the family." I like where I am, and if the raises keep coming, I'll keep liking it. One of my kids is starting college next year, and I need the money to help her out. I get a lot of overtime, particularly when contract deadlines are near. I suppose the rush toward the end of contracts gives some people big headaches, but for me, I don't mind. The work is pretty slow otherwise, and so at least I'm working all the time and then some. But my family wishes my schedule was more predictable.

CONSULTANT: Do you think you'll continue working for EL?

P. J.: I'm not sure I want to answer that. Let's just say that my ratings on the performance appraisal were good, and I expect to see an improvement in my pay. I'll stay for that.

Chalida Montgomery, Technician

CONSULTANT: In general, what are your feelings about the work you do for Electro Logic (EL)?

CHALIDA: Well, I feel my work is quite good, but I also feel that I perform rather boring, tedious tasks. From what my supervisor says, the kinds of things I do are what electrical engineering students do in their last year of classes. I gather their final project is to make a circuit board, and that's what I do, day in and day out.

CONSULTANT: What is it that you would like to do?

CHALIDA: Well, it would be nice to be able to offer some input into some of the designs of these boards. I know I don't have a PhD or anything, but I do have lots of experience. But because I'm a tech, the engineers don't really feel I've got much to offer—even though I build the boards and can tell from the design which one will do what the designer wants it to do. I also would like to maybe supervise other technicians in my department. You know, some kind of advancement would be nice. As it is, lots of techs ask me how to do things, and of course I help, but then they get the credit. Around here, you have to have a piece of paper that says you're educated before they let you officially help other people.

Discussion Questions

1. Using the behavioral guidelines and Figure 6.5 as diagnostic aids, what are the strengths and weaknesses of Electro Logic (EL) from a motivational perspective?
2. What are the high-priority action items you would include in a consulting report to Steve Morgan, president of EL? Focus on specific actions that he could initiate that would better use the abilities of the staff and foster a more motivating work environment.

EXERCISES FOR DIAGNOSING WORK PERFORMANCE PROBLEMS

Proper diagnosis is a critical aspect of effective motivation management. Often, managers become frustrated because they don't understand the causes of observed performance problems. They might experiment with various "cures," but the inefficiency of this trial-and-error process often only increases their frustration level. In addition, the accompanying misunderstanding adds extra strain to the manager-subordinate relationship. This generally makes the performance problem even more pronounced, which in turn prompts the manager to resort to more drastic responses, and a vicious downward spiral ensues.

The performance diagnosis model in Figure 6.7 offers a systematic way for managers and subordinates to pinpoint collaboratively the causes of dissatisfaction and performance problems. It assumes that employees will work hard and be good performers if the work environment encourages these actions. Consequently, rather than jumping to conclusions about poor performance stemming from deficiencies in personality traits or a bad attitude, this diagnostic process helps managers focus their attention on improving the selection, job design, performance evaluation, and reward-allocation systems. In this manner, the specific steps necessary to accomplish work goals and management's expectations are examined to pinpoint why a worker's performance is falling short.

The manager and low-performing subordinate should follow the logical discovery process in the model, step by step. They should begin by examining the current perceptions of performance, as well as the understanding of performance expectations, and then proceed through the model until the performance problems have been identified. The model focuses on seven of these problems.

A. **Perception Problem:** "Do you agree your performance is below expectations?" A perception problem suggests that the manager and subordinate have different views of the subordinate's current performance level. Unless this disagreement is resolved, it is futile to continue the diagnostic process. The entire problem-solving process is based on the premise that both parties recognize the existence of a problem and are interested in solving it. If agreement does not exist, the manager should focus on resolving the discrepancy in perceptions, including clarifying current expectations (Problem 5).

B. **Resources Problem:** "Do you have the resources necessary to do the job well?" Ability has three components, and these should be explored in the order shown in the model. This order reduces a subordinate's defensive reactions. Poor performance may stem from a lack of resource support. Resources include material and personnel support as well as cooperation from interdependent work groups.

C. **Training Problem:** "Is a lack of training interfering with your job performance?" Individuals may be asked to perform tasks that exceed their current skill or knowledge level. Typically, this problem can be overcome through additional training or education.

D. **Aptitude Problem:** "Do you feel this is the right job/blend of work assignments for you?" This is the most difficult of the three ability problems to resolve because it is the most basic. If the resupply (providing additional resources) and retraining solutions have been explored without success, then more drastic measures may be

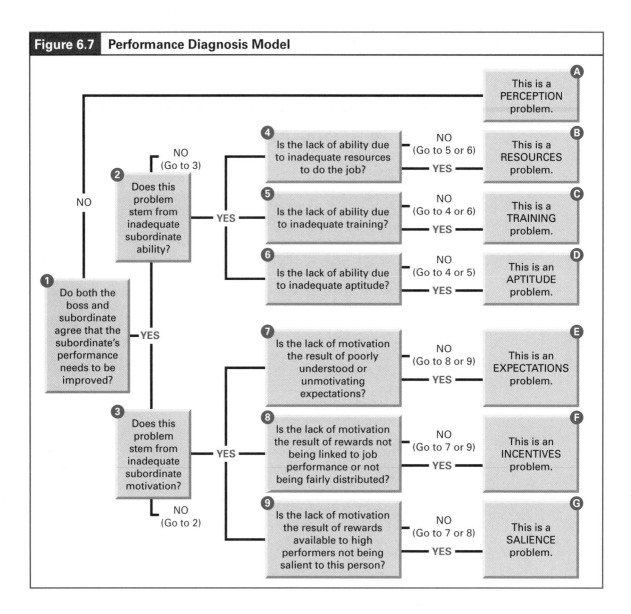

Figure 6.7 Performance Diagnosis Model

A This is a PERCEPTION problem.

④ Is the lack of ability due to inadequate resources to do the job? — NO (Go to 5 or 6) / YES — **B** This is a RESOURCES problem.

② Does this problem stem from inadequate subordinate ability? — NO (Go to 3) / YES

⑤ Is the lack of ability due to inadequate training? — NO (Go to 4 or 6) / YES — **C** This is a TRAINING problem.

⑥ Is the lack of ability due to inadequate aptitude? — NO (Go to 4 or 5) / YES — **D** This is an APTITUDE problem.

① Do both the boss and subordinate agree that the subordinate's performance needs to be improved? — NO / YES

⑦ Is the lack of motivation the result of poorly understood or unmotivating expectations? — NO (Go to 8 or 9) / YES — **E** This is an EXPECTATIONS problem.

③ Does this problem stem from inadequate subordinate motivation? — YES / NO (Go to 2)

⑧ Is the lack of motivation the result of rewards not being linked to job performance or not being fairly distributed? — NO (Go to 7 or 9) / YES — **F** This is an INCENTIVES problem.

⑨ Is the lack of motivation the result of rewards available to high performers not being salient to this person? — NO (Go to 7 or 8) / YES — **G** This is a SALIENCE problem.

required. These include refitting the person's current job requirements, reassigning him or her to another position, or, finally, releasing him or her from the organization.

E. Expectations Problem: "What are your performance expectations for this position? What do you think my expectations are?" This problem results from poor communication regarding job goals or job requirements. In some cases, the stated goals may be different from the desired goals. In other words, the employee is working toward one goal while the supervisor desires another. This often occurs when subordinates are not sufficiently involved in the goal- or standard-setting process. When this results in unrealistic, imposed expectations, motivation suffers.

F. Incentives Problem: "Do you believe rewards are linked to your performance in this position?" Either the individual does not believe that "performance makes a difference" or insufficient performance feedback and reinforcement have been given. The manager should also ask, "Do you feel rewards are being distributed equitably?" This provides an opportunity to discuss subordinates' criteria for judging fairness. Often, unrealistic standards are being used.

G. **Salience Problem:** "Are the performance incentives attractive to you?" Salience refers to the importance an individual attaches to available rewards. Often, the incentives offered to encourage high performance are not highly valued by a particular individual. Managers need to be creative in generating a broad range of rewards and flexible in allowing subordinates to choose among rewards.

Assignment
Option 1:

Read the case, "Joe Chaney," and privately use the diagnostic model (see Figure 6.7) to pinpoint plausible performance problems. Next, discuss in small groups your individual assessments and list specific questions you should ask Joe to accurately identify, from his point of view, the obstacles to his high performance. Finally, brainstorm ideas for plausible solutions. Prepare to represent your group in role-playing a problem-solving interview with Joe.

Option 2:

Administer the Work Performance Assessment survey to several employees. Using the scoring key at the end of this chapter, categorize the obstacles to high performance and satisfaction reported by the respondents. Then get together in small groups, with each group assuming the role of a management task force charged with the responsibility to analyze this employee survey data. Discuss the patterns in the data as well as possible remedies for these problems, using the behavioral guidelines and motivational models in the chapter as guides. Prepare a report on your analysis and recommendations for specific changes.

Joe Chaney

Joe Chaney joined your architectural firm two years ago as a draftsman. He is 35 years old and has been a draftsman since graduating from a two-year technical school right after high school. He is married and has four children. He has worked for four architectural firms in 12 years.

Joe came with mediocre recommendations from his previous employer, but you hired him anyway because you needed help desperately. Your firm's workload has been extremely high due to a local construction boom. The result is that a lot of the practices that contribute to a supportive, well-managed work environment have been overlooked. For instance, you can't remember the last time you conducted a formal performance review or did any career counseling. Furthermore, the tradition of closing the office early on Friday for a social hour was dropped long ago. Unfortunately, the tension in the office runs pretty high some days due to unbearable time pressures and the lack of adequate staff. Night and weekend work have become the norm rather than the exception.

Overall, you have been pleasantly surprised by Joe's performance. Until recently, he worked hard and consistently produced high-quality work. Furthermore, he frequently volunteered for special projects, made lots of suggestions for improving the work environment, and has demonstrated an in-depth practical knowledge of architecture and the construction business. However, during the past few months, he has definitely slacked off. He doesn't seem as excited about his work, and several times you have found him daydreaming at his desk. In addition, he has gotten into several heated arguments with architects about the specifications and proper design procedures for recent projects.

After one of these disagreements, you overheard Joe complaining to his officemate, "No one around here respects my opinion. I'm just a lowly draftsman. I know as much as these hotshot architects, but because I don't have the degree, they ignore my input, and I'm stuck doing the grunt work. Adding insult to injury, my wife has had to get a job to help support our family. I must be the lowest-paid person in this firm." In response to a question from a coworker regarding why he didn't pursue a college degree in architecture,

Joe responded, "Do you have any idea how hard it is to put bread on the table, pay a Seattle mortgage, work overtime, be a reasonably good father and husband, plus go to night school? Come on, be realistic!"

Work Performance Assessment

Respond to the following statements, based on your current work situation.

Rating Scale

1 Strongly disagree

2 Disagree

3 Neutral

4 Agree

5 Strongly agree

1. My supervisor and I agree on the quality of my performance.
2. I feel I have adequate training to perform my current job assignments.
3. I believe that my native skills and abilities are matched very well with my job responsibilities.
4. I believe that I have adequate resources and supplies to do my job well.
5. I understand my boss's expectations and generally feel they are realistic.
6. I believe that rewards are distributed fairly, on the basis of performance.
7. The rewards and opportunities available to me if I perform well are attractive to me personally.
8. My supervisor indicates that I am not performing as well as I should, but I disagree.
9. I could do a much better job if I had more training.
10. I believe that my job is too difficult for my ability level.
11. I believe that my job performance is hindered by a lack of supplies and resources.
12. I believe my boss's expectations are unclear and unrealistic.
13. I believe my boss plays favorites in allocating rewards.
14. I do not find the rewards and opportunities available to high performers very appealing.

EXERCISE FOR RESHAPING UNACCEPTABLE BEHAVIORS

Shaheen Matombo

One of the most challenging aspects of management is transforming inappropriate behaviors into appropriate behaviors. Managers commonly take insufficient action to transform negative actions into positive ones. Some of these insufficient responses include assuming that ignoring an employee's shortcomings will make them go away; praising positive aspects of an individual's performance in hopes that this will encourage him or her to rechannel unproductive energies; discussing problems in vague, general terms in a group meeting, in hopes that the unproductive person will "take a hint" and change; and getting upset with an individual and demanding that he or she "shape up."

Assignment

Assume the role of Andre Tate in the following case. After reading the case, review the applicable behavioral guidelines shown on the Observer's Feedback Form at the end of the chapter. In small groups, discuss how you would resolve this problem. Prepare to role-play your discussion with Shaheen Matombo. After the discussion, assigned observers will provide feedback on your performance, using the Observer's Feedback Form as a guide. Unless you are assigned to play her role, do not read the role instructions for Shaheen prior to the interview.

Andre Tate, Manager

Shaheen has been a member of your staff for only three months. You don't know much about her other than that she is a single parent who has recently entered the workforce after a difficult divorce. She is often 10 to 20 minutes late for work in the morning. You are the manager of a very hectic customer relations office for a utility company. The phones start ringing promptly at 8:00. When she is late for work, you have to answer her phone, and this interrupts your work schedule. This morning, you are particularly annoyed. She is 25 minutes late, and the phones are ringing like crazy. Because you have been forced to answer them, it will be difficult for you to complete an important assignment by the noon deadline. You are getting more upset by the minute.

While you are in the middle of a particularly unpleasant phone conversation with an irate customer, you look out your window and see Shaheen bounding up the steps to the building. You think to yourself, "This is ridiculous, I've got to put a stop to her tardiness. Maybe I should just threaten to fire her unless she shapes up." Upon further reflection, you realize that would be impractical, especially during this period of retrenchment after the rate hike was turned down. Given the rumors about a possible hiring freeze, you know it may be difficult to refill any vacancies.

Also, Shaheen is actually a pretty good worker when she is there. She is conscientious and has a real knack with cranky callers. Unfortunately, it has taken her much longer than expected to learn the computer program for retrieving information on customer accounts. She frequently has to put callers on hold while she asks for help. These interruptions have tended to increase an already tense relationship with the rest of the office staff. She has had some difficulty fitting in socially; the others are much younger and have worked together for several years. Shaheen is the first new hire in a long time, so the others aren't used to breaking someone in. Three of your staff have complained to you about Shaheen's constant interruptions. They feel their productivity is going down as a result. Besides, she seems to expect them to drop whatever they are doing every time she has a question. They had expected their workload to be lighter when a new person was hired, but now they are having second thoughts. (In the past, you have had enough time to train new hires, but your boss has had you tied up on a major project for almost a year.)

Shaheen enters the office obviously flustered and disheveled. She has "I'm sorry" written all over her face. You motion for her to pick up the blinking phone line and then scribble a note on a tablet while you complete your call: "See me in my office at 12:00 sharp!" It's time you got to the bottom of Shaheen's disruptive influence on an otherwise smooth-flowing operation.

Shaheen Matombo, Staff Member

Boy, what a morning! Your babysitter's father died during the night, and she called you from the airport at 6:30 A.M. saying she would be out of town for three or four days. You tried three usually available backups before you finally found someone who could take Keen, your 3-year-old. Then Shayla, your seventh-grader, went through five outfits before she was satisfied that she had just the right look for her first yearbook picture. It's a miracle that Buddy, your oldest, was able to pull himself out of bed after getting only five hours of sleep. On top of football and drama, he's now joined the chess team, and they had their first tournament last night. Why did it have to fall on the night before his final in physics? This morning you wished you had his knack for juggling so many activities. By the time you got the kids delivered, you were already 10 minutes behind schedule. Then there was this incredible accident on the expressway that slowed traffic to a crawl.

As you finally pull off the downtown exit ramp, you notice you're almost 20 minutes late for work. "My kingdom for a cell phone!" you groan. "Although by now I probably couldn't get an open line into the office, anyway." As you desperately scan the side streets for a parking space, you begin to panic. "How am I going to explain this to Andre? He'll be furious. I'm sure he's upset about my chronic lateness. On top of that, he's obviously disappointed with my lack of computer skills, and I'm sure the others complain to him about having to train a newcomer." You're sure that one of the reasons you got the job was that you had completed a computer class at the local community college. Unfortunately, there hadn't been much carryover to the incredibly complex computer program you use at work. (It seems to defy every convention of logic.)

"What am I going to tell him about my being late for work so often?" Unfortunately, there isn't an easy answer. "Maybe it will get better as the kids and I get used to this new routine. It's just very difficult to get the kids to the bus stop and the sitter, commute 20 minutes, and arrive precisely at 8:00. I wonder if he would allow me to come in at 8:30 and only take a half-hour lunch. Staying late wouldn't work because they close down the computers at 5:00, unless there was some paperwork I could do for half an hour."

Then what about the problems with the computer and the other staff members? "Sooner or later he's going to get on my case about those things. Is it my fault I don't think like a computer? Some people might be able to sit down and figure this program out in a couple of hours, but not me. So is that my fault or should someone be giving me more training? I wish the others weren't so cliquish and unwilling to help me out. I wonder why that's the case. It's like they're afraid I'll become as good as they are if they share their experience with me. I wish Andre had more time to help me learn the ropes, but he seems to always be in meetings."

"Well, I'm probably going to catch it this morning. I've never been this late. Maybe I'll be back home full time sooner than I expected."

ACTIVITIES FOR MOTIVATING OTHERS

Suggested Assignments

1. Identify a situation in which you have some responsibility for another person whose performance is significantly below your expectation. Using the Work Performance Assessment Survey included in the Skill Practice section, collect information on the individual's perceptions of the situation. Using the diagnostic model (decision tree) in that section, specifically identify the perceived performance problems. Compare these results with your own views of the situation. Conduct an interview with the individual and discuss the results, highlighting areas of disagreement. Based on this discussion, formulate a plan of action that both parties accept. If inadequate ability is a problem, follow the resupply, retrain, refill, reassign, and release remedial steps. If insufficient effort is a problem, use the steps for reprimanding, redirecting, and rewarding discussed in this chapter as a resource for this discussion. Implement this plan for a period of time and then report on the results.

2. Focus on some aspect of your own work in which you feel performance is below your (or others') expectations. Using the Work Performance Assessment survey (Skill Assessment), identify the specific obstacles to improved performance. Then formulate a plan for overcoming these obstacles, including getting commitments from others. Discuss your plan with individuals affected by it and arrive at a set of actions all parties accept. Implement the plan for a period of time and report on your results. How successful were you in making the changes? Did your performance improve as expected? Based on this experience, identify other aspects of your work that you could improve on in a similar fashion.

3. Identify four or five situations in which you are typically provoked to exhibit punishing behavior. These might involve friends, family members, or work associates. Examine these situations and identify one in which punishment (discipline) is not working. Using the guidelines for reprimanding, redirecting, and rewarding, design a specific plan for shaping the other person's behaviors so you can begin rewarding positive actions. Report on your results. Based on this experience, consider how you might be able to use this strategy in other similar situations.

4. Using the six-step model for creating a motivational work environment (see Table 6.2), design a specific plan for managing a new relationship (e.g., a new subordinate) or a new phase in an old relationship (e.g., friend, family member, or subordinate about to begin work on a new project). Write down specific directions for yourself for implementing each of the six steps. Discuss your plan with this individual

and ask for suggestions for improvement. Make sure your perceptions of the key aspects of the plan are consistent with his or hers. Implement your plan for a period of time and then report on the consequences. Based on this experience, identify changes that would be appropriate in similar situations.

SOURCE: J. Richard Hackman & Greg R. Oldham, *Work Redesign*, 1st © 1980. Electronically reproduced by permission of Pearson Education, Inc., Upper Saddle River, New Jersey.

Application Plan and Evaluation

The intent of this exercise is to help you apply this cluster of skills in a real-life, out-of-class setting. Now that you have become familiar with the behavioral guidelines that form the basis of effective skill performance, you will improve most by trying out those guidelines in an everyday context. Unlike a classroom activity, in which feedback is immediate and others can assist you with their evaluations, this skill application activity is one you must accomplish and evaluate on your own. There are two parts to this activity. Part 1 helps prepare you to apply the skill. Part 2 helps you evaluate and improve on your experience. Be sure to write down answers to each item. Don't short-circuit the process by skipping steps.

Part 1. Planning

1. Write down the two or three aspects of this skill that are most important to you. These may be areas of weakness, areas you most want to improve, or areas that are most salient to a problem you face right now. Identify the specific aspects of this skill that you want to apply.

2. Now identify the setting or the situation in which you will apply this skill. Establish a plan for performance by actually writing down a description of the situation. Who else will be involved? When will you do it? Where will it be done?

   Circumstances:

   Who else?
   When?
   Where?

3. Identify the specific behaviors you will engage in to apply this skill. Operationalize your skill performance.

4. What are the indicators of successful performance? How will you know you have been effective? What will indicate you have performed competently?

Part 2. Evaluation

5. After you have completed your implementation, record the results. What happened? How successful were you? What was the effect on others?

6. How can you improve? What modifications can you make next time? What will you do differently in a similar situation in the future?

7. Looking back on your whole skill practice and application experience, what have you learned? What has been surprising? In what ways might this experience help you in the long term?

Diagnosing Poor Performance and Enhancing Motivation

Scoring Key

SKILL AREA	ITEM	ASSESSMENT	
		PRE-	POST-
Diagnosing performance problems	1	_____	_____
	11	_____	_____
Establishing expectations and setting goals	2	_____	_____
	12	_____	_____
Facilitating performance (Enhancing ability)	3	_____	_____
	13	_____	_____
	20	_____	_____
Linking performance to rewards and discipline	5	_____	_____
	14	_____	_____
	6	_____	_____
	15	_____	_____
Using salient internal and external incentives	7	_____	_____
	16	_____	_____
	8	_____	_____
	17	_____	_____
Distributing rewards equitably	9	_____	_____
	18	_____	_____
Providing timely and straightforward performance feedback	4	_____	_____
	10	_____	_____
	19	_____	_____
Total Score		_____	_____

Comparison Data (N = 5,000 Students)

Compare your scores to three comparison standards:
1. The maximum possible score = 120.
2. The scores of other students in your class.
3. Norm data from more than 5,000 business school students.

Pre-Test				Post-Test
96.33	=	mean	=	103.23
104 or above	=	top quartile	=	112 or above
97–103	=	second quartile	=	104–111
90–96	=	third quartile	=	97–103
89 or below	=	bottom quartile	=	96 or below

Work Performance

Scoring Key

STEP 1: Enter your score from each line below, as follows:

Regular scoring: Enter the number for your response on the survey.
Reverse scoring: Subtract the number of your response from 6 and enter the result.

ITEMS	SCORE		ITEMS	SCORE	
1.	Reverse	_____	8.	Regular	_____
2.	Reverse	_____	9.	Regular	_____
3.	Reverse	_____	10.	Regular	_____
4.	Reverse	_____	11.	Regular	_____
5.	Reverse	_____	12.	Regular	_____
6.	Reverse	_____	13.	Regular	_____
7.	Reverse	_____	14.	Regular	_____

STEP 2: Combine your scores according to the type of performance problem. Problems with scores higher than 7 are obstacles to high performance. Total scores over 50 suggest significant, broad-based motivational deficiencies.

TYPE OF PERFORMANCE PROBLEM	SCORES ON ITEMS		TOTALS OF TWO ITEMS
Perception	1. _____	8. _____	_____
Training	2. _____	9. _____	_____
Aptitude	3. _____	10. _____	_____
Resources	4. _____	11. _____	_____
Expectations	5. _____	12. _____	_____
Incentives	6. _____	13. _____	_____
Reward salience	7. _____	14. _____	_____
		Total Score	_____

Comparison Data (N = 5,000 Students)

Mean score:	29.94
Top quartile:	36 or above
Second quartile:	30–35
Third quartile:	24–29
Bottom quartile:	23 or below

Observer's Feedback Form

RATING

1 = Low

5 = High

Reprimand

_____ 1. Identified the specific inappropriate behavior. Gave examples. Indicated that the action must stop.

_____ 2. Pointed out the impact of the problem on the performance of others, the unit's mission, and so forth.

_____ 3. Asked questions about causes and explored remedies.

Redirect

_____ 4. Described the behaviors or standards expected. Made sure the individual understood and agreed that these are reasonable.

_____ 5. Asked if the individual would comply.

_____ 6. Was appropriately supportive. For example, praised other aspects of the person's work, identified personal and group benefits of compliance, and made sure there were no legitimate obstacles in the way of meeting stated expectations.

Reinforce

_____ 7. Identified rewards that were salient to the individual.

_____ 8. Linked the attainment of desirable outcomes with incremental, continuous improvement.

_____ 9. Rewarded (including using praise) all improvements in performance in a timely and honest manner.

Comments:

7

Managing Conflict

SKILL DEVELOPMENT OBJECTIVES

- DIAGNOSE THE FOCUS AND SOURCE OF CONFLICTS
- UTILIZE APPROPRIATE CONFLICT MANAGEMENT STRATEGIES
- RESOLVE INTERPERSONAL CONFRONTATIONS THROUGH COLLABORATION

DIAGNOSTIC SURVEYS FOR MANAGING CONFLICT

MANAGING INTERPERSONAL CONFLICT

Step 1: Before you read this chapter, respond to the following statements by writing a number from the rating scale that follows in the left-hand column (Pre-Assessment). Your answers should reflect your attitudes and behavior as they are now, not as you would like them to be. Be honest. This instrument is designed to help you discover your level of competency in managing conflict so you can tailor your learning to your specific needs. When you have completed the survey, use the scoring key at the end of the chapter to identify the skill areas discussed in this chapter that are most important for you to master.

Step 2: After you have completed the reading and the exercises in this chapter and, ideally, as many of the Skill Application assignments at the end of this chapter as you can, cover up your first set of answers. Then respond to the same statements again, this time in the right-hand column (Post-Assessment). When you have completed the survey, use the scoring key at the end of the chapter to measure your progress. If your score remains low in specific skill areas, use the behavioral guidelines at the end of the Skill Learning section to guide your further practice.

Rating Scale

1 Strongly disagree
2 Disagree
3 Slightly disagree
4 Slightly agree
5 Agree
6 Strongly agree

Assessment

Pre-   Post-

When I see someone doing something that needs correcting:

_____   _____   1. I avoid making personal accusations and attributing self-serving motives to the other person.

_____   _____   2. When stating my concerns, I present them as my problems.

_____   _____   3. I succinctly describe problems in terms of the behavior that occurred, its consequences, and my feelings about it.

_____   _____   4. I specify the expectations and standards that have been violated.

_____   _____   5. I make a specific request, detailing a more acceptable option.

_____   _____   6. I persist in explaining my point of view until it is understood by the other person.

_____   _____   7. I encourage two-way interaction by inviting the respondent to express his or her perspective and to ask questions.

_____   _____   8. When there are several concerns, I approach the issues incrementally, starting with easy and simple issues and then progressing to those that are difficult and complex.

When someone complains about something I've done:

_____ _____ 9. I look for our common areas of agreement.

_____ _____ 10. I show genuine concern and interest, even when I disagree.

_____ _____ 11. I avoid justifying my actions and becoming defensive.

_____ _____ 12. I seek additional information by asking questions that provide specific and descriptive information.

_____ _____ 13. I focus on one issue at a time.

_____ _____ 14. I find some aspects of the complaint with which I can agree.

_____ _____ 15. I ask the other person to suggest more acceptable behaviors.

_____ _____ 16. I reach agreement on a remedial plan of action.

When two other people are in conflict and I am the mediator:

_____ _____ 17. I acknowledge that conflict exists and treat it as serious and important.

_____ _____ 18. I help create an agenda for a problem-solving meeting by identifying the issues to be discussed, one at a time.

_____ _____ 19. I do not take sides, but remain neutral.

_____ _____ 20. I help focus the discussion on the impact of the conflict on work performance.

_____ _____ 21. I keep the interaction focused on problems rather than on personalities.

_____ _____ 22. I make certain that neither party dominates the conversation.

_____ _____ 23. I help the parties generate multiple alternatives.

_____ _____ 24. I help the parties find areas on which they agree.

STRATEGIES FOR HANDLING CONFLICT

Indicate how often you use each of the following by writing the appropriate number in the blank. Choose a number from a scale of 1 to 5, with 1 being "rarely," 3 being "sometimes," and 5 being "always." After you have completed the survey, use the scoring key at the end of the chapter to tabulate your results.

_____ 1. I argue my position tenaciously.

_____ 2. I put the needs of others above my own.

_____ 3. I arrive at a compromise both parties can accept.

_____ 4. I don't get involved in conflicts.

_____ 5. I investigate issues thoroughly and jointly.

_____ 6. I find fault in other persons' positions.

_____ 7. I foster harmony.

_____ 8. I negotiate to get a portion of what I propose.

_____ 9. I avoid open discussions of controversial subjects.

_____ 10. I openly share information with others in resolving disagreements.

_____ 11. I enjoy winning an argument.

_____ 12. I go along with the suggestions of others.

_____ 13. I look for a middle ground to resolve disagreements.

_____ 14. I keep my true feelings to myself to avoid hard feelings.

_____ 15. I encourage the open sharing of concerns and issues.

_____ 16. I am reluctant to admit I am wrong.

_____ 17. I try to help others avoid "losing face" in a disagreement.

_____ 18. I stress the advantages of "give and take."

_____ 19. I encourage others to take the lead in resolving controversy.

_____ 20. I state my position as only one point of view.

Interpersonal Conflict Management

A conflict over issues is not only likely within top-management teams but also valuable. Such conflict provides executives with a more inclusive range of information, a deeper understanding of the issues, and a richer set of possible solutions. [In our ten-year study] we found that the alternative to conflict is usually not agreement but apathy and disengagement. In fast paced markets, successful strategic decisions are most likely to be made by teams that promote active and broad conflict over issues without sacrificing speed. The key to doing so is to mitigate interpersonal conflict. (Eisenhardt, Kahwajy, & Bourgeois, 1997, pp. 84–85)

One of the leading causes of business failure among major corporations is too much agreement among top management. They have similar training and experience, which means they tend to view conditions the same way and pursue similar goals. The resulting lack of tension between competing perspectives can foster a climate of complacency. This problem is often compounded by boards of directors' failing to play an aggressive oversight role. They avoid conflict with the internal management team who appear unified on key issues and very confident of their positions. What we learn from the study of business failures is that the absence of disagreement is often viewed by managers as a sign of good leadership, when in reality it is a leading indicator of being out of touch with significant changes in the marketplace (Argenti, 1976).

Interpersonal conflict is an essential, ubiquitous part of organizational life. In fact, given the current business trends toward workforce diversity, globalization, and joint ventures, how managers from different organizations and cultures deal with conflict is an increasingly important predictor of organizational success (Seybolt, Derr, & Nielson, 1996; Tjosvold, 1991; Memeth, 2004). Organizations in which there is little disagreement regarding important matters generally fail in competitive environments. Members are either so homogeneous that they are ill-equipped to adapt to changing environmental conditions or so complacent that they see no need to improve the status quo. Conflict is the lifeblood of vibrant, progressive, stimulating organizations. It sparks creativity, stimulates innovation, and encourages personal improvement (Blackard & Gibson, 2002; Pascale, 1990; Wanous & Youtz, 1986).

This view is clearly in line with the management philosophy of Andrew Grove, former president of Intel. "Many managers seem to think it is impossible to tackle anything or anyone head-on, even in business. By contrast, we at Intel believe that it is the essence of corporate health to bring a problem out into the open as soon as possible, even if this entails a confrontation. Dealing with conflicts lies at the heart of managing any business. As a result, confrontation— facing issues about which there is disagreement—can be avoided only at the manager's peril. Workplace politicking grows quietly in the dark, like mushrooms; neither can stand the light of day" (Grove, 1984).

However, we all have ample evidence that conflict often produces harmful results. For example, some people have a very low tolerance for disagreement. Whether this is the result of family background, cultural values, or personality characteristics, interpersonal conflict saps people's energy and demoralizes their spirit. Also, some types of conflicts, regardless of frequency, generally produce dysfunctional outcomes. These include personality conflicts and arguments over things that can't be changed.

As Figure 7.1 shows, scholars generally agree that some conflict is both inevitable and beneficial in effective organizations (Brown, 1983). As illustrated in this figure, holding constant the nature of the conflict and how well it is resolved, a moderate level of conflict appears to be healthy for most organizations.

MIXED FEELINGS ABOUT CONFLICT

With this general observation in mind, it is interesting to note that a well-known American psychologist, Abraham Maslow (1965), has observed a high degree of ambivalence regarding the value of conflict. On the one hand, he notes that managers intellectually appreciate the value of conflict and competition. They agree it is a necessary ingredient of the free-enterprise system. However, their actions demonstrate a personal preference for avoiding

Figure 7.1 **Relationship Between Level of Conflict and Organizational Outcomes**

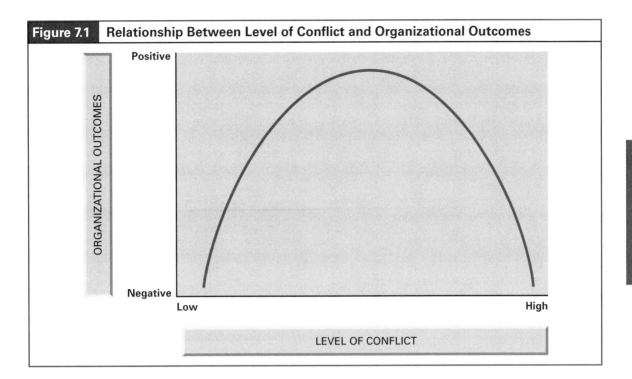

conflicts whenever possible. This ambivalent view of conflict appears to be reflected in the following account:

> In 1984, Ross Perot, an outspoken self-made billionaire, sold Electronic Data Systems (EDS) to General Motors (GM) for $2.5 billion and immediately became GM's largest stockholder and member of the board. GM needed EDS's expertise to coordinate its massive information system. Roger Smith, GM's chairman, also hoped that Perot's fiery spirit would reinvigorate GM's bureaucracy. Almost immediately, Perot became a severe critic of GM policy and practice. He noted that it takes longer for GM to produce a car than it took the country to win WWII. He was especially critical of GM's bureaucracy, claiming it fostered conformity at the expense of getting results. By December 1986, Roger Smith had apparently had enough of Perot's "reinvigoration." Whether his criticisms were true, or functional, the giant automaker paid nearly twice the market value of his stock ($750 million) to silence him and arrange his resignation from the board. (Perot, 1988)

The seemingly inherent tension between the intellectual acceptance of the merits of conflict and the emotional rejection of its enactment is illustrated in a classic study of decision making (Boulding, 1964). Several groups of managers were formed to solve a complex problem. They were told that their performance would be judged by a panel of experts in terms of the quantity and quality of solutions generated. The groups were identical in size and composition, with the exception that half of them included a "confederate." Before the experiment began, the researcher instructed this person to play the role of "devil's advocate." This person was to challenge the group's conclusions, forcing the others to examine critically their assumptions and the logic of their arguments. At the end of the problem-solving period, the recommendations made by both sets of groups were compared. The groups with the devil's advocates had performed significantly better on the task. They had generated more alternatives, and their proposals were judged as superior. After a short break, the groups were reassembled and told that they would be performing a similar task during the next session. However, before they began discussing the next problem, they were given permission to eliminate one member. In every group containing a confederate, he or she was the one asked to leave. The fact that every high-performance group expelled their unique competitive advantage because that member made others feel uncomfortable demonstrates a widely shared reaction to conflict: "I know it has positive outcomes for the performance of the organization, as a whole, but I don't like how it makes me feel, personally."

We believe that much of the ambivalence toward conflict stems from a lack of understanding of the causes of conflict and the variety of modes for managing it effectively, and from a lack of confidence in one's personal skills for handling the tense, emotionally charged environment typical of most interpersonal confrontations. It is natural for an untrained or inexperienced person to avoid threatening situations, and it is generally acknowledged that conflict represents the most severe test of a manager's interpersonal skills. The task of the effective manager, therefore, is to maintain an optimal level of conflict, while keeping conflicts focused on productive purposes (Kelly, 1970; Thomas, 1976).

This view of conflict management is supported by a 10-year study conducted by Kathy Eisenhardt and her colleagues at Stanford University (Eisenhardt et al., 1997). In their *Harvard Business Review* article, they report, "The challenge is to encourage members of management teams to argue without destroying their ability to work together" (p. 78). What makes this possible? These authors identify several key "rules of engagement" for effective conflict management:

❑ Work with more, rather than less, information.
❑ Focus on the facts.
❑ Develop multiple alternatives to enrich the level of debate.
❑ Share commonly agreed-upon goals.
❑ Inject humor into the decision process.
❑ Maintain a balanced power structure.
❑ Resolve issues without forcing consensus.

Thus far, we have determined that: (1) interpersonal conflict in organizations is inevitable; (2) conflicts over issues or facts enhance the practice of management; (3) despite the intellectual acceptance of the value of conflict, there is a widespread tendency to avoid it; and (4) the key to increasing one's comfort level with conflict is to become proficient in managing all forms of interpersonal disputes (both productive and unproductive conflicts).

Following our skill-development orientation, the remainder of this chapter focuses on increasing your competence-based confidence. Drawing upon a large body of research on this subject, it appears that effective conflict managers must be proficient in the use of three essential skills. First, they must be able to accurately diagnose the types of conflict, including their causes. For example, managers need to understand how cultural differences and other forms of demographic diversity can spark conflicts in organizations. Second, having identified the sources of conflict and taken into account the context and personal preferences for dealing with conflict, managers must be able to select an appropriate conflict management strategy. Third, skillful managers must be able to settle interpersonal disputes effectively so that underlying problems are resolved and the relationship between disputants is not damaged. We now turn our attention to these three broad management proficiencies.

Diagnosing the Type of Interpersonal Conflict

Because interpersonal conflicts come in assorted lots, our first skill-building task involves the art of diagnosis. In any type of clinical setting, from medicine to management, it is common knowledge that effective intervention is predicated upon accurate diagnosis. Figure 7.2 presents a categorizing device for diagnosing the *type of conflict*, based on two critical identifying characteristics: focus and source. By understanding the *focus of the conflict*, we gain an appreciation for the substance of the dispute (what is fueling the conflict), and by learning more about the origins, or *source of the conflict*, we better understand how it got started (the igniting spark).

CONFLICT FOCUS

It is common to categorize conflicts in organizations in terms of whether they are primarily focused on *people* or *issues* (Eisenhardt et al., 1997; Jehn & Mannix, 2001). By this distinction we mean: is this a negotiation-like conflict over competing ideas, proposals, interests, or resources; or is this a dispute-like conflict stemming from what has transpired between the parties?

One of the nice features of the distinction between people-focused and issue-focused conflicts is that it helps us understand why some managers believe that conflict is the lifeblood of their organization, while others believe that each and every conflict episode sucks blood from their organization. Research has shown that people-focused conflicts threaten relationships, whereas issue-based conflicts enhance relationships, provided that people are comfortable with it, including feeling able to manage it effectively (de Dreu & Weingart, 2002; Jehn, 1997). Therefore, in general, when we read about the benefits of "productive conflict," the authors are referring to issue-focused conflict.

Although, by definition, all interpersonal conflicts involve people, **people-focused conflict** refers to the "in your face" kind of confrontations in which the

| Figure 7.2 | Categorizing Different Types of Conflict |

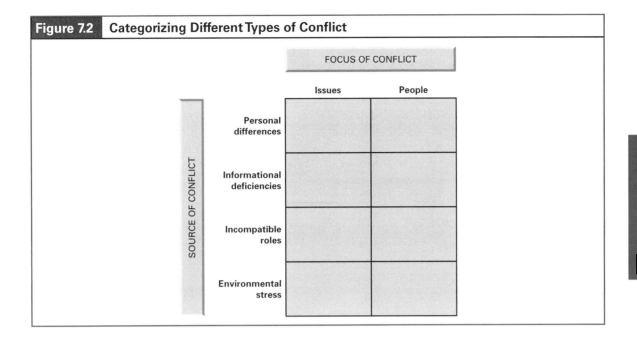

affect level is high and the intense emotional heat is likely fueled by moral indignation. Accusations of harm, demands for justice, and feelings of resentment are the common markers of personal disputes. Hence, personal disputes are extremely difficult to resolve, and the long-term effects of the dispute on interpersonal relations can be devastating. The longer this type of dispute goes on, the larger the gulf between the parties becomes and the more supporters begin showing up, arm in arm, on either side.

You might wonder how likely it is that you will actually become embroiled in a nasty, interpersonal confrontation. Isn't this something that just gets stirred up by spiteful, insecure crackpots and only gets under the skin of defensive, closed-minded people? Although effective application of the skills covered in this book should lessen the likelihood of your interpersonal relationships becoming entangled in the web of personal disputes, the following information is sobering.

In response to the question, "In general, what percentage of management time is wasted on resolving personality conflicts?" Max Messmer, chairman of Accountemps, reports an average response of 18 percent from a large sample of organizations, compared with 9.2 percent a decade earlier. He laments the fact that approximately nine weeks of management time each year is consumed by this nonproductive activity ("The boss as referee," 1996).

Coming at the subject from a different angle, a recent article entitled, "Is Having Partners a Bad Idea?" reported the results of an *Inc.* magazine poll in which

nearly two-thirds of the small business owners surveyed said, notwithstanding the potential benefits, they preferred not adding a partner because of the increased potential for interpersonal conflict. In a second poll reported in this article, researchers at the University of Minnesota uncovered similar misgivings in family businesses. About half of the second-generation family members working in such companies were having second thoughts about the wisdom of joining the firm because, again, they were worried about their business careers being marred by interpersonal conflicts (Gage, 1999).

Whereas we have characterized people-focused conflicts as emotional disputes, **issue-focused conflicts** are more like rational negotiations, which can be thought of as "an interpersonal decision-making process by which two or more people agree how to allocate scarce resources" (Thompson, 2001, p. 2). In issue-based conflicts, manager-negotiators are typically acting as agents, representing the interests of their department, function, or project. Although negotiators have conflicting priorities for how the scarce resources should be utilized, in most day-to-day negotiations within an organization the negotiators recognize the need to find an amicable settlement that appears fair to all parties. Because the negotiation outcome, if not the process itself, is generally public knowledge, the negotiators recognize that there is no such thing as one-time-only negotiations. One veteran manager observed that he uses a simple creed to govern his dealings with others, "It's a small world and a long life"—meaning there is no long-term personal advantage to short-term gains won through unfair means. The importance of conflict "focus" was demonstrated by a longitudinal study of work teams. The teams that were most successful were low on relationship conflict (people-focus) but high on process conflict (issue focus) (Jehn & Mannix, 2001).

Although our discussion of conflict management draws liberally on the negotiations literature, our objective is to prepare readers for highly charged emotional confrontations in which untrained initiators attempt to transfer their frustration to someone else by alleging that great harm has been caused by the offender's self-serving motives or incompetent practices. Being on the receiving end of a "surprise personal attack" is debilitating, and so the unskilled respondent is likely to fight back, escalating the conflict with counteraccusations or defensive retorts. That's why experienced mediators agree that when a disagreement "gets personal," it often becomes intractable.

CONFLICT SOURCE

We now shift our diagnostic lens from understanding the focus, or content, of a conflict ("What's this about?") to the source, or origin, of the conflict ("How did it get started?"). Managers, especially those who feel uncomfortable with conflict, often behave as though interpersonal conflict is the result of personality defects. They label people who are frequently involved in conflicts "troublemakers" or "bad apples" and attempt to transfer or dismiss them as a way of resolving disagreements. While some individuals seem to have a propensity for making trouble and appear to be disagreeable under even the best of circumstances, "sour dispositions" actually account for only a small percentage of organizational conflicts (Hines, 1980; Schmidt & Tannenbaum, 1965).

This proposition is supported by research on performance appraisals (Latham & Wexley, 1994). It has been shown that managers generally attribute poor performance to personal deficiencies in workers, such as laziness, lack of skill, or lack of motivation. However, when workers are asked the causes of their poor performance, they generally explain it in terms of problems in their environment, such as insufficient supplies or uncooperative coworkers. While some face-saving is obviously involved here, this line of research suggests that managers need to guard against the reflexive tendency to assume that bad behaviors imply bad people. In fact, aggressive or harsh behaviors sometimes observed in interpersonal confrontations often reflect the frustrations of people who have good intentions but are unskilled in handling intense, emotional experiences.

In contrast to the personality-defect theory of conflict, we propose four sources of interpersonal conflict in

Table 7.1	Sources of Conflict
Personal differences	Perceptions and expectations
Informational deficiencies	Misinformation and misrepresentation
Role incompatibility	Goals and responsibilities
Environmental stress	Resource scarcity and uncertainty

Table 7.1. These are *personal differences, informational deficiencies, role incompatibility*, and *environmental stress*. **Personal differences** are a common source of conflict because individuals bring different backgrounds to their roles in organizations. Their values and needs have been shaped by different socialization processes, depending on their cultural and family traditions, level of education, breadth of experience, and so forth. As a result, their interpretations of events and their expectations about relationships with others in the organization vary considerably. Conflicts stemming from incompatible personal values and needs are some of the most difficult to resolve. They often become highly emotional and take on moral overtones. Under these conditions, a disagreement about what is *factually correct* easily turns into a bitter argument over *who is morally right*.

The distinction between people-focused conflict and personal differences as a source of conflict may seem a bit confusing. It might help to think of personal differences as a set of lenses that each member of an organization uses to make sense of daily experiences and to make value judgments, in terms of what is good and bad, appropriate and inappropriate. Because these conclusions are likely to become strongly held beliefs that conflict with equally strong beliefs held by coworkers, it is easy to see how these could spark interpersonal conflicts. However, parties to a dispute still have choices regarding what path their dispute will take, in terms of focusing on the issues (e.g., conflicting points of view reflecting different values and needs) or the people (e.g., questioning competence, intent, acceptance, understanding, etc.). It is precisely because conflicts stemming from personal differences tend to become person-focused that effective conflict managers need to understand this analytical distinction so they can help disputants frame their conflict in terms of offending (troublesome) issues, and not offensive (troublemaking) people.

This observation is particularly relevant for managers working in an organizational environment characterized by broad demographic diversity. Why? It has been observed that: (1) a diverse workforce can be a strategic organizational asset, and (2) very different people tend to engage in very intense conflicts—which can become an organizational liability (Lombardo & Eichinger, 1996; Pelled, Eisenhardt, & Xin, 1999). On the positive side, the more heterogeneous the demographic profile of an employee population is, the more diversity of experience and perspective contained in the organization (Cox, 1994). From various studies of diversity in organizations (Cox & Blake, 1991; Morrison, 1996), some of the consistently cited benefits of an effectively managed, diverse workforce include:

❏ Cost savings from reducing turnover rates among minority employees

❏ Improved creativity and problem-solving capabilities due to the broader range of perspectives and cultural mind-sets

❏ Perceptions of fairness and equity in the workplace

❏ Increased flexibility that positively affects motivation and minimizes conflict between work and nonwork demands (e.g., family, personal interests, leisure)

A recent study of diverse teams demonstrates how socially distinct newcomers bring benefits. Although diverse groups expressed less confidence in their performance than homogenous groups, they performed better (Phillips, Liljenquist, & Neale, 2009). But few beneficial changes come without commensurate challenges. The old saying, "To create a spark, strike two unlike substances together," speaks to the notion that a diverse workforce will increase creativity and innovation. This saying also reminds us that "sparks can hurt." That's why it's particularly important to look beneath the surface of interpersonal differences for a better understanding of why people from very different backgrounds often find themselves embroiled in debilitating interpersonal conflicts.

To begin with, people from different ethnic and cultural groups often have very different views about the value of, and justifications for, interpersonal disputes (Adler, 2002; Trompenaars, 1994, 1996). To state this observation more broadly, conflict is largely a culturally defined event (Sillars & Weisberg, 1987; Weldon & Jehn, 1995; Wilmot & Hocker, 2001), in the sense that our cultural background colors our views about what is worth "fighting for" and what constitutes "a fair fight."

In addition, when the everyday business of an organization requires people with very different demographic profiles to interact frequently, it is likely that their interactions will be marred by misunderstanding and mistrust due to a lack of understanding of and appreciation for each other's needs and values. The potential for harmful conflict is even greater when confrontations involve members of majority and minority groups within an organization. This is where "diversity-sensitive" managers can help out by considering questions like: Are both participants from the majority culture of the organization? If one is from a minority culture, to what extent is diversity valued in the organization? To what extent do members of these minority and majority cultures understand and value the benefits of a diverse workforce for our organization? Has this particular minority group or individual had a history of conflict within the organization? If so, are there broader issues regarding the appreciation of personal differences that need to be addressed?

It is not difficult to envision how core differences in employees' personal identities could become manifest in organizational conflicts. For example, if a U.S. firm receives a very attractive offer from the Chinese government to build a major manufacturing facility in that country, it is very likely that a 35-year-old Chinese manager in that firm, who was exiled from China following the 1989 riots in Tiananmen Square, would strongly oppose this initiative. This example illustrates a conflict between a majority and minority member of an organization. It also exemplifies disputes in which differences in personal experiences and values lead one party to support a proposal because it is a good business decision and the other party to oppose the action because it is a bad moral decision.

The second source or cause of conflict among members of an organization is **informational deficiencies**. An important message may not be received, a boss's instructions may be misinterpreted, or decision makers may arrive at different conclusions because they use different databases. Conflicts based on misinformation or misunderstanding tend to be factual; hence, clarifying previous messages or obtaining additional information generally resolves the dispute. This might entail rewording the boss's instructions, reconciling contradictory sources of data, or redistributing copies of misplaced messages. This type of conflict is common in organizations, but it is also easy to resolve. Because value systems are not challenged, such confrontations tend to be less emotional. Once the breakdown in the information system is repaired, disputants are generally able to resolve their disagreement with minimal of resentment.

For example, UOP, Inc., made an agreement with Union Carbide in 1987 that doubled its workforce. Conflicts over operating procedures surfaced immediately between the original employees and the new employees from Union Carbide. This, combined with traditional conflicts between functional groups in the organization, led UOP to begin a new training program in which groups of employees met to discuss quality improvements. "We discovered that the main problem had been a lack of communication," said one senior official. "No one had any idea what other groups were up to, so they all assumed that their way was best" (Caudron, 1992, p. 61).

The complexity inherent in most organizations tends to produce conflict between members whose tasks are interdependent but who occupy incompatible roles. This type of conflict is exemplified by the classic goal conflicts between line and staff, production and sales, and marketing and research and development (R&D). Each unit has different responsibilities in the organization, and as a result each places different priorities on organizational goals (e.g., customer satisfaction, product quality, production efficiency, compliance with government regulations). It is also typical of firms whose multiple product lines compete for scarce resources.

During the early days at Apple Computer, the Apple II division accounted for a large part of the company's revenue. It viewed the newly created Macintosh division as an unwise speculative venture. The natural rivalry was made worse when a champion of the Macintosh referred to the Apple II team as "the dull and boring product division." Because this type of conflict stems from the fundamental incompatibility of the job responsibilities of the disputants, it can often be resolved only through the mediation of a common superior.

Role incompatibility conflicts may overlap with those arising from personal differences or information deficiencies. The personal differences members bring to an organization generally remain dormant until they are triggered by an organizational catalyst, such as interdependent task responsibilities. One reason members often perceive that their assigned roles are incompatible is that they are operating from different bases of information. They communicate with different sets of people, are tied into different reporting systems, and receive instructions from different bosses.

Another major source of conflict is **environmentally induced stress**. Conflicts stemming from personal differences and role incompatibilities are greatly exacerbated by a stressful environment. When an organization is forced to operate on an austere budget, its members are more likely to become embroiled in disputes over domain claims and resource requests. Scarcity tends to lower trust, increase ethnocentrism, and reduce participation in decision making. These are ideal conditions for incubating interpersonal conflict (Cameron, Kim, & Whetten, 1987).

When a large eastern bank announced a major downsizing, the threat to employees' security was so severe that it disrupted long-time, close working relationships. Even friendships were not immune to the effects of the scarcity-induced stress. Long-standing golf foursomes and car pools were disbanded because tension among members was so high.

Another environmental condition that fosters conflict is uncertainty. When individuals are unsure about their status in an organization, they become very anxious and prone to conflict. This type of "frustration conflict" often stems from rapid, repeated change. If task assignments, management philosophy, accounting procedures, and lines of authority are changed frequently, members find it difficult to cope with the resulting stress, and sharp, bitter conflicts can easily erupt over seemingly trivial problems. This type of conflict is generally intense, but it dissipates quickly once a change becomes routinized and individuals' stress levels are lowered.

When a major pet-food manufacturing facility announced that one-third of its managers would have to support a new third shift, the feared disruption of personal and family routines prompted many managers to think about sending out their résumés. In addition, the uncertainty of who was going to be required to work at night was so great that even routine management work was disrupted by posturing and infighting.

Before concluding this discussion of various sources of interpersonal conflicts, it is useful to point out that the seminal research of Geert Hofstede (1980) on cultural values suggests how people from any given cultural background might be drawn into different types of conflict. For example, one of the primary dimensions of cultural values emerging from Hofstede's research was tolerance for uncertainty. Some cultures, such as in Japan, have a high uncertainty avoidance, whereas other cultures, like the United States, are much more uncertainty tolerant. Extrapolating from these findings, if an American firm and a Japanese firm have created a joint venture in an industry known for highly volatile sales (e.g., short-term memory chips), one would expect that the Japanese managers would experience a higher level of uncertainty-induced conflict than their American counterparts. In contrast, because American culture places an extremely high value on individualism (another of Hofstede's key dimensions of cultural values), one would expect that the U.S. managers in this joint venture would experience a higher level of conflict stemming from their role interdependence with their Japanese counterparts.

To illustrate how various types of conflict actually get played out in an organization and how devastating their impact on a firm's performance can be, let's take a look at the troubles encountered by First Boston, one of the top seven investment banks dominating the New York capital market. This venerable firm became embroiled in conflict between two important revenue divisions: trading and investment banking. After the stock market crash in 1987, the investment banking division, which accounted for the bulk of First Boston's profits in the 1980s through mergers and acquisitions, asked that resources be diverted from trading (an unprofitable line) to investment banking. They also asked for allocation of computer costs on the basis of usage instead of splitting the costs in half, since investment banking did not use computers very much. A review committee, including the CEO (a trader by background) reviewed the problem and finally decided to reject the investment banking proposals. This led to the resignations of the head of the investment division and several of the senior staff, including seven leveraged-buyout specialists.

This interdepartmental conflict was exacerbated by increasing frictions between competing subcultures within the firm. In the 1950s, when First Boston began, it was "WASPish" in composition, and its business came chiefly through the "old-boy network." In the 1970s, First Boston recruited a number of innovative "whiz kids"— mostly Jews, Italians, and Cubans. These individuals generated innovative ways to package mergers and acquisitions, which are now the mainstay of the current business in the investment area. These were less aristocratic people, many even wearing jeans to the office. The tension between the new "high flyers" and the "old guard" appeared to color many decisions at First Boston.

As a result of these conflicts, First Boston lost a number of key personnel. "The quitters claim that as the firm has grown, it has become a less pleasant place to work in, with political infighting taking up too much time" ("Catch a Falling Star," 1988).

Selecting the Appropriate Conflict Management Approach

Now that we have examined various types of conflict in terms of their focus and sources, it is natural to shift our attention to the common approaches for managing conflict of any type. As revealed in the Pre-Assessment survey, people's responses to interpersonal confrontations tend to fall into five categories: *forcing, accommodating, avoiding, compromising,* and *collaborating* (Volkema &

Bergmann, 2001). These responses can be organized along two dimensions, as shown in Figure 7.3 (Ruble & Thomas, 1976). These five approaches to conflict reflect different degrees of cooperativeness and assertiveness. A cooperative response is intended to satisfy the needs of the interacting person, whereas an assertive response focuses on the needs of the focal person. The cooperativeness dimension reflects the importance of the relationship, whereas the assertiveness dimension reflects the importance of the issue.

The **forcing response** (assertive, uncooperative) is an attempt to satisfy one's own needs at the expense of the needs of the other individual. This can be done by using formal authority, physical threats, manipulation ploys, or by ignoring the claims of the other party. The blatant use of the authority of one's office ("I'm the boss, so we'll do it my way") or a related form of intimidation is generally evidence of a lack of tolerance or self-confidence. The use of manipulation or feigned ignorance is a much more subtle reflection of an egoistic leadership style. Manipulative leaders often appear to be democratic by proposing that conflicting proposals be referred to a committee for further investigation. However, they ensure that the composition of the committee reflects their interests and preferences so that what appears to be a selection based on merit is actually an authoritarian act. A related ploy some managers use is to ignore a proposal that threatens their personal interests. If the originator inquires about the disposition of his or her memo, the manager pleads ignorance, blames the mail clerk or new secretary, and then suggests that the proposal be redrafted. After several of these encounters, subordinates generally get the message that the boss isn't interested in their ideas.

The problem with the repeated use of this conflict management approach is that it breeds hostility and resentment. While observers may intellectually admire authoritarian or manipulative leaders because they appear to accomplish a great deal, their management styles generally produce a backlash in the long run as people become increasingly unwilling to absorb the emotional costs and work to undermine the power base of the authoritarian leader.

The **accommodating approach** (cooperative, unassertive) satisfies the other party's concerns while neglecting one's own. Unfortunately, as in the case of boards of directors of failing firms who neglect their interests and responsibilities in favor of accommodating the wishes of management, this strategy generally results in both parties "losing." The difficulty with the habitual use of the accommodating approach is that it emphasizes preserving a friendly relationship at the expense of

Figure 7.3   **Two-Dimensional Model of Conflict Behavior**

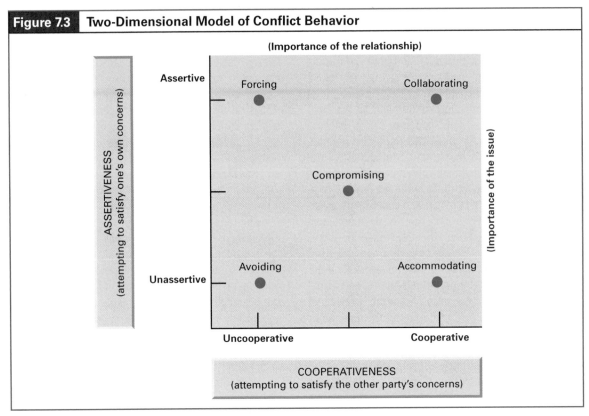

SOURCE: *Adapted from Ruble & Thomas, 1976.*

critically appraising issues and protecting personal rights. This may result in others' taking advantage of you, which lowers your self-esteem as you observe yourself being used by others to accomplish their objectives while you fail to make any progress toward your own.

The **avoiding response** (uncooperative, unassertive) neglects the interests of both parties by sidestepping the conflict or postponing a solution. This is often the response of managers who are emotionally ill-prepared to cope with the stress associated with confrontations, or it might reflect recognition that a relationship is not strong enough to absorb the fallout of an intense conflict. The repeated use of this approach causes considerable frustration for others because issues never seem to get resolved, really tough problems are avoided because of their high potential for conflict, and subordinates engaging in conflict are reprimanded for undermining the harmony of the work group. Sensing a leadership vacuum, people from all directions rush to fill it, creating considerable confusion and animosity in the process.

The **compromising response** is intermediate between assertiveness and cooperativeness. A compromise is an attempt to obtain partial satisfaction for both parties, in the sense that both receive the proverbial "half loaf." To accommodate this, both parties are asked to make sacrifices to obtain a common gain. While this approach has considerable practical appeal to managers, its indiscriminate use is counterproductive. If subordinates are continually told to "split the difference," they may conclude that their managers are more interested in resolving disputes than solving problems. This creates a climate of expediency that encourages game playing, such as asking for twice as much as you need.

A common mistake made in mergers is placing undue emphasis on "being fair to both sides" by compromising on competing corporate policies and practices as well as on which redundant staff members get laid off. When decisions are made on the basis of "spreading the pain evenly" or "using half of your procedures and half of ours," rather than on the basis of merit, then harmony takes priority over value. Ironically, actions taken in the name of "keeping peace in the merged families" often end up being so illogical and impractical that the emerging union is doomed to operate under a pall of constant internal turmoil and conflict.

The **collaborating approach** (cooperative, assertive) is an attempt to address fully the concerns of both parties. It is often referred to as the "problem-solving" mode. In this mode, the intent is to find solutions to the cause of the conflict that are satisfactory to both parties rather than to find fault or assign blame. In this way, both parties can feel that they have "won." This is the only win-win strategy among the five. The avoiding mode results in a lose-lose outcome and the compromising, accommodating, and forcing modes all represent win-lose outcomes. Although the collaborative approach is not appropriate for all situations, when used appropriately, it has the most beneficial effect on the involved parties. It encourages norms of collaboration and trust while acknowledging the value of assertiveness. It encourages individuals to focus their disputes on problems and issues rather than on personalities. Finally, it cultivates the skills necessary for self-governance, so that effective problem solvers feel empowered. The collaborative approach to problem solving and conflict resolution works best in an environment supporting openness, directness, and

equality. In an interview with Steven Jobs after he began, NeXT the editors of *Inc.* magazine quizzed the man they heralded as the "entrepreneur of the decade" regarding the perils of being a celebrity boss. ["It must help you in attracting the best minds to your new computer firm, but once they're there, aren't they intimidated, working for a legend?"]

It all depends on the culture. The culture at NeXT definitely rewards independent thought, and we often have constructive disagreements— at all levels. It doesn't take a new person long to see that people feel fine about openly disagreeing with me. That doesn't mean I can't disagree with them, but it does mean that the best ideas win. Our attitude is that we want the best. Don't get hung up on who owns the idea. Pick the best one, and let's go. (Gendron & Burlingham, 1989)

Table 7.2 shows a comparison of the five conflict management approaches. In this table, the fundamentals

Table 7.2	A Comparison of Five Conflict Management Approaches			
APPROACH	**OBJECTIVE**	**POINT OF VIEW**	**SUPPORTING RATIONALE**	**LIKELY OUTCOME**
1. Forcing	Get your way.	"I know what's right. Don't question my judgment or authority."	It is better to risk causing a few hard feelings than to abandon an issue you are committed to.	You feel vindicated but other party feels defeated and possibly humiliated.
2. Avoiding	Avoid having to deal with conflict.	"I'm neutral on that issue." "Let me think about it." "That's someone else's problem."	Disagreements are inherently bad because they create tension.	Interpersonal problems don't get resolved, causing long-term frustration manifested in a variety of ways.
3. Compromising	Reach an agreement quickly.	"Let's search for a solution we can both live with so we can get on with our work."	Prolonged conflicts distract people from their work and engender bitter feelings.	Participants become conditioned to seek expedient, rather than effective, solutions.
4. Accommodating	Don't upset the other person.	"How can I help you feel good about this encounter?" "My position isn't so important that it is worth risking bad feelings between us."	Maintaining harmonious relationships should be our top priority.	The other person is likely to take advantage of you.
5. Collaborating	Solve the problem together.	"This is my position. What is yours?" "I'm committed to finding the best possible solution." "What do the facts suggest?"	The positions of both parties are equally important (though not necessarily equally valid). Equal emphasis should be placed on the quality of the outcome and the fairness of the decision-making process.	The problem is most likely to be resolved. Also, both parties are committed to the solution and satisfied that they have been treated fairly.

of each approach are laid out, including its objective, how that objective is reflected in terms of an expressed point of view, and a supporting rationale. In addition, the likely outcomes of each approach are summarized.

COMPARING CONFLICT MANAGEMENT AND NEGOTIATION STRATEGIES

Although we have already noted that there is not a one-to-one correspondence between our focus on interpersonal confrontations and the negotiations literature, we believe our understanding of the five conflict management approaches is enriched by the following comparison (Savage, Blair, & Sorenson, 1989; Smith, 1987). **Negotiation strategies** are commonly categorized according to two broad perspectives: *integrative* and *distributive*. Stated succinctly, negotiation perspectives serve as an overarching value, or attitude, held by adversaries, that bound their set of acceptable approaches for resolving their differences and that give meaning to the outcomes of the conflict resolution process.

Negotiators who focus on dividing up a "fixed pie" reflect a **distributive bargaining perspective**, whereas parties using an **integrative perspective** search for collaborative ways of "expanding the pie" by avoiding fixed, incompatible positions (Bazerman & Neale, 1992; Murnighan, 1992, 1993; Thompson, 2001). One way to think about this distinction is that the distributive perspective focuses on the relative, individual scores for both sides (A versus B), whereas the integrative perspective focuses on the combined score (A + B). Hence, distributive negotiators assume an adversarial, competitive posture. They believe that one of the parties can improve only at the other party's expense. In contrast, integrative bargainers use problem-solving techniques to find "win-win" outcomes. They are interested in finding the best solution for both parties, rather than picking between the parties' preferred solutions (de Dreu, Koole, & Steinel, 2000; Fisher & Brown, 1988).

As Table 7.3 shows, four of the five conflict management strategies are distributive in nature. One or both parties must sacrifice something in order for the conflict to be resolved. Compromise occurs when both parties make sacrifices in order to find a common ground. Compromisers are generally more interested in finding an expedient solution than they are in finding an integrative solution. Forcing and accommodating demand that one party give up its position in order for the conflict to be resolved. When parties to a conflict avoid resolution, they do so because they assume that the costs of resolving the

Table 7.3	Comparison Between Negotiation and Conflict Management Strategies	
Negotiation Strategies	Distributive	Integrative
Conflict Management Strategies	Compromising Forcing Accommodating Avoiding	Collaborating

conflict are so high that they are better off not even attempting resolution. The "fixed pie" still exists, but the individuals involved view attempts to divide it as threatening, so they avoid decisions regarding the allocation process altogether.

SELECTION FACTORS

A comparison of alternative approaches inevitably leads to questions like "Which one is the best?" or "Which one should I use in this situation?" Although, in general, the collaborative approach produces the fewest negative side effects, each approach has its place. The appropriateness of a management strategy depends on its congruence with both personal preferences and situational considerations. We will begin by discussing the most limiting consideration: how comfortable do individuals feel actually using each of the conflict management approaches or strategies?

Personal Preferences

As reflected in the "Strategies for Handling Conflict" survey in the Skill Assessment section of this chapter, it is important that we understand our personal preferences for managing conflict. If we don't feel comfortable with a particular approach, we are not likely to use it, no matter how convinced we are that it is the best available tool for a particular conflict situation. Although there are numerous factors that affect our personal preferences for how we manage conflict, three correlates of these choices have been studied extensively: ethnic culture, gender, and personality.

Research on conflict management styles reports that *ethnic culture* is reflected in individual preferences for the five responses we have just discussed (Seybolt et al., 1996; Weldon & Jehn, 1995). For example, it has been shown that individuals from Asian cultures tend to prefer the nonconfrontational styles of accommodating and avoiding (Rahim & Blum, 1994; Ting-Toomey et al., 1991; Xie, Song, & Stringfellow, 1998), whereas, by comparison, Americans and South Africans prefer the forcing approach (Rahim & Blum, 1994; Seybolt et al., 1996; Xie et al., 1998). In general, compromise is the most commonly preferred approach across cultures (Seybolt et al., 1996), possibly because compromising may be viewed as the least costly alternative and the approach that most quickly reaches acceptable levels of fairness to both parties.

The research on the relationship between preferred conflict management style and *gender* is less clear cut. Some studies report that males are more likely to use the forcing response, whereas females tend to select the compromising approach (Kilmann & Thomas, 1977; Ruble & Schneer, 1994). In contrast, other studies found gender to have little influence on an individual's preferred responses to conflict (Korabik, Baril, & Watson, 1993). From a review of the growing literature on conflict styles and gender, Keashly (1994) drew five conclusions:

1. There is little evidence of gender differences in abilities and skills related to conflict management.

2. Evidence suggests that sex-role expectations appear to influence behavior and perceptions of behavior in particular conflict situations.

3. Influences and norms other than sex-role expectations may affect and influence conflict and behavior.

4. The experience and meaning of conflict may differ for women and men.

5. There is a persistence of beliefs in gender-linked behavior even when these behaviors are not found in research.

In summary, there is a widely shared belief that gender differences are correlated with conflict management style preferences, but this perception is only modestly supported by the results of recent research.

The third correlate of personal preferences is *personality type*. One line of research on this topic has linked conflict management style with three distinct personality profiles (Cummings, Harnett, & Stevens, 1971; Porter, 1973).

The *altruistic-nurturing* personality seeks gratification through promoting harmony with others and enhancing their welfare, with little concern for being rewarded in return. This personality type is characterized by trust, optimism, idealism, and loyalty. When altruistic-nurturing individuals encounter conflict, they tend to press for harmony by accommodating the demands of the other party.

The *assertive-directing* personality seeks gratification through self-assertion and directing the activities of others with a clear sense of having earned rewards. Individuals with this personality characteristic tend to be self-confident, enterprising, and persuasive. It is not surprising that the assertive-directing personality tends to challenge the opposition by using the forcing approach to conflict management.

The *analytic-autonomizing* personality seeks gratification through the achievement of self-sufficiency, self-reliance, and logical orderliness. This personality type is cautious, practical, methodical, and principled. Individuals with this type of personality tend to be very cautious when encountering conflict. Initially, they attempt to resolve the problem rationally. However, if the conflict intensifies they will generally withdraw and break contact.

The Advantage of Flexibility

It is important to point out that none of these correlates of personal preferences is deterministic—they suggest general tendencies across various groups of people, but they do not totally determine individual choices. This is an important distinction, because, given the variety of causes, or forms, of conflict, one would suppose that effective conflict management would require the use of more than one approach or strategy.

The research on this matter is illuminating. In a classic study on this topic, 25 executives were asked to describe two conflict situations—one with bad results and one with good (Phillips & Cheston, 1979). These incidents were then categorized in terms of the conflict management approach used. As Figure 7.4 shows, there were 23 incidents of forcing, 12 incidents of problem solving, 5 incidents of compromise, and 12 incidents of avoidance. Admittedly, this was a very small sample of managers, but the fact that there were almost twice as many incidents of forcing as problem solving and nearly five times as many as compromising is noteworthy. It is also interesting that the executives indicated that forcing and compromising were equally as likely to produce good as bad results, whereas problem solving was always linked with positive outcomes, and avoidance generally led to negative results.

It is striking that, despite the fact that forcing was as likely to produce bad as good results, it was by far the most commonly used conflict management mode. Since this approach is clearly not superior in terms of results, one wonders why these senior executives reported a propensity for using it.

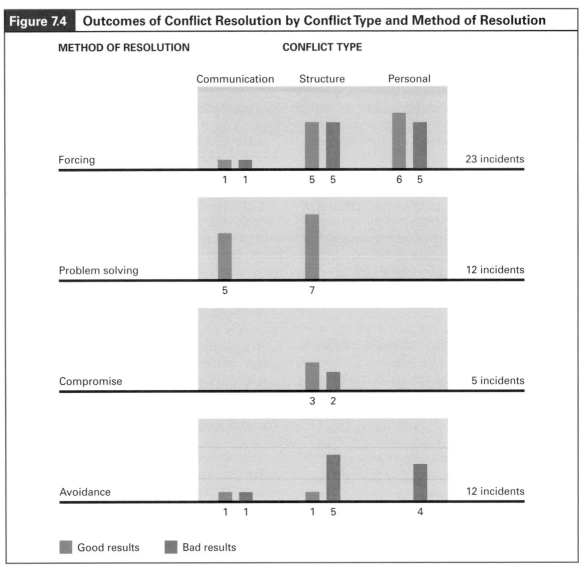

Figure 7.4 Outcomes of Conflict Resolution by Conflict Type and Method of Resolution

METHOD OF RESOLUTION   CONFLICT TYPE

Communication   Structure   Personal

Forcing   23 incidents

1   1   5   5   6   5

Problem solving   12 incidents

5   7

Compromise   5 incidents

3   2

Avoidance   12 incidents

1   1   1   5   4

■ Good results   ■ Bad results

SOURCE: © 1979 by The Regents of the University of California. Reprinted from the California Management Review. Vol. 21, No. 4. By permission of The Regents.

A likely answer is expediency. Evidence for this supposition is provided by a study of the preferred influence strategies of more than 300 managers in three countries (Kipnis & Schmidt, 1983). This study reports that when subordinates refuse or appear reluctant to comply with a request, managers become directive. When resistance in subordinates is encountered, managers tend to fall back on their superior power and insist on compliance. So pervasive was this pattern that the authors of this study proposed an "Iron Law of Power: The greater the discrepancy in power between influence and target, the greater the probability that more directive influence strategies will be used" (p. 7).

A second prominent finding in Figure 7.4 is that some conflict management approaches were never used for certain types of issues. In particular, the managers did not report a single case of problem solving or compromising when personal problems were the source of the conflict. These approaches were used primarily for managing conflicts involving incompatible goals and conflicting reward systems between departments.

Two conclusions can be drawn from the research on the use of different conflict management approaches. First, no one approach is most effective for managing every type of conflict. Second, managers are more effective in dealing with conflicts if they feel comfortable using a variety of approaches (Savage et al., 1989).

These conclusions point out the need to understand the conditions under which each conflict management

Table 7.4 | Matching the Conflict Management Approach with the Situation

SITUATIONAL CONSIDERATIONS	CONFLICT MANAGEMENT APPROACH				
	FORCING	ACCOMMODATING	COMPROMISING	COLLABORATING	AVOIDING
Issue Importance	High	Low	Med	High	Low
Relationship Importance	Low	High	Med	High	Low
Relative Power	High	Low	Equal	Low-High	Equal
Time Constraints	Med-High	Med-High	Low	Low	Med-High

technique is most effective. This knowledge allows one to match the characteristics of a conflict incident with the management techniques best suited for those characteristics. The salient situational circumstances to consider are summarized in Table 7.4.

Situational Considerations

Table 7.4 identifies four important incident-specific circumstances that can be used to select the appropriate conflict management approach. These can be stated in the form of diagnostic questions, with accompanying examples of high and low responses.

1. How important is the disputed issue? (High: Extremely important; Low: Not very important)
2. How important is the relationship? (High: Critical, ongoing, one-of-a-kind, partnership; Low: One-time transaction, for which there are readily available alternatives)
3. What is the relative level of power, or authority, between the disputants? (High: Boss to subordinate; Equal: Peers; Low: Subordinate to boss)
4. To what extent is time a significant constraint in resolving the dispute? (High: Must resolve the dispute quickly; Low: Time is not a salient factor)

The advantage of this table is that it allows you to quickly assess a situation and decide if a particular conflict management approach is suitable. As noted in the following descriptions, it is important to keep in mind that not all of the situational considerations are equally important for selecting a particular approach.

The forcing approach is most appropriate when a conflict involves values or policies and one feels compelled to defend the "correct" position; when a superior-subordinate relationship is involved; when maintaining a close, supportive relationship is not critical;

and when there is a sense of urgency. An example of such a situation might be a manager insisting that a summer intern follow important company safety regulations.

The accommodating approach is most appropriate when the importance of maintaining a good working relationship outweighs all other considerations. While this could be the case regardless of your formal relationship with the other party, it is often perceived as being the only option for subordinates of powerful bosses. The nature of the issues and the amount of time available play a secondary role in determining the choice of this strategy. Accommodation becomes especially appropriate when the issues are not vital to your interests and the problem must be resolved quickly.

Trying to reach a compromise is most appropriate when the issues are complex and moderately important, there are no simple solutions, and both parties have a strong interest in different facets of the problem. The other essential situational requirement is adequate time for negotiation. The classic case is a bargaining session between representatives of management and labor to avert a scheduled strike. While the characteristics of the relationship between the parties are not essential factors, experience has shown that negotiations work best between parties with equal power who are committed to maintaining a good long-term relationship.

The collaborating approach is most appropriate when the issues are critical, maintaining an ongoing supportive relationship between peers is important, and time constraints are not pressing. Although collaboration can also be an effective approach for resolving conflicts between a superior and subordinate, it is important to point out that when a conflict involves peers, the collaborative mode is more appropriate than either the forcing or accommodating approach.

The avoidance approach is most appropriate when one's stake in an issue is not high and there is not a strong interpersonal reason for getting involved, regardless of whether the conflict involves a superior, subordinate, or peer. A severe time constraint becomes a contributing factor because it increases the likelihood of using avoidance, by default. While one might prefer other strategies that have a good chance of resolving problems without damaging relationships, such as compromise and collaboration, these are ruled out because of time pressure.

Now, admittedly, this is a very rational view of how to select the appropriate approach(es) for resolving a conflict. You might wonder if it is realistic to believe that in the heat of an emotional confrontation a person is likely to step back and make this type of deliberate, systematic assessment of the situation. Actually, it is because we share this concern that we are placing so much emphasis on a highly analytical approach to conflict management. Our purpose is to prepare you to effectively manage conflict, which often means overcoming natural tendencies, including allowing one's heightened emotional state to override the need for systematic analysis.

Although we are encouraging you to take a thoughtful, analytical approach to resolving disputes, that doesn't mean you can count on the other parties to the dispute agreeing with your analysis of the situation. For example, when conflicts involve individuals from very different cultural traditions, it is not uncommon for their lack of agreement on how to resolve their differences, or even on how important it is to resolve these differences, to make the prospect of achieving a truly collaborative solution seem remote. Given that several of our proposed diagnostic tools for selecting appropriate conflict management approaches also happen to represent major fault lines between cultural value systems, it is important that you factor into this decision-making process the cultural differences between disputants.

If parties to a conflict hold very different views regarding time, power, ambiguity, the rule of norms, or the importance of relationships, one can expect they will have difficulty agreeing on the appropriate course of action for resolving their dispute (Trompenaars, 1994). Put simply: if you don't agree on *how* you are going to reach an agreement, it doesn't do you much good to discuss *what* that agreement might look like. Therefore, we hope that our ongoing discussion of various sources of differences in perspectives will help you to be sensitive to situations in which it is important to clarify assumptions, interpretations, and expectations early in the conflict management process.

To summarize this section, there are two key factors to take into consideration in selecting a conflict management approach or strategy. First, your choice of alternative approaches will be influenced by your comfort level with the various possibilities—referred to here as your personal preference. In general, personal preferences reflect personal characteristics, such as ethnic culture, gender, and personality. However, given that the use of multiple approaches appears to be a requirement of effective conflict management, it is important to stretch your "comfort zone" and become proficient in the application of the full range of choices. The more you feel comfortable doing this, the more likely it is that you will seriously consider the second key selection factor—matching your choice of conflict management strategy with the salient situational considerations, including issue and relationship importance, relative power, and time constraints. Finally, it is important for parties of a dispute to discuss their assumptions regarding the appropriate process for resolving their differences, especially when they come from very different backgrounds.

Resolving Interpersonal Confrontations Using the Collaborative Approach

We now shift our attention from a consideration of when to use each of the approaches to how one can effectively implement the collaborative approach. We have chosen to focus on this approach for our skill development purposes for two reasons. First, as noted throughout our discussion, collaboration is the best overall approach. In a sense, effective managers treat this approach as their "default option"—unless there is a compelling reason to try something else, they will use this strategy. It is important to underscore the point that the collaborative approach is the appropriate "default option" for both issue-focused and people-focused conflicts. It seems quite natural to think of collaborating with someone with a different point of view regarding a troublesome issue. However, when someone is challenging your competence, motivation, complaining about your "lack of sensitivity," or accusing you of being unfair, it seems like an unnatural act to collaborate with "the enemy." Instead, the natural tendency is to either "run away" (avoid or accommodate) or to "fight fire with fire" (force).

The second reason we are emphasizing the collaborative approach is that it is the hardest approach to implement effectively, under any circumstances. In the study by Kipnis and Schmidt (1983), discussed earlier, most managers expressed general support for the collaborative approach, but when it appeared that things were not going their way, they reverted back to a directive approach. By comparison, it is a fairly simple matter for managers to either give in or impose their will, but resolving differences in a truly collaborative manner is a complicated and taxing process. As a result, when situational conditions indicate that the collaborative approach is most appropriate, unskilled managers often opt for less challenging approaches. To help you gain proficiency in using the collaborative approach, the remainder of this chapter describes behavioral guidelines for effectively resolving interpersonal confrontations in a collaborative manner.

A GENERAL FRAMEWORK FOR COLLABORATIVE PROBLEM SOLVING

The addition of "problem solving" to this title warrants a brief explanation. When two disputants agree to work toward a collaborative solution, they are basically agreeing to share an attitude or value. For example, collaborating disputants would not use asymmetrical sources of advantage (e.g., power, information, resources, etc.) to force the other party to accept a one-sided solution. But skill development requires more than an attitude adjustment—we need to understand the actual competencies required for effective conflict resolution. That is the benefit of incorporating the problem-solving process into our discussion of the collaborative approach. The problem-solving process provides a structured framework for an orderly, deliberate, reasoned approach to dispute resolution that enables disputants to make good on their commitment to work together. The merits of this structured approach are particularly useful when it is applied to people-focused conflicts. In these situations, it is helpful to have a framework to organize your thoughts and to discipline your emotions.

We will begin our discussion of the collaborative problem-solving process by introducing a general, six-step framework adapted from the integrative bargaining literature discussed earlier (Stroh, Northcraft, & Neale, 2002). We will then use this broad outline to develop a more detailed set of problem-solving guidelines.

1. **Establish superordinate goals**. In order to foster a climate of collaboration, both parties to a dispute need to focus on what they share in common. Making more salient their shared goals of increased productivity, lower costs, reduced design time, or improved relations between departments sensitizes the parties to the merits of resolving their differences to avoid jeopardizing their mutual goals. The step is characterized by the general question, "What common goals provide a context for these discussions?"

2. **Separate the people from the problem**. Having clarified the mutual benefits to be gained by successfully resolving a conflict, it is useful to focus attention on the real issue at hand: solving a problem. Interpersonal confrontations are more likely to result in mutual satisfaction if the parties depersonalize their disagreement by suppressing their personal desires for revenge or one-upmanship. In other words, the other party is viewed as the advocate of a point of view, rather than as a rival. The problem solver would say, "That is an unreasonable position" rather than, "You are an unreasonable person."

3. **Focus on interests, not positions.** Positions are demands or assertions; interests constitute the reasons behind the demands. Experience shows that it is easier to establish agreement on interests, given that they tend to be broader and multifaceted. This step involves redefining and broadening problems to make them more tractable. When a variety of issues are examined, parties are better able to understand each other's point of view and place their own views in perspective. A characteristic collaborative statement is, "Help me understand why you advocate that position."

4. **Invent options for mutual gains.** This step focuses on generating unusual, creative solutions. By focusing both parties' attention on brainstorming alternative, mutually agreeable solutions, the interpersonal dynamics naturally shift from competitive to collaborative. In addition, the more options and combinations there are to explore, the greater the probability of finding common ground. This step can be summarized as, "Now that we better understand each other's underlying concerns and objectives, let's brainstorm ways of satisfying both our needs."

5. **Use objective criteria for evaluating alternatives.** No matter how collaborative both parties may be, there are bound to be some incompatible interests. Rather than seizing on these as opportunities for testing wills, it is far more productive to determine what is fair. This requires both parties to examine how fairness should be judged. A shift in thinking from "getting what I want" to "deciding what

makes most sense" fosters an open, reasonable attitude. It encourages parties to avoid overconfidence or overcommitment to their initial position. This approach is characterized by asking, "What is a fair way to evaluate the merits of our arguments?"

6. **Define success in terms of real gains, not imaginary losses.** If a manager seeks a 10 percent raise and receives only 6 percent, that outcome can be viewed as either a 6 percent improvement or a 40 percent shortfall. The first interpretation focuses on gains, the second on losses (in this case, unrealized expectations). The outcome is the same, but the manager's satisfaction with it varies substantially. It is important to recognize that our satisfaction with an outcome is affected by the standards we use to judge it. Recognizing this, the collaborative problem solver facilitates resolution by judging the value of proposed solutions against reasonable standards. This perspective is reflected in the question, "Does this outcome constitute a meaningful improvement over current conditions?"

THE FOUR PHASES OF COLLABORATIVE PROBLEM SOLVING

Notice how the problem-solving approach encourages collaboration by keeping the process focused on *shared problems* and *sharing solutions*. These are important themes to remember, especially when you utilize the collaborative approach to resolve a people-focused conflict. Because of the degree of difficulty inherent in this undertaking, we will continue using the people-focused conflict context in our remaining discussion. For information on how to manage issue-focused conflicts using various negotiation strategies, see Murnighan (1992, 1993) and Thompson (2001).

We have organized our detailed discussion of behavioral guidelines around the four phases of the **problem-solving process**: (1) *problem identification*, (2) *solution generation*, (3) *action plan formulation and agreement*, and (4) *implementation and follow-up*. In the midst of a heated exchange, the first two phases are the most critical steps, as well as the most difficult to implement effectively. If you are able to achieve agreement on what the problem is and how you intend to resolve it, the details of the agreement, including a follow-up plan, should follow naturally. In other words, we are placing our skill-building emphasis where skillful implementation is most critical.

We have also elected to identify specific problem-solving guidelines for each role in a dispute, because by definition, their orientations are discrepant during the initial stages of this process. A dyadic confrontation involves two actors, an **initiator** and a **responder**. For example, a subordinate might complain about not being given a fair share of opportunities to work overtime; or the head of production might complain to the head of sales about frequent changes in order specifications. A dyadic conflict represents a greater challenge for responders because they have responsibility for transforming a complaint into a problem-solving discussion. This requires considerable patience and self-confidence, because unskilled initiators will generally begin the discussion by blaming the responder for the problem. In this situation, an unskilled responder will naturally become defensive and look for an opportunity to "even the score."

If these lose-lose dynamics persist, a **mediator** is generally required to cool down the dispute, reestablish constructive communication, and help the parties reconcile their differences. The presence of a mediator removes some pressure from the responder because an impartial referee provides assistance in moving the confrontation through the problem-solving phases.

The following guidelines provide a model for acting out the initiator, responder, and mediator roles in such a way that problem solving can occur. In our discussion of each role, we will assume that other participants in the conflict are not behaving according to their prescribed guidelines.

Initiator-Problem Identification

I-1 Maintain Personal Ownership of the Problem

It is important to recognize that when you are upset and frustrated, this is your problem, not the other person's. You may feel that your boss or coworker is the source of your problem, but resolving your frustration is your immediate concern. The first step in addressing this concern is acknowledging accountability for your feelings. Suppose someone enters your office with a smelly cigar without asking if it is all right to smoke. The fact that your office is going to stink for the rest of the day may infuriate you, but the odor does not present a problem for your smoking guest. One way to determine ownership of a problem is to identify whose needs are not being met. In this case, your need for a clean working environment is not being met, so the smelly office is your problem.

The advantage of acknowledging ownership of a problem when registering a complaint is that it reduces defensiveness (Adler, Rosenfeld, & Proctor, 2001; Alder & Rodman, 2003). In order for you to get a problem solved, the respondent must not feel threatened by your initial statement of that problem. By beginning the conversation with a request that the responder help solve your problem, you immediately establish a problem-solving atmosphere. For example, you might say, "Bill, do you have a few minutes? I have a problem I need to discuss with you."

I-2 Succinctly Describe Your Problem in Terms of Behaviors, Consequences, and Feelings

A useful model for remembering how to state your problem effectively has been prescribed by Gordon (2000): "I have a problem. When you do X, Y results, and I feel Z." Although we don't advocate the memorization of set formulas for improving communication skills, keeping this model in mind will help you implement three critical elements in your "problem statement."

First, describe the specific behaviors (X) that present a problem for you. This will help you avoid the reflexive tendency when you are upset to give feedback that is evaluative and not specific. One way to do this is to specify the expectations or standards that have been violated. For example, a subordinate may have missed a deadline for completing an assigned task, your boss may gradually be taking over tasks previously delegated to you, or a colleague in the accounting department may have repeatedly failed to provide you with data required for an important presentation.

Second, outline the specific, observable consequences (Y) of these behaviors. Simply telling others that their actions are causing you problems is often sufficient stimulus for change. In fast-paced work environments, people generally become insensitive to the impact of their actions. They don't intend to cause offense, but they become so busy meeting deadlines associated with "getting the product out the door" that they tune out subtle negative feedback from others. When this occurs, bringing to the attention of others the consequences of their behaviors will often prompt them to change.

Unfortunately, not all problems can be resolved this simply. At times, offenders are aware of the negative consequences of their behaviors, yet they persist in them. In such cases, this approach is still useful in stimulating a problem-solving discussion because it presents concerns in a nonthreatening manner. Possibly, the responders' behaviors are constrained by the expectations of their boss or by the fact that the department is currently understaffed. Responders may not be able to change these constraints, but this approach will encourage them to discuss them with you so you can work on the problem together.

Third, describe the feelings (Z) you experience as a result of the problem. It is important that the responder understand that the behavior is not just inconvenient. You need to explain how it is affecting you personally by engendering feelings of frustration, anger, or insecurity. Explain how these feelings are interfering with your work. They may make it more difficult for you to concentrate, to be congenial with customers, to be supportive of your boss, or to be willing to make needed personal sacrifices to meet deadlines.

We recommend using this three-step model as a general guide. The order of the components may vary, and you should not use the same words every time. Obviously, it would get pretty monotonous if everyone in a work group initiated a discussion about an interpersonal issue with the words, "I have a problem." Observe how the key elements in the "XYZ" model are used in different ways in Table 7.5.

I-3 Avoid Drawing Evaluative Conclusions and Attributing Motives to the Respondent

When exchanges between two disputing parties become vengeful, each side often has a different perspective about the justification of the other's actions. Typically, each party believes that it is the victim of the other's aggression. In international conflicts, opposing nations often believe they are acting defensively rather than offensively. Similarly, in smaller-scale conflicts, each side may have distorted views of its own hurt and the motives of the "offender" (Kim & Smith, 1993). Therefore, in presenting your problem, avoid the pitfalls of making accusations, drawing inferences about motivations or intentions, or attributing the responder's undesirable behavior to personal inadequacies. Statements such as, "You are always interrupting me," "You haven't been fair to me since the day I disagreed with you in the board meeting," and "You never have time to listen to our problems and suggestions because you manage your time so poorly" are good for starting arguments but ineffective for initiating a problem-solving process.

Another key to reducing defensiveness is to delay proposing a solution until both parties agree on the nature of the problem. When you become so upset with someone's behavior that you feel it is necessary to initiate a complaint, it is often because the person has seriously violated your ideal role model. For example, you might feel that your manager should have been less dogmatic and listened more during a goal-setting interview. Consequently, you might express your feelings in terms of prescriptions for how the other

Table 7.5	Examples of the "XYZ" Approach to Stating a Problem

Model:

"I have a problem. When you do X (behavior), Y results (consequences), and I feel Z."

Examples:

I have to tell you that I get upset [feelings] when you make jokes about my bad memory in front of other people [behavior]. In fact, I get so angry so that I find myself bringing up your faults to get even [consequences].

I have a problem. When you say you'll be here for our date at six and don't show up until after seven [behavior], the dinner gets ruined, we're late for the show we planned to see [consequences], and I feel hurt because it seems as though I'm just not that important to you [feelings].

The employees want to let management know that we've been having a hard time lately with the short notice you've been giving when you need us to work overtime [behavior]. That probably explains some of the grumbling and lack of cooperation you've mentioned [consequences]. Anyhow, we wanted to make it clear that this policy has really got a lot of the workers feeling pretty resentful [feeling].

SOURCE: *Adapted from Adler, 1977.*

person should behave and suggest a more democratic or sensitive style.

Besides creating defensiveness, the principal disadvantage to initiating problem solving with a suggested remedy is that it hinders the problem-solving process. Before completing the problem-articulation phase, you have immediately jumped to the solution-generation phase, based on the assumption that you know all the reasons for, and constraints on, the other person's behavior. You will jointly produce better, more acceptable, solutions if you present your statement of the problem and discuss it thoroughly before proposing potential solutions.

I-4 Persist Until Understood There are times when the respondent will not clearly receive or acknowledge even the most effectively expressed message. Suppose, for instance, that you share the following problem with a coworker:

> *Something has been bothering me, and I need to share my concerns with you. Frankly, I'm uncomfortable [feeling] with your heavy use of profanity [behavior]. I don't mind an occasional "damn" or "hell," but the other words bother me a lot. Lately I've been avoiding you [consequences], and that's not good because it interferes with our working relationship, so I wanted to let you know how I feel.*

When you share your feelings in this nonevaluative way, it's likely that the other person will understand your position and possibly try to change behavior to suit your needs. On the other hand, there are a number of less satisfying responses that could be made to your comment:

> *Listen, these days everyone talks that way. And besides, you've got your faults, too, you know! [Your coworker becomes defensive, rationalizing and counterattacking.]*
>
> *Yeah, I suppose I do swear a lot. I'll have to work on that someday. [Gets the general drift of your message but fails to comprehend how serious the problem is to you.]*
>
> *Listen, if you're still angry about my forgetting to tell you about that meeting the other day, you can be sure that I'm really sorry. I won't do it again. [Totally misunderstands.]*
>
> *Speaking of avoiding, have you seen Chris lately? I wonder if anything is wrong with him. [Is discomfited by your frustration and changes the subject.]*

In each case, the coworker does not understand or does not wish to acknowledge the problem. In these situations, you must repeat your concern until it has been acknowledged as a problem to be solved. Otherwise, the problem-solving process will terminate at this point and nothing will change. Repeated assertions can take the form of restating the same phrase several times or reiterating your concern with different words or examples that you feel may improve comprehension. To avoid introducing new concerns or shifting from a descriptive to an evaluative mode, keep in mind the "XYZ" formula for feedback. Persistence is most effective when it consists of "variations on a theme," rather than "variation in themes."

I-5 Encourage Two-Way Discussion It is important to establish a problem-solving climate by inviting the respondent to express opinions and ask questions. There may be a reasonable explanation for another's disturbing behavior; the person may have a radically different view of the problem. The sooner this information is introduced into the conversation, the more likely it is that the issue will be resolved. As a rule of thumb, the longer the initiator's opening statement, the longer it will take the two parties to work through their problem. This is because the lengthier the problem statement, the more likely it is to encourage a defensive reaction. The longer we talk, the more worked up we get, and the more likely we are to violate principles of supportive communication. As a result, the other party begins to feel threatened, starts mentally outlining a rebuttal or counterattack, and stops listening empathetically to our concerns. Once these dynamics enter the discussion, the collaborative approach is usually discarded in favor of the accommodating or forcing strategies, depending on the circumstances. When this occurs, it is unlikely that the actors will be able to reach a mutually satisfactory solution to their problem without third-party intervention.

I-6 Manage the Agenda: Approach Multiple or Complex Problems Incrementally

One way to shorten your opening statement is to approach complex problems incrementally. Rather than raising a series of issues all at once, focus initially on a simple or rudimentary problem. Then, as you gain greater appreciation for the other party's perspective and share some problem-solving success, you can discuss more challenging issues. This is especially important when trying to resolve a problem with a person who is important to your work performance but who does not have a long-standing relationship with you. The less familiar you are with the other's opinions and personality, as well as the situational constraints influencing his or her behaviors, the more you should approach a problem-solving discussion as a fact-finding and rapport-building mission. This is best done by focusing your introductory statement on a specific manifestation of a broader problem and presenting it in such a way that it encourages the other party to respond expansively. You can then use this early feedback to shape the remainder of your agenda. For example, "Bill, we had difficulty getting that work order processed on time yesterday. What seemed to be the problem?"

Initiator-Solution Generation

I-7 Focus on Commonalities as the Basis for Requesting a Change

Once a problem is clearly understood, the discussion should shift to the solution-generation phase. Most disputants share at least some personal and organizational goals, believe in many of the same fundamental principles of management, and operate under similar constraints. These commonalities can serve as a useful starting point for generating solutions. The most straightforward approach to changing another's offensive behavior is to make a request. The legitimacy of a request will be enhanced if it is linked to common interests. These might include shared values, such as treating coworkers fairly and following through on commitments, or shared constraints, such as getting reports in on time and operating within budgetary restrictions. This approach is particularly effective when the parties have had difficulty getting along in the past. In these situations, pointing out how a change in the respondent's behavior would positively affect your shared fate will reduce defensiveness: "Jane, one of the things we have all worked hard to build in this audit team is mutual support. We are all pushed to the limit getting this job completed by the third-quarter deadline next week, and the rest of the team members find it difficult to accept your unwillingness to work overtime during this emergency. Because the allocation of next quarter's assignments will be affected by our current performance, would you please reconsider your position?"

Responder-Problem Identification

Now we shall examine the problem-identification phase from the viewpoint of the person who is supposedly the source of the problem. In a work setting, this could be a manager who is making unrealistic demands, a new employee who has violated critical safety regulations, or a coworker who is claiming credit for ideas you generated. The following guidelines for dealing with someone's complaint show how to shape the initiator's behavior so you can have a productive problem-solving experience.

R-1 Establish a Climate for Joint Problem Solving by Showing Genuine Interest and Concern

When a person complains to you, do not treat that complaint lightly. While this may seem self-evident, it is often difficult to focus your attention on someone else's problems when you are in the middle of writing an important project report or concerned about preparing for a meeting scheduled to begin in a few minutes. Consequently, unless the other person's emotional condition necessitates dealing with the problem immediately, it is better to set up a time for another meeting if your current time pressures will make it difficult to concentrate.

In most cases, the initiator will be expecting you to set the tone for the meeting. You will quickly undermine collaboration if you overreact or become defensive. Even if you disagree with the complaint and feel it has no foundation, you need to respond empathetically to the initiator's statement of the problem. This is done by conveying an attitude of interest and receptivity through your posture, tone of voice, and facial expressions.

One of the most difficult aspects of establishing the proper climate for your discussion is responding appropriately to the initiator's emotions. Sometimes you may need to let a person blow off steam before trying to address the substance of a specific complaint. In some cases, the therapeutic effect of being able to express negative emotions to the boss will be enough to satisfy a subordinate. This occurs frequently in high-pressure jobs in which tempers flare easily as a result of the intense stress.

However, an emotional outburst can be very detrimental to problem solving. If an employee begins verbally attacking you or someone else, and it is apparent that the individual is more interested in getting even than in solving an interpersonal problem, you may need to interrupt and interject some ground rules for collaborative problem solving. By explaining calmly to the other person that you are willing to discuss a genuine problem but that you will not tolerate personal attacks or scapegoating, you can quickly determine the initiator's true intentions. In most instances, he or she will apologize, emulate your emotional tone, and begin formulating a useful statement of the problem.

R-2 Seek Additional, Clarifying Information About the Problem by Asking Questions

As shown in Figure 7.5, untrained initiators typically present complaints that are so general and evaluative that they aren't useful problem statements. It is difficult to understand how you should respond to a general, vague comment like "You never listen to me during our meetings," followed by an evaluative, critical comment like "You obviously aren't interested in what I have to say." In addition to not providing detailed descriptions of your offending actions, inflamed initiators often make attributions about your motives and your personal strengths and weaknesses from a few specific incidents. If the two of you are going to transform a personal complaint into a joint problem, you must redirect the conversation from general and evaluative accusations to descriptions of specific behaviors.

The problem is that when you are getting steamed up over what you believe are unfair and unjustified accusations, it is difficult to avoid fighting back. ("Oh yeah, well I haven't wanted to say this about you before, but since you've brought up the subject . . . ") The single best way to keep your mind focused on transforming a personal attack into a jointly identified problem is to limit your responses to questions. If you stick with asking clarifying questions you are going to get better-quality information and you are going to demonstrate your commitment to joint problem solving.

As shown in Figure 7.5, one of the best ways of doing this is to ask for examples ("Can you give me an example of what I did during a staff meeting that led

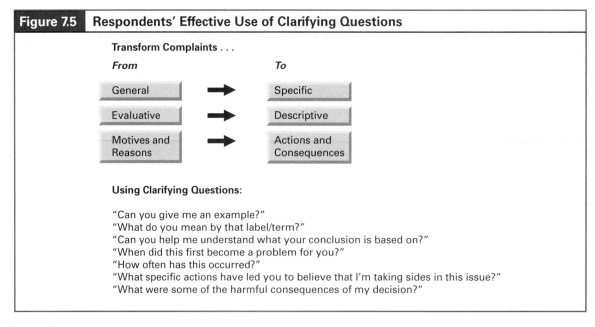

| Figure 7.5 | Respondents' Effective Use of Clarifying Questions |

Transform Complaints . . .

From → *To*

General → Specific

Evaluative → Descriptive

Motives and Reasons → Actions and Consequences

Using Clarifying Questions:

"Can you give me an example?"
"What do you mean by that label/term?"
"Can you help me understand what your conclusion is based on?"
"When did this first become a problem for you?"
"How often has this occurred?"
"What specific actions have led you to believe that I'm taking sides in this issue?"
"What were some of the harmful consequences of my decision?"

you to believe I wasn't listening to what you had to say?"). Building on our discussion of the "XYZ" model in the initiator's guidelines, you might find it useful to ask for examples of your offending actions and their harmful consequences, including damaged feelings ("Can you give me a specific example of my behavior that concerns you?" "When I did that, what were the specific consequences for your work?" "How did you feel when that happened?").

When a complaint is both serious and complex, it is especially critical for you to understand it completely. In these situations, after you have asked several clarifying questions, check your level of understanding by summarizing the initiator's main points and asking if your summary is correct.

Sometimes it is useful to ask for additional complaints: "Are there any other problems in our relationship you'd like to discuss?" If the initiator is just in a griping mood, this is not a good time to probe further; you don't want to encourage this type of behavior. But if the person is seriously concerned about improving your relationship, if your discussion to this point has been helpful, and if you suspect that the initiator is holding back and not talking about the really serious issues, you should probe deeper. Often, people begin by complaining about a minor problem to "test the waters." If you blow up, the conversation is terminated, and the critical issues aren't discussed. However, if you are responsive to a frank discussion about problems, the more serious issues are likely to surface.

R-3 Agree with Some Aspect of the Complaint

This is an important point that is difficult for some people to accept because they wonder how it is possible to agree with something they don't believe is true. They may also be worried about reinforcing complaining behavior. In practice, this step is probably the best test of whether a responder is committed to using the collaborative approach to conflict management rather than the avoiding, forcing, or accommodating approach. People who use the forcing mode will grit their teeth while listening to the initiator, just waiting to find a flaw they can use to launch a counterattack. Or they will simply respond, "I'm sorry, but that's just the way I am. You'll simply have to get used to it." Accommodators will apologize profusely and ask for forgiveness. People who avoid conflicts will acknowledge and agree with the initiator's concerns, but only in a superficial manner because their only concern is how to terminate the awkward conversation quickly.

In contrast, collaborators will demonstrate their concerns for both cooperation and assertiveness by looking for points in the initiator's presentation with which they can genuinely agree. Following the principles of supportive communication, you will find it possible to accept the other person's viewpoint without conceding your own position. Even in the most blatantly malicious and hostile verbal assault (which may be more a reflection of the initiator's insecurity than evidence of your inadequacies), there is generally a grain of truth. A few years ago, a junior faculty member in a business school who was being reviewed for promotion received a very unfair appraisal from one of his senior colleagues. Since the junior member knew that the critic was going through a personal crisis, he could have dismissed the criticism as irrelevant and tendentious. However, one particular phrase— "You are stuck on a narrow line of research"—kept coming back to his mind. There was something there that couldn't be ignored. As a result of turning a vindictive reproach into a valid suggestion, the junior faculty member made a major career decision that produced very positive outcomes. Furthermore, by publicly giving the senior colleague credit for the suggestion, he substantially strengthened the interpersonal relationship.

There are a number of ways you can agree with a message without accepting all of its ramifications (Adler et al., 2001). You can find an element of truth, as in the incident related above. Or you can agree in principle with the argument: "I agree that managers should set a good example" or "I agree that it is important for salesclerks to be at the store when it opens." If you can't find anything substantive with which to agree, you can always agree with the initiator's perception of the situation: "Well, I can see how you would think that. I have known people who deliberately shirked their responsibilities." Or you can agree with the person's feelings: "It is obvious that our earlier discussion greatly upset you."

In none of these cases are you necessarily agreeing with the initiator's conclusions or evaluations, nor are you conceding your position. You are trying to understand, to foster a problem-solving, rather than argumentative, discussion. Generally, initiators prepare for a complaint session by mentally cataloguing all the evidence supporting their point of view. Once the discussion begins, they introduce as much evidence as necessary to make their argument convincing; that is, they keep arguing until you agree. The more evidence that is introduced, the broader the argument becomes and the more difficult it is to begin investigating solutions. Consequently, establishing a basis of agreement is the key to culminating the problem-identification phase of the problem-solving process.

Responder-Solution Generation

R-4 Ask for Suggestions of Acceptable Alternatives Once you are certain you fully understand the initiator's complaint, move on to the solution-generation phase by asking the initiator for recommended solutions. This triggers an important transition in the discussion by shifting attention from the negative to the positive and from the past to the future. It also communicates your regard for the initiator's opinions. This step is a key element in the joint problem-solving process. Some managers listen patiently to a subordinate's complaint, express appreciation for the feedback, say they will rectify the problem, and then terminate the discussion. This leaves the initiator guessing about the outcome of the meeting. Will you take the complaint seriously? Will you really change? If so, will the change resolve the problem? It is important to eliminate this ambiguity by agreeing on a plan of action. If the problem is particularly serious or complex, it is useful to write down specific agreements, including assignments and deadlines, as well as providing for a follow-up meeting to check progress.

Frequently, it is necessary for managers to mediate a dispute (Karambayya & Brett, 1989; Kressel & Pruitt, 1989; Stroh et al., 2002). While this may occur for a variety of reasons, we will assume in this discussion that the manager has been invited to help the initiator and responder resolve their differences. While we will assume that the mediator is the manager of both disputants, this is not a necessary condition for the guidelines we shall propose. For example, a hairstylist in a college-town beauty salon complained to the manager about the way the receptionist was favoring other beauticians who had been there longer. Since this allegation, if true, involved a violation of the manager's policy of allocating walk-in business strictly on the basis of beautician availability, the manager felt it necessary to investigate the complaint. In doing so, she discovered considerable animosity between the two employees, stemming from frequent disagreements regarding the amount of work the stylist had done on a given day. The stylist felt that the receptionist was keeping sloppy records, while the receptionist blamed the problem on the stylist's forgetting to hand in her credit slip when she finished with a customer. The problems between the stylist and the receptionist appeared serious enough to the participants and broad enough in scope that the manager decided to call both parties into her office to help them resolve their differences. The following guidelines are intended to help mediators avoid the common pitfalls associated with this role, which are shown in Table 7.6.

Mediator-Problem Identification

M-1 Acknowledge That a Conflict Exists and Propose a Problem-Solving Approach for Resolving It When a mediator is called in, it means the disputants have failed as problem solvers. Therefore,

Table 7.6	Ten Ways to Fail as a Mediator

1. After you have listened to the argument for a short time, begin to nonverbally communicate your discomfort with the discussion (e.g., sit back, begin to fidget).

2. Communicate your agreement with one of the parties (e.g., through facial expressions, posture, chair position, reinforcing comments).

3. Say that you shouldn't be talking about this kind of thing at work or where others can hear you.

4. Discourage the expression of emotion. Suggest that the discussion would better be held later after both parties have cooled off.

5. Suggest that both parties are wrong. Point out the problems with both points of view.

6. Suggest partway through the discussion that possibly you aren't the person who should be helping solve this problem.

7. See if you can get both parties to attack you.

8. Minimize the seriousness of the problem.

9. Change the subject (e.g., ask for advice to help you solve one of your problems).

10. Express displeasure that the two parties are experiencing conflict (e.g., imply that it might undermine the solidarity of the work group).

Source: *Adapted from Morris & Sashkin, 1976.*

the first requirement of effective mediation is to establish a problem-solving framework. To that end, it is vital that the mediator take seriously the problems between conflicting parties. If they feel they have a serious problem, the mediator should not belittle its significance. Remarks such as, "I'm surprised that two intelligent people like you have not been able to work out your disagreement. We have more important things to do here than get all worked up over such petty issues" will make both parties defensive and interfere with any serious problem-solving efforts. While you might wish that your subordinates could have worked out their disagreement without bothering you, this is not the time to lecture them on self-reliance. Inducing guilt feelings by implying personal failure during an already emotional experience tends to distract the participants from the substantive issues at hand. Seldom is this conducive to problem solving.

One early decision a mediator has to make is whether to convene a joint problem-solving session or meet separately with the parties first. The diagnostic criteria shown in Table 7.7 should help you weigh the trade-offs. First, what is the current position of the disputants? Are both aware that a problem exists? Are they equally motivated to work on solving the problem? The more similar the awareness and motivation of the parties, the more likely it is that a joint session will be productive. If there is a serious discrepancy in awareness and motivation, the mediator should work to reduce that discrepancy through one-on-one meetings before bringing the disputants together.

Second, what is the current relationship between the disputants? Does their work require them to interact frequently? Is a good working relationship critical for their individual job performance? What has their relationship been in the past? What is the difference in their formal status in the organization? As we discussed earlier, joint problem-solving sessions are most productive between individuals of equal status who are required to work together regularly. This does not mean that joint meetings should not be held between a supervisor and subordinate, only that greater care needs to be taken in preparing for such a meeting. Specifically, if a department head becomes involved in a dispute between a worker and a supervisor, the department head should make sure that the worker does not feel this meeting will serve as an excuse for two managers to gang up on an hourly employee.

Separate fact-finding meetings with the disputants prior to a joint meeting are particularly useful when the parties have a history of recurring disputes, especially if these disputes should have been resolved without a mediator. Such a history often suggests a lack of conflict management or problem-solving skills on the part of the disputants, or it might stem from a broader set of issues that are beyond their control. In these situations, individual coaching sessions prior to a joint meeting will increase your understanding of the root causes and

Table 7.7	Choosing a Format for Mediating Conflicts		
FACTORS		HOLD JOINT MEETINGS	HOLD SEPARATE MEETINGS FIRST
Awareness and Motivation			
• Both parties are aware of the problem.		Yes	No
• They are equally motivated to resolve the problem.		Yes	No
• They accept your legitimacy as a mediator.		Yes	No
Nature of the Relationship			
• The parties hold equal status.		Yes	No
• They work together regularly.		Yes	No
• They have an overall good relationship.		Yes	No
Nature of the Problem			
• This is an isolated (not a recurring) problem.		Yes	No
• The complaint is substantive in nature and easily verified.		Yes	No
• The parties agree on the root causes of the problem.		Yes	No
• The parties share common values and work priorities.		Yes	No

improve the individuals' abilities to resolve their differences. Following up these private meetings with a joint problem-solving session in which the mediator coaches the disputants through the process for resolving their conflicts can be a positive learning experience.

Third, what is the nature of the problem? Is the complaint substantive in nature and easily verifiable? If the problem stems from conflicting role responsibilities and the actions of both parties in question are common knowledge, then a joint problem-solving session can begin on a common information and experimental base. However, if the complaint stems from differences in managerial style, values, personality characteristics, and so forth, bringing the parties together immediately following a complaint may seriously undermine the problem-solving process. Complaints that are likely to be interpreted as threats to the self-image of one or both parties (Who am I? What do I stand for?) warrant considerable individual discussion before a joint meeting is called. To avoid individuals feeling as though they are being ambushed in a meeting, you should discuss serious personal complaints with them ahead of time, in private.

M-2 In Seeking Out the Perspective of Both Parties, Maintain a Neutral Posture Regarding the Disputants—If Not the Issues

Effective mediation requires impartiality. If a mediator shows strong personal bias in favor of one party in a joint problem-solving session, the other party may simply walk out. However, such personal bias is more likely to emerge in private conversations with the disputants. Statements such as, "I can't believe he really did that!" and "Everyone seems to be having trouble working with Charlie these days" imply that the mediator is taking sides, and any attempt to appear impartial in a joint meeting will seem like mere window dressing to appease the other party. No matter how well-intentioned or justified these comments might be, they destroy the credibility of the mediator in the long run. In contrast, effective mediators respect both parties' points of view and make sure that both perspectives are expressed adequately.

Occasionally, it is not possible to be impartial on issues. One person may have violated company policy, engaged in unethical competition with a colleague, or broken a personal agreement. In these cases, the challenge of the mediator is to separate the offense from the offender. If a person is clearly in the wrong, the inappropriate behavior needs to be corrected, but in such a way that the individual doesn't feel his or her image and working relationships have been permanently marred. This can be done most effectively when correction occurs in private.

M-3 Serve as a Facilitator, Not as a Judge

When parties must work closely and have a history of chronic interpersonal problems, it is often more important to teach problem-solving skills than to resolve a specific dispute. This is done best when the mediator adopts the posture of facilitator. The role of judge is to render a verdict regarding a problem in the past, not to teach people how to solve problems in the future. While some disputes obviously involve right and wrong actions, most interpersonal problems stem from differences in perspective. In these situations, it is important that the mediator avoid being seduced into "rendering a verdict" by comments such as, "Well, you're the boss; tell us which one is right," or more subtly, "I wonder if I did what was right?" The problem with a mediator's assuming the role of judge is that it sets in motion processes antithetical to effective interpersonal problem solving. The parties focus on persuading the mediator of their innocence and the other party's guilt rather than striving to improve their working relationship with the assistance of the mediator. The disputants work to establish facts about what happened in the past rather than to reach an agreement about what ought to happen in the future. Consequently, a key aspect of effective mediation is helping disputants explore multiple alternatives in a nonjudgmental manner.

M-4 Manage the Discussion to Ensure Fairness—Keep the Discussion Issue Oriented, Not Personality Oriented

It is important that the mediator maintain a problem-solving atmosphere throughout the discussion. This is not to say that strong emotional statements don't have their place. People often associate effective problem solving with a calm, highly rational discussion of the issues and associate a personality attack with a highly emotional outburst. However, it is important not to confuse affect with effect. Placid, cerebral discussions may not solve problems, and impassioned statements don't have to be insulting. The critical point about process is that it should be centered on the issues and the consequences of continued conflict on performance. Even when behavior offensive to one of the parties obviously stems from a personality quirk, the discussion of the problem should be limited to the behavior. Attributions of motives or generalizations from specific events to personal proclivities distract participants from the problem-solving process. It is important that the mediator establish and maintain these ground rules.

It is also important for a mediator to ensure that neither party dominates the discussion. A relatively even balance in the level of inputs improves the quality of the final outcome. It also increases the likelihood that both parties will accept the final decision, because there is a high correlation between feelings about the problem-solving process and attitudes about the final solution. If one party tends to dominate a discussion, the mediator can help balance the exchange by asking the less talkative individual direct questions: "Now that we have heard Bill's view of that incident, how do you see it?" "That's an important point, Brad, so let's make sure Brian agrees. How do you feel, Brian?"

Mediator-Solution Generation

M-5 Explore Options by Focusing on Interests, Not Positions As noted earlier in this section, positions are demands, whereas interests are the underlying needs, values, goals, or concerns behind the demands. Often, conflict resolution is hampered by the perception that incompatible positions necessarily entail irreconcilable differences. Mediation of such conflicts can best be accomplished by examining the interests behind the positions. It is these interests that are the driving force behind the conflict, and these interests are ultimately what people want satisfied.

It is the job of the mediator to discover where interests meet and where they conflict. Interests often remain unstated because they are unclear to the participants. In order to flesh out each party's interests, ask "why" questions: "Why have they taken this position?" "Why does this matter to them?" Understand that there is probably no single, simple answer to these questions. Each side may represent a number of constituents, each with a special interest.

After each side has articulated its underlying interests, help the parties identify areas of agreement and reconcilability. It is common for participants in an intense conflict to feel that they are on opposite sides of all issues—that they have little in common. Helping them recognize that there are areas of agreement and reconcilability often represents a major turning point in resolving long-standing feuds.

M-6 Make Sure All Parties Fully Understand and Support the Solution Agreed Upon, and Establish Follow-Up Procedures The last two phases of the problem-solving process are (1) agreement on an action plan and (2) follow-up. These will be discussed here within the context of the mediator's role, but they are equally relevant to the other roles.

A common mistake of ineffective mediators is terminating discussions prematurely, on the supposition that once a problem has been solved in principle, the disputants can be left to work out the details on their own. Or a mediator may assume that because one party has recommended a solution that appears reasonable and workable, the second disputant will be willing to implement it.

To avoid these mistakes, it is important to stay engaged in the mediation process until both parties have agreed on a detailed plan of action. You might consider using the familiar planning template—Who, What, How, When, and Where—as a checklist for making sure the plan is complete. If you suspect any hesitancy on the part of either disputant, this needs to be explored explicitly ("Tom, I sense that you are somewhat less enthusiastic than Sue about this plan. Is there something that bothers you?").

When you are confident that both parties support the plan, check to make sure they are aware of their respective responsibilities and then propose a mechanism for monitoring progress. For example, you might schedule another formal meeting, or you might stop by both individuals' offices to get a progress report. Without undermining the value of the agreement you've obtained, it is generally a good idea to encourage "good faith" modifications of the proposal to accommodate unforeseen implementation issues. Consider using a follow-up meeting to celebrate the successful resolution of the dispute and to discuss "lessons learned" for future applications.

Summary

Conflict is a difficult and controversial topic. In most cultures, it has negative connotations because it runs counter to the notion that we should get along with people by being kind and friendly. Although many people intellectually understand the value of conflict, they feel uncomfortable when confronted by it. Their discomfort may result from a lack of understanding of the conflict process as well as from a lack of training in how to handle interpersonal confrontations effectively. In this chapter, we have addressed these issues by introducing both analytical and behavioral skills.

A summary model of conflict management, shown in Figure 7.6, contains four elements: (1) diagnosing the sources of conflict and the associated situational considerations; (2) selecting an appropriate conflict management strategy, based on the results of the diagnosis combined with personal preferences; (3) effectively implementing the strategy, in particular the collaborative problem-solving process, which should lead to (4) a successful resolution of the dispute. Note that the final outcome of our model is successful dispute resolution. Given our introductory claim that conflict plays an important role in organizations, our

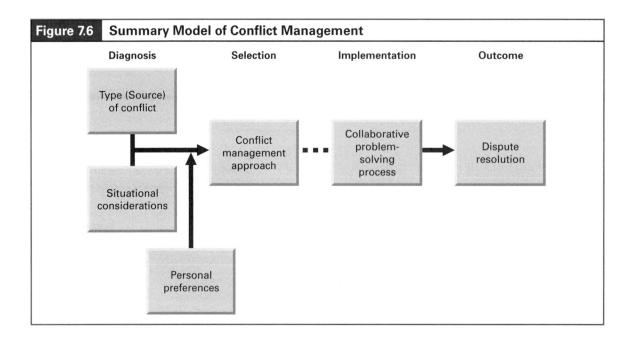

Figure 7.6   **Summary Model of Conflict Management**

Diagnosis   Selection   Implementation   Outcome

- Type (Source) of conflict
- Situational considerations
- Personal preferences
- Conflict management approach
- Collaborative problem-solving process
- Dispute resolution

concluding observation is that the objective of effective conflict management is the successful resolution of disputes, not the elimination of conflict altogether.

The diagnostic element of our summary model contains two important components. First, assessing the source or type of conflict provides insights into the "whys" behind a confrontation. Conflict can be "caused" by a variety of circumstances. We have considered four of these: irreconcilable personal differences, discrepancies in information, role incompatibilities, and environmentally induced stress. These "types" of conflict differ in both frequency and intensity. For example, information-based conflicts occur frequently, but they are easily resolved because disputants have low personal stakes in the outcome. In contrast, conflicts grounded in differences of perceptions and expectations are generally intense and difficult to defuse.

The second important component of the diagnostic process is assessing the relevant situational considerations, so as to determine the feasible set of responses. Important contextual factors that we considered included the importance of the issue, the importance of the relationship, the relative power of the disputants, and the degree to which time was a limiting factor.

The purpose of the diagnostic phase of the model is to wisely choose between the five conflict management approaches: avoiding, compromising, collaborating, forcing, and accommodating. These reflect different degrees of assertiveness and cooperativeness, or the priority given to satisfying one's own concerns versus the concerns of the other party, respectively.

As shown in Figure 7.6, personal preferences, reflecting a person's ethnic culture, gender, and personality play a key role in our conception of effective conflict management. One's personal comfort level with using the various conflict management approaches is both an enabling and a limiting factor. If we feel comfortable with an approach, we are likely to use it effectively. Because effective problem solvers need to feel comfortable using a variety of tools, however, one shouldn't pass over an appropriate tool because its use might be discomforting. For this reason, it is important for conflict managers to stretch their natural "comfort zone" through skill development activities.

That is why, as shown in the figure, we elected to focus on the effective implementation of the specific conflict management approach that is both the most effective, all-purpose tool, and the most difficult to use comfortably and skillfully—collaborative problem solving. It takes little skill to impose your authority on another person, to withdraw from a confrontation, to split the difference between opponents, or to abandon your position at the slightest sign of opposition. Therefore, the behavioral guidelines for resolving an interpersonal confrontation involving complaints and criticisms by using a problem-solving approach have been described in detail.

Behavioral Guidelines

Effective conflict management involves both analytic and behavioral elements. The analytic process involves diagnosing the true causes of a conflict, as well as understanding the key situational considerations and personal preferences that need to be factored into selecting the appropriate conflict management approach. The behavior element of the process involves implementing the chosen strategy effectively to reach a successful resolution of the dispute. Skillful implementation is especially critical for the collaborative problem-solving process advocated in this chapter.

Behavioral guidelines for the diagnosis and selection aspects of conflict management include the following:

1. Collect information on the sources of conflict. Identify the source by examining the focus of the dispute. The four sources, or types of conflict, are personal differences (perception and expectations), information deficiency (misinformation and misinterpretation), role incompatibility (goals and responsibilities), and environmental stress (resource scarcity and uncertainty).

2. Examine relevant situational considerations, including the importance of the issue, the importance of the relationship, the relative power of the disputants, and the degree to which time is a factor.

3. Take into consideration your personal preferences for using the various conflict management approaches. These preferences tend to reflect important elements of your personal identity, including ethnic culture, gender, and personality.

4. Utilize the collaborative approach for managing conflict unless specific conditions dictate the use of an alternative approach.

Behavioral guidelines for effectively implementing the collaborative (problem-solving) approach to conflict management are summarized below. These are organized according to three roles. Guidelines for the problem-identification and solution-generation phases of the problem-solving process are specified for each role. Guidelines for the action plan and follow-up phases are the same for all three roles.

INITIATOR

Problem Identification

1. Maintain personal ownership of the problem.
   - ❏ Succinctly describe your problem in terms of behaviors, consequences, and feelings. ("When you do X, Y happens, and I feel Z.")
   - ❏ Stick to the facts (e.g., use a specific incident to illustrate the expectations or standards violated).

   - ❏ Avoid drawing evaluative conclusions and attributing motives to the respondent.

2. Persist until understood; encourage two-way discussion.
   - ❏ Restate your concerns or give additional examples.
   - ❏ Avoid introducing additional issues or letting frustration sour your emotional tone.
   - ❏ Invite the respondent to ask questions and express another perspective.

3. Manage the agenda carefully.
   - ❏ Approach multiple problems incrementally, proceeding from simple to complex, easy to difficult, concrete to abstract.
   - ❏ Don't become fixated on a single issue. If you reach an impasse, expand the discussion to increase the likelihood of an integrative outcome.

Solution Generation

4. Make a request.
   - ❏ Focus on those things you share in common (principles, goals, constraints) as the basis for recommending preferred alternatives.

RESPONDER

Problem Identification

1. Establish a climate for joint problem solving.
   - ❏ Show genuine concern and interest. Respond empathetically, even if you disagree with the complaint.
   - ❏ Respond appropriately to the initiator's emotions. If necessary, let the person "blow off steam" before addressing the complaint.

2. Seek additional information about the problem.
   - ❏ Ask questions that channel the initiator's statements from general to specific and from evaluative to descriptive.

3. Agree with some aspect of the complaint.
   - ❏ Signal your willingness to consider making changes by agreeing with facts, perceptions, feelings, or principles.

Solution Generation

4. Ask for suggestions and recommendations.
   - ❏ To avoid debating the merits of a single suggestion, brainstorm multiple alternatives.

MEDIATOR
Problem Identification

1. Acknowledge that a conflict exists.
   - ❏ Select the most appropriate setting (one-on-one conference versus group meeting) for coaching and fact-finding.
   - ❏ Propose a problem-solving approach for resolving the dispute.
2. Maintain a neutral posture.
   - ❏ Assume the role of facilitator, not judge. Do not belittle the problem or berate the disputants for their inability to resolve their differences.
   - ❏ Be impartial toward disputants and issues (provided policy has not been violated).
   - ❏ If correction is necessary, do it in private.
3. Manage the discussion to ensure fairness.
   - ❏ Focus discussion on the conflict's impact on performance and the detrimental effect of continued conflict.
   - ❏ Keep the discussion issue oriented, not personality oriented.
   - ❏ Do not allow one party to dominate the discussion. Ask directed questions to maintain balance.

Solution Generation

4. Explore options by focusing on the interests behind stated positions.
   - ❏ Explore the "whys" behind disputants' arguments or demands.
   - ❏ Help disputants see commonalities among their goals, values, and principles.
   - ❏ Use commonalities to generate multiple alternatives.
   - ❏ Maintain a nonjudgmental manner.

ALL ROLES
Action Plan and Follow-Up

1. Ensure that all parties support the agreed-upon plan.
   - ❏ Make sure the plan is adequately detailed (Who, What, How, When, and Where).
   - ❏ Verify understanding of, and commitment to, each specific action.
2. Establish a mechanism for follow-up.
   - ❏ Create benchmarks for measuring progress and ensuring accountability.
   - ❏ Encourage flexibility in adjusting the plan to meet emerging circumstances.

CASE INVOLVING INTERPERSONAL CONFLICT

Educational Pension Investments

Educational Pension Investments (EPI), located in New York, invests pension funds for educational institutions. In 1988, it employed approximately 75 people, 25 of whom were responsible for actual investment activities. The company managed about $1.2 billion of assets and derived an income of about $2.5 million.

The firm was incorporated in 1960 by a group of academic professionals who wanted to control the destiny of their retirement years. They solicited pension funds under the assumption that their investments would be consistent and safe. Through their nearly three decades in the business, they have weathered rapid social and technological change as well as economic volatility. Through it all, they have resisted opportunities to "make it big" and instead stayed with less profitable but relatively secure investments.

Dan Richardson has an MBA from Wharton and is one of the original founders of EPI. He started out working in the research department and has worked in every department since then. The other partners, comfortable with Dan's conservative yet flexible nature, elected him to the position of CEO in the spring of 1975. After that, Dan became known as "the great equalizer." He worked hard to make sure that all the partners were included in decisions and that strong relations were maintained. Over the years, he became the confidant of the other seniors and the mentor of the next generation. He took pride in his "people skills," and EPI's employees looked to Dan for leadership and direction.

Dan's management philosophy is built on the concept of loyalty—loyalty to the organization, loyalty to its members, and loyalty to friends. As he is fond of saying, "My dad was a small town banker. He told me, 'Look out for the other guys and they'll look out for you.' Sounds corny, I know, but I firmly believe in this philosophy."

Dan, bolstered by the support of the other founding members of EPI, continued the practice of consistent and safe investing. This meant maintaining low-risk investment portfolios with moderate income. However, EPI's growth increasingly has not kept pace with other investment opportunities. As a result, Dan has reluctantly begun to consider the merits of a more aggressive investment approach. This consideration was further strengthened by the expressions of several of the younger analysts who were beginning to refer to EPI as "stodgy." Some of them were leaving EPI for positions in more aggressive firms.

One evening, Dan talked about his concern with his racquetball partner and longtime friend, Mike Roth. Mike also happened to be an investment broker. After receiving his MBA from the University of Illinois, Mike went to work for a brokerage firm in New York, beginning his career in the research department. His accomplishments in research brought him recognition throughout the firm. Everyone respected him for his knowledge, his work ethic, and his uncanny ability to predict trends. Mike knew what to do and when to do it. After only two years on the job, he was promoted to the position of portfolio manager. However, he left that firm for greener pastures and had spent the last few years moving from firm to firm.

When Mike heard Dan's concerns about EPI's image and need for an aggressive approach, he suggested to his friend that what EPI needed was some fresh blood, someone who could infuse enthusiasm into the organization—someone like him. He told Dan, "I can help you get things moving. In fact, I've been developing some concepts that would be perfect for EPI."

Dan brought up the idea of hiring Mike at the next staff meeting, but the idea was met with caution and skepticism. "Sure, he's had a brilliant career on paper," said one senior partner. "But he's never stayed in one place long enough to really validate his success. Look at his résumé. During the past seven years, he's been with four different firms, in four different positions."

"That's true," said Dan, "but his references all check out. In fact, he's been described as a rising star, aggressive, productive. He's just what we need to help us explore new opportunities."

"He may have been described as a comer, but I don't feel comfortable with his apparent inability to settle down," said another. "He doesn't seem very loyal or committed to anyone or anything."

Another partner added, "A friend of mine worked with Mike a while back and said that while he is definitely good, he's a real maverick—in terms of both investment philosophy and lifestyle. Is that what we really want at EPI?"

Throughout the discussion, Dan defended Mike's work record. He repeatedly pointed out Mike's impressive performance. He deflected concerns about Mike's reputation by saying that he was a loyal and trusted friend. Largely on Dan's recommendation, the other partners agreed, although somewhat reluctantly, to hire Mike. When Dan offered Mike the job, he promised Mike the freedom and flexibility to operate a segment of the fund as he desired.

Mike took the job and performed his responsibilities at EPI in a superior manner. Indeed, he was largely responsible for increasing the managed assets of the company by 150 percent. However, a price was paid for this increase. From the day he moved in, junior analysts enjoyed working with him very much. They liked his fresh, new approach, and were encouraged by the spectacular results. This caused jealousy among the other partners, who thought Mike was pushing too hard to change the tried-and-true traditions of the firm. It was not uncommon for sharp disagreements to erupt in staff meetings, with one or another partner coming close to storming out of the room. Throughout this time, Dan tried to soothe ruffled feathers and maintain an atmosphere of trust and loyalty.

Mike seemed oblivious to all the turmoil he was causing. He was optimistic about potential growth opportunities. He believed that computer chips, biotechnology, and laser engineering were the "waves of the future." Because of this belief, he wanted to direct the focus of his portfolio toward these emerging technologies. "Investments in small firm stocks in these industries, coupled with an aggressive market timing strategy, should yield a 50 percent increase in performance." He rallied support for this idea not only among the younger members of EPI, but also with the pension fund managers who invested with EPI. Mike championed his position and denigrated the merits of the traditional philosophy. "We should compromise on safety and achieve some real growth while we can," Mike argued. "If we don't, we'll lose the investors' confidence and ultimately lose them."

Most of the senior partners disagreed with Mike, stating that the majority of their investors emphasized security above all else. They also disagreed with the projected profits, stating that "We could go from 8 to 12 percent return on investment (ROI); then again, we could drop to 4 percent. A lot depends on whose data you use." They reminded Mike, "The fundamental approach of the corporation is to provide safe and moderate-income mutual funds for academic pension funds to invest in. That's the philosophy we used to solicit the investments originally, and that's the approach we are obligated to maintain."

Many months passed, and dissension among the managers grew. Mike's frustration over the lack of support among the senior partners began to undermine the day-to-day operations of EPI. He began to criticize detractors in discussions with younger EPI employees. In addition, he assigned research department employees tasks related to technological investments, distracting them from investigating more traditional alternatives. He gradually implemented his ideas within his portfolio, which accounted for approximately 35 percent of EPI's revenues. This disrupted the operations of other managers in EPI because the performance of their funds relied on the timely input of the researchers and other support staff. The other managers bristled when the research staff began tracking the ROI of the various investments on a chart prominently displayed on the conference room wall.

Amidst a rapidly spreading undercurrent of tension, one of the founding partners, Tom Watson, approached Dan one day. Conservative in his ways, Watson was the partner who walks the office and always has time to stop and chat. He began the conversation.

"Dan, I speak for most of the senior staff when I say that we are very troubled by Mike's approach. We've expressed ourselves well enough for Mike to understand, but his actions defy everything we've said. He's a catastrophe just waiting to happen."

"I can understand your concern, Tom," replied Dan. "I'm troubled, too. We have an opportunity to attract new business with some of Mike's new ideas. And the younger staff love working on his projects. But he has stirred up a lot of turmoil."

Tom agreed. "The real issue is that EPI is no longer presenting a unified image. Mike is willfully defying the stated objectives of our organization. And some of our oldest clients don't like that."

"That's true, Tom. On the other hand, some of our newer clients are really encouraged by Mike's approach—and his track record is extremely impressive."

"Come on, Dan. You and I both know that many experts feel the market is overheating. Mike's paper profits could quickly be incinerated if the budget and trade deficits don't turn around. We can't stake the reputation of the firm on a few high-flying technology stocks. Dan, the other senior partners agree. Mike must either conform to the philosophy and management practices of this organization or else resign."

Reflecting on the situation, Dan realized he faced the most difficult challenge of his career. He felt a strong personal investment in helping Mike succeed. Not only had he hired Mike over the objections of several colleagues; he had personally helped him "learn the ropes" at EPI. Beyond that, Dan was haunted by his promise to Mike that he would have the freedom and flexibility to perform the requirements of the position as he pleased. However, this flexibility had clearly caused problems within EPI.

Finally, bowing to the pressure of his peers, Dan called Mike in for a meeting, hoping to find some basis for compromise.

DAN: I gather you know the kinds of concerns the senior partners have expressed regarding your approach.

MIKE: I guess you've talked with Tom. Well, we did have a small disagreement earlier this week.

DAN: The way Tom tells it, you're willfully defying corporate objectives and being insubordinate.

MIKE: Well, it's just like Watson to see progressive change as an attempt to take away his power.

DAN: It's not quite that simple, Mike. When we founded EPI, we all agreed that a conservative stance was best. And right now, with the economic indicators looking soft, many experts agree that it may still be the best alternative.

MIKE: Dan, what are you going to rely on—predictions or performance? These concerns are just smokescreens to deflect attention away from the sub-par records of other portfolio managers. Old views need to be challenged and ultimately discarded. How else are we going to progress and keep up with our competitors?

DAN: I agree we need to change, Mike—but gradually. You have great ideas and terrific instincts, but you can't change a 30-year-old firm overnight. You can help me promote change, but you're pushing so fast, others are digging in their heels. The rate of change is just as important as the direction.

MIKE: You're telling me. And at this rate, it doesn't make much difference which direction we're headed in.

DAN: Come on, Mike. Don't be so cynical. If you'd just stop rubbing people's noses in your performance record and try to see things from their perspective, we could calm things down around here. Then maybe we could start building consensus.

Mike's emotions betray his impatience with the pace of the organization; he becomes agitated.

MIKE: I've always admired your judgment, and I value your friendship, but I honestly think you're kidding yourself. You seem to think you can get this firm to look like it's progressive—shrugging off its stodgy image—without taking any risks or ruffling any feathers. Are you interested in appearance or substance? If you want appearance, then hire a good PR person. If you want substance, then back me up and we'll rewrite the record book. Get off the fence, Dan, before your butt's full of slivers.

DAN: Mike, it simply isn't that easy. I'm not EPI, I'm simply its caretaker. You know we make decisions around here by consensus; that's the backbone of this organization. To move ahead, the confidence of the others has to be won, especially the confidence of the seniors. Frankly, your reputation as a maverick makes it hard to foster confidence in, and loyalty to, your plans.

MIKE: You knew my style when you hired me. Remember how you made it a point to promise me flexibility and autonomy? I'm not getting that any more, Dan. All I'm getting is grief, even though I'm running circles around your conservative cronies.

DAN: Well, that may be true. But your flamboyance . . .

MIKE: Oh, yeah. The sports car, the singles lifestyle, the messy office. But, again, that's appearance, Dan, not substance. Performance is what counts. That's what got me this far, and that's my ticket out. You know I could walk into any firm in town and write my own plan.

DAN: Well, there's no reason to be hasty.

MIKE: Do you honestly believe this can be salvaged? I think not. Maybe it's time for me to be moving on. Isn't that why you called me in here anyway?

Dan, feeling uncomfortable, breaks eye contact and shifts his gaze to the New York skyline. After a long pause, he continues, still gazing out of the window.

DAN: I don't know, Mike. I feel I've failed. My grand experiment in change has polarized the office; we've got two armies at war out there. On the other hand, you really have done a good job here. EPI will no doubt lose a good part of its customer base if you leave. You have a loyal following, with both customers and staff. If you go, so do they—along with our shot at changing our image.

MIKE: It's just like you, Dan, to take this problem personally. Blast it, you take everything personally. Even when I beat you at racquetball. Your heart's in the right place—you just can't ever seem to make the cutthroat hit. You know and I know that EPI needs a change in image. But it doesn't appear to be ready for it yet. And I'm certainly not willing to move slowly.

DAN: Yeah. Maybe. It's just hard to give up . . . [long pause]. Well, why don't we talk more about this after the reception tonight? Come on over and see Joanie and the kids. Besides, I'm dying to show off my new boat.

MIKE: What you see in sailing is beyond me. It's a waste of time, lazily drifting on gentle breezes.

DAN: Save it for later, "Speed King." I've got to get ready for tonight.

Discussion Questions

1. What are the sources of conflict in this case?
2. What approaches to conflict management are used by the actors in this situation? How effective was each?
3. Based on the behavioral guidelines for the collaborative approach, how could Dan have managed this conflict more effectively?

SKILL *PRACTICE*

EXERCISE FOR DIAGNOSING
SOURCES OF CONFLICT

SSS Software Management Problems

In order to manage conflict between others effectively, it is important to be aware of early warning signs. It is also important to understand the underlying causes of disagreements. Conflict that is unmanaged, or managed ineffectively, interferes with work-group performance. A key to managing conflict effectively is recognizing it in its early stages and understanding its roots.

Assignment

Read the memos, faxes, voice mail, and e-mail messages that follow. As you examine each of these documents, look for evidence of organizational conflicts. Identify the two conflicts that you think are most significant for you to address in your role as Chris Perillo. Begin your analysis of these conflicts by identifying their likely sources or causes. Use Figure 7.2 as a diagnostic tool for identifying the type of conflict, based on its source and focus. Prepare to present your analysis, along with supporting evidence from the memos. Also, share your ideas regarding how this analysis of the causes of conflict would influence your approach to resolving the conflict.

SSS Software In-Basket Memos, E-mails, Faxes, and Voice Mails

ITEM 1 – E-MAIL

TO: All Employees
FROM: Roger Steiner, Chief Executive Officer
DATE: October 15

I am pleased to announce that Chris Perillo has been appointed as Vice President of Operations for Health and Financial Services. Chris will immediately assume responsibility for all operations previously managed by Michael Grant. Chris will have end-to-end responsibility for the design, development, integration, and maintenance of custom software for the health and finance/banking industries. This responsibility includes all technical, financial, and staffing issues. Chris will also manage our program of software support and integration for the recently announced merger of three large health maintenance organizations (HMOs). Chris will be responsible for our recently announced project with a consortium of banks and financial firms operating in Tanzania. This project represents an exciting opportunity for us, and Chris's background seems ideally suited to the task.

Chris comes to this position with an undergraduate degree in Computer Science from the California Institute of Technology and an MBA from the University of Virginia. Chris began as a member of our technical/professional staff six years ago and has most recently served for three years as a group manager supporting domestic and international projects for our airlines industry group, including our recent work for the European Airbus consortium.

I am sure you all join me in offering congratulations to Chris for this promotion.

ITEM 2 – E-MAIL

TO: All Managers
FROM: Hal Harris, Vice President, Community and Public Relations
DATE: October 15

For your information, the following article appeared on the front page of the business section of Thursday's *Los Angeles Times*.

In a move that may create problems for SSS Software, Michael Grant and Janice Ramos have left SSS Software and moved to Universal Business Solutions Inc. Industry analysts see the move as another victory for Universal Business Solutions Inc. in their battle with SSS Software for share of the growing software development and integration business. Both Grant and Ramos had been with SSS Software for over seven years. Grant was most recently Vice President of Operations for all SSS Software's work in two industries: health and hospitals, and finance and banking. Ramos brings to Universal Business Solutions Inc. her special expertise in the growing area of international software development and integration.

Hillary Collins, an industry analyst with Merrill Lynch, said "the loss of key staff to a competitor can often create serious problems for a firm such as SSS Software. Grant and Ramos have an insider's understanding of SSS Software's strategic and technical limitations. It will be interesting to see if they can exploit this knowledge to the advantage of Universal Business Solutions Inc."

ITEM 3 – E-MAIL

TO: Chris Perillo
FROM: Paula Sprague, Executive Assistant to Roger Steiner
DATE: October 15

Chris, I know that in your former position as a group manager in the Airline Services Division, you probably have met most of the group managers in the Health and Financial Services Division, but I thought you might like some more personal information about them. These people will be your direct reports on the management team.

Group #1: Bob Miller, 55-year-old white male, married (Anna) with two children and three grandchildren. Active in local Republican politics. Well regarded as a "hands-off" manager heading a high-performing team. Plays golf regularly with Mark McIntyre, John Small, and a couple of VPs from other divisions.

Group #2: Wanda Manners, 38-year-old white female, single with one school-age child. A fitness "nut" and has run in several marathons. Some experience in Germany and Japan. Considered a hard-driving manager with a constant focus on the task at hand. Will be the first person to show up every morning.

Group #3: William Chen, 31-year-old male of Chinese descent, married (Harriet), two young children from his first marriage. Enjoys tennis and is quite good at it. A rising star in the company, he is highly respected by his peers as a "man of action" and a good friend.

Group #4: Leo Jones, 36-year-old white male, married (Janet) with an infant daughter. Recently returned from paternity leave. Has traveled extensively on projects since he speaks three languages. Has liked hockey ever since the time he spent in Montreal. Considered a strong manager who gets the most out of his people.

Group #5: Mark McIntyre, 45-year-old white male, married (Mary Theresa) to an executive in the banking industry. No children. A lot of experience in Germany and Eastern

PRACTICE

Europe. Has been writing a mystery novel. Has always been a good "team player," but several members of his technical staff are not well respected and he hasn't addressed the problem.

Group #6: John Small, 38-year-old white male, recently divorced. Three children living with his wife. A gregarious individual who likes sports. He spent a lot of time in Mexico and Central America before he came to SSS Software. Recently has been doing mostly contract work with the federal government. An average manager, has had some trouble keeping his people on schedule.

Group #7: This position vacant since Janice Ramos left. Roger thinks we ought to fill this position quickly. Get in touch with me if you want information on any in-house candidates for any position.

Group #8: Marcus Harper, 42-year-old African American male, married (Tamara) with two teenage children. Recently won an award in a local photography contest. Considered a strong manager who gets along with peers and works long hours.

Customer Services: Armand Marke, 38-year-old male, divorced. A basketball fan. Originally from Armenia. Previously a group manager. Worked hard to establish the Technical Services Phone Line, but now has pretty much left it alone.

Office Administrator: Michelle Harrison, 41-year-old white female, single. Grew up on a ranch and still rides horses whenever she can. A strict administrator.

There are a number of good folks here, but they don't function well as a management team. I think Michael played favorites, especially with Janice and Leo. There are a few cliques in this group, and I'm not sure how effectively Michael dealt with them. I expect you will find it a challenge to build a cohesive team.

ITEM 4 – E-MAIL

TO: Chris Perillo
FROM: Wanda Manners, Group 2 Manager
DATE: October 15

CONFIDENTIAL AND RESTRICTED

Although I know you are new to your job, I feel it is important that I let you know about some information I just obtained concerning the development work we recently completed for First National Investment. Our project involved the development of asset management software for managing their international funds. This was a very complex project due to the volatile exchange rates and the forecasting tools we needed to develop.

As part of this project, we had to integrate the software and reports with all their existing systems and reporting mechanisms. To do this, we were given access to all of their existing software (much of which was developed by Universal Business Solutions Inc.). Of course, we signed an agreement acknowledging that the software to which we were given access was proprietary and that our access was solely for the purpose of our system integration work associated with the project.

Unfortunately, I have learned that some parts of the software we developed actually "borrow" heavily from complex application programs developed for First National Investment by Universal Business Solutions Inc. It seems obvious to me that one or more of the software developers from Group 5 (that is, Mark McIntyre's group) inappropriately "borrowed" algorithms developed by Universal Business Solutions Inc. I am sure that doing so saved us significant development time on some aspects of the project. It seems very unlikely that First National Investment or Universal Business Solutions Inc. will ever become aware of this issue.

Finally, First National Investment is successfully using the software we developed and is thrilled with the work we did. We brought the project in on time and under budget. You probably know that they have invited us to bid on several other substantial projects.

I'm sorry to bring this delicate matter to your attention, but I thought you should know about it.

ITEM 5A – E-MAIL

TO: Chris Perillo
FROM: Paula Sprague, Executive Assistant to Roger Steiner
DATE: October 15
RE: Letter from C.A.R.E. Services (copies attached)

Roger asked me to work on this C.A.R.E. project and obviously wants some fast action. A lot of the staff are already booked solid for the next couple of weeks. I knew that Elise Soto and Chu Hung Woo have the expertise to do this system and when I checked with them, they were relatively free. I had them pencil in the next two weeks and wanted to let you know. Hopefully, it will take a "hot potato" out of your hands.

ITEM 5B – Copy of Fax

C.A.R.E.
Child and Adolescent Rehabilitative and Educational Services
A United Way Member Agency
200 Main Street
Los Angeles, California 90230

DATE: October 11
Roger Steiner, CEO
SSS Software
13 Miller Way
Los Angeles, California 90224

Dear Roger,

This letter is a follow-up to our conversation after last night's board meeting. I appreciated your comments during the board meeting about the need for sophisticated computer systems in nonprofit organizations and I especially appreciate your generous offer of help to have SSS Software provide assistance to deal with the immediate problem with our accounting system. Since the board voted to fire the computer consultant, I am very worried about getting our reports done in time to meet the state funding cycle.

Thanks again for your offer of help during this crisis.

Sincerely yours,

Janice Polocizwic

Janice Polocizwic
Executive Director

ITEM 5C – COPY OF A LETTER

SSS SOFTWARE
13 Miller Way
Los Angeles, CA 90224

DATE: October 12

Janice Polocizwic
Executive Director, C.A.R.E. Services
200 Main Street
Los Angeles, California 90230

Dear Janice,

I received your fax of October 11. I have asked Paula Sprague, my executive assistant, to line up people to work on your accounting system as soon as possible. You can expect to hear from her shortly.

Sincerely,

Roger Steiner

Roger Steiner
cc: Paula Sprague, Executive Assistant

ITEM 6 – E-MAIL

TO: Michael Grant
FROM: Harry Withers, Group 6 Technical Staff
DATE: October 12

PERSONAL AND CONFIDENTIAL

Our team is having difficulty meeting the submission deadline of November 5 for the Halstrom project. Kim, Fred, Peter, Kyoto, Susan, Mala, and I have been working on the project for several weeks, but we are experiencing some problems and may need additional time. I hesitate to write this letter, but the main problem is that our group manager, John Small, is involved in a relationship with Mala. Mala gets John's support for her ideas and brings them to the team as required components of the project. Needless to say, this has posed some problems for the group. Mala's background is especially valuable for this project, but Kim and Fred, who have both worked very hard on the project, do not want to work with her. In addition, one member of the team has been unavailable recently because of child-care needs. Commitment to the project and team morale have plummeted. However, we'll do our best to get the project finished as soon as possible. Mala will be on vacation the next two weeks, so I'm expecting that some of us can complete it in her absence.

ITEM 7 – VOICE MAIL MESSAGE

Hello, Michael. This is Jim Bishop of United Hospitals. I wanted to talk with you about the quality assurance project that you are working on for us. When Jose Martinez first started talking with us, I was impressed with his friendliness and expertise. But recently, he doesn't seem to be getting much accomplished and has seemed distant and on-edge in conversations. Today, I asked him about the schedule and he seemed very defensive and not entirely in control of his emotions. I am quite concerned about our project. Please give me a call.

ITEM 8 – VOICE MAIL MESSAGE

Hi, Michael. This is Armand. I wanted to talk with you about some issues with the Technical Services Phone Line. I've recently received some complaint letters from Phone Line customers whose complaints have included long delays while waiting for a technician to answer the phone, technicians who are not knowledgeable enough to solve problems, and, on occasion, rude service. Needless to say, I'm quite concerned about these complaints.

I believe that the overall quality of the Phone Line staff is very good, but we continue to be understaffed, even with the recent hires. The new technicians look strong, but are working on the help-line before being fully trained. Antolina, our best tech, often brings her child to work, which is adding to the craziness around here.

I think you should know that we're feeling a lot of stress here. I'll talk with you soon.

ITEM 9 – VOICE MAIL MESSAGE

Hi, Chris, it's Pat. Congratulations on your promotion. They definitely picked the right person. It's great news—for me, too. You've been a terrific mentor so far, so I'm expecting to learn a lot from you in your new position. How about lunch next week?

ITEM 10 – VOICE MAIL MESSAGE

Chris, this is Bob Miller. Just thought you'd like to know that John's joke during our planning meeting has disturbed a few of the women in my group. Frankly, I think the thing's being blown out of proportion, especially since we all know this is a good place for both men and women to work. Give me a call if you want to chat about this.

ITEM 11 – VOICE MAIL MESSAGE

Hello. This is Lorraine Adams from Westside Hospital. I read in today's *Los Angeles Times* that you will be taking over from Michael Grant. We haven't met yet, but your division has recently finished two large million-dollar projects for Westside. Michael Grant and I had some discussion about a small conversion of a piece of existing software to be compatible with the new systems. The original vendor had said that they would do the work, but they have been stalling, and I need to move quickly. Can you see if Harris Wilson, Chu Hung Woo, and Elise Soto are available to do this work as soon as possible? They were on the original project and work well with our people.

Um . . . (long pause) I guess I should tell you that I got a call from Michael offering to do this work. But I think I should stick with SSS Software. Give me a call.

PRACTICE

ITEM 12 – VOICE MAIL MESSAGE

Hi, Chris, this is Roosevelt Moore calling. I'm a member of your technical/professional staff. I used to report to Janice Ramos, but since she left the firm, I thought I'd bring my concerns directly to you. I'd like to arrange some time to talk with you about my experiences since returning from six weeks of paternity leave. Some of my major responsibilities have been turned over to others. I seem to be out of the loop and wonder if my career is at risk. Also, I am afraid that I won't be supported or seriously considered for the opening created by Janice's departure. Frankly, I feel like I'm being screwed for taking my leave. I'd like to talk with you this week.

ITEM 13 – E-MAIL

TO: Michael Grant
FROM: Jose Martinez, Group 1 Technical Staff
DATE: October 12

I would like to set up a meeting with you as soon as possible. I suspect that you will get a call from Jim Bishop of United Hospitals and want to be sure that you hear my side of the story first. I have been working on a customized system design for quality assurance for them using a variation of the J-3 product we developed several years ago. They had a number of special requirements and some quirks in their accounting systems, so I have had to put in especially long hours. I've worked hard to meet their demands, but they keep changing the ground rules. I keep thinking, this is just another J-3 I'm working on, but they have been interfering with an elegant design I have developed. It seems I'm not getting anywhere on this project. Earlier today, I had a difficult discussion with their Controller. He asked for another major change. I've been fighting their deadline and think I am just stretched too thin on this project. Then Jim Bishop asked me if the system was running yet. I was worn out from dealing with the Controller, and I made a sarcastic comment to Jim Bishop. He gave me a funny look and just walked out of the room.

I would like to talk with you about this situation at your earliest convenience.

ITEM 14 – E-MAIL

TO: Chris Perillo
FROM: John Small, Group 6 Manager
DATE: October 15

Welcome aboard, Chris. I look forward to meeting with you. I just wanted to put a bug in your ear about finding a replacement for Janice Ramos. One of my technical staff, Mala Abendano, has the ability and drive to make an excellent group manager. I have encouraged her to apply for the position. I'd be happy to talk with you further about this, at your convenience.

ITEM 15 – E-MAIL

TO: Chris Perillo
FROM: Paula Sprague, Executive Assistant to Roger Steiner
DATE: October 15

Roger asked me to let you know about the large contract we have gotten in Tanzania. It means that a team of four managers will be making a short trip to determine current needs. They will assign their technical staff the tasks of developing a system and software here over the next six months, and then the managers and possibly some team members will be spending about 10 months on site in Tanzania to handle the implementation. Roger thought you might want to hold an initial meeting with some of your managers to check on their interest and willingness to take this sort of assignment. Roger would appreciate an e-mail of your thoughts about the issues to be discussed at this meeting, additional considerations about sending people to Tanzania, and about how you will put together an effective team to work on this project. The October 15 memo I sent to you will provide you with some information you'll need to start making these decisions.

ITEM 16 – E-MAIL

TO: Chris Perillo
FROM: Sharon Shapiro, VP of Human Resources
DATE: October 15
RE: Upcoming meeting

I want to update you on the rippling effect of John Small's sexual joke at last week's planning meeting. Quite a few women have been very upset and have met informally to talk about it. They have decided to call a meeting of all people concerned about this kind of behavior throughout the firm. I plan to attend, so I'll keep you posted.

ITEM 17 – E-MAIL

TO: All SSS Software Managers
FROM: Sharon Shapiro, VP of Human Resources
DATE: October 15
RE: Promotions and External Hires

Year-to-Date (January through September) Promotions and External Hires

| Level | Race | | | | | Sex | | Total |
	White	African American	Asian	Hispanic	Native American	M	F	
Hires into Executive Level	0 (0%)	0 (0%)	0 (0%)	0 (0%)	0 (0%)	0 (0%)	0 (0%)	0
Promotions to Executive Level	0 (0%)	0 (0%)	0 (0%)	0 (0%)	0 (0%)	0 (0%)	0 (0%)	0
Hires into Management Level	2 (67%)	1 (33%)	0 (0%)	0 (0%)	0 (0%)	2 (67%)	1 (33%)	3
Promotions to Management Level	7 (88%)	0 (0%)	1 (12%)	0 (0%)	0 (0%)	7 (88%)	1 (12%)	8
Hires into Technical/ Professional Level	10 (36%)	6 (21%)	10 (36%)	2 (7%)	0 (0%)	14 (50%)	14 (50%)	28

| Level | Race | | | | | Sex | | |
	White	African American	Asian	Hispanic	Native American	M	F	Total
Promotions to Technical/Professional Level	0 (0%)	0 (0%)	0 (0%)	0 (0%)	0 (0%)	0 (0%)	0 (0%)	0
Hires into Non-Management Level	4 (20%)	10 (50%)	2 (10%)	4 (20%)	0 (0%)	6 (30%)	14 (70%)	20
Promotions to Non-Management Level	NA	NA	NA	NA	NA	NA	NA	NA

SSS Software Employee (EEO) Classification Report as of June 30

| Level | Race | | | | | Sex | | |
	White	African American	Asian	Hispanic	Native American	M	F	Total
Executive Level	11 (92%)	0 (0%)	1 (8%)	0 (0%)	0 (0%)	11 (92%)	1 (8%)	12
Management Level	43 (90%)	2 (4%)	2 (4%)	1 (2%)	0 (0%)	38 (79%)	10 (21%)	48
Technical/Professional Level	58 (45%)	20 (15%)	37 (28%)	14 (11%)	1 (1%)	80 (62%)	50 (38%)	130
Non-Management Level	29 (48%)	22 (37%)	4 (7%)	4 (7%)	1 (2%)	12 (20%)	48 (80%)	60
Total	141 (56%)	44 (18%)	44 (18%)	19 (8%)	2 (1%)	141 (56%)	109 (44%)	250

EXERCISES FOR SELECTING AN APPROPRIATE CONFLICT MANAGEMENT STRATEGY

Not all conflicts are alike; therefore, they cannot all be managed in exactly the same way. Effective managers are able to assess accurately the true causes of conflict and to match each type of conflict with an appropriate management strategy.

Assignment

For each of the following brief scenarios, select the most appropriate conflict management strategy. Refer to Table 4 for assistance in matching situational factors with strategies.

Bradley's Barn

You have decided to take your family out to the local steakhouse, Bradley's Barn, to celebrate your son's birthday. You are a single parent, so getting home from work in time to prepare a nice dinner is very difficult. On entering the restaurant, you ask the hostess to seat you in the nonsmoking section because your daughter, Shauna, is allergic to tobacco smoke. On your way to your seat, you notice that the restaurant seems crowded for a Monday night.

After you and your children are seated and have placed your orders, your conversation turns to family plans for the approaching holiday. Interspersed in the general conversation is a light banter with your son about whether or not he is too old to wear "the crown" during dinner—a family tradition on birthdays.

Suddenly you become aware that your daughter is sneezing and her eyes are beginning to water. You look around and notice a lively group of businesspeople seated at the table behind you; they are all smoking. Your impression is that they are celebrating some type of special occasion. Looking back at Shauna, you realize that something has to be done quickly. You ask your son to escort Shauna outside while you rush to the front of the restaurant and find the hostess.

Discussion Questions

1. What are the salient situational factors?
2. What is the most appropriate conflict management strategy?

Avocado Computers

When the head of Avocado Computers ran into production problems with his automated production facility, he hired you away from a competitor. It meant a significant increase in pay and the opportunity to manage a state-of-the-art production facility. What's more, there were very few other female production managers in Silicon Valley. Now you've been on the job a year, and it's been exciting to see your staff start working together as a team to solve problems, improve quality, and finally get the plant up to capacity. In general, Bill, the owner, has also been a plus. He is energetic, fair, and a proven industry leader. You feel fortunate to be in a coveted position, in a "star" firm, in a growth industry.

However, there is one distraction that bugs you. Bill is a real stickler about cleanliness, order, and appearance. He wants the robots all painted the same color, the components within the computer laid out perfectly on a grid, the workers wearing clean smocks, and the floor "clean enough to eat off." You are troubled by this compulsion. "Sure," you think, "it might impress potential corporate clients when they tour the production facility, but is it really that important? After all, who's ever going to look at the inside of their computer? Why should customers care about the color of the robot that built their computers? And who, for Pete's sake, would ever want to have a picnic in a factory?"

Today is your first yearly performance appraisal interview with Bill. In preparation for the meeting, he has sent you a memo outlining "Areas of Strength" and "Areas of Concern." You look with pride at the number of items listed in the first column. It's obvious that Bill likes your work. But you are a bit miffed at the single item of concern: "Needs to maintain a cleaner facility, including employee appearance." You mull over this "demerit" in your mind, wrestling with how to respond in your interview.

Discussion Questions

1. What are the salient situational factors?
2. What is the most appropriate conflict management strategy?

Phelps, Inc.

You are Philip Manual, the head of sales for an office products firm, Phelps, Inc. Your person-nel sell primarily to small businesses in the Los Angeles metropolitan area. Phelps is doing about average for this rapidly growing market. The firm's new president, Jose Ortega, is putting a lot of pressure on you to increase sales. You feel that a major obstacle is the firm's policy on extending credit. Celeste, the head of the credit office, insists that all new customers fill out an extensive credit application. Credit risks must be low; credit terms and collection procedures are tough. You can appreciate her point of view, but you feel it is unrealistic. Your competitors are much more lenient in their credit examinations; they extend credit to higher risks; their credit terms are more favorable; and they are more lenient in collecting overdue payments. Your sales personnel frequently complain that they aren't "playing on a level field" with their competition. When you brought this concern to Jose, he said he wanted you and Celeste to work things out. His instructions didn't give many clues to his priorities on this matter. "Sure, we need to increase sales, but the small business failure in this area is the high-est in the country, so we have to be careful we don't make bad credit decisions."

You decide it's time to have a serious discussion with Celeste. A lot is at stake.

Discussion Questions

1. What are the salient situational factors?
2. What is the most appropriate conflict management strategy?

EXERCISES FOR RESOLVING INTERPERSONAL DISPUTES

The heart of conflict management is resolving intense, emotionally charged confrontations. We have discussed guidelines for utilizing the collaborative (problem-solving) approach to conflict management in these situations. Assuming that the collaborative approach is appropriate for a particular situation, the general guidelines can be used by an initiator, a responder, or a mediator.

Assignment

Following are three situations involving interpersonal conflict and disagreement. After you have finished reading the assigned roles, review the appropriate behavioral guidelines. Do not read any of the role descriptions except those assigned to you.

In the first exercise (Freida Mae Jones), students assigned to play Freida Mae will prac-tice applying the guidelines for the initiator's role. In the second exercise (Can Larry Fit In?), students assigned to play the role of Larry's boss, Melissa, will practice the guidelines for the respondent's role. In the third exercise (Meeting at Hartford Manufacturing Company), students assigned to play the role of Lynn Smith will practice the guidelines for resolving conflicts among subordinates. For each exercise an observer will be assigned to give students playing the roles of Freida Mae, Melissa, or Lynn feedback on their performance, using the Observer's Feedback Form at the end of the chapter as their guide.

Freida Mae Jones

Freida Mae Jones, Assistant Manager, Branch Operations

Freida Mae Jones was born in her grandmother's Georgia farmhouse on June 1, 1949. She was the sixth of George and Ella Jones's 10 children. Mr. and Mrs. Jones moved to New York City when Freida was four because they felt the educational and career opportunities for their children would be better in the North. With the help of some cousins, they settled in a five-room apartment in the Bronx. George worked as a janitor at Lincoln Memorial Hospital, and Ella was a part-time housekeeper in a nearby neighborhood. George and Ella were conservative, strict parents. They kept a close watch on their children's activities and demanded they be home by a certain hour. The Joneses believed that because they were African American, the children would have to perform and behave better than their peers to be successful. They believed their children's education would be the most important factor in their success as adults.

Freida entered Memorial High School, a racially integrated public school, in September 1963. Seventy percent of the student body was Caucasian, 20 percent African American, and 10 percent Hispanic. About 60 percent of the graduates went on to college, of which 4 percent were African American, Hispanic, and male. In her senior year, Freida was the top student in her class. Following school regulations, Freida met with her guidance counselor to discuss plans upon graduation. The counselor advised her to consider training in a "practical" field such as housekeeping, cooking, or sewing, so that she could find a job.

George and Ella Jones were furious when Freida told them what the counselor had advised. Ella said, "Don't they see what they are doing? Freida is the top-rated student in her whole class and they are telling her to become a manual worker. She showed she has a fine mind and can work better than any of her classmates and still she is told not to become anybody in this world. It's really not any different in the North than back home in Georgia, except that they don't try to hide it down South. They want her to throw away her fine mind because she is an African American girl and not a white boy. I'm going to go up to her school tomorrow and talk to the principal."

As a result of Mrs. Jones's visit to the principal, Freida was assisted in applying to 10 Eastern colleges, each of which offered her full scholarships. In September 1966, Freida entered Werbley College, an exclusive private women's college in Massachusetts. In 1970, Freida graduated summa cum laude in history. She decided to return to New York to teach grade school in the city's public school system. Freida was unable to obtain a full-time position, so she substituted. She also enrolled as a part-time student in Columbia University's Graduate School of Education. In 1975, she had attained her master of arts degree in teaching from Columbia but could not find a permanent teaching job. New York City was laying off teachers and had instituted a hiring freeze because of the city's financial problems.

Feeling frustrated about her future as a teacher, Freida decided to get an MBA. She thought there was more opportunity in business than in education. Churchill Business School, a small, prestigious school located in upstate New York, accepted Freida into its MBA program.

Freida completed her MBA in 1977 and accepted an entry-level position at the Industrialist World Bank of Boston in a fast-track management development program. The three-year program introduced her to all facets of bank operations, from telling to loan training and operations management. She was rotated to branch offices throughout New England. After completing the program, she became an assistant manager for branch operations in the West Springfield branch office.

During her second year in the program, Freida had met James Walker, an African American doctoral student in Business Administration at the University of Massachusetts. Her assignment to West Springfield precipitated their decision to get married. They originally anticipated they would marry when James finished his doctorate and could move to Boston. Instead, they decided he would pursue a job in the Springfield-Hartford area.

Freida was not only the first African American but also the first woman to hold an executive position in the West Springfield branch office. Throughout the training program Freida felt somewhat uneasy although she did very well. There were six other African American in the program, five men and one woman, and she found support and comfort in sharing her feelings with them. The group spent much of their free time together. Freida had hoped she would be located near one or more of the group when she went out into the "real world." She felt though she was able to share her feelings about work with James, he did not have as full an appreciation or understanding as her coworkers. However, the nearest group member was located 100 miles away.

Freida's boss in Springfield was Stan Luboda, a 55-year-old native New Englander. Freida felt he treated her differently than he did the other trainees. He always tried to help her and took a lot of time (too much, according to Freida) explaining things to her. Freida felt he was treating her like a child and not like an intelligent and able professional.

"I'm really getting frustrated and angry about what is happening at the bank," Freida said to her husband. "The people don't even realize it, but their prejudice comes through all the time. I feel as if I have to fight constantly just to start off even. Luboda gives Paul Cohen more responsibility than me and we both started at the same time with the same amount of training. He's meeting customers alone and Luboda has accompanied me to each meeting I've had with a customer."

"I run into the same thing at school," said James. "The people don't even know they are doing it. The other day I met with a professor on my dissertation committee. I've known and worked with him for more than three years. He said he wanted to talk with me about a memo he had received. I asked him what it was about and he said the records office wanted to know about my absence during the spring semester. He said I had to sign some forms. He had me confused with Martin Jordan, another African American student. Then he realized it wasn't me, but Jordan he wanted. All I could think was that we all must look alike to him. I was angry. Maybe it was an honest mistake on his part, but whenever something like that happens, and it happens often, it gets me really angry."

"Something like that happened to me," said Freida. "I was using the copy machine, and Luboda's secretary was talking to someone in the hall. She had just gotten a haircut and was saying her hair was now like Freida's—short and kinky—and that she would have to talk to me about how to take care of it. Luckily, my back was to her. I bit my lip and went on with my business. Maybe she was trying to be cute, because I know she saw me standing there, but comments like that are not cute, they are racist."

"I don't know what to do," said James. "I try to keep things in perspective. Unless people interfere with my progress, I try to let it slide. I only have so much energy and it doesn't make sense to waste it on people who don't matter. But that doesn't make it any easier to function in a racist environment. People don't realize that they are being racist. But a lot of times their expectations of African American people or women, or whatever, are different because of skin color or gender. They expect you to be different, although if you were to ask them they would say that they don't. In fact, they would be highly offended if you implied that they were racist or sexist. They don't see themselves that way."

"Luboda is interfering with my progress," said Freida. "The kinds of experiences I have now will have a direct effect on my career advancement. If decisions are being made because I am African American or a woman, then they are racially and sexually biased. It's the same kind of attitude that the guidance counselor had when I was in high school, although not as blatant." In September 1980, Freida decided to speak to Luboda about his treatment of her. She met with him in his office. "Mr. Luboda, there is something I would like to discuss with you, and I feel a little uncomfortable because I'm not sure how you will respond to what I am going to say."

Stan Luboda, Manager, Branch Operations

Stan Luboda is a 55-year-old native New Englander who has managed the Springfield branch for more than a decade and has extensive ties to a tightly knit western Massachusetts community. Stan feels he is liberal and open-minded, and is proud that he recruited Freida Mae Jones, one of only two African American females in the Industrialist World Bank of Boston management development program. Stan feels his working relationship with all of his assistant branch managers is cordial and working smoothly. He has structured the work so that each assistant branch manager is specialized in one part of the business.

He has assigned Paul Cohen to some established accounts as well as having him work on securing new customers, while he has Freida Mae Jones managing the important processing department and supervising a staff of clerical and accounting personnel. While having lunch with Garland Smith, his boss who was visiting from the Boston head office, the subject of why Stan had assigned Cohen the more visible customer contact assignments while assigning Jones to the backroom operations role came up.

"Look Garland, you know I'm not a naive person, and I'm very open-minded, which is why I'm so pleased to have Freida Mae on my staff," said Luboda. "You know the way the world works. There are some things that need to be taken more slowly than others. There are some assignments for which Cohen has been given more responsibility, and there are some assignments for which Jones is given more responsibility than Cohen."

"Don't you think Cohen's career will advance more quickly than Jones's because of the assignments that he gets?" Smith replied.

"That is not true," said Luboda. "Jones's career will not be hurt because she is getting different responsibilities than Cohen. They both need the different kinds of experiences they are getting. And you have to face the reality of the banking business. We are in a conservative business. When we speak to customers, we need to gain their confidence, and we put the best people for the job in the positions to achieve that end. If we don't get their confidence, they can go down the street to our competitors and do business with them. Their services are no different than ours. It's a competitive business in which you need every edge you have. It's going to take time for people to change some of their attitudes about whom they borrow money from or where they put their money. I can't change the way people feel. I am running a business, but believe me, I won't make any decisions that are detrimental to the bank."

SOURCE: *Copyright © Dr. Martin R. Moser, Associate Professor of Management, University of Massachusetts Lowell, Lowell, MA 01854. martin_moser@uml.edu.*

Can Larry Fit In?

Melissa, Office Manager

You are the manager of an auditing team sent to Bangkok, Thailand, to represent a major international accounting firm headquartered in New York. You and Larry, one of your auditors, were sent to Bangkok to set up an auditing operation. Larry is about seven years older than you and has five more years seniority in the firm. Your relationship has become very strained since you were recently designated as the office manager. You feel you were given the promotion because you have established an excellent working relationship with the Thai staff as well as a broad range of international clients. In contrast, Larry has told other members of the staff that your promotion simply reflects the firm's heavy emphasis on affirmative action. He has tried to isolate you from the all-male accounting staff by focusing discussions on sports, local night spots, and so forth.

You are sitting in your office reading some complicated new reporting procedures that have just arrived from the home office. Your concentration is suddenly interrupted by a loud knock on your door. Without waiting for an invitation to enter, Larry bursts into your office. He is obviously very upset, and it is not difficult for you to surmise why he is in such a nasty mood.

You recently posted the audit assignments for the coming month, and you scheduled Larry for a job you knew he wouldn't like. Larry is one of your senior auditors, and the company norm is that they get the choice assignments. This particular job will require him to spend two weeks away from Bangkok in a remote town, working with a company whose records are notoriously messy.

Unfortunately, you have had to assign several of these less desirable audits to Larry recently because you are short of personnel. But that's not the only reason. You have received several complaints from the junior staff (all Thais) recently that Larry treats them in a condescending manner. They feel he is always looking for an opportunity to boss them around, as if he were their supervisor instead of an experienced, supportive mentor. As a result, your whole operation works more smoothly when you can send Larry out of town on a solo project for several days. It keeps him from coming into your office and telling you how to do your job, and the morale of the rest of the auditing staff is significantly higher.

Larry slams the door and proceeds to express his anger over this assignment.

Larry, Senior Auditor

You are really ticked off! Melissa is deliberately trying to undermine your status in the office. She knows that the company norm is that senior auditors get the better jobs. You've paid your dues, and now you expect to be treated with respect. And this isn't the first time this has happened. Since she was made the office manager, she has tried to keep you out of the office as much as possible. It's as if she doesn't want her rival for leadership of the office around. When you were asked to go to Bangkok, you assumed that you would be made the office manager because of your seniority in the firm. You are certain that the decision to pick Melissa is yet another indication of reverse discrimination against white males.

In staff meetings, Melissa has talked about the need to be sensitive to the feelings of the office staff as well as the clients in this multicultural setting. "Where does she come off preaching about sensitivity! What about my feelings, for heaven's sake?" you wonder. This is nothing more than a straightforward power play. She is probably feeling insecure about being the only female accountant in the office and being promoted over someone with more experience. "Sending me out of town," you decide, "is a clear case of 'out of sight, out of mind.'"

Well, it's not going to happen that easily. You are not going to roll over and let her treat you unfairly. It's time for a showdown. If she doesn't agree to change this assignment and apologize for the way she's been treating you, you're going to register a formal complaint with her boss in the New York office. You are prepared to submit your resignation if the situation doesn't improve.

Meeting at Hartford Manufacturing Company

Hartford Manufacturing Company is the largest subsidiary of Connecticut Industries. Since the end of World War I, when it was formed, Hartford Manufacturing has become an industrial leader in the Northeast. Its sales currently average approximately $25 million a year, with an annual growth of approximately six percent. There are more than 850 employees in production, sales and marketing, accounting, engineering, and management.

Lynn Smith is general manager. He has held his position for a little over two years and is well respected by his subordinates. He has the reputation of being firm but fair. Lynn's training in college was in engineering, so he is technically minded, and he frequently likes to walk around the production area to see for himself how things are going. He has also been known to roll up his sleeves and help work on a problem on the shop floor. He is not opposed to rubbing shoulders with even the lowest-level employees. On the other hand, he tries to run a tight company, and employees pretty well stick to their assigned tasks. He holds high expectations for performance, especially from individuals in management positions.

Richard Hooton is the director of production at Hartford Manufacturing. He has been with the company since he was 19 years old, when he worked on the dock. He has worked himself up through the ranks and now, at age 54, is the oldest of the management personnel. Hooton has his own ideas of how things should be run in production, and he is reluctant to tolerate any intervention from anyone, even Lynn Smith. Because he has been with the company so long, he feels he knows it better than anyone else, and he believes he has had a hand in making it the success that it is. His main goal is to keep production running smoothly and efficiently.

Barbara Price is the director of sales and marketing. She joined the company about 18 months ago, after completing her MBA at Dartmouth. Before going back to school for a graduate degree, she held the position of assistant manager of marketing at Connecticut Industries. Price is a very conscientious employee and is anxious to make a name for herself. Her major objective, which she has never hesitated to make public, is to be a general manager some day. Sales at Hartford Manufacturing have increased in the past year to near-record levels under her guidance.

Chuck Kasper is the regional sales director for the New York region. He reports directly to Barbara Price. The New York region represents the largest market for Hartford Manufacturing, and Chuck is considered the most competent salesperson in the company. He has built personal relationships with several major clients in his region, and it appears that some sales occur as much because of Chuck Kasper as because of the products of Hartford Manufacturing. Chuck has been with the company for 12 years, all of them in sales.

This is Friday afternoon, and tomorrow Lynn Smith leaves for Copenhagen at noon to attend an important meeting with potential overseas investors. He will be gone for two weeks. Before he leaves, there are several items in his in-basket that must receive attention. He calls a meeting with Richard Hooton and Barbara Price in his office. Just before the meeting begins, Chuck Kasper calls and asks if he may join the meeting for a few minutes, since he is in town and has something important to discuss that involves both Lynn Smith and Richard Hooton. Smith gives permission for him to join the meeting, since there may not be another chance to meet with Kasper before the trip. The meeting convenes, therefore, with Smith, Hooton, Price, and Kasper all in the room.

Assignment

Groups of four individuals should be formed. Each person should take the role of one of the characters in the management staff of Hartford Manufacturing Company. A fifth person should be assigned to serve as an observer to provide feedback at the end of the meeting, using the Observer's Feedback Form at the end of the chapter as a guide. The letters described in the case that were received by Lynn Smith are shown in Figures 7.7, 7.8, and 7.9. Only the person playing the role of Lynn Smith should read the letters, and no one should read the instructions for another staff member's role. (The letters will be introduced by Lynn Smith during the meeting.)

Figure 7.7

T. J. Koppel, Inc.
General Accountants
8381 Spring Street
Hartford, Connecticut 06127

February 10, 2001

Mr. Lynn Smith
General Manager
Hartford Manufacturing Company
7450 Central Avenue
Hartford, CT 06118

Dear Mr. Smith:

As you requested last month, we have now completed our financial audit of Hartford Manufacturing Company. We find accounting procedures and fiscal control to be very satisfactory. A more detailed report of these matters is attached. However, we did discover during our perusal of company records that the production department has consistently incurred cost overruns during the past two quarters. Cost per unit of production is approximately 5 percent over budget. While this is not a serious problem given the financial solvency of your company, we thought it wise to bring it to your attention.

Respectfully,

T. J. Koppel

TJK: srw

Lynn Smith, General Manager

Three letters arrived today, and you judge them to be sufficiently important to require your attention before you leave on your trip. Each letter represents a problem that requires immediate action, and you need commitments from key staff members to resolve these problems. You are concerned about this meeting because these individuals don't work as well together as you'd like.

For example, Richard Hooton is very difficult to pin down. He always seems suspicious of the motives of others and has a reputation for not making tough decisions. You sometimes wonder how a person could become the head of production in a major manufacturing firm by avoiding controversial issues and blaming others for the results.

Figure 7.8

ZODIAK INDUSTRIES
6377 Atlantic Avenue
Boston, Massachusetts 02112

February 8, 2001

Mr. Lynn Smith
General Manager
Hartford Manufacturing Company
7450 Central Avenue
Hartford, CT 06118

Dear Mr. Smith:

We have been purchasing your products since 1975, and we have been very satisfied with our relations with your sales personnel. However, we have had a problem of late that requires your attention. Your sales representative for the Boston region, Sam St. Clair, has appeared at our company the last three times looking and smelling like he was under the influence of alcohol. Not only that, but our last order was mistakenly recorded, so we received the wrong quantities of products. I'm sure you don't make it a practice to put your company's reputation in the hands of someone like Sam St. Clair, so I suggest you get someone else to cover this region. We cannot tolerate, and I'm sure other companies in Boston cannot tolerate, this kind of relationship. While we judge your products to be excellent, we will be forced to find other sources if some action is not taken.

Sincerely yours,

Miles Andrew
Chief of Purchasing

:ms

PRACTICE

In contrast, Barbara Price is very straightforward. You always know exactly where she stands. The problem is that sometimes she doesn't take enough time to study a problem before making a decision. She tends to be impulsive and anxious to make a decision, whether it's the right one or not. Her general approach to resolving disagreements between departments is to seek expedient compromises. You are particularly disturbed by her approach to the sales incentive problem. You felt strongly that something needed to be done to increase sales during the winter months. You reluctantly agreed to the incentive program because you didn't want to dampen her initiative. But you aren't convinced this is the right answer, because, frankly, you're not yet sure what the real problem is.

Chuck Kasper is your typical, aggressive, "take no prisoners" sales manager. He is hard-charging and uncompromising. He is great in the field because he gets the job done, but he

Figure 7.9

HARTFORD MANUFACTURING COMPANY
7450 Central Avenue
Hartford, Connecticut 06118

"A subsidiary of CONNECTICUT INDUSTRIES"

Memorandum

TO: Lynn Smith, General Manager
FROM: Barbara Price, General Supervisor, Sales and Marketing
DATE: February 11, 2007

Mr. Smith:

In response to your concerns, we have instituted several incentive programs among our sales force to increase sales during these traditionally slow months. We have set up competition among regions, with the salespeople in the top region being honored in the company newsletter and given engraved plaques. We have instituted a "vacation in Hawaii" award for the top salesperson in the company. And we have instituted cash bonuses for any salesperson who gets a new customer order. However, in the last month these incentives have been in operation, sales have not increased at all. In fact, in two regions they have decreased by an average of 5 percent.

What do you suggest now? We have advertised the incentives as lasting through this quarter, but they seem to be doing no good. Not only that, but we cannot afford to provide the incentives within our current budget, and unless sales increase, we will be in the red.

Regretfully, I recommend dropping the program.

sometimes ruffles the feathers of the corporate staff with his uncompromising, "black-and-white" style. He is also fiercely loyal to his sales staff, so you're sure he'll take the complaint about Sam St. Clair hard.

In contrast to the styles of these others, you have tried to use an integrating approach to problem solving: focusing on the facts, treating everyone's inputs equally, and keeping conversations about controversial topics problem-focused. One of your goals since taking over this position two years ago is to foster a "team" approach within your staff.

[*Note*: For more information about how you might approach the issues raised by these letters in your staff meeting, review the collaborating approach in Table 7.2 as well as the mediator's behavioral guidelines at the end of the Skill Learning section of this chapter.]

Richard Hooton, Director of Production

The only times you have had major problems in production were when the young know-it-alls fresh from college have come in and tried to change things. With their scientific management concepts coupled with fuzzy-headed human relations training, they have more often made a mess of things than helped to improve matters. The best production methods have been practiced for years in the company, and you have yet to see anyone who could improve on your system.

On the other hand, you have respect for Lynn Smith as the general manager. Because he has experience and the right kind of training, and is involved in the production part of the organization, he often has given you good advice and has shown special interest. He mostly lets you do what you feel is best, however, and he seldom dictates specific methods for doing things.

Your general approach to problems is to avoid controversy. You feel uncomfortable when production is made the scapegoat for problems in the company. Because this is a manufacturing business, it seems as if everyone tries to pin the blame for problems on the production department. You've felt for years that the firm was getting away from what it does best: mass producing a few standard products. Instead, the trend has been for marketing and sales to push for more and more products, shorter lead times, and greater customization capability. These actions have increased costs and caused significant production delays as well as higher rejection rates.

[*Note*: During the upcoming meeting, you should adopt the avoidance approach shown in Table 7.2. Defend your turf, place blame on others, defer taking a stand, and avoid taking responsibility for making a controversial decision.]

Barbara Price, Director of Sales and Marketing

You are anxious to impress Lynn Smith because you have your eye on a position that is opening up at the end of the year in the parent company, Connecticut Industries. It would mean a promotion for you. A positive recommendation from Lynn Smith would carry a lot of weight in the selection process. Given that both Hartford Manufacturing and Connecticut Industries are largely male dominated, you are pleased with your career advancement so far, and you are hoping to keep it up.

One current concern is Lynn Smith's suggestion some time ago that you look into the problem of slow sales during the winter months. You implemented an incentive plan that was highly recommended by an industry analyst at a recent trade conference. It consists of three separate incentive programs: (1) competition among regions in which the salesperson in the top region would have his or her picture in the company newsletter and receive an engraved plaque, (2) a vacation in Hawaii for the top salesperson in the company, and (3) cash bonuses for salespeople who obtained new customer orders. Unfortunately, these incentives haven't worked. Not only have sales not increased for the company as a whole, but sales for two regions are down an average of five percent. You have told the sales force that the incentives will last through this quarter, but if sales don't improve, your budget will be in the red. You haven't budgeted for the prizes, since you expected the increased sales to more than offset the cost of the incentives.

Obviously, this was a bad idea—it isn't working—and it should be dropped immediately. You are a bit embarrassed about this aborted project. But it is better to cut your losses and try something else rather than continue to support an obvious loser.

In general, you are very confident and self-assured. You feel that the best way to get work done is through negotiation and compromise. What's important is making a decision quickly and efficiently. Maybe everyone doesn't get exactly what he or she wants, but at least they can get on with their work. There are no black and whites in this business—only "grays" that can be traded off to keep the management process from bogging down with "paralysis by analysis." You are impatient over delays caused by intensive studies and investigations of detail. You agree with Tom Peters: action is the hallmark of successful managers.

[*Note*: During this meeting, use the compromise approach shown in Table 7.2. Do whatever is necessary to help the group make a quick decision so you can get on with the pressing demands of your work.]

Chuck Kasper, **Regional Sales Director**

You don't get back to company headquarters often because your customer contacts take up most of your time. You regularly work 50 to 60 hours a week, and you are proud of the job you do. You also feel a special obligation to your customers to provide them with the best product available in the timeliest fashion. This sense of obligation comes not only from your commitment to the company but also from your personal relationships with many of the customers.

Lately, you have been receiving more and more complaints about late deliveries of Hartford Manufacturing's products to your customers. The time between their ordering and delivery is increasing, and some customers have been greatly inconvenienced by the delays. You have made a formal inquiry of production to find out what the problem is. They replied that they are producing as efficiently as possible, and they see nothing wrong with past practices. Richard Hooton's assistant even suggested that this was just another example of the sales force's unrealistic expectations.

Not only will sales be negatively affected if these delays continue, but your reputation with your customers will be damaged. You have promised them that the problem will be quickly solved and that products will begin arriving on time. Since Richard Hooton is so rigid, however, you are almost certain that it will do no good to talk with him. His subordinate probably got his negative attitude from Hooton.

In general, Hooton is a 1960s production worker who is being pulled by the rest of the firm into the new age. Competition is different, technology is different, and management is different, but Richard is reluctant to change. You need shorter lead times, a wider range of products, and the capacity to do some customized work. Sure, this makes production's work harder, but other firms are providing these services with the use of just-in-time management processes, robots, and so forth.

Instead of getting down to the real problems, the home office, in their typical high-handed fashion, announced an incentives plan. This implies that the problem is in the field, not the factory. It made some of your people angry to think they were being pressed to increase their efforts when they weren't receiving the backup support in Hartford to get the job done. Sure, they liked the prizes, but the way the plan was presented made them feel as if they weren't working hard enough. This isn't the first time you have questioned the judgment of Barbara, your boss. She certainly is intelligent and hard-working, but she doesn't seem very interested in what's going on out in the field. Furthermore, she doesn't seem very receptive to "bad news" about sales and customer complaints.

[*Note*: During this meeting, use the forcing approach to conflict management and negotiations shown in Table 7.2. However, don't overplay your part, because you are the senior regional sales manager, and if Barbara continues to move up fast in the organization, you may be in line for her position.]

SKILL *APPLICATION*

ACTIVITIES FOR IMPROVING MANAGING CONFLICT SKILLS

Suggested Assignments

1. Select a specific conflict with which you are very familiar. Using the framework for identifying the sources of conflict discussed in this chapter, analyze this situation carefully. It might be useful to compare your perceptions of the situation with those of informed observers. What type of conflict is this? Why did it occur? Why is it continuing? Next, using the guidelines for selecting an appropriate conflict management strategy, identify the general approach that would be most appropriate for this situation. Consider both the personal preferences of the parties involved and the relevant situational factors. Is this the approach that the parties have been using? If not, attempt to introduce a different perspective into the relationship and explain why you feel it would be more productive. If the parties have been using this approach, discuss with them why it has not been successful thus far. Share information on specific behavioral guidelines or negotiation tactics that might increase the effectiveness of their efforts.

2. Select three individuals whom you know who are from diverse cultural backgrounds and have experience working in American companies. Discuss with them the sources (especially the personal differences) of previous conflicts they have experienced at work. Ask them about their preferences in dealing with conflict situations. What strategies do they prefer to use? How do they generally attempt to resolve disputes? What relevant situational factors influence the way they manage conflict situations with individuals from other cultures and with individuals of their own cultures? With the help of these three persons, identify specific behavioral guidelines for managing conflict more effectively with other persons from their respective cultures.

3. Identify a situation in which another individual is doing something that needs to be corrected. Using the respondent's guidelines for collaborative problem solving, construct a plan for discussing your concerns with this person. Include specific language designed to state your case assertively without causing a defensive reaction. Role-play this interaction with a friend and incorporate any suggestions for improvement. Make your presentation to the individual and report on your results. What was the reaction? Were you successful in balancing assertiveness with support and responsibility? Based on this experience, identify other situations you feel need to be changed and follow a similar procedure.

4. Volunteer to serve as a mediator to resolve a conflict between two individuals or groups. Using the guidelines for implementing the collaborative approach to mediation, outline a plan of action prior to your intervention. Be sure to consider carefully whether or not private meetings with the parties prior to your mediation session are appropriate. Report on the situation and your plan. How did you feel? Which specific actions worked well? What was the outcome? What would you do differently? Based on this experience, revise your plan for use in related situations.

5. Identify a difficult situation involving negotiations. This might involve transactions at work, at home, or in the community. Review the guidelines for integrative bargaining and identify the specific tactics you plan to use. Write down specific questions and responses to likely initiatives from the other party. In particular, anticipate how you might handle the possibility of the other party's using a distributive negotiation strategy. Schedule a negotiation meeting with the party involved and implement your plan. Following the session, debrief the experience with a coworker or friend. What did you learn? How successful were you? What would you do differently? Based on this experience, modify your plan and prepare to implement it in related situations.

Application Plan and Evaluation

The intent of this exercise is to help you apply this cluster of skills in a real-life, out-of-class setting. Now that you have become familiar with the behavioral guidelines that form the basis of effective skill performance, you will improve most by trying out those guidelines in an everyday context. Unlike a classroom activity, in which feedback is immediate and others can assist you with their evaluations, this skill application activity is one you must accomplish and evaluate on your own. There are two parts to this activity. Part 1 helps prepare you to apply the skill. Part 2 helps you evaluate and improve on your experience. Be sure to write down answers to each item. Don't short-circuit the process by skipping steps.

Part 1. Planning

1. Write down the two or three aspects of this skill that are most important to you. These may be areas of weakness, areas you most want to improve, or areas that are most salient to a problem you face right now. Identify the specific aspects of this skill that you want to apply.

2. Now identify the setting or the situation in which you will apply this skill. Establish a plan for performance by actually writing down a description of the situation. Who else will be involved? When will you do it? Where will it be done?

   Circumstances:
   Who else?
   When?
   Where?

3. Identify the specific behaviors you will engage in to apply this skill. Operationalize your skill performance.

4. What are the indicators of successful performance? How will you know you have been effective? What will indicate you have performed competently?

Part 2. Evaluation

5. After you have completed your implementation, record the results. What happened? How successful were you? What was the effect on others?

6. How can you improve? What modifications can you make next time? What will you do differently in a similar situation in the future?

7. Looking back on your whole skill practice and application experience, what have you learned? What has been surprising? In what ways might this experience help you in the long term?

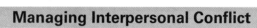

Managing Interpersonal Conflict

Scoring Key

SKILL AREA	ITEM	ASSESSMENT	
		PRE-	POST-
Initiating a complaint	1	_____	_____
	2	_____	_____
	3	_____	_____
	4	_____	_____
	5	_____	_____
	6	_____	_____
	7	_____	_____
	8	_____	_____
Responding to a criticism	9	_____	_____
	10	_____	_____
	11	_____	_____
	12	_____	_____
	13	_____	_____
	14	_____	_____
	15	_____	_____
	16	_____	_____
Mediating a conflict	17	_____	_____
	18	_____	_____
	19	_____	_____
	20	_____	_____
	21	_____	_____
	22	_____	_____
	23	_____	_____
	24	_____	_____
	Total Score	_____	_____

Comparison Data (N = 5,000 Students)

Compare your scores to three comparison standards:
1. The maximum possible score = 144.
2. The scores of other students in your class.
3. Norm group data from more than 5,000 practicing managers and business school students.

Pre-Test				Post-Test
113.20	=	mean	=	122.59
122 or above	=	top quartile	=	133 or above
114–121	=	second quartile	=	123–132
105–113	=	third quartile	=	115–122
104 and below	=	bottom quartile	=	114 or below

Strategies for Handling Conflict

Scoring Key

FORCING		ACCOMMODATING		COMPROMISING	
ITEM	SCORE	ITEM	SCORE	ITEM	SCORE
1	_____	2	_____	3	_____
6	_____	7	_____	8	_____
11	_____	12	_____	13	_____
16	_____	17	_____	18	_____
Total	_____	Total	_____	Total	_____

AVOIDING		INTEGRATING	
ITEM	SCORE	ITEM	SCORE
4	_____	5	_____
9	_____	10	_____
14	_____	15	_____
19	_____	20	_____
Total	_____	Total	_____

Primary conflict management strategy (highest score): _____
Secondary conflict management strategy (next-highest score): _____

SKILL PRACTICE
Exercises for Resolving Interpersonal Disputes

Observer's Feedback Form

RATING

1 = Low
5 = High

Initiator

_____ Maintained personal ownership of the problem, including feelings

_____ Avoided making accusations or attributing motives; stuck to the facts

_____ Succinctly described the problem (behaviors, outcomes, feelings)

_____ Specified expectations or standards violated

_____ Persisted until understood

_____ Encouraged two-way interaction

_____ Approached multiple issues incrementally (proceeded from simple to complex, easy to hard)

_____ Appealed to what the disputants had in common (goals, principles, constraints)

_____ Made a specific request for change

Respondent

_____ Established a climate for joint problem solving

_____ Showed genuine concern and interest

_____ Responded appropriately to the initiator's emotions

_____ Avoided becoming defensive or overreacting

_____ Sought additional information about the problem (shifted general to specific, evaluative to descriptive)

_____ Focused on one issue at a time, gradually broadened the scope of the discussion, searched for integrative solution

_____ Agreed with some aspect of the complaint (facts, perceptions, feelings, or principles)

_____ Asked for suggestions for making changes

_____ Proposed a specific plan of action

Mediator

_____ Acknowledged that a conflict exists; treated the conflict and disputants seriously

_____ Broke down complex issues, separated the critical from the peripheral; began with a relatively easy problem

_____ Helped disputants avoid entrenched positions by exploring underlying interests

_____ Remained neutral (facilitator, not judge) and impartial toward issues and disputants

_____ Kept the interaction issue oriented (e.g., pointed out the effect of the conflict on performance)

_____ Made sure that neither party dominated conversation, asked questions to maintain balance

_____ Kept conflict in perspective by emphasizing areas of agreement

_____ Helped generate multiple alternatives, drawn from common goals, values, or principles

_____ Made sure that both parties were satisfied and committed to the proposed resolution

Comments:

Part III

Group Skills

8

Empowering and Delegating

SKILL DEVELOPMENT OBJECTIVES

- EMPOWER OTHERS
- EMPOWER YOURSELF
- DELEGATE EFFECTIVELY

DIAGNOSTIC SURVEYS FOR EMPOWERING AND DELEGATING

EFFECTIVE EMPOWERMENT AND DELEGATION

Step 1: Before you read the material in this chapter, please respond to the following statements by writing a number from the rating scale below in the left-hand column (Pre-Assessment). Your answers should reflect your attitudes and behaviors as they are now, not as you would like them to be. Be honest. This instrument is designed to help you discover your level of competency in empowering and delegating so you can tailor your learning to your specific needs. When you have completed the survey, use the scoring key at the end of the chapter to identify the skill areas discussed in this chapter that are most important for you to master.

Step 2: After you have completed the reading and the exercises in this chapter and, ideally, as many as you can of the Skill Application assignments at the end of this chapter, cover up your first set of answers. Then respond to the same statements again, this time in the right-hand column (Post-Assessment). When you have completed the survey, use the scoring key at the end of the chapter to measure your progress. If your score remains low in specific skill areas, use the behavioral guidelines at the end of the Skill Learning section to guide further practice.

Rating Scale

1 Strongly disagree
2 Disagree
3 Slightly disagree
4 Slightly agree
5 Agree
6 Strongly agree

Assessment

Pre-   Post-

In situations in which I have an opportunity to engage others in accomplishing work:

_____   _____   1. I help people develop personal mastery in their work by involving them first in less complex tasks, and then in more difficult tasks.

_____   _____   2. I help people feel competent in their work by recognizing and celebrating their small successes.

_____   _____   3. I serve as an example of successful task accomplishment.

_____   _____   4. I identify other successful people who can serve as role models.

_____   _____   5. I frequently praise, encourage, and express approval of other people.

_____   _____   6. I provide regular feedback and needed support to other people.

_____   _____   7. I try to foster friendships and informal interaction.

_____   _____   8. I highlight the important impact that a person's work will have on others and on goals.

_____   _____   9. I try to provide all the information that people need to accomplish their tasks.

_____ _____ 10. As I become aware of it, I pass along relevant information to people on a continuous basis.

_____ _____ 11. I ensure that people have the necessary resources (equipment, space, and time) to succeed.

_____ _____ 12. I help people get access to needed resources that I may not have available personally.

_____ _____ 13. I help people become involved in teams in order to increase their participation.

_____ _____ 14. I encourage teams to make decisions and implement their own recommendations.

_____ _____ 15. I foster confidence by being fair and equitable in my decisions.

_____ _____ 16. I exhibit caring and personal concern for each person with whom I have dealings.

When delegating work to others:

_____ _____ 17. I specify clearly the results I desire.

_____ _____ 18. I specify clearly the level of initiative I want others to take (e.g., wait for directions, do part of the task and then report, do the whole task and then report, etc.).

_____ _____ 19. I allow participation by those accepting assignments regarding when and how work will be done.

_____ _____ 20. I make certain that the amount of authority I give matches the amount of responsibility I expect for producing results.

_____ _____ 21. I work within existing organizational structures when delegating assignments, and I never bypass someone without informing him or her.

_____ _____ 22. I identify constraints and limitations that people will face but also provide needed support.

_____ _____ 23. I maintain accountability for results, not for methods used.

_____ _____ 24. I delegate consistently—not just when I'm overloaded.

_____ _____ 25. I avoid upward delegation by asking people to recommend solutions, rather than merely asking for advice or answers, when a problem is encountered.

_____ _____ 26. I make clear the consequences of success and failure.

PERSONAL EMPOWERMENT ASSESSMENT

This instrument helps identify the extent to which you are empowered in your own work. You should respond to the items based on your own job, or, if you are in school, the work you do as a student. The items listed below describe different orientations people can have with respect to their work roles. Using the following scale, indicate the extent to which you believe each is true of you:

Rating Scale

1 Very strongly disagree
2 Strongly disagree
3 Disagree
4 Neutral
5 Agree
6 Strongly agree
7 Very strongly agree

Assessment

_____ 1. The work that I do is very important to me.

_____ 2. I am confident about my ability to do my work.

_____ 3. I have significant autonomy in determining how I do my job.

_____ 4. I have significant impact on what happens in my work unit.

_____ 5. I trust my coworkers to be completely honest with me.

_____ 6. My work activities are personally meaningful to me.

_____ 7. My work is within the scope of my competence and capabilities.

_____ 8. I can decide how to go about doing my own work.

_____ 9. I have a great deal of control over what happens in my work unit.

_____ 10. I trust my coworkers to share important information with me.

_____ 11. I care about what I do in my work.

_____ 12. I am confident in my capabilities to successfully perform my work.

_____ 13. I have considerable opportunity for independence and freedom in how I do my work.

_____ 14. I have significant influence over what happens in my work unit.

_____ 15. I trust my coworkers to keep the promises they make.

_____ 16. The work I do has special meaning and importance to me.

_____ 17. I have mastered the skills necessary to do my work.

_____ 18. I have a chance to use personal initiative in carrying out my work.

_____ 19. My opinion counts in my work unit's decision making.

_____ 20. I believe that my coworkers care about my well-being.

Empowering and Delegating

Many management books are oriented toward helping managers know how to control others' behavior. They focus on how managers can increase employees' performance, engender conformity, or motivate employees to achieve certain objectives. This book, too, includes skills that will help you motivate people to do what you want them to do (see the chapter on Motivating Others) or achieve power and influence over them (see the Gaining Power and Influence chapter). The present chapter, however, focuses on a skill called **empowerment** and on a special form of empowerment called **delegation**.

Empowerment is based on a set of assumptions that are in contrast to those normally made by managers. Empowerment means providing freedom for people to do successfully what they want to do, rather than getting them to do what you want them to do. Managers who empower people remove controls, constraints, and boundaries for them instead of motivating, directing, or stimulating their behavior. Rather than being a "push" strategy, in which managers induce employees to respond in desirable ways through incentives and influence techniques, empowerment is a "pull" strategy. It focuses on ways that managers can design a work situation so that it energizes and provides intrinsic encouragement to employees. In the context of such a strategy, workers accomplish tasks because they are intrinsically attracted by them, not because of an extrinsic reward system or influence technique.

Empowering others, however, can lead to dilemmas. On the one hand, evidence shows that empowered employees are more productive, more satisfied, and more innovative, and that they create higher-quality products and services than unempowered employees (Greenberger & Stasser, 1991; Kanter, 1983; Sashkin, 1982, 1984; Spreitzer, 1992). Organizations are more effective when an empowered workforce exists (Conger & Kanungo, 1988; Gecas, 1989; Thomas & Velthouse, 1990). On the other hand, empowerment means giving up control and letting others make decisions, set goals, accomplish results, and receive rewards. It means that other people probably will get credit for success. Managers with high needs for power and control (see McClelland, 1975) face a challenge when they are expected to sacrifice their needs for someone else's gain. They may ask themselves: "Why should others get the goodies when I am in charge? Why should I allow others to exercise power, and even facilitate their acquiring more power, when I naturally want to receive rewards and recognition myself?"

The answer is that although empowering others is neither easy nor natural (we aren't born knowing how to do it), it need not require a great amount of self-sacrifice. You don't need to sacrifice desired rewards, recognition, or effectiveness in order to be a skillful empowering manager. On the contrary, through real empowerment, managers actually multiply their own effectiveness. They and their organizations become more effective than they could have been otherwise. Nevertheless, for most managers, empowerment is a skill that must be developed and practiced, because despite the high visibility of the concept of empowerment in popular literature, its actual practice is all too rare in modern management.

Evidence for this assertion comes from a national survey by the Louis Harris organization, reported in *Business Week* for January 18, 1993. According to this survey, feelings of powerlessness and alienation among workers rose sharply through the 1990s and, according to more recent Harris polls, have not reversed themselves in the twenty-first century (Harris Poll, 2002). The percentage of workers answering "yes" to the questions in Table 8.1 illustrates this trend.

In this chapter, we begin by discussing the core dimensions of empowerment and, in particular, how to effectively accomplish empowerment. In the second part of this section, we discuss a special situation in which empowerment is essential: the delegation of responsibility. We conclude with a summary model of empowerment and delegation and a list of behavioral guidelines for successfully empowering and delegating to others.

A Management Dilemma Involving Empowerment

One of the most well-researched findings in organization and management science over the last four decades has shown that when environments are predictable and stable, organizations can function as routine, controlled, mechanistic units. Under such conditions, workers can be expected to follow rules and procedures and to engage in standardized, formalized behavior. Managers can maintain control and issue top-down mandates regarding the strategy and direction to be pursued by the organization.

Table 8.1	Powerlessness and Alienation Survey			
QUESTION		**1972**	**1985**	**1992**
What I think doesn't count very much anymore.		50%	62%	62%
Most people with power take advantage of people like myself.		43%	65%	71%
The people in charge don't really care what happens to me.		46%	65%	71%
I'm left out of things going on around me.		25%	48%	48%

However, the modern business environment is often described using terms such as *hyperturbulence, complexity, speed, competition*, and *revolutionary change*. Under such conditions, prescriptions for organizational and management effectiveness call for a flexible, autonomous, entrepreneurial workforce (DeGraff & Lawrence, 2002; Drucker, 1988; Quinn, 2005), rather than one that relies on management for direction and control. Less-centralized decision making, less top-down direction, and less-autocratic leadership are all prescribed as prerequisites for high-performing modern organizations.

When environments are unstable and unpredictable —when they change a lot or in unpredictable ways— organizations must be more flexible and organic. Workers are expected to be adaptable and self-managing. Managers must involve others in decision making and facilitate broad participation and accountability (Eisenhart & Galunic, 1993; Lawrence & Lorsch, 1967). The workers flexibility must match the flexibility of the environment (Ashby, 1956).

Our own research has shown, however, that instead of becoming adaptable, flexible, autonomous, and self-managing, individuals in rapidly changing, complex environments tend to behave in opposite ways than they should in order to succeed. Both managers and employees tend to become less flexible, less adaptable, less autonomous, less self-managing, and more stable, more rigid, and more defensive when they face turbulence and change (Cameron, Whetten, & Kim, 1987; Cameron, Kim, & Whetten, 1987; Cameron, 1998).

In our research on how organizations are managed when they face decline, turbulence, downsizing, and change, we have identified 12 negative attributes or attitudes, which we label the **dirty dozen.** Table 8.2 summarizes these negative attitudes.

THE DIRTY DOZEN

Among the dirty dozen attributes is a "threat-rigidity" response (Staw, Sandelands, & Dutton, 1981; Weick, 1993), in which people become conservative when faced with uncertainty. They hunker down and become self-protective and increasingly rely on old, first-learned habits and past behaviors. In reaction to a perceived threat, they do that which they know how to do best or that which has worked best in the past. Despite new circumstances in which old behaviors may not be effective, there is an escalating commitment to habitual behavior. People consider fewer options, look for information that confirms their previous biases, and become more narrow-minded in their perspectives.

In addition, less communication occurs among workers. When individuals in organizations are divulging information, they become vulnerable by putting their personal expertise or untested ideas at risk. This sense of vulnerability magnifies the feeling of uncertainty brought about by changing conditions. Under such circumstances, people are less likely to become contributing team members and to try out new, innovative ideas. Fear and conflict increase, while trust, morale, and productivity decrease. A "mean mood" is typical of most interactions, as loyalty and commitment to the organization erode. The tendency in such circumstances is for most important decisions to be made at the top of the organizational hierarchy because managers at the top feel an increasing need to be in control and to be closer to decisions. On the other hand, people at lower organizational levels become hesitant to make decisions without getting approval from a superior.

How can we ever expect a workforce in the modern, changing environment to develop the prescribed characteristics for effectiveness—that is, to be adaptable, flexible, autonomous, and self-managing? If people become more rigid and resistant in uncertain times rather than more independent and flexible, how can we ever foster effective performance?

The answer to these questions is to use empowerment. If managers are skilled at empowering workers, the inertia that drives organizations toward dysfunctional dirty dozen attitudes is counteracted. Workers

Table 8.2	The Dirty Dozen: Outcomes of Stress in Organizations
ATTRIBUTE	**EXPLANATION**
Centralization	Decision making is pulled toward the top of the organization. Less power is shared.
Threat-rigidity response	Conservative, self-protective behaviors predominate. Old habits are relied upon. Change is resisted.
Loss of innovativeness	Trial and error learning stops. Low tolerance for risk and creativity occurs.
Decreasing morale	In-fighting and a mean mood permeate the organization. It isn't fun.
Politicized environment	Special interest groups organize and become vocal. Everything is negotiated.
Loss of trust	Leaders lose the confidence of subordinates. Distrust predominates among employees.
Increased conflict	Infighting and competition occur. Self-centeredness predominates over the good of the organization.
Restricted communication	Only good news is passed upward. Information is not widely shared and is held close to the vest.
Lack of teamwork	Individualism and disconnectedness inhibit teamwork. Lack of coordination occurs.
Loss of loyalty	Commitment to the organization and to the leader erodes. Focus is on defending oneself.
Scapegoating leaders	Leadership anemia occurs as leaders are criticized, priorities become less clear, and a siege mentality occurs.
Short-term perspective	A crisis mentality is adopted. Long-term planning and flexibility are avoided.

SOURCE: Adapted from: *Cameron et al., 1987.*

LEARNING

become more effective, even in the face of trying times. Empowerment is a key to unlocking the potential of a successful workforce in an era of chaotic change and escalating competitive conditions.

But what is empowerment? What does it mean to be an empowered worker? What is the set of management skills associated with empowerment?

The Meaning of Empowerment

To empower means to enable; it means to help people develop a sense of self-confidence; it means to help people overcome feelings of powerlessness or helplessness; it means to energize people to take action; it means to mobilize intrinsic motivation to accomplish a task. Empowered people not only possess the wherewithal to accomplish something, but they also think of themselves differently than they did before they were empowered.

Empowerment is different from merely giving power to someone. Like empowerment, power connotes the ability to get things done. But power and empowerment are not the same things. Table 8.3 contrasts the concepts of power and empowerment so as to highlight their differences. People may have power and

also be empowered. However, although one can give someone else power, one must accept empowerment for oneself. You cannot empower me; you can only create the circumstances in which I can empower myself.

As explained in the chapter on Gaining Power and Influence, the acquisition of power is based on several personal factors and certain position attributes. In each case, other people need to acknowledge your power, follow your lead, and acquiesce to your influence in order for you to have power. The underlying source of your power is other people. For example, you may have power because you have more resources or political support than someone else. Thus, you can reward others and have *reward power*. Alternatively, you may have the ability to penalize or sanction others as a result of your strength or support so you have *sanctioning power*. Your title or position may give you power over others, thus giving you *traditional power*. You may possess more knowledge or information than others, giving you *expertise power*. Or, you may be personally attractive or charismatic, thus having *referent power*. French and Raven (1960) identified these five factors as being the primary bases of power. Regardless of whether these are the five factors or whether there are others, each can be conveyed to

Table 8.3	The Difference Between Power and Empowerment	
POWER	**EMPOWERMENT**
External source	Internal source
Ultimately, few people have it	Ultimately, everyone can have it
The capacity to have others do what you want	The capacity to have others do what they want
To get more implies taking it away from someone else	To get more does not affect how much others have
Leads to competition	Leads to cooperation

another person. Each depends on others acknowledging it. Each can be delegated to someone else.

In the case of empowerment, however, people can be empowered even if no one acknowledges their personal attributes or positions. Victor Frankl, Nelson Mandela, and Mahatma Gandhi are examples of individuals who, despite the absence of the attributes of power, maintained complete empowerment in dismal circumstances (i.e., in prison and in bigoted environments). This is because the source of empowerment is internal. Its source is within the individual, not as a result of social acceptance, political support, or title. One accepts empowerment for oneself.

In addition, if I become more powerful, that generally means you become less powerful. If I have the power to get someone to do what I want, but that differs from what you want, my power and your power come into conflict. That's why, ultimately, relatively few people have power. Power gets concentrated among a few in most organizations. Furthermore, power struggles are almost universal in organizations and even small groups. Who gets enough power to have his or her way is a common problem, and it almost always leads toward conflict. Power games become a clash of wills or a battle to see who will win and reign supreme. On the other hand, every person can be empowered without affecting any other person's position or stature. It merely leads to each of us being enabled to accomplish what we choose. Empowerment, in fact, is more likely to lead to cooperation and collaboration than to conflict.

Historical Roots of Empowerment

The word *empowerment* came into vogue in the 1980s and 1990s but has since taken on the image of a faddish and even outdated concept (Abrahamson, 1996; Block, 1987). In our own consulting and executive education teaching, many managers will respond when introducing the concept of empowerment, "We already tried that." Or "That's a 1990s term, isn't it?"

Because the concept of empowerment was so widely used in so many different contexts, it tended to become almost any management practice relating to employee involvement. Empowerment became associated with everything from team-building to entrepreneurship to flexible benefits. The word became so overused that its precise meaning became obscured. It may be helpful, therefore, to provide a brief background of the roots of empowerment because it is by no means a new concept. This should help us avoid confusing empowerment with other related management behaviors.

Empowerment has roots in the disciplines of psychology, sociology, and theology dating back for centuries. In the field of psychology, Adler (1927) developed the concept of *mastery motivation*, emphasizing the striving that people have for competence in dealing with their world. Similar concepts introduced several decades ago include *effectance motivation*, an intrinsic motivation to make things happen (White, 1959); *psychological reactance*, which refers to seeking freedom from constraints (Brehm, 1966); *competence motivation*, a striving to encounter and master challenges (Harter, 1978); and *personal causation*, a drive to experience free agency (DeCharms, 1979). In each of these studies, the root concepts are similar to the notion of empowerment discussed in this chapter; that is, the inclination of people to experience self-control, self-importance, and self-liberation.

In sociology, notions of empowerment have been fundamental to most rights movements (e.g., Civil Rights, Women's Rights, Gay Rights) (see Bookman & Morgan, 1988; Solomon, 1976), in which people campaign for freedom and control of their own circumstances. Moreover, much of the writing attacking societal problems through social change has centered fundamentally on the empowerment of groups of people (Alinsky, 1971; Marx, 1844). That is, people seek social change in order to increase their access to an empowered condition.

In theology, issues of free will versus determinism, self-will versus submissiveness, predestination versus faith and works, and humanism versus positivism have been hotly debated for centuries. At their root, they are all variations on a theme of empowerment versus helplessness. The more recent literature on "liberation theology" (Friere & Faundez, 1989) emphasizes the empowerment of individuals to take charge of their own destinies, rather than relying solely and completely on the dictates of an all-controlling, supernatural force. This does not mean that people who believe in a Supreme Being cannot feel empowered; rather, empowered people couple a sense of self-mastery and self-determination with their faith in God.

Empowerment is not a new concept. It has appeared in various forms throughout modern management literature. In the 1950s, for example, management literature was filled with prescriptions that managers should be friendly to employees (human relations); in the 1960s, that managers should be sensitive to the needs and motivations of people (sensitivity training); in the 1970s, that managers should ask employees for help (employee involvement); in the 1980s, that managers should form teams and hold meetings (quality circles), and in the 1990s, that employees should become entrepreneurial and flexible. All of these emphases were associated with the notion of empowerment. Despite the continuing emphasis on various versions of employee involvement and empowerment, however, the ability to empower employees is still not common in most managers' repertoire of skills. Empowerment is more rarely seen than prescribed (Quinn & Spreitzer, 1997).

Dimensions of Empowerment

In one of the best empirical studies of empowerment Spreitzer (1992) identified four dimensions of empowerment. We have added one dimension to her model, based on the research of Mishra (1992). In this section, we explain these five key dimensions of empowerment. In order for managers to empower others successfully, they must engender these five qualities in those they intend to empower. Skillful empowerment means producing (1) a sense of *self-efficacy*, (2) a sense of *self-determination*, (3) a sense of *personal consequence*, (4) a sense of *meaning*, and (5) a sense of *trust* (see Table 8.4). When these five dimensions of empowerment are present, empirical evidence is clear: individuals perform better and organizations perform better than normal.

When managers are able to foster these five attributes in others, they create a condition that is highly

Table 8.4	Five Core Dimensions of Empowerment	
DIMENSION	**EXPLANATION**
Self-efficacy	A sense of personal competence
Self-determination	A sense of personal choice
Personal consequence	A sense of having impact
Meaning	A sense of value in activity
Trust	A sense of security

empowering, or that makes it easy for others to become empowered. No one can force another to be empowered, of course, but fostering an environment where these five factors are present makes it likely that people will accept empowerment for themselves. Empowered people can not only more effectively accomplish tasks, but also think differently about themselves. They are more confident, they feel more freedom, they feel more important, and they feel more comfortable in their work and work setting.

After explaining these five dimensions, we provide guidelines for engendering each one.

SELF-EFFICACY

When people are empowered, they have a sense of **self-efficacy**, or the feeling that they possess the capability and competence to perform a task successfully. Empowered people not only feel *competent*, they feel *confident* that they can perform adequately. They are more self-assured. They feel a sense of personal mastery and believe they can learn and grow to meet new challenges (see Bandura, 1989; Bennis & Nanus, 1985; Conger & Kanungo, 1988; Gecas, 1989; Zimmerman, 1990). Some writers believe that this is the most important element in empowerment because having a sense of self-efficacy determines whether people will try and persist in attempting to accomplish a difficult task.

The strength of people's conviction in their own effectiveness is likely to affect whether they would even try to cope with given situations. . . . They get involved in activities and behave assuredly when they judge themselves capable of handling situations that would otherwise be intimidating. . . . Efficacy expectations determine how much effort people will expend and how long they will persist in the face of obstacles and aversive experiences. (Bandura, 1977, pp. 193–194)

Our colleague Roger Goddard and his associates found that a sense of efficacy among students in a classroom—what he referred to as "collective efficacy"—is a more powerful predictor of success in school than any other single factor (Goddard, Hoy, & Hoy, 2002). That is, when students believe in themselves, when they have confidence that they can succeed and when they have faith that a successful outcome will occur, they are significantly higher performers in their academic work. Their grades are higher, their test scores are higher in math and reading, and their absenteeism and tardiness are lower. Collective efficacy is a more important factor in determining these outcomes than race; gender; socioeconomic status; attending a large or small, inner-city or suburban school; or ethnic makeup of the class.

A great deal of additional research has been done on the consequences of self-efficacy and its opposite, powerlessness, in relation to physical and psychological health. For example, self-efficacy has been found to be a significant factor in overcoming phobias and anxieties (Bandura, 1986), alcohol and drug abuse (Seeman & Anderson, 1983), eating disorders (Schneider & Agras, 1985), smoking addiction (DiClemente, 1985), depression (Seligman, 1975), as well as increasing tolerance for pain (Neufeld & Thomas, 1977). Recovery from illness and injury, as well as coping with job loss or disruptions, is more effective and more rapid among people who have developed a strong sense of self-efficacy, because they are more physically and psychologically resilient and are better able to change negative behaviors (Gecas, Seff, & Ray, 1988; Schwalbe & Gecas, 1988).

Bandura (1977) suggested that three conditions are necessary for people to feel a sense of self-efficacy: (1) a belief that they have the ability to perform a task, (2) a belief that they are capable of putting forth the necessary effort, and (3) a belief that no outside obstacles will prevent them from accomplishing the task. In other words, people feel empowered when they develop a sense of self-efficacy by having a basic level of competence and capability, a willingness to put forth effort to accomplish a task, and the absence of overwhelming inhibitors to success. We will suggest ways later for enhancing self-efficacy.

SELF-DETERMINATION

Empowered people also have a sense of **self-determination**. Whereas self-efficacy refers to a sense of competence, self-determination refers to feelings of *having a choice*. "To be self-determining means to experience a sense of choice in initiating and regulating one's own actions" (Deci, Connell, & Ryan, 1989, p. 580). People feel self-determined when they can voluntarily and intentionally involve themselves in tasks, rather than being forced or prohibited from involvement. Their actions are a consequence of personal freedom and autonomy. Empowered individuals have alternatives and a sense of freedom; therefore, they develop a sense of responsibility for and ownership of their activities (Rappoport, Swift, & Hess, 1984; Rose & Black, 1985; Staples, 1990; Zimmerman, 1990). They see themselves as proactive self-starters. They are able to take initiative on their own accord, make independent decisions, and try out new ideas (Conger & Kanungo, 1988; Thomas & Valthouse, 1990; Vogt & Murrell, 1990). Rather than feeling that their actions are predetermined, externally controlled, or inevitable, they experience themselves as the locus of control. In any task or situation, a sense of self-determination can be engendered and enhanced, so people do not have to have high internal locus of control scores to feel a sense of empowerment.

Research shows that a strong sense of self-determination is associated with less alienation in the work environment (Maddux, 2002), more work satisfaction (Organ & Green, 1974), higher levels of work performance (Anderson, Hellreigel, & Slocum, 1977), more entrepreneurial and innovative activity (Hammer & Vardi, 1981), high levels of job involvement (Runyon, 1973), and less job strain (Gemmill & Heisler, 1972). In medical research, recovery from severe illness has been found to be associated with having the patient "reject the traditional passive role and insist on being an active participant in his own therapy" (Gecas, 1989, p. 298). People who are helped to feel that they can have personal impact on what happens to them, even with regard to the effects of disease, are more likely to experience positive outcomes than those who lack this feeling.

Self-determination is associated most directly with having choices about the *methods* used to accomplish a task, the amount of *effort* to be expended, the *pace* of the work, and the *time frame* in which it is to be accomplished. Empowered individuals have a feeling of ownership for tasks because they can determine how tasks are accomplished, when they are accomplished, and how quickly they are completed. Having a choice is the critical component of self-determination. Later we will offer specific suggestions for fostering self-determination.

PERSONAL CONSEQUENCE

Empowered people have a sense that when they act, they can produce a result. Think of an assembly line job where a worker screws a nut on a bolt, but if he makes an error, someone down the line will correct it. Such a person will have little sense that he can have any effect on the outcome of the product or that his efforts have an effect on the end product. He will feel little personal control over the outcome. On the other hand, people with a sense of personal consequence believe that expending effort produce a result. Personal consequence is "an individual's beliefs at a given point in time in his or her ability to effect a change in a desired direction" (Greenberger, Stasser, Cummings, & Dunham, 1989, p. 165). It is the conviction that through one's own actions, a person can influence what happens. A sense of personal consequence, then, refers to a perception of *impact*.

Empowered individuals do not believe that obstacles in the external environment control their actions; rather, they believe that those obstacles can be controlled. They have a feeling of *active control*—which allows them to bring their environment into alignment with their wishes—as opposed to *passive control*—in which their wishes are brought into alignment with environmental demands (see Greenberger & Stasser, 1991; Rappoport et al., 1984; Rothbaum, Weisz, & Snyder, 1982; Thomas & Velthouse, 1990; Zimmerman & Rappoport, 1988). Instead of being reactive to what they see around them, people with a sense of personal consequence try to maintain command over what they see. For individuals to feel empowered, they must not only feel that what they do produces an effect, but that they can produce the effect themselves. That is, they must feel that they are in control of producing the consequence in order for that consequence to be associated with a sense of empowerment.

Having a sense of personal consequence is related to internal locus of control discussed in the chapter on Self-Awareness. (You completed that instrument earlier in the book.) Unlike internal locus of control, however, a sense of personal consequence can be developed in association with a particular task. Managers can help other people develop this sense of having control over their work outcomes. Internal locus of control is a more fundamental and difficult-to-change personality attribute. This is, most people have developed an orientation toward internal or external locus of control, which characterizes their general approach to life. In helping people succeed in specific tasks, however, those who successfully empower others help them develop a sense that they can produce a desired result. Some ideas for how to foster a sense of consequence are discussed later.

Research on personal control suggests that people are intrinsically motivated to seek personal control (White, 1959). They fight to maintain a sense of control of themselves and their situations. Prisoners of war, for example, have been known to do strange things such as refusing to eat certain foods, not walking in a certain place, or developing secret communication codes, in order to maintain a sense of personal control. A certain amount of personal control is necessary for people to maintain psychological and physical well-being. When people lose personal control, we usually label them as insane and psychopathic.

Even small losses of personal control can be harmful physically and emotionally. For example, loss of control has been found to lead to depression, stress, anxiety, low morale, loss of productivity, burnout, learned helplessness, and even increased death rates (see Greenberger & Stasser, 1991; Langer, 1983). Having a sense of personal control, then, appears necessary for health as well as for empowerment. On the other hand, even the most empowered people are not able to control totally everything that happens to them. No one is in complete control of the outcomes in his or her life. Nevertheless, empowerment helps people increase the number of personal outcomes that they can control. Often, this is as much a matter of identifying areas in which personal consequence is possible as it is of manipulating or changing the external environment to increase control over it.

MEANING

Empowered people have a sense of meaning. They value the purpose or goals of the activity in which they are engaged. Their own ideals and standards are perceived as consistent with what they are doing. The activity "counts" in their own value system. Not only do they feel that they can produce a result, but empowered individuals believe in and care about what they produce. They invest psychic or spiritual energy in the activity, and they feel a sense of personal significance from their involvement. They experience personal connectedness and personal integrity as a result of engaging in the activity (Bennis & Nanus, 1985; Block, 1987; Conger & Kanungo, 1988; Manz & Sims, 1989). Meaningfulness, then, refers to a perception of *value*.

Activities infused with meaning create a sense of purpose, passion, or mission for people. They provide a source of energy and enthusiasm, rather than draining energy and enthusiasm from people. Merely getting paid, helping an organization earn money, or just doing a job does not create a sense of meaning for most people. Something more fundamental, more personal, and more value-laden must be linked to the activity. It must be associated with something more human. Almost all people want to feel that they are spending their time on something that will produce lasting benefit, that will make the world a better place, or that is associated with a personal value.

Acquiring personal benefit from an activity does not guarantee meaning. For example, service to others may bring no personal reward, yet it may be far more meaningful than work that produces a hefty paycheck. Involvement in activities without meaning, on the other hand, creates dissonance and annoyance, and produces a sense of disengagement from the work. People become bored or exhausted. Other incentives—such as rules, supervision, or extra pay—are required to get people to invest in the work. Unfortunately, these extra incentives are costly to organizations and represent non-value-added expenses that constrain organizational efficiency and effectiveness. It costs companies a lot of money to require work that has little or no meaning to workers. Self-estrangement results from lack of meaning; vigor and stimulation result from meaningful work (see Brief & Nord, 1990; Hackman & Oldham, 1980; Kahn, 1990; Thomas & Velthouse, 1990).

Research on meaningfulness in work has found that when individuals engage in work that they feel is meaningful, they are more committed to it and more involved in it. They have a higher concentration of energy and are more persistent in pursuing desired goals than when a sense of meaningfulness is low. People feel more excitement and passion for their work and have a greater sense of personal significance and self-worth because of their association with activities that are meaningful. Individuals empowered with a sense of meaningfulness also have been found to be more innovative, upwardly influential, and personally effective than those with low meaningfulness scores (Bramucci, 1977; Deci & Ryan, 1987; Pratt & Ashforth, 2003; Spreitzer, 1992; Vogt & Murrell, 1990; Wrzesniewski, 2003).

TRUST

Finally, empowered people have a sense of trust. They are confident that they will be treated fairly and equitably. They maintain an assurance that even if they are in subordinate positions, the ultimate outcome of their actions will be justice and goodness as opposed to harm or damage. Usually, this means they have confidence that those holding authority or power positions will not harm or injure them, and that they will be treated impartially. However, even in circumstances in which individuals holding power positions do not demonstrate integrity and fairness, empowered people still maintain a sense of assurance. Trust means, in other words, having a sense of *personal security*. Trust also implies that individuals place themselves in a position of vulnerability (Zand, 1972), and have faith that, ultimately, no harm will come to them as a result of that trust (Barber, 1983; Deutsch, 1973; Luhmann, 1979; Mishra, 1992).

How can a person maintain trust and a sense of security even when caught in a circumstance that seems unfair, inequitable, or even dangerous? In his attempts to gain independence for India, for example, Gandhi determined that he would burn the passes that the British government required be carried by all native Indians but not by British citizens. Gandhi called a meeting and publicly announced his intent to resist this law by burning the passes of each of his Indian supporters. In a now-famous incident, after Gandhi burned several of the passes, the British police intervened by clubbing him with nightsticks. Despite the beating, Gandhi continued to burn passes. Where is the trust or sense of security in this case? How can Gandhi be empowered in the process of being beaten by the police? In what did Gandhi have trust? Was Gandhi empowered or not? Gandhi's sense of security came not from the British authorities but from his faith in the principles that he espoused. His sense of security was associated with his belief that doing the right thing always leads, ultimately, to the right consequence.

Research on trust has found that trusting individuals are more apt to replace superficiality and facades with directness and intimacy; they are more apt to be open, honest, and congruent rather than deceptive or shallow. They are more search-oriented and self-determining, more self-assured and willing to learn. They have a larger capacity for interdependent relationships, and they display a greater degree of cooperation and risk-taking in groups than do those with low trust. Trusting people are more willing to try to get along with others and to be a contributing part of a team. They are also more self-disclosing, more honest in their own communication, and more able to listen carefully to others. They have less resistance to change and are better able to cope with unexpected traumas than are those with low levels of trust. Individuals who trust others are more likely to be trustworthy themselves and to maintain high personal ethical standards (see Gibb & Gibb, 1969; Golembiewski & McConkie, 1975; Mishra, 1992).

Because "trusting environments allow individuals to unfold and flourish" (Golembiewski & McConkie, 1975, p. 134), empowerment is closely tied to a sense of trust. Having a feeling that the behavior of others is consistent and reliable, that information can be held in confidence, and that promises will be kept all are a part of developing a sense of empowerment in people. Trusting others allows people to act in a confident and straightforward manner, without wasting energy on self-protection, trying to uncover hidden agendas, or playing politics. In brief, a sense of trust empowers people to feel secure.

REVIEW OF EMPOWERMENT DIMENSIONS

The main point of our discussion thus far is to make the point that fostering the five attributes of empowerment in individuals—*self-efficacy* (a sense of competence), *self-determination* (a sense of choice), *personal consequence* (a sense of impact), *meaning* (a sense of value), and *trust* (a sense of security)—produces very positive outcomes. Research findings associated with each of the five dimensions of empowerment indicate that both personal and organizational advantages result when people feel empowered. Negative consequences occur, on the other hand, when people experience the opposite of empowerment, such as powerlessness, helplessness, and alienation. Helping people feel a certain way about themselves and their work helps them to be more effective in the behaviors they display.

Some authors have gone so far as to claim that helping others develop this feeling of empowerment is at the very root of managerial effectiveness. Without it, they claim, neither managers nor organizations can be successful in the long term (Bennis & Nanus, 1985; Block, 1987; Conger, 1989; Kanter, 1983; Quinn & Spreitzer, 1997). As a psychological state, however, empowerment is never under the complete control of a manager. Individuals can refuse to feel empowered. In fact, some cynical students (but few practicing managers) have stated that empowering people is naïve since many people will not accept empowerment and will try to get along as a "free rider." Many people, they say, are not inclined to want empowerment.

This Theory X–like assumption is neither consistent with our own experience with thousands of practicing managers nor with the empirical research. People who don't want to get involved or who reject opportunities for empowerment—free-riders—exist in teams or classes, for example, when they do not value the outcome that has been assigned (absence of a sense of value), they believe that someone else will produce the result without their input (absence of a sense of personal consequence), or they don't believe that they have anything to contribute (absence of self-efficacy). When the five dimensions of empowerment are present, on the other hand, almost all people will become actively engaged. Research by Hackman and Oldham (1980) found that more than 80 percent of workers have high "growth need strength," or a desire to grow and contribute in their jobs. Providing opportunities for empowerment to people helps respond to this inherent need for growth and contribution.

A sense of empowerment can be influenced significantly by the conditions in which people find themselves. For that reason, the next section of this chapter discusses specific actions managers can take to facilitate empowerment in others.

How to Develop Empowerment

People are most in need of empowerment when they are faced with situations they perceive to be threatening, unclear, overly controlled, coercive, or isolating; when they experience inappropriate feelings of dependency or inadequacy; when they feel stifled in their ability to do what they would like to do; when they are uncertain about how to behave; when they feel that some negative consequence is imminent; and when they feel unrewarded and unappreciated.

Ironically, most large organizations engender these kinds of feelings in people, because, as Block (1987) noted, bureaucracy encourages dependency and submission. Rules, routines, and traditions define what can be done, stifling and supplanting initiative and discretion. In such circumstances, the formal organization—not the individual—is the recipient of empowerment. Therefore, in large organizations, empowerment is especially needed.

But empowerment is also key in environments outside of vast bureaucracies. For example, studies demonstrate positive effects of empowerment on child development, learning in school, coping with personal stress, and changing personal habits (see Ozer & Bandura, 1990).

Despite the applicability of empowerment in many different contexts including school and family life, our discussion considers ways in which managers can empower those with whom they work. We focus on empowerment mainly as a management skill, even though people in other roles, such as parents, teachers, coaches, tutors, and friends, can also benefit by developing the skills of empowerment.

LEARNING

Research by Kanter (1983), Hackman and Oldham (1980), Bandura (1986), Quinn and Spreitzer (1997), Wrzesniewski (2003), and others has produced at least nine specific prescriptions for fostering empowerment; that is, producing a sense of competence, choice, impact, value, and security. These include: (1) articulating a clear vision and goals, (2) fostering personal mastery experiences, (3) modeling, (4) providing support, (5) creating emotional arousal, (6) providing necessary information, (7) providing necessary resources, (8) connecting to outcomes, and (9) creating confidence. Each of these prescriptions is discussed below. Figure 8.1 illustrates their relationships to the five core dimensions of empowerment.

Some of these prescriptions are similar to the guidelines found in the chapters on Building Relationships by Communicating Supportively, Gaining Power and Influence, and Motivating Others. Because a completely separate and unique set of managerial skills does not exist for communicating with, influencing, and motivating others, some commonality and overlap is inevitable. On the other hand, the context of empowerment sheds a different light on some of the guidelines you have read about before.

ARTICULATING A CLEAR VISION AND GOALS

Creating an environment in which individuals can feel empowered requires that they be guided by a clearly articulated vision of where the organization is going and how they can contribute as individuals. We all desire to know the purpose of the activities in which we engage, what the ultimate objective is, and how we fit into that objective. The worst circumstance we can experience is one with a total lack of direction, where people do whatever comes to mind, or where no common objective or goal is evident. This is the classical condition—labeled *anomie*—that leads to anarchy, chaos, and even death (Durkheim, 1963). To avoid such chaotic conditions, a clear vision and an established set of goals must be articulated so that behavior remains congruent with organizational purposes.

Cameron and Quinn (2006); Martin, Feldman, Hatch, and Sitkin (1983); and others have reported that several studies confirm that the most effective way to articulate a vision in a clear and energizing way is by using word pictures, stories, metaphors, and real-life examples. That is, individuals are more likely to

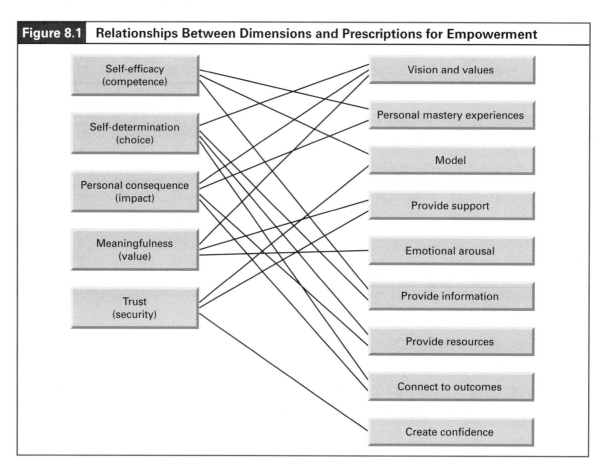

Figure 8.1 Relationships Between Dimensions and Prescriptions for Empowerment

Self-efficacy (competence)	Vision and values
Self-determination (choice)	Personal mastery experiences
Personal consequence (impact)	Model
Meaningfulness (value)	Provide support
Trust (security)	Emotional arousal
	Provide information
	Provide resources
	Connect to outcomes
	Create confidence

understand a vision if it has both right brain (intuitive, pictorial, story-based) as well as left brain (logical, reasonable, performance-based) elements associated with it. Not only do people understand communication more clearly when it contains stories and examples as well as descriptions, but they develop more of a sense of self-determination ("I can see the alternatives available"), a sense of personal consequence ("I can see how I can influence the outcomes"), and a sense of meaning ("I can see why this is so important").

Empowerment is also enhanced as specific behavioral goals are identified that help guide individuals' behavior as they work on their tasks. Goals specify desired outcomes as well as accountability. Locke and Latham (1990) identified the attributes of the most effective goals, and the acronym **SMART goals** best summarizes these attributes.

❏ *Specific goals*—those that are identifiable, behavioral, and observable.
❏ *Measurable goals*—those that have outcome criteria associated with them, that can be assessed objectively, and where the degree of successful accomplishment can be determined. One can evaluate the accomplishment of measurable goals.
❏ *Aligned goals*—those that are congruent with the overall purposes and vision of the organization. Their accomplishment contributes to the broader good.
❏ *Realistic goals*—realistic goals, those that are not so far above the capacity of the individual that they become discouraging at best and considered nonsense at worst. Realistic does not mean easily achieved, because research is clear that difficult goals—stretch goals—are better motivators of behavior and predict higher levels of accomplishment than do easy goals (Locke & Latham, 1990).
❏ *Time-bound goals*—that is, a time for accomplishing the goals is specified. Goals that have no ending point are not effective; a deadline for achievement is clear.

The point is: individuals are empowered as they are provided a clear vision of the future and some specific, behavioral goals that help clarify how they can get there.

FOSTERING PERSONAL MASTERY EXPERIENCES

Bandura (1986) found that the single most important thing a manager can do to empower other people is to help them experience personal mastery over some challenge or problem. By successfully accomplishing a task, defeating an opponent, or resolving a problem, people develop a sense of mastery. Personal mastery can be fostered by providing people with the opportunity to accomplish successively more difficult tasks that eventually lead to the accomplishment of desirable goals. The key is to start with easy tasks and then progress by small steps to more difficult tasks until the person experiences a sense of mastery over an entire complex of problems.

Managers can help others feel increasingly empowered by helping them develop an awareness that they can succeed. One way to do this is by breaking apart large tasks and giving workers only one part at a time. The manager watches for small successes achieved by workers and then highlights and celebrates them. Jobs can be expanded incrementally so that tasks become broader and more complex as workers master the basic elements. Other people are given further problem-solving responsibility as they succeed in resolving rudimentary difficulties. Managers can also provide opportunities for people to direct or lead others in a project, task force, or committee.

When managers adopt a **small-wins strategy**, individuals get opportunities to succeed in small ways, even though an overall challenge may be formidable (Weick, 1984). Small wins can occur when large problems are divided up into limited units that can be attacked individually. Small wins may seem insignificant by themselves, but they generate a sense of movement, progress, and success. The recognition and celebration of small wins generate momentum that leads people to feel empowered and capable.

Lee Iacocca used this strategy to turn around a failing Chrysler Corporation in the early 1980s. An analysis of his speeches to the top management team at Chrysler over a period of five years reveals that even though Chrysler was losing money, costs were too high, and quality was a major problem, Iacocca continued to celebrate small successes. (A transcript of these speeches is contained in the Skill Analysis section of the chapter on Leading Positive Change.) For example, he regularly announced that a certain amount of money was saved, a particular improvement was produced, a certain executive was hired away from the competition, or a compliment was received from a Wall Street analyst, even though the firm was losing a billion dollars a year. A great deal of emphasis was placed on succeeding at small things, all of which were aimed at eventually toppling the much larger challenge of company survival. In this case, continual small wins led to a big achievement.

MODELING

Another way to empower people is to model or demonstrate the correct behavior that they are to perform. Observing someone else succeed at challenging activities, Bandura (1977) found, provides a forceful impetus for others to believe that they, too, can succeed. It helps people presume that a task is do-able, that a job is within their capabilities, and that success is possible.

The manager may serve as the role model by demonstrating desired behaviors. On the other hand, it may not be possible for a manager to model desired behaviors personally for every single person with whom he or she interacts. The manager may not see an employee often enough to show him or her how to accomplish work or to frequently demonstrate success. Alternatively, however, managers may be able to draw people's attention to other individuals who have been successful in similar circumstances. They might make it possible for people to associate with senior or visible role models who could serve as examples, and they could provide opportunities for workers to be coached by these successful people. They can partner their people with mentors who can discuss their own past experiences that were similar to those of the person being mentored.

In other words, empowering people involves making available examples of past success. This is consistent with the learning model upon which this book is based. The Skill Analysis step of the learning model exemplifies appropriate and inappropriate behavior engaged in by others. It provides a model of people who have succeeded in accomplishing the desired skill. This modeling function helps foster a sense of empowerment in individuals who are trying to develop and improve management skills by showing ways in which such skills can be showcased successfully.

Think of what happens when a barrier is broken. In track and field athletics, for example, once John Thomas broke the seven-foot high jump mark and Roger Bannister broke the four-minute mile record, a host of other athletes quickly exceeded that standard. But before the first person broke those barriers, they were considered insurmountable. It took someone to demonstrate that the standard could be exceeded in order for others to experience the empowerment necessary to replicate the accomplishment themselves.

PROVIDING SUPPORT

A fourth technique for helping others experience empowerment is providing them with social and emotional support. If people are to feel empowered, managers should praise them, encourage them, express approval of them, back them, and reassure them. Kanter (1983) and Bandura (1986) each found that a crucial part of empowerment is having responsive and supportive managers. Managers seeking to empower others should find ways to praise others' performance regularly. They can write letters or notes to workers, to members of their unit, or even to their family indicating that the person's good work has been noticed. They can provide feedback to people about their abilities and competencies. They can arrange for opportunities for individuals to receive social support from others by becoming part of a team or social unit. They can express confidence in people by monitoring them less closely or by allowing longer time intervals to elapse before requiring them to report results. Managers can hold regular ceremonies where individuals' achievements are recognized. It may simply be a matter of listening to people and trying to understand their feelings and points of view.

Managers can empower others, then, by engendering a feeling that they are accepted, that they are a valued asset, and that they are an integral part of the overall organizational mission or objective. This support can come from either the manager or colleagues.

Cameron, Freeman, and Mishra (1991), for example, described a variety of support activities undertaken by a highly effective manager who was forced to lay off workers due to a corporate downsizing mandate. Understandably, the layoffs resulted in undermined employee trust, increased skepticism, and an escalated sense of powerlessness. Because the announcement came down from the parent company, workers felt that they had lost the ability to control their own destinies. In short, they felt unempowered. Following the layoff, the manager held personal meetings with each remaining employee to reaffirm his or her value to the organization. People were told in a straightforward manner that they were considered valuable human resources, not human liabilities, to the company. A special "Build with Pride" week was held in which outsiders—the press, government officials, family members, school classes—were invited to tour the facility and provide feedback (which, by the way, consistently took the form of praise) to the employees for the products and services they were producing. An impromptu hot dog roast was held one lunch hour to recognize and celebrate the extra-mile efforts of one group of employees in the facility. People were assured that counseling, training, and assistance would be provided when job assignments changed or positions were merged as a result of the downsizing. In general, this notable manager attempted to re-empower his workforce by providing social and emotional support in a variety of ways. He helped provide the assistance people needed to cope with the uncertainty resulting from this uncontrollable event. Predictably, both organizational and individual performance results did not deteriorate after downsizing. Instead, contrary to what happens in most organizations that downsize, performance actually improved.

EMOTIONAL AROUSAL

Emotional arousal means replacing negative emotions such as fear, anxiety, or crabbiness with positive emotions such as excitement, passion, or anticipation. To empower people, managers help make the work environment fun and attractive. They ensure that the purpose behind the work is clear. They ensure that people's right brain (the side that controls emotions and passions) is involved in the work as well as their left brain (the side that controls logic and analysis). They provide positive energy to people. Bandura (1977) found that the absence of positive emotional arousal makes it difficult, if not impossible, for individuals to feel empowered. Baker, Cross, and Wooten (2003), on the other hand, found that positively energizing people enhances performance markedly and is even more important than providing people with powerful positions or special information in their work. Positive energy is easy to detect in people. When we interact with some people they seem to give us life and vigor. Other people seem to be life-depleting or negatively energizing. Emotional arousal is associated with being a positive energy source for people.

The visible celebrations of employee accomplishments and motivational events in marketing firms such as Mary Kay Cosmetics, Shaklee Products, and Amway are well known. However, emotional arousal doesn't simply mean tooting horns, increasing the decibel levels, listening to speeches, or superficially creating excitement. Instead, emotional arousal occurs more likely when what individuals are doing is connected to values they hold dear. To feel a sense of empowerment, workers must see how what they are doing every day is associated with their basic beliefs. Employees can get more excited, for example, about working for the betterment of humankind, for the improvement of the quality of people's lives, and for personal growth and development, than they can for a 10 percent return to institutional investors. This is not to say that revenue for stockholders is unimportant. But emotional arousal is associated more with personal values than with organizational profitability.

Managers can also increase workers' sense of empowerment by holding periodic social gatherings to foster friendships among coworkers. In their official communications, they can occasionally include a joke or lighthearted message to relieve tension. They can use superlatives in providing feedback or describing successes (e.g., say "terrific" instead of "good"; "awesome" instead of "acceptable"). They can make sure that employees are clear about how their work will affect the company's customers. They can help identify external threats or challenges that need to be met.

Successful emotional arousal is often associated with athletic teams. Chuck Coonradt (1985) observed that "people are willing to pay for the privilege of working harder than they will work when they are paid." That is, individuals will actually pay money in order to work at a more demanding level than the level at which they work when they are receiving a salary. Here is one example:

> In the frozen food business, people are hired to work in refrigerated warehouses in terrible working conditions at near-zero temperatures. But the unions and OSHA have done much to make conditions bearable. Companies are required to provide insulated clothing and boots. They are required to provide hot drinks within so many feet of cold work areas. Workers must have a ten-minute break every hour. It's tough to get people to work in those kinds of conditions. Yet, whenever a winter snowstorm passes over . . . the mountains, followed by clearing skies and plunging temperatures, there is a sudden jump in employee absenteeism, particularly among young workers. Instead of staying home to avoid the freezing temperatures, they migrate up the local canyons to test the new and famous powder snow. . . . Equipped with hundreds of dollars of equipment, they gladly take a reduction in pay for the day off and a chance to buy a $40 pass to spend the day outside in subfreezing temperatures. There are no hot-drink vending machines on the slopes, nor does anyone demand a ten-minute break every hour. (Coonradt, 1985, p. 1)

Thus, people actually end up working harder, in worse conditions—and paying for the privilege—than when they are at work getting paid. Why is this so? Why does recreation produce such energy, such commitment, and such a sense of empowerment?

Part of the explanation relates to the emotional arousal that results from several characteristics of sports. For example, all recreation has a clear *goal* (e.g., winning, exceeding a personal best). Without a clearly defined goal, no one gets excited. That goal is always pitted against a standard that people care about (e.g., winning the NCAA championship, bowling a 300 game). In recreation, the *scorekeeping* and *feedback* systems are objective, self-administered, and continuous. In a basketball game, for example, everyone knows that a free throw always counts one point, that the winner is the team that makes the most baskets, and that there is never a time when everyone can't find out the exact score of the game. One reason why people get so excited watching athletic events is because of the scorekeeping and feedback systems. In recreation, the *out-of-bounds* is clearly identified. Everyone knows the consequence of kicking a soccer ball over the end line, of hitting a ball to the left side of third base, or of stepping over the end of the takeoff board in the long jump. They are all out-of-bounds, and everyone knows that out-of-bounds behavior stops action.

Managers can help empower people through emotional arousal, not just by being a cheerleader, delivering charismatic speeches, and keeping the work climate fun, but also by capitalizing on some of the principles of recreation that create excitement: clear goals; objective, self-administered, and continuous scorekeeping and feedback; and clearly defined out-of-bounds behavior.

PROVIDING INFORMATION

Kanter (1983) identified information as one of the most crucial managerial "power tools." Acquiring information, particularly information that is viewed as central or strategic in an organization, can be used to build a power base and to make oneself indispensable and influential in that organization. On the other hand, when managers provide their people with more, rather than less information, those people gain a sense of empowerment and are more likely to work productively, successfully, and in harmony with the manager's wishes. The manager actually enhances his or her power base by involving others in the pursuit of desirable outcomes. With more information, people tend to experience more self-determination, personal control, and trust. The resulting sense of empowerment enhances the probability that subordinates will not resist the manager, defend against his or her power, or work at protecting themselves. Rather, they are likely to collaborate with the empowering manager.

Therefore, a manager who wishes to increase an employee's sense of empowerment will make sure that the employee is given all task-relevant information needed to carry out an assignment. The empowering manager will make available, on an ongoing basis, pertinent technical information and data collected by others.

Such a manager keeps workers informed about what is happening in other areas of the organization that might affect what the worker is doing. Managers will keep employees informed of policy-making meetings and senior-level discussions related to their area of responsibility. Workers can be given access to sources closest to the information they need: for example, senior level people in the organization, customers, or the market research staff. Historical or "context" information can be shared in order to give the worker as broad a background as possible. Managers should make certain that employees have information about the effects of their own behavior on others and on the organization's goals.

To be sure, it is possible to overload people with information and to create anxiety and burnout with too much data. But our experience has been that most people suffer from too little information instead of too much. Furthermore, if the information is relevant in this context, overload is less likely to occur. Spreitzer (1992) found, for example, that people who received relevant information about costs, customers, and strategy felt significantly more empowered than those who did not. Block (1987) argued:

> *Sharing as much information as possible is the opposite of the military notion that only those who "need to know" should be informed. Our goal is to let people know our plans, ideas, and changes as soon as possible. . . . If we are trying to create the mindset that everyone is responsible for the success of this business, then our people need complete information.* (p. 90)

Our own research further confirms the importance of providing information to enhance empowerment (Cameron, Freeman, & Mishra, 1993). In one study, for example, we interviewed CEOs of large, well-known companies every six months to assess organizational changes and strategies they were using to cope with declining revenues. In one firm, not much progress was being made in improving the financial outlook. The CEO was very careful to share information on financial, productivity, cost, and climate indicators in the company only with his senior management team. No one else in the firm had access to that information. A change of CEO, however, led to a dramatic change in information-sharing policy. The new CEO began to provide information to every single employee in the firm who desired it. No data were treated as the sole possession of senior management. The sweepers had the same access as the vice presidents. The resulting empowerment that employees experienced led to dramatic results. Employee-initiated improvements increased markedly, morale and commitment surged, and the resulting financial turnaround made the CEO look like a genius. He attributed his success to his willingness to empower employees by sharing the information they needed to know to improve.

PROVIDING RESOURCES

In addition to providing information, empowerment is also fostered by providing people with other kinds of resources that help them accomplish their tasks. In this sense, managers who empower others act more like blocking backs on a football team than quarterbacks. They are less directors and commanders than they are resource providers (creating time to throw a pass or make a handoff) and obstacle eliminators (blocking on-rushing defensive linemen). One of the primary missions of empowering managers, then, is to help others accomplish their objectives.

Managers attempting to enhance other people's empowerment by providing them with needed resources will ensure that they receive adequate and ongoing training and development experiences. Sufficient technical and administrative support will be provided to ensure success. Managers will give their people space, time, or equipment that may not be readily available otherwise. They will ensure that these people have access to communication or interpersonal networks that will make their jobs easier. Individuals can also be given discretion to spend money or commit resources to activities that they consider important.

It is unrealistic, of course, to assume that everyone can have everything he or she desires. Very few successful organizations have excess resources to be distributed at will. On the other hand, the most important resources that empowering managers can provide are those that help people achieve control over their own work and lives; that is, foster a sense of self-efficacy and self-determination. When individuals feel that they have what they need to be successful and that they have the freedom to pursue what they want to accomplish, performance is significantly higher than when these types of resources are not available (Spreitzer, 1992). One of the best examples of using resources to empower comes from Carl Sewell, one of the most successful car salesmen in the United States,

who described his approach to empowerment through providing resources:

> Not many people get to see our service repair shop—our insurance company wants to keep traffic there to a minimum—but those who do always comment on its cleanliness. And, in fact, it's immaculate. Why? Because, while customers rarely see it, our technicians do. They live and work there every day. Where would you like to spend your day—in a place that's dirty or one that's spotless? But it's more than just aesthetics. If we make the technicians' work environment more professional, more pleasant, more efficient, if we provide them with the very best equipment and tools, we're going to be able to hire the best technicians. . . . All this gives them another reason for working for us instead of our competition. (Sewell, 1990, p. 53)

One reason Carl Sewell has been so dramatically successful is that he provides each individual with everything necessary to accomplish desired goals. This is true whether Sewell is dealing with mechanics or top salespersons, and whether his company is selling Cadillacs and Lexuses or Hyundais and Geos. It is not only *need*-to-have resources that Sewell provides, but also some *nice*-to-have resources. The point is: "Resources lead to empowerment."

CONNECTING TO OUTCOMES

One of the important lessons learned by U.S. manufacturing companies as a result of the Japanese entrance into the North American automobile and consumer electronics industries is that workers experience more empowerment when they can see the outcomes of their work. It was often a surprise to U.S. companies, for example, that their Japanese counterparts regularly visited customers in their homes or place of business, regularly observed how the products that the workers produced were used, and regularly received feedback directly from end users. This connection to the ultimate customer helped workers feel more empowered as well as provided a valuable source of improvement ideas. The importance of connecting workers with customers was confirmed, as mentioned in the chapter on Motivating Others, by Hackman and Oldham's (1980) research on job design and job enrichment. These investigators found that people are motivated at work when they can interact with ultimate customers in order to see the effects of their work.

A related idea is to provide employees with the authority to resolve problems on the spot. Studies at IBM, Ford Motor Company, Carl Sewell's auto dealerships, and other companies indicated that allowing employees to address customer concerns at the time the complaint was registered positively affected both employee and customer. When employees were given discretion to resolve a problem, respond immediately to a customer's complaint, fix the error instantly, or commit a certain level of company resources in pursuing customer satisfaction, not only was customer satisfaction dramatically increased (an average improvement of 300 percent), but workers felt far more empowered as well. Employees were given the necessary authority to go along with their responsibility for customer satisfaction, and they were provided with an opportunity to affect outcomes directly.

Hackman, Oldham, Janson, and Purdy (1975) suggested that another of the highly effective ways to enhance employee motivation and satisfaction is to create **task identity**, that is, the opportunity to accomplish a whole task. Individuals become frustrated and lack a sense of empowerment when they work on only part of a task, never see the end result of their work, and are blocked from observing the impact that their job creates. One of us has a colleague who quit a very lucrative job in a prestigious Wall Street firm because he became frustrated with his inability to see the results of his work. He was regularly given assignments to accomplish the first few steps in a complicated job and then had to hand the work off to a senior executive who completed the work and received most of the recognition. Not only was this colleague denied deserved rewards, but more important to him, he was unable to feel that he had completed a whole job. Task identity and the resulting sense of empowerment were completely lacking.

Having task identity implies that individuals can plan, implement, and evaluate the success of their efforts. The effects of what is accomplished can be assessed as well as the outcome. To feel empowered, in other words, I want to know whether I successfully completed my assigned job as well as whether that job made any difference to the overall success of my work unit. The more clear that connection is, the more I will feel empowered.

In sum, clarifying the connections between individuals' work and their outcomes and effects fosters empowerment by helping others develop a sense of self-efficacy (they feel more capable and competent) and a sense of personal consequence (a sense of having personal impact).

CREATING CONFIDENCE

One additional technique to be mentioned here—among many others—for engendering empowerment is to create a sense of confidence among workers in the trustworthiness of the manager. Rather than being on guard and suspicious, workers are secure in their feeling that the manager and the organization are honorable. This confidence helps drive out uncertainty, insecurity, and ambiguity in the relationships between employees and the manager.

There are at least two reasons why individuals feel more empowered as they develop greater confidence in their manager. First, the wasteful, unproductive behaviors associated with mistrust and suspicion are avoided. When people distrust one another, they don't listen, they don't communicate clearly, they don't try hard, and they don't collaborate. On the other hand, when trust exists, individuals are free to experiment, to learn, and to contribute without fear of retribution. Second, individuals who are admirable and honorable always create positive energy for others and make them feel more capable. Not without reason do universities trumpet the number of Nobel Prize winners on their faculties, the past Heisman trophy winners on their football teams, the number of outstanding faculty members in their business schools, and the notable achievements of their best students. Although other members of the university may have nothing to do with the achievements being publicized, they gain an enhanced self-image and a sense of empowerment because they are affiliated with the same organization. For the same reasons, creating confidence in a manager helps employees develop a sense of empowerment.

In creating such a sense of confidence and trustworthiness, five factors are especially important: (1) *reliability*, (2) *fairness*, (3) *caring*, (4) *openness*, and (5) *competence*. Managers create confidence, and thereby engender empowerment in others, as they display these five characteristics which are associated with being honorable.

❏ *Reliability.* Managers who wish their people to develop confidence in them need to exhibit reliability. Managers' behavior must be consistent, dependable, and stable. Their actions are congruent with their words and attitudes.

❏ *Fairness.* Good managers also need to be fair and must not take wrongful advantage of anyone. They are equitable in their actions. Workers are clear about the criteria used by the manager in making judgments as well as how the manager applies those criteria. Managers must make clear the standards by which workers will be judged and ensure that those standards are applied in an unbiased way.

❏ *Caring*. Managers must show a sense of personal concern for others and help each one feel important to the manager. Managers validate the points of view of other people and avoid denigrating them as individuals. When correction is needed, caring managers focus on the mistake or the behavior, not on the individual's personal characteristics.

❏ *Openness*. Confidence-building managers are open in their relationships. No harmful secrets exist, and relevant information is shared openly and honestly with employees. This does not suggest that a manager cannot keep confidences. But it does mean that other people should not have to worry about hidden agendas that could negatively affect them because their manager is straightforward and honest.

❏ *Competence*. People should be made aware of the manager's competence. They need to be assured that the manager has the necessary ability, experience, and knowledge to perform tasks and to solve problems. Without flaunting their expertise, skillful managers inspire a feeling on the part of employees that their confidence in the expertise and proficiency of their leader is not misplaced.

The power of creating confidence in others is illustrated by several CEOs who were interviewed regarding their keys to successful organizational change. Each CEO had managed a downsizing or redesign of his organization and was attempting to maintain a healthy, productive workforce in the midst of turmoil. The key role of trust and confidence in management is hard to miss (see Cameron et al., 1993; Mishra, 1992).

If they don't believe what I'm telling them, if they think it's all a bunch of bull, don't expect them to go out there and work a little harder. They won't work a little different. They're not going to be receptive to change unless they understand and trust the things that we're talking about are true. I think trust is the biggest single issue.

I had a boss one time who said, "What you do speaks so much louder than what you say." I've always stuck that in the back of my mind. I believe that. The people watch very closely what you do. And, boy, you cannot underestimate that.

What's most important in my organization is this: being truthful. Don't b.s. anyone. Tell them what it is. Right or wrong or different. Tell them the truth.

My people are all 150 percent dedicated to helping one another. Because not one of them can do it alone, they need each other badly. But here comes the openness and trust. You have to talk about those things. I don't think you can go in and accomplish things without talking about what the barriers are going to be in trying to make a change or set a new direction.

Successful managers create confidence in themselves among their colleagues. They are authentic, honorable, and trustworthy.

REVIEW OF EMPOWERMENT PRINCIPLES

Table 8.5 summarizes the list of actions that we have discussed on the previous pages in relation to the nine prescriptions for empowerment. It provides a list of things managers can do to empower other people. Not all of these suggestions are relevant in every circumstance or with every person, of course, but developing the skill of empowerment at least partly depends on knowing what alternatives are available to empower people, as well as knowing how to implement them. This list is not comprehensive; other activities may be equally effective in empowering people. But the nine prescriptions and the suggestions associated with each of them represent actions that you will want to practice as you try to improve your competence in the skill of empowerment. The Skill Practice section of this chapter provides an opportunity for you to do this.

Research suggests that empowered individuals are most inclined to empower others. For that reason, we included an Assessment instrument at the beginning of this chapter that measures the extent to which you experience empowerment in your own work. Your scores on the instrument entitled Personal Empowerment Assessment indicate how much your own work is empowering for you in terms of self-efficacy, self-determination, personal control, meaning, and trust. Knowing what provides a sense of empowerment for you can be helpful as you consider ways in which you, in turn, can empower others. The other instrument that you completed in the Skill Assessment section

Table 8.5 Practical Suggestions for Empowering Others

Articulate a Clear Vision and Goals

- Create a picture of a desired future.
- Use word pictures and emotional language to describe the vision.
- Identify specific actions and strategies that will lead to the vision.
- Establish SMART goals.
- Associate the vision and goals with personal values.

Foster Personal Mastery Experiences

- Break apart large tasks and assign one part at a time.
- Assign simple tasks before difficult tasks.
- Highlight and celebrate small wins.
- Incrementally expand job responsibilities.
- Give increasingly more responsibility to solve problems.

Model Successful Behaviors

- Demonstrate successful task accomplishment.
- Point out other people who have succeeded.
- Facilitate interaction with other role models.
- Find a coach.
- Establish a mentor relationship.

Provide Support

- Praise, encourage, express approval for, and reassure.
- Send letters or notes of praise to family members or coworkers.
- Regularly provide feedback.
- Foster informal social activities to build cohesion.
- Supervise less closely and provide time-slack.
- Hold recognition ceremonies.

Arouse Positive Emotions

- Foster activities to encourage friendship formation.
- Periodically send light-hearted messages.
- Use superlatives in giving feedback.
- Highlight compatibility between important personal values and organizational goals.
- Clarify impact on the ultimate customer.
- Foster attributes of recreation in work: clear goals, effective scorekeeping and feedback systems, and out-of-bounds behavior.

Provide Information

- Provide all task-relevant information.
- Continuously provide technical information and objective data.
- Pass along relevant cross-unit and cross-functional information.
- Provide access to information or people with senior responsibility.

Table 8.5	Practical Suggestions for Empowering Others

- Provide access to information from its source.
- Clarify effects of actions on customers.

Provide Resources

- Provide training and development experiences.
- Provide technical and administrative support.
- Provide needed time, space, or equipment.
- Ensure access to relevant information networks.
- Provide more discretion to commit resources.

Connect to Outcomes

- Provide a chance to interact directly with those receiving the service or output.
- Provide authority to resolve problems on the spot.
- Provide immediate, unfiltered, direct feedback on results.
- Create task identity, or the opportunity to accomplish a complete task.
- Clarify and measure effects as well as direct outcomes.

Create Confidence

- Exhibit reliability and consistency.
- Exhibit fairness and equity.
- Exhibit caring and personal concern.
- Exhibit openness and honesty.
- Exhibit competence and expertise.

(Effective Empowerment and Delegation) identified the extent to which you behave in ways that empower people with whom you work and the extent to which you delegate work effectively. How much you actually engage in the behaviors discussed above is assessed, as well as the extent to which you are an effective delegator.

Inhibitors to Empowerment

If the data are clear that empowering people produces superior results, and if techniques for enhancing empowerment are clear, why then is empowerment in organizations so rare? Why do a majority of people feel that they are alienated from their work, unengaged, and flourishing (Cameron, Dutton, & Quinn, 2003)? In his book on managerial empowerment, Peter Block (1987) noted that empowerment is very difficult to accomplish:

Many, increasingly aware of the price we pay for too many controls, have had the belief that if some of these controls were removed, a tremendous amount of positive energy in service of the organization would be released. While in many cases this has happened, too often our attempts at giving people more responsibility have been unwelcome and met with persistent reluctance. Many managers have tried repeatedly to open the door of participation to their people, only to find them reluctant to walk through it. [In a study of managers who were offered total responsibility for their work areas], about 20 percent of the managers took the responsibility and ran with it, about 50 percent of the managers cautiously tested the sincerity of the offer and then over a period of six months began to make their own decisions. The frustrating part of the effort was that the other 30 percent absolutely refused to take the reins. They clutched tightly to their dependency and continued to complain that top management did not really mean it, they were not given enough people or resources to really do their job, and the unique characteristics of their particular location made efforts at participative management unreasonable. (p. 154)

As Block noted, many managers and employees are reluctant to accept empowerment, but they are even more reluctant to offer empowerment. One reason for this is the personal attitudes of managers. Several management surveys, for example, have examined the reasons managers have for not being willing to empower their employees (Byham, 1988; Newman & Warren, 1977; Preston & Zimmerer, 1978). These reasons can be organized into three broad categories.

ATTITUDES ABOUT SUBORDINATES

Managers who avoid empowering others often believe their subordinates are not competent enough to accomplish the work, aren't interested in taking on more responsibility, are already overloaded and unable to accept more responsibility, would require too much time to train, or shouldn't be involved in tasks or responsibilities typically performed by the boss. They feel that the problem of nonempowerment lies with the employees, not with themselves. This is typical of the classic distinction between Theory X managers and Theory Y managers first pointed out by Douglas McGregor (1960), which was discussed in the chapter on Motivating Others. Most managers, McGregor claimed, are characterized by these kinds of assumptions—that is, that workers try to avoid work and cannot be trusted to take initiative to perform work on their own. The rationale is: I'm willing to empower my people, but they just won't accept the responsibility. On the other hand, as pointed out above, these assumptions are far more typical of managers who use them as an excuse to avoid empowering than they are of people in general. A vast majority of people seek empowerment.

PERSONAL INSECURITIES

Some managers fear they will lose the recognition and rewards associated with successful task accomplishment if they empower others. They are unwilling to share their expertise or "trade secrets" for fear of losing power or position. They have an intolerance for ambiguity, which leads them to feel that they personally must know all the details about projects assigned to them. They prefer working on tasks by themselves rather than getting others involved, or they are unwilling to absorb the costs associated with subordinates

making mistakes. The rationale is: I'm willing to empower people, but when I do, they either mess things up or try to grab all the glory. Unfortunately, when people try to be the heroes, obtain all the glory for themselves, or avoid involving other people, they almost never accomplish what they could have by capitalizing on the expertise and energy of others. The empirical data are abundant showing that empowered teams do better than even the most competent individual (see the chapter on Building Effective Teams and Teamwork).

NEED FOR CONTROL

Nonempowering managers also often have a high need to be in charge and to direct and govern what is going on. They presume that an absence of clear direction and goals from the boss and a slackening of controls will lead to confusion, frustration, and failure on the part of employees. They feel that direction from the top is mandatory. Moreover, they often see short-lived, disappointing results from pep talks, work teams, suggestion systems, job enrichment programs, and other fix-it activities ("We tried that, and it didn't work"). The rationale is: I'm willing to empower people, but they require clear directions and a clear set of guidelines; otherwise, the lack of instructions leads to confusion. Whereas it is true that clear goals and specific directions enhance performance, self-established goals are always more motivating than those prescribed by someone else. Thus, people will perform better if they are empowered to establish their own goals rather than to have the manager superimpose them as a prerequisite to success.

The rationale associated with each of these inhibitors may be partially true, of course, but they nevertheless inhibit managers from achieving the success associated with skillful empowerment. Even if managers demonstrate the willingness and courage to empower others, success still requires skillful implementation. Incompetent empowerment, in fact, can undermine rather than enhance the effectiveness of an organization and its employees. For example, such incompetent empowerment as giving employees freedom without clear directions or resources has been found to lead to psychological casualties among individuals, as manifested by increased depression (Alloy, Peterson, Abrahamson, & Seligman, 1984), heightened stress (Averill, 1973), decreased performance and job satisfaction (Greenberger et al., 1989), lowered alertness, and even increased mortality (Langer & Rodin, 1976). Of course, these negative consequences are not solely associated with incompetent empowerment. They have been noted, nevertheless, in situations in which attempted empowerment was ineffective and unskillful.

For example, when managers associated empowerment with behaviors such as "simply letting go," refusing to clarify expectations, abdicating responsibility, having an absence of ground rules, or giving inflexible or inconsistent directions—none of which are consistent with skillful empowerment—the results were not only unsuccessful, but even harmful. Because of the negative psychological and physiological consequences for workers resulting from nonempowerment or from incompetent empowerment, Sashkin (1984) labeled skillful empowerment "an ethical imperative" for managers.

Delegating Work

The situation in which empowerment is most needed is when other people must become involved in accomplishing work. Obviously, if a person is doing a task alone, knowing how to empower others is largely irrelevant. On the other hand, it is impossible for a manager to perform all the work needed to carry out an organization's mission, so work and the responsibility to carry it out must be delegated to others. All managers, therefore, are required to empower their employees if they are to accomplish the tasks of the organization. Without delegation and the empowerment that must accompany it, no organization and no manager can enjoy long-term success. Delegation involves the assignment of work to other people, and it is an activity inherently associated with all managerial positions.

In this section, we discuss the nature of delegation as well as ways in which delegation can be most effectively empowered. Delegation normally refers to the assignment of a task. It is work-focused. Empowerment, on the other hand, may involve nonwork activities, emotions, and relationships. It involves the way people think about themselves. We have previously discussed ways in which managers can affect people's sense of being empowered. We will now discuss ways in which managers can get work accomplished effectively through empowered delegation.

We begin by pointing out that although delegation is commonly practiced by managers, it is by no means always competently performed. In fact, one of the grand masters of management, Lester Urwick (1944, p. 51), claimed that the "lack of courage to delegate properly, and of knowledge of how to do it, is one of the most general causes of failures in organizations." Moreover, as pointed out by Leana (1987), researchers have paid little attention to delegation, and less is known about the relationships between delegation and management effectiveness than many other common management skills (Locke & Schweiger, 1979).

ADVANTAGES OF EMPOWERED DELEGATION

Learning to become a competent delegator who can simultaneously empower others has several important advantages for managers. It obviously helps managers accomplish more work than they could accomplish otherwise and can be used as a time-management tool to free up discretionary time. On the other hand, if delegation occurs only when managers are overloaded, those receiving the delegated tasks may feel resentful and sense that they are being treated only as objects to meet the managers' ends. In such cases, they will experience a sense of disempowerment. However, skillful use of empowered delegation can provide significant benefits to organizations, managers, and individuals receiving assigned tasks. Table 8.6 summarizes these advantages.

Table 8.6	Advantages of Delegation
ADVANTAGE	**EXPLANATION**
Time	Increases the discretionary time of the manager
Development	Develops knowledge and capabilities of delegates
Trust	Demonstrates trust and confidence in delegates
Commitment	Enhances commitment of delegates
Information	Improves decision making with better information
Efficiency	Enhances efficiency and timeliness of decisions
Coordination	Fosters work integration by manager coordination

Empowered delegation can help develop subordinates' capabilities and knowledge so that their effectiveness is increased. It can be a technique to encourage personal mastery experiences. Delegation can also be used to demonstrate trust and confidence in the person receiving the assignment. Mishra (1992) and Gambetta (1988) summarized research showing that individuals who felt trusted by their managers were significantly more effective than those who didn't feel that way. Empowered delegation can be used to enhance the commitment of individuals receiving work. Beginning with the classic study of participation by Coch and French (1948), research has consistently demonstrated a positive relationship between having an opportunity to participate in work and subsequent satisfaction, productivity, commitment, acceptance of change, and desire for more work.

Empowered delegation can also be used to improve the quality of decision making by bringing to bear more information, closer to the source of the problem, than the manager has alone. Delegating tasks to those who have direct access to relevant information can enhance efficiency (i.e., require less time and fewer resources) as well as effectiveness (i.e., result in a better decision).

Finally, empowered delegation can increase the coordination and integration of work by funneling information and final accountability through a single source. Empowering managers, in other words, can ensure that no cross-purposes occur in delegation and that different tasks are not producing contradictory effects. Competently administered, empowered delegation can produce all five dimensions of empowerment: a sense of competence, choice, impact, value, and security.

On the other hand, when delegation is ineffectively performed, several negative consequences can result that not only inhibit empowerment but also subvert the ability to get work accomplished at all. For example, instead of freeing up time, ineffective delegation may require even more time to supervise, evaluate, correct, and arbitrate disagreements among employees. Employees may find themselves spending a longer time to accomplish a task because of lack of know-how, experience, or information. Stress levels and interpersonal conflict may increase when tasks, accountability, or expectations are unclear. Managers may find themselves out of touch with what is really going on with employees, may lose control, and may find goals being pursued that are incompatible with the rest of the organization. Chaos, rather than coordination, can result. Subordinates may also begin to

expect that they should be involved in all decisions and that any decision the manager makes alone is autocratic and unfair.

In this section, we identify ways in which the positive outcomes of delegation can be cultivated and the potential negative outcomes of poor delegation avoided. Empowerment and delegation must be linked in the accomplishment of work. We will present guidelines for deciding *when* to delegate, *to whom* to delegate, and, finally, *how* to delegate.

DECIDING WHEN TO DELEGATE

Empowered delegating involves deciding, first of all, when to delegate tasks to others and when to perform them oneself. When should subordinates be assigned to design and perform work or make decisions? To determine when delegation is most appropriate, managers should ask five basic questions (Vroom & Yetton, 1973; Vroom & Jago, 1974). Research indicates that when delegation occurs based on these questions, successful results are almost four times more likely than when these questions are not considered. These questions are equally applicable whether assigned work is to be delegated to a team or to a single subordinate.

1. *Do subordinates have the necessary (or superior) information or expertise?* In many cases, subordinates may actually be better qualified than their managers to make decisions and perform tasks because they are more familiar with customer preferences, hidden costs, work processes, and so forth, due to being closer to actual day-to-day operations.

2. *Is the commitment of subordinates critical to successful implementation?* Participation in the decision-making process increases commitment to the final decision. When employees have some latitude in performing a task (i.e., what work they do, and how and when they do it), they generally must be involved in the decision-making process to ensure their cooperation. Whereas participation usually will increase the time required to make a decision, it will substantially decrease the time required to implement it.

3. *Will subordinates' capabilities be expanded by this assignment?* Delegation can quickly get a bad name in a work team if it is viewed as a mechanism used by the boss to get rid of undesirable tasks. Therefore, delegation should be consistent, not just when overloads occur.

It should reflect an overall management philosophy emphasizing employee development. Enhancing the abilities and interests of subordinates should be a central motive in delegating tasks.

4. *Do subordinates share with management and each other common values and perspectives?* If subordinates do not share a similar point of view with one another and with their manager, unacceptable solutions, inappropriate means, and outright errors may be perpetuated. In turn, this produces a need for closer supervision and frequent monitoring. Articulating a clear mission and objective for subordinates is crucial. In particular, managers must be clear about why the work is to be done. Coonradt (1985) found that important people are always told why, but less important people are merely told what, how, or when. Telling subordinates why the work is meaningful creates a common perspective.

5. *Is there sufficient time to do an effective job of delegating?* It takes time to save time. To avoid misunderstanding, managers must spend sufficient time explaining the task and discussing acceptable procedures and options. Time must be available for adequate training, for questions and answers, and for opportunities to check on progress.

Empowered delegation depends on a positive answer to each of the preceding questions. If any of these conditions is not present when delegation is being considered, the probability is greater that it will not be effective. More time will be required, lower quality will result, more frustration will be experienced, and less empowerment will occur. However, a negative answer to any of the preceding questions does not necessarily mean that effective delegation is forever precluded because managers can change situations so that subordinates get more information, develop common perspectives, have adequate time to receive delegation, and so forth.

DECIDING TO WHOM TO DELEGATE

Having decided to delegate a task, managers must then consider whether to involve only a single individual or a team of subordinates. If the decision is made to form a team, it is also important to decide how much authority to give the members of the team. For example, managers should determine if the team will only investigate the problem and explore alternatives or if it will make the final decision. Managers must also outline whether or not they will participate in the team's deliberations. Figure 8.2 presents a model for helping managers decide who should receive delegated tasks—individuals or teams—and whether the manager should be an active participant in a team if it is formed.

Figure 8.2 is constructed as a "tree diagram" that allows a manager to ask questions and, as a result of the answer to each question, move along a path until a final alternative is selected (Huber, 1980; Vroom & Jago, 1974). Here is how it works:

If you were a manager determining whether to involve others in accomplishing a task or making a decision, you should look over the considerations below the question, "Should I involve others in the task or the decision?" If you decide that subordinates do not possess relevant information or skills, that their acceptance is not important, that no personal development can occur for members of the team, that time is tight, or that conflicts will arise among subordinates, you should answer "no" to this question. The tree then prescribes that you perform the task or make the decision yourself. However, if you answer "yes" to this question, you then move on to the next question: "Should I direct my subordinates to form a team?" Look over the five considerations below that question and then continue through the model. Any of the considerations below a question can result in a "no" answer. The most participative and empowering alternative is to delegate work to a team and then participate as an equal member of the team. The least empowering response, of course, is to do the work yourself.

DECIDING HOW TO DELEGATE EFFECTIVELY

When a decision has been made to delegate a task, and the appropriate recipients of the delegation have been identified, empowered delegation has just begun. Positive outcomes of empowered delegation are contingent upon managers following 10 proven principles throughout the process.

1. *Begin with the end in mind.* Managers must articulate clearly the desired results intended from the delegated task. Being clear about what is to be accomplished and why it is important is a necessary prerequisite for empowered delegation. In fact, unless people know why a task is important and what is to be achieved by performing it, they are unlikely to

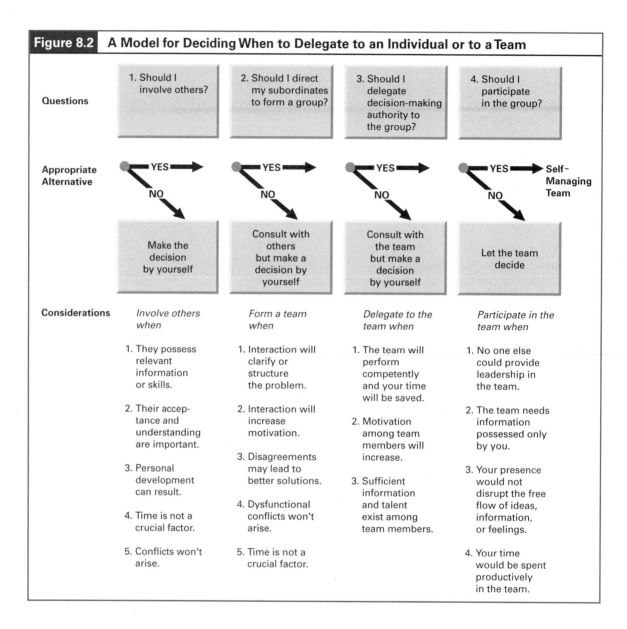

Figure 8.2   A Model for Deciding When to Delegate to an Individual or to a Team

Questions	1. Should I involve others?	2. Should I direct my subordinates to form a group?	3. Should I delegate decision-making authority to the group?	4. Should I participate in the group?
Appropriate Alternative	YES → / NO ↓	YES → / NO ↓	YES → / NO ↓	YES → Self-Managing Team / NO ↓
	Make the decision by yourself	Consult with others but make a decision by yourself	Consult with the team but make a decision by yourself	Let the team decide
Considerations	*Involve others when*	*Form a team when*	*Delegate to the team when*	*Participate in the team when*
	1. They possess relevant information or skills.	1. Interaction will clarify or structure the problem.	1. The team will perform competently and your time will be saved.	1. No one else could provide leadership in the team.
	2. Their acceptance and understanding are important.	2. Interaction will increase motivation.	2. Motivation among team members will increase.	2. The team needs information possessed only by you.
	3. Personal development can result.	3. Disagreements may lead to better solutions.	3. Sufficient information and talent exist among team members.	3. Your presence would not disrupt the free flow of ideas, information, or feelings.
	4. Time is not a crucial factor.	4. Dysfunctional conflicts won't arise.		4. Your time would be spent productively in the team.
	5. Conflicts won't arise.	5. Time is not a crucial factor.		

act at all. No voluntary action ever persists unless these two elements are present. We don't stick with work, school, assignments, or other activities unless we have an idea of the purposes and intended outcomes involved. At a minimum, recipients of delegation will infer or fabricate a purpose or desired outcome, or the task will not be performed at all. To ensure that the ends desired by a manager are likewise perceived as desirable by others, the manager should point out the personal benefits to be achieved, the connection of task accomplishment to the organization's mission, or the important values represented by the task (e.g., service, learning, growth).

2. *Delegate completely.* In addition to the desired ends, managers must clearly specify the constraints under which the tasks will be performed. Every organization has rules and procedures, resource constraints, or boundaries that limit the kind of action that can be taken. These should be clarified when the task is delegated. In particular, managers must be clear about deadlines and the time frame for reporting back. When should the task be completed, who should receive the report, and to whom is accountability being assigned? No empowerment can occur without employees knowing what these boundaries are. Managers also must specify precisely the level of initiative

expected. No other oversight in the delegation process causes more confusion than the failure to delineate expectations regarding the level of initiative expected or permitted. At least five levels of initiative are possible, each of which may vary in terms of the amount of empowerment available to subordinates. These initiative levels differ in terms of the amount of control permitted over the timing and content of the delegated task. The five alternatives are:

❑ *Wait to be told what to do.* Take action only after specific directions are given. This is the least empowering form of delegation because it permits no initiative on the part of the subordinate. There is no control over timing, that is, when the task is to be accomplished, or content, that is, what is to be done.

❑ *Ask what to do.* Some discretion is provided to subordinates in that they have some control over the timing of the task, but not its content. Subordinates may formulate ideas for approaching the task, but because no action can be taken until the manager gives approval, empowerment is highly constrained.

❑ *Recommend, then take action.* This alternative is more empowering because subordinates are given some freedom over both the timing and the content of the delegated task. However, at least three different types of recommendations are possible, each with a different level of empowerment. One is for subordinates to simply gather information, present it to the manager, and let him or her decide what needs to be done. Another is for subordinates to determine alternative courses of action for each part of the task, leaving the manager to choose which course will be followed. Still another possibility is to outline a course of action for accomplishing the entire task and have the whole package approved at once. Progressively more empowerment is associated with each of these three recommendation types.

❑ *Act, then report results immediately.* Subordinates are given the freedom to act on their own initiative, but they are required to report to the manager immediately upon completion to ensure that their actions are correct and compatible with other organizational work. Subordinates may be permitted to perform only one part of a task at a time, reporting the results of each individual step. Or, they may be given the discretion to perform the entire task, reporting only when the final result has been accomplished. The latter alternative, of course, is the most empowering. But it may not be possible unless subordinates possess the necessary ability, information, experience, or maturity.

❑ *Initiate action, and report only routinely.* Subordinates receive complete control over timing and over content of the tasks assigned. Reporting occurs only in a routine fashion to maintain coordination. With sufficient ability, information, experience, and maturity among subordinates, this level of initiative is not only the most empowering but also the likeliest to produce high satisfaction and motivation among subordinates (Hackman & Oldham, 1980).

The important point for managers to remember is that they must be very clear about which of these levels of initiative they expect of their subordinates.

3. *Allow participation in the delegation of assignments.* Subordinates are more likely to accept delegated tasks willingly, perform them competently, and experience empowerment when they help decide what tasks are to be delegated to them and when. Often, managers cannot give subordinates complete choice about such matters, but providing opportunities to decide when tasks will be completed, how accountability will be determined, when work will begin, or what methods and resources will be used in task accomplishment increases employees' empowerment. Such participation should not be manipulative; that is, opportunities for participation should not be provided merely to convince subordinates of decisions already made. Rather, managers should promote participation when task requirements allow it and when acceptance and personal development can result.

Bernard (1938) formulated an "acceptance theory of authority" in which he proposed that people will accept and fulfill assignments only if four conditions are met. First, subordinates must *understand* what they are being asked to do. Second, subordinates must perceive that the assignment is *consistent* with the purpose of the organization. Third, subordinates must believe that the assignment is *compatible* with their own interests. Fourth, subordinates must be *able* to perform the assignment.

Bernard's theory underscores the importance of two-way communication during the delegation process. Not only should subordinates be encouraged to ask questions and seek information regarding delegated assignments, but they should also feel free to express ideas about the parameters of the work to be delegated. Expecting subordinates to seek answers to questions or providing guidance on every aspect of the delegated assignment can perpetuate overdependence if the manager answers every detailed question or provides continual advice. On the other hand, managers who remain available for consultation and idea interchange, foster two-way communication, and encourage a climate of openness and sharing make the delegation process empowering.

4. *Establish parity between authority and responsibility.* The oldest and most general rule of thumb in delegation is to match the amount of responsibility given with the amount of authority provided. Commonly, managers assign responsibility for work to subordinates without furnishing a corresponding amount of discretion to make decisions and authority to implement those decisions. If subordinates are to be successful, they must have as much authority as they need to accomplish the tasks assigned to them. An important part of developing a sense of self-determination and a sense of personal control—both critical dimensions of empowerment—is ensuring this match. Of course, managers also must take care not to delegate more authority than responsibility, thereby giving subordinates more authority, discretion, resources, or information than they can use. Such a mismatch leads to lack of accountability, potential abuses of power, and confusion on the part of subordinates. For example, without the necessary responsibility, providing a child with a loaded gun, or a $50 bill in a candy shop, could result in actions that would not lead to desirable outcomes.

Although managers cannot delegate *ultimate* accountability for delegated tasks, they can delegate *prime* accountability. This means that "the buck stops," eventually, at the manager's desk. Final blame for failure cannot be given away. This is ultimate accountability. On the other hand, managers can delegate prime accountability, which means that subordinates can be given responsibility for producing desired short-term results. Their accountability is to the manager who delegated to them. Giving subordinates prime accountability is an important part of empowered delegation.

5. *Work within the organizational structure.* Another general rule of empowered delegation is to delegate to the lowest organizational level at which a job can be done. The people who are closest to the actual work being performed or the decision being made should be involved. They are usually the ones with the largest, most accurate fund of information. By definition, this increases efficiency (lower labor and information collection costs), and it frequently increases effectiveness (better understanding of problems). Whereas managers have a broader overall view of problems, the detailed knowledge needed to accomplish many tasks is most likely to reside with those who are lower in the organizational hierarchy.

In delegating a task down more than one level in an organization, it is important that the organizational chain of command be followed. In other words, delegation must occur *through* subordinates, not *around* them. If a senior manager circumvents the formal hierarchy, bypassing a manager to communicate directly with that manager's subordinate, the manager becomes unempowered. The subordinate now becomes accountable to the senior manager, not the manager with direct responsibility for the subordinate. The entire accountability system is thus destroyed. Following the chain of command by involving those at affected levels of the hierarchy in delegation is important for empowered delegation.

All individuals affected by a decision must be informed that it has been delegated. This applies to cross-functional coordination as well as hierarchical coordination. If a subordinate has been delegated responsibility, others who may have needed information, who may influence the results, or who may implement the recommendations must be notified of the delegation. If delegation occurs but no one knows about it, authority is essentially nullified.

6. *Provide adequate support for delegated tasks.* When authority is delegated to subordinates, managers must provide as much support to them as possible. As discussed earlier, this

involves making public announcements and presenting clearly stated expectations. It also means continuously providing relevant information and resources to help subordinates accomplish tasks. Reports, recent news clippings, customer data, articles, and even random thoughts that pertain to the delegated task should be passed on as they become available. This support not only aids task accomplishment but also communicates interest and concern for subordinates. Managers should help subordinates learn where to acquire needed resources, since the manager alone cannot be the sole source of all the support that subordinates will need.

Agreeing on the limits of resource use is also important. Since unlimited access to resources is never possible, managers must be clear about the limit beyond which no further resources can be used. Formulating a budget or establishing a set of specifications is a common way to specify limits.

Another form of support that managers can provide is to bestow credit—but not blame—publicly. Even though prime accountability has been delegated, pointing out mistakes or faults in front of others embarrasses workers, creates defensiveness, fosters the impression that the manager is trying to pass the buck and get rid of final accountability, and guarantees that workers will be less willing to initiate action on their own in the future. Correcting mistakes, critiquing work, and providing negative feedback on task performance of subordinates should be done in private, where the probability of problem solving and training can be enhanced.

7. *Focus accountability on results.* Once tasks are delegated and authority is provided, managers generally should avoid closely monitoring the way in which subordinates accomplish tasks. Excessive supervision of methods destroys the five dimensions of empowerment: self-efficacy, self-determination, personal control, meaningfulness, and trust. Successful accomplishment of a task, after all, rather than use of the manager's preferred procedures, is the primary goal of delegation. To be sure, harmful or unethical means for accomplishing tasks cannot be tolerated, nor can methods be used that obstruct other employees or subvert organizational rules. For the most part, though, managers should focus primarily on results achieved by subordinates, rather than on the techniques used to achieve those results.

In order for accountability to be maintained, there must be agreement on acceptable levels of performance. Managers must clearly specify what level of performance is expected, what constitutes unacceptable performance, and what requirements are associated with the result. Without such specifications, it becomes difficult for managers not to worry about means as well as ends. By allowing subordinates to exercise initiative regarding how to tackle a task, their sense of empowerment is enhanced, and innovation and originality are more likely as well.

8. *Delegate consistently.* The time for managers to delegate is before they have to. Sometimes, when managers have time to do work themselves, they do just that, even though that work could and should be delegated. Two problems result. First, delegation becomes simply a method for relieving the manager's workload and stress. A primary reason for delegation—empowering subordinates—is forgotten. Employees begin to feel that they are merely "pressure valves" for managers rather than valued team members. Secondly, when delegation occurs only under pressure, there is no time for training, providing needed information, or engaging in two-way discussions. Clarity of task assignments may be impaired. Workers' mistakes and failures increase, and managers are tempted to perform tasks alone, in order to ensure quality. When managers delay delegating until they are overloaded, they create pressure on themselves to perform delegatable tasks personally, thereby increasing their own overload.

Another key to consistent delegation is for managers to delegate both pleasant and unpleasant tasks. Sometimes managers keep for themselves the tasks they like to perform and pass less-desirable work along to subordinates. It is easy to see the detrimental consequences this has on morale, motivation, and performance. When individuals feel that they are being used only to perform "dirty work," follow-through on delegated tasks is less likely. On the other hand, managers must not be afraid to share difficult or unpleasant tasks with subordinates. Playing the role of martyr by refusing to involve others in disagreeable tasks or drudgery creates unrealistic expectations for employees and isolates managers. Consistency of delegation, then, means that managers delegate tasks continuously, not just when overworked, and that they delegate both pleasant and unpleasant tasks.

9. *Avoid upward delegation.* Although it is crucial for subordinates to participate in the delegation process in order to become empowered, managers must conscientiously resist all so-called upward delegation, in which subordinates seek to shift responsibility for delegated tasks back onto the shoulders of the superior who did the initial delegating. Managers who fail to forestall upward delegation will find their time being tied up doing subordinates' work rather than their own.

Suppose a worker comes to a manager after delegation has occurred and says, "We have a problem. This assignment just isn't turning out very well. What do you suggest I do?" If the manager replies, "Gee, I'm not sure. Let me think about it, and I'll get back to you," the original delegated task has now been shifted from the employee back to the manager. Note that the manager has promised to report to the employee, that is, to maintain prime accountability, and the employee is now in a position to follow up on the manager's commitment, that is, supervising the manager. Thus, the subordinate has become the manager, and the manager the subordinate. Managers, in the hope of being helpful to, and supportive of their subordinates, often get caught in the trap of upward delegation.

One way to avoid upward delegation is to insist that workers always take the initiative for developing their own solutions. Instead of promising the subordinate a report on the manager's deliberations, a more appropriate response would have been, "What do you recommend?" "What alternatives do you think we should consider?" "What have you done so far?" "What do you think would be a good first step?" Rather than sharing problems and asking for advice, subordinates should be required to share *proposed solutions* or to ask permission to implement them. Managers should refuse to solve delegated tasks. That is why specifying the expected level of initiative (see Rule 2) is so important. Not only does this avoid upward delegation, but it also helps

managers train employees to become competent problem solvers and to avoid working on tasks for which someone else has prime accountability. Yielding to upward delegation does not empower subordinates but, rather, makes them more dependent.

10. *Clarify consequences.* Subordinates should be made aware of the consequences of the tasks being delegated to them. They are more likely to accept delegation and be motivated to take initiative if it is clear what the rewards for success will be, what the opportunities might be, what the impact on the ultimate customer or the organization's mission may be, and so on. In particular, managers should help employees understand the connection between successful performance and financial rewards, opportunities for advancement, learning and developmental opportunities, informal recognition, and so forth. Most specific delegated assignments do not result in a direct payoff from the formal reward system, of course. But associating some desirable consequence—as minor as a pat on the back or a congratulatory mention in a staff meeting or as major as a financial bonus or incentive—enhances successful delegation.

Clarifying consequences also can help ensure an understanding that delegation not only implies task accomplishment, but enhancement of interpersonal relationships as well. Relationships with others in the organization, on the team, or with the manager individually should be strengthened as a result of task accomplishment. Accomplishing assignments in the course of damaging or destroying relationships creates more long-term costs than any organization can bear. Therefore, a desirable consequence of any delegation experience is the enhancement of interpersonal relationships and a strengthening of the organization.

REVIEW OF DELEGATION PRINCIPLES

The 10 principles summarizing *how* to delegate, preceded by the five criteria for determining *when* to delegate, and the four questions for identifying *to whom* to delegate, provide guidelines for ensuring not only that subordinates will experience a sense of empowerment but that other positive consequences will result as well. In particular, research results clearly show that empowered delegation leads to the following consequences:

- Delegated tasks are readily accepted by subordinates.
- Delegated tasks are successfully completed.
- Morale and motivation remain high.
- Workers' problem-solving abilities are increased.
- Managers have more discretionary time.
- Interpersonal relationships are strengthened.
- Organizational coordination and efficiency are enhanced.

Figure 8.3 summarizes the relationships among these principles.

International Caveats

Empowerment and empowered delegation are sometimes misinterpreted as a soft approach to management, an abrogation of responsibility by leaders, an invitation to the inmates to run the asylum, and a prescription for chaos. Strong leadership, visionary managers, and take-charge bosses are usually the ones we read about in the newspapers and business magazines. A great deal of attention is given to people who "take command of the situation" and "stay out front of the troops." With such a definition, empowerment is not a popular alternative in many cultures where, for example, an emphasis on *universalism, individualism, specificity,* and *ascription* are dominant. (Recall from Chapter 1 that the Trompenaars [1996, 1998] model differentiates cultures on the basis of seven dimensions: *universalism* versus *particularism, individualism* versus *communitarianism, neutrality* versus *affectivity, specificity* versus *diffuseness, achievement* versus *ascription, internal* versus *external* control, and *past, present,* or *future* time orientation.)

Empowerment is sometimes viewed as contrary to some of these values in that maintaining consistency with rules and procedures (universalism) rather than encouraging experimentation and team innovation may

LEARNING

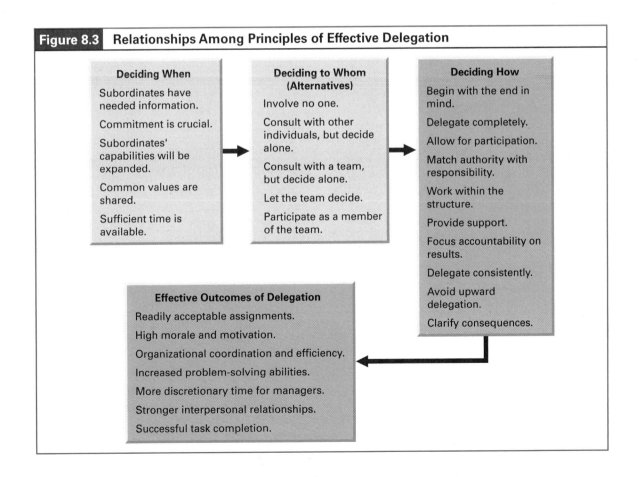

Figure 8.3 Relationships Among Principles of Effective Delegation

Deciding When
Subordinates have needed information.
Commitment is crucial.
Subordinates' capabilities will be expanded.
Common values are shared.
Sufficient time is available.

Deciding to Whom (Alternatives)
Involve no one.
Consult with other individuals, but decide alone.
Consult with a team, but decide alone.
Let the team decide.
Participate as a member of the team.

Deciding How
Begin with the end in mind.
Delegate completely.
Allow for participation.
Match authority with responsibility.
Work within the structure.
Provide support.
Focus accountability on results.
Delegate consistently.
Avoid upward delegation.
Clarify consequences.

Effective Outcomes of Delegation
Readily acceptable assignments.
High morale and motivation.
Organizational coordination and efficiency.
Increased problem-solving abilities.
More discretionary time for managers.
Stronger interpersonal relationships.
Successful task completion.

seem to make empowerment less desirable. Focusing on individual performance (individualism) rather than team or collective effort may be viewed as contrary to empowerment. Involving only a limited amount of the self in the work setting or task assignment (specificity) rather than engaging multiple roles and in-depth relationships with individuals with whom one is working also may be interpreted as inconsistent with empowerment and empowered delegation. A focus on ascribed status, title, and traditional position (ascription) rather than a blurring of hierarchical lines and focusing on merit or contribution also appears to contradict the aims of empowerment. Hence, empowerment may seem to be a concept that is more acceptable in cultures with a strong orientation toward particularism, collectivity, diffuseness, and achievement orientation.

On the other hand, the principles of empowerment and empowered delegation that we have discussed in this chapter are applicable across most, if not all, cultures. It is a misconception to believe that these principles do not work effectively in Eastern cultures as well as Western cultures, in Western Europe as well as South America, in Africa as well as the Polynesian Islands. Principles of empowerment are relevant to old and young, male and female, foreign and domestic. This is because the five principles of empowerment are connected to fundamental human needs that transcend national or ethnic cultures. Virtually everyone has needs for, and performs better when they are exposed to, an environment in which they: (1) feel capable, confident, and competent, (2) experience freedom, discretion, and choice, (3) believe they can make a difference, have an impact, and achieve a desired result, (4) sense meaning, value, and a higher purpose in their activities, and (5) trust that they will not be harmed or abused, but honored and respected. In other words, the keys to effective empowerment are also keys to effective human performance at a very fundamental level. Strong leaders are not lone rangers so much as they are savvy individuals who know how to mobilize those they lead and manage. Therefore, whereas individual differences must certainly be taken into account, and the pace at which empowerment and empowered delegation can be fully implemented may vary with the circumstances, these principles of empowerment are essential to effective managerial performance.

Summary

Empowerment means helping to develop in others a sense of self-efficacy, self-determinism, personal control, meaning, and trust. The current business environment is not particularly compatible with the principles of managerial empowerment. Because of the turbulent, complex, competitive circumstances that many organizations face, managers frequently experience a tendency to be less, rather than more, empowering. When managers feel threatened, they become rigid and seek more control over other people, not less. However, without empowered employees, organizations cannot succeed in the long run. Learning how to be a competent empowering manager is therefore a critical skill for individuals who probably will face a predilection not to practice empowerment.

Nine prescriptions that managers can use to empower others were discussed. We also offered a series of principles and criteria for ensuring empowered delegation, which results in better acceptance of delegated tasks by subordinates, enhanced motivation and morale, improved coordination and efficiency, better development of subordinates, increased discretionary time, strengthened relationships, and successful task performance. Producing a sense of empowerment in others and delegating in a way that empowers subordinates also brings desirable outcomes for organizations as well as employees. Empowered employees are more productive, psychologically and physically healthy, proactive and innovative, persistent in work, trustworthy, interpersonally effective, intrinsically motivated, and have higher morale and commitment than employees who are not empowered. Figure 8.4 illustrates the relationships among the various elements of empowerment and delegation.

Behavioral Guidelines

As you practice empowering others and carry out empowered delegating, you will want to use the following guidelines as cues. *To ensure empowerment in others, follow these guidelines*

1. Foster self-efficacy or a sense of competence by fostering personal mastery experiences and pointing out successful role models.
2. Foster self-determination or a sense of personal choice by providing alternatives and information to people.
3. Foster personal consequence or a sense of personal impact by allowing people to see the effects of their work on end users or on those affected by the results.
4. Foster meaningfulness or a sense of value by clarifying vision and values and connecting to something of inherent value.

Figure 8.4

Figure 8.4 | **Relationships Among the Elements of Empowerment and Empowered Delegation**

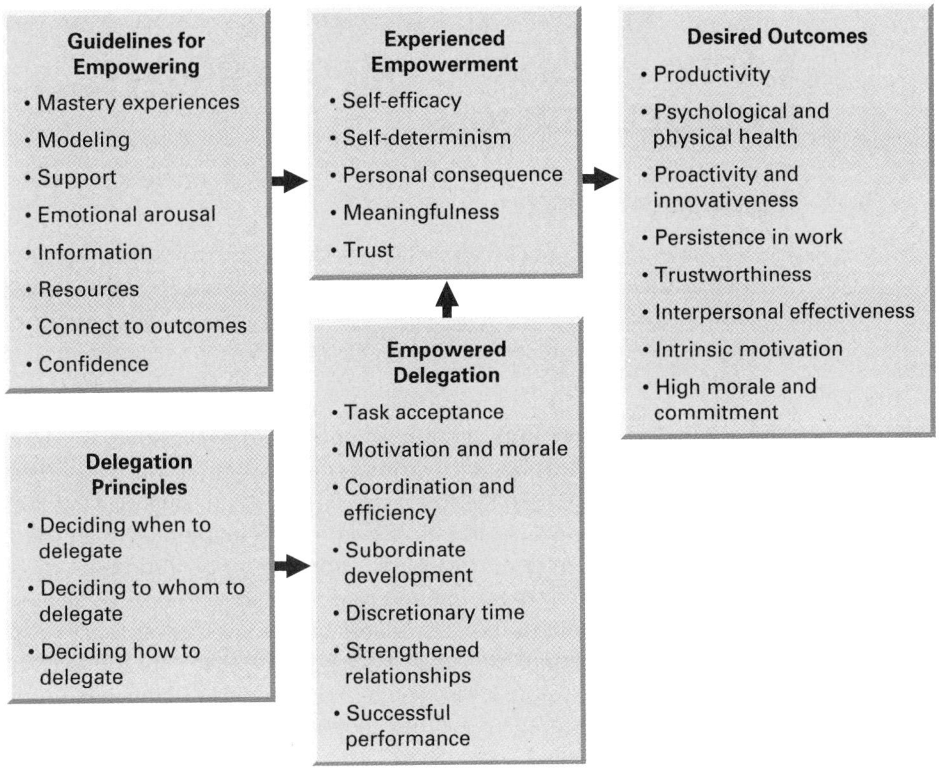

Guidelines for Empowering
- Mastery experiences
- Modeling
- Support
- Emotional arousal
- Information
- Resources
- Connect to outcomes
- Confidence

Experienced Empowerment
- Self-efficacy
- Self-determinism
- Personal consequence
- Meaningfulness
- Trust

Desired Outcomes
- Productivity
- Psychological and physical health
- Proactivity and innovativeness
- Persistence in work
- Trustworthiness
- Interpersonal effectiveness
- Intrinsic motivation
- High morale and commitment

Delegation Principles
- Deciding when to delegate
- Deciding to whom to delegate
- Deciding how to delegate

Empowered Delegation
- Task acceptance
- Motivation and morale
- Coordination and efficiency
- Subordinate development
- Discretionary time
- Strengthened relationships
- Successful performance

LEARNING

5. Foster trust or a sense of security by providing support and creating confidence, primarily by being consistent, honest, open, and fair.

6. Delegate work effectively by using the guidelines provided in the chapter to determine to whom the work should be delegated and when it should be delegated.

CASES INVOLVING EMPOWERMENT AND DELEGATION

Minding the Store

On January 1, Ruth Cummings was formally named branch manager for the Saks Fifth Avenue store in a suburb of Denver. Her boss, Ken Hoffman, gave her this assignment on her first day: "Ruth, I'm putting you in charge of this store. Your job will be to run it so that it becomes one of the best stores in the system. I have a lot of confidence in you, so don't let me down."

One of the first things Ruth did was to hire an administrative assistant to handle inventories. Because this was such an important part of the job, she agreed to pay her assistant slightly more than the top retail clerks were making. She felt that having an administrative assistant would free her to handle marketing, sales, and personnel matters—areas she felt were crucial if the store was to be a success.

Within the week, however, she received a call from Hoffman: "Say, Ruth, I heard that you hired an administrative assistant to handle inventories. Don't you think that is a bit risky? Besides, I think paying an assistant more than your top sales clerk is damaging to morale in the store. I wish you had cleared this with me before you made the move. It sets a bad precedent for the other stores, and it makes me look like I don't know what is going on in the branches."

Three weeks later, Ruth appeared on a local noontime talk show to discuss new trends in fashion. She had worked hard to make contact with the hosts of the show, and she felt that public exposure like this would increase the visibility of her store. Although the TV spot lasted only 10 minutes, she was pleased with her performance and with the chance to get public exposure.

Later that night at home, she received another phone call from Hoffman: "Don't you know the policy of Saks? Any TV appearances made on behalf of the store are to be cleared through the main office. Normally, we like to have representatives from the main store appear on these kinds of shows because they can do a better job of plugging our merchandise. It's too bad that you didn't notify someone of your intentions. This could be very embarrassing for me."

Just before Easter, Ruth was approached in the store by one of the sales clerks. A customer had asked to charge approximately $3,000 worth of china as a gift for his wife. He had been a customer of the store for several years and Ruth had seen him on several occasions, but store rules indicated that no charge could be made for more than $1,000 for any reason. She told the customer that she was not authorized to okay a charge of that amount, but that if he would visit the main store in Denver, maybe arrangements could be made.

Later in the day, an irate Hoffman called again: "What in the world are you thinking about, Ruth? Today we had a customer come into the main store and say that you wouldn't make a sale to him because the charge was too much. Do you know how long he has been a customer of ours? Do you know how much he spends in the store every year? I certainly hope we have not lost him as a customer because of your blunder. This makes me very upset. You've just got to learn to use your head."

Ruth thought about the conversation for several days and finally decided that she needed to see Ken Hoffman. She called his secretary to schedule an appointment for the following day.

Discussion Questions

1. What guidelines related to empowerment were violated by Ken Hoffman? By Ruth Cummings?
2. What guidelines related to delegation were violated by Ken Hoffman? By Ruth Cummings?
3. What should Ruth Cummings and Ken Hoffman discuss in their meeting? Identify specific agenda items that should be raised.
4. What are the questions that Ruth should ask Ken to help her acquire the necessary elements of empowerment? What questions should Ken ask Ruth to be better able to ensure her success?
5. If you were an outside consultant attending the meeting, what advice would you give Ken? What advice would you give Ruth?

Changing the Portfolio

You are head of a staff unit reporting to the vice president of finance. He has asked you to provide a report on the firm's current portfolio, including recommendations for changes in the current selection criteria. Doubts have been raised about the efficiency of the existing system given the current market conditions, and there is considerable dissatisfaction with prevailing rates of return.

You plan to write the report, but at the moment you are perplexed about the approach to take. Your own specialty is the bond market, and it is clear to you that detailed knowledge of the equity market, which you lack, would greatly enhance the value of the report. Fortunately, four members of your staff are specialists in different segments of the equity market. Together, they possess a vast amount of knowledge about the intricacies of investment. However, they seldom agree on the best way to achieve anything when it comes to investment philosophy and strategy.

You have six weeks before the report is due. You have already begun to familiarize yourself with the firm's current portfolio and have been provided by management with a specific set of constraints that any portfolio must satisfy. Your immediate problem is to come up with some alternatives to the firm's present practices and to select the most promising for detailed analysis in your report.

Discussion Questions

1. Should this decision be made by you alone? Why or why not?
2. If you answered the question, "Should I involve others?" affirmatively, which alternative in Figure 8.2 should be used in making a decision? Justify your choice.
3. What are the most important considerations in deciding whom to involve in this task?
4. If others are to become involved, how much empowerment should they have? What would you do specifically to achieve the appropriate level of empowerment?

SKILL *PRACTICE*

EXERCISES FOR EMPOWERMENT

Executive Development Associates

Assume that you are Mary Ann O'Connell, General Manager at Executive Development Associates. Your firm provides outplacement, training and development, career planning, and head-hunting services for a large number of *Fortune* 500 companies. You have been at the corporate board meeting for the last three days in the Rocky Mountains, and you relied on your secretary to screen out all but the most important or urgent messages. You slipped into the office on the way home from the airport Monday evening, just to check your electronic messages and your mail. Aside from a host of phone calls to return, here is the collection of messages that your secretary retrieved from your e-mail file and mail box.

Assignment

1. For each message, outline specifically the plan you will implement to empower others effectively to solve these problems. Determine who should be involved, what level of initiative should be taken, what actions you can take to ensure empowerment, how accountability should be maintained, and so on.

2. Write out the actions you'd take in response to each item. A worksheet has been provided on the next page to remind you of what you should consider as you record your responses.

3. After you have completed your own responses to each item, form a team of fellow students and share your plans. Provide feedback to one another on what is especially good, what could be improved, and what could be added to each person's action plan. In particular, what principles of empowerment are included, which are omitted, and which are contradicted?

Solving Problems Through Empowerment Worksheet

For each message, write out your plan of action. This plan should include answers to the questions listed below. Not every question is relevant to each message, but most are, and they can guide your action plan. After you have formed your own responses, form a team of fellow students and share these plans in turn. Provide feedback to one another on what is especially good, what could be improved, and what could be added to each action plan.

1. Who should be involved in resolving this issue? Will you form a team?

2. What kinds of personal mastery experiences can be provided for whomever you involve? Can you model successful behavior?

3. What kinds of support, information, and resources can be provided?

4. How will you create emotional arousal and create confidence in others?

5. What are the main considerations in deciding if you should delegate each task?

6. If you opt for delegation, what will you do to:

   Begin with the end in mind?
   Delegate completely?
   Allow participation?
   Match authority with responsibility?
   Work within the structure?
   Provide support?
   Maintain accountability?
   Ensure consistency of delegation?
   Avoid upward delegation?
   Clarify consequences?

INTEROFFICE MEMORANDUM

Data Processing Center

DATE: 15 June
TO: Mary Ann O'Connell,
         General Manager
FROM: Roosevelt Monroe,
         for the Data Processing Staff

After looking over last quarter's audit, it is clear that the number of complaints our group is receiving from individuals throughout the company is escalating. The problem is an obvious one to us. It is, simply, that several incompatible software systems have evolved over the last several years in various departments, and it is becoming increasingly difficult to coordinate across units. As you know, some data have to be retyped two or three times into different systems because of these incompatibilities.

The trouble is, our own employees, not to mention our customers, are becoming increasingly impatient with our slow turnaround time. They focus squarely on our group as the bottleneck. We think the rising complaint numbers in the quarterly audit are misleading, however, and they divert us from the real cause of the problem.

We're writing this memo to you to collectively urge you to address this issue as soon as possible. At a minimum, it should be discussed at our upcoming staff meeting on Tuesday. So far, the data processing staff is taking the blame for not getting data processed fast enough, yet it is really the fault of the system, not our unit.

We'll look forward to hearing from you on Tuesday.

INTEROFFICE MEMORANDUM

Human Resources Department

DATE: 15 June
TO: Mary Ann
FROM: Lucy

I was excited by your speech at the senior management meeting last week in which you established a new challenge for all senior executives. With the new competitive environment that we face, the vision that you articulated for our future is both exciting and challenging and, I think, an important step forward. It really makes clear the key success factors that should drive our business.

In particular, I think your directive for all senior executives to disseminate the vision throughout the organization to their own subordinates is a good way to get the message delivered. However, you made a statement in your speech that has me troubled. You said, "We used to pay you on the basis of new accounts generated, quarterly earnings, customer satisfaction ratings, and new product designs. Our new barometer is going to be how you're doing in disseminating the vision throughout your own units."

Frankly, I'm perplexed as to how we'll ever measure this directive. As the one who has to administer the appraisal and compensation systems, I'm not sure what criteria we'll look for or what indicators we'll use to determine success. I'm afraid that we'll create dissatisfaction if we don't have something specific outlined. Our people, especially those who may not perform, will think it is purely arbitrary. Do you really mean to have us change the appraisal and compensation systems to include this new criterion? How do you propose we measure effective performance? What would you like me to do to support your statement? Did you mean to make the statement that you did?

This is rather urgent because I have a staff meeting Tuesday afternoon, and I promised to have a response by then. I've already stalled until I had a chance to talk to you.

COPY OF A LETTER

Midwest State University

24 May

Dear Ms. O'Connell:

I am happy to be joining Executive Development Associates after several years at Midwest State University. As you know, leaving Midwest State has been quite traumatic for me, and that is what motivated me to make a request of you. I'm convinced that the reason I didn't receive tenure at Midwest State is because the expectations were never clear about what my responsibilities were and what the criteria were for success.

I know your company is very professional and employees are pretty much on their own, but I'm feeling a need to get some specific performance requirements outlined for me. I'm sure that I can be a good addition to your company, but I want to be clear about what your expectations are.

I have set a meeting with you on Tuesday through your secretary. Would you please outline a specific set of responsibilities and expectations for my job as instructor in the training and development department? If possible, I'd like it in writing to avoid any misunderstanding. Regardless, I'll look forward to talking to you Tuesday.

Thank you for your consideration.

Sincerely,

Lester Frost

INTEROFFICE MEMORANDUM

Training and Development

DATE: Monday, A.M.
TO: Mary Ann
FROM: Pam
RE: Tom Kinnir's Jury Duty

I know you're just getting back, but we've got an emergency on our hands.

I was just notified this morning by Tom that he has been selected for jury duty and that (can you believe it) he is being sequestered! Holy cow, Mary Ann, this couldn't come at a worse time. As our expert on activity-based costing, Tom is the only guy we have who can teach the topic. So what's the trouble, you say? The trouble is that we have over 100 corporate trainers showing up here for a seminar on Friday, and the seminar isn't prepared yet. Tom said that he has some notes and a few transparencies on his desk, but he had planned to spend this entire week designing and preparing it. Not only don't any of us know the topic very well, but we're not even sure what information we need, what data still needs to be gathered, who's got what, and how we go about filling in. Help! We're counting on this seminar to make budget this quarter, and we're feeling a little ticked off at Tom for waiting until the last minute. What do we do next?

By the way, how were the Rocky Mountains???

INTEROFFICE MEMORANDUM

Outplacement Department

DATE: Monday, A.M.
TO: Mary Ann O'Connell
FROM: Aneil Mishra
RE: Pending Plant Closure

You may have missed the news over the weekend. It was announced in the paper that Detroit Manufacturing has filed for Chapter 11 protection and that they're closing their Toledo plant. That means about 4,000 people will be out of work.

If we want the business, we've got to get moving right away. They will be looking at proposals from outplacement firms next week. We've got to get our proposal together, identify staff, determine a budget, and prepare a presentation in the next day or two.

Sound's like a great opportunity. I'll stop by tomorrow when you get back.

Empowering Ourselves

In this exercise, your task is to identify ways in which the empowerment of members of the graduating students this year in your own institution can be enhanced. You should use the principles of empowerment in the chapter to identify specific ways in which the empowerment of this group of people can be increased. What can be done, practically speaking, to effect empowerment?

Make certain that you don't merely identify what others could do, what the administration could implement, or what hypothetically could occur. Rather, identify very practical and realistic factors that could empower this graduating class. What could they do as a group? What could you do? What personal responsibility could they take for their own empowerment?

Do not treat this exercise as hypothetical or fantasy. Actually identify behaviors that you can implement that will enhance empowerment. Use the suggestions in the text as well as others that you add to those lists.

	Things That Can Be Done to Enhance the Empowerment of the Graduating Class
Self-Efficacy (personal competence)	
Self-Determination (personal choice)	
Personal Consequence (personal impact)	
Meaningfulness (personal value)	
Trust (personal security)	

Now form a team with three or four colleagues. Share your ideas with the group. For each dimension of empowerment, identify the most powerful ideas you hear from the team members. Add at least one new idea to your list. Also, identify when and how you'll actually implement your list. Use your team to help specify actual behaviors that you can implement.

Deciding to Delegate

Delegation is one of the most deceiving management skills because it seems so easy to accomplish. Just tell someone what to do, and they'll do it, right? Unfortunately, highly competent delegators are rare, and this exercise is designed to help you determine when and how to delegate more effectively. To accomplish this exercise you'll need to use the framework in Figure 8.2.

For each of the two scenarios that follow, ask the following questions:

❏ *Should I involve others or make the decision by myself?*
❏ *If I involve others, should I direct them to form a team, or should I consult them individually and make the decision by myself?*
❏ *If I form a team, should I delegate decision-making authority to the team, or should I consult with the team but make the decision by myself?*
❏ *If I delegate to the team, should I participate in the team, or should I let the team decide?*

After you have made a decision about how to handle each of these two scenarios, form a team of colleagues. Share your decision and your rationale with the team. Reach a consensus regarding the most appropriate strategy to use in each of these two cases. For

PRACTICE ◆

comparison purposes, an analysis by experts for the Emergency Request case is contained at the end of the chapter. It is provided only to enhance your team discussion. No comparative analysis is provided for the Biological Warfare case.

An Emergency Request

You are a general plant supervisor and seven product lines involving four of your eight foremen must be disrupted to satisfy an emergency request from an important client. You naturally wish to minimize the disruption. No additional personnel are available, and time limits to complete the new project are restrictive. The plant is new and is the only industrial plant in an economically depressed area dominated by farming. You can count on everyone pulling his or her own weight. The wages in the plant are substantially above farm wages, and the workers' jobs depend on the profitability of this plant—the first new industrial development in the area in 15 years. Your subordinates are relatively inexperienced, and you have been supervising them more closely than you might if the plant had been in a well-established industrial area and your subordinates were more experienced. The changes involve only standard procedures and are routine for someone of your experience. Effective supervision poses no problems. Your problem is how to reschedule the work to meet this emergency within the time limit with minimum disruption of the existing product lines. Your experience in such matters should enable you to figure out a way of meeting the request that will minimize the disruption of existing product lines.

Biological Warfare

You are the executive vice president of a small pharmaceutical manufacturer. You have the opportunity to bid on a contract for the Defense Department pertaining to biological warfare. The contract is outside the mainstream of your business; however, it could make economic sense, since you do have unused capacity in one of your plants, and the manufacturing processes are not dissimilar. You have written the document to accompany the bid and now have the problem of determining the dollar value of the quotation you think will win the job for your company. If the bid is too high, you will undoubtedly lose to one of your competitors. If it is too low, you could lose money on the program. There are many factors to consider in making this decision, including the cost of the new raw materials and the additional administrative burden of relationships with a new client, not to speak of factors that are likely to influence the bids of your competitors, such as how much they need this particular contract. You have been busy assembling the necessary data to make this decision, but there remain several unknowns, one of which involves the manager of the plant in which the new products will be manufactured. Of all your subordinates, only he can estimate the costs of adapting the present equipment to its new purpose, and his cooperation and support will be necessary if the specifications of the contract are to be met. However, in an initial discussion with him when you first learned of the possibility of the contract, he seemed adamantly opposed to the idea. His experience has not particularly equipped him to evaluate projects like this one, so you were not overly influenced by his opinions. From the nature of his arguments, you inferred that his opposition was ideological rather than economic. You recall that he was once involved in a local peace organization and was one of the most vocal opponents in the company to the Vietnam and the Persian Gulf Wars.

ACTIVITIES FOR EMPOWERMENT
AND DELEGATION

Suggested Assignments

1. Teach someone else (your spouse, a colleague, your boss) how to empower others and delegate effectively. Include the principles in Table 8.5 in your discussion. Use your own examples and illustrations.

2. Interview a manager about his or her empowerment practices. Try to determine what is especially effective, what doesn't work, what comes off as condescending, and what motivates people to perform. Identify the extent to which the manager knows and uses the principles discussed in the Skill Learning section of this chapter.

3. Think of a situation you now face with which you would like some help. It may be a task you want to accomplish, a tough decision you need to make, or a team you want to form. Make sure you think of something that requires the involvement of other people. Write down specific things you can do to empower other people to help you. How can you help them do what they want to do, while simultaneously having them do what you want them to do?

4. Schedule a meeting with a manager who is not very good at empowerment. (Finding such a person shouldn't be difficult, because most leaders tend to be more authoritarian and bureaucratic than empowering.) As a student who has learned about and practiced empowerment and delegation, share what you have learned and offer suggestions that could help this manager improve.

Application Plan and Evaluation

The intent of this exercise is to help you apply this cluster of skills in a real-life, out-of-class setting. Now that you have become familiar with the behavioral guidelines that form the basis of effective skill performance, you will improve most by trying out those guidelines in an everyday context. Unlike a classroom activity, in which feedback is immediate and others can assist you with their evaluations, this skill application activity is one you must accomplish and evaluate on your own. There are two parts to this activity. Part 1 helps prepare you to apply the skill. Part 2 helps you evaluate and improve on your experience. Be sure to write down answers to each item. Don't short-circuit the process by skipping steps.

Part 1. Planning

1. Write down the two or three aspects of this skill that are most important to you. These may be areas of weakness, areas you most want to improve, or areas that are most salient to a problem you face right now. Identify the specific aspects of this skill that you want to apply.

2. Now identify the setting or the situation in which you will apply this skill. Establish a plan for performance by actually writing down a description of the situation. Who else will be involved? When will you do it? Where will it be done?

   Circumstances:
   Who else?
   When?
   Where?

3. Identify the specific behaviors in which you will engage to apply this skill. Operationalize your skill performance.

4. What are the indicators of successful performance? How will you know you have been effective? What will indicate you have performed competently?

Part 2. Evaluation

5. After you have completed your implementation, record the results. What happened? How successful were you? What was the effect on others?

6. How can you improve? What modifications can you make next time? What will you do differently in a similar situation in the future?

7. Looking back on your whole skill practice and application experience, what have you learned? What has been surprising? In what ways might this experience help you in the long term?

Effective Empowerment and Delegation

Scoring Key

Skill Area	Items	Assessment	
		Pre-	Post-
Personal mastery experiences	1, 2	_____	_____
Modeling	3, 4	_____	_____
Providing support	5, 6	_____	_____
Arousing positive emotions	7, 8	_____	_____
Providing information	9, 10	_____	_____
Providing resources	11, 12	_____	_____
Organizing teams	13, 14	_____	_____
Creating confidence	15, 16	_____	_____
Delegating work	17–26	_____	_____
Total Score		_____	_____

Comparison Data (N = 5,000 Students)

Compare your scores to three standards:
1. The maximum possible score = 156.
2. The scores of other students in the class.
3. Norm data from more than 5,000 business school students.

Pre-Test				Post-Test
129.54	=	mean	=	138.03
139 or above	=	top quartile	=	149 or above
130–138	=	second quartile	=	140–148
121–129	=	third quartile	=	129–139
120 or below	=	bottom quartile	=	128 or below

Personal Empowerment

Scoring Key

Skill Area	Items	Mean (Total ÷ 4)
Self-efficacy (competence)	2, 7, 12, 17	_____
Self-determination (choice)	3, 8, 13, 18	_____
Personal consequence (impact)	4, 9, 14, 19	_____
Meaningfulness (value)	1, 6, 11, 16	_____
Trust (security)	5, 10, 15, 20	_____

Comparison Data (N = 4500 students)

Skill Area	Mean	Top Quartile	Third Quartile	Second Quartile	Bottom Quartile
Self-efficacy (competence)	6.14	6.75 or above	6.25–6.74	5.75–6.24	5.74 or below
Self-determination (choice)	5.87	6.50 or above	6.00–6.49	5.25–5.99	5.24 or below
Personal control (impact)	5.61	6.50 or above	5.75–6.49	5.00–5.74	4.99 or below
Meaningfulness (value)	5.90	6.75 or above	6.00–6.74	5.50–5.99	5.49 or below
Trust (security)	5.50	6.25 or above	5.75–6.24	5.00–5.74	4.99 or below

SKILL PRACTICE
Deciding to Delegate: Analysis of "An Emergency Request"

Question:	Analysis:
Is it a group or individual problem?	Group because the task affects subordinates.
Is there a quality requirement?	Yes, because one way is better than another.
Does the manager have needed information?	Yes; the manager has experience.
Is the problem structured or unstructured?	Structured, because routine changes are required.
Do subordinates have to accept the decision?	No, because they have no discretion in implementation.
Are subordinates likely to accept the decision?	Yes, because close supervision is accepted.
Does everyone share a common goal?	Yes; all want the firm to be profitable.
Is conflict among subordinates likely?	No, since there is no investment in a prior alternative.
Do subordinates have needed information?	No; subordinates are inexperienced.

Choice: Make an individual decision if time is the important factor. If training of subordinates is the important factor, form a team and participate in the team's discussions.

QUESTION:	*ANALYSIS:*
Is it a group or individual problem?	Group because the task affects many employees.
Is there a quality requirement?	Yes, because one bid may clearly be better than another.
Does the manager have needed information?	No; the manager must obtain information from others.
Is the problem structured or unstructured?	Structured, because standard routines are involved.
Do subordinates have to accept the decision?	Yes, because they will have discretion in implementation.
Are subordinates likely to accept the decision?	Yes, probably, because of the benefit to the firm.
Does everyone share a common goal?	No; whereas all want the firm to be profitable, some are ideologically opposed to this kind of business.
Is conflict among subordinates likely?	Yes, since ideological factors may become relevant.
Do subordinates have needed information?	No; subordinates are inexperienced.

Choice: Make a decision by yourself, without sharing the problem with subordinates, after having obtained the necessary information. You may or may not share the problem with subordinates to discuss alternatives, but regardless, the decision should be yours alone.

SKILL *ASSESSMENT*

- Team Development Behaviors
- Diagnosing the Need for Team Building

SKILL *LEARNING*

- Developing Teams and Teamwork
- The Advantages of Teams
- Team Development
- Leading Teams
- Team Membership
- Summary
- Behavioral Guidelines

SKILL *ANALYSIS*

- She Loves a Challenge!
- The Cash Register Incident

SKILL *PRACTICE*

- Team Diagnosis and Team Development Exercise
- Winning the War on Talent
- Team Performance Exercise

SKILL *APPLICATION*

- Suggested Assignments
- Application Plan and Evaluation

SCORING KEYS AND *COMPARISON DATA*

9

Building Effective Teams and Teamwork

SKILL DEVELOPMENT OBJECTIVES

- DIAGNOSE AND FACILITATE TEAM DEVELOPMENT
- BUILD HIGH-PERFORMANCE TEAMS
- FACILITATE TEAM LEADERSHIP
- FOSTER EFFECTIVE TEAM MEMBERSHIP

DIAGNOSTIC SURVEYS FOR BUILDING EFFECTIVE TEAMS

TEAM DEVELOPMENT BEHAVIORS

Step 1: Before you read the material in this chapter, please respond to the following statements by writing a number from the rating scale below in the left-hand column (Pre-Assessment). Your answers should reflect your attitudes and behavior as they are now, not as you would like them to be. Be honest. This instrument is designed to help you discover your level of competency in building effective teams so you can tailor your learning to your specific needs. When you have completed the survey, use the scoring key at the end of the chapter to identify the skill areas discussed in this chapter that are most important for you to master.

Step 2: After you have completed the reading and the exercises in this chapter and, ideally, as many as you can of the Skill Application assignments at the end of this chapter, cover up your first set of answers. Then respond to the same statements again, this time in the right-hand column (Post-Assessment). When you have completed the survey, use the scoring key at the end of the chapter to measure your progress. If your score remains low in specific skill areas, use the behavioral guidelines at the end of the Skill Learning section to guide further practice.

Rating Scale

1 Strongly disagree
2 Disagree
3 Slightly disagree
4 Slightly agree
5 Agree
6 Strongly agree

Assessment

Pre-   Post-

When I am in the role of leader in a team:

_____ _____ 1. I know how to establish credibility and influence among team members.

_____ _____ 2. I behave congruently with my stated values and I demonstrate a high degree of integrity.

_____ _____ 3. I am clear and consistent about what I want to achieve.

_____ _____ 4. I create positive energy by being optimistic and complimentary of others.

_____ _____ 5. I build a common base of agreement in the team before moving forward with task accomplishment.

_____ _____ 6. I encourage and coach team members to help them improve.

_____ _____ 7. I share information with team members and encourage participation.

_____ _____ 8. I articulate a clear, motivating vision of what the team can achieve, along with specific short-term goals.

When I am in the role of team member:

_____ _____ 9. I know a variety of ways to facilitate task accomplishment in the team.

_____ _____ 10. I know a variety of ways to help build strong relationships and cohesion among team members.

_____ _____ 11. I confront and help to overcome negative, dysfunctional, or blocking behaviors by others.

_____ _____ 12. I shift roles from facilitating task accomplishment to helping build trusting relationships among members, depending on what the team needs to move forward.

When I desire to make my team perform well, regardless of whether I am a leader or member:

_____ _____ 13. I am knowledgeable about the different stages of team development experienced by most teams.

_____ _____ 14. I help establish clear expectations and purpose as well as help team members feel comfortable with one another at the outset of a team.

_____ _____ 15. I encourage team members to become as committed to the success of the team as to their own personal success.

_____ _____ 16. I help team members become committed to the team's vision and goals.

_____ _____ 17. I help the team avoid groupthink by making sure that sufficient diversity of opinions are expressed in the team.

_____ _____ 18. I can diagnose and capitalize on my team's core competencies, or unique strengths.

_____ _____ 19. I encourage the team to continuously improve as well as to seek for dramatic innovations.

_____ _____ 20. I encourage exceptionally high standards of performance and outcomes that far exceed expectations.

DIAGNOSING THE NEED FOR TEAM BUILDING

Teamwork has been found to dramatically affect organizational performance. Some managers have credited teams with helping them to achieve incredible results. On the other hand, teams don't work all the time in all organizations. Therefore, managers must decide when teams should be organized. To determine the extent to which teams should be built in your organization, complete the instrument below.

Think of an organization in which you participate (or will participate) that produces a product or service. Answer these questions with that organization in mind. Write a number from a scale of 1 to 5 in the blank at the left; 1 indicates that there is little evidence; 5 indicates there is a lot of evidence. Comparison data is provided at the end of the chapter.

_____ 1. Output has declined or is lower than desired.

_____ 2. Complaints, grievances, or low morale are present or are increasing.

_____ 3. Conflicts or hostility between members is present or is increasing.

_____ 4. Some people are confused about assignments, or their relationships with other people are unclear.

_____ 5. Lack of clear goals and lack of commitment to goals exist.

6. Apathy or lack of interest and involvement by members is in evidence.

_____ 7. Insufficient innovation, risk taking, imagination, or initiative exists.

_____   8. Ineffective and inefficient meetings are common.

_____   9. Working relationships across levels and units are unsatisfactory.

_____   10. Lack of coordination among functions is apparent.

_____   11. Poor communication exists; people are afraid to speak up; listening isn't occurring; and information isn't being shared.

_____   12. Lack of trust exists among members and between members and senior leaders.

_____   13. Decisions are made that some members don't understand, or with which they don't agree.

_____   14. People feel that good work is not rewarded or that rewards are unfairly administered.

_____   15. People are not encouraged to work together for the good of the organization.

_____   16. Customers and suppliers are not part of organizational decision making.

_____   17. People work too slowly and there is too much redundancy in the work being done.

_____   18. Issues and challenges that require the input of more than one person are being faced.

_____   19. People must coordinate their activities in order for the work to be accomplished.

_____   20. Difficult challenges that no single person can resolve or diagnose are being faced.

SOURCE: _Adapted from Diagnosing the Need for Team Building, William G. Dyer. (1987)_ Team Building: Issues and Alternatives. _Reading, MA: Addison Wesley. Reprinted with permission of Addison Wesley._

Developing Teams and Teamwork

Near the home of one of the authors of this book, scores of Canada geese spend the winter. They fly over the house to the nature pond nearby almost every morning. What is distinctive about these flights is that the geese always fly in a V pattern. The reason for this pattern is that the flapping wings of the geese in front create an updraft for the geese that follow. This V pattern increases the range of the geese collectively by 71 percent compared to flying alone. On long flights, after the lead goose has flown at the front of the V for a while, it drops back to take a place in the V where the flying is easier. Another goose then takes over the lead position, where the flying is most strenuous. If a goose begins to fly out of formation, it is not long before it returns to the V because of the resistance it experiences when not supported by the wing flapping of the other geese.

Another noticeable feature of these geese is the loud honking that occurs when they fly. Canada geese never fly quietly. One can always tell when they are in the air because of the noise. The reason for the honking is not random, however. It occurs among geese in the rear of the formation in order to encourage the lead goose. The leader doesn't honk—just those who are supporting and urging on the leader. If a goose is shot, becomes ill, or falls out of formation, two geese break ranks and follow the wounded or ill goose to the ground. There they remain, nurturing their companion, until it is either well enough to return to the flock or it dies.

This remarkable phenomenon serves as an apt metaphor for our chapter on teamwork. The lessons garnered from the flying V formation help highlight important attributes of effective teams and skillful teamwork. For example:

- ❏ *Effective teams have interdependent members.* Like geese, the productivity and efficiency of an entire unit is determined by the coordinated, interactive efforts of all its members.
- ❏ *Effective teams help members be more efficient working together than alone.* Like geese, effective teams outperform even the best individual's performance.

- ❏ *Effective teams function so well that they create their own magnetism.* Like geese, team members desire to affiliate with a team because of the advantages they receive from membership.
- ❏ *Effective teams do not always have the same leader.* As with geese, leadership responsibility often rotates and is shared broadly as teams develop over time.
- ❏ *In effective teams, members care for and nurture one another.* No member is devalued or unappreciated. All are treated as an integral part of the team.
- ❏ *Effective teams have members who cheer for and bolster the leader, and vice versa.* Mutual encouragement is given and received by each member.
- ❏ *Effective teams have a high level of trust among members.* Members demonstrate integrity and are interested in others' success as well as their own.

Because any metaphor can be carried to extremes, we don't wish to overemphasize the similarities between Canada geese and work teams. On the other hand, these seven attributes of effective teams do serve as the nucleus of this chapter. They will help us identify ways for you to improve your abilities to lead a team, to be an effective team member, and to foster effective team processes. Our intent is to identify proven techniques and skills that will help you function more effectively in team settings.

One important reason for this emphasis on teams is that participation in teams is fun for most people. There is something inherently attractive about being engaged in teamwork. Consider, for example, the two advertisements that appeared next to one another in a metropolitan newspaper, both seeking to fill the same type of position. They are reproduced in Figure 9.1. While neither advertisement is negative or inappropriate, they are noticeably different. Which job would you rather take? Which firm would you rather work for? For most of us, the team-focused job seems much more desirable. This chapter focuses on helping you to flourish in these kinds of team settings.

Figure 9.1	A Team-Oriented and a Traditional Advertisement for a Position

Our Team Needs One Good Multiskilled Maintenance Associate

Our Team is down one good player. Join our group of multiskilled Maintenance Associates who work together to support our assembly teams at American Automotive Manufacturing.

We are looking for a versatile person with skills in one or more of the following: ability to set up and operate various welding machinery, knowledge in electric arc and M.I.G. welding, willingness to work on detailed projects for extended time periods, and general overall knowledge of the automobile manufacturing process. Willingness to learn all maintenance skills a must. You must be a real team player, have excellent interpersonal skills, and be motivated to work in a highly participative environment.

Send qualifications to:

AMM

American Automotive Manufacturing
P.O. Box 616
Ft. Wayne, Indiana 48606
Include phone number. We respond to all applicants.

Maintenance Technician/Welder

Leading automotive manufacturer looking for Maintenance Technician/Welder. Position requires the ability to set up and operate various welding machinery and a general knowledge of the automobile production process. Vocational school graduates or 3–5 years of on-the-job experience required. Competitive salary, full benefits, and tuition reimbursement offered.

Interviews Monday, May 6, at the Holiday Inn South, 3000 Semple Road, 9:00 A.M. to 7:00 P.M. Please bring pay stub as proof of last employment.

NMC

National Motors Corporation
5169 Blane Hill Center
Springfield, Illinois 62707

The Advantages of Teams

Whether one is a manager, a subordinate, a student, or a homemaker, it is almost impossible to avoid being a member of a team. Some form of teamwork permeates most people's daily lives. Most of us are members of discussion groups, friendship groups, neighborhood groups, sports teams, or even families in which tasks are accomplished and interpersonal interaction occurs. Teams, in other words, are simply groups of people who are interdependent in the tasks they perform, affect one another's behavior through interaction, and see themselves as a unique entity. What we discuss in this chapter is applicable to team activity in most kinds of settings, although we focus mainly on teams and teamwork in employing organizations rather than in homes, classrooms, or in the world of sports. The principles of effective team performance, team leadership, and team participation we address here, however, are virtually the same across all these kinds of teams.

For example, empowered teams, autonomous work groups, semiautonomous teams, self-managing teams, self-determining teams, crews, platoons, cross-functional teams, top management teams, quality circles, project teams, task forces, virtual teams, emergency response teams, and committees are all examples of the various manifestations of teams and teamwork that appear in the scholarly literature, and research has been conducted on each of these forms of teams. Our focus is on helping you develop skills that are relevant in most or all these kinds of situations, whether as a team leader or a team member.

Developing team skills is important because of the tremendous explosion in the use of teams in work organizations over the last decade. For example, 79 percent of *Fortune* 1000 companies reported that they used self-managing work teams, and 91 percent reported that employee work groups were being utilized (Lawler, 1998; Lawler, Mohrman, & Ledford, 1995). More than two thirds of college students participate in an organized team, and almost no one can graduate from a business school anymore without participating in a team project or a group activity. Teams are ubiquitous in both work life and at school. Possessing the ability to lead and manage teams and teamwork, in other words, has become a commonplace requirement in most organizations. In one survey, the most desired skill of new employees was found to be the ability to work in a team (Wellins, Byham, & Wilson, 1991).

One noted management consultant, Tom Peters (1987), even asserted:

> Are there any limits to the use of teams? Can we find places or circumstances where a team structure doesn't make sense? Answer: No, as far as I can determine. That's unequivocal, and meant to be. Some situations may seem to lend themselves more to team-based management than others. Nonetheless, I observe that the power of the team is so great that it is often wise to violate apparent common sense and force a team structure on almost anything. (p. 306)

One reason for the escalation in the desirability of teamwork is that increasing amounts of data show improvements in productivity, quality, and morale when teams are utilized. Many companies have attributed their improvements in performance directly to the institution of teams in the workplace (Cohen & Bailey, 1997; Guzzo & Dickson, 1996; Hamilton, Nickerson, & Owan, 2003; Katzenbach & Smith, 1993; Senge, 1991). For example, by using teams in their organizations:

- ❏ Shenandoah Life Insurance Company in Roanoke, Virginia, saved $200,000 annually because of reduced staffing needs, while increasing its volume 33 percent.
- ❏ Westinghouse Furniture Systems increased productivity 74 percent in three years.
- ❏ AAL increased productivity by 20 percent, cut personnel by 10 percent, and handled 10 percent more transactions.
- ❏ Federal Express cut service errors by 13 percent.
- ❏ Carrier reduced unit turnaround time from two weeks to two days.
- ❏ Volvo's Kalamar facility reduced defects by 90 percent.
- ❏ General Electric's Salisbury, North Carolina, plant increased productivity by 250 percent compared to other GE plants producing the same product.
- ❏ Corning cellular ceramics plant decreased defect rates from 1,800 parts per million to 9 parts per million.
- ❏ AT&T's Richmond operator service increased service quality by 12 percent.

- ❏ Dana Corporation's Minneapolis valve plant trimmed customer lead time from six months to six weeks.
- ❏ General Mills plants became 40 percent more productive than plants operating without teams.
- ❏ A garment-making plant increased its productivity 14 percent by adopting a team-based production system.

Table 9.1 reports the positive relationships between employee involvement in teams and several dimensions of organizational and worker effectiveness. Lawler, Mohrman, and Ledford (1995) found that among firms that were actively using teams, both organizational and individual effectiveness were above average and improving in virtually all categories of performance. In firms without teams or in which teams were infrequently used, effectiveness was average or low in all categories.

Of course, a variety of factors can affect the performance and usefulness of teams. Teams are not inherently effective just because they exist. A *Sports Illustrated* cover story, for example, labeled the Los Angeles Clippers NBA basketball team the worst team in the history of professional sports from inception to the year 2000 (Lidz, 2000)—evidence that just because a group of talented people get together does not mean that an effective team can be created. Hackman (1993) identified a set of common inhibitors to effective team performance, including rewarding and recognizing individuals instead of the team, not maintaining stability of membership over time, not providing team members with autonomy, not fostering interdependence among team members, and failing to orient all team members. In contradiction to Peters' comments about the universal utility of teams, Verespei (1990) observed:

> All too often corporate chieftains read the success stories and ordain their companies to adopt work teams—NOW. Work teams don't always work and may even be the wrong solution to the situation in question.

The instrument, called "*Diagnosing the Need for Team Building*" in the Skill Assessment section of this chapter, helps identify the extent to which the work teams in which you are involved are performing effectively, and the extent to which they need team building. Often, teams can take too long to make decisions, they can drive out effective action by becoming too insular, and they can create confusion, conflict, and frustration

Table 9.1	Impact of Involvement in Teams on Organizations and Workers	
PERFORMANCE CRITERIA	**PERCENT INDICATING IMPROVEMENT**	
Changed management style to more participatory	78	
Improved organizational processes and procedures	75	
Improved management decision making	69	
Increased employee trust in management	66	
Improved implementation of technology	60	
Elimination of layers of management supervision	50	
Improved safety and health	48	
Improved union-management relations	47	
PERFORMANCE CRITERIA	**PERCENT INDICATING POSITIVE IMPACT**	
Quality of products and services	70	
Customer service	67	
Worker satisfaction	66	
Employee quality of work life	63	
Productivity	61	
Competitiveness	50	
Profitability	45	
Absenteeism	23	
Turnover	22	

(N = 439 of the *Fortune* 1000 firms)

SOURCE: *Impact of* involvement in teams on organizations and workers, Lawler, E. E., Mohman, S. A., & Ledford, G. E. (1992). Creating high performance organizations: Practices and results of employee involvement and total quality in Fortune 1000 companies. Reprinted with permission of John Wiley & Sons, Inc.

for their members. All of us have been irritated by being members of an inefficient team, a team dominated by a single person, a team with slothful members, or a team in which standards are compromised in order to get agreement from everyone. The common adage that "a camel is a horse designed by a team" illustrates one of the many potential liabilities of a team.

On the other hand, a great deal of research has been conducted to identify the factors associated with high performance in teams. Factors such as team composition (e.g., heterogeneity of members, size of the team, familiarity among team members), team motivation (e.g., team potency, team goals, team feedback), team type (e.g., virtual teams, cockpit crews, quality circles) and team structure (e.g., team member autonomy, team norms, team decision-making processes) have been studied to determine how best to form and lead teams (see comprehensive reviews by Cohen & Bailey, 1997; Guzzo & Dickson, 1996; Hackman, 2003).

Several thousand studies of groups and teams have appeared in just the last decade. Self-managing work teams, problem-solving teams, therapy groups, task forces, interpersonal growth groups, student project teams, and many other kinds of teams have been studied extensively. Studies have ranged from teams meeting for just one session to teams whose longevity extends over several years. Membership in teams has varied widely, ranging from children to aged people, top executives to line workers, students to instructors, volunteers to prison inmates, professional athletes to playground toddlers. The analyses have included a variety of predictors of performance such as team-member roles, unconscious cognitive processes, group dynamics, problem-solving strategies, communication patterns, leadership actions, interpersonal needs, decision-making quality, innovativeness, and productivity (e.g., Ancona & Caldwell, 1992; Gladstein, 1984; Senge, 1991; Wellins et al., 1991).

We will not spend time in this chapter reviewing the extensive literature associated with teams, nor the multitude of factors that have been associated with team performance. Instead, we focus on a few key skills that will help you lead and participate effectively in most kinds of teams. We particularly focus here on teams that are faced with a task to accomplish. This may be a work team at your job, a project team composed of fellow students, an ad hoc team discussing an issue, or a self-managing team in a service organization. Regardless of the form of the team, you will want to improve your skills in helping the team become a high-performing unit. We will concentrate first on helping you understand the development of teams and how to diagnose the key issues present in each of four stages of team development. Then we focus on helping you improve your capability to lead teams in these various stages, and to become a more effective member of a team.

AN EXAMPLE OF AN EFFECTIVE TEAM

To illustrate some of the principles we discuss in this chapter, we briefly describe one of the most effective team efforts we know about. It is the team formed to plan and conduct the logistical support for the United States' engagement in the 1990 Persian Gulf War (Desert Storm)—the original conflict motivated by Iraq's threatened invasion of Kuwait. General Gus Pagonis was the designated leader of this team, which was organized as a result of the first President George Bush's announcement that the United States would send troops to Saudi Arabia in order to confront the Iraqi aggression into Kuwait.

The tasks Pagonis faced were daunting. He was charged with building a team that could transport more than half a million people and their personal belongings to the other side of the world, on short notice. But transporting the people was only part of the challenge. Supporting them once they arrived, moving them into position for a surprise attack, supporting their battle plans, and then getting them and their equipment back home in record time were even greater challenges.

More than 122 million meals had to be planned, moved, and served—approximately the number eaten by all the residents of Wyoming and Vermont in three months. Fuel (1.3 billion gallons) had to be pumped—about the same amount used in Montana, North Dakota, and Idaho in a year—in order to support soldiers driving 52 million miles. Tanks, planes, ammunition, carpenters, cashiers, morticians, social workers,

doctors, and a host of support personnel had to be transported, coordinated, fed, and housed. More than 500 new traffic signs had to be constructed and installed in order to help individuals speaking several different languages navigate the relatively featureless terrain of Saudi Arabia. Five hundred tons of mail had to be sorted and processed each day. More than 70,000 contracts with suppliers had to be negotiated and executed. All green-colored equipment—more than 12,000 tracked vehicles and 117,000 wheeled vehicles—had to be repainted desert brown and then repainted green when shipped home. Soldiers had to be trained to fit in with an unfamiliar culture that was intolerant of typical soldier-relaxation activity. Supplies had to be distributed at a moment's notice to several different locations, some of them behind enemy lines, in the heat of battle. Traffic control was monumental, as evidenced by one key checkpoint near the front where 18 vehicles per minute passed, seven days a week, 24 hours a day, for six weeks. More than 60,000 enemy prisoners of war had to be transported, cared for, and detained.

Because the war ended far sooner than predicted, an even more daunting challenge presented itself—getting all those supplies and personnel back home. Most of the equipment, ammunition, and food had to be brought back home because it had been unpacked but was mostly unused. That required thorough scrubbing to remove microorganisms or pests and reshrinkwrapping a huge amount of supplies. Since large, bulk containers had been broken up into smaller units during the war, it took twice as long to gather and ship materials out of Saudi Arabia as it did to ship them in. Yet, personnel were eager to return home at the end of the campaign, so the pressure for speed was at least as great as at the outset of the war. In short, Pagonis' team faced a set of tasks that had never before been accomplished on that scale, and they were to do it in a time frame that would have been laughable if it weren't factual.

The team building and teamwork skills used to accomplish these tasks was detailed in Pagonis' 1993 book, *Moving Mountains*. Pagonis was awarded a third star during Desert Storm as a result of his outstanding leadership in the field of battle. He helped plan and execute the famous "end run" that took the Iraqi army completely by surprise. Most observers now agree that it was the success of the logistics team that really won the Persian Gulf War for the United States in 1991 and saved tens of thousands, if not hundreds of thousands, of lives. We use excerpts from his description of this team's functioning to illustrate principles of effective team building and team leadership in the sections that follow.

Team Development

Regardless of whether you play the role of team leader or team member, in order to function effectively in a team it is important that you understand that all teams progress through stages of development. These stages cause the dynamics within the team to change, the relationships among team members to shift, and effective leader behaviors to be modified. In this section we outline the four major stages that teams pass through from early stages of development—when a team is still struggling to become a coherent entity—to a more mature stage of development—when the team has become a highly effective, smoothly functioning unit. The skill we want you to develop is to be able to diagnose the stage of your team's development so that you will know what kinds of behaviors will most effectively enhance your team's performance.

Evidence of predictable patterns of team development has been available since the early part of this century (Dewey, 1933; Freud, 1921). In fact, despite the variety in composition, purpose, and longevity of the teams investigated in a large array of studies, the stages of group and team development have been strikingly similar (Cameron & Whetten, 1984; Hackman, 2003; Quinn & Cameron, 1983). The research shows that teams tend to develop through four separate, sequential stages. These stages were first labeled by Tuckman (1965) as **forming, norming, storming,** and **performing.** Because of their rhyme and parsimony, these labels are still widely used today. (Tuckman's second and third stages are reversed in this chapter based on the research of Greiner, 1972, and Cameron & Whetten, 1981.)

Table 9.2 summarizes the four main stages of team development. In order for teams to be effective and for team members to benefit most from team membership, teams must progress through the first three stages of development to achieve Stage 4. In each separate stage, unique challenges and issues predominate, and it is by successfully diagnosing and managing these issues and challenges that a team matures and becomes more effective. For each of the four stages, we first identify major team member issues and questions, then we identify the management responses that help the team effectively transcend that stage of development.

THE FORMING STAGE

When team members first come together, they are much like an audience at the outset of a concert. They are not a team but an aggregation of individuals sharing a common setting. Something must happen for them to feel that they are a cohesive unit. When you meet with a group of people for the first time, for example, chances are that you do not feel integrated with the group right away. Several questions are probably on your mind, such as:

❏ Who are these other people?
❏ What is expected of me?
❏ Who is going to lead?
❏ What is supposed to happen?

The questions uppermost in the minds of participants in a new team have to do with establishing a sense of security and direction, getting oriented, and

Table 9.2	Four Stages of Team Development
STAGE	EXPLANATION
Forming	The team is faced with the need to become acquainted with its members, its purpose, and its boundaries. Relationships must be formed and trust established. Clarity of direction is needed from team leaders.
Norming	The team is faced with creating cohesion and unity, differentiating roles, identifying expectations for members, and enhancing commitment. Providing supportive feedback and fostering commitment to a vision are needed from team leaders.
Storming	The team is faced with disagreements, counterdependence, and the need to manage conflict. Challenges include violations of team norms and expectations and overcoming groupthink. Focusing on process improvement, recognizing team achievement, and fostering win/win relationships are needed from team leaders.
Performing	The team is faced with the need for continuous improvement, innovation, speed, and capitalizing on core competencies. Sponsoring team members' new ideas, orchestrating their implementation, and fostering extraordinary performance are needed from the team leaders.

becoming comfortable with the new situation. Sometimes, new team members can articulate these questions, while at other times they are little more than general feelings of discomfort or disconnectedness. Uncertainty and ambiguity tend to predominate as individuals seek some type of understanding and structure. Because there is no shared history with the team, there is no unity among members. Thus, the typical interpersonal relationships that predominate in this stage are:

❑ Silence
❑ Self-consciousness
❑ Dependence
❑ Superficiality

Even though some individuals may enter a team situation with great enthusiasm and anticipation, they are usually hesitant to demonstrate their emotions to others until they begin to feel at ease. Moreover, without knowing the rules and boundaries, it feels risky to speak out or to even ask questions. Seldom are new members willing to actively query a leader when a team first meets together, even though uncertainty prevails. When a leader asks questions of team members, rarely does someone jump at the chance to give an answer. When answers are given, they are likely to be brief. Little interaction occurs among team members themselves, most communication is targeted at the team leader or person in charge, and each individual is generally thinking more of himself or herself than of the team. Interactions tend to be formal and guarded. Congruent behaviors are masked in the interest of self-protection.

Individuals cannot begin to feel like a team until they become familiar with the rules and boundaries of their setting. They don't know whom to trust, who will take initiative, what constitutes normal behavior, or what kinds of interactions are appropriate. They are not yet a real team but only a collection of individuals. Therefore, the task of the team in this stage is less focused on producing an output than on developing the team itself. Helping team members become comfortable with one another takes precedence over task accomplishment. A team faces the following kinds of task issues in its first stage of development:

❑ Orienting members and getting questions answered
❑ Establishing trust
❑ Establishing relationships with the leader(s)
❑ Establishing clarity of purpose, norms, procedures, and expectations

This stage may be brief, but it is not a time to rely on free and open discussion and consensus decision making to accomplish an outcome. Direction, clarity, and structure are needed instead. The first task is to ensure that all team members know one another and that their questions are answered. Because relatively little participation may occur during this stage, the temptation may be to rush ahead or to short-circuit introductions and instructions. However, teams tend to flounder later if the challenges of this stage are not adequately managed.

In the case of the Persian Gulf logistics team, the first critical task was to make certain that objectives, rules and regulations, time frames, and resources were clearly laid out. Each member of the team had to become comfortable with his or her team membership:

The team got down to work with a redoubled sense of urgency. They were soon fully familiar with the plan that had been roughed out. We quickly got to a joint understanding of what I took to be our role in the theater. Our session . . . was very successful, mainly because from the outset we had a well-defined structure for invention. We worked toward several clearly expressed goals, and there was an imposed time limit to keep us on track. And finally, our various experiences were complementary. We needed each other and we knew it. (Pagonis, 1993, pp. 82–83)

THE NORMING STAGE

Once team members have become oriented, achieved clarity about the team's goals, and accepted their place in the team, the main challenge of the team is to create a cohesive unit or a "sense of team." Norms, rules, and expectations are clarified in the first stage, but an underlying team culture and informal relationships among members must also be developed. The need to move the team from a group of individuals sharing a common goal to a highly cohesive unit is the motivation that leads the team to a new stage of development—the norming stage. The more team members interact with one another, the more they develop common behaviors and perspectives. They experience a certain amount of pressure to conform to the expectations of other team members, so the team begins to develop a character and culture of its own. We all have experienced strong peer pressure, the clearest example of the dynamics in this stage of team development. A new cohesive team culture affects the amount of work done by the team, its style of communicating, approaches to problem solving, and even team member dress.

The major focus of team members, in other words, shifts from overcoming uncertainty in the forming stage to developing the norms of a unified group. Typical questions in team members' minds during this stage include:

❏ What are the norms and values of the team?
❏ How can I best get along with everyone else?
❏ How can I show my support to others?
❏ How can I fit in?

During the norming stage, team members become contented with team membership and begin to value the team's goals more than their own personal goals. Individual needs are met through the team's accomplishments. The team, rather than the leader or a single person, takes responsibility for solving problems, confronting and correcting mistakes, and ensuring success. Agreement and a willingness to go along characterize the climate of the team. Individuals experience feelings of loyalty to the team, and the interpersonal relationships that most characterize team members include:

❏ Cooperativeness
❏ Conformity to standards and expectations
❏ Heightened interpersonal attraction
❏ Ignoring disagreements

This norming stage is a time when effective teams encourage relationship-building roles. Participation by all team members is encouraged, and the team takes responsibility for ensuring that it:

❏ Maintains unity and cohesion
❏ Facilitates participation and empowerment
❏ Shows support to team members
❏ Provides feedback on team and team member performance

A major problem may arise in this stage of development, however, especially if the team refuses to move on. That problem is an increasing inability to engender diversity and varied perspectives in the team. Whereas team members may feel extremely satisfied with their tightly bonded unit, the team risks a danger of developing groupthink (Janis, 1972). Groupthink occurs when the cohesiveness and inertia developed in a team drives out good decision making and problem solving. The preservation of the team takes precedence over accurate decisions or high-quality task accomplishment. Not

enough differentiation and challenge to the team's mind-set occurs.

Irv Janis (1972) conducted research in which he chronicled several high-performing teams that in one instance performed in a stellar fashion, but performed disastrously in another instance. His classic example was the cabinet of President John F. Kennedy. This team worked through what is often considered one of the best sets of decisions ever made in handling the Cuban Missile Crisis, in which the former Soviet Union was inhibited from placing warhead missiles in Cuba by means of a high-stakes confrontation by Kennedy and his cabinet. This was also the same team, however, that earlier had made the disastrous decisions related to the Bay of Pigs fiasco, in which a planned overthrow of Fidel Castro's government in Cuba became a logistical nightmare, a confluence of indecision, and an embarrassing defeat for the same subsequently high-functioning team.

What was the difference? Why did the same team do so well in one circumstance and so poorly in another? Janis' answer is groupthink. Groupthink typically occurs when the following attributes develop in teams that are stuck in the norming stage.

❏ *Illusion of invulnerability*. Members feel assured that the team's past success will continue. ("Because of our track record, we cannot fail.")
❏ *Shared stereotypes*. Members dismiss disconfirming information by discrediting its source. ("These people just don't understand these things.")
❏ *Rationalization*. Members rationalize away threats to an emerging consensus. ("This is the reason they don't agree with us.")
❏ *Illusion of morality*. Members believe that they, as moral individuals, are not likely to make wrong decisions. ("This team would never knowingly make a bad decision or do anything immoral.")
❏ *Self-censorship*. Members keep silent about misgivings and try to minimize doubts. ("I must be wrong if others think that way.")
❏ *Direct pressure*. Sanctions are imposed on members who explore deviant viewpoints. ("If you don't agree, why don't you leave the team?")
❏ *Mind guarding*. Members protect the team from being exposed to disturbing ideas. ("Don't listen to them. We need to keep the rabble rousers at bay.")

❏ *Illusion of unanimity.* Members conclude that the team must have reached a consensus since the most vocal members are in agreement. ("If Dave and Melissa agree, there must be a consensus.")

The problem with groupthink is that it leads teams to commit more errors than normal. For example, consider the following commonly observed scenario. Not wanting to make a serious judgment error, a leader convenes a meeting of his or her team. In the process of discussing an issue, the leader expresses a preference for one option. Other team members, wanting to appear supportive, present arguments justifying the decision. One or two members tentatively suggest alternatives, but they are strongly overruled by the majority. The decision is carried out with even greater conviction than normal because everyone is in agreement, but the consequences are disastrous. How did this happen? While the leader brought the team together to avoid making a bad decision, the presence of groupthink actually made a bad decision more likely. Without the social support provided by the team, the leader may have been more cautious in implementing a personally preferred but uncertain decision.

To manage this tendency to develop groupthink, the team must move through the norming stage into the storming stage. The team must develop attributes that will foster diversity, heterogeneity, and even conflict in the team's processes. In particular, Janis makes the following suggestions for addressing groupthink:

❏ *Critical evaluators.* At least one team member should be assigned to perform the role of critic or evaluator of the team's decisions.

❏ *Open discussion.* The team leader should not express an opinion at the outset of the team meeting but should encourage open discussion of differing perspectives by team members.

❏ *Subgroups.* Multiple subgroups in the team may be formed to develop independent proposals.

❏ *Outside experts.* Invite outside experts to listen to the rationale for the team's decision and critique it.

❏ *Devil's advocate.* Assign at least one team member to play devil's advocate during the discussion if it seems that too much homogeneity exists in the team's discussion.

❏ *Second-chance meetings.* Sleep on the team's decision and revisit it afresh the next day. The expression of team members' second thoughts should be encouraged.

In other words, teams in the norming stage become cohesive and highly integrated entities, and this may create a tendency to preserve high involvement and good feeling at the expense of all else. Having a cohesive family feeling is necessary to pull the separate members together and to create a singular identity. However, it can prove disastrous if important information is filtered out, contrary points of view are squelched, or nonconformity in any form is punished. Effective teams must also move on to the next stage, the storming stage of development.

THE STORMING STAGE

Whereas the comfortable climate that team members develop in the norming stage can lead to an excessive amount of agreement and homogeneity, it also can lead to the opposite phenomenon. That is, once team members begin to feel comfortable with the team, they often begin to explore different roles. Some may tend toward task facilitation, for example, while others may tend toward relationship building. This differentiation of team members' roles invariably leads the team into a stage of potential conflict and counterdependence—a storming stage.

Playing different roles causes team members to develop different perspectives and to develop ideas that challenge the leadership and direction of the team. Virtually every effective team goes through a stage in which team members question the legitimacy of the team's direction, the leader, the roles of other team members, the opinions or decisions of others, and the task objectives. Up to now, the team was largely characterized by harmony and consensus. Individual differences were suppressed in order to create a sense of team. However, such a condition will not last forever without team members becoming uncomfortable about losing their individual identity, subjugating their feelings, or stifling differing perspectives. The team's long-term success, therefore, will depend on how well it manages the storming stage of development. Typical questions that arise in team members' minds during this stage are:

❏ How will we handle dissension?
❏ How can we make decisions amidst disagreement?
❏ How will we communicate negative information?
❏ Do I want to maintain my membership in the team?

An old Middle Eastern proverb states: "All sunshine makes a desert." Similarly, team development implies that some struggles must occur, some discomfort must be experienced, and some obstacles must be overcome for the team to prosper. The team must learn to deal with adversity—especially that produced by its own members. Tendencies toward groupthink must be attacked head-on. If team members are more interested in keeping peace than in solving problems and accomplishing tasks, the team will never become effective. No one wants to remain in a team that will not allow for individuality and uniqueness and that wants to maintain harmony more than it wants to accomplish its goals. Consequently, harmony is sometimes sacrificed as the team attacks problems and accomplishes objectives.

Of course, team members do not cease to care about one another, and they remain committed to the team and its success. But they do begin to take sides on issues, to find that they are more compatible with some team members than others, and to align themselves with certain points of view. This leads to:

- ❏ Coalitions or cliques being formed
- ❏ Competition among team members
- ❏ Disagreement with the leader
- ❏ Challenging others' points of view

During Desert Storm, for example, a relatively rigid military command hierarchy—along with the urgency of the mission to be performed—inhibited large deviations from established norms and rules, but small aberrations began to emerge as Pagonis' team developed. Logistics team members painted personal logos on some tanks and trucks, insider code names were given to people and locations as a bit of sarcasm, and challenges to top-brass mandates became more common in briefing rooms. This testing of norms and boundaries is sometimes merely an expression of a need for individuality, while in other instances it is a product of strong feelings that the team can be improved. The main task issues to be addressed by the team in this stage include:

- ❏ Managing conflict
- ❏ Legitimizing productive expressions of individuality
- ❏ Turning counterdependence into interdependence
- ❏ Fostering consensus-building processes

Conflict, coalition formation, and counterdependence create conditions that may lead to the norms and values of the team being questioned. Rather than being stifled or resisted, however, effective teams encourage members to turn those challenges into constructive suggestions for improvement. It is important for team members to feel that they can legitimately express their personal uniqueness and idiosyncrasies, so long as they are not destructive to the overall team. It is clear from research on teams that when they face difficult or complex problems, teams are more effective if membership is heterogeneous than if all team members act, believe, and see things the same way (Campion, Medsker, & Higgs, 1993; Hackman, 2003). Diversity is productive in fostering creativity, individuality, and solutions to difficult problems (Cox, 1994). It has been said that "teams make complex problems simple." The trouble is, "teams also make simple problems complex," so diversity and heterogeneity are not universally appropriate. The first two stages of team development, in fact, are purposeful in minimizing diversity and heterogeneity. In this stage, however, maintaining flexibility in the team implies that tolerance for individuality is acceptable and that changes and improvements are promoted. General Pagonis' philosophy about the way to manage differences was to encourage their expression:

The key is to be open to different experiences and perspectives. If you can't tolerate different kinds of people, you're not likely to learn from different kinds of perspectives. Effective leaders encourage contrary opinions, an important source of vitality. This is especially true in the military where good ideas come in an incredible variety of packages. (Pagonis, 1993, p. 24)

In the storming stage of development, tensions arise between forces pushing the team toward cohesion and forces pushing it toward differentiation. At the same time strong bonds of team unity have been fostered, individuals begin differentiating themselves from one another and adopting unique roles in the team. They become complementary. This complementarity of roles may actually foster team cohesion and productivity rather than conflict, however, if the team:

- ❏ Identifies an external enemy (rather than one another) as a target for competition
- ❏ Reinforces team commitment with recognition of team-level performance
- ❏ Maintains visibility of vision and superordinate goals
- ❏ Turns students into teachers by having team members teach the group's values and vision to others

Pagonis' logistics team illustrates the value of the first three suggestions above—identifying an external enemy, team-level recognition, and vision.

In the presence of the enemy, our strength was flexibility, both as individuals and as a group. Organizations must be flexible enough to adjust and conform when their environments change. But the flexibility can degenerate into chaos in the absence of well-established goals. . . . Once everyone in the organization understands the goals of the organization, then each person sets out several objectives by which to attain those goals within his or her own sphere of activity. . . . When it works, cooperation and collegiality are enhanced, and in-fighting and suboptimization are minimized. (Pagonis, 1993, p. 83)

The fourth suggestion above is illustrated well by a process used effectively by Xerox Corporation to address stiff competition from external competitors—mainly Canon. Figure 9.2 illustrates a process implemented by Xerox where students were turned into teachers in order to ensure that a common vision and common processes were implemented throughout the company. To ensure that all units and all managers were working in harmony, the company divided itself into hierarchical family teams. A four-step process was then implemented:

1. *Learn.* Core principles, vision, and values were taught and discussed.
2. *Apply.* Action plans were formed and an improvement agenda was implemented.
3. *Teach.* The principles and successful experiences were taught to the next-lower family team.
4. *Inspect.* The performance and action plans of this lower family team were measured and monitored.

Teams were exposed to the desired information four times: when they learned it, when they applied it, when they taught it, and when they inspected it. More importantly, because team members were engaged in teaching others, their commitment to the team, even in light of differentiated roles, was enhanced.

THE PERFORMING STAGE

The performing stage of development represents highly effective and efficient team functioning. Because the team has worked through the issues embedded in each of the previous stages of development, it is able to work

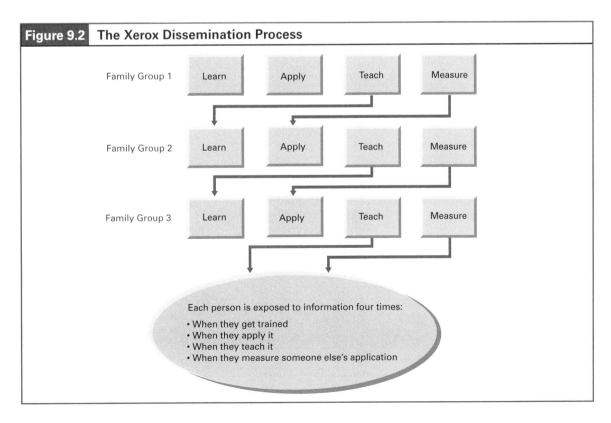

Figure 9.2 The Xerox Dissemination Process

Family Group 1 — Learn → Apply → Teach → Measure

Family Group 2 — Learn → Apply → Teach → Measure

Family Group 3 — Learn → Apply → Teach → Measure

Each person is exposed to information four times:
- When they get trained
- When they apply it
- When they teach it
- When they measure someone else's application

at a high level of performance. The team has overcome issues of skepticism, uncertainty, nonparticipativeness, dependence, and self-centeredness typical of the first, or forming stage of development. It has developed a clear mission, personal commitment to the team, a high degree of loyalty and morale, and has overcome tendencies toward groupthink that can occur in the norming stage. It has fostered differentiation and variety while also overcoming tendencies toward counterdependence, conflict, polarization, and disharmony typical of the storming stage. It now has the potential to develop the attributes of a high-performing team.

A listing of attributes of high-performance teams is provided in Table 9.3, based on research summarized

Table 9.3	Some Attributes of High-Performing Teams

- *Performance outcomes*

  High-performing teams do things. They produce something; they don't just discuss it. Without accomplishment, teams dissolve and become ineffective over time.

- *Specific, shared purpose and vision*

  The more specific the purpose, the more commitment, trust, and coordination can occur. Individuals don't work for themselves; they work for one another in pursuit of the shared purpose. The shared purpose can also be the same as a motivating vision of what the team should achieve.

- *Mutual, internal accountability*

  The sense of internal accountability is far greater than any accountability imposed by a boss or outsider. Self-evaluation and accountability characterize a high-performing team.

- *Blurring of formal distinctions*

  Team members do whatever is needed to contribute to the task, regardless of previous positions or titles. Team membership and team roles are more predominant than outside status.

- *Coordinated, shared work roles*

  Individuals always work in coordination with others on the team. The desired output is a single group product, not a set of individual products.

- *Inefficiency leading to efficiency*

  Because teams allow for lots of participation and sharing, mutual influence about purpose, and blurring of roles, they may initially be inefficient. As the team develops, because they come to know one another so well and can anticipate each other's moves, they become much more efficient than single people working alone.

- *Extraordinarily high quality*

  Teams produce outcomes above and beyond current standards of performance. They surprise and delight their various constituencies with quality levels not expected and never before obtained. An intolerance of mediocrity exists, so standards of performance are very high.

- *Creative continuous improvement*

  Large-scale innovations as well as never-ending small improvements characterize the team's processes and activities. Dissatisfaction with the status quo leads to a constant flow of new ideas, experimentation, and a quest for progress.

- *High credibility and trust*

  Team members trust one another implicitly, defend members who are not present, and form interdependent relationships with one another. Personal integrity and honesty characterize team activities and team member interactions.

- *Clarity of core competence*

  The unique talents and strategic advantages of the team and its members are clear. The ways in which these competencies can be utilized to further the team's objectives are well understood. Extraneous activities and deflections from the team's core mission are given low priority.

SOURCE: *Adapted from Hackman, 1990, 2003; Katzenbach & Smith, 1993; Lawler, 1998, 2003.*

in Cohen and Bailey (1997), Guzzo and Dickson (1996), Hackman (1990; 2003), Katzenbach and Smith (1993), Parker (1996), and Yeatts and Hyten (1998). These attributes are those that produce the benefits enumerated earlier in the chapter (e.g., productivity improvements, quality achievements, speed, and cost reductions). By and large, teams produce the dramatic successes in organizations reported in the best-practice literature only if they reach the performing stage of development.

The team in the performing stage is not, of course, free of challenges. The common issues that tend to dominate members of high-performing teams are:

❏ How can we help our members thrive?
❏ How can we foster continuous improvement and creativity?
❏ How can we build on our core competence?
❏ How can we maintain a high level of energy in the team?

Team members' questions in this stage change from being static to being dynamic. They shift in focus from merely accomplishing objectives to fostering change and improvement and achieving extraordinarily positive performance. Continuous improvement replaces accomplishment as an objective. Up to this point, the team has been trying to manage and resolve issues that lead to three key outcomes: (1) accomplishing tasks or objectives, (2) coordinating and integrating team members' roles, and (3) assuring the personal well-being of all team members. It can now turn its attention to achieving a level of performance above the ordinary. The interpersonal relationships of team members are characterized by:

❏ High mutual trust
❏ Unconditional commitment to the team
❏ Mutual training and development
❏ Entrepreneurship

Team members in this stage exhibit a sense of shared responsibility and concern for one another as they carry out their work. Their relationships are not limited merely to accomplishing a task together, but also extend to ensuring that each team member is learning, developing, and flourishing. Coaching and assisting one another is common. In General Pagonis' high-performing team, for example, team members were continuously teaching one another and helping the team and its individual members become more competent.

I arranged to take a day or two away from headquarters with a group of key people from the command [the team]. We use this brief respite from our everyday activities to take a long look at what our organization is doing. These sessions . . . gave us a chance to work as a group, in a focused way. . . . From Day One, I held large, open classes where we discussed scenarios and potential solutions. I would pose a question to the group: "O.K., you have a ship that docked at Ad Dammam this morning. It's ready to be unloaded, and the onboard crane breaks. What's our response?" Collectively, the group would work toward one of several solutions. . . . These group sessions served several useful purposes at once. Obviously, they brought potential challenges into the open so we could better prepare for them. . . . Equally important, they promoted collaborative discussion across ranks and disciplines. (Pagonis, 1993, pp. 101, 177)

In addition to multifaceted relationships and unconditional commitment to one another, high-performing team members also take responsibility individually for continuously improving the team and its processes. Experimentation, trial-and-error learning, freewheeling discussions of new possibilities, and personal responsibility by everyone for upgrading performance is typical. The team adopts a set of behaviors that help to foster and perpetuate this stage of development, including:

❏ Capitalizing on core competence
❏ Fostering innovation and continuous improvement
❏ Enhancing flourishing relationships
❏ Encouraging positive deviance

The most effective teams in this stage develop the capacity to perform beyond the norm. They achieve outcomes that are extraordinary. They extend the boundaries of what is possible. They become positively deviant. After having moved through the first three stages of development in the Persian Gulf War, for example, General Pagonis' logistics team moved into a stage characterized by activities that extended beyond the norm. On one occasion, for example, Pagonis directed two team members to generate a solution to the problem of how to provide combat troops with decent meals on the front lines.

Imagine that you've been at some remote and desolate desert site for weeks, or even months, consuming dehydrated or vacuum-packed military rations. One day, unannounced, an odd-looking vehicle with the word "Wolf-mobile" painted on it comes driving into your camp. The side panels open up, and a smiling crew inside offers to cook you a hamburger to order. "Side of fries? How about a Coke?" Morale shot up everywhere the Wolfmobiles pulled in—a little bit of home in the desert. (Pagonis, 1993, p. 129)

This incident illustrates the major opportunity associated in the fourth stage of development—to help team members expand their focus from merely accomplishing their work and maintaining good interpersonal relationships to upgrading and elevating the team's performance. This level of performance unlocks positive energy and makes it impossible to ever return to a lower level of performance again.

An example of the power of high-performing teams and their effects of members is a story told by our friend Bob Quinn (2005) in which an upper-level executive in a major manufacturing organization was expressing frustration with his company. "The trouble with my firm," lamented the executive, "is that they cannot stand excellence." He illustrated his frustration by recounting the following incident.

One day in his plant, a major problem occurred on the assembly line, and the line had to be shut down and repaired. The issue was serious and required personnel from multiple shifts to come to the plant to work on the problem. As a gesture of goodwill on his part, this executive purchased lunch—pizza, hot dogs, and soft drinks—for these employees who were going the extra mile for the company. They completed the task at the highest levels of quality and in record time. Sometime later, a representative from the finance department entered the office of this executive, slapped a piece of paper down on the desk, and exclaimed, "We can't pay this bill for the food. You know that it is against corporate policy to purchase food for employees from your budget. This bill will not be reimbursed." Of course, no one could fault the finance department representative—he was simply doing his job and reinforcing the rules. Flabbergasted, however, the executive responded: "Look, I cannot do the same things we have always done and expect different results. I have to break rules once in a while in the service of achieving excellence or extraordinary performance. Buying lunch made all the difference to these employees. It's what accounted for our success."

"This incident just proves," stated the executive, "that my firm cannot stand excellence. They cannot tolerate being extraordinary." Our friend Bob offered this executive some advice. He simply proposed that the executive give up and conform to the rules and expectations. Stop trying to achieve extraordinary levels of success. The executive's reply was telling, however, and illustrates the power of high-performing teams in this fourth stage of development. His reply was: "I can't quit trying. Once I have experience excellence, normal performance is just not good enough anymore. I can't stand still and not to strive for extraordinary results."

Teams in this fourth stage of development are not all outstanding, of course, and unfortunately, are quite rare, yet their power and influence on team members is transformational. Once a person experiences this kind of excellence, team performance stuck in the first three stages of development will never be satisfactory again. Some of the prescriptions for achieving these levels of extraordinary success are highlighted in the sections below as we discuss skills involved in leading teams and in being an effective member of teams.

Leading Teams

In highly effective teams, members' behavior is interdependent, and personal goals are subservient to the accomplishment of the team goal. A commitment to and desire for team membership is present. Even though individuals may be formally designated as a team, if they act so as to bring exclusive credit to themselves, to accomplish their own objectives instead of the team's objective, or to maintain independence from others, they are not truly a team, regardless of the name of the group. A key challenge, then, is to find ways to create the elements of a highly effective team—interdependence, efficiency, magnetism, shared responsibility, positive energy, mutual encouragement, and trust—when individuals may have had no prior commitment to one another or to a common task.

One important factor in creating effective teams, of course, is the role of the leader. As pointed out by Hackman (2003), however, it is not the style of the leader that makes a difference. Multiple leadership styles can be effective, and no one style has particular advantages over others. Rather, it is the skills and capabilities of the leader, or the tools and techniques put into practice that account for effective versus ineffective team performance. We highlight two especially critical aspects of team leadership here. Not only are these two aspects of team leadership observable in General Pagonis, but they have emerged in the scholarly literature as critical factors in leading almost any kind of team (Edmonson, 1999; Hackman, 1990). The first is developing credibility and influence among team members. The second is establishing a motivating vision and goals for the team.

DEVELOPING CREDIBILITY

Effective leaders have the respect and commitment of team members. That is, they develop credibility (Kouzes & Posner, 1987). Establishing credibility and the capacity to influence team members are the first key challenges faced by leaders of teams. Except in rare circumstances (e.g., in a crisis), leading a team by command or direct control is much less effective than leading through influence and indirect control (Druskat & Wheeler, 2000; Hackman, 1987). Consequently, we focus on ways that you can be effective by working *with* team members rather than working *on* team members. Giving directions, articulating goals, or trying to motivate team members are all wasted efforts if you have not established credibility and respect. General Pagonis described this leadership challenge in the following way:

I have found, time and time again in commands around the world, that my troops are more invested in their work and better motivated when they understand and buy into the ultimate goals of the operation. Reason counts for far more than rank, when it comes to motivation. And motivation is the root of all organizational progress. Over the years I have developed a very distinctive leadership style. Gus Pagonis' command style, like everyone else's, is unique. This meant that I had choices to make. Would I rather have the world's best port operation officer, if he was someone who didn't already know

my style? Or would I rather have the world's second best port operation officer who knew my style intimately and was comfortable with it? The answer was obvious; we couldn't waste time fighting our own systems. Equally important, we couldn't afford the time that would be wasted as a new person tried to impress me, or get on my good side. We needed an instant body of leaders, strengthened by a united front. We needed to know that we could depend on one another unconditionally. We needed the confidence that the mission, and not personal advancement, would always be paramount in the mind of each participant. (Pagonis, 1993, p. 78, 84)

In earlier chapters we identified ways to enhance a manager's influence (Chapter 5) and trust (Chapter 8), which are components of credibility. In this chapter we highlight additional behaviors you can use to help establish leadership credibility in a team. Team members, of course, will not follow a person whom they don't trust, who is hypocritical or dishonest, or whose motives appear to be personal aggrandizement instead of the welfare of the team. In fact, Posner and Kouzes (1987) identified credibility as the single most important requirement for leadership effectiveness. Once credibility has been established, then goals for the team can be articulated and the team can move toward high performance. The seven behaviors summarized in Table 9.4 are keys to building and maintaining credibility and influence among team members. Whereas they are simple and straightforward, much scholarly evidence exists that support their efficacy (see Cialdini, 1995; Druskat & Wheeler, 2000; Hackman, 2003; Katzenbach & Smith, 1993; Kramer, 1999; Manz & Sims, 1987; Turner, 2000).

Table 9.4   Ways to Build Team Leader Credibility
Team leaders build credibility with their team members by:
• Demonstrating integrity, representing authenticity, and displaying congruence.
• Being clear and consistent about what they want to achieve.
• Creating positive energy by being optimistic and complimentary.
• Building a base of agreement among team members before moving on, with a focus on task accomplishment.
• Managing agreement and disagreement among team members by using one-sided and two-sided arguments appropriately—one-sided in situations when all team members agree, two-sided when consensus is not preexisting.
• Encouraging and coaching team members to help them improve.
• Sharing information about the team itself, providing perspective from external sources, and encouraging participation.

LEARNING

1. *Demonstrate integrity.* Chief among the behaviors that create leadership credibility is the demonstration of integrity. Integrity means that you do what you say, you behave congruently with your values, and you are believable in what you espouse. Some people call this "walking the talk" or "talking the walk." Credibility is dependent on having team members believe that the leader is trustworthy, that hidden agendas or unspoken motives are absent, and that the leader demonstrates justice and fairness. Individuals who appear to say one thing and do another, who are not honest in their feedback, or who do not follow through with promises are perceived to lack integrity and are ineffective as leaders of teams.

2. *Be clear and consistent.* Expressing certainty about what you want and where you are going, without being dogmatic or stubborn, helps produce confidence on the part of others. Being wishy-washy or inconsistent in your viewpoints inhibits credibility. The electorate in most countries throughout the world rate their politicians as very low in credibility because most candidates appear to be inconsistent in their statements, changing perspectives depending on the audience (Cialdini, 1995). Credible people, on the other hand, can be trusted to be consistent and predictable. A passionate point of view, it is said, is worth 50 IQ points. That's because being clear about what you want reduces uncertainty, fosters clarity, and creates consistency that leads to trust of the part of team members. Articulating and reinforcing an unwavering and persistent point of view is much more effective than changing opinions or preferences depending on whether or not others agree with you.

3. *Create positive energy.* Stay optimistic and complimentary. Most teams do not perform effectively when there is a climate of criticism, cynicism, or negativity. Criticizing team members, past leaders, others outside the team, or even being critical of the circumstances in which the team finds itself are usually not effective ways to help a team perform well. Individuals and teams perform better when positive energy exists—optimism, compliments, celebrations of success, and recognition of progress. This does not mean being unrealistic or a "Pollyanna." Instead, it means that when you are seen as a source of positive energy and enthusiasm, you have more credibility and influence among team members. People are more attracted to positive than negative forces for the same reason they are more likely to say "yes" to a request if they have said "yes" to previous requests (Cialdini, 1995). Team members are more likely to be agreeable and committed to your agenda if you, as the leader, are agreeable and optimistic.

4. *Use commonality and reciprocity.* If you express views in the team that are held in common with team members, they are more likely to agree with your later statements. If you want to foster team change, or move the team toward an outcome that appears to be risky or uncomfortable, begin by expressing views with which other team members agree. It can be as simple as "I know you all have very busy schedules." Or, "We have a lot of diversity of opinion in our team on this issue." These kinds of statements work because of the principle of reciprocity. Team members have a tendency to agree with you more if they have received something from you in advance, even if that is merely your agreement with their point of view. After you have expressed agreement with them, you can then lead them toward goals or targets that may stretch them or that may be uncomfortable or uncertain. Your credibility will have been established if your initial statements are seen as consistent with the values and perspectives of other team members. This is also a fundamental strategy in effective negotiations.

5. *Manage agreement and disagreement.* When team members initially agree with you, you are more effective if you use a one-sided argument. That is, present only one point of view and support it with evidence. When team members tend to disagree with you at the outset, use two-sided arguments. That is, first present both sides of the case and then show how your own point of view is superior to the contrary perspective. Keep in mind that when team members agree with you, the first statements you make tend to hold more weight and are remembered the longest. When they disagree with you, the last statements made tend to carry the most weight.

6. *Encourage and coach.* Providing encouragement to team members has been found to be among the most powerful predictors of effective

team leadership. Encouragement means to help others develop courage—to tackle uncertainty, to achieve beyond their current performance, to disrupt the status quo. Encouraging team members not only involves compliments and supportive statements, it also involves coaching and assistance. Coaching, as pointed out in Chapter 4, means helping to show the way, providing information or advice, and assisting team members with task requirements. It doesn't mean that the team leader becomes controlling or takes over. It means that coaches help others perform well while not being actively involved themselves. Effective encouragement, then, is more than cheerleading. It involves giving both positively reinforcing comments and helpful advice or direction.

7. *Share information.* Credible team leaders are knowledgeable, mainly about the preferences and talents that reside in the team and about the task facing the team. Building credibility means coming to understand the perspectives of team members as well as a sense of their talents and resources. Coming to know your team members well is crucial for successful leadership. One way to do this is to use the principle of "frequent checking." This merely involves asking questions and checking with team members regularly to determine levels of agreement, obstacles, dissatisfactions, needs, and interpersonal or team issues. Credibility is also built by having knowledge about the tasks and the external environment facing the team. This kind of knowledge can be achieved by playing the roles of "ambassador" and "scout" for the team, representing the team to outsiders, and obtaining information from external sources. Importantly, however, credibility grows as knowledge is shared. Being the source from which others can acquire needed information builds credibility and influence, so sharing is crucial. Of course, no leader can be an expert on all topics relevant to the team, but effective leaders continually increase and expand their storehouse of knowledge about the team and its environment.

As stated by General Pagonis:

Keeping [team members] abreast of your actions, as well as the rationale behind those actions, puts everybody on an equal information footing. I believe that information

is power, but only if it is shared. . . . Very early on I had gotten in the habit of sneaking John Carr into these briefing sessions with CINC [General Schwarzkopf and others] by having Carr flip my slides in and out of the overhead projector. That way, he stayed as smart and as current about the CINC's plans as I did. (Pagonis, 1993, p. 88, 131)

ESTABLISH SMART GOALS AND EVEREST GOALS

Once team members have confidence in the leader, it is then possible for that leader to identify goals that the team can achieve and levels of performance to which team members can aspire. Katzenbach and Smith (1993), in an outstanding study of high-performing teams, reinforced this point of view:

The best teams invest a tremendous amount of time and effort exploring, shaping, and agreeing on a goal that belongs to them collectively and individually. . . . With enough time and sincere attention, one or more broad, meaningful aspirations invariably arise that motivate teams to provide a fundamental reason for their extra effort. (p. 50)

There are two kinds of goals that characterize high-performing teams, and leaders must identify and espouse both kinds. The first are called **SMART goals** and the second are called **Everest goals.** The purpose for establishing clear goals is so that every person on the team can give a similar answer to the question: What are we trying to achieve? Leaders who clearly articulate the desired outcomes for and with the team are more likely to experience high performance from the team. Goal-directed performance, in fact, always exceeds performance disassociated with goals (Locke, 1990). Figure 9.3 illustrates this point.

It shows that when people are given *no goals* ("Here is your task. Go do it."), their performance tends to be low, even though most people will perform at a minimum level even when they are not certain of the standard that they should achieve. However, being provided with an *easy goal* ("The average is 10 per day, but you can shoot for 4.") leads to even lower performance. People tend to work toward the standard that has been established, and when it is easy, they slack off. Establishing *general goals* ("Do your best.") result in improved performance over easy goals, but identifying *difficult goals* ("The average is 10 per day, but you

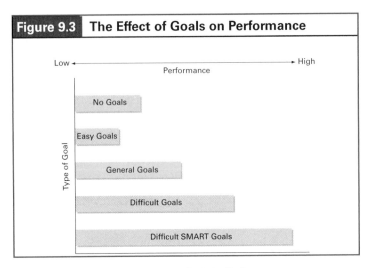

Figure 9.3	The Effect of Goals on Performance

Low ◄─────── Performance ─────────► High

Type of Goal

- No Goals
- Easy Goals
- General Goals
- Difficult Goals
- Difficult SMART Goals

SOURCE: *University of Michigan, Positive Organizational Scholarship: Kim Cameron.*

should shoot for 12.") produces far higher levels of performance. The kinds of goals that produce the highest levels of performance, however are difficult goals that possess five characteristics. The acronym SMART identifies these attributes. SMART goals are:

- ❏ **S**pecific—The goal is clear, and precise targets and standards are identified.
- ❏ **M**easurable—The goal can be assessed and quantified. The extent to which the goal has been achieved is obvious.
- ❏ **A**ligned—The goal is supportive of and consistent with the goals of the broader organization. People are not pursuing their own objectives independent of their team.
- ❏ **R**ealistic—While being difficult and causing performance to stretch, the goal is not foolhardy or a fantasy.
- ❏ **T**ime-bound—An end point is identified or a completion date established so that goal achievement is not open-ended.

Consider the difference between goal statements such as "We will be the best in our industry," compared to a goal statement that is SMART: "We will achieve a 5 percent improvement in the on-time delivery of our products by the end of the quarter." The latter provides a more motivating goal in that it is specific, measurable, aligned with key outcomes, realistic, and time-bound. It gives people something they can easily understand and shoot for. It is important to keep in mind, however, that articulating motivating goals and identifying the methods to achieve them are different. The former specifies the target. The latter specifies the means for achieving the target. The former is

crucial to successful team leadership. The latter is often lethal. Pagonis' team illustrates this well:

> *I never tell a subordinate how to carry out a specific goal. Dictating terms to a subordinate undermines innovation, decreases the subordinate's willingness to take responsibility for his or her actions, increases the potential for suboptimization of resources, and increases the chances that the command will be dysfunctional if circumstances change dramatically. Our first month in the theater only underscored my sense that our [team] would have to be incredibly elastic. (Pagonis, 1993, p. 119)*

The second type of goal that effective team leaders articulate is called an Everest goal. An Everest goal goes beyond normal goal setting. It represents an ultimate achievement, an extraordinary accomplishment, or a beyond-the-norm outcome. Achieving it requires everything one can give. Like setting your sights on getting to the summit of Mount Everest, an Everest goal is clear and compelling: serves as a unifying focal point; builds team spirit; engages people; and creates positive energy and excitement. An Everest goal is stimulating because it connects to a profound passion. People get it right away, with little explanation. An Everest goal is visionary, not just tactical or strategic, and it leaves people better for having engaged in its pursuit. It requires extraordinary effort to achieve, and maybe a little luck.

Examples of Everest goals include Henry Ford's goal of democratizing the automobile industry so that his workers could afford to purchase cars in the 1920s; Masaru Ibuka's goal of helping Sony to become the company that overcame the image of poor Japanese quality in the 1960s and 1970s; Steven Jobs' goal of one person, one computer throughout the world in the 1980s; or Sam Walton's goal in the 1990s of having Wal-Mart become the first trillion-dollar company.

Team leaders can identify stretch targets, of course, such as: "We will be #1 or #2 in our industry," or "We will be the world's best software team," or "We will achieve 100 percent customer satisfaction." These are very difficult goals to achieve and certainly extend beyond the norm. However, Everest goals have a very important attribute that supplements these goal statements. This attribute is illustrated by the following quotation from a climber who finally made it to the top of Mount Everest after three failed attempts:

I realized something on that night in the dark on Everest. What I realized was that real winning had nothing to do with beating someone else, or crossing the finish line first, or standing on top. Winning wasn't anything external at all. It was an internal satisfaction, a deep inner sense of pride and joy. Success can only be measured within ourselves, by ourselves. It has nothing to do with other people's perception of our achievements. It has everything to do with our own perceptions of our efforts . . . Success isn't standing on the podium, or hearing the cheers of others, or standing on the summit at all. It's giving it your all. . . . I think that in anything in life, if you give it everything you possibly can, you really do succeed. . . . Our business in life is not to get ahead of others but to get ahead of ourselves, to break our own records, to outstrip our yesterday by our today, to do our work with more force than ever before. We took comfort in the words of Gandhi: 'Full effort is full victory'. . .

I have come to understand that for me this notion of success is upside down. In fact, a traditional end—the summit, an Olympic gold medal, or wealth—only serves as a navigational tool, a marker to give the process direction. The end for me is a greater depth and breadth of character. I measure this in terms of greater integrity, better business and communication skills, and a higher personal motivation to become stronger. More simply, my aim is to become as internally knowledgeable and as externally aware as possible. The process, the experience, the struggle, the hard-won lessons, these are ends in themselves. (Clarke & Hobson, 2005, pp. 168, 169)

Everest goals are not merely stretch targets, but they possess the ability to elevate human performance far beyond the norm. People achieve what they could not previously have thought possible. They thrive personally in ways that would not have been feasible otherwise. Typical Everest goals:

❏ Capture deep inner commitment of people because they are tied to something about which they care deeply

❏ Require supreme effort and a passionate commitment

❏ Depend on complete honesty and authenticity, since achieving them cannot be accomplished by trying to be something artificial or false

❏ Motivate learning and wisdom, allowing people to learn new things about themselves and their capabilities in the pursuit of the goal

❏ Enhance positive human relationships—it is impossible to achieve an Everest goal alone, so they require support and interdependence with others

❏ Lead people beyond probabilities into the realm of possibilities, so that previously unconsidered levels of accomplishment become realistic

Identifying such a goal, of course, is neither automatic nor easy. Such goals don't just roll off the tips of our tongues. Most people identify few of these in a lifetime. These goals are often connected to: (1) producing a human benefit for others, (2) a core personal value, (3) producing an impact that extends beyond the immediate, even over a lifetime, (4) virtues such as love, faith, integrity, compassion, hope, or (5) producing a ripple effect, so that the achievement is reproduced over and over again. Establishing Everest goals requires that you get in touch with your personal values, your core mission or purpose in life, and that which provides you profound meaning. Everest goals help you reach those ultimate aspirations.

In summary, being an effective leader of a team requires two key skills: (1) developing credibility among team members and (2) articulating SMART goals and Everest goals for the team. Whereas these are obviously not the only skills that effective team leaders possess, without these two core capabilities, it is unlikely that the teams you lead will be successful.

INTERNATIONAL CAVEATS

We have pointed out throughout the book that individuals in different cultures exhibit differences in values and orientations (Trompenaars, 1996, 1998). Diagnosing, understanding, and capitalizing on individual differences, we repeat, is a crucial skill of competent managers. The seven value orientations identified by Trompenaars provide a useful tool for identifying those individual differences. That is, you can understand differences among people by assessing them on the extent to which they emphasize one value orientation over its opposite: *universalism* versus *particularism*, *individualism* versus *communitarianism*, *neutrality* versus *affectivity*, *specificity* versus *diffuseness*, *achievement* versus *ascription*, *internal* versus *external* control, and *past*, *present*, or *future* time orientation. The first chapter in this book provides a more detailed explanation of these value dimensions.

Individual differences may require that some modification be made in these team leadership behaviors. For example, if you are leading a team with members from cultures that tend to have a *collectivist* (e.g., Mexico, Japan, France, Philippines) as opposed to an *individualist* orientation, team members will expect to be involved in the creation and articulation of the goals. They will be less comfortable with the goals coming from a single leader, regardless of his or her credibility and influence. Consequently, the Everest goal and its accompanying SMART goals should be designed with active participation of team members. Similarly, team members from countries where a *neutral* (e.g., Korea, China, Japan, New Zealand) as opposed to an *affective* culture predominates, may be less energized by language filled with superlatives and passion. Their orientation toward task accomplishment and factual data may mute their responses to emotional language. Consequently, being sensitive to the wording of your Everest goal statement will help make it more motivating.

On the other hand, the differences in cultural values among different nationalities are not so great as to negate the overall effectiveness of the two key skills mentioned above—building credibility and articulating two types of goals. The data from thousands of managers worldwide supports the effectiveness of these two key skills for team leaders, regardless of national differences (see Trompenaars & Hampden-Turner, 1998). You may need to be sensitive to the potential need to modify your behaviors based on the composition of your team, but team composition will not have as strong an influence on team effectiveness as the leadership skills you display. (For one review of team composition influences, see Guzzo & Dickson, 1996.)

Team Membership

Most of the time, most of us will not serve as the leader of the teams in which we participate. Whereas you will want to prepare for the leadership roles you will play in the future, the vast majority of the time you will be an active member of a team, working for the common good of the group, rather than the person in charge. You will be valuable to your team because of the contributions you make in nonleadership roles. Fortunately, you can be at least as effective as a member of a team as you can be as the team's leader in having an effect on its performance. One of the most amazing statements made by General Pagonis as he reviewed the outcomes of Desert Storm related to the performance of his team, even when he was not the active leader:

> *I meet with skepticism, even disbelief, when I tell people that I didn't issue a single order during the ground war. This is only slightly a stretch of the truth. Yes, people sought and got guidance. But the people in my command knew exactly what they were supposed to do in almost every conceivable circumstance. They had been trained and encouraged to think on their feet. I felt they could even deal with the inconceivable. (Pagonis, 1993, p. 148)*

Team members were not only guided by an overarching goal and a clear understanding of what they were to accomplish, but they had become an extraordinarily high-performing team because of the roles played by team members. Pagonis described it this way: "Truth be told, we spent less of our time as logisticians, and more of our time as managers, fixers, firefighters, father confessors, and cheerleaders. There was simply nobody else around to play those roles" (p. 87). In this section, we point out two main skills associated with team membership—playing advantageous roles, and providing helpful feedback to others. Once again, these skills are not complicated, but they have been found to be highly effective in helping team members foster team success (see Parker, 1996).

ADVANTAGEOUS ROLES

Work teams face two main challenges: accomplishing the task that has been assigned and building unity and collaboration among the team members. As a member of a team you can enhance or inhibit those two challenges at least as much as you can as the team leader. All of us have experienced teams that just seemed to click, that were able to get results quickly and effectively, and were fun to be in. Those dynamics don't happen by chance but depend on certain key roles played by team members.

A great deal of research has been done on the power of group pressure and the influence of team members on one another. The classic Solomon Asch experiments (1951) were among the first to highlight the influence of team members on one another. The Asch experiments showed, for example, that when other team members verbalized agreement with a statement that was obviously false—say, "The federal government controls the stock market"—the person being observed also tended to verbalize agreement with the

obviously false statement. Team members' behavior dramatically influenced the behaviors of one another. Most teams don't operate on the basis of blatant pressure tactics, of course, but team performance can be markedly enhanced by having team members play certain roles that facilitate task accomplishment and group cohesion.

Two main types of roles exist that enhance team performance: ***task-facilitating roles*** and ***relationship-building roles*** (Schein, 1976). It is difficult for team members to emphasize both types of roles equally, and most people tend to contribute in one area more than the other. That is, some team members tend to be more task-focused whereas others tend to be more relationship-focused. Task-facilitating roles are those that help the team accomplish its outcomes or objectives. Table 9.5 identifies the most common task-facilitating roles. They include:

LEARNING

Table 9.5	Task-Facilitating Roles
ROLE	**EXAMPLES**
Direction giving	"This is the way we were instructed to approach our task."
	"Everyone write down your ideas, then share them."
Information seeking	"What did you mean by that?"
	"Does anyone else have more information about this?"
Information giving	"Here are some relevant data."
	"I want to share some information that may be helpful."
Elaborating	"Building on your idea, here is an additional alternative."
	"An example of what you just said is . . . "
Urging	"We have only 10 minutes left, so we need to move more quickly."
	"We can't quit now. We're close to finalizing our proposal."
Monitoring	"You maintain accountability for the first recommendation, and I'll handle the second."
	"Here are some criteria we can use to judge our success."
Process analyzing	"It seems as if the energy level in the team is beginning to decline."
	"I've noticed that the females are participating less than the males in our team."
Reality testing	"Let's see if this is really practical."
	"Do you think this is workable given our resources?"
Enforcing	"We're beginning to wander in our comments; let's stay on task."
	"Since we agreed not to interrupt one another, I suggest we stick to our pact."
Summarizing	"It seems to me that these are the conclusions we have reached."
	"In summary, you have made three points . . . "

- *Direction giving.* Identifying ways to proceed or alternatives to pursue and clarifying goals and objectives.
- *Information seeking.* Asking questions, analyzing knowledge gaps, requesting opinions, beliefs, and perspectives.
- *Information giving.* Providing data, offering facts and judgments, and highlighting conclusions.
- *Elaborating.* Building on the ideas expressed by others; providing examples and illustrations.
- *Urging.* Imploring team members to stay on task and to achieve team goals.
- *Monitoring.* Checking on progress, developing measures of success and helping to maintain accountability for results.
- *Process analyzing.* Analyzing processes and procedures used by the team in order to improve efficiency and timeliness.
- *Reality testing.* Exploring whether ideas presented are practical or workable; grounding comments in reality.
- *Enforcing.* Helping to reinforce team rules, reinforcing standards, and maintaining agreed-upon procedures.
- *Summarizing.* Combining ideas and summing up points made in the team; helping members understand the conclusions that have been reached.

Performing task-facilitating roles helps the team work more efficiently and effectively in achieving its objectives. Without having at least one team member displaying task-facilitating behaviors, teams tend to take longer to achieve their objectives and have difficulty staying focused. In your role as a team member, you will find it useful to sometimes play the role of task facilitator. Sometimes keeping the team "on task" is the most important thing you can do. These roles are especially important when: progress toward goal accomplishment is slow, when the team is being deflected from its task, when time pressures exist, when the assignment is complex or ambiguous and it is not clear how to proceed, or when no one else is helping the team move toward task accomplishment. One doesn't have to be a task master to be an effective facilitator of outcomes. In fact, just recognizing that the team is in need of task facilitation is a big part of being an effective team member. In most effective teams, you will find several members performing these task-facilitation roles.

In addition to task accomplishment, high-performing teams also have a certain amount of interpersonal cohesion and collaboration. An overwhelming amount of evidence exists to suggest that high-performing teams are cohesive, interdependent, and have positive affect among team members (Cohen & Bailey, 1997; Druskat & Wolff, 1999; Gully, Divine, & Whitney, 1995; Mullen & Copper, 1994; Parker, 1996). Relationship-building roles are those that emphasize the interpersonal aspects of the team. They focus on assisting team members to feel good about one another, enjoy the team's work, and maintain a tension-free climate. These roles are especially important when disagreement is prevalent, tension is high, or team members are not contributing to the team's performance. Table 9.6 identifies the most common relationship-building roles:

- *Supporting.* Praising the ideas of others, showing friendliness, and pointing out others' contributions.
- *Harmonizing.* Mediating differences between others, and finding a common ground in disputes and conflicting points of view.
- *Tension relieving.* Using jokes and humor to reduce tension and put others at ease.
- *Confronting.* Challenging unproductive or disruptive behaviors; helping to ensure proper behavior in the team.
- *Energizing.* Motivating others toward greater effort; exuding enthusiasm.
- *Developing.* Assisting others to learn, grow, and achieve; orienting and coaching members of the team.
- *Consensus building.* Helping build solidarity among team members, encouraging agreement, and helping interactions to be smooth.
- *Empathizing.* Reflecting group feelings and expressing empathy and support for team members.

All of us have been on a team, or in a class, when a fellow participant was funny, actively engaging with others, or especially supportive of others on the team or in the class. The chemistry of the group just seems to improve under such conditions. It becomes easier to work and more enjoyable to be a team member. A certain amount of magnetism and positive energy exists. People tend to take more responsibility, collaborate more readily, and try harder to find consensual outcomes. These are the results that are intended by performing relationship-building roles. They are not designed to deflect attention away from the task,

Table 9.6	**Relationship-Building Roles**
ROLE	**EXAMPLES**
Supporting	"Your ideas are terrific!"
	"I really appreciate your honesty and openness. It's refreshing."
Harmonizing	"I hear the two of you saying essentially the same thing."
	"The disagreements being expressed don't seem to be all that crucial."
Tension relieving	"Hey folks, let's lighten up!"
	"This reminds me of the new conference table we bought. It sleeps 12."
Confronting	"How does your comment address the topic we are discussing?"
	"You are not taking as much responsibility as the other team members."
Energizing	"Your insights are terrific!"
	"This team is the most enjoyable group I've been in for a long time."
Developing	"How can I help you?"
	"Let me give you some assistance with that."
Consensus building	"It seems like we're all saying pretty much the same thing."
	"Can we all at least agree on point number 1, even if we disagree on the rest?"
Empathizing	"I know how you feel."
	"This must be a very sensitive topic for you given your personal experience."

but they assist the team in working more effectively together.

Without both task-facilitating and relationship-building roles, teams struggle to perform effectively. Some members must ensure that the team accomplishes its tasks, while others must ensure that members remain bonded together interpersonally. These are usually not the same individuals, and at certain points in time, different roles may become more dominant than others. The key is to have a balance between task-oriented roles and relationship-building roles displayed in the team. The downfall of many teams is that they become unidimensional—for example, they emphasize task accomplishment exclusively—and do not give equal attention to both types of roles.

Of course, each role can also have a downside if performed ineffectively or in inappropriate circumstances. For example, *elaborating* may be disruptive if the team is trying to reach a quick decision; *tension relieving* may be annoying if the team is trying to be serious; *enforcing* may create resistance when the team is already experiencing high levels of pressure; *consensus building* may mask real differences of opinion and tension among team members. However, it is even more likely that team members will display other unproductive roles rather than inappropriately play

task or relationship roles. Unproductive roles inhibit the team or its members from achieving what they could have achieved, and they destroy morale and cohesion. They are called **blocking roles.** We point out a few of them here because, as you analyze the teams to which you belong, you may recognize these roles being performed and be able to confront them. Among the common blocking roles are:

- ❏ *Dominating.* Excessive talking, interrupting, or cutting others off.
- ❏ *Overanalyzing.* Splitting hairs and examining every detail excessively.
- ❏ *Stalling.* Not allowing the group to reach a decision or finalize a task by sidetracking the discussion, being unwilling to agree, repeating old arguments, and so on.
- ❏ *Remaining passive.* Not being willing to engage in the team's task. Staying on the fringe or refusing to interact with other team members. Expecting others to do the team's work.
- ❏ *Overgeneralizing.* Blowing something out of proportion and drawing unfounded conclusions.
- ❏ *Faultfinding.* Being unwilling to see the merits of others' ideas or criticizing others excessively.

- *Premature decision making.* Making decisions before goals are stated, information is shared, alternatives are discussed, or problems are defined.
- *Presenting opinions as facts.* Failing to examine the legitimacy of proposals and labeling personal opinions as truth.
- *Rejecting.* Rejecting ideas based on the person who stated them rather than on their merits.
- *Pulling rank.* Using status, expertise, or title to get ideas accepted rather than discussing and examining their value.
- *Resisting.* Blocking all attempts to change, to improve, or to make progress. Being disagreeable and negative about virtually all suggestions from other team members.
- *Deflecting.* Not staying focused on the topic of the team's discussion. Changing the subject of discussion or making comments that deflect attention away from the main points.

Each of these blocking roles has the potential to inhibit a team from efficiently and effectively accomplishing its task by crushing morale, destroying consensus, creating conflict, hampering progress, and making ill-informed decisions. Effective team members recognize when blocking roles are displayed, confront and isolate dysfunctional members, and provide feedback to those who are inhibiting effective team performance. Knowing the most effective ways in which that feedback can be delivered is the second key skill of team members.

PROVIDING FEEDBACK

It is not easy to provide feedback to someone who is behaving inappropriately or disruptively. Whereas it is much easier to provide positive feedback or give compliments, helping others correct their negative behavior or pointing out the dysfunctions of blocking roles is difficult. Most of us are afraid of offending others, of making the problem worse, or of creating conflict that may destroy team unity. (The chapter on building positive relationships by supportively communicating addressed this issue in detail.) While no set of behaviors are guaranteed to be effective in every situation or with every individual, of course, certain principles for providing feedback—usually negative feedback—have been found to be especially effective (Dew, 1998; Hayes, 1997; Yeatts & Hyten, 1998). They are summarized in Table 9.7.

- *Focus feedback on behavior rather than persons.* Individuals can control and change their behavior. They cannot change their personalities or physical characteristics. For example, "Your comments are not on the topic" is more effective than "You are completely naïve."
- *Focus feedback on observations rather than inferences and on descriptions rather than judgments.* Facts and objective evidence are more trustworthy and acceptable than opinions and conjectures. For example, "The data don't support your point" is more effective than "You just don't get it, do you?"
- *Focus feedback on behavior related to a specific situation, preferably to the "here-and-now," rather than on abstract or past behavior.* It will merely frustrate people if they cannot pinpoint a specific incident or behavior to which you are referring. Similarly, people cannot change something that has already happened and is "water under the bridge." For example, "You have yet

Table 9.7	Rules for Effective Team Feedback	
EFFECTIVE FEEDBACK	INEFFECTIVE FEEDBACK
Focus on behaviors	Focus on the person
Focus on observations	Focus on inferences
Focus on descriptions	Focus on evaluations
Focus on a specific situation or incident	Focus on abstract or general situations
Focus on the here-and-now	Focus on the past
Focus on sharing ideas and information	Focus on giving advice
Give feedback that is valuable to the receiver	Give feedback that provides an emotional release
Give feedback at an appropriate time and place	Give feedback when it is convenient for you

to agree with anyone's comments" is more effective than "You have always been a problem in this team."

❏ *Focus feedback on sharing ideas and information rather than giving advice.* Explore alternatives together. Unless requested, avoid giving direct instructions and demands. Instead, help recipients identify changes and improvements themselves. For example, "How do you suggest we can break this logjam and move forward?" is more effective than "This is what we must do now."

❏ *Focus feedback on the amount of information that the recipient can use, rather than on the amount you might like to give.* Information overload causes people to stop listening. Not enough information leads to frustration and misunderstanding. For example, "You seem to have reached a conclusion before all the facts have been presented" is more effective than "Here are some data you should consider, and here are some more, and here are some more, and here are some more."

❏ *Focus feedback on the value it may have to the receiver, not on the emotional release it provides for you.* Feedback should be for the good of the recipient, not merely for you to let off steam. For example, "I must say that your excessive talking is very troublesome to me and not helpful to the group" is more effective than "You are being a jerk and are a big cause of our team's difficulty in making any progress."

❏ *Focus feedback on time and place so that personal data can be shared at appropriate times.* The more specific feedback is, or the more it can be anchored in a specific context, the more helpful it can be. For example, "During a break I would like to chat with you about something" is more effective than "You think your title gives you the right to force the rest of us to agree with you, but it's just making us angry."

INTERNATIONAL CAVEATS

These team member skills may require some modification in different international settings or with teams comprised of international members (Trompenaars & Hampen-Turner, 1998). Whereas the team member skills discussed above have been found to be effective in a global context, it is naïve to expect that everyone will react the same way to team member roles.

For example, in cultures that emphasize *affectivity* (e.g., Iran, Spain, France, Italy, Mexico), personal confrontations and emotional displays are more acceptable than in cultures that are more *neutral* (e.g., Korea, China, Singapore, Japan), where personal references are more offensive. Humor and displaying enthusiastic behavior is also more acceptable in affective cultures than neutral cultures. Similarly, status differences are likely to play a more dominant role in *ascription*-oriented cultures (e.g., Czech Republic, Egypt, Spain, Korea), than in *achievement*-oriented cultures (e.g., United States, Norway, Canada, Australia, United Kingdom), in which knowledge and skills tend to be more important. Appealing to data and facts in the latter cultures will carry more weight than in the former cultures. Some misunderstanding may also arise, for example, in cultures emphasizing different *time frames*. Whereas some cultures emphasize just-in-time, short-term time frames (e.g., United States), others emphasize long-term future time frames (e.g., Japan). The story is told of the Japanese proposal to purchase Yosemite National Park in California. The first thing the Japanese submitted was a 250-year business plan. The reaction of the California authorities was, "Wow, that's 1,000 quarterly reports." The urgency to move a team forward toward task accomplishment, in other words, may be seen differently by different cultural groups. Some cultures (e.g., Japan) are more comfortable spending substantial amounts of time on relationship-building activities before moving toward task accomplishment.

Summary

All of us are members of multiple teams—at work, at home, and in the community. Teams are becoming increasingly prevalent in the workplace and in the classroom because they have been shown to be powerful tools to improve the performance of individuals and organizations. Consequently, it is important to become proficient in leading and participating in teams. It is obvious that merely putting people together and giving them an assigned task does not make them into a team. Students often complain about an excessive amount of teamwork in business schools, but most of it is less real teamwork than a repetitive experience of aggregating people together and assigning them a task. In this chapter we have reviewed three types of team skills: diagnosing and facilitating team development, leading a team, and being an effective team member. Figure 9.4 illustrates the relationship of these three key skills to high performing team performance. These three skills are ones that you have no doubt engaged in

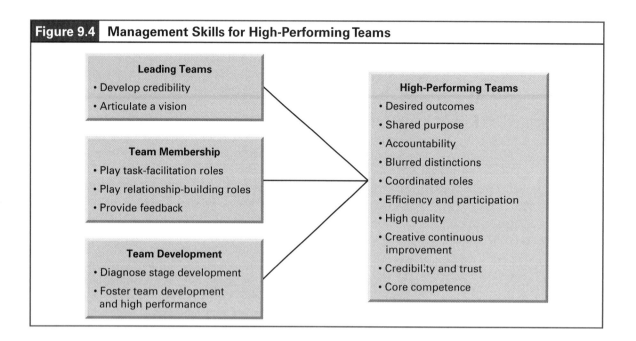

Figure 9.4 Management Skills for High-Performing Teams

Leading Teams
- Develop credibility
- Articulate a vision

Team Membership
- Play task-facilitation roles
- Play relationship-building roles
- Provide feedback

Team Development
- Diagnose stage development
- Foster team development and high performance

High-Performing Teams
- Desired outcomes
- Shared purpose
- Accountability
- Blurred distinctions
- Coordinated roles
- Efficiency and participation
- High quality
- Creative continuous improvement
- Credibility and trust
- Core competence

before, but to be a skillful manager, you will need to hone your ability to perform each of these skill activities competently.

Behavioral Guidelines

1. Learn to diagnose the stage in which your team is operating in order to help facilitate team development and perform your role appropriately. Know the key characteristics of the forming, norming, storming, and performing stages of development.

2. Provide structure and clarity in the forming stage, support and encouragement in the norming stage, independence and exploration in the storming stage, and foster innovation and positive deviance in the performing stage.

3. When leading a team, first develop credibility as a prerequisite to having team members follow you.

4. Based on your established credibility, establish two types of goals for and with your team: SMART goals and Everest goals.

5. As a team member, facilitate task performance in your team by encouraging the performance of different roles listed in Table 9.5.

6. As a team member, facilitate the development of good relationships in your team by encouraging the performance of different roles listed in Table 9.6.

7. When encountering team members who block the team's performance with disruptive behaviors, confront the behavior directly and/or isolate the disruptive member.

8. Provide effective feedback to unhelpful team members that has characteristics listed in Table 9.7.

CASES INVOLVING BUILDING EFFECTIVE TEAMS

She Loves a Challenge!

As the new director of Admissions at a prestigious university in Turkey, Dr. Shaheen's first task was to encourage her staff to communicate with each other and work together as a team. Here is an account of how Dr. Shaheen achieved this. Although based on a true account, all names and descriptions have been changed.

The president of the university was keen to discuss Dr. Marie Shaheen's new position but she was on her way to London and would not be able to discuss the matter in any great detail until she returned. Dr. Shaheen was planning to pursue a second thesis and had arranged to meet with her PhD supervisor, but the president announced her appointment in her absence, forcing Dr. Shaheen to return home to prepare for the coming academic year. Dr. Shaheen had been assigned to head one of the most important departments in any institution of higher education, a department that was not functioning as well as it should and that needed a strong leader.

All departments in any educational institution are important, especially those that require personnel to be in direct contact with students, parents, and educators. The department that Dr. Shaheen now headed was Admissions, and she considered it to be the backbone of the university. The main objective of the department was to promote the university's image and to encourage students to apply for a place at the university. Therefore, a coordinated effort was required across the department, and personnel were expected to possess excellent communication and interpersonal skills.

Admissions is the very first office that students, parents, and visitors come into contact with. Accordingly, it is crucial that all members of the office share the same goals, attitude, and mission. Dr. Shaheen believed that the department's success depended on how effectively the personnel developed and utilized their communication skills. Consequently, Dr. Shaheen had to figure out the strengths and weaknesses of all the personnel in her department.

Upon Dr. Shaheen's appointment as director, there were four employees in the office: May, Mehdi, Chirine, and Aisha. Apart from introducing herself and asking the employees to introduce themselves, during the first week Dr. Shaheen simply observed their performance and the office dynamics. She found that the dominant culture was "I" and not "we." There was no productive interaction, and it was evident that there was absolutely no team spirit. She needed to convey that team spirit was a prerequisite for teamwork and mutual respect and trust. Dr. Shaheen realized the scope of the challenge ahead of her, but she had a deep sense of commitment to the institution, and her loyalty and self-motivation meant that she wanted to do the best thing by her new team and the university.

Dr. Shaheen took refuge in her office to contemplate and prepare her plan of action. As she thought about the strategy she would need to ensure that her new goals would be met, she pondered on the characteristics of each of the employees she had inherited. She was reminded of something she had previously read by

Barbara Coloroso: people are more inclined to think in terms of "me, mine, and more," but with a bit of encouragement and support people could begin to think in terms of "us, ours, and enough." This self-centered thinking was typical of the Admissions staff, and Dr. Shaheen was definitely not going to ignore the problem at hand.

The department lacked synergy, which was triggered by low morale and lack of trust. Dr. Shaheen noticed this and decided to meet with each employee and then have a group meeting. The one-on-one sessions with each of the staff members were quite informative. Ironically, both overlaps and contradictions came to light. Each of the staff members had issues with the others that had steadily intensified over the past few months. Each employee explained that problems had arisen repeatedly but that no one ever took the time to investigate or to solve the matters.

During the group meeting, May, Mehdi, Chirine, and Aisha were all asked to be honest and "lay their cards on the table" so that they could move on and carry out their jobs without distraction. The meeting was quite tense, and Dr. Shaheen noticed that negative feelings between staff members had been allowed to accumulate and were never resolved. However, the meeting proved to be fruitful, and it was very healthy to have them talk about their grievances and to have them listen to one another. They were aware of Dr. Shaheen's presence and mindful that she was attentive and patient with their outbursts. Deep down, they were very grateful that someone was concerned enough to take the time to talk and listen to them in the attempt to enhance their relationship with one another in the office.

After a lengthy assembly, Dr. Shaheen set her ground rules. She emphasized that gossip would not be tolerated and that if there were any problems, even with her, that they should approach her personally; her door would always be open. She told them, "We are here to be as productive as possible as we have a great responsibility to fulfill." Dr. Shaheen went on to explain that "we need to trust one another so that we can share and cooperate for the welfare of the office." She was also determined to be an advocate of participative management and management by walking around (MBWA). Dr. Shaheen emphasized her willingness to encourage employee involvement and told them that she welcomed all constructive feedback. "You are the people on the ground and your direct contact with students can be an enlightening experience if you work hand-in-hand." Dr. Shaheen then reminded them that the acronym TEAM means "Together Everyone Achieves More."

Moreover, the mission of the institution was revised and the goals of the office specified. Thereafter, duties were delegated according to seniority and accountability was made clear. Meetings would be held on a regular basis to inform the staff of plans and activities and to share information, as well as to listen to recommendations and input. Furthermore, Dr. Shaheen stated that they needed to demonstrate more commitment, and it was only through this sense of belonging that they would experience self-satisfaction.

Dr. Shaheen did not expect things to be easy. "There will be obstacles; there will be resistance; there will be lack of cooperation from other offices; however, if we unify and solidify our efforts, we can overcome those hurdles," she explained, "we have the option to choose our attitude; let's go for the positive preference." Dr. Shaheen continued, "I can't succeed alone, I need you all to help me and as they say 'one hand alone can't clap,' so let's make a lot of noise together and we can make a real difference."

Dr. Shaheen was delighted to notice the signs of relaxation on their faces, and they all expressed their willingness to work together. For the next couple of weeks, Dr. Shaheen carefully observed the interaction in the office. Moreover, she encouraged them to come and speak to her about anything that was bothering them. She was delighted to sense the positive attitudes. As she sat in her office, Dr. Shaheen felt satisfied with her efforts in creating a more harmonious work environment. It was important that her staff members understood the importance of team work and communication and how this, in turn, improved the quality of their work.

The office required more personnel, and so three new employees were recruited: Ahmad, George, and Nawal. On their first day, a meeting was held with all seven staff members and the department's framework was explained, this time not by Dr. Shaheen, but by each of the experienced office staff—May, Mehdi, Chirine, and Aisha.

Discussion Questions

1. Identify each of the four stages of team development and explain how Dr. Shaheen described each to the staff.
2. Dr. Shaheen stressed both team spirit and teamwork. What is the difference?
3. Describe the MBWA concept. What does Dr. Shaheen's use of this concept tell you about her personality? Do you think the results were productive?
4. How did Dr. Shaheen motivate her employees? If you were a consultant observing Dr. Shaheen's performance, what more would you recommend?

The Cash Register Incident

Read the following scenario by yourself. Then complete a three-step exercise, the first two steps by yourself, and the third step with a team. A time limit is associated with each step.

> *A store owner had just turned off the lights in the store when a man appeared and demanded money. The owner opened a cash register. The contents of the cash register were scooped up, and the man sped away. A member of the police force was notified promptly.*

Step 1: After reading these instructions, close your book. Without looking at the scenario, rewrite it as accurately as you can. Describe the incident as best you can using your own words.

Step 2: Assume that you observed the incident described in the paragraph above. Later, a reporter asks you questions about what you read in order to write an article for the local newspaper. Answer the questions from the reporter by yourself. Do not talk with anyone else about your answers. Put a Y, N, or DK in the response column. Since reporters are always pressed for time, take no more than two minutes to complete step 2.

	Answer
Y	Yes, or true
N	No, or false
DK	Don't know, or there is no way to tell

Step 3: The reporter wants to interview your entire team together. As a team, discuss the answers to each question and reach a consensus decision—that is, one with which everyone on the team agrees. Do not vote or engage in horse-trading. The reporter wants to know what you all agree upon. Complete your team discussion in 10 minutes.

Statements About the Incident

"As a reporter, I am interested in what happened in this incident. Can you tell me what occurred? I'd like you to address the following eleven questions."

Statement

Alone   *Team*

1. Did a man appear after the owner turned off his store lights?
2. Was the robber a man?
3. Is it true that the man did not demand money?

———   ——— 4. The man who opened the cash register was the owner, right?

———   ——— 5. Did the store owner scoop up the contents of the cash register?

———   ——— 6. OK, so someone opened the cash register, right?

———   ——— 7. Let me get this straight, after the man who demanded the money scooped up the contents of the cash register, he ran away?

———   ——— 8. The contents of the cash register contained money, but you don't know how much?

9. Did the robber demand money of the owner?

———   ——— 10. OK, by way of summary, the incident concerns a series of events in which only three persons are involved: the owner of the store, a man who demanded money, and a member of the police force?

———   ——— 11. Let me be sure I understand. Is it true that the following events occurred: Someone demanded money, the cash register was opened, its contents were scooped up, and a man dashed out of the store?

When you have finished your team decision making and mock interview with the reporter, the instructor will provide correct answers. Calculate how many answers you got right as an individual, and then calculate how many right answers your team achieved. Also go back and compare your own description of the incident with the actual wording of the scenario. How did you do? How accurate were you in your description?

Discussion Questions

1. How many individuals did better than the team as a whole? (In general, more than 80 percent of people do worse than the team.)
2. What changes would be needed in order for your team score to be even better?
3. How do you explain the superior performance of most teams over even the best individuals?
4. Under what conditions would individuals do better than teams in making decisions?

EXERCISES IN BUILDING EFFECTIVE TEAMS

Team Diagnosis and Team Development Exercise

In order to help you develop the ability to diagnose team stage development, consider a team in which you are now a member. If you belong to a team as part of this class, select that one. You may also select a team at your employment, in your church or community, or a team in another class in school. Complete the following three-step exercise:

Step 1: Use the following questions to help you determine the stage of development in which your team is operating. Create a score for your team for each stage of development. Identify the stage in which the team seems to operate the most.

Step 2: Identify what actions or interventions would lead your team to the next higher stage of development. Specify what dynamics need to change, what team members need to do, and/or how the team leader could foster more advanced team development.

Step 3: Share your scores and your suggestions with others in class in a small-group setting, and add at least one good idea from someone else's diagnosis to your own design. Use the following scale in your rating of your team right now.

Rating Scale

1 Not typical at all of my team
2 Not very typical of my team
3 Somewhat typical of my team
4 Very typical of my team

Stage 1

_____   1. Not everyone is clear about the objectives and goals of the team.

_____   2. Not everyone is personally acquainted with everyone else in the team.

_____   3. Only a few team members actively participate.

_____   4. Interactions among team members are very safe or somewhat superficial.

_____   5. Trust among all team members has not yet been established.

_____   6. Many team members seem to need direction from the leader in order to participate.

Stage 2

_____   7. All team members know and agree with the objectives and goals of the team.

_____   8. Team members all know one another.

_____   9. Team members are very cooperative and actively participate in the activities of the team.

_____   10. Interactions among team members are friendly, personal, and nonsuperficial.

_____ 11. A comfortable level of trust has been established among team members.

_____ 12. A strong unity exists in the team, and team members feel very much a part of a special group.

Stage 3

_____ 13. Disagreements and differing points of view are openly expressed by team members.

_____ 14. Competition exists among some team members.

_____ 15. Some team members do not follow the rules or the team norms.

_____ 16. Subgroups or coalitions exist within the team.

_____ 17. Some issues create major disagreements when discussed by the team, with some members on one side and others on the other side.

_____ 18. The authority or competence of the team leader is being questioned or challenged.

Stage 4

_____ 19. Team members are committed to the team and actively cooperate to improve the team's performance.

_____ 20. Team members feel free to try out new ideas, experiment, share something crazy, or do novel things.

_____ 21. A high level of energy is displayed by team members and expectations for performance are very high.

_____ 22. Team members do not always agree, but a high level of trust exists and each person is given respect, so disagreements are resolved productively.

_____ 23. Team members are committed to helping one another succeed and improve, so self-aggrandizement is at a minimum.

_____ 24. The team can make fast decisions without sacrificing quality.

Scoring

Add up the scores for the items in each stage of team development. Generally, one stage clearly stands out as having the highest scores. Team stages develop sequentially, so the highest stage in which scores occur is usually the dominant stage of development. Based on these scores, identify ways to move the team to the next level.

Total of Stage 1 items _____

Total of Stage 2 items _____

Total of Stage 3 items _____

Total of Stage 4 items _____

Winning the War on Talent

In this exercise, you will form teams of six members. Your team will have an overall objective to achieve, and each team member will have individual objectives. The exercise is accomplished in seven steps and it should take a total of 50 minutes to complete steps 1 through 6.

Step 1: In your team, read the scenario on the next page about the problem of attracting and retaining talented employees in twenty-first century organizations. Your team objective is to generate two innovative but workable ideas for how to retain good teachers in the public school system. You will have 15 minutes to develop the ideas.

Step 2: When each team has completed the assignment, each is given two minutes to present the two ideas. These ideas will be evaluated, and a winning team will be selected based on the following criteria:

- ❏ The ideas are workable and affordable.
- ❏ The ideas are interesting, innovative, and unusual.
- ❏ The ideas have a good chance of making a difference if they are implemented.

Step 3: In addition to the team assignment, each team member is assigned to play three team member roles during the discussion. A role assignment schedule is listed below. Team members may select the roles they wish to play, or an instructor can assign the roles. One purpose of this individual assignment is to give team members practice in playing either task-facilitation roles or relationship-building roles in a team setting, so you should take these assignments seriously. Remember, however, that you have only 15 minutes. When your team has completed its task, each team member will rate the effectiveness of every other team member in how well they played their roles and how much they helped the team accomplish its task. You will have five minutes to complete the ratings.

TEAM MEMBER NAME	ROLES	PERFORMANCE RATING (1) LOW–(10) HIGH PERFORMANCE FEEDBACK
1	Direction giving Urging Enforcing	
2	Information seeking Information giving Elaborating	
3	Monitoring Reality testing Summarizing	
4	Process analyzing Supporting Confronting	
5	Harmonizing Tension relieving Energizing	
6	Developing Consensus building Empathizing	

Step 4: Each team member uses the form above to rate the performance of, and provide feedback to, every other member of the team. In completing the form, make sure you focus on how well each person performed his or her assigned roles. Identify at least one thing you noticed about the performance of each team member so that you can provide personal feedback to each one. Remember that the overall purpose of this exercise is to give you practice in playing effective roles in teams and providing feedback to team members. You are given five minutes for this rating task.

Step 5: When each team has completed its task, one representative from each team is selected to form a judging team. This judging team evaluates the quality of the ideas produced by each team. A winning team is announced as a result of their deliberations. (Other class members will want to observe and rate the performance of this judging team and its members as they make their selection.) The judging team will be given 10 minutes to select the winning team.

Step 6: Teams meet again so that personal feedback can be given. Each team member takes a total of three minutes to give feedback to the other members of his or her team based on the evaluation form above. A total of 20 minutes will be required to provide this feedback.

Step 7: Hold a class discussion about what you observed regarding team members' roles. Especially, reflect on your own experience trying to play those roles and what seemed to be most effective in facilitating task accomplishment and in building team cohesion.

The Problem Scenario

Almost to a person, the chief concern expressed by senior executives in most "old economy" firms is how to attract and retain managerial talent. With the economy expected to grow at almost three times the growth of the job market, finding competent employees will be a continuing challenge for the next several years. The allure of dot.com firms, high-growth companies, and high-risk–high-return ventures has created an incredibly difficult environment for organizations whose chief competitive advantage is intellectual capital and human talent. Headhunters, venture capitalists, and even firms' customers are aggressively trying to lure away management talent any way they can. A recent survey of Wall Street investment bankers revealed that more than half had been approached by an Internet company. Armed with venture capital dollars and business plans promising swift public offerings, it is easy to see why many are succeeding in attracting managerial talent away from traditional companies. Compensation packages in the seven figures are not unusual.

In this highly competitive environment where intellectual capital is at a premium, consider the difficulty faced by not-for-profit organizations, local or state governments, arts organizations, or educational institutions whose budgets are constrained far below the high-priced world of the "new economy." How will they compete for talent when they cannot come close to the salaries of firms whose market capitalization exceeds the GDP of many African countries?

In particular, the U.S. public education system has suffered tremendously in this environment. Currently the United States spends more per child than any other country, and the costs of education are increasing far faster than the consumer price index. However, it is well known that more than a quarter of public school students drop out before high school graduation, and of those who remain, the percent passing proficiency exams is woefully low—in some school districts, less than 10 percent. The average tenure of public school teachers is less than seven years, and that number is dropping rapidly as these knowledge workers can find positions elsewhere at triple and quadruple their school salaries. Add to that the difficulties escalating in the classroom resulting from students in single-parent homes, marginal economic circumstances, threats of violence, and behavioral disruptions, and it is clear why teaching is a difficult profession, even if monetary compensation were higher.

Numerous alternatives have been proposed, but few have addressed the problem of teacher attraction and retention. Your task as a team is to identify two answers to the question: How can we attract and retain teachers in the public schools of the United States? You may want to consider what is being done in the school systems in other countries or in highly effective school systems in America.

Team Performance Exercise

The purpose of this exercise is to help you practice the dynamics of team formation, development, and effective performance. The most important part of the exercise is having you practice effective team leadership and team membership, and accurately diagnosing the stages of team development so you can behave appropriately.

Your instructor will form you into teams of five members each. Your task as a team is to create a five-pointed star in the form that you drew when you were a child (see Figure 9.5). You will do this with a piece of rope that has been tied at the ends to form a circle. Here is how this exercise will occur:

1. You will find a 50-foot piece of rope on the floor. Each member of your team will surround the rope and take hold of it with both hands. Once you have taken hold of the rope, you cannot let go until the exercise has been completed.

2. You will be given five minutes to plan how you are going to create the star, with all the appropriate crisscrosses. You may not move at all during this five-minute planning period. You must stay exactly where you are. Practicing is not permitted.

3. Once you have finished the five-minute planning session, you may not talk out loud again. The task must be completed in complete silence. You may not communicate verbally with any other member of your team. Only nonverbal communication is permitted. Remember, once you have taken hold of the rope, you cannot let go with either hand.

4. When the instructor gives the signal, you will start moving in order to create your five-sided star. When you have finished, you will place the rope down on the floor in exactly the position in which you are standing. You may not rearrange or move the rope on the floor. The rope should accurately represent your team members' positions.

5. The quality of your results will be evaluated by the instructor and the winning team announced.

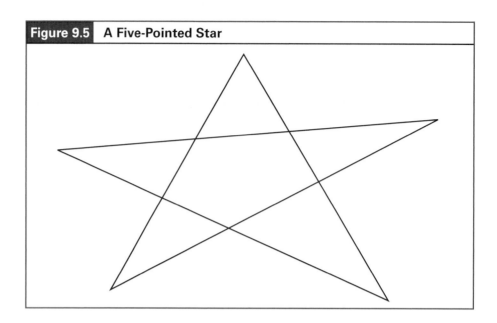

Figure 9.5 A Five-Pointed Star

When you have finished the task, discuss the following questions:

1. As a team, what was especially effective, and what was especially ineffective in planning for task accomplishment in advance?

2. What hints about initial stages of team development were utilized?

3. What happened to your team dynamics over the duration of the activity? Did they change from one stage to another? Did you end up as a high-performing team?

4. What team leadership and membership roles did each of your team members play? Which were the most effective?

5. What were the differences between teams that accomplished the task the most quickly and with the highest quality compared to the others?

6. How did you make up for the inability to communicate as a team during the task?

7. What do you wish you could do differently to be more efficient and more effective if you were to do another task together?

ACTIVITIES FOR BUILDING EFFECTIVE TEAMS

Suggested Assignments

1. Teach someone else how to determine which stage of development a team is in and what behaviors are most effective in each separate stage.

2. Analyze the characteristics of a team in which you are a member. Determine in what ways its functioning could be improved. Based on the attributes of high-performance teams, identify what could be done to improve its performance.

3. Conduct a role analysis of a real team meeting in which members are trying to make a decision, solve a problem, or examine an issue. Who performed what roles? Which team members were most helpful? Which team members were least helpful? Provide feedback to the team on what roles you saw being played, what roles were missing, and what improvements could have made the team more effective.

4. Write out a formal vision statement for a team you are leading. Make certain that the vision possesses the attributes of effective, energizing vision statements discussed in the chapter. Identify specifically what you can do to get team members to commit to that vision.

5. Do an in-depth analysis of an effective team leader you know. Focus specifically on the ways in which he or she has developed credibility and continues to influence team members. Identify what followers say about credibility, not just the leader.

6. Teach someone, or coach someone, on how to become an effective leader of a team, and how to become an effective team member. Demonstrate or exemplify the skills you teach that person.

7. For a team in which you participate, identify the basic services that it must deliver, the performance services that it should deliver, and the excitement services that it could deliver to its customers if it were not only to satisfy, but also to surprise and delight them.

APPLICATION

Application Plan and Evaluation

The intent of this exercise is to help you apply this cluster of skills in a real-life, out-of-class setting. Now that you have become familiar with the behavioral guidelines that form the basis of effective skill performance, you will improve most by trying out those guidelines in an everyday context. Unlike a classroom activity, in which feedback is immediate and others can assist you with their evaluations, this skill application activity is one you must accomplish and evaluate on your own. There are two parts to this activity. Part 1 helps prepare you to apply the skill. Part 2 helps you evaluate and improve on your experience. Be sure to write down answers to each item. Don't short-circuit the process by skipping steps.

Part 1. Planning

1. Write down the two or three aspects of this skill that are most important to you. These may be areas of weakness, areas you most want to improve, or areas that are most salient to a problem you face right now. Identify the specific aspects of this skill that you want to apply.

2. Now identify the setting or the situation in which you will apply this skill. Establish a plan for performance by actually writing down a description of the situation. Who else will be involved? When will you do it? Where will it be done?

   Circumstances:

   Who else?

   When?

   Where?

3. Identify the specific behaviors in which you will engage to apply this skill. Operationalize your skill performance.

4. What are the indicators of successful performance? How will you know you have been effective? What will indicate you have performed competently?

Part 2. Evaluation

5. After you have completed your implementation, record the results. What happened? How successful were you? What was the effect on others?

6. How can you improve? What modifications can you make next time? What will you do differently in a similar situation in the future?

7. Looking back on your whole skill practice and application experience, what have you learned? What has been surprising? In what ways might this experience help you in the long term?

Team Development Behaviors

Scoring Key

SKILL AREA	ITEMS	ASSESSMENT	
		PRE-	POST-
Leading the team	1–8	_____	_____
Being an effective team member	9–12	_____	_____
Diagnosing and facilitating team development	13–20	_____	_____
Total Score		_____	_____

Comparison Data (N = 5,000 Students)

Compare your scores to three standards:
1. The maximum possible score = 120.
2. The scores of other students in the class.
3. Norm data from more than 5,000 business school students.

Pre-Test				**Post-Test**
96.97	=	mean	=	104.07
105 or above	=	top quartile	=	113 or above
98–104	=	second quartile	=	106–112
90–97	=	third quartile	=	98–105
89 or below	=	bottom quartile	=	97 or below

Diagnosing the Need for Team Building

Comparison Data (N = 5,000 Students)

Mean score: 54.22
Top quartile: 70 or above
Second quartile: 53–69
Third quartile: 39–52
Bottom quartile: 38 or below

SKILL *ASSESSMENT* ▶

- Leading Positive Change
- Reflected Best-Self Feedback Exercise
- Machiavellianism Scale—MACH IV

SKILL *LEARNING* ■

- Leading Positive Change
- Ubiquitous and Escalating Change
- The Need for Frameworks
- Tendencies Toward Stability
- A Framework for Leading Positive Change
- Summary
- Behavioral Guidelines

SKILL *ANALYSIS* ▶

- Corporate Vision Statements
- Lee Iacocca's Transformation of Chrysler—1979–1984

SKILL *PRACTICE* ◆

- Reflected Best-Self Portrait
- Positive Organizational Diagnosis Exercise
- A Positive Change Agenda

SKILL *APPLICATION* ●

- Suggested Assignments
- Application Plan and Evaluation

SCORING KEYS AND *COMPARISON DATA* ■

10

Leading Positive Change

SKILL DEVELOPMENT OBJECTIVES

- LEARN HOW TO CREATE POSITIVE DEVIANCE IN ORGANIZATIONS
- DEVELOP THE CAPABILITY TO LEAD POSITIVE CHANGE
- ACQUIRE THE ABILITY TO MOBILIZE THE CAPABILITIES OF OTHERS IN ACHIEVING POSITIVE CHANGE

DIAGNOSTIC SURVEYS FOR LEADING POSITIVE CHANGE

LEADING POSITIVE CHANGE

Step 1: Before you read the material in this chapter, please respond to the following statements by writing a number from the rating scale below in the left-hand column (Pre-Assessment). Your answers should reflect your attitudes and behavior as they are now, not as you would like them to be. Be honest. This instrument is designed to help you discover your level of competency in problem solving and creativity so you can tailor your learning to your specific needs. When you have completed the survey, use the scoring key at the end of the chapter to identify the skill areas discussed in this chapter that are most important for you to master.

Step 2: After you have completed the reading and the exercises in this chapter and, ideally, as many as you can of the Skill Application assignments at the end of this chapter, cover up your first set of answers. Then respond to the same statements again, this time in the right-hand column (Post-Assessment). When you have completed the survey, use the scoring key at the end of the chapter to measure your progress. If your score remains low in specific skill areas, use the behavioral guidelines at the end of the Skill Learning section to guide further practice.

Rating Scale

1 Strongly disagree
2 Disagree
3 Slightly disagree
4 Slightly agree
5 Agree
6 Strongly agree

Assessment

Pre-   Post-

When I am in a leadership position required to lead change:

_____ _____ 1. I create positive energy in others when I interact with them.

_____ _____ 2. I know how to unlock the positive energy in other people.

_____ _____ 3. I express compassion toward people who are facing pain or difficulty.

_____ _____ 4. I help promote compassionate responses in others when it is appropriate.

_____ _____ 5. I emphasize a higher purpose or meaning associated with the change I am leading.

_____ _____ 6. I forgive others for the harm they may have produced or the mistakes they made.

_____ _____ 7. I maintain high standards of performance, even though I am quick to forgive.

_____ _____ 8. The language I use encourages virtuous actions by people.

_____ _____ 9. I express gratitude frequently and conspicuously, even for small acts.

_____ _____ 10. I keep track of things that go right, not just things that go wrong.

_____ _____ 11. I frequently give other people positive feedback.

_____ _____ 12. I emphasize building on strengths, not just overcoming weaknesses.

_____ _____ 13. I use a lot more positive comments than negative comments.

_____ _____ 14. I compare my own (or my group's) performance against the highest standards.

_____ _____ 15. When I communicate a vision, I capture people's hearts as well as their heads.

_____ _____ 16. I work to close abundance gaps—the difference between good performance and great performance.

_____ _____ 17. I exemplify absolute integrity.

_____ _____ 18. I know how to get people to commit to my vision of positive change.

_____ _____ 19. I take advantage of a small-wins strategy in all my change initiatives.

_____ _____ 20. I have developed a teachable point of view for subjects I care about.

REFLECTED BEST-SELF FEEDBACK™ EXERCISE*

All of us can recall our own extraordinary moments, those moments when we felt that our best self was brought to light, affirmed by others, and put into practice. These memories are seared into our minds as moments in which we have felt alive, true to our deepest selves, and pursuing our full potential as human beings. Over time, we collect these experiences into a portrait of who we are when we are at our personal best. To help compose a best-self portrait, it is important to draw on the perceptions of significant others who have unique and valuable insights into our strengths and enduring talents. The Reflected Best-Self Feedback Exercise creates an opportunity for us to receive feedback regarding who we are when we are at our best. A detailed explanation of this exercise, including the research that supports its effectiveness in helping people become better leaders, can be found at: www.bus.umich.edu/positive. Look under POS teaching and learning tools.

In this exercise, you will gather information about yourself from other people who know you well. In the Skill Practice section of the chapter, you will be asked to develop a best self-portrait based on this feedback. The first step is to gather the information. Here is how you go about it.

Identify 20 people who know you well. These may be colleagues (former or current), friends (old or recent), family members, neighbors, class members, or anyone who has had extended contact with you. Think about who will give you an honest opinion. The more diverse the group, the better. Also, realize that due to time constraints, everyone may not be able to respond. You need at least 10 responses to complete this part of the assignment, so ask enough people to ensure at least 10 responses, but try for 20.

Compose the feedback request (see the example request below), and send it to the 20 people you select. While this request may seem awkward or difficult for you, people have found this assessment to be a profound learning activity, and other people are quite willing to participate in this exercise. You will find that this actually strengthens your relationships in many instances.

SOURCE: *Roberts et al., 2005.*

A SAMPLE E-MAIL REQUEST FOR FEEDBACK

I am taking a course that requires me to construct a profile of my unique strengths. I have been asked to contact 20 people who know me well. I would like to invite you to help me

_____

* This assessment is not available online.

with this exercise. I am to request that each person provide me with three stories of when I was at my best.

This will require that you think about your interactions with me and identify times when you saw me at my very best. Please provide examples so I can understand the situation and the characteristics you are describing. I have attached some examples of what these stories could look like. Please use these only as a guide.

Feedback Examples:

1. *One of your greatest strengths is:* The ability to get people to work together and give all they have to a task.

For example, I think of the time that: We were doing the Alpha project. We were getting behind and the stress was building. We started to close down and get very focused on just meeting our deadline. You noticed that we were not doing our best work and stopped the group to rethink our approach. You asked whether we wanted to just satisfy the requirements or whether we wanted to really do good and important work. You reminded us of what we were capable of doing and how each of us could contribute to a better outcome. No one else in that room would have thought to do that. As a result, we did meet the deadline and created a result we all feel proud of.

2. *One of your greatest strengths is:* Being happy all the time.

For example, I think of the time that: We had just lost the league championship game, and we were all really down in the dumps. All of us knew we could have played better, and we were really in a funk. You were the one who pumped us up and made us feel better—not in a superficial or silly way, but by expressing genuine pleasure at having a chance to play and being together as friends. I really admire you for being able to see the good in a situation and being such a positive person.

3. *One of your greatest strengths is:* The capacity to persist in the face of adversity.

For example, I think of the time that: We were past our deadline on a major report. Frank quit and we were left short-handed. Instead of getting discouraged, you became more focused than I have ever seen anyone get. I think you went 48 hours without sleep. I was amazed that you could produce such a quality product under those conditions.

Your feedback to me: Please provide me with three examples of the strengths you observed by completing the following statements.

1. *One of your greatest strengths is:*
   For example, I think of the time that:
2. *One of your greatest strengths is:*
   For example, I think of the time that:
3. *One of your greatest strengths is:*
   For example, I think of the time that:

Please e-mail your responses to me by [insert a date]. Thank you very much for your cooperation. I will be sure to share with you what I learn.

When you have obtained this feedback, you will be guided in developing a best-self portrait in the Skill Practice section of this chapter.

SOURCE: *Adapted from Quinn, Dutton, & Spreitzer, 2003.*

MACHIAVELLIANISM SCALE—MACH IV

Listed on the next page are a number of statements. Each represents a commonly held opinion, but there are no right or wrong answers. Indicate the extent to which you agree or disagree with each item using this scale. Comparison data is provided at the end of the chapter.

+3   Agree strongly
+2   Agree somewhat
+1   Agree slightly
−1   Disagree slightly
−2   Disagree somewhat
−3   Disagree strongly

If you find that the numbers to be used in answering do not adequately indicate your own opinion, use the one which is closest to the way you feel.

1.	Never tell anyone the real reason you did something unless it is useful to do so.	+3 +2 +1 −1 −2 −3
2.	The best way to handle people is to tell them what they want to hear.	+3 +2 +1 −1 −2 −3
3.	One should take action only when sure it is morally right.	+3 +2 +1 −1 −2 −3
4.	Most people are basically good and kind.	+3 +2 +1 −1 −2 −3
5.	It is safest to assume that all people have a vicious streak and it will come out when they are given a chance.	+3 +2 +1 −1 −2 −3
6.	Honesty is the best policy in all cases.	+3 +2 +1 −1 −2 −3
7.	There is no excuse for lying to someone else.	+3 +2 +1 −1 −2 −3
8.	Generally speaking, people won't work hard unless they're forced to do so.	+3 +2 +1 −1 −2 −3
9.	All in all, it is better to be humble and honest than to be important and dishonest.	+3 +2 +1 −1 −2 −3
10.	When you ask someone to do something for you, it is best to give the real reasons for wanting it rather than giving reasons which carry more weight.	+3 +2 +1 −1 −2 −3
11.	Most people who get ahead in the world lead clean, moral lives.	+3 +2 +1 −1 −2 −3
12.	Anyone who completely trusts anyone else is asking for trouble.	+3 +2 +1 −1 −2 −3
13.	The biggest difference between most criminals and other people is that the criminals are stupid enough to get caught.	+3 +2 +1 −1 −2 −3
14.	Most people are brave.	+3 +2 +1 −1 −2 −3
15.	It is wise to flatter important people.	+3 +2 +1 −1 −2 −3
16.	It is possible to be good in all respects.	+3 +2 +1 −1 −2 −3
17.	Barnum was wrong when he said that there's a sucker born every minute.	+3 +2 +1 −1 −2 −3
18.	It is hard to get ahead without cutting corners here and there.	+3 +2 +1 −1 −2 −3
19.	People suffering from incurable diseases should have the choice of being put painlessly to death.	+3 +2 +1 −1 −2 −3
20.	Most people forget more easily the death of their father than the loss of their property.	+3 +2 +1 −1 −2 −3

SOURCE: *MACH IV Scale, R. Christie et al., "Machiavellianism" in Wrightsman, L. and Cook, S. (1965) Factor analysis and attitude.*

SKILL *LEARNING*

Leading Positive Change

The word **leadership** is often used as a catch-all term to describe almost any desirable behavior by a manager. "Good leadership" is frequently the explanation given for the success of almost any positive organizational performance—from stock price increases to upward national economic trends to happy employees. Magazine covers trumpet the remarkable achievements of leaders, and the person at the top is almost always credited as being the cause of the success or failure. Coaches are fired when players don't perform, CEOs lose their jobs when customers choose a competitor, and presidents are voted out of office when the economy goes south. Contrarily, leaders are often given hero status when their organizations succeed (e.g., Gandhi, Welch, Buffett). The leader as scapegoat, and hero, is an image that is alive and well in modern society. Rationally speaking, however, most of us recognize that there is much more to organizational success than the leader's behavior, but we also recognize that leadership is one of the most important influences in helping organizations perform well (Cameron & Lavine, 2006; Pfeffer, 1998).

Some writers have differentiated between the concepts of leadership and management (Kotter, 1999; Tichy, 1993, 1997). *Leadership* has often been described as what individuals do under conditions of change. When organizations are dynamic and undergoing transformation, people exhibit leadership. *Management,* on the other hand, has traditionally been associated with the status quo. Maintaining stability is the job of the manager. Leaders have been said to focus on setting direction, initiating change, and creating something new. Managers have been said to focus on maintaining steadiness, controlling variation, and refining current performance. Leadership has been equated with dynamism, vibrancy, and charisma; management with predictability, equilibrium, and control. Hence, leadership is often defined as "doing the right things," whereas management is often defined as "doing things right."

Recent research is clear, however, that such distinctions between leadership and management, which may have been appropriate in previous decades, are no longer useful (Cameron & Lavine, 2006; Cameron & Quinn,1999; Quinn, 2000, 2004). Managers cannot be successful without being good leaders, and leaders cannot be successful without being good managers. No longer do organizations and individuals have the luxury of holding on to the status quo; worrying about doing things right without also doing the right things; keeping the system stable without also leading change and improvement; maintaining current performance without also creating something new; concentrating on equilibrium and control without also concentrating on vibrancy and charisma. Effective management and leadership are largely inseparable. The skills required to do one are also required for the other. No organization in a postindustrial, hyperturbulent, twenty-first-century environment will survive without individuals capable of providing both management and leadership. Leading change and managing stability, establishing vision and accomplishing objectives, breaking the rules and monitoring conformance, although paradoxical, all are required to be successful. Individuals who are effective managers are also effective leaders much of the time. The skills required to be effective as a leader and as a manager are essentially identical.

On the other hand, Quinn (2004) has reminded us that no person is a leader all of the time. Leadership is a *temporary* condition in which certain skills and competencies are displayed. When they are demonstrated, leadership is present. When they are not demonstrated, leadership is absent. In other words, regardless of a person's title or formal position, people may act as leaders or not, depending on the behaviors they display. Most of the time people are not displaying leadership behaviors. People choose to enter a state of leadership when they choose to adopt a certain mind-set and implement certain key skills.

> *Understanding that leadership is a temporary, dynamic state brings us to a radical redefinition of how we think about, enact, and develop leadership. We come to discover that most of the time, most people, including CEOs, presidents, and prime ministers, are not leaders. We discover that anyone can be a leader. Most of the time, none of us are leaders.* (Quinn, 2004, xx)

In this chapter, we focus on the most common activity that demonstrates leadership—leading change.

It is while engaging in this task that the temporary state of leadership is most likely to be revealed. That is, despite the heroic image of leaders, every person can develop the skills needed to lead change. No one was born as either a leader or absent the abilities that would enable him or her to be a leader. Everyone can, and most everyone does, become a leader at some point. On the other hand, effectively leading change involves a complex and difficult-to-master set of skills, so assistance is required in order to do it successfully. That is because of the difficulties associated with change.

Ubiquitous and Escalating Change

It is not news that we live in a dynamic, turbulent, and even chaotic world. Almost no one would try to predict with any degree of certainty what the world will be like in ten years. Things change too fast. We know that the technology currently exists, for example, to put the equivalent of a full-size computer in a wristwatch, or inject the equivalent of a laptop computer into the bloodstream. New computers are beginning to be etched on molecules instead of silicon wafers. The half-life of any technology you can name—from complex computers to nuclear devices to software—is less than six months. Anything can be reproduced in less than a half a year.

The mapping of the human genome is probably the greatest source for change, for not only can we now change a banana into an agent to inoculate people against malaria, but new organ development and physiological regulation promise to dramatically alter population life styles. As of this writing, more than 100 whole animals have been patented. Patents have exploded from an overwhelming 4,000 applications in 1991, up to 22,000 in 1995, and in 2008 they mushroomed to 500,000 per year, with exponential growth expected to continue. Whereas it took ten years to produce a generic alternative to a normal pharmaceutical drug in 1965, the time was cut in half by 1980, cut in half again by 1990, and by the year 2000, generic alternatives could be produced for almost any pharmaceutical compound in about a week. In 1980 it took a year to assemble 12,000 DNA base pairs; by 1999 it took less than a minute, and by the end of 2000, 1,000 base pairs could be assembled in less than one second. Currently, computers are being configured that can sequence every major disease in a single day. Who can predict the changes that will result? Hence, not only is change ubiquitous and constant, but almost everyone predicts that it will escalate exponentially (see Enrique, 2000).

The Need for Frameworks

Frameworks or theories help provide stability and order in the midst of constant change. To illustrate the importance of frameworks, consider a simple experiment conducted by Nobel laureate Herbert A. Simon. Experimental subjects were shown a chess board as it appeared midgame. Some of these individuals were experienced chess players, some were novices. They were allowed to observe the chess board for ten seconds, and then the board was wiped clean. The subjects were asked to replace the pieces on the board exactly as they had appeared before the board was cleared. This experiment was actually conducted on a computer, so wiping the chess board clean was simple, and multiple trials could be generated for each person. Each trial showed a different configuration of a chess game midway through.

The question being investigated was: Which group was best at replacing the chess pieces, the novices or the experienced players? After looking at the board for ten seconds, which individuals would be most accurate in placing each piece in its previous location? An argument could be made for either group. On the one hand, the minds of novices would not be cluttered by preconceptions. They would look at the board with a fresh view. It is similar to the answer to the question: When is the best time to teach a person a new language, age 3 or age 30? The fact that 3-year-olds can learn a new language more quickly than 30-year-olds suggests that novices might also be better at this task because of their lack of preconceptions. On the other hand, the contrary argument is that experience ought to count for something, and the familiarity of experienced players with the chess board should allow them to be more successful.

The results of the experiment were dramatic. Novices accurately replaced the pieces less than five percent of the time. Experienced players were accurate more than 80 percent of the time. When experienced chess players looked at the board they saw familiar patterns, or what might be called frameworks. They said things like this: "This looks like the Leningrad defense, except this bishop is out of place and these two pawns are arranged differently." Experienced players identified the patterns quickly, and then they paid attention to the few exceptions on the board. Novices, on the other hand, needed to pay attention to every single piece as if it were an exception, since no pattern (or framework) was available to guide their decisions.

Frameworks serve the same function for managers. They clarify complex or ambiguous situations. Individuals who are familiar with frameworks can manage complex situations effectively because they can respond to fewer exceptions. Individuals without frameworks are left to react to every piece of information as a unique event or an exception. The best managers possess the most, and the most useful, frameworks. When they encounter a new situation, they do not become overwhelmed or stressed because they have frameworks that can help simplify and clarify the unfamiliar.

Tendencies Toward Stability

Organizations are designed like frameworks that allow exceptions to be managed effectively. They are intended to create stability, steadiness, and predictable conditions. They try to constrain as much change as possible. That is, organizations help specify what is expected of employees, who reports to whom, what the goals are, what procedures are to be employed, what rules apply, how the work gets done, and so on. These elements are all intended to reduce the ambiguity of changing conditions and to create predictability for employees so that the uncertainties of environmental change do not overwhelm them. Managers are obliged to try to ensure that steady, stable conditions are fostered.

Leading change, therefore, is contradictory to the common requirements of ensuring predictability and constancy. It disrupts the permanence of the system and creates more uncertainly. The skill of leading change, therefore, runs contrary to what organizations are fundamentally designed to do. Even more important, leading *positive* change is different from simply leading ordinary change in an organization. Change will always be widespread and constant, but leading positive change in organizations is unusual and difficult, and it requires special know-how and a special skill set.

To illustrate the difference between leading commonplace change and positive change, consider the continuum in Figure 10.1 (Cameron, 2003a). It shows a line depicting normal, healthy performance in the middle, with unhealthy, negative performance on the left and unusually positive performance on the right. Most organizations and most managers strive to maintain performance in the middle of the continuum. People and organizations strive to be healthy, effective, efficient, reliable, compatible, and ethical. It is in the middle of the continuum where things are most comfortable.

We usually refer to the left end of the continuum as **negative deviance**. To call someone a "deviant" usually means that he or she needs correction or treatment. Most managers strive to get deviant people to behave within a normal range. If they don't, if they continue to behave badly, they get transferred, punished, or fired. With few exceptions (e.g., athletes and heroic figures) the same pressure toward normal behavior exists on the right side of the continuum as

---

Figure 10.1 A Continuum of Negative and Positive Deviance

Individual:	Negative Deviance	Normal	Positive Deviance
Physiological (*Medical research*)	Illness	Health	Wellness
Psychological (*Psychological research*)	Illness	Health	Flow

Organizational and Managerial:
(*Management and organizational research*)

	Negative Deviance	Normal	Positive Deviance
Revenues	Unprofitable	Profitable	Generous
Effectiveness	Ineffective	Effective	Excellent
Efficiency	Inefficient	Efficient	Extraordinary
Quality	Error-prone	Reliable	Flawless
Ethics	Unethical	Ethical	Virtuous
Relationships	Conflictual	Compatible	Caring
Adaptation	Threat-rigidity	Coping	Flourishing

Deficit gaps   Abundance gaps

Source: Cameron, 2003b.

well as the left. Pressure is always brought to bear to get people to behave in predictable, normal ways.

Think, for example, of people you have encountered who are positively deviant at work—flawless performers, flourishing in everything they do, and constantly extraordinary. They're too perfect. They make people feel uncomfortable. They make others feel guilty. They are rate-busters. We accuse them of showing up other people. There is a lot of pressure to get them back in line or within a normal range of performance. Most of the time we insist that others stay in the middle range. Being on either the right side or the left side of the continuum is usually interpreted as against the rules.

Not surprisingly, we know a lot more about the left side of the continuum than the right side. Consider the top line of Figure 10.1, for example, and think of your own physical health. If you're ill, you usually get treatment from a medical professional who provides medication or therapy until you return to normal health. When you're healthy you stop seeing the doctor and the doctor stops treating you. About 90 percent of all medical research has focused on how to get people from the left side of the continuum—illness—to the middle of the continuum—health. Yet, everyone knows that a condition exists on the right side of the continuum which is better than just being healthy. It is exemplified by people who can run a marathon, do 400 pushups, or compete at Olympic fitness levels. They are positively deviant on the health continuum. Much less serious attention in medical science has been paid to how people can reach this state of **positive deviance**. Leading positive change (from the middle point to the right side) is more uncertain than leading change from the left side to the middle point.

Similarly, the second line of the figure refers to psychological health. On the left is illness—depression, anxiety, burnout, paranoia, and so forth—and the middle depicts normal psychological functioning—being emotionally healthy or reasonably happy. Seligman (2002) reported that more than 99 percent of psychological research in the last 50 years has focused on the left and middle points on the continuum—that is, how to treat people who are ill in order to get them to a state of normality or health. Again, however, a positively deviant psychological condition is also possible. It is sometimes characterized by a state of "**flow**" (Csikszentmihalyi, 1990)—where people's minds are totally engaged in a challenging task so that they lose track of time, physical appetites, and outside influences—or they experience especially positive emotions (Fredrickson, 2003) such as joy, excitement, or love. Most people have experienced

at some time being "in the zone," during which more of their brain capacity is used than at normal times. Such conditions represent positively deviant psychological states. A new movement in psychology studies positively deviant psychological states, and we will summarize some of those findings below. Most managers and most organizations, however, are in business to create normal behavior, not to foster deviant behavior. This is illustrated by the lower lines in Figure 10.1, which refer to organizations and managers.

The figure lists conditions ranging from unprofitable, ineffective, inefficient, and error-prone performance on the left side, to profitable, effective, efficient, and reliable performance in the middle. For the most part, leaders and managers are charged with the responsibility to ensure that their organizations are operating in the middle range. They are consumed with the problems and challenges that threaten their organizations from the left side of the continuum (e.g., unethical behavior, dissatisfied employees or customers, financial losses, and so on.) Most leaders and managers are content if they can get their organizations to that middle state—profitable, effective, reliable. In fact, almost all organizational and managerial research has focused on how to ensure that organizations can perform in the normal range. We don't have very good language to describe the right side of the organizational continuum. Instead of just being profitable, positively deviant organizations might strive to be generous, using their resources to do good. Instead of just being effective, efficient, reliable, they might strive to be benevolent, flourishing, and flawless.

The right side of the continuum is referred to as an **abundance approach** to performance. The left side of the continuum is referred to as a **deficit approach** to performance (Cameron & Lavine, 2006). Much more attention has been paid to solving problems, surmounting obstacles, battling competitors, eliminating errors, making a profit, and closing deficit gaps compared to identifying the flourishing and life-giving aspects of organizations, or closing abundance gaps. Our colleague Jim Walsh (1999) found, for example, that words such as "win," "beat," and "competition" have dominated the business press over the past two decades, whereas words such as "virtue," "caring," and "compassion" have seldom appeared at all. Less is known, therefore, about the right side of the continuum in Figure 10.1 and the concepts that characterize it. Most research on leadership, management, and organizations, therefore, has remained fixed on the left and center points of the continuum. Yet, it is on the right end that the skill of leading positive change becomes relevant. It is on that side of the continuum that our discussion will focus in this chapter.

Focusing on the right side of the continuum—or on abundance gaps—unlocks something called the heliotropic effect. This is a natural tendency in every living system to be inclined toward positive energy—toward light—and away from negative energy or from the dark. The reason is that light is life-giving and energy creating. Abundance creates positive energy. Deficits often do not. All living systems are inclined toward that which gives life, so abundance approaches to change enable the heliotropic effect to occur.

For example, with individuals, the heliotropic effect may be manifest physiologically as the *placebo effect*. A variety of studies have shown that if a person holds positive beliefs that a medication will be effective, it will, in fact, produce the desired effect about 60 percent of the time. Psychologically, the heliotropic effect is manifest as the *Pygmalion effect*. That is, not only does a person's biological system respond to his or her own positive expectations, but the expectations of others also can produce a heliotropic effect. A large amount of evidence suggests that when someone holds positive expectations for you—especially if that person is important to you—your behavior is altered positively.

The heliotropic effect is also manifest emotionally. Many studies have documented the fact that people with positive emotional states and optimistic outlooks experience fewer illness and accidents and, in fact, actually enjoy a longer and higher quality of life. Depressed, anxious, or angry people get sick more often than happy, joyful, upbeat people, even when exposed to the same number of cold viruses, and they tend more often to be in the wrong place at the wrong time and experience accidents.

The heliotropic effect can manifest itself in visualization. When people visualize themselves as succeeding—they see themselves hitting the ball, clearing the bar, making the shot, getting the right answer, or recovering from illness—they tend to succeed significantly more than otherwise. This heliotropic effect is explained in more detail in Cameron and Lavine (2006).

A Framework for Leading Positive Change

Leading positive change is a management skill that focuses on unlocking positive human potential. Positive change enables individuals to experience appreciation, collaboration, vitality, and meaningfulness in their work. It focuses on creating abundance and human well-being. It fosters positive deviance. It acknowledges that positive change engages the heart as well as the mind.

A Case Example An example of this kind of change occurred in a New England hospital that faced a crisis of leadership when the popular vice president of operations was forced to resign (Cameron & Caza, 2002). Most employees viewed him as the most innovative and effective administrator in the hospital and as the chief exemplar of positive energy and change. Upon his resignation, the organization was thrown into turmoil. Conflict, backbiting, criticism, and adversarial feelings permeated the system. Eventually, a group of employees appealed to the board of directors to replace the current president and CEO with this ousted vice president. Little confidence was expressed in the current leadership, and the hospital's performance was deteriorating. Their lobbying efforts were eventually successful in that the president and CEO resigned under pressure, and the popular vice president was hired back as president and CEO.

Within six months of his return, however, the decimated financial circumstances at the hospital led to an announced downsizing aimed at reducing the workforce by 10 percent. The hospital faced millions of dollars in losses. This newly hired CEO had to eliminate the jobs of some of the very same people who supported his return. The most likely results of this action were an escalation in the negative effects of downsizing loss of loyalty and morale, perceptions of injustice and duplicity, blaming and accusations. Based on research on the effects of downsizing, a continuation of the tumultuous, antagonistic climate was almost guaranteed (Cameron, Whetten, & Kim, 1987).

Instead, the opposite results occurred. Upon his return, the new CEO made a concerted effort to lead positive change in the organization, not merely manage the required change. He institutionalized forgiveness, optimism, trust, and integrity. Throughout the organization, stories of compassionate acts of kindness and virtue were almost daily fare. One typical example involved a nurse who was diagnosed with terminal cancer. Respondents reported that when word spread of the man's illness, doctors and staff members from every area in the hospital donated vacation days and personal leave time so that he would continue to collect a salary even though he could not work. Ironically, the pool of days expired just before he died, so he was never terminated, and he received a salary right up to his last day.

Employees also reported that the personal and organizational damage done by the announced downsizing—friends losing jobs, budgets being cut—had been formally forgiven. Employees released grudges and moved on toward an optimistic future. One indication was the language used throughout the organization, which commonly included words such as love, hope, compassion, forgiveness, and humility, especially in reference to the leadership that announced the downsizing actions.

We are in a very competitive health care market, so we have differentiated ourselves through our compassionate and caring culture. . . . I know it sounds trite, but we really do love our patients. . . . People love working here, and their family members love us too. . . . Even when we downsized, [our leader] maintained the highest levels of integrity. He told the truth, and he shared everything. He got the support of everyone by his genuineness and personal concern. . . . It wasn't hard to forgive. (Representative responses from a focus group interview of employees, 2002)

Even the redesigned physical architecture of the hospital reflected its positive approach to change, being designed to foster a more humane climate for patients and to communicate the virtuousness of the organization. For example, the maternity ward installed double beds (which didn't previously exist) so husbands could sleep with their wives rather than sitting in a chair all night; numerous communal rooms were created for family and friend gatherings; hallways and floors were all carpeted; volunteer pets were brought in to comfort and cheer up patients; original paintings on walls displayed optimistic and inspiring themes; nurses' stations were all within eyesight of patients' beds; Jacuzzis were installed in the maternity ward; special meals were prepared to fit patients' dietary preferences; and so on. Employees indicate that the leadership of positive change—not merely the management of change—was the key to their recovery and thriving. Special language, activities, and processes were important parts of employees' explanations for the organization's renewal. Figure 10.2 illustrates the financial turnaround associated with the hospital's concentrated focus on virtuousness.

A Framework of Positive Change This chapter reviews the five key management skills and activities required to effectively lead positive change. They include: (1) establishing a climate of positivity, (2) creating readiness for change, (3) articulating a vision of abundance, (4) generating commitment to the vision, and (5) institutionalizing the positive

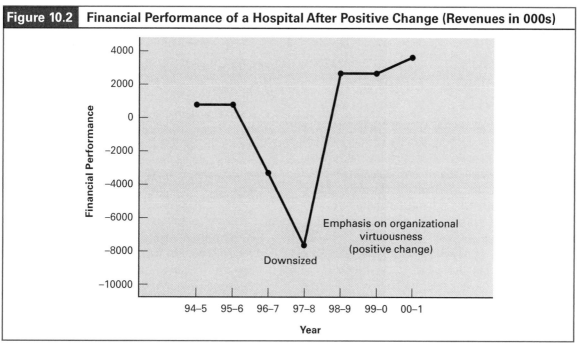

Figure 10.2 | **Financial Performance of a Hospital After Positive Change (Revenues in 000s)**

SOURCE: *Cameron, Bright, & Caza, 2003.*

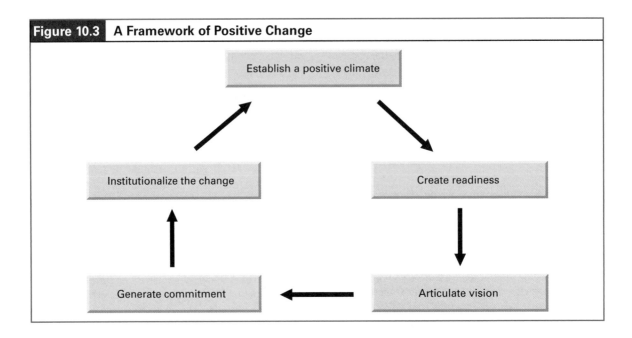

Figure 10.3 A Framework of Positive Change

Establish a positive climate

Institutionalize the change

Create readiness

Generate commitment

Articulate vision

change (Cameron & Ulrich, 1986). Figure 10.3 summarizes these steps, and we discuss them below. Leaders of positive change are not all CEOs, of course, nor are they in titled or powerful positions. On the contrary, the most important leadership demonstrated in organizations usually occurs in departments, divisions, and teams and by individuals who take it upon themselves to enter a temporary state of leadership (Meyerson, 2001; Quinn, 2004). These principles apply as much to the first-time manager, in other words, as to the experienced executive.

ESTABLISHING A CLIMATE OF POSITIVITY

The first and most crucial step in leading positive change is to set the stage for positive change by establishing a climate of positivity. Because constant change is typical of all organizations, most managers most of the time focus on the negative or problematic aspects of change. A leader who will focus on positive change is both rare and valuable. Not everyone masters it, although everyone can.

Baumeister, Bratslavsky, Finkenauer, and Vohs (2001) pointed out that negative occurrences, bad events, and disapproving feedback are more influential and longer lasting in people than positive, encouraging, and upbeat occurrences. For example, if someone breaks into your home and steals $1,000, it will affect you more, and will be more long-lasting in its effects,

than if someone sends you a $1,000 gift. If three people compliment you on your appearance and one person is critical, the one criticism will carry more weight than the three compliments. In other words, according to Baumeister's review of the literature, "bad is stronger than good." People tend to pay more attention to negative than positive phenomena, and for good reason. Ignoring a negative threat could cost you your life. Not attending to negative events could prove dangerous. Ignoring a positive, pleasant experience, on the other hand, would only result in regret. Consequently, managers and organizations—constantly confronted by problems, threats, and obstacles—have a tendency to focus on the negative much more than the positive. Managers must consciously choose to pay attention to the positive, uplifting, and flourishing side of the continuum in Figure 10.1, otherwise negative tendencies overwhelm the positive. Leading positive change, in other words, is going against the grain. It is not necessarily a natural thing to do. It requires skill and practice.

Mahatma Gandhi's statement illustrates the necessity of positivity, even though it is difficult:

Keep your thoughts positive, because your thoughts become your words. Keep your words positive, because your words become your behavior. Keep your behavior positive, because your behavior becomes your habits. Keep your habits positive because your habits become your values. Keep your values positive, because your values become your destiny. (Gold, 2002)

In order to establish a climate of positivity in an organization, managers must help establish at least three necessary conditions: (1) positive energy networks, (2) a climate of compassion, forgiveness, and gratitude, and (3) attention to strengths and the best self.

Create Positive Energy Networks

Have you ever been around a person who just makes you feel good? You leave every interaction happier, more energized, and uplifted? In contrast, do you know people who are constantly critical, negative, and discouraging? They seem to deplete your own reserve of positive energy? Recent research has discovered that people can be identified as "positive energizers" or "negative energizers" in their relationships with others (Baker, Cross, & Wooten, 2003). **Positive energizers** are those who strengthen and create vitality and liveliness in others. **Negative energizers** are people who deplete the good feelings and enthusiasm in other people and make them feel diminished, devalued, or drained. Research shows that positive energizers are higher performers, enable others to perform better, and help their own organizations succeed more than negative energizers (Baker et al., 2003). People who drain energy from others tend to be critical, express negative views, fail to engage others, and are more self-centered than positive energizers. Being a positive energizer is associated with being sensitive in interpersonal relationships, trustworthy, supportive to others in comments, actively (not passively) engaged in social interactions, flexible and tolerant in thinking, and unselfish. They are not necessarily charismatic, giddy, or just Pollyannaish. Rather, positive energy creators are optimistic and giving, and others feel better by being around them.

Here is why that is so important in leading positive change. Research by Wayne Baker (2001) has investigated the kinds of networks that exist in organizations. Most research investigates two kinds of networks—information networks and influence networks. If you are at the center of an information network, that means more information and communication flow through you than anyone else. You have access to a greater amount of information than others. Predictably, people at the center of an information network have higher performance and are more successful in their careers than people on the periphery. The same can be said for people at the center of influence networks. Influential people are not always people with the most prestigious titles, but they tend to be people who can influence others to get things done (see Chapter 5 on power and influence). Recent research has discovered, however, that **positive energy networks** are far more powerful in predicting success than information or influence networks. In fact, being a positive energizer in an organization is four times more predictive of success than being at the center of an information network or even being the person with an important title or senior position. Displaying positive energy, in other words, tends to be a very powerful predictor of personal as well as organizational success.

Effective managers identify positive energizers and then make certain that networks of people are formed who associate with these energizers. Positive energizers are placed in positions where others can interact with them and be influenced by them. The research findings are clear that people who interact with positive energizers perform better, as well as do the positive energizers themselves, so make sure you and others rub shoulders with them often. In addition to forming positive energy networks, effective managers will also foster positive energy in other people by: (1) exemplifying or role modeling positive energy themselves, (2) recognizing and rewarding people who exemplify positive energy, and (3) providing opportunities for individuals to form friendships at work (which usually are positive energy creators).

Ensure a Climate of Compassion, Forgiveness, and Gratitude

A second aspect of a climate of positivity is the appropriate display of compassion, forgiveness, and gratitude in organizations. These terms may sound a bit saccharine and soft—even out of place in a serious discussion of developing management skills for the competitive world of business. Yet, recent research has found them to be very important predictors of organizational success. Companies that scored higher on these attributes performed significantly better than others (Cameron, 2003b). That is, when managers fostered compassionate behavior among employees, forgiveness for missteps and mistakes, and gratitude resulting from positive occurrences, their firms excelled in profitability, productivity, quality, innovation, and customer retention. Managers who reinforced these virtues were more successful in producing bottom-line results.

Paying attention to these concepts simply acknowledges that employees at work have human concerns—they feel pain, experience difficulty, and encounter injustice in their work and personal lives. Think of people you know, for example, who are currently managing a severe family illness, experiencing a failed relationship, coping with hostile and unpleasant coworkers or associates, or facing overload and burnout. Many organizations don't allow personal problems to get in the way of getting the job done. Human concerns take a backseat to work-related concerns. Regardless of what is happening personally, responsibilities and performance expectations remain the same. To lead positive change, however, managers must build a climate in which human concerns are acknowledged and where healing and restoration can occur. Because change always creates pain, discomfort, and disruption, leaders of positive change are sensitive to the human concerns that can sabotage many change efforts. Without a reserve of goodwill and positive feelings, almost all change fails. Therefore, unlocking people's inherent tendency to feel compassion, to forgive mistakes, and to express gratitude helps build the human capital and reserve needed to successfully lead positive change. How might that occur?

Compassion   Kanov and colleagues (2003) found that **compassion** is built in organizations when managers foster three things: **collective noticing, collective feeling**, and **collective responding**. When people are suffering or experiencing difficulty, the first step is to notice or simply become aware of what is occurring. An iron-clad rule exists at Cisco Systems, for example, where CEO John Chambers must be notified within 48 hours of the death or serious illness of any Cisco employee or family member. People are on the lookout for colleagues who need help.

The second step is to enable the expression of collective emotion. Planned events where people can share feelings (for example, grief, support, or love) help build a climate of compassion. For example, a memorial service for a recently deceased executive at which the CEO shed tears was a powerful signal to organization members that responding compassionately to human suffering was important to the organization (Frost, 2003).

The third step is collective responding, meaning that the manager ensures that an appropriate response is made when healing or restoration is needed. In the aftermath of the 11 September 2001 tragedy, many examples of compassion—and noncompassion—were witnessed in organizations around the country. While some leaders modeled caring and compassion in the responses they fostered, others stifled the healing process (see Dutton, Frost, Worline, Lilius, & Kanov, 2002).

Forgiveness   Most managers assume that **forgiveness** has no place in the work setting. Because of high

quality standards, the need to eliminate mistakes, and a requirement to "do it right the first time," managers assume that they cannot afford to let errors go unpunished. Forgiving mistakes will just encourage people to be careless and unthinking, they conclude. However, forgiveness and high standards are not incompatible. That is because forgiveness is not the same as pardoning, condoning, excusing, forgetting, denying, minimizing, or trusting (Enright & Coyle, 1998). To forgive does not mean relieving the offender of a penalty (i.e., pardoning), or saying that the offense is OK, not serious, or forgotten (i.e., condoned, excused, denied, minimized). The memory of the offense need not be erased for forgiveness to occur. Instead, forgiveness in an organization involves the capacity to abandon justified resentment, bitterness, and blame, and, instead, to adopt positive, forward-looking approaches in response to harm or damage (Cameron & Caza, 2002).

For example, because minor offenses and disagreements occur in almost all human interactions, especially in close relationships, most people are practiced forgivers. Without forgiveness, relationships could not endure and organizations would disintegrate into squabbles, conflicts, and hostilities. One explanation for the successful formation of the European Economic Union is forgiveness, for example (Glynn, 1994). Collectively speaking, the French, Dutch, and British forgave the Germans for the atrocities of World War II, as did other damaged nations. Likewise, the reciprocal forgiveness demonstrated by the United States and Japan after World War II helps explain the flourishing economic and social interchange that developed in subsequent decades. On the other hand, the lack of peace in certain war-torn areas of the world can be at least partly explained by the refusal of organizations and nations to forgive one another for past trespasses (Helmick & Petersen, 2001).

The importance of forgiveness in organizations, and societies, is illustrated by Nobel laureate Desmond Tutu in his description of postapartheid South Africa:

> *Ultimately, you discover that without forgiveness, there is no future. We recognize that the past cannot be remade through punishment. . . . There is no point in exacting vengeance now, knowing that it will be the cause for future vengeance by the offspring of those we punish. Vengeance leads only to revenge. Vengeance destroys those it claims and those who become intoxicated with it . . . therefore, forgiveness is an absolute necessity for continued human existence. (Tutu, 1998, p. xiii; 1999, p. 155)*

Forgiveness is enhanced in organizations when managers:

1. Acknowledge the trauma, harm, and injustice that their organization members have experienced, but they define the occurrence of hurtful events as an opportunity to move forward toward a new goal.

2. Associate the outcomes of the organization (e.g., its products and services) with a higher purpose that provides personal meaning for organization members. This higher purpose replaces a focus on self (e.g., retribution, self-pity) with a focus on a higher objective.

3. Maintain high standards and communicate the fact that forgiveness is not synonymous with tolerance for error or lowered expectations. Use forgiveness to facilitate excellence by refusing to focus on the negative and, instead, focus on achieving excellence.

4. Provide support by communicating that human development and human welfare are as important in the organization's priorities as the financial bottom line. This kind of support helps employees catch sight of a way to move past the injury.

5. Pay attention to language, so that terms such as forgiveness, compassion, humility, courage, and love are acceptable; this language provides a humanistic foundation upon which most forgiveness occurs.

An analysis of the several organizations' successful turnaround after the trauma of downsizing reveals these five steps being demonstrated in institutionalizing forgiveness.

Gratitude Observing acts of compassion and forgiveness—not to mention being the recipient of them—creates a sense of gratitude in people. **Gratitude** is crucial in organizations because it leads to reciprocal behavior, equity, and justice (e.g., returning a favor, doing good in return for receiving good, being fair). Simmel referred to gratitude as "the moral memory of mankind . . . if every grateful action . . . were suddenly eliminated, society (at least as we know it) would break apart" (1950, p. 388).

Feelings of gratitude have been found to have dramatic effects on individual and organizational performance. For example, Emmons (2003) induced feelings of gratitude in students by assigning them to keep journals as part of a semester-long assignment. Some of the students were required to keep "gratitude journals" on a daily or weekly basis. That is, they wrote down events or incidents that happened during the day (or week) for which they were grateful. Other students were assigned to write down events or incidents that were frustrating, and still other students were assigned to write down events or incidents that were merely neutral. Students keeping gratitude journals, compared to frustrated students and neutral students, experienced fewer physical symptoms such as headaches, colds, and so on; felt better about their lives as a whole; were more optimistic about the coming week; had higher states of alertness, attentiveness, determination, and energy; reported fewer hassles in their lives; engaged in more helping behavior toward other people; experienced better sleep quality; and had a sense of being more connected to others. In addition, they were absent and tardy less often and had higher grade point averages. Feelings of gratitude had significant impact on student classroom performance as well as people's personal lives.

McCraty and Childre (2004) helped explain one reason why the positive effect of gratitude occurs in people's lives. They studied heart rhythms of people when they experienced frustrating or stressful work conditions, and compared those heart rhythms to changes that occurred when people were induced into a gratitude condition. Figure 10.4 shows the differences. For the first 100 seconds, the erratic and disordered heartbeat pattern shows a condition of frustration and stress, whereas for the next 100 seconds the heartbeat pattern shows a condition of appreciation and gratitude. It is easy to see why performance and health are enhanced by gratitude.

Emmons also found that expressions of gratitude by one person tend to motivate others to express gratitude, so a self-perpetuating, virtuous cycle occurs when gratitude is expressed. Gratitude elicits positive behaviors on the part of other people (e.g., they are more likely to loan money, provide compassionate support, as well as behave reciprocally). For example, a handwritten "thank you" on a restaurant bill by the server elicits about 11 percent higher tips, and visits by case workers and social workers are 80 percent higher if they are thanked for coming (McCullough, Emmons, & Tsang, 2002). People respond positively to expressions of gratitude. Thus, not only does gratitude help people *feel* good but *do* good as well.

Managers engender gratitude in an organization simply by expressing gratitude frequently and conspicuously themselves, even for small acts and small successes, and by keeping track of things that go right (not just things that go wrong) and expressing gratitude

LEARNING

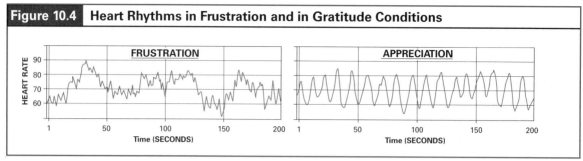

Figure 10.4 Heart Rhythms in Frustration and in Gratitude Conditions

These are actual heart rhythm patterns resulting from in an induced state of frustration followed by an induced gratitude condition.

SOURCE: *McCraty & Childre, (2004) "The Grateful Heart." In Emmons, R. A. and Mc Cullough, M. E. (Eds.). The Psychology of Gratitude (pp. 230–255) New York: Oxford University Press.*

for them. Elaborate programs are not needed, just frequent thank yous.

Pay Attention to Strengths and the Best Self

Identifying people's strengths (or what they do right) and then building on them creates more benefit than identifying weaknesses (or what people do wrong) and trying to correct them. For example, managers who spend more time with their strongest performers (rather than their weakest performers) achieved double the productivity. In organizations where workers have a chance to "do what they do best every day," productivity is one-and-a-half times greater than in normal organizations. People who are given feedback on their strengths are significantly more likely to feel highly engaged and to be more productive than people who are given feedback on their weaknesses. Students who are given feedback on their talents have fewer days of absenteeism, are tardy less often, and have higher GPAs than students who get no feedback on their talents. The strongest readers make more improvement in a speed-reading class designed to improve reading than the poor readers (Clifton & Harter, 2003).

Another illustration of this principle that building on positive strengths is more effective than concentrating on overcoming weaknesses is a classic study of (American) bowling (Kirschenbaum, 1984). To explain the study, let's assume that we decided to take a group of people to a bowling alley. The objective is to help these folks improve their bowling scores. We ask them all to bowl three games, and as they bowl, we videotape each person. Then, we ask that the entire group practice bowling for the next six months in order to improve their scores. However, to assist them, we will show them videotape of the three games we filmed. For half the group, we show them only video footage of when they rolled strikes, or

knocked all the pins down. For the other half of the group, we show them only video footage of when they did not roll strikes, or they did not knock all the pins down. Half the people are trying to capitalize on what they did right. Half the group is trying to correct mistakes. After six months of practice, we bring all the people back together and ask them to bowl three more games. We would discover that there is a statistically significant difference between the two groups. One group would bowl significantly better than the other. Which would you predict would do the best?

The research indicates that those who watched their past successes—they saw footage of their strikes—improved significantly more than those who watched footage of mistakes. That's because when we start out almost any activity, we mostly make mistakes. Yet, we tend to learn how to do it right over time. We tend to make more and more strikes, hit the ball down the center of the fairway, swish the free throw, or improve our public speaking ability, even though we make a lot of mistakes in the beginning. In other words, focusing on the positive will bring superior results to focusing on the negative. The trouble is, most people, most of the time, are inclined to pay attention to what's wrong, the problems, the negative feedback, or the failures they experience. The research, however, demonstrates the potency of the positive.

An even more dramatic finding resulted from a study of top management teams engaged in strategic planning for their organizations. Losada and Heaphy (2003) studied 60 teams of senior executives who met to set objectives, refine budgets, and identify plans for the upcoming year. The research focused on investigating why some teams, and their organizations, performed better than others. The teams used in the research were executives and top managers in well-recognized corporations.

The teams were categorized into three groups based on six measures of performance, such as firm profitability, productivity, managerial capability, and so on. The three groups were: those that performed well, those that performed about average, and those that performed poorly. To explain differences among the groups, the communication patterns of the teams were carefully monitored and analyzed. The single most important factor in predicting success—which was four times more powerful in predicting success than any other factor—was the ratio of positive comments to negative comments. Positive comments are those that express appreciation, support, helpfulness, or compliments. Negative comments express criticism, disapproval, or blame. The results of the research were dramatic. In high-performing teams, the ratio of positive to negative comments was 5:1. Five times more positive comments were made than negative comments. In medium-performing teams, the ratio was 1:1. In low-performing teams, the ratio was 0.36:1. In other words, in low-performing teams, there were three negative comments for every positive comment.

What these results show is that high-performing teams have an abundance of positive comments compared to negative comments. Effective teams are far more complimentary and supportive than ineffective teams. It's not that correction and criticism are entirely absent—it's not Pollyanna or rose-colored glasses all the time—but the positive outweighs the negative by a ratio of 5 to 1. Teams that performed moderately well had about an equal number of positive and negative comments, and teams that performed poorly had more negative than positive comments. The same ratio, by the way, has been found in successful marriages. Marriages that are strong also have a ratio of 5 to 1 positive interactions. Marriages that end in divorce have more negative than positive comments (Gottman, 1994).

Obviously, the management skill demonstrated by effective leaders of positive change is to bias their communication toward positive, supportive comments rather than negative and corrective comments. Remember, however, that the ratio is not 100:1 or 5:0. That is, critical, confrontive, and corrective comments need to be present and cannot be ignored. It's just that effective managers are, by and large, more focused on positive than negative communication.

Reflected Best-Self Feedback
One technique that managers can use to enhance positivity and focus on strengths is called **"reflected best-self feedback"** (Quinn, Dutton, & Spreitzer, 2003) It is a technique developed and used extensively at the University of Michigan Business School and recently adopted at the Harvard Business School, MIT, and several major corporations. It is designed to provide people with feedback on their strengths and unique capabilities. This kind of information is not frequently given to people, if ever, but receiving it allows individuals to build on their unique strengths in a positive way. Figure 10.5 illustrates the kind of feedback resulting from this exercise.

Begin at the bottom of the figure. Most of us have a lot of weaknesses—areas that are underdeveloped, areas in which we are uninformed, areas in which we have little skill. Most feedback systems provide information on what those areas are and how we compare to other people's capabilities in the same areas. Those are labeled **weaknesses** in Figure 10.5. We also all have areas in which we perform competently. We do fine—not stellar, but good enough. Those are areas of **competence**. A third category is areas of well-developed skill. We're outstanding performers in some areas. We have special capabilities or talents, and we do better than most people. These are areas of **strength**. Finally, we all have areas that are unique to us. If we don't contribute what we have, or if we don't share our capacities and gifts, no one else has the ability to do so. Our talent or skill is special. We refer to this area as **uniquenesses**. Research indicates that capitalizing on our strengths and uniquenesses produces more success than trying to work on and overcome weaknesses—even though weaknesses may be more numerous and more obvious (Clifton & Harter, 2003).

You engaged in the reflected best-self feedback process as part of the Skill Pre-Assessment section of this chapter. In this technique each person is asked to identify 20 other individuals who are acquaintances. These can be friends, coworkers, neighbors, or family members. Each of these acquaintances is asked to write three stories responding to this question: "When you have seen me at my best, or when you have seen me make a real contribution, what strengths did I display?" In other words, the 20 people write three stories about when the person was his or her best self. Those 60 stories identify the key strengths and unique talents of the individual—information that is both rare and extremely valuable. This information is analyzed by the person receiving the stories and summarized into a few key themes. Those themes represent the best-self strengths and uniquenesses of the person. The feedback comes in the form of incidents and stories, not numbers or trend lines, so it is connected directly to behaviors that the person has displayed in the past and which can be repeated and

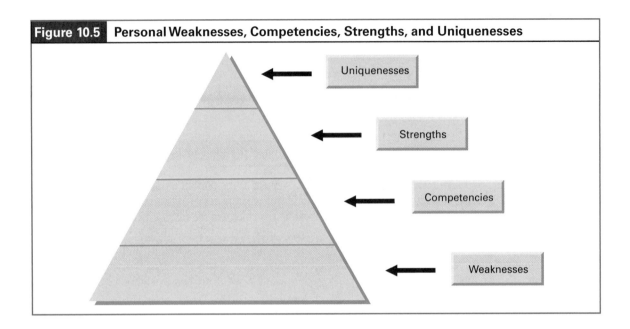

| Figure 10.5 | Personal Weaknesses, Competencies, Strengths, and Uniquenesses |

enhanced in the future. It captures emotions and feelings as well as intentional actions. These are the strengths and uniquenesses that can be built upon and enhanced. This kind of feedback does not even mention weaknesses or shortcomings. It does not motivate people to overcome areas of deficiency. Rather, it emphasizes the positive and helps people develop strategies to capitalize on it.

Of course, completely ignoring weaknesses and inadequacies is not healthy either. Focusing exclusively on the positive and disregarding critical weaknesses is not apt to be healthy in the long run. It's just that most individuals, and most organizations, concentrate almost exclusively on the negative and are likely to ignore, or at least short-change, the positive. The reflective best-self feedback technique is a way to counterbalance that tendency.

Summary Not everyone, and maybe even very few people, live or work in a positive organizational climate in which people flourish and experience positive energy. The role of the leader of positive change, therefore, is to facilitate and engender these characteristics. Table 10.1 summarizes some specific behaviors that can be implemented.

Being a source of positive energy and building positive energy networks leads to higher levels of personal success and organizational success. Similarly, the expression of compassion, forgiveness, and gratitude in organizations is also associated with superior performance, personally and organizationally. And, focusing on

strengths and talents—celebrating successes, complimenting what is going right, recognizing what folks do well—produces superior performance as well. Therefore, as the first step in leading positive change, establishing a positive climate is a crucial prerequisite. Without it, resistance and negativity are almost certain to present major obstacles. The tendency of most people is to focus on the problems, challenges, and negative issues associated with change. With a positive climate, however, positive change is much more likely to be successful. Figure 10.6 shows the relationship among these three aspects of positive climate.

Receiving feedback on strengths and successes produces feelings of gratitude and compassion, which, in turn, leads to being positively energized. Each factor, in turn, affects performance directly, as well as in combination with the other factors.

CREATING READINESS FOR CHANGE

In addition to establishing a climate of positivity, individuals must feel a need for the change and to understand its importance and urgency. A positive climate is a crucial foundation, but leading positive change requires engaging individuals in the actual process of change. The second step in leading positive change, therefore, is to create readiness among those to be involved in the change. Many techniques are available, but three are mentioned here.

Table 10.1	Establishing a Climate of Positivity

1. Create positive energy networks.

- Place positive energizers in places where others can interact with them and be influenced by them.
- Model positive energy yourself.
- Recognize and reward positive energizers.
- Provide opportunities for people to form close friendships at work.

2. Ensure a climate of compassion, forgiveness, and gratitude.

- Enable collective noticing of human concerns.
- Enable the expression of collective emotion.
- Enable the collective responding to difficulty, pain, or distress.
- Publicly and personally acknowledge trauma and harm.
- Identify higher purpose outcomes that people can point toward.
- Maintain high standards and look toward the future after mistakes.
- Provide personal support to people who have been harmed.
- Pay attention to language so that virtuous words are acceptable.
- Express gratitude frequently and conspicuously, even for small acts.
- Keep track of things that go right (not just that go wrong).

3. Identify and give people feedback on their strengths and unique competencies.

- Implement a reflected best-self feedback process.
- Spend the most time with the strongest performers.
- Work to capitalize on strengths rather than focusing on overcoming weaknesses.
- Use five positive comments for every negative comment in your interactions with others.

Figure 10.6	Relationships Among Factors in a Climate of Positivity

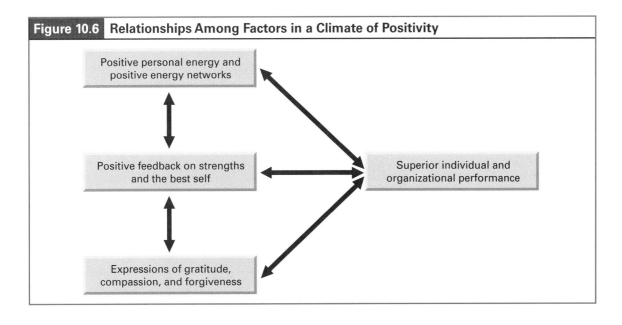

Benchmark Best Practice, and Compare Current Performance to the Highest Standards

One way to create readiness for change is to compare current levels of performance to the highest standards you can find. Identifying who else performs at spectacular levels helps set a standard toward which people can aspire. It identifies a target of opportunity. This is referred to as **benchmarking**, and it involves finding best practice, studying it in detail, and then planning to exceed that performance. "Shooting ahead of the duck" is the principle. Identifying best practice doesn't mean copying it. It means learning from it and exceeding it. Planned performance goes beyond the best practice, otherwise benchmarking is merely mimicking. Several different kinds of best practice standards are available for comparison.

- ❑ **Comparative standards**, or comparing current performance to similar individuals or organizations (e.g., "Here is how we are doing relative to our best competitors.")
- ❑ **Goal standards**, or comparing current performance to the publicly stated goals (e.g., "Here is how we are doing compared to the goals we have established.")
- ❑ **Improvement standards**, or comparing current performance with improvements made in the past (e.g., "Here is how we are doing compared to our improvement trends of the past year.")
- ❑ **Ideal standards**, or comparing current performance with an idea or perfect standard (e.g., "Here is how we are doing relative to a zero defect standard.")
- ❑ **Stakeholder expectations**, or comparing current performance with the expectations of customers, employees, or other stakeholders (e.g., "Here is how we are doing in meeting customer demands.")

Which standard of comparison is most appropriate depends, of course, on what opportunities exist, which standard has the most legitimacy with organization members, and which standard is perceived to be reachable. The purpose of these comparisons is to highlight the opportunities available by finding a higher level of performance and showing the possibility of achieving it.

Identifying benchmark standards also helps ensure that new information, new ideas, and new perspectives will be imported, and that standards not considered possible before may become realistic. Studying others who may be doing the same job better than you may be accomplished by sponsoring visitors, holding learning events (symposia and colloquia) or conferences, creating study teams, and scheduling visits to other sites. The objective is to unfreeze people from reliance on past practice by learning that there may be a better way.

Institute Symbolic Events

Leaders of positive change must signal the end of the old way of doing things and the beginning of a new way of doing things by means of symbols. This means that an event is used to signify a positive change or a new future. The symbolic event should be tangible and clearly identified with the positive change.

For example, during the 1980s Chrysler was experiencing very dark days. The company was bankrupt, and no one knew for sure if it would survive. Lee Iacocca was hired to be the new CEO. Tens of thousands of cars sat idle in the "sales bank" (Chrysler's term for cars parked in vacant lots) waiting to be sold. In his first closed-door speech to senior executives, Iacocca announced that the sales bank would be abolished. All cars in the sales bank would be sold at "distressed prices." "But," he said, "I want to keep one. You know what people do when they pay off the mortgage; they burn it on the front lawn. I want to burn that last car on the front lawn of headquarters, so the whole world knows it's over!" (Cameron, 1985). A symbolic event was held, in fact, in which the last car in the sales bank was burned, symbolizing a new future under Iacocca.

In that same speech, Iacocca asked all top managers to take out a piece of paper and write down all they had achieved in Chrysler during the past 12 months. After they had done so, they were instructed to tear up that paper and throw it away. They were to take out another piece of paper and write down all the things they were going to achieve in the next 12 months for the company. That was the document Iacocca instructed them to hang on their wall and explain to their coworkers. Symbolically, Iacocca was communicating the message: "You may have succeeded in the past, but the future is where we will now put our emphasis." The symbolic imagery communicated that message far more powerfully than merely stating it in a speech. The point is, symbolic images capture hearts as well as heads, and that resource is required for positive change to occur.

Create a New Language

Another way to create readiness for change is to help organization members begin to use different language to describe old realities. When new language is used, perspectives change. For example, a key goal for the theme park division at Disney Corporation is to provide the best service in the world. The trouble is, most of Disney's theme park employees in the summer months are college students working at temporary jobs and not particularly invested in being a park sweeper or concession stand cashier. Disney addresses this challenge by making sure that all new employees at Disney are taught that they have been hired by central casting, not the personnel department. They are cast members, not employees. They wear costumes, not uniforms. They serve guests and audience members, not tourists. They work in attractions, not rides or arcades. They have roles in the show and play characters (even as groundskeepers), not merely work a job. During working hours, they are onstage and must go offstage to relax, eat, or socialize.

The intent of this alternative language is to change the way these employees think about their work, to place them in a mind-set that they wouldn't have considered otherwise. At Disney, summer employees are in show business—on stage, playing a role, performing for an audience. Changing language helps unfreeze old interpretations and helps create new ones. Another example is CNN. When the network was first formed, employees were fined $100 if they ever spoke the word "foreign." The reason: at a worldwide news organization, no one is foreign. Thinking globally requires that language change, and foreign became a forbidden word. Leading positive change requires that optimistic words replace pessimistic words, and language that blocks progress is shunned. Intel, for example, forbids phrases such as "It can't be done"; "It won't work"; "It's just like an idea we already tried"; "It will never get approved." These phrases are all "creativity killers," and they inhibit positive change, innovation, and improvement.

Bennis and Nanus (1984) observed that the most successful leaders in education, government, business, the arts, and the military are those who have developed a special language. Most notable is the absence in their vocabularies of the word *failure*. These individuals simply haven't allowed themselves, or others around them, to accept the possibility of failure. Alternative descriptors are used, such as temporary slowdown, false start, miscue, error, blooper, stumble, foul-up, obstacle, disappointment, or nonsuccess. These leaders use an alternative language in order to interpret reality for their organizations, to foster a willingness to try again, and to foster an inclination toward positive change. This language communicates the fact that failure is not an option. Success is just around the corner.

Summary

Creating readiness is a step designed to mobilize individuals in the organization to actively engage in the positive change process. It involves more than merely unfreezing people. Making people uncomfortable is a frequent prescription for getting people ready for change, and it often works. Making people uncomfortable, however, usually involves creating fear, crisis, or negative conditions. There is no doubt, of course, that change also creates its own discomfort. Interpersonal relationships, power and status, and routine ways of behaving are disrupted by change, so change is usually interpreted as anything but a positive condition. Leading positive change, on the other hand, focuses on ways to create readiness in ways that unlock positive motivations rather than resistance, and provides optimistic alternatives rather than fear. Benchmarking best practice, positive symbols, and new language are three practical ways to do it, as summarized in Table 10.2.

Establishing a climate of positivity and creating readiness for change does little good, of course, if there is not a clear idea of where the positive change is heading. That is why the third step in the framework refers to articulating a clear, motivating vision of abundance.

ARTICULATING A VISION OF ABUNDANCE

Positive change seldom occurs without a leader articulating a **vision of abundance** (see Figure 10.1). By abundance we mean a vision of a positive future, a flourishing condition, and a legacy about which people care passionately. This kind of vision helps unleash human wellsprings of potential since it addresses a basic human desire—to do something that makes a difference, something that outlasts one's own life, and something that has enduring impact. Visions of abundance are different from visions of goal achievement or effectiveness—such as earning a certain percent profit, becoming number one in the marketplace, or receiving personal recognition. Rather, these are visions that speak to the heart as well as the head.

For example, the vision of Richard Bogomolny, the CEO of Finast Supermarkets in Cleveland, Ohio, was to

Table 10.2	Creating Readiness in Others to Pursue Positive Change

1. Benchmark best practice, and compare current performance to the highest standards.

   • Use comparable others as standards.

   • Use stated goals as standards.

   • Use past improvement as a standard.

   • Use an ideal as a standard.

   • Use others' expectations as a standard.

2. Institute symbolic events to signal the positive change.

   • Interpret events or activities as indicators of the beginning of a new era.

   • Manage people's interpretations and mental images of incidents so that they reinforce the intended change.

   • Pay as much attention to the meaning of change as the substance of the change.

3. Create a new language that illustrates the positive change.

   • Use words associated with the change that capture people's imagination.

   • Use passionate and inspiring language.

   • Use words that communicate and reinforce a new direction.

improve the quality of life for residents of blighted areas of Cleveland who would otherwise never have access to a reasonably priced grocery store with competitive prices. He invested in new, state-of-the-art supermarkets in poor urban neighborhoods, stocking shelves with ethnic foods that were not popular in suburban stores, and providing an environment of safety and cleanliness along with offering prices competitive with suburban shopping centers. Finast stores have now become the social gathering places for entire neighborhoods, have provided training and employment for the chronically unemployed, and, at the same time, have become a highly profitable investment for the company (Bollier, 1996). Without the leader's clear statement of a vision of abundance, the overwhelming tendencies toward addressing obstacles, problem solving, and negative feedback drive out positive change.

Most organizations have some kind of mission statement or have established goals, but a **vision statement** is something different. Visions include the universalistic values and principles that will guide behavior. They provide a sense of direction. They help identify what the future holds. They provide glimpses of possibilities, not just probabilities. They evoke deeper meaning than mission statements or goals. They provide optimism and hope.

For example, goals that call for a 20 percent increase in ROI, an improvement in product quality,

timelier responses to customers, or lower costs all are valuable and important to organizations. Yet, they are not visions. They are examples of targets that the organization wants to achieve. Visions, on the other hand, are focused on helping individuals' *think* differently about themselves and about their future. They possess several important characteristics that are central to the positive change process.

Include Left-Brain and Right-Brain Features

Many years ago, neurosurgeons discovered that the brain consists of two hemispheres that can actually work independently when surgically separated. The left hemisphere controls the right side of the body, but it also controls rational cognitive activities such as sequential thinking, logic, deduction, numeric thought, and so on. Activities such as reading, solving math problems, and rational analysis are dominated by *left-brain thinking.*

The right hemisphere, on the other hand, controls the left side of the body as well as nonrational cognitive activities such as intuition, creativity, fantasy, emotions, pictorial images, and imagination. Composing music, storytelling, and artistic creation are most likely tied to *right-brained thinking.*

Of course, neither hemisphere operates autonomously from the other, and both kinds of mental activity are required in complex tasks. But that is precisely the point. Vision statements of leaders must contain rational targets, goals, and action plans (left-brain components), as well as metaphors, colorful language, and imagination (right-brain components). Unfortunately, most managers and most organizations emphasize the left-brain side in their mission statement or strategic planning documents (they focus, for example, on increased market share, becoming number one in the industry, or raising quality standards). Fewer paint pictures of the future, use exciting language, and speak to the imaginations of members. In the Skill Analysis section of this chapter, several corporate vision statements are provided for you to analyze. Note the differences among them in the relative emphasis on right-brain versus left-brain thinking.

Articulating the *left-brained* side of the vision is facilitated by answering the following questions:

❏ What are our most important strengths as an organization? Where do we have a strategic advantage?
❏ What major problems and obstacles do we face? What stands in the way of significant improvement?
❏ What are the primary resources that we need? What information is required?
❏ Who are our key customers? What must be done to respond to their expectations?
❏ What measurable outcomes will we accomplish? What are the criteria to be monitored?

Articulating the *right-brained* side of the vision is aided by answering the following questions:

❏ What is the best we can achieve? What represents peak performance?
❏ What stories or events can we tell that characterize what we stand for?
❏ What metaphors or analogies can we use that will identify what the future of our organization will look like?
❏ What symbols are appropriate for helping capture people's imaginations?
❏ What colorful and inspirational language can exemplify what we believe in?

The most motivating vision statements—for example, Churchill's "Never Give In" speech, Kennedy's "Ask Not What Your Country Can Do for You" speech, Mandela's "A Dream for Which I Am Prepared to Die" speech, Martin Luther King's "I Have a Dream" speech—all contain both left-brained and right-brained elements. Leaders of positive change pay attention to both in articulating their vision statements.

Make Vision Statements Interesting

Murray Davis (1971) published a now-classic article on what causes some kinds of information to be judged interesting or uninteresting. The truth or veracity of the information has little to do with that judgment, according to Davis. Rather, what's interesting depends on the extent to which the information contradicts weakly held assumptions and challenges the status quo. If new information is consistent with what is already known, people tend to dismiss it as common sense. If new information is obviously contradictory to strongly held assumptions, or if it blatantly challenges the core values of the organization's members, it is labeled ridiculous, silly, or blasphemous. Information that helps create new ways to view the future, that challenges the current state of things (but not core values), is viewed as interesting. New insights are created and people are drawn to the information because it makes them think, or it uncovers a new way to think.

Inspiring vision statements are interesting. They contain challenges and prods that confront and alter the ways people think about the past and the future. They are not outlandish or cavalier in their message, just provocative. For example, Ralph Peterson, CEO of CH2MHill (a large environmental and engineering firm) indicated that "corporate immortality" was the ultimate objective of the company, meaning that the firm was in business to create outcomes that would last well beyond the lifetime of any individual. Jeffrey Schwartz, CEO of Timberland, the shoe and clothing company, espoused a vision related to doing good in order to do well—organizational virtuousness is equally important to organizational profitability. Tom Gloucer, CEO of Reuters, espoused the vision that Reuters would become the fastest company in the world. Ross Perot, while serving on the board of directors at General Motors, articulated his vision of the new GM if he were at the helm. "From this point forward, GM'ers will fight in the marketplace, not with each other. Starting today, GM'ers will work together using brains, wits, creative abilities, and initiative as substitutes for money. Starting today, as GM goes through a transformation, all sacrifices will start at the top" (1988).

These examples are not intended to illustrate the best vision statements, of course, nor even vision statements that energize you personally. But, in each case, they carried a strong and motivating message for those in the organizations mentioned. They helped paint a mental picture. One of the chief reasons is that these vision statements are interesting. They identify a message that people care about but which challenges the normal perception of things. The statements confront the status quo and provide a new way to think about what people do in the organization every day. The fact that they are interesting is what captures attention and positive energy.

Include Passion and Principles

Effective visions are grounded in core values that organization members believe in, and about which they feel passionate. Such vision statements increase people's desire to affiliate with the organization if they care deeply about the company's core principles. The principles espoused in the vision, therefore, must be personal. A vision focused on "increasing productivity" is less energizing and inspiring than a vision based on "changing people's lives." "Achieving profitability" is less magnetic than "making people happy." Furthermore, such principles are best phrased using superlatives. Notice the difference in how you feel about the following comparisons: "phenomenal performance" versus "successful." Or, "passionately engaged" versus "committed." Or, "explosive growth" versus "good progress." Or, "awesome products" versus "useful items." Visions based on the former phrases engender more enthusiasm and passion than those based on the latter phrases.

Consider as an example of such language the vision statement of John Sculley, former CEO of Apple Computer Company:

> We are all part of a journey to create an extraordinary corporation. The things we intend to do in the years ahead have never been done before. . . . One person, one computer is still our dream. . . . We have a passion for changing the world. We want to make personal computers a way of life in work, education, and the home. Apple people are paradigm shifters. . . . We want to be the catalyst for discovering new ways for people to do things. . . . Apple's way starts with a passion to create awesome products with a lot of distinctive value built in. . . . We have chosen directions for Apple that will lead us to wonderful ideas we haven't as yet dreamed. (Sculley, 1987)

Two specific hints for articulating inspiring, passionate, principle-centered visions include:

1. Ensure that the vision statement reinforces *core values* about which you feel strongly. Instead of focusing on end results such as profit growth, expanded market share, customer satisfaction measures, or goal accomplishment, for example, the vision statement should relate to something fundamental about which people can feel passionate. This is likely to be associated with human flourishing, interpersonal relationships, or an ultimate good—that is, things that make life worth living. These are things that outlast a single person's lifetime, or that create a ripple effect so that the impact extends far beyond the immediate situation. Outcomes such as assistance to mankind, helping to make life or work more rewarding, increasing the freedom of individuals, or improving the quality of life all are more attractive and motivational than instrumental outcomes. People can become passionate about these kinds of aspirations.

2. The vision statement must be straightforward and simple. A common error of leaders is to be too complicated, too lengthy, or too multifaceted in their vision statement. Most great leaders acknowledge that they have only three or four major objectives in mind. Their visions help people focus. Ronald Reagan, Michael Eisner (Disney), Jack Welch (GE), Bill Gates (Microsoft), Jim Hackett (Steelcase) all are well-known examples of leaders who publicly espoused a simple and straightforward vision—usually with only three or four key parts. Contrast that with the former CEO and chairman of Whirlpool Corporation who wrote a 15-page document outlining his vision for the company. Employees complained that they couldn't understand exactly what he wanted or where the company was going. It was difficult to sign up for 15 pages! One senior manager dismissed the document by stating, "He simply has too much vision!" It was only when the vision statement was condensed to four key points that it became credible in the organization.

Attach the Vision to a Symbol

Effective vision statements are associated with a symbol. This is more than a symbolic event that helps create readiness for change. Rather, people must associate the vision with something tangible they see or hear. Not only does the vision identify expectations and direction for individuals in their day-to-day activities, but they should be reminded of it regularly by the presence of a symbol. That symbol may be a logo, a phrase from a speech, a flag, a physical structure, or any number of things that can serve as a reminder of where the vision is taking the organization.

The turnaround at Ford Motor Company after William Clay Ford took over was symbolized by the resurrection of the blue Ford oval on the headquarters building. Chrysler returned to the classic Chrysler logo instead of the five-pointed star. Malden Mills reconstructed a plant that had been devastated by fire on the same property to symbolize human commitment and corporate compassion. The replacement structures for the World Trade Center towers are targeted specifically to symbolize a positive and uplifting future after the devastating tragedy. Logos such as the golden arches, Nike Swoosh, or Mickey Mouse are carefully publicized, even protected, because of the symbolic messages that they communicate about the companies they represent.

One of us served as a dean in a Midwest business school for a time, and a key responsibility was to articulate a motivating and energizing vision in order to set a new direction for the school. The vision being articulated focused on enhancing the school's reputation, engendering a spirit of entrepreneurship and innovation, and building a sense of pride in scholarly excellence. Speeches were made about these aspirations—we have all heard these kinds of talks—but speeches given by the dean seldom if ever have lasting impact. A symbol was needed to make the vision real and to serve as a constant reminder. That symbol was the construction of a new building, designed by the world's most famous architect. The new building symbolized a best-in-class, one-of-a-kind structure, and it signified that the school would be an innovative, entrepreneurial, out-of-the-box kind of place. Pride in being unique in the world was an important symbolic message. To get a sense of how a building could serve as a symbol of such things, look at the final building model in Figure 10.7.

You can see that this design can communicate strong messages to both internal and external constituencies. It was interpreted as representing the twenty-first century rather than the eighteenth or nineteenth century (which are more typical of most ivy-covered college campuses in America). It was used to represent innovation and the entrepreneurial spirit. It communicates humaneness, comfort, and interaction. It symbolizes movement, fluidity, and dynamism. It epitomizes best-in-class. The building was designed to

Figure 10.7 | **An Example: A Symbol of Positive Organizational Change**

foster lots of interaction, representing the fact that learning is mainly a social activity. It touches the whole person—emotions and spirit as well as intellect. It stimulates extraordinary thinking (Cameron, 2003b). Speeches about a vision, in other words, were not nearly as powerful as a visible symbol that could be experienced every day by the people who saw it.

Table 10.3 summarizes some specific behaviors you can use in articulating a high-impact vision of abundance.

GENERATING COMMITMENT TO THE VISION

Once this vision of abundance has been articulated, it is necessary for leaders to help organization members commit to that vision, to sign up, to adopt the vision as their own, and to work toward its accomplishment. The whole intent of a vision is to mobilize the energy and human potential of individuals who are to implement and be affected by it. Among the ways to generate commitment to a vision are four discussed below. Others are discussed in depth in the chapters on motivation, empowerment, and teamwork.

Apply Principles of Recreation

An interesting truism was identified by Chuck Coonradt (1985): "*People will pay for the privilege of working harder than they will work when they are paid.*" Think about that for a minute. "People will pay for the privilege of working harder than they will work when they are paid." In other words, under certain circumstances, individuals are more committed to doing

Table 10.3	Articulating a Vision of Abundance

1. Focus on creating positive deviance rather than correcting negative deviance.

   • Focus on possibilities more than probabilities.

   • Focus on extraordinary, spectacular achievement rather than just winning or being seen as successful.

2. Include left-brain images by asking questions such as:

   • What are our most important strengths as an organization?

   • Where do we have a strategic advantage?

   • What major problems and obstacles do we face?

   • What stands in the way of significant improvement?

   • What are the primary resources that we need?

   • What information is required?

   • Who are our key customers?

   • What must be done to respond to customers' expectations?

   • What measurable outcomes will we accomplish?

   • What are the criteria to be monitored?

3. Include right-brain images by asking questions such as:

   • What is the best we can achieve?

   • What represents peak performance?

   • What stories or events can we tell that characterize what we stand for?

   • What metaphors or analogies can we use that will identify what the future of our organization will look like?

   • What symbols are appropriate for helping capture people's imaginations?

   • What colorful and inspirational language can exemplify what we believe in?

4. Make the vision interesting by challenging weakly held assumptions.

5. Ensure credibility of the vision through demonstrating:

   • Integrity in adhering to a consistent set of principles.

   • Knowledge regarding the implications of the vision.

   • Enthusiasm and personal passion for the vision.

   • Association with core personal values.

   • A straightforward and simple message.

   • Exciting and energizing language.

6. Attach the vision to a symbol to constantly remind people of the vision.

   • Create visual images such as logos, flags, or signs.

   • Make certain that the visual symbol is closely associated with the vision so it remains a constant reminder.

work that actually costs them money than they are to doing work for which they receive remuneration. Sometimes people will pay to work when they will not work when they are paid. How can that be? In what circumstances might that be the case?

Consider the following hypothetical example. Suppose you live in Utah in the winter and, as you arrive at work, you find that the furnace is out of order. As the temperature falls to 65 degrees Fahrenheit you put on a coat. At 60 degrees you complain that it is too cold to work. At 55 degrees you leave, confident that no one could expect you to perform in such adverse conditions. Then you put on your $300 ski outfit, grab your $750 skis and boots, race off to the slopes in order to pay $75 for a lift ticket, $25 for gas, and $30 for a junk-food lunch. You will spend all day long in 10-degree weather working much harder skiing than you would have worked at the firm where you could have been paid. If this sounds unusual, consider the skyrocketing absenteeism rates in companies and schools when the first big snow falls in ski areas, when the surf is up in cities close to the beach, or the first day of hunting or fishing season. People regularly choose to pay to work harder than they would consider working when they are paid.

Well, you say, that's because it's fun. It's recreation. And you're right. But there is no reason why the work performed in a regular job cannot be characterized by the same principles that characterize recreation. In other words, what causes people to *want* to engage in recreational work can also be what causes them to be equally committed to their occupational work. At least five characteristics are typical of **recreational work** (Coonradt, 1985).

1. Goals are clearly defined
2. Scorekeeping is objective, self-administered, peer-audited, and compared to past performance
3. Feedback is frequent
4. Personal choice is present; rules are consistent and don't change until the season is over
5. A competitive environment is present

Consider the game of (American) football. Each year the University of Michigan averages about 106,000 fans per game, every one of whom knows exactly what the goal is—to score more points than the opponent. There is no need for a periodic performance appraisal system, because the score changes only when a team crosses the goal line or kicks a field goal. There is no guessing about how to get ahead. Feedback is not only frequent, it is continuous. If the clock goes down, they stop the game. No one would consider playing if the time and the score were not kept continuously. Within the rules of the game, every participant and fan has personal choice. Players can go full speed or not; fans can cheer or not; the team can run the ball or pass. No one forces people to perform a role that they don't want to perform. Coordination and control occur because everyone knows the rules, and the rules don't change. Off-side is off-side, a first down is a first down, and a touchdown is a touchdown. When a receiver is wide

open and makes an easy catch in the end zone, no one could imagine an NCAA committee deliberating about how many points the score is worth. No one would say, "Easy catch; wide open; worth only 4.5 points." No one would stand for that, and 106,000 people would go crazy. The rules simply don't change in recreation. Plus, the environment is one of competition—both against an opponent and against personal past performance. The stimulation of competing against something is fun. Playing against someone who is markedly less skilled—beating them 100 to 0, is not as much fun.

Despite the inherent motivation and commitment associated with these principles, many leaders behave inconsistently with them. Their vision is not stated clearly and precisely. There is no objective, self-administered evaluation system. The scorekeeping system is controlled hierarchically, by managers one step above, instead of being peer-audited and continuous, as in recreation. Criteria of evaluation are vague and inconsistently administered. Organization feedback often comes only when quarterly earnings statements are tabulated, and then it is often focused on what went wrong. Personal freedom is too often constrained, as evidenced by the elaborate bureaucratic structures that typify most large organizations. It is not unusual to have the criteria of success change in the middle of the game, especially if a new manager takes over. And, most employees never see how what they do makes any difference at all in obtaining the ultimate goal, or winning against a competitor.

The point is, one way for leaders to generate commitment to the vision is to identify clear, consistent goals associated with the vision; identify the criteria that will indicate progress toward reaching the vision which each organization member can monitor; provide mechanisms for frequent feedback to organization members; give individuals personal choice and the maximum discretion possible; maintain a consistency and stability of the rules of the game and expectations; and identify a competitive standard against which performance can be evaluated. Like commitment to recreation, commitment to visions, if based on similar principles, will also become strong and long-lasting.

Ensure Public Commitments

Another well-documented way to enhance commitment to a vision is to have people state their commitments aloud, in public. Individuals are motivated to behave consistently with their public declarations (Salancik, 1977). The internal need for congruence ensures that public statements will be followed by consistent actions. After making public pronouncements, individuals are more committed and more consistent in their behavior to that which they have espoused (Baker, 2001; Cialdini, 2000).

For example, during World War II, good cuts of meat were in short supply in the United States. Lewin (1951) found that a significant difference existed between the commitment level of shoppers who promised out loud to buy more plentiful but less desirable cuts of meat (e.g., liver, kidneys, brains) compared to those who made the same promise in private. In another study, students were divided in a college class into two groups. All students set goals for how much they would read and what kinds of scores they would get on exams. Only half the students were allowed to state these goals publicly to the rest of the class. By midsemester, the students who stated their goals publicly averaged 86 percent improvement. The nonpublic goal-setting students averaged 14 percent improvement.

When the Tennessee Valley Authority (TVA) was attempting to build a dam in the late 1940s, it found that local farmers vehemently resisted the efforts because of the land that would be flooded. To overcome this resistance and elicit farmers' commitment to the project, the TVA made local farmers members of the board that would supervise the construction efforts. These local farmers began to make public statements on behalf of the TVA project and, over time, became strongly committed to it (Selznick, 1949).

This point is, leaders of positive change look for opportunities to have others make public statements in favor of the vision, or to restate the vision themselves. Assigning individuals to represent the vision to outside groups or to other employees, or forming discussion groups so that others can help refine or clarify the vision, are examples of how opportunities for public statements can be fostered in order to enhance commitment.

Institute a Small-Wins Strategy

People become committed to change when they see progress being made or success being achieved. We are all more committed to winners than to losers. Fans attend more games when the team has a good record than when it has a poor record. The number of people claiming to have voted for a winning candidate always exceeds by a large margin the actual number of votes received. In other words, when we see success, or progress being made, we are more committed to respond positively, to continue that path, and to offer our support.

Leaders of positive change create this kind of support by identifying small wins—a strategy that was discussed in Chapter 2 on managing stress, as well as being mentioned in discussions of problem solving and

empowerment. This small-wins strategy is applicable in a variety of skill-building activities, so we repeat part of the discussion here. The key message is that surfacing and publicizing small wins creates commitment and builds momentum for desired change (Weick, 1981). For example, we have observed leaders, when beginning a major change initiative, starting with small changes such as a new coat of paint, abolishing reserved parking spaces, adding a display case for awards, flying a flag, holding regular social events, instituting a suggestion system, and so on. Each of these small changes (and hundreds more) is designed to create commitment to the visualized change.

A small-wins strategy, in other words, is designed to create a sense of momentum by creating minor, quick changes. As a refresher, the basic rule of thumb for small wins is: *Find something that is easy to change. Change it. Publicize it, or recognize it publicly. Then, find a second thing that's easy to change, and repeat the process.*

Small wins create commitment because: (1) they reduce the importance of any one change ("It is no big deal to make this change."); (2) they reduce demands on any group or individual ("There isn't a lot to do."); (3) they improve the confidence of participants ("At least I can do that."); (4) they help avoid resistance or retaliation ("Even if they disagree, it's only a small loss."); (5) they attract allies and create a bandwagon effect ("I want to be associated with this success."); (6) they create the image of progress ("Things seem to be moving forward."); (7) if they don't work they only create a small flop ("No major harm is done and no long-lasting effects occur."); (8) they provide initiatives in multiple arenas ("Resistance cannot be coordinated or organized in a single area.") (Weick, 1993).

Communicate the Vision

Effective leaders of positive change communicate the vision, then they communicate it again, then again, and then again. If leaders stop communicating the vision, or if they change themes as they address organization members, the members tend to think that the vision isn't important anymore. Unless leaders continually and consistently articulate and rearticulate the vision, it loses its power and commitment erodes. Being accused of repetition is much less serious than being accused of neglect. Persistent and continuous delivery of the vision message is required, but surprisingly, it is a frequent shortcoming of leaders. They give a speech or hand out a sheet on which the vision is written; then they think their job is complete. In reality, it has only begun. No one ever heard Nelson Mandela speak in South Africa, for example, without having him rearticulate his vision of human dignity and equal treatment for all persons.

Communicating the vision must also occur using a variety of methods. This means referring to the vision in public statements, newsletters, celebrations and ceremonies, speeches, memos, and everyday interactions. Leaders model the vision in their personal behavior. There should be no questions, by observing and listening to leaders, what the vision is. For example, Jan Carlzon, the former president of Scandinavian Airlines (SAS), took control of the airline when it was losing $20 million a year. In the first year he increased revenues by $80 million and led his company to being voted "the best airline in the world" by *Fortune* magazine. Here is what he said about communicating his vision.

Good leaders spend more time communicating than anything else. From my first day at SAS I've made communicating, particularly with our employees, a top priority. In fact, during the first year I spent exactly half my working hours out in the field talking to SAS people. The word going around was that any time three employees gathered, Jan Carlzon would probably show up and begin talking with them.

When we began reorganizing SAS, our critics scoffed at our efforts as mere promotional gimmicks. They claimed we had become too marketing oriented, but in fact we hadn't increased our marketing budget one cent. Rather, we were spending our money more effectively on messages that were easily understood. (Carlzon, 1987, pp. 88, 92)

Creating commitment is enhanced, in other words, by applying principles of recreational work, providing opportunities for public statements of commitment, instituting small wins, and communicating the vision frequently, consistently, and broadly. In essence, as summarized in Table 10.4, leaders will achieve commitment to that which they *say*, that

Table 10.4	Generating Commitment to the Vision

1. Apply principles of recreation to the work associated with the vision:
   - Clearly define goals.
   - Ensure that scorekeeping is objective, self-administered, peer-audited, and compared to past performance.
   - Ensure frequent (or continuous) feedback.
   - Provide opportunity for personal choice.
   - Ensure that rules are consistent and don't change.
   - Provide a competitive environment.
2. Provide opportunities for people to publicly commit to the vision.
   - Hold events where people can verbalize their commitment.
   - Ask people to teach others about, or recruit others to sign up for, the vision.
3. Institute a strategy of small wins.
   - Find something easy to change.
   - Change it.
   - Publicize it.
   - Repeat the process multiple times.
4. Communicate the vision frequently.
   - Never give a public speech or presentation without mentioning the vision.
   - Make certain that all your written messages contain references to the vision.
   - Avoid changing messages.

which they *do*, and that which they *reward*, but without consistency and frequency, not necessarily to that which they *want*.

INSTITUTIONALIZING THE POSITIVE CHANGE

The final challenge for leaders of positive change is to make the change a part of ongoing organizational life. General officers in the United States Army refer to this step as **"creating irreversible momentum"**; that is, ensuring that the positive change gains such momentum that it cannot be thwarted (U.S. Army, 2003). The challenge is to separate the vision from the visionary, to get others to own and become champions of the change, to create processes that reinforce the positive change without having to continually rely on the leader. The objective is to ensure that even if the leader leaves, the positive change will continue because of the sustainable impetus put in place. If Bill Gates was incarcerated for unfair business competition, Jan Carlzon got in an airplane crash, Lee Iacocca was run over by a car, or Jack Welch was electrocuted by a faulty refrigerator wire, Microsoft, SAS, Chrysler, and General Electric would not have missed a step. The positive changes championed by these leaders would still have been pursued because they had become embedded in their organizations' cultures. They were institutionalized and had gained irreversible momentum.

Institutionalizing change doesn't happen quickly, of course, and the four previous steps in positive change—establishing a climate of positivity, creating readiness, articulating a vision, and generating commitment—all must be successfully accomplished first. However, institutionalization is the necessary final step if the organization is to successfully achieve positive change. How do leaders institutionalize their positive changes? Three hints are provided.

Turn Students into Teachers

Most of the time we assume that it is the leader's responsibility to articulate the vision of abundance, and everyone else listens to it and accepts it. Teachers teach what students need to know and students learn it for the exam. The chief gives direction and the rest of us follow.

The most effective leaders, however, provide an opportunity for everyone in the organization to articulate the vision, or to teach others about the desired positive change. This process requires that every person develop "a teachable point of view" (Tichy, 1997). Developing one's own teachable point of view means that individuals come to believe in something, and they can clearly explain what it is and why. In other words, people get to the point where they can articulate the vision in their own words. They are given opportunities to teach others what they understand the positive change to be. They are required to develop their own perspective on the positive change in a way that it can be explained and illustrated to someone else. They are transformed from students or listeners into teachers or visionaries.

Researchers at the National Training Laboratories in Bethel, Maine, developed a "learning stair" (see Figure 10.8). Their studies found that people remember 5 percent of what they hear in a lecture, 10 percent of what they read, 20 percent of what they view in a video, 30 percent of what they observe being demonstrated, 50 percent of what they discuss in a group, 75 percent of what they apply, and 90 percent of what they teach to others. That is, by teaching someone else about the vision or the intended positive change, individuals remember it, become committed to it, and make it a part of their own personal agenda.

One manifestation of this principle was at Xerox under Rex Kern, a remarkable leader who turned that company around in the late 1980s and early 1990s. Kern's focus was on rapidly institutionalizing a positive change process by turning students into teachers. He spent time sharing his vision of positive change with his top leadership team. Then these leaders were required to apply what they heard; that is, to implement personal action agendas and make personal changes. Then, most importantly, they were required to teach the positive change vision to someone else. Who would they teach? They taught the next level of leaders in the firm. They were also required to assess or monitor the positive change. This was in order to identify measurable indicators, milestones, and hard data to ensure that the positive change was really taking place. It was a way to guard against lip service with no real substance. What did they assess? It was the action agendas and managerial experiments implemented by the leaders they taught. The process continued down through all the organizational levels. Each person, in other words, was exposed to the vision four times: when they learned it from their leader; when they applied it; when they taught it; and when they assessed it. Within a year, Xerox achieved stunning results. It is widely acknowledged that this process was key in turning Xerox around as a company and in labeling Rex Kern

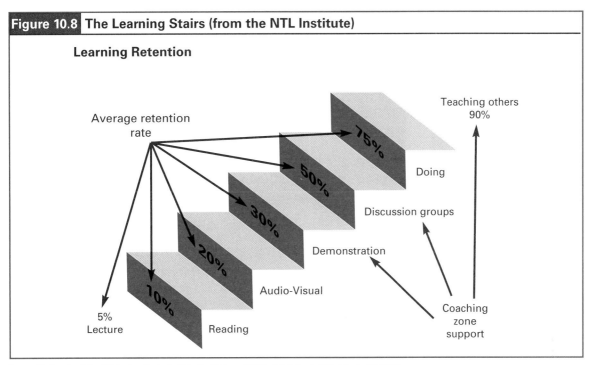

Figure 10.8 The Learning Stairs (from the NTL Institute)

Learning Retention

Average retention rate

Teaching others 90%

75%

Doing

50%

Discussion groups

30%

Demonstration

20%

Audio-Visual

10%

5% Lecture

Reading

Coaching zone support

Source: *The Learning Stairs; NTL Institute for Applied Behavioral Science, 1091 South Bell Street, #300, Arlington VA 22202.*

as one of the great corporate leaders of the twentieth century.

This is similar to the process used by certain divisions within Hewlett-Packard. These divisions require engineers to spend time recruiting on college campuses. Having engineers actually recruit students—from disciplines in business, mathematics, physical sciences, arts and humanities, as well as engineering—is risky because engineers are not trained recruiters. However, the strategy pays off because HP engineers are required to articulate the vision, publicly praise Hewlett-Packard, and teach interested job candidates about the company. Former HP "students" are required to become the "teachers." These engineers may not convince many rookie recruits, but by articulating the HP Way, they internalize it themselves. As a result, Hewlett-Packard has the lowest turnover rate in the industry among engineers, one of its stated core competencies.

Build Human Capital

For positive change to have staying power, for it to last beyond the lifetime of the leader, people throughout the organization must have developed the capability to lead the vision themselves, to institute positive change, and to carry on under their own initiative. In other words, well-developed human capital is always

the chief predictor of growth in financial capital. The skill set of the people is the bedrock upon which organizational success is built. No company can make money over time without well-developed human capital—meaning capable and skilled employees. Institutionalizing positive change occurs as individuals throughout the organization develop the capacity to lead positive change themselves. This can happen in many ways, of course, but a good example of the core principle is illustrated by a large Asian company in which we conducted research.

This particular company requires that each time a senior manager is promoted, he or she is required to take a three-month leave of absence. The person must actually leave work for three full months. For one of the months the manager is required to intensively study religion or ethics, and then document it, usually with a written report. For another month the individual is required to study history or a major historical figure, and then document it. The third month must be spent studying business, broadly defined. So, at the end of three months, three documents have been prepared. If, after the three months, the business has run smoothly with no major hitches, then the promotion occurs. That is, the promotion occurs at the end of the three-month leave, not before. Why would a large company implement such a strange promotion system at substantial risk and expense? Why not just send the manager to a week-long executive education program at a university?

The reason is that this is part of the process for institutionalizing the vision of the company. A key value in the company relates to developing human capital, in addition to financial capital and physical capital. They know that human capital is the key driver of long-term success. The three-month leave of absence, of course, provides a chance for self-development, personal enrichment, and broadened perspective. Senior managers are required to study religion or ethics because all business decisions are based on some set of values or standards. The firm wants to make certain that these people have spent time intelligently thinking through their own value system. To avoid the trap of becoming short-term in orientation, studying history helps broaden viewpoints and helps assure that the mistakes of the past aren't repeated. Studying business principles helps expand the knowledge base and competence of the managers. Most importantly, however, the leave of absence is really a test. The key value in this company is that human capital must be developed if success is to be achieved, so the leave of absence serves as a test of whether the manager has really developed his or her employees. If the organization performs less well when subordinates are in charge, then the manager is not prepared to be promoted. All managers have the responsibility to help develop others to be as competent as they are in leading positive change, and managers are held accountable for that development.

The point is, a key to ensuring that positive change continues is to have capable people in place. Providing organization members with developmental opportunities—that is, chances to increase their own skill set—is an investment in the long-term future of the organization and in the continuing success of positive change.

Metrics, Measurement, Milestones

A third aspect of institutionalization is the establishment of **metrics** (or specific indicators of success), **measures** (or methods for assessing levels of success), and **milestones** (or benchmarks to determine when detectable progress will have occurred). These three factors help ensure accountability for change, make it clear whether or not progress is being made, and provide visible indicators that the change is successful. The adage "You get what you measure" is an illustration of this principle. Change becomes institutionalized when it becomes a part of what people are held accountable to achieve. When it is clear

what the measures are, people tend to respond to those measures. If I am measured on my test scores in a class but not on the extra reading I do, I will likely spend more effort and time studying for the exams than reading extra materials. It is only when I am measured on different criteria that I shift my focus. Consequently, institutionalizing positive change means that clear metrics are identified, a measurement system is put into place, and a milestone is identified for when the change must have been accomplished.

As an illustration of these points is Jan Carlzon's (1987) approach to institutionalizing his vision in the once-struggling Scandinavian Airlines.

> *Employees at all levels must understand exactly what the target is and how best to achieve it. Once the frontline personnel . . . have taken on the responsibility of making specific decisions, these employees must have an accurate feedback system for determining whether the decisions they are making are, in fact, the ones that will accomplish the company's overall goals. . . . The necessity of measuring results is particularly crucial for those employees who affect customer service but don't have face-to-face contact with these customers. Ticket agents get immediate feedback on their job performance hundreds of times a day from the customers they serve. However, other workers such as baggage handlers have no such advantages. In fact, loading and unloading cargo is probably the most thankless job we have at SAS. . . . The baggage handlers never come into contact with the passenger, and so they never get positive or negative feedback from them. Lacking this, they need clear targets and other means of measuring how well they are meeting their goals. (pp. 108–109)*

The keys to establishing effective metrics, measures, and milestones for positive change are:

1. Identify two or three metrics or indicators that specify the result that is to be achieved. (A common mistake is to measure too many things. The key is to focus on a few core items.) These should not be metrics associated with effort or methods, but they should focus on results or outcomes. Specifically, they should address the outcomes desired from the vision of abundance.

At SAS Airlines, one metric includes the elapsed time between the plane pulling up to the gate and the first bag being delivered on the carousel.

2. Determine a measurement system. Data should be collected at certain time intervals in particular ways. This may be reports, surveys, or face-to-face meetings. At SAS, daily logs are kept of baggage handler performance. These measures do not focus on hours worked or how many bags are handled. They focus on the key outcomes desired, namely, speed and accuracy of delivery.

3. Milestones are specified, meaning that at a certain point in time, a measurable amount of progress will have been achieved. For example, by the end of the month baggage handler timeliness will have improved one percent. By the end of the year, it will have improved 15 percent. Milestones simply create a time frame for keeping track of real progress.

Institutionalizing a vision of abundance and positive change, in sum, depends on making it a part of daily life and the habitual behavior displayed by individuals throughout the organization. No positive change can survive if it depends solely on the leader. Therefore, helping people develop a teachable point of view about the positive change and providing opportunities for them to teach, building human capital through developing others' leadership skills, and instituting metrics, measurements, and milestones to ensure accountability all are actions that can help ensure successful institutionalization of positive change. Specific behaviors associated with these strategies are summarized in Table 10.5.

Summary

Most approaches to change focus on overcoming challenges, addressing obstacles, and solving problems. This chapter identifies an alternative approach to change in which the goal is to create abundance and extraordinarily positive change. It provides techniques and hints designed to help you achieve the best of the human condition or the highest potential of teams and organizations.

Leading positive change—that is, aiming for abundance-focused or positive targets rather than deficit-based or problem-centered targets—unlocks something called the *heliotropic effect*. To explain the heliotropic effect, let us pose this question: What happens over time when you put a plant in a window? The answer, of course, is that the plant begins to lean toward the light. That is, a natural inclination exists in every living system toward positive energy—toward light—and away from negative energy or from the dark. The reason is that light is life-giving and energy creating and all living systems are inclined toward that which gives life.

When you are able to foster positive change in organizations, you unleash the heliotropic effect and achieve outcomes that would be impossible otherwise. Fostering virtuousness, positive energy, strengths, aspirational targets, and inspiring language, for example,

Table 10.5 Institutionalizing the Vision and Creating Irreversible Momentum
1. Turn students into teachers.
• Provide opportunities for people to develop a teachable point of view.
• Make certain that others are required to articulate the vision themselves.
2. Build human capital.
• Ensure training and development opportunities for others so they can be leaders of positive change.
• Encourage the formation of networks and friendships that provide support.
3. Identify metrics, measures, and milestones.
• Identify when measurable progress will be achieved.
• Identify what the specific criteria will be for evaluating success.
• Determine how successful achievement of the vision will be ascertained.
• Maintain accountability for the success of the positive change.

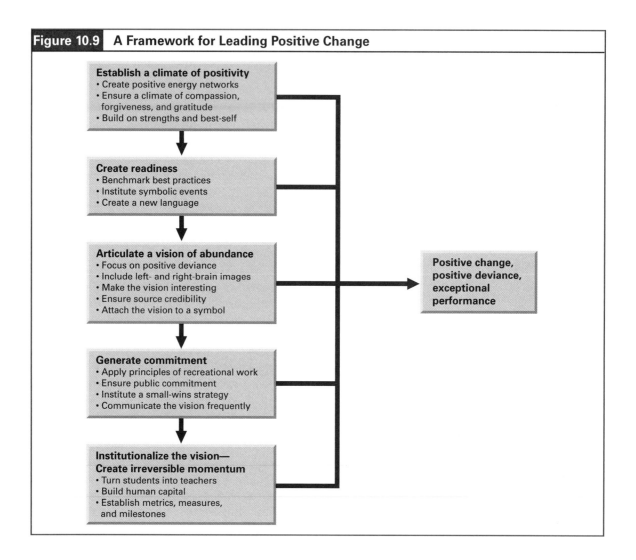

Figure 10.9 A Framework for Leading Positive Change

Establish a climate of positivity
• Create positive energy networks
• Ensure a climate of compassion, forgiveness, and gratitude
• Build on strengths and best-self

Create readiness
• Benchmark best practices
• Institute symbolic events
• Create a new language

Articulate a vision of abundance
• Focus on positive deviance
• Include left- and right-brain images
• Make the vision interesting
• Ensure source credibility
• Attach the vision to a symbol

Generate commitment
• Apply principles of recreational work
• Ensure public commitment
• Institute a small-wins strategy
• Communicate the vision frequently

Institutionalize the vision— Create irreversible momentum
• Turn students into teachers
• Build human capital
• Establish metrics, measures, and milestones

Positive change, positive deviance, exceptional performance

are among the ways to unlock the heliotropic effect. This effect has been demonstrated in a variety of ways within organizations and individuals—physiologically, psychologically, emotionally, visually, and socially (see Cooperrider, 1990; Cameron, 2003b; Bright, Cameron, & Caza, 2006). It is also documented in a study by Cameron and Lavine (2006).

In this chapter we provided a simple and easily remembered framework for accomplishing positive change and unleashing the power of the heliotropic effect. Five sets of skills and activities were explained: (1) establishing a climate of positivity, (2) creating readiness for change, (3) articulating a vision of abundance, (4) generating commitment to the vision, and (5) institutionalizing the positive change. Specific behavioral guidelines for implementing this approach to change are provided next.

Behavioral Guidelines

Figure 10.9 summarizes the skill set involved in leading positive change. Because change is so pervasive in organizations, every leader must manage change much of the time. However, positive change cuts across the grain and goes against the tendencies of most leaders. Negative, problem-focused concerns consume most leaders and managers. Leading positive change requires a different skill set. The following are the behavioral guidelines for achieving positive change:

1. Establish a climate of positivity by creating positive energy networks; ensuring a climate of compassion, forgiveness, and gratitude; and identifying and giving feedback to people on their strengths and unique competencies.

2. Create readiness in others to pursue positive change by benchmarking best practice, and comparing current performance to the highest standards; instituting symbolic events to signal positive change; and creating a new language that illustrates the positive change.

3. Articulate a vision of abundance by focusing on creating positive deviance rather than correcting negative deviance; including right-brain as well as left-brain images; making the vision interesting by challenging weakly held assumptions; and ensuring credibility of the vision and the visionary.

4. Generate commitment to the vision by applying principles of recreational work associated with the vision; providing opportunities for people to publicly commit to the vision; instituting a strategy of small wins; and communicating the vision frequently.

5. Institutionalize the vision, or create irreversible momentum by turning students into teachers, helping people develop teachable points of view, and articulating the vision themselves; building human capital among others; and identifying metrics, measures, and milestones for success.

SKILL *ANALYSIS*

CASES INVOLVING LEADING POSITIVE CHANGE

Corporate Vision Statements

Here are examples of four vision statements by well-known leaders of companies in the United States—Google, Toyota, Johnson & Johnson, and Microsoft. Each of these leaders was, at the time, considered to be among the most successful change leaders in the world. Analyze their statements in light of the principles discussed in the Skill Learning section of this chapter. How effective are each of these vision statements? What would be your prediction about the success of these firms based on the statements of their leaders?

Ten Things Google Has Found to Be True

1. Focus on the user and all else will follow.

Since the beginning, we've focused on providing the best user experience possible. Whether we're designing a new Internet browser or a new tweak to the look of the homepage, we take great care to ensure that they will ultimately serve **you** rather than our own internal goal or bottom line. Our homepage interface is clear and simple, and pages load instantly. Placement in search results is never sold to anyone, and advertising is not only clearly marked as such, it offers relevant content and is not distracting. And when we build new tools and applications, we believe they should work so well you don't have to consider how they might have been designed differently.

2. It's best to do one thing really, really well.

We do search. With one of the world's largest research groups focused exclusively on solving search problems, we know what we do well, and how we could do it better. Through continued iteration on difficult problems, we've been able to solve complex issues and provide continuous improvements to a service that already makes finding information a fast and seamless experience for millions of people. Our dedication to improving search helps us apply what we've learned to new products, like Gmail and Google Maps. Our hope is to bring the power of search to previously unexplored areas, and to help people access and use even more of the ever-expanding information in their lives

3. Fast is better than slow.

We know your time is valuable, so when you're seeking an answer on the web you want it right away—and we aim to please. We may be the only people in the world who can say our goal is to have people leave our homepage as quickly as possible. By shaving excess bits and bytes from our pages and increasing the efficiency of our serving environment, we've broken our own speed records many times over, so that the average response time on a search result is a fraction of a second. We keep speed in mind with each new product we release, whether it's a mobile application or Google Chrome, a browser designed to be fast enough for the modern web. And we continue to work on making it all go even faster.

4. Democracy on the web works.

Google search works because it relies on the millions of individuals posting links on websites to help determine which other sites offer content of value. We assess the importance of every web page using more than 200 signals and a variety of techniques, including our patented PageRank™ algorithm, which analyzes which sites have been "voted" to be the best sources of information by other pages across the web. As the web gets bigger, this approach actually improves, as each new site is another point of information and another vote to be counted. In the same vein, we are active in open source software development, where innovation takes place through the collective effort of many programmers.

5. You don't need to be at your desk to need an answer.

The world is increasingly mobile: people want access to information wherever they are, whenever they need it. We're pioneering new technologies and offering new solutions for mobile services that help people all over the globe to do any number of tasks on their phone, from checking email and calendar events to watching videos, not to mention the several different ways to access Google search on a phone. In addition, we're hoping to fuel greater innovation for mobile users everywhere with Android, a free, open source mobile platform. Android brings the openness that shaped the Internet to the mobile world. Not only does Android benefit consumers, who have more choice and innovative new mobile experiences, but it opens up revenue opportunities for carriers, manufacturers and developers.

6. You can make money without doing evil.

Google is a business. The revenue we generate is derived from offering search technology to companies and from the sale of advertising displayed on our site and on other sites across the web. Hundreds of thousands of advertisers worldwide use AdWords to promote their products; hundreds of thousands of publishers take advantage of our AdSense program to deliver ads relevant to their site content. To ensure that we're ultimately serving all our users (whether they are advertisers or not), we have a set of guiding principles for our advertising programs and practices:

- We don't allow ads to be displayed on our results pages unless they are relevant where they are shown. And we firmly believe that ads can provide useful information if, and only if, they are relevant to what you wish to find—so it's possible that certain searches won't lead to any ads at all.

- We believe that advertising can be effective without being flashy. We don't accept pop-up advertising, which interferes with your ability to see the content you've requested. We've found that text ads that are relevant to the person reading them draw much higher click-through rates than ads appearing randomly. Any advertiser, whether small or large, can take advantage of this highly targeted medium.

- Advertising on Google is always clearly identified as a "Sponsored Link," so it does not compromise the integrity of our search results. We never manipulate rankings to put our partners higher in our search results and no one can buy better PageRank. Our users trust our objectivity and no short-term gain could ever justify breaching that trust.

7. There's always more information out there.

Once we'd indexed more of the HTML pages on the Internet than any other search service, our engineers turned their attention to information that was not as readily accessible. Sometimes it was just a matter of integrating new databases into search,

ANALYSIS

such as adding a phone number and address lookup and a business directory. Other efforts required a bit more creativity, like adding the ability to search news archives, patents, academic journals, billions of images and millions of books. And our researchers continue looking into ways to bring all the world's information to people seeking answers.

8. The need for information crosses all borders.

Our company was founded in California, but our mission is to facilitate access to information for the entire world, and in every language. To that end, we have offices in dozens of countries, maintain more than 150 Internet domains, and serve more than half of our results to people living outside the United States. We offer Google's search interface in more than 110 languages, offer people the ability to restrict results to content written in their own language, and aim to provide the rest of our applications and products in as many languages as possible. Using our translation tools, people can discover content written on the other side of the world in languages they don't speak. With these tools and the help of volunteer translators, we have been able to greatly improve both the variety and quality of services we can offer in even the most far-flung corners of the globe.

9. You can be serious without a suit.

Our founders built Google around the idea that work should be challenging, and the challenge should be fun. We believe that great, creative things are more likely to happen with the right company culture—and that doesn't just mean lava lamps and rubber balls. There is an emphasis on team achievements and pride in individual accomplishments that contribute to our overall success. We put great stock in our employees—energetic, passionate people from diverse backgrounds with creative approaches to work, play and life. Our atmosphere may be casual, but as new ideas emerge in a café line, at a team meeting or at the gym, they are traded, tested and put into practice with dizzying speed—and they may be the launch pad for a new project destined for worldwide use.

10. Great just isn't good enough.

We see being great at something as a starting point, not an endpoint. We set ourselves goals we know we can't reach yet, because we know that by stretching to meet them we can get further than we expected. Through innovation and iteration, we aim to take things that work well and improve upon them in unexpected ways. For example, when one of our engineers saw that search worked well for properly spelled words, he wondered about how it handled typos. That led him to create an intuitive and more helpful spell checker.

Even if you don't know exactly what you're looking for, finding an answer on the web is our problem, not yours. We try to anticipate needs not yet articulated by our global audience, and meet them with products and services that set new standards. When we launched Gmail, it had more storage space than any email service available. In retrospect offering that seems obvious—but that's because now we have new standards for email storage. Those are the kinds of changes we seek to make, and we're always looking for new places where we can make a difference. Ultimately, our constant dissatisfaction with the way things are becomes the driving force behind everything we do.

Update: We first wrote these "10 things" several years ago. From time to time we revisit this list to see if it still holds true. We hope it does—and you can hold us to that. (September 2009)

SOURCE: *Used by permission. google.com/corporate/tenthings.html*

Toyota's Mission and Guiding Principles

Established in 1990, revised in 1997. (Translation from original Japanese.)

1. Honor the language and spirit of the law of every nation and undertake open and fair corporate activities to be a good corporate citizen of the world.

2. Respect the culture and customs of every nation and contribute to economic and social development through corporate activities in the communities.

3. Dedicate ourselves to providing clean and safe products and to enhancing the quality of life everywhere through all our activities.

4. Create and develop advanced technologies and provide outstanding products and services that fulfill the needs of customers worldwide.

5. Foster a corporate culture that enhances individual creativity and teamwork value, while honoring mutual trust and respect between labor and management.

6. Pursue growth in harmony with the global community through innovative management.

7. Work with business partners in research and creation to achieve stable, long-term growth and mutual benefits, while keeping ourselves open to new partnerships.

Five Main Principles of Toyota

- Always be faithful to your duties, thereby contributing to the Company and to the overall good.

- Always be studious and creative, striving to stay ahead of the times.

- Always be practical and avoid frivolousness.

- Always strive to build a homelike atmosphere at work that is warm and friendly.

- Always have respect for God, and remember to be grateful at all times.

SOURCE: *www2.toyota.co.jp/en/vision/philosophy/index.html*

Johnson & Johnson
Our Credo
James Burke, CEO

We believe our first responsibility is to the doctors, nurses and patients,
to mothers and all others who use our products and services.

In meeting their needs everything we do must be of high quality.
We must constantly strive to reduce our costs in order to maintain reasonable prices.
Customers' orders must be serviced promptly and accurately.
Our suppliers and distributors must have an opportunity to make a fair profit.

We are responsible to our employees,
the men and women who work with us throughout the world.
Everyone must be considered as an individual.
We must respect their dignity and recognize their merit.
They must have a sense of security in their jobs.
Compensation must be fair and adequate, and working
conditions clean, orderly and safe.
We must be mindful of ways to help our employees
fulfill their family responsibilities.

Employees must feel free to make suggestions and complaints.
There must be equal opportunity for employment, development
and advancement for those qualified.
We must provide competent management,
and their actions must be just and ethical.

We are responsible to the communities in which we live and work
and to the world community as well.
We must be good citizens—support good works and charities
and bear our fair share of taxes.
We must encourage civic improvements and better health and education.
We must maintain in good order the property we are privileged to use,
protecting the environment and natural resources.

Our final responsibility is to our stockholders.
Business must make a sound profit.
We must experiment with new ideas.
Research must be carried on, innovative programs developed and mistakes paid for.
New equipment must be purchased, new facilities provided
and new products launched.
Reserves must be created to provide for adverse times.
When we operate according to these principles, the stockholders
should realize a fair return.

Johnson & Johnson

SOURCE: *Courtesy of Johnson & Johnson.*

Microsoft

Bill Gates
2004 Excerpts

Microsoft was built on innovation, and our future depends on it. We are in an extraordinary position to deliver even greater value to customers through a broad set of technologies, designed to complement each other and many third-party products and services. This is what we mean by *integrated innovation,* which is key to our business strategy.

To drive innovation, Microsoft has a long-term commitment to research and development. Our investment to date has brought about many of the successful products we offer today, and has built an increasingly valuable store of intellectual property. In fiscal 2004, we applied for more than 2,000 patents on some of our recent innovations. During the coming year, we plan to file for another 3,000 patents, which will make us one of the largest patent filers in the world. Our innovations are available for broad use in others' products through our patent licensing programs.

A key focus of our innovation is security. Beyond the advances in Windows XP SP2, we are developing advanced technologies that will help isolate computers from Internet attacks and make them more resilient when they are attacked. We are making it easier for customers to keep their systems updated with our latest, most secure software.

In addition, we are collaborating with other industry leaders to develop more effective community responses to security threats, and working closely with governments around the world to bring cybercriminals to justice. Through this broad, multipronged approach, our goal is to help bring significant improvements in security, and help preserve the benefits of technology for everyone.

Our innovation is also focused on exciting market opportunities across our businesses, which we believe hold great potential for growth over the next several years.

As we innovate in technology, we are equally focused on crisp execution. In particular, we are working to deliver an unparalleled customer and partner experience. Across the company, we have created new listening, feedback, and response systems to help us get closer to customers and respond quickly and appropriately. Using automated error-reporting technologies, we have fixed a large majority of the computer crashes and hangs reported by customers, and our strengthened field response system has favorably resolved most nontechnical issues reported by customers.

Microsoft competes vigorously, and we always will. At the same time, we are committed to maintaining positive relationships within our industry, including with competitors, and to forging strong relationships with governments. We are also committed to helping make technology safer and easier to use. We work to help protect the safety of children online, for example, through our partnership with the International Centre for Missing and Exploited Children. We are deeply engaged in industry efforts to protect peoples' privacy online, counter the problem of identify theft, and curb the spam epidemic.

SOURCE: *2004 Annual Report. Reprinted with permission from Microsoft Corporation.*

Discussion Questions

First answer the following questions by yourself, and then form a team of colleagues and share your answers. Reach consensus regarding a rank ordering.

Step 1: Rank order these four firms based on these famous leaders' statements about their companies (1 = the best, and 4 = the worst).

	Google	Toyota	J&J	Microsoft
1. Which of the vision statements do you think represents the most effective positive leadership?	____	____	____	____
2. Based on these statements, what is your prediction about future success in each firm in the next 10 years, from most to least successful? Ignore the health of the industry itself—e.g., computers, autos, software, pharmaceuticals—and predict how each firm will do in its own industry based on these statements.	____	____	____	____
3. Which statement has the clearest and most inspiring vision for the future?	____	____	____	____
4. Which statement do you believe has been institutionalized the most thoroughly, and the least thoroughly?	____	____	____	____

Step 2: Based on what you now know about leading positive change, what advice would you give each of these leaders if you were to make suggestions about how to more effectively create readiness for change, articulate a vision of abundance, generate commitment and so on.

ANALYSIS

Lee Iacocca's Transformation of Chrysler—1979–1984

This is a transcription of speeches by Chairman Lee Iacocca to Chrysler's top management team from the time he became CEO and chairman in 1979 until the dramatic transformation had been completed in 1984. The previously confidential videotapes were compiled and edited by Professor Kim S. Cameron at the University of Michigan and are used to exemplify the leadership of change. These speeches were intended by Mr. Iacocca only for an internal and confidential audience, not for the press, stockholders, or the general public. Duplication without permission of the University of Michigan Business School is strictly forbidden.

The transcript begins with the new president of Ford, Paul Bergmoser, explaining the state of the company and of the economy in 1979. He then introduced Mr. Iacocca to the top management team for the first time. The entire transcript from that point on is from Mr. Iacocca.

1979
Paul Bergmoser, President:

I don't have to tell you that we are meeting at a very critical time in the Corporation's history. You don't need a recitation of the problems that are facing us. At the same time that the volumes and penetrations are down, we are up against the most costly product program in Chrysler history. There is no margin for error as we plan for next year 1980. Our first slide today gives you a perspective of the current situation. It shows how we are doing thus far in 1979. I said thus far—the year isn't over yet. In our presentation to the government, we predicted we would lose a billion seventy-one million. That is about where we will come out if we move the sales bank, move the imports, get our manufacturing efficiencies, and meet all the commitments between now and December 31. In some areas we are coming in on target, others we are off. For example, our market share was less than we expected largely because the market went haywire. Consumers begin to lose confidence when our problems hit the headlines. We are looking at a sluggish economy, double-digit inflation, high interest rates that put a lot of pressure on both dealers and retail customers. Much has been written and much has been unspoken about the Chrysler crisis and its causes. A considerable amount of the rhetoric has dealt with past management as being one of the primary causes of that situation. Let me tell you how I stand on the matter at the moment. All of you fellows have survived personnel reductions and corporate reorganizations. You are, in the eyes of the outsider, now the new management. That goes for me, I am new, but every one of you is just as new in terms of the New Chrysler Corporation. We will be judged by what we do in 1980 and '81. We have stated to the government and to the world at large that those will be the years when Chrysler will recover from its current record loss position. We will not live to see 1981 if we don't do the job in 1980. So, in my view, it no longer serves any purpose to look back and reference your problems to the past management. Let Mr. Iacocca and let me handle the past. You will be a success or you will be a failure on the basis of what you do in 1980.

It is going to be a real tough year, a very tough year, perhaps, the toughest in the history of your corporate life! If you don't feel like being on my team in this fight, you had better come and see me very soon now, because I am counting on each and every one of you to do the job better than it has ever been done before. If the objectives are too tough, too hard, and too disciplined, come and see me now, because I need the help of every one of you. I am confident that we can carry it through. Now, fellows, in time, I think people are going to look back on this management team with respect and admiration for the job they have done. This is the New Chrysler Corporation. And I want to introduce the man who is providing the leadership and direction for all of us to carry out our day-to-day tasks, Chairman Lee Iacocca. Lee!

Lee Iacocca, CEO and Chairman:

As I said in my opening statement to Congress, this has not been a vintage year for me, for Chrysler, for the auto industry, or for the whole damn country. And, I guess that some of you must feel the same way. As Paul said, we lost a lot of money. Over a billion dollars is a lot of money. Our market penetration at the moment is down to what you might call deplorable levels. Some of our customers, or maybe I should say, some of our former customers, aren't really that confident that we are going to make it. Still, there are some good things to say about 1979. I believe it has been a year in which we did more than just survive. We reduced our fixed cost. We did proceed to put in place a product plan that will help us return to profitability. We took steps to improve our profit margins. In short, we invested a lot of time and money in our future.

First, I would like to give you an assessment of what is happening with our request for the loan guarantees* in Washington, and then second I want to expand on the concept of the "New Chrysler Corporation" mentioned by Paul in his presentation. There has been a lot of talk about our chances for getting legislation out of the Congress in time to help the Chrysler Corporation. Well, I want to tell you first hand that things, as of this afternoon at least, do look good. The energy picture is muddled and threatening as ever. I just saw in the paper this afternoon that Saudi Arabia is going to go for six dollars a barrel increase. That means the rest will go for seven or eight, and that's got to be bad news. The continuing crisis in Iran; production cut backs by other OPEC nations, Libya, Iraq and these way-out guys; and the lack of a sound, reasonable national energy policy right here; all of those put together are really what you would call bad news, not good news. But, what we have to do is survive, and more than survive, become profitable as soon as we can. And as Paul said, it won't be real easy. In fact, the first six months of 1980 will be pure hell, in my opinion, and I might as well tell it to you that way. There will be demanding challenges facing all of you, and me, in the months ahead. So this brings me to my second point today that I want to cover briefly.

When I say these are challenges facing us, I want you to know that the "us" is you and me. And, it is the new Chrysler Corporation. From the day that President Carter signs into law the Chrysler Loan Guarantee Program, a new era begins at Chrysler. And don't make any mistake about it, there will be a great deal to accomplish from that day forward. Much will be asked of you, and much will be expected of you. To begin with, we will have to re-launch Chrysler. We have to rebuild confidence, first amongst ourselves, then the rest of the Chrysler family, and most important with our customers. And this will not be easy. But, the early signals clearly show that it can be done. In spite of a dismal market this year, we have achieved some significant and positive results. We did take a hundred and thirty thousand orders for vehicles in November. We did move twenty thousand out of our sales bank.** And, I have to mention sales bank one more time, because it may be the last time you will hear me say it. That thing is in its death throes. I got to thinking on the way over here that we have plans to move those last ten thousand at distressed prices, and forget that we ever built them. And, I thought, I want him to keep one. And I want to do what they do when you finally pay off the mortgage, you burn it on the front lawn. I want to burn that last damn one on the front lawn of headquarters, so, the whole world knows it is over!

For the next ninety days each of you in this room has to play salesman. And, to do that, all you have to do is get in one of our cars, and expose it, and demonstrate it to somebody.

---

*Chrysler had appealed to the federal government to guarantee its bank loans, because the amount to be borrowed was more than the value of the company at the time.

**The sales bank refers to the excess inventory of unsold cars.

Those are our four new cars, and that market still is pretty good, even though it is down a little. And, those four cars—if you have driven them lately—are not just commercial, they are fine cars that everybody in this room should be proud of. They are good looking cars. They've got good features, and they don't rattle and leak as much as their predecessors the year before. At the new Chrysler Corporation we will build them better, and we will back them better. If we don't, nothing else is going to matter anyway, and we will have no one to blame but ourselves. What will be required to do these kind of things, to keep them as promises and not let them become just sales gimmicks, is hard work and dedication and, most of all, the realization that the new Chrysler Corporation is a team. A team that openly discusses its problems and freely exchanges ideas on how to improve our efforts and willingly accepts responsibility for performance. What will be required to rebuild confidence in this company is an active participation in its survival effort.

Over the next months the new Chrysler Corporation will be engaged in efforts to raise a lot of capital. But, with the products we have, with the improvements we have made, with the plans for the future, being as exciting as I believe they are—that money is going to be available to us. Count on it. In fact, what is happening with this corporation right now is unprecedented in the history of our industry and maybe the whole country. Just think of it. The UAW is willing now to reopen its contract settlement in order to participate in the effort of the new Chrysler Corporation and to make it profitable. Mayor Coleman Young has indicated that Detroit is willing to offer a hundred and fifty million dollars in Chrysler support. We expect a minimum of three hundred million dollars from Canada. I say three hundred million, but it could be as much as a $1.2 billion for Canadian operations so that we can go first class in a couple of programs we have planned. Other states with Chrysler plants and operations have expressed a willingness to help and their commitment comes up to about a hundred million dollars. We are confident that the Japanese banks will restore our letter of credit agreement under which we can continue to import vehicles from Mitsubishi. We are also offering right now, or will be very shortly I should say, a preferred stock offering to Chrysler suppliers and dealers. If we are as good as we think we are, we will sell four hundred million dollars of equity stock to our family, suppliers and dealers. If we are not good salesman, we sell two hundred. So the number is two hundred to four hundred million dollars. By mid-January we will discuss the role of the suppliers and the dealers in this offer. Our dealers' lobbying efforts in Washington in our behalf were nothing short of sensational, and I think that they will be a big part of turning this Congress around.

Before you go home for the holidays, I would like to ask you to do this. In just a few short minutes, I want you to ask yourselves, honestly, what have you done to help this company, your company, during the last twelve months. Put it down. Don't fight with it. Just put it down. Then throw it away. If you want to read it to your wife or your kids, fine but then throw it away. Then, after you have done that the more important part is get another piece of paper, a clean sheet of paper. Put down the things that you plan to do for your company, and for yourself, in the next twelve months, the year 1980. We will get the vote of confidence we need from the government. That is, I think, assured. It will then be up to all of us in the new Chrysler family to share that confidence, first amongst ourselves right in this room, then to spread it through all the family members, and eventually to the biggest family of them all, our customers out there. What I am saying to you is that we have all of the essentials in place. The basics are here. And more important, we have got the people, the team, to do it. Let me make it clear that this new Chrysler is not a mixed bag of hanger-ons mixed in with a little new talent from some other corporations. It is not that at all. It is a new, unified team that starts a new decade. Remember, on New Year's Eve January 1st, we start a new ten-year look.

One final thought to all of you. Somebody wrote a hit song called, "We Are Family," and Willie Stargell picked it up as a model to inspire his team to win the World Series

Championship. Well, the reason that I mentioned it to you is that we, the new Chrysler Corporation, are Family. Else, how is it possible to raise a billion and a half dollars from our own constituents? We do have a lot to do, and it is going to be tough. But because we are family, we can do it. So, that is all we have to say to you today except, have a nice Christmas all of you, and let's start the New Year with a Bang!

1980

While the economy was coming down around our ears, we put together a financing package to raise better than two billion dollars in non-guaranteed funds. We put together an operating plan that showed we can continue as a growing concern without any government help after 1983. Secretary Miller and Mr. Volcker said, it was by a long shot, the most complicated package in the entire history of American business. It involved the governments of five nations, local governments, more than four hundred lenders, and all the constituents of a very big industrial company—suppliers, dealers, employees, and the shareholders. We put the package together in record time. Within two weeks of the deadline that we set for ourselves, the Treasury Department, the Loan Guarantee Board, and some hardnosed consultants have scrutinized—and believe me they have scrutinized—all of our plans, every aspect of our business. And the hardheads, and the hard noses, came out and said they liked what they saw. No matter what you read in the press, that is what they ended up saying. They said that our operating plan code was realistic and feasible. They said that we demonstrated that we can continue as a growing concern, and that, simply stated, is why they gave us a guarantee. The guarantees give us a fighting chance we need to complete our rebuilding program.

In the meanwhile, we need to keep on doing right all of the other things that are so essential to our future. We talked about what that involved last December here, and I would like to take just a minute to look at the report card and see how we faired since we last met as a group. First, we talked about people. That is the strength of any business organization. We have kept almost, not all, but almost all of our top-flight people. We have been able to move some into key spots like Jack Withrow in engineering. We have attracted some very impressive new people at the organization to supplement our present staff. Don Dellerosa came on board as Vice President of Design. I worked with him for a long time. He is the best designer of small cars in the world. Dick Dow came on board as Executive VP of Diversified Operations. Dick has been in charge of production at VW-America, and before that he was at GM, where he was the youngest plant manager in their history. Dave Platt came on as Vice President of Procurement and Supply. He is experienced. He will make sure all of our suppliers meet their quality targets. I could go on and on, but the management, I am trying to say, is strong.

We have the plans and programs to meet our objectives, so I hope that everybody in this room knows and understands them. We have a great management team. I think it's the best in the business. We have the sales program. We are improving quality. Ford and GM will have to catch us from now on. We have the innovations to set us apart from the competition. We have the products that deliver the value that customers want today. So, in spite all of the difficulties created for us, and all the obstacles put in our way, our plans are finally starting to come together. We see some real daylight.

The Loan Guarantee Board looked at a lot of factors when they considered our application—cost projections, industry volume, the debt load, the product plans. But when I talked to them privately, the most important consideration of all was whether this Chrysler Team had the guts, and the capacity, and the ability to see this program through to the end and to bring Chrysler back to profitability. The guy who asked me that most is a guy I admire a lot—Paul Volcker, of the Federal Reserve. He asked, "Are you really sure you have got the right people to stick it out?" They looked hard at us, at you really. They looked at what you have accomplished so far, and what's left to do. They must have seen

ANALYSIS

winners in some of you because they decided to put the country's money on you. Which is a big gamble. They put a billion and a half on the line.

1982

Good evening. We announced our 1981 results this morning. For the total year we lost four hundred and seventy-six million. That is a little less than the analysts said that we would lose. They said that we would lose, for sure, five hundred million. One year ago— if you just stop to think about what was in the news four months ago—all of the smart money on Wall Street was betting that Volcker's scandalous interest rates, the advent of GM's new competition the 'J' car, and the total collapse of the car and truck market would certainly wipe out Chrysler in 1981. This was their year to die. The smart money was wrong again, because we not only survived this worse depression in the history of the automobile industry, but I think that you will agree we have come through as a stronger and more competitive company.

We continued our program to cut costs and become even more productive in the year '81. We performed major surgery to bring our cost under control. We looked at all of our operations, plant-by-plant and job-by-job, and over the last two years we have consolidated these operations. We have now closed a full twenty plants. We have cut our fixed cost by well over a half billion dollars in the last four months. And we have reduced our salaried employees by half, from about forty thousand to twenty-one thousand. Our break even is now half of what it was two years ago. We twenty thousand are doing the work of those forty thousand, but we are selling more cars and building more cars. What the hell were we doing wrong? Since the first of this year—we have taken several important actions to build an extra cash cushion to ride out the recession and protect our future programs. Last Friday we reached an agreement to sell Chrysler Defense, that is the tank business, to General Dynamics for three hundred and forty-eight point five million dollars. I have to say to you; gentlemen and ladies, that decision was a tough call. Chrysler Defense is a strong subsidiary with some great people, a lot of whom worked for this company for a lot of years. We have forty years of history tied up in the tank business. We were part of the Arsenal of Democracy in World War Two. I can tell you, our guys did design and build the best damn battle tank in the entire world. They had some very exciting and profitable new products on the drawing board, and we had some of the best talent in this organization running that place. Nobody wanted to give all of that up. But, in today's economic climate, we had to balance our attachment to that company against the need to build a substantial cash cushion with which to ride out this very serious economic depression that we are in. Our charter is to concentrate on cars and trucks. That is why we got the Loan Guarantees, and that is why we are here. Our job is to build the best cars and trucks, and take on the Japanese, even if just to be patriotic, but that's our job.

Here is our problem put as simply as I know how to put it. Today, it costs us exactly seventy-nine hundred dollars to build the average Chrysler car, and we sell them on an average for seventy-five hundred. We make our money today on Chrysler Financial, on Mexico, and on parts sales. We had better start to learn how to make money on cars and trucks, because that, again, is our business. We have to live within our budgets in '82, as tight as they are with no cost overruns, and that's nobody!

Now let me end with this note. We have all come through a hellish couple of years. I know we all feel that way, I do. But together, we have established Chrysler as a leader in the rebuilding of the American auto industry, and maybe of the entire American Industry. Together, we have set an example of what determined Americans can accomplish in the face of great adversity. We are on the edge of success. We are not quite there, but we are on the real sharp edge of success. If the management, the Union, all of our employees, and the dealers and the suppliers—all continue to work together towards our common goals, we can put the finishing touches on maybe the greatest chapter in the history of American business.

1983

We really are poised, no matter what the economy throws at us, no matter what the Japanese or Ford or General Motors throw at us, not only to stay in business but to prosper and do very, very, well. I also said to you late in July in a meeting with President Carter, that we now own our company again. I announced that we were paying off the loans, and that means that we are all alone now, and we can make our own decisions and we can make our own mistakes.

We have got to get this quality thing behind us. We have come a long, long, way. Warranty is down thirty eight percent the last couple of years, and our quality is up, but the track is fast, as you know. Ford is doing better on things gone wrong, and GM and we are a little worse than they are and Japan is still out-doing us all. So, we can have five and fifties, and we can have good power trains, and we can have five year warranties, and think about ten year warranties, but we have got to get rid of some of this crap we are doing. We've got some problems, but they are not big problems, I don't think.

I like to think that the officers, the first team, let's call it, the varsity, is good enough that each of us in the top senior management has ten charges out there. I can look around the room, and I feel that ten of you are my protégés. I watch to see what you are doing. I look at your future, and I get to know you well, and I take care of you, because you take of the company and me. At our level, this level, everybody is on the team. Everybody has gotten the message. Nobody believes there is an old way of doing it. Well, you have got your work cut out for you, and here is your assignment. It is a very general one, but it is the only thing that will make this company click. Out of the three hundred odd of you in here, each of you must accept as your charges ten subordinates. Ten times three hundred is three thousand, and that's the group we are looking at. The next three thousand has got to get the word. That is the only way we are going to continue to build on the progress that we have made, and we have made some fantastic progress. I hope that you are feeling that you are a big part of it, because you are. Every one of you, look to yourself, and look within yourself. When you manage, a good manager is a multiplier and a motivator. That is all he is. He can multiply himself, every day, wherever he is. People look up to him, and people work, because they know what their objective is, and they go out and hustle, and they do it because the boss is leading them and motivating them. Now, if you would just do that, we have got a big year ahead of us. While we are counting the two billion dollars back home, you will be really putting the seed corn in where it counts. Multiply yourselves times ten and nothing will stop us.

When the press asked me, what is the greatest thing you got out of the last five years, I say: "Hot a hell of a lot. It got tiring." But I did take one thing. It is the realization that six hundred thousand people, pulled in the same directions. Pulled the oars in the same way. Everybody felt they were getting the fair shake, the old equality of sacrifice. It is amazing how we can move a mountain. So, if you see anybody pulling apart, or they don't want to be on a team, you have got to straighten them out. I will end on this note. I will assure you that just as we are paying you for having reduced warranty costs, less engineering changes, and better market share, the new barometer will be how you are doing with your little nest of ten people. Some of you, I know, have twenty or thirty, but start with ten. I can settle for that right now if everybody in the room signed up for it.

1984

I would think that in the next five years, we start a new era. We have got to talk innovation in product, and we have got to talk innovation in service, and in manufacturing processes. I think that is going to be key to how well this corporation does. I think that we are on the threshold of doing great things together. I think that anytime any company, for whatever the reason, reports the one and a half plus billion dollars in six months, you should all be damned proud. As one of the reporters already said, "That is their peak." Two analysts followed it up yesterday, and said "Chrysler will never make over eight hundred million dollars again in a three month period." They make it sound like I was a fluke. Well, we are going to show them that it is no fluke. True, it has been driven by volume, driven by rich mixes, but it has been driven by productivity improvements, and quality improvements, and having the right products for the market—rich convertibles and T–115s [minivans] that are a smash.

But the two areas that are not market driven but are management driven are the two you are not doing hot on. That is quality and market share. Market share, if you include T–115s, is doing pretty damn well. But we are not going to get to twelve percent. And quality is a disappointment. GM has caught up with us. The Japanese are way beyond us. And Ford is losing us in their dust right now. I take nothing from you or this managing team, but you have got to look at the whole cart now. Why is it, on the two toughies, competing head to head every day in the market, even with voluntary restraints on the part of the Japanese, against GM and Ford, we can't seem to meet our quality objectives, and in market share we are flunking out. Now, when I say it that way, we have come a long way from three years ago. Were shipping crap, frankly. And now you can be proud of what you are shipping. I am glad to hear it, I hope we don't do it every day, but I am glad to hear from time to time we shut a line down to get the message across that quality is not only the first priority but it could well be in the next twelve to twenty-four months our only priority.

We are going to have to join up with new technology, and we are going to have to cut out a position for ourselves at Chrysler in electronics, certainly new materials and composites of all kinds. That is on our strategy list. I asked one of our top people why can't I just order on a requisition tomorrow, a sports car, and I would like to do it in twenty-four months. You say, I can't do that. I say why? You say, we don't know how. But, what the hell, it is a car, and they're selling like hotcakes. We don't know how? Well, you have got to ask yourself, why not? You can't just claim that it's money. We've got plenty of money if we want to do something like that. While they are all reacting on our T–115, we have got to react back to them in some of these markets. Those aren't little niche markets. That may be the market of the future for young people.

Discussion Questions

1. In 1979, with the company in such bad shape and the economy so dismal, how did Iacocca create a climate of positivity? What symbols are used? What small wins were identified? What is interesting about his language?
2. In 1980, how did Iacocca ensure credibility? Who is the enemy? What is interesting about his language?
3. In 1982, how did Iacocca maintain positivity? What is the vision for the company? What symbolic events are used? How is commitment developed?
4. In 1983, how is the vision institutionalized? How does Iacocca personally exemplify the principles he espouses?
5. In 1984, given the dramatic turnaround of the company, why doesn't Iacocca celebrate? What is his motivation? Why does he mix confrontation and challenge in his positive message?

EXERCISES IN LEADING
POSITIVE CHANGE

Reflected Best-Self Portrait

In the Skill Assessment section of this chapter you were asked to identify 20 people who could provide feedback to you regarding when you were at your very best. Now that you have obtained that feedback on your strengths, you will want to analyze that data to create a best-self portrait. Read all of your feedback and take notes on the key insights. Look for commonalities across the individuals who provided you with feedback. Create themes where you find commonalities, and link the examples to them. You may find it useful to use a table such as the following.

COMMONALITY/THEME	EXAMPLES GIVEN	MY INTERPRETATION
1. Creative	1. Innovative builder of new projects at work. 2. Found new solutions for old problems. 3. Guided the team in transforming itself.	My ideas tend to be interesting and creative. I tend to bring new ideas to people with whom I work. I am innovative in my approach to problem solving.
2.	1. 2. 3.	
3.	1. 2. 3.	

Step 1: Now, create a portrait of your best self that captures the wisdom in your data. Identify when you are at your very best and what attributes and capabilities you display at your best. Write at least one paragraph describing yourself in third person using your best-self feedback as the data. The person you are reading about in this feedback is like this at his or her best. . . . Here are some reflective questions that you may want to consider as you craft your self portrait.

❑ What have you learned about your own key strengths and uniquenesses?

❑ What was surprising to you about your feedback?

❑ What circumstances bring out your best?

❑ How do you intend to follow up or capitalize on this feedback?

❑ What career or life implications does this feedback hold?

❑ What has changed, or could change, as a result of obtaining this feedback?

Write up your conclusions and your commitments as a result of reading through the feedback. Writing will have a clarifying and focusing effect, and you are not likely to get this

PRACTICE

kind of data very often in your life. Don't miss the opportunity to craft something meaningful for yourself.

Step 2: Read your best-self portrait with a team of colleagues. Get verbal feedback from them about what you have written. That is, your colleagues will help you clarify and become specific about your best-self attributes.

SOURCE: *www.bus.umich.edu/positive*

Positive Organizational Diagnosis Exercise

Step 1: Select an organization that you can diagnose. If you are not currently working in one, volunteering in one, or leading one, select your own school or university. Your objective is to identify the strengths, peak experiences, and examples of positive deviance in the organization (rather than the problems and challenges). These kinds of data are seldom gathered in organizations, and people are not often asked to provide this kind of data. However, in every organization, something works well. When cued to do so, people can always identify things that are spectacular about their organization. Furthermore, the questions we ask and the language we use helps determine our vision of the future. People are more comfortable moving into the unknown future when they carry parts of the past forward. That is, when they have experienced success in the past, they are more willing to pursue a vision of the future, knowing that they have achieved extraordinary success some time in the past. They are confident that they can do it again.

Here are some examples of questions you should ask in diagnosing the positive aspects of an organization, a group, or even your own family.

- ❑ *Best-in-Class:* Put yourself in clients' or customers' shoes. What would they say makes this organization the best there is?
- ❑ *Careers:* What do you love about this organization that makes you want to come to work each day?
- ❑ *Leadership:* Who are the leaders in your organization you admire the most, and why? What do they do?
- ❑ *Communication:* When did you have an extremely satisfying and productive interchange with someone you care deeply about?
- ❑ *Teamwork:* When have you experienced delight at extraordinary cooperation and teamwork that emerged in this organization?
- ❑ *Culture:* What is especially fun, energizing, revitalizing about your culture? What turns you on?
- ❑ *Aspiration:* What are your highest aspirations for this organization? What do you really hope for?
- ❑ *Work:* What is the best you have ever seen accomplished in the work here? What was achieved that exceeded everyone's expectations?

When you ask these kinds of questions, you will detect more enthusiasm being displayed by the person responding, and you will note an unleashing of positive energy. This is in contrast to more typical questions used in organizational diagnosis:

- ❏ What are your major problems and challenges?
- ❏ Where are your deficits?
- ❏ What is troublesome to people in this organization?
- ❏ What needs fixing?
- ❏ In what areas are you missing your targets?
- ❏ Who is doing better than you are, and why?

Craft your own interview format for conducting a positive diagnosis of an organization, a group, or a family. Use the positive questions above as a guide. Interview a representative sample of people in that organization (or all the members of your family).

Step 2: Now, write up the equivalent of a best-self portrait for the organization. Address these questions regarding the organization.

- ❏ What are the strengths and unique qualities of this organization?
- ❏ In what ways can it capitalize on its competencies?
- ❏ What is the vision that drives the organization?
- ❏ What recommendations do you have for positive change?

A Positive Change Agenda

Write out a detailed plan for leading positive change in an organization in which you are participating. You need not be the formal leader of that organization, since most real change is initiated from places within the organization rather than the leader's office. Most great leaders simply capitalize on the ideas and agendas of their people.

In crafting your plan, address the following questions with very specific and actionable ideas. Do not simply say something like: "I'll treat people better." That is not specific enough and does not identify an action. Instead, say, "I will compliment someone every day." That's more doable and measurable.

1. In what ways will you work to create a positive climate? What will you actually do?
2. In what specific ways will you create readiness in others to pursue positive change?
3. What is your specific vision of abundance? How will you communicate it so that it is accepted and energizing to people?
4. How will you generate commitment to that vision among others? Identify specific actions.
5. What will you do to institutionalize and create irreversible momentum for your positive change?

Now, identify the specific things you will need to do personally to exemplify and model your positive change? How will you enhance your own credibility?

SKILL *APPLICATION*

ACTIVITIES FOR LEADING POSITIVE CHANGE

Suggested Assignments

1. Find someone you know well who is working in an organization. Teach him or her the principles of leading positive change. Use the concepts, principles, techniques, and exercises provided in this chapter. Describe what you taught and record the results in your journal.

2. Give genuine positive feedback on a regular and consistent basis to one or more of your colleagues. Do it at least daily. Observe the extent to which your relationship changes over the next month.

3. Do a systematic analysis of the things that occur in your life for which you are grateful. What is going right, and what makes life worth living? Consider your job, family, school, and social life. Keep a "gratitude journal" for at least a semester (a three-month period). Make an entry in it at least once a week. Note what else changes in your life compared to before you began the journal.

4. Identify at least one person in your circle of acquaintances who is positively energizing to you. When you are around this person, you simply feel better. Make certain that you interact with that person on a frequent and consistent basis.

5. Identify an example of best practice. That is, find someone or some organization that is unique in being the best there is at something. Try to identify what it is that accounts for that extraordinary performance. What factors could be generalized to others or to other settings?

6. Establish an abundance agenda that you aspire to accomplish this year. Make it compatible with the top priorities in your life. Specify the behavioral action steps, the reporting and accounting mechanisms, and the criteria of success that you will implement. Share this plan with others you know so that you have an incentive to pursue it even after you finish this class.

7. Identify a symbol that can serve as a constant reminder of your own—or your organization's—vision of abundance. Select something that is positively energizing and that can remind you every time you see it that you are pursuing a meaningful, uplifting vision.

8. Establish a close mentoring relationship with someone with whom you work or go to school. Your mentor may be a professor, a senior manager, or someone who has been around longer than you have. That relationship should build your self-esteem and be energizing to you. Make certain, however, that the relationship is reciprocal, not one-way.

Application Plan and Evaluation

The intent of this exercise is to help you apply this cluster of skills in a real-life, out-of-class setting. Now that you have become familiar with the behavioral guidelines that form the basis of effective skill performance, you will improve most by trying out those guidelines in an everyday context. Unlike a classroom activity, in which feedback is immediate and others can assist you with their evaluations, this skill application activity is one you must accomplish and evaluate on your own. There are two parts to this activity. Part 1 helps prepare you to apply the skill. Part 2 helps you evaluate and improve on your experience. Be sure to write down answers to each item. Don't short-circuit the process by skipping steps.

Part 1. Planning

1. Write down the two or three aspects of this skill that are most important to you. These may be areas of weakness, areas of strength, or areas that are most salient to a situation you face right now. Identify the specific aspects of this skill that you want to apply.

2. Now identify the setting or the situation in which you will apply this skill. Establish a plan for performance by actually writing down a description of the situation. Who else will be involved? When will you do it? Where will it be done?

    Circumstances:
    Who else?
    When?
    Where?

3. Identify the specific behaviors in which you will engage to apply this skill. Operationalize your skill performance.

4. What are the indicators of successful performance? How will you know you have been effective? What will indicate you have performed competently?

Part 2. Evaluation

5. After you have completed your implementation, record the results. What happened? How successful were you? What was the effect on others?

6. How can you improve? What modifications can you make next time? What will you do differently in a similar situation in the future?

7. Looking back on your whole skill practice and application experience, what have you learned? What has been surprising? In what ways might this experience help you in the long term?

SCORING KEYS AND COMPARISON DATA

Leading Positive Change Assessment

Scoring Key

SUBSCALES	ITEMS
Personal capability to lead positive change	2, 3, 5, 6, 7, 9, 10, 12, 13, 16, 17, 20
Ability to mobilize others toward positive change	1, 4, 8, 11
Capacity to create positive deviance in organizations	14, 15, 18, 19

Comparison Data (N = 5,000 Students)

Compare your scores to three standards:
1. The maximum possible score = 100.
2. The scores of other students in the class.
3. Norm data from more than 5,000 business school students.

Pre-Test				Post-Test
98.33	=	mean	=	105.24
106 or above	=	top quartile	=	114 or above
99–105	=	second quartile	=	107–113
92–98	=	third quartile	=	99–106
91 or below	=	bottom quartile	=	98 or below

Reflected Best-Self Feedback™ Exercise

This exercise does not have a solution or comparison data. Answers will vary among students.

Machiavellianism Scale—MACH IV

Scoring Key

This scale measures individuals' general orientation toward dealing with other people, especially the extent to which they tend to manipulate others in interpersonal situations. High scores on this scale are the opposite of the qualities needed for effective leadership of positive change. That is, authenticity, genuineness, optimism, gratitude, humility, and emotional sensitivity are all characteristics of effective leaders of positive change, but this scale measures the extent to which people are cynical, distrustful, and manipulative.

INSTRUCTIONS: In computing your total score, be certain to consider positive and negative values in the response scale. To compute your total score, you will need to REVERSE the scores for the following items. That is, +3 becomes −3, +2 becomes −2, +1 becomes −1, and so on. Reverse score items: 3, 4, 6, 7, 9, 10, 11, 14, and 16.

The lowest possible score is −60, and the highest possible score is +60. A score of 0 is the neutral point.

The three subscales in this instrument are:

Duplicity:	Items 1, 2, 3, 6, 7, 9, 10, 15, 17	(reverse score: 3, 6, 7, 9, 10)
Negativism:	Items 5, 8, 12, 13, 18, 19, 20	
Distrust:	Items 4, 11, 12, 14, 16	(reverse score: 4, 11, 14, 16)

Comparison Data (N = 5,000 Students)

Mean score:	−17.18
Top quartile:	−8 or above
Third quartile:	−18 to −9
Second quartile:	−27 to −19
Bottom quartile:	−28 or below

In a 2000 survey published in *USA Today,* Lee Iacocca was rated as the greatest salesperson of our time. The other five, listed in order, were: Bill Gates, Bill Clinton, Ronald Reagan, Michael Dell, and Ted Turner. In other words, Iacocca was viewed the quintessential example of positive influence.

Some facts that may be helpful as you analyze the case are:

1979: The name of the company was changed to symbolically signal a new era. The "sales bank" was simply excess inventory, and Chrysler really did burn the last car on the front lawn of headquarters. This was the first time in U.S. history when loan guarantees had been requested, and at the time of the speech, no support had been received whatsoever from the federal government or from Congress. It was only through the persuasive influence of Iacocca that the loan guarantees were granted.

1980: Iacocca's salary was $1 per year. The "why" was to build credibility. Consider how much of the time Iacocca spends on the right-brain aspects of his speeches versus the left-brain side. Normally laying people off and hiring new employees would antagonize current workers. Why did Iacocca's announcement have the opposite effect?

1982: Iacocca makes a loss of $476 million sound like a big win. How? Why did he sell the tank business? What did he do with the money? Did he pay off the creditors? He delivers a strong message: "I'll put my money where my mouth is." Why does he refer to patriotism?

1983: Iacocca is incredibly close to the customer, as evidenced by his knowledge of the hood-release problem. Can CEOs really do that? This speech has a great deal to do with institutionalizing the vision. How does he do that?

1984: Up to that point in history, no company had ever earned more than $1.6 billion in six months. This was an incredible achievement. Why, then, doesn't Iacocca celebrate? He is creating readiness for change all over again, and he treats change as a cyclical affair, not a one-time, linear achievement. His wife died in 1984; he was asked to run for president, then Congress; he chaired the Statue of Liberty celebration; so Chrysler faltered for the rest of the decade. But near the end of the 1990s, Iacocca again took the reins and pulled off another dramatic transformation of a sinking company. Chrysler, which pundits predicted would not survive through the 1990s, once again became an iconic car company. However, a decade after Lee Iacocca left, Chrysler was sold to Daimler, a German company that makes Mercedes-Benz automobiles. The attempt to merge these two car companies was so disastrous that the entire financial value of Chrysler was destroyed over the next five years. Chrysler was divested by Daimler in 2007, and in 2009 the company declared bankruptcy. By selling its major assets to Fiat that year, the bankruptcy lasted less than two months, and the company's financial future is hopeful but not yet assured.

Part IV

Specific Communication Skills

A

Making Oral and Written Presentations

SKILL DEVELOPMENT OBJECTIVES

- MAKE IMPACTFUL AND ENGAGING ORAL PRESENTATIONS
- WRITE CLEARLY AND PERSUASIVELY
- RESPOND APPROPRIATELY TO QUESTIONS AND CHALLENGES

Making Oral and Written Presentations

Taylor Billingsley was hired as a sales representative in the Apex Communications Corporation in 1972. With training and hard work, she advanced through the levels of the corporation, finally landing the position of senior vice president in charge of personnel. Although she had anticipated this position would require some adjustments, she was surprised at the kinds of challenges she faced during her first few weeks on the job. Taylor had a lot of ideas about how to make the personnel division work more efficiently, but she realized almost immediately she had to convince others to adopt them. In addition, she had to establish her own credibility—to make her employees and interested outsiders understand and appreciate her personal commitments and management style.

In the first few days on the job, Taylor had several opportunities to communicate her philosophy and expectations during a number of meetings with the departments in her division. Some of these meetings were formal, such as when she first accepted the position; others were more informal, including lunch meetings with the division heads. Immediately following the announcement of her appointment, she also wrote a memo to her division heads and their employees outlining some of her ideas for moving the department forward. In separate memos she addressed the personnel development and financial benefits departments, introducing a new project and encouraging them to move ahead full speed to develop a new policy on research teams.

Then Taylor began a round of visits with people who worked in her division. She talked individually with several workers and responded to the questions posed by informal groups. She was asked to write up her evaluation of morale among workers in her division and forward it to the corporate chief executive officer. The latest financial reports released by the company's controller's office revealed that quarterly figures were down unexpectedly; it seemed certain costs had risen dramatically. Taylor was concerned and adjusted a report she had written for a scheduled meeting with the region's top executives to reflect these new developments. Later, she spoke to an assembled employee group in the cafeteria in an effort to calm their fears about job cuts. At another facility located in a tough urban environment, the task proved more difficult. Workers were outspokenly critical of the company and challenged much of the information she presented. Following these meetings, Taylor was the featured dinner speaker at a regional Chamber of Commerce meeting.

Taylor Billingsley was experiencing the challenges of management in her new position. During her first two weeks, she addressed dozens of groups on a broad range of subjects; she wrote even more reports and memos. In most of this communication, Taylor was not simply presenting facts. Instead, she was conveying support, pointing a new direction, generating enthusiasm, communicating a sense of caring, building goodwill, and underscoring the value of teamwork. Some situations called for polite, ceremonial messages; others were confrontational. Some covered familiar material; others stretched her ability to find the right words to convey her ideas. At the end of her first two weeks, Taylor began to appreciate the importance of communication skills.

Managers have to master the basic elements of public communication and be flexible enough to adapt them to varying situations (Barrett, 1977; Mambert, 1976; Peoples, 1988; Sanford & Yeager, 1963; Wilcox, 1967). Like Taylor Billingsley, you may find yourself addressing many different audiences through speeches and in writing. Like Taylor Billingsley, you will probably discover very quickly your effectiveness as a manager depends in large part upon your ability to communicate with your coworkers and customers. Unfortunately, new managers are often lacking in these skills. According to a survey of major business recruiters, the biggest deficiencies in college graduates were the lack of good oral communication and writing skills (*Endicott Report*, 1992). Researchers have observed elaborate training programs are ineffective if basic skills, such as writing, are not present (Maruca, 1996). Considering that speaking and writing skills are central to good management and many new employees are also relatively weak in these areas, we should turn our attention to how managers can improve these two critical skills. Let's focus first on the core ingredients of good communication and then examine the specific requirements of speaking and writing.

Essential Elements of Effective Presentations

How can one person meet all of the communication demands confronting a good manager? There are five basic steps to making effective presentations—we'll label them the Five *S*'s. These five *S*'s are sequential in the sense that each step builds upon the preceding steps. Good communication depends heavily on adequate forethought and preparation. As shown in Figure A.1, the first three steps involve preparation, the fourth and fifth focus on the spoken or written presentation itself. Adequate preparation is the cornerstone of effective communication (Collins and Devanna, 1990; Gelles-Cole, 1985; Wells, 1989).

1. Formulate a *strategy* for the specific audience and occasion. This is the phase in which you develop your purposes in relationship to the audience and situation.

2. Develop a clear *structure*. This step translates your broad strategy into specific content.

3. *Support* your ideas with examples, illustrations, and other material adapted to your audience. This will reinforce your ideas.

4. Prepare your material to create a presentation *style* that will enhance your ideas. How you present your ideas is often as important as what you present.

5. *Supplement* your presentation with confident, informed responses to questions and challenges. Your performance in a spontaneous, free-flowing discussion or exchange of memos should be as impressive and informative as your prepared presentation.

We have maintained throughout this book that effective personal performance is a function of skill, knowledge, and practice. This is especially the case with communication. The key to gaining confidence in making oral and written presentations is preparation and practice. If you follow the basic five steps, you should be on your way to delivering effective messages. Specific guidelines for implementing these five steps are presented in the following sections.

FORMULATE A SPECIFIC STRATEGY

Identify Your Purpose

Michael Sheehan, a leading communications consultant whose clients include CEOs of major firms and presidential candidates, lists as his number one rule for effective communication: "Know your objective, know your audience. It sounds easy, but it's really the hardest art of communications" (Reingold, 2004). In line with this recommendation, before collecting information or writing notes, you should clarify your general purpose for speaking or writing. Are you trying to motivate, inform, persuade, demonstrate, or teach? Your general purpose is to inform if you are providing information, demonstrating a technique, or delivering a report. When your purpose is to inform, you are concerned with the transmission and retention of ideas and facts. On the other hand, if you are motivating workers for higher production, convincing others to adopt your ideas, or stimulating pride in the company, your general purpose is to persuade. Persuasion requires the use of motivational language, convincing argument, and audience adaptation. Your general purpose may affect how you structure your message and how you supplement your ideas as well as your style of presentation. That is why it is important to identify your general purpose first.

Your specific purpose should be easier to determine once you have identified your general purpose (see Figure A.2). You can discover your specific purpose by asking, "What do I want my listeners to learn?" or "What behaviors or attitudes do I want my listeners to adopt?" You may answer, "I want my listeners or readers to learn the six steps in our new accounting procedure" or "I want them to spend more time with customers." Each of these is a specific purpose. It determines how

---

Figure A.1 — The Five *S*'s Approach to an Effective Presentation

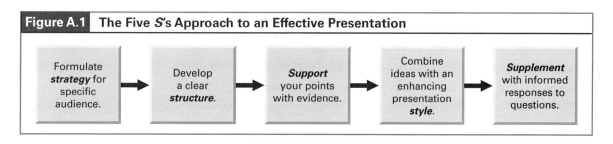

Formulate **strategy** for specific audience. → Develop a clear **structure**. → **Support** your points with evidence. → Combine ideas with an enhancing presentation **style**. → **Supplement** with informed responses to questions.

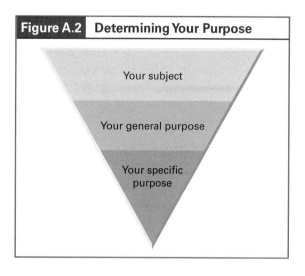

Figure A.2	Determining Your Purpose

Your subject

Your general purpose

Your specific purpose

you will tailor the remainder of your preparation to your audience and the demands of the situation.

Tailor Your Message to Your Specific Audience

The success of your communication is partially dependent on your audience's understanding and receptivity.

The key to developing an audience-appropriate message is to understand their knowledge of the topic, their attitude toward your message, and their expectations of your presentation. If they already know what you are trying to teach them, they'll become bored and possibly hostile. Start with what they already know, then expand on it. If you are teaching a new accounting procedure, begin with the one your listeners currently use, then add the new steps. Remember audiences retain more information if the material is associated with something they already know, rephrased and repeated, reinforced with visual aids, and limited to three to five new ideas. Motivated listeners retain more, so, early in your message, explain how they can use the information.

Your audience's attitudes toward your message are also critical to consider. Hostile receivers don't learn as readily as eager receivers. If your audience is hostile, start by setting realistic goals. If you try to do too much, you might trigger a boomerang effect in which your audience becomes even more hostile. Emphasize common ground by sharing similar values or parallel goals. For example, you might point out that increased profits are good for everyone in the company or everyone has a stake in improving plant conditions.

For hostile or uncommitted listeners it is important to develop a two-sided message (see Table A.1). Present both sides of the issue. Use strong arguments built on logic and extensive evidence (Sprague & Stuart, 1996). Choose neutral language as you develop your ideas. In these situations, it is also important to build your credibility. Show yourself to be calm, fair, reasonable, and well informed. Use humor directed at yourself to ease tension (Sprague & Stuart, 1996).

Meet the Demands of the Situation

Your receivers' expectations of your presentation are also important. The situation frequently determines expectations, such as the level of formality. Some situations clearly demand more formal presentations.

Table A.1	One-Sided Versus Two-Sided Messages

You should use a one-sided message when:

• Your audience already favors your position.

• Your audience is not well educated in general or on the topic.

• You require a public commitment from your audience.

You should use a two-sided message when:

• Your audience initially disagrees with your position.

• Your audience is well educated in general or on the topic.

• Your audience will experience counterpersuasion on the topic.

Research suggests the best way to present a two-sided message is to first give the arguments that support your position. Organize those arguments beginning with the weakest and ending with the strongest. Then, present the argument of your opposition. Organize the opposition arguments beginning with the strongest and ending with the weakest. In this way, you take advantage of your listeners' tendency to remember the most recent thing they hear: your strong argument and your opponent's weak argument.

Source: *Adapted from Sproule, 1991.*

If you are expected to address a board meeting, you should prepare carefully. On the other hand, if you are asked for your off-the-cuff comments, a prepared speech is not appropriate or practical. In this case, it is permissible to present more spontaneous remarks. Written communication also involves certain expectations. Invitations to a company picnic can be posted on bulletin boards, but invitations to a board of directors meeting are sent individually. Some situations are tricky. For example, television often appears informal; however, you should carefully think out your comments. Banquets and ceremonies may encourage an informal, friendly atmosphere, but don't be fooled. These aren't the same settings as one-on-one or small-group events.

The settings of business presentations can create a number of constraints you must anticipate. (Remember forethought and preparation are keys to effective communication.) Consider these common occurrences. A meeting schedule runs over so your 20-minute presentation must be condensed to 5 minutes. Be prepared with a short version that highlights information that will serve your strategy. After presenting your committee's proposal for changing customer service procedures, which the committee has studied for three months, an influential nonmember distributes an outline of a competing proposal. Be prepared to answer specific criticisms of your proposal while maintaining a tone of cordial professionalism.

Language is also affected by the situation. More formal language choices and more correct sentence structure are demanded by formal situations. Slang, colloquialisms, contractions, and less rigid grammar can add to the ease of informal settings. Determine your audience's expectations and adapt your language to them. Most experts agree your language should be one step more intense than your audience's.

DEVELOP A CLEAR STRUCTURE

Begin with a Forecast

In general, an effective introduction does three things. First, it catches the listeners' attention and sets a tone for the message. Second, it provides your listeners with a reason for listening or reading. Finally, it gives them a road map or quick sketch of the message.

At a supervisor's meeting, you might start out your talk on a new plan for production changes this way: "Do you realize we have not changed our basic production process in four years? In that time, seven new competitors have entered the market, and we've lost 9 percent of market share. But with three changes, we can get more production, which will generate 3 percent more profits and pay raises in the next fiscal year. First, we reorganize Bay 2; second, we install a track between the parts room and the assembly line; and, third, we set up a phone connection between the parts room and the assembly line. Let me spend a few minutes filling out the details of each change and explaining why these changes will save us money."

This introduction gets your audience's attention because it portrays the immediacy of the problem and shows why your listeners have an important stake in what you have to say. By setting the larger context of increased competition, you intensify their reason for listening and counter possible resistance to change, which is common in organizations.

Choose an Appropriate Organizational Pattern

Organization is critical because it affects comprehension of the message. Learners retain more when messages are organized. Organization also affects your credibility as a speaker or writer. A person who is organized is viewed more positively than one who is not—and organization affects attitude change. Your receivers are more likely to be influenced by your viewpoint if it is organized. Finally, an organized message is more likely to be retained, and thus to influence the listener.

There are many patterns of organization to choose from (see Table A.2). In general, you should order your thoughts using continua such as time, direction, causal process, problem-solving sequence, complexity, space, or familiarity. A related technique is to organize your material as a series of answers to typical questions. Another common technique is called *sandwiching*. This involves three steps. First, you emphasize the advantages of the plan. Second, you realistically assess the risks or concerns associated with it. Third, you reinforce the benefits by showing how they outweigh the costs, demonstrate how risks can be minimized with proposed safeguards, or show how resistance to change can be overcome.

As you plan your message consider your listeners' orientation. The main question to ask is; "What does my audience already know or think?" Start from that point, then move closer to the desired knowledge or point of view.

Written and spoken communication vary in the amount of detailed information that can be conveyed in a single effort. Because a memo or report can be reread, the receiver doesn't have to remember all the information. However, speeches can't be reheard. It's more important to limit the amount of information presented orally. How many points can you make in a speech?

LEARNING

Table A.2	Common Patterns of Organization
STRATEGY	**EXPLANATION**
Chronological	Traces the order of events in a time sequence (such as past, present, and future, or first step, second step, and third step).
Spatial	Arranges major points in terms of physical distance (such as north, central, and south) or direction from each other (such as internal and external).
Causal	Develops ideas from cause (such as diagnosing a disease from its causes) to effect or results to cause (such as from its symptoms to the disease).
Topical	Enumerates aspects of the topic (such as size, color, shape, or texture).
Monroe's Motivated Sequence	Follows a five-step process: 1. Gaining attention 2. Showing a need 3. Presenting a solution 4. Visualizing the results when the solution is implemented 5. Calling for action to implement the solution
Familiarity-acceptance order	Begins with what the listener knows or believes and moves on to new ideas.
Inquiry order	Develops the topic in steps the same way you acquire the information or solve a problem.
Question-answer	Raises and answers a series of listeners' questions.
Problem-solution	First establishes that a problem exists then develops a plan to solve the problem.
Elimination order	Surveys all the available solutions and systematically eliminates each possibility until one remains.

Three main points are preferred by most speakers, but many listeners can remember up to five main points. Seven chunks of information is about the limit of a person's immediate short-term memory at any one time. Since people must remember what you have said if they are to act on it, dividing your speech into no more than five major chunks should make your ideas easier to remember (Miller, 1967). If your presentation is long, consider using visual aids, such as PowerPoint slides or handouts, to reinforce the message.

Use Transitions or Signposts to Signal Your Progress

It is important to give your audience a "road map" at the beginning of your message. Don't stop there. Continue to help them follow you through it. To do this, signal when you're moving from one idea to another by summarizing the first idea, then forecasting the new idea. This is especially important in oral communication, since listeners will only hear your message once; it is critical you provide signposts during your speech. You should indicate major transitions between ideas, such as: "We've just seen how the two standard types of data storage operate, now let's look at the advantages and disadvantages of each storage system." In written form, you can signal transitions by indenting, numbering, or using bullets to highlight information. You can call your reader's attention to key words with italicized or bold print.

Conclude on a High Note

Two important psychological concepts are at work in communication—primacy and recency. Primacy is the first impression received and recency is the last. People tend to remember the first and last things they read or hear in messages. It's easy to understand why the most important parts of any presentation are the first and last impressions it creates. You establish an initial feeling in your introduction that colors the rest of the presentation, and the impression created during the conclusion influences the audience's overall evaluation of your message. Since these are the most important segments of your presentation, they warrant the most preparation. You should plan your message with the beginning and end in mind, that is, consider your specific purpose statement as you develop your introduction and conclusion. Some people write the conclusion first because this allows them to organize the rest of their material so it naturally flows into the conclusion.

Reach closure at the end of your speech or written message by summarizing your ideas for a final time. Research shows this kind of reinforcement helps listeners retain information. Normally, people remember less than 20 percent of what they hear or read. If you preview the information in your introduction, reinforce it in internal summaries, and then summarize in the conclusion, you will increase the odds that your audience will remember your ideas.

The last statements you make after your summary should create a sense of closure and add to the memorability of your message. These statements can take a variety of forms. You can call for action, reinforce your audience's commitment to action, or establish feelings of goodwill (see Table A.3 for further suggestions). For example, you might emphasize legitimacy by highlighting several authoritative quotes, emphasize the "I'm here to help" theme, predict conditions in the future, underscore the utility of your proposal by emphasizing its impact on the bottom line, or use an emotional appeal to increase commitment and loyalty.

SUPPORT YOUR POINTS
Choose a Variety of Support

There are many reasons to use supporting materials, or evidence, as you develop your message. Most research concludes that supporting material makes a great difference in the impact of ideas. This is true even if you are not well known to your receivers or if they find your credibility moderate to low. What kind of support should you choose? Table A.4 illustrates some of the many kinds of supporting materials available. Messages are strongest when they are built upon a variety of supporting materials. For example, reinforce statistics on profit sharing with a specific instance, such as how those numbers will affect a person on the assembly line.

Consider Your Listeners When Choosing Your Support

The kinds of supporting materials you choose partially depends on your audience. If the evidence is new to them, it will have more impact. Videotapes, recordings,

Table A.3	Types of Introductions and Conclusions

When you select an introduction or conclusion, ask yourself if it orients your audience to your purposes and clearly signals the beginning or ending of your speech.

1. Refer to the subject or occasion.
2. Use a personal reference or greeting.
3. Ask a rhetorical question.
4. Make a startling statement.
5. Use a quotation.
6. Tell a humorous story.
7. Use an illustration.
8. Issue a challenge or appeal.
9. Use suspense.
10. Appeal to the listener's self-interest.
11. Employ a visual aid.
12. Refer to a recent incident.
13. Compliment the audience or a member of the audience.
14. Refer to the preceding speaker.
15. Request a specific action.

Table A.4	Types of Supporting Materials
Examples	Specific instances that illustrate the point or clarify the idea: For example, "Our plants in Detroit and Sacramento use Quality Circles."
Statistics	Numbers that express relationships of magnitude, segments, or trends: For example, "Currently, a full 32% of our workforce is involved in Quality Circle decision-making, and that is up 17% over the past two years."
Testimony	The opinions or conclusions of others, particularly experts: For example, "After studying our plants, professor Henry Wilson of the Harvard School of Business observed American workers are not group motivated. He concluded 'American workers cannot be expected to respond well to Quality Circles for that reason.'"

or photos also have greater impact. People who are highly dogmatic are more affected by evidence than those who are not so dogmatic. People are likely to believe evidence that agrees with their own position more than evidence that does not. So their initial position determines the extent to which they will find evidence believable. If your receivers find the source or types of evidence to be believable or credible, it will be more effective (see Table A.5).

Use Visual Aids as Support

There are as many reasons to use visual aids as there are types of visual aids (see Table A.6). Visual aids help people process and retain data (Seiler, 1971). In addition to enhancing comprehension and memory, visual aids can heighten the persuasive impact of your ideas if they engage receivers actively in the communicative exchange. Your credibility and your persuasiveness are enhanced by good visual aids. With these functions in mind, remember visual aids should be simple, clear, and professional (see Table A.7). The purpose of a visual aid is to augment your presentation, not replace it or distract from it. Unfortunately, this last point is lost by many professionals who treat presentations as slide shows in which screen displays and even sound effects—not the presenter—become the center of attention.

Table A.5	Using Supporting Materials

There is a great deal of research on the use of supporting materials or evidence in oral presentations. The following patterns seem to emerge:

1. If you have low to moderate credibility, evidence will probably increase your persuasive effectiveness.

2. There seems to be minimal difference between emotional and logical evidence.

3. Using evidence is usually better than not using it.

4. There seems to be little difference between biased sources and objective sources in their final impact on audiences.

5. Good speech delivery may improve the potency of evidence when sources of the evidence are unknown or have low credibility.

6. Evidence can reinforce the long-term effectiveness of persuasion.

7. Evidence is most effective when listeners are not familiar with it.

8. People are more likely to believe evidence that agrees with their own position.

9. Highly dogmatic people are more affected by evidence than are less dogmatic people.

10. Evidence produces more attitude change when the course and source qualifications are provided.

11. Speakers with low credibility are seen as more credible when they cite evidence.

12. Using irrelevant evidence or poorly qualified sources may produce an effect opposite to what the speaker intends.

Source: *From Persuasion: Reception, and Responsibility 6th edition by Larson.* © 1992. Reprinted with the permission of Wadsworth, a division of Thomson Learning: www.thomsonrights.com. Fax 800 730-2215.

Table A.6 Functions of Visual Aids

According to research, using effective visual aids in an oral presentation:

- Makes your presentation up to 50% more memorable.
- Significantly clarifies complex or detailed information.
- Portrays you as more professional and better prepared.
- Speeds up group decision making.
- Shortens meeting time by up to 28%.
- Makes your message 43% more persuasive.

Sources: *Osborn & Osborn, 1991, and Gronbeck et al., 1992.*

Computer-aided graphics make it easier than ever to supplement your main ideas with visual materials. They also make it easier to create cluttered, excessive visual and sound images that distract the audience from your strategic message. Select and design visual aids to reinforce your strategy and ideas, and to make them clearer. Keep in mind each type of visual aid communicates information in a different way. In general, visual aids such as slides, photographs, and posters can help an audience *feel* the way you do. They enhance the emotional dimension of a presentation. On the other hand, descriptive or written materials help an audience *think* the way you do. Numbers and charts reinforce cognitive processes; photographs reinforce affective processes. Use tables and graphs to highlight relationships and patterns, not to convey comprehensive data. If necessary, use supplemental handouts of comprehensive tables and charts.

USE AN ENHANCING STYLE

Up to this point, the preparation of oral and written messages is very similar. Whether you intend to deliver

Table A.7 Checklist for Using Visual Aids

As you prepare your visual aids, ask yourself the following questions:

- ❏ Can I avoid making the visual aid the most important aspect of my speech? Will it be more than just an ornament?
- ❏ Can I translate complex numbers into bar or line graphs for easier comprehension?
- ❏ Am I comfortable with using the visual aid? Have I practiced with it so using it is natural, and it does not break the flow of ideas in my speech?
- ❏ Is it large enough to be seen by everyone without straining?
- ❏ Is all the printing short and neat?
- ❏ Is the visual aid colorful and involving? Studies show color highlights aid recall of information.
- ❏ Are my visual aids professional: neat, attractive, and accurate?
- ❏ Have I made the necessary arrangements for special visual aids in advance?
- ❏ Can I use the visual aid without blocking my audience's view of it? Will I be able to maintain good eye contact with my listeners while using the visual aid?
- ❏ Can I avoid reaching across my body or waving the visual aid in front of my face?
- ❏ Can I avoid distracting my listeners by keeping the visual aid covered or out of sight before and after I use it?
- ❏ What will I do if the visual aid fails to work? Am I prepared for unexpected contingencies such as a burned-out projector bulb or a room that cannot be darkened?
- ❏ Have I planned for assistance or volunteers in advance if they are needed?
- ❏ Will a pointer be needed?
- ❏ Will all charts be secured so I don't have to hunt for them on the floor in the middle of my speech?
- ❏ Am I using a variety of visual aids to increase my listeners' interest?
- ❏ If I'm using handouts, can I adjust to the distraction caused by passing them around? Can I compete with listeners who will read the handout rather than listen to me?
- ❏ Can I speak over the noise of a projector or other machine?

a speech or write a memo, you need to develop your strategy by identifying your purposes, structuring your message, and supporting your ideas with evidence. The fourth step requires separate treatment of oral and written messages because they are stylistically very different forms of communication. We'll first focus on oral presentations.

STYLE IN ORAL COMMUNICATION

Prepare Your Notes

The mark of effective presenters is the appearance of effortlessness. Some speakers have such command of their material it appears they are ad libbing. Most of us prefer such a conversational style (see Table A.8), but don't be fooled by appearances. Hours of preparation and practice preceded the actual performance. You've already been introduced to the three steps of preparation, but how do you develop the fourth stage of your preparation for oral communication?

After you have carefully considered your strategy, structure, and support, you should prepare your speaking notes. To do this, simply write your key points in a

Table A.8	Differences Between Public Speaking and Conversation

Folk wisdom holds that giving a speech is just like talking to another person. While it is true most people prefer a conversational style of public speaking, there are at least three noteworthy differences between giving speeches and holding conversations:

1. Public speaking is more highly structured. It requires more detailed planning and development. Specific time limits may be imposed, and the speaker does not have the advantage of being able to respond individually to listeners.

2. Public speaking requires more formal language. Slang, jargon, and poor grammar all lower speaker credibility, even in informal speech situations. Listeners usually react negatively to poor language choices. In fact, many studies show some kinds of language, such as obscene language, dramatically lower a speaker's credibility.

3. Public speaking requires a different method of delivery. The speaker's voice must be adjusted in volume and projection, posture is more correct, and distracting mannerisms and verbal habits are avoided.

Source: *Adapted from Lucas, 1989.*

rough outline following the organizational pattern you have chosen. What you do next depends on your method of presentation. Most often, you will speak in a conversational manner that is not memorized or read; this is referred to as extemporaneous speaking. Extemporaneous presentation is desirable because it is natural and flexible; it applies to most situations. To prepare, copy key words on note cards to stimulate your memory; standard pages are often distracting. Write out quotations, statistics, or anything that requires exact wording. Highlight places where you intend to use visual aids, pause for questions, or present an exhibit. To rehearse, go through the speech, phrasing your ideas in language that seems natural. You may find yourself phrasing ideas with different words each time. That is okay. It will increase the conversational quality of your speech because your words will be typical of oral style and natural expression. It will help you develop flexibility, allowing you to adjust to different wording and flow of ideas.

If the occasion is formal and demands precise wording or exquisite prose, you should prepare a word-for-word manuscript to memorize or read. Then you should rehearse with the manuscript, trying to achieve as much natural flow in the dialogue as possible. This form of presentation is rare, but it may be required for discussing legal and financial issues, making announcements to the press, or conducting special ceremonies. Otherwise, avoid using written scripts and memorization for presentations because they disrupt the natural flow of conversational style and break eye contact with your listeners. Because manuscripts are prepared in written form first, they usually take on the style of written language. Unless you are a practiced speechwriter, your manuscript will sound like written rather than oral speech (see Table A.9).

Practice Your Presentation

It is a good idea to rehearse your presentation under simulated conditions—in a similar room, with listeners who can give you suggestions for improvement. Time your presentation so you know if it is necessary to cut or expand your ideas. Research shows practicing a speech for short periods of time over the course of several days is more successful in reducing anxiety and improving memory than concentrated practice. So give the speech to yourself during breakfast, at your morning coffee break, as you walk to a midafternoon meeting, and before bed. Distributed practice is more efficient and yields better results than massed practice.

Table A.9 Differences Between Oral and Written Styles

Why do we instantly recognize a memorized speech? Why does a meeting transcript sound funny? The answer to both questions is oral style differs from written style. Memorized speeches from manuscripts reveal their written style, and conversations that are read reveal their oral style. Oral style differs from written style in the following ways:

1. The average sentence length is shorter (about 16 words) in conversations.

2. Vocabulary is more limited in speaking than in writing. "I" and "you" make up almost 8% of the words used in speaking; fewer than 50 words make up almost half of the total vocabulary we use when we speak.

3. Spoken vocabulary consists of more short words.

4. Speakers use more words referring to themselves such as "I," "me," and "we"; listeners rate this as more interesting.

5. More qualifying terms (such as "much," "many," and "a lot") and allness terms (such as "none," "never," and "always") are used in speaking.

6. More phrases and terms indicating hesitation are apparent in speaking, such as "it seems to me," "apparently," "in my opinion," and "maybe."

7. Fewer precise numbers are used in speaking.

8. Speakers use more contractions and colloquial expressions such as "can't," "wouldn't," "wow," and "chill out."

One final note on language: There is some evidence that we use lexical diversity as a cue to a speaker's socioeconomic status, competence, and perceived similarity.

Source: *Copyright 1978 From* Oral and Written Style *by L. Einhorn. Reproduced by permission of Taylor & Francis Group, LLC. www.taylorandfrancis.com.*

LEARNING

Practice Using Your Visual Aids

This will help you get used to managing them and give you some idea of how long your speech will take with the visual aids. Prepare for the totally unexpected. What if the roar of an overhead plane drowns out your voice? What if the microphone goes dead, a window blows open, or the room becomes extremely hot? Compensate for minor disruptions by slowing your rate, raising your volume a little, and continuing. You will encourage listeners to listen to your message rather than be temporarily distracted. For other disruptions, a good rule of thumb is to respond the same way you would if you were in the audience. Take off your jacket if it is too hot, close the window, raise your voice if listeners can't hear you, or pause to allow a complex idea to sink in.

As you practice, think about how you will channel your anxiety. Most speakers report feeling anxious before they speak; it's normal. To manage your anxiety, channel it into positive energy. Prepare well in advance for the speech—develop your ideas, support them, and practice your delivery. Even if you are anxious, you will have something important to say. It may help to visualize the speaking situation. Close your eyes, relax, and think about how it's going to feel and what your audience will look like as they watch you. Expect to feel a little momentary panic as you get up to speak; it will evaporate as you progress into the speech. Remember to think about your ideas rather than how nervous you feel. Focus on your message. Also remember anxiety about speaking never really goes away. Most experienced speakers still get podium panic. The advantage of experience is you learn how to cope by converting your anxiety into energy and enthusiasm. That gives you an extra sparkle as you speak. Above all, don't tell your listeners you are nervous. This will divert their attention from your ideas to your anxiety. Usually, listeners can't tell a speaker is nervous—only speakers know, and they should keep that secret.

Convey Controlled Enthusiasm for Your Subject

When a survey was given to 1,200 people asking them to identify the characteristics of effective presentations (Peoples, 1988), the results contained adjectives such as flexible, cooperative, audience-oriented, pleasant, and interesting. What was striking about these results is that only the last item on the list of 12 outstanding characteristics was specifically related to the content of the presentations. This suggests the preceding discussion of effective format, while necessary, is not sufficient to guarantee your success. Put another way, a rambling, poorly organized presentation will surely produce an overall negative evaluation. On the other hand, a well-organized, highly logical, and easy-to-follow presentation that is poorly delivered will also be viewed negatively. This study suggests style is extremely important in oral communication.

Years of research on student evaluations of classroom teaching performance have consistently shown that enthusiasm is the hallmark of a good teacher. Students will forgive other deficiencies if the teacher obviously loves the subject and is genuinely interested in conveying that appreciation to the students. The same holds true for presenters. Your posture, tone of voice, and facial expressions are all critical indicators of your attitude. Speak standing if you can, move occasionally, and use gestures to convey an attitude of earnestness. Remember, your audience will become infected with your enthusiasm.

Although enthusiasm is important, it must be controlled. Do not confuse enthusiasm with loudness. A good rule is to use vigorous but conversational tones of voice and inflections. Avoid bellowing or preaching at your listeners. Be sure you can be easily heard and your tone is sufficiently emphatic to convey meaning effectively. In general, your speech should resemble an animated or lively conversation.

Use Delivery to Enhance Your Message

Another key to maintaining audience attention is effective delivery. Eye contact is the most important tool for establishing audience involvement. It makes listeners feel as if they are involved in a one-on-one, semiprivate discussion with you. In this culture, we value directness and honesty. One of the expressions of these values is direct eye contact. Effective eye contact means looking directly at members of the audience, one at a time, on a random, rotating basis. Generally, the smaller the group, the longer you can look at each person. Maintaining eye contact is also your primary source of audience feedback as you are presenting. If your audience appears puzzled, you may need to pause and review your key ideas.

It is important to use physical space and body movement to enhance your message. Remember presentations are like movies, not snapshots. Alternate moving and standing still, speaking and listening, doing and thinking. Intersperse your lecture with chalkboard use, demonstration, audience participation, and audiovisual aids so no single activity occupies a large portion of the presentation. Add some spice to your presentation by including personal anecdotes, references to members of the group, unusual facts, vital information, and vibrant images. Whenever appropriate, arrange the podium area to accommodate physical movement. Physical movement can be used to punctuate important points, signal transitions, build rapport with a person who asks a question, heighten the interest of particular segments of the audience, and help your listeners stay alert by refocusing their attention.

Other aspects of physical space affect the quality of your presentation. If possible, arrange the podium area and seating in the room to remove distractions. In more intimate settings, group participants so there is less space between them. Eliminate unnecessary or distracting materials from the podium, such as unused equipment, signs, and displays. Keep your visual aids covered until they are used and keep the chalkboard clean. Focus your listeners' attention on you and your message.

You can use space to convey intimacy or distance. Position yourself roughly in the middle of your audience from left to right and in a spot where you can comfortably maintain eye contact. With this in mind, you can deliberately alter your presentation style to build rapport with members of the audience. Move closer if you intend to build intimacy or tension; move to a comfortable distance when your ideas are neutral.

Gestures can also add to a presentation. They should appear to be spontaneous and natural in order to enhance, rather than distract from, your message. They should be relaxed, not rigid. Use them to accentuate your normal mode of expression. To some extent, when you concentrate on your message, not your movements, the appropriate gestures will come naturally. Remember your gestures should be smooth, relatively slow, and not too low (below your waist), too high (above your shoulders), or too wide (more than two feet from your body). If you are using a podium, step slightly behind or to the side of the podium so it does not block your listeners' view of your movement. The general rules for gestures change as your audience becomes larger. You must adapt to large groups by making larger, more dramatic gestures.

Avoid any gestures or movements that distract from your message. Irrelevant movement such as jingling change in a pocket, toying with notes, shifting from foot to foot, twisting hair, or adjusting eyeglasses are annoying. In fact, any movement repeated too often creates a distraction. Practice using a variety of body movements to illustrate or describe, enumerate, add emphasis, or direct attention. For variety, some gestures should involve the entire upper body, not just your dominant hand.

STYLE IN WRITTEN COMMUNICATION

Like oral communication, written communication is a skill; it can be learned. Written communication follows the same three preparation steps as oral communication. The writer determines strategies, structure, and support before actually putting pen to paper. As with effective presentations, good writing draws on careful analysis of the audience and situation. In a business setting, "every document is a response to a problem or opportunity requiring that some consensus be achieved or action taken" (Poor, 1992, p. 38).

There are significant differences between oral and written communication style. Although it lacks the interpersonal dimension of immediacy, written communication offers one tremendous advantage over oral communication—it lasts. Written documents can be retained, studied, duplicated, and filed for the future. This means they are essentially capable of conveying much more detailed information. While written communication offers these advantages, it also makes different demands on the communicator; written communication demands precision.

Develop Mechanical Precision in Your Writing

Your professional image is judged by the appearance of your written communication. Cross outs, erasures, typographical errors, or other sloppiness detract from your written message, just as awkward mannerisms can distract from your oral message. Grammatical precision is also required—misspellings, punctuation errors, and poor grammar are marks of uneducated writers. This is certainly not an image you want to convey. You may expect a secretary or clerical worker to catch and correct all these things, and many times that happens. However, when you sign or otherwise endorse the final product, you alone are accountable for any errors it contains. It is essential to develop the habit of proofreading final drafts before you sign them.

Violations of the rules of grammar and punctuation may affect more than just your credibility. They can also disrupt your reader. If the reader is distracted by typos, confusing grammar, or ambiguous pronouns, your ideas may become lost; such errors can cripple the impact of your message. Some recruiters toss out résumés that contain mechanical errors. Their reasoning is if job applicants can't take the time to proofread a short résumé, they may be sloppy on the job, too. Some readers are insulted by poor grammar; others automatically consider themselves superior to the writer. While these may not be logical reactions, they occur, and more important, they block your effectiveness. You may argue correct grammar and punctuation are not vital. Maybe not, but you take a chance every time you present careless work to another reader. Consider the campaign of Charles Day for a seat on local government. His campaign flyers, delivered house to house, carried the banner, "Vote Charles Day for School Bord." Would you want a man who apparently can't spell make decisions on academic matters for your neighborhood schools? The impression is if you don't have the time or incentive to check your own writing, you won't pay attention to details in the work of others.

Practice Factual Precision in Your Writing

Getting the facts right is important. If you send a memo calling for a meeting but record an incorrect meeting date, you'll suffer the consequences of inconveniencing others. Accuracy is critical, but that's just the beginning. It's up to the writer to create sentences that make the meaning unmistakably clear to the reader. Many times writers know the facts but omit important details in writing. Omission occurs when you have all the facts or circumstances but as you write, you assume the reader knows the facts. Write with your reader in mind. This assumes you have analyzed who your readers are and understand what information they need and expect. What basic information is important for readers to know in order to understand your message? Instead of starting with the central part of the message, provide the background first, such as: "In response to your memo of February 2, requesting corrections to our policy on grievances, we have taken three actions. First . . . " If you're not sure what to include, ask someone who doesn't know the details of the situation to read what you have written.

Ambiguity is another barrier to clear writing. Many times we write as we speak, throwing in phrases as we would speak them. Unlike speakers, writers can't use nonverbal cues to convey specific meanings or associations. Since readers may not have the advantage of asking questions or getting immediate feedback, they are left to determine associations for themselves. Consider how ambiguity creates a lack of precise factual meaning in this memo:

> *The next meeting of the department is scheduled for next week. Matt Olsen has told Leo Robinson to report on the union elections. His report will follow announcements. We will elect new officers at our upcoming meeting.*

LEARNING

This memo doesn't pass the standard test of clear writing. If the memo was sent on Friday and received on Monday, which week contains the meeting? Who is giving the report? The pronoun "his" causes confusion since it could refer to either Matt Olsen or Leo Robinson. Which "upcoming meeting" will result in the election of officers? Will it be the meeting called by the memo or another "upcoming meeting"? Because it can breed confusion, annoyance, and wasted time, such a sloppy memo can have an adverse effect on the relationship between the writer and recipients that can affect their subsequent communication. Seen in this light, the memos a manager routinely writes are an important factor in managing relationships strategically and productively.

Construct Written Messages with Verbal Precision

Achieving verbal precision is different from mechanical or factual precision. Verbal precision is based on the accuracy of the words chosen to express the ideas. In an ideal world, words would provide the exact meaning you intended, but words can't replicate reality. Rather, words are symbols of objects and ideas. Add to this inexact representation the reader's own subtle shadings of meaning, and you can see why it's difficult to achieve verbal precision. Put another way, a word has two levels of meaning: its denotation, or the meaning agreed upon by most people who use the word, and its connotation, or the personal dimension of meaning brought to the word by the receiver.

Communication depends on a blend of both denotative and connotative meanings. Consider the noun *Greenpeace*. Its denotative reference is to a specific international environmental organization. The connotative meaning varies widely. For many environmentalists, Greenpeace is leading a worthy crusade. However, for some governments and companies, the organization is, at best, a nuisance. These are the connotative references of a single word. Consider the difficulty in creating the right blend of denotative and connotative meaning in entire documents. You need to be aware of both types of meaning of the words you use. Frequently, you may recognize your own connotative meaning but be unaware of how others may react. While connotation is often a personal matter, you can attempt to judge this meaning by thinking from your receivers' viewpoint. What is their most likely reaction?

The key to verbal precision in writing is clarity. The fundamental questions you must ask yourself are: "Does the word or phrase convey my meaning without confusion?" or "Could anyone reading this memo for the first time understand the ideas directly and simply?" A secondary question is whether the written message conveys unintentional meanings stimulated by connotative meanings of words or phrases. The impact of connotations once more underlines the importance of knowing your audience and of being aware of what is appropriate for one audience or another.

Pay Attention to Tone

The tone of your writing is directly related to your diction, or word choices. For example, compare these two statements: "Our company will purchase the product" and "We'll buy it." The second sounds more informal because it uses pronouns and a contraction. In general, longer words and sentences tend to convey a more formal tone.

Using the appropriate level of formality in your writing calls for you to analyze the nature of the writing situation. An invitation to a reception for the company's board of directors calls for formal language. When you are writing to strangers or up the chain of command, it is safer to be formal. When you are communicating across or down the chain, you may often be informal. However, a letter of reprimand to a subordinate should be formal in tone.

Tone in business writing goes beyond its relative formality. It reflects on the nature of the writer as a person and therefore affects how the reader feels about the writer. Its impact can be significant and often unexpected. For example, a terse letter may be interpreted as sarcastic or angry even if the writer did not intend sarcasm or anger. Consider a customer who writes a long letter expressing problems with a product. What would the customer think if this response were mailed back: "Thank you for your letter of January 12. We always enjoy hearing from our customers." Although this response has the trappings of courtesy, it seems insincere and perhaps sarcastic. It hardly seems that the respondent read the customer's letter—there is nothing about its contents—or that the letter was "enjoyed." Although the response shows factual and mechanical precision, the tone is inappropriate and potentially damaging to the relationship with this customer.

In most cases, even disappointing news can be expressed in a positive way. Consider an employer who responds to a job applicant by writing, "In a company as well respected as ours, we rarely have time to consider applications such as yours." Not only is the news bad, the arrogant tone also needlessly humiliates the applicant. A response with a more positive tone might be: "We read your application with interest but currently do not have any openings in your specialties. Best wishes with your continued search." The news is still bad, but the polite tone shows respect for the applicant and promotes a professional image for the company.

Compare the following sentence and its more positive version: "Because of recent heavy demand, we will be unable to ship the items you ordered until July 15," and "Although recent demand has been heavy, we will be able to ship the items you ordered July 15." A slight variation in wording here changes a tone of helplessness to one of helpfulness.

Under most business writing conditions, you should be cordial. You should express tact and friendliness appropriate to your relationship with the reader. This attitude will have a positive effect on your word choices, which in turn will more likely convey an appropriate tone.

One area of modern business writing where failing to pay attention to tone has cost many bad feelings and lost time is e-mail. By its nature, e-mail encourages rapid-fire exchanges, especially when busy workers face an in-box filled with messages, many of which are ill-considered and unclear. E-mail is not a phone conversation in which tone of voice and other cues can clarify your meaning and in which you can read the listener's vocal cues. However, many e-mailers seem to forget the difference. They don't state the context of their message; they don't give needed background information; they don't organize their message; they don't make careful word choices that convey a cordial tone. By not taking the time to consider their message in light of the situation and the receiver, e-mailers can convey inappropriately demanding tones or disapproving tones if their requests aren't met promptly. The antagonism created by the poor tone of e-mail messages can delay solving the business problem at hand and negatively affect the work relationships of the e-mailers.

Use the Proper Format

Like it or not, first impressions count, even in written communication. Sloppiness suggests the writer doesn't take the message seriously; odd or unconventional formats hint the writer is ignorant or unprofessional. You should become acquainted with the physical layout of letters, memos, proposals, and other common forms of written business communication. Others expect you to have this basic knowledge; many handbooks and computer software programs are available to guide you in the development of these formats. Some companies have style guides that precisely prescribe the formats for all documents representing the company.

While there are several acceptable formats for written communication such as business letters, the reader should be able to pick up specific information at a glance. In the business letter, this information includes: the intended recipient of the letter, the sender, the sender's address for return correspondence, any enclosures, and recipients of copies of the letter. All of this information is separate from the body of the letter and should be clearly visible.

Because memos are intended to communicate within an organization, their format is different from that of letters. Instead of business letterhead, memo letterhead is used. Basic information can also be obtained at a glance. The top of the memo should include: To, From, Date, and Subject headings. Usually, salutations and closings are not considered necessary within an organization.

Proposals are much lengthier and require special attention to supporting information such as tables, graphs, and charts. The best ways to represent such data can be found in readily available resources on business writing.

Whatever the final format, there is one objective in all written business communication: Your message should be simple, direct, and clear. Anything that interrupts your reader's movement through your writing limits its effectiveness. Any imprecision—a mechanical blunder, a factual omission, or a strange word—calls attention to itself and, like an odd gesture in spoken communication, diverts attention away from your ideas. As a writer, you must aim at clear, direct transmission of your message.

SUPPLEMENT YOUR PRESENTATION BY RESPONDING TO QUESTIONS AND CHALLENGES

Prepare Thoroughly to Handle Questions

Answering questions and responding to objections is a vital part of the communication process because it allows us to interact directly with our listeners. We can learn about how our listeners are thinking and their responses to our ideas from their questions; it's a two-way street.

The key to formulating effective responses is the same as the key to developing good speeches—careful preparation. Read broadly and talk with experts in your field. Don't read just the material that supports your point of view but also read what the opposition is saying. The best defense can be a good offense, and this is no exception. Ask your colleagues to critique your material, discuss their questions and objections with them, and collect supporting documentation or evidence. You can also practice your responses. Begin by considering what your listeners might ask or find someone opposed to your position who will list questions for you. Then, practice your responses to these questions.

Despite your best efforts, you may get an overwhelmingly hostile response from your listeners. Don't be afraid to take a stand that disagrees with them. People may not agree with you but they will respect your sincerity. If someone throws you a curve, don't apologize or bluff your way through with an inadequate response. Be honest and direct, tell them if you don't have the answer. Invite them to discuss the problem further at a later time and follow up on your invitation. The next time someone asks the same question, you will be prepared.

Respond to Objections in an Orderly Manner

In general, answer questions as succinctly as possible. Rambling answers may make it appear as though you are hedging or unsure. They also suggest an inability to think concisely. You can answer objections in four steps:

1. *Restate the objection.* This gives you time to think, shows your interest, and makes sure everyone understands the question. Restatement recognizes the objection and clarifies it for everyone in the audience.

2. *State your position.* Give a concise, direct statement of what you believe to make it clear where you stand.

3. *Offer support for your position.* This is the critical part of the response. Provide evidence that shows your position is the right one.

4. *Indicate the significance of your rebuttal.* Show the impact of adopting your position. Offer reasons for doing so.

Following the four steps we've outlined, a good response to an objection might take this form:

1. Joe has stated a management-by-objectives system won't work in our factory because supervisors don't want input from the cutting floor (restatement of the objection).

2. I think a management-by-objectives system will work and it will increase worker satisfaction (statement of your position).

3. I'm basing my position on a group of studies done in our Newark plant last year. Output increased 0.5 percent during the first month, and more importantly, workers reported more job satisfaction. They had fewer sick days, too (support for the position).

4. If our plant is similar to the Newark plant— and I think it is—then I believe our supervisors will notice the same gains here. Until Joe can provide us with a reason to stick with the current system, I think we ought to give the new one a try—we stand to get more output and better job satisfaction (significance of rebuttal).

Practice this format until it becomes automatic. It builds up your own case while responding to the objection. Since this format rationally shores up your position, it increases your credibility as well. And, it increases the chances that others will agree with you.

Maintain Control of the Situation

You need to balance being sensitive to feedback and flexible enough to respond to legitimate concerns with avoiding prolonged, unproductive interchanges. Recognizing everyone's right to ask questions or offer alternative positions is important because it grants audience members respect. On the other hand, you also have every right to decide what is relevant for consideration. You shouldn't allow one or two members of your audience to dictate the pace or direction of your presentation. This places you in a position of weakness that undermines your credibility. If you should alter your position, make certain the majority of your listeners view it as a responsible shift rather than an effort to placate a minority voice.

Keep exchanges on an intellectual level. Arguments and rebuttals can degenerate into name-calling in which little is settled. Effective communication is more likely to occur when the calm voice of reason dominates than when you squabble with your listeners.

You'll soon learn people don't always ask questions just because they want information. Some people crave attention; others may sabotage your position if they perceive your ideas as a threat. Planning for these possibilities will give you more options; foresight enables you to respond appropriately. You might answer hostile questions with further questions, drawing out your interrogator and regaining the offensive. Or you might broaden the discussion. Don't get trapped into an argument with one person. Involve others to determine if this is an isolated concern or a legitimate issue. Finally, you might express your willingness to discuss special or detailed issues but defer extensive discussion until the end of your presentation.

Summary and Behavioral Guidelines

A key aspect of management is communication, and formal presentations are an essential communication tool. Therefore, effective managers must be able to create effective informative and persuasive messages. You can enhance your speaking and writing with thorough preparation and repeated practice. This chapter has outlined a number of guidelines based on the Five *S*'s model:

1. Formulate a *strategy* for the specific audience and occasion.
2. Develop a clear *structure*.
3. *Support* your points with evidence adapted to your audience.
4. Practice presenting your material in a *style* that will enhance your ideas.
5. *Supplement* your presentation by effectively responding to questions and challenges.

Strategy

1. Identify your general and specific purposes.
2. Tailor your message to your audience.
   - ❏ Understand their needs, desires, knowledge level, and attitude toward your topic.
   - ❏ Make sure your approach is audience-centered.
   - ❏ Present both sides of the issue if your audience is hostile or uncommitted.
3. Meet the demands of the situation.
   - ❏ More formal situations demand formal language and sentence structure.
   - ❏ Informal situations allow slang and less rigid language use.

Structure

4. Begin with a forecast of your main ideas.
   - ❏ Catch your audience's attention as you begin.
   - ❏ Provide them with a reason for listening or reading.
   - ❏ Give them an outline of the message so they can follow along.

5. Choose your organizational pattern carefully.
   - ❏ Start with what your listeners already know or think.
   - ❏ Use organization to increase your credibility.
   - ❏ Move from familiar to unfamiliar, simple to complex, old to new, or use other continua for organizing your thoughts.
   - ❏ Make no more than three to five main points in oral communication.
6. Use transitions to signal your progress.
7. Conclude on a high note.
   - ❏ Take advantage of greater audience attention at the conclusion of your message.
   - ❏ Reach closure by reinforcing through a summary of your ideas.
   - ❏ Use your last statements to call for action, reinforce the commitment to action, or establish a feeling of goodwill.

Support

8. Choose a variety of support.
   - ❏ The most effective support is not well known to your listeners.
   - ❏ Support increases your credibility.
   - ❏ You may use a wide variety of supporting material.
9. Consider your audience when choosing your support.
   - ❏ New evidence and live videotapes have more impact.
   - ❏ The audience's initial position determines the extent to which they find evidence believable.
   - ❏ Using evidence is better than not using evidence.
10. Use visual aids as support.
    - ❏ Visual aids have a dramatic impact on comprehension and retention.
    - ❏ Visual aids also enhance persuasion.
    - ❏ Keep visual aids simple and effective.

Style in Oral Communication

11. Prepare your notes.
    - ❏ Remember, the crucial effect is conversational style.
    - ❏ Extemporaneous presentation requires limited notes combined with frequent delivery practice.
    - ❏ Formal occasions demand precise wording that requires a manuscript or memorized speech.

LEARNING

12. Practice your presentation.
    - ❏ Use distributed practice rather than massed practice.
    - ❏ Practice using your visual aids and plan for the unexpected.
    - ❏ Plan to channel your speaking anxiety.
13. Convey controlled enthusiasm for your subject.
    - ❏ Effective speakers communicate excitement about their topics.
    - ❏ Your posture, tone of voice, and facial expressions all indicate your attitude.
    - ❏ Your speech should resemble an animated conversation.
14. Engage your audience with effective delivery.
    - ❏ Eye contact is the most critical tool.
    - ❏ Use physical space and body movement to enliven your message.
    - ❏ Use space to convey intimacy or distance.
    - ❏ Use gestures to accentuate your normal mode of expression.
    - ❏ Avoid any movement that distracts from your message.

Style in Written Communication

15. Develop mechanical precision in your writing.
    - ❏ Project a professional image.
    - ❏ Errors may distract your readers and disrupt the impact of your message.
16. Practice factual precision in your writing.
    - ❏ Accuracy ensures your meaning will be communicated clearly.
    - ❏ Ambiguity prevents factual precision.
17. Construct written messages with verbal precision.
    - ❏ Words cannot replicate reality.
    - ❏ Consider denotative and connotative meanings of words as you write them.
    - ❏ The key to verbal precision is clarity.

18. Pay attention to tone.
    - ❏ Tone is directly related to word choice.
    - ❏ Adjust the tone of your message to the formality of the situation.
    - ❏ Tone affects how readers feel about the writer.
    - ❏ Writing should express appropriate cordiality.
    - ❏ Positive phrasing is preferable to negativity.
19. Use the proper format.
    - ❏ You are responsible for creating an impression of professionalism.
    - ❏ Business letters, memos, and proposals all have special formats.

Supplement: Questions and Answers

20. Anticipate questions and thoroughly prepare responses.
    - ❏ Rehearse answers to difficult questions.
    - ❏ Handle hostile listeners with honesty and directness.
21. Respond to objections in an orderly fashion.
    - ❏ Restate the objection.
    - ❏ State your position.
    - ❏ Offer support for your position.
    - ❏ Indicate the significance of your rebuttal.
22. Maintain control of the situation.
    - ❏ Balance the demands of specific individuals with the interest of the group.
    - ❏ Keep exchanges on an intellectual level.
    - ❏ Plan for the questioner who has a personal agenda.

EXERCISES FOR MAKING EFFECTIVE ORAL AND WRITTEN PRESENTATIONS

Speaking as a Leader

As illustrated in the opening case about Taylor Billingsley at Apex Communications, one of the major challenges facing leaders is the requirement to deliver a wide range of presentations. Effective communicators must be skilled at both informing and inspiring. They must be able to hold their own with hostile audiences as well as to impress content experts and instill confidence in novices. They must be skilled at building consensus, pointing out new directions, and explaining complex topics. This exercise, adapted from Richard Linowes, provides an opportunity to practice speaking on a variety of leadership topics.

Assignment

To practice playing this important leadership role, prepare a talk and a memo on one of the following topics. Your speech should last from three to five minutes, unless you are otherwise instructed. Your memo should not exceed two pages. Create a context for your communication by assuming a management role in a familiar organization. Before beginning, explain the details of the context to your audience (either orally or in a written summary). Briefly explain your organizational position, the makeup of the audience, and their expectations of your presentation. (For the memo, attach a one-page background statement.) The specific content of your communication is less important than how well it is prepared and how persuasively it is delivered. Prepare to respond to questions and challenges.

In preparing your presentation, review the behavioral guidelines at the end of the Skill Learning section. The checklist in this exercise may also be useful. You will receive feedback based on the criteria shown in the Observer's Feedback Form.

Topics for Leadership Talks

1. **Taking Charge of an Established Group.** The speaker is a manager newly assigned to a group that has worked together under other managers for some time.

2. **Announcing a New Project.** The speaker is announcing a new undertaking to members of his or her department and is calling on all to rally behind the effort.

3. **Calling for Better Customer Service.** The speaker is motivating all employees to be as attentive and responsive as possible to customers.

4. **Calling for Excellence and High-Quality Work.** The speaker is motivating all employees to perform their jobs with a commitment to meeting the highest possible standards.

5. **Announcing the Need for Cost Reductions.** The speaker is requesting everyone look for ways to cut expenditures and immediately begin to slash spending.

6. **Commending a Job Well Done.** The speaker is extolling a group of people who have worked very hard for an extended period to produce outstanding results.

7. **Calming a Frightened Group of People.** The speaker is endeavoring to restore calm and confidence to those who feel panic in the face of distressing business developments.

PRACTICE

8. **Addressing a Challenging Opposition.** The speaker is presenting a heartfelt belief to a critical, even hostile, audience.

9. **Mediating Between Opposing Parties.** The speaker is serving as judge or arbiter between two groups who are bitterly opposed on a key issue.

10. **Taking Responsibility for Error.** The speaker is a spokesperson for an institution whose actions have produced an unfortunate result that affects the audience.

11. **Reprimanding Unacceptable Behavior.** The speaker is rebuffing certain individuals who have failed to perform up to required levels.

12. **Petitioning for Special Allowances.** The speaker is presenting the case for an institution seeking certain rights that must be authorized by some external body.

Checklist for Developing Effective Presentations

1. What are my general and specific objectives?
2. What is the context of my communication? (My audience, the situation, etc.)
3. How will I open and close the communication?
4. How will I organize my information?
5. How will I get and keep the attention of my audience?
6. What supporting materials will I use?
7. What visual aids (graphs, charts, objects, etc.) will I use?
8. How will I tailor the presentation to my audience?
9. What format will I use in my presentation?
10. What questions or responses will likely occur?

Quality Circles at Battle Creek Foods

A management tool made popular in Japan is widely used in U.S. firms. Ironically, Edward Deming, an American, first brought the notion of "statistical quality control," a management tool, to the Japanese in the early post-World War II years. The Japanese combined these ideas with the assumption the person who performs a job is the one who best knows how to identify and correct its problems. As a result, the Japanese, with Deming's help, developed the "quality circle." A quality circle is a group of people (usually about 10) who meet periodically to discuss and develop solutions to problems related to quality, productivity, or product cost.

The purpose of this exercise is to give you an opportunity to make a presentation on this important topic.

Assignment

You are the director of personnel at Battle Creek Foods, a leading manufacturer of breakfast cereal. Productivity has been sagging industrywide, and your organization is starting to see its effect on profitability. In response, you have been asked by the corporate executive committee to make a 20-minute oral presentation (or prepare a five-page memo) on quality circles. The committee has heard that QCs have been initiated at several plants by your leading competitor, and it would like your recommendation as to whether Battle Creek Foods should follow suit. The committee's only previous exposure to QCs is what each member has read in the popular press. Using the following reference material, prepare a presentation on quality circles. Explain the QC structure and process, and the advantages and disadvantages of QCs. The final section of the presentation should include a recommendation regarding their adoption at your plants. Prepare to respond to questions and challenges.

In preparing your presentation, refer to the behavioral guidelines for effective presentations at the end of the Skill Learning section and the checklist in the preceding exercise. You will receive feedback based on the Observer's Feedback Form.

A Look at Some of the Evidence

Quality circles, on balance, appear to be making a positive contribution to product quality, profits, morale, and even improved employee attendance (DuBrin, 1985, pp. 174–185). The widespread attention QCs have received in recent years has led logically to their evaluation by both businesspeople and researchers. Here we will rely on several types of evaluation methods, sampling first the positive evidence, and then the negative.

Favorable Outcomes with QCs

Honeywell, a high-technology electronics firm, has become a pioneer in the application of QCs in North America. Honeywell currently operates several hundred QCs in the United States. Typically, about a half-dozen assembly workers are brought together every two weeks by a first-level supervisor or team leader. "We feel this type of participatory management program not only increases productivity," says Joseph Riordan, director of Honeywell Corporate Productivity Services, "but it also upgrades the quality of work life for employees. Line workers feel they are more a part of the action. As a result, we find the quality of work improves and absenteeism is reduced. With this kind of involvement, we have, in many cases, been able to increase the capacity of a line without the addition of tooling or extra shifts."

Honeywell used the quality circle method to manage the problem of winning a renewable bid for a government contract. "Here was a situation," Riordan relates, "where we already had cut our rejects down, where all of the learning had effectively gone out of the process." The problem was assigned to the quality circle representing that particular work area. "They came up with a suggestion for further automating the process that enabled us to improve our competitive position by about 20 percent and win the contract."

In an attempt to determine the appropriateness of QCs to North American firms, a team of researchers set up a one-year field experiment at a metal fabricating facility of an electronics firm.

Eleven quality circles, averaging nine production employees each, were established. Performance was measured by a computerized monitoring system created from the company's existing employee performance reporting system. Both quantity and quality measurements were taken. Employee attitudes were also assessed, using the Motivating Potential Score (MPS) of the Hackman-Oldham Job Diagnostic Survey.

The major result of the circle program was its positive impact on reject rate, as shown in the top half of Figure A.3. Reject rates per capita for quality circle participants dropped by one-third to one-half of the former rates by the time the program had run three months. Surprisingly, the reject rates for the control group increased during the same period.

An explanation offered by the researchers for these results is circle members tackled the issues of internal communication as a top priority item. For example, one of the initial projects implemented by the QCs was improving training manuals and procedures, including translating materials into a worker's native language if the worker desired. Careful attention to better training in fundamentals prevented many errors.

Circle members also made fewer errors. In addition, the defective parts the circle members did make tended to be less expensive to scrap or rework into usable parts. The explanation given for these results is circle training instructs employees how to prioritize problems on the basis of dollar impact on the company. The cost savings

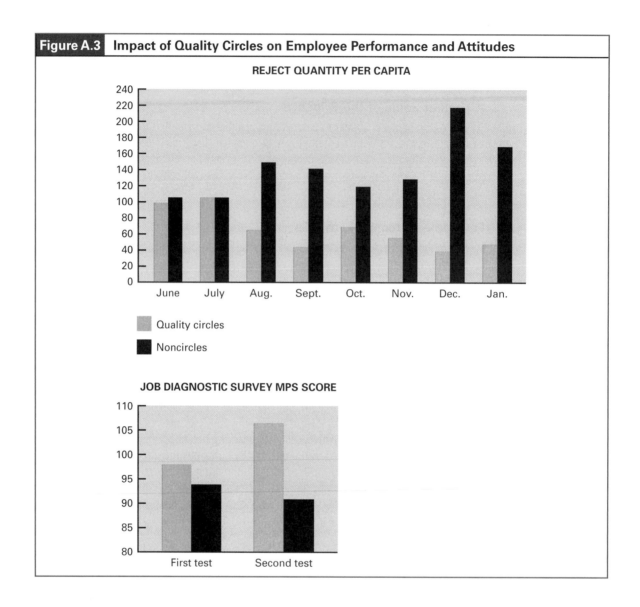

Figure A.3 Impact of Quality Circles on Employee Performance and Attitudes

REJECT QUANTITY PER CAPITA

Quality circles

Noncircles

JOB DIAGNOSTIC SURVEY MPS SCORE

generated by the lower reject rate represented a 300 percent return on the cost of investment in the program.

The impact of QCs on participants' level of work satisfaction was equally impressive. Results shown in Figure A.3 indicate the Motivating Potential Score (MPS) for the circle participants increased, while the control group showed a decrease. No other changes were present in the work environment that would impact the experimental group differently than the control group. The researchers therefore concluded the improvement in employee job attitudes could be attributed to the circle training program and the problem-solving activity. The job characteristic most influenced by the quality activity was skill variety: the extent to which a job requires a variety of skills.

Negative Outcomes with Quality Circles

Despite the favorable outcomes reported, many negative results have also been reported. A review of the results of the first surge of QC activity in the United States revealed as many as 75 percent of initially successful programs were no longer in operation after a few years. Even Lockheed, one of the American pioneers in this method, had decreased its involvement with quality circles. Robert Cole, a recognized authority on the Japanese workforce, made these pessimistic remarks:

> *[The] fact is that the circles do not work very well in many Japanese companies. Even in those plants recognized as having the best operating programs, management knows that perhaps only one-third of the circles are working well, with another third borderline, and one-third simply making no contribution at all. For all of the rhetoric of voluntarism, in a number of companies the workers clearly perceive circle activity as coercive. Japanese companies face a continuing struggle to revitalize circle activity to ensure that it does not degenerate into ritualistic behavior.*

A study of quality circles in 29 companies, conducted by Matthew Goodfellow, found only eight of them to be cost-effective in terms of gains in productivity. Management consultant Woodruff Imberman investigated the 21 unsuccessful QC efforts and found four major causes of failure. First, in many firms, the employees intensely disliked management. Their antagonism carried over into the quality circles, which some employees perceived to be a management ploy to reduce overtime and trim the workforce by increasing productivity.

Second, most organizations did a poor job of selling the QCs. Instead of conducting individual discussions with employees, they relied on flip charts, booklets, and formal management presentations. The workers were left wondering, "What's in it for me?"

Third, the supervisors chosen to lead the circles received some training in human relations and group dynamics, but they felt little of this information satisfied the specific needs of their own departments.

Fourth, most of the 21 firms regarded the QC programs merely as a way of improving the efficiency of production techniques. They did not realize QCs cannot succeed unless top management is willing to shift its philosophy toward emphasizing good relations among employees and between management and workforce. This last point hints at the importance of establishing the conditions that allow a quality circle program to succeed.

Key Elements of a Successful Program

Quality circle programs show some variation from company to company, whether these companies are engaged in manufacturing or service. They may differ in how frequently they meet, how much authority is granted to the team leader or supervisor, whether they use a group facilitator in addition to a supervisor, and how much coordination there is with the existing quality-control department. Based on the judgments of several observers, the successful programs have certain elements in common.

Quality circles work best in firms where good employee-management relations already exist. QCs are not likely to succeed in organizations suffering from acrimonious union-management conflict or high levels of distrust between employees and management.

Top management is committed to the program. Without commitment from top management, the initiation of a QC program is inadvisable. Instead, the director of a circle project should first prepare reports on other companies where QCs have been successful and present them to top management.

Circle leaders use a participative leadership style. Laurie Fitzgerald, a QC consultant, advocates the "leader as a worker for the members" concept. When the circle leader takes on a highly authoritarian role, the members are usually unresponsive.

The right people and the right area are selected. For quality circles to be effective, the program manager has to be enthusiastic, persistent, and hardworking. The facilitator or team leader must be energetic and cooperative. Also, another important step in getting the program off the ground is to select an area of the company where one can expect cooperation and enthusiasm from participants.

Program goals are stated explicitly. Objectives should be made clear in order to avoid confusion or unreasonable expectations from the circle program. Among the goals of QC programs are improving product quality, increasing productivity, improving communications between workers and supervisors, decreasing product costs, improving the quality of work life, and preparing people for future supervisory assignments.

The program is well publicized throughout the firm. Once the program is started, information about it should be disseminated widely throughout the company. Better communication results in less resistance and fewer negative rumors about the program. The content of the communication should be open and positive.

The program starts slowly and grows slowly. A gradual introduction of the program helps expose people to new concepts and helps reduce doubts about its intention and potential merit.

The QC program is customized to meet the needs of the firm. A subtle source of failure in some QC programs is the use of a canned set of procedures that don't fit local circumstances. A QC participant whose work is data processing may have difficulty with the translation of a case from the aerospace industry. A workable compromise is to use standard training as a framework and build on it with the unique problems of the firm in question.

Quality circles are used as a method of employee development. A key purpose of these circles is to foster personal development of the participating workers. If managers intend to install a QC as a tool for their own selfish gain, they would do better not to begin.

Management is willing to grant recognition for ideas originating in the circles. If management attempts to manipulate the circle volunteers or take away from them the credit for improvements, the program will most likely backfire. More will be lost than gained.

Membership is voluntary. As with job enrichment and all forms of participative management, employee preference is an influential factor. Employees who desire to contribute their ideas will generally perform better than employees who are arbitrarily assigned to a QC.

Achievements of quality circles are recognized as results of group, not individual, effort. Recognizing them as such decreases showing off and competitiveness and increases cooperation and interdependence within the group or department. Quality circles, not individual employees, should receive credit for innovations and suggestions for improvement.

Ample training is provided. Program volunteers generally need some training in conference techniques or group dynamics. At a minimum, the circle leader will need skills in group participation methods. Otherwise, he or she will wind up lecturing about topics such as quality improvement and productivity improvement. Leaders and participants will also need training in the use of whatever statistical and problem-solving methods are to be used. Following are eight major problem-solving techniques and their purposes:

1. Brainstorming is used to identify all problems, even those beyond the control of circle members.
2. A check-sheet is used to log problems within the circle's sphere of influence within a certain time frame.
3. A Pareto chart graphically illustrates check-sheet data to identify the most serious problems; that is, the 20 percent of the problems that cause 80 percent of the major mistakes.
4. A cause-and-effect diagram graphically illustrates the cause of a particular problem.

5. Histograms or bar charts are graphed to show the frequency and magnitude of specific problems.

6. Scatter diagrams or "measles charts" identify major defect locations, which show up as dense dot clusters on the pictures of products.

7. Graph-and-control charts monitor a production process and are compared with production samples.

8. Stratification, generally accomplished by inspecting the same products from different production areas, randomizes the sampling process.

Creativity is encouraged. As illustrated above, brainstorming or variations thereof fit naturally into the quality circle method and philosophy. Maintaining an attitude of "anything goes" is particularly important, even if rough ideas must be refined later. If half-processed ideas are shot down by the leader or other members, idea generation will extinguish quickly.

Projects are related to members' actual job responsibilities. Quality circles are not arenas for amateur speculation about other people's work. People make suggestions about improving the quality of work for which they are already responsible. They should, however, be willing to incorporate information from suppliers and customers.

The Arguments For and Against Quality Circles

A major argument for quality circles is they represent a low-cost, efficient vehicle for unleashing the creative potential of employees. In the process, highly desirable ends are achieved, such as improvements in the quality of both products and work life. Quality circles, in fact, are considered part of the quality of work life movement.

Another favorable feature of these circles is they are perceived positively by all—management, workers, unions, and stockholders. A firm contemplating implementing such a program thus runs no risk of either internal or external opposition. (It is conceivable, however, that opposition will be forthcoming if management fails to act on quality circle suggestions.)

Quality circles contribute to organizational effectiveness in another important way. They have emerged as a useful method of developing present and future managers. Recently, a major computing manufacturing firm established a quality circle program. After the program had been operating for two years, the director of training observed the supervisors who were quality circle leaders were significantly more self-confident, knowledgeable, and poised than other supervisors who were attending the regular training program. The director believed the supervisors' involvement in the QC training programs and activities had been the major contributor to this difference.

One major criticism of quality circles is many of them are not cost-effective. Furthermore, even more pessimistic is the criticism that the reported successes of QCs may be attributable to factors other than the actual quality circle program. One explanation is the attention paid to employees by management may be the force behind the gains in productivity and morale (the well-known Hawthorne effect). Another possible explanation of the successes of quality circle programs is the gains are due to improved group dynamics and problem-solving techniques. Therefore, an entire QC program need not be conducted just to achieve these gains.

A discouraging argument has been advanced that quality circles may not be suited to North American workers. Matsushita Electric, a leading user of the quality circle method in Japan, does not use circles in its U.S. plant (located in Chicago) because it does not consider the American worker suited to circle activities. Perhaps Matsushita management believes Americans are too self-oriented to be group oriented.

PRACTICE

Quality circles may prove to be breeding grounds for friction and role confusion between the quality-control department and the groups themselves. Unless management carefully defines the relationship of quality circles vis-à-vis the quality-control department, much duplication of effort (and therefore waste of resources) will inevitably result.

Exclusive reliance upon volunteers for the circles may result in the loss of potentially valuable ideas. Many nonassertive people may shy away from participation in the circles despite their having valid ideas for product improvement.

Some employees who volunteer to join quality circles may do so for the wrong reasons. The circle may develop the reputation of being "a good way to get away from the line for a while and enjoy a coffee break and a good bull session." (To counter such an abuse of the quality-circle program, QC group members might monitor the quality of input from their own group members.)

Guidelines for Action

An early strategic step in implementing a quality circle is to clarify relationships between the circle and the formal quality-control department. Otherwise, the quality-control department may perceive the circle as a redundancy or threat. One effective arrangement is for the quality circle to complement the quality-control department; the QC department thus does not become subject to the loss of authority.

Membership in the circle should be voluntary and on a rotating basis. In many instances, a team member will soon run out of fresh ideas for quality improvement. Rotating membership will result in a wider sampling of ideas being generated. Experience suggests that group size should be limited to nine.

Quality circles should be implemented on a pilot basis. As the circle produces results and wins the acceptance of managers and employees alike, it can be expanded as the demand for its output increases.

Do not emphasize quick financial returns or productivity increases from the output of the quality circles. The program should be seen as a long-range project that will raise the quality consciousness of the organization. (Nevertheless, as noted in the report from Honeywell, immediate positive results are often forthcoming.)

Management must make good use of many of the suggestions coming from the quality circle yet still define the limits of the power and authority of the circle. On the one hand, if none of the circle's suggestions are adopted, the circle will lose its effectiveness as an agent for change. Circle members will become discouraged because of their lack of clout. On the other hand, if the circle has too much power and authority, it will be seen as a governing body for technical change. Under the latter circumstances, people may use the circle for political purposes. An individual who wants to get a technical modification authorized may try to influence a member of the quality circle to suggest modification during a circle meeting.

Training in group dynamics and methods of participative management will be particularly helpful. It may also prove helpful at the outset to appoint a group facilitator (an internal or external consultant) who can help the group run more smoothly.

Observer's Feedback Form

RATING

1 = Low
5 = High

Strategy

_____ 1. Identified the general and specific purposes.

_____ 2. Tailored the message to the audience's needs, attitudes, knowledge level, and so forth.

_____ 3. Met the expectations of the audience by using appropriate language and style.

Structure

_____ 4. Began with a forecast of the main ideas and captivated the audience's interest by giving them an important reason to listen.

_____ 5. Chose an appropriate organizational structure; for example, moved from familiar to unfamiliar and simple to complex.

_____ 6. Used transitions, including internal summaries, to signal progress.

_____ 7. Concluded on a high note; reinforced major points; summarized key actions.

Support

_____ 8. Used a variety of supporting information, examples, and so forth, to increase the credibility and understanding of major points.

_____ 9. Used supporting material (both the content and format of evidence and illustrations) appropriate for the audience.

_____ 10. Used effective, simple visual aids to enhance comprehension and retention of the message.

Style in Oral Communication

_____ 11. Used notes to create a conversational style.

_____ 12. Presentation had obviously been well-rehearsed, including the use of visual aids, and so forth.

_____ 13. Conveyed controlled enthusiasm for the subject through the tone of voice, posture, and facial expressions.

_____ 14. Engaged the audience through effective eye contact, physical arrangement of the room, and appropriate gestures.

Style in Written Communication

_____ 15. Document was mechanically precise; that is, it contained no errors that detracted from the message.

_____ 16. Document was factually precise; that is, the content was accurate.

_____ 17. The choice of words communicated the message clearly and unambiguously.

_____ 18. The tone matched the topic and the audience (e.g., formality, emotion, directness).

_____ 19. Used the appropriate format for the type of correspondence.

Supplement: Questions and Answers

_____ 20. Handled questions and challenges thoughtfully, candidly, and assertively.

_____ 21. Responded to objections in an orderly manner; for example, restated the objection, restated your position, offered further support for your position, and explained the significance of your rebuttal.

_____ 22. Maintained control of the meeting by balancing the demands of specific individuals with the interests of the group and keeping the discussion focused on the issues.

SKILL *LEARNING*

- Planning and Conducting Interviews
- Specific Types of Organizational Interviews
- Summary and Behavioral Guidelines

SKILL *PRACTICE*

- Evaluating the New Employee-Orientation Program
- Performance Appraisal Interview with Chris Jakobsen
- Employment-Selection Interview at
  Smith Farley Insurance

Conducting
Interviews

SKILL DEVELOPMENT OBJECTIVES

- ADOPT GENERAL GUIDELINES FOR EFFECTIVE INTERVIEWS
- APPLY APPROPRIATE GUIDELINES FOR INFORMATION-GATHERING INTERVIEWS
- UTILIZE APPROPRIATE GUIDELINES FOR EMPLOYMENT-SELECTION INTERVIEWS
- IMPLEMENT APPROPRIATE GUIDELINES FOR PERFORMANCE-APPRAISAL INTERVIEWS

Planning and Conducting Interviews

Except for conversations, interviews are perhaps the most frequently occurring form of communication (Sincoff & Goyer, 1984); they certainly occur regularly in organizations. Individuals interview to obtain a position; they interview to gather information to perform their jobs; and managers interview subordinates to review their performance and provide counseling and coaching.

Interviews are so common they are often taken for granted. People view interviews as simply conversations during which information is gathered. While interviews are similar to conversations, there are important differences. An **interview** is a specialized form of communication conducted for a specific task-related purpose (Downs, Smeyak, & Martin, 1980; Lopez, 1975). Indeed, one reason why some managers perform poorly as interviewers is they treat this "purposeful communication" too casually, as though it were merely a conversation. As a result of poor planning and lack of attention to managing the interview process, they fail to accomplish their purpose and often alienate the interviewee in the process.

These outcomes are illustrated in the following counseling interview between Joe Van Orden, director of management services, and Kyle Isenbarger, a management consultant on his staff (DuBrin, 1981).

> JOE: Kyle, I have scheduled this meeting with you because I want to talk about certain aspects of your work. My comments are not all favorable.
>
> KYLE: Since you have formal authority over me, I guess I don't have much choice. Go ahead.
>
> JOE: I'm not a judge reading a verdict to you. I want your input.
>
> KYLE: But you called the meeting; go ahead with your complaints. Particularly any with foundation. I remember once when we were having lunch you told me you didn't like the fact I wore a brown suit with a blue shirt. I would put that in the category of unfounded.
>
> JOE: I'm glad you brought up appearance. I think you present a substandard impression to clients. A consultant is supposed to look sharp, particularly at the rates we charge clients. You often present the impression you cannot afford good clothing. Your pants are baggy. Your ties are unstylish and often food-stained.
>
> KYLE: The firm may charge those high rates, but the money I receive does not allow me to purchase fancy clothing. Besides, I have very little interest in trying to dazzle clients with my clothing. I have heard no complaints from them.
>
> JOE: Nevertheless, I think your appearance should be more businesslike. Now, let's talk about another concern. A routine audit of your expense account shows a practice I think is improper. You charged one client for a Thursday night dinner for three consecutive weeks, yet your airline ticket receipt shows you returned home at three in the afternoon each week. That kind of behavior is unprofessional. How do you explain your charges for these phantom dinners?
>
> KYLE: The flight ticket may say 3 P.M., but with our unpredictable weather, the flight could very well be delayed. If I eat at the airport, then my wife won't have to run the risk of preparing a dinner for me that goes to waste. Food is very expensive.
>
> JOE: But how can you eat dinner at 3 P.M. at the airport?
>
> KYLE: I consider any meal after one in the afternoon to be dinner.
>
> JOE: Okay for now. I want to comment on your reports to clients. They are much more careless than they should be. I know you are capable of more meticulous work. I saw an article you prepared for publication that was first-rate and professional. Yet on one report you misspelled the name of the client company. That's unacceptable.
>
> KYLE: A good secretary should have caught that mistake. Besides, I never claimed I was able to write perfect reports. There are only so many hours in the working day to spend on writing up reports.

Effective interviews don't just happen. Like other purposeful communication activities, interviews must be properly planned and executed. To help you become an effective interviewer, this supplement includes a series of guidelines, organized according to the schema shown in Figure B.1. First, we present broad guidelines for planning and conducting interviews in general. These guidelines are divided into two steps: planning the interview and conducting the interview. Following this discussion, we will give more specific guidelines for conducting specialized interviews with limited purposes: gathering information, selecting new employees, and reviewing subordinate performance.

PLANNING THE INTERVIEW

Establish the Purpose and Agenda

As is the case with any kind of planned communication event, you need to define clearly your purpose for holding the interview. In an interview, as in an oral presentation, ask yourself what it is you want to accomplish. Do you want to gather information? Persuade? Counsel? Evaluate? Not only do you need to consider what you want to accomplish in terms of the *content* of the interview, you must also consider the *relationship* you want to develop with the other participant. Consider who your interview partner is and how what you say will affect the already existing relationship. This resembles the process of adapting

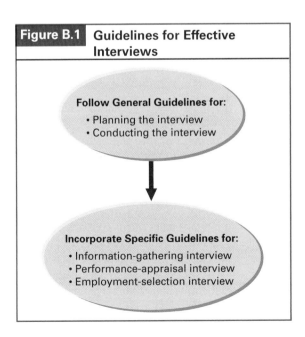

Figure B.1 Guidelines for Effective Interviews

Follow General Guidelines for:
• Planning the interview
• Conducting the interview

Incorporate Specific Guidelines for:
• Information-gathering interview
• Performance-appraisal interview
• Employment-selection interview

your message to your audience in an oral presentation but is somewhat easier since there is only one member in your interview "audience." Also consider the situation in which the interview will occur. Are participants under pressures of deadlines? Can you arrange not to be interrupted?

Once you've determined your purpose, develop an agenda. Consider what kinds of information you need to obtain with respect to your purpose. Based on this, write out a list of topics that need to be covered in the interview. While these topics do not have to be listed in any particular order, you may want to prioritize them.

Create Good Questions That Encourage Information Sharing

Questions arise out of your purpose and agenda and are the fundamental means by which you obtain information in an interview. Any interviewer can ask questions; only well-prepared interviewers ask effective questions—ones that elicit the information they need. Make sure the questions are worded clearly and they ask for the information you want. Adapting to your interviewee is critical. Phrase your questions in language the interviewee can understand and in ways that will enhance your relationship with that person.

Different types of questions can be used for different effects and different types of information-gathering purposes. **Open questions** such as, "How is your work going?" or "How has the new regulation affected department morale?" elicit general information. Use open questions when you want to let the interviewee talk without restriction. They allow interviewees freedom to discuss how they feel, what their priorities are, and how much they know about a topic. Thus, open questions are useful for developing rapport. Remembering the answers to open questions is a problem, particularly if the interviewee talks on and on. Open questions are also time-consuming, and using them too often makes it difficult for the interviewer to control the interview. However, if you are looking for broad, general information, ask open questions.

If, on the other hand, you need specific information, ask closed questions. **Closed questions** such as, "Where were you last employed?" or "Would you rather work on Project A or Project Z?" restrict the possible answers an interviewee can give. They are appropriate when you have limited time or want to clarify a point made in an answer to an open question. Table B.1 suggests when to use open or closed questions.

Table B.1 When to Use Open and Closed Questions

Use open questions when you want to:

- Discover the interviewee's priorities.

- Discover the interviewee's frame of reference.

- Let the interviewee talk through his or her opinions without constraints.

- Ascertain the depth of the interviewee's knowledge.

- Ascertain how articulate the interviewee is.

Use closed questions when you want to:

- Save time, energy, and money.

- Maintain control over the interview situation.

- Obtain very specific information from the interviewee.

- Encourage the interviewee to reconstruct a specific event.

- Encourage a shy person to talk.

- Avoid extensive explanations on the part of the interviewee.

- Clarify a point made in answer to an open question.

Source: *Adapted from Downs, Smeyak, & Martin, 1980.*

As you plan your questions, pay close attention to how the questions are worded. Often, an unprepared interviewer will ask questions that are difficult to answer or prevent open, honest answers. One example is the **double-barreled question**:

- ❏ If there's anything that would make you stay, what would it be?
- ❏ If you had no choice but to use this system, how would you use it productively?
- ❏ Why should we adopt this insurance plan when none of our competitors has adopted it?

Each of these questions assumes a condition that the interviewee may not agree with but then calls for the interviewee to support or defend the condition. The first question assumes the interviewee is looking for a reason to stay; the second assumes the system can be used productively; the third suggests something is wrong with the plan. Such questions may lead to hypothetical answers that don't reflect the interviewee's honest position.

Another potentially problematic question is the **false bipolar question**. A bipolar question offers the interviewee two choices: "Did you vote yes or no on the union contract?" This can be a legitimate and appropriate question. However, suppose you asked this question: "Do you approve or disapprove of overtime work?" Most people do not totally approve or disapprove of overtime work; yet this question forces interviewees to choose from limited, or false, options, neither of which likely represents their true stand on the issue. Thus, if you use bipolar questions, make sure the options you offer are the only two possible options; otherwise, you will obtain inaccurate information.

A final type of problematic question is the **leading question**, in which you let the interviewee know the answer you want to hear by how you phrase the question:

- ❏ Don't you think using this plan will alleviate the problems we've been having?
- ❏ Are you in favor of this policy like all your coworkers?
- ❏ Of course, you want the best for your family, don't you?

It would not take an astute interviewee very long to figure out what you wanted to hear, and so you are likely to get biased responses. Leading questions can be useful when a biased answer is intended and desired. For instance, the question "Of course you want the best for your family, don't you?" would be useful in a sales interview if the interviewer tries to persuade a potential buyer to buy a set of encyclopedias. However, if you do not realize you have asked a leading question, you will not know whether you are receiving a biased answer, which can create a serious problem. Table B.2 offers ways to reword these three types of badly constructed questions.

Structure the Interview Using Interviewing Aids

After determining the purpose and agenda, and after formulating your questions, the next step in preparing for an interview is to develop a structure. To do this, you need to think about three things: the interview guide, the questioning sequence, and transitions. The interview guide is an outline of the topics and subtopics you want to cover, usually with specific questions listed under each heading. In other words, it is the finalized version of the agenda. Alternative interview guide formats will be discussed later.

While you are constructing the interview guide, you will also need to be concerned with the sequence of questions; that is, how they will interconnect. The two most common types of question sequences are the **funnel sequence** and the **inverted funnel sequence**.

The funnel sequence begins with general questions and then moves toward increasingly specific questions. The inverted funnel sequence reverses this order,

Table B.2 Rewording Badly Constructed Questions

DOUBLE-BARRELED QUESTION	PROBLEM	BETTER QUESTION
1. If there's anything that would make you stay, what would it be?	The question ignores the reason behind the interviewee's decision and implies it can be changed.	Why do you want to leave our organization? (Let interviewee respond.) Is there anything I can do to change your mind?
2. If you had no choice but to use this system, how would you use it productively?	The question avoids an open analysis of the system and forces the interviewee to defend it.	What do you feel are the benefits of this system? (Let interviewee respond.) What do you feel are the disadvantages of this system?
3. Why should we adopt this insurance plan when none of our competitors has adopted it?	The question raises a suspicion something is wrong with the plan and urges the interviewee to put the suspicion to rest rather than to evaluate the plan.	Do you think we should adopt this insurance plan? (Let interviewee respond.) Do you think it offers us new benefits? (Let interviewee respond.) Have any of our competitors adopted it?

FALSE BIPOLAR QUESTION	PROBLEM	BETTER QUESTION
1. Do you prefer working with people or working alone?	The question assumes there are only two possible choices.	Do you work well with other people? (Can be followed with appropriate probe.)
2. Do you approve or disapprove of the union contract?	The question assumes there are only two ways to view the issue.	What are your feelings concerning the union contract?

LEADING QUESTION	PROBLEM	BETTER QUESTION
1. Don't you think using this plan will alleviate the problems we've been having?	The question identifies the expected answer, making it difficult for the interviewee to disagree.	Do you think this plan will be useful in alleviating the problems we've been having?
2. Are you in favor of this policy like all your coworkers?	The question places interviewee in the position of siding with the "right" side.	What is your attitude toward this policy?
3. Of course, you want the best for your family, don't you?	The question associates response with a desirable goal (getting the best for the family), making it difficult for the interviewee to say no.	This product offers you some real advantages. Could I take some of your time to tell you about them?

Table B.3	Funnel and Inverted Funnel Question Sequences

Funnel: From General to Specific

How do you feel about the new regulations concerning smoking in the building?

Are these regulations fair?

How are these regulations curtailing smoking among employees?

Inverted Funnel: From Specific to General

How are the new smoking regulations curtailing smoking among employees?

Do you think these regulations are fair?

In general, how do you feel about these new regulations?

Use the funnel sequence when:

• You want to discover the interviewee's frame of reference.

• You want to avoid leading the interviewee.

• You want to maximize your ability to probe issues.

• The interviewee is willing to talk about the issues.

Use the interverted funnel sequence when:

• You want to get at specific facts before general reactions.

• You want to motivate a reluctant interviewee.

• You want to jog the interviewee's memory.

Source: *Adapted from Downs et al., 1980.*

beginning with specific questions and moving toward more open questions toward the end. Table B.3 shows examples of these two sequences. Your choice of which sequence to use depends on what you want to accomplish in the interview. Table B.3 also summarizes when you should use each of these sequences, depending on your goals.

After establishing the sequence of your questions, you should consider what kinds of transitions you can use to help the interviewee follow along. The transitions in an interview perform the same function as transitions in an oral presentation: They help listeners maintain focus and keep them aware of where the speaker is in terms of the overall organization. Transitions are difficult to prepare ahead in unstructured interviews, yet a good interviewer will keep in mind transitions should be used when a topic change occurs. A simple statement such as, "I see what you're saying about that situation. Do you think you could help me with another issue?" allows you to move from one topic into the next. You may also use a brief summary of the interviewee's responses to wrap up one topic before moving to the next one.

Plan the Setting to Enhance Rapport

The interview location can have a major impact on the interview atmosphere and interview outcome. If you hold the interview in your office or an organizational meeting room, you will create a formal atmosphere. On the other hand, if you conduct the interview in a more neutral area, such as a restaurant, the climate will be more relaxed. The choice of setting depends on your goals for the interview. The most important point to remember about the setting is that, if at all possible, you should try to hold the interview in a setting that will be conducive to encouraging the kind of communication you seek.

Anticipate Problems and Prepare Responses

As you prepare for an interview, you should consider what kinds of problems you might encounter. Imagine how the interviewee might respond to what you have to ask, and prepare for his or her objections and questions. Consider the personality of the interviewee and how you might have to adapt to either draw the person out or to control his or her tendency to dominate. Anticipate how much time you will need to ask your questions and how much time your interviewee has to give you. Each interview will offer unique problems. If you can plan for some of these situations, you will be able to handle them better during the actual interview than if you had not considered them at all.

Table B.4 provides a checklist for helping prepare for an interview.

CONDUCTING THE INTERVIEW

Couple thorough preparation with sensitive implementation. Because an interview is an interpersonal communication situation, in this section we will first briefly review the concept of supportive communication as it applies to interviews. Then we will look at the three stages of the interview—the introduction, body, and conclusion—and discuss the functions of each. We will offer suggestions for developing the necessary skills to conduct an interview effectively. Finally, we will discuss ways of recording the interview information.

Establish and Maintain a Supportive Communication Climate

The climate of the interview refers to the tone of the interview and the general atmosphere in which the interview occurs. An interview, like any other interpersonal communication event, should be a supportive interaction, one in which participants feel free to communicate accurately. As the interviewer, you set the climate of the interview in the introduction when you begin to build rapport with the interviewee. In general, you should seek to build a comfortable, open climate, free of incongruence. Maintaining a supportive and productive climate requires you constantly analyze and adapt to the interaction as it occurs. When you sense the climate is no longer supportive, move away from the content level of the interview and address the relational level. Consider this excerpt from an information-gathering interview:

INTERVIEWER: Thanks for taking the time to speak with me today.

INTERVIEWEE: Oh, it's no problem at all. What can I do for you?

INTERVIEWER: Well, I was wondering if you could tell me a little about the incident that occurred on the shop floor last week. First, do you have any idea how it started?

INTERVIEWEE: No, not really. I was doing my job and then, all of a sudden, the two of them were at it.

INTERVIEWER: I see. You didn't hear them talking before they began to fight?

INTERVIEWEE: No. Like I said, it seemed to start out of the blue.

INTERVIEWER: Weren't you paying attention?

INTERVIEWEE: How was I to know they were going to fight?!

Table B.4	Interview Preparation Checklist
1. Have I determined my general purpose?
2. Have I written out my specific purposes and agenda?
a. Do I know exactly what I want to accomplish in terms of content?
b. Do I know exactly what I want to accomplish in terms of the relationship with the interviewee?
3. Do my questions all relate to my purposes and agenda?
4. Are my questions clearly worded in language the interviewee can understand?
5. Are my questions worded in an unbiased manner?
6. Have I chosen an appropriate interview structure for the situation?
7. Have I chosen an appropriate question sequence for the interview situation?
8. Have I developed potential transitions to be used in the interview?
9. Have I chosen a physical setting suited to the topics and the interviewee?
10. Have I planned ways to deal with problems that could develop during the interview?

By now, the questions are obviously beginning to irritate the interviewee. The interviewer has continued to probe an issue that the interviewee seems to think has already been covered sufficiently. The interviewer should move away from this one point and attempt to ease the interviewee's discomfort before continuing.

> INTERVIEWER: You're right. You really weren't in a position to anticipate this situation. Perhaps, though, you could describe to me what happened after the fight.

At this point, the interviewee may be hesitant to disclose fully. The interviewer may have to continue to strengthen relational support until the interviewee appears to be comfortable in answering the questions.

A supportive climate is not maintained solely by verbal behaviors. Listening analytically is also essential to maintaining the climate of an interview. If you do not show you are listening and responding to what the interviewee is saying, he or she will not want to continue talking with you. In general, you should listen for *comprehension* of the content of the interview, for *empathy* with the interviewee, and for *evaluation* of information and feelings (Stewart & Cash, 1985).

Introduce the Interview

Supportive communication begins immediately in the introduction, where you establish the tone and set the climate of the interview. You should greet the interviewee in such a way as to build positive rapport. The impressions created in the initial minutes of an interview are crucial to its success (Stewart & Cash, 1985). Therefore, you should try to convey as favorable an impression as possible. After the greeting, you need to motivate the interviewee to participate willingly in the interview. Some common ways of doing this are to ask for the interviewee's help or tell the interviewee why he or she was chosen as a source of information. Finally, the introduction should contain an orientation to the total interview. You should tell an interviewee: (1) the purpose of the interview, (2) how he or she will help meet that purpose, and (3) how the information obtained during the interview will be used. The introduction should end with a transition into the body of the interview. Using a transition statement, such as, "Now then, let me begin by asking . . . " or "Now that you understand what's going to happen during the next few minutes, let's move on to the questions" tells the interviewee the "real" interview is about to begin.

Conduct the Body of the Interview

Generally, the body of the interview will follow your interview guide, which is a predetermined sequence of questions. There are three types of guides: structured, semistructured, and unstructured. If the interview guide is structured, you will simply read the questions on the guide and record the interviewee's answers. A semistructured guide lists several recommended questions under each topic. The interviewer then selects the most appropriate questions for a specific candidate. A sample interview guide for a semistructured employment interview is shown in Table B.5.

If the interview guide is unstructured, then you will use the guide only as an agenda. For example, an unstructured interview guide for a termination interview might simply list a few general topics for discussion, for example, "What did he or she like and dislike about the work and the company?" "Why is he or she leaving?" "Any suggestions for improvement?" Particularly in an unstructured interview, an interviewee will need encouragement to answer your questions as fully as possible. In order to encourage complete answers, you will need to follow his or her initial responses with probing questions. Probing well depends directly on your ability to listen well and analyze the content and relational information the interviewee offers you. Probing questions are rarely planned ahead because you cannot predict how the interviewee will respond to your questions. You will want to probe when you feel that, for whatever reason, you are receiving an inadequate response to your question.

The kind of probing you do will depend on the responses given by your interviewee and the kind of information you are looking for. If you feel the response is superficial or inadequate due to lack of information, you should use an **elaboration probe**, such as:

- ❏ "Tell me more about that issue."
- ❏ "Why do you suppose it happened that way?"
- ❏ "Was there anything else going on at the time?"

If you need to clarify the information given by the interviewee, use a **clarification probe**, such as:

- ❏ "What does job satisfaction mean to you?"
- ❏ "You said you are unhappy with this policy. Can you tell me specifically what aspects make you feel this way?"
- ❏ "Earlier you mentioned you enjoyed working with people. Can you provide a specific example?"

Table B.5	Sample Interview Questions for an Employment Interview	
EDUCATION	**WORK EXPERIENCE**	**SELF-EVALUATION**
• What was there about your major that appealed to you?	• How did you obtain your current job?	• What do you know about our industry or company?
• What was your most rewarding experience in college?	• What duties occupy most of your time?	• What interests you about our product or service?
• What subjects were the most difficult for you to master? Why?	• What part of your work do you like the most and the least?	• What is your long-term career objective?
• If you were starting college all over again, what courses would you take?	• What has been your greatest frustration and your greatest joy?	• What are your greatest strengths and weaknesses?
• What difficulties did you experience in getting along with other students and faculty?	• What things about your supervisor did you like and dislike?	• What have you done that has demonstrated initiative and willingness to work hard?
• What did you learn from your extracurricular activities?	• What criticisms of your work have you received?	• What do you think determines a person's progress in a good company?
		• What are your plans for self-improvement during this year?
		• What are the three most important things in your life?

A **reflective probe** is also used when you want elaboration or clarification. It is nondirective in nature and generally mirrors or repeats some aspect of the answer the interviewee just gave you:

❏ "You think, then, this policy will work?"
❏ "Are you saying your supervisor doesn't offer the kind of supervision you need?"
❏ "Is it correct to assume you would be willing to relocate?"

If the interviewee does not answer your question, you may need to use a **repetition probe**. Simply paraphrase the question or repeat it verbatim. If you want the interviewee to keep on talking freely, use *silence* to encourage him or her to do so. Silence tends to communicate you expect more from the interviewee. Be careful not to wait too long, though; give an interviewee enough time to think but not enough time to become uncomfortable. Responses such as "I see," "Hmmmm," and "Okay, go on" are nondirective and nonevaluative ways of encouraging the interviewee to speak. Table B.6 summarizes these probes and when to use them.

The effective use of probing questions is perhaps the most important skill an interviewer can develop.

It is also the most difficult to develop. Too often, an interviewer leaves an interview and thinks about all the things that could have been discussed if only the topic had been followed up with appropriate probes. Or perhaps the interview was ineffective because the interviewer probed into irrelevant topics and thus spent too much time gathering relatively useless information. An effective interviewer needs to learn when to probe and when to stop. If you have planned appropriately, you will be aware of the issues you want to cover and at what depth. Follow your interviewee's cues as well as your agenda in determining when and how much to probe issues.

Conclude the Interview

The third stage of the interview is the conclusion. When you conclude an interview, you should accomplish four purposes. First, be sure you indicate explicitly the interview is about to end. Say something such as, "Well, that's all the questions I have" or "You've been very helpful." This helps the interviewee understand if he or she has any questions, they should be asked now. Second, try to summarize the information you obtained. This serves as a check on the accuracy of the information you have just obtained: the interviewee can correct

Table B.6	**Types of Probes and When to Use Them**

• Use an *elaboration* probe when an answer seems superficial or inadequate in some way:
INTERVIEWER: How have you been able to adapt to your new job responsibilities?
INTERVIEWEE: Well, each day I find myself challenged by something new.
INTERVIEWER: Why don't you tell me more about a specific challenge.
• Use a *clarification* probe when you need to clarify information given by the interviewee:
INTERVIEWER: How do you feel about working overtime?
INTERVIEWEE: Well, it's okay some of the time.
INTERVIEWER: Can you tell me specifically when you would be willing to work overtime?
• Use a *reflective* probe when you want elaboration or clarification but want to obtain it in a nondirective manner:
INTERVIEWER: So how are you adapting to your new responsibilities?
INTERVIEWEE: Well, each day I find myself challenged by something new.
INTERVIEWER: Really? Something new each day?
• Use a *repetition* probe when the interviewee doesn't answer your question:
INTERVIEWER: What do you believe to be the most difficult aspect of your job?
INTERVIEWEE: Well, that's not an easy question. My supervisor says I have problems with meeting productivity quotas.
INTERVIEWER: But what do *you* believe to be the most difficult aspect of your job?
• Use *silence* when you want to encourage the interviewee to continue talking:
INTERVIEWER: Do you think we should continue our policy concerning absenteeism?
INTERVIEWEE: Yes, I do.
INTERVIEWER: (pauses for 10 seconds)
INTERVIEWEE: Yes, I think it's good policy because . . .

your impressions if they seem to be in error. Third, let the interviewee know what's going to happen next: Will you need to meet again? Will you make a report? Finally, make sure you continue to build the relationship by expressing appreciation for his or her time and thoughtful responses.

Record the Information

While you may have planned the interview perfectly and asked all the right questions and probes, if you cannot remember accurately the information obtained, the interview cannot be considered a success. After all, you prepared and conducted the interview to get information, not simply because you wanted to have a conversation with someone. The first point you need to recognize concerning remembering interview information is simple: Memory alone will not work. Relying solely on memory leaves open the possibility of forgetting the information or adjusting it to meet your own

needs. Even if you summarize the interview as soon as it is over, you run the risk of reinterpreting the information in ways the interviewee did not mean. However, if summarizing the interview is your preferred choice, make sure you write your summary immediately after the interview. Additionally, you might want to use your interview guide as a basis for summarizing: Review your questions and write out the interviewee's answers.

A better way to remember information is to take notes during the interview. Make sure you advise the interviewee you will take notes. Take notes as unobtrusively as possible so as not to make the interviewee uncomfortable. Learn how to write notes while still maintaining eye contact with the interviewee. This is a difficult skill to master, but it can be done; journalists use this skill frequently with great success. Develop your own shorthand so you are, in fact, taking notes and not recording the interview verbatim. If you need a verbatim account of the interview, then you should use a tape recorder. First ask the interviewee if he or she minds being tape-recorded. Keep the recorder out of sight if possible so neither you nor the interviewee feels threatened by it. One final way to help you remember the interview information is to have a second interviewer participate in the interview. After the interview, your discussion will function as a check on each other's memory of what occurred.

Specific Types of Organizational Interviews

The information presented in the preceding sections will help you plan and conduct almost any type of interview. However, there are some special types to plan and consider. In this section, we will briefly describe the most common types of organizational interviews and apply the general principles presented earlier to specific issues and circumstances.

INFORMATION-GATHERING INTERVIEWS

The information-gathering interview is the one most frequently held in organizations and is also the one that is most like a conversation. You might conduct this type of interview when you need to gather facts about an issue or to help in a problem-solving situation. If you treat these fact-finding missions as interviews, you will be in a better position to gather accurate, useful information because you will take the time to plan ahead. Clearly, you need to follow the planning steps discussed above: decide on a general purpose and create an agenda; develop questions; develop the structure of the interview; plan the setting; and anticipate problems.

Furthermore, the information-gathering interview is the only interview for which you can choose the expert. In other organizational interviews, such as the selection interview or the performance-appraisal interview, you have little choice of whom you will see. However, when you want to gather information about some topic or problem, you choose the interviewee. This choice is based on two factors: who *can* give you the information you need and who is *willing* to give you this information (Stano & Reinsch, 1982). Too often, interviewers will talk to interviewees who are willing but who do not have the necessary information. For instance, suppose your organization is considering the implementation of a flextime work schedule and you have been assigned to write a feasibility report. While you may get some interesting opinions from a colleague on the advantages of such a schedule, it would be better if you could find an expert on flextime for your interview. On the other hand, if you wanted to find out how well received such a change would be, then you would talk to colleagues rather than an expert.

The nature of an information-gathering interview is such that the interviewee may not realize he or she is being interviewed. Thus, it may be difficult to keep the interviewee on track and responsive to your questions. More so than in any other interview, you as the interviewer must remain flexible and adaptive to your interviewee. Choose a physical setting that will encourage talk and provide an appropriate climate. The funnel sequence works well in information-gathering interviews because of its ability to immediately elicit general information and the interviewee's feelings on the subject. However, the inverted funnel may be a better choice if you will be interviewing a number of people on the same topic and you need to maintain consistency in evaluating their responses.

EMPLOYMENT-SELECTION INTERVIEWS

The employment interview is used to help current organizational members choose new members. During the selection interview, the interviewer tries to assess whether job candidates will fit into the organization and if they have the appropriate skills for the job. In addition, the interviewer often tries to sell the organization itself to the interviewee. Questions asked during the selection interview address four general topics: prior work experience, education and training, personality characteristics, and related activities and interests. The nature of the job and the interviewee will dictate which topics will be emphasized.

As Table B.7 shows, there are three sources of information you should review when creating questions for a selection interview:

Table B.7	**Formulating Selection Interview Questions**

- ❑ Use the *job description* to formulate questions concerning task-related skills and personality characteristics.

- ❑ Use the selection interview *evaluation form* to formulate questions that can help you assess the applicant on the basis of your organization's general criteria for employees.

- ❑ Use the applicant's *résumé* and *cover letter* to formulate questions concerning the applicant's specific skills and prior work experience.

1. Review the *job description* to assess the technical skills and experience needed by the person. Also review the job environment to determine the desirable personal qualities required. Create your questions based on these reviews; avoid asking merely generic questions.

2. Look at the *evaluation form* your company uses to assess prospective employees. Make sure some of your questions deal with the topics on this evaluation form. For instance, if one of the topics on this form is communication skills, create questions that specifically address this subject. In this case, you may want to ask the applicant about his or her writing skills and how he or she has used them in the past.

3. One final piece of information you should use for developing questions for a selection interview is the applicant's *résumé* and *cover letter*. Read these documents carefully. If there are gaps in time between jobs, ask the applicant about them. If the information on the résumé is too general, develop questions to get at the specifics. Remember most people create résumés with a very specific goal in mind: to obtain an interview. Therefore, the information tends to be a summary of all the good aspects of that person's career to date. Additionally, all information tends to be written in glowing language. Be prepared to reach beyond this language to obtain clarifying information. For example, suppose you came across this line in a cover letter: "I've had years of experience in leadership positions." Clearly, you would want to ask this applicant for more specific information: "How many years?" "What kinds of positions were these?" "What were your specific leadership responsibilities?"

In constructing interview questions, be sure to include some that focus on specific experiences. For instance, you might want to ask something such as, "Can you tell me about a time when you successfully met a goal you set?" The interviewee may be reluctant to be specific, but you should probe until the interviewee offers you useful, specific, behavioral information.

Why is behavioral information so important? Many experts believe the best way to assess future job performance is to assess past behavior: Past behavior predicts future performance. If you can find out how the interviewee behaved in real situations in the past that are similar to those he or she is likely to face in

your organization, you can determine if his or her style will fit into your organization and work well with other members.

Take care that you ask a balanced series of questions: Ask for negative information as well as positive. This will help you obtain a well-rounded picture of the interviewee and also expose hidden bias. For instance, you might want to follow the positive question with something like: "Well, now tell me about a time when you failed to meet a goal you set." Again, make sure the person gives you specific behavioral information.

In conclusion, remember your primary purpose in a selection interview is to find a person who is qualified for a particular opening in your organization. Table B.8 details a six-step process (using the acronym PEOPLE) used by a major firm to help interviewers accomplish this purpose. It follows the general interviewing model outlined in the first half of this supplement.

PERFORMANCE-APPRAISAL INTERVIEWS

The performance-appraisal interview is usually part of a larger professional appraisal system. The goal of this system is to evaluate a member of an organization and often to provide feedback to a subordinate concerning ways to improve job performance. While every organization differs in the specifics of carrying out the performance-appraisal system, there are some common aspects.

Generally, prior to the performance-appraisal interview, written evaluations are prepared by the subordinate, the superior, or both people. There are any number of types of evaluation forms, including an essay form, on which the manager writes a description of the subordinate's work, with no real set format; *forced-choice ratings*, in which the manager chooses a statement from many which describes the subordinate in one area; or a *graphic rating scale*, in which the manager rates the subordinate on various areas on a 1–7 numerical scale. In most cases, though, you will be asked to back up your assessment of the subordinate with specific and concrete information. For instance, if you are using a graphic rating scale and indicate the employee performed unsatisfactorily, you should write out in objective terms why you have made this assessment. The subordinate has a right to know, and you have the responsibility to back up your decisions with evidence.

It is the responsibility of the interviewer to prepare the structure of the performance-appraisal interview. The interviewer should set a definite time and place for the

Table B.8	Selection Interview Format (PEOPLE-Oriented Process)

P = Prepare

1. Review application, résumé, transcripts, and other background information.

2. Prepare both general and individual-specific questions.

3. Prepare suitable physical arrangements.

E = Establish Rapport

1. Try to make applicant comfortable.

2. Convey genuine interest.

3. Communicate supportive attitude with voice and manner.

O = Obtain Information

1. Ask questions.

2. Probe.

3. Listen carefully.

4. Observe the person (dress, mannerisms, body language).

P = Provide Information

1. Describe current and future job opportunities.

2. Sell positive features of firm.

3. Respond to applicant's questions.

L = Lead to Close

1. Clarify responses.

2. Provide opportunity for final applicant input.

3. Explain what happens next.

E = Evaluate

1. Assess match between technical qualifications and job requirements.

2. Judge personal qualities (leadership, maturity, team orientation).

3. Make a recommendation.

interview, considering the effects these choices will have on the interview and the interviewee. The interviewer must decide on the general purpose of the interview and the agenda. Common topics that are often brought up in performance-appraisal interviews include job knowledge, job performance, job goals, career goals and opportunities, and interpersonal skills.

The difficult aspect of the performance-appraisal interview is that people tend to shy away from evaluating others or being evaluated in face-to-face situations. Both participants in a performance-appraisal interview may be apprehensive. As the interviewer, you need to reassure the interviewee that you are conducting the performance-appraisal interview as a means of assisting in the interviewee's development. Keep in mind that people do not like to be criticized, and balance your criticisms with reassurances and commendations.

In conducting a performance-appraisal interview, you must decide beforehand on your objectives. The objectives should then dictate the form of the interview. In general, three types of appraisal interviews seek to meet specific objectives (Maier, 1958), and a fourth type can be used to meet multiple objectives (Beer, 1987). These interview types are summarized in Table B.9.

The first type of appraisal interview is called the *tell-and-sell* interview. This approach is evaluative in nature. First, you *tell* the subordinate how you have

Table B.9	Types of Performance-Appraisal Interviews
Tell-and-Sell Interview	
Used for purely evaluative purposes. Manager tells the employee the evaluation and then persuades the employee to follow recommendations for improvement.	
Tell-and-Listen Interview	
Used for purely evaluative purposes. Manager tells the employee the evaluation and then listens to the employee's reactions to the evaluation in a nonjudgmental manner.	
Problem-Solving Interview	
Used for employee-development purposes. Manager does not offer evaluation but lets employee decide his or her weak areas and works with employee to develop plan for improvement.	
Mixed-Model Interview	
Used for both evaluative and development purposes. Manager begins interview with problem-solving session and concludes with a more directive tell-and-sell approach.	

evaluated him or her, and then you *sell* the subordinate on the ways you have chosen to improve his or her performance. This type of interview should be used when you must be very clear about your expectations. This format is also effective with young employees who find it difficult to evaluate themselves, with very loyal employees or those who strongly identify with the organization or the appraiser, and with employees who do not want to have a say in how to develop their job and role in the organization (Downs et al., 1980).

If, however, you want to let the subordinate respond to your evaluation, you would use the *tell-and-listen* appraisal format. In this interview, you first *tell* the employee your evaluation; then you *listen* to his or her reactions without displaying any agreement or disagreement. The objective of this interview is evaluative, but you also want to hear the subordinate's viewpoints and work with the subordinate to help him or her accept your evaluation. Active listening directed at helping the subordinate work through his or her feelings about the evaluation and past performance will help you successfully complete a tell-and-listen appraisal. This type of interview works best with people who have a high need to participate in their jobs, with interviewees who are relatively close in status to the interviewer, and with subordinates who are highly educated (Downs et al., 1980).

The third general type of performance appraisal is the *problem-solving* interview. In this interview, evaluating the person is no longer the goal. Rather, the appraiser's role is to help the employee develop a plan for improving his or her performance. The performance deficiencies are determined by the subordinate, not the supervisor. Your goal as the interviewer is to avoid judgments and evaluations; rather, you offer suggestions for solutions to the problems defined by the interviewee. You form a partnership with the subordinate to solve the problems he or she brings up.

Finally, if your objectives are to both perform an evaluation and offer developmental coaching, you could choose to use a *mixed-model* interview (Beer, 1987). In this type of appraisal interview, you begin with a problem-solving framework and end the interview with a more directive tell-and-sell approach. In this way, you can both help a subordinate meet the development goals as well as offer your own evaluation and plan for development.

No matter which type of interview you choose, a performance-appraisal interview should contain all the elements of a general interview: build rapport and orient the interviewee to the subject; conduct the body of the interview in a supportive manner; conclude by specifying what is going to happen. Additionally, the performance-appraisal interview generally includes a discussion of a specific plan for improvement or change.

Summary and Behavioral Guidelines

While many people consider interviewing a process that just happens, we have argued that effective interviewing requires planning and thought. The steps shown in Figure B.1 provide a framework for enhancing your interviewing skills. The first step, thorough preparation, is essential for a successful interview. Planning involves deciding on your purposes, questions, structure, setting, and responses to anticipated problems. During the actual interview, work toward establishing and maintaining a supportive and productive climate. Keep in mind every interview should have an introduction, body, and conclusion and you need to develop ways to record the information you obtain during the interview.

There are a variety of organizational interviews, but the most common are the information-gathering interview, the employment-selection interview, and the performance-appraisal interview. Each of these interviews has very different objectives and specific means to reach them. Be flexible in how you conduct these interviews. As in any communication activity, you should adapt to the situation, your personality, and the person with whom you are conversing.

Interviewing is a vital management skill. When done well, an interview can provide you with information not otherwise available. This information can then better inform the decisions you make as you act out your role in the organization.

Following are general behavioral guidelines for planning and conducting interviews. Specific guidelines for specialized interviews are incorporated into the Observer's Feedback Forms in the Skill Practice exercises.

Planning the Interview

1. Specify your purposes and plan an agenda.
   - ❑ Determine your general purpose: to gather information, persuade, discipline, or evaluate.
   - ❑ Compose an agenda, prioritizing all topics.
2. Formulate questions.
   - ❑ Determine the type of questions (closed or open) that are consistent with the objectives.
   - ❑ Write specific questions for each topic on the agenda.
   - ❑ Use appropriate language in your questions.
   - ❑ Avoid biased or leading questions.
3. Develop the interview guide.
   - ❑ Select the appropriate format: structured, semistructured, or unstructured.
   - ❑ Use either the funnel or inverted funnel question sequence.
   - ❑ Formulate transition statements between topics.
4. Select a setting that is consistent with your objectives.
5. Identify potential complications that might occur during the interview and develop contingency plans.

Conducting the Interview

6. Establish and maintain a supportive climate.
   - ❑ Greet interviewee and initiate a brief social conversation.
   - ❑ Foster a positive communications climate by constant analysis of, and adaptation to, the interview process.
   - ❑ Use effective listening skills and nonverbal language (eye contact, posture, and gestures) to foster cooperation.
7. Introduce the interview.
   - ❑ State the purpose of the interview.
   - ❑ Clarify interviewee's and interviewer's roles.
   - ❑ Specify the time frame of the interview.
   - ❑ Indicate how the information will be used.
   - ❑ Use a transition to signal the beginning of the interview.
8. Conduct the interview.
   - ❑ Use the interview guide to manage the flow of the interview.
   - ❑ Use probing questions when elaboration or clarification are required.
   - ❑ Be flexible and adapt to the flow of the interview.
9. Conclude the interview.
   - ❑ Signal the interview is about to end.
   - ❑ Summarize the information you have collected.
   - ❑ Clarify details or technical information.
   - ❑ Review what will happen as a result of the interview.
   - ❑ Strengthen the relationship by expressing appreciation.
10. Record the interview content, using the appropriate format.
    - ❑ Write a summary immediately after the interview.
    - ❑ Take notes during the interview (sustaining eye contact).
    - ❑ Use a tape recorder (with the interviewee's permission).
    - ❑ Use a second interviewer to improve your recall.

EXERCISES FOR CONDUCTING SPECIAL-PURPOSE INTERVIEWS

Evaluating the New Employee-Orientation Program

You work for a high-tech electronics firm that was recently purchased by a large, multibusiness conglomerate. Your company produces components for highly sophisticated communications equipment used by the government. This is an exciting, but somewhat confusing, period in the company's history. The new parent company, BETA Products, is known as a Japanese-like firm. It emphasizes high productivity, along with employee commitment and loyalty.

BETA is sending a human resources management team to inspect your organization in two weeks. In advance, they have sent a list of programs they want to review, including your new employee-orientation program. Your boss, the vice president of human resources, has given you the assignment of preparing a 30-minute briefing on this program to the BETA task force. Specifically, she has asked you to interview representatives of various groups in your organization to determine their perceptions of the program's merits and shortcomings.

Currently, when a new employee enters your organization, he or she goes through an extensive orientation session. During this session, the new employee meets with a member of the Human Resources Department to learn about company policies and procedures and receive the Employee's Handbook. This session can last from two to three hours, depending on the participants. At the end of the session, the new employee is assigned a mentor, a member of the new employees department who has been with the organization for at least one year. The role of the mentor is to help the new employee become familiar with his or her new job and coworkers. The mentor is expected to meet with the new employee on a semiregular basis for at least six months. The relationship can continue if both parties agree. This orientation program has been used for about three years but has never been formally evaluated.

Assignment

To complete this assignment, you have scheduled interviews with several department heads, mentors, and current trainees. Prepare the interview you would conduct with the person from whom you are assigned to gather information about the orientation program. Before beginning this task, review the behavioral guidelines for planning an effective interview at the end of the Skill Learning section. You should also consult Tables B.1 through B.3, and Table B.6. In small groups, compare your questions with others. What did you leave out? What questions need to be reworded? What types of probes may be needed? After this discussion, split up into triads and take turns serving as the interviewer, interviewee, and observer. Do not look at the following role descriptions while planning this exercise. An observer will give feedback using the Observer's Feedback Form as a guide.

Role Descriptions for Interviewees
Trainee

You've just found out you are going to be interviewed on the mentor program with which you've been involved for three months. You've been quite happy with the program and would like to see it continued; in fact, someday, you want to be a mentor to new employees.

Many of your friends have pointed out you have a tendency to talk too fast, talk a lot, and tend to dominate a conversation. You realize when you get nervous or involved in an issue, you do talk a lot. You are certainly nervous about this interview because you are very involved in the program and you've heard through the grapevine the program might be cut. You feel that would be terrible. You really want to let the interviewer know how much you've learned from your mentor and the whole orientation program. What you have to say is important, and you want to make sure the interviewer hears all the good things you have to say about the program.

You are particularly positive about the program because it contrasts with your experience from your former job. In that organization, you were merely given a cursory overview of the company benefits through a videotape presentation. Furthermore, because there was no standardized mentoring program, new employees were left to fend for themselves. They were given no clear picture of what the company expected of them, no encouragement, and no sense of involvement in a group effort. As a result, a great deal of confusion and misunderstanding resulted. Here, in contrast, you have appreciated being able to get answers to your questions from one person. Overall, you feel as though this approach enabled you to become proficient in your job very quickly.

Department Head

You've just found out you are going to be interviewed on the mentor program, and it couldn't have come at a worse time. You've just lost one of your best employees, and you have been scrambling to try to find a replacement. You're really not interested in spending time to think about this interview or participate in it. You'd rather use the time on employment interviews to find a new assistant.

In fact, you tend to be uncomfortable in interviews of any kind. Because you tend to be shy, this kind of one-on-one formal conversation always makes you feel uncomfortable. You don't mind it so much when you are the interviewer—at least then you have some control over the situation. But you don't feel you've ever been a really good interviewee. The direct questions always make you feel as if you are on trial; as a result, you withdraw and appear to be uncooperative, even defensive.

You think the interviewer should be talking to people more directly involved in the program. You really don't have much to do with it anyway, except for matching up people. The program seems to work okay, but no doubt trainees would learn just as quickly if they sought out their own mentors. You know many of your staff members feel the program is worthwhile, so you'll back it up, albeit reluctantly. However, you would much rather write an evaluation of the program than have to talk about it to a relative stranger.

Mentor

You've just found out you are going to be interviewed on the mentor program, a program with which you've been involved for six months. When you first became a mentor, you were excited about the possibilities. Now, however, experience has shown the program is a waste of time. Too often, the trainees use their mentors as a crutch, both at work and in their social lives. The program inspires a dependency you find counterproductive and time wasting.

You've found yourself in the position of practically taking over trainees' jobs because they got used to relying on your expertise. You've thought this might simply be a result of your own personality—too willing to help, perhaps—but you've also noticed this behavior in other mentors and trainees.

Furthermore, you haven't noticed any significant difference in productivity between people who have gone through the program and people who haven't. In fact, because of the development of social relationships, your feeling is that productivity has probably declined: there is too much gossip and goofing off and not enough concentration on tasks.

You think the company ought to abandon the program. While a brief orientation might be useful to new hires, you no longer can justify the amount of time you put into the program, given the results. Even this evaluation of the program is taking up your valuable time.

Observer's Feedback Form

RATING

1 = Low
5 = High

Introduction

1. Did interviewer

_____ use a friendly greeting?

_____ begin to build rapport?

_____ state purpose?

_____ orient interviewee?

_____ refer to taking notes or recording interview?

Body

2. Did interviewer

_____ use appropriate question sequence?

_____ use a variety of question types?

_____ use internal summaries and transitions?

_____ respond to interviewee with good secondary questions (probes)?

_____ use silence when appropriate?

_____ maintain rapport with interviewee?

_____ handle problematic interviewee well?

Closing

3. Did interviewer

_____ sum up?

_____ maintain/encourage good interpersonal relationship?

_____ indicate what would happen with information?

_____ set up another meeting, if appropriate?

_____ thank interviewee?

Nonverbals

4. Did interviewer

_____ wear appropriate clothing?

_____ maintain eye contact with interviewee?

_____ use purposeful gestures?

_____ use appropriate tone of voice?

_____ maintain good posture?

_____ look enthusiastic and interested in what interviewee had to say?

	take notes inconspicuously?
_____	avoid verbal pauses such as uh, uhm, and so forth?

Comments:

Performance-Appraisal Interview with Chris Jakobsen

Background Information for Pat Ginelli

You are vice president of the Commercial Loan Division at Firstbank, a medium-sized, state-licensed bank. You have been with Firstbank for four years and have conducted a number of performance-appraisal interviews. During your tenure, you have increased your division's profits by 45 percent. Your goal is to increase this level by another 15 percent before the end of next year. In order to do so, you need to have aggressive, dynamic, and dedicated loan officers working for you.

Chris Jakobsen has been with Firstbank for three years. This will be your first review of Chris's performance because he was transferred to your department five months ago to fill a loan officer position vacated by Helen Smith, who had worked in the Personal Loan Division. You agreed to the transfer after reviewing Chris's credentials and past performance appraisal forms. Chris appeared to be qualified for the position, and the performance appraisal reports indicated that Chris's work was rated from above average to outstanding.

Unfortunately, you have been extremely disappointed with Chris's performance in your department. For a longtime bank employee, he seems surprisingly unfamiliar with standard procedures and protocol. Last week, he told a customer there shouldn't be any problem getting approval for her loan application. She wanted to open a boutique in a renovated building downtown. However, the review committee turned it down because the building hadn't met code yet.

There are several other deficiencies in Chris's performance. In contrast to Helen, Chris seems inattentive to detail. He has frequently left out important information on loan applications, causing needless delays in processing. Furthermore, he doesn't seem to be able to keep up with the workload. It takes him twice as long as it should to handle routine paperwork, and he seems totally ill at ease with your department's computerized information system. Due to a favorable investment environment and the recent opening of a local industrial park, your group's workload is up 50 percent from a year ago. You simply can't tolerate having to take extra time to make sure Chris is doing things right the first time.

In Chris's favor, he is extremely punctual and his attendance has been perfect. He also keeps a very neat work area and takes pride in his own appearance. Furthermore, as a native of the community and an active civic leader, he has very good contacts in the business community. It is also clear that everyone likes Chris. He is jovial and easygoing. He has a quick wit that livens up even the most routine and dull staff meeting. He loves treating coworkers during happy hour after work. Unfortunately, he sometimes loses perspective and gets carried away. Indeed, you've wondered at times how this free spirit ended up in a bank job. Certainly his attitude runs counter to your more formal and reserved personality, but it's hard to deny he has charm and class.

In general, Chris seems to have plenty of potential, but at best his current work performance is only average (an "expected" rating on your company's form). He just hasn't applied himself to his new position. You wonder if this is the right work for him or if perhaps he hasn't had adequate training. You spent some time orienting Chris to the group and assigned Jim, a veteran of the department, to act as his mentor. But, in retrospect, the local business boom has made it difficult for you and Jim to help Chris learn the ropes. Your days seem to be filled up with meetings with local investors and city planners. Still, it bugs you that he never asks questions. If he needs help with the technical aspects of the job, why doesn't he ever ask for assistance?

You have scheduled the interview with Chris for later in the day in your office. You know your review will make him very unhappy and probably put him on the defensive. He obviously has high aspirations for advancing in the bank and has received pretty positive feedback in the past. You've got to figure out some way to get him to improve. Your department is short-handed as it is, and everyone must contribute his or her share.

As you contemplate the unpleasant task ahead, you reflect, "Boy, I certainly miss Helen. I never had to have this type of conversation with her."

Assignment for Pat Ginelli

In preparation for this interview, complete a draft of the performance evaluation form in Exhibit 1 (the form is located after Chris's assignment). In keeping with standard practice, you have given a blank copy of the form to Chris and asked him to do a self-evaluation. He will bring his completed form to the interview.

After you have completed your draft, identify the type of performance-appraisal interview you feel is most appropriate for this situation (see Table B.9). Also, review the behavioral guidelines at the end of the Skill Learning section. Then formulate a series of questions consistent with your overall strategy. Finally, anticipate questions and objections Chris might initiate and prepare responses. Compare your plans in small groups and make revisions. Use the Interview Checklist in Table B.4 to guide your discussion.

Upon completion of your small-group discussion, prepare to conduct the interview with Chris. Do not look at the background information for Chris's role prior to the interview. An observer will use the Observer's Feedback Form to give you feedback.

Background Information for Chris Jakobsen

You have been with Firstbank, a medium-sized, state-licensed bank, for three years. For most of that time, you worked in the Personal Loan Division as a loan officer. You liked your job, your clients, and the people with whom you worked. You had hoped your first move at Firstbank would be a promotion within the Personal Loan Division. However, five months ago, you were transferred to the Commercial Loan Division to replace a loan officer who had worked in that position for 10 years. You did not really want to transfer, but you realized the move would, in fact, put you in a better position for the next upward move. Your former supervisor indicated you would not have to stay in this position very long if you kept receiving good ratings on your performance appraisal forms, and you have always received outstanding or above-average ratings. He argued you really needed to gain exposure to other departments in the bank as well as to other managers. Your new boss, Pat Ginelli, is a real rising star in the bank.

You expect your new supervisor, Pat, is going to be pretty tough on you. You feel frustrated and upset because you don't think there has been any change in your effort or commitment. Since you have been in the department, Pat's attitude toward you has seemed very distant and formal. You know Pat thinks the person you replaced was an excellent worker who contributed greatly to Pat's goal of achieving a 15 percent increase in profits this year. But certainly she doesn't expect you to immediately pick up where a 10-year veteran left off.

Then there's the problem of training. She promised to give you a thorough orientation when you arrived, but instead you were shunted off to Jim. He seemed sincere and interested in helping out, and he told you to come and ask questions whenever you needed help. However, when you asked about the department's loan-application procedure, he made you feel like an idiot for asking such a basic question, and you've never gone back. Furthermore, Pat always seems to be in meetings. You realize she is bringing in important business for the bank, so you feel it would be inappropriate to distract her with your basic questions.

This lack of assistance has caused you to make some mistakes. These have primarily been due to the change in procedures between the Personal and Commercial Loan departments. You had much more autonomy and authority over there, probably because the loans were much smaller. In addition, there are many more government regulations to worry about over here. Besides, you really miss the close contact with people that was built into your old job. That's why you took your first job in the bank. You have always been a very people-oriented person and received great satisfaction from helping them. Now, you just seem to be buried in paperwork and committee meetings. Some days, you regret accepting the offer to transfer. You're not sure this stepping-stone to advancement is worth the lost enjoyment you received in your former position.

Assignment for Chris Jakobsen

Your interview with Pat is scheduled for her office. In preparation for the interview, Pat has asked you to complete a copy of the performance-appraisal form as a self-evaluation. Prior to the interview, complete the form in Exhibit 1. Do not review the background information for Pat's role.

Exhibit 1 Interview with Chris Jakobsen

Employee Performance Appraisal

DATA COMPLETED

NAME Chris Jakobsen
DATE OF BIRTH 6/22/65
YEARS OF EMPLOYMENT 3
OFFICE LOCATION BRANCH 4 DEPARTMENTAL 9
DEPARTMENT Commercial

PRESENT JOB TITLE Loan Officer
CONVERSION CODE 32
YEARS IN PRESENT POSITION 6 months
SOC. SEC. NO. 555–33–9999
EDUCATION B.A.—Business

Select the statement under each of the following categories that best describes the individual.

Quality of Work

General excellence of output with consideration to accuracy—thoroughness—dependability—without close supervision.

_____ Exceptionally high quality. Consistently accurate, precise, quick to detect errors in own and others' work.

_____ Work sometimes superior and usually accurate. Negligible amount needs to be redone. Work regularly meets standards.

_____ A careful worker. A small amount of work needs to be redone. Corrections made in reasonable time. Usually meets normal standards.

_____ Work frequently below acceptable quality. Inclined to be careless. Moderate amount of work needs to be redone. Excessive time to correct.

PRACTICE

_____ Work often almost worthless. Seldom meets normal standards. Excessive amount needs to be redone.

Quantity of Work

Consider the amount of useful work over the period of time since the last appraisal. Compare the output of work to the standard you have set for the job.

_____ Output consistently exceeds standards. Unusually fast worker. Exceptional amount of output.

_____ Maintains a high rate of production. Frequently exceeds standards. More than normal effort.

_____ Output is regular. Meets standards consistently. Works at steady average speed.

_____ Frequently turns out less-than-normal amount of work. A low producer.

_____ A consistently low producer. Excessively slow worker. Unacceptable output.

Cooperation

Consider the employee's attitude toward the work, the employee's coworkers, and supervisors. Does the employee appreciate the need to understand and help solve problems with others?

_____ Always congenial and cooperative. Enthusiastic and cheerfully helpful in emergencies. Well-liked by associates.

_____ Cooperates well. Understands and complies with all rules. Usually demonstrates a good attitude. Liked by associates.

_____ Usually courteous and cooperative. Follows orders but at times needs reminding. Gets along well with associates.

_____ Does only what is specifically requested. Sometimes complains about following instructions. Reluctant to help others.

_____ Unfriendly and uncooperative. Refuses to help others.

Knowledge of the Job

The degree to which the employee has learned and understands the various procedures of the job and their objectives.

_____ Exceptional understanding of all phases. Demonstrates unusual desire to acquire information.

_____ Thorough knowledge in most phases. Has interest and potential toward personal growth.

_____ Adequate knowledge for normal performance. Will not voluntarily seek development.

_____ Insufficient knowledge of job. Resists criticism and instruction.

_____ No comprehension of the requirements of job.

Dependability

The reliability of the employee in performing assigned tasks accurately and within the allotted time.

_____ Exceptional. Can be left on own and will establish priorities to meet deadlines.

_____ Very reliable. Minimal supervision required to complete assignments.

_____ Dependable in most assignments. Normal supervision required. A profitable worker.

_____ Needs frequent follow-up. Excessive prodding necessary.

_____ Chronic procrastinator. Control required is out of all proportion.

Attendance and Punctuality

Consider the employee's record, reliability, and ability to conduct the job within the unit's work rules.

_____ Unusual compliance and understanding of work discipline. Routine usually exceeds normal.

_____ Excellent. Complete conformity with rules but cheerfully volunteers time during peak loads.

_____ Normally dependable. Rarely needs reminding of accepted rules.

_____ Needs close supervision in this area. Inclined to backslide without strict discipline.

_____ Unreliable. Resists normal rules. Frequently wants special privileges.

Knowledge of Company Policy and Objectives

Acceptance, understanding, and promotion of company policies and objectives in the area of the employee's job responsibilities.

_____ Thorough appreciation and implementation of all policies. Extraordinary ability to express objectives and encourage others to meet them.

_____ Reflects knowledge of almost all policies related to this position.

_____ Acceptable but fairly superficial understanding of job objectives.

_____ Limited insight into job or company goals. Mentally restricted.

_____ Not enough information or understanding to permit minimum efficiency.

Initiative and Judgment

The ability and interest to suggest and develop new ideas and methods; the degree to which these suggestions and normal decisions and actions are sound.

_____ Ingenious self-starter. Superior ability to think intelligently.

_____ Very resourceful. Clear thinker—usually makes thoughtful decisions.

_____ Fairly progressive, with normal sense. Often needs to be motivated.

_____ Rarely makes suggestions. Decisions need to be checked before implementation.

_____ Needs detailed instructions and close supervision. Tendency to assume and misinterpret.

Supervisory or Technical Potential

Consider the employee's ability to teach and increase skills of others, to motivate and lead, to organize and assign work, and to communicate ideas.

_____ An accomplished leader who can earn respect and inspire others to perform. An articulate and artful communicator, planner, and organizer.

_____ Has the ability to reach and will lead by example rather than technique. Speaks and writes well and can organize and plan with help.

_____ Fairly well informed on job-related subjects but has some difficulty communicating with others. Nothing distinctive about spoken or written word.

_____ Little ability to implement. Seems uninterested in teaching or helping others. Careless speech and writing habits.

_____ Unable to be objective or reason logically. Inarticulate and stilted in expression.

PRACTICE

Overall Rating

There are five alternatives in each category. The first alternative is worth 5 points, the last alternative is worth 1 point. Place a number from 1–5 by each of the selected alternatives and total the score for all nine categories. Then select the appropriate overall rating.

_____ Outstanding (45–39)

_____ Above Expected (38–32)

_____ Expected (31–23)

_____ Below Expected (22–16)

_____ Unsatisfactory (15–9)

Observer's Feedback Form

RATING

1 = Low

5 = High

Introduction

1. Did interviewer

_____ use appropriate greeting?

_____ build rapport?

_____ orient interviewee to the interview?

_____ refer to taking notes?

Body

2. Did interviewer

_____ praise individual's strengths?

_____ focus on specific concerns?

_____ compare perceptions of the problems?

_____ probe for underlying causes?

_____ reach agreement on performance expectations and goals?

_____ discuss specific plans of action for improving deficiencies?

_____ make specific references to the appraisal form?

Conclusion

3. Did interviewer

_____ provide opportunity for interviewee to make suggestions and ask questions?

_____ summarize interview?

_____ specify when next appraisal interview will be held?

Nonverbals

4. Did interviewer

_____ use nonverbal behaviors to maintain open climate and good rapport?

_____ avoid use of uhs and uhms?

_____ maintain good posture?

_____ maintain eye contact?

Comments:

Employment-Selection Interview at Smith Farley Insurance

Smith Farley is a rapidly growing insurance firm located in Peoria, Illinois. It offers general lines of insurance, including auto, fire, life, and health. It prides itself on its competitive rates, excellent agent relations, and fast claim service. Employees of the firm appreciate its no-layoff policy, generous pay and benefits, and family-oriented culture. Next to Caterpillar, it is the largest employer in the community, a source of employee pride.

Smith Farley has taken the lead in computerizing the insurance business. Agents and claim handlers conduct much of their business using laptop computers in their offices and in the field. Furthermore, the agents' and claim handlers' offices are all networked with one another as well as with the regional offices. This permits rapid transfer of information, including rate changes, new applications, and claims.

To support this massive computer system, the firm has installed state-of-the-art computer hardware in its 10 regional office centers. In addition, the company has a large software development and maintenance department, which has doubled in size in the past five years and now employs 800 programmers. These programmers are generally recruited directly from college. Although they need no previous experience, any relevant experience can help new programmers move quickly into management or senior technical positions.

Programmer/analysts use typical programming languages to develop computer applications for the insurance business (e.g., new claim-handler and customer application forms), for the corporate headquarters staff (e.g., accounting and personnel records), and the computer system itself (internal procedures and controls). Data processing positions range from extremely technical design of complex computer networks to routine maintenance of existing programs.

All new programmers are put through a 16-week school in which they are oriented to the company and the data processing department, brought up to speed on the relevant programming languages and tools, and socialized into the corporate culture. To meet the heavy demand for computer applications, the data processing department has been authorized to hire two cohorts of 60 programmers a year.

To attract programmers to the firm, Smith Farley offers above-average starting salaries and rapid promotions during the first five years. After that, individuals can continue to pursue the technical career option, which leads to a senior analyst's position that pays about $10,000 above industry average, or they can move into management. The consistently high performance of the firm and its ongoing expansion of data processing afford ample opportunity for promotion into senior positions.

You are J. R. Henderson, a 20-year employee of Smith Farley. For the past 10 years you have been working in the personnel department, primarily interviewing job candidates for the data processing department. You enjoy your work—the constant contact with young, enthusiastic college graduates is invigorating—but sometimes you find the heavy travel schedule taxing.

For example, during the next week you will be traveling to three cities: first to nearby Bloomington, then to New Orleans and Atlanta. In addition to the regular campus interviews you have scheduled in these areas, you have received several résumés in response to local newspaper ads. In sifting through these inquiries, three résumés caught your interest. You have made arrangements to interview all three applicants during this trip.

Assignment

Review Exhibits 1 through 5 and prepare a list of questions you would ask these three job candidates. Using the Interview Guide planning form at the end of the chapter, review the general questions you should ask all three. In addition, identify several specific questions you would like to ask the candidate(s) you are assigned, based on their résumés and cover letters.

Review your proposed questions in small groups. What points did you overlook? What questions need to be reworded or discarded?

Using the questions you think are most appropriate, be prepared to conduct selection interviews with these job candidates in class. Prior to each interview, think about the questions each candidate is likely to ask you about the company, the community of Peoria, and the specific jobs available. In addition, identify your "selling points"—the specific features of the company, the community, and the jobs you think each candidate would find most attractive. Also review the general behavioral guidelines and the six-step PEOPLE approach to selection interviews (Table B.8). Remember: The interviewing process influences the content of the information exchanged.

Following the interview, take a few minutes and grade the interviewee on each of the seven criteria on the Interview Guide (5 = high, 1 = low). Justify your grades with specific comments. Then make an oral report to the observer assigned to your interview; include a recommendation. (Assume the observer is the director of recruiting for your firm.) After your report, for those criteria related to the interview itself (as compared with the background of the assigned role), discuss your observations with the interviewee. Following this discussion, an observer will give you feedback on your performance as an interviewer using the Observer's Feedback Form as a guide.

Exhibit 1 Smith Farley Insurance Job Posting

A. POSITIONS OPEN

1. *Programmer/Analyst*—Auto & Life Company Data Processing Trainee openings leading to Programmer/Analyst positions at the conclusion of *16-week* training program. The DP Trainee is trained in the programming skills necessary to either develop new or to revise data-processing programs that help administer over 10 million auto, life, fire, and health insurance policies.

2. *Analyst*—Computer Operations Support Trainee opening leading to *Analyst* positions at conclusion of a *nine-month* training program. Computer Operations Support is responsible for technical operations support for the Regional Data Processing Offices, including: developing operator procedures, developing and administering training, problem resolution, and coordinating implementation of new systems and major changes for Regional Data Processing Offices.

B. MAJORS CONSIDERED

We are recruiting for three Data Processing Departments (Auto Data Processing, Life Data Processing, and Computer Operations Support), each having different requirements, which are as follows:

1. *Auto Data Processing:* Strongly prefer applied computer science, computer technology, and MIS majors, but will consider other majors with 12–15 hours of computer science academic background. Strongly prefer *3.0 overall GPA.*

   Logical analysis, problem-solving skills, and communication skills are important for expected job performance. Candidates should possess course work in *COBOL, C, C++,* and/or *Java.*

2. *Life Data Processing:* Most college majors are acceptable (i.e., mathematics, business or related majors, English, music, and science).

   Student must have a sincere interest in and aptitude for data processing. Only students with a *3.5 overall GPA* will be considered.

3. *Computer Operations Support:* Most business majors are acceptable (i.e., business, business administration, finance, economics, accounting, etc., with 6–10 hours of computer science academic background). Prefer a *3.0 overall GPA.*

Student must have a sincere interest in and aptitude for data processing.

C. CITIZENSHIP REQUIREMENTS

Must be citizens or permanent residents.

D. LOCATION

These positions will be located at the corporate headquarters in Peoria, Illinois.

Exhibit 2 Interview Guide for Data Processing (DP)

APPLICANT'S NAME _____   SCHOOL _____

INTERVIEW DATE _____   GPA _____

LOCATION _____ TIME ____   MAJOR _____

CRITERION	FOCUS	GENERAL QUESTIONS	APPLICANT-SPECIFIC QUESTIONS
Aptitude/ Knowledge	Determine if exposure to and retention of a high-level computer language and development methods are adequate.	Of the DP courses you have had, which was the most beneficial and why? Explain in detail the most difficult DP assignment you have had. How do you rate yourself as a programmer? Why?	
Interest/ Experience	Determine if interest and record of success in DP studies or work has been sustained (2+ years).	How did you first get interested in DP? What about it do you like the most? The least? Can you give me an example of a DP-related experience you have had that was satisfying? Not satisfying? What is your professional goal?	
Ability to work with others	Determine success of achieving results in team effort.	Do you feel you work more effectively on a one-to-one basis or in a group? Describe a situation in which you worked as a member of a team. What approach did you take to get people together and establish a common approach to the task?	

(Continued)

PRACTICE ◆

CRITERION	FOCUS	GENERAL QUESTIONS	APPLICANT-SPECIFIC QUESTIONS
Commitment/ Initiative	Determine level of success in achieving task completion in light of task complexity, adversity, load, level of knowledge, and so forth.	What approaches do you use to get people to accept your ideas or goals? What is a big obstacle you had to overcome to get where you are today? Do you consider yourself a self-starter or are you better at implementing the plans of others?	
Communication	Determine quality of written/spoken word.	Would you rather write a report or give a verbal report? Why? Do you think you are a good listener? What qualities do you need to be a good listener? How do you handle a situation when you are explaining something and the other person doesn't understand?	
Problem solving/ Decision making	Determine if applicant has a record of addressing relatively complex projects.	In your opinion, what are the most difficult problems with which a programmer/ analyst must deal? What particular strengths do you have that allow you to deal with these problems? What design methods do you use to create a program? Describe how to use them. Describe the most complex program you have ever written.	
Other:	Stability Maturity Leadership Personal appearance		

Exhibit 3 Résumé

William L. Henderson II

Campus
700 North Camden #107
Normal, IL 61761
(309) 454–6178

Home
1915 Western Hills
Arlington Heights, IL 60004
(312) 255–5738

OBJECTIVE	*Analyst/Data Processing*
EDUCATION	Illinois Wesleyan University, Bloomington, Illinois Expected Degree 2007 Major: Computer Science Major GPA: 3.75 Business Administration GPA: 3.03
EDUCATIONAL HIGHLIGHTS	Dean's List Spring Semester 2007 ACM Award Spring Semester 2007
STUDENT ACTIVITIES	*ILLINOIS WESLEYAN UNIVERSITY* Member of Gamma Ray Social Fraternity (3 years) Pledge Class President; In-House Activities; Intramurals; Offset Chairman; Social Committee. Member of Varsity Football Team (2 years)
WORK SUMMARY (Part time during college)	CENTRAL STATES INSURANCE, Bloomington, IL Auto/Divisional Programming—Corporate *Position:* DP—Intern ILLINOIS WESLEYAN UNIVERSITY, Bloomington, IL Office of Admissions *Position:* Admissions Counselor Aid Computer Lab *Position:* Lab Assistant
(Summers)	PREMIER CHECK PRINTERS, INC., Des Plaines, IL Printing presses (2 years) *Position:* Press Assistant/Operation SOFTWARE, ETC., Arlington Heights, IL Sales, Inventory, Shipping, Ordering, Partial Management *Position:* Salesman
AVAILABILITY	June 2008
REFERENCES	References available upon request

Exhibit 4 Résumé

Bryan E. Jensen
4364 Peachtree Place
Lilburn, Georgia 30247
Home (404) 381-8909

OBJECTIVE	*Project Leader/Systems Analyst* with supervision potential
BACKGROUND	Anticipated the decline in manufacturing jobs and retrained in computer science. Presently have two associate degrees and four years of in-depth experience. Accepted temporary position at Caterpillar to gain experience. The economic recession in the Midwest prompted my relocation to Atlanta. Accepted my present position to broaden my experience. I am now seeking a permanent career position with a midwest employer located in a "smaller" city. I will be an asset to a progressive company. I am well motivated, resourceful, versatile, work well with others, and accept responsibility readily.

HARDWARE	IBM 370—Models 3090E, 3083, 3084, 4341; IBM PC/XT; 486, Power PC
SOFTWARE	Case Tools: Knowledgeware GAMMA
	Databases: IMS-DL/I, DBII—SQL, Access, Oracle
	Communications: IMS—MFS, TSO—ISPF
	Languages: C, C++, Java
	Related: BTS, DDLTO, Fileaid-IMS, Datavatage, IMS-Online, SPUFI, QMF, OS/MVS-XA, JES2, Fileaid, Panvalet, Infopac, SDSF, JES-Master, Design/I, All-In-One, Diagram Master, Excel, Word PowerPoint, Dreamweaver
EXPERIENCE 03/07–	*Continental Service Corporation*, Macon, Georgia (Corporate) Senior Systems Analyst/Team Leader
	Guided planning, estimating, analysis, and development of major areas of IMB DB/DC Billing System. It has a 2.5 million customer base and is located in 42 states. Use Method/I life cycle/ methodology. Utilized Pacdesign (Yourdon) for system design and Pacbase for completion of deliverables and code generation.
01/04–03/07	*Federal Reserve Bank*, Savannah, Georgia (Corporate) Project Leader (10/06–03/07)
	Supervised eight analysts and programmers through the implementation of a billing system for Federal Reserve Districts throughout the United States. Presented written and verbal status reports, employee-performance reviews, and time-planning estimates/schedules to upper management.
	(09/05–10/06)
	Led development of IMS DB/DC billing system. Analyzed requirements to produce data-flow diagrams and logical data model. Participated in team presentation of system. Created program specifications. Investigated and resolved code-generation problems. Provided support to other team members.
	(01/05–08/05)
	Received Merit Award for outstanding performance. Designed, programmed, and tested accounting interface to all corporate IBM and branch Unisys applications. Provided training and support during parallel test and acceptance of accounting system. Redirected installation efforts for an accounting deposit module that had fallen behind. Provided production support of newly implemented accounting system.
	(04/04–12/04)
	Installed accounting software from tape. Modified all JCL to district standards. Installed and modified job-submission system. Documented and instructed the users on the system and the results of each job.
	(01/04–03/04)
	Designed, wrote, tested, and documented IMB DB/DC programs for system used to report the dollar amount of checks as they clear the Reserve.
03/03–12/03	*Caterpillar Tractor Company*, Chicago, Illinois (Corp.) Programmer

Programmed, tested, and documented IMS DB/DC programs from specifications for Man and Material Management System. (Due to be laid off 01/04)

04/97–06/01   Skilled Trades Machinist (last position held—layoff)

EDUCATION   Illinois Central College; East Peoria, Illinois—2001, Associate in Applied Science, Data Processing Technology Bradley University; Peoria, Illinois (1998–1999) Fifteen hours past Associate toward Manufacturing B.S. Illinois Central College; East Peoria, Illinois— 1995, Associates in Applied Science, Manufacturing Technology.

PERSONAL   Married, one child. Enjoy outdoor activities. Well motivated. References available upon request.

Exhibit 5 Résumé

Mary Lynn Smith
3922 North Blair Street
New Orleans, Louisiana 70117
(504) 945–6077

CAREER OBJECTIVES

Entry-level position in artificial intelligence research with an industrial firm and eventual managerial capacity in such a firm.

EDUCATION

Dillard University, Division of Natural Sciences, New Orleans, LA.
B.S. degree, Mathematics major with Computer Science minor, May 1999,
G.P.A.: 3.58/4.0 (overall), 3.82/4.0 (major)

Courses in Mathematics:

Calculus I, II, III	Complex Variables	
Modern Algebra I & II	Real Algebra	Differential Equations
Advanced Calculus	Linear Algebra	Engineering Statistics

Courses in Computer Science:

Computer Fundamentals	BASIC	Advanced BASIC
Systems Analysis	Pascal	FORTRAN

HONORS AND ACTIVITIES

University academic scholarship, University and National Dean's Lists, Kappa Beta Alpha and Beta Kappa Tau Honor Societies, Kappa Delta Pi Mathematics Society, and Dillard University Concert Choir.

WORK EXPERIENCE

Computer Services, Inc., Systems Operator/Payroll Processor, Summer, 2007.
—Performed system backups, file verification, programming, and payroll processing.
—Verified payroll figures and prepared tax reports.

Black Computer Operators Association, Teacher, 8/06.
—Prepared the South New Orleans Computer Science Team for a national competition.

The South New Orleans Team placed first in the national competition.

Washington Elementary School, Summer Mini Camp, Teacher, 7/06–8/06.
—Taught children how to use computers and educational software.

Observer's Feedback Form

RATING

1 = Low

5 = High

Opening

1. Did interviewer

_____ use appropriate greeting?

_____ build rapport?

_____ orient interviewee to the interview?

_____ use appropriate transition to body of interview?

Body

2. Did interviewer

_____ clearly define structure of the interview?

_____ use transitions between topics?

_____ ask questions based on available information and needs?

_____ probe when necessary?

_____ solicit behavioral examples?

Closing

3. Did interviewer

_____ offer organizational or job information?

_____ invite questions?

_____ answer interviewee's questions appropriately and specifically?

_____ state when and how interviewee will be contacted?

Nonverbal

4. Did interviewer

_____ act poised?

_____ dress appropriately?

_____ speak articulately?

_____ act enthusiastically?

_____ use appropriate language style?

_____ maintain eye contact?

_____ use purposeful gestures?

Comments:

C
Conducting Meetings

SKILL DEVELOPMENT OBJECTIVES

- IMPLEMENT GUIDELINES FOR PLANNING AND CONDUCTING EFFECTIVE MEETINGS
- ENHANCE THE VALUE OF MEETINGS ATTENDED

Conducting Effective Meetings: A Short Guide for Meeting Managers and Meeting Participants

Becoming a skillful planner and conductor of meetings—a meeting manager—is a prerequisite for managerial and organizational effectiveness. There are several reasons this skill is a crucial one. One reason is because so much of a manager's time is spent in meetings. A 3M Company study, done in the late 1980s, found meetings occupy a large percentage of a manager's workweek. These researchers found the number of meetings had doubled over the last decade. As you move up the hierarchy, meeting demands increase substantially. The more senior the manager is, the more meetings he or she attends (3M, 1994).

A second reason is meetings are a significant cost. This research found the compensation for managers "just being there" had nearly tripled. About 15 percent of most companies' personnel budget was spent on meeting matters. And in the last decade these demands have increased substantially. With flatter organizations and an emphasis on teams and teamwork, the number of meetings has grown exponentially.

A third reason becoming a skillful meeting manager is crucial is meetings are the place where most corporate decisions are actually made, or reviewed. Hence, the matter of decision quality—the amount of useful results from the meeting—becomes crucial for the health of the organization. The skilled meeting master can "produce" a meeting that results in high-quality decisions—not her or his decisions, but decisions that truly reflect the group's.

A fourth reason relates to the concept of whole life, as opposed to work life. In these days of the boundaryless organization, skills that are useful at work are also useful and important away from work. Many people spend a substantial portion of their time in non-work-oriented meetings. For example, any community volunteer work; church activity; or participation in art councils, youth programs, and civic associations requires a lot of meetings. Failure here can have a great impact on our social fabric. Robert Putnam of Harvard University has developed a thesis about the decline in "social capital" in American society (Putnam, 2000). Collective activities seem to be on the decline across a wide range of organizations. One of the reasons for this decline is unorganized meetings that frustrate participants rather than help them contribute to the organization's goals. Folks may figure they just do not want to waste their time.

Because meetings are such a pervasive activity both in and out of work settings, being a skillful meeting manager has important rewards beyond those associated with team building. Meeting groups, if properly managed, can make higher-quality decisions than individuals. The phrase "if properly managed" is the key. If not properly managed, meetings become the supreme organizational and civic time waster. They can actually set the organization back by making rotten decisions when problematic processes such as folly (Tuchman, 1984), groupthink (Janis, 1983), the Abilene paradox (Harvey, 1974), the garbage can model of organizational choice (Cohen, March, & Olsen, 1972), or the "boiled frog syndrome" (Tichy & Devanna, 1986) come into play.

The Five *P*s of Effective Meetings

Effective meeting managers know the five steps in preparing for and conducting meetings: (1) purpose, (2) participants, (3) plan, (4) participation, and (5) perspective.

1. Purpose

Purpose refers to the reason for which a meeting is held. There are three functions a meeting performs—to make announcements, to make decisions, and to brainstorm. Of these three, only the second two count as reasons for actually holding a meeting. When information can be conveyed by a memo or phone call, when people are not prepared, when key people cannot attend, when the cost of a meeting is higher than the potential payoff, and when there is no advantage to holding a meeting, no meeting should be called (3M, 1994). In short, if there are no decisions to be made, nor any brainstorming to do, cancel the meeting.

Productive meetings *result* from good decision making and brainstorming. A meeting should be called when one or more of the following conditions applies:

We are grateful to John Tropman, who prepared this section based on the material the authors had in the previous editions.

- *Information sharing.* When all needed information is not held by any single person, when ideas will be stimulated by getting people together, and when it is not clear what information is needed or available.

- *Commitment building.* When individuals need to become committed to a course of action and when they are involved in its planning and implementation.

- *Information disseminating and feedback.* When many people must receive the same message in the same way, e-mail is good. However, when the real issue is not the dissemination, but gauging the reaction and allowing for "ventilation," then a meeting is very helpful.

- *Problem solving.* Groups outperform the best individuals in accomplishing complex tasks and making high-quality decisions where various policies or information are needed. Therefore, meetings should be called to manage complex problems and outline the options for decisions through brainstorming.

2. Participants

The second *P*, **participants**, refers to the individuals invited to attend a meeting. In conducting an effective meeting, it is important to determine the *size, composition*, and *skills* of the participants. Meetings can fail because too many or too few participants attend or because the wrong mix of people is present. If a meeting is too large, discussion may be superficial and diffuse; few people will be able to participate. If a meeting is too small, not enough information will be shared and problems will not be adequately solved. Odd numbers of participants work best because even numbers have a higher propensity of causing the group to polarize.

Meeting composition refers to three main dualistic dimensions:

- Homogeneity–Heterogeneity
- Competition–Cooperation
- Task–Process

A homogeneous group is composed of members with similar backgrounds, personalities, knowledge, or values. Homogeneous groups produce less conflict and disagreement, but their outcomes may be mundane and unimaginative. On the other hand, heterogeneous groups produce more differences among individuals, which leads to criticisms and disputes, but potentially to more novel, complex solutions to problems as well.

With regard to the competition–cooperation dimension, research on its effect in problem-solving meetings is compelling. Groups whose members are working toward a common goal and who adopt a cooperative stance toward one another perform more effectively and produce higher levels of member satisfaction than groups whose members are striving to fulfill individual needs or are pursuing competing goals. Cooperative groups also demonstrate more effective interpersonal communication, more complete divisions of labor, higher levels of involvement, and better task performance.

On the task–process dimension, meetings are more effective if they have participants who generate a balance of both task and process. Task-oriented participants are "all business." They have little tolerance for joking or for discussions of feelings and friendships. The task is accomplished efficiently, but satisfaction may be low. Process-oriented participants emphasize esprit de corps and participation. They are sensitive to participants' feelings and satisfaction. They may sacrifice accomplishment in favor of members' enjoyment. (This usually turns out to be a bad choice; the greatest enjoyment comes from accomplishment.) For meeting participants, one tip is not to refrain from using your default (or usual) style (task or process) but, rather, "Do what is not being done." If there is a lot of process going on, you can emphasize task. If there is an "all task" mind-set, then add a bit of process.

Skills address the competencies participants bring to the meeting. We can think of *general* and *specific* skill sets. In general, the four generic skill sets Cohen, March, and Olsen (1972) identify should be present in the meeting *at the same time.* First are the problem knowers—participants who have some sense of the problem under discussion. Second are the solution providers—participants who are creative and imaginative, but may not know the problems. Third are the resource controllers—participants who sign off on money, people, and resources needed for most decisions; therefore, they need to be in the loop. Finally, there are people called "decision-makers-looking-for-work"—the "organizational archbishops" who "bless" or affirm decisions. If all these skill sets are in the same room at the same time, and the process is a good one, the likelihood of a high-quality decision (timely, creative, participative) is great. In terms of specific skills, the particular knowledge that might be needed in a particular situation can be ascertained as one plans for the meeting, using the rule of halves, which will be mentioned later in this chapter. It is true individuals may double up—and fit more than one of these categories. That is fine. Just be sure you have them all.

3. Planning

The third *P*, **planning**, refers to preparation of the meeting agenda. Often, the justification for a meeting is clear (e.g., we need to determine how to get fuel to troops at the front), and the appropriate individuals are in attendance, but the meeting still seems to flounder, wander aimlessly, or is unable to produce a final decision. Such meetings often begin with the leader saying, "We have a problem I think we all need to sit down and discuss." The leader's erroneous assumption is because a problem exists and all participants understand it, the meeting will be successful. Unfortunately, participants may come to the meeting unprepared, may be unaware of critical information, may be unclear about their specific roles, and may be confused about how to achieve the objective. Conversely, the meeting planner may try to cram too much into a single meeting, schedule too many presentations, handle too many documents, or cover too much business. Research suggests there are a number of rules for planning meetings effectively (Tropman, 1996). The following is a list of the most important:

The Rule of Halves All agenda items for an upcoming meeting must be in the hands of the agenda scheduler no later than one-half of the time interval between the last meeting and the upcoming meeting. If meetings are held weekly, the person constructing the agenda should gather agenda items for the next meeting by the halfway mark in the week. This allows time to sort and cluster items, handle some items one-on-one outside the meeting, and produce and distribute an agenda in advance of the meeting. It also allows for the assembling of special skills, as driven by the developing agenda.

The Rule of Sixths Approximately two-thirds of the agenda should be focused on current agenda items. The remaining third should be subdivided into two-sixths. One of those sixths of meeting time should be spent on past agenda items and follow-up. The remaining sixth of the meeting should be spent on brainstorming for the future. Continuity is thus maintained and agenda items don't slip through the cracks.

The Reports Rule Meetings go better if the usual round of "reports" does *not* occur. Rather, the information that is contained in the "reports" is reorganized into specific items—announcement, decision, brainstorming.

The Rule of Three-Fourths Packets of information, including minutes from the past meeting and an agenda, should be sent to meeting participants at the three-quarter point between meetings. For example, if a weekly meeting is scheduled, the packet should be sent out approximately two days before the next meeting.

The Agenda Rule Agendas for meetings should be written with action verbs or sentence summaries, not with single words. Rather than saying "Minutes," for example, use "Approve Minutes." Rather than "Production Report," use "Determine Production Schedule." This provides clarity and impetus for what the meeting should accomplish. Figure C.1 illustrates this process.

The Rule of Thirds All meetings are divided into three parts: (1) a start-up period in which less difficult items are covered, latecomers arrive, and people get on board; (2) a heavy work period in which the most difficult items are considered; and (3) a decompression period in which the meeting begins to wind down. *Instructional items* should be handled in the first period, *items for decision* should be handled in the second period, and *items for discussion* should be handled in the third period.

Executive Summary Rule Reports circulated to meeting participants should always contain executive summaries or options memos. An executive summary highlights key points and conclusions of the report. An

Figure C.1	The Weekly Meeting	
1. Approve Minutes		2:00–2:05
2. Announcements		2:05–2:10
	New desks ordered	
	$1,000 each to your account	
3. Retreat Location (Action)		2:10–2:15
	Key West seems best	
4a. Vendor Selection (Action)		2:15–2:25
	A new vendor for gaskets	
	would like some business	
4b. Disposal of Broken Gaskets (Action)		2:25–2:35
	Trash? Sell abroad/fix?	
5. Permission to Ship (Action)		2:35–3:00
	Ship part with scratch?	
	Give discount?	
6. Improving Quality (Brains)		3:00–3:38
7. Adjourn		3:38–3:40

Source: *John Tropman.*

options memo summarizes alternatives to be discussed and decided on. This eliminates the need to sift through many pages to find relevant information and to spend meeting time shuffling through the report.

The Agenda Bell Rule This rule is a more specific rule about when certain types of agenda items should be covered. Agenda items should be considered in order of ascending controversiality, then attention should be turned to discussion and decompression items. Figure C.2 shows a typical agenda bell for a meeting.

The Agenda Integrity Rule All items on the agenda should be discussed, and items not on the agenda should not be discussed. This rule helps ensure meeting participants do not sidetrack the meeting with items that are tangential, for which no one has prepared, or for which insufficient information is available.

The Temporal Integrity Rule This rule is simple: Start on time and end on time. Follow a time schedule in the meeting itself. This ensures all agenda items are given adequate time, latecomers are not rewarded by having the meeting wait for them, and people can count on finishing at a certain point.

The Minutes Rule Minutes of meetings should have three characteristics: agenda relevance (information recorded is related to an agenda item), content relevance (minutes should be written in a form that follows the agenda so it is easy to find pertinent material with a quick review), and decision focus (minutes should reflect decisions, conclusions, and actions agreed upon, rather than the processes by which the decisions are reached). After a brief summary of each item, skip a line and place the action or result in a box. Here is where names are named, times are timed, and so on. The key item is easy for everyone to see.

These 10 rules of meeting preparation help to ensure that when individuals arrive for a meeting and the meeting begins, a structure and plan will be in place to make the meeting productive and efficient.

4. Participation

The fourth *P*, **participation**, refers to the actual process of meetings and the methods used to ensure meetings involve everyone present.

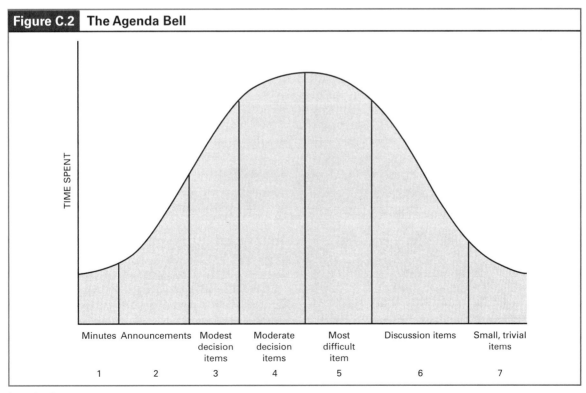

Figure C.2 The Agenda Bell

TIME SPENT

Minutes	Announcements	Modest decision items	Moderate decision items	Most difficult item	Discussion items	Small, trivial items
1	2	3	4	5	6	7

Source: *John Tropman.*

Provide Introductions Meeting participants should be introduced to each other and helped to feel comfortable together, especially if controversial issues are to be considered.

Establish Ground Rules It should be made clear what amount of participation is expected, what variations from the agenda will be tolerated, and what the time frame will be. Establishing a structure for the meeting at the outset helps keep the meeting on track.

Establish Decision Rules Decision rules are norms that make participants comfortable. Establish them at the beginning of the meeting. Because there are no neutral decision rules, meeting managers usually have to use several at once—a complex intellectual task. The most common are the extensive rule, the intensive rule, the involvement rule, the expert rule, and the power rule.

The *extensive rule* is majority rule. Each meeting participant votes on alternatives, and the alternatives with a majority of the votes wins. However, there are variations of this rule, which should be noted:

- ❏ *Highest total.* When more than two alternatives are being considered, none may get a majority of the votes. The alternative with the highest number of votes is adopted.
- ❏ *Straw vote.* A nonbinding vote is taken to get a sense of the participants' feelings toward various alternatives. This may happen several times before a decision is reached in order to eliminate nonsupported alternatives from consideration.
- ❏ *Weighted rating.* Meeting participants can divide 100 points among alternatives, so the strength of their support can be tallied. If four alternatives exist, for example, a participant can give 90 points to one and 5 points to two others. The alternative with the most points wins.
- ❏ *Ranking.* Alternatives are rank ordered, and the alternative receiving the highest average ranking is adopted.

If the *intensive rule* is used, those who care most win. Through discussion, rather than voting, individuals who feel deeply can share that feeling with the group. Groups will try to be as accommodating as possible. However, problems occur if the majority cares a lot, but not "most," or if there are two groups that care deeply but differently. It requires a lot of imagination and attempts to come up with a solution that pleases the "shallow feelers" and the "deep feelers."

In the *involvement rule*, the person or subgroup that has to carry out any action gets to pick, or has it their way. Their downstream involvement gives them a particular view, which may not always be for the overall best. Using the *expert rule,* the participant with the law or science on his or her side wins. But neither law nor science is infallible by any means. Using the *power rule* means the boss wins.

Any one of these rules can work, but quality decisions with the greatest buy-in (and hence, sticking power) usually come from consensus. Consensus, in this case, means a decision is taken that meets, and can be shown to meet, each of the rules—it satisfied the greatest number of those who feel strongly, those who must carry it out, the experts, and the boss.

Sometimes it is necessary to proceed "in principle." Although agreement cannot be reached on all specific details, certain general principles can be agreed upon. The priniciples, rather than the entire proposal, are accepted. For example, you and your partner may decide in principle to have Italian food Friday night. Details (such as if you will go out, and if not, who will do the cooking) might remain unresolved for the moment while a range of details is explored.

Use a Variety of Media To maintain the interest of meeting participants, use various media to present information. Handouts, overhead transparencies, slides, flip charts, videos, and blackboard diagrams are all helpful in maintaining interest and increasing the efficiency with which information is presented and processed. Participants should be able to use at least two of their senses during a meeting (for example, seeing and hearing).

Encourage and Establish Participation Participation in a meeting should be equitable among participants, which does not mean everyone must make exactly the same number of comments. Those with more information or those with vested interests in the topic will participate more. However, it is important to control the overparticipator or the person who dominates the discussion, as well as encourage those who may have something to contribute but may not be inclined to share it. Equity should also be maintained among different points of view, so representatives of one side of an argument don't dominate the discussion. Ways to promote discussion among meeting participants include the following:

- ❏ Ask open-ended questions rather than questions that can be answered with a "yes" or a "no."

- Ask questions using the language of the participants rather than using jargon or recondite terminology.

- Encourage participants to share personal experiences that relate to the topic being considered.

- Use examples from your own experience to clarify points.

- Make eye contact with those to whom you are talking and summarize their points when they finish their statements.

- Ask group members for their reactions to points made by other meeting participants.

- When appropriate, involve others in answering a question asked of you.

- Remember communication comes in a strand of two parts—the report part (information) and the rapport part (connection and feeling). Be sure to attend to both parts.

- As the leader, make certain you facilitate the discussion rather than dominate it.

Summarize   Close the meeting by summarizing the decisions reached, tasks assigned, progress accomplished, key points discussed, and what was learned in the meeting. Review action items that will be reported on at the next meeting. Help meeting participants feel a sense of accomplishment for having spent their time in the meeting. This may be a good time to anticipate the next meeting by identifying when minutes and the next meeting's agenda will be distributed and what preparation will be required.

5. Perspective

The last *P* is **perspective**. Perspective directs us to view the meetings from a distance. It means evaluating each meeting and, every so often, the decisions of and process of the meeting series. At the end of each meeting, for example, you can use KSS methodology to do a quick and simple assessment. Pass out a piece of paper to each participant. Ask each participant to respond under each of the three letters—*K*, *S*, and *S*. *K* means "keep"—What went well about this meeting that we should keep or expand. *S* means "stop"—What about this meeting is nonproductive and should be stopped or phased out. *S* means "start"—What about this meeting is not happening and should be started. You may get the usual irreverent responses (for example, "better doughnuts"), but if you look for serious patterns of feedback, you can constantly improve the meeting series. The next week, give the participants

the results (in summary form) and let them know how you are using their feedback to improve the meeting.

Suggestions for Group Members

So far in this discussion of effective meeting management, we have focused on the role of the meeting manager—the person who calls, plans, and serves as the meeting's "conductor." This role is key to the success of any group activity. However, meeting participants also bear responsibility for the meeting's effectiveness. It is important for each participant to appreciate the impact of her or his contribution, both in shaping the short-term outcomes of meetings and affecting long-term career opportunities. The success of the meeting is the responsibility of everyone present, and even those not present, in the sense that these latter folks have the responsibility to let their views be known in advance. The best meetings are those in which meeting managers and other participants each take some responsibility for meeting leadership.

Following are several pointers for contributing to the effectiveness of meeting from a non-manager's perspective.

1. *Determine if you need to attend the meeting.* Don't attend merely because you have been invited. If you have doubts about whether the meeting's agenda applies to you, discuss with the meeting manager why he or she believes your presence is important. Under the rule of three-fourths, you will know what is coming up in fairly specific detail. This information should help.

2. *Prepare.* Acquaint yourself with the agenda, and prepare any reports or information that will facilitate *others'* understanding of the issues. Come prepared with questions that will help you understand the issues.

3. *Be on time.* Stragglers not only waste the time of other participants by delaying the meeting or by requiring summaries of what has happened, but they also hinder effective team building and hurt morale.

4. *Ask for clarification on points that are unclear or ambiguous.* Often, you will find others in this room have the same questions but were too timid to speak out.

5. *When giving information, be precise and to the point.* Don't bore everyone with anecdotes and details that add little to your point.

6. *Listen.* Keep eye contact with whomever is speaking, and try to ascertain the underlying ideas behind the comments. Be sensitive to the effects of your nonverbal behavior on speakers, such as slouching, doodling, or reading.

7. *Be supportive of other group members.* Following the guidelines on supportive communication, acknowledge and build on the comments of others. ("As Jane was saying . . . ")

8. *Assure equitable participation.* Take the lead in involving others so everyone's talents are used. This is especially important if you know that critical information from particular points of view are not being included in the discussion. This can be rectified by encouraging those who rarely participate. ("Jim, your unit worked on something like this last year. What was your experience like?")

9. *Make disagreements principle-based.* If it is necessary to disagree with, or challenge, the comments of others, follow the guidelines for collaborative conflict management in the text. For example, base your comments on commonly held principles or values. ("That's an interesting idea, Bill, but how does it compare with the president's emphasis on cost cutting?")

10. *Act and react in a way that will enhance the group performance.* Leave your personal agendas at the door and work toward the goals of the group.

Summary and Behavioral Guidelines

Meetings are a pervasive part of organizational life, especially for managers. Few important initiatives are forged without extensive and intensive group efforts. However, meetings are one of the most maligned aspects of organizational membership. To avoid poorly managed meetings, a Five-Ps approach was presented.

1. **Purpose** Use meetings to accomplish the following purposes:
   - ❏ Decisions
      - ❏ A complex problem needs to be resolved using the expertise of several people.
      - ❏ Group members' commitment to a decision, or to each other, needs to be enhanced.
   - ❏ Brainstorming
   - ❏ Ideas about a problem need to be explored, such as:
      - ❏ Precipitating and predisposing causes
      - ❏ What is the root cause?
      - ❏ Are there more effective and efficient ways we could approach this problem?
      - ❏ What is the evidence?
      - ❏ What does the evidence prove?
   - ❏ Announcements
      - ❏ Information needs to be shared simultaneously among several people.

2. **Participants** Make decisions regarding who and how many to invite based on the following:
   - ❏ The size of the group should be comparable with the task. (For interactive groups, five to seven participants tend to work best.)
   - ❏ A balance between individuals with strong task orientations and others with strong group-process orientations should be sought.
   - ❏ Individuals should share some common goals or values.
   - ❏ All relevant experience and knowledge need to be represented.
   - ❏ The group's composition should reflect the goals of the meeting. (Homogeneity encourages solidarity and commitment; heterogeneity fosters creativity and innovation.)
   - ❏ Be sure the general skills of problem knowing, problem solving, resource controlling, and key decision makers are on board.

3. **Plan** In preparing for the meeting, be sure to do the following:
   - ❏ Provide for adequate physical space, audiovisual equipment, and so on.
   - ❏ Establish priorities by sequencing agenda items and allotting time to each item.
   - ❏ Prepare and distribute an agenda before, or at the beginning of, the meeting.
   - ❏ Choose the most appropriate decision-making format structure for each item (for example, ordinary group discussion, brainstorming, or one of several consensus-building techniques).

4. **Process** In managing the group dynamics, specify the target time length, and highlight specific tasks by doing the following:
   - ❏ Establish process ground rules, such as how decisions will be made.
   - ❏ Allow members to become acquainted (if necessary) and make them feel comfortable.
   - ❏ When critical thinking is important, refrain from expressing strong personal opinions. Also, assign the role of critical evaluator to a group member.
   - ❏ Sustain the flow of the meeting by using informational displays.

- ❏ Encourage the group not to stray from assigned tasks.
- ❏ Manage the discussion to achieve equitable participation.
- ❏ Discourage the premature evaluation of ideas.
- ❏ Prevent "social loafing" by assigning specific responsibilities and stressing the importance of group tasks.
- ❏ Discourage "conceptual misers"—those who opt for the "quick fix."
- ❏ Counteract the natural tendency for groups to make risky decisions by touching base with participants prior to the meeting so discussion-induced trends can be detected. (The rule of halves helps with getting this information.)
- ❏ Deal with disruptive members by using supportive communication and collaborative conflict management skills.
- ❏ Conclude the meeting by summarizing what was accomplished, reviewing assignments, and making preparations for subsequent meetings, if necessary.

5. **Perspective** Evaluate each meeting using the KSS (Keep, Stop, Start) methodology by asking the following:
   - ❏ What went well in this meeting that we should keep?
   - ❏ What was nonproductive that we should stop or phase out?
   - ❏ What didn't happen in this meeting that we want to start in the future?

6. **Group Members** Foster constructive group dynamics as a participant by doing the following:
   - ❏ Take time to prepare for the meeting, and gain a clear understanding of the purposes of the meeting.
   - ❏ Respect other group members by arriving on time and leaving personal agendas at the door.
   - ❏ Listen to other group members, be supportive of them, and clarify and build upon points made by others.
   - ❏ Encourage participation by all members.

EXERCISES FOR CONDUCTING MEETINGS

Preparing and Conducting a Team Meeting at SSS Software

Part 1

Refer to the SSS Software In-Basket exercise at the end of this section. Assume the role of Chris Perillo. Since you are new to your position, you decide to hold a meeting with some or all of your direct reports tomorrow afternoon (Tuesday). You want to be brought up to date as well as to handle the items of business introduced in your e-mail, phone messages, and memos.

1. Review each of the 16 items in the SSS Software In-Basket exercise. This is the "business" to be covered in this meeting.
2. Determine the *purpose* of the meeting, the *participants* (who should attend), the *plan* (write an agenda; establish a time limit for the meeting) as well as the meeting *process* you will use, using the appropriate Behavioral Guidelines.

Part 2

3. Now select the nine other individuals who will be attending the meeting and assign them their roles in the Health and Financial Services Group. Each team member should realistically play the role assigned to him or her, even if not much specific information exists for the role in the memos. Each team member should play the role as though he or she were attending the first team meeting with a new leader. Each person should be prepared to make recommendations for each in-basket item pertaining to their role. The team should consist of:

Chris Perillo, Vice President
Bob Miller, Group 1 Manager
Wanda Manners, Group 2 Manager
William Chen, Group 3 Manager
Leo Jones, Group 4 Manager
Mark McIntyre, Group 5 Manager
John Small, Group 6 Manager
Marcus Harper, Group 8 Manager
Armand Marke, Customer Service Manager
Michelle Harrison, Office Administrator

4. At the conclusion of the meeting, assigned observers will provide feedback, using the Meeting Evaluation Worksheet as a guide.

Role Diagnosis

This exercise is intended to help you identify and practice effective role performance in meetings.

Listed on the next page are a set of roles organized into three categories. As you are observing a team meeting, put check marks by the roles performed by the team members you are observing each time they make a comment or display behaviors that match one of the roles listed on the next page. If you are analyzing your own team after it has completed its meeting, put names of team members next to the roles they played. (See the chapters on Building Effective Teams and Teamwork for more information about these roles.)

Task-Facilitating Roles
Direction-giving
Information-seeking
Information-giving
Elaborating
Coordinating
Monitoring
Process-analyzing
Reality-testing
Enforcing
Summarizing

Process (Relationship-Building) Roles
Supporting
Harmonizing
Tension-relieving
Energizing
Developing
Facilitating
Processing

Blocking Roles
Overanalyzing
Overgeneralizing
Fault finding
Premature decision making
Presenting opinions as facts
Rejecting
Pulling rank
Dominating
Stalling

What suggestions do you have for improvement in the team members' performance? Identify some specific suggestions for more effective role performance in the meeting. Who could have done more and who could have done less? Why?

Meeting Evaluation Worksheet

It is important individuals planning, conducting, and participating in meetings are asked periodically to evaluate the effectiveness of the time spent meeting together. The following worksheet can be used for this purpose.

To gain experience evaluating meetings, use the following questions to assess the effectiveness of a class or work-related project or staff meeting:

1. What is the specific purpose of the meeting?
2. Who was invited to attend? How were they contacted? Was the way in which the meeting announced appropriate (e.g., face-to-face, e-mail, secretary phone call)?

3. Was the agenda that was constructed consistent with the following rules?
   - ❏ The Agenda Rule (use action words)
   - ❏ The Rule of Sixths (two-thirds current items, one-third past and future items)
   - ❏ The Rule of Thirds (one-third warm up, one-third work, one-third wind down)
   - ❏ The Reports Rule (reports nonexistent; content reordered into specific items—announcements, decision, and brainstorm issues)
   - ❏ The Agenda Bell Rule (agenda ordered according to a bell-shaped "level of difficulty" process)
   - ❏ The Temporal Integrity Rule (start and stop on time)
   - ❏ The Minutes Rule (someone assigned to keep minutes)

4. What was done especially well in preparing for this meeting?

5. To what extent were the rules of effective meeting process followed in the meeting? Rate each step in terms of its effectiveness in the team meeting:

	Ineffective	Effective
1. Review purpose	_____	_____
2. Make introductions	_____	_____
3. Establish ground rules	_____	_____
4. Use informational displays	_____	_____
5. Ensure participation	_____	_____
6. Summarize conclusions	_____	_____

6. What could have been improved upon? What was omitted?

SSS Software In-Basket Memos, E-Mails, Faxes, and Voice Mails

ITEM 1 – E-MAIL

TO: All Employees
FROM: Roger Steiner, Chief Executive Officer
DATE: October 15

I am pleased to announce that Chris Perillo has been appointed as Vice President of Operations for Health and Financial Services. Chris will immediately assume responsibility for all operations previously managed by Michael Grant. Chris will have end-to-end responsibility for the design, development, integration, and maintenance of custom software for the health and finance/banking industries. This responsibility includes all technical, financial, and staffing issues. Chris will also manage our program of software support and integration for the recently announced merger of three large health maintenance organizations (HMOs). Chris will be responsible for our recently announced project with a consortium of banks and financial firms operating in Tanzania. This project represents an exciting opportunity for us, and Chris's background seems ideally suited to the task.

Chris comes to this position with an undergraduate degree in Computer Science from the California Institute of Technology and an MBA from the University of Virginia. Chris began as a member of our technical/professional staff six years ago and has most recently served for three years as a group manager supporting domestic and international projects for our airlines industry group, including our recent work for the European Airbus consortium.

I am sure you all join me in offering congratulations to Chris for this promotion.

ITEM 2 – E-MAIL

TO: All Managers

FROM: Hal Harris, Vice President, Community and Public Relations

DATE: October 15

For your information, the following article appeared on the front page of the business section of Thursday's *Los Angeles Times*.

> *In a move that may create problems for SSS Software, Michael Grant and Janice Ramos have left SSS Software and moved to Universal Business Solutions Inc. Industry analysts see the move as another victory for Universal Business Solutions Inc. in their battle with SSS Software for share of the growing software development and integration business. Both Grant and Ramos had been with SSS Software for over seven years. Grant was most recently Vice President of Operations for all SSS Software's work in two industries: health and hospitals, and finance and banking. Ramos brings to Universal Business Solutions Inc. her special expertise in the growing area of international software development and integration.*

Hillary Collins, an industry analyst with Merrill Lynch, said "the loss of key staff to a competitor can often create serious problems for a firm such as SSS Software. Grant and Ramos have an insider's understanding of SSS Software's strategic and technical limitations. It will be interesting to see if they can exploit this knowledge to the advantage of Universal Business Solutions Inc."

ITEM 3 – E-MAIL

TO: Chris Perillo

FROM: Paula Sprague, Executive Assistant to Roger Steiner

DATE: October 15

Chris, I know in your former position as a group manager in the Airline Services Division, you probably have met most of the group managers in the Health and Financial Services Division, but I thought you might like some more personal information about them. These people will be your direct reports on the management team.

Group #1: Bob Miller, 55-year-old white male, married (Anna) with two children and three grandchildren. Active in local Republican politics. Well regarded as a "hands-off" manager heading a high-performing team. Plays golf regularly with Mark McIntyre, John Small, and a couple of VPs from other divisions.

Group #2: Wanda Manners, 38-year-old white female, single with one school-age child. A fitness "nut" has run in several marathons. Some experience in Germany and Japan. Considered a hard-driving manager with a constant focus on the task at hand. Will be the first person to show up every morning.

Group #3: William Chen, 31-year-old male of Chinese descent, married (Harriet), two young children from his first marriage. Enjoys tennis and is quite good at it. A rising star in the company, he is highly respected by his peers as a "man of action" and a good friend.

Group #4: Leo Jones, 36-year-old white male, married (Janet) with an infant daughter. Recently returned from paternity leave. Has traveled extensively on projects, since he speaks three languages. Has liked hockey ever since the time he spent in Montreal. Considered a strong manager who gets the most out of his people.

Group #5: Mark McIntyre, 45-year-old white male, married (Mary Theresa) to an executive in the banking industry. No children. A lot of experience in Germany and Eastern Europe. Has been writing a mystery novel. Has always been a good "team player," but several members of his technical staff are not well respected and he hasn't addressed the problem.

Group #6: John Small, 38-year-old white male, recently divorced. Three children living with his wife. A gregarious individual who likes sports. He spent a lot of time in Mexico and Central America before he came to SSS Software. Recently has been doing mostly contract work with the federal government. An average manager, has had some trouble keeping his people on schedule.

Group #7: This position vacant since Janice Ramos left. Roger thinks we ought to fill this position quickly. Get in touch with me if you want information on any in-house candidates for any position.

Group #8: Marcus Harper, 42-year-old African American male, married (Tamara) with two teenage children. Recently won an award in a local photography contest. Considered a strong manager who gets along with peers and works long hours.

Customer Services: Armand Marke, 38-year-old male, divorced. A basketball fan. Originally from Armenia. Previously a group manager. Worked hard to establish the Technical Services Phone Line, but now has pretty much left it alone.

Office Administrator: Michelle Harrison, 41-year-old white female, single. Grew up on a ranch and still rides horses whenever she can. A strict administrator.

There are a number of good folks here, but they don't function well as a management team. I think Michael played favorites, especially with Janice and Leo. There are a few cliques in this group, and I'm not sure how effectively Michael dealt with them. I expect you will find it a challenge to build a cohesive team.

ITEM 4 – E-MAIL

TO: Chris Perillo
FROM: Wanda Manners, Group 2 Manager
DATE: October 15

CONFIDENTIAL AND RESTRICTED

Although I know you are new to your job, I feel it is important I let you know about some information I just obtained concerning the development work we recently completed for First National Investment. Our project involved the development of asset management software for managing their international funds. This was a very complex project due to the volatile exchange rates and the forecasting tools we needed to develop.

As part of this project, we had to integrate the software and reports with all their existing systems and reporting mechanisms. To do this, we were given access to all of their existing software (much of which was developed by Universal Business Solutions Inc.). Of course, we signed an agreement acknowledging the software to which we were given access was proprietary and our access was solely for the purpose of our system integration work associated with the project.

Unfortunately, I have learned some parts of the software we developed actually "borrow" heavily from complex application programs developed for First National Investment by Universal Business Solutions Inc. It seems obvious to me one or more of the software developers from Group 5 (that is, Mark McIntyre's group) inappropriately "borrowed" algorithms developed by Universal Business Solutions Inc. I am sure that doing so saved us significant development time on some aspects of the project. It seems very unlikely First National Investment or Universal Business Solutions Inc. will ever become aware of this issue.

Finally, First National Investment is successfully using the software we developed and is thrilled with the work we did. We brought the project in on time and under budget. You probably know they have invited us to bid on several other substantial projects.

I'm sorry to bring this delicate matter to your attention, but I thought you should know about it.

ITEM 5A – E-MAIL

TO: Chris Perillo
FROM: Paula Sprague, Executive Assistant to Roger Steiner
DATE: October 15
RE: Letter from C.A.R.E. Services (copies attached)

Roger asked me to work on this C.A.R.E. project and obviously wants some fast action. A lot of the staff are already booked solid for the next couple of weeks. I knew Elise Soto and Chu Hung Woo have the expertise to do this system and when I checked with them, they were relatively free. I had them pencil in the next two weeks and wanted to let you know. Hopefully, it will take a "hot potato" out of your hands.

ITEM 5B – COPY OF FAX

C.A.R.E.
Child and Adolescent Rehabilitative and Educational Services
A United Way Member Agency
200 Main Street
Los Angeles, California 90230

DATE: October 11

Roger Steiner, CEO
SSS Software
13 Miller Way
Los Angeles, California 90224

Dear Roger,

This letter is a follow-up to our conversation after last night's board meeting. I appreciated your comments during the board meeting about the need for sophisticated computer systems in nonprofit organizations and I especially appreciate your generous offer of assistance to have SSS Software provide assistance to deal with the immediate problem with our accounting system. Since the board voted to fire the computer consultant, I am very worried about getting our reports done in time to meet the state funding cycle.

Thanks again for your offer of help during this crisis.

Sincerely yours,

Janice Polocizwic

Janice Polocizwic
Executive Director

ITEM 5C – COPY OF A LETTER

SSS SOFTWARE
13 Miller Way
Los Angeles, CA 90224

DATE: October 12

Janice Polocizwic
Executive Director, C.A.R.E. Services
200 Main Street
Los Angeles, California 90230

Dear Janice,

I received your fax of October 11. I have asked Paula Sprague, my executive assistant, to line up people to work on your accounting system as soon as possible. You can expect to hear from her shortly.

Sincerely,

Roger Steiner

Roger Steiner
cc: Paula Sprague, Executive Assistant

ITEM 6 – E-MAIL

TO: Michael Grant
FROM: Harry Withers, Group 6 Technical Staff
DATE: October 12

PERSONAL AND CONFIDENTIAL

Our team is having difficulty meeting the submission deadline of November 5 for the Halstrom project. Kim, Fred, Peter, Kyoto, Susan, Mala, and I have been working on the project for several weeks, but we are experiencing some problems and may need additional time. I hesitate to write this letter, but the main problem is our group manager, John Small, is involved in a relationship with Mala. Mala gets John's support for her ideas and brings them to the team as required components of the project. Needless to say, this has posed some problems for the group. Mala's background is especially valuable for this project, but Kim and Fred, who have both worked very hard on the project, do not want to work with her. In addition, one member of the team has been unavailable recently because of child-care needs. Commitment to the project and team morale have plummeted. However, we'll do our best to get the project finished as soon as possible. Mala will be on vacation the next two weeks, so I'm expecting some of us can complete it in her absence.

ITEM 7 – VOICE MAIL MESSAGE

Hello, Michael. This is Jim Bishop of United Hospitals. I wanted to talk with you about the quality assurance project you are working on for us. When Jose Martinez first started talking with us, I was impressed with his friendliness and expertise. But recently, he doesn't seem to be getting much accomplished and has seemed distant and on edge in conversations. Today, I asked him about the schedule and he seemed very defensive and not entirely in control of his emotions. I am quite concerned about our project. Please give me a call.

ITEM 8 – VOICE MAIL MESSAGE

Hi, Michael. This is Armand. I wanted to talk with you about some issues with the Technical Services Phone Line. I've recently received some complaint letters from Phone Line customers whose complaints have included long delays while waiting for a technician to answer the phone, technicians who are not knowledgeable enough to solve problems, and, on occasion, rude service. Needless to say, I'm quite concerned about these complaints.

I believe the overall quality of the Phone Line staff is very good, but we continue to be understaffed, even with the recent hires. The new technicians look strong, but are working on the help-line before being fully trained. Antolina, our best tech, often brings her child to work, which is adding to the craziness around here.

I think you should know we're feeling a lot of stress here. I'll talk with you soon.

ITEM 9 – VOICE MAIL MESSAGE

Hi, Chris, it's Pat. Congratulations on your promotion. They definitely picked the right person. It's great news—for me, too. You've been a terrific mentor so far, so I'm expecting to learn a lot from you in your new position. How about lunch next week?

ITEM 10 – VOICE MAIL MESSAGE

Chris, this is Bob Miller. Just thought you'd like to know John's joke during our planning meeting has disturbed a few of the women in my group. Frankly, I think the thing's being blown out of proportion, especially since we all know this is a good place for both men and women to work. Give me a call if you want to chat about this.

ITEM 11 – VOICE MAIL MESSAGE

Hello. This is Lorraine Adams from Westside Hospital. I read in today's *Los Angeles Times* you will be taking over for Michael Grant. We haven't met yet, but your division has

PRACTICE

recently finished two large million-dollar projects for Westside. Michael Grant and I had some discussion about a small conversion of a piece of existing software to be compatible with the new systems. The original vendor had said they would do the work, but they have been stalling, and I need to move quickly. Can you see if Harris Wilson, Chu Hung Woo, and Elise Soto are available to do this work as soon as possible? They were on the original project and work well with our people.

Um . . . (long pause) I guess I should tell you I got a call from Michael offering to do this work. But I think I should stick with SSS Software. Give me a call.

ITEM 12 – VOICE MAIL MESSAGE

Hi, Chris, this is Roosevelt Moore calling. I'm a member of your technical/professional staff. I used to report to Janice Ramos, but since she left the firm, I thought I'd bring my concerns directly to you. I'd like to arrange some time to talk with you about my experiences since returning from six weeks of paternity leave. Some of my major responsibilities have been turned over to others. I seem to be out of the loop and wonder if my career is at risk. Also, I am afraid I won't be supported or seriously considered for the opening created by Janice's departure. Frankly, I feel like I'm being screwed for taking my leave. I'd like to talk with you this week.

ITEM 13 – E-MAIL

TO: Michael Grant
FROM: Jose Martinez, Group 1 Technical Staff
DATE: October 12

I would like to set up a meeting with you as soon as possible. I suspect you will get a call from Jim Bishop of United Hospitals and want to be sure you hear my side of the story first. I have been working on a customized system design for quality assurance for them using a variation of the J–3 product we developed several years ago. They had a number of special requirements and some quirks in their accounting systems, so I have had to put in especially long hours. I've worked hard to meet their demands, but they keep changing the ground rules. I keep thinking, this is just another J–3 I'm working on, but they have been interfering with an elegant design I have developed. It seems I'm not getting anywhere on this project. Earlier today, I had a difficult discussion with their controller. He asked for another major change. I've been fighting their deadline and think I am just stretched too thin on this project. Then Jim Bishop asked me if the system was running yet. I was worn out from dealing with the controller, and I made a sarcastic comment to Jim Bishop. He gave me a funny look and just walked out of the room.

I would like to talk with you about this situation at your earliest convenience.

ITEM 14 – E-MAIL

TO: Chris Perillo
FROM: John Small, Group 6 Manager
DATE: October 15

Welcome aboard, Chris. I look forward to meeting with you. I just wanted to put a bug in your ear about finding a replacement for Janice Ramos. One of my technical staff,

Mala Abendano, has the ability and drive to make an excellent group manager. I have encouraged her to apply for the position. I'd be happy to talk with you further about this, at your convenience.

ITEM 15 – E-MAIL

TO: Chris Perillo

FROM: Paula Sprague, Executive Assistant to Roger Steiner

DATE: October 15

Roger asked me to let you know about the large contract we have gotten in Tanzania. It means a team of four managers will be making a short trip to determine current needs. They will assign their technical staff the tasks of developing a system and software here over the next six months, and then the managers and possibly some team members will be spending about 10 months on site in Tanzania to handle the implementation. Roger thought you might want to hold an initial meeting with some of your managers to check on their interest and willingness to take this sort of assignment. Roger would appreciate an e-mail of your thoughts about the issues to be discussed at this meeting, additional considerations about sending people to Tanzania, and about how you will put together an effective team to work on this project. The October 15 memo I sent to you will provide you with some information you'll need to start making these decisions.

ITEM 16 – E-MAIL

TO: Chris Perillo

FROM: Sharon Shapiro, VP of Human Resources

DATE: October 15

RE: Upcoming meeting

I want to update you on the rippling effect of John Small's sexual joke at last week's planning meeting. Quite a few women have been very upset and have met informally to talk about it. They have decided to call a meeting of all people concerned about this kind of behavior throughout the firm. I plan to attend, so I'll keep you posted.

ITEM 17 – E-MAIL

TO: All SSS Software Managers

FROM: Sharon Shapiro, VP of Human Resources

DATE: October 15

RE: Promotions and External Hires

YEAR-TO-DATE (JANUARY THROUGH SEPTEMBER) PROMOTIONS AND EXTERNAL HIRES

Level		Race				Sex		
	White	African American	Asian	Hispanic	Native American	M	F	Total
Hires into Executive Level	0 (0%)	0 (0%)	0 (0%)	0 (0%)	0 (0%)	0 (0%)	0 (0%)	0

Level	White	African American	Asian	Hispanic	Native American	M	F	Total
			Race				Sex	
Promotions to Executive Level	0	0	0	0	0	0	0	0
	(0%)	(0%)	(0%)	(0%)	(0%)	(0%)	(0%)	
Hires into Management Level	2	1	0	0	0	2	1	3
	(67%)	(33%)	(0%)	(0%)	(0%)	(67%)	(33%)	
Promotions to Management Level	7	0	1	0	0	7	1	8
	(88%)	(0%)	(12%)	(0%)	(0%)	(88%)	(12%)	
Hires into Technical/ Professional Level	10	6	10	2	0	14	14	28
	(36%)	(21%)	(36%)	(7%)	(0%)	(50%)	(50%)	
Promotions to Technical/ Professional Level	0	0	0	0	0	0	0	0
	(0%)	(0%)	(0%)	(0%)	(0%)	(0%)	(0%)	
Hires into Non-management Level	4	10	2	4	0	6	14	20
	(20%)	(50%)	(10%)	(20%)	(0%)	(30%)	(70%)	
Promotions to Nonmanagement Level	NA	NA	NA	NA	NA	NA	NA	NA

SSS SOFTWARE EMPLOYEE (EEO) CLASSIFICATION REPORT AS OF JUNE 30

Level	White	African American	Asian	Hispanic	Native American	M	F	Total
			Race				Sex	
Executive Level	11	0	1	0	0	11	1	12
	(92%)	(0%)	(8%)	(0%)	(0%)	(92%)	(8%)	
Management Level	43	2	2	1	0	38	10	48
	(90%)	(4%)	(4%)	(2%)	(0%)	(79%)	(21%)	
Technical/ Professional Level	58	20	37	14	1	80	50	130
	(45%)	(15%)	(28%)	(11%)	(1%)	(62%)	(38%)	

| Level | Race | | | | | Sex | | |
	White	African American	Asian	Hispanic	Native American	M	F	Total
Non-management Level	29	22	4	4	1	12	48	60
	(48%)	(37%)	(7%)	(7%)	(2%)	(20%)	(80%)	
Total	141	44	44	19	2	141	109	250
	(56%)	(18%)	(18%)	(8%)	(1%)	(56%)	(44%)	

NOTE: The SSS Software exercise is used with permission. Copyright © 1995 by Susan Schor, Joseph Seltzer, and James Smither. All rights reserved.

A

ability: the product of aptitude multiplied by training and opportunity. p. 349

abundance approach: the right side of the performance continuum, characterized by concepts such as striving for excellence and being ethically virtuous, which are especially relevant to the skill of leading positive change. p. 563

accommodating approach: a response to conflict that tries to preserve a friendly interpersonal relationship by satisfying the other party's concerns while ignoring one's own. It generally ends with both parties losing. p. 405

achievement orientation: an emphasis on personal accomplishment and merit as the basis for getting ahead, used in contrast to an ascription orientation. One of the key dimensions that identifies international culture differences. p. 89

advising response: a response that provides direction, evaluation, personal opinion, or instructions. p. 279

affectivity orientation: an emphasis on open displays of emotion and feeling as being acceptable, used in contrast to a neutral orientation. One of the key dimensions that identifies international culture differences. p. 286

alarm stage: initial response to stress characterized by increases in anxiety, fear, sorrow, or depression. p. 136

ambidextrous thinking: the use of both the left and right sides of the brain, indicative of the most creative problem solvers. p. 215

analytical problem solving: a method of solving problems that involves four steps: (1) defining the problem; (2) generating alternative solutions; (3) evaluating and selecting an alternative; and (4) implementing and following up on the solution. p. 209

anticipatory stressor: the anxious expectation of unfamiliar, uncertain, or disagreeable events. p. 142

appropriately challenging goals: one of the factors affecting the motivating potential of stated goals—hard goals tend to be more motivating than easy goals. p. 356

ascription orientation: an emphasis on attributes such as age, gender, or family background as the basis for getting ahead, used in contrast to achievement orientation. One of the key dimensions that identifies international culture differences. p. 89

attraction: also referred to as personal attraction, "likability" stemming from agreeable behavior and attractive physical appearance; a combination of behaviors normally associated with friendships that has been shown to contribute to managerial success. p. 311

autonomy: the freedom to choose how and when to do a particular task; one of the characteristics of an intrinsically satisfying job. p. 153

avoiding response: an unassertive, uncooperative reaction to conflict that neglects the interests of both parties by sidestepping the issue. The resulting frustration may engender power struggles as others rush to fill the leadership vacuum. p. 406

B

benchmarking: comparing current levels of performance to the highest standards available, by finding best practice, studying it in detail, and planning to exceed it. p. 574

bias against thinking: the inclination to avoid mental work, one indication of the conceptual block, complacency. p. 215

blocking roles: behaviors that stand in the way of or inhibit the effective performance of a team, or that subvert team member effectiveness. p. 537

brainstorming: a technique designed to help people solve problems by generating alternative solutions without prematurely evaluating and rejecting them. p. 221

C

centrality: the attribute of a position in which the occupant is a key member of informal networks of task-related and interpersonal relationships. The resulting access to information, resources, and the personal commitment of others is an important source of power. p. 315

clarification probe: question(s) designed to clarify information given by the interviewee. p. 281

closed questions: interview questions designed to elicit specific information from interviewees by restricting the possible answers the interviewee can give. Useful when time is limited and/or when answers to open questions need clarifying. p. 643

coaching: interpersonal communication used by managers to pass along advice and information or to set standards for subordinates. p. 267

cognitive style: the manner in which an individual gathers and evaluates information he/she receives. p. 96

collaborating approach: the cooperative, assertive, problem-solving mode of responding to conflict. It focuses on finding solutions to the basic problems and issues that are acceptable to both parties rather than on finding fault and assigning blame. Of the conflict management approaches, this is the only win-win strategy. p. 407

collective feeling: a feature of compassionate organizations, in which managers plan events where people can share feelings such as grief, support, or love. p. 568

collective noticing: a feature of compassionate organizations, in which managers notice or simply become aware when employees suffer or experience difficulty. p. 568

collective responding: a feature of compassionate organizations, in which managers ensure an appropriate response is made when healing or restoration is needed. p. 568

collectivism orientation: an emphasis on the predominance of groups, families, or collectives over individuals, used in contrast to individualism orientation. One of the key dimensions that identifies international culture differences. Also referred to as communitarianism. p. 89

commitment: the conceptual block that results when an individual endorses a particular point of view, definition, or solution. p. 210

comparative standards: standards that compare current performance to similar individuals or organizations, one of several different kinds of best practice standards. p. 574

compassion: in an organization, the capacity to foster collective noticing, feeling, and responding. p. 568

competence: areas in which a person performs fine—not stellar, but good enough. p. 571

complacency: the conceptual block that occurs not because of poor thinking habits or inappropriate assumptions but because of fear, ignorance, self-satisfaction, or mental laziness. p. 214

compression: the conceptual block that results from an individual's looking at a problem too narrowly, screening out too much relevant data, or making assumptions that inhibit solving the problem. p. 212

compromising response: a reaction to conflict that attempts to find satisfaction for both parties by "splitting the difference." If overused, it sends the message that settling disputes is more important than solving problems. p. 406

conceptual blocks: mental obstacles that restrict the way a problem is defined and limit the number of alternative solutions that might otherwise be considered. p. 205

conformity level: the second level of values maturity, at which moral reasoning is based on agreement with and support of society's conventions and expectations. p. 92

congruence: exactly matching the communication, verbally and nonverbally, to what an individual is thinking and feeling. p. 269

conjunctive communication: connection of responses to previous messages in such a way that conversation flows smoothly. p. 276

consistent goals: one of the factors affecting the motivating potential of stated goals—it is difficult to pursue goals that are inconsistent or incompatible. p. 356

constancy: the conceptual block that results from using only one way to look at a problem—to approach, define, describe, or solve it. p. 208

continuous improvement: small, incremental changes team members initiate. p. 526

core competence: an aggregation of individual team member skills, including knowledge, styles, communication patterns, and ways of behaving. p. 526

core self-evaluation: a concept that captures the essential aspects of personality; it accounts for the five personality dimensions (neuroticism, extroversion, conscientiousness, agreeableness, and openness). p. 84

counseling: interpersonal communication used to help subordinates recognize their own problems rather than offering advice, direction, or a right answer. p. 267

creating irreversible momentum: ensuring positive change gains such momentum that it becomes institutionalized and cannot be thwarted. p. 584

creative problem solving: a method of solving problems that involves four stages: preparation, incubation, illumination, and verification. p. 216

D

deep breathing: relaxation technique of taking several successive, slow deep breaths, then exhaling completely. p. 167

defensiveness: focusing on self-defense rather than listening; occurs when an individual feels threatened or punished by the communication. p. 268

deficit approach: the left side of the performance continuum, characterized by concepts such as solving problems and making a profit, which has garnered much more attention than the abundance approach but is less relevant to the skill of leading positive change. p. 563

deflecting response: a response that switches the focus from the communicator's subject to one selected by the listener; or simply the change of subject by the listener. p. 280

delegation: assignment of responsibility for tasks to subordinates. p. 465

descriptive communication: objective description of the event or behavior that needs modification; description of the reaction to the behavior or its consequences; and suggestion of a more acceptable alternative. p. 270

diffuseness orientation: an emphasis on integrating work, family, and personal roles in a society, used in contrast to specificity orientation. One of the key dimensions that identifies international culture differences. p. 89

dignity (and liberty): the ethical decision principle that a decision is right and proper if it preserves the basic humanity of individuals and provides the opportunity for them to have greater freedom. p. 95

direct analogies: a Synectic problem-solving technique in which individuals apply facts, technology, and previous experience to solving a problem. p. 218

dirty dozen: twelve negative attributes found in companies facing decline, turbulence, downsizing, and change. p. 466

disciplining: a motivational strategy by which a manager reacts negatively to an employee's undesirable behavior in order to discourage further occurrences. Disciplining may be useful up to a point but does not encourage exceptional performance. p. 361

disconfirmation: a "put-down"; or the feeling resulting from communication that demeans or belittles the recipient and threatens his or her sense of self-worth. p. 268

disjunctive communication: responses that are disconnected from what was stated before. It can result from (1) a lack of equal opportunity to speak; (2) long pauses in a speech or before a response; or (3) when one person decides the topic of conversation. p. 276

disowned communication: attribution to an unknown person, group, or some external source; allows the communicator to avoid responsibility for the message and therefore avoid investing in the interaction. p. 277

distributive bargaining perspective: negotiation tactic that requires both parties to sacrifice something to resolve the conflict—to divide up a "fixed pie." (Contrast with the integrative approach.) p. 408

double-barreled question: a problematic question that actually consists of two questions that should be asked separately in order to avoid confusing the interviewee. p. 644

E

effort: an important source of power suggesting personal commitment. p. 312

elaboration probe: question(s) designed to pursue a topic further when an interviewee has responded with superficial or inadequate information. pp. 281, 648

emotional intelligence: the ability to manage oneself emotionally and to manage relationships with others. p. 83

empowerment: the use of acquired power to give others power in order to accomplish objectives; it strikes a balance between lack of power and abuse of power. p. 465

enactive strategy: a method of managing stress that creates a new environment by eliminating the stressors. p. 138

encounter stressor: the type of stressor that results from interpersonal conflict. p. 140

environmentally induced stress: conflict-fostering tension induced by such organizational factors as budget tightening or uncertainty caused by rapid, repeated change. p. 404

equity: workers' perceptions of the fairness of rewards based on the comparison of what they are getting out of the work relationship (outcomes) to what they are putting into it (input). p. 370

ethical decision making: a well-developed set of moral principles used when making decisions. p. 94

evaluative communication: a statement that makes a judgment about or places a label on other individuals or on their behavior. p. 270

Everest goals: goals that represent an ultimate achievement, an extraordinary accomplishment, or a beyond-the-norm outcome. p. 531

expertise: cognitive ability resulting from formal training and education or from on-the-job experience; an important source of power in a technological society. p. 310

extrinsic outcomes: rewards for performances that are controlled by someone other than the employee—usually the supervisor—such as appreciation, job security, or good working conditions. (Compare with internal motivators.) p. 364

F

false bipolar question: a poorly worded interview question, implying the choices are mutually exclusive, when in fact, the respondents are more likely to have mixed feelings (e.g., do you approve or disapprove of overtime work?). p. 644

fantasy analogies: a synetic problem-solving technique in which individuals ask, "In my wildest dreams, how would I wish the problem to be resolved?" p. 218

feedback: information regularly received by individuals from superiors about their performance on a job. Knowledge of results permits workers to understand how their efforts have contributed to organizational goals. pp. 153, 356

flexibility: the freedom to exercise one's judgment—an important prerequisite for gaining power in a position—particularly in tasks that are high in variety and novelty. p. 317

flexibility of thought: the diversity of ideas or concepts generated. p. 221

flexible communication: the result of the willingness of the coach or counselor to accept the existence of additional data or other alternatives and to acknowledge that other individuals may be able to make significant contributions both to the problem solution and to the relationship. p. 274

flow: a psychological state in which a person's mind is so totally engaged in a challenging task that he or she often loses track of time, physical appetites, and outside influences. p. 563

fluency of thought: the number of ideas or concepts produced in a given length of time. p. 221

forcing response: an assertive, uncooperative response to conflict that uses the exercise of authority to satisfy one's own needs at the expense of another's. p. 405

forgiveness: in an organization, the capacity to abandon justified resentment, bitterness, and blame, and instead, to adopt positive, forward-looking approaches in response to harm or damage. p. 568

forming stage: first stage of team development in which the team is oriented to each other and establishes clarity of purpose. p. 520

frameworks: familiar patterns that managers can use to clarify complex or ambiguous situations. p. 561

funnel sequence: a sequence of interview questions that begins with general questions and moves toward more and more specific questions. p. 645

G

goal characteristics: effective goals are specific, consistent, and appropriately challenging. p. 356

goal setting: the foundation of an effective motivational program, which consists of (1) including employees in the goal-setting process; (2) setting specific, consistent, and challenging goals; and (3) providing feedback. p. 355

goal-setting process: the critical consideration is that goals must be understood and accepted if they are to be effective. p. 355

goal standards: standards that compare current performance to publicly stated goals, one of several different kinds of best practice standards. p. 574

gratitude: in an organization, the frequent expression of thankfulness that leads to reciprocal behavior, equity, and justice. p. 569

groupthink: one of the pitfalls in group decision making that occurs when the pressure to reach consensus interferes with critical thinking. When the leader or the majority appear to prefer a particular solution, holders of dissenting views are reluctant to speak out. p. 227

H

hardiness: a combination of the three characteristics of a highly stress-resistant personality—control, commitment, and challenge. p. 161

hierarchical-needs model: a general theory of motivation, positing that behavior is oriented toward need fulfillment, and that human needs tend to be arranged hierarchically (i.e., lower-level needs must be fulfilled before higher-order needs become salient). p. 367

human capital: a person's abilities and competencies ("I know the answer to the question"). Compare with social capital. p. 310

I

idea champion: person who comes up with the innovative solutions to problems. p. 229

ideal standards: standards that compare current performance to an ideal or perfect standard, one of several different kinds of best practice standards. p. 574

ignoring: a manager's neglect of both the performance and the satisfaction of employees. Such a lack of effective leadership can paralyze a work unit. p. 353

ignoring commonalities: a manifestation of the commitment block—the failure to identify similarities among seemingly disparate situations or data. p. 211

illumination stage: in creative thought, the third stage, which occurs when an insight is recognized and a creative solution is articulated. p. 217

imagery and fantasy: a relaxation technique using visualization to change the focus of one's thoughts. p. 167

imagination creativity: the pursuit of new ideas, breakthroughs, and radical approaches to problem solving. p. 201

imperviousness in communication: the failure of the communicator to acknowledge the feelings or opinions of the listener. p. 274

imposing: a manager's exploitation of employees by assigning tasks with the sole emphasis on performance and without regard to their job satisfaction—usually disastrous in the long term. p. 353

improvement creativity: the pursuit of incremental improvements on existing ideas. p. 203

improvement standards: standards that compare current performance to improvements made in the past, one of several different kinds of best practice standards. p. 574

incongruence: a mismatch between what one is experiencing and what one is aware of, or a mismatch between what one feels and what one communicates. p. 269

incubation creativity: the pursuit of creativity through teamwork, involvement, and coordination among individuals. p. 203

incubation stage: an early stage in creative thought in which mostly unconscious mental activity combines unrelated thoughts in pursuit of a solution to a problem. p. 217

indifference: a type of communication in which the other person's existence or importance is not acknowledged. p. 274

individualism orientation: an emphasis on the self, uniqueness, and individuality, used in contrast to collectivism orientation. One of the key dimensions that identifies international cultural differences. p. 89

indulging: a manager's emphasis on employee satisfaction to the exclusion of employee performance; the resulting country club atmosphere hinders productivity. p. 352

informational deficiencies: breakdowns in organizational communication. Conflicts based on the resulting misunderstandings tend to be common but easy to resolve. p. 403

initiator role: the part played in a conflict management model by the individual who first registers a complaint with another person who is the "responder." p. 414

innovation: large, visible, discontinuous changes; breakthroughs. p. 196

innovativeness: fostering new ideas among individuals by methods such as placing them in teams and separating them at least temporarily from the normal pressures of organizational life. p. 467

instrumental values: those values that prescribe desirable standards of conduct or methods to reach a goal. p. 90

integrating: a motivation strategy that emphasizes job performance and job satisfaction equally—a challenging strategy for a manager to implement, but one that can result in both high productivity and high morale of employees. p. 353

integrative perspective: negotiation tactic in which the focus is on collaborative ways of "expanding the pie" by avoiding fixed, incompatible positions. (Contrast with distributive approach.) p. 408

internal locus: the viewpoint of an individual who attributes the success or failure of particular behavior to his/her own actions. p. 100

interpersonal competence: the ability to manage conflict, to build and manage high-performance teams, to conduct efficient meetings, to coach and counsel employees, to provide negative feedback in constructive ways, to influence others' opinions, and to motivate and energize employees. p. 152

interview: a specialized form of communication conducted for a specific, task-related purpose. p. 642

intrinsic outcomes: job characteristics inherent in the job itself, over which the manager has no control, and that determine whether or not a particular employee will find that job interesting and satisfying. (Compare with external motivators.) p. 364

invalidating communication: that which denies the other person the possibility of contributing to the communication. p. 273

inverted funnel sequence: a sequence of interview questions that begins with specific questions and moves toward more and more general questions. p. 645

investment creativity: the pursuit of rapid goal achievement and competitiveness. p. 203

issue-focused conflict: interpersonal conflicts that are substantive, or content, oriented. See people-focused conflict. p. 401

issue selling: influence strategy characterized by being the champion or representative of an issue. p. 325

J

Janusian thinking: thinking contradictory thoughts at the same time; conceiving two opposing ideas to be true concurrently. p. 220

L

leadership: a temporary, dynamic condition that can be developed and demonstrated by any person willing to choose to adopt a certain mind-set and implement certain key skills and competencies. p. 560

leading positive change: a management skill that focuses on unlocking positive human potential, creating abundance and human well-being, and acknowledging that positive change engages the heart as well as the mind. p. 564

leading question: a tricky interview question that includes the desired answer in the question itself. While useful in a sales interview, it can lead to biased answers in other types of interviews. p. 644

learning stair: a model, developed by researchers at the National Training Laboratories in Bethel, Maine, that grades learning retention; at the lowest level, people remember only 5 percent of what they hear in a lecture, while at the highest level, people remember 90 percent of what they teach to others. p. 584

learning style: the way in which individuals perceive, interpret, and respond to information. Four main learning styles exist. p. 154

left-hemisphere thinking: brain activity concerned with logical, analytic, linear, or sequential tasks. p. 215

legitimacy: conformity with an organization's value system and practices, which increases one's acceptance and thus one's influence in that organization. p. 314

life balance: the development of resiliency in all areas of one's life in order to handle stress that cannot be eliminated. p. 156

locus of control: the second dimension of orientation toward change; the viewpoint from which an individual judges the extent to which he/she controls his/her own destiny. p. 100

M

manifest needs model: a general theory of motivation, positing that individuals can be classified according to the strengths of their various needs, which are often divergent and conflicting. p. 367

measures: methods for assessing levels of success. p. 586

mediator role: the conflict management role played by the third party who intervenes in a dispute between an "initiator" and a "responder." p. 414

metrics: specific indicators of success. p. 586

milestones: benchmarks to determine when detectable progress will have occurred. p. 586

morphological synthesis: a four-step process intended to expand the number of creative alternatives available for solving a problem. It involves combining the different attributes of a problem together in unique ways. p. 223

motivation: a combination of desire and commitment demonstrated by effort. p. 349

muscle relaxation: technique of relaxation by easing the tension in successive muscle groups. p. 166

N

need for achievement: an expressed desire for accomplishment and recognition. p. 367

need for affiliation: an expressed desire for social relations. p. 368

need for control: the desire to maintain for oneself a satisfactory balance of power and influence in relationships. p. 484

need for power: an expressed desire for control, or influence, over others. p. 368

negative deviance: change toward illness, error, conflict, and the like, usually depicted as a shift to the left along the continuum that shows normal, healthy performance in the middle. p. 562

negative energizers: people who deplete the good feelings and enthusiasm in others and make them feel diminished, devalued, or criticized. p. 567

negotiation strategies: two broad approaches or perspectives used for resolving differences or allocating scarce resources—integrative and distributive. p. 408

neutral orientation: an emphasis on rational and stoic approaches to problem solving, used in contrast to an affective orientation. One of the key dimensions that identifies international cultural differences. p. 89

noninquisitiveness: the failure to ask questions, obtain information or search for data; an example of the complacency block. p. 214

norming stage: the second stage of a team's development in which expectations become clear, a group identity is formed, and the norms become clear and accepted. p. 520

O

open questions: interview questions designed to elicit general information from interviewees—how they feel, what their priorities are, and how much they know about a topic. Useful for establishing rapport, they can be time-consuming. p. 643

orchestrator: person who brings together cross-functional groups and necessary political support to facilitate implementation of a creative idea. p. 229

organizational culture: the values and basic assumptions that typify an organization. It refers to the most basic elements of an organization, or "just the way things are around here." p. 90

orientation toward change: an individual's adaptability to ever-increasing levels of ambiguity and turbulence. p. 84

owning communication: statements for which a person takes responsibility, acknowledging that he or she is the source of the message; an indication of supportive communication. p. 277

P

participants: individuals invited to attend a meeting. p. 675

participation: the actual process of meetings and the methods used to ensure that meetings involve everyone present. The involvement of individuals—in addition to a single leader—in an activity. p. 677

particularism orientation: an emphasis on relationships and close personal connections to govern behavior, used in contrast to universalism orientation. One of the key dimensions that identifies international cultural differences. p. 89

people-focused conflict: interpersonal conflict that is personal (e.g., a clash between different personalities or interpersonal styles). See issue-focused conflict. p. 400

perceptual stereotyping: defining a problem by using preconceptions based on past experience, thus preventing the problem from being viewed in novel ways. p. 211

performance: the product of ability multiplied by motivation. p. 349

performing stage: stage of a team when it is able to function as a highly effective and efficient unit. p. 520

personal analogies: recommended as part of Synectics, whereby individuals try to identify themselves as the problem, asking the question, "If I were the problem, what would I like? What would satisfy me?" p. 218

personal differences: variations among individuals' values and needs that have been shaped by different socialization processes. Interpersonal conflicts stemming from such incompatibilities are the most difficult for a manager to resolve. p. 402

personal management interview program (PMI): a regularly scheduled, one-on-one meeting between a manager and his or her subordinates. p. 283

personal values: an individual's standards that define what is good/bad, worthwhile/worthless, desirable/undesirable, true/false, moral/immoral. p. 83

perspective: the evaluation of a meeting from a distance. p. 679

planning: preparation for the meeting agenda. p. 676

positive deviance: change toward excellence, perfection, psychological "flow," and the like, usually depicted as a shift to the light along the continuum that shows normal, healthy performance in the middle. p. 563

positive energizers: people who strengthen and create vitality and liveliness in others. p. 567

positive energy networks: interconnected groups of vitality and liveliness creators, being a member of which has been shown to be more predictive of success than being at the center of an information network or influence network. p. 567

positive interpersonal relationships: relationships that create positive energy and physiological, emotional, intellectual, and social consequences. p. 260

preparation stage: a stage in creative thought that includes gathering data, defining the problem, generating alternatives, and consciously examining all available information. p. 217

principled level: the third and highest level of values maturity in which an individual judges right from wrong by following internalized principles developed from personal experience. p. 92

proactive strategy: a method of managing stress that initiates action in order to resist the negative effects of stress. p. 138

probing response: a response that asks a question about what the communicator just said or about a topic selected by the listener. p. 281

problem-solving process: an approach to conflict resolution that focuses on identifying underlying problems, or issues, and brainstorming solutions. p. 414

process: a sequential set of activities designed to lead to a specific outcome. p. 81

process improvement: stage in process management where process itself is changed so as to foster advancement. p. 520

purpose: the reason a meeting is held, including information sharing, commitment building, information disseminating, and problem solving and decision making. p. 674

Q

quality circles: A problem-solving process originating in Japan in which teams who meet to discuss issues and make recommendations to upper management. p. 632

R

reactive strategy: a method for managing stress that copes with the stressors immediately, temporarily reducing their effects. p. 138

reason: the influence strategy that relies on persuasion and appeals to rational consideration of the inherent merits of the request in order to gain compliance. It is explicit and direct, not manipulative. p. 322

reassigning: moving the poor performer to a position more consonant with his or her skill level and aptitude. p. 351

reciprocity: an influence strategy through which a manager uses bargaining as a tool for exacting a subordinate's compliance. This approach operates on the principle of self-interest and respect for the value of the interpersonal relationship. p. 322

recreational work: work that people willingly engage in due to characteristics such as clearly defined goals, objective evaluations, frequent feedback, the presence of personal choice, consistent rules, and a competitive environment. p. 581

redirection: a behavior-shaping process that follows a reprimand and gives the offender the opportunity to receive a future reward by modifying his or her behavior. p. 363

refitting: adapting the requirements of a job to an employee's abilities in order to improve poor performance. p. 351

reflected best-self feedback: a technique that managers can use to enhance positivity and focus on strengths, by providing people with feedback on their strengths and unique capabilities rather than their weaknesses. p. 571

reflecting response: a response that serves two purposes: (1) to confirm a message that was heard and (2) to communicate understanding and acceptance of the other person. p. 282

reflection probe: nondirective question(s) used for either elaboration or clarification of information; it generally mirrors or repeats some aspect of the interviewee's last answer. p. 281

reflective probe: a response to a communicator by reflecting back in one's own words what the communicator said. The purpose is to clarify the message and help the communicator feel open and safe in sharing more messages. p. 649

reframing: stress-reduction technique of redefining a situation as manageable. p. 167

rehearsal: relaxation technique of trying out stressful scenarios and alternative reactions. p. 167

reinforce: when rewards are linked to desired behaviors they are said to reinforce those behaviors (i.e., increase their frequency). p. 364

relational algorithm: a blockbusting technique for combining unrelated attributes in problem solving by connecting words to force a relationship between two elements in a problem. p. 223

relationship-building roles: those that emphasize the interpersonal aspects of the team. p. 535

relevance: the characteristic of a position whose tasks relate most closely to the dominant competitive goals of an organization and therefore enhance the power of the occupant. p. 319

repetition probe: a repeated or paraphrased question used if the interviewee has not directly answered a question the first time. pp. 281, 649

reprimand: a behavior-shaping approach used to transform unacceptable behaviors into acceptable ones; the discipline should be prompt and it should focus on the specific behavior. p. 363

resiliency: one's capacity to cope with stress. p. 156

resistance stage: response to stress in which defense mechanisms predominate. p. 136

respectful communication: treating subordinates as worthwhile, competent, and insightful by emphasizing joint problem solving rather than projecting a superior position. p. 274

responder role: the part played in a conflict management model by the person who is supposedly the source of the "initiator's" problem. p. 414

resupplying: managerial option for overcoming an employee's lack-of-ability problem that focuses on supplying the support needed to do the job. p. 351

retraining: a management tool for overcoming the problem of an employee's poor performance, especially needed in rapidly changing technical work environments. p. 351

retribution: an influence strategy that involves a threat—the denial of expected rewards or the imposition of punishment. It usually triggers an aversive response in the subordinate and the breakdown of the interpersonal relationship. p. 320

reverse the definition: a tool for improving and expanding problem definition by reversing the way you think of the problem. p. 219

rewarding: the motivational strategy that links desired behaviors with employee-valued outcomes. Such positive reinforcement gives an employee more incentive for exceptional accomplishment than does disciplining. p. 361

right-hemisphere thinking: mental activity concerned with intuition, synthesis, playfulness, and qualitative judgment. p. 215

rigidity in communication: a type of message that portrays the communication as absolute, unequivocal, or unquestionable. p. 273

role incompatibility: the conflict-producing difference between workers whose tasks are interdependent but whose priorities differ because their responsibilities within the organization differ. The mediation of a common superior is usually the best solution. p. 404

rule breaker: the person who goes beyond organizational boundaries and barriers to ensure success of the creative solution. p. 229

S

self-awareness: a knowledge of one's own personality and individuality. p. 79

self-centered level: the first level of values maturity. It contains two stages of values development, moral reasoning and instrumental values, which are based on personal needs or wants and the consequences of an act. p. 92

self-determination: feelings of having a choice. p. 470

self-disclosure: revealing to others ambiguous or inconsistent aspects of oneself, a process necessary for growth. p. 81

self-efficacy: empowered feeling of possessing the capability and competence to perform a task successfully. p. 469

sensitive line: an invisible boundary around one's self-image, which, if threatened, will evoke a strong defensive reaction. p. 80

separating figure from ground: the ability to filter out inaccurate, misleading, or irrelevant information so the problem can be defined accurately and alternative solutions can be generated. p. 214

situational stressor: the type of stressor that arises from an individual's environment or circumstances, such as unfavorable working conditions. p. 140

skill variety: an attribute of a job that uses an individual's talents and abilities to the maximum and thus makes the job seem worthwhile and important. p. 153

small-wins strategy: a strategy for individuals to use for coping with stress; it involves celebrating each small successful step, especially changes that are easy to implement and that build momentum, in the attack on a large project. p. 475

SMART goals: goals that are specific, measurable, aligned, realistic, and time-bound. pp. 475, 531

social capital: a person's social connections ("I know someone who knows the answer to the question"). Compare with human capital. p. 310

source credibility: a judgment about the extent to which information can be believed, three attributes of which are trustworthiness, expertise, and dynamism. p. 588

specific goals: goals that are measurable, unambiguous, and behavioral. p. 356

specificity orientation: an emphasis on separating work, family, and personal roles in a society, used in contrast to diffusion orientation. One of the key dimensions that identifies international cultural differences. p. 89

sponsor: person who helps provide the resources, environment, and encouragement that the idea champion needs in order to work. p. 229

stakeholder expectations: a best-practice standard in which current performance is compared with the expectations of customers, employers, or other stakeholders. p. 574

storming stage: team development stage in which members question the team's direction, the leader, roles of other members, and task objectives. p. 520

strength: areas in which a person is an outstanding performer, has special capabilities or talents, and does better than most people. p. 571

stressors: stimuli that cause physiological and psychological reactions in individuals. p. 142

subdivision: the breaking apart of a problem into smaller parts. p. 222

superiority-oriented communication: a message that gives the impression that the communicator is informed while others are ignorant, adequate while others are inadequate, competent while others are incompetent, or powerful while others are impotent. p. 273

supportive communication: communication that helps managers share information accurately and honestly without jeopardizing interpersonal relationships. p. 264

symbolic analogies: symbols or images that are imposed on the problem; recommended as part of Synectics. p. 218

Synectics: a technique for improving creative problem solving by putting something you don't know in terms of something you do know. p. 218

T

task-facilitating roles: those that help the team accomplish its outcome objectives. p. 535

task identity: an attribute of a job that enables an individual to perform a complete job from beginning to end. pp. 153, 480

task significance: the degree to which the performance of a task affects the work or lives of other people. The greater its significance, the more meaningful the job is to the worker. p. 153

terminal values: those values that designate desirable ends or goals for an individual. p. 90

thinking languages: the various ways in which a problem can be considered, from verbal to nonverbal or symbolic languages as well as through sensory and visual imagery. Using only one thinking language is one indication of the constancy block. p. 209

threat-rigidity response: the tendency of almost all individuals, groups, and organizations to become rigid, meaning conservative and self-protective, when faced with a threat. p. 81

time stressor: the type of stressor generally caused by having too much to do in too little time. p. 139

tolerance of ambiguity: an individual's ability to cope with ambiguous, fast-changing, or unpredictable situations in which information is incomplete, unclear, or complex. p. 84

two-way communication: the result of respectfulness and flexibility. p. 275

Type A personality: a hard-driving, hostile, intense, highly competitive personality. p. 162

U

uniquenesses: areas in which a person has special capacities, gifts, talents, or skills. p. 571

universalism: the ethical decision principle that a decision is right and proper if everyone would be expected to behave in the same way under the same circumstances. p. 89

V

validating communication: a message that helps people feel recognized, understood, accepted, and valued. It is respectful, flexible, two-way, and based on agreement. p. 273

values maturity: the level of moral development displayed by individuals. p. 91

verification stage: the final stage in creative thought in which the creative solution is evaluated relative to some standard of acceptability. p. 217

vertical thinking: defining a problem in a single way and then pursuing that definition without deviation until a solution is reached. p. 208

visibility: the power-enhancing attribute of a position that can usually be measured by the number of influential people one interacts with in the organization. p. 318

vision of abundance: an image of a positive future, a flourishing condition, and a legacy about which people care passionately, which a leader articulates in order to promote positive change. p. 575

vision statement: a leadership document that outlines an organization's guiding values and principles, provides a sense of direction and possibilities, and inspires optimism and hope for a better future. p. 576

W

weaknesses: areas in which a person is underdeveloped, uninformed, or has little skill. p. 571

work design: the process of matching job characteristics and workers' skills and interests. p. 364

APPENDIX II
REFERENCES

INTRODUCTION REFERENCES

American Management Association. (2000). Managerial skills and competence. National survey by AMA, March–April 2000. (N = 921)

Andersen Consulting Company. (2000). *Skills needed for the e-business environment.* Chicago: Author.

Bandura, A. (1977). *A social learning theory.* Englewood Cliffs, NJ: Prentice Hall.

Bass, B. (1990). *Handbook of leadership: Theory, research, and managerial applications,* 3rd ed. New York: Macmillan.

Blimes, L., K. Wetzker, and P. Xhonneux. (1997 February 10). Value in human resources. *Financial Times.*

Boyatzis, R. E. (1996). Consequences and rejuvenation of competency-based human resource and organization development. In Richard Woodman and William A. Pasmore (Eds.), *Research in organizational change and development,* Vol. 9. Greenwich, CT: JAI Press.

Boyatzis, R. E. (2000). Developing emotional intelligence. In C. Cherniss and D. Goleman (Eds.), *Development in emotional intelligence.* New York: Bantam.

Boyatzis, R. E. (2005). Self-directed change and learning as a necessary meta-competency for success and effectiveness in the 21st century. In R. Sims and J. G. Veres (Eds.), *Keys to employee success in the coming decades.* Westport, CT: Greenwood Publishing.

Boyatzis, R. E., S. S. Cowen, and D. A. Kolb. (1995). *Innovation in professional education: Steps on a journey from teaching to learning.* San Francisco: Jossey-Bass.

Boyatzis, R. E., D. Leonard, K. Rhee, and J. V. Wheeler. (1996). Competencies can be developed, but not in the way we thought. *Capability, 2:* 25–41.

Brodbeck, F., et al. (2000). Cultural variation of leadership prototypes across 22 countries. *Journal of Occupational and Organizational Psychology, 73:* 1–50.

Burnaska, R. F. (1976). The effects of behavioral modeling training upon managers' behavior and employees' perceptions. *Personnel Psychology, 29:* 329–335.

Cameron, Kim S., and Robert E. Quinn. (2006). *Diagnosing and changing organizational culture.* San Francisco: Jossey-Bass.

Cameron, K. S., R. E. Quinn, J. DeGraff, and A. V. Thakor. (2006). *Competing values leadership: Creating value in organizations.* New York: Edward Elgar.

Cameron, K., and M. Tschirhart. (1988). Managerial competencies and organizational effectiveness. Working paper, School of Business Administration, University of Michigan.

Cameron, K. S., and D. O. Ulrich. (1986). Transformational leadership in colleges and universities. In J. Smart (Ed.), *Higher education: Handbook of theory and research* Vol. 2 (pp. 1–42). New York: Agathon.

Cameron, K. S., and D. A. Whetten. (1984). A model for teaching management skills. *Organizational Behavior Teaching Journal, 8:* 21–27.

Cohen, P. A. (1984). College grades and adult achievement: A research synthesis. *Research in Higher Education, 20:* 281–291.

Cox, T. H. (1994). *Cultural diversity in organizations: Theory, research, and practice.* San Francisco: Barrett-Koehler.

Cox, T. H., and R. L. Beal. (1997). *Developing competency to manage diversity.* San Francisco: Barrett-Koehler.

Curtis, D. B., J. L. Winsor, and D. Stephens. (1989). National preferences in business and communication education. *Communication Education, 38:* 6–15.

Davis, T. W., and F. Luthans. (1980). A social learning approach to organizational behavior. *Academy of Management Review, 5:* 281–290.

Goleman, D. (1998). *Working with emotional intelligence.* New York: Bantam.

Greenberg, E. (1999). Broadcast Transcript, National Public Radio Morning Edition, October 26.

Hanson, G. (1986). *Determinants of firm performance: An integration of economic and organizational factors.* Unpublished doctoral dissertation, University of Michigan Business School.

Holt, J. (1964). *How children fail.* New York: Pitman.

Huselid, M. A. (1995). The impact of human resource management practices on turnover, productivity, and corporate financial performance. *Academy of Management Journal, 38:* 647.

Huselid, M. A., and B. E. Becker. (1997). The impact of high-performance work systems, implementing effectiveness, and alignment with strategy on shareholder wealth. *Academy of Management Best Papers Proceedings:* 144–148.

Katzenbach, J. R. (1995). *Real change leaders: How you can create growth and high performance in your company.* New York: New York Times Business, Random House.

Kolb, D. A. (1984). *Experiential learning: Experience as the source of learning and development.* Englewood Cliffs, NJ: Prentice Hall.

Latham, G. P., and L. P. Saari, (1979). Application of social learning theory to training supervisors through behavioral modeling. *Journal of Applied Psychology, 64:* 239–246.

Leonard, D. (1996). *The impact of learning goals on self-directed change in management development and education.* Unpublished doctoral dissertation, Weatherhead School of Management, Case Western Reserve University.

Luthans, F., S. A. Rosenkrantz, and H. W. Hennessey. (1985). What do successful managers really do? An observation study of managerial activities. *Journal of Applied Behavioral Science, 21:* 255–270.

Mintzberg, H. (1975). The manager's job: Folklore and fact. *Harvard Business Review, 53:* 49–71.

Moorehead, B. (n.d.). http://www.snopes.com/politics/soapbox/paradox.asp.

Moses, J. L., and R. J. Ritchie. (1976). Supervisory relationships training: A behavioral evaluation of a behavioral modeling program. *Personnel Psychology, 29:* 337–343.

Nair, K. (1994). *A higher standard of leadership.* San Francisco: Barrett-Koehler.

Pfeffer, J. (1998). *The human equation: Building profits by putting people first.* Boston Harvard Business School Press.

Pfeffer, J., and J. F. Veiga. (1999). Putting people first for organizational success. *Academy of Management Executive, 13:* 37–48.

Porras, J. I., and B. Anderson. (1991). Improving managerial effectiveness through modeling-based training. *Organizational Dynamics, 9:* 60–77.

Quinn, R. E. (2000). *Change the world.* San Francisco: Jossey-Bass.

Quinn, R. E., and J. Rohrbaugh. (1983). A special model of effectiveness criteria: Towards a competing values approach to organizational analysis. *Management Science, 29:* 363–377.

Rhee, K. (1997). *Journey of Discovery: A longitudinal study of learning during a graduate professional program.* Unpublished doctoral dissertation, Weatherhead School of Management, Case Western Reserve University.

Rigby, D. (1998). *Management tools and techniques.* Boston: Bain and Company.

Smith, P. E. (1976). Management modeling training to improve morale and customer satisfaction. *Personnel Psychology, 29:* 351–359.

Staw, B. M., L. Sandelands, and J. Dutton. (1981). Threat-rigidity effects in organizational behavior: A multi-level analysis. *Administrative Science Quarterly, 26:* 501–524.

Tichy, N. M. (1993). *Control your destiny or someone else will.* New York: Doubleday.

Tichy, N. M. (1999). *The leadership engine.* New York: Harper Business.

Trompenaars, F., and C. Hampden-Turner. (1998). *Riding the waves of culture.* Understanding diversity in global business. New York: McGraw-Hill.

U.S. Office of the Comptroller of the Currency. (1990). http://www.occ.treas.gov.

Vance, C. M. (1993). *Mastering management education.* Newbury Park, CA: Sage.

Van Velsor, E., and L. Jean Britain. (1995). Why executives derail: Perspectives across time and culture. *Academy of Management Executive, 9:* 62–72.

Weick, K. E. (1995). *Sensemaking in organizations.* Thousand Oaks, CA: Sage.

Welbourne, T., and A. Andrews. (1996). Predicting performance of initial public offering firms: Should HRM be in the equation? *Academy of Management Journal, 39:* 891–919.

Wheeler, J. V. (1999). *Organizational and environmental supports and opportunities for self-directed learning following graduate education.* Unpublished doctoral dissertation, Weatherhead School of Management, Case Western Reserve University.

Whetten, D. A., and K. S. Cameron. (1983). Management skill training: A needed addition to the management curriculum. *Organizational Behavior Teaching Journal, 8:* 10–15.

CHAPTER 1 REFERENCES

Agor, W. H. (1985). Intuition as a brain skill in management. *Public Personnel Management, 14:* 15–25.

Alexander, K. L. (2000, February 22). No Mr. Nice Guy for Disney. *USA Today:* B1–B2.

Allan, H., and J. Waclawski. (1999). Influence behaviors and managerial effectiveness in lateral relations. *Human Resource Development Quarterly, 10:* 3–34.

Allport, G., R. Gordon, and P. Vernon. (1931, 1960). *The study of values manual.* Boston: Houghton Mifflin.

Allport, G., P. Vernon, and G. Lindzey. (1960). *Study of values.* Boston: Houghton Mifflin.

Anderson, C., and C. E. Schneider. (1978). Locus of control, leader behavior, and leader performance among management students. *Academy of Management Journal, 21:* 690–698.

Andrews, K. (1989, September–October). Ethics in practice. *Harvard Business Review:* 99–104.

Armstrong, S. J. (2000). The influence of cognitive style on performance in management education. *Educational Psychology, 20:* 323–339.

Armstrong-Stassen, M. (1998). Downsizing the federal government: A longitudinal study of managers' reactions. *Revue Canadienne des Sciences de l'Administration, 15:* 310–321.

Bar-On, R. (1997). *Bar-On emotional quotient inventory: Users manual.* Toronto: Multi-Health Systems.

Bernardi, R. (1997). The relationships among locus of control, perceptions of stress, and performance. *Journal of Applied Business Research, 13:* 108.

Berscheid, E., and E. H. Walster. (1978). *Interpersonal attraction.* Reading, MA: Addison-Wesley.

Bigoness, W., and G. Blakely. (1996). A cross-national study of managerial values. *Journal of International Business Studies, 27:* 739–752.

Bilsky, W., and S. H. Schwartz. (1994). Values and personality. *European Journal of Personality, 8:* 163–181.

Bonnett, C., and A. Furnham. (1991). Who wants to be an entrepreneur? *Journal of Economic Psychology, 66:* 125–138.

Bono, J. E., and T. A. Judge. (2003). Core self-evaluations: A review of the trait and its role in job satisfaction and job performance. *European Journal of Personality, 17:* 5–18.

Boone, C., and B. de Brabander. (1997). Self-reports and CEO locus of control research: A note. *Organizational Studies, 18:* 949–971.

Boyatzis, R. E. (1998). Self-directed change and learning as a necessary meta-competency for success and effectiveness in the 21st century. In R. Sims and J. G. Veres (Eds.), *Keys to employee success in the coming decade.* Westport, CT: Greenwood.

Boyatzis, R. E. (1982). *The competent manager: A model for effective performance.* New York: Wiley.

Boyatzis, R. E., D. Goleman, and K. Rhee. (2000). Clustering competence in emotional intelligence: Insights from the Emotional Intelligence Inventory. In R. Bar-On and J. D. A. Parker (Eds.), *Handbook of emotional intelligence* (pp. 343–352). San Francisco: Jossey-Bass.

Brown, N. W. (1997). Description of personality similarities and differences of a sample of black and white female engineering students. *Psychological Reports, 81:* 603–610.

Budner, S. (1962). Intolerance of ambiguity as a personality variable. *Journal of Personality, 30:* 29–50.

Cable, D., and T. A. Judge. (1996). Person-organization fit, job choice decisions, and organizational entry. *Organizational Behavior and Human Decision Processes, 67:* 294–311.

Cameron, K. S., and R. E. Quinn. (2006). *Diagnosing and changing organizational culture.* San Francisco: Jossey-Bass.

Cassidy, S. (2004). Learning styles: An overview of theories, models, and measures. *Educational Psychology, 24:* 419–444.

Cavanaugh, G. F. (1980). *American business values in transition.* Englewood Cliffs, NJ: Prentice-Hall.

Cervone, D. (1997). Social-cognitive mechanisms and personality coherence: Self-knowledge, situational beliefs, and cross-situational coherence in perceived self-efficacy. *Psychological Science, 8:* 156–165.

Chan, D. (1966). Cognitive misfit of problem-solving style at work: A facet of person-organization fit. *Organizational Behavior and Human Decision Processes, 68:* 194–207.

Chenhall, R., and D. Morris. (1991). The effect of cognitive style and sponsorship bias on the treatment of opportunity costs in resource allocation decisions. *Accounting, Organizations, and Society, 16:* 27–46.

Clare, D. A., and D. G. Sanford. (1979). Mapping personal value space: A study of managers in four organizations. *Human Relations, 32:* 659–666.

Coleman, D., G. Irving, and C. Cooper. (1999). Another look at the locus of control-organizational commitment relationship: It depends on the form of commitment. *Journal of Organizational Behavior, 20:* 995–1001.

Cools, E., and H. Van den Broeck. (2007). Development and validation of the Cognitive Style Indicator. *Journal of Psychology, 14:* 359–387.

Covey, S. R. (1989). *The seven habits of highly effective people.* New York: Simon & Schuster.

Cox, T. H. (1994). *Cultural diversity in organizations.* San Francisco: Barrett-Koehler.

Cromie, S., I. Callaghan, and M. Jansen. (1992). The entrepreneurial tendencies of managers. *British Journal of Management, 3:* 1–5.

Darrow, B. (1998, November 16). Michael Dell. *Computer Reseller News:* 124–125.

Dollinger, S. J., F. T. L. Leong, and S. K. Ulicni. (1996). On traits and values: With special reference to openness to experience. *Journal of Research in Personality, 30:* 23–41.

Eckstrom, R. B., J. W. French, and H. H. Harmon. (1979). Cognitive factors: Their identification and replication. *Multivariate Behavioral Research Monographs, 72:* 3–84.

Elliott, A. L., and R. J. Schroth. (2002). *How companies lie: Why Enron is just the tip of the iceberg.* New York: Crown Business.

Elsayed-Elkhouly, S. M., and R. Buda. (1997). A cross–cultural comparison of value systems of Egyptians, Americans, Africans, and Arab executives. *International Journal of Commerce and Management, 7:* 102–119.

Erez, A., and T. A. Judge. (2001). Relationship of core self–evaluations to goal setting, motivation, and performance. *Journal of Applied Psychology, 86:* 1270–1279.

Feist, G. J., and F. Barron. (1996). Emotional intelligence and academic intelligence in career and life success. Presented at the American Psychological Association Meeting, San Francisco.

Fisher, S. G., W. D. K. Macrosson, and M. R. Yusuff. (1996). Team performance and human values. *Psychological Reports, 79:* 1019–1024.

Fisher, S. G., W. D. K. Macrosson, and C. A. Walker. (1995). FIRO-B: The power of love and the love of power. *Psychological Reports, 76:* 195–206.

Freud, S. (1956). *Collected papers* (Vols. 3 and 4). London: Hogarth.

Gilligan, C. (1979). Women's place in man's lifecycle. *Harvard Educational Review, 49:* 431–446.

Gilligan, C. (1980). Moral development in late adolescence: A critique and reconstruction of Kohlberg's theory. *Human Development, 23:* 77–104.

Gilligan, C. (1982). In a different voice: Women's conceptions of self and morality. *Harvard Educational Review, 47:* 481–517.

Gilligan, C. (1988). Two moral orientations: Gender differences and similarities. *Merrill-Palmer Quarterly, 34:* 223–237.

Goleman, D. (1995). *Emotional intelligence.* New York: Bantam.

Goleman, D. (1998). What makes a leader? *Harvard Business Review, 76:* 92–102.

Goleman, D. (1998). *Working with emotional intelligence.* New York: Bantam.

Haase, R. F., D. Yul Lee, and D. L. Banks. (1979). Cognitive correlates of polychronicity. *Perceptual and Motor Skills, 49:* 271–282.

Hammer, T. H., and Y. Vardi. (1981). Locus of control and career self-management among nonsupervisory employees in industrial settings. *Journal of Vocational Behavior, 18:* 13–29.

Harris, S. (1981, October 6). Know yourself? It's a paradox. *Associated Press.*

Harter, S. (1990). Causes, correlates, and the functional role of global self-worth. In R. J. Sternberg and J. Kolligan (Eds.), *Competence reconsidered.* (pp. 67–97). New Haven: Yale University Press.

Hayes, J., and C. W. Allinson. (1994). Cognitive style and its relevance for management practice. *British Journal of Management, 5:* 53–71.

Henderson, J. C., and Paul C. Nutt. (1980). The influence of decision style on decision making behavior. *Management Science, 26:* 371–386.

Hendricks, J. A. (1985, May–June). Locus of control: Implications for managers and accountants. *Cost and Management:* 25–29.

Hewett, T. T., G. E. O'Brien, and J. Hornik. (1974). The effects of work organization, leadership style, and member compatibility upon the productivity of small groups working on a manipulative task. *Organizational Behavior and Human Performance, 11:* 283–301.

Jacobson, C. M. (1993). Cognitive styles of creativity: Relations of scores on the Kirton Adaptation-Innovation Inventory and the Myers-Briggs Type Indicator among managers in the USA. *Psychological Reports, 72:* 1131–1138.

Johnston, C. S. (1995). The Rokeach Value Survey: Underlying structure and multidimensional scaling. *Journal of Psychology, 129:* 583–597.

Judge, T. A., and J. E. Bono. (2001). Relationship of core self-evaluations traits—self-esteem, generalized self-efficacy, locus of control, and emotional stability—with job satisfaction and job performance: A meta-analysis. *Journal of Applied Psychology, 86:* 80–92.

Judge, T. A., A. Erez, J. E. Bono, and C. J. Thoreson. (2002). Are measures of self-esteem, neuroticism, locus of control, and generalized self-efficacy indicators of a common core construct? *Journal of Personality and Social Psychology, 83:* 693–710.

Judge, T. A., A. Erez, J. E. Bono, and C. J. Thoreson. (2003). The core self-evaluation scale: Development of a measure. *Personnel Psychology, 56:* 303–331.

Kirton, M. J. (2003). *Adaptation–innovation in the context of diversity and change.* London: Routledge.

Kohlberg, L. (1969). The cognitive-developmental approach to socialization. In D. A. Goslin (Ed.), *Handbook of socialization theory and research.* Chicago: Rand McNally.

Kohlberg, L. (1976). Moral stages and moralization, the cognitive-developmental approach. In T. Lickona (Ed.), *Moral development and behavior.* New York: Holt, Rinehart & Winston.

Kohlberg, L. (1981). *Essays in moral development,* Vol. 1. New York: Harper & Row, pp. 409–412.

Kohlberg, L., and R. A. Ryncarz. (1990). Beyond justice reasoning: Moral development and consideration of a seventh stage. In C. Alexander and E. J. Langer (Eds.), *Higher stages of human development.* New York: Oxford University Press.

Kolb, D. A., R. E. Boyatzis, and C. Mainemelis. (2000). Experiential learning theory: Previous research and new directions. In R. J. Sternberg and L. F. Zhang (Eds.), *Perspectives on cognitive, learning, and thinking styles.* Mahwah, NJ: Lawrence Erlbaum.

Kren, L. (1992). The moderating effects of locus of control on performance incentives and participation. *Human Relations, 45:* 991–1012.

Lickona, T. (1976). Critical issues in the study of moral development and behavior. In T. Lickona (Ed.), *Moral development and behavior: Theory, research, and social issues.* New York: Holt, Rinehart & Winston.

Liddel, W. W., and John W. Slocum Jr. (1976). The effects of individual-role compatibility upon group performance: An extension of Schutz's FIRO theory. *Academy of Management Journal, 19:* 413–426.

Locke, E. A., K. McClear, and D. Knight. (1996). Self-esteem at work. *International Review of Industrial/Organizational Psychology, 11:* 1–32.

Maslow, A. H. (1962). *Toward a psychology of being.* Princeton, NJ: D. Von Nostrand.

Milgram, S. (1963). Behavioral study of obedience. *Journal of Abnormal and Social Psychology, 67:* 371–378.

Miller, D., M. F. R. Kets de Vries, and J. M. Toulouse. (1982). Top executive locus of control and its relationship to strategy-making, structure, and environment. *Academy of Management Journal, 25:* 237–253.

Mitchell, L. E. (2002). *Corporate irresponsibility: America's newest export.* New Haven: Yale University Press.

Moore, T. (1987, March 30). Personality tests are back. *Fortune:* 74–82.

Newton, T., and A. Keenan. (1990). The moderating effect of Type A behavior pattern and locus of control upon the relationship between change in job demands and change in psychological strain. *Human Relations, 43:* 1229–1255.

Nwachukwu, S. L. S., and S. J. Vitell. (1997). The influence of corporate culture on managerial ethical judgments. *Journal of Business Ethics, 16:* 757–776.

O'Reilly, B. (1999). The mechanic who fixed Continental. *Fortune, 140:* 176–186.

Parker, V., and K. Kram. (1993). Women mentoring women. *Business Horizons, 36:* 101–102.

Phillips, J., and S. Gully. (1997). Role of goal orientation, ability, need for achievement, and locus of control in self-efficacy and goal-setting processes. *Journal of Applied Psychology, 82:* 792–802.

Posner, B., and J. Kouzes. (1993). Values congruence and differences between the interplay of personal and organizational values. *Journal of Business Ethics, 12:* 341–347.

Rest, J. R. (1979). *Revised manual for the Defining Issues Test: An objective test of moral judgment development.* Minneapolis: Minnesota Moral Research Projects.

Rice, Michelle. (1999). Rugged mountains and lifelong connections: Adrian Manger. *Australian CPA, 69:* 36–37.

Rogers, C. R. (1961). *On becoming a person.* Boston: Houghton Mifflin.

Rokeach, M. (1973). *The nature of human values.* New York: Free Press.

Rosenthal, R. (1977). The PONS Test: Measuring sensitivity to nonverbal cues. In P. McReynolds (Ed.), *Advancement on psychological assessment.* San Francisco: Jossey-Bass.

Rotter, J. B. (1966). Generalized expectancies for internal versus external control of reinforcement. *Psychological Monographs, 80:* 1–28.

Ryan, L. R. (1970). *Clinical interpretation of the FIRO-B.* Palo Alto, CA: Consulting Psychologists Press.

Salovey, P., and J. Mayer. (1990). Emotional intelligence. *Imagination, Cognition, and Personality, 9:* 185–211.

Schein, E. H. (1960). Interpersonal communication, group solidarity, and social influence. *Sociometry, 23:* 148–161.

Seeman, M. (1982). On the personal consequences of alienation in work. *American Sociological Review, 32:* 273–285.

Snarey, J. R., and G. E. Vaillant. (1985). How lower- and working-class youth become middle-class adults: The association between ego defense mechanisms and upward social mobility. *Child Development, 56:* 899–910.

Sosik, J., and L. E. Megerian. (1999). Understanding leader emotional intelligence and performance: The role of self–other agreement on transformational leadership perceptions. *Group and Organization Management, 24:* 367–390.

Spector, P. E. (1982). Behavior in organizations as a function of employee's locus of control. *Psychological Bulletin, 47:* 487–489.

Spencer, L. M., and S. M. Spencer. (1993). *Competence at work: Models for superior performance.* New York: Wiley.

Sternberg, R. J. (1996). *Successful intelligence.* New York: Simon & Schuster.

Sternberg, R. J., and L. F. Zhang (Eds.). (2000). *Perspectives on cognitive, learning, and thinking styles.* Mahwah, NJ: Lawrence Erlbaum.

Sweeney, P., D. McFarlin, and J. Cotton. (1991). Locus of control as a moderator of the relationship between perceived influence and procedural justice. *Human Relations, 44:* 333–342.

Teoh, H. Y., and S. L. Foo. (1997). Moderating effects of tolerance for ambiguity and risk–taking propensity on the role conflict–perceived performance relationship: Evidence from Singaporean entrepreneurs. *Journal of Business Venturing, 12:* 67–81.

Timothy, A., C. Thoresen, V. Pucik, and T. Welbourne. (1999). Managerial coping with organizational change: A dispositional perspective. *Journal of Applied Psychology, 84:* 107–122.

Trompenaars, F. (1996). Resolving international conflict: Culture and business strategy. *Business Strategy Review, 7:* 51–68.

Trompenaars, F., and C. Hampton-Turner. (1998). *Riding the waves of culture.* New York: McGraw-Hill.

Tubbs, W. (1994). The roots of stress-death and juvenile delinquency in Japan: Disciplinary ambivalence and perceived locus of control. *Journal of Business Ethics, 13:* 507–522.

Vance, C. M., K. S. Groves, Y. Paik, and H. Kindler. (2007). Understanding and measuring linear–nonlinear thinking style for enhanced management education and professional practice. *Academy of Management Learning and Education Journal, 6:* 167–185.

Watson, D. (2000). *Mood and temperament.* New York: Guilford.

Weick, K. E. (1993). The collapse of sensemaking in organizations. *Administrative Science Quarterly, 38:* 628–652.

Weick, K. E., and K. Sutcliffe. (2000). High reliability: The power of mindfulness. *Leader to Leader, 17:* 33–38.

Wheeler, R. W., and J. M. Davis. (1979). Decision making as a function of locus of control and cognitive dissonance. *Psychological Reports, 44:* 499–502.

CHAPTER 2 REFERENCES

Adler, C. M., and J. J. Hillhouse (1996). Stress, health, and immunity: A review of the literature. In Thomas W. Miller (Ed.), *Theory and assessment of stressful life events.* Madison, CT: International University Press.

Adler, J. (2005). *My prescription for anti-depressive living.* New York: Regan.

Adler, J. (1999, June 14). Stress, *Newsweek;* 56–61.

Adler, V. (1989). Little control equals lots of stress. *Psychology Today, 23:* 18–19.

American Institute of Stress. (2000). www.stress.org/problem.htm.

Anderson, C. R. (1977). Locus of control, coping behaviors and performance in a stress setting: A longitudinal study. *Journal of Applied Psychology, 62:* 446–451.

Auerbach, S. M. (1998). *Stress management: Psychological foundations.* Upper Saddle River, NJ: Prentice Hall.

Balzer, W. K., M. E. Doherty, and R. O'Connor. (1989). Effects of cognitive feedback on performance. *Psychological Bulletin, 106:* 410–433.

Bandura, A. (1997). *Self-efficacy: The exercise of control.* New York: W. H. Freeman.

Beary, J. F., and H. Benson. (1977). A simple psychophysiologic technique which elicits the hypometabolic changes in the relaxation response. *Psychosomatic Medicine, 36:* 115–120.

Bell, C. R. (1998). *Managers as mentors.* San Francisco: Barrett-Koehler.

Benson, H. (1975). *The relaxation response.* New York: William Morrow.

Bramwell, S. T., M. Masuda, N. N. Wagner, and T. H. Holmes. (1975). Psychosocial factors in athletic injuries. *Journal of Human Stress, 1:* 6.

Brockner, J., and B. M. Weisenfeld. (1993). Living on the edge: The effects of layoffs on those who remain. In J. Keith Murnighan (Ed.), *Social psychology in organizations: Advances in theory and research.* Englewood Cliffs, NJ: Prentice Hall.

Cameron, K. S. (1998). Strategic organizational downsizing: An extreme case. *Research in Organizational Behavior, 20:* 185–229.

Cameron, K. S. (1994). Strategies for successful organizational downsizing. *Human Resource Management Journal, 33:* 189–212.

Cameron, K. S., S. J. Freeman, and A. K. Mishra. (1991). Best practices in white-collar downsizing: Managing contradictions. *Academy of Management Executive, 5:* 57–73.

Cameron, K. S., M. U. Kim, and D. A. Whetten. (1987). Organizational effects of decline and turbulence. *Administrative Science Quarterly, 32:* 222–240.

Cameron, K. S., D. A. Whetten, and M. U. Kim. (1987). Organizational dysfunctions of decline. *Academy of Management Journal, 30:* 126–138.

Cantor, N., and J. F. Kihlstrom. (1987). *Personality and social intelligence*. Englewood Cliffs, NJ: Prentice Hall.

Coddington, R. D., and J. R. Troxell. (1980). The effect of emotional factors on football injury rates: A pilot study. *Journal of Human Stress, 6:* 3–5.

Cooper, C. L., and M. J. Davidson. (1982). The high cost of stress on women managers. *Organizational Dynamics, 11:* 44–53.

Cooper, C. L. (1998). *Theories of organizational stress*. New York: Oxford University Press.

Cooper, M. J., and M. M. Aygen. (1979). A relaxation technique in the management of hypocholesterolemia. *Journal of Human Stress, 5:* 24–27.

Cordes, C. L., and T. W. Dougherty. (1993). Review and an integration of research on job burnout. *Academy of Management Review, 18:* 621–656.

Covey, S. (1989). *Seven habits of highly effective people*. New York: Wiley.

Cowley, C. (2000, June 14). Stress-busters: What works. *Newsweek:* 60.

Curtis, J. D., and R. A. Detert. (1981). *How to relax: A holistic approach to stress management*. Palo Alto: Mayfield Publishing Co.

Davidson, J. (1995). *Managing your time*. Indianapolis: Alpha Books.

Davis, M., E. Eshelman, and M. McKay. (1980). *The relaxation and stress reduction workbook*. Richmond, CA: New Harbinger Publications.

Deepak, M. D. (1995). *Creating health: How to wake up the body's intelligence*. New York: Houghton Mifflin.

Dellbeck, M., and S. Shatkin. (1991). *Scientific research on the transcendental meditation process*. Fairfield, IA: Maharishi International University of Management Press.

Dyer, W. G. (1987). *Teambuilding*. Reading, MA: Addison-Wesley.

Eliot, R. S., and D. L. Breo. (1984). *Is it worth dying for?* New York: Bantam Books.

Farnham, A. (1991, October 7). Who beats stress and how? *Fortune:* 71–86.

Fisher, C., and R. Gitelson. (1983). A meta-analysis of the correlates of role conflict and role ambiguity. *Journal of Applied Psychology, 68:* 320–333.

French, J. R. R., and R. D. Caplan. (1972). Organizational stress and individual strain. In A. J. Marrow (Ed.), *The failure of success*. New York: AMACOM.

Friedman, M., and R. H. Rosenman. (1974). *Type A behavior and your heart*. New York: Knopf.

Friedman, M., and D. Ulmer. (1984). *Treating type A behavior and your heart*. New York: Alfred A. Knopf, 84–85.

Friedman, M. (1996). *Type A behavior: Its diagnosis and treatment*. New York: Kluwer Academic Publishers.

Gardner, H. (1993). *Multiple intelligences: The theory in practice*. New York: Basic Books.

Gittell, J., K. Cameron, and S. Lim. (2006). Relationships, layoffs, and organizational resilience. *Journal of Applied Behavioral Science*.

Goldberg, H. (1976). *The hazards of being male*. New York: Nash.

Goleman, D. (1998). *Working with emotional intelligence*. New York: Bantam Books.

Gordon, A. (1959). *A day at the beach*. Copyright © 1959 by Arthur Gordon. All rights reserved. Reprinted by permission of the author. First published in the *Reader's Digest*.

Greenberg, J. (1987). *Comprehensive stress management*, 2nd ed. Dubuque, IA: William C. Brown Publishers.

Greenberger, D. B., and S. Stasser. (1991). The role of situational and dispositional factors in the enhancement of personal control in organizations. *Research in Organizational Behavior, 13:* 111–145.

Griest, J. H., et al. (1979). Running as treatment for depression. *Comparative Psychology, 20:* 41–56.

Hackman, J. R., G. R. Oldham, R. Janson, and K. Purdy. (1975). A new strategy for job enrichment. *California Management Review, 17:* 57–71.

Hackman, R. J., and G. R. Oldham. (1980). *Work redesign*. Reading, MA: Addison-Wesley.

Hall, D. T. (1976). *Careers in organizations*. Santa Monica, CA: Goodyear.

Hendricks, W. (1996). *Coaching, mentoring, and managing*. Franklin Lakes, NJ: Career Press.

Hepburn, G. C., C. A. McLoughlin, and J. Barling. (1997). Coping with chronic work stress. In B. H. Gottlieb (Ed.), *Coping with chronic stress*. (pp. 343–366). New York: Plenum.

Hobson, C. J., J. Kamen, J. Szostek, C. M. Nethercutt, J. W. Tiedmann, and S. Wojnarowicz. (1998). Stressful life events: A revision and update of the Social Readjustment Rating Scale. *International Journal of Stress Management, 5:* 1–23.

Holmes, T. H., and R. H. Rahe. (1967). The social readjustment rating scale. *Journal of Psychosomatic Research, 11:* 213–218.

Holmes, T. H., and R. H. Rahe. (1970). The social readjustment rating scale. *Journal of Psychosomatic Research, 14:* 121–132.

Hubbard, J. R., and E. A. Workman. (1998). *Handbook of stress medicine: An organ system approach*. Boca Raton, FL: CRC Press.

Ivancevich, J., and D. Ganster. (1987). *Job stress: From theory to suggestions*. New York: Haworth.

Ivancevich, J. M., and M. T. Matteson. (1980). *Stress & work: A managerial perspective*. Glenview, IL: Scott Foresman.

Jourard, S. M. (1964). *The transparent self*. Princeton, NJ: Von Nostrand.

Judge, T. A., and J. E. Bono. (2001). Relationship of core self-evaluations traits—self-esteem, generalized self-efficacy, locus of control, and emotional stability—with job satisfaction and job performance: A meta-analysis. *Journal of Applied Psychology, 86:* 80–92.

Kahn, R. L., et al. (1964). *Organizational stress: Studies in role conflict and ambiguity*. New York: Wiley.

Kahn, R. L., and P. Byosiere. (1992). Stress in organizations. In Marvin Dunnette and L. M. Hough (Eds.), *Handbook of industrial and organizational psychology* (pp. 571–650). Palo Alto: Consulting Psychologists.

Karasek, R. A., T. Theorell, J. E. Schwartz, P. L. Schnall, C. F. Pieper, and J. L. Michela. (1988). Job characteristics in relation to the prevalence of myocardial infarction in the U.S. Health

Examination Survey and the Health and Nutrition Examination Survey. *American Journal of Public Health, 78:* 910–918.

Katzenbach, J. R., and D. K. Smith. (1993). *The wisdom of teams.* Boston: Harvard Business School Press.

Kobasa, S. C. (1979). Stressful life events, personality, and health: An inquiry into hardiness. *Journal of Personality and Social Psychology, 37:* 1–12.

Kobasa, S. (1982). Commitment and coping in stress resistance among lawyers. *Journal of Personality and Social Psychology, 42:* 707–717.

Kram, K. (1985). *Mentoring at work.* Glenview, IL: Scott Foresman.

Kuhn, A., and R. D. Beam. (1982). *The logic of organizations.* San Francisco: Jossey-Bass.

Lakein, D. (1989). *How to get control of your time and your life.* New York: McKay.

Latack, J., A. J. Kinicki, and G. Prussia. (1995). An integrative process model of coping with job loss. *Academy of Management Review, 20:* 311–342.

Lawler, E. E., S. A. Mohrman, and G. E. Ledford. (1992). *Employee involvement and total quality management.* San Francisco: Jossey-Bass.

Lehrer, P. M. (1996). *The Hatherleigh guide to issues in modern therapy.* New York: Hatherleigh Press.

Levinson, J. D. (1978). *Seasons of a man's life.* New York: Knopf.

Lewin, K. (1951). *Field theory in social science.* New York: Harper & Row.

Likert, R. (1967). *The human organization.* New York: McGraw-Hill.

Locke, E., and G. Latham. (1990). *A theory of goal setting and task performance.* Englewood Cliffs, NJ: Prentice Hall.

Lusch, R. F., and R. R. Serpkenci. (1990). Personal differences, job tension, job outcomes, and store performance: A study of retail managers. *Journal of Marketing, 54:* 85–101.

Maddi, S., and S. C. Kobasa. (1984). *The hardy executive: Health under stress.* Homewood, IL: Dow Jones-Irwin.

Masten, A. S., and M. J. Reed. (2002). Resilience in development. In C. R. Snyder, and S. J. Lopez (Eds.), *Handbook of positive psychology* (pp. 74–88). New York: Oxford University Press.

McNichols, T. J. (1973). *The case of the missing time.* Evanston, IL: Northwestern University Kellogg School of Business.

Mednick, M. T. (1982). Woman and the psychology of achievement: Implications for personal and social change. In H. J. Bernardin (Ed.), *Women in the workforce.* New York: Praeger.

Milgram, S. (1963). Behavioral study of obedience. *Journal of Abnormal and Social Psychology, 63:* 371–378.

Mintzberg, H. (1973). *The nature of managerial work.* New York: Harper & Row.

Mishra, A. K. (1992). *Organizational responses to crisis.* Unpublished doctoral dissertation, University of Michigan School of Business Administration.

Murphy, L. R. (1996). Stress management in work settings: A critical review of health effects. *American Journal of Health Promotion, 11:* 112–135.

Northwestern National Life Insurance Company (NNL). (1992). *Employee burnout: Causes and cures.* Minneapolis, MN: Author.

Orme-Johnson, D. W. (1973). Autonomic stability and transcendental meditation. *Psychosomatic Medicine, 35:* 341–349.

Peters, T. (1988). *Thriving on chaos.* New York: Knopf.

Pfeffer, J. (1998). *The human equation: Building profits by putting people first.* Boston: Harvard Business School Press.

Pilling, B. K., and S. Eroglu. (1994). An empirical examination of the impact of salesperson empathy and professionalism and merchandise salability on retail buyer's evaluations. *Journal of Personal Selling and Sales Management, 14:* 55–58.

Rahe, R. H., D. H. Ryman, and H. W. Ward. (1980). Simplified scaling for life change events. *Journal of Human Stress, 6:* 22–27.

Rosenthal, R. (1977). The PONS Test: Measuring sensitivity to nonverbal cues. In P. McReynolds (Ed.), *Advances in psychological measurement.* San Francisco: Jossey-Bass.

Rostad, F. G., and B. C. Long. (1996). Exercise as a coping strategy for stress: A review. *International Journal of Sport Psychology, 27:* 197–222.

Saarni, C. (1997). Emotional competence and self-regulation in childhood. In P. Savoey and D. J. Sluyter (Eds.), *Emotional development and emotional intelligence.* New York: Basic Books.

Schein, E. H. (1960). Interpersonal communication, group solidarity, and social influence. *Sociometry, 23:* 148–161.

Selye, H. (1976). *The stress of life,* 2nd ed. New York: McGraw-Hill.

Shoda, Y., W. Mischel, and P. K. Peake. (1990). Predicting adolescent cognitive and self-regulatory competencies from preschool delay of gratification: Identifying diagnostic conditions. *Developmental Psychology, 26:* 978–986.

Siegman, A. W., and T. W. Smith (Eds.). (1994). *Anger, hostility, and the heart.* Mahwah, NJ: Lawrence Erlbaum and Associates.

Singh, J. (1993). Boundary role ambiguity: Facts, determinants, and impacts. *Journal of Marketing, 57:* 11–30.

Singh, J. (1998). Striking balance in boundary-spanning positions: An investigation of some unconventional influences of role stressors and job characteristics on job outcomes or salespeople. *Journal of Marketing, 62:* 69–86.

Sorenson, M. J. (1998). *Breaking the chain of low self-esteem.* Stone Mountain, GA: Wolf Publications.

Spencer, L. M., and S. M. Spencer. (1993). *Competence at work: Models for superior performance.* New York: Wiley.

Stalk, G., and T. M. Hout. (1990). *Competing against time.* New York: Free Press.

Staw, B. M., L. Sandelands, and J. Dutton. (1981). Threat-rigidity effects in organizational behavior. *Administrative Science Quarterly, 26:* 501–524.

Sternberg, R. (1997). *Successful intelligence.* New York: Simon & Schuster.

Stone, R. A., and J. Deleo. (1976). Psychotherapeutic control of hypertension. *New England Journal of Medicine, 294:* 80–84.

Sutcliffe, K., and T. Vogus. (2003). Organizing resilience. In K. S. Cameron, J. E. Dutton, and R. E. Quinn (Eds.), *Positive organizational scholarship.* San Francisco: Barrett-Koehler.

Thoits, P. A. (1995). Stress, coping, and social support processes: Where are we? What next? *Journal of Health and Social Behavior, 36:* 53–79.

Trompenaars, F. (1996). Resolving international conflict: Culture and business strategy. *Business Strategy Review, 7:* 51–68.

Trompenaars, F., and C. Hampden-Turner. (1998). *Riding the waves of culture.* New York: McGraw-Hill.

Turkington, C. (1998). *Stress management for busy people.* New York: McGraw-Hill.

Vinton, D. E. (1992). A new look at time, speed, and the manager. *Academy of Management Executive, 6:* 1–16.

Weick, K. (1984). Small wins. *American Psychologist, 39:* 40–49.

Weick, K. E. (1993a). The collapse of sensemaking in organizations. *Administrative Science Quarterly, 38:* 628–652.

Weick, K. E. (1993b). The KOR experiment. Working paper, University of Michigan School of Business Administration.

Weick, K. E. (1995). *Sensemaking in organizations.* Beverly Hills, CA: Sage.

William, R., and V. Williams. (1998). *Anger kills: 17 strategies to control the hostility that can harm your health.* New York: Harper Collins.

Wolff, H. G., S. G. Wolf, and C. C. Hare (Eds.). (1950). *Life stress and bodily disease.* Baltimore: Williams and Wilkins.

Yogi, M. (1994). *Science of being and art of living: Transcendental meditation.* New Haven, CT: Meridian Books.

CHAPTER 3 REFERENCES

Adams, J. L. (2001). *Conceptual blockbusting: A guide to better ideas.* Cambridge, MA: Perseus Publishing.

Albert, R. S., and M. A. Runco. (1999). A history of research on creativity. In R. J. Sternberg (Ed.), *Handbook of creativity.* Cambridge: Cambridge University Press.

Amabile, T. M. (1988). A model of creativity and innovation in organizations. In L. L. Cummings and B. M. Staw (Eds.), *Research in Organizational Behavior, 10:* 123–167.

Basadur, M. S. (1979). *Training in creative problem solving: Effects of deferred judgment and problem finding and solving in an industrial research organization.* Unpublished doctoral dissertation, University of Cincinnati.

Ben-Amos, P. (1986). Artistic creativity in Benin Kingdom. *African Arts, 19:* 60–63.

Black, J. S., and H. B. Gregersen. (1997). Participative decision making: An integration of multiple dimensions. *Human Relations, 50:* 859–878.

Blasko, V. J., and M. P. Mokwa. (1986). Creativity in advertising: A Janusian perspective. *Journal of Advertising, 15:* 43–50.

Bodycombe, D. J. (1977). *The mammoth puzzle carnival.* New York: Carroll & Graf.

Cameron, K. S., R. E. Quinn, J. DeGraff, and A. V. Thakor. (2006). *Competing values leadership: Creating values in organizations.* New York: Edward Elgar.

Chu, Y-K. (1970). Oriented views of creativity. In A. Angloff and B. Shapiro (Eds.), *Psi factors in creativity* (pp. 35–50). New York: Parapsychology Foundation.

Cialdini, R. B. (2001). *Influence: Science and practice.* Needham Heights, MA: Allyn and Bacon.

Collins, M. A., and T. M. Amabile. (1999). Motivation and creativity. In R. J. Sternberg (Ed.), *Handbook of creativity.* Cambridge, UK: Cambridge University Press.

Covey, S. R. (1998) "Creative orientation." *Executive Excellence, 1:* 13–14.

Crovitz, H. F. (1970). *Galton's walk.* New York: Harper & Row.

Csikszentmihalyi, M. (1996). *Creativity: Flow and the psychology of discovery and invention.* New York: Harper Collins.

de Bono, E. (1968). *New think.* New York: Basic Books.

de Bono, E. (1973). *CoRT thinking.* Blanford, England: Direct Educational Services.

de Bono, E. (1992). *Serious creativity.* New York: Harper Collins.

de Bono, E. (2000). *New thinking for the new millennium.* New York: New Millennium Press.

DeGraff, J., and K. A. Lawrence. (2002). *Creativity at work: Developing the right practices to make innovation happen.* San Francisco: Jossey-Bass.

Dutton, J. E., and S. J. Ashford. (1993). Selling issues to top management. *Academy of Management Review, 18:* 397–421.

Einstein, A. (1919). Fundamental ideas and methods of relativity theory, presented in their development. (© 1919, G. Holton). Unpublished manuscript.

Ettlie, J. E., and R. D. O'Keefe. (1982). Innovative attitudes, values, and intentions in organizations. *Journal of Management Studies, 19:* 163–182.

Feldman, D. H. (1999). The development of creativity. In R. J. Sternberg (Ed.), *Handbook of creativity.* Cambridge, UK: Cambridge University Press.

Festinger, L. (1957). *A theory of cognitive dissonance.* Stanford: Stanford University Press.

Finke, R. A., T. B. Ward, and S. M. Smith. (1992). *Creative cognition: Theory, research, and applications.* Cambridge, MA: MIT Press.

Getzels, J. W., and M. Csikszentmihalyi. (1976). *The creative vision: A longitudinal study of problem finding.* New York: Wiley.

Gladwell, M. (2005). *Blink.* Boston: Little, Brown.

Goll, I., and A. M. A. Rasheed. (1997). Rational decision making and firm performance: The moderating role of environment. *Strategic Management Journal, 18:* 583–591.

Gordon, W. J. J. (1961). *Synectics: The development of creative capacity.* New York: Collier.

Hawn, C. (2004, January). If he's so smart . . . *Fast Company:* 68–74.

Heider, F. (1946). Attitudes and cognitive organization. *Journal of Psychology, 21:* 107–112.

Hermann, N. (1981). The creative brain. *Training and Development Journal, 35:* 11–16.

Hudspith, S. (1985). *The neurological correlates of creative thought.* Unpublished PhD Dissertation, University of Southern California.

Hyatt, J. (1989, February). The odyssey of an excellent man. *Inc.:* 63–68. Copyright © 1989 by Goldhirsch Group, Inc. Reprinted with permission of the publishers, 38 Commercial Wharf, Boston, MA 02110.

Interaction Associates. (1971). *Tools for change.* San Francisco: Author.

Janis, I. L. (1971). *Groupthink.* New York: Free Press.

Janis, I. L., and L. Mann. (1977). *Decision making: A psychological analysis of conflict, choice, and commitment.* New York: Free Press. Copyright © 1977 by the Free Press. Reprinted with the permission of the Free Press, an imprint of Simon & Schuster.

Juran, J. (1988). *Juran on planning management.* New York: Free Press.

Koberg, D., and J. Bagnall. (2003). *The universal traveler: A soft system guidebook to creativity, problem solving, and the process of design.* Los Altos, CA: William Kaufmann.

Koestler, A. (1964). *The act of creation.* New York: Dell.

Koopman, P. L., J. W. Broekhuijsen, and A. F. M. Wierdsma. (1998). Complex decision making in organizations. In P. J. D. Drenth and H. Thierry (Eds.), *Handbook of work and organizational psychology*, Vol. 4 (pp. 357–386). Hove, England: Psychology Press/Erlbaum.

Kuo, Y-Y. (1996). Toaistic psychology of creativity. *Journal of Creative Behavior, 30:* 197–212.

Maduro, R. (1976). *Artistic creativity in a Brahmin painter community* (Monograph 14). Berkeley: University of California Center for South and Southeast Asia Cultures.

March, J. G. (1994). *A primer on decision making: How decisions happen.* New York: Free Press.

March, J. G. (Ed.). (1999). *The pursuit of organizational intelligence.* New York: Blackwell.

March, J. G., and H. A. Simon. (1958). *Organizations.* New York: Wiley.

Markoff, J. (1988, November 2). For scientists using supercomputers, visual imagery speeds discoveries. New York Times News Service, *Ann Arbor News*, D3.

Martindale, C. (1999). Biological bases of creativity. In R. J. Sternberg (Ed.), *Handbook of creativity.* Cambridge, UK: Cambridge University Press.

McKim, R. H. (1997). *Thinking visually: A strategy manual for problem solving.* Parsippany, NJ: Dale Seymour Publications.

McMillan, I. (1985). Progress in research on corporate venturing. Working paper, Center for Entrepreneurial Studies, New York University.

Medawar, P. B. (1967). *The art of the soluble.* London: Methuen.

Miller, S. J., D. J. Hickson, and D. C. Wilson. (1996). Decision making in organizations. In S. R. Clegg and C. Hardy (Eds.), *Handbook of organizational studies* (pp. 293–312). London: Sage.

Mitroff, I. I. (1998). *Smart thinking for crazy times: The art of solving the right problems.* San Francisco: Barrett-Koehler.

Mumford, M. D., W. A. Baughman, M. A. Maher, D. P. Costanza, and E. P. Supinski. (1997). Process-based measures of creative problem solving skills. *Creativity Research Journal, 10:* 59–71.

Nayak, P. R., and J. M. Ketteringham. (1986). *Breakthroughs!* New York: Rawson Associates.

Nemeth, C. J. (1986). Differential contributions of majority and minority influence. *Psychological Review, 93:* 23–32.

Newcomb, T. (1954). An approach to the study of communicative acts. *Psychological Review, 60:* 393–404.

Nickerson, R. S. (1999). Enhancing creativity. In R. J. Sternberg (Ed.), *Handbook of creativity.* Cambridge: Cambridge University Press.

Osborn, A. (1953). *Applied imagination.* New York: Scribner.

Poincare, H. (1921). *The foundation of science.* New York: Science Press.

Raudsepp, E. (1981). *How creative are you?* New York: Perigee Books/G.P. Putnam's Sons. Copyright © 1981 by Eugene Raudsepp. Reprinted with the permission of the author, c/o Dominick Abel Literary Agency, Inc.

Raudsepp, E., and G. P. Hough. (1977). *Creative growth games.* New York: Putnam.

Ribot, T. A. (1906). *Essay on the creative imagination.* Chicago: Open Court.

Riley, S. (1998). *Critical thinking and problem solving.* Upper Saddle River, NJ: Simon & Schuster.

Rothenberg, A. (1979). *The emerging goddess.* Chicago: University of Chicago Press.

Rothenberg, A. (1991). Creativity, health, and alcoholism. *Creativity Research Journal, 3:* 179–202.

Rothenberg, A., and C. Hausman. (2000). Metaphor and creativity. In M. A. Runco (Ed.), *Creativity research handbook*, Vol. 2. Cresskill, NJ: Hampton.

Roukes, N. (1988). *Design synectics: Stimulating creativity in design.* Berkeley, CA: Davis Publications.

Scope, E. E. (1999). *A meta-analysis of research on creativity: The effects of instructional variables.* Ann Arbor, MI: Dissertation Abstracts International, Section A: Humanities and Social Sciences.

Scott, O. J. (1974). *The creative ordeal: The story of Raytheon.* New York: Atheneum.

Siau, K. L. (1995). Group creativity and technology. *Journal of Creative Behavior, 29:* 201–216.

Smith, G. F. (1998). Idea-generation techniques: A formulary of active ingredients. *Journal of Creative Behavior, 32:* 107–133.

Starko, A. J. (2001). *Creativity in the classroom: Schools of curious delight.* Mahwah, NJ: Lawrence Erlbaum.

Sternberg, R. J. (Ed.). (1999). *Handbook of creativity.* Cambridge: Cambridge University Press.

Tichy, N. (1983). *Strategic human resource management.* New York: Wiley.

Trompenaars, F., and C. Hampden-Turner. (1987). *Riding the waves of culture: Understanding cultural diversity in business.* Yarmouth, ME: Nicholas Brealey Publishing.

Trompenaars, F., and C. Hampden-Turner. (2004). *Managing people across cultures.* Mankato, MN: Capstone Publishing.

Tushman, M. L., and P. Anderson. (1997). *Managing strategic innovation and change.* New York: Oxford University Press.

Van de Ven, A. (1997). Technological innovation, learning, and leadership. In R. Garud, P. Rattan Nayyar, and Z. Baruch Shapira (Eds.), *Technological innovation: Oversights and foresights.* Cambridge: Cambridge University Press.

von Oech, R. (1986). *A kick in the seat of the pants.* New York: Harper & Row.

Vroom, V. H., and P. W. Yetton. (1973). *Leadership and decision making.* Pittsburgh: University of Pittsburgh Press.

Vygotsky, L. (1962). *Thought and language.* Cambridge, MA: MIT Press.

Wallas, G. (1926). *The art of thought.* London: C. A. Watts.

Ward, T. B., S. M. Smith, and R. A. Finke. (1999). Creative cognition. In R. J. Sternberg (Ed.), *Handbook of creativity.* Cambridge: Cambridge University Press.

Weick, K. E. (1979). *The social psychology of organizing.* Reading, MA: Addison-Wesley.

Weick, K. E. (1984). Small wins. *American Psychologist, 39*: 40–49.

Weick, K. E. (1995). *Sensemaking in organizations.* Beverly Hills, CA: Sage.

Williams, W. M., and L. T. Yang. (1999). Organizational creativity. In R. J. Sternberg (Ed.), *Handbook of creativity.* Cambridge, UK: Cambridge University Press.

Wonder, J., and J. Blake. (1992). Creativity East and West: Intuition versus logic. *Journal of Creative Behavior, 26:* 172–185.

Zeitz, P. (1999). *The art and craft of problem solving.* New York: Wiley.

Zhou, J., and C. E. Shalley. (2003). Research on employee creativity: A critical review and directions or future research. *Research in Personnel and Human Resources Management, 22:* 165–217.

CHAPTER 4 REFERENCES

Argyris, C. (1991). Teaching smart people how to learn. *Harvard Business Review, 63:* 99–109.

Athos, A. and J. Gabarro. (1978). *Interpersonal behavior.* Englewood Cliffs, NJ: Prentice Hall.

Baker, W. (2000). *Achieving success through social capital.* San Francisco: Jossey-Bass.

Barnlund, D. C. (1968). *Interpersonal communication: Survey and studies.* Boston: Houghton Mifflin.

Beebe, S. A., S. J. Beebe, and M. V. Redmond. (1996). *Interpersonal communication.* Boston: Allyn & Bacon.

Boss, W. L. (1983). Team building and the problem of regression: The personal management interview as an intervention. *Journal of Applied Behavioral Science, 19:* 67–83.

Bostrom, R. N. (1997). The process of listening. In O. D. W. Hargie (Ed.), *The handbook of communication skills.* London: Routledge.

Bowman, G. W. (1964). What helps or harms promotability? *Harvard Business Review, 42:* 14.

Brownell, J. (1986). *Building active listening skills.* Englewood Cliffs, NJ: Prentice Hall.

Brownell, J. (1990). Perceptions of effective listeners. *Journal of Business Communication, 27:* 401–415.

Cameron, K. S. (1994). Strategies for successful organizational downsizing. *Human Resource Management Journal, 33:* 89–122.

Carrell, L. J., and S. C. Willmington. (1996). A comparison of self-report and performance data in assessing speaking and listening competence. *Communication Reports, 9:* 185–191.

Council of Communication Management. (1996). Electronic communication is important, but face-to-face communication is still rated high. *Communication World, 13:* 12–13.

Covey, S. R. (1989). *The seven habits of highly effective people.* New York: Simon & Schuster.

Crocker, J. (1978). Speech communication instruction based on employers' perceptions of the importance of selected communication skills for employees on the job. Paper presented at the Speech Communication Association meeting, Minneapolis, Minn.

Cupach, W. R., and B. H. Spitzberg. (1994). *The dark side of interpersonal communication.* Hillsdale, NJ: Lawrence Erlbaum.

Dutton, J. E. (2003). *Energize your workplace: How to create and sustain high quality relationships at work.* San Francisco: Jossey-Bass.

Dyer, W. G. (1972). Congruence. In *The sensitive manipulator.* Provo, UT: Brigham Young University Press.

Fredrickson, B. L. (2001). The role of positive emotions in positive psychology: The broaden-and-build theory of positive emotions. *American Psychologist, 56:* 218–226.

Gackenbach, J. (1998). *Psychology and the Internet: Intrapersonal, interpersonal, and transpersonal implications.* New York: Academic Press.

Geddie, T. (1999). Moving communication across cultures. *Communication World, 16:* 37–40.

Gibb, J. R. (1961). Defensive communication. *Journal of Communication, 11:* 141–148.

Gittell, J. H. (2003). A theory of relational coordination. In K. S. Cameron, J. E. Dutton, and R. E. Quinn (Eds.), *Positive organizational scholarship.* San Francisco: Barrett-Koehler.

Gittell, J. H., K. S. Cameron, and S. Lim. (2006). Relationships, layoffs, and organizational resilience: Airline industry responses to September 11th. *Journal of Applied Behavioral Science, 42:* 300–329.

Glasser, W. (1965). *Reality therapy: A new approach to psychiatry.* New York: Harper & Row.

Glasser, W. (2000). *Reality therapy in action.* New York: Harper Collins.

Golen, S. (1990). A factor analysis of barriers to effective listening. *Journal of Business Communication, 27:* 25–35.

Gordon, R. D. (1988). The difference between feeling defensive and feeling understood. *Journal of Business Communication, 25:* 53–64.

Gudykunst, W. B., and S. Ting-Toomey. (1988). *Culture and interpersonal communication.* Newbury Park, CA: Sage.

Gudykunst, W. B., S. Ting-Toomey, and T. Nishida. (1996). *Communication in personal relationships across cultures.* Thousand Oaks, CA: Sage.

Haas, J. W., and C. L. Arnold. (1995). An examination of the role of listening in judgments of communication competence in coworkers. *Journal of Business Communication, 32:* 123–139.

Haney, W. V. (1992). *Communication and interpersonal relations.* Homewood, IL: Irwin.

Hanson, G. (1986). *Determinants of firm performance: An integration of economic and organizational factors.* Unpublished doctoral dissertation, University of Michigan Business School.

Hargie, O. D. W. (1997). Communication as skilled performance. In O. D. W. Hargie (Ed.), *The handbook of communication skills.* London: Routledge.

Heaphy, E. D., and J. E. Dutton. (2006). Embodying social interactions: Integrating physiology into the study of positive connections and relationships at work. *Academy of Management Review* (in press).

Huseman, R. C., J. M. Lahiff, and J. D. Hatfield. (1976). *Interpersonal communication in organizations.* Boston: Holbrook Press.

Hyman, R. (1989). The psychology of deception. *Annual Review of Psychology, 40:* 133–154.

James, W., cited in D. R. Laing (1965). Mystification, confusion, and conflict. In I. Boszormenya-Nagy and J. L. Franco (Eds.), *Intensive family therapy.* New York: Harper & Row.

Knapp, M. L., and A. L. Vangelisti. (1996). *Interpersonal communication and human relationships.* Boston: Allyn & Bacon.

Kramer, D. A. (2000). Wisdom as a classical source of human strength: Conceptualization and empirical inquiry. *Journal of Social and Clinical Psychology, 19:* 83–101.

Kramer, R. (1997). *Leading by listening: An empirical test of Carl Rogers' theory of human relationship using interpersonal assessments of leaders by followers.* Ann Arbor, MI: Dissertation Abstracts International Section A: Humanities and Social Sciences, Volume 58.

Loomis, F. (1939). *The consultation room.* New York: Knopf.

Losada, M., and E. Heaphy. (2004). The role of positivity and connectivity in the performance of business teams. *American Behavioral Scientist, 47:* 740–765.

Maier, N. R. F., A. R. Solem, and A. A. Maier. (1973). Counseling, interviewing, and job contacts. In N. R. F. Maier (Ed.), *Psychology of industrial organizations.* Boston: Houghton Mifflin.

McGregor, D. (1960). *The human side of enterprise.* New York: McGraw-Hill.

Ouchi, W. (1981). *Theory Z.* Reading, MA: Addison-Wesley.

Peters, T. (1988). *Thriving on chaos.* New York: Knopf.

Pfeffer, J. (1998). *The human equation: Building profits by putting people first.* Boston: Harvard Business School Press.

Randle, C. W. (1956). How to identify promotable executives. *Harvard Business Review, 34:* 122.

Reis, H., and S. L. Gable. (2003). Toward a positive psychology of relationships. In C. L. M. Keyes and J. Haidt. *Flourishing: Positive psychology and the life well-lived* (pp. 129–160). Washington, DC: American Psychological Association.

Rogers, C. W. (1961). *On becoming a person.* Boston: Houghton Mifflin.

Rogers, C., and R. Farson. (1976). *Active listening.* Chicago: Industrial Relations Center.

Rosen, S. (1998). A lump of clay. *Communication World, 15:* 58–59.

Schnake, M. E., M. P. Dumler, D. S. Cochran, and T. R. Barnett. (1990). Effects of differences in superior and subordinate perceptions of superiors' communication practices. *Journal of Business Communication, 27:* 37–50.

Sieburg, E. (1969). *Dysfunctional communication and interpersonal responsiveness in small groups.* Unpublished doctoral dissertation, University of Denver.

Sieburg, E. (1978). *Confirming and disconfirming organizational communication.* Working paper, University of Denver.

Spitzberg, B. H. (1994). The dark side of (in)competence. In William R. Cupach and Brian H. Spitzberg (Eds.), *The dark side of interpersonal communication.* Hillsdale, NJ: Lawrence Erlbaum.

Steil, L. K. (1980). *Your listening profile.* Minneapolis: Sperry Corporation.

Steil, L., L. Barker, and K. Watson. (1983). *Effective listening: Key to your success.* New York: Addison-Wesley.

Sternberg, R. J. (1990). *Wisdom: Its nature, origins, and development.* Cambridge: Cambridge University Press.

Synopsis Communication Consulting of London. (1998). *The human factor: New rules for the digital workplace.* London: Author.

Szligyi, A. D., and M. J. Wallace. (1983). *Organizational behavior and human performance.* Glenview, IL: Scott Foresman.

Time. (2000, June 19). Embarrassing miscue: 31.

Thorton, B. B. (1966). As you were saying: The number one problem. *Personnel Journal, 45:* 237–238.

Triandis, H. C. (1994). *Culture and social behavior.* New York: McGraw-Hill.

Trompenaars, F. (1996). Resolving international conflict: Culture and business strategy. *Business Strategy Review, 7:* 51–68.

Trompenaars, F., and C. Hampden-Turner. (1998). *Riding the waves of culture.* New York: McGraw-Hill.

Wiemann, J. M. (1977). Explanation and test of a model of communication competence. *Human Communication Research, 3:* 145–213.

Wolvin, A., and C. Coakley. (1988). *Listening.* Dubuque, IA: W. C. Brown.

CHAPTER 5 REFERENCES

Adler, P. S., and S. Kwon. (2002). Social capital: Prospects for a new concept. *Academy of Management Review, 27:* 17–40.

Allen, R. W., D. L. Madison, L. W. Porter, P. A. Renwick, and B. T. Mayer. (1979). Organizational politics: Tactics and characteristics of actors. *California Management Review, 22:* 77–83.

Allinson, C. W., S. J. Armstrong, and J. Hayes. (2001). The effects of cognitive style on leader-member exchange: A study of manager-subordinate dyads. *Journal of Occupational and Organizational Psychology, 74:* 201–220.

Anderson, C., O. P. John, D. Keltner, and A. M. Kring. (2001). Who attains social status? Effects of personality and physical attractiveness in social groups. *Journal of Personality and Social Psychology, 81:* 116–132.

Agle, B. R., N. J. Nagarajan, J. A. Sonnenfeld, and D. Srinivasan. (2006). Does CEO charisma matter? An empirical analysis of the relationships among organizational performance, environmental uncertainty, and top management team perceptions of CEO charisma. *Academy of Management Journal, 49:* 161–174.

Bacharach, S. B. (2005, May). Making things happen by mastering the game of day-to-day politics. *Fast Company*: 93.

Baum, L., and J. A. Byre. (1986, April). Executive secretary: A new rung on the corporate ladder; but hitching her star to the boss can work both ways. *BusinessWeek:* 74.

Bennis, W., and B. Nanus. (2003). *Leaders: Strategies for taking charge*, 2nd ed. New York: Harper Collins.

Bies, R. J., and T. M. Tripp. (1998). Two faces of the powerless: Coping with tyranny in organizations. In R. M. Kramer, and M. A. Neale (Eds.), *Power and influence in organizations.* Thousand Oaks, CA: Sage.

Bolman, L. G., and T. E. Deal. (1997). *Reframing organizations: Artistry, choice, and leadership.* San Francisco: Jossey-Bass.

Breen, B. (2001, November). Trickle-up leadership. *Fast Company:* 70.

Buell, B., and A. L. Cowan. (1985, August). Learning how to play the corporate power game. *BusinessWeek:* 54–55.

Bunderson, J. S. (2002). Team member functional background and involvement in management teams. *Academy of Management Proceedings, OB:* 11–16.

Bunderson, J. S. (2003). Team member functional background and involvement in management teams: Direct effects and the moderating role of power centralization. *Academy of Management Journal, 46:* 458–474.

Bunker, K. A., K. E. Kram, and S. Ting. (2002). The young and the clueless. *Harvard Business Review, 80:* 80–87.

Burt, R. S. (1997). The contingent value of social capital. *Administrative Science Quarterly, 42:* 339–365.

Canfield, F. E., and J. J. LaGaipa. (1970). Friendship expectations at different stages in the development of friendship. Paper read at the annual meeting of the Southeastern Psychological Association, Louisville.

Chiu, L. H. (1972). A cross-cultural comparison of cognitive styles in Chinese and American children. *International Journal of Psychology, 8:* 235–242.

Chiu, L. (2001). Locus of control differences between American and Chinese adolescents. *Journal of Social Psychology, 128:* 411–413.

Choi, I., R. E. Nisbett, and A. Norenzayan. (1999). Causal attribution across cultures: Variation and universality. *Psychological Bulletin, 125:* 47–63.

Cialdini, R. B. (2001). *Influence: Science and practice,* 4th ed. Boston: Allyn & Bacon.

Cohen, A. R., and D. L. Bradford. (2003). Influence without authority: The use of alliances, reciprocity, and exchange to accomplish work. In B. M. Staw (Ed.), *Psychological dimensions of organizational behavior,* 3rd ed. (pp. 359–367). Englewood Cliffs, NJ: Prentice Hall.

Conger, J. A., and R. N. Kanungo. (1998). *Charismatic leadership in organizations.* Thousand Oaks, CA: Sage.

Conner, J., and D. Ulrich. (1996). Human resource roles: Creating value, not rhetoric. *Human Resource Planning, 19:* 38–49.

Cuming, P. (1984). *The power handbook.* Boston: CBI Publishing Co.

Daly, J. P. (1995). Explaining changes to employees: The influence of justifications and change outcomes on employees' fairness judgments. *Journal of Applied Behavioral Science, 31:* 415–428.

Deal, T. E., and A. A. Kennedy. (1982). *Corporate cultures: The rites and rituals of corporate life.* Reading, MA: Addison-Wesley.

DeGeorge, R. T. (1999). *Business ethics.* Upper Saddle River, NJ: Prentice Hall.

Dilenschneider, R. L. (1990). *Power and influence: Mastering the art of persuasion.* New York: Prentice Hall.

Dilenschneider, R. (2007). *Power and influence: The rules have changed.* New York: McGraw-Hill.

Dirks, K. T., and D. L. Ferrin. (2001). The role of trust in organizational settings. *Organization Science, 12:* 450–467.

Dutton, J. E., and S. J. Ashford. (1993). Selling issues to top management. *Academy of Management Review, 18(3):* 397–428.

Dutton, J. E., and R. B. Duncan. (1987). The creation of momentum for change through the process of strategic issue diagnosis. *Strategic Management Journal, 83(3):* 279–295.

Dyer, W. G. (1972). Congruence. In *The sensitive manipulator.* Provo, UT: Brigham Young University Press.

Emerson, R. M. (1962). Power-dependence relations. *American Sociological Review, 27:* 31–40.

Erez, A., V. F. Misangyi, D. E. Johnson, M. A. LePine, and K. C. Halverson. (2008). Stirring the hearts of followers: Charismatic leadership as the transferal of affect. *Journal of Applied Psychology, 93:* 602–616.

Fisher, A. (2005, March 7). Starting a new job? Don't blow it. *Fortune:* 48.

Furman, W. (2001). Working models of friendship. *Journal of Social and Personal Relationships, 18:* 583–602.

Gabarro, J. J., and J. P. Kotter. (1980). Managing your boss. *Harvard Business Review, 58:* 92–100.

Gabarro, J. J., and J. P. Kotter. (2007). Managing your boss. In K. P. Coyne, E. J. Coyne, L. Bossidy, J. J. Gabarro, and J. P. Kotter (Eds.). *Managing UP,* 2nd ed. (HBR Article Collection). Boston: *Harvard Business Review.*

Gardner, J. (1990). *On leadership.* New York: Free Press.

Gelman, E. (1985, September). Playing office politics. *Newsweek:* 56.

Giamatti, A. B. (1981). *The university and public interest.* New York: Atheneum.

Grove, A. (1983). *High output management.* London: Souvenir Press.

Hinings, C. R., D. J. Hickson, J. M. Pennings, and R. E. Schneck. (1974). Structural conditions of intraorganizational power. *Administrative Science Quarterly, 21:* 22–44.

Hoerr, J. (1985, December). Human resource managers aren't corporate nobodies anymore. *BusinessWeek:* 58.

Hogg, M. A. (2001). A social identity theory of leadership. *Personality and Social Psychology Review, 5:* 184–200.

Hosmer, L. T. (1995). Trust: The connecting link between organizational theory and philosophical ethics. *Academy of Management Review, 20:* 379–403.

Hosoda, M., E. F. Stone-Romero, and G. Coats. (2003). The effects of physical attractiveness on job-related outcomes: A meta-analysis of experimental studies. *Personnel Psychology, 56:* 431–462.

Kanter, R. (1979). Power failures in management circuits. *Harvard Business Review, 57:* 65–75. Copyright © 1979 by The President and Fellows of Harvard College. Reprinted with the permission of *Harvard Business Review.* All rights reserved.

Kaplan, R. E., and M. Mazique. (1983). *Trade routes: The manager's network of relationships* (Technical Report #22). Greensboro, NC: Center for Creative Leadership.

Kipnis, D. (1987). Psychology and behavioral technology. *American Psychologist, 42:* 30–36.

Kipnis, D., and S. M. Schmidt. (1988). Upward-influence styles: Relationship with performance evaluations, salary, and stress. *Administrative Science Quarterly, 33:* 528–542.

Kipnis, D., S. M. Schmidt, and I. Wilkinson. (1980). Intraorganizational influence tactics: Explorations in getting one's way. *Journal of Applied Psychology, 65:* 440–452.

Korda, M. (1991). *Power: How to get it, how to use it.* New York: Warner Books.

Kotter, J. P. (1977). Power, dependence and effective management. *Harvard Business Review, 55:* 125–136.

Labich, K. (1995, February 20). Kissing off corporate America. *Fortune, 131:* 44–52.

Langlois, J. H., L. Kalakanis, A. J. Rubenstein, A. Larson, M. Hallam, and M. Smoot. (2000). Maxims of myths of beauty? A meta-analytic and theoretical review. *Psychological Bulletin 126:* 390–423.

Lawrence, R. R., and J. W. Lorsch. (1986). *Organization and environment: Managing differentiation and integration.* Boston: Harvard University Press.

Leger, D. M. (2000, May). Help! I'm the new boss. *Fortune:* 281–284.

Marwell, G., and D. R. Schmitt, (1967). Dimensions of compliance-gaining strategies: A dimensional analysis. *Sociometry, 30:* 350–364.

May, R. (1998). *Power and innocence: A search for the sources of violence.* New York: Norton.

McCall, M. M., Jr., and M. M. Lombardo. (1983). What makes a top executive? *Psychology Today, 26:* 28–31. Copyright © 1983 by Sussex Publishers Inc. Reprinted with the permission of *Psychology Today.*

McClelland, D. C., and D. H. Burnham. (2003). Power is the great motivator. *Motivating People, 81:* 117–126.

Mechanic, D. (1962). Sources of power of lower participants in complex organizations. *Administrative Science Quarterly, 7:* 349–364.

Miller, R. (1985). Three who made a difference. *Management Review, 74:* 16–19.

Morris, M. W., J. M. Podolny, and S. Ariel. (2000). Missing relations: Incorporating relational constructs into models of culture. In P. C. Earley and H. Singh (Eds.), *Innovation in international and cross-cultural management* (pp. 52–90). Thousand Oaks, CA: Sage.

Mulder, M., L. Koppelaar, R. V. de Jong, and J. Verhage. (1986). Organizational field study. *Journal of Applied Psychology, 7:* 566–570.

Mulgan, G. (1998). *Connexity: How to live in a connected world.* Boston: Harvard Business School Press.

Pascale, R. (1985). The paradox of "corporate culture": Reconciling ourselves to socialization. *California Management Review, 27:* 26–41.

Perrow, C. (1970). Departmental power and perspectives in industrial firms. In M. N. Zold, (Ed.), *Power in organizations.* Nashville, TN: Vanderbilt University Press.

Peters, T. (1978). Symbols, patterns, and settings: An optimistic case for getting things done. *Organizational Dynamics, 7:* 3–22.

Pfeffer, J. (1977). Power and resource allocation in organizations. In B. Staw and G. Salancik (Eds.), *New direction in organizational behavior.* Chicago: St. Clair Press.

Pfeffer, J. (1981). *Power in organizations.* Marshfield, MA: Pitman.

Pfeffer, J. (1994). *Power and influence in organizations.* Boston: Harvard Business School Press.

Pfeffer, J., and A. Konrad. (1991). The effects of individual power on earnings. *Work and Occupations, 18:* 385–414.

Schein, E. H. (1999). *The corporate culture survival guide: Sense and nonsense about culture change.* San Francisco: Jossey-Bass.

Schmidt, S., and D. Kipnis. (1987). The perils of persistence. *Psychology Today, 21:* 32–33.

Shipper, F., and J. E. Dillard. (2000). A study of impending derailment and recovery of middle managers across career stages. *Human Resource Management, 39:* 331–345.

Sparrowe, R. T., R. C. Liden, and M. L. Kraimer. (2001). Social networks and the performance of individuals and groups. *Academy of Management Journal, 44:* 316–325.

Stewart, T. A. (1992, May 18). The search for the organization of tomorrow. *Fortune:* 92–98.

Tedeschi, J. T. (1974). Attributions, liking and power. In T. L. Huston (Ed.), *Foundations of interpersonal attraction.* New York: Academic Press.

Thompson, L. (2001). *The mind and heart of the negotiator.* Upper Saddle River, NJ: Prentice Hall.

Triandis, H. (1994). *Culture and social behavior.* New York: McGraw-Hill.

Trompenaars, F. (1996). Resolving international conflict: Culture and business strategy. *Business Strategy Review, 7:* 51–68.

Tully, S. (1993, February 8). The modular corporation. *Fortune:* 106–114.

Yukl, G. (2002). *Leadership in organizations,* 5th ed. Upper Saddle River, NJ: Prentice Hall.

CHAPTER 6 REFERENCES

Abbott, R. K. (1997). Flexible compensation: Past, present, and future. *Compensation & Benefits Management, 13:* 18–24.

Adria, M. (2000). Making the most of e-mail. *Academy of Management Executive, 14:* 153–154.

Alderfer, C. P. (1977). A critique of Salancik and Pfeffer's examination of need-satisfaction theories. *Administrative Science Quarterly, 22:* 658–672.

Atkinson, J. W. (1992). Motivational determinants of thematic apperception? In C. P. Smith (Ed.), *Motivation and personality: Handbook of thematic content analysis.* New York: Cambridge University Press.

Bennis, W. (1984). The four competencies of leadership. *Training and Development Journal, 38:* 15–19.

Bennis, W. (2003). *On becoming a leader.* Cambridge, MA: Perseus Books Group.

Birch, D., and J. Veroff. (1966). *Motivation: A study of action.* Monterey, CA: Brooks-Cole.

Bitter, M. E., and W. L. Gardner. (1995). A mid-range theory of the leader/member attribution process in professional service organizations: The role of the organizational environment and impression management. In M. J. Martinko (Ed.), *Attribution theory: An organizational perspective*. Delray Beach, FL: St. Lucie Press.

Boehle, S., K. Dobbs, and D. Stamps. (2000). Two views of distance learning. *Training, 37:* 34.

Butler, T., and J. Waldroop. (1999, September–October). Job sculpting: The art of retaining your best people. *Harvard Business Review:* 144–152.

Choi, I., R. E. Nisbett, and A. Norenzayan. (1999). Causal attribution across cultures: Variation and universality. *Psychological Bulletin, 125:* 47–63.

Cook, A. (2005, May). Money's a sure-fire motivator—Isn't it? *Promotions and Incentives:* 56–59.

Cropanzano, R., and R. Folger. (1996). Procedural justice and worker motivation. In R. M. Steers, L. W. Porter, and G. A. Bigley (Eds.), *Motivation and leadership at work*. New York: McGraw-Hill.

Davidson, O. B., and D. Eden. (2000). Remedial self-fulfilling prophecy: Two field experiments to prevent golem effects among disadvantaged women. *Journal of Applied Psychology 85:* 386–398.

Fisher, A. (2005, March 7). Starting a new job? Don't blow it. *Fortune:* 5.

Ganzach, Y. (1998). Intelligence and job satisfaction. *Academy of Management Journal, 41:* 526–536.

Gerhart, B. A. (2003). *Compensation: Theory, evidence, and strategic implications*. Thousand Oaks, CA: Sage.

Graham, M. E., and C. O. Trevor. (2000). Managing new pay program introductions to enhance the competitiveness of multinational corporations (MNCS). *Competitiveness Review, 10:* 136–154.

Hackman, J. R., and G. R. Oldham. (1980). *Work redesign*. Reading, MA: Addison-Wesley.

Harter, J. K., F. L. Schmidt, and T. L. Hayes. (2002). Business-unit-level relationship between employee satisfaction, employee engagement, and business outcomes: A meta-analysis. *Journal of Applied Psychology, 87:* 268–279.

House, R. J., and T. R. Mitchell. (1974). Path-goal theory of leadership. *Journal of Contemporary Business, 3:* 81–97.

Jackson, P. (2000). Interview with Phil Jackson by Bob Costas. MSNBC.

Janssen, O. (2001). Fairness perceptions as a moderator in the curvilinear relationships between job demands, and job performance and job satisfaction. *Academy of Management Journal, 44:* 1039–1050.

Jay, A. (1967). *Management and Machiavelli, an inquiry into the politics of corporate life*. New York: Holt, Rinehart & Winston.

Kerr, S. (1995). On the folly of rewarding A, while hoping for B. *Academy of Management Executive, 9(1):* 7–14.

Kerr, S. (1996, July 22). Risky business: The new pay game. *Fortune:* 94–97.

Kleiman, C. (2005, June 14). Awards for workers get better as they get personal. *Chicago Tribune:* 2.

Knight, D., C. C. Durham, and E. A. Locke. (2001). The relationship of term goals, incentives, and efficacy to strategic risk, tactical implementation, and performance. *Academy of Management Journal, 44:* 326–338.

Komaki, J., T. Coombs, and S. Schepman. (1996). Motivational implications of reinforcement theory. In R. M. Steers, L. W. Porter, and G. A. Bigley (Eds.), *Motivation and leadership at work*. New York: McGraw-Hill.

Kopelman, R. E. (1985, Summer). Job redesign and productivity: A review of evidence. *National Productivity Review:* 237–255.

Kotter, J. (1996, August 5). Kill complacency. *Fortune:* 168–170.

Latham, G., M. Erez, and E. Locke. (1988). Resolving scientific disputes by the joint design of crucial experiments by the antagonists: Application to the Erez-Latham disputes regarding participation in goal setting. *Journal of Applied Psychology, 73:* 753–772.

Lawler, E. E. (1987). The design of effective reward systems. In J. Lorsch (Ed.), *Handbook of organizational behavior*. Englewood Cliffs, NJ: Prentice Hall.

Lawler, E. E. (1988). Gainsharing theory and research: Findings and future directions. In W. A. Pasmore and E. R. Woodman (Eds.), *Research in organizational change and development* (Vol. 2). Greenwich, CT: JAI Press.

Lawler, E. E. (2000a). *Strategic pay*. San Francisco: Jossey-Bass.

Lawler, E. E., III. (2000b). *Pay strategies for the new economy*. San Francisco: Jossey-Bass.

LeDue, A. I., Jr. (1980). Motivation of programmers. *Data Base, 3:* 5.

Levering, R., and M. Moskowitz. (2003, January 20). 100 best companies to work for. *Fortune, 147:* 127.

Locke, E. A., and G. P. Latham. (2002, September). Building a practically useful theory of goal setting and task motivation. *American Psychologist, 57:* 705–717.

Luthans, F., and A. D. Stajkovic. (1999). Reinforce for performance: The need to go beyond pay and even rewards. *Academy of Management Executive, 13(2):* 49–57.

Maslow, A. H. (1970). *Motivation and personality,* 2nd ed. New York: Harper & Row.

McCauley, L. (1999). Next stop—the 21st century. *Fast Company, 27:* 108–112.

McClelland, D. (1971). *Assessing human motivation*. New York: General Learning Press.

McClelland, D. C., J. W. Arkinson, R. A. Clark, and E. L. Lowell. (1953). *The achievement motive*. New York: Appleton-Century-Crofts.

McClelland, D. C., and D. H. Burnham. (2003). Power is the great motivator. *Harvard Business Review, 81:* 117–126.

McGregor, D. (1960). *The human side of enterprise*. New York: McGraw-Hill.

Michener, H. A., J. A. Fleishman, and J. J. Vaske. (1976). A test of the bargaining theory of coalition formulation in four-person groups. *Journal of Personality and Social Psychology, 34:* 1114–1126.

Moe, M. T., and H. Blodget. (2000, May 23). *The knowledge web. Part 4: corporate e-learning—feeding hungry minds*. Merrill Lynch & Co.

Murlis, H., and A. Wright. (1985). Rewarding the performance of the eager beaver. *Personnel Management, 17:* 28–31.

Murray, B., and B. Gerhart. (1998). An empirical analysis of a skill-based pay program and plant performance outcomes. *Academy of Management Journal, 41:* 68–78.

Nelson, B. (2000). Are performance appraisals obsolete? *Compensation and Benefits Review, 32:* 39–42.

Nelson, N. (2005). *The power of appreciation in business: How an obsession with value increases performance, productivity, and profits.* Malibu, CA: MindLab Publishing.

Nelton, S. (1988, March). Motivating for success. *Nation's Business:* 25.

News-Gazette. (1987, January): 6.

Parker, G. (2001). Establishing remuneration practices across culturally diverse environments. *Compensation & Benefits Management, 17:* 23–27.

Perry, M. (2000, January). Working in the dark. *Training Media Review:* 13–14.

Peters, T., and R. H. Waterman. (1982). *In search of excellence.* New York: Warner Books.

Pfeffer, J. (1995). Producing sustainable competitive advantage through the effective management of people. *Academy of Management Executive, 9:* 55–71.

Quick, T. L. (1977). *Person to person managing.* New York: St. Martin's Press.

Quick, T. L. (1991). Motivation: Help your star performers shine even brighter. *Sales and Marketing Management, 143:* 96.

Reese, S. (1999, July). Getting your money's worth from training. *Business and Health:* 26–29.

Schriesheim, C. A., and L. L. Neider. (1996). Path-goal leadership theory: The long and winding road. *Leadership Quarterly, 7:* 317–321.

Shamir, B., R. J. House, and M. B. Arthur. (1993). The motivational effects of charismatic leadership: A self-concept based theory. *Organization Science, 4 (4):* 577–594.

Stajkovic, A. D., and F. Luthans. (2001). Differential effects of incentive motivators on work performance. *Academy of Management Journal, 4:* 580–500.

Steers, R. M., L. W. Porter, and G. A. Bigley. (1996). *Motivation and leadership at work.* New York: McGraw-Hill.

Sue-Chan, C., and M. Ong. (2002). Goal assignment and performance: Assessing the mediating roles of goal commitment and self-efficacy and the moderating role of power distance. *Organizational Behavior and Human Decision Processes, 89:* 1140–1161.

Taylor, W. C. (1995). At Verifone it's a dog's life (and they love it?). *Fast Company, 1:* 115.

Thompson, D. W. (1978). *Managing people: Influencing behavior.* St. Louis, MO: C. V. Mosby Co.

Tichy, N. (1997, April). Bob Knowling's change manual. *Fast Company:* 76.

Tomlinson, A. (2002, March 25). T&D spending up in U.S. as Canada lags behind. *Canadian HR Reporter, 15:* 1–18.

Triandis, H. C. (1994). *Culture and social behavior.* New York: McGraw-Hill.

Vroom, V. (1964). *Work and motivation.* New York: Wiley.

Weiner, B. (2000). Intrapersonal and interpersonal theories of motivation from an attributional perspective. *Educational Psychology Review, 12:* 1–14.

Wood, R., and A. Bandura. (1989). Social cognitive theory of organizational management. *Academy of Management Review, 14(3):* 361–383.

Zingheim, P. K., and J. R. Schuster. (1995). Introduction: How are the new pay tools being deployed? *Compensation and Benefits Review* (July–August): 10–11.

CHAPTER 7 REFERENCES

Adler, N. J. (2002). *International dimensions of organizational behavior,* 4th ed. Cincinnati, OH: South-Western.

Adler, R. B. (1977). Satisfying personal needs: Managing conflicts, making requests, and saying no. In *Confidence in communication: A guide to assertive and social skills.* New York: Holt, Rinehart & Winston.

Adler, R. B., L. B. Rosenfeld, and R. F. Proctor. (2001). *Interplay: The process of interpersonal communication.* Fort Worth, TX: Harcourt, Inc.

Alder, R. B., and G. Rodman. (2003). *Understanding human communication,* 8th ed. New York: Oxford University Press.

Argenti, J. (1976). *Corporate collapse: The causes and symptoms.* New York: Wiley.

Bazerman, M. H., and M. A. Neale. (1992). *Negotiating rationally.* New York: Free Press.

Blackard, K., and J. Gibson. (2002). *Capitalizing on conflict: Strategies and practices for turning conflict into synergy in organizations: A manager's handbook.* Palo Alto, CA: Davis-Black Publishing.

The boss as referee. [Accountemps survey]. (1996, September). *CMA Management Accounting Magazine, 70 (7):* 32.

Boulding, E. (1964). Further reflections on conflict management. In R. L. Kahn and E. Boulding (Eds.), *Power and conflict in organizations.* New York: Basic Books.

Brown, L. D. (1983). *Managing conflict at organizational interfaces.* Reading, MA: Addison-Wesley.

Cameron, K. S., M. U. Kim, and D. A. Whetten. (1987). Organizational effects of decline and turbulence. *Administrative Science Quarterly, 32:* 222–240.

Catch a falling star. (1988, April 23). *The Economist,* 88–90.

Caudron, S. (1992). Subculture strife hinders productivity. *Personnel Journal, 71(2):* 60–64.

Cox, T. H. (1994). *Cultural diversity in organizations: Theory, research, and practice.* San Francisco: Barrett-Koehler.

Cox, T. H., and Blake, S. (1991). Managing cultural diversity: Implications for organizational competitiveness. *Academy of Management Executive, 5(3):* 45–56.

Cummings, L. L., D. L. Harnett, and O. J. Stevens. (1971). Risk, fate, conciliation, and trust: An international study of attitudinal differences among executives. *Academy of Management Journal, 14:* 285–304.

de Dreu, C. K. W., S. L. Koole, and W. Steinel. (2000). Unfixing the fixed pie: A motivated information-processing approach to integrative negotiation. *Journal of Personality and Social Psychology, 79:* 975–987.

de Dreu, C. K. W., and L. R. Weingart. (2002). Task versus relationship conflict: A meta-analysis. *Academy of Management Proceedings, CM:* B1–B6.

Eisenhardt, K. M., J. L. Kahwajy, and L. J. Bourgeois III. (1997, July–August). How management teams can have a good fight. *Harvard Business Review:* 77–85.

Fisher, R., and S. Brown. (1988). *Getting together: Building a relationship that gets to yes.* Boston: Houghton Mifflin.

Gage, D. (1999, December). Is having partners a bad idea? *IndustryWeek*, Growing Companies Edition: 46–47.

Gendron, G., and B. O. Burlingham. (1989, April). The entrepreneur of the decade: An interview with Steve Jobs. *Inc.:* 123.

The GM system is like a blanket of fog. (1988, February 15). *Fortune:* 48–49.

Gordon, T. (2000). *Parent effectiveness training.* New York: Three Rivers Press.

Grove, A. (1984, July). How to make confrontation work for you. *Fortune:* 74.

Hines, J. S. (1980). *Conflict and conflict management.* Athens: University of Georgia Press.

Hofstede, G. (1980, Summer). Motivation, leadership, and organization: Do American theories apply abroad? *Organizational Dynamics:* 42–63.

Jehn, K. A. (1997). A qualitative analysis of conflict types and dimensions of organizational groups. *Administrative Science Quarterly, 41:* 530–557.

Jehn, K., and E. A. Mannix. (2001). The dynamic nature of conflict: A longitudinal study of intragroup conflict and group performance. *Academy of Management Journal, 44:* 238–251.

Karambayya, R., and J. M. Brett. (1989). Managers handling disputes: Third party roles and perceptions of fairness. *Academy of Management Journal, 32:* 687–704.

Keashly, L. (1994). Gender and conflict: What does psychological research tell us? In A. Taylor and J. B. Miller (Eds.), *Conflict and gender.* Cresskill, NJ: Hampton Press.

Kelly, J. (1970, July–August). Make conflict work for you. *Harvard Business Review, 48:* 103–113.

Kilmann, R. H., and K. W. Thomas. (1977). Developing a forced-choice measure of conflict-handling behavior: The MODE instrument. *Educational and Psychological Measurement, 37:* 309–325.

Kim, S. H., and R. H. Smith. (1993). Revenge and conflict escalation. *Negotiation Journal. 9:* 37–44.

Kipnis, D., and S. Schmidt. (1983). An influence perspective in bargaining within organizations. In M. H. Bazerman, and R. J. Lewicki (Eds.), *Bargaining inside organizations.* Beverly Hills, CA: Sage.

Korabik, D., G. L. Baril, and C. Watson. (1993). Managers' conflict management style and leadership effectiveness: The moderating effects of gender. *Sex Roles, 29(5/6):* 405–420.

Kressel, K., and D. G. Pruitt. (1989). *Mediation research: The process and effectiveness of third party intervention.* San Francisco: Jossey-Bass.

Latham, G., and K. Wexley. (1994). *Increasing productivity through performance appraisal.* Reading, MA: Addison-Wesley.

Lombardo, M. M., and R. W. Eichinger. (1996). *The Career ARCHITECT Development Planner.* Minneapolis: Lominger Ltd.

Maslow, A. (1965). *Eupsychian management.* Homewood, IL: Irwin.

Memeth, C. J., B. Personnaz, M. Personnaz, and J. A. Goucalo. (2004). The liberating role of conflict in group creativity: A study in two countries. *European Journal of Social Psychology, 34:* 365–374.

Morris, W., and M. Sashkin. (1976). *Organizational behavior in action.* St. Paul, MN: West Publishing.

Morrison, A. M. (1996). *The new leaders: Leadership diversity in America.* San Francisco: Jossey-Bass.

Murnighan, J. K. (1992). *Bargaining games: A new approach to strategic thinking in negotiations.* New York: William Morrow.

Murnighan, J. K. (1993). *The dynamics of bargaining games.* Upper Saddle River, NJ: Prentice Hall.

Pascale, R. (1990, February). Creating contention without causing conflict. *Business Month:* 69–71.

Pelled, L. H., K. M. Eisenhardt, and K. R. Xin. (1999). Exploring the black box: An analysis of work group diversity, conflict, and performance. *Administrative Science Quarterly, 44:* 1–28.

Perot, H. R. (1988, February). How I would turn around GM. *Fortune:* 48–49.

Phillips, E., and R. Cheston. (1979). Conflict resolution: What works. *California Management Review, 21:* 76–83.

Phillips, K. W., K. A. Liljenquist, and M. A. Neale. (2009). Is the pain worth the gain? The advantages and liabilities of agreeing with socially distinct newcomers. *Personality and Social Psychology Bulletin, 35:* 336–350.

Porter, E. H. (1973). *Manual of administration and interpretation for strength deployment inventory.* La Jolla, CA: Personal Strengths Assessment Service.

Rahim, M. A., and A. A. Blum. (1994). *Global perspectives on organizational conflict.* Westport, CT: Praeger.

Ruble, T., and J. A. Schneer. (1994). Gender differences in conflict-handling styles: Less than meets the eye? In A. Taylor, and J. B. Miller, (Eds.), *Conflict and gender.* Cresskill, NJ: Hampton Press.

Ruble, T., and K. Thomas. (1976). Support for a two-dimensional model of conflict behavior. *Organizational Behavior and Human Performance, 16:* 145.

Savage, G. T., J. D. Blair, and R. L. Sorenson. (1989). Consider both relationships and substance when negotiating strategically. *Academy of Management Executive, 3:* 37–48.

Schmidt, W. H., and R. Tannenbaum. (1965, November–December). Management of differences. *Harvard Business Review, 38:* 107–115.

Seybolt, P. M., C. B. Derr, and T. R. Nielson. (1996). Linkages between national culture, gender, and conflict management styles. Working paper, University of Utah.

Sillars, A., and J. Weisberg. (1987). Conflict as a social skill. In M. E. Roloff and G. R. Miller (Eds.), *Interpersonal processes: New directions in communication research.* Beverly Hills, CA: Sage.

Smith, W. P. (1987). Conflict and negotiation: Trends and emerging issues. *Journal of Applied Social Psychology, 17:* 631–677.

Stroh, L. K., G. Northcraft, and M. Neale. (2002). *Organizational behavior: A management challenge,* 3rd ed. Mahwah, NJ: Lawrence Erlbaum Associates.

Thomas, K. (1976). Conflict and conflict management. In M. D. Dunnette (Ed.), *Handbook of industrial and organizational psychology*. London: Routledge and Kegan Paul.

Thompson, L. (2001). *The mind and heart of the negotiator*, 2nd ed. Upper Saddle River, NJ: Prentice Hall.

Ting-Toomey, S., G. Gao, P. Trubisky, Z. Yang, H. S. Kim, S. L. Lin, and T. Nishida. (1991). Culture, face maintenance, and styles of handling interpersonal conflict: A study in five cultures. *International Journal of Conflict Management, 2:* 275–296.

Tjosvold, D. (1991). *The conflict positive organization*. Reading, MA: Addison-Wesley.

Trompenaars, F. (1994). *Riding the waves of culture: Understanding diversity in global business*. New York: Irwin.

Trompenaars, F. (1996). Resolving international conflict: Culture and business strategy. *Business Strategy Review, 7:* 51–68.

Volkema, R. J., and T. J. Bergmann. (2001). Conflict styles as indicators of behavioral patterns in interpersonal conflicts. *Journal of Social Psychology, 135:* 5–15.

Wanous, J. P., and A. Youtz. (1986). Solution diversity and the quality of group decisions. *Academy of Management Journal, 1:* 149–159.

Weldon, E., and K. A. Jehn. (1995). Examining crosscultural differences in conflict management behavior: Strategy for future research. *International Journal of Conflict Management, 6:* 387–403.

Wilmot, W. W., and J. L. Hocker. (2001). *Interpersonal conflict*. New York: McGraw-Hill.

Xie, J., X. M. Song, and A. Stringfellow. (1998). Interfunctional conflict, conflict resolution styles, and new product success: A four-culture comparison. *Management Science, 44:* S192–S206.

CHAPTER 8 REFERENCES

Abrahamson, E. (1996). Management fashion. *Academy of Management Review, 21:* 254–285.

Adler, A. (1927). *Understanding human nature*. Garden City, NY: Garden City Publishing.

Alinsky, S. D. (1971). *Rules for radicals: A pragmatic primer for realistic radicals*. New York: Vintage Books.

Alloy, L. B., C. Peterson, L. Y. Abrahamson, and M. E. P. Seligman. (1984). Attributional style and the generality of learned helplessness. *Journal of Personality and Social Psychology, 46:* 681–687.

Anderson, C., D. Hellriegel, and J. Slocum. (1977). Managerial response to environmentally induced stress. *Academy of Management Journal, 20:* 260–272.

Ashby, R. (1956). *Design for the brain*. London: Science Paperbacks.

Averill, J. R. (1973). Personal control over aversive stimuli and its relationships to stress. *Psychological Bulletin, 80:* 286–303.

Baker, W., R. Cross, and M. Wooten. (2003). Positive organizational network analysis and energizing relationships. In K. S. Cameron, J. E. Dutton, and R. E. Quinn (Eds.), *Positive Organizational Scholarship* (pp. 328–342). San Francisco: Barrett-Koehler.

Bandura, A. (1977). Self-efficacy: Toward a unifying theory of behavioral change. *Psychological Review, 84:* 191–215.

Bandura, A. (1986). *Social foundations of thought and action: A social cognitive theory*. Englewood Cliffs, NJ: Prentice Hall.

Bandura, A. (1989). Human agency in social cognition theory. *American Psychologist, 44:* 1175–1184.

Barber, B. (1983). *The logic and limits of trust*. New Brunswick, NJ: Rutgers University Press.

Bennis, W., and B. Nanus. (1985). *Leaders: The strategies for taking charge*. New York: Harper & Row.

Bernard, C. I. (1938). *The functions of the executive*. Cambridge, MA: Harvard University Press.

Block, P. (1987). *The empowered manager: Positive political skills at work*. San Francisco: Jossey-Bass.

Bookman, A., and S. Morgan. (1988). *Women and the politics of empowerment*. Philadelphia: Temple University Press.

Bramucci, R. (1977). A factorial examination of the self-empowerment construct. Unpublished doctoral dissertation, University of Oregon.

Brehm, J. W. (1966). *Response to loss of freedom: A theory of psychological reactance*. New York: Academic Press.

Brief, A., and W. Nord. (1990). *Meanings of occupational work*. Lexington, MA: Lexington Books.

Byham, W. C. (1988). *Zapp! The lightening of empowerment*. New York: Harmony Books.

Cameron, K. S. (1998). Strategic organizational downsizing: An extreme case. *Research in Organizational Behavior, 20:* 185–229.

Cameron, K. S., J. E. Dutton, and R. E. Quinn. (2003). *Positive organizational scholarship*. San Francisco: Barrett-Koehler.

Cameron, K. S., S. J. Freeman, and A. K. Mishra. (1991). Best practices in white-collar downsizing: Managing contradictions. *Academy of Management Executive, 5:* 57–73.

Cameron, K. S., S. J. Freeman, and A. K. Mishra. (1993). Organization downsizing and redesign. In G. P. Huber, and W. Glick (Eds.), *Organizational change and design*. New York: Oxford University Press.

Cameron, K. S., M. U. Kim, and D. A. Whetten. (1987). Organizational effects of decline and turbulence. *Administrative Science Quarterly, 32:* 222–240.

Cameron, K. S., D. A. Whetten, and M. U. Kim. (1987). Organizational dysfunctions of decline. *Academy of Management Journal, 30:* 126–138.

Cameron, K. S., and R. E. Quinn. (2006). *Diagnosing and changing organizational culture*. San Francisco: Jossey-Bass.

Coch, L., and J. R. P. French. (1948). Overcoming resistance to change. *Human Relations, 11:* 512–532.

Conger, J. A. (1989). Leadership: The art of empowering others. *Academy of Management Executive, 3:* 17–24.

Conger, J. A., and R. N. Kanungo. (1988). The empowerment process. *Academy of Management Review, 13:* 471–482.

Coonradt, C. A. (1985). *The game of work*. Salt Lake City: Shadow Mountain Press.

DeCharms, R. (1979). Personal causation and perceived control. In L. C. Perlmuter and R. A. Monty (Eds.), *Choice and perceived control*. Hillsdale, NJ: Erlbaum.

Deci, E. L., and R. M. Ryan. (1987). The support of autonomy and control of behavior. *Journal of Personality and Social Psychology, 53:* 1024–1037.

Deci, E. L., J. P. Connell, and R. M. Ryan. (1989). Self-determination in a work organization. *Journal of Applied Psychology, 74:* 580–590.

DeGraff, J., and K. A. Lawrence. (2002). *Creativity at work: Developing the right practices to make innovation happen.* San Francisco: Jossey-Bass.

Deutsch, M. (1973). *The resolution of conflict: Constructive and destructive processes.* New Haven, CT: Yale University Press.

DiClemente, C. C. (1985). Perceived efficacy in smoking cessation. Paper presented at the Annual meeting of the American Association for the Advancement of Science, Los Angeles.

Drucker, P. (1988, January–February). The coming of the new organization. *Harvard Business Review:* 45–53.

Durkheim, E. (1964). *The division of labor in society.* New York: Free Press.

Eisenhart, K. M., and D. Charlie Galunic. (1993). Renewing the strategy-structure-performance paradigm. *Research in organizational behavior.* Greenwich, CT: JAI Press.

French, J. P. R., Jr., and B. Raven. (1960). The bases of social power. In D. Cartwright and A. Zander (Eds.), *Group dynamics* (pp. 607–623). New York: Harper & Row.

Freire, P., and A. Faundez. (1989). *Learning to question: A pedagogy of liberation.* New York: Continuum Publishing.

Gambetta, D. (1988). *Trust: Making and breaking cooperative relations.* Cambridge, MA: Basil Blackwell.

Gecas, V. (1989). The social psychology of self-efficacy. *Annual Review of Sociology, 15:* 291–316.

Gecas, V., M. A. Seff, and M. P. Ray. (1988). Injury and depression: The mediating effects of self concept. Paper presented at the Pacific Sociological Association Meetings, Las Vegas.

Gemmill, G. R., and W. J. Heisler. (1972). Fatalism as a factor in managerial job satisfaction. *Personnel Psychology, 25:* 241–250.

Gibb, J. R., and L. M. Gibb. (1969). Role freedom in a TORI group. In A. Burton (Ed.), *Encounter theory and practice of encounter groups.* San Francisco: Jossey-Bass.

Goddard, R. D., W. K. Hoy, and A. W. Hoy. (2003). Collective efficacy beliefs: Theoretical developments, empirical evidence, and future directions. *Educational Researcher, 33:* 3–13.

Golembiewski, R. T., and M. McConkie. (1975). The centrality of trust in group processes. In C. Cooper (Ed.), *Theories of group processes.* New York: Wiley.

Greenberger, D. B., and S. Stasser. (1991). The role of situational and dispositional factors in the enhancement of personal control in organizations. *Research in Organizational Behavior,* Vol. 13, (pp. 111–145). Greenwich, CT: JAI Press.

Greenberger, D. B., S. Stasser, L. L. Cummings, and R. B. Dunham. (1989). The impact of personal control on performance and satisfaction. *Organizational Behavior and Human Decision Processes, 43:* 29–51.

Hackman, J. R., and G. R. Oldham. (1980). *Work design.* Reading, MA: Addison-Wesley.

Hackman, J. R., G. R. Oldham, R. Janson, and K. Purdy. (1975). A new strategy for job enrichment. *California Management Review, 17:* 57–71.

Hammer, T. H., and Y. Vardi. (1981). Locus of control and career self-management among nonsupervisory employees in industrial settings. *Journal of Vocational Behavior, 18:* 13–29.

Harris, L. (2002). *Harris Poll #31.* New York: Harris Interactive.

Harter, S. (1978). Effectance motivation reconsidered: Toward a developmental model. *Human Development, 21:* 34–64.

Huber, G. P. (1980). *Managerial decision making.* Glenview, IL: Scott Foresman.

Kahn, W. A. (1990). Psychological conditions of personal engagement and disengagement at work. *Academy of Management Journal, 33:* 692–724.

Kanter, R. (1983). *The change masters.* New York: Simon & Schuster.

Langer, E. J. (1983). *The psychology of control.* Beverly Hills, CA: Sage.

Langer, E. J., and J. Rodin. (1976). The effects of choice and enhanced personal responsibility. *Journal of Personality and Social Psychology, 34:* 191–198.

Lawler, E. E. (1992) *The ultimate advantage: Creating the high involvement organization.* San Francisco: Jossey-Bass.

Lawrence, P., and J. Lorsch. (1967). *Organizations and environments.* Homewood, IL: Irwin.

Leana, C. R. (1987). Power relinquishment versus power sharing: Theoretical clarification and empirical comparison on delegation and participation. *Journal of Applied Psychology, 72:* 228–233.

Locke, E. A., and D. M. Schweiger. (1979). Participation in decision making: One more look. In B. M. Staw and L. L. Cummings (Eds.), *Research in organizational behavior,* Vol. 1 (pp. 265–340). Greenwich, CT: JAI Press.

Luhmann, N. (1979). *Trust and power.* New York: Wiley.

Maddux, J. E. (2002). Self-efficacy. In C. R. Snyder and S. J. Lopez, *Handbook of positive psychology* (pp. 277–287). New York: Oxford.

Manz, C. C., and H. Sims. (1989). *Super-leadership: Teaching others to lead themselves.* Englewood Cliffs, NJ: Prentice Hall.

Martin, J., M. Feldman, M. J. Hatch, and S. Sitkin. (1983). The uniqueness paradox of organizational stories. *Administrative Science Quarterly, 28:* 438–452.

Marx, K. (1844). *Early writings.* Edited and translated by T. B. Bottomore. New York: McGraw-Hill.

McClellend, D. (1975). *Power: The inner experience.* New York: Irvington.

Mishra, A. K. (1992). Organizational response to crisis: The role of mutual trust and top management teams. Unpublished doctoral dissertation, University of Michigan.

Neufeld, R. W. J., and P. Thomas. (1977) Effects of perceived efficacy of a prophylactic controlling mechanism on self-control under painful stimulation. *Canadian Journal of Behavioral Science, 9:* 224–232.

Newman, W. H., and K. Warren. (1977). *The process of management.* Englewood Cliffs, NJ: Prentice Hall.

Organ, D., and C. N. Greene. (1974). Role ambiguity, locus of control, and work satisfaction. *Journal of Applied Psychology, 59:* 101–112.

Ozer, E. M., and A. Bandura. (1990). Mechanisms governing empowerment effects: A self-efficacy analysis. *Journal of Personality and Social Psychology, 58:* 472–486.

Pratt, M. G., and B. E. Ashforth. (2003). Fostering meaningfulness in working and at work. In K. S. Cameron, J. E. Dutton, and R. E. Quinn (Eds.), *Positive organizational scholarship* (pp. 309–327). San Francisco: Barrett-Koehler.

Preston, P., and T. W. Zimmerer. (1978). *Management for supervisors.* Englewood Cliffs, NJ: Prentice Hall.

Quinn, R. E. (2005). *Building the bridge as you walk on it.* San Francisco: Jossey-Bass.

Quinn, R. E., and G. Spreitzer. (1997). The road to empowerment: Seven questions every leader should consider. *Organizational Dynamics, 25:* 37–49.

Rappoport, J., C. Swift, and R. Hess. (1984). *Studies in empowerment: Steps toward understanding and action.* New York: Haworth Press.

Rose, S. M., and B. L. Black. (1985). *Advocacy and empowerment: Mental health care in the community.* Boston: Routledge and Kegan Paul.

Rothbaum, F., J. R. Weisz, and S. S. Snyder. (1982). Changing the world and changing the self: A two-process model of perceived control. *Journal of Personality and Social Psychology, 42:* 5–37.

Runyon, K. E. (1973). Some interaction between personality variables and management style. *Journal of Applied Psychology, 57:* 288–294.

Sashkin, M. (1982). *A manager's guide to participative management.* New York: American Management Association.

Sashkin, M. (1984). Participative management is an ethical imperative. *Organizational Dynamics, 12:* 4–22.

Schneider, J. A., and W. W. Agras. (1985). A cognitive behavioral treatment of bulimia. *British Journal of Psychiatry, 146:* 66–69.

Schwalbe, M. L., and V. Gecas. (1988). Social psychological consequences of job-related disabilities. In J. T. Mortimer and K. M. Borman (Eds.), *Work experience and psychological development through life span.* Boulder, CO: Westview.

Seeman, M., and C. S. Anderson. (1983). Alienation and alcohol. *American Sociological Review, 48:* 60–77.

Seligman, M. E. P. (1975). *Helplessness: On depression, development, and death.* San Francisco: Freeman.

Sewell, Carl. (1990). *Customers for life.* New York: Pocket Books.

Solomon, B. B. (1976). *Black empowerment: Social work in oppressed communities.* New York: Columbia University Press.

Spreitzer, G. M. (1992). *When organizations dare: The dynamics of individual empowerment in the workplace.* Unpublished doctoral dissertation, University of Michigan.

Staples, L. H. (1990). Powerful ideas about empowerment. *Administration in Social Work, 14:* 29–42.

Staw, B., L. Sandelands, and J. Dutton. (1981). Threat-rigidity effects in organizational behavior: A multilevel analysis. *Administrative Science Quarterly, 26:* 501–524.

Thomas, K. W., and B. A. Velthouse. (1990). Cognitive elements of empowerment: An interpretive model of intrinsic task motivation. *Academy of Management Review, 15:* 666–681.

Trompenaars, F. (1996). Resolving international conflict: Culture and business strategy. *Business Strategy Review, 7:* 51–68.

Trompenaars, F., and C. Hampden-Turner. (1998). *Riding the waves of culture.* New York: McGraw-Hill.

Urwick, L. (1944). *Elements of administration.* New York: Harper and Brothers.

Vogt, J. F., and K. L. Murrell. (1990). *Empowerment in organizations.* San Diego: University Associates.

Vroom, V. H., and A. G. Jago. (1974). Decision making as social process: Normative and descriptive models of leader behavior. *Decision Sciences, 5:* 743–769.

Vroom, V. H., and P. W. Yetton. (1973). *Leadership and decision making.* Pittsburgh: University of Pittsburgh Press.

Weick, K. E. (1979). *The social psychology of organizing.* Reading, MA: Addison-Wesley.

Weick, K. E. (1984). Small wins. *American Psychologist, 39:* 40–49.

Weick, K. E. (1993). Collapse of sense-making in organizations. *Administrative Science Quarterly, 38:* 628–652.

White, R. W. (1959). Motivation reconsidered: The concept of competence. *Psychological Review, 66:* 297–333.

Wrzesniewski, A. (2003). Finding positive meaning in work. In K. S. Cameron, J. E. Dutton, and R. E. Quinn (Eds.), *Positive organizational scholarship* (pp. 296–308). San Francisco: Barrett-Koehler.

Zand, D. E. (1972). Trust and managerial problem solving. *Administrative Science Quarterly, 17:* 229–239.

Zimmerman, M. A., and J. Rappaport. (1988). Citizen participation, perceived control, and psychological empowerment. *American Journal of Community Psychology, 16:* 725–750.

Zimmerman, M. A. (1990). Taking aim on empowerment research: On the distinction between individual and psychological conceptions. *American Journal of Community Psychology, 18:* 169–177.

CHAPTER 9 REFERENCES

Ancona, D. G., and D. Caldwell. (1992). Bridging the boundary: External activity and performance in organizational teams. *Administrative Science Quarterly, 27:* 459–489.

Asch, S. E. (1951). Effects of group pressure upon the modification and distortion of judgments. In H. Guetzkow (Ed.), *Groups, leadership, and men.* Pittsburgh: Carnegie Press.

Cameron, K. S., and D. A. Whetten. (1981). Perceptions of organizational effectiveness in organizational life cycles. *Administrative Science Quarterly, 27:* 524–544.

Cameron, K. S., and D. A. Whetten. (1984). Organizational life cycle approaches: Overview and applications to higher education. *Review of Higher Education, 6:* 60–102.

Campion, M. A., G. J. Medsker, and A. C. Higgs. (1993). Relations between work group characteristics and effectiveness: Implications for designing effective work groups. *Personnel Psychology, 46:* 823–850.

Cialdini, R. B. (1995). *Influence: Science and practice,* 3rd ed. Glenview, IL: Scott Foresman.

Clarke, J., and A. Hobson. (2005). *Above all else: The Everest dream.* Toronto: Stewart Publishing.

Cohen, S. G., and D. E. Bailey. (1997). What makes teams work: Group effectiveness research from the shop floor to the executive suite. *Journal of Management, 23:* 239–290.

Cox, T. H. (1994). *Cultural diversity in organizations: Theory, research, and practice.* San Francisco: Barrett-Koehler.

Dew, J. R. (1998). *Managing in a team environment.* Westport, CT: Quorum.

Dewey, J. (1933). *How we think.* Boston: Heath.

Druskat, V., and J. Wheeler. (2000). Effective leadership of self-managing teams: Behaviors that make a difference. Working paper, Weatherhead School of Management, Case Western Reserve University.

Druskat, V., and S. Wolff. (1999). The link between emotions and team effectiveness: How teams engage members and build effective task processes. *Academy of Management Best Paper Proceedings*, Organizational Behavior Division.

Dyer, W. G. (1987). *Team building: Issues and alternatives.* Reading, MA: Addison-Wesley.

Edmonson, A. (1999). Psychological safety and learning behavior in work teams. *Administrative Science Quarterly, 44:* 350–383.

Freud, S. (1921). *Group psychology and the analysis of the ego.* London: Hogarth Press.

Gladstein, D. (1984). Group in context: A model of task group effectiveness. *Administrative Science Quarterly, 29:* 497–517.

Greiner, L. (1972, July–August). Evolution and revolution as organizations grow. *Harvard Business Review:* 37–46.

Gully, S. M., D. S. Divine, and D. J. Whitney. (1995). A meta-analysis of cohesion and performance: Effects of level of analysis and task interdependence. *Small Group Research, 26:* 497–520.

Guzzo, R. A., and M. W. Dickson. (1996). Teams in organizations: Recent research on performance and effectiveness. *Annual Review of Psychology, 47:* 307–338.

Hackman, J. R. (1987). The design of work teams. In J. W. Lorsch (Ed.), *Handbook of organizational behavior.* Englewood Cliffs, NJ: Prentice Hall.

Hackman, J. R. (1990). *Groups that work (and those that don't).* San Francisco: Jossey-Bass.

Hackman, J. R. (1993). Teams and group failure. Presentation at the Interdisciplinary College on Organization Studies, University of Michigan, October.

Hackman, J. R. (2003). *Leading teams.* Cambridge, MA: Harvard Business School Press.

Hamilton, B. H., J. A. Nickerson, and H. Owan. (2003). Team incentives and worker heterogeneity: An empirical analysis of the impact of teams on productivity and participation. *Journal of Political Economy, 111:* 465–497.

Hayes, N. (1997). *Successful team management.* Boston: International Thompson Business Press.

Janis, I. (1972). *Victims of groupthink.* Boston: Houghton Mifflin.

Katzenbach, J. R., and D. K. Smith. (1993). *The wisdom of teams.* Boston: Harvard Business School Press.

Kouzes, J., and B. Posner. (1987). *The leadership challenge.* San Francisco: Jossey-Bass.

Kramer, R. M. (1999). Trust and distrust in organizations: Emerging perspectives, enduring questions. *Annual Review of Psychology, 50:* 569–598.

Lawler, E. E. (1998). *Strategies for high performance organizations.* San Francisco: Jossey-Bass.

Lawler, E. E. (2003). *Treat people right.* San Francisco: Jossey-Bass.

Lawler, E. E., S. A. Mohrman, and G. E. Ledford. (1995). *Creating high performance organizations: Practices and results of employee involvement and total quality management in* Fortune *1000 companies.* San Francisco: Jossey-Bass.

Lidz, F. (2000). Up and down in Beverly Hills. *Sports Illustrated, 92(16):* 60–68.

Locke, E. (1990). *A theory of goal setting and task performance.* Upper Saddle River, NJ: Prentice Hall.

Manz, C., and H. Sims. (1987). Leading workers to lead themselves: The external leadership of self-managing work teams. *Administrative Science Quarterly, 32:* 106–128.

Mullen, B., and C. Copper. (1994). The relation between group cohesiveness and performance: An integration. *Psychological Bulletin, 115:* 210–227.

Pagonis, W. G. (1993). *Moving mountains.* Cambridge, MA: Harvard Business School Press.

Parker, G. M. (1996). *Team players and teamwork: The new competitive business strategy.* San Francisco: Jossey-Bass.

Peters, T. (1987). *Thriving on chaos.* New York: Knopf.

Quinn, R. E. (2005). *Building the bridge as you walk on it.* San Francisco: Jossey-Bass.

Quinn, R. E., and K. S. Cameron. (1983). Organizational life cycles and shifting criteria of effectiveness: Some preliminary evidence. *Management Science, 29:* 33–51.

Schein, E. H. (1976). What to observe in a group. In C. R. Mill and L. C. Porter (Eds.), *Reading book for human relations training.* Bethel, ME: NTL Institute.

Senge, P. (1991). *The fifth discipline.* New York: Doubleday.

Trompenaars, F. (1996). Resolving international conflict: Culture and business strategy. *Business Strategy Review, 7:* 51–68.

Trompenaars, F., and C. Hampden-Turner. (1998). *Riding the waves of culture.* New York: McGraw-Hill.

Tuckman, B. W. (1965). Developmental sequence in small groups. *Psychological Bulletin, 63:* 384–399.

Turner, M. E. (Ed.). (2000). *Groups at work: Advances in theory and research.* New York: Lawrence Erlbaum.

Verespei, M. A. (1990, June 18). Yea, teams? Not always. *Industry Week:* 103–105.

Wellins, R. S., W. C. Byham, and J. M. Wilson. (1991). *Empowered teams.* San Francisco: Jossey-Bass.

Yeatts, D. E., and C. Hyten (1998). *High performing self-managing work teams: A comparison of theory to practice.* Thousand Oaks, CA: Sage.

CHAPTER 10 REFERENCES

Baker, W. (2001). *Achieving success through social capital.* San Francisco: Jossey-Bass.

Baker, W., R. Cross, and M. Wooten. (2003). Positive organizational network analysis and energizing relationships. In K. S. Cameron, J. E. Dutton, and R. E. Quinn (Eds.), *Positive organizational scholarship: Foundations of a new discipline* (pp. 328–342). San Francisco: Barrett-Koehler.

Baumeister, R. F., E. Bratslavsky, C. Finkenauer, and K. D. Vohs. (2001). Bad is stronger than good. *Review of General Psychology, 5:* 323–370.

Bennis, W., and B. Nanus. (1985). *Leaders: The strategies for taking charge.* New York: Harper & Row.

Bollier, D. (1996). *Aiming higher: Twenty-five stories of how companies prosper by combining sound management and social vision.* New York: Amacom.

Bright, D. S., K. S. Cameron, and A. Caza. (2006). The ethos of virtuousness in downsized organizations. *Journal of Business Ethics, 64:* 249–269.

Cameron, K. S. (1985). Iacocca's transformation of Chrysler; Excerpts from Lee Iacocca's speeches to his top management team, 1979–1984. (In possession of the author.)

Cameron, K. S. (2003a). Ethics, virtuousness, and constant change. In N. M. Tichy and A. R. McGill (Eds.), *The ethical challenge* (pp. 185–193). San Francisco: Jossey-Bass.

Cameron, K. S. (2003b). Organizational virtuousness and performance. In K. S. Cameron, J. E. Dutton, and R. E. Quinn (Eds.), *Positive organizational scholarship: Foundations of a new discipline* (pp. 48–65). San Francisco: Barrett-Koehler.

Cameron, K. S., and A. Caza. (2002). Organizational and leadership virtues and the role of forgiveness. *Journal of Leadership and Organizational Studies, 9:* 33–48.

Cameron, K. S., and M. Lavine. (2006). *Making the impossible possible: Leading extraordinary performance—The Rocky Flats story.* San Francisco: Barrett-Koehler.

Cameron, K. S., and R. E. Quinn. (1999). *Diagnosing and changing organizational culture.* Reading, MA: Addison-Wesley.

Cameron, K. S., and D. O. Ulrich. (1986). Transformational leadership in colleges and universities. *Higher Education: Handbook of Theory and Research, 2:* 1–42.

Cameron, K. S., D. A. Whetten, and M. U. Kim. (1987). Organizational effects of decline and turbulence. *Administration Science Quarterly, 32:* 222–240.

Carlzon, J. (1987). *Moments of truth.* Cambridge, MA: Ballinger.

Christie, R., and S. Lehman. (1970). The structure of Machiavellian orientations. In R. Christie and F. Geis (Eds.), *Studies in Machiavellianism* (pp. 359–387). New York: Academic Press.

Cialdini, R. B. (2000). *Influence: The science of persuasion.* New York: Allyn & Bacon.

Clifton, D. O., and J. K. Harter. (2003). Investing in strengths. In K. S. Cameron, J. E. Dutton, and R. E. Quinn (Eds.), *Positive organizational scholarship: Foundations of a new discipline* (pp. 111–121). San Francisco: Barrett-Koehler.

Coonradt, C. (1985). *The game of work.* Salt Lake City: Shadow Mountain Press.

Csikszentmihalyi, M. (1990). *Flow: The psychology of optimal experience.* New York: Harper Perennial.

Davis, M. (1971). That's interesting! *Philosophy of the Social Sciences, 1:* 309–344.

Dutton, J. E., P. J. Frost, M. C. Worline, J. M. Lilius, and J. M. Kanov. (2002, *January*). Leading in times of trauma. *Harvard Business Review:* 54–61.

Emmons, R. A. (2003). Acts of gratitude in organizations. In K. S. Cameron, J. E. Dutton, and R. E. Quinn (Eds.), *Positive organizational scholarship: Foundations of a new discipline* (pp. 81–93). San Francisco: Barrett-Koehler.

Enright, R. D., and C. Coyle. (1998). Researching the process model of forgiveness within psychological interventions. In E. L. Worthington (Ed.), *Dimensions of forgiveness* (pp. 139–161). Philadelphia: Templeton Foundation Press.

Enrique, J. (2000). *As the future catches you.* New York: Crown Business.

Fredrickson, B. L. (2003). Positive emotions and upward spirals in organizations. In K. S. Cameron, J. E. Dutton, and R. E. Quinn (Eds.), *Positive organizational scholarship: Foundations of a new discipline* (pp. 163–175). San Francisco: Barrett-Koehler.

Frost, P. J. (2003). *Toxic emotions at work: How compassionate managers handle pain and conflict.* Cambridge, MA: Harvard Business School Press.

Glynn, P. (1994). Toward a politics of forgiveness. *American Enterprise, 5:* 48–53.

Gold, T. (2002). *Open your mind, open your life.* Springfield, IL: Andrews McNeel Publishing.

Gottman, J. (1994). *Why marriages succeed and fail.* New York: Simon & Schuster.

Helmick, R. G., and R. L. Petersen. (2001). *Forgiveness and reconciliation: Religion, public policy, and conflict.* Philadelphia: Templeton Foundation Press.

Kanov, J. M., S. Maitlis, M. C. Worline, J. E. Dutton, and P. J. Frost. (2003). Compassion in organizational life. *American Behavioral Scientist:* 1–54.

Kirschenbaum, D. (1984). Self-regulation and sport psychology: Nurturing and emerging symbiosis. *Journal of Sport Psychology, 8:* 26–34.

Kotter, J. (1999). *John Kotter on what leaders really do.* Cambridge, MA: Harvard Business School Press.

Lewin, K. (1951). *Field theory in social science.* New York: Harper & Row.

Losada, M., and E. Heaphy. (2003). The role of positivity and connectivity in the performance of business teams: A nonlinear dynamics model. *American Behavioral Scientist, 47:* 740–765.

McCraty, R., and Childre, D. (2004). The grateful heart. In R. A. Emmons and M. E. McCullough (Eds.), *The psychology of gratitude* (pp. 230–255). New York: Oxford University Press.

McCullough, M. E., R. A. Emmons, and J. Tsang. (2002). The grateful disposition: A conceptual and empirical topography. *Journal of Personality and Social Psychology, 82:* 112–127.

Meyerson, D. (2001). *Tempered radicals.* Cambridge, MA: Harvard Business School Press.

Perot, H. R. (1988). A vision for General Motors. Internal company document. General Motors Corporation, Detroit, MI.

Pfeffer, J. (1998). *The human equation: Building profits by putting people first.* Boston: Harvard Business School Press.

Quinn, R. E. (2000). *Change the world.* San Francisco: Jossey-Bass.

Quinn, R. E. (2004). *Building the bridge as you walk on it.* San Francisco: Jossey-Bass.

Quinn, R. E., J. E. Dutton, and G. M. Spreitzer. (2003). Reflected best-self exercise: Assignment and instructions for participants. Center for Positive Organizational Scholarship, Ross School of Business, University of Michigan. Product #001B.

Roberts, L. M., G. Spreitzer, J. Dutton, R. Quinn, E. Heaphy, and B. Barker. (2005). How to play to your strengths. *Harvard Business Review, 83:* 75–80.

Salancik, G. R. (1977). Commitment of control of organizational behavior and belief. In B. M. Staw and G. R. Salancik (Eds.),

News directions in organizational behavior. Chicago: St. Clair Press.

Sculley, J. (1987). Apple's identity and goals. Internal company document. Apple Computer, Inc., Cupertino, CA.

Seligman, M. E. P. (2002). *Authentic happiness*. New York: Free Press.

Selznick, P. (1949). *TVA and the grass roots*. Berkeley: University of California Press.

Simmel, G. (1950). *The sociology of Georg Simmel*. Glencoe, IL: Free Press.

Tichy, N. M. (1993). *Control your destiny or someone else will*. New York: Doubleday.

Tichy, N. M. (1997). *The leadership engine*. New York: Harper Collins.

Tutu, D. (1998). Without forgiveness there is no future. In R. D. Enright and J. North (Eds.), *Exploring forgiveness*. Madison: University of Wisconsin Press.

Tutu, D. (1999). *No future without forgiveness*. New York: Doubleday.

U. S. Army Strategic Leadership Program. (2003). Personal communication. Boston, MA.

Walsh, J. P. (1999). Business must talk about its social role. In T. Dickson (Ed.), *Mastering strategy* (pp. 289–294). London: Financial Times/Prentice Hall.

Weick, K. E. (1981). Small wins: Redefining the scale of social problems. *American Psychologist, 39:* 40–49.

Weick, K. E. (1993, Winter). Small wins in organizational life. *Dividend:* 20–24.

SUPPLEMENT A REFERENCES

Barrett, H. (1977). *Practical uses of speech communication,* 4th ed. New York: Holt, Rinehart & Winston.

Collins, E., and M. Devanna. (1990). *The portable MBA*. New York: Wiley.

Dubrin, A. J. (1985). *Contemporary applied management*. Plano, TX: Business Publications, Inc.

Endicott Report. (1992). Baton Rouge: Louisiana State University Press.

Gelles-Cole, S. (1985). *The complete guide to executive manners*. New York: Rawson.

Gronbeck, B. E., et al. (1992). *Principles of speech communication,* 11th ed. New York: Harper Collins.

Lucas, S. (1989). *The art of public speaking*, 3rd ed. New York: Random House.

Mambert, W. A. (1976). *Effective presentation*. New York: Wiley.

Maruca, R. F. (1996). Looking for better productivity? *Harvard Business Review, 74:* 9–10.

Miller, G. A. (1967). *The psychology of communication*. Baltimore: Penguin.

Osborn, M., and S. Osborn. (1991). *Public speaking*. Boston: Houghton Mifflin.

Peoples, D. A. (1988). *Presentations plus*. New York: Wiley.

Poor, E. (1992). *The executive writer: A guide to managing words, ideas, and people*. New York: Grove Weidenfeld.

Reingold, J. (2004, October). The man behind the curtain. *Fast Company:* 100–104.

Sproule, M. (1991). *Speechmaking: An introduction to rhetorical competence*. Dubuque, IA: William C. Brown.

Sanford, W. P., and W. H. Yeager. (1963). *Principles of effective speaking*, 6th ed. New York: Ronald Press.

Seiler, W. J. (1971). The effects of visual materials on attitudes, credibility, and retention. *Speech Monographs, 38:* 331–334.

Sprague, J., and D. Stuart. (1996). *The speaker's handbook,* 4th ed. Fort Worth, TX: Harcourt Brace College Publishers.

Wells, W. (1989). *Communications in business,* 5th ed. Belmont, CA: Wadsworth.

Wilcox, R. P. (1967). *Oral reporting in business and industry*. Upper Saddle River, NJ: Prentice Hall.

SUPPLEMENT B REFERENCES

Beer, M. (1987). *Meetings: How to make them work for you*. New York: Van Nostrand Reinholdt.

Downs, C. W., G. P. Smeyak, and E. Martin. (1980). *Professional interviewing*. New York: Harper & Row.

DuBrin, A. J. (1981). *Human relations: A job-oriented approach,* 2nd ed. Reston, VA: Reston Publishing Company.

Lopez, R. M. (1975). *Personnel interviewing*. New York: McGraw-Hill.

Maier, N. R. F. (1958, March–April). Three types of appraisal interviews. *Personnel:* 27–40.

Sincoff, M. Z., and R. S. Goyer. (1984). *Interviewing*. New York: Macmillan.

Stano, M. E., and N. L. Reinsch, Jr. (1982). *Communication in interviews*. Upper Saddle River, NJ: Prentice Hall.

Stewart, C. J., and W. B. Cash, Jr. (1985). *Interviewing: Principles and practice,* 4th ed. Dubuque, IA: Brown.

SUPPLEMENT C REFERENCES

Cohen, M., J. March and J. Olsen. (1972). A garbage can model of organizational choice. *Administrative Science Quarterly, 17:* 1–15.

DeBono, E. (1985). *The six thinking hats*. Boston: Little, Brown.

De Tocqueville, A. (1841). *Democracy in America*. New York: Langley.

Harvey, J. (1974, Summer). The abilene paradox. *Organizational Dynamics:* 63–80.

Janis, I. (1972). *Victims of groupthink*. Boston: Houghton Mifflin.

Janis, I. (1983). *Groupthink: Psychological studies of policy decisions and fiascoes*. Boston: Houghton Mifflin.

Putnam, R. (2000). *Bowling alone*. New York: Simon & Schuster.

Rothman, J., J. Erlich, and J. Tropman. (2000). Strategies of community intervention, 6th ed. Itasca, IL: F. E. Peacock.

3M Meeting Management Team. (1994). *Mastering meetings*. New York: McGraw-Hill.

Tichy, N., and M. Devanna. (1986). *The transformational leader*. New York: Wiley.

Tropman, J., J. Erlich, and J. Rothman. (2000). *Tactics of community intervention,* 4th ed. Itasca, IL: F. E. Peacock.

Tropman, J. E. (1996). *Effective meetings,* 2nd ed. Thousand Oaks, CA: Sage.

Tuchman, B. (1984). *The march of folly: From Troy to Vietnam*. New York: Knopf.

NAME INDEX

Page numbers followed by an f or t represent figures and tables respectively.

DeGeorge, R., 307
DeGraff, J., 33, 200, 201, 226, 466
Deleo, J., 165
Dell Computer, 112, 234
Dell, Michael, 112, 580
Derr, C., 398
Detert, R., 165
Deutsch, M., 472
Devanna, M., 615, 674
Dew, J., 538
Dewey, J., 520
Dickson, M., 517, 518, 527, 534
DiClemente, C., 470
Dilenschneider, R., 306
Dillard, J., 307
Dirks, K., 315
Disney Corporation, 575
Disney, Walt, 202, 203
Disraeli, Benjamin, 274
Divine, D., 536
Dobbs, K., 351
Doherty, M. E., 140
Dollinger, S. J., 91
Downs, C., 642, 654
Drucker, P., 466
Drucker, Peter, 25, 98
Druskat, V., 529, 536
DuBrin, A., 633, 642
Duncan, R., 325
Dunlap, Al, 307
Dunn, Keith, 239–243
Durham, C., 356
Durkheim, E., 474
Dutt, James, L., 318
Dutton, J., 43, 81, 135, 163, 199, 260,
    325, 466, 483, 568, 571
Dyer, W., 166, 269, 322, 358

E
EBay, 235
Eden, D., 356
Edison, Thomas, 25
Edmonson, A., 529
Eichinger, R., 403
Einstein, Albert, 221
Eisenhardt, K., 398, 400, 403
Eisner, Michael, 578
Elsayed-Elkhouly, S. M., 91
Emerson, R., 327
Emmons, R., 569
Enright, R., 568
Enrique, J., 561
Enron, 94, 235
Equity Funding, 94
Eroglu, S., 152
Eshelman, E., 165, 180

F
Farnham, A., 150, 151, 153
Farson, R., 278–279
Federal Express, 517
Feldman, D., 209, 223, 474
Ferrin, D., 315
Festinger, L., 208
Finast Supermarkets, 575–576
Finke, R., 206, 217, 222, 223
Firestone, 94
First Boston, 405
First Chicago, 145
Fisher, C., 139, 140, 315, 354
Fisher, Irving, 25
Fisher, R., 408
Fisher, S. G., 90, 91
Fleishman, J., 349
Fleming, Sir Alexander, 212
Foerstner, George, 209–210, 214
Ford, Henry, 158, 235, 532

Ford Motor Co., 29, 94, 196, 480, 579
Ford, William Clay, 579
Frankl, Victor, 468
Fredrickson, B., 260, 563
Freeman, S. J., 153, 476, 478
French, J. R. R., 96, 139, 140, 153,
    467, 486
Freud, S., 80, 520
Friedman, M., 162, 163
Fromm, Erich, 80
Fry, Art, 210, 212, 214, 229
Furman, W., 311

G
Gabarro, Jack, 282, 313
Gable, S., 260
Gackenbach, J., 261
Gage, D., 401
Galunic, D. C., 466
Gambetta, D., 486
Gandhi, Mahatma, 145, 203, 468, 472,
    533, 560
Ganzach, Y., 364
Gardner, H., 151, 348
Gardner, John, 305
Gates, Bill, 578, 584, 594–595, 610
Gecas, V., 465, 469, 470
Geddie, T., 278
Gehry, Frank, 239
Gelles-Cole, S., 615
Gelman, E., 305, 316, 318
Gemmill, G., 470
Gendron, G., 407
Geneen, Harold, 314
General Electric, 95, 104, 196, 206,
    314, 366, 584
General Electric Aircraft, 158
General Mills, 517
General Motors, 28–29, 154, 166, 305,
    399, 577
Gerhart, B., 349, 359
Getzels, J., 206
Giamatti, A. Bartlett, 330
Gibb, J., 268, 472
Gibb, L., 472
Gilligan, C., 94
Gitelson, R., 139, 140
Gittell, J., 161, 260
Gladstein, D., 518
Gladwell, Malcolm, 196
Glasser, W., 277
Gloucer, Tom, 577
Glucksman, Lewis, 306
Glynn, P., 568
Goddard, Roger, 470
Goldberg, H., 163
Goleman, D., 34, 81, 84, 85, 86, 87,
    151, 152
Golembiewski, R., 472, 473
Golen, S., 262, 264
Goll, I., 196
Goodson, Gene, 228
Google, 590–592
Gordon, E., 415
Gordon, R., 268
Gordon, W. J. J., 218
Gottman, J., 571
Goyer, R., 642
Graham, M., 360
Greenberg, Eric, 37, 159, 165
Greenberger, D. B., 153, 465,
    471, 484
Greene, C., 470
Gregersen, H., 199
Greiner, L., 520
Griest, J. H., 159
Grove, A., 311, 398
Gudykunst, W., 286

Gully, S., 536
Guzzo, R., 517, 518, 527, 534

H
Haas, J., 278
Haase, R. F., 99
Hackett, Jim, 578
Hackman, J. R., 153, 154, 364, 472,
    473, 474, 479, 480, 489, 517,
    518, 520, 524, 527, 528,
    529, 633
Hall, D. T., 142
Hamilton, B., 517
Hammarskjold, Dag, 151
Hammer, T., 101, 470
Hampden-Turner, C., 44, 88, 140, 224,
    534
Haney, W., 262
Hanson, G., 28, 266
Hare, C. C., 141
Hargie, O., 261
Harnett, D., 409
Harris, J. R., 94, 95
Harris, S., 81, 104
Harter, J., 570, 571
Harter, S., 102, 352, 468
Harvey, J., 674
Harvey, William, 218
Hatfield, J., 278
Hausman, C., 221
Hayes, J., 83, 312
Hayes, N., 538
Hayes, T., 352
Heaphy, E., 260, 281, 570
Heider, F., 208
Heisler, W., 470
Hellreigel, C., 470
Helmick, R., 568
Hendricks, W., 100, 165
Hepburn, G., 135, 158
Hermann, N., 215
Hess, R., 470
Hewlett-Packard, 235, 316, 585
Hickson, D., 199, 200, 317
Higgs, A., 524
Hillhouse, J. J., 137, 142, 158,
    159, 160
Hinings, C., 317
Hitler, Adolf, 207, 275
Hobson, A., 533
Hobson, C. J., 141–142
Hocker, J., 403
Hoerr, J., 319
Hofstede, Geert, 404
Hogg, M., 311
Holmes, T. H., 141–142
Holt, J., 45
Honda, 203
Hosoda, M., 312
House, R., 357
Hout, T. M., 139
Hoy, A., 470
Hoy, W., 470
Hubbard, J., 134, 160
Huber, G., 487
Hudspith, S., 215
Huseman, R., 278
Hyman, R., 269
Hyten, C., 527, 538

I
Iacocca, Lee, 475, 574, 584, 596–602,
    610–611
Ibuka, Masaru, 532–533
Ideo, 202
In Search of Excellence, 371–372
Intel Corporation, 318, 398, 575
Interaction Associates, 217

Intermountain Health Care, 348
Ivancevich, J., 161

J
Jackson, Phil, 348
Jago, A., 486, 487
James, William, 274
Janis, I., 227, 522, 523, 674
Jansky, Karl, 209
Janson, R., 153, 480
Jay, Anthony, 350
Jehn, K., 400, 402, 403, 408
Jesus, 218
Jobs, Steve, 202, 234, 306, 407, 533
Johnson & Johnson, 158, 590, 593–594
Johnson Controls, 228
Johnston, C. S., 91
Jones, Jean C., 318
Jones, Tom, 314
Jourard, S. M., 163
Judge, T. A., 83, 84, 90, 91,
    101–103, 161
Juran, J., 196

K
Kahn, R., 137, 139, 472
Kahwajy, J., 398
Kallmer, Kathleen, 318
Kanov, J., 568
Kanter, Rosabeth, 306–307, 308, 310,
    315, 325, 333, 465, 473, 474,
    476, 478
Kanungo, R., 311, 465, 469, 470, 471
Kaplan, R., 316, 319
Karambayya, R., 420
Karasek, R. A., 153
Katzenbach, J., 38, 166, 517, 526, 527,
    529, 531
Keashly, L., 409
Kekule, Fredrich, 212
Kelleher, Herb, 113, 313
Kelley, R. E., 81
Kelly, J., 400
Kennedy, A., 314
Kennedy, John, F., 26, 522, 577
Kentucky Fried Chicken, 209
Kern, Rex, 584–585
Kerr, S., 360
Kerr, William Rolfe, 145t
Kettering, Charles, 197
Ketteringham, J., 207, 210, 211, 212,
    214, 215
Kihlstrom, J. F., 151
Kilmann, R., 409
Kim, M. U., 81, 82, 140, 404,
    466, 564
Kim, S., 415
Kinicki, A. J., 142
Kipnis, D., 320, 324, 410, 412
Knapp, M., 269
Knight, D., 102, 356
Knowling, Bob, 352–353
Kobasa, S., 142, 161
Koberg, D., 223
Koestler, A., 209, 212
Kohlberg, L., 91–94, 95
Kolb, D. A., 34, 36, 97, 98
Konrad, A., 316
Koole, S., 408
Koopman, P., 196
Kopelman, R., 366
Korabik, D., 409
Korda, M., 306
Kotter, John, 305, 310, 313, 353, 560
Kouzes, J., 90, 529
Kraimer, M., 316
Kram, K., 83, 165, 307
Kramer, R., 278, 529

Page numbers followed by an f or t represent figures and tables respectively.

COMBINED INDEX

Page numbers followed by an f or t represent figures and tables respectively.

Clarke, J., 533
Clark, R., 367
Clifton, D., 570, 571
Closed questions, for interviews, 643–644
CNN, 575
Coaching, on communication, 266–268
Coats, G., 312
Coch, L., 490
Cockcroft, John, D., 211
Coddington, R. D., 142
Cognitive style, 83, 96–98, 97t
    creating style, 97–98
    indicator, 74
    knowing style, 96–97
    planning style, 97
Cohen, A., 322
Cohen, M., 674, 675
Cohen, P. A., 34
Cohen, S., 517, 518, 527, 536
Collaboration, in conflict management, 407–408, 412, 413–424
Collaboration, in stress management, 150–152
Collectivism, 88t, 89
Collins, E., 615
Collins, M. A., 216
Commitment, as conceptual block, 210–212
Commonalities, ignoring, as conceptual block, 211–212
Communication, and empowerment, 466, 467
Communication, supportive. See also Interviews, conducting
    accuracy and, 262–264
    attributes of, 264–266, 265t
    barriers to, 286
    behavioral guidelines for, 287
    coaching and counseling for, 266–268
    and congruence, 269–270
    conjunctive, 276–277
    consequences of ineffective, 264
    descriptive, 270–272
    effective, importance of, 261–262
    and electronic communication, 261
    international caveats for, 285–286
    and interpersonal relationships, 260–261
    listening and responding, 278–282, 294–295
    obstacles to, 268, 268t
    owned, 277–278
    personal management interview (PMI), 282–285
    problem oriented, 272–273
    pronunciations, inconsistent, 263t
    scoring key for, 298–300
    skill analysis for, 288–290
    skill application for, 296–297
    skill assessment for, 256–259
    skill practice for, 291–295
    specific, 275–276
    studies of, 261–262
    validating, 273–275
Communist prison camp, exercise on, 106–107
Compassion, and leadership, 567–568
Competing Values Framework, 38–39, 201
Compromising, in conflict management, 406, 407t, 411, 411t
Computerized exam, exercise on, 107–108
Conceptual blocks
    commitment as, 210–212
    complacency as, 214–216

compression as, 212–214
constancy as, 208–210
defined, 205
exercises to assess, 237–243
and mental filtering, 205–206
as mental obstacles, 230
overcoming, 216–221, 230
review of, 216
Conclusions, for a presentation, 619t
Conflict management
    ambivalent view of, 398–400
    approaches to, 405–408, 411–413
    behavioral guidelines for, 424–426
    collaborative problem solving and, 412–426
    conflict focus, 402
    and cultural diversity, 403–404, 408–409
    and environmentally induced stress, 404–405
    flexibility in, 409–411
    and gender, 409
    and informational deficiencies, 403–404
    interpersonal, 398
    issue-focused, 401–402
    model for, 423–424
    and negotiation strategies, 407t
    people-focused, 400–401
    and personal differences, 402–403
    personal preferences for, 408–409, 424
    and role incompatibility, 404
    rules of engagement for, 400
    scoring key for, 457–459
    situational considerations for, 411–412, 411t
    skill analysis for, 427–431
    skill application for, 453–455
    skill assessment for, 396–397
    skill practice for, 432–452
    XYZ approach to, 415–416, 418–419, 416t
Conger, J., 311, 465, 469, 470, 471, 473
Congruence, and communication, 269–270
Connell, J., 470
Conner, J., 319
Conscientiousness, 102
Constancy, as conceptual block, 208–210
Constraints, artificial, as conceptual block, 212–213
Continental Airlines, 113–114
Cook, A., 367
Coolidge, Calvin, 199
Coonradt, Chuck, 477, 487, 579–581
Cooper, C., 100, 136, 149
Cooper, M., 165
Cordes, C. L., 140, 142, 165
Core self-evaluation, 83–84, 101–103
Core Self-Evaluation Scale, 77–78, 125
Core Self-Evaluation Survey, 103
Corning, 517
Council of Communication Management, 261
Counseling, on communication, 266–268
Courtney, Henry, 229
Covey, S., 81, 143, 151
Cowan, A., 305
Cowley, J., 161
Cox, T. H., 44, 82, 403, 524
Coyle, C., 568
Creating style, 97–98
Creativity, and problem solving, 196–231

Credibility, and teamwork, 529–531
Creon, King, 307
Crocker, J., 261, 278
Cross, R., 477, 567
Crovitz, H., 223
Csikszentmihalyi, M., 206, 217, 563
Cuban Missile Crisis, 522
Culture. See also Diversity
    affectivity in, 140
    and communication, 263
    and conflict management, 412
    egalitarian, 140
    hierarchical, 140
    personal, learning plan for, 114–116
    and power, 306
    as predictive factor in stress, 140
    sensitivity for, 44
    and teamwork, 534
    values of different, 83–85
Cuming, P., 322
Cummings, L., 409, 471
Cupach, W., 268, 273
Curtis, J., 32, 165
Customer relationships, establishing, 153
Customer Undeniably Deserves Attention (CUDA), 242

D
Dalkon Shield, 94
Daly, J., 325
Dana Corporation, 228, 517
Davidson, J., 143, 149, 150
Davidson, O., 356
Davis, Murray, 577
Davis, T. W., 35, 101, 165, 181
Dawidowicz, Bogdan, 305
Deal, T., 310, 314
De Bono, Edward, 206, 208
DeButts, John, 314
DeCharms, R., 468
Deci, E., 470, 472
Decision dilemmas, exercise on, 108–110
De Dreu, C., 400, 408
Deepak, M., 165, 167
Defensiveness, and communication, 268
Defensiveness, and self-awareness, 81
Defining Issues Test, 70–73, 121–123
Definitions, reversing, 219–221
Deflecting response, 280
DeGeorge, R., 307
DeGraff, J., 33, 200, 201, 226, 466
Delegation. See also Empowerment
    advantages of, 485–486, 485t
    behavioral guidelines for, 494–495
    principles for, 493f
    process for, 487–492, 488f
    relationship to empowerment, 495f
    scoring key for, 507
    skill analysis for, 496–497
    skill application for, 505–506
    skill assessment for, 462–464
    skill practice for, 498–502
    timing for, 486–487, 488f
Deleo, J., 165
Dellbeck, M., 165
Dell Computer, 112, 234
Dell, Michael, 112, 580
Derr, C., 398
Desert Storm. See Persian Gulf War
Detert, R., 165
Deutsch, M., 472
Devanna, M., 615, 674
Deviance, negative and positive, 562–563, 568f
Dewey, J., 520
Dew, J., 538
Dickson, M., 517, 518, 527, 534

DiClemente, C., 470
Dietary control, to combat stress, 159–160
Dilenschneider, R., 306
Dillard, J., 307
Dirks, K., 315
Disconfirmation, and communication, 268, 268t
Disney Corporation, 575
Disney, Walt, 202, 203
Disraeli, Benjamin, 274
Distance learning, 351
Diversity
    differences vs. distinctions, 82–83
    growth of, in workplace, 104
    and individual differences, 43–44
    and self-awareness, 83–84, 85f
    and Trompenaars model, 44
Divine, D., 536
Dobbs, K., 351
Doctor's dilemma, exercise on, 72, 122
Doherty, M. E., 140
Dollinger, S. J., 91
Dominant response pattern, 43
Double-barreled questions, for interviews, 644, 645t
Downs, C., 642, 654
Drucker, P., 466
Drucker, Peter, 25, 98
Druskat, V., 529, 536
DuBrin, A., 633, 642
Duncan, R., 325
Dunlap, Al, 307
Dunn, Keith, 239–243
Durham, C., 356
Durkheim, E., 474
Dutt, James, L., 318
Dutton, J., 43, 81, 135, 163, 199, 260, 325, 466, 483, 568, 571
Dyer, W., 166, 269, 322, 358

E
EBay, 235
Eden, D., 356
Edison, Thomas, 25
Edmonson, A., 529
Effort, as power source, 312–314
Egalitarian communication, 274
Eichinger, R., 403
Einstein, Albert, 221
Eisenhardt, K., 398, 400, 403
Eisner, Michael, 578
Elaboration probe, for interviews, 648, 650t
Elaboration, used in problem solving, 219
Elsayed-Elkhouly, S. M., 91
E-mail, tone for, 627
Embedded pattern puzzle, 214f, 252
Emerson, R., 327
Emmons, R., 569
Emotional bank account, 151
Emotional competence, 84–86
Emotional Competence Inventory, 85
Emotional Intelligence, 85
Emotional intelligence (EQ)
    assessment for, 119–121
    capabilities of those with, 85–86
    compared to IQ, 86–87
    and cultural diversity, 44
    defined, 84
    vs. emotional competence, 87
    EQ-I measure, 85
    as factor in success, 83, 84
    falling scores of, 34
    improving, 45
    refining concept of, 83–85
    skill assessment for, 69–70
    and stress management, 150–152